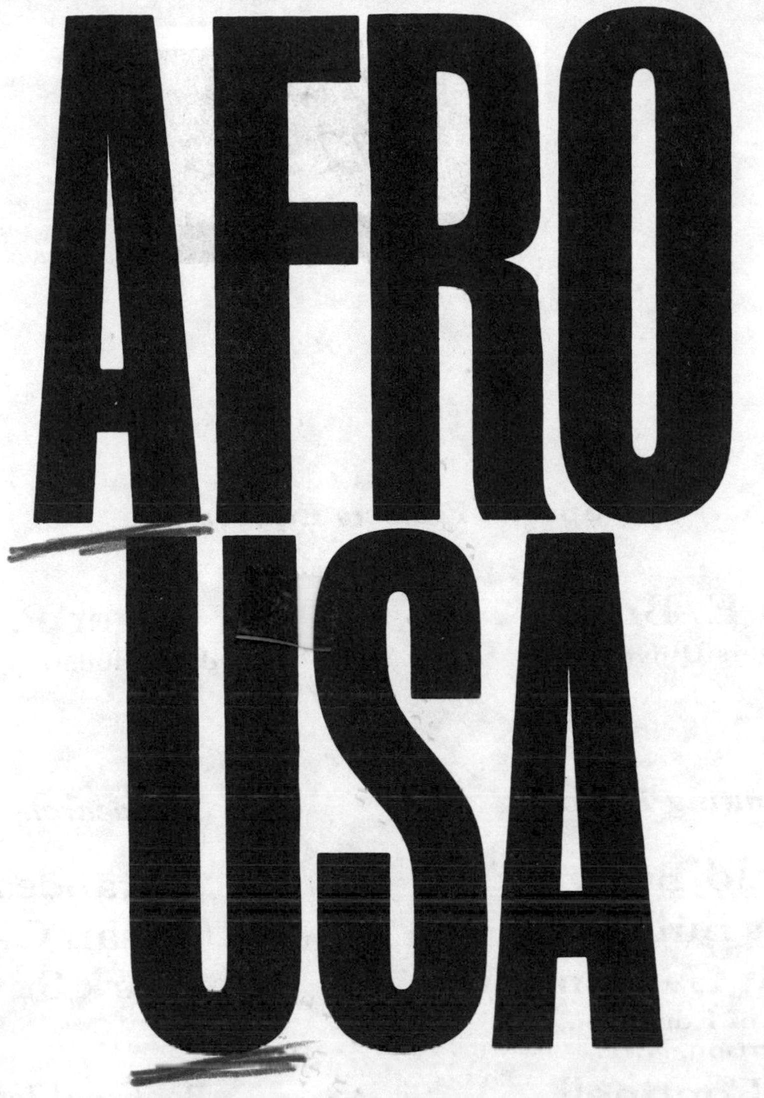

a reference work on the black experience

Compiled and Edited by:

Harry A. Ploski, Ph.D.
New York University

and

Ernest Kaiser
Bibliographer, Schomburg Collection of Negro History and Literature and contributing editor FREEDOMWAYS magazine.

AFRO-U.S.A.
is a special deluxe presentation of the regular edition
of the prestigious new revised *Negro Almanac.*

Published by Bellwether Publishing Company Inc. for exclusive distribution by FP Sales Inc.

Special Projects Editors:

John E. Brown
Rutgers University

Roger P. Nelson
Board of Education, New York City

Contributing Editors

Donald Brown
Barbara Bulkostein
Joseph Carbone
Board of Education,
Harrison, N. Y.
F. J. Fontinell
Middleton A. "Spike" Harris
Negro History Associates
Rev. J. Clinton Hoggard
Department of Foreign Missions,
A.M.E. Zion Church
Warren Marr II
Public Relations Department NAACP
Richard Rosenthal
News Age
Clinton Utterbach

Research Assistants

Frances Davis
Susan Carpenter
Mark Stroock III

Book and Jacket Design

Bob Bilek
Charles Zednicek
Oldrich Holubar

Special Photographic Work

Ed Druck
Bill Mackey

Library of Congress Catalog Card Number: 70-151238

PUBLISHERS NOTE

AFRO U.S.A. IS BASED UPON AN ENLARGED AND EXPANDED VERSION of the prestigious *Negro Almanac,* first published in 1967 and since cited by Library Journal, in conjunction with the American Library Association, as one of the outstanding reference works of the past decade. Like its predecessor, the volume examines the black man's role in the settlement and growth of the United States, and goes on to consider his contemporary situation in light of his current position within the framework of American society. It contains biographical data on an imposing roster of historical and contemporary personalities—men and women of achievement from all walks of life. It is generously stocked with valuable statistical material—including tables, charts and graphs—all of which provide their own technical insights into the scope and importance of the black experience in the United States. AFRO U.S.A. also explores the significance of modern black militancy, seeking not only to discover its historical roots, but also to assess its contemporary importance, without bias or partisanship. Its strength, then, lies both in the breadth of its concept and the depth of its analysis. To achieve our objective, we have drawn freely from a multiplicity of sources, not only from existing scholarship, but also from government material which has been restyled and, where necessary, reinterpreted. Innumerable sources for checking factual material were utilized. In many instances, much of the material is original from the standpoint of never having been previously compiled.

Information on the wide variety and extensive range of topics which have been covered here can only be obtained from multiple sources in a few specialized library collections and, as such, is relatively inaccessible to all but the most trained researchers. By laying the groundwork for a far broader dissemination of such information in an enlarged format, we hope to provide the widest possible audience with an accurate, comprehensive and well-documented study of the black man's culture in the United States, and around the world as well.

ACKNOWLEDGMENTS

THE COOPERATION FORTHCOMING FROM A NUMBER OF OUTSIDE sources has aided us immeasurably in the creation of this set. Several organizations have demonstrated far more than conventional courtesy in making their facilities and findings available to us and, as such, deserve a special note of commendation. Heading the list is the Schomburg Collection of Negro History and Literature, along with such staff members as Mrs. Jean Blackwell Hutson (curator); Mrs. Cora V. Eubanks; Mr. Stan Biddle, and Mr. Richard Waters. Mr. Wendell Wray and Mr. Gene Michael of the Countee Cullen branch also gave unstintingly of their time and talents.

Our thanks are also extended to the U.S. Department of Labor, the Census Bureau, the Pentagon, and the entire military establishment, including the service academies. In like measure, we are grateful to Mr. James C. Evans for his help in obtaining material for the military affairs section, and to Mrs. Sarah Jackson of the National Archives.

The Southern Regional Council and the Metropolitan Applied Research Center proved particularly helpful in providing information on black voting patterns and black elected officials, and the U.S. Civil Rights Commission was likewise of great assistance in compiling a wide assortment of statistics. We are also grateful to the American Oil Company for its assistance in the compilation of our "landmarks" section. Our thanks are extended as well to the Golden State Mutual Life Insurance Company of Los Angeles for their prompt attention to our requests for permission to reproduce much of the art work and biographical data visible in the fine arts section.

A final word is due Mrs. Virginia Cherry for the special editorial assistance she rendered at every stage of manuscript preparation.

CONTENTS

Page

Page

Oceanica Classis

CHRONOLOGY: A HISTORICAL REVIEW

Major Events in Negro History (1492-1954)
A Review of the Civil Rights Revolution (1954-1964)
Urban Violence and Black Power (1964-1970)
The March of News (1965-1970)
Deaths of Prominent Negroes (1969-1970)

Negro history in the Western Hemisphere most probably begins with the discovery of the New World by Christopher Columbus in 1492. Negroes are known to have participated meaningfully in a number of later explorations made by Europeans in various parts of the United States and Spanish America. Facts such as these at once fashion a new dimension for Negro history within the mainstream of American history. Inasmuch as one of the primary purposes of this volume is to record comprehensively the historical achievements of the Negro, it becomes most important to offer the reader a chronological account through which he can conveniently familiarize himself with the broad sweep of American Negro history. The years covered here are 1492–1954.

1492 The New World

Negroes are among the first explorers to come to the New World. Pedro Alonso Niño, identified by some scholars as a Negro, arrives with Columbus; other Negroes accompany Balboa, Ponce de Leon, Cortes, Pizarro and Menendez on their travels and explorations.

1517 Latin America; the Caribbean

Bishop Las Casas persuades the Spanish Crown to allow Spanish settlers a quota of 12 Negro slaves each, thus encouraging immigration to Latin America and the Caribbean.

1526 South Carolina

Negro slaves in a Spanish-ruled colony revolt and flee to the Indians.

1538 Arizona-New Mexico

Estevanico, a Negro explorer, leads an expedition from Mexico into the territory of the American Southwest; is credited with the discovery of what is today Arizona and New Mexico.

1600 Latin America

Historical records indicate that, by 1600, 900,000 slaves have been brought to Latin America; in the next century, 2,750,000 slaves are added to that total.

1612 Colombia, South America

Spanish Jesuit Peter Claver, known among Catholic saints as the "Friend of the Negroes", brings some 300,000 Negroes into the Catholic Church. Claver remains in this apostolate for 40 years.

1619 Jamestown, Virginia

Negro history in "English America" begins with the arrival of 20 Negro slaves aboard a Dutch vessel (August 20).

1624 Jamestown, Virginia

Baptism of William Tucker, the first Negro child born in the English colonies.

1642 Virginia

Virginia passes a fugitive slave order penalizing people who lend refuge to runaways. Offenders are fined 20 pounds worth of tobacco for every night they harbor runaways. Attempts are made to discourage slaves by threatening them with branding. The letter "R" is burned into the flesh of anyone caught after a second escape attempt.

1651 North Hampton County, Virginia

Anthony Johnson, himself a Negro, imports five servants and thus qualifies to receive a 200-acre land grant along the Pawgoteague River in Virginia. Other Negroes soon join Johnson and attempt to launch an independent black community. At its height, the separate settlement has 12 black homesteads with sizable holdings.

1662 Virginia

The colony passes a law which provides that the status of children—bound or free —will be determined by the condition of the mother.

1663 Gloucester, Virginia

The first major conspiracy involving Negro slaves and white indentured servants is betrayed by a house servant.

1663 Maryland

The settlers pass a law stipulating that all imported Negroes are to be given the status of slaves. Free white women who marry such slaves are to assume this status during the lives of their spouses, and children of the union are likewise classified as slaves. Ironically, children born of white servant women and Negroes are regarded as free by a later law (1681).

1670 Virginia

The colony declares that all non-Christians imported to the territory, "by shipping" are to be slaves for life, whereas those who have entered by a land route are to serve until the age of 30 if they begin as "boys and girls," and for 12 years if they are adult men and women when their period of servitude commences.

1688 Germantown, Pennsylvania

Signing of the Germantown Mennonite Anti-Slavery Resolution, the first formal protest made against slavery in the Western Hemisphere.

1704 New York City

Elias Neau, a Frenchman, opens a school for Negro slaves.

1705 Virginia

The Assembly declares that "no Negro, mulatto, or Indian shall presume to take upon him, act in or exercise any office, ecclesiastic, civil or military." Negroes are forbidden to serve as witnesses in court cases, and are condemned to lifelong servitude, unless they have either been Christians in their native land, or free men in a Christian country.

1712 New York City

An early slave revolt claims the lives of nine whites, and results in the execution of 21 Negroes. Six others commit suicide.

1723 Virginia

The colony enacts laws to limit the increase of free Negroes to those who are born into this class, or manumitted by special acts of the legislature. Such laws are so effective that, by 1782, there are only 2,800 free Negroes in the territory. This same year, free Negroes are denied the right to vote and forbidden to carry weapons of any sort.

1735 New York

Dutch burgher John Van Zandt whips his slave to death for being picked up outside of his quarters. Van Zandt is tried by a coroner's jury which asserts that the slave was killed "by the visitation of God."

1739 Stono, South Carolina

An early slave revolt led by Cato results in the death of 30 whites and many more slaves. Some, however, escape to freedom.

1740 South Carolina

The colony passes a slave code which forbids slaves from raising livestock, provides that any animals owned by slaves be forfeited, and fixes severe penalties for slaves who make "false appeals" to the governor on the grounds that they have been placed in bondage illegally.

1741 New York

A series of arsonist acts throughout the city prompts a massive white backlash which results in the burning of 11 Negroes and the hanging of 18 others. Public suspicion of slaves stems solely from their presence, rather than from any circumstantial or direct proof of their connection with the crimes.

1744 Virginia

The colony amends its 1705 law declaring that Negroes cannot serve as witnesses in court cases; it decides, instead, to admit "any free Negro, mulatto or Indian being a Christian," as a witness in a criminal or civil suit *involving another Negro* (not a white person), mulatto, or Indian.

1746 Deerfield, Massachusetts

Slave poet Lucy Terry pens "Bars Fight", a commemorative poem recreating the Deerfield Massacre. Miss Terry, generally considered the first Negro poet in America, later tried unsuccessfully to convince the Board of Trustees at Williams College to admit her son to the school.

1747 South Carolina

The Assembly commends Negro slaves for demonstrating "great faithfulness and courage in repelling attacks of His Majesty's enemies." It then makes cautious provisions for utilizing black recruits in the events of danger or emergency. No more than half of all able-bodied slaves aged 16-60 is authorized to enlist; once mustered in, slaves are to be divided among the companies so that they never constitute more than one-third of the white men in the company.

1750 Framingham, Massachusetts

Crispus Attucks, later to become one of the first heroes of the American Revolution, escapes from his master.

1752 Mount Vernon

There are 18 slaves at Mount Vernon at the time George Washington acquires the estate there. Under Washington, the number grows to 200. At his death, the President provides for their manumission. Washington's record shows a concern for their physical welfare, but affords little proof of equal concern for their mental or moral betterment.

1754 Philadelphia

Quaker John Woolman publishes *Some Considerations on the Keeping of Negroes*, an exhortation to fellow members of the Society of Friends to consider manumitting their slaves on grounds of morality. Three years later, some Quakers take formal action against members who ignore this plea and continue to own slaves. In Philadelphia, Quakers dealing in the slave trade are barred from making contributions for financial upkeep. In New England, Quakers who import slaves are similarly penalized; in London, the suggestion is made that they be expelled from the Society.

1760 New York City

Jupiter Hammon, believed to be the first Negro poet in the colonies, publishes *Salvation By Christ With Penitential Cries*.

1760 Rhode Island

Despite the exhortations of some members and official statements from other Quaker communities, Quaker policy is not uniform on the slavery issue. One group in Rhode Island continues to be active in the slave trade. It is known, too, that a few Quakers in the Carolinas and Virginia refused to relinquish slaves.

1767 Charleston, South Carolina

Birth of Denmark Vesey, a sailor and carpenter so opposed to slavery that he made elaborate preparations for a slave uprising which was betrayed and thus led to Vesey's capture, trial and hanging on July 3, 1822.

1770 Boston, Massachusetts

Crispus Attucks is shot and killed during the Boston Massacre.

1770 Philadelphia, Pennsylvania

Led by Anthony Benezet, the Quakers open a school for Negroes.

1770 Charleston, South Carolina

Birth of Morris Brown, later a bishop of the AME Church. Though exempt from most of the restrictions applied to Negroes early in his career, Brown lost his credibility in the white community after the Vesey conspiracy, and was forced to flee, reaching Philadelphia in 1823. He died in 1849.

1773 Savannah, Georgia

George Lisle and Andrew Bryan organize the first Negro Baptist church in the state.

1775 Philadelphia

Organization of the first abolitionist society in the United States.

1775 Fort Ticonderoga

Negro patriots join Ethan Allan and the Green Mountain Boys in the capture of Fort Ticonderoga.

1775 Bunker Hill

Peter Salem, Salem Poor and others are among the first Negroes to fight heroically at Bunker Hill.

1775 Philadelphia

The Continental Congress bars Negroes from the American Revolutionary army.

Peter Salem (extreme right, partially hidden) at the Battle of Bunker Hill

General Washington crossed the Delaware on Christmas Day, 1776. With him were two Negroes, Oliver Cromwell and Prince Whipple.

1775 Virginia

Lord Dunmore, British governor of Virginia, offers freedom to all male slaves who join the loyalist forces.

1775 Philadelphia

General George Washington, originally opposed to the enlistment of Negroes, is alarmed by the response to the Dunmore proclamation, and orders recruiting officers to accept free Negroes for service. The Continental Congress later approves Washington's action.

1776 Philadelphia

Adoption of the amended form of the Declaration of Independence, which eliminates the Jefferson proposal denouncing slavery. (See page 61.)

1776 Delaware River

Two Negroes—Prince Whipple and Oliver Cromwell—cross the Delaware with Washington en route to a surprise attack of the British and their Hessian mercenaries in Trenton, New Jersey.

1778 Rhode Island

Formation of a black battalion consisting of 300 former slaves who are compensated on a par with their white comrades-in arms and promised their freedom after the war. In August, the battalion plunges into action against the Hessians, killing more than 1,000 of the enemy. The battalion later sees action under Colonel Green at Ponts Bridge in New York.

1779 New York

Alexander Hamilton endorses the plan of South Carolina's Henry Laurens to use slaves as soldiers. "I have not the least doubt that the Negroes will make very excellent soldiers," says Hamilton, ". . . for their natural faculties are as good as ours." Apart from the biological argument, Hamilton alerts the Continental Congress to the fact that the enemy will probably make use of Negroes if the Americans fail to capitalize on the opportunity. In Hamilton's words: ". . . the best way to counteract the temptations they will hold out, will be to offer them ourselves."

1780 Charles City County, Virginia

Birth of black Baptist missionary Lott Carey who purchases his freedom in 1813, becomes a preacher at the First Baptist Church in Richmond and, in 1819, begins service with the Baptist Board of Foreign Missions. Carey later organizes and pastors the First Baptist Church of Liberia. In 1822, the American Colonization Society sponsors his trip to Liberia with 28 colonists, among the founders of the state. Carey dies defending the colony in 1828.

1782 Virginia

Thomas Jefferson's *Notes on Virginia* exhibits a curious mixture of perceptive understanding and alarming naivete with the regard to the Negro. On the one hand, Jefferson sees that "the whole commerce between master and slave is a perpetual exercise of the most boisterous passions"; on the other, he invents the fantasy that "their griefs are transient."

1783 Saratoga, New York

The famed "Black Regiment" is deactivated at the close of the Revolutionary War.

1785 Wilmington, North Carolina

Birth of black abolitionist David Walker who in 1827 establishes a second-hand clothing business in Boston and, two years later, writes *Walker's Appeal*, an open call to revolt in the South. The document creates such a furor among slaveowners that at least one Southern legislature makes circulation of it a capital offense.

1786 Virginia

James, the slave of William Armistead, is freed by the state in recognition of his spying services for General Lafayette.

1787 Philadelphia

Negro preachers Richard Allen and Absalom Jones organize the Free African Society.

1787 Northwest Territory

Congress forbids the extension of slavery into this area by virtue of the Northwest Ordinance.

1787 Philadelphia

Prince Hall organizes the first Negro Masonic lodge in America—African Lodge No. 459.

1787 New York City

Opening of the African Free School.

1791 District of Columbia

On the recommendation of Thomas Jefferson, Benjamin Banneker—astronomer, inventor, mathematician and gazetteer—is appointed to serve as a member of the commission charged with laying out plans for the city of Washington.

1793 Virginia

Passage of a state law which forbids free Negroes from entering the state.

1793 South Carolina

Twenty-three free Negro men and women from Canada—and some white supporters—sign a petition protesting the state poll tax of free Negroes.

1793 Philadelphia

Passage of the Fugitive Slave Act which makes it criminal to harbor a slave, or prevent his arrest.

1793 Mulberry Grove, Georgia

Eli Whitney patents his invention of the cotton gin.

1794 Philadelphia

Dedication of the First African Church of St. Thomas, the first Negro Episcopal congregation in the United States.

1794 Philadelphia

Organization by Richard Allen of the Bethel Church, a Negro Methodist Episcopal Church. Allen and Absalom Jones are well known to the citizens of Philadelphia, having been commended by the mayor for organizing Negroes to minister to the sick and bury the dead during an outbreak of yellow fever.

The cotton gin made slave labor more "essential" in the South.

1795 Virgina

George Washington advertises for the return of one of his slaves although he stipulates that the notice for his retrieval not be run North of Virginia. This same year, John Adams writes: "I have never owned a Negro or any other slave (even) when it has cost me thousands of dollars for the labor and sustenance of free men, which I might have saved by the purchase of Negroes at times when they were very cheap."

1796 Tennessee

Admission of Tennessee to the Union as a slave state. The state's constitution, however, does not deny suffrage to free Negroes.

1796 New York City

Organization of the Zion Methodist Church.

1797 North Carolina

Congress refuses to accept the first recorded anti-slavery petition seeking redress against a North Carolina law which requires that slaves, although freed by their Quaker masters, be returned to the state and to their former condition.

1797 Hurley, New York
Chapel Hill, North Carolina

Births of Sojourner Truth and George Moses Horton. Miss Truth, freed in 1827, feels herself singled out for a divinely inspired crusade involving emancipation and women's liberation. During the Civil War, she is a nurse; later, she is a touring lecturer. Janitor George Moses Horton writes love poems for students and later publishes a book of verse. Horton is freed after the Civil War and finishes a second volume, *Naked Genius*.

1798 Washington, D.C.

Secretary of the Navy Stoddert forbids the deployment of Negro sailors on men-of-war, thus disrupting a non-racial enlistment policy which has been operative for many years. Nevertheless, a few Negroes slip past the ban, including William Brown, a "powder monkey" on the *Constellation* and George Diggs, quartermaster of the schooner *Experiment*.

1799 Mount Vernon, Virginia

George Washington, first president of the United States, declares: ". . . it is my will and desire that all the slaves which I hold in my own right, shall receive their freedom."

1800 Richmond, Virginia

Betrayal of Gabriel Prosser's plan to lead thousands of slaves in an attack on Richmond. Gabriel and 15 of his followers are later hanged.

1800 Southampton, Virginia

Birth of Nat Turner, a brilliant and moody slave, allegedly subject to visions, hallucinations and other psychic disturbances which contributed to his conception of himself as a Moses-like figure leading his people from bondage. Turner and seven others launch a spectacular orgy of bloodletting in the summer of 1831, killing more than 50 whites and spreading terror throughout the country. After hiding for several weeks, Turner is tracked down, tried and hanged in Jerusalem.

1803 New York City

Negroes of New York actually succeed in burning parts of the city and in destroying several homes. Some are arrested, but others remain at large until they are caught and convicted of arson.

1804 Ohio

The Ohio legislature enacts the first of the "Black Laws" restricting the rights and movements of Negroes. Other Northern states soon follow suit. (Illinois, Indiana and Oregon later have anti-immigration clauses in their state constitutions.)

1805 New York City

Birth of the great Negro tragedian, Ira Aldridge. Educated in the African Free School, Aldridge made his stage debut in a play called *Pizarro,* later studied in Scotland, played Othello in London, and toured Ireland and the Continent. In his prime, Aldridge was ranked among the world's great actors.

1807 New Jersey

The state alters its 1776 Constitution by limiting the vote to free white males, thus extending previous restrictions which had established the proper age and property qualifications as the only conditions to be met before residents would be allowed to vote.

1807 London, England

British parliament abolishes the slave trade.

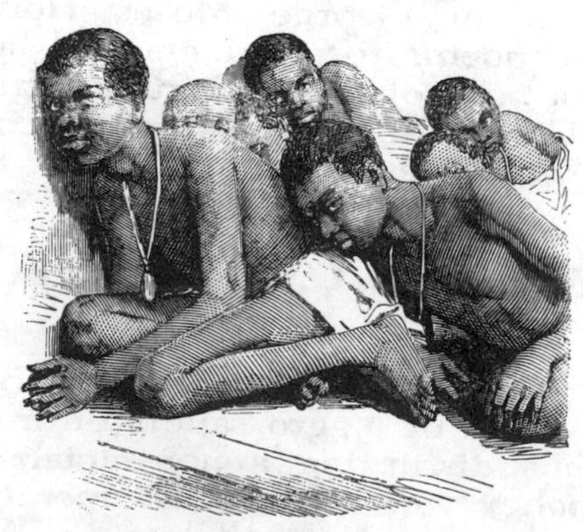

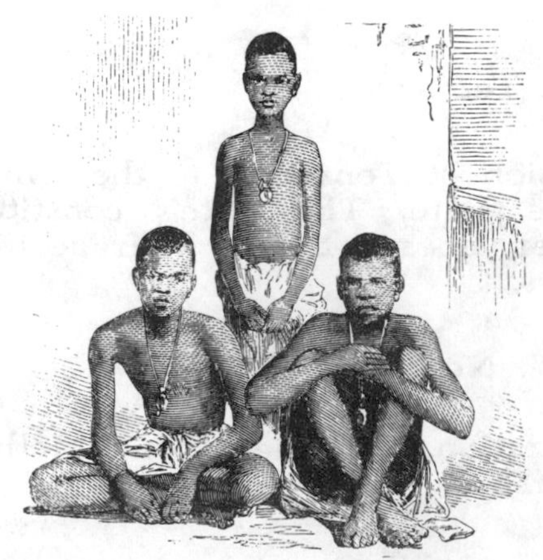

Although the slave trade was declared illegal in 1807, slaverunning continued. These people were taken from a captured slave schooner.

1807 Washington, D.C.

Congress bars the importation of any *new* slaves into the territory of the United States (effective January 1, 1808).

1808 United States

As of this year, the one in which the Congressional ban on the importation of slaves is scheduled to take effect, there are one million slaves in the country.

1809 Maryland

Birth into slavery of author/educator James W. C. Pennington, whose education is assisted by a Pennsylvania Quaker and who goes on, as a freedman, to become an eloquent orator, president of the Hartford Central Association of Congregational Ministers, and representative to the 1843 Anti-Slavery Convention in London.

1809 Hardin County, Kentucky

Birth of Abraham Lincoln.

1810 Washington, D.C.

President Madison tells Congress that some Americans are still violating the laws of humanity and their own country by carrying on trade in enslaved Africans. Madison encourages Congress to devise "further means of suppressing the evil."

1810 Salem, Massachusetts

Birth of anti-slavery leader Charles Lenox Remond who, in 1838, is appointed an agent for the Massachusetts Anti-Slavery Society and, two years later, attends the world Anti-Slavery Convention in London. During the Civil War, Remond joins his colleague and fellow abolitionist Frederick Douglass in recruiting black volunteers for the 54th Massachusetts.

1811 Delaware

The state forbids the immigration of free Negroes, and stipulates that it considers any native-born free Negro who has been out of Delaware for more than six months to be a nonresident.

1811 Louisiana

U.S. troops suppress a slave uprising in two parishes some 35 miles from New Orleans. The revolt is led by Charles Deslandes.

1812 Louisiana

Admission of Louisiana to the Union as a slave state. State law enables freedmen to serve in the state militia.

1813 New York City

Birth of James McCune Smith, a black physician and writer who is educated in New York's African Free School, studies at the University of Glasgow in Scotland and eventually opens a pharmacy in New York. Smith also serves for 23 years on the staff of the Colored Orphan Asylum. A contributor to many abolitionist periodicals and an author whose work covered a wide range of topics, Smith is regarded by Henry Highland Garnet as the most scholarly Negro of his day.

1815 Kent County, Maryland

Birth into slavery of educator/clergyman Henry Highland Garnet who escapes to New York in 1824, dividing his time there between preaching and abolition. In 1843, Garnet calls upon slaves to rise up against their masters, but the National Convention of Free People of Color at which he delivers this address rejects his proposal. Frederick Douglass is an especially outspoken opponent. Garnet later goes into missionary work, and is appointed Minister to Liberia in 1881.

1816 Louisiana

State law prohibits slaves from testifying against whites and free Negroes, except in cases where the latter are ostensibly involved in slave uprisings.

1816 Philadelphia

Organization of the African Methodist Episcopal Church.

1816 Washington, D.C.

Organization of the American Colonization Society, which seeks to transport free Negroes back to Africa. (Protest meetings are subsequently held by many such Negroes in opposition to the Society's efforts "to exile us from the land of our nativity.")

1818 Connecticut

Disfranchisement of Negroes in this state.

1818 Philadelphia

Free Negroes form the Pennsylvania Augustine Society—"for the education of people of colour."

1819 Alabama

Alabama enters the Union as a slave state, although its constitution provides the legislature with the power to abolish slavery and compensate slaveowners. Other liberal measures include jury trials for slaves figuring in crimes above petty larceny, and penalties for malicious killing of slaves.

1820 Washington, D.C.

The Missouri Compromise provides for Missouri's entry into the Union as a slave state, and Maine's entry as a free state. There are thus 12 slave and 12 free states in the United States. All territory north of 36° 30′ is declared free; all territory south of that line open to slavery.

1820 New York City

The "Mayflower of Liberia" sails for the west coast of Africa (Sierra Leone) with 86 Negroes on board.

1821 New York City

Founding of the African Methodist Episcopal Zion Church, with James Varick as its first bishop.

1821 New York

The State Constitutional Convention alters the voting requirements of the 1777 N.Y. Convention by establishing higher property and longer residence requirements for Negroes.

1822 Charleston, South Carolina

Betrayal of the Denmark Vesey conspiracy, one of the most elaborate on record. Vesey and 36 of his collaborators are hanged, while an additional 130 Negroes and four whites are arrested.

1822 Rhode Island

The state constitution of Rhode Island deprives free Negroes of the right to vote.

1825 Maryland

Josiah Henson, prototype for the original "Uncle Tom," leads a group of slaves to freedom in Kentucky. Henson later crosses the border into Canada, and becomes leader of a community of ex-slaves in present-day Ontario.

1827 New York City

Freedom's Journal, the first Negro newspaper, begins publication on March 16. "In the spirit of candor and humility we intend . . . to lay our case before the public with a view to arrest the progress of prejudice, and to shield ourselves against its consequent evils."

1827 New York

Slavery is abolished in New York State on July 4.

1829 Boston

Publication by David Walker, a free Negro, of a militant anti-slavery pamphlet (*An Appeal to the Colored People of the World*) which is distributed throughout the country and arouses a furor among slaveholders.

1830 North Carolina

Masters fearing violation of state law manumit more than 400 slaves to Quaker residents of North Carolina, who retain theoretical ownership but allow slaves virtual freedom until they can afford to transport them to free states.

1830 Washington, D.C.

The U.S. Census Bureau reports that 3,777 Negro heads of families own slaves, mostly in Louisiana, Maryland, Virginia, North Carolina and South Carolina.

1830 Philadelphia

Chaired by Richard Allen, the first National Negro Convention meets from September 20-24 at Philadelphia's Bethel Church, launching a church-affiliated program to improve the social status of the American Negro.

1831 Boston

The *Liberator*, an abolitionist organ, is founded by William Garrison. "I am in earnest—I will not equivocate—I will not excuse—I will not retreat a single inch—AND I WILL BE HEARD."

1831 Southampton County, Virginia

Nat Turner leads the greatest slave rebellion in history, with some 60 whites killed and the entire South thrown into panic. Turner is captured on October 30, and hanged in Jerusalem (Virginia) 12 days later.

1831 Philadelphia

Convocation of the first Annual Convention of the People of Color at Wesleyan Church, where delegates from five states resolve to study black conditions, explore settlement possibilities in Canada, and raise money for an industrial college in New Haven. Delegates oppose the American Colonization Society and recommend annual meetings.

1832 Boston

The New England Anti-Slavery Society is established by 12 whites at the African Baptist Church on Boston's Beacon Hill.

1833 Philadelphia

Negro and white abolitionists organize the American Anti-Slavery Society.

1833 Canterbury, Connecticut

Prudence Crandall, a white liberal, is arrested for conducting an academy for Negro girls.

1833 Ohio

Founding in Ohio of Oberlin College, integrated from the outset and a leader in the abolitionist cause. By the time the Civil War erupts, Negroes constitute fully one-third of Oberlin's students.

1834 Abbeville, South Carolina

Birth of Henry McNeal Turner, writer and clergyman who serves as an army chaplain during the Civil War and goes on to become one of the most ardent spokesmen for the repatriation of Negroes in Africa. Turner promotes the cause of exodus by frequent travels to West Africa, where he introduces the Methodist religion.

1834 British Empire

Slavery is abolished in the British Empire.

1834 South Carolina

South Carolina enacts a law prohibiting the teaching of free Negro or slave children.

1837 Alton, Illinois

Elijah P. Lovejoy is murdered by a mob in Alton after refusing to stop publishing anti-slavery material.

1838 New York City

The first Negro periodical—*Mirror of Liberty*—is published by David Ruggles, a Negro abolitionist.

1839 Warsaw, New York

Founding of the first anti-slavery political organization, the Liberty Party, with Negro abolitionists Samuel Ringgold Ward and Henry Highland Garnet among its leading supporters.

1839 Montauk, Long Island

The slave ship *Amistad* is brought into Montauk by a group of Africans who have revolted against their captors. The young African leader Cinque and his followers are defended before the Supreme Court by former President John Quincy Adams, and are awarded their freedom.

1839 Washington, D.C.

The State Department rejects a Negro's application for a passport on the grounds that Negroes are not citizens.

1840 Indiana

The state forbids racial intermarriages and sets fines of $1,000-$5,000 and prison terms of 10-20 years from violators. Clerks who issue licenses and ministers who perform ceremonies are also implicated.

1841 Hampton, Virginia

Slaves revolt on the vessel *Creole* en route from Hampton, Virginia to New Orleans. Overpowering the crew and

Captain Ferrer is slain aboard the slave ship Amistad *off the Cuban coast in July 1839.*

sailing the ship to the Bahamas, the slaves are granted asylum and freedom.

1841 Massachusetts

Frederick Douglass begins his career as a lecturer with the Massachusetts Anti-Slavery Society.

1842 Boston

The capture of George Latimore in Boston precipitates the first of several famous fugitive slave cases straining North-South relations. Latimore is later purchased from his master by Boston abolitionists.

1843 Buffalo, New York

Henry Highland Garnet calls for a slave revolt and general strike while addressing the National Convention of Colored Men.

1843 Buffalo

Garnet, Samuel R. Ward and Charles B. Ray participate in the Liberty Party convention—thus becoming the first Negroes to take part in a national political gathering.

1843 New York City

Sojourner Truth takes to the platform as an anti-slavery lecturer.

1844 Philadelphia

Birth of Richard Greener, the first Negro to receive a degree from Harvard (1870). Active as a teacher and editor, Greener is admitted to the South Carolina bar in 1876, and becomes dean of Howard's Law School three years later.

1844 California

Jim Beckwourth discovers a pass through the Sierra Nevadas to California and the Pacific Ocean.

1845 Worcester, Massachusetts

Macon B. Allen becomes the first Negro formally admitted to the bar in the United States.

1846 New York

Abolitionist Gerritt Smith's plan to parcel up thousands of acres of his land in New York fails to attract prospective Negro farmers. Lack of capital among Negroes and the infertility of the land itself combine to doom the project.

1847 St. Louis, Missouri

Dred Scott first files suit for his freedom in the Circuit Court of St. Louis.

1847 Rochester, New York

Frederick Douglass publishes the first issue of his abolitionist newspaper, *The North Star*.

1848 Buffalo

The convention of the Free Soil Party

is attended by a number of Negro abolitionists.

1849 Maryland

Harriet Tubman, soon to be a conductor on the "Underground Railroad," escapes from slavery in Maryland. (Miss Tubman later returns to the South no less than 19 times, and helps transport more than 300 slaves to freedom.)

1849 Boston

Benjamin Roberts files the first school integration suit on behalf of his daughter. The Massachusetts Supreme Court rejects the suit, and establishes a "separate but equal" precedent.

1850 Washington, D.C.

The Compromise of 1850 strengthens the 1793 Fugitive Slave Act. Federal officers are now offered a fee for the slaves they apprehend.

1850 New York

Samuel R. Ward becomes president of the American League of Colored Laborers, a prospective union of skilled black workers who will develop black craftsmen and encourage black-owned business.

1852 Rochester

Frederick Douglass delivers his scathing "What to the Slave is the Fourth of July?" oration—". . . your celebration a sham; your boasted liberty an unholy license; your national greatness, swelling vanity; . . ."

1852 Boston

Publication of the first edition of Harriet Beecher Stowe's controversial work, *Uncle Tom's Cabin*.

1852 Cincinnati

Some 200 of the 3500 Cincinnati Negroes are prosperous property owners whose aggregate worth is $500,000 and who pay real estate taxes on their accumulated wealth.

The Fugitive Slave Law, part of the Compromise of 1850, was more strenuously enforced than its predecessor—the Fugitive Slave Act of 1793.

WORDS
composed and respectfully dedicated, in token of confident esteem to
FREDERICK DOUGLASS
A Graduate from the
"PECULIAR INSTITUTION"
For his fearless advocacy, signal ability and wonderful success in behalf of
HIS BROTHERS IN BONDS.
(and to the FUGITIVES FROM SLAVERY in the)
FREE STATES & CANADAS.
by their friend
JESSE HUTCHINSON JUN^R.

BOSTON, Published by HENRY PRENTISS 33 Court St.

Entered according to act of congress in the year 1845 by Henry Prentiss in the clerks office of the district court of Massachusetts

1853 London

William Wells Brown publishes *Clotel,* the first novel written by an American Negro.

1854 Oxford, Pennsylvania

Lincoln University, the first Negro college, is founded as Ashmum Institute.

1854 Boston

Anthony Burns, a fugitive slave, is arrested and escorted through the streets of Boston prior to being returned to his master, who refuses an offer of $1,200 made by Boston citizens attempting to purchase his freedom.

1854 Washington, D.C.

The Kansas-Nebraska Act admits the territories of Kansas and Nebraska to the Union without slavery restrictions, in direct contradiction to the provisions of the Missouri Compromise.

1854 Paris, France

James Augustine Healy, later the first American Negro Roman Catholic bishop, is ordained a priest in Notre Dame Cathedral.

1855 Ohio

John Mercer Langston is elected clerk of Brownhelm township, Lorain County, Ohio, the first Negro to win elective office in the history of the United States.

1856 Ohio

Wilberforce University is founded by the Methodist Episcopal Church.

1856 Washington, D.C.

Senator Summer of Massachusetts is severely beaten on the Senate floor by a racist member of the House, Representative Brooks of South Carolina. Summer is in the midst of attacking slaveowners and those who favor pro-slavery legislation.

John Brown on his way to the gallows.

A group of slaves listens attentively as a Union soldier reads the text of the Emancipation Proclamation.

1857 Washington, D.C.

The Dred Scott decision handed down by the U.S. Supreme Court opens federal territory to slavery and denies citizenship rights to American Negroes. (Scott is later freed by his new owner.)

1858 Chatham, Canada

Twelve whites and 34 Negroes attend John Brown's anti-slavery convention.

1859 Harpers Ferry

John Brown and his band (13 whites, five Negroes) attack Harpers Ferry. Two of the Negroes are killed; two are captured, and one escapes. (Brown is later hanged at Charles Town, West Virginia.)

1860 Washington, D.C.

Abraham Lincoln is elected president.

1861 The United States of America

Civil War—with slavery one of the major issues—threatens to dissolve the Union.

1861 Washington, D.C.

The Secretary of the Navy authorizes the enlistment of Negro slaves in this branch of service.

1862 New York

Formation of the National Freedmen's Relief Association, one of many groups dedicated to assist the Negro slave in making the transition to freedom. Groups in Philadelphia, Cincinnati and Chicago are eventually consolidated as the American Freedmen's Aid Commission.

1862 Washington, D.C.

President Lincoln proposes a plan for gradual, compensated emancipation.

1862 Charleston, South Carolina

Negro pilot Robert Smalls, later a Reconstruction Congressman, sails the *Planter,* a Confederate steamer, out of Charleston harbor, and turns the ship over to Union forces as war booty.

Robert Smalls and the captured gunboat Planter.

1862 Washington, D.C.

Congress authorizes the enlistment of Negroes for military service.

1863 Washington, D.C.

President Lincoln issues the Emancipation Proclamation.

1865 Washington, D.C.

John Rock becomes the first Negro admitted to practice before the Supreme Court.

1865 Washington, D.C.

Congress ratifies the 13th Amendment, and establishes the Freedmen's Bureau.

1865 Washington, D.C.

Death of Abraham Lincoln.

1865 Mississippi

Passage of the "Black Codes."

1865 Montgomery, Alabama

Jefferson Davis authorizes the Confederacy to fill its military quota by enlisting Negroes in numbers not to exceed 25% of the able-bodied slave population. The measure comes one month before Appomattox, and is too late to have any material impact on the outcome of the war.

1866 Massachusetts

Edward G. Walker and Charles L. Mitchell are elected to the Massachusetts House of Representatives, thus becoming the first Negroes to serve in a legislative assembly in the United States.

1866 Washington, D.C.

A bill is introduced in the District to provide for Negro suffrage. White voters are asked to indicate their sentiments in a referendum. Over 6500 vote against extension of the franchise to blacks; only 35 favor it.

1866 Tennessee

Opening of Fisk University in Nashville.

1866 Washington, D.C.

Passage of the Civil Rights Bill of 1866 despite President Andrew Johnson's veto.

1867 Atlanta, Georgia
Washington, D.C.

Opening of Morehouse College and Howard University, respectively.

1867 Washington, D.C.

Congress passes the First Reconstruction Act, providing for military rule in the South, pending the reorganization of state governments loyal to the Union.

1868 Washington, D.C.

Ratification of the 14th Amendment which establishes the concept of "equal protection" for all citizens under the laws of the U.S. Constitution.

1868 Louisiana

Ex-slave Oscar J. Dunn becomes lieutenant governor of Louisiana—at that time the highest elective office ever held by an American Negro.

1868 Louisiana

Readmission of Louisiana's Senator and Representatives to the U.S. government. The move follows the systematic terror initiated by the Ku Klux Klan against members of the Republican Party and emancipated blacks. Killings, lynchings and beatings are recorded in several Louisiana parishes.

1869 Haiti

Ebenezer Don Carlos Bassett, believed to be the first Negro to receive an appointment in the diplomatic service, becomes Minister to Haiti.

1870 Washington, D.C.

Joseph H. Rainey is seated as the first Negro in the House of Representatives.

1870 Washington, D.C.

Hiram Revels, the first Negro senator in the history of the U.S., delivers his first speech before the Senate on March 16—". . . I maintain that the past record of my race is a true index of the feelings which today animate them. . . . They aim not to elevate themselves by sacrificing one single interest of their white fellow-citizens."

1870 Washington, D.C.

Ratification of the 15th Amendment, guaranteeing to *all* citizens the right to vote.

1871 Washington, D.C.

Congress enacts the "Ku Klux Klan" Act designed to enforce the provisions of the 14th Amendment.

1871 Nashville

The renowned Fisk Jubilee Singers go on an international tour to raise money for the college and to expose Negro spirituals to wider and ever-growing audiences.

1872 Washington, D.C.

Charlotte E. Ray becomes the first Negro woman to graduate from a university law school (Howard) in the United States.

1872 Louisiana

P. B. S. Pinchback becomes acting governor of the state upon the impeachment of the incumbent.

1874 Washington, D.C.

Rev. Patrick F. Healy, S.J., is named president of Georgetown, the oldest Catholic university in the United States.

1875 Washington, D.C.

Congress passes the Civil Rights Bill of 1875, prohibiting discrimination in such public accommodations as hotels, theatres and amusement parks. A key piece of legislation in the post-Civil War era, it seeks to "mete out equal and exact justice to all, of whatever nativity, race, color, or persuasions, religious or political, . . ."

1876 Washington, D.C.

The Supreme Court, in *U.S.* v. *Cruikshank*, declares that the 14th Amendment provides Negroes with equal protection under the law, but does not add anything "to the rights which one citizen has under the Constitution against another." The Court rules that "the right of suffrage is not a necessary attribute of national citizenship."

1881 Washington, D.C.

Ex-senator Blanche K. Bruce is appointed Register of the Treasury after refusing two other minor federal appointments, one a ministerial post in Brazil.

1881 Tennessee

Tennessee passes a "Jim Crow" railroad law which sets a trend soon taken up by Florida (1887); Mississippi (1888); Texas (1889); Louisiana (1890), and a host of other Southern and Border states.

1881 Tuskegee, Alabama

Booker T. Washington opens Tuskegee Institute.

1883 Lynn, Massachusetts

The shoe-lasting machine of Jan Matzeliger, a Negro from Dutch Guiana, so revolutionizes the industry that Lynn becomes the "shoe-capital of the world."

1883 Washington, D.C.

The Supreme Court declares the Civil Rights Act of 1875 unconstitutional.

1884 Washington, D.C.

Former Negro Reconstruction Congressman John Roy Lynch is elected temporary chairman of the Republican convention—the first Negro to preside over a national political gathering.

1886 Salisbury, North Carolina

The founding of Livingstone College.

1888 Richmond Washington, D.C.

Founding of two Negro banks—The Savings Bank of the Grand Fountain United Order of True Reformers in Virginia and the Capital Savings Bank in the nation's capital.

1889 Haiti

Frederick Douglass is appointed United States Minister to Haiti.

1890 Mississippi

The Mississippi Constitutional Convention begins the systematic exclusion of Negroes from the political arena in the South by adopting literacy and other complex "understanding" tests as prerequisites to voting. Seven other Southern states follow suit by 1910.

1891 Chicago, Illinois

The incorporation of Provident Hospital —with the first training school for Negro nurses in the United States.

1892 St. Louis

Georgia Populists strive to unite poor black and white farmers in the South who, according to gubernatorial candidate Tom Watson, are kept apart by landed interests. Watson argues that wealthy Southerners perpetuate racial antagonisms so that poor whites and their black counterparts will resent each other, rather than cooperate for mutually advantageous ends.

1895 Atlanta, Georgia

Booker T. Washington delivers his famous "Atlanta Compromise" address at the Cotton Exposition—"To those of my race who depend on bettering their condition in a foreign land, or who underestimate the importance of cultivating friendly relations with the Southern white man . . . I would say: 'Cast down your bucket where you are . . .'"

1896 Washington, D.C.

The Supreme Court in the *Plessy* v. *Ferguson* decision upholds the doctrine of "separate but equal"—paving the way for the segregation of Negroes in all walks of life.

1898 Santiago, Cuba

Four Negro regiments in the regular army compile an outstanding combat record in and around Santiago during the Spanish-American War.

A Negro cavalry unit supports the Rough Rider attack near Santiago, Cuba in 1898.

This "Silent Protest Parade" was held in New York City by Negroes demonstrating against lynchings.

1898 Louisiana

Addition of a "grandfather clause" to the State Constitution of Louisiana enables poor whites to qualify for the franchise, even as it effectively curtails black registration. In 1896, there were over 130,000 black voters on the Louisiana rolls; four years later, the number is reduced to barely 5,000.

1900 London

W. E. B. DuBois attends the conference of the African and New World Intellectuals, where he delivers an address incorporating his famous dictum: "The problem of the 20th century is the problem of the color line." DuBois also attends the first Pan-African Congress, an international body of concerned African nations protesting Western imperialism and promoting the concept of self-government among colonized peoples.

1900 Boston

Founding of the National Negro Business League.

1901 Washington, D.C.

Congressman George White delivers his farewell address in the House of Representatives "in behalf of an outraged, heart-broken, bruised, and bleeding, but God-fearing people, faithful, industrious, loyal people—rising people, full of potential force."

1904 Atlanta

Financier Andrew Carnegie brings together a parcel of prominent Negro leaders, including Booker T. Washington, and W. E. B. DuBois, who discuss the advancement of "the Interests of the Negro Race." The personal and ideological clash between the two men is evident at the meeting, though there is agreement that the group should press for "absolute civil, political, and public equality." The group shows little fire in advancing familiar proposals for black self-help.

1905 Buffalo

Militant Negro intellectuals from 14 states organize the Niagara Movement, (a forerunner of the NAACP) in opposition to the conciliatory policies of Booker T. Washington, as expressed in his 1895 Atlanta speech. Delegates to the convention demand the abolition of all distinctions based on race.

1908 Washington, D.C.

The first Negro sorority, Alpha Kappa Alpha, is founded at Howard University.

1909 New York City

The National Association for the Advancement of Colored People (NAACP) is founded in New York on the 100th anniversary of Lincoln's birth. The signers of the original charter of incorporation include Jane Addams, John Dewey, Dr. W. E. B. DuBois, William Dean Howells, and Lincoln Steffens.

1909 North Pole

Matthew Henson, a Negro member of Admiral Peary's expedition, places the flag of the United States at the North Pole.

1910 New York City

Founding of the National Urban League, with Eugene Kinckle Jones as its first executive secretary.

1910 New York

The first number of *Crisis* Magazine, edited by W. E. B. DuBois, appears. Only 1,000 copies are in print. Before the end of the decade, circulation of the magazine has increased one hundred fold. Among the articles in the first number is one penned by DuBois in which he maintains that individuals should be free to marry whomever they choose. The article concedes, however, that such an enlightened policy would cause a social calamity in the U.S.

1913 Washington, D.C.

President Woodrow Wilson refuses to appoint a National Race Commission to study the social and economic status of Negroes, rejecting a proposal sponsored by Oswald Garrison Villard. The President also appoints white foreign service officers to Haiti and Santo Domingo, among the few consular posts open to Negroes by custom and practice.

1914 New York City

Joel E. Spingarn of the NAACP institutes the Spingarn awards, to be given annually to American Negroes for unique and distinguished achievement.

1915 Southern states

Dr. Carter G. Woodson establishes the Association for the Study of Negro Life and History, and also launches the *Journal of Negro History*, with himself as its editor.

1915 Alabama

Revival of the Ku Klux Klan in the South, beginning in Alabama and spreading to Oklahoma, California, Oregon, Indiana, and Ohio. (Membership in the organization reaches four million in the 1920's.)

1915 Southern states

Beginning of the "Great Migration" during which two million Southern Negroes move to industrial centers in the North.

1915 Washington, D.C.

U.S. Supreme Court in *Guinn* v. *United States* declares the "grandfather clause" in the Oklahoma constitution unconstitutional.

1917 New York City

Some 10,000 Negroes parade down Fifth Avenue in protest against lynchings in the South. The marchers include NAACP leaders W. E. B. DuBois and James Weldon Johnson.

1917 New York

Joel Spingarn presses the War Department to establish an officers' training camp for Negroes, thus alienating many of his NAACP colleagues who feel that such a camp only perpetuates segregation and, in effect, gives substance to the notion of black inferiority. Others concede that the move is prudent, since it is the only way for black officers to be trained. The organization ultimately puts itself on record as being in favor of separate camps.

1919 Atlantic City

Samuel Gompers of the AFL delivers an address to the federation's annual conference in which he vows to remove "every class and race distinction" from the movement, and pledges himself to the total abolition of all discrimination in union membership. Gompers professes to see a new era in the struggle for Negro rights "as well as an advance in the history of political and economic liberty in America."

1919 Paris

W. E. B. DuBois organizes the first Pan-African Congress at the Grand Hotel—"The Natives of Africa must have the right to participate in the government as fast as their development permits . . ."

1920 New York City

Marcus Garvey opens the national convention of the Universal Negro Improvement Association (UNIA) at Liberty Hall in Harlem. The UNIA, a pioneer black nationalist group, reaches the peak of its influence from 1920 to 1921.

1922 Washington, D.C.

Republican Senators vote to abandon the Dyer Anti-Lynching Bill which provides severe penalties and fines for "any state or municipal officer" convicted of negligence in affording protection to individuals in custody who are attacked by a mob bent on lynching, torture, or physical intimidation. The Bill had also provided for compensation to the families of victims.

1924 New York

New York's Emmanuel Cellar introduces legislation to provide for the formation of a blue-ribbon panel to study the racial question. The idea is met with disdain from the black press, particularly the Chicago *Defender* which editorializes: "We have been commissioned to death . . . We have too many studies and reports already." The *Defender* asserts that Negroes need only to look after their own interests through the creation of a strong party vehicle and potent political leadership in the halls of Congress.

1926 Washington, D.C.

Twenty-three Negroes are lynched the very same year President Coolidge tells Congress that the country must provide "for the amelioration of race prejudice and the extension to all elements of equal opportunity and equal protection under the laws, which are guaranteed by the Constitution."

1926 New York

Controversy rages in the black intelligentsia pursuant to the publication of *Nigger Heaven* by white writer Carl van Vechten. The book glamorizes the free-wheeling style of Harlem life amid the general contention that blacks are less ashamed of sex and more morally honest than whites. DuBois finds the assumptions deplorable; James Weldon Johnson, on the other hand, believes the treatment is neither scandalous nor insulting.

1926 Washington, D.C.

Negro History Week is introduced by Dr. Carter G. Woodson and the Association for the Study of Negro Life and History.

1927 Washington, D.C.

The U.S. Supreme Court strikes down the Texas law barring Negroes from voting in the "white primary" (*Nixon v. Herndon*).

1928 Illinois

The election of Oscar De Priest—the first Negro Congressman from a Northern state.

1929 New York

Chicago's Oscar De Priest tells an audience of 2,500 gathered at a rally at Harlem's Abyssinian Baptist Church that Negroes will never make substantial progress until they elect political leaders whose fortunes are dependent on their ability to fight for black interests in Congress. De Priest concludes: ". . . no one can really lead you but one who has been Jim Crowed as you have."

1930 Washington, D.C.

The NAACP mounts a strong lobby against Senate confirmation of the Supreme Court nomination of John H. Parker, one-time self-admitted opponent of the franchise for Negroes. The organization not only blocks the confirmation of Parker, but also helps unseat three of the Senators who voted for him in later Congressional elections.

1933 Washington, D.C.

At the height of the Depression, black gospel preacher Solomon Lightfoot Michaux founds the Good Neighbor League, a private philanthropic group that feeds thousands of indigent persons at its Happy New Cafe. Michaux endorses FDR for the presidency over incumbent Herbert Hoover, thus confirming the popular black shift away from the Republican party, first signalled by the election of Congressman De Priest in Chicago.

1934 Chicago

Arthur Mitchell becomes the first Negro Democrat of the 20th century to be elected to Congress.

1935 New York City

Founding by Mary McLeod Bethune of the National Council of Negro Women.

1935 Washington, D.C.

Supreme Court Justice Roberts upholds the Texas law that prevents Negroes from voting in the Texas Democratic primary. The decision comes as a setback to the NAACP, which has waged several effective legal battles to equalize the ballot potential of the Negro voter.

1936 Berlin, Germany

Jesse Owens wins four gold medals in the 1936 Olympics.

1937 Virgin Islands

William H. Hastie is confirmed as judge of the Federal District Court in the Virgin Islands—thereby becoming the first Negro to serve as a federal judge in the history of the United States.

1937 Chicago

Joe Louis becomes heavyweight champion of the world, defeating Jim Braddock for the title.

1938 Pennsylvania

Crystal Bird Fauset of Philadelphia, the first Negro woman state legislator, is elected to the Pennsylvania House of Representatives.

1939 Washington, D.C.

Marian Anderson, denied the use of Constitution Hall by the Daughters of the American Revolution, sings on Easter Sunday before 75,000 people assembled at the Lincoln Memorial.

1939 New York City

Jane Bolin is appointed judge of the Court of Domestic Relations in New York City—thus becoming the first Negro woman judge in the United States.

1939 New York

Incorporation of the NAACP Legal Defense and Educational Fund.

1939 Miami, Florida

Intimidation and cross-burnings by the Ku Klux Klan in the black ghetto of Miami fail to discourage most of the city's registered Negroes from appearing at the polls. The Klan parades with effigies of Negroes who will allegedly be slain for daring to vote.

1940 New York

Publication of *Native Son* by Richard Wright.

1940 Virginia

The Virginia legislature chooses "Carry Me Back to Ole Virginny," written by Negro composer James A. Bland, as the official state song.

1940 Washington, D.C.

Appointment of Benjamin O. Davis, Sr. as the first Negro general in the history of the U.S. Armed Forces.

1940 Washington, D.C.

FDR announces that black strength in the armed forces will be proportionate to Negro population totals. Several branches of the military service and several occupational specialties are to be opened to Negroes, but Roosevelt rules out troop integration because it will be "destructive to morale and detrimental to . . . preparation for national defense."

1941 Washington, D.C.

Dr. Robert Weaver is appointed director of the government office charged with integrating Negroes into the National Defense program.

1941 Washington, D.C.

The Supreme Court—in a case brought by U.S. Congressman Arthur Mitchell—rules that separate facilities in railroad travel must be *substantially* equal.

1941 Washington, D.C.

Negro threat to stage massive protest march on nation's capital results in the issuance of Executive Order 8802, prohibiting discrimination in the defense establishment. "There shall be no discrimination in the employment of workers in defense industries or Government because of race, creed, color, or national origin. . . ."

1941 Pearl Harbor

Dorie Miller, messman aboard the *USS Arizona,* mans a machine gun during the Pearl Harbor attack; downs four enemy planes, and wins the Navy Cross.

1942 Chicago

William L. Dawson—now the senior Negro Congressman in the United States—is first elected to Congress.

1942 Washington, D.C.

The Justice Department threatens to file suit against a number of Negro newspapers which it believes are guilty of systematic denunciation of Washington racial policies in the Armed Services. When the Department labels such criticism seditious, the NAACP steps in to suggest guidelines which will satisfy the Justice

Benjamin O. Davis, Sr., the first black general, as he looked at the time of his appointment.

Department. The clear alternative is suppression of the black press should it remain unruly.

1942 Chicago

Founding of the Congress of Racial Equality (CORE), a civil rights group dedicated to a direct-action, non-violent program.

1944 New York City

Election of Adam Clayton Powell, Jr., the first Negro Congressman from the East.

1945 Kentucky

Benjamin O. Davis, Jr. is named commander of Godman Field.

1945 New York

The first state Fair Employment Practices Commission (FEPC) is established in New York.

1947 Atlanta

The Southern Regional Council releases figures which demonstrate that only 12% (c. 600,000) of the Negroes in the Deep South are qualified to vote. In the states of Louisiana, Alabama, and Mississippi, the figures are approximately 3%. In Tennessee, more than one in four adult Negroes is entitled to exercise the franchise.

1947 Washington, D.C.

The Truman committee on civil rights formally condemns racial injustice in America in the widely quoted report "To Secure These Rights."

1947 Tuskegee, Alabama

Tuskegee statistics indicate that 3,426 Negroes have been lynched in the United States in the period 1882-1947. Of these, 1,217 were lynched in the decade 1890-1900.

1948 Washington, D.C.

Supreme Court in *Shelley* v. *Kraemer* rules that federal and state courts may not enforce restrictive covenants.

1948 Washington, D.C.

President Truman issues Executive Order 9981 directing "equality of treatment and opportunity" in the Armed Forces.

1948 New York

Ralph Bunche is confirmed by the United Nations Security Council as Acting UN mediator in Palestine.

1948 California

The California Supreme Court declares the state statute banning racial intermarriage unconstitutional.

1949 Connecticut

The state becomes the first in the Union to extend the jurisdiction of the Civil Rights Commission into the domain of public housing.

1949 Washington, D.C.

Congressman William L. Dawson becomes the first Negro to head a Congressional committee when he is named Chairman of the House Committee on Government Operations.

1950 Chicago

Gwendolyn Brooks is awarded a Pulitzer prize for poetry—the first and, to date, only Negro so honored.

1950 New York City

Edith Sampson is appointed an alternate delegate to the United Nations.

1950 Oslo, Norway

Ralph Bunche is named winner of the Nobel Peace prize.

1951 Korea

Pfc. William Thompson is awarded the Congressional Medal of Honor during the Korean War—thus becoming the first Negro since the Spanish-American War to win the nation's highest military citation.

1951 New York City

Ralph Bunche is appointed Undersecretary to the United Nations.

1952 Tuskegee

A Tuskegee report indicates that, for the first time in its 71 years of tabulation, no lynchings have occurred in the United States.

1953 New York City

Hulan Jack is sworn in as Borough President of Manhattan.

1953 District of Columbia

D.C. Commissioners order the abolition of segregation in several district agencies. The fire department is among those which escape the mandate.

1954 Washington, D.C.

President Dwight D. Eisenhower nominates J. Ernest Wilkins of Chicago to be Assistant Secretary of Labor.

1954 Washington, D.C.

The U. S. Department of Defense releases summer figures which indicate that Negro units no longer exist in the Armed Services. Schools are shown to be operating under new guidelines of desegregation which only a few diehards resist. DOD efficiency in combating reactionary elements draws the plaudits of several organizations and liberal observers.

Ralph Bunche (l.), shown here with Roy Wilkins of the NAACP.

A REVIEW OF THE CIVIL RIGHTS REVOLUTION: 1954–1964

A major turning point in the course of Negro history in the United States was reached when the Supreme Court in *Brown* v. *Board of Education* (May 17, 1954) ruled that racial segregation in the public schools of the nation was unconstitutional. This great legal victory signaled for the Negro an unprecedented opportunity to begin anew the painstaking process of what has always been for him a distant goal: total integration into the cultural fabric of the United States. Since the Supreme Court decision, the Negro himself has added a new dimension to the civil rights picture in the United States: his own preparedness to campaign actively and aggressively for the rights granted him by the courts. This new militancy is at the heart of what is called the civil rights revolution. It is the thread which runs through the events reviewed here—testifying to the transition of the Negro from a more passive to a more active role in the struggle for first-class citizenship.

Brown v. Board of Education—(1954)

When the Supreme Court in 1954 came to address itself to the momentous problem of school segregation in the United States, it was dealing with a practice which was so solidly entrenched that fully 40% of the country's school enrollment was affected by it. (No less than 17 Southern and Border states and the District of Columbia actually *required* segregation, while three others exercised a local option to permit it in certain areas.)

The *Brown* v. *Board of Education* case was one of five presented to the Supreme Court in the fall of 1952, the others having originated in Delaware, South Carolina, Virginia and the District of Columbia. The Court heard the cases and then, at the end of the June term, scheduled them for reargument the following October.

In the interim, however, Chief Justice Fred Vinson died, necessitating the appointment of a successor to occupy this all-important post. Former California governor Earl Warren, named to head the High Court, was unquestionably instrumental in clarifying the issue as to whether segregation itself denied the equal protection of the laws.

On May 17, 1954, he delivered the opinion of the Court declaring that segregation in the public schools was unconstitutional, the inconclusive language of the 14th Amendment notwithstanding. The opinion was unanimous; not even a separate concurrence was written.

"We conclude," Warren said, "that in the field of public education the doctrine of 'separate but equal' (Ed. Note: the dictum of the *Plessy* v. *Ferguson* decision of 1896) has no place. Separate educational facilities are inherenty unequal."

The Montgomery Bus Boycott—(1955-1956)

The Montgomery bus boycott was a 382-day-long protest movement in which "direct action" was effectively used for the first time in the South with the primary objective of dramatizing the effects of racial discrimination on a Negro community—in this case, one in Alabama.

The journalist Louis Lomax dates the Negro revolt "from the moment" Mrs. Rosa Parks refused to "move to the rear" of the Cleveland Avenue bus in downtown Montgomery, Alabama on December 1, 1955. Mrs. Parks was thought by many to be a tool of the local NAACP and even accused in some quarters of being a Communist agent. In point of fact, she turned out to be an individual Negro who had simply decided to contest the long-standing Jim Crow ordinance which required Negroes to occupy seats in the rear, and thus reserved seats in the front for whites only.

The arrest of Mrs. Parks was a "last straw" to the Negro community which, within 24 hours, had decided to call a bus boycott, and keep some 17,000 Negroes from riding this public conveyance indefinitely. The task of organizing the boycott fell to Martin Luther King, Jr., then an unheralded 27-year-old clergyman with little experience in the techniques of mass protest. Dr. King coordinated the activities of the boycotters by forming the Montgomery Improvement Association (MIA),

Negroes and whites board a public transit bus in Montgomery after the Supreme Court ruling against Alabama's "Jim Crow" laws.

a church-oriented agency which acted as a clearinghouse and information center for all interested in supporting the boycott.

The MIA soon decided to expand its base of operations and conduct an entire campaign around the central notion of improving the Negro's economic lot at the hands of municipal government. Negroes sought a larger share in the job pool for bus drivers, especially in areas where they formed a substantial or commanding portion of the local population. For their part, local authorities were outraged by such a vigorous show of determined resistance from Negro citizens, and sued immediately to have the boycott declared illegal. Arrest and stalemate ensued until December 13, 1956, at which time the U.S. Supreme Court ruled that Alabama laws requiring segregated seating on public conveyances were unconstitutional. Terrorists sought for a time to undermine the court order, but moderates on both sides ultimately prevailed, and bus service was restored for all on an integrated basis.

The bus boycott had numerous concrete results, and several important psychological ones. For one thing, it established Martin Luther King, Jr. as a new voice in the ranks of Negro leadership; for another, it opened the eyes of the urban Negro to the strength he could command when united behind a coordinated program for the assertion of his rights as a citizen. What happened in Montgomery proved to be symptomatic of what was soon to follow in several other cities across the South.

Near Integration at the University of Alabama: Autherine Lucy—(1956)

The Autherine Lucy debacle at the University of Alabama in 1956 was the first major instance of a federal-state clash over the issue of school segregation. In February of that year, Miss Lucy, a 26-year-old library science student, was admitted to the university by virtue of a federal court order, and then barred by university officials in the wake of an outbreak of mob violence. Miss Lucy then filed contempt-of-court proceedings against the trustees and president of the school; against the Dean of Women for

barring her from the dining halls and dormitories, and against four other men (none connected with the university) for participating in the riots. Alabama authorities eventually prevailed in their decision to expel Miss Lucy for making "outrageous" charges against them in her suit for reinstatement. (Alabama remained segregated until 1963, at which time two Negro students gained admission to the school.)

Southern Congressmen Resist the Supreme Court—(1956)

On March 11, 1956, 96 Southern Congressmen drafted a proclamation in which they challenged the right of the Supreme Court to encroach upon the educational systems prevalent in their states. Citing the *Plessy* v. *Ferguson* decision of 1896, and reiterating that the 14th Amendment made no express mention of education, this legislative bloc served notice of its intention to "use all lawful means to bring about a reversal of this decision which is contrary to the Constitution and to prevent the use of force in its implementation."

The Prayer Pilgrimage—(1957)

The Prayer Pilgrimage to Washington, D.C.—the first large-scale Negro demonstration in the nation's capital in the postwar era—took place on May 17, 1957, the third anniversary of the Supreme Court decision outlawing segregation in the public schools. The pilgrimage was organized in order to dramatize to the President, to Congress and to the nation's major political parties the great need for *implementing* the Court's decision. It was also designed to demonstrate Negro unity; to protest violence against "Freedom Fighters" in the South, and to urge the passage of pending civil rights legislation (The Civil Rights Act of 1957).

A crowd of 15,000 from more than 30 states assembled on the steps of the Lincoln Memorial, where it heard a series of orations, Scripture readings, and speeches, the most important of which was delivered by the Rev. Martin Luther King, Jr., already well on the road to becoming the most influential Negro leader of the decade.

The Little Rock Crisis—(1957)

The intransigence of the South against the "law of the land" was amply demonstrated in the Little Rock case of 1957 involving nine children who sought to integrate Central High School in the state capital. When Governor Orval Faubus summoned National Guardsmen to turn away the Negro pupils, he maintained that they were acting "not as segregationists or integrationists but as soldiers."

At Little Rock, however, a direct challenge was posed to the federal government which had already approved a desegregation plan submitted by the local school board. When the Negro students were forced to withdraw from the premises of the school—in direct defiance of a federal district court order—President Eisenhower, for the first time since Reconstruction, sent in federal troops to protect the rights of the beleaguered students. Some 1,000 paratroopers descended on Little Rock, and were joined by 10,000 National Guardsmen under the command of Major General Edwin A. Walker.

The nine children entered Central High School on the morning of September 25 with an escort of paratroopers. The soldiers remained on call for the entire school year, inasmuch as Governor Faubus refused to assume the responsibility for maintaining order in the community. Later, Faubus and the forces of segregation failed to get a requested 2½-year postponement of the integration timetable set up for the school.

Little Rock high schools were then closed for the 1958-1959 school term but, when the school-closing laws were declared unconstitutional by a federal court, the doors of Central High School swung open once again for members of all races.

The Sit-in Movement—(1960)

Joseph McNeil, Ezell Blair, Jr. and two of their classmates—four college freshmen from North Carolina A. & T.—sat down at a lunch counter in a Woolworth store on February 1, 1950 and, in so doing, launched one of the most ingenious and effective tactics of protest seen in the South during the past decade. Within three months, thousands of Negro and white students were "trained" to take their seats at lunch counters, submit to the inevitable heckling and harassment

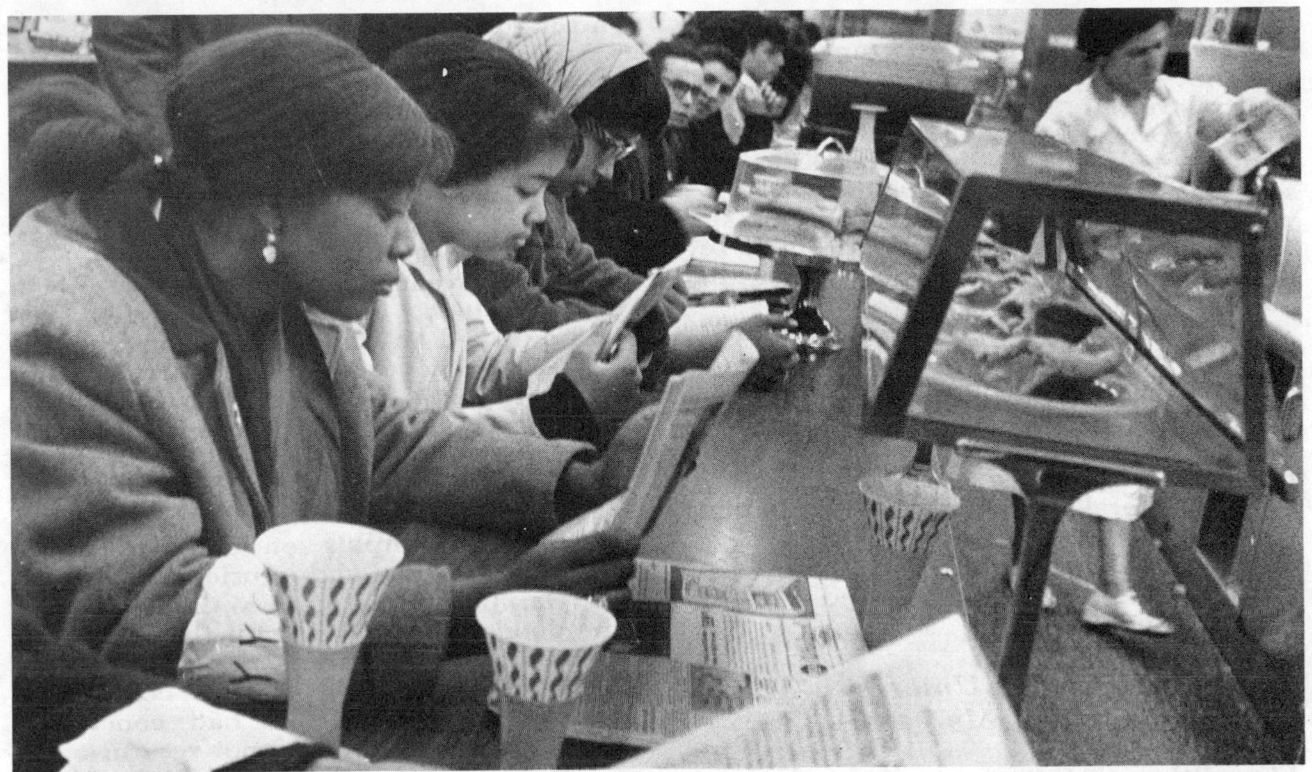

Lunch counters like this one at Woolworth's were desegregated by means of the sit-down tactic developed by young Negro college students.

that ensued; "sit tight, and refuse to fight."

Three months later, the lunch counter at the Woolworth's in Greensboro was open to the public, regardless of race. By the end of the year, hotels, movie theatres, libraries, super markets, amusement parks and a host of other similar establishments had lowered their barriers against Negroes, and begun the slow, arduous process of allowing them a greater measure of mobility.

The Freedom Rides—(1961)

The freedom rides took their cue from the sit-in demonstrations which swept the South in 1960. Beginning in the nation's capital, a group of CORE freedom riders set out for New Orleans on May 4, 1961—with stops en route in Virginia, North and South Carolina, Georgia, Alabama and Mississippi. When they reached Anniston and, later, Birmingham, they were savagely beaten, stomped, and slashed with chains, while one of their buses was stoned and burned.

Later that May, a bi-racial group left Atlanta for Montgomery, where it intended to protest bus-terminal segregation. Before federal marshals could arrive in the Alabama capital city to offer the riders protection, they were assaulted and further threatened. Attorney General Robert Kennedy quickly petitioned the Interstate Commerce Commission to outlaw segregation in all trains, buses and terminals—an order which became effective on November 1.

The order notwithstanding, a group of freedom riders in McComb, Mississippi was charged with "breach of the peace" violations when it attempted to desegregate the bus terminal—*after* the ICC ruling had ostensibly gone into effect. By December, however, the "Freedom Riders" had merged their operation with the then-budding movement to launch full-scale assaults on patterns of segregation in selected cities across the South.

The Albany Movement—(1962)

Albany, Georgia became a major civil rights battleground in the summer of 1962. It was in this city that Negro leaders attempted, for the first time, to liquidate discrimination in all public facilities —buses, libraries, parks, playgrounds, swimming pools, etc. The coordinated, city-wide campaign was sponsored by SCLC, SNCC, and elements of CORE and the NAACP.

For all its historic importance, Albany was not a noteworthy success in the civil rights struggle, despite the fact that numerous protest marches were organized, and the jails were filled. (Dr. King himself was arrested for "parading without a permit," and chose to serve out his sentence, only to be released within a few hours after an anonymous donor had paid his fine.)

City officials and police authorities slowed down the tempo of Albany by minimizing the instances in which violence was allowed to erupt. Division in the Negro leadership ranks was also a factor in taking the edge off the movement's overall momentum. At Albany, time worked in favor of the white segregationist and, as the months dragged on, the city gradually disappeared from the national limelight.

Integration at the University of Mississippi: James Meredith—(1962)

Meredith v. *Mississippi*, although not a legal citation, does serve to describe the clash between a 29-year-old Negro Air Force veteran and university authorities on the all-white campus of "Ole Miss."

In June 1962, the United States Court of Appeals for the Fifth Circuit found that Meredith's application for enrollment at the University of Mississippi had been rejected solely on racial grounds, and hence directed his admission to the school. After frantic legal maneuvers designed to keep him from enrolling, Meredith underwent a grueling 10-day ordeal during which, among other things, he was blocked in the school doorway by Mississippi governor Ross Barnett, and later prevented from entering the college administrative offices. On September 30, President John F. Kennedy federalized the Mississippi National Guard, and dispatched a detachment of U. S. Army troops to Memphis on stand-by alert. After two deaths, and injuries to scores of people, James Meredith walked through the doors of "Ole Miss" for the first time.

Having finished one semester at Mississippi, Meredith held a press conference and announced that he had concluded that "the 'Negro' should not return. . . ."

"However," he continued, "I have decided that I, J. H. Meredith, will register for the second semester."

Meredith graduated on August 18, 1963.

University of Mississippi students are stopped at the door of their dormitory by members of the National Guard during the Meredith crisis.

The Birmingham Crisis—(1963)

Birmingham, Alabama is, in the words of at least one civil rights leader, "a watershed in the Negro nonviolent revolution." It was in this city in 1963 that the plight of the Negro in the South was dramatized to the nation at large with greater impact than at any time in the previous decade.

The Negro leaders who converged on Birmingham had set for themselves a number of minimum goals, including: removal of racial restrictions in stores and restaurants; adoption of non-racial hiring practices in certain job areas; formation of a bi-racial committee to negotiate even further desegregation at a later date.

On Good Friday, April 12, Martin Luther King, Jr. and a group of ministers attempted a march into the heart of the city, but were met and arrested there by Commissioner "Bull" Connor and members of his police force. Day after day, demonstrations were followed by arrests until, on May 3, fire hoses and police dogs were called into play in a desperate effort to discourage the marchers. Federal mediators were sent in to effect a truce, and were joined in their efforts by the business community, wary of the loss in profits which would follow a sustained boycott. The boycotts, the pray-ins at the Sixteenth Street Baptist Church, and the freedom songs gradually communicated the Negro's deep sense of frustration and his explosive bent of mind.

After a temporary truce, violence again flared when the Negro ghetto was shaken with two bomb-blasts—one of which demolished the home of Reverend A. D. King, younger brother of Martin Luther King, Jr., while the other rocked the headquarters of the Negro integrationists, the A. G. Gaston Motel. The bombings only succeeded in triggering another three-hour riot, in which houses and blocks of stores were burned, police vehicles smashed, and police officers attacked.

President Kennedy alerted federal troops, whereupon city officials and law enforcement groups made another concerted effort to reach a truce which in some manner would take into appropriate account the demands of the Negro community.

With the advent of a "moderate" city administration, progress was made toward an easing of racial tensions—at least until the morning of September 15. On that Sunday, a bomb exploded in the Sixteenth Street Baptist Church during a childrens' Bible class, killing four girls ranging in age from 11 to 14, and injuring scores of other innocent children. Later that day, two other youths were slain.

From that point on, no other outbreaks of violence occurred in Birmingham, and the city was quiet. But the fuse that had been lit there spread to other large urban centers across the nation, and the battleground in the civil rights revolution once again changed its major setting —this time from the South to the urban Northern ghetto.

The Medgar Evers Murder—(1963)

Medgar Evers, 37 year-old NAACP leader, was gunned down in the doorway of his home in Jackson, Mississippi on June 13, 1963, in a manner and fashion not unlike the one in which John F. Kennedy met his death a few months later in Dallas, Texas. In the Evers case, a white Mississippian from Greenwood, Byron de la Beckwith, was arrested 11 days after the shooting, and charged with the murder. Thirteen days after that, the Beckwith case ended in a mistrial when the jury could not agree on a verdict. (It was divided 7-5 for acquittal.)

The March On Washington—(1963)

The largest single protest demonstration in the history of the United States occurred on August 28, 1963 on the occasion of the March on Washington. More than 200,000 Americans of all races, colors and creeds, and from all walks of life, converged on Washington, D.C., to stage a civil rights protest on the steps of the Lincoln Memorial.

In general, the March represented the attempt of Negro leaders to dramatize to the nation at large the scope of Negro discontent and the enormous appeal which the idea of an open, desegregated society had for millions of Americans. Moreover, the extent of the effectiveness of non-violence on a large scale had also to be tested, and it was thought that no more appropriate gesture could be found than a freedom march in which members of all groups—the church, organized labor, business, professional, and entertainment circles—could take part.

The March was essentially the work of the established civil rights groups, including the NAACP, CORE, SCLC, SNCC, and many others. A. Philip Randolph, the venerable "elder statesman" of the movement, is generally regarded as the chief architect of the march, although he credits Bayard Rustin, a Negro intellectual who had formerly worked as a field secretary with CORE, with having been "Mr. March on Washington." Rustin was the logistics expert of the march and its prime coordinator. He was, however, assisted in his endeavors by a huge braintrust of advisers and fellow strategists.

Among the principal speakers for this memorable day were: James Farmer, head of CORE; Roy Wilkins, executive secretary of the National Association for the Advancement of Colored People (NAACP); Randolph himself, and John Lewis, president of the Student Nonviolent Coordinating Committee. (Lewis, originally intending to deliver a vitriolic address, was ultimately persuaded to temper his remarks to suit the occasion.)

The most compelling and spellbinding oration of the afternoon, however, was delivered by Martin Luther King, Jr. of the Southern Christian Leadership Conference (SCLC).

Reactions to the March were varied. Some felt that its chief effect was to weaken the aims of the protest movement by sapping the energies of its participants in a gesture which, in the final analysis, could only have had dramatic impact, rather than any practical advantage. Others praised the March in long-range terms as a valuable tool for persuading "waverers" to commit themselves more fully to the civil rights struggle.

Generally speaking, the March was greeted with enthusiasm in the foreign press, where it was variously praised for its "perfect discipline," and for the fact that it was "the greatest demonstration in support of racial equality the world has ever seen."

BAYARD RUSTIN: CHIEF ORGANIZER OF THE MARCH

Negro intellectual Bayard Rustin was the organizing genius behind the March on Washington. A native of Pennsylvania, Rustin studied abroad, and began participating in demonstrations as early as 1947. During the 1940's, he also served as field secretary for the Congress of Racial Equality (CORE) and, from 1955 to 1960, worked as an advisor to Dr. Martin Luther King, Jr. Active in pacifist causes as well, Rustin is executive secretary of the War Resisters League.

A resident of New York City, Rustin does considerable travelling in conjunction with his attempts to enlist the support of various liberal and labor-union groups in the fight for civil rights.

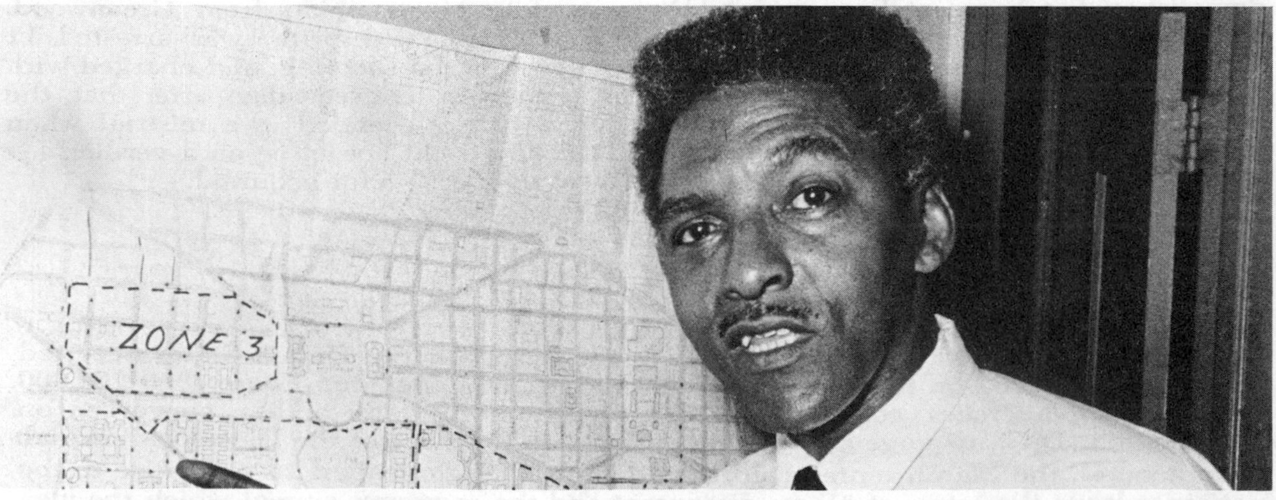

Bayard Rustin plots strategy in his New York office.

Three Civil Rights Martyrs—(1964)

The bodies of Michael Schwerner, 24; Andrew Goodman, 20; and James E. Chaney, 21—three civil rights workers who were reported missing in Mississippi on the night of June 21, 1964—were found buried near Philadelphia, Mississippi on August 4 of that year.

The crime, one of the most brutal in the nation's history, went unpunished. Twenty-one white men, including the sheriff and deputy sheriff of Neshoba County, Mississippi, were arrested on federal charges of conspiracy to violate the Civil Rights Code and violation of an 1870 statute providing for a maximum penalty of 10 years in prison and up to a $5,000 fine. (They could not be indicted for murder since murder is not a federal crime.)

On Sunday, October 25, 1964, a memorial tribute to the three slain workers was staged at Carnegie Hall in New York City, and the Medgar W. Evers Award was presented posthumously by A. Philip Randolph to the parents of Michael Schwerner, Andrew Goodman and James Chaney.

Charges against 19° f the men were dismissed on December 10, 1964 by U. S. which indicated that a Ku Klux Klan-inspired plot had led to the murder of the three civil rights workers.

The Nobel Peace Prize: Martin Luther King—(1964)

The announcement of Martin Luther King's reception of the 1964 Nobel Peace Prize signaled a moment of enormous pride and immense jubilation for the American Negro. For the first time, there was a degree of official international recognition connected with his struggle. There was a sense that the nonviolent aspects of the civil rights revolution had captured the attention of the world.

Dr. King received his award in Oslo, Norway on December 10, 1964. At 35, he became the youngest man in history to have won the coveted distinction.

Martin Luther King, Jr. (left) receives the Nobel Peace Prize from Gunnar Jahn, chairman of the Nobel Prize committee.

THE MARCH OF NEWS (1965-1970)

Negro newsmakers have come to occupy an increasingly important place in the national spotlight during the past decade, and news events of special interest to Negro citizens are reported on the front pages of our nation's newspapers with greater frequency than ever before. These events and stories have been compiled both to illustrate this phenomenon, and to help capture the prevailing mood of the nation as a whole on the civil rights question.

JANUARY 2-23

On January 2, Rev. Martin Luther King, Jr. announces his intention to call for demonstrations if Alabama Negroes are not permitted to register and vote in appropriate numbers. Twelve Negroes, including Dr. King himself, book rooms on January 18 at Selma's Hotel Albert, thus becoming the first Negroes accepted by this formerly all-white hotel. While signing the register, Dr. King is accosted by a white segregationist who is later fined $100 and given a 60-day jail sentence. On January 19, Sheriff James G. Clark arrests 62 Negroes in Selma after they refuse to enter the Dallas County courthouse through an alley door. Clark and his deputies arrest 150 other Negro voter-registration applicants the very next day. A federal district court order issued on January 23 bars law enforcement officials from interfering with voter registration and warns against violence.

JANUARY 4

The U. S. House of Representatives votes to seat five white Congressmen elected from Mississippi. Some 600 Negroes from this state assemble in protest outside the House chamber.

JANUARY 15

A Jackson, Mississippi federal grand jury hands down indictments for the June 1964 slaying of three civil rights workers —James E. Chaney, Andrew Goodman, and Michael Schwerner. The following day, 18 men (including two law enforcement officers from the state of Mississippi) are arrested.

FEBRUARY 1-4

Rev. Martin Luther King, Jr. and some 770 Negroes are arrested in Selma, Alabama during protest demonstrations against discrimination in Negro voter registration (February 1). Dr. King remains in jail for four days before posting bond. During this time, more than 3,000 persons are arrested. On February 4, a federal district court orders the county board of registrars to refrain from using an unduly difficult literacy test on voter applicants, or from rejecting their applications on petty technicalities.

The Selma Story

Martin Luther King and thousands of civil rights supporters made a five-day, 54-mile march from Selma to the Alabama state capital of Montgomery from March 21-25, 1965, in an effort to dramatize the denial of voting rights to Negroes who had attempted to register in Selma.

When the march ended in front of the State Capitol building, the number of participants had swelled to 25,000. Dr. King addressed the throng, and later sought to present an equal rights petition to Governor George C. Wallace, who twice turned away a delegation before finally meeting with it on March 30.

The march, which captured national headlines, was first attempted on March 7, 1965, at which time some 200 Alabama state troopers and possemen of the Dallas County Sheriff's office halted the 525 Negro marchers by charging into their ranks—using tear gas, nightsticks and whips in a reputed effort to enforce Governor Wallace's order banning the demonstration. Seventeen Negroes were hospitalized, and 67 others treated for injuries of varying severity, including exposure to tear gas.

On March 8, Governor Wallace denied that the police had made an intemperate display of force, and maintained further that police action in dispersing marchers had undoubtedly saved many Negro lives. Dr. King then returned to Selma to lead another March on Montgomery.

On March 9, President Lyndon B. Johnson stated that he was certain that all Americans "joined in deploring the brutality with which a number of Negro citizens of Alabama were treated when

State troopers charge into a line of demonstrators grouped for the first Selma march which was banned by Governor George Wallace of Alabama.

they sought to dramatize their deep and sincere interest in attaining the precious right to vote."

On the same day, 1500 Negroes and whites, among them hundreds of Northern clergymen and civil rights workers, began a second march to Montgomery, with Martin Luther King in the front rank. By that time, however, Federal Judge Frank M. Johnson, Jr. had already issued a restraining order against the march. The demonstrators again turned back, although they were allowed to pass a few minutes in prayer before doing so.

After the second march, Community Relations Service head LeRoy Collins, on the scene as a special emissary of President Johnson, worked out an arrangement with Dr. King, according to which the marchers would stop as soon as they encountered any signs of resistance.

On March 17, Judge Johnson upheld the right of Negro demonstrators to stage the march as originally planned, and enjoined Governor Wallace and other Alabama officials from intimidating the participants in any way. Furthermore, the judge ordered the governor to provide police protection for the march.

Governor Wallace in turn told President Johnson that Alabama was "financially unable to bear the burden" of mobilizing the National Guard. The President ordered an additional contingent of regular troops sent into Alabama.

After the march had begun, some 2,900 of the original 3,200 participants returned to Selma on the evening of March 21. Thereafter, in accordance with a court order, the number of marchers was limited to 300 each day.

On March 28, three days after the march, Martin Luther King appeared on nationwide television, and advocated a withdrawal of federal support of activities in Alabama, including a boycott of Alabama products.

FEBRUARY 9

President Lyndon B. Johnson and Dr. King meet in the White House to discuss the latter's proposed guarantees for Negro voting rights. Among these is a proposal for the enforcement of legislation by federal registrars appointed by the chief executive.

FEBRUARY 16

Three Negroes and a white woman from Canada (described by police as pro-Castro left-wingers) are arrested in New York City on charges of plotting to blow up the Statue of Liberty, the Liberty Bell and the Washington Monument.

FEBRUARY 18

Some 300 school-boycotting Negro students sweep through the streets of downtown Brooklyn, New York, hurling bricks at policemen and breaking store windows. The following day, an estimated 5,500 students are absent from 27 schools.

FEBRUARY 21

Malcolm X, 39-year-old black nationalist leader and former member of the Black Muslim cult, is shot to death in the Audubon Ballroom, New York City, as he is about to deliver an address before a rally of several hundred followers.

After the murder, Black Muslim headquarters in New York City and San Francisco are burned, and most Muslim leaders are placed under heavy police guard. Three Negroes—Talmadge Hayer, Norman 3X Butler and Thomas 15X Johnson—are later taken into custody, and charged with first-degree murder. The trio is convicted and sentenced to life imprisonment on March 10, 1966.

(Suspended from the Black Muslims by Elijah Muhammad after he had referred to President John F. Kennedy's assassination as a case of "chickens coming home to roost," Malcolm X had retired for a time to the Middle East, where he had engaged in a serious study of the Moslem faith before returning to the United States and founding his own nationalist group, the Organization of Afro-American Unity.)

Dr. Martin Luther King, Jr. leads the Selma-to-Montgomery marchers on the last leg of their journey to the Alabama state capital. To his left is Mrs. King; to his right, Ralph J. Bunche, fellow winner of the Nobel Peace Prize.

Malcolm X addresses a rally of his followers in New York City. The black nationalist leader was murdered in 1965.

FEBRUARY 25

U. S. District Court Judge W. Harold Cox dismisses a federal indictment against 17 of the men accused of conspiracy in the June 1964 murder of three civil rights workers in Philadelphia, Mississippi. (See January 15 entry.)

FEBRUARY 26

Jimmie Lee Jackson, a 26-year-old Negro, dies in Selma, eight days after having been clubbed and shot during a night march in Marion, Alabama.

MARCH 9-15

Three white Unitarian ministers are beaten on March 9 in Selma, Alabama while assisting in the civil rights drive being directed by Rev. Martin Luther King, Jr. Rev. James J. Reeb, a 38-year-old white Boston minister, is critically injured and dies [illegible]rmingham hospital on March 11. A federal judge arranges with law-enforcement officials in Selma to allow more than 2,000 white and Negro sympathizers to hold memorial services there on March 15.

MARCH 13

Colonel Al Lingo, head of the Alabama Highway Patrol, admits that Jimmie Lee Jackson (see February 26 entry) was shot in Marion by a state trooper.

MARCH 13-17

President Johnson meets with Governor George C. Wallace to discuss racial unrest in Selma, Alabama. The president later addresses the nation, calling for assurances that "the right of peaceful assembly will be permitted in Alabama"—particularly in connection with protests against the denial of the right to vote. On March 14, Governor Wallace agrees that all eligible citizens in the state should be allowed to vote.

MARCH 16-17

Some 600 civil rights demonstrators (including over 200 white students from Northern colleges) are dispersed in Montgomery, Alabama. Eight persons are injured as police resort to the use of ropes, nightsticks, and electric cattle-prods. Later in the day (March 16), a second march of some 1,000 persons, holding a parade permit, is held under the protection of the police. That night, Martin Luther King, Jr. calls for a mass protest meeting on the steps of the county courthouse. The following day, some 1,600 demonstrators assemble at the appointed place after first having obtained the necessary permit. Later meetings between Dr. King and county and federal officials result in an agreement by the police to end the harassment of well-disciplined demonstrations.

MARCH 21-25

Civil rights leaders undertake a 54-mile march from Selma to the state capital in Montgomery, Alabama, after having been blocked by state troopers in two earlier attempts. Governor George C. Wallace of Alabama is ordered by a federal court to refrain from "harassing or threatening" the demonstrators. Hundreds of Army troops and National Guardsmen are on hand to protect the 25,000 marchers led by Nobel Peace Prize winners Martin Luther King, Jr. and Ralph Bunche. The governor refuses at first to receive a delegation bearing an equal rights petition, but eventually consents to do so.

MARCH 26-30

President Johnson announces the arrest of four Ku Klux Klan members in connection with the murder of Mrs. Viola Gregg Liuzzo, a 39-year-old white civil rights worker from Detroit slain on a Lowndes County highway during the Selma-to-Montgomery Freedom March. The president goes on to declare war on the Klan, calling it a "hooded society of bigots." Robert M. Shelton, Jr., Imperial Wizard of the United Klans of America, Inc., answers the president's charges by branding him "a damn liar." On March 30, the House Un-American Activities Committee votes to open a full investigation of the activities of the Klan. The Committee chairman, a Louisiana Democrat, asserts that the Klan is perpetrating "shocking crimes."

APRIL 1-2

Martin Luther King, Jr. announces plans for an economic boycott of Alabama during a meeting of the executive board of the Southern Christian Leadership Conference (SCLC) in Baltimore. The three-stage program outlined by King calls for:

1. Suspension by the business community of all plant location and expansion in Alabama
2. Withdrawal of federal tax funds from Alabama banks coupled with an appeal to private institutions, churches, and labor unions to make certain their investments are not used to support racism in the state
3. A boycott of Alabama-produced goods

President Johnson warns against full execution of such a program, maintaining that it would endanger the security of innocent people.

APRIL 13

A grand jury in Selma, Alabama indicts three white men for the murder of Rev. James J. Reeb. (See March 9-15 entry.) They are: William S. Hoggle, Namon O. Hoggle (his brother), and Elmer L. Cook.

APRIL 23

Martin Luther King, Jr. leads a three-mile civil rights demonstration in Boston, parading from the predominantly Negro section of Roxbury to the Boston Common. There, he tells a crowd of 20,000 that America cannot afford to become a nation of "onlookers" in the struggle against segregation.

APRIL 29

The autumn of 1967 is set by the federal government as a deadline for integration at all grade levels of public schools seeking to qualify for federal funds. In addition, Commissioner of Education Francis Keppel states that school districts must also show a "good faith substantial start" toward desegregation by September of 1965. (This is defined as desegregation of at least four of the first 12 grades.)

MAY 3-7

A mistrial is declared in the trial of Collie Leroy Wilkins, a Ku Klux Klansman charged with the murder of Mrs. Viola Gregg Liuzzo. (See entry dated March 26.) The all-male, all-white jury is hopelessly deadlocked after two days of deliberation, the vote being split 10-2 in favor of conviction.

At the opening of the trial (May 3), FBI informer and undercover agent Gary Thomas Rowe, Jr., who was allegedly in the car at the time of the murder, testifies that Wilkins and a fellow passenger fired shots at Mrs. Liuzzo after driving their own car alongside hers. The FBI presents the weapons as evidence, indicating that tests prove the bullets which killed Mrs. Liuzzo were fired from them. The defense attorney, however, attempts to discredit Rowe as a witness by maintaining that he has broken the oath of secrecy associated with membership in the Ku Klux Klan (Rowe had joined the organization as part of his assignment) and, therefore, cannot be believed. Moreover, witnesses are produced who testify they have seen Wilkins elsewhere at the approximate time of the shooting. In closing, the defense attorney maintains that what happened to Mrs. Liuzzo was her own fault since she was riding in a vehicle with a Negro passenger. The jury is instructed that it can convict Wilkins on a lesser charge than first-degree murder, and quickly settles on a charge of first-degree manslaughter.

MAY 16-31

On May 23, following a May 16 meeting between city officials and the Negro Bogalusa Civic and Voters League, the mayor of Bogalusa announces that the city will repeal all segregation ordinances. Street demonstrations continue through the following week, culminating in the eruption of violence from May 29 to May 31. Demonstrations are subsequently banned.

MAY 26

The Senate passes the Voting Rights Bill, 77-19.

MAY 30

Vivian Malone becomes the first Negro to graduate from the University of Alabama.

JUNE 6

Louisiana law-enforcement officials express growing concern over the activities of the Deacons for Defense and Justice, an armed Negro group with the professed aim of protecting Negroes from terrorism by whites. Members of the group are reported to have twice fired on whites who were caught harassing Negroes.

JUNE 10-16

Mass demonstrations, marches to city hall and other gestures of protest begin in Chicago on June 10—drawing attention to the slow pace of desegregation in the city's public school system. On June 11, 225 persons are arrested, including comedian Dick Gregory and CORE director James Farmer. Within four days, the arrest total reaches 530. On June 16, a final march culminates in a meeting between Chicago mayor Richard Daley and a delegation led by the Rev. John Porter, leader of the Chicago branch of the NAACP.

JUNE 17

Pope Paul VI names John Patrick Cody of New Orleans, a staunch advocate of civil rights, to the post of Archbishop of Chicago, the nation's largest Roman Catholic see.

JUNE 18

More than 850 persons are arrested in Jackson, Mississippi after five days of protest demonstrations there.

JULY 1-19

Between July 1 and July 5, the Congress of Racial Equality (CORE) lays the groundwork for a "major assault" in Bogalusa, Louisiana, scene of alleged police brutality against Negroes. On July 7, a march is made on the Bogalusa city hall to present desegregation demands. The following day, during a second march, a white man attacks two Negroes, one of whom shoots and seriously wounds the man. On July 10, a federal district court judge enjoins Bogalusa authorities from blocking civil rights demonstrations, and orders protection for Negroes who are being harassed by whites. Marches resume on July 11 with James

Watts: scene of one of the worst urban riots in U.S. history.

Farmer of CORE in the vanguard. On July 12, Louisiana Governor John J. McKeithen flies to Bogalusa and appeals for a 30-day cooling-off period. On July 19, as the marches still continue, the Justice Department files criminal and civil contempt actions against Bogalusa officials. On July 22, the governor announces the formation of a 40-member bi-racial committee.

JULY 2

Title VII of the 1964 Civil Rights Act prohibiting job discrimination in private business goes into effect.

JULY 11

A special report submitted to President Johnson on the 1964 Civil Rights Act indicates that it has been even more effective than its sponsors had anticipated.

JULY 13

Thurgood Marshall is nominated as Solicitor General of the United States, the first Negro to hold this office.

JULY 20

The House Un-American Activities Committee subpoenas more than 160 witnesses to testify on the Ku Klux Klan during closed hearings.

JULY 24-26

Martin Luther King, Jr. and the Southern Christian Leadership Conference (SCLC) conduct a civil rights campaign in Chicago—leading 18 rallies and church services in Negro neighborhoods, as well as in the primarily white suburb of Winnetka. On July 26, King and some 10,000 to 20,000 marchers assemble at the city hall, where King assails the city's *de facto* segregation patterns.

AUGUST 6

President Johnson signs the 1965 Voting Rights Act, providing for the registration by federal examiners of those Negro voters turned away by state officials.

AUGUST 8

Some 700 members of the Ku Klux Klan stage a silent march and memorial service in Americus, Georgia for a white youth slain in a racial conflict.

AUGUST 11-21

A six-day orgy of looting, burning and rioting plunges the predominantly Negro section of Watts, Los Angeles into a state of virtual anarchy. Thousands of National Guardsmen and state police are rushed in to quell the rioting which is traced to the arrest and alleged mistreatment of a Negro youth by white policemen on charges of drunken driving. The death toll is 35; 883 are injured; 3,598 arrested. Fire damage: 175 million dollars. Property damage: 46 million dollars.

AUGUST 20

President Johnson denounces the Los Angeles rioters, comparing them in one sense to Ku Klux Klan extremists. He declares that the existence of legitimate grievances in such communities as Watts is no justification for lawlessness. "We cannot . . . in one breath demand laws to protect the rights of all our citizens, and then turn our back . . . and . . . allow laws to be broken that protect the safety of our citizens."

SEPTEMBER 27-30

An all-white Alabama jury acquits part-time deputy sheriff Thomas L. Coleman of manslaughter charges in connection with the slaying of Jonathan M. Daniels, 26, a white Episcopal seminarian and civil rights worker from Keene, New Hampshire (September 30). State Attorney General Richmond Flowers calls the verdict "appalling" and a "license to kill."

(On September 27, Flowers took over the prosecution and asked for a postponement on the grounds that his star witness, Rev. Richard Morrisroe, was still hospitalized from injuries received during the same incident in which Daniels had been killed. Circuit Judge T. Werth Thagard denied the request. On September 28, Flowers' assistant opened the case and told the court that testimony to the effect that the two clergymen were armed was "a lie." When the prosecution maintained that it could not proceed with its case unless Rev. Morrisroe were present, the judge placed the case in the hands of circuit and county solicitors. A law enforcement official testified that Coleman, who admitted to the shootings, had fired only because he was under the impression that one of the clergymen was reaching for a knife.)

OCTOBER 2

Pope Paul appoints the first Negro bishop in the U. S. in the 20th century. He is the Very Rev. Harold R. Perry (Auxiliary Bishop of New Orleans).

OCTOBER 19

The House Un-American Activities Committee opens public hearings in the nation's capital on the activities of the Ku Klux Klan. Robert M. Shelton, Jr., Imperial Wizard of the largest Klan group, invokes his constitutional rights and refuses to answer any of the committee's questions. Federal investigators charge Klan leaders with misappropriation of funds, and the frequent use of violence against individuals and groups they consider to be enemies.

OCTOBER 22

An all-white Alabama jury acquits Ku Klux Klansman Collie Leroy Wilkins in the slaying of Mrs. Viola Gregg Liuzzo. (See entries dated April 26-30; May 3-7.) The verdict is greeted with a storm of applause in the courthouse.

The first Wilkins trial (see entry dated May 3-7) ended in a hung jury. At the second trial, the prosecution was handled by State Attorney General Richmond Flowers who said of Wilkins: "The blood of this man's sins, if you do not find him guilty, will stain the very soul of our county for an eternity." Flowers attempted to disqualify the jury after several members admitted they felt civil rights workers were inferior human beings. The Alabama Supreme Court, however, ruled against him, with the result that six self-styled white supremacists and eight present or former members of the White Citizens Council were selected to pass judgment on the case.

NOVEMBER 23

A federal court in Montgomery, Alabama nullifies state court injunctions against the enrollment of federally registered voters in six Alabama counties.

DECEMBER 2

Segregationist Hubert D. Strange, 23, is convicted by a state court in Anniston, Alabama of second-degree murder in the slaying of Willie Brewster, a 38-year-old Negro. Strange is sentenced to 10 years in prison by an all-white jury.

DECEMBER 3

An all-white jury convicts Collie Leroy Wilkins, 22, Eugene Thomas, 42, and

William Orville Eaton, 42, on charges of conspiracy in the murder of Mrs. Viola Gregg Liuzzo. (See entries dated March 26; May 3; October 22.) Convictions are based on an 1870 federal civil rights law.

DECEMBER 10

A Selma, Alabama jury acquits three white businessmen charged with the murder of Rev. James J. Reeb, a Boston clergyman slain in Selma civil rights demonstrations. (See entries dated March 11; April 13.)

1966

JANUARY 2

Kivie Kaplan, a Boston industrialist and philanthropist, succeeds Arthur B. Spingarn as the president of the National Association for the Advancement of Colored People (NAACP).

JANUARY 3

Floyd McKissick is named national director of the Congress of Racial Equality (CORE), succeeding James Farmer who announces his intention to head a new anti-poverty group, the Center for Community Action Education.

JANUARY 4

Tuskegee student Sammy Younge, 21, is shot to death in downtown Tuskegee by a white service-station attendant.

JANUARY 10

Julian Bond, elected to the Georgia legislature, is denied his seat for opposing U. S. involvement in the Vietnam war.

JANUARY 13

President Johnson's State of the Union Message contains proposals for legislation to prohibit discrimination in housing and in jury selection. The president also vows to offer civil rights workers in the South full federal protection.

JANUARY 13

Robert Weaver is named head of the Department of Housing and Urban Development (HUD)—the first Negro appointed to serve in a presidential cabinet in U. S. history.

Robert Weaver: First Negro in a Presidential Cabinet

Robert Weaver became the first Negro appointed to a presidential cabinet when Lyndon B. Johnson named him to head the newly created Department of Housing and Urban Development (HUD) on January 13, 1966.

Previously, Weaver had served as head of the Housing and Home Finance Agency (HHFA).

Robert Weaver was born on December 29, 1907 in Washington, D. C. where he attended Dunbar High School and worked during his teens as an electrician. Encountering discrimination when he attempted to join a union, he decided instead to concentrate on economics, and eventually received his Ph. D. in that field from Harvard University. (Weaver's grandfather, Dr. Robert Tanner Freeman, was the first American Negro to earn a doctor's degree in dentistry at Harvard.)

In 1933, Weaver became an aide to Secretary of the Interior Harold Ickes, a member of President Franklin D. Roosevelt's first "New Deal" cabinet. At this time, Roosevelt was gathering about him a select group of young, university-trained Negroes who came to be known as the "Black Cabinet."

In 1934, Weaver became advisor in the Department of the Interior, and a consultant in the Housing Division of the Public Works Administration (PWA). It was through the work of this agency that the first public housing and slum-clearing projects were undertaken as part of the emergency works program put into effect during the Depression.

Four years later, Weaver became special assistant to Nathan Straus, Administrator of the U. S. Housing Authority.

During the 1940's and 1950's, Weaver concentrated his energies on the field of education. (He had already been a professor of economics at the Agricultural and Technical College of North Carolina in Greensboro from 1931 to 1932.) In 1947, he became a lecturer at Northwestern University in Evanston, Illinois and, following this, a visiting professor at Teachers College, Columbia University and at the New York University School of Education. During this period, he was also a professor of economics at the New School for Social Research.

From 1949 to 1955. he was Director of

the Opportunity Fellowships Program of the John Hay Whitney Foundation; served as a member of the National Selection Committee for Fulbright Fellowships; was chairman of the Fellowship Committee of the Julius Rosenwald Fund, and a consultant to the Ford Foundation.

In 1955, Weaver was named Deputy State Rent Commissioner by New York's Governor Averell Harriman. By the end of the year, he had become State Rent Commissioner and the first Negro to hold state cabinet rank in New York. Still later, he served as vice chairman of the New York City Housing and Redevelopment Board, a three-man body which supervised New York's urban renewal and middle-income housing programs.

Weaver is married to the former Ella Haith, now assistant professor of speech at Brooklyn College. The Weavers have no children of their own, their adopted son having died.

Robert Weaver

JANUARY 15

President Johnson names Lisle Carter, a Negro, as an assistant secretary in the Department of Health, Education and Welfare (HEW).

JANUARY 25

Constance Baker Motley, former NAACP lawyer and Borough President of Manhattan, becomes the first Negro woman to be named to a federal judgeship in the history of the United States.

JANUARY 25

Governor Edward Breathitt of Kentucky signs a civil rights law, the first of its kind adopted by any state south of the Ohio River. The measure goes even further than the 1964 Civil Rights Act in banning discrimination in places of public accommodation.

FEBRUARY 7

A federal court finds Lowndes County, Alabama guilty of "gross, systematic exclusion of members of the Negro race from jury duty." County officials are ordered to prepare a new jury list, one taking into account the added fact that an Alabama law barring women from juries has been declared unconstitutional. Lowndes County is also ordered to desegregate its school system within two years, to close 24 Negro schools staffed with only one teacher each, and to introduce remedial programs designed to close the educational gap between white and Negro pupils.

FEBRUARY 10

A federal court upholds the right of the Georgia legislature to refuse to seat Julian Bond for his stand on the Vietnam war. (See January 10 entry.)

FEBRUARY 15

The United States Civil Rights Commission reports that the majority of Southern school districts are evading integration while still adhering to federal guidelines for desegregation. The commission proposes federal legislation to outlaw the harassment of Negro families sending their children to predominantly white schools.

FEBRUARY 24

The House of Representatives ends its hearings on Ku Klux Klan activities. Its findings do not lead to any indictments.

The Ku Klux Klan

The Ku Klux Klan was founded in Pulaski, Tennessee as a secret society to terrorize Southern Negroes. The original Constitution or "Prescript" of the organization was ratified in 1867, and revised the following year.

This "Prescript" does not contain the actual words *Ku Klux Klan*, which is probably derived from the Greek word *kuklos* (meaning band or circle), but rather substitutes three asterisks for this name. *Ku Klux* seems to have been suggested by a member of the original group, and the word *Klan* added for further alliteration.

Members of the organization were required to submit to a series of initiation rites, ending with the recital of the following final oath:

> "I ——— of my own free will and accord, and in the presence of Almighty God, do solemnly swear or affirm, that I will never reveal to any one not a member of the Order of the * * *, by any intimation, sign, symbol, word or act, or in any other manner whatever, any of the secrets, signs, grips, passwords, or mysteries of the Order of the * * *, or that I am a member of the same, or that I know any one who *is* a member; and that I will abide by the Prescript and Edicts of the Order of the * * *. So help me God. . ."

The Klan was disbanded in 1869, and is not to be confused with Ku Klux Klan, Inc., which was organized in 1915.

MARCH 1

Wyatt Tee Walker, former chief of staff to Martin Luther King, Jr. and now the top executive of a Yonkers, New York publishing firm, is named Special Assistant on Urban Affairs to Governor Nelson Rockefeller of New York.

MARCH 7

The U. S. Supreme Court upholds the crucial provisions of the Voting Rights Act of 1965.

MARCH 7

The Office of Education, Department of Health, Education and Welfare (HEW), issues tighter guidelines to end discrimination in schools and hospitals, threatening to cut off federal funds in both areas. Harold Howe II declares an end to the era of "paper compliance."

MARCH 15

A renewed outbreak of violence in Watts results in two deaths, injury to 26 people, 34 arrests and damage to 15 buildings. Government studies indicate little change in the economic prospects of the average Watts citizen, with unemployment still running around 35%.

MARCH 25

The U. S. Supreme Court outlaws the poll tax for all elections, a ruling which complements the 24th Amendment to the U. S. Constitution, barring such a tax in federal elections.

MARCH 28

Thirteen Ku Klux Klansmen are arrested by the FBI in connection with the slaying earlier in the year of Vernon F. Dahmer, a Negro civil rights leader in Hattiesburg, Mississippi.

APRIL 1-24

The first World Festival of Negro Arts is held in Dakar, Senegal. Negro art the world over is brought for exhibit, with several American Negro artists being awarded prizes for their work.

First World Festival of Negro Arts

Cultural history was made between April 1 and April 24, 1966 when the first World Festival of Negro Arts opened in Dakar, capital and showcase city of the West African republic of Senegal.

The choice of Dakar, Africa's westernmost city and the point nearest to the Western Hemisphere, once again confirmed its position as an important crossroads linking Africa, Europe and the "New World."

For the first time, masterpieces of Negro art—from the bronzes of Benin to the royal Bakuba wood carvings of the

Congo—were selected from museums all over the world, and shown in a single exhibit.

Concerts—often of the open-air variety—were given by African choirs, and by singers of Negro spirituals from the United States. American jazz recordings, as well as traditional and religious African chants, were also utilized to portray the Negro's role in the development of music.

Another collection highlighted contemporary sculpture, oil painting, gouache, engraving, the decorative arts, illustrated books, and tapestries—all of which were chosen for exhibit by participating states. Still a third comprehensive exhibit laid stress on the Negro's contribution to world literature.

Prizes were offered for music, as well as for films (i.e. educational, artistic and scientific documentaries) created by and about Negroes.

The most interest-provoking aspects of the Festival were the gala nightly performances of ballets, musical compositions, and plays at the Daniel Sorano National Theater. These proved so successful that they were then rescheduled for daytime performances in the municipal stadium for the benefit of the general public.

The sponsors of the Festival were the Government of Senegal, UNESCO, and the Society for the Study of African Culture. Guest of honor was the Republic of Nigeria.

Participating artists appeared as representatives of their respective countries, rather than purely as individuals. A conference on Negro art, attended by leading figures in the art world, brought the Festival to a fitting conclusion.

AMERICAN NEGRO PRIZEWINNERS AT FESTIVAL

Category	*Designee*	*Selection*	*Position*
Drama	Leroi Jones	The Slave	Second
Poetry	Robert Hayden	Ballad of Remembrance	First
Reportage	Louis Lomax	The Negro Revolt	Second
General Essay	Ralph Ellison	Shadow and Act	Second
Social Science Essay	Kenneth B. Clark	Dark Ghetto	First
	Robert C. Weaver	The Urban Complex	Second
Illustration—Engraving	William Majors	—	First
Recordings	Mahalia Jackson	Greatest Hits	First
Jazz	Louis Armstrong	Hello, Dolly!	First
Best Film	—	Nothing But A Man	First
Best Actress	Abbey Lincoln	Nothing But A Man	First
Best Actor	Ivan Dixon	Nothing But A Man	First

APRIL 29

President Johnson sends his third civil rights bill to Congress—this one making the racial murder of a civil rights worker, a student seeking education, or a citizen attempting to vote a federal crime punishable by life imprisonment. The Johnson bill is also designed to force the desegregation of schools and other public facilities, and to outlaw discrimination on racial and religious grounds in the sale, rental or occupancy of *all* housing.

MAY 4

Better than 80% of Alabama's more than 235,000 registered Negroes turn out for the Democratic primary election in which Lurleen Wallace is nominated by the party to succeed her husband as governor of the state. Sheriffs James Clark (Selma) and Al Lingo (Birmingham) fail in their bid for renomination.

MAY 16

Stokely Carmichael is named as the new head of the Student Nonviolent Coordinating Committee (SNCC), replacing John Lewis, while Mrs. Ruby Smith Robinson is appointed to fill the post of James Forman as SNCC executive secretary. The shakeup is interpreted to mean that the organization is charting an even more militant course—one leading to the possible founding of an all-Negro political party in the South.

JUNE 6

James Meredith is shot from ambush shortly after beginning a 220-mile voting-rights pilgrimmage from Memphis, Tennessee to Jackson, Mississippi. Aubrey James Norvell, 40, is arrested at the scene and taken to jail where, according to authorities, he admits to the shooting. Meredith suffers multiple injuries, but recovers.

JUNE 22

A federal grand jury in Biloxi, Mississippi returns indictments against 15 alleged members of the Ku Klux Klan in connection with the January 10 slaying of Vernon F. Dahmer, a Negro active in promoting voter-registration.

JUNE 26

The Mississippi March begun by James Meredith ends with a rally in front of the state capitol in Jackson. Addresses are delivered by Meredith himself, by Martin Luther King, Jr., and by Stokely Carmichael who urges the 15,000 Negroes in attendance to "build a power base . . . so strong that we will bring them (whites) to their knees every time they mess with us." (The "Meredith March Against Fear," taken up on June 7 by an assortment of civil rights groups, covers 260 miles, and results in the registration of about 4,000 Negroes.)

JULY 1-4

The national convention of the Congress of Racial Equality (CORE) votes to adopt a resolution endorsing the concept of "black power" as enunciated by Stokely Carmichael during the "Meredith March." CORE National Director Floyd McKissick says: "As long as the white man has all the power and money, nothing will happen, because we have nothing. The only way to achieve meaningful change is to take power."

JULY 4-9

The National Association for the Advancement of Colored People (NAACP) disassociates itself from the "black power" doctrine. Its position is backed by Vice President Hubert Humphrey who says: "We must reject calls for racism whether they come from a throat that is white or one that is black."

JULY 10

Martin Luther King, Jr. launches a drive to make Chicago an "open city," addressing a predominantly Negro crowd of 30,000 to 45,000 at Soldier Field. The rally is sponsored by the Coordinating Council of Committee Organizations (CCCO), a coalition consisting of some 45 local civil rights groups.

JULY 12-15

Three nights of rioting sweep Chicago's West Side Negro district in the wake of a police decision to shut off a fire hydrant which had been open illegally to give Negro children relief from the stifling heat. Two Negroes are killed; scores of police and civilians are wounded, and 372 persons are arrested.

JULY 18-23

Shooting, fire-bombing and looting sweeps through the Negro area of Hough on Cleveland's East Side. Four are killed, and 50 are injured amid widespread property damage. Most of the 164 persons arrested are charged with looting.

JULY 22

John Lewis resigns from the Student Nonviolent Coordinating Committee, vowing to remain active in the civil rights movement.

JULY 29-31

Martin Luther King launches demonstrations in a Southwest Side Chicago neighborhood as part of the "open city" campaign begun by his Southern Christian Leadership Conference (SCLC). Jeering whites pelt marchers with rocks and bottles before being driven off by police. In the Gage Park section, some 300 white hecklers overturn five cars belonging to Negro demonstrators.

AUGUST 5

Martin Luther King is stoned in Chicago as he leads a march of 600 demonstrators through crowds of angry white residents in the Gage Park section of Chicago's Southwest Side. Near rioting ensues between 4,000 whites and 960 policemen, including 160 members of a riot-control force. King leaves Chicago on August 6, but pledges to "keep coming back until we are safe from harassment."

AUGUST 9

By a vote of 259-157, the House of Representatives passes and sends to the Senate an amended version of the Administration's proposed Civil Rights Bill of 1966. Most of the long debate centers around the bill's controversial "open-housing" section embodied in Title IV. The Mathias Amendment, added to the bill, exempts some 60% of the nation's housing from its anti-discrimination provisions. Other sections of the bill concern jury selection; interference with the civil rights of individuals, and initiation of court action to desegregate schools and public accommodations.

SEPTEMBER 13

New York Assemblyman Percy Sutton is elected president of the Borough of Manhattan, succeeding Mrs. Constance Baker Motley who is sworn in as a federal judge on September 9. A native of Texas, Sutton once served as president of the New York branch of the National Association for the Advancement of Colored People (NAACP), and was elected to the New York State Assembly in 1964. He presided over the 1966 Democratic party state convention, during which Frank O'Connor was nominated for the governorship.

Adam Clayton Powell holds a press conference on the isle of Bimini during his "exile".

1967

JANUARY-MARCH 1967

Representative Adam Clayton Powell, Jr. of New York is stripped of his chairmanship of the House Committee on Education and Labor, and then barred from assuming his seat in the 90th Congress. A Congressional committee investigating the case later proposes public censure, loss of seniority, and a $40,000 fine, stipulating, however, that he be returned to his seat. Congress, on the other hand, votes for exclusion, whereupon Powell and his lawyers indicate their intention to challenge the constitutionality of this decision in federal court. James Meredith then announces his decision to run against Powell on the Republican ticket in the special runoff election for the vacant seat, then withdraws. Powell is reelected with 86% of the vote cast in the April 15 special election.

FEBRUARY 15

President Johnson requests that Congress consider and pass new civil rights legislation in the area pertaining to the sale and rental of housing. In his special message, Johnson outlines the scope of the proposed bill, specifying that it be designed to end discrimination in jury selection, to permit the Equal Employment Opportunity Commission (EEOC) to issue cease-and-desist orders, to extend the life of the U.S. Commission on Civil Rights, and to authorize 2.7 million dollars in appropriations for the Community Relations Service. Violators are to be subject to court orders and fines issued by the Secretary of Housing and Urban Development. The law is also to address itself to the matter of the civil rights of individuals, particularly insofar as it will enable them to file damage suits in cases where they are being victimized by discrimination. Civil rights workers, too, would be in a position to seek injunctions to combat discriminatory practices.

FEBRUARY 23

Congressional probers recommend that New York's Adam Clayton Powell be stripped of his seniority, publicly censured, and subjected to a $40,000 fine for "gross misconduct." The committee charges that Powell has misused $46,000 in funds, and maintained his wife on the payroll in absentia while she had no ostensible function.

FEBRUARY 27

A federal grand jury returns federal conspiracy indictments against 19 men in connection with the 1964 slayings of civil rights workers Michael Schwerner, Andrew Goodman and James Earl Chaney. Another 12 men are indicted in connection with the 1966 firebombing of black leader Vernon Dahmer.

MARCH 1-8

Representative Powell is barred from the 90th Congress by a vote of 307-116, and immediately files suit in U. S. District Court to combat his ouster. Powell argues that he has met all Constitutional requirements for House membership, i.e., citizenship, age, and residency. The Congressman also charges that his constituency is left without representation, and hence subject to discrimination.

MARCH 7-13

James Meredith announces he will run against Adam Powell, calling the impending special election "one of the most important in the history of this country." Though he declares himself an independent Democrat, Meredith plans to run on the Democratic ticket. Meredith withdraws on March 13 after meeting with CORE leader Floyd McKissick and Charles Evers, NAACP field secretary from Mississippi.

MARCH 22

A three-judge federal court in Montgomery, Alabama orders the state board of education and the governor to begin desegregation of public schools in the fall term. This is the first instance in which an entire state is under a single injunction to end discrimination.

MARCH 29

The 5th Circuit Court of Appeals upholds the legality of revised federal school desegregation guidelines in an 8-4 ruling which calls for the desegregation of all students, teachers, school transportation facilities and school-related activities in six Deep South states. The guidelines establish rough percentage goals to be used in determining compliance with the Civil Rights Act of 1964.

APRIL 7-11

Adam Clayton Powell appeals a U.S. District Court dismissal of his suit seeking reinstatement in the House. The Court declares it has no jurisdiction in the matter, and is unable to tell Congress how to govern itself. Powell next seeks and receives a popular mandate, being returned to office by more than 74% of the Harlem electorate in a special election.

The Congressman conducts his campaign from his Bimini retreat—partly because he would risk possible arrest on contempt charges if he were to return to New York, but also as a means of demonstrating his enormous popularity.

He is a landslide winner in the special runoff election for the 18th Congressional District which has been left unrepresented since Powell's exclusion from the House. Powell wins 27,900 votes to 4,091 for Republican candidate Lucille Pickett Williams and only 427 for Rev. Erwin Yearling, Conservative Party standard bearer.

APRIL 11-24

Demonstrations escalate in Louisville, Kentucky following rejection of a proposed open-housing ordinance by the city's Board of Aldermen. In the vanguard of the march are Rev. A. D. Williams King and comedian/activist Dick Gregory. White youth harassing the marchers chant "We Want Wallace," and carry banners saying "We Don't Want Any Niggers." On April 13, a band of some 75 whites burn a cross on the lawn of the Southern Junior High School. A circuit court judge issues a restraining order seeking to curb the marches, but attorneys for the demonstrators petition to dissolve the injunction. Police use tear gas and smoke bombs to disperse whites who interfere with the march, and arrest black demonstrators for violating the injunction. Demonstrations are extended into affluent white suburbs and exclusive East Side sections of Louisville; arrests, trials and convictions follow in their wake. On April 24, county and city leaders agree to hold "hard bargaining sessions" to resolve the problems.

APRIL 15-24

Ignoring the criticisms of some of his black colleagues, Martin Luther King, Jr. signals his full-fledged entry into the peace movement by leading thousands of demonstrators through New York's Central Park to the UN building, where he and other prominent leaders deliver a series of forceful addresses attacking U.S. policy in Vietnam. More than 100,000 attend the rally, only one of several staged at campuses and in cities across the U. S. King later announces the formation of Negotiation Now, a pressure group dedicated to the project of accumulating one million signatures for a peace petition to be submitted to the President.

APRIL 16-26

Racial tumult overtakes the predominantly black section of Hough in Cleveland, where window-smashing, looting, and bottle-throwing lead to four arrests. On April 26, Martin Luther King, Jr. calls Cleveland a racially divided city ripe for violence unless something is done to relieve tensions in the high-density East Side (Hough) where Negroes are fed up with substandard housing. King tells the local administration to get tough with poverty, rats, slums and poor education.

MAY 3

A federal district court in Montgomery overturns the Alabama statute countering federal guidelines for school desegregation. The court rules that no state may nullify the action of "a federal department or agency without initiating Court action" reviewable by the U. S. Supreme Court.

MAY 10-13

A Negro delivery man, Benjamin Brown, on his way to a restaurant, is shot and killed during riots on the campus of Jackson State College. The man, within full view of police, is left at the scene unattended until he is taken to the University Hospital by Negro bystanders. Rioters are apparently "not rioting over any specific grievance," according to Kenneth Dean, director of the Mississippi Council on Human Relations. Police, unable to contain the demonstrators whose ranks are swelled by participants from nearby Tougaloo College, are reinforced by more than 1,000 National Guardsmen.

MAY-12-16

H. Rap Brown replaces Stokely Carmichael as chairman of the Student Nonviolent Coordinating Committee. Brown calls a news conference to announce that SNCC's black power policy will remain intact, and pledges to build a strong anti-draft program and movement among black youth. Carmichael vows to stay on at SNCC as field secretary in Washington, D.C.

JUNE 2-5

Scores of persons are injured, and 75-100 are arrested in an outbreak of rioting in Boston's predominantly Negro section of Roxbury. The disturbance occurs in the

Thurgood Marshall is the first Negro nominated to serve on the Supreme Court. His wife offers congratulations.

wake of an attempt by welfare mothers to barricade themselves inside a building as a protest against departmental policies and police rudeness. Police who try to enter the building are struck by stones and bottles; others inside the building form a flying wedge and charge out the center, only to be bombarded by various missiles.

JUNE 6
The NAACP's Legal Defense Fund director/counsel Jack Greenberg announces the creation of a new educational project to inform Negroes of their rights in housing, health, employment etc. The program, known as the Division of Legal Information and Community Service and funded by a matching $300,000 Rockefeller grant, is headed by Jean Fairfax.

JUNE 11-13
Violence breaks out in Tampa, Florida after police shoot and kill a black robbery suspect. City officials bring the disorders under control after they enlist the aid of 100 black youths to circulate in ghetto neighborhoods and help cool tempers. After three nights of violence, 65-80 arrests are reported, and property damage is estimated at 1.5 million dollars.

JUNE 12-15
More than 300 persons are arrested in Cincinnati racial disturbances which include incidents of looting and arson. H. Rap Brown arrives in the city on June 15, advising city fathers to remove National Guard patrols and "honkie cops" and urging that 12 imprisoned Negroes be released. The cause of the rioting, originally identified as a protest aired against a death sentence imposed on a black convict, turns out to be the familiar litany of grievances associated with urban unrest, primarily police brutality and lack of job opportunity.

JUNE 13
Thurgood Marshall is appointed an associate justice of the Supreme Court, the

first Negro so designated. President Johnson calls Marshall "the right man," the Court "the right place" and the appointment "the right thing to do."

JUNE 14
Nine prominent civil rights leaders, meeting secretly in Suffern, New York, announce plans to ease racial tensions in Cleveland, a city they regard as one in which "underlying causes of unrest and despair" have reached crisis proportions. One of the leaders, Martin Luther King, Jr., confirms SCLC's previously announced plans for initiating organized civil rights action during the summer, and singles out the bread industry for a selective buying campaign. The NAACP's Roy Wilkins expresses reservations about King's plans to "stir up trouble," although he hastens to add that slums, poor schools, and lack of jobs are the real causes of trouble. The FBI's J. Edgar Hoover faults King for issuing an "open invitation" to summer violence by naming cities where it is likely to occur.

JUNE 12-17
The "long hot summer" begins in earnest in Newark, New Jersey, scene of the most devastating riot to sweep an urban center since the 1965 Watts uprising. While many whites assume the violence is premeditated rather than spontaneous, observers ranging from Attorney General Ramsey Clark to New Jersey governor Richard Hughes find no evidence of conspiracy or intercity planning. Clark asserts that the law enforcement capabilities of the federal government in riot-torn cities are minimal; Hughes takes charge of police and National Guard operations to prevent "criminal elements who are burning and maiming and killing" from taking control of the city. Though one statistic seems encouraging—only 2% of the city's population allegedly takes part in the violence—others are harrowing: 23 dead, including six women and two children; damage over 10 million dollars; 1,000 people injured, and 1,600 under arrest.

JUNE 18-22
Stokely Carmichael is arrested as he joins a crowd of 200-500 persons gathered in the Dixie Hill section of Atlanta to protest the arrest of a citizen accused of "malicious mischief." Carmichael tells the crowd that the police has "everybody marked, ready to shoot" and exhorts them to take to the streets. State Senator Leroy Johnson tries to organize a youth patrol to cool tempers, but the move does not prevent a confrontation between police and crowds gathered in a shopping center. There, one Negro is killed, and three others are injured. Carmichael is convicted on June 22 of fomenting a riot, and sentenced to 50 days in jail.

JUNE 19
U.S. District Court Judge J. Skelly Wright rules that *de facto* segregation of Negroes in the District of Columbia is unconstitutional, and orders the public school system to abolish the "track system," i.e., the assignment of some children to special courses for gifted students. Wright orders the complete desegregation of D.C. schools by the fall.

JUNE 24
James Meredith and four others resume the "march against fear" in Mississippi mainly, as Meredith says, to complete unfinished business, to demonstrate that local police can protect Negroes if they choose to and because "the Negro has a whole history of failure and incompletions," based on the fear which he seeks to expose and extinguish.

JUNE 27-30
Three days of rioting in Buffalo result in more than 85 injuries, 205 arrests, and property damage estimated at $100,000.

JULY 10-15
The 58th NAACP convention is a tense and at times bitter affair in which Executive Director Roy Wilkins defends black militants for shaking up the establishment, but warns against the endorsement of the kind of radicalization that will force whites out of the movement altogether.

JULY 19
The House of Representatives passes legislation which declares it a federal crime to cross state lines or to use interstate facilities for the purpose of inciting a riot. The bill is aimed at alleged professional agitators who travel from city to city to inflame the people. New York's Emanuel Celler finds the bill "neither preventive nor curative," and fears it will only arouse Negro hostilities even further.

JULY 20-23
Despite objections by Governor Hughes, a four-day conclave of black leaders, many of them black power advocates, convenes

in Newark. Militancy and a call for separate nationhood dominates the meeting, as most delegates concur with the estimate offered by one participant, Alfred Black of the Newark Human Relations Commission: "The Negro today is either a radical or an Uncle Tom. There is no middle-ground."

JULY 23-30

Hard on the heels of the Newark conflagration comes another week of incendiary violence in Detroit, the nation's fifth largest city. Before order is restored, 43 persons—33 of them black—are dead, and 22 million dollars worth of property is destroyed. More than 2,000 are injured; more than 5,000 are homeless, and 7,200 persons are arrested, many of them held in custody in makeshift jails. Paratroopers, state troopers, National Guardsmen — a veritable army of occupation—are needed to deal with what is variously termed an armed insurrection, a mammoth riot, a monumental civil disorder. Governor Romney asks the President to declare the city a disaster area. Labor leader Walter Reuther calls Detroit no different from any other large American city in which the "have nots of America" strike out against armed authority and the affluent society in reaction against "the ugly economic facts" which feed "their frustrations and their sense of hopelessness."

JULY 25-28

"You better get yourselves some guns. The only thing honkies respect is guns." These words, attributed to SNCC leader H. Rap Brown, are cited as the cause of the rioting and arson that inflicts wholesale damage on the black business section of Cambridge, Maryland. Gov. Spiro Agnew later tours the district and tells the press that Brown is responsible for the trouble. The governor orders 700 National Guardsmen to take up positions in Cambridge. On July 28, the governor calls the city "sick" and obviously segregated.

JULY 27

President Johnson appoints a blue-ribbon panel to "investigate the origins of the recent disorders in our cities." The president instructs the commission to leave aside political considerations and concern itself solely with the health and safety of American society and its citizens. The president imposes only three guidelines on

Helmeted police riot grounds remove a wounded victim of the 1967 Newark riot.

the panel, three basic questions which he deems it indispensable to answer: a) what happened, b) why did it happen, and c) how can it be prevented from happening again.

AUGUST 10

The National Advisory Commission on Civil Disorders urges President Johnson to increase the number of Negroes in the Army and Air National Guard. The panel also recommends increased riot-control training for the Guard, as well as a review of promotion procedures. The recommendations, delivered in a letter to LBJ, are forwarded to Defense Secretary Robert McNamara.

AUGUST 14-22

H. Rap Brown is indicted *in absentia* by a Dorchester County grand jury on charges of inciting to riot, arson, and other related actions inimical to the public peace. Brown is arrested in New York on August 19 and charged with carrying a gun across state lines while under indictment. After strenuous objections are voiced by his white lawyer, William Kunstler, Brown's bail is reduced to $15,000 on August 22, and he is released in time to address a crowd of 100 Negroes on the steps of the Foley Square courthouse. Pointing to whites nearby, Brown says: "That's your enemy out there. And you better not forget, because I ain't going to."

AUGUST 14-21

The Student Nonviolent Coordinating Committee (SNCC) publishes an article in its newsletter denouncing Zionism and charging Israelis with inflicting atrocities against the Arabs. The article accuses Israel of practicing segregation against Arabs still in their country, and of assigning second-class status to dark-skinned Jews. Author Harry Golden and folk-singer Theodore Bikel resign from SNCC following the charges posted in the article. The article is later defended by SNCC as being anti-Zionist, not anti-Semitic.

AUGUST 16

The House passes an amended Administration bill to defend persons exercising federally protected civil rights. The vote is 326-93.

AUGUST 19-23

Nearly 450 persons are arrested during five days of looting, arson, and vandalism in New Haven. No serious injuries are reported, and no shots are fired by police despite frequent curfew violations. New Haven Mayor Richard C. Lee declares: "We've done a lot, but for every one thing we've done, there are five that we haven't."

SEPTEMBER 6

President Johnson discloses he will nominate Walter E. Washington to head the newly reorganized municipal government of Washington, D.C. Washington is the first Negro to govern a major American city.

SEPTEMBER 19

An open-housing ordinance is introduced in the Milwaukee Common Council following weeks of open-housing demonstrations led by the militant Catholic priest, Rev. James E. Groppi. Committeemen fail to agree on specific provisions of the ordinance.

OCTOBER 3-5

Black power at the polls is evidenced by the Democratic primary victory of Rep. Carl Stokes, who unseats incumbent Ralph Locher in the race for Cleveland mayor. Wealthy black lawyer and businessman A. W. Willis, Jr. is less successful, however, running a poor fourth in a nonpartisan election for mayor of Memphis on October 5.

OCTOBER 6

The Equal Employment Opportunity Commission (EEOC) declares that there is widespread discrimination against Negroes in the nation's drug industry. EEOC Chairman Clifford Alexander meets with Food & Drugs Commissioner James L. Goddard and 24 representatives of industry whose companies account for 70% of the drug business. Alexander threatens to institute the "complaint process" unless hiring and upgrading of Negroes commences immediately.

OCTOBER 20

An all-white Mississippi federal jury of five men and seven women returns a verdict of guilty in the 1964 murder trial of 3 civil rights workers near Philadelphia. Seven men are convicted of conspiracy; eight, however, are acquitted, and three are declared to be victims of mistrial. Among the guilty are chief deputy sheriff Cecil Price and Sam Bowers, imperial wizard of the Ku Klux Klan.

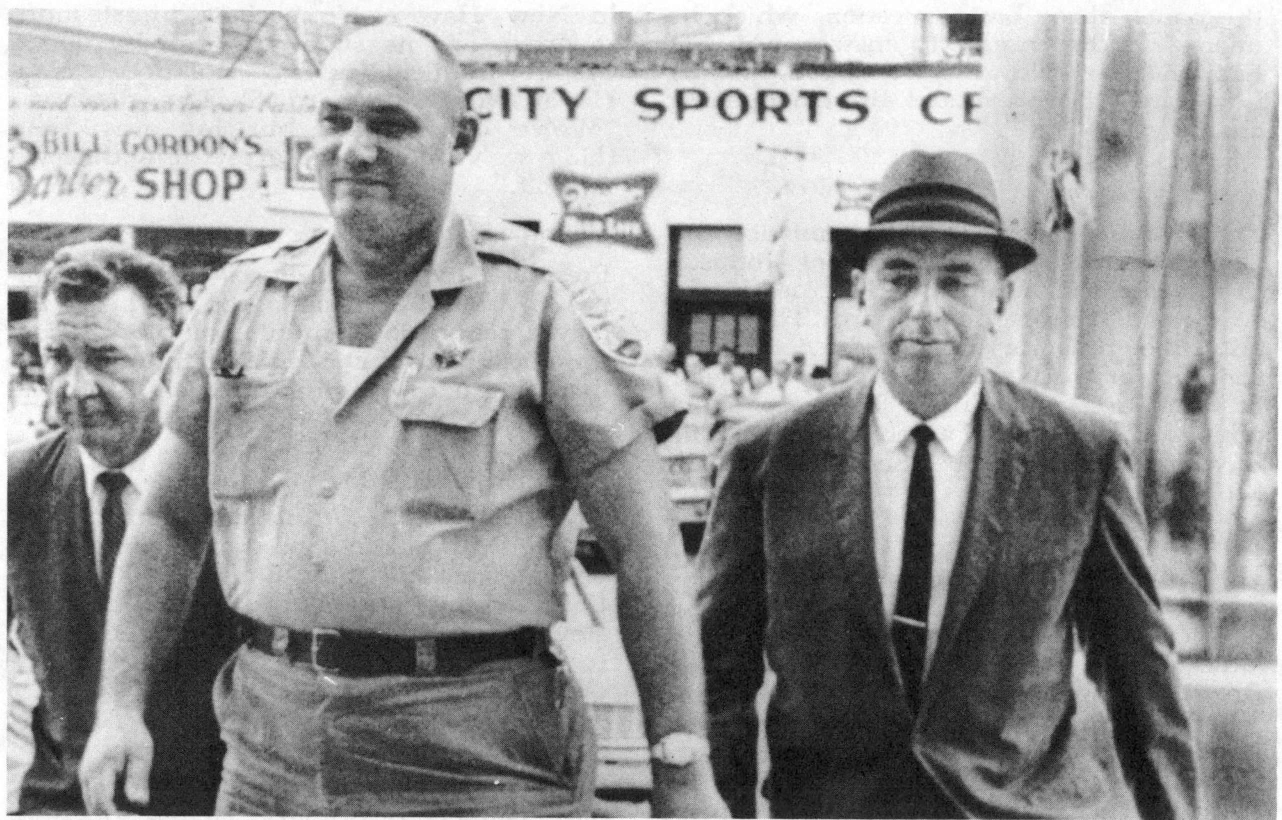

Mississippi Sheriff Lawrence Rainey was accused of conspiracy in the murder of three civil rights workers in 1964.

NOVEMBER 7
Black candidates Richard Hatcher and Carl Stokes capture the mayoralty of Gary, Indiana and Cleveland, Ohio, respectively.

NOVEMBER 28
Martin Luther King, Jr. announces significant victories for SCLC's Operation Breadbasket, a program of skillful buying and selective pressure designed to convince white chain stores operating in ghetto neighborhoods to hire and upgrade more blacks.

DECEMBER 4
Martin Luther King, Jr. announces plans for a massive civil disobedience campaign scheduled for Washington, D.C. in the spring of 1968 and designed to apply pressure on Congress and the Johnson Administration to end poverty by providing jobs and income for all of America's citizens.

DECEMBER 27
Roy Innis is named to succeed Lincoln Lynch as associate national director of CORE. Innis, a militant black nationalist, was formerly chairman of CORE's New York (Harlem) chapter.

1968

JANUARY 4

Black poet/playwright Leroi Jones is sentenced to 2½-3 years in prison and fined $1,000 for illegal possession of firearms during the July 1967 riots in Newark. Two others are sentenced with Jones, but their terms are far less severe.

JANUARY 8

NAACP executive director Roy Wilkins concedes that his organization's membership decreased by 3% in 1967, with a consequent loss in operating revenue as well. Wilkins attributes the decline to the problems of central cities, and the violence which invariably produces a loss of sympathy for all black organizations. He ignores reference to the appeal of other militant black groups at odds with NAACP strategy.

JANUARY 8-13

Adam Clayton Powell, rejected by the House in 1967 after having been excluded from that body due to irregularities in the use of Congressional funds, goes on a speaking tour of California campuses, exhorting his white listeners "to join the black revolution" and classifying black power as "the saving grace of the U.S."

JANUARY 24

President Johnson appeals to Congress to enact his pending 1967 civil rights proposals in the areas of housing, jobs, jury selection, and federal protection of persons exercising their civil rights. The President recognizes that minorities in America are subject to social, educational, and economic disparities, not merely the equities or inequities of law. He places heavy stress on the denial of equal justice and opportunity as the primary factors behind the tragedy of urban riots, but he insists that such lawlessness must be curbed, if only because its prime victims are ghetto residents themselves.

FEBRUARY 5-26

Three black youths are shot to death and more than 30 people are wounded in a racial outburst involving police and students at Orangeburg's South Carolina State College. The violence is the culmination of student protest against the segregation of a local bowling alley. Students begin the protests on February 5 and continue them the next evening when 15 are arrested on trespassing charges. One policeman and seven students are injured and hospitalized. On February 7, the campus is sealed off and classes are suspended in the wake of rock and bottle-throwing incidents. The three students shot on February 8 are fired on by police who mistakenly believe one of their troopers has been shot when, in reality, he has been knocked down by a piece of lumber heaved by a demonstrator. On February 9, Governor McNair orders a curfew, and attributes the violence to "black power" advocates, including Cleveland Sellers, state coordinator for SNCC. Sellers, under arrest, is held on $50,000 bond. On February 11, local Negroes call for the removal of the National Guard, and announce plans for a boycott of white business. The city fathers counter by establishing a Human Relations Commission which resolves to prevent further outbreaks by determining the causes of the present one. On February 13, the NAACP criticizes the commission for failing to consult with it before appointing the Negro members. On February 24, the Southern Regional Council issues a report analyzing the Orangeburg upheaval and tracing it to such things as: the emotional appeal of Black Power to young blacks, white overreaction to this euphoria, the tendency of blacks to see violence as being more and more necessary in the face of continued failure to enforce federal laws (in this case, the 1964 Civil Rights Act), and the expectation by whites that police power and military force must be utilized to cope with all forms of public demonstrations. The analysis does not prevent later violence after the resumption of classes at the College on February 26.

FEBRUARY 15-17

McGeorge Bundy of the Ford Foundation says his organization will work to eliminate racial prejudice even if it is forced to lend its support to black separatists. The Foundation announces grants to three experimental projects in school decentralization in New York City—the IS 201 complex, and Ocean-Hill Brownsville in Brooklyn, and Two Bridges in lower New York.

FEBRUARY 29

The President's National Advisory Commission on Civil Disorders issues an exhaustive report on the causes of the civil disorder that disrupted the nation in 1967. The commission identifies the major cause of the rioting as the existence of two separate societies in America—"one black, one white, separate and unequal." It charges that white racism, more than anything else, was the chief catalyst in the already explosive mixture of discrimination, poverty and frustration that ignited so many urban ghettos in the tragic summer of 1967. It reminds white America how deeply it is implicated in the existence of the ghetto. "White institutions created it, white institutions maintain it, and white society condones it." To overcome this terrible and crushing legacy, the Commission implores the nation to initiate a massive and sustained commitment to action and reform, and appeals for unprecedented levels of "funding and performance" in housing, education, employment, welfare, law enforcement, and the mass media.

MARCH 11

The Senate passes the Civil Rights Bill of 1968, prompting President Johnson to hail the "nation's commitment to human rights under law." Among its major provisions are sweeping housing and anti-riot measures which go far beyond the federal protections offered to civil rights workers in the 1967 House version of the bill.

MARCH 12

Though he was victorious in the primary, Charles Evers is defeated by a 2-1 margin in the special runoff election for the Congressional seat in Mississippi's Third District. His rival, Charles Griffin, outpolls him 87,761 to 43,083. Evers carries two of the district's 12 counties, Jefferson and Claiborne.

MARCH 18

The Department of Health, Education and Welfare (HEW) extends its school desegregation guidelines to Northern schools. It calls upon the elimination of such concrete examples of unequal treatment as overcrowded classes, lower per-pupil expenditures, less-qualified teachers, and inadequate textbooks.

MARCH 22-24

Adam Clayton Powell returns to New York City and surrenders on criminal contempt-of-court charges. On March 24, Powell tells his congregation at Abyssinian Baptist Church that nonviolence is no longer the most effective strategy in the civil rights struggle. Powell says black leadership is in the hands of a "new breed," dedicated to retaliatory violence. His words: "Think big, think black, and think like a child of God."

MARCH 28-29

A teen-aged black youth is slain in Memphis after a protest march led by Martin Luther King, Jr. deteriorates into violence and looting. The march culminates six weeks of labor strike activity involving the sanitation workers of the city, 90% of whom are black. The workers seek a pay raise, a dues checkoff system, seniority rights, health and hospitalization insurance and recognition of the American Federation of State, County and Municipal Employees as bargaining agents. City officials, including the mayor, contend the strike is illegal under the terms of a State Supreme Court decision banning strikes by public employees. Civil rights leaders and black ministers call for a boycott of downtown business and urge massive civil disobedience to express support for the strikers. Such action broadens the thrust of the strike and transforms it into a general civil rights action. On the day of the march, disturbances begin almost immediately. Some black students who have been refused the right to leave school and participate in the march begin pelting police with bricks; others smash department store windows along Beale Street and steal merchandise. Still, most of the marchers (estimates vary from 6,000 to 20,000) are peaceful until city and county police join the National Guard in quelling the disturbances. After Dr. King is spirited away to safety at a nearby hotel, tear gas is fired at the crowds, and more than 150 persons are arrested, 40 of them on looting charges.

APRIL 4-11

The nation and the world are shocked by the terrible news of the assassination of Martin Luther King, Jr. by a sniper's bullet in Memphis. The killing triggers a wave of violence in such urban centers as Washington, D.C., Chicago, Baltimore and Kansas City, where disorders, lootings, burnings, and shootings are most pronounced. Some 46 persons are killed in the aftermath of the slaying, and thousands of others are either injured or arrested. Local law enforcement officials are unable to maintain order, necessitating the activation of some 34,000 National Guard troops. Felled by a single bullet fired from a distance of only 50-100 yards from the point of impact, Dr. King was pronounced dead at St. Joseph's Hospital at 7:05 p.m. CST, barely an hour after he had been hit. Attorney General Ramsey Clark, on hand to conduct the preliminary investigation in person, declares that the early evidence points to the crime as being the work of a single assassin. Witnesses report seeing a white man running from the doorway of a rooming house at 420 South Main Street minutes after the shooting. On April 5, Rev. Ralph Abernathy is named to succeed King, and discloses that SCLC's first public gesture will be to lead the march King himself was planning. Three days later, Coretta Scott King takes her place in the front ranks of the marchers, locking arms with two of the 42,000 people on hand for the demonstration. King's body is put on public view at Ebenezer Baptist Church on April 6. He is buried at South View Cemetery on April 9 after funeral services are held at the church and a general memorial service is conducted at Morehouse

The trajectory of the shot fatal to Dr. Martin Luther King, Jr.

College, his alma mater. There is an eerie magnificence and a sublime dignity to the last gesture in the proceedings before interment when the King coffin is carried through the streets on a faded green farm wagon pulled by two Georgia mules. In accordance with a request of Mrs. King, the tape-recorded voice of King echoes through the crowd at the funeral service as a last reminder of the man and a vivid testimony to his courage: "Say . . . that I tried to love and serve humanity . . . say that I was a drum major for peace . . . for righteousness . . ." Tributes, words of sympathy, of warning, of apprehension pour in from all over the world: from the Vatican, from Africa, from Red China, from the leaders of the Western world, and the black and white leaders of America.

APRIL 10-11

The assassination moves the House to submit to the President a Senate-passed civil rights bill prohibiting racial discrimination in the sale or rental of 80% of the nation's housing. The President signs the measure on April 11, and counsels the nation to stay on the road to progress by recognizing "the process of law."

APRIL 16

An accord is reached in the Memphis sanitationmen's strike, the issue which brought Martin Luther King, Jr. to the beleaguered Southern city which turned out to be his place of doom. Most of the workers' demands are met, including dues checkoff, recognition of a bargaining agent, and an immediate pay raise.

APRIL 23

Roman Catholic bishops call on the faithful to "declare war" on racism in housing, education, and employment. The National Conference on Catholic Bishops appropriates $25,000 to "Operation Connection," an interfaith group raising money to finance black-sponsored programs in five cities.

MAY 11-JUNE 10

Nine caravans of poor people begin arriving in Washington, D.C., the vanguard of the Poor People's Campaign. The Defense Department alerts "selected troop units" to help D.C. police in the event of violence. On Mother's Day, May 12, Mrs. Martin Luther King, Jr. leads a march of welfare mothers from 20 cities, and declares at a subsequent rally that she will try to enlist the support of all the nation's women "in a campaign of conscience." The next day, Ralph Abernathy, clad in blue denims and using carpenter's tools, presides at the christening of Resurrection City, the ply-

Dr. King is carried to his final resting place on a mule-driven cart.

The mule train – symbol of the 1968 Poor People's March.

wood shantytown erected within walking distance of the White House and the Capital. Demonstrations follow almost immediately as the SCLC staff leadership begins to put pressure on Congress and the Administration to declare its dedication to the goal of eliminating poverty in the U.S. Meanwhile, bad weather contributes to the mounting internal crises being faced by residents of the city. Inadequate cooking, bathing and sanitation facilities create health hazards for some, and induce others to leave the campsite. Bayard Rustin, called in to lead a special Solidarity Day March on June 19, resigns on June 7 following a dispute among staff hierarchy as to the exact nature of Rustin's role. The controversy stems from Rustin's association with reformist sentiments and pressure on Abernathy from other quarters to adopt a more revolutionary stance. Abernathy explains that Rustin does not intend to press for jobs, a minimum guaranteed income, major housing and welfare reform and an end to the war in Vietnam. Rustin's replacement, Sterling Tucker of the Washington Urban League, drafts a revised list of demands which include the establishment of strong federal gun control laws and a commitment to de-escalate the Vietnam war. On the positive side, Abernathy is able to report, as the campaign draws to a close, that certain gains have been recorded. The Department of Agriculture, for instance, agrees to "provide food to the neediest counties in this country"; the Senate approves an amendment removing restrictions on the Agriculture Department's use of contingency funds for this purpose; the Senate approves a bill to increase low-income housing construction; and the OEO allocates 25 million dollars for expanded programs, including one encouraging participation of the poor.

MAY 27-30

Violence sweeping the streets of Louisville results in the deaths of two Negroes and the activation of over 1,000 National Guardsmen to quiet the disturbances. Cause of the upheaval is the attempt by a patrolman to disperse a street-corner rally being held to protest the reinstatement of an unpopular policeman.

JUNE 5-8

Senator Robert Kennedy is shot and killed in Los Angeles moments after leaving a rally in celebration of his victory over

Robert Kennedy moments before he was assassinated. Over his left shoulder stands bodyguard Rosey Grier.

Eugene McCarthy in the California Democratic primary. Seized almost immediately after the shooting is Sirhan Sirhan, a young Jordanian resident of the Los Angeles area who is disarmed by Roosevelt Grier, one of the black bodyguards and aides who had been accompanying Kennedy throughout his California campaign to protect him from excitable crowds. (The other two are Rafer Johnson, former Olympic decathlon champion, and Deacon Jones, Los Angeles footballer.) Kennedy is flown by presidential jet to New York on June 6. Among the passengers consoling his grieving widow Ethel are Mrs. Martin Luther King, Jr. and Mrs. Medgar Evers, both of whom have seen their own husbands fall victim to the assassin's bullet. Late in the night of June 8, Kennedy is buried at Arlington National Cemetery under floodlights and only a few feet from the remains of his brother, former President John F. Kennedy.

JUNE 8

James Earl Ray, assassin of Dr. Martin Luther King, Jr. is arrested at a London airport on June 8, the same day on which Senator Kennedy is buried at Arlington. Four days later, the U.S. applies for extradition, thus ending what is said to have been the most extensive manhunt in U.S. history. Ray had been under indictment as Eric Starvo Galt since April 23, and was first indicted under his real name on May 7. After Ray's capture, rumors of conspiracy again multiply, but Attorney General Ramsey Clark continues to make numerous public statements discounting them.

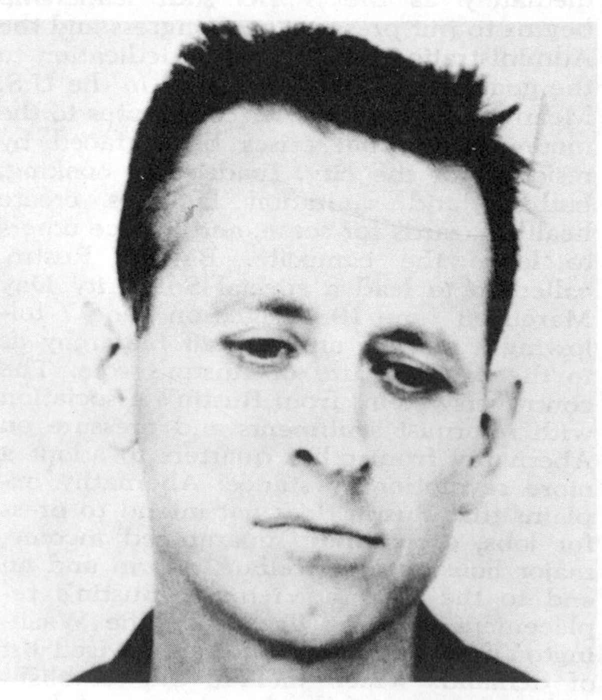

James Earl Ray

JUNE 25-27

Ralph Abernathy is sentenced to 20 days in jail for leading an unlawful assembly at the foot of Capitol Hill. From his cell, he issues a letter encouraging the clergy to join in a demonstration the next day. The letter, reminiscent of Dr. King's Letter from a Birmingham Jail, is distributed nationally, but less than 25 clergymen respond. Abernathy announces his intention to fast for spiritual strength.

JULY 8

CORE National Director Floyd McKissick takes a leave of absence from the organization, whereupon Roy Innis assumes the directorship. Innis pledges to tighten up the organization and give it a single direction.

JULY 16

Black comedian Dick Gregory is released from Olympia, Washington jail after being held for six weeks following his conviction on charges of illegal net fishing during a 1966 Indian fishing-rights demonstration. While in custody, Gregory fasted for six weeks in order to call attention to the civil rights struggle of the Indian minority.

JULY 23-27

A racial outburst in Cleveland's Glenville district results in the death of 11 persons, eight of them black (including three labelled as nationalists), and three white policemen. Black mayor Carl Stokes helps restore order with relative rapidity after a night of burnings and lootings which result in over a million dollars worth of property damage. Over 3,000 National Guardsmen are on the scene, but they are not widely utilized. Blame for the attack is laid to Ahmed (Fred) Evans, 37-year-old anti-poverty worker and head of the Black Nationalists of New Libya. At the height of the shoot-out, followers of Evans occupy several Glenville buildings, exchanging gunfire with police reinforcements. Stokes later confers with black community leaders who agree to help organize citizen's patrols and assist regular police to maintain order. The distressed areas are cordoned off, but the renewed outbreak of looting and violence forces Stokes to send in Guard units once more, albeit sparingly. Within a day, calm is restored, and the Stokes 9 p.m.-6 a.m. curfew is lifted. On June 26, Ahmed Evans is arraigned on three charges of first degree murder; a day later, Stokes offers an analysis of the incident in which he claims it is "uniquely different" from those experienced elsewhere in the country. In this case, Stokes feels that the episode was part of a deliberate, premeditated attempt to attack police in a revolutionary manner. SNCC program director Phil Hutchings confirms this estimate in a New York press conference.

JULY 27

The Kerner Commission releases preliminary findings which indicate a sharp rise in the number of Negroes who accept urban riots as a justifiable or inevitable response to conditions prevailing in the nation's ghettos. One study totally rejects the so-called "riff-raff" theory, i.e., the assumption that the riots were caused by a small dissatisfied portion of the black community subjected to outside agitation.

AUGUST 1

President Johnson signs into law the Housing and Urban Development Act of 1968 which authorizes more than five billion dollars worth of funds for a three-year program aimed at providing 1.7 million units of new or rehabilitated housing for families with low-income status. The bill sets up a homeownership assistance program that will provide eligible low-income purchasers with an interest-rate subsidy. Other subsidies cover construction or rehabilitation of rental and cooperative housing.

AUGUST 6

Representatives of the Poor People's Campaign put in various appearances at the convention headquarters of various Republican Presidential hopefuls, receiving an enthusiastic welcome from New York's Governor Rockefeller, a lukewarm reception from the Nixon entourage, and a flat rejection from California's Governor Reagan who bars them from his news conference. Claiming to represent the "51st state—that of poverty," Abernathy calls for a platform "to end poverty and injustice in America," and declares that Rockefeller is the last hope of the party to capture "the black vote."

AUGUST 7-8

Two days of looting, fire bombing and shooting in the black section of Miami culminate in Florida Governor Claude Kirk's decision to summon the National Guard to quell disorders. Despite Ralph Abernathy's plea for "an end to this violence," crowds of Negroes battle police in the eight-block area which the latter have cordoned off. On August 8, three Negroes are killed in gun battles with law enforcement officials. Although Dade County Mayor Chuck Hall accuses outsiders of instigating the trouble, particularly to gain exposure before a nationwide audience, the 10% rate of unemployment, particularly among blacks in the 16-22 age bracket, is certainly a factor producing the explosive situation.

AUGUST 29

Ralph Abernathy, appearing with his Poor People's entourage, addresses an August 29 rally at Grant Park, and accuses Democratic officials of rebuffing his requests to address the convention and offering little encouragement or support for Poor People campaigners. Abernathy demands a personal apology from Democratic nominee Hubert Humphrey. Elsewhere on the streets, comedian Dick Gregory and 300 other demonstrators marching toward the convention site are halted by police, who arrest 150 persons and disperse the others by using tear gas.

AUGUST 29

Dr. Nathan Wright announces that white newsmen will be barred from the Third National Conference on Black Power due to the allegedly false stories they filed at the previous conference. During the four-day meeting, some 4,000 delegates approve more than 100 formal proposals in such areas as politics, education and economics. One of them calls for a national Negro party.

SEPTEMBER 4

More than 150 whites, many of them said to be off-duty patrolmen, allegedly attack a handful of Black Panthers and white sympathizers who are standing in a hallway of Brooklyn's Criminal Court building. The policemen, said to be members of a right-wing group within the department, are reported to have proclaimed themselves "the white tigers" and to have swung blackjacks while stomping the outnumbered group. Mayor Lindsay orders an investigation, but no arrests are made, nor is disciplinary action taken.

SEPTEMBER 8-27

Black Panther Huey Newton is tried and convicted of manslaughter in the October 28, 1967 fatal shooting of a white patrolman. Nearly three weeks later, Newton is sentenced to 2-15 years imprisonment. Both the trial and the conviction serve to introduce the nation at large to a new and formidable organization of black militants: the Black Panthers. Who they are and what they represent is the subject of occasionally hysterical inquiry. Their numbers are relentlessly sought out, but carefully concealed—if indeed they are known to anyone. "Them that says don't know; them that knows don't say" is a clever Malcolm X retort applied to the persistent question.

SEPTEMBER 9

Opening day of the N. Y. teachers' strike which immobilizes the public school system in the city and keeps a million pupils out of the schools for several weeks. The dispute carries strong racial overtones, centering as it does on the Ocean-Hill Brownsville School Demonstration District, a predominantly black and Puerto Rican district in Brooklyn, most of whose 500 teachers are white. Teachers, fearing student and community harassment, and administrators, seeking to implement the notion of community control or involvement in the operation of the schools, clash head on over jurisdiction, procedures, tenure, seniority, the right to teach, etc. The union vows to remain out on strike until its members are assured they cannot be arbitrarily dismissed; the community, on the other hand, feels the teachers show callous disregard for the needs of the children, plus a disturbing unwillingness to submit to some form of periodic evaluation or quality control. Battle lines in the dispute crystallize around three basic positions: complete retention of the status quo, creation of a decentralized system recognizing neighborhood or local residential patterns, the establishment of full-fledged community control based on local self-determination in matters pertaining to funding, hiring and firing, and direction of curriculum.

SEPTEMBER 10

The Gallup poll reports that 50% of union members interviewed in the South favor Governor Wallace over both major party nominees, Humphrey (29%) and Nixon (16%). The poll shows that labor's traditional support of the Democratic nominee is being overridden by increasing blue-collar disenchantment with the pace of black progress in the labor market and with the social strength of the black movement.

SEPTEMBER 17-24

News that Eldridge Cleaver has been asked to deliver a series of 10 lectures at the Berkeley campus of UCLA touches off a furious battle between radical student supporters of the idea and conservatives who denounce the Black Panther leader as an "advocate of racism and violence." Governor Reagan is among those who oppose Cleaver; the Board of Regents takes the stand that he should be allowed to appear as a one-time guest lecturer; students demand that all conditions restricting his appearance be rescinded. Cleaver eventually delivers a single lecture entitled "The Roots of Racism." The lecture is well received, and is regarded as scholarly and moderate.

OCTOBER 8

Some 250 Washington, D.C. Negroes protest the fatal shooting of a black pedestrian by a motorcycle policeman who had reportedly tried to stop the victim on a jaywalking charge. Demonstrators set fires and block traffic until police reinforcements disperse them with tear gas. The patrolman is eventually charged by a federal grand jury and exonerated of guilt.

OCTOBER 14

Gary Mayor Richard Hatcher and Detroit Congressman John Conyers, members of an all-black National Committee of Inquiry, propose that black voters withhold their support of Democratic nominee Hubert Humphrey unless he takes an unequivocal stand on the war in Vietnam and agrees in advance to support programs designed to cope meaningfully with problems indigenous to all black communities across the nation.

NOVEMBER 13

Five black gunmen allegedly invade the headquarters of the New England Grass Roots Organization (NEGRO), shooting to death three officials involved with the self-help association and wounding two others. Later news reports indicate that the men, both victims and intruders, are involved in a consortium of black organizations which has received almost two million dollars from the Labor Department to institute a job training program. The Labor Department ultimately cancels the contract, disclosing that only 12 trainees have in fact been hired by the consortium.

NOVEMBER 13-19

Two gunbattles involving Panthers in California keep the feud between the Party and the police in the national spotlight. On November 13, in Berkeley, one Panther and one patrolman are injured in a shooting fracas after police stop a car whose driver is accused of a traffic viola-

George Wallace, the splinter candidate in the 1968 Presidential election.

tion; six days later, three police are wounded in a gunfight with eight Negroes wanted for questioning in a service station holdup. The eight Negroes are in possession of a panel truck identified as a vehicle of "The Black Panther Black Community News Service."

NOVEMBER 27-29

Eldridge Cleaver, Black Panther Minister of Information and Presidential candidate of the Peace and Freedom Party, is sought by police as a parole violator on a fugitive warrant issued in San Francisco. Cleaver is believed to have left the U. S. for Montreal to attend an international conference of anti-war militants. Local officials ask the FBI to join in the manhunt.

DECEMBER 1-5

Three members of the Panthers are arrested on charges of carrying out a machinegun attack on a Jersey City police station on November 29. A Panther spokesman claims that a Dec. 1 bombing of party headquarters in Newark is in response to the Jersey City attack. A police sergeant cites the arrest of seven Newark Panthers on November 28 as the cause of the precinct attack. Amid such frequent speculation and wholesale accusations on both sides, little explanation can be offered save the conscientious reporting of the kaleidoscopic incidents and the conflicting versions of what happened.

1969

JANUARY 3

After long and entangled debate concerning his qualifications and conduct, the House of Representatives votes to seat Adam Clayton Powell, although it fines him $25,000 for alleged misuse of payroll funds and travel allowances, and demotes him to freshman status by stripping him of his seniority rank.

JANUARY 29

Barely a week after his inauguration, President Nixon stirs the apprehensions of the liberal alliance by postponing for 60 days a deadline that would have cut off federal funds for five Southern school districts who have failed to abolish segregated schooling. HEW secretary Robert Finch asks for more time to study the cases, but others interpret the moves as a calculated and familiar stall.

FEBRUARY 6

President Nixon admits he is not regarded as "a friend by many of our black citizens," professing instead a desire to be a "friend to all the people." At his press conference, he reaffirms his reluctance to cut off federal funds to school districts refusing to foster integration.

MARCH 10

Confessed murderer James Earl Ray is sentenced to 99 years for the slaying of Dr. Martin Luther King, Jr. The Department of Justice brings no evidence to bear that Ray was part of a larger conspiracy, although it leaves open that possibility by continuing its investigation.

MARCH 30

An apparent shoot-out between a black separatist group and members of the police results in the death of one patrolman, the wounding of a second patrolman and other injuries to four civilians. Later, some 135 persons are arrested, but order is restored and the apprehension of a repeat performance of the 1967 Detroit holocaust dies away.

APRIL 8

The Justice Department moves against Cannon Mills, a Southern textile company which it accuses of bias in employment and housing. The move marks the first time the government has exerted legal pressure in the question of company-owned housing facilities which are segregated by design.

APRIL 9

Harvard-trained Clifford Alexander, Jr. resigns as chairman of the Equal Employment Opportunity Commission (EEOC), citing "a crippling lack of administration support" as the main grounds for his departure. Mr. Alexander alludes specifically to a threat made by Republican Senator Dirksen to have him ousted for harassing businessmen on the issue of job discrimination.

APRIL 19-20

Student members of the campus Afro-American Society seize a student center at Cornell University, protesting, among other things, the alleged harassment of black co-eds and the burning of a cross on campus. Whites try unsuccessfully to remove them, and four are injured in the brief skirmish. After the administration yields to their demands, students relinquish control of the building and leave peacefully, though with weapons poised for action. Campus radicals cheer; most students and faculty are shocked or appalled.

Armed black students emerge from the student union building at Cornell.

APRIL 22-26
More than 700 striking Charleston hospital workers are led by Rev. Ralph Abernathy of the Southern Christian Leadership Conference (SCLC) in a march designed to dramatize their deplorable working conditions and draw national support for their unionizing efforts. Mrs. Martin Luther King, Jr. lends her presence to support the strikers. On April 26, 100 black students are thrown in jail when they try to march down the city's main street in support of the workers. National Guardsmen and state troopers on duty in the city arrest over 200 people.

MAY 2
The Department of Health, Education and Welfare (HEW) authorizes Antioch College to operate an all-Negro black studies program on the condition that nonblacks are excluded only on the ground that their background is not "relevant" to the courses, not because of arbitrary distinctions based on race, color, or national origin.

MAY 6
Howard Lee is elected mayor of Chapel Hill, North Carolina, the first black man to hold such an office in a predominantly white North Carolinian city.

MAY 13
Charles Evers joins a host of successful black candidates who win assorted political posts in the state of Mississippi. Evers defeats a white incumbent in an election free from violence and harassment, and becomes mayor of Fayette.

MAY 28
Los Angeles City Councilman Thomas Bradley, a heavy favorite, is upset by incumbent mayor Sam Yorty in a mayoralty election that is riddled with unsavory campaign tactics and blatant appeals to prejudice. Yorty resorts to unsubstantiated smears and guilt-by-association moves which polarize the voting community and heighten racial tension.

JUNE 6-20
Testimony released in a federal court in Houston, Texas indicates that the telephones of Martin Luther King, Jr. and Elijah Muhammad have been tapped by the FBI, despite the fact that President Johnson had ordered a halt to all wiretaps in 1965. The loophole in the order stems from the Attorney General's discretion in reported cases of "national security." Former Attorney General Ramsey Clark labels

as misleading the statement by FBI director J. Edgar Hoover that Robert Kennedy ordered wiretaps on Dr. King.

JUNE 16
The Supreme Court slaps down the House of Representative suspension of Harlem Congressman Adam Clayton Powell, and terms that action a violation of the U. S. Constitution which establishes only the proper age, a residency requirement, and U. S. citizenship as grounds for possible representation of a constituency.

JUNE 20
Rev. Ralph Abernathy is thrown into jail on charges of inciting to riot in the aftermath of a brick and bottle-throwing episode which involves police and National Guard near a Negro church in Charleston. The violence erupts at a rally supporting the continuing strike and persistent demands of the city's adamant hospital workers.

JULY 3
The Nixon Administration affirms its intention to hold Southern school districts to the September deadline for school desegregation, but its exemption of some districts from the mandate on grounds that they have "bonafide . . . problems" causes the NAACP's Roy Wilkins to accuse the government of breaking the law.

JULY 6
James Forman of the National Black Economic Development Conference receives a check for $15,000 from the Washington Square United Methodist Church in New York City. The church is the first predominantly white organization to come up with some money in the aftermath of Forman's earlier demand made on American churches that they owe 500 million dollars in reparations for helping to perpetuate slavery.

JULY 9
The Justice Department accuses the Chicago Board of Education and the state board in Georgia of practicing segregation. The latter group is said to be maintaining a dual system which is unconstitutional, while the former is singled out for segregating faculty.

JULY 18
The 113-day old Charleston hospital strike comes to a close. Its most notable achievement is the cooperation achieved between labor and civil rights groups seeking union representation and racial justice.

JULY 29
Black candidates win four of five seats on the county commission of Alabama's Greene County, and also capture two of the five school board seats in a special election victory which Ralph Abernathy calls "the most significant achievement by black men since the Emancipation."

AUGUST 1
The Justice Department files suit against the state of Georgia to end segregation in its schools, in the first desegregation suit against an entire state. Governor Lester G. Maddox condemns the action as criminal and declares the state will "win the war against these tyrants."

AUGUST 18-23
President Nixon nominates Southern judicial conservative Clement Haynsworth, Jr. to occupy the seat vacated by departing Justice Abe Fortas. Investigation of Haynsworth's holdings reveals that the judge tried a 1963 case involving a textile concern depending for supplies on a vending-machine company in which he owned stock.

Judge Clement Hansworth

AUGUST 20
Bobby Seale's defense attorney accuses the Justice Department of initiating a national campaign to intimidate and harass the Black Panther Party. Seale, being held on

$25,000 bail, is under indictment for the May 1969 slaying of an alleged Panther informer in Connecticut.

AUGUST 21-25
The 600 delegates at the National Welfare Rights Organization convention in Detroit assail President Nixon's $1600 annual minimum family assistance figure as inadequate, and call for a figure of $3,200.

AUGUST 25-29
Five construction sites in Pittsburgh are closed by several hundred black construction workers and members of the Black Construction Coalition to protest "discriminatory hiring practices." Four hundred angry white workers stage counter-demonstrations on August 28 and 29 to protest the work stoppage agreed to by the construction project owner while negotiations for a black job training project were in progress.

AUGUST 26-27
Civil rights lawyers in the Nixon Administration make known their dissatisfaction with the government's request in the application of desegregation guidelines. The lawyers say that the Nixon braintrust is instituting a slowdown in virtually all areas of civil rights enforcement. When news reaches them that the government has called for a delay in Mississippi school integration, more than half of the Justice Department's Civil Rights Division joins in protest against the decision.

AUGUST 28
Work is suspended on major Pittsburgh construction projects as the city seeks to deal with black demands for more and better jobs in construction. White construction workers lead counter-demonstrations chanting "Wallace in 1972."

SEPTEMBER 2
After a comparatively quiet summer, the nation is stunned at the news that Hartford, Connecticut is the scene of widespread ghetto disorders including firebombings and snipings. Scores of people are placed under arrest, and a dusk-to-dawn curfew is imposed.

SEPTEMBER 2
Governor Nelson Rockefeller of New York urges a federal take-over of all welfare costs at the meeting of the National Governors Conference in Colorado Springs.

SEPTEMBER 3
The Episcopal Church's House of Deputies votes James Forman's Black Economic Development Conference $200,000, part of the 500 million dollars the organization has demanded for injustices to the black man.

SEPTEMBER 3
General Leonard F. Chapman, Jr., Marine Corps Commander, orders an end to discrimination against blacks in promotions, assignments, and social activities on marine posts.

SEPTEMBER 12
A 105-page report by the U.S. Commission on Civil Rights, chaired by Father Theodore Hesburgh, president of Notre Dame University, charges the Nixon administration with choosing the wrong school desegregation policy and covering its actions with overly optimistic statistics.

SEPTEMBER 12
Black militant Robert F. Williams lands in Detroit and is arrested in connection with a kidnapping charge. The kidnapping was supposed to have occurred in North Carolina eight years previously. Since that time Williams had been in self-imposed exile in Cuba, China, and Africa.

SEPTEMBER 23
Labor Secretary George P. Shultz orders federally assisted construction projects in Philadelphia to follow the guidelines for minority hiring suggested in the so-called "Philadelphia Plan."

OCTOBER 17
Dr. Clifton Reginald Wharton, Jr., a black economist from New York City, is elected president of Michigan State University. Dr. Wharton becomes the first black to head a major public and predominantly white university.

OCTOBER 29
The Supreme Court orders an end to all school segregation "at once." The decision replaces the Warren court's doctrine of "all deliberate speed," and is regarded as a setback for the Nixon administration.

OCTOBER 29
Judge Julius J. Hoffman orders Bobby Seale, on trial for conspiracy to incite to riot in Chicago, gagged and chained after Seale disrupts court proceeding by jumping up and shouting insults at the judge.

NOVEMBER 4
Carl B. Stokes is reelected mayor of Cleve-

land. He is the first black mayor of a major American city.

NOVEMBER 5

Black Panther leader Bobby Seale is sentenced to four years in prison for contempt of court by Chicago 7 judge Julius Hoffman.

NOVEMBER 21

The Senate rejects the nomination of Clement F. Haynsworth, Jr. of South Carolina to the Supreme Court by a vote of 55 to 45.

1970

JANUARY 3

Mississippi Governor John Bell Williams announces his intention to submit to the state legislature a proposal to authorize income tax credits of up to $500 a year for contributors to "private" educational institutions. The plan is designed to create a "workable alternative" to school desegregation. That same day, HEW reports that a comprehensive survey indicates that 61% of the nation's black students and 65.6% of its white students were attending segregated schools as of 1968.

JANUARY 5-6

Negro children are enrolled in three formerly all-white Mississippi districts under the watchful eyes of federal marshals and Justice Department officials. Scores of white parents picket the schools, while others keep their children home, relying on the new private schools which have been chartered to circumvent desegregation. HEW Secretary Robert Finch supports a countermove to cut off tax exemptions for the 300-400 "private schools" which have opened in the South since the 1964 Civil Rights Act was enacted.

JANUARY 10-23

Four Southern governors—Maddox of Georgia, Brewer of Alabama, McKeithen of Louisiana, and Kirk of Florida—promise to reject all busing plans designed for their states by the federal government or the courts. Each moves independently to block the busing order. Maddox asks the legislature to abolish compulsory attendance; McKeithen reveals no plan, but describes himself as one "drawing the line in the dust"; Brewer denies the courts have the constitutional authority to order busing as a device to achieve racial balance and promises to use his full executive powers to prevent it; Kirk vows to issue an executive order to block further desegregation of Florida schools.

JANUARY 12

The Supreme Court refuses to review the ruling of an Ohio State Court which upholds an equal employment plan comparable to the Nixon Administration's "Philadelphia Plan." The plan requires state contractors to give assurances that they will employ a specified number of black workers in projects constructed with federal funds or sponsored *in toto* by the federal government. The Ohio contractor who brought suit in the case had refused to provide such assurances.

JANUARY 13

A three-judge federal court orders the Internal Revenue Service to refuse tax-exemption status for more segregated private academies in Mississippi. Those already in existence are immune from the ruling.

JANUARY 14

The U.S. Supreme Court overturns a December 1, 1969 Circuit Court of Appeals ruling which sets September 1, 1970 as a pupil desegregation deadline date for six Southern states. The Court sets Feb. 1, 1970 as the new deadline, rejecting a Justice Department bid for postponement. Four justices concur without reservation in reaffirming the conclusion of the Court's October 29, 1969 ruling in *Alexander* vs. *Holmes Board of Education* (see that entry). The words "at once" are requoted from the Alexander decision.

JANUARY 15

Though the day is not yet a national holiday, the anniversary of the birth of Martin Luther King, Jr. is celebrated with impressive ceremonies, eulogies and church services in many parts of the country. Public schools are closed in many cities; in others, they are kept open for formal study of Dr. King's work and utterances. In Atlanta, Mrs. Coretta Scott King dedicates the Martin Luther King, Jr. Memorial Center, which includes his home, the Ebenezer Baptist Church, and the crypt where his remains are housed.

JANUARY 16

Black Panther Warren Kimbro, head of the party's New Haven chapter, pleads guilty to second-degree murder in the killing of alleged Panther informer Alex Rackley. Kimbro faces a possible life term.

JANUARY 19

Florida Governor Claude Kirk petitions the Supreme Court for a rehearing of its January 14 ruling ordering immediate school desegregation. Kirk claims the state is "financially and physically unable" to meet the Court's deadline, and says he will instruct school districts not to change their calendar in mid-year. Two attorneys representing school districts in Louisiana inform the Court that they are encountering insurmountable difficulties in complying with the Court order.

JANUARY 19-20

The nomination to the Supreme Court of G. Harrold Carswell draws the immediate fire of civil rights advocates, including Leroy Clark, former head of operations in North Florida for the NAACP Legal Defense and Education Fund. Clark brands Carswell "the most openly and blatantly segregationist" federal judge before which he has appeared. Joseph Rauh chides the President for submitting "an unknown, whose principal qualification . . . seems to be his opposition to Negro rights."

JANUARY 20

A Los Angeles District Court judge orders the Pasadena school district to submit a desegregation plan for its public schools no later than February 16, 1970. Pasadena is the first Northern school district pressed by the federal government to produce an educational plan in which no single school has a majority of non-white students. The plan is slated to take effect in September 1970.

JANUARY 21

A Chicago coroner's jury finds no grounds for holding the police responsible for murder in the December 4, 1969 deaths of Panthers Fred Hampton and Mark Clark. The jurors maintain that the shootings were a justifiable defense against the gunfire with which police were allegedly greeted during their pre-dawn raid of Hampton's apartment.

G. Harrold Carswell

JANUARY 21-27

Civil rights organizations and labor groups begin a salvo of criticism against the Carswell Supreme Court nomination. On January 21, the NAACP leads off by condemning his "pro-segregation record." Two days later, the SCLC's Ralph Abernathy sends a telegram to Senate leaders pleading for "reassurance to the black community that there is . . . understanding and support . . . for our needs." AFL-CIO president George Meany calls the appointment "a slap in the face to the nation's Negro citizens." Testifying before the Senate Judiciary Committee on January 27, Carswell states: "I am not a racist. I have no notions, secretive or otherwise, of racial superiority." The statement contrasts sharply with a 1948 remark that Carswell would yield to no man "in the firm, vigorous belief in the principles of white supremacy." Carswell is also accused of helping form a private golf club in 1956 in an effort to prevent desegregation.

FEBRUARY 1

Three districts in Louisiana, two in Mississippi and one in Florida comply with the Supreme Court order setting February 1 as the date for establishing integration. About 15 others are granted delays by district court judges, whereas 20 districts choose to disobey the order either by closing schools, or supporting parent-organized boycotts. Vice President Agnew announces a Presidential plan to appoint a cabinet-level committee to advise the districts on how best to implement the court's order without causing wholesale disruption. Elsewhere, South Carolina (January 27) announces that it will comply with the desegregation mandate.

FEBRUARY 2-3

Pretrial hearings open for 13 Black Panthers charged with conspiring to bomb public facilities in New York City. Despite warnings by trial judge John Murtaugh, fist fighting erupts on the second day of the hearings and Murtaugh threatens to impose disciplinary measures to maintain order.

FEBRUARY 5-9

Senators John Stennis and Strom Thurmond demand that Northern school districts be obliged to observe federal desegregation guidelines in the same way as their Southern counterparts. On February 9, Connecticut Senator Abraham Ribicoff endorses the Stennis Amendment, a rider to the House-passed education bill then before the Senate. The Stennis bill is a virtual reduplication of the text of the 1969 New York State bill prohibiting the assignment of students to schools according to race. Ribicoff condemns Northern liberals who blame the South for resistance to integration while, at the same time, failing to recognize and assail similar policies in the North. He chides Northern communities for their "systematic and consistent" denial of educational opportunity to black children.

FEBRUARY 6

Some ⅓ of Denver buses slated to put into effect the city's plan to achieve racial balance by busing the city's school children are destroyed by dynamite bombs which are believed to have been set by fanatic opponents of busing.

FEBRUARY 7

The NAACP asks the U.S. government to examine and ban a fourth-grade Alabama history textbook that "glorifies the Ku Klux Klan," claiming that the vigilante organization appeared only sporadically, and then only to prevent carpetbaggers from taking refuge behind unjust laws.

FEBRUARY 11-16

Black neurosurgeon Dr. Thomas W. Matthew, head of the National Economic Growth and Reconstruction Organization (NEGRO) criticizes the NAACP for its continued harassment of Supreme Court nominee G. Harrold Carswell. Matthew endorses Carswell, citing his "public renunciation of racist views." The Senate Judiciary Committee clears the Carswell nomination on February 16.

FEBRUARY 11-17

School integration is ordered in Los Angeles (February 11) and Pontiac (February 17). In Los Angeles, a Superior Court judge instructs the school system to present a formula by June 1 for integrating the district's 555 schools by no later than September 1971. In Pontiac, Michigan, the community is ordered by a federal judge to integrate its schools at the student, faculty and administrative levels by the fall of 1970.

FEBRUARY 16

President Nixon establishes a Cabinet-level task force to assist and counsel local school districts which have been ordered to desegregate their schools immediately. The objective is to spare the public school system undue disruption while, at the same time, insuring compliance with the law.

FEBRUARY 16

Joe Frazier knocks out Jimmy Ellis to assume undisputed possession of the heavyweight championship of the world. After the match, Frazier indicates he will retire unless a match can be arranged with Muhammad Ali, the former title holder.

FEBRUARY 17

Leon E. Panetta, director of the Office for Civil Rights in the Department of Health, Education and Welfare (HEW), resigns in protest against the Nixon Administration's lax enforcement of the nation's civil rights laws. Panetta states that, though Nixon himself may be sincere in bringing about greater unity among Americans, he is surrounded by others who are perfectly willing to subvert that goal if it is necessary to win the next election.

FEBRUARY 18

The U.S. Senate passes, by a 56-36 margin, an amendment to deny federal funds to *all school districts* whose racial imbalance stems from residential segregation. Mississippi Senator Stennis hails the move as an endorsement of his proposal to force Northern districts to grapple with the same guidelines and policies which are being imposed on the South. The text of Stennis amendment reads as follows:

> "It is the policy of the U.S. that guidelines and criteria pursuant to Title VI of the Civil Rights Act of 1964 and Section 182 of the Elementary and Secondary Amendments of 1966 shall be applied uniformly in all regions of the U.S. in dealing with conditions of segregation by race, whether de jure or de facto, in the schools of the local educational agencies of any state without regard to the origin or cause of such segregation."

FEBRUARY 18

Hearings on the extension of the 1965 Voting Rights Act open in Congress with the NAACP's Clarence Mitchell seeking to reinstate the government's power to veto allegedly discriminatory voting laws in the South. The House amendments to the law seek to curb the government's veto power, a policy which would reduce the pressure on these states to conform to federally approved voting guidelines. The use of federal registrars and the reliance on the enforcement power of the attorney general's office have added almost 900,000 Negroes to the voting rolls in the South.

FEBRUARY 19

Southerners in the House and Senate incorporate into two appropriations bills four riders designed to restore "freedom-of-choice" school plans and to prevent the federal government from resorting to busing as a vehicle to promote racial balance.

FEBRUARY 21-23

Texas Governor Preston Smith recommends a statewide referendum to give voters the opportunity to declare approval or rejection of public school busing. Governors Maddox and McKeithen sign bills prohibiting busing and student/teacher transfers to achieve racial balance; Governor Brewer calls a special session of the legislature to sponsor a similar bill for Alabama.

FEBRUARY 21-25

Three gasoline bombs explode in front of the New York home of State Supreme Court Justice John Murtaugh, presiding judge at the Panther hearings. Though no one is injured, there is some property damage and a warning scrawled on the pavement. "Free the Panther 21." On February 25, Murtaugh halts the hearings, demanding from the defendants a written pledge to observe American courtroom procedures.

FEBRUARY 28

The Senate approves the education appropriations bill after first voting down three Southern riders aimed at diluting the government's power to enforce school desegregation laws. The Senate succeeds entirely in blocking Southern efforts to reinstate "freedom of choice" plans. The Mathias amendment weakens the restrictive language of the House's anti-busing amendment by making it conform to the requirements of the Constitution, which already required integration.

MARCH 2-5

Presidential adviser Daniel Moynihan attempts to explain his controversial White House memorandum in which he proposes to the President the introduction of an era of "benign neglect" toward race problems in general. Moynihan asserts his purpose in drafting the document is (a) to review the progress of a decade and (b) to suggest ways to consolidate those gains, rather than becoming involved in the extremist rhetoric of the militant Black Panthers or equally subversive right-wing fanatics. Despite his attempt to explain his position as a rejection of demagoguery and an appeal to reason and objectivity, civil rights leaders, educators and Congressmen remind the ex-Harvard educator that the Negro is still deprived in many areas of American life and can hardly be expected to endorse a program of neglect and inattention.

MARCH 3

State troopers intervene with riot guns and tear gas to disperse an angry mob, armed with ax handles and baseball bats, which smashes windows and menaces a bus transporting 39 Negro students to an all-white school in Lamar, South Carolina. Two empty buses are overturned; both troopers and mob members are injured, none severely.

MARCH 4-7

White House aide John D. Ehrlichman says he is opposed to school integration if its real purpose is to foster social integration without an accompanying improvement in the calibre of education. Sociologist James S. Coleman, however, suggests that integration is the most effective instrument yet discovered to upgrade the education of poor black children.

MARCH 6

The Mississippi State Senate clears a tax relief bill designed to grant financial support to white parents who intend to enroll their children in private academies.

MARCH 9

The U.S. Supreme Court orders the Memphis school system, consisting of 74,000 black students and 60,000 whites, to end racial segregation, and remands the case to a lower court where it issues instructions to develop an effective desegregation plan.

MARCH 21

Federal Reserve Board member Andrew Brimmer, a leading black economist, declares that there is "a deepening schism" in the black community, despite the economic gains which are being recorded. Upon studying the figures further, Brimmer concludes that the gap is widening between the able and the less able, between the more prepared and those with few skills. In Brimmer's view, this accounts, in part, for the growing militancy at the bottom end of the scale, where the disparity is most keenly felt.

MARCH 24

President Nixon's long-awaited statement on school desegregation (see Documents section, 1970 entry) affirms his "personal belief" that the 1954 Supreme Court decision (*Brown* v. *Board of Education*) is right "in both constitutional and human terms." The President vows to bring the full force of his office and authority to bear toward eliminating *de jure* segregation, but balks at applying the same standard to the question of *de facto* segregation, stating that the courts have not yet provided clear-cut mandates in this domain. Nixon, however, rejects the concept of school busing and offers instead financial aid to upgrade ghetto schools. Most civil rights groups regard the statement as bland, evasive, and retrogressive.

MARCH 25

Self-imposed exile Stokely Carmichael testifies before a closed session of the Senate Internal Security Subcommittee in Washington, D.C. Carmichael discusses his travels and associations in Cuba, Africa, Red China, and Puerto Rico, and explains that his return is linked to his desire to curb drug abuse in the black community. Some observers brand the sessions "an inquisition," others are vexed that they were uninformed about schedules for the proceedings.

MARCH 30

The Metropolitan Applied Research Center, and the Voter Education Project of the Southern Regional Council announce results of a nationwide survey into the number of black elected officials in the U.S. The survey shows there are 48 mayors, 575 other city officials, 362 school board members, 168 legislators, 114 judges, and 99 law enforcement officials. Still, less than 1% of the nation's elected officials are black. Remarkably, however, 38% of those who are black have been elected in the South.

APRIL 6

A motion to return the nomination of G. Harrold Carswell to committee is foiled in the Senate by a 52-44 vote. President Nixon, angered at the recommital attempt, accuses Carswell opponents of trying to usurp his power under the Constitution.

APRIL 7

HEW Secretary Finch predicts the number of Negro children in schools with whites will double by the fall of 1970. Finch maintains that busing will be one of the practices used to enforce desegregation, claiming that 90% of the South's schools already utilize buses for comparable functions. The secretary admits, however, that the decision as to whether discrimination is *de facto* or *de jure* will have to be rendered on an individual basis.

APRIL 7

The recessed pretrial hearings of 13 Black Panthers are resumed in a courtroom atmosphere of calm and restraint on both sides. Justice Murtaugh, unable to obtain a signed pledge from the defendants to uphold the decorum of the court, proceeds nonetheless with the legal issues at hand.

APRIL 7

The Detroit school board approves a busing plan for some 3,000 high school students and announces the initiation of a decentralization plan aimed at dispersing white minority students among the city's secondary schools. In Detroit, 63% of the system's 294,000 students are non-white, as are 42% of the teachers.

APRIL 8

In what is regarded as a major Administration defeat, Supreme Court nominee G. Harrold Carswell is rejected by the Senate in a 51-45 vote. Among the key swing senators who influence the outcome are Winston Prouty of Vermont and Margaret Chase Smith of Maine. Instrumental in the defeat of Carswell are the quiet and diplomatic moves of Senator Edward A. Brooke. Brooke's gentle prodding of Republican colleagues and his constant reminders that Carswell's record not only stamps him as racially biased but as judicially intemperate are held as vital factors influencing some of the last-minute shifts which upended Carswell.

APRIL 11

The Commission on Civil Rights criticizes President Nixon's March 24 policy statement as inadequate, overcautious, and indicative of a possible retreat in the area of school integration. The panel maintains that de jure segregation is not confined to the South, and indicates that the President could apply great pressure to eliminate it in this area of the country as well.

APRIL 20

Sociologist Kenneth Clark, director of the Metropolitan Applied Research Center, testifies that segregation is even more damaging to white school children than to those from minority groups. Clark maintains that the President's March 24 statement constitutes an important withdrawal from the situation, a failure to assess its moral, ethical and educational implications, and a slackening of the momentum generated by the courts and by some segments of society.

APRIL 20

Resumption in Ellicott City of the trial of H. Rap Brown, charged with arson and

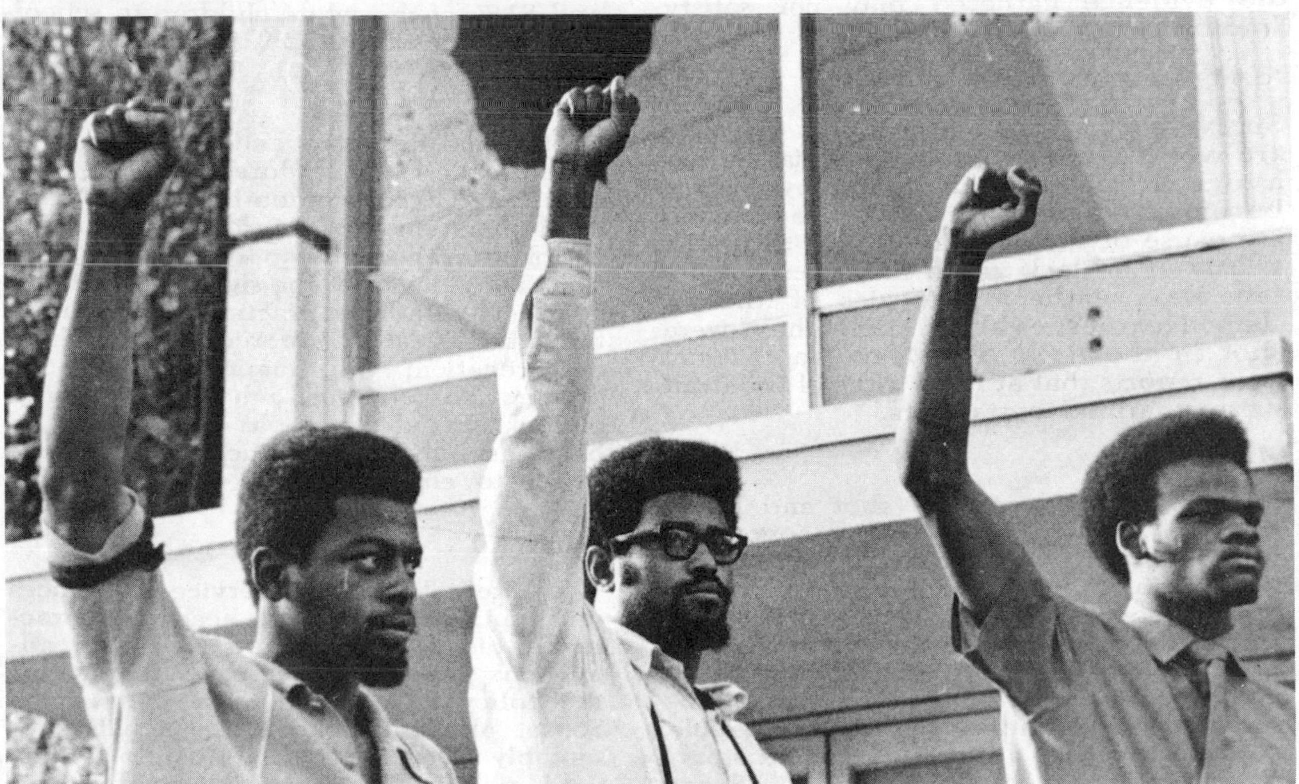

Raised black fists answer the shattered windows of Jackson State.

inciting to riot. Though Brown is not present, his defense lawyer maintains he is alive. One possible reason for his disappearance: the killing of two of his friends by an explosive device on March 9. A second bombing in Cambridge on March 11 may also have contributed to his disappearance.

APRIL 22-23

A student strike is called at Yale in support of the eight Black Panthers awaiting trial in New Haven. Yale president Kingman Brewster asserts that he is "skeptical" that such black revolutionaries can achieve a fair trial in the U.S.

MAY 4

A warrant is issued for the arrest of H. Rap Brown who again fails to appear in court to resume his trial. Brown's bond is forfeited, and the FBI is asked to join Maryland authorities in the search. Days later, Brown's name is added to the list of the nation's 10 most-wanted fugitives.

MAY 8

All charges against seven Panthers indicted on January 30 on charges of instigating a shootout with Chicago police are dropped. The State Attorney admits that the evidence gathered may not satisfy "judicial standards of proof."

MAY 12

Six Negroes are shot and 20 other people are wounded in Augusta, Georgia, during a night of violence punctuated by looting, burning and sniper activity. The immediate cause of the violence is said to be the killing of a black youth in a county jail a few days earlier. Autopsies of the six slain Negroes establish that they were shot in the back. The New York *Times* later reports that at least three of the dead were unarmed bystanders.

MAY 14-17

Two black students are shot and killed after a night of violence outside a women's dormitory at Jackson State College in Mississippi. Witnesses charge that police simply move in and indiscriminately blast the residence hall with shotguns. President Nixon dispatches Justice Department officials to ferret out the facts, but contradictory explanations make it impossible to piece together a wholly coherent story. On May 17, the Mississippi United Front vows to provide students and other groups with independent protection.

MAY 23

A five-day, 110-mile march against repression ends in downtown Atlanta with a rally by the SCLC and the NAACP. Speakers include Ralph Abernathy, Mrs. Coretta King, and Senator George McGovern. Jointly, they condemn racism, the Vietnam war, student killings at Kent State and Jackson State, and alleged police brutality in Augusta.

JUNE 13

The NAACP announces a $50,000 grant to a panel of independent citizens created in December 1969 to study clashes between the Black Panthers and the police in various cities across the U.S. The commission, hoping for funds from the Ford Foundation, is disappointed at the lack of interest shown by this group, and confesses it will be unable to function until it can raise its budget to $150,000.

JUNE 22

The Fourth Circuit Court of Appeals rejects a school desegregation proposal offered by the Norfolk school district. The Court finds the plan retains the traditional racial characteristics of the city's public schools—86% of the black children in schools that are more than 92% black, and 81% of the white children in schools that are more than 92% white.

JUNE 29

Spottswood Robinson and a host of other black leaders who address the 61st annual NAACP convention brand the Nixon Administration anti Negro and catalog a list of grievances to support their contention. These include: the signing of defense contracts with firms practicing discrimination; the retreat on enforcement of school desegregation; the nominations of Supreme Court Justices whose record and outlook brand them as insensitive to black aspirations, and the systematic attempt to emasculate the Voting Rights Act.

JULY 10

The Internal Revenue Service announces its intention to tax private academies practicing racial discrimination in their admissions policies. The greatest impact of the policy is expected to be felt in the South, although schools there will presumably receive ample time to adjust their policies should they be branded racist. Thus, the new policy promises these schools sufficient flexibility to avoid immediate revocation of their tax-exempt status.

JULY 19

Whitney Young refuses to follow the hard line taken by the NAACP in denouncing Administration policy toward the Negro. Instead, Young characterizes that policy as "pro-political," designed exclusively to win political votes from a beguiled majority. To offset this "white magic" policy, Young encourages the total spectrum of black groups—from the Panthers to the Baptists—to enter the arena of decision-making by forging a coalition of agreement on vital issues affecting the total black community.

AUGUST 7

A dramatic shootout outside the San Rafael courthouse results in the death of Superior Court Judge Harold Haley and three other men—all black prisoners on trial. The shootout follows a daring escape plan in which weapons are smuggled into the courtroom while the court is in session by a 17-year-old youth. The prisoners take control of the court, seize the judge and members of the jury at gunpoint, and try to effect their escape. Police reinforcements open fire on the escape van, killing its driver and the other fugitives. The judge, too, is slain by a shotgun blast from the weapon of one of the fugitives. Later investigation traces the sale of the weapons used in the shootout to Angela Davis, controversial UCLA professor and long-time defender of the so-called "Soledad Brothers." Miss Davis, a self-admitted Communist, has been the center of considerable dispute over her right to teach at UCLA. Though dismissed by the Board of Regents, she has strong faculty and student backing, and benefits from a court decision invalidating dismissal for political beliefs. After the shootout, Miss Davis disappears. In accordance with California law, she is charged with murder and kidnapping. The FBI places her on its list of the 10 most wanted fugitives in the nation.

SEPTEMBER 22

Suburban commuters from Glen Cove air their views in a "speak-out" on the local high school problem, i.e., the persistent outbreak of racial violence involving black and white students. Riders of the Long Island Railroad are told by School Superintendent Robert Finley that "we've got to get our story to the people . . . especially . . . people who are too tired to attend night meetings." The New York *Times* reports the story and writes: "The race problem drew many questions, but there were no black commuters in the car." The superintendent alludes to the likely existence of white vigilante groups who regard it as their duty to protect their children, by a pseudo-occupation of school grounds if necessary. Protection is also a key concept in the thinking of some black leaders (none of whom are represented on the train). Popular CORE leader Howard Davis pressures police into an arrest when he insists on the right to protect his own—and by extension black—children in the school. (The school shows a total enrollment of 1600, of whom 10% are black and 2% are Spanish-speaking.) The Finley discussion ranges over a number of topics, including the weekend incidents which precipitated the violence that left 25 students injured. Clear from the discussion—however well-intentioned and concerned it may be—is the fact that it is not reaching or convincing many of those actually involved in the turmoil. At issue is the endemic generation gap, the real leaders of the black community, and the assumptions implicit in the middle-class way of life. Dr. Finley announces his intention to hire security guards and professional restroom monitors; no protests are lodged regarding any possible strain on the school budget. The episode is of significance as a barometer measuring the emotional stresses evident in suburban communities where the presence of a substantial portion of black children is frequently regarded by many whites as an intrusion and a problem.

OCTOBER 1

A three-judge federal court convening in Buffalo declares void New York State's anti-busing law which made it illegal for appointed school boards to reshuffle pupil assignment plans for the purpose of achieving racial balance. The law had been copied by several Southern school districts to forestall desegregation. Earlier, Gov. Ronald Reagan had signed into California law a bill prohibiting the busing of students "for any . . . reason without the written permission of the parent or guardian."

OCTOBER 12

Rev. Theodore M. Hesburgh, Chairman of the U.S. Commission on Civil Rights, announces in a 1,115-page report that there has been a "major breakdown" in the enforcement of national mandates outlawing racial discrimination. The Commission maintains that the absence of pressures from the White House contributes to the general breakdown in the enforcement of pertinent laws.

OCTOBER 13

Angela Davis is arrested in New York and arraigned in federal court on charges of unlawful flight to avoid prosecution for her alleged role in a California kidnap-escape plot. Seized with Miss Davis is David R. Poindexter, a 36-year-old Chicago Negro accused of knowingly aiding a fugitive.

NOVEMBER 30

Senator Abraham Ribicoff of Connecticut introduces legislation to bring about total integration of the nation's schools, both urban and suburban. The target date: 1982.

DECEMBER 7

James Farmer resigns as assistant secretary for administration of the Department of Health, Education, and Welfare. Farmer declines to criticize Nixon Administration policies.

DECEMBER 17

A Pentagon task force reports "frustration and anger" among black troops stationed in Germany. At stake is the morale of black troops subjected to racial indignities by the civilian population.

1971

JANUARY 4

Rev. Leon Howard Sullivan is elected to the Board of Directors of General Motors, the first black man to participate in the direction of a U.S. auto company.

JANUARY 5

Bethlehem Steel is charged with job bias through the use of a seniority system which effectively discriminates against blacks. Bethlehem denies the charge, but agrees to establish new hiring, training, and promotion quotas for black employees.

FEBRUARY 4

Eight black federal employees file suit in federal court claiming that the principal test qualifying college graduates for civil service posts is "culturally and racially discriminatory." Defendants in the suit include HUD Secretary George Romney.

MARCH 8

Joe Frazier scores a unanimous 15-round decision over Muhammad Ali and becomes undisputed heavyweight champion of the world.

MARCH 11

Whitney M. Young, Jr., Executive Director of the Urban League since 1961, died in Lagos, Nigeria of an apparent heart attack at the age of 49. Mr. Young was in Africa to attend a conference aimed at increasing understanding between black Africans and Americans. His untimely death came at the height of an impressive and illustrious career in which he distinguished himself as a voice of conciliation between black and white communities at a time when racial polarization was splitting the nation. Young nonetheless chafed at the notion that he was non-militant and rather moderate. He believed that anyone in the civil rights movement, by the very nature of his direction, was a radical, and that violent confrontation tended to obfuscate the real issues involved in the movement. "Personally," said Young, "I am not non-violent, but I'm not a fool either. I can count. I know you can't fight a tank with a beer can or destroy a regiment with a switch. White racists are not afraid of our firepower, but they are afraid of our brain, our political and our economic power." For biographical material on Young, see page 215.

URBAN VIOLENCE AND BLACK POWER (1964-1970)

The racial revolt of the 1950's was largely a civil rights struggle involving thousands of aroused Southern Negroes who followed non-violent leaders like Martin Luther King, Jr. and legal allies like the NAACP in an assertive quest to broaden their Constitutional privileges and immunities. Sit-ins, marches, court cases, protest demonstrations—these were the ingredients of that struggle. Beginning in 1964, the racial battleground shifted dramatically out of the South and into the Northern ghetto, where the conditions of daily life were more important to residents and to leaders than the extension of basic citizenship rights. Southern towns like Selma invaded the headlines on occasion after the 1964 Harlem riots, but the main focus of black activity since 1964 has been the urban ghetto. The civil rights leader is under increasing pressure nowadays to yield to the black militant, or at least to accord him an indisputable place in the strategy sessions which will determine the thrust of black activism throughout the 1970s.

The Harlem Riot—(1964)

The Harlem riot broke out in the summer of 1964, two days after the shooting of a 15-year-old Negro youth by an off-duty patrolman in the Yorkville section of they culminated in the near annihilation of Newark and Detroit. Crowds of Negroes roamed through the streets, breaking windows, looting stores, menacing policemen and threatening the few white people found in the area. They faced helmeted police patrols who fired volley after volley into the night air in a futile attempt to disperse the crowds. In comparison with what was to come, the Harlem casualty figures were paltry. One man died, and 144 were injured. Prophetically, though, things had exploded in Harlem, the prototype black ghetto in the consciousness of white America. Few cared then that virtually every major American city was structured in the same way New York was, with an invisible wall encircling the black ghetto and buttressing white city dwellers from exposure to, and contact with, their black counterparts.

The Watts Riot—(1965)

The Watts section of southwest Los Angeles, a 20-square-mile Negro ghetto with an estimated population of 90,000, was the scene of one of the worst riots in the history of the United States, August 11-16, 1965.

Thirty-five people were killed, and property damage due to looting, arson, etc. reached the staggering total of 200 million dollars. Negro deaths numbered 28.

Stores were looted; entire city blocks burned to the ground; buses and ambulances stoned; and firemen, policemen and airplanes shot at in a 150-block area which, after six days, lay under a virtual state of siege.

The incident which sparked the outburst occurred on August 11 when state highway patrolmen chased an automobile around a six-block area, and arrested its driver on a charge of drunken driving.

A crowd gathered as word of the arrest spread, and rumors of brutality were passed on by eyewitnesses. Rocks were thrown, and police summoned to disperse the rioters, who soon began stoning cars and smashing windows. A semblance of order was restored by 3 a.m. the next morning, but rioting again broke out on the evening of August 12.

Los Angeles Mayor Samuel Yorty and Chief of Police William Parker summoned the National Guard to assist beleaguered police and deputies. Between August 13 and August 16, 12,634 Guardsmen, 1,430 city police, 1,017 county sheriff's deputies and 68 state highway patrolmen served on riot duty.

CAUSES OF THE RIOT

A number of causes were advanced to explain what had triggered the riots. Among those mentioned were:

1. poverty in general, and lack of job opportunity
2. racial humiliation, failure to accept the dignity of the Negro
3. lack of Negro leadership
4. the civil rights movement
5. police brutality
6. a heat wave
7. the criminal element

Whatever the causes, whatever the weight attributed to any combination of them, one thing was obvious: they demonstrated the axiom that violence is an inevitable result of a failure to come to grips with the root causes underlying social discontent.

Statistics told part of the story. Two-thirds of Watts residents have less than a high school education; one-eighth of them are technically illiterate. Only 13% of the homes in the area have been built since 1939—the remainder being in various stages of disrepair and decay. Three out of every 10 children come from broken homes, and drop out of school at a rate 2.2 times above the city's average. These children grow up among an assortment of social outcasts—prison parolees, prostitutes, narcotics addicts and the like.

Negro psychiatrist J. Alfred Cannon offered this summation:

"They have developed a feeling of potency. They feel the whole world is watching now. And out of the violence, no matter how wrong the acts were, they have developed a sense of pride."

The rallying cry of the mob ("Get Whitey") revealed another aspect of the problem. Aggressive "Get Whitey" cries were counterbalanced by the protective signs of "Brother" or "Blood" which appeared in the windows of Negro shopkeepers. In the view of some observers, however, "Whitey"—i.e. the white policeman, the white merchant, the white social worker—was attacked mainly because he was a symbol of the Negro's

***The Newark Riot*—(1967)**

The immediate cause of Newark's ghastly and tragic uprising in the summer of 1967 was a single arrest and the false rumors it generated. On the evening of July 12, black cabdriver John Smith tried to hurry past a prowl car patrolling in a Negro neighborhood. Carrying a passenger, Smith darted by the slow-moving vehicle, was cut off by police, and hauled down to the station following a heated argument. (It developed that he was an illegal driver since his license had been revoked for numerous violations and accidents.) Central Ward witnesses who saw police dragging a limp and stiff body into the station concluded hastily that a hackie had been beaten up and killed. (In truth, Smith's injuries were serious enough to require a doctor's treatment.) He seems to have been roughed up to such an extent that he could not have cooperated peacefully with arresting officers even if he were so disposed.

The second day of rioting in Watts

The news of death on the ghetto grapevine, however, escalated the tension and pushed residents and police toward open confrontation. By midnight, rocks and bottles were clattering against the walls of the stationhouse. Inside, the police girded for action; outside, the grapevine telegraphed a message calling for more manpower and other reinforcements.

Meanwhile, civil rights leaders, black militants, community officials, and police authorities attempted to sort out the facts and quiet the hostility and hysteria of the gathering throng. As black participants at the meeting were attempting to persuade police to initiate an investigation to determine just how Smith had been injured, the unruly people outside became a matter of such pressing concern that spokesmen were sent outside to disperse the crowd. During the next melee, Molotov cocktails were hurled against the wall of the stationhouse, starting minor fires. These were quickly extinguished, but they were ominous enough to persuade the police to set up a line of defense in front of the station.

Once the leaders sensed they could not disperse the crowd, they decided shrewdly to attempt to organize a spontaneous march on City Hall to protest Smith's arrest and demand a thorough investigation. Some of the crowd positioned itself for such a march; others, however, milled around, disgruntled and unappeased. People in the line of march were struck by rocks; windows continued to be shattered; a car was set afire. Seeing the situation deteriorating still further, police rushed the crowd and sent it fleeing in all directions. Late-night reports of the episode carried references to a few isolated lootings, but otherwise indicated that the disturbances had run their course.

Police chief Dominick Spina, however, sensed the seriousness of the situation, and realized that tensions had been aroused beyond a simple rage outburst. The next evening, a "Police Brutality Protest Rally" was organized by assorted black power advocates, including the Black Muslims, the United Afro-American Association, and other fervent black nationalists. Together, they planned to picket the Fourth Precinct Station.

Despite the announcement that the Smith incident would be investigated, the people remained unsatisfied. In short order, the police station was again under a virtual state of siege, whereupon police once again charged into the crowds, hurrying them off into the night. They did not, however, return to their homes or quiet their anger.

In the early morning hours of Friday, July 14, Mayor Hugh Addonizio finally conceded the situation was beyond his control, and sent in an urgent request to New Jersey Governor Richard J. Hughes for state police and National Guard units.

After daybreak, more than 2,600 National Guard reinforcements were deployed throughout the area. Arrests were made systematically, and roadblocks effectively deterred entrance into, or flight from, the area. Command of the anti-riot operations was assumed by the governor who declared Newark a city in open rebellion and defined the restoration of order as his first priority. Hughes ordered all guns and ammunition confiscated from stores that were selling them, imposed three separate curfews, and toured the area accompanied by a protective task force which arrested looters on sight.

Despite the apparent logic and the systematic procedures of the police and the National Guard, neither the armored personnel carriers, the .50 caliber rifles, nor the other war equipment could offset the defiance of looters and the tenacity of snipers. Their persistence unquestionably prolonged the emergency, even as white fury compounded the tragedies.

A three-year-old girl lost the sight of one eye and the hearing of one ear when she was hit by a police bullet fired at fleeing snipers; a 73-year-old man was felled by another police bullet fired as part of a sortie aimed at a group of looters who had attracted a crowd of milling spectators. The imprudent spectators, too, were quickly dispersed by the barrage of bullets, and innocent people were exposed to danger and injury simply by being on the scene. A garage mechanic was shot in the side while jacking up a car; a man standing on a porch was hit in the eye by a bullet; a 10-year-old boy driving in the family car was shot through the head.

Later testimony before the House of Representatives uncovered a hideous skein of events in which it became apparent that the amount of sniper fire was being grossly exaggerated and that, in many cases, it was more likely that frightened Guardsmen and fidgety police were exchanging gunfire.

Other incidents of incredible brutality, anonymous killing, and savage behavior were too numerous to report, and equally grisly and mindless. The statisticians compiled their precise reports after state police and Guardsmen were recalled on July 17. They read as follows: 23 dead (21 of them black and two of them—a policeman and a fireman—white). Of these, six were black women, and two black children. Damage was over 10 million dollars, about 20% of it to buildings and fixtures, and the overwhelming majority due to stock loss at super markets, liquor stores, clothing shops, etc. More than 1,000 people were injured, and another 1,600 under arrest. Among them was black poet/activist Leroi Jones who was snatched from a Volkswagen, beaten up, and hauled off to jail after being relieved of two .32 caliber pistols.

And Newark was only the first city to burn in 1967 . . .

The Detroit Riot—(1967)

The Detroit riot was traceable to much the same origins as the Newark uprising, stemming, on the surface at least, from an arrest which attracted widespread attention on the streets of the ghetto. It began at 3:45 a.m. Sunday morning July 22 when the police raided a so-called "blind pig," an after-hours drinking and gambling spot which happened to be crowded with patrons attending a party being thrown in honor of a group of black servicemen, two of whom were recent returnees from Vietnam. It took over an hour before all 82 patrons could be arrested. As they were being carted off, however, a crowd of about 200 gathered, and a mood of ugly resentment soon prevailed.

Shortly after 5 a.m., an empty bottle smashed into a police car, and a litter basket was hurled through a store window. Police reinforcements were summoned as riot tensions mounted, but few police were on duty in the immediate riot area. By 6 a.m., hundreds of irate blacks were already massed on the street, and assorted window-smashing and looting had begun along 12th Street, a high-density area of sub-standard and deteriorating housing.

The special police units which arrived on the scene did not interfere with looters, and only some of them attempted to form an effective cordon containing the riot. Police and media attempted to downplay the disorder, and maintain a "business as usual" facade for Detroit that Sunday.

By 8:30 a.m. black representative John Conyers had been notified of the trouble, and was in the process of cruising through the area, asking people to stay at home or to disperse. His efforts, by his own admission, were largely futile. A jovial atmosphere reigned in many places as looters rushed into stores and carried off whatever they could.

By early afternoon, Mayor Cavanaugh had met with community and political leaders at police headquarters. All had determined that reinforcements would be needed to halt the spread of looting to main thoroughfares beyond the 12th Street area. At 4:20 p.m., Cavanaugh summoned the National Guard. Units conducting their regular weekend drill in the city were on the streets by 7 p.m. Less than an hour later, Cavanaugh imposed a 9 p.m.-5 a.m. curfew.

The Cavanaugh curfew had little material effect on the situation. Looters continued to raid supermarkets recklessly, and streetfights, beatings, knifings, and gun battles were common. A 23-year-old white woman was hit at close range after she and her husband had dropped off two Negro friends; less than two hours later, she was dead. A 45-year-old white man collaborating with black companions was shot from a car by the owner of the supermarket he was looting. A 68-year-old white shoe repairman was beaten to death by a black youth for interfering with looters cleaning out a nearby store. Fallen power lines killed a white fireman and a black homeowner.

By 2 a.m. Monday, 8,000 National Guardsmen were on their way to bolster the 800 State Police officers and 1200 National Guardsmen already on duty. By this time, Governor Romney and Mayor Cavanaugh had both decided to request federal assistance. The Attorney General's office replied that, if state and local police could not control the situation, he (the governor) would have to declare a "state of insurrection." Romney declined to follow this course once he realized that insurance companies would be relieved of financial responsibility for the damages pursuant to such a declaration.

President Johnson then authorized the sending of a paratrooper task force which arrived at Selfridge Air Force Base near the city at about 4 p.m. Monday. Romney, Cavanaugh and other government officials then toured the city until 7:15 p.m. What they saw prompted them to conclude that the dispatch of federal troops into the city was still premature.

Still, during the Monday daylight hours, nine people had been killed by gunshot fire throughout the city. A black man, 23, was allegedly shot to death by a white man who stopped his car in front of the Negro's house, engaged him in an argument, and then carried out a threat to shotgun him to death.

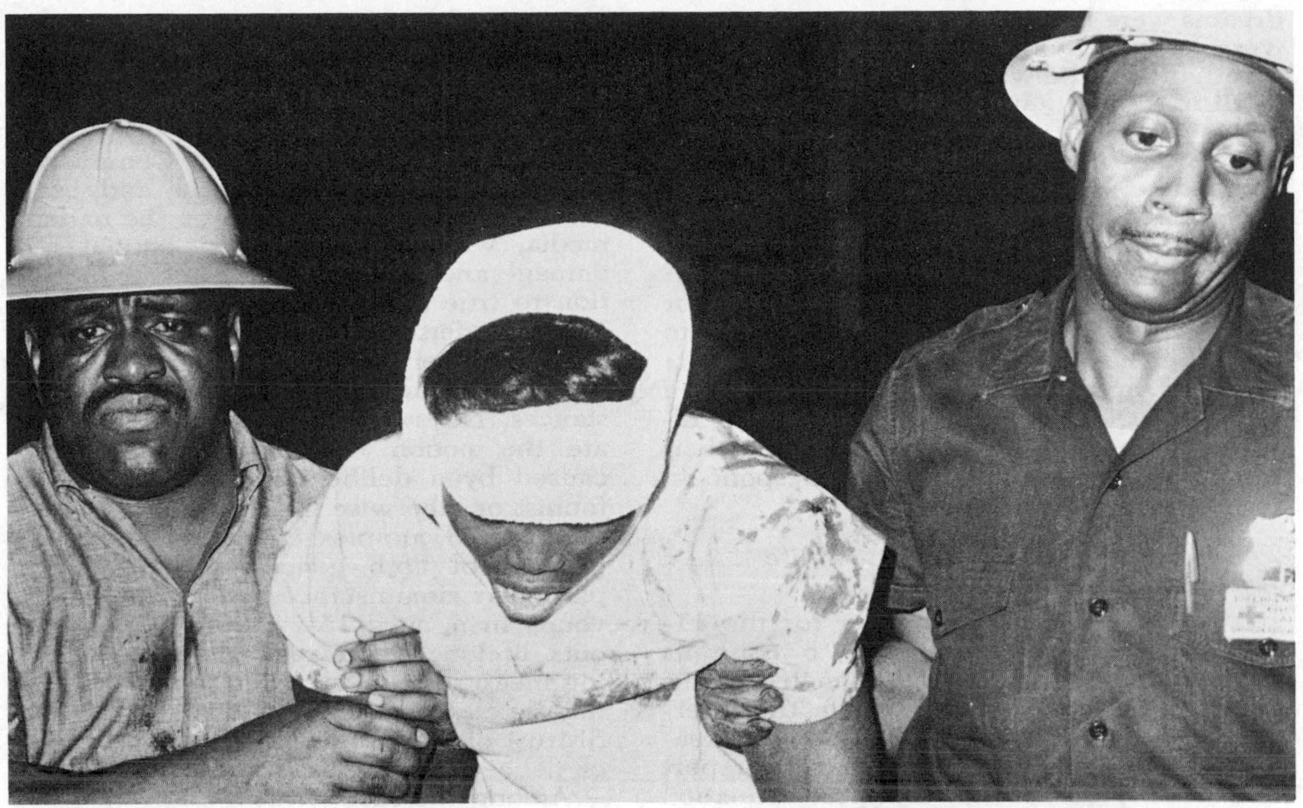

Riot police take command of the Newark riot.

By 11:30 p.m., federal observers (primarily Cyrus Vance and General John L. Throckmorton) advised President Johnson to authorize the use of paratroopers. The president signed the executive order federalizing the Guard, and thus committed the jittery men to what amounted to a complex battle situation.

By 4 a.m., Tuesday morning, indiscriminate firing based on faulty rumors was a hazardous reality in the most active riot areas of the city. One Negro guard who had scattered a small group which sought to loot a supermarket was struck down by a spray of bullets fired in his direction without analysis of the situation. Such incidents left Guardsmen, police, and residents panic-stricken and dangerously irrational. It also left many bystanders, pedestrians, and children dead in their tracks.

Some moves were initiated to dissipate the hysteria by encouraging contact between troops and residents. As soon as the former began cleaning up the streets, collecting garbage, and tracing lost persons, the latter responded with sandwiches, soup, and gestures of good cheer.

Nevertheless, instances of prudent camaraderie were more often than not outweighed by incidents of blind and disastrous overreaction.

At the Algiers Motel, three youths were slain by law enforcement officers who have since been exonerated, but who certainly participated in a major shoot-out around the hotel premises. The prosecution implied there had been a pistol whipping, but the defense argued that the actions of the police had been dictated by the tense hazards of the situation.

The casualties in the Detroit riot outstripped those of Newark. Altogether, 43 persons were killed, 33 of them black and 10 white. Two of the 17 looters who died were white; the rest, black. Fifteen citizens (four whites), one white National Guardsmen, one white fireman, and one black private guard fell victim to gunshot wounds. Property damage soared to 22 million dollars, not counting business stock, private furnishings, churches, and charitable institutions, many of whom were covered by insurance.

In toto, over 7,000 persons were arrested —3,000 on the second day of the riot and over 4,000 by midnight Monday. Some were kept in makeshift jails in such places as buses and underground garages.

When the curfew was finally lifted and the National Guard removed from the city on Saturday, July 29, what remained in many places was a charred mess of tangled rubble and water-logged ashes. For some, dreams were broken; for others, nightmares were seemingly shattered. Some blacks who had lost the work of a lifetime sobbed in dismay and gave up hope; conversely, others who had never accumulated many possessions seemed relieved of rage and inclined to build.

For the white establishment—whether a Henry Ford or a Walter Reuther—another day of reckoning had passed, with many still too timid or too angry to press for real change. Reuther found the words to describe the needs dramatized by Detroit: "Those Americans (who) do not feel a part of society . . . don't behave like responsible people. Only when they get their fair share of America will they respond in terms of responsibility."

The Kerner Report—(1968): *White America Analyzes*

It did not require a full year for the 11-member Kerner Commission to issue its provocative report on the mangled status of black society in the U. S. in the aftermath of the urban riots of 1967. One reason for the early appearance of the report may have been the fear that procrastination might only serve as fuel for a possible repetition of the holocaust. Another was assuredly the elementary recognition that the causes of the rioting were implicit in the situations and conditions of ghetto life, and these were not, after all, mysteriously unknown factors.

In gathering the facts, the Commission discovered that mass hysteria and exaggeration had reached as far as the nation's media, which had rendered estimates of damage and destruction far out of proportion to true figures. There were, in truth, 164 disorders—eight of them "major," 33 of them "serious" and the rest hardly worthy of attention under normal circumstances. No evidence existed to substantiate the notion that the uprisings were caused by a deliberate conspiracy, Communist or otherwise. Each riot had its own unique and complex character, and was a product of both general grievances and particular circumstances. Most rioters were young men, aged 15-24, high school dropouts, lifelong ghetto residents with a growing measure of racial pride, hostility to the middle-class (black or white) and a basic distrust of the political system and the role of police enforcers.

Among the facts which were cited and exhaustively documented were: a distressing crime rate (sometimes 35 times higher

Detroit rioters meet the fixed bayonets of the National Guard.

than in white neighborhoods), the lack of health facilities and municipal services (infant mortality among blacks was reported to be 58% higher than among whites; poor garbage collection and sanitation provisions helped account for 14,000 cases of rat bite in 1965 alone), and the increasing compression of poor black citizens within the urban ghetto itself. These problems were compounded by poor educational opportunity, inadequate recreational facilities, biased administration of justice, discriminatory credit and consumer practices, feeble welfare programs, and incredibly high unemployment. In other words, it was not possible to contemplate wholesale escape, nor was it likely that internal change could be undertaken effectively without wholesale assistance.

The recommendations outlined by the Commission called for a program "equal to the dimension of the problems." Such proposals did not take into account matters of obvious caste or political opposition; instead, they concentrated strictly on the issues and the policies which exacerbated tensions and produced an atmosphere of popular readiness to riot.

In the employment sector, the Commission recommended the creation of two million jobs over the next three years, half by government, and half by private enterprise. The panel also advised the federal government to reimburse private employers for the extra costs of training hard-core unemployables or ghetto youths, or to issue tax credits as additional incentive to the business sector.

Federal support was also invoked in the area of education, where it was recommended that schools cooperating voluntarily in the elimination of *de facto* segregation be rewarded with additional federal aid, just as schools sabotaging the law be deprived of such aid. Adult-education and anti-illiteracy programs were also stressed, as was the notion that ghetto and poverty schools be "dramatically" upgraded. Higher education for poor students was similarly propounded.

Housing was another priority commanding the attention of the Commission. Here, the panel confirmed President Lyndon B. Johnson's figures that 6 million new low- and moderate-income homes were needed, but reduced by five years the feasible time estimated to construct them. According to the commission, 600,000 units were needed in the first year alone.

Welfare was another thorny issue with which the panel came to grips. Here, the group asserted that the federal government should bear a minimum of 90% of all welfare costs, and establish uniform national standards of assistance guaranteeing every American family an income at least as high as the poverty level. Ideally, however, the solution was "to develop a national system of income supplementation."

Police training and attitudes were also singled out as matters of overall social concern. More black recruitment was recommended, as was increased police protection for the ghetto areas. The latter could probably best be afforded by special training in riot prevention and control, rather than by the more dangerous procedure of stockpiling lethal weapons of the type used by an actual army in the field.

The proposals constituted an irrefutable admission that the nation was in fact racially polarized, that it was in fact riddled with white racism, and that blacks were now so aroused and so explosive that, whenever it suited their strategy or their mood, they would not shy away from open racial warfare. Nevertheless, a fundamental gulf remained between the Kerner's Commission analysis of the situation (with which black militants generally concurred) and the action which had to be generated to alleviate its most distressing aspects. To the militants, it was clear that, though the message was couched in urgent, indeed "shocking" terms, it was still being directed to a sluggish and unresponsive source: the U. S. Government, Congress, the Establishment . . .

From "Burn Baby Burn" to "Build Baby Build"—(1969)

None of these sources was really responsible for making the year 1969 a comparatively cool summer. It could be argued, from a fatalistic point of view at least, that black discontent and frustration had simply reached a pitch of frenzy which had to subside, just as a convulsive attack of epilepsy runs its course for no precisely discernible reason. Far more encouraging and constructive explanations for the cessation of violence could be advanced, however. For one thing, both ghetto residents and black middle-class leaders recognized the excruciating reality that the riots only destroyed their own turf and left many homeless, totally unprotected, and utterly devoid of marketable resources. Even militants who argue that the ghetto is a separate state, or colonial enclave, concede that social intercourse and responsible exchange is necessary in the ghetto if it is to prosper, let alone survive.

Somewhere deep in the psyche of the

Many blacks who saw the ruins of the cities, united to help rebuild them.

black community, deeper even than the rage and the anguish over being suppressed or neglected, lay the realization that no amount of oppression had managed to crush it. It was as if many black citizens could sense how dependent the white world had become on manipulating them by confining them to a largely decaying and unrewarding world. From that understanding of their position and from the sense of potency derived from the cataclysmic events they had caused, many blacks discovered a feeling of hope and anticipation which gave their lives a forceful and dynamic meaning. Some whites encouraged this new-found sense of self and volunteered to foster it in whatever way they could; others lapsed into the familiar lame denunciations of black self-help as a cover for revolutionary intentions. Not that the black movement was utterly devoid of extremist tacticians who had lost faith in the white man's ability or resolve to wade into the problem.

In the main, however, most leaders and citizens sought an alternative to war and confrontation. Not all were equally communicative about it, nor were all pursuing a program so balanced and "normal" that one could avoid criticism of aspects of it. The Panthers, for example, opened ghetto clinics, and instituted school lunch pro-

grams, but they also sponsored propaganda sessions which many white critics labelled as "brainwashing" and hate campaigns. Yet, even here, it was obvious that the store-front teacher was engaged in an important mission: endowing the ghetto child with a feeling of self-worth, the power to function, and the necessity for conscientious habits of learning. Political rhetoric, in other words, was supplemented by intellectual training and mental development. Someone showed that he cared.

Among the adults, sophistication and finesse were equally evident. Many blacks realized that they often had the political muscle to put black candidates into responsible office and cooperated in the achievement of that goal because of its obvious advantages. Even black militants "cooled it" when a black candidate announced his intentions to run for office, presumably not because political favors were to be peddled, but because racial solidarity demanded it. In the job area, blacks pressured business leaders, industrial titans, and labor union officials to expand job training and employment opportunities. This was particularly evident in the construction industry, where black representation has always been kept to a token minimum. The NAACP and the workers themselves demanded a fair share of all jobs on government-sponsored construction, and were prepared to undermine operations legally, or sabotage them with demonstrations, until some reasonable accord was reached and enforced.

In the white community, movement was also discernible. Many leaders responded to the apprehension that future violence could be geographically isolated, particularly if spontaneous uprisings became calculated instances of violence exported to the suburbs by revolutionary diehards; the more enlightened members of the liberal alliance felt pangs of conscience and a moral obligation to sponsor job-training programs and business opportunities for black ghetto residents. Government money and bank loans were the major source of this brand of constructive assistance. New plant construction, recreation facilities, the Model Cities Program — all relieved nagging grievances and tried to improve the caliber of life in the ghetto.

Dialogue also helped somewhat—blacks talking to blacks, as well as with whites. The police restraint and the widespread effective use of police community-relations programs contributed greatly to a deescalation of tensions. Volunteer patrols manned by black members of the community also sprang up in Watts, Detroit and Newark, fostering close ties with the majority of youth and monitoring the movements of potential troublemakers.

Beyond all of this, however, hope stemmed from the young black's increasing determination to build his society, rather than promote his own extermination. Restlessness was frequently replaced by ambition; pride and hope were healthy substitutes for self-contempt and despondency. The mood was one of determination to reach a goal, regardless of whether the white community — government, industry and labor — welcomed it with open arms. Black hands were reaching out, but not for handouts.

Black Power—(1966-1970): *Black America Acts*

Black minds were also reaching out — far beyond the Kerner report and the liberal alliance. The solution of black power advocates was to mobilize the forces of protest latent within the ghetto, to rally them around a set of communicable goals, and to weld together a coalition of self-interest groups dedicated to the proposition that black power was the embodiment of the long-term solution to the race problem in the United States. In reality, the term black power was comprehensible to most whites, although they pretended only to be appalled by it. Secretly, they viewed it as a formula for displacing them by force, in a bloodbath if necessary, rather than as a program for promoting tangible goals in a black-oriented setting. Since its inception, the black power movement has been able to establish a doctrinaire footing, to debate tangible priorities, and to invent coherent techniques to achieve its objectives. Black power advocates concentrate on the development of institutions which will have as their primary function the creation of goods, services and improvement mechanisms for the preponderant masses of black people.

ORIGINS AND DEFINITIONS

"Black power" is said to have been introduced as a concept by Stokely Carmichael of the Student Nonviolent Coordinating Committee (SNCC). In coining the term, Carmichael accomplished three things:

1. He created a memorable and potent slogan around which young militants and diehard separatists could rally.

2. He captured the attention and crystallized the apprehension of the white population.

3. He created a profound schism in the

ranks of the civil rights groups themselves, specifically between the radicals on the one hand, and the moderates on the other.

Historically, the term is now associated with the Mississippi march undertaken by James H. Meredith in June 1966. Bushwhacked on June 6, Meredith eventually recovered from his gunshot wounds, and later delivered a passionate address in Jackson, Mississippi (the state capital), where the rallying cry of "black power" first began to show signs of overshadowing the nonviolent theme in the civil rights revolution.

In the days following the Mississippi march, many civil rights leaders analyzed and condemned the concept of "black power." Martin Luther King, Jr., for example, whose philosophy of nonviolence appeared to be antithetical to the position taken by the advocates of "black power," said:

"I happen to believe that a doctrine of Black Supremacy is as evil as White Supremacy. I don't think that anything can be more tragic in the Civil Rights movement than the attitude that the Black Man can solve his problems by himself."

On July 5, the National Association for the Advancement of Colored People (NAACP) heard its executive secretary, Roy Wilkins, denounce "black power" at its annual convention in Los Angeles.

"No matter how endlessly they try to explain it, the term 'black power' means antiwhite power. In a racially pluralistic society, the concept, the formation and the exercise of an ethnically tagged power means opposition to other ethnic powers.

"In the black-white relationship, it means that every other ethnic power is the rival and the antagonist of 'black power.' It has to mean 'going it alone.' It has to mean separatism .

The National Urban League, the last of the civil rights groups to comment on the controversy, issued a press release on July 11, disassociating itself from "black power," both semantically and philosophically.

"The National Urban League does not intend to invent slogans, however appealing they may be to the press. What we will continue to do through our unique structure, is expand and develop positive programs of action which bring jobs to the unemployed, housing to the dispossessed, education to the deprived, and necessary voter education to the disenfranchised. The Urban League is dedicated to an interracial approach to solving the problems faced by the nation. We are equally dedicated to the expansion of the services and programs which have helped hundreds of thousands of people find jobs and get the training, education, and counseling they need. Our interracial staff is at work in 76 cities with programs, not slogans."

The Congress of Racial Equality (CORE), on the other hand, adopted a resolution at one of its conventions endorsing the concept of "black power" in these terms:

"Black Power is not hatred. It is a means to bring the Black Americans into the covenant of Brotherhood. Black Power is not Black Supremacy; it is a unified Black Voice reflecting racial pride in the tradition of our heterogenous nation."

Stokely Carmichael has also elaborated further on the subject:

"Black power seems to me a number of things. Number one, that black people in this country are oppressed for one reason—and that's because of their color, and that's what this country has to face . . . their rally cry must be the issue around which they are oppressed, as it was for unions. The workers came together, they were oppressed because they were workers. And we must come together around the issue that oppressed us — which is our blackness. Unions — they needed power to stop their oppression. We need power to stop ours. So it's black power. And black power just means black people coming together and getting people to represent their needs and to stop that oppression."

Some observers have explained "black power" in terms of the collective frame of mind inevitable in a people emerging from a long period of inferior status. Others find that "black power" reflects a new ethnic integrity among Negroes. Still others interpret it as a phenomenon embracing many deep-seated, anti-white emotions, and see in it further a rejection of existing political and social institutions, a voluntary form of separatism nurtured by personal pride, and a desire to meet violence with counterviolence.

THE CONFERENCES

The Second National Conference on Black Power was held in Newark from July 20-23, 1967, an outgrowth of a meeting which had taken place in the Rayburn House Office Building in Washington, D. C. on September 3, 1966. (This meeting, known as the First National Conference on Black Power, was convened in Washington, D.C. by Congressman Adam Clayton Powell. It was attended by 169 delegates from 37 cities; 18 states and 64 organizations.)

The largest and most broadly representative gathering of black Americans ever to attend such a meeting poured into Newark —more than 1,000 strong from 36 states and 42 cities. Its atmosphere and style were distinctly different from any previously scheduled meeting of national consequence involving black leaders. For one thing, white authorities—the Administration and the press — were not given ringside seats at the event, nor were their opinions and analyses solicited. The meeting was a closed-circuit black affair, a four-day private parley that took place at the conference headquarters of Cathedral House in the heart of Newark's Episcopal Diocese.

Dr. Nathan Wright, director of urban work for the diocese and chairman of the conference, opened the meeting by observing that "black people constitute the greatest unused resource in the world" and, as such, are compelled to work together "for black unity." Unless they could gain the power and the self direction to control their lives, they would be faced, in Dr. Wright's view, with the distinct possibility of perishing as a viable entity.

The serious nature of the issues produced a shroud of secrecy which enveloped the participants in the 14 workshops organized to grapple with the theme and establish key points of programmatic accord. The black representatives clearly wished to keep their divergent opinions private until they could hammer out some form of unified approach to a particular aspect of the problem.

The goals spelled out by various groups were admittedly outside the "contemporary grail of integration." In part, they constituted what conference public relations officer Chuck Stone called a "reaffirmation of pride in blackness, or negritude," and a rejection of the restricted goals and concepts of the traditional civil rights movement.

The spectrum of black organizations represented at the meeting ranged from so-called conservative groups like the NAACP, the SCLC and the Urban League to the so-called orthodox radicals (CORE and SNCC) to the more abrasive and occasionally strident paramilitary groups (Ron Karenga's US of Los Angeles and Charles 37X Kenyatta's Mau Mau of New York).

The sporadic reports of violence bubbling up in several American cities lent added vigor to the proclamations of the paramilitary groups who advocated organized military training for black youth, and self-defense courses for all black families, castigation of Christianity as a selfish and corrupt religion preaching love and practicing hate and materialism, and rejection of the word "Negro" for the word "black." Other resolutions called for the formal partitioning of the U. S. into two separate nations, the refusal of blacks to accept induction into the Armed Forces, the censure of all Congressmen who voted to unseat Congressman Adam Clayton Powell, and the support of a black boycott of the 1968 Olympics in the event Muhammad Ali's title remained unrestored.

Black churches also came under fire. Those not actively committed to the "black revolution" were to be boycotted. Black publications were instructed to rid their pages of all ads for skin conditioners and hair straighteners. A call also went forth for the establishment of black universities to create "professional black revolutionaries," and for formal recognition by the nation at large of charismatic black leaders such as Malcolm X. In what must have been a provision applauded by the Muslims, blacks were urged to disown all notions of birth control, which was regarded as a white trick to insure a numerical majority and hence a flagrantly genocidal tactic.

Some of the participants and the eyewitnesses were clearly in an ugly mood toward white newsmen and cameramen attempting to cover the conference. Fisticuffs erupted at times; unruly youths engaged in shoving matches or rammed home a fist or two to express their furious dissatisfaction with the purported intrusion of unwanted whites. Dr. Wright, overwhelmed but undaunted, mused philosophically: "No pain . . . no progress." At the same time, he conceded that the situation was fraught with potential peril.

At the Third National Conference on Black Power, held in Philadelphia in the last week of August 1968, more than 3,000 delegates were in attendance. Chairman Wright again advised that the purpose of the meeting was to attempt to save "this nation from an out-of-joint white world." This conference specifically barred white reporters from workshops and discussions, and drew a tight security net on all participants. In general, Wright revealed that the discussions were revolving around the question of "a political course of action," i.e., whether the group would propose a boycott of the 1968 Presidential election or come up with plans to establish a Third Party movement.

Not all resolutions of the Conference were made public. Among those released to the press were:

- Neutrality in the Nigeria-Biafra war and a statement only that both sides move for a settlement
- Immediate withdrawal of U.S. forces from Vietnam
- Boycott of the draft by all eligible black youths
- Implementation of the goal of creating a black urban army in the city's ghettos for the protection of black citizens
- Denunciation of the term "ghetto."

In 1969, delegates to the black power confab took a different approach, scheduling the meeting for Hamilton, Bermuda, and viewing it as an attempt to create an international black power organization. Delegates who attended came from the U. S., Africa, Canada and the Caribbean. Some of the delegates were refused entry into Bermuda, including Omar Ahmed of New York, a vice-chairman of the Conference. Conference chairman Chuck Stone, successor to Nathan Wright, rushed to Ahmed's defense in a strongly worded statement which deplored "the selective racism of the white-controlled Bermuda government in denying certain Black Americans the right to attend this week's conference . . ."

Stone also announced that there would be two other Black Power Conferences in 1969: one in Los Angeles (August 29-31) and one over Thanksgiving, "either in Mississippi or Georgia." The Los Angeles conference was later postponed.

As in the previous year, the resolutions offered by the Black Power Conference dwindled in number. They included:

- An end to media distortion of the black population
- A return of all documents, art and artifacts relating to black people from the world's museums
- A protest against the trial of black Canadian students
- A call for immediate withdrawal from Vietnam and a boycott of draft induction by black youths.

The 1970 conference was held in Atlanta amid the continuing rhetoric that its aim was to develop institutions that would promote the liberation of black people. Significantly, the term black power was removed from the title of the conference, and the scope of the group was broadened to further upgrade the identity of other-than-American black people. Hence, the name: the Congress of African People.

The meeting was attended by delegates from North America, Latin America, the Caribbean and Africa. The internationalist outlook of the participants was apparent in the tendency to identify people by region, rather than by nation.

Committee chairman Haywood Henry explained that one reason for the supranational designation was the desire to concentrate "on the creation of instruments" to help eliminate the oppression faced by black people regardless of their land of origin.

Henry, a member of Harvard's black studies department and chairman of the Black Affairs Council, defined the problem basically as one of organization. "Historically," he said, "black people have lacked the . . . vehicles to carry out mandates of the national and international black communities."

Black nationalist poet/playwright Leroi Jones concurred that the conference had to be far more than just an exalted gabfest in which revolutionary ideas were glibly enunciated before tumbling into oblivion.

What was clear from five years of conferences, meetings, encounters, confrontations, violent upheavals, and position papers was that black power was a new driving force in the black community, not just a clever slogan that achieved momentary fashion and then faded into oblivion. Every black leader has had more than just an incidental curiosity about its real meaning; each has somehow been subject to its demands even as he has sought to harness and comprehend its implications.

THE HAMILTON THESIS

The most potent analysis of the black power movement over the years has been supplied by Dr. Charles V. Hamilton, political science professor at Roosevelt University in Chicago and co-author (with Stokely Carmichael) of *Black Power: The Politics of Liberation in America.* Hamilton foresaw the danger that the slogan "Black Power" would contribute to both calculated acts of instrumental violence and spontaneous acts of expressive violence. Nevertheless, he felt such outpourings need not invalidate the basic concept. For Hamilton, black power clearly meant ". . . a new, different way to create institutions of legitimacy for black Americans" and ". . . a way to create confidence in one's self and group to overcome alienation."

Hamilton viewed black power as a "clear *alternative* to acts of expressive or instrumental violence, because it means the legitimate involvement of masses of black people in activities and institutions which affect their lives. Black Power is not only interested in an equitable distribution of goods and services, it is also vitally concerned with an equitable distribution of decision-making powers."

Hamilton has admitted that control of black communities by black people may not bring immediate improvements (in fact, he freely concedes it may even lead to some temporary setbacks), but he feels there is no greater psychological advantage to be gained from the application of any other program.

There are, however, practical advantages to be gained in providing black people with control. For one thing, they will, in Hamilton's view, come to appreciate the problems inherent in the very idea of making progress and thus develop an understanding for the word "delay." Delay is far easier to tolerate when one is aware that it has not originated with the white man's trickery. The control exercised in this setting would conceivably enable long-term improvements to gather momentum.

Under the circumstances, black power advocates prefer ghettos to integration, concentration to dispersal, schools they can control to schools which are integrated at great expense and inconvenience. A good all-black school, they argue, is better than a poor integrated one. Though they may theoretically concede that a good integrated school is the best school, they believe they can only achieve this end (if they bother to think of it at all) by progressing through a good black school first. They, too, are reluctant to expect schools to bear the burden of integrating the nation. They want black parents to participate in school activities in such a way that teachers can be freed of clerical and administrative chores interfering with student-teacher interaction. They do not believe black parents will attend or participate in white-dominated PTA meetings.

Guerrilla warfare is another theme with which Hamilton deals, professing to be aware of no less than 27 black groups preparing some form of armed revolution. In his view, however, such groups are so heavily infiltrated that the move to armed revolution will probably stagnate. This does not mean, however, that acts of terrorism will be totally curbed.

Hamilton has postulated four categories into which all black organizations and leaders fall. They are: the political bargainers, the moral crusaders, the alienated reformers, and the alienated revolutionaries. The "bargainers," such as the NAACP and the Urban League, believe in the two-party system and are working within it to achieve the equitable distribution of goods and services through better jobs, more efficient schools, decent housing, and the "integration" of black people into the American mainstream. The "bargainers" accept the melting-pot thesis, the expansion of the middle class, and the continuation of the alliance between white liberals, black professionals, labor and religious leaders.

The SCLC crusaders like Dr. King, Ralph Abernathy and Jesse Jackson aim to alter society by reforming its conscience and extracting from it an abiding recognition of moral obligation.

The "reformers" include CORE (and SNCC when it was operative) and other groups who seek to bypass or dismantle the existing machinery of government to establish direct links between Washington and urban ghettos. Reformers view municipal government as corrupt and show contempt for political machines. They draw their support from young college-age people, often with middle-class origins, but are also backed by many middle-age and middle-income groups who sympathize with riots, and argue that black power rhetoric is a response to the apathy and indifference of much of white America.

The "revolutionaries" and "nationalists" like the Panthers and Stokely Carmichael believe in the inevitability of violence, see riots as preparatory skirmishes for warfare, and are planning systematically for black independence, presumably in a separate state of U.S. territory. Followers of the revolutionary line emphasize black culture as an exclusive commodity of the black population, and identify strongly with the political and economic aspirations of such West African countries as Ghana and Guinea.

Black power, then, is an ideology which attacks certain social institutions and proposes new ones to replace them; it is an ethic which judges men and decides goals; it is a series of strategic arrangements designed to achieve goals that benefit the Negro; it is a philosophy which seeks to impart to the Negro a sense of his manhood and undeniable importance. It is the black man today.

DEATHS OF PROMINENT NEGROES (1969-1970)

The years 1969 and 1970 marked the deaths of several important black celebrities, and other figures active in public or academic life. No attempt has been made here to list prominent African leaders-who have died, or been assassinated, within the past two years. References to men like Prime Minister Abubakar Tafawa Balewa of Nigeria or Tom Mboya of Kenya can be found in the African section of this volume.

1969

Jazz immortal COLEMAN HAWKINS, a peerless saxophonist, died at age 64 of pneumonia after a lengthy bout with illness. "Hawk," as he was known to jazz buffs, reached the peak of his popularity in the early 1940's but his warm and rhythmic playing (among his most unforgettable numbers was *Body and Soul*) was fit for all seasons and all styles, from Ben Webster to John Coltrane.

Veteran black actor REX INGRAM, 73, died of a heart attack in Hollywood. Ingram's booming voice and commanding stage presence were utilized to good advantage in such prominent plays as *The Emperor Jones, Cabin in the Sky* and *Porgy*.

REV. A. D. KING, 38, younger brother of Martin Luther King, Jr. died accidentally in his pool in Atlanta. After brother Martin's death, King became co-pastor of Ebenezer Baptist Church in Atlanta. Earlier, he had been active on the civil rights front in Birmingham and Louisville.

Black folksinger and balladeer JOSH WHITE, 61, died during heart surgery in Manhasset, New York. A native of Greenville, South Carolina, White first hit the charts in 1941 with a best-selling record album of songs from the Georgia prison farms, *Chain Gang*.

Singer ROY HAMILTON, 40, died in New Rochelle, New York on July 20. Among Hamilton's most popular hits were: *You'll Never Walk Alone* and *Unchained Melody*.

1970

Writer/educator LOU LOMAX, 47, visiting professor of the humanities and writer in residence for the 1970-1971 term at Hofstra University, was killed in an automobile crash on July 30, 1970. Lomax was the author of three books, including a study on the lives of Malcolm X and Martin Luther King, Jr. He also wrote a highly acclaimed television documentary on black extremism, *The Hate That Hate Produced*.

MAURICE STOKES, 36, struck down with paralysis at the height of his professional basketball career, died of a heart attack in Cincinnati after many years of a gallant uphill struggle to recuperate. A three-time NBA All-Star, Stokes was among the rebounding and scoring leaders of the game in 1958, when he suffered a severe fall while on the playing court, and later collapsed with what was diagnosed as paralysis caused by brain swelling.

JOHNNY HODGES, 63-year-old saxophone sideman with Duke Ellington through the golden years of the latter's band career, died of a heart attack in Manhattan. Hodges had been a jazz great for over 40 years.

Black actor JAMES EDWARDS, best known for his role in a 1949 Hollywood film *Home of the Brave,* died of a heart attack in San Francisco at age 51. Edwards was cast in several other prominent films, including *The Caine Mutiny, The Manchurian Candidate* and *Member of the Wedding*. Still, none of these afforded him the recognition he received for his portrayal of a mental patient in the World War II film (*Home of the Brave*) which dealt seriously with the theme of American racism.

Popular organist and record star EARL GRANT, 39, died in an automobile crash in the New Mexico desert. Grant, son of an Oklahoma Baptist minister, won singing competitions as a soldier at Fort Bliss, Texas in the 1950's and later became a highly paid professional who toured the world. His instrumental version of *Ebb Tide* sold in the millions.

MRS. LISLE CARTER, 60-year-old lawyer and social worker, died in New York of cancer. From 1935 to 1945, Mrs. Carter served under Governor Thomas E. Dewey as the first black woman district attorney in New York. Later, she was a consultant to the Economic and Social Council of the United Nations and for the International Council of Women.

BURTON I. GORDIN, executive director of the Michigan Civil Rights Commission, is shot to death in a downtown Detroit garage. Police ascertain no immediate motive for the slaying.

FRANK SILVERA, actor, producer and director, is accidentally electrocuted in Pasadena, California. Silvera began his acting career in 1934, and played in several roles which were not racially motivated. He often appeared as a Mexican.

Rock star JIMI HENDRIX, 27, dies in London of complications possibly stemming from the presence of drugs in his system, although not from an overdose, as first reported. Born in Seattle on November 27, 1942, Hendrix climbed to the top of the rock world with a unique style blended of a grating, blues-laden voice, a pulsating electric guitar he could play with his teeth, and erotic body motions which overwhelmed his youthful audiences.

FELTON CLARK, 66-year-old Negro educator, dies in New Orleans, Louisiana. Clark was president of Southern University from 1938 to 1969.

LEON M. JORDAN, member of the Missouri House of Representatives, is shot and killed on a Kansas City street while walking to his car. Jordan, a political moderate, represented the 11th District in Kansas City and was being opposed in the Democratic primary by Lee A. Bohannon, described in the New York *Times* as a "25-year-old black militant." Jordan worked his way into politics from a career in the police department. He was the first black police lieutenant in Kansas City.

BENJAMIN O. DAVIS, SR., dies November 26, 1970 at the Great Lakes Naval Hospital in North Chicago, Illinois. Davis, 93, was the first Negro to serve as a general in the U.S. Armed Forces.

WARREN R. COLEMAN, 67, radio, stage and film actor (Kingfish on the "Amos and Andy" program) died in Massachusetts.

ROBERT P. DANIEL, 65, president of Virginia State College, died in Virginia.

FRANKIE LYMON, popular 27-year-old singer, died of drug overdose.

SUSIE MONROE, 89, died in Philadelphia. Miss Monroe served as a state representative for the last two years of her life.

ALLAN MORRISON, 51, former New York editor for *Jet* and *Ebony* magazines, died in New York City.

KENNETH M. PHIPPS, 51, New York Criminal Court Judge, died of a heart attack.

IRA DE AUGUSTINE RIED, 67, sociologist and head of the Dept. of Sociology at Haverford College from 1947 to 1966, died in Bryn Mawr, Pa.

RUTH LOGAN ROBERTS, 76, a leader in many Negro and welfare groups, died in a nursing home in New York City.

MALLIE ROBINSON, 78, mother of Jackie Robinson, died in Pasadena, Calif.

WALTER C. ROBINSON, SR., 75, publisher of the *Chattanooga Observer* which he had founded, died after a long illness.

CALVIN L. SMITH, 61, Illinois state representative, former deputy coroner of Cook County and pres. of the Chicago Pharmacists Assn., died in Chicago of a heart attack.

WALTER E. TURPIN, 58, novelist professor of English at Morgan State College, Baltimore, Md., died after an operation. Author of the novels *These Low Grounds, O Canaan* and *The Rootless* and co-author with Nick Aaron Ford of *Better Skills for Better Writing*.

IN CONGRESS, JULY 4, 1776.

A DECLARATION

BY THE REPRESENTATIVES OF THE

UNITED STATES OF AMERICA,

IN GENERAL CONGRESS ASSEMBLED.

WHEN in the Course of human Events, it becomes necessary for one People to dissolve the Political Bands which have connected them with another, and to assume among the Powers of the Earth, the separate and equal Station to which the Laws of Nature and of Nature's God entitle them, a decent Respect to the Opinions of Mankind requires that they should declare the causes which impel them to the Separation.

WE hold these Truths to be self-evident, that all Men are created equal, that they are endowed by their Creator with certain unalienable Rights, that among these are Life, Liberty, and the Pursuit of Happiness---That to secure these Rights, Governments are instituted among Men, deriving their just Powers from the Consent of the Governed, that whenever any Form of Government becomes destructive of these Ends, it is the Right of the People to alter or to abolish it, and to institute new Government, laying its Foundation on such Principles, and organizing its Powers in such Form, as to them shall seem most likely to effect their Safety and Happiness. Prudence, indeed, will dictate that Governments long established should not be changed for light and transient Causes; and accordingly all Experience hath shewn, that Mankind are more disposed to suffer, while Evils are sufferable, than to right themselves by abolishing the Forms to which they are accustomed. But when a long Train of Abuses and Usurpations, pursuing invariably the same Object, evinces a Design to reduce them under absolute Despotism, it is their Right, it is their Duty, to throw off such Government, and to provide new Guards for their future Security. Such has been the patient Sufferance of these Colonies; and such is now the Necessity which constrains them to alter their former Systems of Government. The History of the present King of Great-Britain is a History of repeated Injuries and Usurpations, all having in direct Object the Establishment of an absolute Tyranny over these States. To prove this, let Facts be submitted to a candid World.

HE has refused his Assent to Laws, the most wholesome and necessary for the public Good.

HE has forbidden his Governors to pass Laws of immediate and pressing Importance, unless suspended in their Operation till his Assent should be obtained; and when so suspended, he has utterly neglected to attend to them.

HE has refused to pass other Laws for the Accommodation of large Districts of People, unless those People would relinquish the Right of Representation in the Legislature, a Right inestimable to them, and formidable to Tyrants only.

HE has called together Legislative Bodies at Places unusual, uncomfortable, and distant from the Depository of their public Records, for the sole Purpose of fatiguing them into Compliance with his Measures.

HE has dissolved Representative Houses repeatedly, for opposing with manly Firmness his Invasions on the Rights of the People.

HE has refused for a long Time, after such Dissolutions, to cause others to be elected; whereby the Legislative Powers, incapable of Annihilation, have returned to the People at large for their exercise; the State remaining in the mean time exposed to all the Dangers of Invasion from without, and Convulsions within.

HE has endeavoured to prevent the Population of these States; for that Purpose obstructing the Laws for Naturalization of Foreigners; refusing to pass others to encourage their Migrations hither, and raising the Conditions of new Appropriations of Lands.

HE has obstructed the Administration of Justice, by refusing his Assent to Laws for establishing Judiciary Powers.

HE has made Judges dependent on his Will alone, for the Tenure of their Offices, and the Amount and Payment of their Salaries.

HE has erected a Multitude of new Offices, and sent hither Swarms of Officers to harrass our People, and eat out their Substance.

HE has kept among us, in Times of Peace, Standing Armies, without the consent of our Legislatures.

HE has affected to render the Military independent of and superior to the Civil Power.

HE has combined with others to subject us to a Jurisdiction foreign to our Constitution, and unacknowledged by our Laws; giving his Assent to their Acts of pretended Legislation:

FOR quartering large Bodies of Armed Troops among us:

FOR protecting them, by a mock Trial, from Punishment for any Murders which they should commit on the Inhabitants of these States:

FOR cutting off our Trade with all Parts of the World:

FOR imposing Taxes on us without our Consent:

FOR depriving us, in many Cases, of the Benefits of Trial by Jury:

FOR transporting us beyond Seas to be tried for pretended Offences:

FOR abolishing the free System of English Laws in a neighbouring Province, establishing therein an arbitrary Government, and enlarging its Boundaries, so as to render it at once an Example and fit Instrument for introducing the same absolute Rule into these Colonies:

FOR taking away our Charters, abolishing our most valuable Laws, and altering fundamentally the Forms of our Governments:

FOR suspending our own Legislatures, and declaring themselves invested with Power to legislate for us in all Cases whatsoever.

HE has abdicated Government here, by declaring us out of his Protection and waging War against us.

HE has plundered our Seas, ravaged our Coasts, burnt our Towns, and destroyed the Lives of our People.

HE is, at this Time, transporting large Armies of foreign Mercenaries to compleat the Works of Death, Desolation, and Tyranny, already begun with circumstances of Cruelty and Perfidy, scarcely paralleled in the most barbarous Ages, and totally unworthy the Head of a civilized Nation.

HE has constrained our fellow Citizens taken Captive on the high Seas to bear Arms against their Country, to become the Executioners of their Friends and Brethren, or to fall themselves by their Hands.

HE has excited domestic Insurrections amongst us, and has endeavoured to bring on the Inhabitants of our Frontiers, the merciless Indian Savages, whose known Rule of Warfare, is an undistinguished Destruction, of all Ages, Sexes and Conditions.

IN every stage of these Oppressions we have Petitioned for Redress in the most humble Terms: Our repeated Petitions have been answered only by repeated Injury. A Prince, whose Character is thus marked by every act which may define a Tyrant, is unfit to be the Ruler of a free People.

NOR have we been wanting in Attentions to our British Brethren. We have warned them from Time to Time of Attempts by their Legislature to extend an unwarrantable Jurisdiction over us. We have reminded them of the Circumstances of our Emigration and Settlement here. We have appealed to their native Justice and Magnanimity, and we have conjured them by the Ties of our common Kindred to disavow these Usurpations, which, would inevitably interrupt our Connections and Correspondence. They too have been deaf to the Voice of Justice and of Consanguinity. We must, therefore, acquiesce in the Necessity, which denounces our Separation, and hold them, as we hold the rest of Mankind, Enemies in War, in Peace, Friends.

WE, therefore, the Representatives of the UNITED STATES OF AMERICA, in GENERAL CONGRESS, Assembled, appealing to the Supreme Judge of the World for the Rectitude of our Intentions, do, in the Name, and by Authority of the good People of these Colonies, solemnly Publish and Declare, That these United Colonies are, and of Right ought to be, FREE AND INDEPENDENT STATES; that they are absolved from all Allegiance to the British Crown, and that all political Connection between them and the State of Great-Britain, is and ought to be totally dissolved; and that as FREE AND INDEPENDENT STATES, they have full Power to levy War, conclude Peace, contract Alliances, establish Commerce, and to do all other Acts and Things which INDEPENDENT STATES may of right do. And for the support of this Declaration, with a firm Reliance on the Protection of divine Providence, we mutually pledge to each other our Lives, our Fortunes, and our sacred Honor.

Signed by ORDER *and in* BEHALF *of the* CONGRESS,

JOHN HANCOCK, PRESIDENT.

ATTEST.
CHARLES THOMSON, SECRETARY.

PHILADELPHIA: PRINTED BY JOHN DUNLAP.

SIGNIFICANT DOCUMENTS IN AMERICAN HISTORY

A documentary survey of the black man in American life (1688-1970)

The documents included in this section—whether they be resolutions, legislative enactments, amendments to the Constitution, executive proclamations, or presidential speeches—have all been chosen because they bear a special relevance to the context of Negro history in the United States. Some—like the Declaration of Independence, the Constitution, the Emancipation Proclamation—are household words which are an implicit part of every American's heritage; others, though less known, deserve comparable status. In themselves, they offer eloquent testimony to the impact of the Negro on American history—as slave, as freedman and, ultimately, as full-fledged American citizen.

THE GERMANTOWN MENNONITE RESOLUTION AGAINST SLAVERY (1688)

The Germantown Mennonite Resolution Against Slavery represents the earliest such protest formally voiced in Colonial America. It was passed 69 years after the introduction of the first Negro slaves in America—at a time when the number of slaves in the Colonies was comparatively small. It was not until 1775, however, that the Quakers, a religious group similarly opposed to the institution, formed the first antislavery society in the Colonies.

This is to the monthly meeting held at Richard Worrell's:

These are the reasons why we are against the traffic of men-body, as followeth: Is there any that would be done or handled at this manner? viz., to be sold or made a slave for all the time of his life? How fearful and faint-hearted are many at sea, when they see a strange vessel, being afraid it should be a Turk, and they should be taken, and sold for slaves into Turkey. Now, what is *this* better done, than Turks do? Yea, rather it is worse for them, which say they are

Christians; for we hear that the most part of such negers are brought hither against their will and consent, and that many of them are stolen. Now, though they are black, we cannot conceive there is more liberty to have them slaves, as it is to have other white ones. There is a saying, that we should do to all men like as we will be done ourselves; making no difference of what generation, descent, or colour they are. And those who steal or rob men, and those who buy or purchase them, are they not all alike? Here is liberty of conscience, which is right and reasonable; here ought to be likewise liberty of the body, except of evil-doers, which is another case. But to bring men hither, or to rob and sell them against their will, we stand against. In Europe there are many oppressed for conscience-sake; and here there are those oppressed which are of a black colour. And we who know that men must not commit adultery—some do commit adultery *in* others, separating wives from their husbands, and giving them to others: and some sell the children of these poor creatures to other men. Ah! do consider well this thing, you who do it, if you would be done at this manner—and if it is done according to Christianity! You surpass Holland and Germany in this thing. This makes an ill report in all those countries of Europe, where they hear of [it], that the Quakers do here handel men as they handel there the cattle. And for that reason some have no mind or inclination to come hither. And who shall maintain this your cause, or plead for it? Truly, we cannot do so, except you shall inform us better hereof, viz.: that Christians have liberty to practice these things. Pray, what thing in the world can be done worse towards us, than if men should rob or steal us away, and sell us for slaves to strange countries; separating husbands from their wives and children. Being now this is not done in the manner we would be done at; therefore, we contradict, and are against this traffic of men-body. And we who profess that it is not lawful to steal, must, like-

The first slaves in the English colonies of mainland America arrived at Jamestown in 1619.

wise, avoid to purchase such things as are stolen, but rather help to stop this robbing and stealing, if possible. And such men ought to be delivered out of the hands of the robbers, and set free as in Europe. Then is Pennsylvania to have a good report, instead, it hath now a bad one, for this sake, in other countries; Especially whereas the Europeans are desirous to know in what manner *the Quakers* do rule in *their* province; and most of them do look upon us with an envious eye. But if this is done well, what shall we say is done evil?

If once these slaves (which they say are so wicked and stubborn men,) should join themselves—fight for their freedom, and handel their masters and mistresses, as they did handel them before; will these masters and mistresses take the sword at hand and war against these poor slaves, like, as we are able to believe, some will not refuse to do? Or, have these poor negers not as much right to fight for their freedom, as you have to keep them slaves?

Now consider well this thing, if it is good or bad. And in case you find it to be good to handel these blacks in that manner, we desire and require you hereby lovingly, that you may inform us herein, which at this time never was done, viz., that Christians have such a liberty to do so. To the end we shall be satisfied on this point, and satisfy likewise our good friends and acquaintances in our native country, to whom it is a terror, or fearful thing, that men should be handelled so in Pennsylvania.

This is from our meeting at Germantown, held ye 18th of the 2d month, 1688, to be delivered to the monthly meeting at Richard Worrell's.

Garret Henderich,
Derick op de Graeff,
Francis Daniel Pastorius,
Abram op de Graeff.

THE DECLARATION OF INDEPENDENCE (1776)

The final version of the Declaration of Independence, as accepted by Congress, did not contain the following paragraph written by Thomas Jefferson as part of an initial draft of the document.

He has waged cruel war against human nature itself, violating its most sacred rights of life and liberty in the persons of a distant people who never offended him, captivating and carrying them into slavery in another hemisphere, or to incur miserable death in their transportation thither. This piratical warfare, the opprobrium of infidel powers, is the warfare of the Christian king of Great Britain. Determined to keep open a market where MEN should be bought and sold, he has prostituted his negative for suppressing every legislative attempt to prohibit or to restrain this execrable commerce; and that this assemblage of horrors might want no fact of distinguished die, he is now exciting these very people to rise in arms among us, and to purchase that liberty of which he *deprived them, by murdering the people upon whom* he *also obtruded them; thus paying off former crimes committed against the* liberties *of one people, with crimes which he urges them to commit against the* lives *of another.*

The omission of this passage reflected the awareness on the part of some Congressmen that a number of New England merchants were profitably engaged in the slave trade. Other legislators were simply in favor of slavery as an institution, and felt that the inclusion of such sentiments would prejudice the case for its continuation.

Many historians and critics have understandably concluded that the elimination of the above passage offers adequate proof that the American Negro, unlike his white counterpart, was never meant to share in the fruits of independence and equality in his adopted homeland.

When in the Course of human events, it becomes necessary for one people to dissolve the political bands which have connected them with another, and to assume among the Powers of the earth, the separate and equal station to which the Laws of Nature and of Nature's God entitle them, a decent respect to the opinions of mankind requires that they should declare the causes which impel them to the separation.

We hold these truths to be self-evident, that all men are created equal, that they are endowed by their Creator with certain unalienable Rights, that among these are Life, Liberty and the pursuit of Happiness. That to secure these rights, Governments are instituted among Men, deriving their just powers from the consent of the governed, That whenever any Form of Government becomes destructive of these ends, it is the Right of the People to alter or to abolish it, and to institute new Government, laying its foundation on such principles and organizing its powers in such form, as to them shall seem most likely to effect their Safety and Happiness. Prudence, indeed, will dictate that Governments long established should not be changed for light and transient causes; and accordingly all experience hath shown, that mankind are more disposed to suffer, while evils are sufferable, than to right themselves by abolishing the forms to which they are accustomed. But when a long train of abuses and usurpations, pursuing invariably the same Object evinces a design to reduce them under absolute Despotism, it is their right, it is their duty, to throw off such Government, and to provide new Guards for their future security.—Such has been the patient sufferance of these Colonies; and such is now the necessity which constrains them to alter their former Systems of Government. The history of the present King of Great Britain is a history of repeated injuries and usurpations, all having in direct object the establishment of an absolute Tyranny over these States. To prove this, let Facts be submitted to a candid world.

He has refused his Assent to Laws, the most wholesome and necessary for the public good.

He has forbidden his Governors to pass Laws of immediate and pressing importance, unless suspended in their operation till his Assent should be obtained; and when so suspended, he has utterly neglected to attend to them.

He has refused to pass other Laws for the accommodation of large districts of people, unless those people would relinquish the right of Representation in the Legislature, a right inestimable to them and formidable to tyrants only.

He has called together legislative bodies at places unusual, uncomfortable, and distant from the depository of their Public Records, for the sole purpose of fatiguing them into compliance with his measures.

He has dissolved Representative Houses repeatedly, for opposing with manly firmness his invasions on the rights of the people.

He has refused for a long time, after such dissolutions, to cause others to be elected; whereby the Legislative Powers, incapable of Annihilation, have returned to the People at large for their exercise; the State remaining in the mean time exposed to all the dangers of invasion from without, and convulsions within.

He has endeavoured to prevent the population of these States; for that purpose obstructing the Laws of Naturalization of Foreigners; refusing to pass others to encourage their migration hither, and raising the conditions of new Appropriations of Lands.

He has obstructed the Administration of Justice, by refusing his Assent to Laws for establishing Judiciary Powers.

He has made Judges dependent on his Will alone, for the tenure of their offices, and the amount and payment of their salaries.

He has erected a multitude of New Offices, and sent hither swarms of Officers to harass our People, and eat out their substance.

He has kept among us, in times of peace, Standing Armies without the Consent of our legislature.

He has affected to render the Military independent of and superior to the Civil Power.

He has combined with others to subject us to a jurisdiction foreign to our constitution, and unacknowledged by our laws; giving his Assent to their acts of pretended legislation:

For quartering large bodies of armed troops among us:

For protecting them, by a mock Trial, from Punishment for any Murders which they should commit on the Inhabitants of these States:

For cutting off our Trade with all parts of the world:

For imposing taxes on us without our Consent:

For depriving us in many cases, of the benefits of Trial by Jury:

For transporting us beyond Seas to be tried for pretended offences:

For abolishing the free System of English Laws in a neighbouring Province, establishing therein an Arbitrary government, and enlarging its Boundaries so as to render it at once an example and fit instrument for introducing the same absolute rule into these Colonies:

For taking away our Charters, abolishing our most valuable Laws, and altering fundamentally the Forms of our Governments:

For suspending our own Legislature, and declaring themselves invested with Power to legislate for us in all cases whatsoever.

He has abdicated Government here, by declaring us out of his Protection and waging War against us.

He has plundered our seas, ravaged our Coasts, burnt our towns, and destroyed the lives of our people.

He is at this time transporting large armies of foreign mercenaries to compleat the works of death, desolation and tyranny, already begun with circumstances of Cruelty & perfidy scarcely paralleled in the most barbarous ages, and totally unworthy the Head of a civilized nation.

He has constrained our fellow Citizens taken Captive on the high Seas to bear Arms against their Country, to become the executioners of their friends and Brethren, or to fall themselves by their Hands.

He has excited domestic insurrections amongst us, and has endeavoured to bring on the inhabitants of our frontiers, the merciless Indian Savages, whose known rule of warfare, is an undistinguished destruction of all ages, sexes and conditions.

In every stage of these Oppressions We have Petitioned for Redress in the most humble terms: Our repeated Petitions have been answered only by repeated injury. A Prince, whose character is thus marked by every act which may define a Tyrant, is unfit to be the ruler of a free People.

Nor have We been wanting in attention to our British brethren. We have warned them from time to time of attempts by their legislature to extend an unwarrantable jurisdiction over us. We have reminded them of the circumstances of our emigration and settlement here. We have appealed to their native justice and magnanimity, and we have conjured them by the ties of our common kindred to disavow these usurpations, which would inevitably interrupt our connections and correspondence. They too have been deaf to the voice of justice and of consanguinity. We must, therefore, acquiesce in the necessity, which denounces our Separation, and hold them, as we hold the rest of mankind, Enemies in War, in Peace Friends.

We, therefore, the Representatives of the united States of America, in General Congress, Assembled, appealing to the Supreme Judge of the world for the rectitude of our intentions, do, in the Name, and by Authority of the good People of these Colonies, solemnly publish and declare, That these United Colonies are, and of Right ought to be Free and Independent States; that they are Absolved from all Allegiance to the British Crown, and that all political connection between them and the State of Great Britain, is and ought to be totally dissolved; and that as Free and Independent States, they have full Power to levy War, conclude Peace, contract Alliances, establish Commerce, and to do all other Acts and Things which Independent States may of right do. And for the support of this Declaration, with a firm reliance on the Protection of Divine Providence, we mutually pledge to each other our Lives, our Fortunes and our sacred Honor.

JOHN HANCOCK.

Massachusetts-Bay
SAML. ADAMS,
JOHN ADAMS,
ROBT. TREAT PAINE,
ELBRIDGE GERRY.

New Hampshire
JOSIAH BARTLETT,
WM. WHIPPLF,
MATTHEW THORNTON.

Connecticut
ROGER SHERMAN,
SAM'EL HUNTINGTON,
WM. WILLIAMS,
OLIVER WOLCOTT.

GEO. READ,
THO. M'KEAN.

Georgia
BUTTON GWINNETT,
LYMAN HALL,
GEO. WALTON.

New York
WM. FLOYD,
PHIL. LIVINGSTON,
FRANS. LEWIS,
LEWIS MORRIS.

South Carolina
EDWARD RUTLEDGE,
THOS. HEYWARD, JUNR.,
THOMAS LYNCH, JUNR.,
ARTHUR MIDDLETON.

Rhode Island
STEP. HOPKINS,
WILLIAM ELLERY.

Pennsylvania
ROBT. MORRIS,
BENJAMIN RUSH,
BENJA. FRANKLIN,
JOHN MORTON,
GEO. CLYMER,
JAS. SMITH,
GEO. TAYLOR,
JAMES WILSON,
GEO. ROSS.

Delaware
CAESAR RODNEY,

North Carolina
WM. HOOPER,
JOSEPH HEWES,
JOHN PENN.

Maryland
SAMUEL CHASE,
WM. PACA,
THOS. STONE,
CHARLES CARROLL
of Carrollton.

New Jersey
RICHD. STOCKTON,
JNO. WITHERSPOON,
FRAS. HOPKINSON,
JOHN HART,
ABRA. CLARK.

Virginia
GEORGE WYTHE,
RICHARD HENRY LEE,
TH. JEFFERSON,
BENJA. HARRISON,
THS. NELSON, JR.,
FRANCIS LIGHTFOOT LEE,
CARTER BRAXTON.

THE CONSTITUTION OF THE UNITED STATES (1787)

Although the editors have chosen to print the Constitution and the Bill of Rights in their entirety, they are more concerned—within the framework of this volume—with two passages in particular: Sections 2 and 9 of Article I. Section 2, containing the so-called "three-fifths compromise" (see paragraph three, section 2, first sentence set in italic), in effect defines the Negro ("other Persons") as three-fifths of the white man ("free Persons"). Section 9 (the first two paragraphs of which are also in italic) provides both for the extension of the slave trade for a 20-year period, and for the return of runaway slaves. Such passages attest to the strong element of conservatism that existed in the United States in the critical period following the Revolutionary War.

WE THE PEOPLE of the United States, in Order to form a more perfect Union, establish Justice, insure domestic Tranquility, provide for the common defence, promote the general Welfare, and secure the Blessings of Liberty to ourselves and our Posterity, do ordain and establish this Constitution for the United States of America.

ART. I

Sec. 1. All legislative Powers herein granted shall be vested in a Congress of the United States, which shall consist of a Senate and House of Representatives.

Sec. 2. The House of Representatives shall be composed of Members chosen every second Year by the People of the several States, and the Electors in each State shall have the Qualifications requisite for Electors of the most numerous Branch of the State Legislature.

No Person shall be a Representative who shall not have attained to the Age of twenty-five Years, and been seven Years a Citizen of the United States, and who shall not, when elected, be an Inhabitant of that State in which he shall be chosen.

Representatives and direct Taxes shall be apportioned among the several States which may be included within this Union, according to their respective Numbers, which shall be determined by adding to the whole Number of free Persons, including those bound to Service for a Term of Years, and excluding Indians not taxed, three fifths of all other Persons. The actual Enumeration shall be made within three Years after the first Meeting of the Congress of the United States, and within every subsequent Term of ten Years, in such Manner as they shall by Law direct. The Number of Representatives shall not exceed one for every thirty Thousand, but each State shall have at Least one Representative; and until such enumeration shall be made, the State of New Hampshire shall be entitled to chuse three, Massachusetts eight, Rhode-Island and Providence Plantations one, Connecticut five, New-York six, New Jersey four, Pennsylvania eight, Delaware one, Maryland six, Virginia ten, North Carolina five, South Carolina five, and Georgia three.

When vacancies happen in the Representation from any State, the Executive Authority thereof shall issue Writs of Election to fill such Vacancies.

The House of Representatives shall chuse their Speaker and other Officers; and shall have the sole Power of Impeachment.

Sec. 3. The Senate of the United States shall be composed of two Senators from each State, chosen by the Legislature thereof, for six Years; and each Senator shall have one Vote.

Immediately after they shall be assembled in Consequence of the first Election, they shall be divided as equally as may be into three Classes. The Seats of the Senators of the first Class shall be vacated at the Expiration of the second Year, of the second Class at the Expiration of the fourth Year, and of the third Class at the Expiration of the sixth Year, so that one third may be chosen every second Year; and if Vacancies happen by Resignation, or otherwise, during the Recess of the Legislature of any State, the Executive thereof may make temporary Appointments until the next Meeting of the Legislature, which shall then fill such Vacancies.

No Person shall be a Senator who shall not have attained to the Age of thirty Years, and been nine Years a Citizen of the United States, and who shall not, when elected, be an Inhabitant of that State for which he shall be chosen.

The Vice President of the United States shall be President of the Senate, but shall have no Vote, unless they be equally divided.

The Senate shall chuse their other Officers, and also a President pro-tempore, in the Absence of the Vice President, or when he shall exercise the Office of President of the United States.

The Senate shall have the sole Power to try all Impeachments. When sitting for that Purpose, they shall be on Oath or Affirmation. When the President of the United States is tried, the Chief Justice shall preside: And no Person shall be convicted without the Concurrence of two thirds of the Members present.

Judgment in Cases of Impeachment shall not extend further than to removal from Office, and disqualification to hold and enjoy any Office of honor, Trust or Profit under the United States: but the Party convicted shall nevertheless be liable and subject to Indictment, Trial, Judgment and Punishment, according to Law.

Sec. 4. The Times, Places and Manner of holding Elections for Senators and Representatives, shall be prescribed in each State by the Legislature thereof; but the Congress may at any time by Law make or alter such Regulations, except as to the Places of chusing Senators.

The Congress shall assemble at least once in every Year, and such Meeting shall be on the first Monday in December, unless they shall by Law appoint a different Day.

Sec. 5. Each House shall be the Judge of the Elections, Returns and Qualifications of its own Members, and a Majority of each shall constitute a Quorum to do Business; but a smaller Number may adjourn from day to day, and may be authorized to compel the Attendance of absent Members, in such Manner, and under such Penalties as each House may provide.

Each House may determine the Rules of its Proceedings, punish its Members for disorderly Behaviour, and, with the Concurrence of two thirds, expel a Member.

Each House shall keep a Journal of its Proceedings, and from time to time publish the same, excepting such Parts as may in their Judgment require Secrecy; and the Yeas and Nays of the Members of either House on any question shall, at the Desire of one fifth of those Present, be entered on the Journal.

Neither House, during the Session of Congress, shall, without the Consent of the other, adjourn for more than three days, nor to any other Place than that in which the two Houses shall be sitting.

Sec. 6. The Senators and Representatives shall receive a Compensation for their Services, to be ascertained by Law, and paid out of the Treasury of the United States. They shall in all Cases, except Treason, felony and Breach of the Peace, be privileged from Arrest during their Attendance at the Session of their respective Houses, and in going to and returning from the same; and for any speech or Debate in either House, they shall not be questioned in any other Place.

No Senator or Representative shall, during the Time for which he was elected, be appointed to any civil Office under the Authority of the United States which shall have been created, or the Emoluments whereof shall have been encreased during such time; and no Person holding any Office under the United States, shall be a Member of either

House during his Continuance in Office.

Sec. 7. All Bills for raising Revenue shall originate in the House of Representatives; but the Senate may propose or concur with Amendments as on other Bills.

Every Bill which shall have passed the House of Representatives and the Senate, shall, before it become a Law, be presented to the President of the United States; If he approve he shall sign it, but if not he shall return it, with his Objections to that House in which it shall have originated, who shall enter the Objections at large on their Journal, and proceed to reconsider it. If after such Reconsideration two thirds of that House shall agree to pass the Bill, it shall be sent, together with the Objections, to the other House, by which it shall likewise be reconsidered, and if approved by two thirds of that House, it shall become a Law. But in all such Cases the Votes of both Houses shall be determined by yeas and Nays, and the Names of the Persons voting for and against the Bill shall be entered on the Journal of each House respectively. If any Bill shall not be returned by the President within ten Days (Sundays excepted) after it shall have been presented to him, the Same shall be a Law, in like Manner as if he had signed it, unless the Congress by their Adjournment prevent its Return, in which Case it shall not be a Law.

Every Order, Resolution, or Vote to which the Concurrence of the Senate and House of Representatives may be necessary (except on a question of Adjournment) shall be presented to the President of the United States; and before the Same shall take Effect, shall be approved by him, or being disapproved by him, shall be repassed by two thirds of the Senate and House of Representatives, according to the Rules and Limitations prescribed in the Case of a Bill.

Sec. 8. The Congress shall have Power To lay and collect Taxes, Duties, Imposts and Excises, to pay the Debts and provide for the common Defence and general Welfare of the United States; but all Duties, Imposts and Excises shall be uniform throughout the United States;

To borrow Money on the credit of the United States;

To regulate Commerce with foreign Nations, and among the several States, and with the Indian Tribes;

To establish an uniform Rule of Naturalization, and uniform Laws on the subject of Bankruptcies throughout the United States;

To coin Money, regulate the Value thereof, and of foreign Coin, and fix the Standard of Weights and Measures;

To provide for the Punishment of counterfeiting and Securities and current Coin of the United States;

To establish Post Offices and post Roads;

To promote the Progress of Science an useful Arts, by securing for limited Times to Authors and Inventors the exclusive Right to their respective Writings and Discoveries;

To constitute Tribunals inferior to the supreme Court;

To define and punish Piracies and Felonies committed on the high Seas, and Offences against the Law of Nations;

To declare War, grant Letters of Marque and Reprisal, and make Rules concerning Captures on Land and Water;

To raise and support Armies, but no Appropriation of Money to that Use shall be for a longer Term than two Years;

To provide and maintain a Navy;

To make Rules for the Government and Regulation of the land and naval Forces;

To provide for calling forth the Militia to execute the Laws of the Union, suppress Insurrections and repel Invasions;

To provide for organizing, arming, and disciplining, the Militia, and for governing such Part of them as may be employed in the Service of the United States, reserving to the States respectively, the Appointment of the Officers, and the Authority of training the Militia according to the discipline prescribed by Congress;

To exercise exclusive Legislation in all Cases whatsoever, over such District (not exceeding ten Miles square) as may, by Cession of particular States, and the Acceptance of Congress, become the Seat of the Government of the United States, and to exercise like Authority over all Places purchased by the Consent of the Legislature of the State in which the Same shall be, for the Erection of Forts, Magazines, Arsenals, dock-Yards, and other needful Buildings;—And

To make all Laws which shall be necessary and proper for carrying into Execution the foregoing Powers, and all other Powers vested by this Constitution in the Government of the United States, or in any Department or Officer thereof.

Sec. 9. *The Migration or Importation of such Persons as any of the States now existing shall think proper to admit, shall*

Alexander Hamilton

not be prohibited by the Congress prior to the Year one thousand eight hundred and eight, but a Tax or duty may be imposed on such Importation, not exceeding ten dollars for each Person.

The Privilege of the Writ of Habeas Corpus shall not be suspended, unless when in Cases of Rebellion or Invasion the public Safety may require it.

No Bill of Attainder or ex post facto Law shall be passed.

No Capitation, or other direct, Tax shall be laid, unless in Proportion to the Census or Enumeration before directed to be taken.

No Tax or Duty shall be laid on Articles exported from any State.

No Preference shall be given by any Regulation of Commerce or Revenue to the Ports of one State over those of another: nor shall Vessels bound to, or from, one State, be obliged to enter, clear, or pay Duties in another.

No Money shall be drawn from the Treasury, but in Consequence of Appropriations made by Law; and a regular Statement and Account of the Receipts and Expenditures of all public Money shall be published from time to time.

No Title of Nobility shall be granted by the United States: And no Person holding any Office of Profit or Trust under them, shall, without the Consent of the Congress, accept of any present, Emolument, Office, or Title, of any kind whatever, from any King, Prince or foreign State.

Sec. 10. No State shall enter into any Treaty, Alliance, or Confederation; grant Letters of Marque and Reprisal; coin Money; emit Bills of Credit; make any Thing but gold and silver Coin a Tender in Payment of Debts; pass any Bill of Attainder, ex post facto Law, or Law impairing the Obligation of Contracts, or grant any Title of Nobility.

No State shall, without the Consent of the Congress, lay any Imposts or Duties on Imports or Exports, except what may be absolutely necessary for executing its inspection Laws: and the net Produce of all duties and Imposts, laid by any State on Imports or Exports, shall be for the Use of the Treasury of the United States; and all such Laws shall be subject to the Revision and Controul of the Congress.

No State shall, without the Consent of Congress, lay any Duty of Tonnage, keep Troops, or Ships of War in time of Peace, enter into any Agreement or Compact with another State, or with a foreign Power, or engage in War, unless actually invaded, or in such imminent Danger as will not admit of delay.

Art. II

Sec. 1. The executive Power shall be vested in a President of the United States of America. He shall hold his Office during the Term of four Years, and, together with the Vice President, chosen for the same Term, be elected, as follows

Each State shall appoint, in such Manner as the Legislature thereof may direct, a Number of Electors, equal to the whole Number of Senators and Representatives to which the State may be entitled in the Congress: but no Senator or Representative, or Person holding an Office of Trust or Profit under the United States, shall be appointed an Elector.

The electors shall meet in their respective States, and vote by Ballot for two Persons, of whom one at least shall not be an inhabitant of the same State with themselves. And they shall make a List of all the Persons voted for, and of the Number of Votes for each; which List they shall sign and certify, and transmit sealed to the Seat of the Government of the United States, directed to the President of the Senate. The President of the Senate shall, in the Presence of the Senate and House of Representatives, open all the Certificates, and the Votes shall then be counted. The Person having the greatest Number of Votes shall be the President, if such Number be a Majority of the whole Number of Electors appointed; and if there be more than one who have such Majority, and have an equal Number of Votes, then the House of Representatives shall immediately chuse by Ballot one of them for President; and if no person have a Majority, then from the five highest on the List the said House shall in like Manner chuse the President. But in chusing the President, the Votes shall be taken by States, the Representation from each State having one Vote; A quorum for this Purpose shall consist of a Member or Members from two thirds of the States, and a Majority of all the states shall be necessary to a choice. In every case, after the choice of the president, the person having the greatest number of Votes of the Electors shall be the Vice President. If there should remain two or more who have equal Votes, the Senate shall chuse from them by Ballot the Vice President.

The Congress may determine the Time of chusing the Electors, and the Day on which they shall give their Votes; which Day shall be the same throughout the

United States.

No Person except a natural born Citizen, or a Citizen of the United States, at the time of the Adoption of this Constitution, shall be eligible to the Office of President; neither shall any Person be eligible to that Office who shall not have attained to the Age of thirty five Years, and been fourteen Years a Resident within the United States.

In Case of the Removal of the President from Office, or of his Death, resignation, or Inability to discharge the Powers and Duties of the said Office, the Same shall devolve on the Vice President, and the Congress may by Law provide for the Case of Removal, Death, Resignation or Inability, both of the President and Vice President, declaring what Officer shall then act as President, and such Officer shall act accordingly, until the Disability be removed, or a President shall be elected.

The President shall, at stated Times, receive for his Services, a Compensation, which shall neither be encreased nor diminished during the Period for which he shall have been elected, and he shall not receive within that Period any other Emolument from the United States, or any of them.

Before he enter on the execution of his Office, he shall take the following Oath or Affirmation:—"I do solemnly swear (or affirm) that I will faithfully execute the Office of President of the United States, and will to the best of my Ability, preserve, protect and defend the Constitution of the United States."

Sec. 2. The President shall be Commander in Chief of the Army and Navy of the United States, and of the Militia of the several States, when called into the actual Service of the United States; he may require the Opinion, in writing, of the principal Officer in each of the executive Departments, upon any Subject relating to the Duties of their respective Offices, and he shall have Power to grant Reprieves and Pardons for Offences against the United States, except in cases of Impeachment.

He shall have Power, by and with the Advice and Consent of the Senate, to make Treaties, provided two thirds of the Senators present concur; and he shall nominate, and by and with the Advice and Consent of the Senate, shall appoint Ambassadors, other public Ministers and Consuls, Judges of the supreme Court, and all other Offices of the United States, whose Appointments are not herein otherwise provided for, and which shall be established by Law; but the Congress may by Law vest the Appointment of such inferior Officers, as they think proper, in the President alone, in the Courts of Law, or in the Heads of Departments.

The President shall have Power to fill up all Vacancies that may happen during the Recess of the Senate, by granting Commissions which shall expire at the end of their next Session.

Sec. 3. He shall from time to time give to the Congress Information of the State of the Union, and recommend to their Consideration such Measures as he shall judge necessary and expedient; he may, on extraordinary Occasions, convene both Houses, or either of them, and in Case of Disagreement between them, with Respect to the Time of Adjournment, he may adjourn them to such Time as he shall think proper; he shall receive Ambassadors and other public Ministers; he shall take care that the Laws be faithfully executed, and shall Commission all the Officers of the United States.

Sec. 4. The President, Vice President and all civil Officers of the United States, shall be removed from Office on Impeachment for, and Conviction of, Treason, Bribery, or other high Crimes and Misdemeanors.

ART. III

Sec. 1. The judicial Power of the United States, shall be vested in one supreme Court. And in such inferior Courts as the Congress may from time to time ordain and establish. The Judges, both of the supreme and inferior Courts, shall hold their Offices during good Behaviour, and shall, at stated Times, receive for their Services, a Compensation which shall not be diminished during their Continuance in Office.

Sec. 2. The judicial Power shall extend to all Cases, in Law and Equity, arising under this Constitution, the Laws of the United States, and Treaties made, or which shall be made, under their Authority;—to all Cases affecting Ambassadors, other public Ministers and Consuls;—to all Cases of admiralty and maritime Jurisdiction;—to Controversies to which the United States shall be a Party;—to Controversies between two or more States; —between a State and Citizens of another State;—between Citizens of different states,—between Citizens of the same State claiming Lands under Grants of different States, and between a State, or the Citizens thereof, and foreign States,

Citizens or Subjects.

In all Cases affecting Ambassadors, other public Ministers and Consuls, and those in which a State shall be Party, the supreme Court shall have original Jurisdiction. In all the other Cases before mentioned, the supreme Court shall have appellate Jurisdiction, both as to Law and Fact, with such Exceptions, and under such Regulations as the Congress shall make.

The Trial of all Crimes, except in Cases of Impeachment, shall be by Jury; and such Trial shall be held in the State where the said Crimes shall have been committed; but when not committed within any State, the Trial shall be at such Place or Places as the Congress may by Law have directed.

Sec. 3. Treason against the United States, shall consist only in levying War against them, or in adhering to their Enemies, giving them Aid and Comfort. No Person shall be convicted of Treason unless on the Testimony of two Witnesses to the same overt Act, or on Confession in open Court.

The Congress shall have Power to declare the Punishment of Treason, but no Attainder of Treason shall work Corruption of Blood, or Forfeiture except during the Life of the Person attainted.

Art. IV

Sec. 1. Full Faith and Credit shall be given in each state to the Public Acts, Records, and judicial Proceedings of every other State. And the Congress may by general Laws prescribe the Manner in which such Acts, Records and Proceedings shall be proved, and the Effect thereof.

Sec. 2. The Citizens of each State shall be entitled to all Privileges and Immunities of Citizens in the several States.

A Person charged in any State with Treason, Felony, or other Crime, who shall flee from Justice, and be found in another State, shall on Demand of the executive authority of the State from which he fled, be delivered up, to be removed to the State having Jurisdiction of the Crime.

No Person held to Service or Labour in one State, under the Laws thereof, escaping into another, shall, in Consequence of any Law or Regulation therein, be discharged from such Service or Labour, but shall be delivered up on Claim of the Party to whom such Service or Labour may be due.

Sec. 3. New States may be admitted by the Congress into this Union; but no new States shall be formed or erected within the Jurisdiction of any other State; nor any State be formed by the Junction of two or more States, or Parts of States, without the Consent of the Legislatures of the States concerned as well as of the Congress.

The Congress shall have Power to dispose of and make all needful Rules and Regulations respecting the Territory or other Property belonging to the United States; and nothing in this Constitution shall be so construed as to Prejudice any Claims of the United States, or of any particular State.

Sec. 4. The United States shall guarantee to every State in this Union a Republican Form of Government, and shall protect each of them against Invasion; and on Application of the Legislature, or of the Executive (when the Legislature cannot be convened) against domestic Violence.

Art. V

The Congress, whenever two thirds of both Houses shall deem it necessary, shall propose Amendments to this Constitution, or, on the Application of the Legislatures of two thirds of the several States, shall call a Convention for proposing Amendments, which, in either Case, shall be valid to all Intents and Purposes, as Part of this Constitution, when ratified by the Legislatures of three fourths of the several States, or by Conventions in three fourths thereof, as the one or the other Mode of Ratification may be proposed by the Congress; Provided that no Amendment which may be made prior to the Year One thousand eight hundred and eight shall in any Manner affect the first and fourth Clauses in the Ninth Section of the first Article; and that no State, without its Consent, shall be deprived of its equal Suffrage in the Senate.

Art. VI

All Debts contracted and Engagements entered into, before the Adoption of this Constitution, shall be as valid against the United States under this Constitution, as under the Confederation.

This Constitution, and the Laws of the United States which shall be made in Pursuance thereof; and all Treaties made, or which shall be made, under the authority of the United States, shall be the supreme Law of the Land; and the Judges in every State shall be bound thereby, any Thing in the Constitution or Laws of any State to the Contrary notwithstanding.

The Senators and Representatives before mentioned, and the Members of the several State Legislatures, and all executive and judicial Officers, both of the United States and of the several States, shall be bound by Oath or Affirmation, to support this Constitution; but no religious Test shall ever be required as a Qualification to any Office or public Trust under the United States.

ART. VII

The Ratification of the Conventions of Nine States, shall be sufficient for the Establishment of this Constitution between the States so ratifying the Same.

Done in Convention by the Unanimous Consent of the States present the Seventeenth Day of September in the Year of our Lord one thousand seven hundred and Eighty seven and of the Independence of the United States of America the Twelfth. In witness whereof We have hereunto subscribed our Names,

G° WASHINGTON—Presid[t]
and deputy from Virginia

New Hampshire	JOHN LANGDON NICHOLAS GILMAN
Massachusetts	NATHANIEL GORHAM RUFUS KING
Connecticut	W[M] SAM[L] JOHNSON ROGER SHERMAN
New York	ALEXANDER HAMILTON
New Jersey	WIL: LIVINGSTON DAVID BREARLEY W[M] PATERSON JONA: DAYTON
Pennsylvania	B FRANKLIN THOMAS MIFFLIN ROB[T] MORRIS GEO. CLYMER THO[S] FITZSIMONS JARED INGERSOLL JAMES WILSON GOUV MORRIS
Delaware	GEO: READ GUNNING BEDFORD jun JOHN DICKINSON RICHARD BASSETT JACO: BROOM
Maryland	JAMES M[C]HENRY DAN OF S[T] THO[S] JENIFER DAN[L] CARROLL
Virginia	JOHN BLAIR— JAMES MADISON JR
North Carolina	W[M] BLOUNT RICH[D] DOBBS SPAIGHT HU WILLIAMSON
South Carolina	J. RUTLEDGE CHARLES COTESWORTH PINCKNEY CHARLES PINCKNEY PIERCE BUTLER
Georgia	WILLIAM FEW ABR BALDWIN

THE BILL OF RIGHTS (1791)

ART. I

Congress shall make no law respecting an establishment of religion, or prohibiting the free exercise thereof; or abridging the freedom of speech, or of the press; or the right of the people peaceably to assemble, and to petition the government for a redress of grievances.

ART. II

A well regulated Militia, being necessary to the security of a free State, the right of the people to keep and bear Arms, shall not be infringed.

ART. III

No Soldier, shall, in time of peace be quartered in any house, without the consent of the Owner, nor in time of war, but in a manner to be prescribed by law.

ART. IV

The right of the people to be secure in their persons, houses, papers, and effects, against unreasonable searches and seizures, shall not be violated, and no Warrants shall issue, but upon probable cause, supported by Oath or affirmation, and particularly describing the place to be searched, and the persons or things to be seized.

ART. V

No person shall be held to answer for a capital, or otherwise infamous crime, unless on a presentment or indictment of a Grand Jury, except in cases arising in the land or naval forces, or in the Militia, when in actual service in time of War or public danger; nor shall any person be subject for the same offence to be twice put in jeopardy of life or limb; nor shall be compelled in any criminal case to be a witness against himself, nor be deprived of life, liberty, or property, without due process of law; nor shall private property be taken for public use, without just compensation.

ART. VI

In all criminal prosecutions, the accused shall enjoy the right to a speedy and public trial, by an impartial jury of the State and district wherein the crime shall have been committed, which district shall have been previously ascertained by law, and to be informed of the nature and cause of the accusation; to be confronted with the witnesses against him; to have compulsory process for obtaining witnesses in his favor, and to have the Assistance of Counsel for his defence.

ART. VII

In Suits at common law, where the value in controversy shall exceed twenty dollars, the right of trial by jury shall be perserved, and no fact tried by a jury, shall be otherwise re-examined in any Court of the United States, than according to the rules of the common law.

ART. VIII

Excessive bail shall not be required, nor excessive fines imposed, nor cruel and unusual punishments inflicted.

ART. IX

The enumeration in the Constitution, of certain rights, shall not be construed to deny or disparage others retained by the people.

ART. X

The powers not delegated to the United States by the Constitution, nor prohibited by it to the States, are reserved to the States respectively, or to the people.

GEORGE WASHINGTON'S LAST WILL AND TESTAMENT: THE FIRST PRESIDENT FREES HIS SLAVES (1799)

During the 18th century, Negro slavery was a firmly entrenched institution of American life, particularly in the South where it was justified mainly as an economic necessity. This argument notwithstanding, it was Washington's decision, at the writing of his last will and testament in 1799, to free all those slaves which he held in his "own right." Washington's will also reflected his concern for the financial welfare and educational support of his former charges.

IN THE NAME OF GOD AMEN

I George Washington of Mount Vernon—a citizen of the United States,—and lately President of the same, do make, ordain and declare this Instrument; which is written with my own hand and every page thereof subscribed with my name, to be my last Will & Testament, revoking all others. . . . Upon the decease of my wife, it is my Will & desire that all the Slaves which I hold in *my own right*, shall receive their freedom. . . . And whereas among those who will receive freedom according to this devise, there may be some, who from old age or bodily infirmities, and others who on account of their infancy, that will be unable to support themselves; it is my Will and desire that all who come under the first & second description shall be comfortably cloathed & fed by my heirs while they live;—and that such of the latter description as have no parents living, or if living are unable, or unwilling to provide for them, shall be bound by the Court until they shall arrive at the age of twenty five years;—and in cases where no record can be produced, whereby their ages can be ascertained, the judgment of the Court upon its own view of the subject, shall be adequate and final. —The Negros thus bound, are (by their Masters or Mistresses) to be taught to read & write; and to be brought up to some useful occupation, agreeably to the Laws of the Commonwealth of Virginia, providing for the support of Orphan and other poor Children.—And I do hereby expressly forbid the Sale, or transportation out of the said Commonwealth of any Slave I may die possessed of, under any pretence whatsoever.—And I do moreover most pointedly, and most solemnly enjoin it upon my Executors hereafter named, or the Survivors of them, to see that *this* clause respecting Slaves, and every part thereof be religiously fulfilled at the Epoch at which it is directed to take place; without evasion, neglect or delay, after the Crops which may then be on the ground are harvested, particularly as it respects the aged and infirm;—Seeing that a regular and permanent fund be established for their Support so long as there are subjects requiring it; not trusting to the uncertain provision to be made by individuals.— And to my Mulatto man William (calling himself William Lee) I give immediate freedom; or if he should prefer it (on account of the accidents which have befallen him, and which have rendered him incapable of walking or of any active employment) to remain in the situation he now is, it shall be optional in him to do so: In either case however, I allow him an annuity of thirty dollars during his natural life, which shall be independent of the victuals and cloaths he has been accustomed to receive, if he chuses the last alternative; but in full, with his freedom, if he prefers the first; & this I give him as a testimony of my sense of his attachment to me, and for his faithful services during the Revolutionary War.

THE ACT TO PROHIBIT THE IMPORTATION OF SLAVES (1807)

The Act of 1807 (which actually went into effect on January 1, 1808, and thereby did not interfere with the provisions of Article I, Section 9 of the U. S. Constitution) sought to end the slave trade by prohibiting the importation of "men-body' 'onto the North American mainland. The act, however, was not rigidly enforced, despite the appeals of Presidents Martin Van Buren and John Tyler. Evidence of this can be found in the fact that, between 1808 and 1860, some 250,000 slaves were illegally imported into the United States.

Captive African Negroes were transported to the New World under the most adverse conditions imaginable, and were often brutalized by crew members aboard slave ships.

ACT TO PROHIBIT THE IMPORTATION OF SLAVES

March 2, 1807

An Act to prohibit the importation of Slaves into any port or place within the jurisdiction of the United States, from and after the first day of January, in the year of our Lord one thousand eight hundred and eight.

Be it enacted, That from and after the first day of January, one thousand eight hundred and eight, it shall not be lawful to import or bring into the United States or the territories thereof from any foreign kingdom, place, or country, any negro, mulatto, or person of colour, as a slave, or to be held to service or labour.

Sec. 2. That no citizen of the United States, or any other person, shall, from and after the first day of January, in the year of our Lord one thousand eight hundred and eight, for himself, or themselves, or any other person whatsoever, either as master, factor, or owner, build, fit, equip, load or to otherwise prepare any ship or vessel, in any port or place within the jurisdiction of the United States, nor shall cause any ship or vessel to sail from any port or place within the same, for the purpose of procuring any negro, mulatto, or person of colour, from any foreign kingdom, place, or country, to be transported to any port or place whatsoever within the jurisdiction of the United States, to be held, sold, or disposed of as slaves, or to be held to service or labour: and if any ship or vessel shall be so fitted out for the purpose aforesaid, or shall be caused to sail so as aforesaid, every such ship or vessel, her tackle, apparel, and furniture, shall be forfeited to the United States, and shall be liable to be seized, prosecuted, and condemned in any of the circuit courts or district courts, for the district where the said ship or vessel may be found or seized. . . .

Sec. 4. If any citizen or citizens of the United States, or any person resident within the jurisdiction of the same, shall, from and after the first day of January, one thousand eight hundred and eight, take on board, receive or transport from any of the coasts or kingdoms of Africa, or from any other foreign kingdom, place, or country, any negro, mulatto, or person of colour in any ship or vessel, for the purpose of selling them in any port or place within the jurisdiction of the United States as slaves, or be to held to service or labour, or shall be in any ways aiding or abetting therein, such citizen or citizens, or person, shall severally forfeit and pay five thousand dollars, one moiety thereof to the use of any person or persons who shall sue for and prosecute the same to effect. . .

Sec. 6. That if any person or persons whatsoever, shall, from and after the first day of January, one thousand eight hundred and eight, purchase or sell any negro, mulatto, or person, of colour, for a slave, or to be held to service or labour, who shall have been imported, or brought from any foreign kingdom, place, or country, or from the dominions of any foreign state, immediately adjoining to the United States, after the last day of December, one thousand eight hundred and seven, knowing at the time of such purchase or sale, such negro, mulatto, or person of colour, was so brought within the jurisdiction of the United States, as aforesaid, such purchaser and seller shall severally forfeit and pay for every negro, mulatto, or person of colour, so purchased or sold as aforesaid, eight hundred dollars. . . .

Sec. 7. That if any ship or vessel shall be found, from and after the first day of January, one thousand eight hundred and eight, in any river, port, bay, or harbor, or on the high seas, within the jurisdictional limits of the United States, or hovering on the coast thereof, having on board any negro, mulatto, or person of colour, for the purpose of selling them as slaves, or with intent to land the same, in any port or place within the jurisdiction of the United States, contrary to the prohibition of the act, every such ship or vessel, together with her tackle, apparel, and furniture, and the goods or effects which shall be found on board the same, shall be forfeited to the use of the United States, and may be seized, prosecuted, and condemned, in any court of the United States, having jurisdiction thereof. And it shall be lawful for the President of the United States, and he is hereby authorized, should he deem it expedient, to cause any of the armed vessels of the United States to be manned and employed to cruise on any part of the coast of the United States, or territories thereof, where he may judge attempts will be made to violate the provisions of this act, and to instruct and direct the commanders of armed vessels of the United States, to seize, take, and bring into any port of the United States all such ships or vessels, and moreover to seize, take, or bring into any port of the U. S. all ships or vessel of the U. S. wheresoever found on the high seas, contravening the provisions of this act, to be proceeded against according to law. . . .

THE MISSOURI COMPROMISE (1819-1821)

Under the terms of the Missouri Compromise (1819-1821), Missouri was admitted to the Union as a slave state. (It was followed in short order by Maine, a free state.) However, slavery was prohibited from that time onward in all Louisiana Territory lying north of latitude 36° 30′. For a certain period, the Compromise appeased both pro and antislavery spokesmen. However, the question of slavery once again vaulted into the national spotlight with the outbreak of the Mexican War, which gave promise of greatly increasing the potential territory open to slavery. (See Compromise of 1850 entry.)

1. The Tallmadge Amendment
February 13, 1819

And provided also, That the further introduction of slavery or involuntary servitude be prohibited, except for the punishment of crimes, whereof the party shall be duly convicted; and that all children of slaves, born within the said state, after the admission thereof into the Union, shall be free but may be held to service until the age of twenty-five years.

2. The Taylor Amendment
January 26, 1820

The reading of the bill proceeded as far as the fourth section; when

Mr. Taylor, of New York, proposed to amend the bill by incorporating in that section the following provision:

Section 4, line 25, insert the following after the word "States"; "And shall ordain and establish, that there shall be neither slavery nor involuntary servitude in the said State, otherwise than in the punishment of crimes, whereof the party shall have been duly convicted: *Provided, always,* That any person escaping into the same, from whom labor or service is lawfully claimed in any other State, such fugitive may be lawfully reclaimed, and conveyed to the person claiming his or her labor or service as aforesaid: *And provided, also,* That the said provision shall not be construed to alter the condition or civil rights of any person now held to service or labor in the said Territory."

3. The Thomas Amendment
February 17, 1820

And be it further enacted, That, in all that territory ceded by France to the United States, under the name of Louisiana, which lies north of thirty-six degrees and thirty minutes north latitude, excepting only such part thereof as is included within the limits of the State contemplated by this act, slavery and involuntary servitude, otherwise than in the punishment of crimes whereof the party shall have been duly convicted, shall be and is hereby forever prohibited: *Provided always,* That any person escaping into the same, from whom labor or service is lawfully claimed in any State or Territory of the United States, such fugitive may be lawfully reclaimed, and conveyed to the person claiming his or her labor or service, as aforesaid.

4. Missouri Enabling Act
March 6, 1820

An Act to authorize the people of the Missouri territory to form a constitution and state government, and for the admission of such state into the Union on an equal footing with the original states, and to prohibit slavery in certain territories.

Be it enacted That the inhabitants of that portion of the Missouri territory included within the boundaries hereinafter designated, be, and they are hereby, authorized to form for themselves a constitution and state government, and to assume such name as they shall deem proper; and the said state, when formed, shall be admitted into the Union, upon an equal footing with the original states, in all respects whatsoever.

Sec. 2. That the said state shall consist of all the territory included within the following boundaries, to wit: Beginning in the middle of the Mississippi river, on the parallel of thirty-six degrees of north latitude; thence west, along that parallel of latitude, to the St. Francois river; thence up, and following the course of that river, in the middle of the main channel thereof, to the parallel of latitude of thirty-six degrees and thirty minutes; thence west, along the same, to a point where the said parallel is intersected by a meridian line passing through the middle of the mouth of the Kansas river, where the same empties into the Missouri river, thence, from the point aforesaid north, along the said meridian line, to the intersection of the parallel of latitude which passes through the rapids of the river Des Moines, making the said line to correspond with the Indian boundary line; thence east, from the point of intersection last aforesaid, along the said parallel of latitude, to the middle of the channel of the main fork of the said river Des Moines; thence down and along the middle of the main channel of the said river Des Moines, to the mouth of the same, where it empties into the Mississippi river; thence, due east, to the middle of the main channel of the Mississippi river; thence down, and following the course of the Mississippi river, in the middle of the main channel thereof, to the place of beginning: . . .

Sec. 3. That all free white male citizens of the United States, who shall have arrived at the age of twenty-one years, and have resided in said territory three months previous to the day of election, and all other persons qualified to vote for representatives to the general assembly of the said territory, shall be qualified to be elected, and they are hereby qualified and authorized to vote, and choose representatives to form a convention. . . .

Sec. 8. That in all that territory ceded by France to the United States, under the name of Louisiana, which lies north of thirty-six degrees and thirty minutes north latitude, not included within the limits of the state, contemplated by this act, slavery and involuntary servitude, otherwise than in the punishment of crimes, whereof the parties shall have been duly convicted, shall be, and is hereby, forever prohibited: *Provided always,* That any person escaping into the same, from whom labour or service is lawfully claimed, in any state or territory of the United States, such fugitive may be lawfully reclaimed and conveyed to the person claiming his or her labour or service as aforesaid.

5. The Constitution of Missouri
July 19, 1820

Sec. 26. The general assembly shall not have power to pass laws—

1. For the emancipation of slaves without the consent of their owners; or without paying them, before such emancipation, a full equivalent for such slaves so emancipated; and,

2. To prevent *bona-fide* immigrants to this State, or actual settlers therein, from bringing from any of the United States, or from any of their Territories, such persons as may there be deemed to be slaves, so long as any persons of the same description are allowed to be held as slaves by the laws of this State.

They shall have power to pass laws—

1. To prevent *bona-fide* immigrants to this State of any slaves who may have committed any high crime in any other State or Territory;

2. To prohibit the introduction of any slave for the purpose of speculation, or as an article of trade or merchandise;

3. To prohibit the introduction of any slave, or the offspring of any slave, who heretofore may have been, or who hereafter may be, imported from any foreign country into the United States, or any Territory thereof, in contravention of any existing statute of the United States; and,

4. To permit the owners of slaves to emancipate them, saving the right of creditors, where the person so emancipating will give security that the slave so emancipated shall not become a public charge.

It shall be their duty, as soon as may be, to pass such laws as may be necessary

1. To prevent free negroes end [and] mulattoes from coming to and settling in this State, under any pretext whatsoever; and,

2. To oblige the owners of slaves to treat them with humanity, and to abstain from all injuries to them extending to life or limb.

6. Resolution for the Admission of Missouri
March 2, 1821

Resolution *providing for the admission of the State of Missouri into the Union, on a certain condition.*

Resolved, That Missouri shall be admitted into this union on an equal footing with the original states, in all respects whatever, upon the fundamental condition, that the fourth clause of the twenty-sixth section of the third article of the constitution submitted on the part of said state to Congress, shall never be construed to authorize the passage of any law, and that no law shall be passed in conformity thereto, by which any citizen, of either of the states in this Union, shall be excluded from the enjoyment of any of the privileges and immunities to which such citizen is entitled under the constitution of the United States: *Provided,* That the legislature of the said state, by a solemn public act, shall declare the assent of the said state to the said fundamental condition, and shall transmit to the President of the United States, on or before the fourth Monday in November next, an authentic copy of the said act; upon the receipt whereof, the President, by proclamation, shall announce the fact; whereupon, and without any further proceeding on the part of Congress, the admission of the said state into this Union shall be considered as complete.

THE INAUGURAL EDITION OF FREEDOM'S JOURNAL: THE FIRST NEGRO NEWSPAPER IN THE U.S.A. (1827)

Freedom's Journal, *owned and edited by Samuel Cornish and John B. Russwurm, put its first issue on the streets of New York City in 1827. This editorial, printed here in its entirety, devoted itself to slavery and discrimination.*

TO OUR PATRONS

In presenting our first number to our Patrons, we feel all the diffidence of persons entering upon a new and untried line of business. But a moment's reflection upon the noble objects, which we have in view by the publication of this Journal; the expediency of its appearance at this time, when so many schemes are in action concerning our people—encourage us to come boldly before an enlightened publick. For we believe, that a paper devoted to the dissimination of useful knowledge among our brethren, and to their moral and religious improve-

Mastheads for three of the most famous abolitionist journals in the pre-Civil War era.

ment, must meet with the cordial approbation of every friend to humanity.

The peculiarities of this Journal, renders it important that we should advertise to the world our motives by which we are actuated, and the objects which we contemplate.

We wish to plead our own cause. Too long have others spoken for us. Too long has the publick been deceived by misrepresentations, in things which concern us dearly, though in the estimation of some mere trifles; for though there are many in society who exercise towards us benevolent feelings; still (with sorrow we confess it) there are others who make it their business to enlarge upon the least trifle, which tends to the discredit of any person of colour; and pronounce anathemas and denôunce our whole body for the misconduct of this guilty one. We are aware that there are many instances of vice among us, but we avow that it is because no one has taught its subjects to be virtuous; many instances of poverty, because no sufficient efforts accommodated to minds contracted by slavery, and deprived of early education have been made, to teach them how to husband their hard earnings, and to secure to themselves comfort.

Education being an object of the highest importance to the welfare of society, we shall endeavour to present just and adequate views of it, and to urge upon our brethren the necessity and expediency of training their children, while young, to habits of industry, and thus forming them for becoming useful members of society. It is surely time that we should awake from this lethargy of years, and make a concentrated effort for the education of our youth. We form a spoke in the human wheel, and it is necessary that we should understand our pendence on the different parts, and theirs on us, in order to perform our part with propriety.

Though not desiring of dictating, we shall feel it our incumbent duty to dwell occasionally upon the general principles and rules of economy. The world has grown too enlightened, to estimate any man's character by his personal appearance. Though all men acknowledge the excellency of Franklin's maxims, yet comparatively few practise upon them. We may deplore when it is too late, the neglect of these self-evident truths, but it avails little to mourn. Ours will be the task of admonishing our brethren on these points.

The civil rights of a people being of the greatest value, it shall ever be our duty to vindicate our brethren, when oppressed; and to lay the case before the publick. We shall also urge upon our brethren, (who are qualified by the laws of the different states) the expediency of using their elective franchise; and of making an independent use of the same. We wish them not to become the tools of party.

And as much time is frequently lost, and wrong principles instilled, by the perusal of works of trivial importance, we shall consider it a part of our duty to recommend to our young readers, such authors as will not only enlarge their stock of useful knowledge, but such as will also serve to stimulate them to higher attainments in science.

We trust also, that through the columns of the FREEDOM'S JOURNAL, many practical pieces, having for their bases, the improvement of our brethren, will be presented to them, from the pens of many of our respected friends, who have kindly promised their assistance.

It is our earnest wish to make our Journal a medium of intercourse between our brethren in the different states of this great confederacy: that through its columns an expression of our sentiments, on many interesting subjects which concern us, may be offered to the publick: that plans which apparently are beneficial may be candidly discussed and properly weighed; if worth, receive our cordial approbation; if not, our marked disapprobation.

Useful knowledge of every kind, and everything that relates to Africa, shall find a ready admission into our columns; and as that vast continent becomes daily more known, we trust that many things will come to light, proving that the natives of it are neither so ignorant nor stupid as they have generally been supposed to be.

And while these important subjects shall occupy the columns of the FREEDOM'S JOURNAL, we would not be unmindful of our brethren who are still in the iron fetters of bondage. They are our kindred by all the ties of nature; and though but little can be effected by us, still let our sympathies be poured forth, and our prayers in their behalf, ascend to Him who is able to succour them.

From the press and the pulpit we have suffered much by being incorrectly represented. Men whom we equally love and

William Lloyd Garrison

admire have not hesitated to represent us disadvantageously, without becoming personally acquainted with the true state of things, nor discerning between virtue and vice among us. The virtuous part of our people feel themselves sorely aggrieved under the existing state of things—they are not appreciated.

Our vices and our degradation are ever arrayed against us, but our virtues are passed by unnoticed. And what is still more lamentable, our friends, to whom we concede all the principles of humanity and religion, from these very causes seem to have fallen into the current of popular feeling and are imperceptibly floating on the stream—actually living in the practice of prejudice, while they abjure it in theory, and feel it not in their hearts. Is it not very desirable that such should know more of our actual condition; and of our efforts and feelings, that in forming or advocating plans for our amelioration, they may do it more understandingly? In the spirit of candor and humility we intend by a simple representation of facts to lay our case before the public, with a view to arrest the progress of prejudice, and to shield ourselves against the consequent evils. We wish to conciliate all and to irritate none, yet we must be firm and unwavering in our principles, and persevering in our efforts.

If ignorance, poverty and degradation have hitherto been our unhappy lot; has the Eternal decree gone forth, that our race alone are to remain in this state, while knowledge and civilization are shedding their enlivening rays over the rest of the human family? The recent travels of Denham and Clapperton in the interior of Africa, and the interesting narrative which they have published; the establishment of the republic of Hayti after years of sanguinary warfare; its subsequent progress in all the arts of civilization; and the advancement of liberal ideas in South America, where despotism has given place to free governments, and where many of our brethren now fill important civil and military stations, prove the contrary.

The interesting fact that there are FIVE HUNDRED THOUSAND free persons of colour, one half of whom might peruse, and the whole be benefitted by the publication of the Journal; that no publication, as yet, has been devoted exclusively to their improvement—that many selections from approved standard authors, which are within the reach of few, may occasionally be made—and more important still, that this large body of our citizens have no public channel—all serve to prove the real necessity, at present, for the appearance of the FREEDOM'S JOURNAL.

It shall ever be our desire so to conduct the editorial department of our paper as to give offence to none of our patrons; as nothing is farther from us than to make it the advocate of any partial views, either in politics or religion. What few days we can number, have been devoted to the improvement of our brethren; and it is our earnest wish that the remainder may be spent in the same delightful service.

In conclusion, whatever concerns us as a people, will ever find a ready admission into the FREEDOM'S JOURNAL, interwoven with all the principal news of the day.

And while every thing in our power shall be performed to support the character of our Journal, we would respectfully invite our numerous friends to assist by their communications, and our coloured brethren to strengthen our hands by their subscriptions, as our labour is one of common cause, and worthy of their consideration and support. And we most earnestly solicit the latter, that if at any time we should seem to be zealous, or too pointed in the inculcation of any important lesson, they will remember, that they are equally interested in the cause in which we are engaged, and attribute our zeal to the peculiarities of our situation; and our earnest engagedness in their well-being.

THE LIBERATOR: THE MOST FAMOUS ABOLITIONIST NEWSPAPER IN THE UNITED STATES (1831)

The Liberator *was published weekly in Boston, Massachusetts from 1831 to 1865. Most of its subscribers were Negroes, although its founder, William Lloyd Garrison ("I have a system to destroy, and I have no time to waste") was himself white.*

A key organ of abolitionist propaganda, The Liberator *succeeded in shifting the sentiment of much of the nation away from the notion of gradual emancipation, and more toward that of total abolition.*

. . . During my recent tour for the purpose of exciting the minds of the people by a series of discourses on the subject of slavery, every place that I visited gave fresh evidence of the fact, that a greater revolution in public sentiment was to be effected in the free states—and particularly in New England—than at the south. I found contempt more bitter, opposition more active, detraction more relentless, prejudice more stubborn, and apathy more frozen, than among slave owners themselves. Of course, there were individual exceptions to the contrary. This state of things afflicted, but did not dishearten me. I determined, at every hazard, to lift up the standard of emancipation in the eyes of the nation, within sight of Bunker Hill and in the birth place of liberty. That standard is now unfurled; and long may if float, unhurt by the spoliations of time or the missiles of a desperate foe—yea, till every chain be broken, and every bondman set free! Let Southern oppressors tremble—let their secret abettors tremble—let their Northern apologists tremble—let all the enemies of the persecuted blacks tremble. . . .

I am aware, that many object to the severity of my language; but is there not cause for severity? I will be as harsh as truth, and as uncompromising as justice. On this subject, I do not wish to think, or speak, or write, with moderation. No! No! Tell a man whose house is on fire, to give a moderate alarm; tell him to moderately rescue his wife from the hands of the ravisher; tell the mother to gradually extricate her babe from the fire into which it has fallen;—but urge me not to use moderation in a cause like the present. I am in earnest—I will not equivocate—I will not excuse—I will not retreat a single inch—AND I WILL BE HEARD. . . .

WILLIAM LLOYD GARRISON

THE NORTH STAR: THE ABOLITIONIST ORGAN OF FREDERICK DOUGLASS (1847)

Frederick Douglass, a leading Negro spokesman in the abolitionist movement, founded his newspaper on December 3, 1847 in Rochester, New York. Douglass conceded that he would plead the cause of the Negro before all else, but did not exclude the possibility that several other major topics might also occupy the editorial spotlight from time to time.

TO OUR OPPRESSED COUNTRYMEN

We solemnly dedicate the *North Star* to the cause of our long oppressed and plundered fellow countrymen. May God bless the offering to your good! It shall fearlessly assert your rights, faithfully proclaim your wrongs, and earnestly demand for you instant and even-handed justice. Giving no quarter to slavery at the South, it will hold no truce with oppressors at the North. While it shall boldly advocate emancipation for our enslaved brethren, it will omit no opportunity to gain for the nominally free, complete enfranchisement. Every effort to injure or degrade you or your cause—originating wheresoever, or with whomsoever—shall find in it a constant, unswerving and inflexible foe.

We shall energetically assail the ramparts of Slavery and Prejudice, be they composed of church or state, and seek the destruction of every refuge of lies, under which tyranny may aim to conceal and protect itself. . . .

While our paper shall be mainly Anti-Slavery, its columns shall be freely opened to the candid and decorous discussions of all measures and topics of a moral and humane character, which may serve to enlighten, improve, and elevate mankind. Temperance, Peace, Capital Punishment, Education,—all subjects claiming the attention of the public mind may be freely and fully discussed here.

While advocating your rights, the *North Star* will strive to throw light on your duties: while it will not fail to make known your virtues, it will not shun to discover your faults. To be faithful to our foes it must be faithful to ourselves, in all things.

Remember that we are one, that our

cause is one, and that we must help each other, if we would succeed. We have drunk to the dregs the bitter cup of slavery; we have worn the heavy yoke; we have sighed beneath our bonds, and writhed beneath the bloody lash;—cruel mementoes of our oneness are indelibly marked in our living flesh. We are one with you under the ban of prejudice and proscription—one with you under the slander of inferiority—one with you in social and political disfranchisement. What you suffer, we suffer; what you endure, we endure. We are indissolubly united, and must fall or flourish together. . . .

We shall be the advocates of learning, from the very want of it, and shall most readily yield the deference due to men of education among us; but shall always bear in mind to accord most merit to those who have labored hardest, and overcome most, in the praiseworthy pursuit of knowledge, remembering "that the whole need not a physician, but they that are sick," and that "the strong ought to bear the infirmities of the weak."

Brethren, the first number of the paper is before you. It is dedicated to your cause. Through the kindness of our friends in England, we are in possession of an excellent printing press, types, and all other materials necessary for printing a paper. Shall this gift be blest to our good, or shall it result in our injury? It is for you to say. With your aid, cooperation and assistance, our enterprise will be entirely successful. We pledge ourselves that no effort on our part shall be wanting, and that no subscriber shall lose his subscription—"The *North Star* Shall Live."

The North Star, December 3, 1847

THE COMPROMISE OF 1850

The Compromise of 1850 was occasioned by a revival of the slavery question pursuant to the Mexican War. Henry Clay, chief architect of the compromise, made five key points upon which the document is based:

1. *That California be admitted to the Union as a free state.*
2. *That territorial governments be established in New Mexico and Utah without any immediate decision as to whether they would be slave or free.*
3. *That a stricter fugitive slave law be passed.*
4. *That the slave trade be abolished in the District of Columbia.*
5. *That the Texas-New Mexico boundary be settled, and that the federal government liquidate any debts incurred by Texas.*

Clay's Resolutions
January 29, 1850

1. *Resolved*, That California, with suitable boundaries, ought, upon her application to be admitted as one of the States of this Union, without the imposition by Congress of any restriction in respect to the exclusion or introduction of slavery within those boundaries.

2. *Resolved*, That as slavery does not exist by law, and is not likely to be introduced into any of the territory acquired by the United States from the republic of Mexico, it is inexpedient for Congress to provide by law either for its introduction into, or exclusion from, any part of the said territory; and that appropriate territorial governments ought to be established by Congress in all of the said territory, not assigned as the boundaries of the proposed State of California, without the adoption of any restriction or condition on the subject of slavery.

3. *Resolved*, That the western boundary of the State of Texas ought to be fixed on the Rio del Norte, commencing one marine league from its mouth, and running up that river to the southern line of New Mexico; thence with that line eastwardly, and so continuing in the same direction to the line as established between the United States and Spain, excluding any portion of New Mexico, whether lying on the east or west of that river.

4. *Resolved*, That it be proposed to the State of Texas, that the United States will provide for the payment of all that portion of the legitimate and bona fide

public debt of that State contracted prior to its annexation to the United States, and for which the duties on foreign imports were pledged by the said State to its creditors, not exceeding the sum of—— dollars, in consideration of the said duties so pledged having been no longer applicable to that object after the said annexation, but having thenceforward become payable to the United States; and upon the condition, also, that the said State of Texas shall, by some solemn and authentic act of her legislature or of a convention, relinquish to the United States any claim which it has to any part of New Mexico.

5. *Resolved,* That it is inexpedient to abolish slavery in the District of Columbia whilst that institution continues to exist in the State of Maryland, without the consent of that State, without the consent of the people of the District, and without just compensation to the owners of slaves within the District.

6. *But, resolved,* That it is expedient to prohibit, within the District, the slave trade in slaves brought into it from States or places beyond the limits of the District, either to be sold therein as merchandise, or to be transported to other markets without the District of Columbia.

7. *Resolved,* That more effectual provision ought to be made by law, according to the requirement of the constitution, for the restitution and delivery of persons bound to service or labor in any State, who may escape into any other State or Territory in the Union. And,

8. *Resolved,* That Congress has no power to promote or obstruct the trade in slaves between the slaveholding States; but that the admission or exclusion of slaves brought from one into another of them, depends exclusively upon their own particular laws.

The Texas and New Mexico Act
September 9, 1850

An Act proposing to the State of Texas the Establishment of her Northern and Western Boundaries, the Relinquishment by the said State of all Territory claimed by her exterior to said Boundaries, and of all her claims upon the United States, and to establish a territorial Government for New Mexico.

First. The State of Texas will agree that her boundary on the north shall commence at the point at which the meridian of one hundred degrees west from Greenwich is intersected by the parallel of thirty-six degrees thirty minutes north latitude, and shall run from said point due west to the meridian of one hundred and three degrees west from Greenwich; thence her boundary shall run due south to the thirty-second degree of north latitude; thence on the said parallel of thirty-two degrees of north latitude to the Rio Bravo del Norte, and thence with the channel of said river to the Gulf of Mexico.

Second. The State of Texas cedes to the United States all her claim to territory exterior to the limits and boundaries which she agrees to establish by the first article of this agreement.

Third. The State of Texas relinquishes all claim upon the United States for liability of the debts of Texas, and for compensation or indemnity for the surrender to the United States of her ships, forts, arsenals, custom-houses, custom-house revenue, arms and munitions of war, and public buildings with their sites, which became the property of the United States at the time of the annexation.

Fourth. The United States, in consideration of said establishment of boundaries, cession of claim to territory, and relinquishment of claims, will pay to the State of Texas the sum of ten millions of dollars in a stock bearing five per cent interest, and redeemable at the end of fourteen years, the interest payable half yearly at the treasury of the United States. . . .

Fugitive Slave Act
(September 18, 1850)

An Act to amend, and supplementary to, the Act entitled "An Act respecting Fugitives from Justice, and Persons escaping from the Service of their Masters," approved—[February 12, 1793].

. . . Sec. 5. That it shall be the duty of all marshals and deputy marshals to obey and execute all warrants and precepts issued under the provisions of this act, when to them directed; and should any marshal or deputy marshal refuse to receive such warrant, or other process, when tendered, or to use all proper means diligently to execute the same, he shall, on conviction thereof, be fined in the sum of one thousand dollars, to the use of such claimant, . . . and after arrest of such fugitive, by such marshal or his deputy, or whilst at any time in his custody under the provisions of this act, should such fugitive escape, whether with or without the assent of such marshal or his deputy, such marshal shall be liable, on his official bond, to be prosecuted for the benefit of such claimant, for the full value of the service or labor of said fugitive in the State, Territory, or District whence he escaped: and the better to enable the said commissioners, when thus appointed, to execute their duties faithfully and efficiently, in conformity with the requirements of the Constitution of the United States and of this act, they are hereby authorized and empowered, within their counties respectively, to appoint, . . . any one or more suitable persons, from time to time, to execute all such warrants and other process as may be issued by them in the lawful performance of their respective duties;

SEC. 6. That when a person held to service or labor in any State or Territory of the United States, has heretofore or shall hereafter escape into another State or Territory of the United States, the person or persons to whom such service or labor may be due, . . . may pursue and reclaim such fugitive person, either by procuring a warrant from some one of the courts, judges, or commissioners aforesaid, of the proper circuit, district, or county, for the apprehension of such fugitive from service or labor, or by seizing and arresting such fugitive, where the same can be done without process, and by taking, or causing such person to be taken, forthwith before such court, judge, or commissioner, whose duty it shall be to hear and determine the case of such claimant in a summary manner; and upon satisfactory proof being made, by deposi-

PRACTICAL ILLUSTRATION OF THE FUGITIVE SLAVE LAW.

The Fugitive Slave Act of 1850 stiffened the penalties for harboring runaways, thus sharpening hostilities between Northern abolitionists and Southern slaveholders.

tion or affidavit, in writing, to be taken and certified by such court, judge, or commissioner, or by other satisfactory testimony, duly taken and certified by some court, . . . and with proof, also by affidavit, of the identity of the person whose service or labor is claimed to be due as aforesaid, that the person so arrested does in fact owe service or labor to the person or persons claiming him or her, in the State or Territory from which such fugitive may have escaped as aforesaid, and that said person escaped, to make out and deliver to such claimant, his or her agent or attorney, a certificate setting forth the substantial facts as to the service or labor due from such fugitive to the claimant, and of his or her escape from the State or Territory in which he or she was arrested, with authority to such claimant, . . . to use such reasonable force and restraint as may be necessary, under the circumstances of the case, to take and remove such fugitive person back to the State or Territory whence he or she may have escaped as aforesaid.

SEC. 7. That any persons who shall knowingly and willingly obstruct, hinder, or prevent such claimant, his agent or attorney, or any person or persons lawfully assisting him, her, or them, from arresting such a fugitive from service or labor, either with or without process as aforesaid, or shall rescue, or attempt to rescue, such fugitive from service or labor, from the custody of such claimant, . . . or other person or persons lawfully assisting as aforesaid, when so arrested, . . . or shall aid, abet, or assist such person so owing service or labor as aforesaid, directly or indirectly, to escape from such claimant, . . . or shall harbor or conceal such fugitive, so as to prevent the discovery and arrest of such person, after notice or knowledge of the fact that such person was a fugitive from service or labor . . . shall, for either of said offences, be subject to a fine not exceeding one thousand dollars, and imprisonment not exceeding six months . . . ; and shall moreover forfeit and pay, by way of civil damages to the party injured by such illegal conduct, the sum of one thousand dollars, for each fugitive so lost as aforesaid. . . .

SEC. 9. That, upon affidavit made by the claimant of such fugitive, . . . that he has reason to apprehend that such fugitive will be rescued by force from his or their possession before he can be taken beyond the limits of the State in which the arrest is made, it shall be the duty of the officer making the arrest to retain such fugitive in his custody, and to remove him to the State whence he fled, and there to deliver him to said claimant, his agent, or attorney. And to this end, the officer aforesaid is hereby authorized and required to employ so many persons as he may deem necessary to overcome such force, and to retain them in his service so long as circumstances may require.

ACT ABOLISHING THE SLAVE TRADE IN THE DISTRICT OF COLUMBIA
September 20, 1850

An Act to suppress the Slave Trade in the District of Columbia.

Be it enacted . . . , That from and after January 1, 1851, it shall not be lawful to bring into the District of Columbia any slave whatever, for the purpose of being sold, or for the purpose of being placed in depot, to be subsequently transferred to any other State or place to be sold as merchandize. And if any slave shall be brought into the said District by its owner, or by the authority or consent of its owner, contrary to the provisions of this act, such slave shall thereupon become liberated and free.

WHAT TO THE SLAVES IS THE FOURTH OF JULY?: FREDERICK DOUGLASS' INDEPENDENCE DAY ADDRESS (1852)

Perceiving full well the irony implicit in his delivering an address which commemorated the coming of independence to the United States, Frederick Douglass lost little time in laying bare the contradiction inherent in allowing slavery to exist within a society professedly dedicated to individual freedom.

Fellow Citizens: Pardon me, and allow me to ask, why am I called upon to speak here today? What have I or those I represent to do with your national independence? Are the great principles of political freedom and of natural justice, embodied in that Declaration of Independence, extended to us? And am I, therefore, called upon to bring our humble offering to the national altar, and to confess the benefits, and express devout gratitude for the blessings resulting from your independence to us?

Would to God, both for your sakes and ours, that an affirmative answer could be truthfully returned to these questions. Then would my task be light, and my burden easy and delightful. For who is there so cold that a nation's sympathy could not warm him? Who so obdurate and dead to the claims of gratitude, that would not thankfully acknowledge such priceless benefits? Who so stolid and selfish that would not give his voice to swell the halleluiahs of a nation's jubilee, when the chains of servitude had been torn from his limbs? I am not that man. . . .

I am not included within the pale of this glorious anniversary! Your high independence only reveals the immeasurable distance between us. The blessings in which you this day rejoice are not enjoyed in common. The rich inheritance of justice, liberty, prosperity, and independence bequeathed by your fathers is shared by you, not by me. The sunlight that brought life and healing to you has brought stripes and death to me. This Fourth of July is *yours,* not *mine. You* may rejoice, *I* must mourn. To drag a man in fetters into the grand illuminated temple of liberty, and call upon him to join you in joyous anthems, were inhuman mockery and sacrilegious irony. Do you mean, citizens, to mock me, by asking me to speak today? . . .

Fellow citizens, above your national, tumultuous joy, I hear the mournful wail of millions, whose chains, heavy and grievous yesterday, are today rendered more intolerable by the jubilant shouts that reach them. If I do forget, if I do not remember those bleeding children of sorrow this day, "may my right hand forget her cunning, and may my tongue cleave to the roof of my mouth!" To forget them, to pass lightly over their wrongs, and to chime in with the popular theme, would be treason most scandalous and shocking, and would make me a reproach before God and the world. My subject, then, fellow citizens, is "American Slavery." I shall see this day and its popular characteristics from the slave's point of view. Standing here, identified with the American bondman, making his wrongs mine, I do not hesitate to declare, with all my soul, that the character and conduct of this nation never looked blacker to me than on this Fourth of July. Whether we turn to the declarations of the past, or to the professions of the present, the conduct of the nation seems equally hideous and revolting. America is false to the past, false to the present, and solemnly binds herself to be false to the future. Standing with God and the crushed and bleeding slave on this occasion, I will, in the name of humanity, which is outraged, in the name of liberty, which is fettered, in the name of the Constitution and the Bible, which are disregarded and trampled upon, dare to call in question and to denounce, with all the emphasis I can command, everything that serves to perpetuate slavery—the great sin and shame of America! "I will not equivocate; I will not excuse"; I will use the severest language I can command, and yet not one word shall escape me that any man, whose judgment is not blinded by prejudice, or who is not at heart a slave-holder, shall not confess to be right and just.

But I fancy I hear some of my audience say it is just in this circumstance that you and your brother Abolitionists fail to make a favorable impression on the public mind. Would you argue more and denounce less, would you persuade more and rebuke less, your cause would be much more likely to succeed. But, I submit, where all is plain there is nothing to be argued. What point in the anti-slavery creed would you have me argue? On what branch of the subject do the people of this country need light? Must I undertake to prove that the slave is a man? That point is conceded already. Nobody doubts it. The slave-holders themselves acknowledge it in the enactment of laws for their government. They acknowledge it when they punish disobedience on the part of the slave. There are seventy-two crimes in the State of Virginia, which, if committed by a black man (no matter how ignorant he be), subject him to the punishment of death; while only two of these same crimes will subject a white man to like punishment. What is this but the acknowledgment that the slave is a moral, intellectual, and responsible being? The manhood of the slave is conceded. It is admitted in the fact that Southern statute-books are covered with enactments, forbidding, under severe fines and penalties, the teaching of the slave to read and write. When you can point to any such laws in reference to the beasts of the field, then I may consent to argue the manhood of the slave. When the dogs in your streets, when the fowls of the air, when the cattle on your hills, when the fish of the sea, and the reptiles that crawl, shall be unable to distinguish the slave from a brute, then I will argue with you that the slave is a man!

For the present it is enough to affirm the equal manhood of the Negro race. Is it not astonishing that, while we are plowing, planting, and reaping, using all kinds of mechanical tools, erecting houses, constructing bridges, building ships, working in metals of brass, iron, copper, silver, and gold; that while we are reading, writing, and cyphering, acting as clerks, merchants, and secretaries, having among us lawyers, doctors, ministers, poets, authors, editors, orators, and teachers; that while we are engaged in all the enterprises common to other men—digging gold in California, capturing the whale in the Pacific, feeding sheep and cattle on the hillside, living, moving, acting, thinking, planning, living in families as husbands, wives, and children, and above all, confessing and worshipping the Christian God, and looking hopefully for life and immortality beyond the grave—we are called upon to prove that we are men?

Would you have me argue that man is entitled to liberty? That he is the rightful owner of his own body? You have already declared it. Must I argue the wrongfulness of slavery? Is that a question for republicans? Is it to be settled by the rules of logic and argumentation, as a matter beset with great difficulty, involving a doubtful application of the principle of justice, hard to understand? How should I look today in the presence of Americans, dividing and subdividing a discourse, to show that men have a natural right to freedom, speaking of it relatively and positively, negatively and affirmatively? To do so would be to make myself ridiculous, and to offer an insult to your understanding. There is not a man beneath the canopy of heaven who does not know that slavery is wrong *for him.*

What! Am I to argue that it is wrong to make men brutes, to rob them of their liberty, to work them without wages, to keep them ignorant of their relations to their fellow men, to beat them with sticks, to flay their flesh with the last, to load their limbs with irons, to hunt them with dogs, to sell them at auction, to sunder their families, to knock out their teeth, to burn their flesh, to starve them into obedience and submission to their masters? Must I argue that a system thus marked with blood and stained with pollution is wrong? No; I will not. I have better employment for my time and strength than such arguments would imply.

What, then, remains to be argued? Is it that slavery is not divine; that God did not establish it; that our doctors of divinity are mistaken? There is blasphemy in the thought. That which is inhuman cannot be divine. Who can reason on such a proposition? They that can, may; I cannot. The time for such argument is past.

At a time like this, scorching irony, not convincing argument, is needed. Oh! had I the ability, and could I reach the nation's ear, I would today pour out a fiery stream of biting ridicule, blasting reproach, withering sarcasm, and stern rebuke. For it is not light that is needed, but fire; it is not the gentle shower, but thunder. We need the storm, the whirlwind, and the earthquake. The feeling of the nation must be quickened; the conscience of the nation must be roused; the propriety of the nation must be startled; the hypocrisy of the nation must be exposed; and its crimes against God and man must be denounced.

What to the American slave is your Fourth of July? I answer, a day that reveals to him more than all other days of the year, the gross injustice and cruelty to which he is the constant victim. To him your celebration is a sham; your boasted liberty an unholy license; your national greatness, swelling vanity; your sounds of rejoicing are empty and heartless; your denunciation of tyrants, brass-fronted impudence; your shouts of liberty and equality, hollow mockery; your prayers and hymns, your sermons and thanksgivings, with all your religious parade and solemnity, are to him mere bombast, fraud, deception, impiety, and hypocrisy—a thin veil to cover up crimes which would disgrace a nation of savages. There is not a nation of the earth guilty of practices more shocking and bloody than are the people of these United States at this very hour.

Go where you may, search where you will, roam through all the monarchies and despotisms of the Old World, travel through South America, search out every abuse and when you have found the last, lay your facts by the side of the everyday practices of this nation, and you will say with me that, for revolting barbarity and shameless hypocrisy, America reigns without a rival.

THE KANSAS-NEBRASKA ACT (1854)

The Kansas-Nebraska Act repealed the Missouri Compromise, placing in the hands of the territories themselves the ultimate decision as to whether or not they would be slave or free.

An Act to Organize the Territories of Nebraska and Kansas.

Be it enacted . . . , That all that part of the territory of the United States included within the following limits, except such portions thereof as are hereinafter expressly exempted from the operations of this act, to wit: beginning at a point in the Missouri River where the fortieth parallel of north latitude crosses the same; thence west on said parallel to the east boundary of the Territory of. Utah, on the summit of the Rocky Mountains; thence on said summit northward to the forty-ninth parallel of north latitude; thence east on said parallel to the western boundary of the territory of Minnesota; thence southward on said boundary to the Missouri River; thence down the main channel of said river to the place of beginning, be, and the same is hereby, created into a temporary government by the name of the Territory of Nebraska; and when admitted as a State or States, the said Territory, or any portion of the same, shall be received into the Union with or without slavery, as their constitution may prescribe at the time of their admission: . . .

SEC. 14. *And be it further enacted,* . . . That the Constitution, and all laws of the United States which are not locally inapplicable, shall have the same force and effect within the said Territory of Nebraska as elsewhere within the United States, except the eighth section of the act preparatory to the admission of Missouri into the Union, approved March 6, 1820, which, being inconsistent with the principle of non-intervention by Congress with slavery in the States and Territories, as recognized by the legislation of eighteen hundred and fifty, commonly called the Compromise Measures, is hereby declared inoperative and void; it being the true intent and meaning of this act not to legislate slavery into any Territory or State, nor to exclude it therefrom, but to leave the people thereof perfectly free to form and regulate their domestic institutions in their own way, subject only to the Constitution of the United States: *Provided,* That nothing herein contained shall be construed to revive or put in force any law or regulation which may have existed prior to the act of March 6, 1820, either protecting, establishing, prohibiting, or abolishing slavery. . . .

SEC. 19. *And be it further enacted,* That all that part of the Territory of the United States included within the following limits, except such portions thereof as are hereinafter expressly exempted from the operations of this act, to wit, beginning at a point on the western boundary of the State of Missouri, where the thirty-seventh parallel of north latitude crosses the same; thence west on said parallel to the eastern boundary of New Mexico; thence north on said boundary to latitude thirty-eight; thence following said boundary westward to the east boundary of the Territory of Utah, on the summit of the Rocky Mountains; thence northward on said summit to the fortieth parallel of latitude; thence east on said parallel to the western boundary of the State of Missouri; thence south with the western boundary of said state to the place of beginning, be, and the same is hereby, created into a temporary government by the name of the Territory of Kansas; and when admitted as a State or States, the said Territory, or any portion of the same, shall be received into the Union with or without slavery, as their constitution may prescribe at the time of their admission: . .

EMANCIPATION
NEW YORK
MAINE
MASSACHUSETTS
CONNECTICUT
NEW HAMPSHIRE
RHODE ISLAND
MARYLAND
DELAWARE
VERMONT
KENTUCKY
VIRGINIA
W. VIRGINIA
GEORGIA
N. CAROLINA
S. CAROLINA
FLORIDA
LOUISIANA
TEXAS
ALABAMA
TENNESSEE
MISSISSIPPI
MISSOURI
ARKANSAS
CALIFORNIA
OREGON
NEVADA
COLORADO
NEBRASKA
MICHIGAN
KANSAS
MINNESOTA
IOWA
WISCONSIN
ILLINOIS
INDIANA
OHIO
NEW JERSEY
PENNSYLVANIA
Proclamation
Whereas
NOW THEREFORE I
ABRAHAM LINCOLN
PRESIDENT OF THE UNITED STATES,
BY VIRTUE OF THE POWER IN ME VESTED AS
COMMANDER IN CHIEF OF THE ARMY AND NAVY
United States
Arkansas, Texas, Louisiana
Florida, Georgia, South Carolina, North Carolina and Virginia
Mississippi, Alabama
West Virginia
United States
United States
Constitution
Almighty God.
United States
CASHIER
PUBLIC SCHOOL
GIVE THANKS ALL YE PEOPLE, GIVE THANKS TO THE LORD.

THE EMANCIPATION PROCLAMATION (1863)

The Emancipation Proclamation, drafted in 1862 and put into effect on January 1, 1863, freed the slaves in those states that had seceded from the Union. *All other slaves—and there were some 800,000 unaffected by the provisions of this act—were not yet free.*

BY THE PRESIDENT OF THE UNITED STATES OF AMERICA:
A Proclamation.

Whereas on the 22d day of September, A.D. 1862, a proclamation was issued by the President of the United States, containing, among other things, the following, to wit:

"That on the 1st day of January, A.D. 1863, all persons held as slaves within any State or designated part of a State the people whereof shall then be in rebellion against the United States shall be then, thenceforward, and forever free; and the executive government of the United States, including the military and naval authority thereof, will recognize and maintain the freedom of such persons and will do no act or acts to repress such persons, or any of them, in any efforts they may make for their actual freedom.

"That the executive will on the 1st day of January aforesaid, by proclamation, designate the States and parts of States, if any, in which the people thereof, respectively, shall then be in rebellion against the United States; and the fact that any State or the people thereof shall on that day be in good faith represented in the Congress of the United States by members chosen thereto at elections wherein a majority of the qualified voters of such States shall have participated shall, in the absence of strong countervailing testimony, be deemed conclusive evidence that such State and the people thereof are not then in rebellion against the United States."

Now, therefore, I, Abraham Lincoln, President of the United States, by virtue of the power in me vested as Commander in-Chief of the Army and Navy of the United States in time of actual armed rebellion against the authority and government of the United States, and as a fit and necessary war measure for suppressing said rebellion, do, on this 1st day of January, A.D. 1863, and in accordance with my purpose so to do, publicly proclaimed for the full period of one hundred days from the first day above mentioned, order and designate as the States and parts of States wherein the people thereof, respectively, are this day in rebellion against the United States the following, to wit:

Arkansas, Texas, Louisiana (except the parishes of St. Bernard, Plaquemines, Jefferson, St. John, St. Charles, St. James, Ascension, Assumption, Terrebonne, Lafourche, St. Mary, St. Martin, and Orleans, including the city of New Orleans), Mississippi, Alabama, Florida, Georgia, South Carolina, North Carolina, and Virginia (except the forty-eight counties designated as West Virginia, and also the counties of Berkeley, Accomac, Northhampton, Elizabeth City, York, Princess Anne, and Norfolk, including the cities of Norfolk and Portsmouth), and which excepted parts are for the present left precisely as if this proclamation were not issued.

And by virtue of the power and for the purpose aforesaid, I do order and declare that all persons held as slaves within said designated States and parts of States are, and henceforward shall be, free; and that the Executive Government of the United States, including the military and naval authorities thereof, will recognize and maintain the freedom of said persons.

And I hereby enjoin upon the people so declared to be free to abstain from all violence, unless in necessary self-defense; and I recommend to them that, in all cases when allowed, they labor faithfully for reasonable wages.

And I further declare and make known that such persons of suitable condition will be received into the armed service of the United States to garrison forts, positions, stations, and other places, and to man vessels of all sorts in said service.

And upon this act, sincerely believed to be an act of justice, warranted by the Constitution upon military necessity, I invoke the considerate judgment of mankind and the gracious favor of Almighty God.

THE FREEDMEN'S BUREAU (1865)

The Freedmen's Bureau, brought into being in 1865, was designed to provide basic health and educational services for freedmen, and to administer all land abandoned in the South. The life of the bureau was extended after the war, despite the veto of President Andrew Johnson.

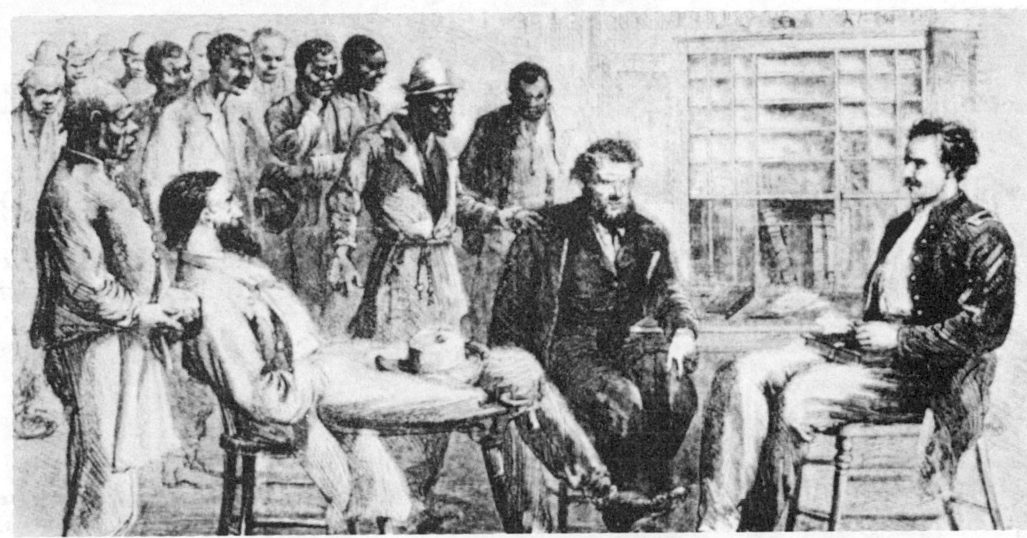

Negroes flocked to this branch of the Freedmen's Bureau located in Memphis, Tennessee. The Bureau was in existence from 1865 to 1872.

An Act to Establish a Bureau for the Relief of Freemen and Refugees.

Be it enacted, That there is hereby established in the War Department, to continue during the present war of rebellion, and for one year thereafter, a bureau of refugees, freedmen, and abandoned lands, to which shall be committed, as hereinafter provided, the supervision and management of all abandoned lands, and the control of all subjects relating to refugees and freedmen from rebel states, or from any district of country within the territory embraced in the operations of the army, under such rules and regulations as may be prescribed by the head of the bureau and approved by the President. The said bureau shall be under the management and control of a commissioner to be appointed by the President, by and with the advice and consent of the Senate. . . .

SEC. 2. That the Secretary of War may direct such issues of provisions, clothing, and fuel, as he may deem needful for the immediate and temporary shelter and supply of destitute and suffering refugees and freedmen and their wives and children, under such rules and regulations as he may direct.

SEC. 3. That the President may, by and with the advice and consent of the Senate, appoint an assistant commissioner for each of the states declared to be in insurrection, not exceeding ten in number, who shall, under the direction of the commissioner, aid in the execution of the provisions of this act; . . . And any military officer may be detailed and assigned to duty under this act without increase of pay or allowances. . . .

SEC. 4. That the commissioner, under the direction of the President, shall have authority to set apart, for the use of loyal refugees and freedmen, such tracts of land within the insurrectionary states as shall have been abandoned, or to which the United States shall have acquired title by confiscation or sale, or otherwise, and to every male citizen, whether refugee or freedman, as aforesaid, there shall be assigned not more than forty acres of such land, and the person to whom it was so assigned shall be protected in the use and enjoyment of the land for the term of three years at an annual rent not exceeding six per centum upon the value of such land, as it was appraised by the state authorities in the year eighteen hundred and sixty, for the purpose of taxation, and in case no such appraisal can be found, then the rental shall be based upon the estimated value of the land in said year, to be ascertained in such manner as the commissioner may by regulation prescribe. At the end of said term, or at any time during said term, the occupants of any parcels so assigned may purchase the land and receive such title thereto as the United States can convey, upon paying therefor the value of the land, as ascertained and fixed for the purpose of determining the annual rent aforesaid. . . .

THE THIRTEENTH AMENDMENT (1865)

Brief and to the point, the 13th Amendment to the U. S. Constitution abolishes slavery "within the United States," thus completing the job begun by the Emancipation Proclamation.

RATIFIED DECEMBER 18, 1865

Section 1. Neither slavery nor involuntary servitude, except as a punishment for crime whereof the party shall have been duly convicted, shall exist within the United States, or any place subject to their jurisdiction.

Section 2. Congress shall have power to enforce this article by appropriate legislation.

THE CIVIL RIGHTS ACT (1866)

The Civil Rights Act of 1866 was designed to protect the freedman from the Black Codes and other repressive legislation. This measure conferred citizenship upon Negroes, and set the stage for the more inclusive 14th Amendment.

An Act to protect all Persons in the United States in their Civil Rights, and furnish the Means of their Vindication.

Be it enacted, That all persons born in the United States and not subject to any foreign power, excluding Indians not taxed, are hereby declared to be citizens of the United States; and such citizens, of every race and color, without regard to any previous condition of slavery or involuntary servitude, except as a punishment for crime whereof the party shall have been duly convicted, shall have the same right, in every State and Territory in the United States, to make and enforce contracts, to sue, be parties, and give evidence, to inherit, purchase, lease, sell, hold, and convey real and personal property and to full and equal benefit of all laws and proceedings for the security of person and property, as is enjoyed by white citizens, and shall be subject to like punishment, pains, and penalties, and to none other, any law, statute, ordinance, regulation, or custom, to the contrary notwithstanding.

SEC. 2. *And be it further enacted,* That any person who, under color of any law, statute, ordinance, regulation, or custom, shall subject, or cause to be subjected, any inhabitant of any State or Territory to the deprivation of any right secured or protected by this act, or to different punishment, pains, or penalties on account of such person having at any time been held in a condition of slavery or involuntary servituude, except as a punishment for crime whereof the party shall have been duly convicted, or by reason of his color or race, than is prescribed for the punishment of white persons, shall be deemed guilty of a misdemeanor, and, on conviction, shall be punished by fine not exceeding one thousand dollars, or imprisonment not exceeding one year, or both, in the discretion of the court.

SEC. 3. *And be it further enacted,* That the district courts of the United States, . . . shall have, exclusively of the courts of the several States, cognizance of all crimes and offences committed against the provisions of this act, and also, concurrently with the circuit courts of the United States, of all causes, civil and criminal, affecting persons who are denied or cannot enforce in the courts or judicial tribunals of the State or locality where they may be any of the rights secured to them by the first section of this act. . . .

SEC. 4. *And be it further enacted,* That the district attorneys, marshals, and deputy marshals of the United States, the commissioners appointed by the Circuit and territorial courts of the United States, with powers of arresting, imprisoning, or bailing offenders against the laws of the United States, the officers and agents of the Freedmen's Bureau, and every other officer who may be specially empowered by the President of the United States, shall be, and they are hereby, specially authorized and required, at the expense of the United States, to institute proceedings against all and every person who shall violate the provisions of this act, and cause him or them to be arrested and imprisoned, or bailed, as the case may be, for trial before such court of the United States or territorial court as by this act has cognizance of the offence. . . .

SEC. 8. *And be it further enacted,* That whenever the President of the United States shall have reason to believe that offences have been or are likely to be committed against the provisions of this act within any judicial district, it shall be lawful for him, in his discretion, to direct the judge, marshal, and district attorney of such district to attend at such place within the district, and for such time as he may designate, for the purpose of the more speedy arrest and trial of persons charged with a violation of this act; and it shall be the duty of every judge or other officer, when any such requisition shall be received by him, to attend at the place and for the time therein designated.

SEC. 9. *And be it further enacted,* That it shall be lawful for the President of the United States, or such person as he may empower for that purpose, to employ such part of the land or naval forces of the United States, or of the militia, as shall be necessary to prevent the violation and enforce the due execution of this act.

SEC. 10. *And be it further enacted,* That upon all questions of law arising in any cause under the provisions of this act a final appeal may be taken to the Supreme Court of the United States.

THE FIRST RECONSTRUCTION ACT (1867)

The First Reconstruction Act of 1867 contained the general principles which governed Congressional Reconstruction. President Andrew Johnson vetoed the bill in vain, inasmuch as the Radical Republicans were able to muster the two-thirds majority necessary to override his veto.

An Act to provide for the more efficient Government of the Rebel States

WHEREAS no legal State governments or adequate protection for life or property now exists in the rebel States of Virginia, North Carolina, South Carolina, Georgia, Mississippi, Alabama, Louisiana, Florida, Texas, and Arkansas; and whereas it is necessary that peace and good order should be enforced in said States until loyal and republican State governments can be legally established: Therefore,

Be it enacted, That said rebel States shall be divided into military districts and made subject to the military authority of the United States as hereinafter prescribed, and for that purpose Virginia shall constitute the first district; North Carolina and South Carolina the second district; Georgia, Alabama, and Florida the third district; Mississippi and Arkansas the fourth district; and Louisiana and Texas the fifth district.

SEC. 2. That it shall be the duty of the President to assign to the command of each of said districts an officer of the army, not below the rank of brigadier-general, and to detail a sufficient military force to enable such officer to perform his duties and enforce his authority within the district to which he is assigned.

SEC. 3. That it shall be the duty of each officer assigned as aforesaid, to protect all persons in their rights of persons and property, to suppress insurrection, disorder, and violence, and to punish, or cause to be punished, all disturbers of the public peace and criminals; and to this end he may allow local civil tribunals to take jurisdiction of and to try offenders, or, when in his judgment it may be necessary for the trial of offenders, he shall have power to organize military commissions or tribunals for that purpose, and all interference under color of State authority with the exercise of military authority under this act, shall be null and void.

SEC. 4. That all persons put under military arrest by virtue of this act shall be tried without unnecessary delay, and no cruel or unusual punishment shall be inflicted, and no sentence of any military commission or tribunal hereby authorized, affecting the life or liberty of any

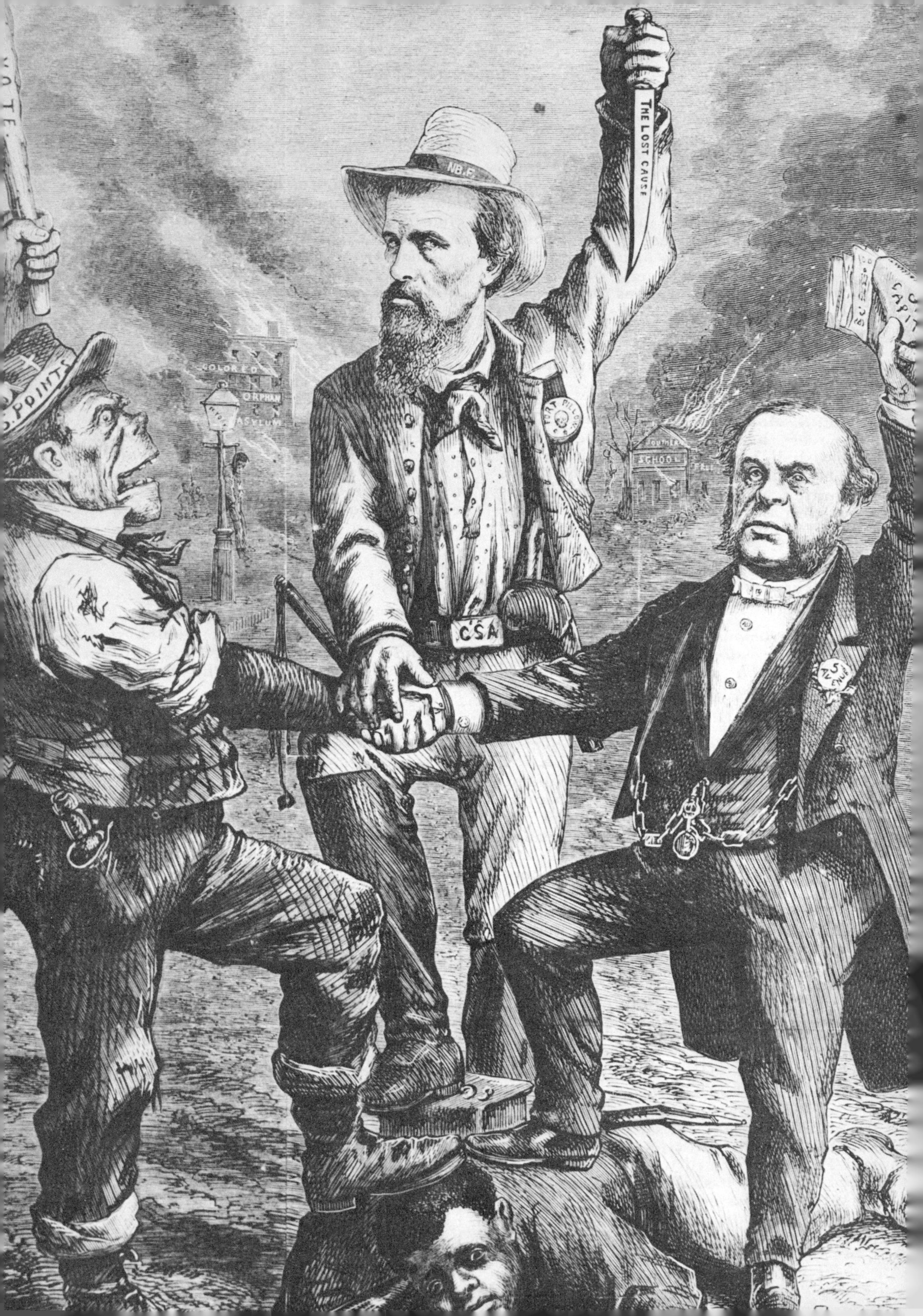
THE LOST CAUSE
N.B.F.
FORT PILLOW
CSA
COLORED ORPHAN ASYLUM
SCHOOL

person, shall be executed until it is approved by the officer in command of the district, and the laws and regulations for the government of the army shall not be affected by this act, except in so far as they conflict with its provisions: *Provided,* That no sentence of death under the provisions of this act shall be carried into effect without the approval of the President.

SEC. 5. That when the people of any one of said rebel States shall have formed a constitution of government in conformity with the Constitution of the United States in all respects, framed by a convention of delegates elected by the male citizens of said State, twenty-one years old and upward, of whatever race, color, or previous condition, who have been resident in said State for one year previous to the day of such election, except such as may be disfranchised for participation in the rebellion or for felony at common law, and when such constitution shall provide that the elective franchise shall be enjoyed by all such persons as have the qualifications herein stated for electors of delegates, and when such constitution shall be ratified by a majority of the persons voting on the question of ratification who are qualified as electors for delegates, and when such constitution shall have been submitted to Congress for examination and approval, and Congress shall have approved the same, and when said State, by a vote of its legislature elected said constitution, shall have adopted the amendment to the Constitution of the United States, proposed by the Thirty-ninth Congress, and known as article fourteen, and when said article shall have become a part of the Constitution of the United States said State shall be declared entitled to representation in Congress, and senators and representatives shall be admitted therefrom on their taking the oath prescribed by law, and then and thereafter the preceding sections of this act shall be inoperative in said State: *Provided,* That no person excluded from the privilege of holding office by said proposed amendment to the Constitution of the United States, shall be eligible to election as a member of the convention to frame a constitution for any of said rebel States, nor shall any such person vote for members of such convention.

SEC. 6. That, until the people of said rebel States shall be by law admitted to representation in the Congress of the United States, any civil governments which may exist therein shall be deemed provisional only, and in all respects subject to the paramount authority of the United States at any time to abolish, modify, control, or supersede the same; and in all elections to any office under such provisional governments all persons shall be entitled to vote, and none others, who are entitled to vote, under the provisions of the fifth section of this act; and no persons shall be eligible to any office under any such provisional governments who would be disqualified from holding office under the provisions of the third *article* of said constitutional amendment.

THE FOURTEENTH AMENDMENT (1868)

The 14th Amendment defined U. S. citizenship, and reversed the traditional federal-state relationship by providing for the intervention of the federal government in cases where state governments were accused of violating the Constitutional rights of the individual.

RATIFIED JULY 23, 1868

Section 1. All persons born or naturalized in the United States, and subject to the jurisdiction thereof, are citizens of the United States and of the State wherein they reside. No state shall make or enforce any law which shall abridge the privileges or immunities of citizens of the United States; nor shall any State deprive any person of life, liberty, or property, without due process of law; nor deny to any person within its jurisdiction the equal protection of the laws.

Section 2. Representatives shall be apportioned among the several States according to their respective numbers, counting the whole number of persons in each State, excluding Indians not taxed. But when the right to vote at any election for the choice of electors for President and Vice President of the United States, Representatives in Congress, the Executive and Judicial officers of a State, or the members of the Legislature thereof, is denied to any of the male inhabitants of such State, being twenty-one

Sooner or later all the people of the world will have to discover a way to live together in peace, and thereby transform this pending cosmic elegy into a creative psalm of brotherhood.

If this is to be achieved, man must evolve for all human conflict a method which rejects revenge, aggression and retaliation. The foundation of such a method is love.

The tortuous road which has led from Montgomery, Ala. to Oslo bears witness to this truth. This is a road over which millions of Negroes are traveling to find a new sense of dignity. This same road has opened for all Americans a new era of progress and hope.

It has led to a new civil rights bill, and it will, I am convinced, be widened and lengthened into a superhighway of justice as Negro and white men in increasing numbers create alliance to overcome their common problems.

I accept this award today with an abiding faith in America and an audacious faith in the future of mankind. I refuse to accept the idea that the "isness" of man's present nature makes him morally incapable of reaching up for the eternal "oughtness" that forever confronts him.

I refuse to accept the idea that man is mere flotsam and jetsam in the river of life which surrounds him. I refuse to accept the view that mankind is so tragically bound to the starless midnight of racism and war that the bright daybreak of peace and brotherhood can never become a reality.

I refuse to accept the cynical notion that nation after nation must spiral down a militaristic stairway into the hell of thermonuclear destruction.

I believe that unarmed truth and unconditional love will have the final word in reality. This is why right temporarily defeated is stronger than evil triumphant.

I believe that even amid today's mortar bursts and whining bullets, there is still hope for a brighter tomorrow.

I believe that wounded justice, lying prostrate on the blood-flowing streets of our nations, can be lifted from this dust of shame to reign supreme among the children of men.

I have the audacity to believe that people everywhere can have three meals a day for their bodies, education and culture for their minds, and dignity, equality and freedom for their spirits. I believe that what self-centered men have torn down men other-centered can build up.

I still believe that one day mankind will bow before the altars of God and be crowned triumphant over war and bloodshed, and nonviolent redemptive good will proclaim the rule of the land. "And the lion and the lamb shall lie down together and none shall be afraid." I still believe that we shall overcome.

This faith can give us courage to face the uncertainties of the future. It will give our tired feet new strength as we continue our forward stride toward the city of freedom.

When our days become dreary with low-hovering clouds and our nights become darker than a thousand midnights, we will know that we are living in the creative turmoil of a genuine civilization struggling to be born.

Today I come to Oslo as a trustee, inspired and with renewed dedication to humanity. I accept this prize on behalf of all men who love peace and brotherhood. I say I come as a trustee, for in the depths of my heart I am aware that this prize is much more than an honor to me personally.

Every time I take a flight I am always mindful of the many people who make a successful journey possible—the known pilots and the unknown ground crew.

So you honor the dedicated pilots of our struggle who have sat at the controls as the freedom movement soared into orbit. You honor, once again, Chief (Albert) Luthuli of South Africa, whose struggles with and for his people, are still met with the most brutal expression of man's inhumanity to man.

You honor the ground crew without whose labor and sacrifices the jetflights to freedom could never have left the earth.

Most of these people will never make the headlines and their names will not appear in Who's Who. Yet the years have rolled past and when the blazing light of truth is focused on this marvelous age in which we live—men and women will know and children will be taught that we have a finer land, a better people, a more noble civilization—because these humble children of God were willing to suffer for righteousness sake.

I think Alfred Nobel would know what I mean when I say that I accept this award in the spirit of a curator of some precious heirloom which he holds in trust for its true owners—all those to whom beauty is truth and truth beauty—and in whose eyes the beauty of genuine brotherhood and peace is more precious than diamonds or silver or gold.

of any of the accommodations, advantages, facilities, or privileges in said section enumerated, or by aiding or inciting such denial, shall, for every such offense, forfeit and pay the sum of five hundred dollars to the person aggrieved thereby, . . . and shall also, for every such offense, be deemed guilty of a misdemeanor, and, upon conviction thereof, shall be fined not less than five hundred nor more than one thousand dollars, or shall be imprisoned not less than thirty days nor more than one year . . .

SEC. 3. That the district and circuit courts of the United States shall have, exclusively of the courts of the several States, cognizance of all crimes and offenses against, and violations of, the provisions of this act . . .

SEC. 4. That no citizen possessing all other qualifications which are or may be prescribed by law shall be disqualified for service as grand or petit juror in any court of the United States, or of any State, on account of race, color, or previous condition of servitude; and any officer or other person charged with any duty in the selection or summoning of jurors who shall exclude or fail to summon any citizen for the cause aforesaid shall, on conviction thereof, be deemed guilty of a misdemeanor, and be fined not more than five thousand dollars.

SEC. 5. That all cases arising under the provisions of this act . . . shall be renewable by the Supreme Court of the United States, without regard to the sum in controversy. . . .

BOOKER T. WASHINGTON'S "ATLANTA COMPROMISE" SPEECH (1895)

Booker T. Washington, at one time the sole voice in the movement for Negro advancement, is often criticized today for having encouraged the Negro to cultivate a spirit of "peaceful co-existence" with the white Southerner. Washington advocated technical and industrial self-help programs for the Negro, even if they tended to discount the importance of his cultivating intellectual and aesthetic values as well.

Mr. President and Gentlemen of the Board of Directors and Citizens:

One third of the population of the South is of the Negro race. No enterprise seeking the material, civil, or moral welfare of this section can disregard this element of our population and reach the highest success. I but convey to you, Mr. President and Directors, the sentiment of the masses of my race when I say that in no way have the value and manhood of the American Negro been more fittingly and generously recognized than by the managers of this magnificent Exposition at every stage of its progress. It is a recognition that will do more to cement the friendship of the two races than any occurrence since the dawn of our freedom.

Not only this, but the opportunity here afforded will awaken among us a new era of industrial progress. Ignorant and inexperienced, it is not strange that in the first years of our new life we began at the top instead of at the bottom; that a seat in Congress or the State Legislature was more sought than real estate or industrial skill; that the political convention or stump speaking had more attractions than starting a dairy farm or truck garden.

A ship lost at sea for many days suddenly sighted a friendly vessel. From the mast of the unfortunate vessel was seen a signal: "Water, water; we die of thirst!" The answer from the friendly vessel at once came back: "Cast down your bucket where you are." A second time the signal, "Water, water; send us water!" ran up from the distressed vessel, and was answered: "Cast down your bucket where you are." And a third and fourth signal for water was answered: "Cast down your bucket where you are." The captain of the distressed vessel, at last heeding the injunction, cast down his bucket, and it came up full of fresh, sparkling water from the mouth of the Amazon River. To those of my race who depend on bettering their condition in a foreign land, or who underestimate the importance of cultivating friendly relations with the Southern white man, who is their next door neighbor, I would say: "Cast down your bucket where you are"—cast it down in making friends in every manly way of the people of all races by whom we are surrounded.

Cast it down in agriculture, mechanics, in commerce, in domestic service, and in the professions. And in this connection it is well to bear in mind that whatever other sins the South may be called to bear, when it comes to business, pure and simple, it is in the South that the Negro is given a man's chance in the commercial world, and in nothing is this Exposition more eloquent than in emphasizing this chance. Our greatest danger is, that in the great leap from slavery to freedom we may overlook the fact that the masses of us are to live by the productions of our hands, and fail to keep in mind that we shall prosper in proportion as we learn to dignify and glorify common labor, and put brains and skill into the common occupations of life; shall prosper in proportion as we learn to draw the line between the superficial and the substantial, the ornamental gewgaws of life and the useful. No race can prosper till it learns that there is as much dignity in tilling a field as in writing a poem. It is at the bottom of life we must begin, and not at the top. Nor should we permit our grievances to overshadow our opportunities.

To those of the white race who look to the incoming of those of foreign birth and strange tongue and habits for the prosperity of the South, were I permitted, I would repeat what I say to my own race, "Cast down your bucket where you are." Cast it down among the 8,000,000 Negroes whose habits you know, whose fidelity and love you have tested in days when to have proved treacherous meant the ruin of your firesides. Cast down your bucket among these people who have, without strikes and labor wars, tilled your fields, cleared your forests, builded your railroads and cities, and brought forth treasures from the bowels of the earth, and helped make possible this magnificent representation of the progress of the South. Casting down your bucket among my people, helping and encouraging them as you are doing on these grounds, and, with education of head, hand and heart, you will find that they will buy your surplus land, make blossom the waste place in your fields, and run your factories. While doing this, you can be sure in the future, as in the past, that you and your families will be surrounded by the most patient, faithful, law-abiding, and unresentful people that the world has seen. As we have proved our loyalty to you in the past, in nursing your children, watching by the sick bed of your mothers and fathers, and often following them with tear-dimmed eyes to their graves, so in the future, in our humble way, we shall stand by you with a devotion that no foreigner can approach, ready to lay down our lives, if need be, in defense of yours, interlacing our industrial, commercial, civil, and religious life with yours in a way that shall make the interests of both races one. In all things that are purely social we can be as separate as the fingers, yet one as the hand in all things essential to mutual progress.

There is no defense or security for any of us except in the highest intelligence and development of all. If anywhere there are efforts tending to curtail the fullest growth of the Negro, let these efforts be turned into stimulating, encouraging, and making him the most useful and intelligent citizen. Effort or means so invested will pay a thousand per cent interest. These efforts will be twice blessed—"blessing him that gives and him that takes."

There is no escape through law of man or God from the inevitable:

"The laws of changeless justice bind
Oppressor with oppressed;
And close as sin and suffering joined
We march to fate abreast."

Nearly sixteen millions of hands will aid you in pulling the load upwards, or they will pull against you the load downwards. We shall constitute one-third and more of the ignorance and crime of the South, or one-third its intelligence and progress; we shall contribute one-third to the business and industrial prosperity of the South, or we shall prove a veritable body of death, stagnating, depressing, retarding every effort to advance the body politic.

Gentlemen of the Exposition, as we present to you our humble effort at an exhibition of our progress, you must not expect overmuch. Starting thirty years ago with ownership here and there in a few quilts and pumpkins and chickens (gathered from miscellaneous sources), remember the path that has led from these to the invention and production of agricultural implements, buggies, steam engines, newspapers, books, statuary, carving, paintings, the management of drug stores and banks, has not been trodden without contact with thorns and thistles. While we take pride in what we exhibit as a result of our independent efforts, we do not for a moment forget that our part in this exhibition would fall far short of your expectations but for the constant help that has come to our educational life, not only from the Southern States, but especially from Northern philanthropists, who have made their gifts a constant stream of blessing and encouragement.

The wisest among my race understand that the agitation of questions of social equality is the extremist folly, and that progress in the enjoyment of all the privileges that will come to us must be the result of severe and constant struggle rather than of artificial forcing. No race that has anything to contribute to the markets of the world is long in any degree ostracized. It is important and right that all privileges of the law be ours, but it is vastly more important that we be prepared for the exercise of those privileges. The opportunity to earn a dollar in a factory just now is worth infinitely more than the opportunity to spend a dollar in an opera house.

In conclusion, may I repeat that nothing in thirty years has given us more hope and encouragement, and drawn us so near to you of the white race, as this opportunity offered by the Exposition; and here bending, as it were, over the altar that represents the results of the struggles of your race and mine, both starting practically empty-handed three decades ago, I pledge that, in your effort to work out the great and intricate problem which God has laid at the doors of the South, you shall have at all time the patient, sympathetic help of my race; only let this be constantly in mind that, while from representations in these buildings of the product of field, of forest, of mine, of factory, letters, and art, much good will come, yet far above and beyond material benefits will be that higher good, that let us pray God will come, in a blotting out of sectional differences and racial animosities and suspicions, in a determination to administer absolute justice, in a willing obedience among all classes to the mandates of law. This, coupled with our material prosperity, will bring into our beloved South a new heaven and a new earth.

THE UNIVERSAL NEGRO IMPROVEMENT ASSOCIATION: SPEECH AT LIBERTY HALL, NEW YORK CITY (1922)

The Universal Negro Improvement Association (UNIA) was founded by Marcus Garvey—a West Indian Negro who, in the decade following World War I, won a large following in the United States. Garveyism was the precursor of present-day Negro nationalist movements. It represented a sharp repudiation of Washington's ideas, as did the work of Negro scholar W.E.B. DuBois, one of the founding fathers of the NAACP.

Over five years ago the Universal Negro Improvement Association placed itself before the world as the movement through which the new and rising Negro would give expression of his feelings. This Association adopts an attitude not of hostility to other races and peoples of the world, but an attitude of self-respect. . . . . . Wheresoever human rights are denied to any group, wheresoever justice is denied to any group, there the U.N.I.A. finds a cause. And at this time among all the peoples of the world, the group that suffers most from injustice, the group that is denied most of those rights that belong to all humanity, is the black group . . . even so under the leadership of the U.N.I.A., we are marshaling the 400,000,000 Negroes of the world to fight for the emancipation of the race and of the redemption of the country of our fathers.

We represent a new line of thought among Negroes. Whether you call it advanced thought or reactionary thought, I do not care. If it is reactionary for people to seek independence in government, then we are reactionary. If it is advanced thought for people to seek liberty and freedom, then we represent the advanced school of thought among the Negroes of this country. We of the U.N.I.A. believe that what is good for the other folks is good for us. If government is something that is worth while; if government is something that is appreciable and helpful and protective to others, then we also want to experiment in government. We do not mean a government that will make us citizens without rights or subjects without consideration. We mean a kind of government that will place our race in control, even as other races are in control of their own government.

. . . The U.N.I.A. is not advocating the cause of church building, because we have a sufficiently large number of churches among us to minister to the spiritual needs of the people, and we are not going to compete with those who are engaged in so splendid a work; we are not engaged in building any new social institutions, . . . because there are enough social workers engaged in those praiseworthy efforts. We are not engaged in politics because we have enough local politicians, . . . and the political situation is well taken care of. We are not engaged in domestic politics, in church building or in social uplift work, but we are engaged in nation building.

In advocating the principles of this Association we find we have been very much misunderstood and very much misrepresented by men from within our own race, as well as others from without. Any reform movement that seeks to bring about changes for the benefit of humanity is bound to be misrepresented by those who have always taken it upon themselves to administer to, and lead the unfortunate. . . .

. . . The Universal Negro Improvement Association stands for the Bigger Brotherhood; the Universal Negro Improvement Association stands for human rights, not only for Negroes, but for all races. The Universal Negro Improvement Association believes in the rights of not only the black race, but the white race, the yellow race and the brown race. The Universal Negro Improvement Association believes that the white man has as much right to be considered, the yellow man has as much right to be considered, the brown man has as much right to be considered as the black man of Africa. In view of the fact that the black man of Africa has contributed as much to the world as the white man of Europe, and the brown man and yellow man of Asia, we of the Universal Negro Improvement Association demand that the white, yellow and brown races give to the black man his place in the civilization of the world. We ask for nothing more than the rights of 400,000,000 Negroes. We are not seeking, as I said before, to destroy or disrupt the society of the government of other races, but we are determined that 400,000,000 of us shall unite ourselves to free our motherland from the grasp of the invader. . . .

The Universal Negro Improvement Association is not seeking to build up another government within the bounds or borders of the United States of America. The Universal Negro Improvement Association is not seeking to disrupt any organized system of government, but the Association is determined to bring Negroes together for the building up of a nation of their own. And why? Because we have been forced to it. We have been forced to it throughout the world; not only in America, not only in Europe, not only in the British Empire, but wheresoever the black man happens to find himself, he has been forced to do for himself.

To talk about Government is a little more than some of our people can appreciate. . . . The average man . . . seems to say, "Why should there be need for any other government?" We are French, English or American. But we of the U.N.I.A. have studied seriously this question of nationality among Negroes—this American nationality, this British nationality, this French, Italian or Spanish nationality, and have discovered that it counts for nought when that nationality comes in conflict with the racial idealism of the group that rules. When our interests clash with those of the ruling faction, then we find that we have absolutely no rights. In times of peace, when everything is all right, Negroes have a hard time, wherever we go, wheresoever we find ourselves, getting those rights that belong to us in common with others whom we claim as fellow citizens; getting that consideration that should be ours by right of the constitution, by right of the law; but in the time of trouble they make us all partners in the cause, as happened in the last war. . . .

We have saved many nations in this manner, and we have lost our lives doing that before. Hundreds of thousands—nay, millions of black men, lie buried under the ground due to that old-time camouflage of saving the nation. We saved the British empire; we saved the French empire; we saved this glorious country more than once; and all that we have received for our sacrifices, all that we have received for what we have done, even in giving up our lives, is just what you are receiving now, just what I am receiving now.

You and I fare no better in America, in the British Empire, or any other part of the white world; we fare no better than any black man wheresoever he shows his head. . . .

The U.N.I.A. is reversing the old-time order of things. We refuse to be followers anymore. We are leading ourselves. That

Marcus Garvey was one of the pioneer advocates of what has now come to be termed "Negro nationalism." Garvey's name flared into prominence during the early 1920's, but he was deported to Jamaica in 1927, and died in obscurity in England 13 years later.

means, if any saving is to be done, . . . we are going to seek a method of saving Africa first. Why? And why Africa? Because Africa has become the grand prize of the nations. Africa has become the big game of the nation hunters. Today Africa looms as the greatest commercial, industrial and political prize in the world.

The difference between the Universal Negro Improvement Association and the other movements of this country, and probably the world, is that the Universal Negro Improvement Association seeks independence of government, while the other organizations seek to make the Negro a secondary part of existing governments. We differ from the organizations in America because they seek to subordinate the Negro as a secondary consideration in a great civilization, knowing that in America the Negro will never reach his highest ambition, knowing that the Negro in America will never get his constitutional rights. All those organizations which are fostering the improvement of Negroes in the British Empire know that the Negro in the British Empire will never reach the height of his constitutional rights. What do I mean by constitutional rights in America? If the black man is to reach the height of his ambition in this country—if the black man is to get all of his constitutional rights in America—then the black man should have the same chance in the nation as any other man to become president of the nation, or a street cleaner in New York. If the black man in the British Empire is to have all his constitutional rights it means that the Negro in the British Empire should have at least the same right to become premier of Great Britain as he has to become street cleaner in the city of London. Are they prepared to give us such political equality? You and I can live in the United States of America for 100 more years, and our generations may live for 200 years or for 5000 more years, and so long as there is a black and white population, when the majority is on the side of the white race, you and I will never get political justice or get political equality in this country. Then why should a black man with rising ambition, after preparing himself in every possible way to give expression to that highest ambition, allow himself to be kept down by racial prejudice within a country? If I am as educated as the next man, if I am as prepared as the next man, if I have passed through the best schools and colleges and universities as the other fellow, why should I not have a fair chance to compete with the other fellow for the biggest position in the nation? . . . .

We are not preaching a propaganda of hate against anybody. We love the white man; we love all humanity. . . . The white man is as necessary to the existence of the Negro as the Negro is necessary to his existence. There is a common relationship that we cannot escape. Africa has certain things that Europe wants, and Europe has certain things that Africa wants, . . . it is impossible for us to escape it. Africa has oil, diamonds, copper, gold and rubber and all the minerals that Europe wants, and there must be some kind of relationship between Africa and Europe for a fair exchange, so we cannot afford to hate anybody.

The question often asked is what does it require to redeem a race and free a country? If it takes man power, if it takes scientific intelligence, if it takes education of any kind, or if it takes blood, then the 400,000,000 Negroes of the world have it.

It took the combined power of the Allies to put down the mad determination of the Kaiser to impose German will upon the world and upon humanity. Among those who suppressed his mad ambition were two million Negroes who have not yet forgotten how to drive men across the firing line. . . . when so many white men refused to answer to the call and dodged behind all kinds of excuses, 400,000 black men were ready without a question. It was because we were told it was a war of democracy; it was a war for the liberation of the weaker peoples of the world. We heard the cry of Woodrow Wilson, not because we liked him so, but because the things he said were of such a nature that they appealed to us as men. Wheresoever the cause of humanity stands in need of assistance, there you will find the Negro ever ready to serve.

He has done it from the time of Christ up to now. When the whole world turned its back upon the Christ, the man who was said to be the Son of God, when the world cried out "Crucify Him," when the world spurned Him and spat upon Him, it was a black man, Simon, the Cyrenian, who took up the cross. Why? Because the cause of humanity appealed to him. When the black man saw the suffering Jew, struggling under the heavy cross, he was willing to go to His assistance, and he bore that cross up to the heights of Calvary. In the spirit of Simon, the Cyrenian, 1900 years ago, we answered the call of Woodrow Wilson, the call to a larger humanity, and it was for that that we willingly rushed into the war. . . .

We shall march out, yes, as black American citizens, as black British subjects, as black French citizens, as black Italians or as black Spaniards, but we shall march out with a greater loyalty, the loyalty of race. We shall march out in answer to the cry of our fathers, who cry out to us for the redemption of our own country, our motherland, Africa.

We shall march out, not forgetting the blessings of America. We shall march out, not forgetting the blessings of civilization. We shall march out with a history of peace before and behind us, and surely that history shall be our breastplate, for how can man fight better than knowing that the cause for which he fights is righteous? . . . Glorious shall be the battle when the time comes to fight for our people and our race.

We should say to the millions who are in Africa to hold the fort, for we are coming 400,000,000 strong.

EXECUTIVE ORDER 8802 (1941)

Executive Order 8802, signed by President Franklin D. Roosevelt, eliminated discriminatory practices in the defense industry during World War II. Since then, such orders have often been supplemented by comprehensive legislation designed to cope with the very grievances outlined by men like Garvey.

. . . . . . I do hereby reaffirm the policy of the United States that there shall be no discrimination in the employment of workers in defense industries or Government because of race, creed, color, or national origin, and I do hereby declare that it is the duty of employers and of labor organizations, in furtherance of said policy and of this order, to provide for the full and equitable participation of all workers in defense industries, without discrimination because of race, creed, color, or national origin . . . . .

EXECUTIVE ORDER 9981 (1948)

Executive Order 9981, signed by President Harry S. Truman, ended segregation in the Armed Forces of the United States.

WHEREAS it is essential that there be maintained in the armed services of the United States the highest standards of democracy, with equality of treatment and opportunity for all those who serve in our country's defense:

NOW, THEREFORE, by virtue of the authority vested in me as President of the United States, by the Constitution and the statutes of the United States, and as Commander in Chief of the armed services, it is hereby ordered as follows:

1. It is hereby declared to be the policy of the President that there shall be equality of treatment and opportunity for all persons in the armed services without regard to race, color, religion or national origin. This policy shall be put into effect as rapidly as possible, having due regard to the time required to effectuate any necessary changes without impairing efficienty or morals.

2. There shall be created in the National Military Establishment an advisory committee to be known as the President's Committee on Equality of Treatment and Opportunity in the Armed Services, which shall be composed of seven members to be designated by the President.

3. The Committee is authorized on behalf of the President to examine into the rules, procedures and practices of the armed services in order to determine in what respect such rules, procedures and practices may be altered or improved with a view to carrying out the policy of this order. The Committee shall confer and advise with the Secretary of Defense, the Secretary of the Army, the Secretary of the Air Force, and shall make such recommendations to the President and to said Secretaries as in the judgment of the Committee will effectuate the policy hereof.

4. All executive departments and agencies of the Federal Government are authorized and directed to cooperate with the Committee in its work, and to furnish the Committee such information or the services of such persons as the Committee may require in the performance of its duties.

5. When requested by the Committee to do so, persons in the armed services or in any of the executive departments and agencies of the Federal Government shall testify before the Committee and shall make available for the use of the Committee such documents and other information as the Committee may require.

6. The Committee shall continue to exist until such time as the President shall terminate its existence by Executive order.

THE CIVIL RIGHTS ACTS OF 1957 AND 1960

The Civil Rights Acts of 1957 and 1960, both passed during the Eisenhower Administration, represented the first comprehensive federal legislation in this area in the 20th century. (Both these documents are presented in summary form.)

Provisions of the Act of 1957

Title I

Created an executive Commission on Civil Rights composed of six members, not more than three from the same political party, to be appointed by the President with the advice and consent of the Senate.

Established rules of procedure for the Commission.

Authorized the Commission to receive in executive session any testimony that might defame or incriminate anyone.

Provided that penalties for unauthorized persons who released information from executive hearings of the Commission would apply only to persons whose services were paid for by the Government.

Barred the Commission from issuing subpenas for witnesses who were found, resided or transacted business outside the state in which the hearing would be held.

Placed the pay for Commissioners at $50 per day—plus $12 per day for expenses away from home.

Empowered the Commission to investigate allegations that U.S. citizens were being deprived of their right to vote and have that vote counted by reason of color, race, religion, or national origin; to study and collect information concerning legal developments constituting a denial of equal protection of the laws under the Constitution; to appraise the laws and policies of the Federal Government with respect to equal protection of the laws.

Directed the Commission to submit interim reports to the President and Congress and a final report of its activities, findings and recommendations not later than two years following enactment of the bill.

Authorized the President, with the advice and consent of the Senate, to appoint a full-time staff director of the Commission whose pay would not exceed $22,500 a year.

Barred the Commission from accepting or utilizing the services of voluntary or uncompensated personnel.

Title II

Authorized the President to appoint, with the advice and consent of the Senate, one additional Assistant Attorney General in the Department of Justice.

Title III

Extended the jurisdiction of the district courts to include any civil action begun to recover damages or secure equitable relief under any act of Congress providing for the protection of civil rights, including the right to vote.

Repealed a statute of 1866 giving the President power to employ troops to enforce or to prevent violation of civil rights legislation.

Title IV

Prohibited attempts to intimidate or prevent persons from voting in general or primary elections for federal offices.

Empowered the Attorney General to seek an injunction when an individual was deprived or about to be deprived of his right to vote.

Gave the district courts jurisdiction over such proceedings, without requiring that administrative remedies be exhausted.

Provided that any person cited for contempt should be defended by counsel and allowed to compel witnesses to appear.

Title V

Provided that in all criminal contempt cases arising from the provisions of the Civil Rights Act of 1957, the accused, upon conviction, would be punished by fine or imprisonment or both.

Placed the maximum fine for an individual under those provisions at $1,000 or six months in jail.

Allowed the judge to decide whether a defendant in a criminal contempt case involving voting rights would be tried with or without a jury.

Provided that in the event a criminal contempt case was tried before a judge without a jury and the sentence upon conviction was more than $300 or more than 45 days in jail, the defendant could demand and receive a jury trial.

Stated that the section would not apply to contempts committed in the presence of the court or so near as to interfere directly with the administration of justice, nor to the behavior or misconduct of any officer of the court in respect to the process of the court.

Provided that any U.S. citizen over 21, who had resided for one year within a judicial district would be competent to serve as a grand or petit juror unless: (1) he had been convicted of a crime punishable by imprisonment for more than one year and his civil rights not restored; (2) he was unable to read, write, speak and understand the English language; (3) he was incapable, either physically or mentally, to give efficient jury service.

Provisions of the Act of 1960

Title I

Provided that persons who obstructed or interfered with any order issued by a federal court, or attempted to do so, by threats or force, could be punished by a fine of up to $1,000, imprisonment of up to one year, or both. Such acts could also be prevented by private suits seeking court injunctions against them.

Title II

Made it a federal crime to cross state lines to avoid prosecution or punishment for, or giving evidence on, the bombing or burning of any building, facility or vehicle, or an attempt to do so. Penalties could be a fine of up to $5,000, or imprisonment of up to five years, or both.

Made it a federal crime to transport or possess explosives with the knowledge or intent that they would be used to blow up any vehicle or building. Allowed the presumption, after any bombing occurred, that the explosives used were transported across state lines (therefore allowing the FBI to investigate any bombing case), but stipulated that this would have to be proved before the person could be convicted. Penalties could be imprisonment of up to one year and/or $10,000 fine; if personal injury resulted, 10 years and/or $10,000 fine; if death resulted, life imprisonment or a death penalty if recommended by a jury.

Made it a federal crime to use interstate facilities, such as telephones, to threaten a bombing or give a false bomb-scare, punishable by imprisonment of up to one year or a fine of up to $1,000, or both.

Title III

Required that voting records and registration papers for all federal elections, including primaries, must be preserved for 22 months. Penalties for failing to comply or for stealing, destroying or mutilating the records could be a fine of up to $1,000, and/or imprisonment for one year.

Directed that the records, upon written application, be turned over to the Attorney General "or his representative" at the office of the records' custodian.

Unless directed otherwise by a court, the Justice Department representative must not disclose the content of the records except to Congress, a government agency, or in a court proceeding.

Title IV

Empowered the Civil Rights Commission, which was extended for two years in 1959, to administer oaths and take sworn statements.

Title V

Stated that arrangements might be made to provide for the education of children of members of the armed forces when the schools those children regularly attended had been closed to avoid integration and the U.S. Commissioner of Education had decided that no other educational agency would provide for their schooling. Amended the laws on aid to impacted school districts (PL 81-815, PL 81-874) to this effect.

Title VI

Provided that after the Attorney General won a civil suit brought under the 1957 Civil Rights Act to protect Negroes' right to vote, he could then ask the court to hold another adversary proceeding and make a separate finding that there was a "pattern or practice" of depriving Negroes of the right to vote in the area involved in the suit.

If a court found such a "pattern or

practice," any Negro living in that area could apply to the court to issue an order declaring him qualified to vote if he proved (1) he was qualified to vote under state law; (2) he had tried to register after the "pattern or practice" finding; and (3) he had not been allowed to register or had been found unqualified by someone acting under color of law. The court would have to hear the Negro's application within 10 days and its order would be effective for as long a period as that for which he would have been qualified to vote if registered under state law.

State officials would be notified of the order, and they would then be bound to permit the person to vote. Disobedience would be subject to contempt proceedings.

To carry out these provisions, the court may appoint one or more voting referees, who must be qualified voters in the judicial district. The referees would receive the applications, take evidence, and report their findings to the court. The referee must take the Negro's application and proof in an *ex parte* proceeding (without cross-examination by opponents) and the court may set the time and place for the referee's hearing.

The court may fix a time limit of up to 10 days, in which state officials may challenge the referee's report. Challenges on points of law must be accompanied by a memorandum and on points of fact by a verified copy of a public record or an affidavit by those with personal knowledge of the controverting evidence. Either the court or the referee may decide the challenges in accordance with court-directed procedures. Hearings on issues of fact could be held only when the affidavits show there is a real issue of fact.

If a Negro has applied for a court certificate 20 or more days before the election, his application is challenged, and the case is not decided by election day, the court must allow him to vote provisionally, provided he is "entitled to vote under state law," and impound his ballot pending a decision on his application. If he applies within 20 days before the election, the court has the option of whether or not to let him vote.

The court would not be limited in its powers to enforce its decree that these Negroes be allowed to vote and their votes be counted and may authorize the referee to take action to enforce it.

The referees would have the powers conferred on court masters by rule 53 (c) of the Federal Rules of Civil Procedure. (Rule 53(c) gives masters the right to subpena records, administer oaths and cross-examine witnesses.)

In any suit instituted under these provisions, the state would be held responsible for the actions of its officials and, in the event state officials resign and are not replaced, the state itself could be sued.

EXECUTIVE ORDER 10730 (1957)

Executive Order 10730, signed by President Dwight D. Eisenhower, ended segregation in Little Rock's Central High School.

WHEREAS on September 23, 1957, I issued Proclamation No. 3204 reading in part as follows:

WHEREAS certain persons in the State of Arkansas, individually and in unlawful assemblages, combinations, and conspiracies, have wilfully obstructed the enforcement of orders of the United States District Court for the Eastern District of Arkansas with respect to matters relating to enrollment and attendance at public schools, particularly at Central High School, located in Little Rock School District, Little Rock, Arkansas; and

WHEREAS such wilful obstruction of justice hinders the execution of the laws of that State and of the United States, and makes it impracticable to enforce such laws by the ordinary course of judicial proceedings; and

WHEREAS such obstructions of justice constitutes a denial of the equal protection of the laws secured by the Constitution of the United States and impedes the course of justice under those laws;

NOW, THEREFORE, I, DWIGHT D. EISENHOWER, President of the United States, under and by virtue of the authority vested in me by the Constitution and Statutes of the United States, including Chapter 15 of Title 10 of the United States Code, particularly sections 332, 333 and 334 thereof, do command all

priate to carry out the purposes of this Order, any or all of the units of the National Guard of the United States and of the Air National Guard of the United States within the State of Arkansas to serve in the active military service of the United States for an indefinite period and until relieved by appropriate orders.
persons engaged in such obstruction of justice to cease and desist therefrom, and to disperse forthwith, and

WHEREAS the command contained in that Proclamation has not been obeyed and wilful obstruction of enforcement of said court orders still exists and threatens to continue:

NOW, THEREFORE, by virtue of the authority vested in me by the Constitution and Statutes of the United States, including Chapter 15 of Title 10, particularly sections 332, 333 and 334 thereof, and section 301 of Title 3 of the United States Code, it is hereby ordered as follows:

SECTION 1. I hereby authorize and direct the Secretary of Defense to order into the active military service of the United States as he may deem appropriate

SEC. 2. The Secretary of Defense is authorized and directed to take all appropriate steps to enforce any orders of the United States District Court for the Eastern District of Arkansas for the removal of obstruction of justice in the State of Arkansas with respect to matters relating to enrollment and attendance at public schools in the Little Rock School District, Little Rock, Arkansas. In carrying out the provisions of this section, the Secretary of Defense is authorized to use the units, and members thereof, ordered into the active military service of the United States pursuant to Section 1 of this Order.

SEC. 3. In furtherance of the enforcement of the aforementioned orders of the United States District Court for the Eastern District of Arkansas, the Secretary of Defense is authorized to use such of the armed forces of the United States as he may deem necessary.

SEC. 4. The Secretary of Defense is authorized to delegate to the Secretary of the Army or the Secretary of the Air Force, or both, any of the authority conferred upon him by this Order.

EXECUTIVE ORDER 11053 (1962)

Executive Order 11053, signed by President John F. Kennedy, authorized the use of federal troops in integrating the University of Mississippi.

WHEREAS on September 30, 1962, I issued Proclamation No. 3497 reading in part as follows:

WHEREAS the Governor of the State of Mississippi and certain law enforcement officers and other officials of that State, and other persons, individually and in unlawful opposing and obstructing the enforcement of orders entered by the United States District Court for the Southern District of Mississippi and the United States Court of Appeals for the Fifth Circuit; and

WHEREAS such unlawful assemblies, combinations, and conspiracies oppose and obstruct the execution of the laws of the United States, impede the course of justice under those laws and make it impracticable to enforce those laws in the State of Mississippi by the ordinary course of judicial proceedings; and

WHEREAS I have expressly called the attention of the Governor of Mississippi to the perilous situation that exists and to his duties in the premises, and have requested but have not received from him adequate assurances that the orders of the courts of the United States will be obeyed and that law and order will be maintained:

NOW, THEREFORE, I, JOHN F. KENNEDY, President of the United States, under and by virtue of the authority vested in me by the Constitution and laws of the United States, including Chapter 15 of Title 10 of the United States Code, particularly sections 332, 333 and 334 thereof, do command all persons engaged in such obstructions of justice to cease and desist therefrom and to disperse and retire peaceably forthwith; and

WHEREAS the commands contained in that proclamation have not been obeyed and obstruction of enforcement of those court orders still exists and threatens to continue:

NOW, THEREFORE, by virtue of the

authority vested in me by the Constitution and laws of the United States, including Chapter 15 of Title 10, particularly Sections 332, 333 and 334 thereof, and Section 301 of Title 3 of the United States Code, it is hereby ordered as follows:

Section 1. The Secretary of Defense is authorized and directed to take all appropriate steps to enforce all orders of the United States District Court for the Southern District of Mississippi and the United States Court of Appeals for the Fifth Circuit and to remove all obstructions of justice in the State of Mississippi.

Sec. 2. In furtherance of the enforcement of the aforementioned orders of the United States District Court for the Southern District of Mississippi and the United States Court of Appeals for the Fifth Circuit, the Secretary of Defense is authorized to use such of the armed forces of the United States as he may deem necessary.

Sec. 3. I hereby authorize the Secretary of Defense to call into the active military service of the United States, as he may deem appropriate to carry out the purposes of this order, any or all of the units of the Army National Guard and of the Air National Guard of the State of Mississippi to serve in the active military service of the United States for an indefinite period and until relieved by appropriate orders. In carrying out the provisions of Section 1, the Secretary of Defense is authorized to use the units, and members thereof, ordered into the active military service of the United States pursuant to this section.

Sec. 4. The Secretary of Defense is authorized to delegate to the Secretary of the Army or the Secretary of the Air Force, or both, any of the authority conferred upon him by this order.

THE BIRMINGHAM MANIFESTO (1963)

In 1963, a series of events in Birmingham, Alabama dramatized the Negro's plight to the nation at large. Negro citizens were arrested en masse *during peaceful demonstrations which were subsequently quelled by local police using dogs and by firemen using hoses. The Manifesto, dated April 3, 1963, embodied the hope of the Negro community in Birmingham that law, order, and peace would somehow prevail.*

The patience of an oppressed people cannot endure forever. The Negro citizens of Birmingham for the last several years have hoped in vain for some evidence . . . [of the] . . . resolution of our just grievances.

Birmingham is part of the United States and we are bona fide citizens. Yet the history of Birmingham reveals that very little of the democratic process touches the life of the Negro in Birmingham. We have been segregated racially, exploited economically, and dominated politically. Under the leadership of the Alabama Christian Movement for Human Rights, we sought relief by petition for the repeal of city ordinances requiring segregation and the institution of a merit hiring policy in city employment. We were rebuffed. We then turned to the system of the courts. We weathered set-back after set-back, with all of its costliness, finally winning the terminal, bus, parks and airport cases. The bus decision has been implemented begrudgingly and the parks decision prompted the closing of all municipally-owned recreational facilities with the exception of the zoo and Legion Field. . . .

We have always been a peaceful people, bearing our oppression with superhuman effort. Yet we have been the victims of repeated violence, not only that inflicted by the hoodlum element but also that inflicted by the blatant misuse of police power. . . . For years, while our homes and churches were being bombed, we heard nothing but the rantings and ravings of racist city officials.

The Negro protest for equality and justice has been a voice crying in the wilderness. Most of Birmingham has remained silent, probably out of fear. In the meanwhile, our city has acquired the dubious reputation of being the worst big city in race relations in the United States. Last fall, for a flickering moment, it appeared that sincere community leaders from religion, business and industry discerned the inevitable confrontation in race relations approaching. Their concern for the city's image and commonweal of all its citizens did not run deep enough. Solemn promises were made, pending a postponement of direct action, that we would be joined in a suit seeking the relief of segregation ordinances. Some merchants agreed to desegregate their rest-rooms as a good faith start, some actually complying, only to retreat shortly thereafter. We hold in our hands now, broken faith and broken promises. We believe in the American Dream of democracy, in the Jeffersonian doctrine that "all men are created equal and are endowed by their Creator with certain inalienable rights, among these being life, liberty and the pursuit of happiness."

Twice since September we have deferred our direct action thrust in order that a change in city government would not be made in the hysteria of a community crisis. We act today in full concert with our Hebraic-Christian tradition, the law of morality and the Constitution of our nation. The absence of justice and progress in Birmingham demands that we make a moral witness to give our community a chance to survive. We demonstrate our faith that we believe that the beloved community can come to Birmingham. We appeal to the citizenry of Birmingham, Negro and white, to join us in this witness for decency, morality, self-respect and human dignity. Your individual and corporate support can hasten the day of "liberty and justice for all." This is Birmingham's moment of truth in which every citizen can play his part in her larger destiny. . . .

LETTER FROM A BIRMINGHAM JAIL (1963)

In the spring of 1963, Martin Luther King, Jr. was hauled off to jail in the aftermath of the Birmingham confrontation with Public Safety Commissioner "Bull" Connor and municipal authorities. Beatings, hosings, and the unleasing of vicious dogs could not deter thousands of demonstrating Negroes from risking serious injury, even death, in peaceful parades into the heart of downtown Birmingham. When King was criticized by a group of white clergymen who blamed him for precipitaing the violence, he penned a subdued, but passionate letter of reply to his colleagues, smuggling it out on toilet tissue, the margins of newspapers, indeed any scrap of paper available to him. Excerpts of the letter, printed below, indicate more than just extreme despair and anxiety; they offer eloquent testimony to the flaming moral concern for oppressed humanity which was King's legacy to his fellow Americans.

We have waited for more than 340 years for our constitutional and God-given rights. The nations of Asia and Africa are moving with jetlike speed toward the goal of political independence, and we still creep at horse-and-buggy pace toward the gaining of a cup of coffee at a lunch counter. I guess it is easy for those who have never felt the stinging darts of segregation to say "wait."

But when you have seen vicious mobs lynch your mothers and fathers at will and drown your sisters and brothers at whim; when you have seen hate-filled policemen curse, kick, brutalize and even kill your black brothers and sisters; when you suddenly find your tongue twisted and your speech stammering as you seek to explain to your six-year-old daughter why she can't go to the public amusement park that has just been advertised on television, and see tears welling up in her little eyes when she is told that "Funtown" is closed to colored children, and see the depressing clouds of inferiority begin to form in her little mental sky, and see her begin to distort her little personality by unconsciously developing a bitterness toward white people; when you are humiliated day in and day out by nagging signs reading "white" and "colored," when your first name becomes "nigger" and your middle name becomes "boy" (however old you are) and your last name becomes "John," and when your wife and mother are never given the respected title "Mrs."; when you are harried by day and haunted by night by the fact that you are a Negro, living constantly at tiptoe stance, never quite knowing what to expect next, and plagued with inner fears and outer resentments; when you are forever fighting a degenerating sense of "nobodyness"—then you will understand why we find it difficult to wait.

In your statement you asserted that our actions, even though peaceful, must be condemned because they precipitate violence. Isn't this like condemning the robbed man because his possession of money precipitated the evil act of robbery? Isn't this like condemning Socrates because his unswerving commitment to truth and his philosophical delvings precipitated the misguided popular mind to make him drink the hemlock? Isn't this like condemning Jesus because his unique

God-consciousness and never-ceasing devotion to God's will precipitated the evil act of the Crucifixion?

The question is not whether we will be extremist but what kind of extremist will we be. Will we be extremists for hate or will we be extremists for love? Will we be extremists for the preservation of injustice—or will we be extremists for the cause of justice? In that dramatic scene on Calvary's hill, three men were crucified for the same crime—the crime of extremism. Two were extremists for immorality, and thus fell below their environment. The other, Jesus Christ, was an extremist for love, truth and goodness, and thereby rose above his environment. So, after all, maybe the South, the nation and the world are in dire need of creative extremists.

Before the Pilgrims landed at Plymouth, we were here. Before the pen of Jefferson etched across the pages of history the majestic words of the Declaration of Independence, we were here. For more than two centuries, our foreparents labored in this country without wages; they made cotton "king," and they built the homes of their masters in the midst of brutal injustice and shameful humiliation —and yet out of a bottomless vitality, they continued to thrive and develop. If the inexpressible cruelties of slavery could not stop us, the opposition we now face will surely fail. We will win our freedom because the sacred heritage of our nation and the eternal will of God are embodied in our echoing demands.

A DIGEST OF THE CIVIL RIGHTS ACT OF 1964

The Civil Rights Act of 1964 is subdivided into 11 titles, as follows:

TITLE I—VOTING
TITLE II—PUBLIC ACCOMMODATIONS
TITLE III—PUBLIC FACILITIES
TITLE IV—PUBLIC SCHOOLS
TITLE V—CIVIL RIGHTS COMMISSION
TITLE VI—FEDERAL AID
TITLE VII—EMPLOYMENT
TITLE VIII—STATISTICS
TITLE IX—COURTS
TITLE X—CONCILIATORY SERVICES
TITLE XI—MISCELLANEOUS

Title 1 (voting) prohibits registrars to apply different standards for Negro and white voting applicants, and prevents registrars from disqualifying applicants due to trivial mistakes made on their forms. It also establishes written literacy tests (except for the blind), and provides that an applicant be given a copy of the questions and his answers, should he desire to have it. A sixth-grade education is considered to be a sufficient basis for the presumption of literacy.

Title II (public accommodations) prohibits discrimination in the use of public accommodations—i.e., hotels, motels, restaurants, gasoline stations, and places of amusement whose operations involve interstate commerce. The constitutionality of this title has already been upheld by the Supreme Court of the United States in two test cases, both of which were decided on December 14, 1964. These are: *Heart of Atlanta* v. *United States*, (see page 193, and *Katzenbach* v. *Mc-*

Clung (379 U.S. 802, 803). Title II also enables the Attorney General to bring suit in a federal court against all persons or groups found to be resisting enforcement of its provisions.

Title III (public facilities) is designed to guarantee that Negroes be accorded equal access to, and treatment in, all public-owned and -operated facilities, including parks, stadiums, and swimming pools. As in the case of Title II, this section makes it possible for the Attorney General to bring suit for its enforcement if private individuals are unable to do so.

Title IV (public schools) authorizes the federal government to provide technical and financial aid to all school districts engaged in the process of desegregation. Once again, the Attorney General is empowered to sue for school desegregation, provided private citizens are not in a position to do so.

Title V (Civil Rights Commission) extends the tenure of the Civil Rights Commission until January 31, 1968.

Title VI (federal aid) guarantees that no person shall be subject to any form of racial discrimination in any program which is receiving federal financial aid. It also empowers federal agencies to take appropriate steps to counteract any such discrimination, particularly by denying federal funds to any state or local agencies which practice discrimination.

Title VII (employment) prohibits discrimination on the part of employers or unions with more than 100 employees or members during the first year from the date the Act takes effect. Four years from that date, the number of employees for both unions and employers is to be reduced to 25. This title also establishes a commission to investigate charges of discrimination in employment or employee organizations and, where necessary, to take appropriate steps in mediating such charges. Where a "pattern or practice" of resistance to the provisions of this title becomes definitely identifiable, the Attorney General is empowered to bring suit before a three-judge federal court.

Title VIII (statistics) directs the Census Bureau to compile voting statistics by race in areas of the country designated by the Civil Rights Commission.

Title IX (courts) allows higher federal courts to prevent lower federal courts from sending a civil rights case back to a state or local court—particularly when such a step by the lower court might compromise the case of an appellant. This reverses a former trend whereby the decision of such a federal court to return a case to a state or local court could not be voided.

Title X (conciliatory services) establishes a Community Relations Service (CRS) in the Department of Commerce for the purpose of mediating racial disputes at the local level. The CRS generally intervenes only after it has received a request to do so from appropriate local officials.

Title XI (miscellaneous) assures the right of jury trial in criminal contempt cases which grow out of any part of the act, save Title I. This title in no way supercedes state laws which already afford protection similar to that which is offered in the provisions of the Civil Rights Act. Furthermore, it provides that the Civil Rights Act as a whole will not be affected by the possible invalidation of any single portion of it.

(President Lyndon B. Johnson announced the signing of the bill in a nationwide television address made in July 1964.)

MY FELLOW AMERICANS:

I am about to sign into law the Civil Rights Act of 1964. I want to take this occasion to talk to you about what that law means to every American.

One hundred and eighty-eight years ago this week a small band of valiant men began a long struggle for freedom.

They pledged their lives, their fortunes and their sacred honor not only to found a nation but to forge an ideal of freedom, not only for political independence but for personal liberty, not only to eliminate foreign rule but to establish the rule of justice in the affairs of men.

That struggle was a turning point in our history.

Today in far corners of distant continents the ideals of those American patriots still shape the struggles of men who hunger for freedom.

This is a proud triumph. Yet those who founded our country knew that freedom would be secure only if each generation thought to renew and enlarge its meaning.

From the Minutemen at Concord to the soldiers in Vietnam, each generation has been equal to that trust.

Americans of every race and color have worked to build a nation of widening opportunities.

Now, our generation of Americans, has been called on to continue the unending search for justice within our own borders.

We believe that all men are created equal—yet many are denied equal treatment.

We believe that all men have certain unalienable rights—yet many Americans do not enjoy those rights.

We believe that all men are entitled to the blessings of liberty—yet millions are being deprived of those blessings, not because of their own failures, but because of the color of their skin.

The reasons are deeply imbedded in history and tradition and the nature of man. We can understand without rancor or hatred how this all happened. But it cannot continue. . . .

We must not approach the observance and enforcement of this law in a vengeful spirit. Its purpose is not to punish. Its purpose is not to divide but to end divisions, divisions which have lasted all too long.

Its purpose is national not regional. Its purpose is to promote a more abiding commitment to freedom, a more constant pursuit of justice and a deeper respect for human dignity.

We will achieve these goals because most Americans are law-abiding citizens who want to do what is right. This is why the Civil Rights Act relies first on voluntary compliance, then on the efforts of local communities and states to secure the rights of citizens.

It provides for the national authority to step in only when others cannot or will not do the job.

This Civil Rights Act is a challenge to all of us to go to work in our communities and our states, in our homes and in our hearts to eliminate the last vestiges of injustice in our beloved country. . . .

My fellow citizens, we have come now to a time of testing. We must not fail. . .

PRESIDENT JOHNSON'S VOTING RIGHTS ADDRESS: WE SHALL OVERCOME

In an address delivered before a joint session of Congress on March 15, 1965, President Johnson placed the full weight of his office behind the passage of legislation needed to enforce the 15th Amendment, which guarantees all Americans the right to vote. The speech takes its name from the following lines:

> *". . . it's not just Negroes, but really it's all of us who must overcome the crippling legacy of bigotry and injustice. And we shall overcome." (Emphasis supplied.)*

Mr. Speaker, Mr. President, members of the Congress, I speak tonight for the dignity of man and the destiny of democracy.

I urge every member of both parties, Americans of all religions and of all colors, from every section of this country, to join me in that cause.

At times, history and fate meet at a single time in a single place to shape a turning point in man's unending search for freedom.

So it was at Lexington and Concord. So it was a century ago at Appomattox. So it was last week in Selma, Ala.

There, long suffering men and women peacefully protested the denial of their rights as Americans. Many were brutally assaulted. One good man—a man of God—was killed. . . .

There is no Negro problem. There is no Southern problem. There is no Northern problem. There is only an American

Our fathers believed that if this noble view of the rights of man was to flourish it must be rooted in democracy. The most basic right of all was the right to choose your own leaders.

The history of this country in large measure is the history of expansion of that right to all of our people. Many of the issues of civil rights are very complex and most difficult. But about this there can and should be no argument: every American citizen must have an equal right to vote. . . .

Wednesday, I will send to Congress a law designed to eliminate illegal barriers to the right to vote. . . .

This bill will strike down restrictions to voting in all elections, Federal, state and local, which have been used to deny Negroes the right to vote.

This bill will establish a simple, uniform standard which cannot be used, however ingenious the effort, to flout our Constitution. It will provide for citizens to be registered by officials of the United States Government, if the state officials refuse to register them.

It will eliminate tedious, unnecessary lawsuits which delay the right to vote.

Finally, this legislation will insure that properly registered individuals are not prohibited from voting.

I will welcome the suggestions from all the members of Congress—I have no doubt that I will get some—on ways and means to strengthen this law and to make it effective.

But experience has plainly shown that this is the only path to carry out the command of the Constitution. To those who seek to avoid action by their national Government in their home communities, who want to and who seek to maintain purely local control over elections, the answer is simple: Open your polling places to all your people.

Allow men and women to register and vote whatever the color of their skin. . . .

There is no constitutional issue here. The command of the Constitution is plain. There is no moral issue. It is wrong—deadly wrong—to deny any of your fellow Americans the right to vote in this country.

There is no issue of states rights, or national rights. There is only the struggle for human rights. . . .

So I ask you to join me in working long hours and nights and weekends, if necessary, to pass this bill.

And I don't make that request lightly, for from the window where I sit with the problems of our country I recognize that from outside this chamber is the outraged conscience of a nation, the grave concern of many nations and the harsh judgment of history on our acts.

But even if we pass this bill the battle will not be over.

What happened in Selma is part of a far larger movement which reaches into every section and state of America. It is the effort of American Negroes to secure for themselves the full blessings of American life.

Their cause must be our cause too. Because it's not just Negroes, but really it's all of us who must overcome the crippling legacy of bigotry and injustice. And we shall overcome. . . .

A century has passed—more than 100 years—since equality was promised, and yet the Negro is not equal.

A century has passed since the day of promise, and the promise is unkept. The time of justice has now come, and I tell you that I believe sincerely that no force can hold it back. It is right in the eyes of man and God that it should come, and when it does, I think that day will brighten the lives of every American.

For Negroes are not the only victims. How many white children have gone uneducated? How many white families have lived in stark poverty? How many white lives have been scarred by fear, because

There is really no part of America where the promise of equality has been fully kept. In Buffalo as well as in Birmingham, in Philadelphia as well as Selma, Americans are struggling for the fruits of freedom. This is one nation. What happens in Selma and Cincinnati is a matter of legitimate concern to every American. . . .

And I have not the slightest doubt that good men from everywhere in this country, from the Great Lakes to the Gulf of Mexico, from the Golden Gate to the harbors along the Atlantic, will rally now together in this cause to vindicate the freedom of all Americans.

For all of us owe this duty and I believe that all of us will respond to it. Your President makes that request of every American.

The real hero of this struggle is the American Negro. His actions and protests, his courage to risk safety, and even to risk his life, have awakened the conscience of this nation. His demonstrations have been designed to call attention to injustice, designed to provoke change; designed to stir reform.

He has called upon us to make good the promise of America. And who among us can say that we would have made the same progress were it not for his persistent bravery and his faith in American democracy?

For at the real heart of the battle for equality is a deep-seated belief in the democratic process. Equality depends, not on the force of arms or tear gas, but depends upon the force of moral right—not on recourse to violence, but on respect for law and order.

There have been many pressures upon your President and there will be others as the days come and go. But I pledge you tonight that we intend to fight this battle where it should be fought—in the courts, and in the Congress, and in the hearts of men.

We must preserve the right of free speech and the right of free assembly.

But the right of free speech does not carry with it—as has been said—the right to holler fire in a crowded theatre.

We must preserve the right to free assembly. But free assembly does not carry with it the right to block public thoroughfares to traffic.

We do have a right to protest. And a right to march under conditions that do not infringe the constitutional rights of our neighbors. And I intend to protect all those rights as long as I am permitted to serve in this office.

We will guard against violence, knowing it strikes from our hands the very weapons which we seek—progress, obedience to law, and belief in American values. . . .

The bill I am presenting to you will be known as a civil rights bill.

But in a larger sense, most of the program I am recommending is a civil rights program. Its obiect is to open the city of hope to all people of all races, because all Americans just must have the right to vote, and we are going to give them that right.

All Americans must have the privileges of citizenship, regardless of race, and they are going to have those privileges of citizenship regardless of race.

But I would like to caution you and remind you that to exercise these privileges takes much more than just legal right. It requires a trained mind and a healthy body. It requires a decent home and the chance to find a job and the opportunity to escape from the clutches of poverty.

Of course people cannot contribute to the nation if they are never taught to read or write; if their bodies are stunted from hunger; if their sickness goes untended; if their life is spent in hopeless poverty, just drawing a welfare check.

So we want to open the gates to opportunity. But we're also going to give all our people, black and white, the help that they need to walk through those gates. . . .

I want to be the President who helped to feed the hungry and to prepare them to be taxpayers instead of tax eaters.

Above the pyramid on the great seal of the United States it says in Latin, "God has favored our undertaking." God will not favor everything that we do. It is rather our duty to divine His will. But I cannot help believe that He truly understands and that He really favors the undertaking that we begin here tonight.

THE VOTING RIGHTS ACT OF 1965

The 1965 Voting Rights Law was an outgrowth of the protest demonstrations organized by Negroes to draw attention to discriminatory voter-registration practices in several Southern states. These were particularly prevalent in Alabama, Arkansas, Mississippi, Texas and Virginia, which, until passage of the 24th Amendment to the U.S. Constitution, still required payment of a poll tax as a prerequisite for voting in national elections.

The 1965 law abolished literacy, knowledge and character tests as qualifications for voting in those states where less than one-half of the eligible population had voted, or been entitled to vote, in November 1964. It empowered federal registrars to register potential voters in any county where such tests have been suspended, and where, in the judgment of the Attorney General of the United States, registrars are indeed necessary to enforce the 15th Amendment. The Attorney General also has the right to take whatever legal action he deems necessary to eliminate any equivalent of the poll tax.

The text of the act follows:

Be it enacted by the Senate and House of Representatives of the United States of America in Congress assembled, That this Act shall be known as the "Voting Rights Act of 1965".

SEC. 2. No voting qualification or prerequisite to voting, or standard, practice, or procedure shall be imposed or applied by any State or political subdivision to deny or abridge the right of any citizen of the United States to vote on account of race or color.

SEC. 3. (a) Whenever the Attorney General institutes a proceeding under any statute to enforce the guarantees of the fifteenth amendment in any State or political subdivision the court shall authorize the appointment of Federal examiners by the United States Civil Service Commission in accordance with section 6 to serve for such period of time and for such political subdivisions as the court shall determine is appropriate to enforce the guarantees of the fifteenth amendment (1) as part of any interlocutory order if the court determines that the appointment of such examiners is necessary to enforce such guarantees or (2) as part of any final judgment if the court finds that violations of the fifteenth amendment justifying equitable relief have occurred in such State or subdivision: *Provided,* That the court need not authorize the appointment of examiners if any incidents of denial or abridgement of the right to vote on account of race or color (1) have been few in number and have been promptly and effectively corrected by State or local action, (2) the continuing effect of such incidents has been eliminated, and (3) there is no reasonable probability of their recurrence in the future.

(b) If in a proceeding instituted by the Attorney General under any statute to enforce the guarantees of the fifteenth amendment in any State or political subdivision the court finds that a test or device has been used for the purpose or with the effect of denying or abridging the right of any citizen of the United States to vote on account of race or color, it shall suspend the use of tests and devices in such State or political subdivisions as the court shall determine is appropriate and for such period as it deems necessary.

(c) If in any proceeding instituted by the Attorney General under any statute to enforce the guarantees of the fifteenth amendment in any State or political subdivision the court finds that violations of the fifteenth amendment justifying equitable relief have occurred within the territory of such State or political subdivision, the court, in addition to such relief as it may grant, shall retain jurisdiction for such period as it may deem appropriate and during such period no voting qualification or prerequisite to voting, or standard, practice, or procedure with respect to voting different from that in force or effect at the time the proceeding was commenced shall be enforced unless and until the court finds that such qualification, prerequisite, standard, practice, or procedure does not have the purpose and will not have the effect of denying or abridging the right to vote on account of race or color: *Provided,* That such qualification, prerequisite, standard, practice, or procedure may be enforced if the qualification, prerequisite, standard, practice, or procedure has been submitted by the chief legal officer or other appropriate official of such State or subdivision to the Attorney General and the Attorney General has not interposed an objection within sixty days after such submission, except that neither the court's finding nor the Attorney General's failure to object shall bar a subsequent action to enjoin enforcement of such qualification, prerequisite, standard, practice, or procedure.

SEC. 4. (a) To assure that the right of citizens of the United States to vote is not denied or abridged on account of race or color, no citizen shall be denied the right to vote in any Federal, State, or local election because of his failure to comply with any test or device in any State with respect to which the determinations have been made under subsection (b) or in any political subdivision with respect to which such determinations have been made as a separate unit, unless the United States District Court for the District of Columbia in an action for a declaratory judgment brought by such State or subdivision against the United States has determined that no such test or device has been used during the five years preceding the filing of the action for the purpose or with the effect of denying or abridging the right to vote on account of race or color: *Provided,* That no such declaratory judgment shall issue with respect to any plaintiff for a period of five years after the entry of a final judgment of any court of the United States, other than the denial of a declaratory judgment under this section, whether entered prior to or after the enactment of this Act, determining that denials or abridgments of the right to vote on account of race or color through the use of such tests or devices have occurred anywhere in the territory of such plaintiff.

(e) (1) Congress hereby declares that to secure the rights under the fourteenth amendment of persons educated in American-flag schools in which the predominant classroom language was other than English, it is necessary to prohibit the States from conditioning the right to vote of such persons on ability to read, write, understand, or interpret any matter in the English language.

(2) No person who demonstrates that he has successfully completed the sixth primary grade in a public school in, or a private school accredited by, any State or territory, the District of Columbia, or the Commonwealth of Puerto Rico in which the predominant classroom language was other than English, shall be denied the right to vote in any Federal, State, or local election because of his inability to read, write, understand, or interpret any matter in the English language, except that in States in which State law provides that a different level of education is presumptive of literacy, he shall demonstrate that he has successfully completed an equivalent level of education in a public school in, or a private school accredited by, any State or territory, the District of Columbia, or the Commonwealth of Puerto Rico in which the predominant classroom language was other than English.

SEC. 5. Whenever a State or political subdivision with respect to which the prohibitions set forth in section 4(a) are in effect shall enact or seek to administer any voting qualification or prerequisite to voting, or standard, practice, or procedure with respect to voting different from that in force or effect on November 1, 1964, such State or subdivision may institute an action in the United States District Court for the District of Columbia for a declaratory judgment that such qualification, prerequisite, standard, practice, or procedure does not have the purpose and will not have the effect of denying or abridging the right to vote on account of race or color, and unless and until the court enters such judgment no person shall be denied the right to vote for failure to comply with such qualification, prerequisite, standard, practice, or procedure.

SEC. 6. Whenever (a) a court has authorized the appointment of examiners pursuant to the provisions of section 3(a), or (b) unless a declaratory judgment has been rendered under section 4(a), the Attorney General certifies with respect to any political subdivision named in, or included within the scope of, determinations made under section 4(b) that (1) he has received complaints in writing from twenty or more residents of such political subdivision alleging that they have been denied the right to vote under color of law on account of race or color, and that he believes such complaints to be meritorious, or (2) that in his judgment (considering, among other factors, whether the ratio of nonwhite persons to white persons registered to vote within such subdivision appears to him to be reasonably attributable to violations of the fifteenth amendment or whether substantial evidence exists that bona fide efforts are being made within such subdivision to comply with the fifteenth amendment), the appointment of examiners is otherwise necessary to enforce the guarantees of the fifteenth amendment, the Civil Service Commission shall appoint as many examiners for such subdivision as it may deem appropriate to prepare and maintain lists of persons eligible to vote in Federal, State, and local elections.

SEC. 7. (a) The examiners for each political subdivision shall, at such places as the Civil Service Commission shall by regulation designate, examine applicants concerning their qualifications for voting. An application to an examiner shall be in such form as the Commission may require and shall contain allegations that the applicant is not otherwise registered to vote.

(b) Any person whom the examiner finds, in accordance with instructions received under section 9(b), to have the qualifications prescribed by State law not inconsistent with the Constitution and laws of the United States shall promptly be placed on a list of eligible voters.

(c) The examiner shall issue to each person whose name appears on such a list a certificate evidencing his eligibility to vote.

(d) A person whose name appears on such a list shall be removed therefrom by an examiner if (1) such person has been successfully challenged in accordance with the procedure prescribed in section 9, or (2) he has been determined by an examiner to have lost his eligibility to vote under State law not inconsistent with the Constitution and the laws of the United States.

SEC. 8. Whenever an examiner is serving under this Act in any political subdivision, the Civil Service Commission may assign, at the request of the Attorney General, one or more persons, who may be officers of the United States, (1) to enter and attend at any place for holding an election in such subdivision for the purpose of observing whether persons who are entitled to vote are being permitted to vote, and (2) to enter and attend at any place for tabulating the votes cast at any election held in such subdivision for the purpose of observing whether votes cast by persons entitled to vote are being properly tabulated. Such persons so assigned shall report to an examiner appointed for such political subdivision, to the Attorney General, and if the appointment of examiners has been authorized pursuant to section 3(a), to the court.

SEC. 9. (a) Any challenge to a listing on an eligibility list prepared by an examiner shall be heard and determined by a hearing officer appointed by and responsible to the Civil Service Commission and under such rules as the Commission shall by regulation prescribe.

SEC. 10. (a) The Congress finds that the requirement of the payment of a poll tax as a precondition to voting (i) precludes persons of limited means from voting or imposes unreasonable financial hardship upon such persons as a precondition to their exercise of the franchise, (ii) does not bear a reasonable relationship to any legitimate State interest in the conduct of elections, and (iii) in some areas has the purpose or effect of denying persons the right to vote because of race or color. Upon the basis of these findings, Congress declares that the constitutional right of citizens to vote is denied or abridged in some areas by the requirement of the payment of a poll tax as a precondition to voting.

SEC. 11. (a) No person acting under color of law shall fail or refuse to permit any person to vote who is entitled to vote under any provision of this Act or is otherwise qualified to vote, or willfully fail or refuse to tabulate, count, and report such person's vote.

(b) No person, whether acting under color of law or otherwise, shall intimidate, threaten, or coerce, or attempt to intimidate, threaten, or coerce any person for voting or attempting to vote, or intimidate, threaten, or coerce, or attempt to intimidate, threaten, or coerce any person for urging or aiding any person to vote or attempt to vote, or intimidate, threaten, or coerce any person for exercising any powers or duties under section 3(a), 6, 8, 9, 10, or 12(e).

(c) Whoever knowingly or willfully gives false information as to his name, address, or period of residence in the voting district for the purpose of establishing his eligibility to register or vote, or conspires with another individual for the purpose of encouraging his false registration to vote or illegal voting, or pays or offers to pay or accepts payment either for registration to vote or for voting shall be fined not more than $10,000 or imprisoned not more than five years, or both: *Provided, however,* That this provision shall be applicable only to general, special, or primary elections held solely or in part for the purpose of selecting or electing any candidate for the office of President, Vice President, presidential elector, Member of the United States Senate, Member of the United States House of Representatives, or Delegates or Commissioners from the territories or possessions, or Resident Commissioner of the Commonwealth of Puerto Rico.

(d) Whoever, in any matter within the jurisdiction of an examiner or hearing officer knowingly and willfully falsifies or conceals a material fact, or makes any false, fictitious, or fraudulent statements or representations, or makes or uses any false writing or document knowing the same to contain any false, fictitious, or fraudulent statement or entry, shall be fined not more than $10,000 or imprisoned not more than five years, or both.

SEC. 12. (a) Whoever shall deprive or attempt to deprive any person of any right secured by section 2, 3, 4, 5, 7, or 10 or shall violate section 11 (a) or (b), shall be fined not more than $5,000, or imprisoned not more than five years, or both.

(b) Whoever, within a year following an election in a political subdivision in which an examiner has been appointed (1) destroys, defaces, mutilates, or otherwise alters the marking of a paper ballot which has been cast in such election, or (2) alters any official record of voting in such election tabulated from a voting machine or otherwise, shall be fined not more than $5,000, or imprisoned not more than five years, or both.

(c) Whoever conspires to violate the provisions of subsection (a) or (b) of this section, or interferes with any right secured by section 2, 3, 4, 5, 7, 10, or 11 (a) or (b) shall be fined not more than $5,000, or imprisoned not more than five years, or both.

(d) Whenever any person has engaged or there are reasonable grounds to believe that any person is about to engage in any act or practice prohibited by section 2, 3, 4, 5, 7, 10, 11, or subsection (b) of this section, the Attorney General may institute for the United States, or in the name of the United States, an action for preventive relief, including an application for a temporary or permanent injunction, restraining order, or other order, and including an order directed to the State and State or local election officials to require them (1) to permit persons listed under this Act to vote and (2) to count such votes.

(e) Whenever in any political subdivision in which there are examiners appointed pursuant to this Act any persons allege to such an examiner within forty-eight hours after the closing of the polls that notwithstanding (1) their listing under this Act or registration by an appropriate election official and (2) their eligibility to vote, they have not been permitted to vote in such election, the examiner shall forthwith notify the Attorney General if such allegations in his opinion appear to be well founded. Upon receipt of such notification, the Attorney General may forthwith file with the district court an application for an order providing for the marking, casting, and counting of the ballots of such persons and requiring the inclusion of their votes in the total vote before the results of such election shall be deemed final and any force or effect given thereto. The district court shall hear and determine such matters immediately after the filing of such application. The remedy provided in this subsection shall not preclude any remedy available under State or Federal law.

(f) The district courts of the United States shall have jurisdiction of proceedings instituted pursuant to this section and shall exercise the same without regard to whether a person asserting rights under the provisions of this Act shall have exhausted any administrative or other remedies that may be provided by law.

SEC. 14. (a) All cases of criminal contempt arising under the provisions of this Act shall be governed by section 151 of the Civil Rights Act of 1957 (42 U.S.C. 1995).

(b) No court other than the District Court for the District of Columbia or a court of appeals in any proceeding under section 9 shall have jurisdiction to issue any declaratory judgment pursuant to section 4 or section 5 or any restraining order or temporary or permanent injunction against the execution or enforcement of any provision of this Act or any action of any Federal officer or employee pursuant hereto.

(c) (1) The terms "vote" or "voting" shall include all action necessary to make a vote effective in any primary, special, or general election, including, but not limited to, registration, listing pursuant to this Act, or other action required by law prerequisite to voting, casting a ballot, and having such ballot counted properly and included in the appropriate totals of votes cast with respect to candidates for public or party office and propositions for which votes are received in an election.

SEC. 16. The Attorney General and the Secretary of Defense, jointly, shall make a full and complete study to determine whether, under the laws or practices of any State or States, there are preconditions to voting, which might tend to result in discrimination against citizens serving in the Armed Forces of the United States seeking to vote. Such officials shall, jointly, make a report to the Congress not later than June 30, 1966, containing the results of such study, together with a list of any States in which such preconditions exist, and shall include in such report such recommendations for legislation as they deem advisable to prevent discrimination in voting against citizens serving in the Armed Forces of the United States.

BLACK PANTHER MANIFESTO (1966)

The tightly knit, close-fisted Black Panther Party relies on a strict and uncompromising regimen to mold its members into a unified and cohesive revolutionary force. Like the Muslims, the Party denounces all intoxicants, drugs and artificial stimulants "while doing party work." The intellectual fare of every party member is the 10-point program (supplemented by daily reading of political developments), which every member is obliged to know and understand, presumably even to commit to memory. Military training and political education courses are mandatory; strict adherence to central directives is also prescribed. Grants, poverty funds, and other "outside money" may not be accepted by chapters, branches, or members of the party unless National Headquarters first lends its approval. Apart from policy, there is the matter of consistent ideology. This is embodied in the 10-point program drafted in 1966 and enumerated below.

1. We want freedom. We want power to determine the destiny of our Black Community.

We believe that black people will not be free until we are able to determine our destiny.

2. We want full employment for our people.

We believe that the federal government is responsible and obligated to give every man employment or a guaranteed income. We believe that if the white American businessman will not give full employment, then the means of production should be taken from the businessmen and placed in the community so that the people of the community can organize and employ all of its people and give a high standard of living.

3. We want an end to the robbery by the CAPITALIST of our Black Community.

We believe that this racist government has robbed us and now we are demanding the overdue debt of forty acres and two mules. Forty acres and two mules was promised 100 years ago as restitution for slave labor and mass murder of black people. We will accept the payment in currency which will be distributed to our many communities. The Germans are now aiding the Jews in Israel for the genocide of the Jewish people. The Germans murdered six million Jews. The American racist has taken part in the slaughter of over fifty million black people, therefore, we feel that this is a modest demand that we make.

4. We want decent housing, fit for shelter of human beings.

We believe that if the white landlords will not give decent housing to our black community, then the housing and the land should be made into cooperatives so that our community, with government aid, can build and make decent housing for its people.

5. We want education for our people that exposes the true nature of this decadent American society. We want education that teaches us our true history and our role in the present-day society.

We believe in an educational system that will give to our people a knowledge of self. If a man does not have knowledge of himself and his position in society and the world, then he has little chance to relate to anything else.

6. We want all black men to be exempt from military service.

We believe that Black people should not be forced to fight in the military service to defend a racist government that does not protect us. We will not fight and kill other people of color in the world who, like black people, are being victimized by the white racist government of America. We will protect ourselves from the force and violence of the racist police and the racist military, by whatever means necessary.

7. We want an immediate end to POLICE BRUTALITY and MURDER of black people.

We believe we can end police brutality in our black community by organizing black self-defense groups that are dedicated to defending our black community from racist police oppression and brutality. The Second Amendment to the Constitution of the United States gives a right to bear arms. We therefore believe that all black people should arm themselves for self-defense.

8. We want freedom for all black men held in federal, state, county and city prisons and jails.

We believe that all black people should be released from the many jails and prisons because they have not received a fair and impartial trial.

9. We want all black people when brought to trial to be tried in court by a jury of their peer group or people from their black communities, as defined by the constitution of the United States.

We believe that the courts should follow the United States Constitution so that black people will receive fair trials. The 14th Amendment of the U.S. Constitution gives a man a right to be tried by his peer group. A peer is a person from a similar economic, social, religious, geographical, environmental, historical and racial background. To do this the court will be forced to select a jury from the black community from which the black defendant came. We have been, and are being tried by all-white juries that have no understanding of the "average reasoning man" of the black community.

10. We want land, bread, housing, education, clothing, justice and peace. And as our major political objective, a United Nations-supervised plebiscite to be held throughout the black colony in which only black colonial subjects will be allowed to participate, for the purpose of determining the will of black people as to their national destiny.

When, in the course of human events, it becomes necessary for one people to dissolve the political bands which have connected them with another, and to assume, among the powers of the earth, the separate and equal station to which the laws of nature and nature's God entitle them, a decent respect to the opinions of mankind requires that they should declare the causes which impel them to the separation.

We hold these truths to be self-evident, that all men are created equal; that they are endowed by their Creator with certain unalienable rights; that among these are life, liberty, and the pursuit of happiness. **That, to secure these rights, governments are instituted among men, deriving their just powers from the consent of the governed; that, whenever any form of government becomes destructive of these ends, it is the right of the people to alter or to abolish it, and to institute a new government, laying its foundation on such principles, and organizing its powers in such form, as to them shall seem most likely to effect their safety and happiness.** Prudence, indeed, will dictate that governments long established should not be changed for light and transient causes; and, accordingly, all experience hath shown, that mankind are more disposed to suffer, while evils are sufferable, than to right themselves by abolishing the forms to which they are accustomed. **But, when a long train of abuses and usurpations, pursuing invariably the same object, evinces a design to reduce them under absolute despotism, it is their right, it is their duty, to throw off such government, and to provide new guards for their future security.**

THE CIVIL RIGHTS ACT OF 1968: PROVISION FOR OPEN HOUSING

Just as the 1964 Civil Rights Bill reflected the nation's belatedly noble attempt to pay tribute to the memory of an assassinated President, John F. Kennedy, so too did the 1968 Civil Rights Act represent a memorial gesture in honor of an assassinated national figure, Martin Luther King, Jr. In both cases. it was Lyndon B. Johnson who presided over the formal passage of the legislation. As originally drafted in the House, the bill was impotent and uninspiring; in the Senate, however, liberal Democrats and Republicans shaped an open-housing provision with some teeth in it and created an expanded package covering the Constitutional rights of Indians and containing two anti-riot clauses. Had it not been for King's death, however, chances are that the conservative mood of the 1968 House would have prevailed, and the bill would have been shelved. With the death of Dr. King, however, the issue became, in the words of House Speaker John McCormack, one of "human dignity," rather than political partisanship. Within a week of King's death, the bill passed the House by a 249-171 margin. NAACP lobbyists for the bill were delighted; black militants, on the other hand, branded the legislation a colossal hoax. To the moderates, the opening of 80% of the nation's housing to Negroes represented the key to unlocking the prison of the ghetto; to the militants, however, 80% of the nation's housing was out of the economic reach of most ghetto residents and so nothing more than an unattainable luxury.

DISCRIMINATION IN THE SALE OR RENTAL OF HOUSING

Sec. 804. As made applicable by section 803 and except as exempted by sections 803(b) and 807, it shall be unlawful—

(a) To refuse to sell or rent after the making of a bona fide offer, or to refuse to negotiate for the sale or rental of, or otherwise make unavailable or deny, a dwelling to any person because of race, color, religion, or national origin.

(b) To discriminate against any person in the terms, conditions, or privileges of sale or rental of a dwelling, or in the provision of services or facilities in connection therewith, because of race, color, religion, or national origin.

(c) To make, print, or publish, or cause to be made, printed, or published any notice, statement, or advertisement, with respect to the sale or rental of a dwelling that indicates any preference, limitation, or discrimination based on race, color, religion, or national origin, or an intention to make any such preference, limitation, or discrimination.

(d) To represent to any person because of race, color, religion, or national origin that any dwelling is not available for inspection, sale, or rental when such dwelling is in fact so available.

(e) For profit, to induce or attempt to induce any person to sell or rent any dwelling by representations regarding the entry or prospective entry into the neighborhood of a person or persons of a particular race, color, religion, or national origin.

TITLE I—INTERFERENCE WITH FEDERALLY PROTECTED ACTIVITIES

(b) Whoever, whether or not acting under color of law, by force or threat of force willfully injures, intimidates or interferes with, or attempts to injure, intimidate or interfere with—

(1) any person because he is or has been, or in order to intimidate such person or any other person or any class of persons from—

(A) voting or qualifying to vote, qualifying or campaigning as a candidate for elective office, or qualifying or acting as a poll watcher, or any legally authorized election official, in any primary, special, or general election; . . .

(2) any person because of his race, color, religion or national origin . . .

(3) during or incident to a riot or civil disorder, any person engaged in a business in commerce or affecting commerce . . . shall be fined not more than $1,000, or imprisoned not more than one year, or both; and if bodily injury results shall be fined not more than $10,000, or imprisoned not more than ten years, or both; and if death results shall be subject to imprisonment for any term of years or for life.

Chapter 102—RIOTS

(a) (1) Whoever travels in interstate or foreign commerce or uses any facility of interstate or foreign commerce, including, but not limited to, the mail, telegraph, telephone, radio, or television, with intent—

(A) to incite a riot; or

(B) to organize, promote, encourage, participate in, or carry on a riot; or

(C) to commit any act of violence in furtherance of a riot; . . . shall be fined not more than $10,000, or imprisoned not more than five years, or both.

TITLE II—RIGHTS OF INDIANS

Sec. 202. No Indian tribe in exercising powers of self-government shall—

(1) make or enforce any law prohibiting the free exercise of religion, or abridging the freedom of speech, or of the press, or the right of the people peaceably to assemble and to petition for a redress of grievances;

(2) violate the right of the people to be secure in their persons, houses, papers, and effects against unreasonable search and seizures, nor issue warrants, but upon probable cause, supported by oath or affirmation, and particularly describing the place to be searched and the person or thing to be seized;

(3) subject any person for the same offense to be twice put in jeopardy;

(4) compel any person in any criminal case to be a witness against himself;

(5) take any private property for a public use without just compensation; . . .

TITLE IX—PREVENTION OF INTIMIDATION IN FAIR HOUSING CASES

Sec. 901. Whoever, whether or not acting under color of law, by force or threat of force willfully injures, intimidates or interferes with, or attempts to injure, intimidate or interfere with—

(a) any person because of his race, color, religion or national origin and because he is or has been selling, purchasing, renting, financing, occupying, or contracting or negotiating for the sale . . . of any dwelling . . . shall be fined not more than $1,000, or imprisoned not more than one year, or both; and if bodily injury results shall be fined not more than $10,000, or imprisoned not more than ten years, or both; and if death results shall be subject to imprisonment for any term of years or for life.

THE BLACK MANIFESTO (1969)

On Sunday May 4, 1969, James Forman strode down the center aisle of New York's Riverside Church, planted himself in front of the congregation at the communion service, and boldly announced that the National Black Economic Development Conference was demanding 500 million dollars from America's churches and synagogues as "reparations" for the injustices suffered by blacks under slavery and capitalism. A murmur tinged with fear, excitement and mortification swept through the congregation which had hardly expected such a revolutionary introduction to the work it had in fact sponsored under the Interreligious Foundation for Community Organization (IFCO). Forman had simply crystallized the thinking of many black leaders who had met in Detroit in April 1968 to discuss the economic aspects of black power. At the close of the meeting, the Black Economic Development Conference was a viable entity, and the "reparations" principle was a stated ingredient of its program. The Manifesto, in fact, contained several plausible projects, including the establishment of a Southern land bank and the construction of a new black university in the South. Forman's use of shock treatment to promote such ideas may have alienated many moderates, even as it drew outright rejection from the New York Archdiocese and a variety of Jewish groups. The National Council of Churches, however, did not dismiss the Manifesto because of its unorthodox presentation, choosing instead to reaffirm its sense of sharing "the aspirations of the black people of this country." The Episcopal Church later went a step further, earmarking $200,000 at its convention for the interdenominational National Committee of Black Churchmen, a loosely knit church group endorsing the Forman plan. Early in 1970, the Massachusetts Conference of the United Church of Christ granted the newly created Black Ecumenical Commission (another caucus of black clergymen) one million dollars to finance unspecified programs in the area of race relations and development. Thus, in the words of one minister, the Protestants were "taking care of our own."

We the black people assembled in Detroit, Michigan for the National Black Economic Development Conference are fully aware that we have been forced to come together because racist white America has exploited our resources, our minds, our bodies, our labor. For centuries we have been forced to live as colonized people inside the United States, victimized by the most vicious, racist system in the world. We have helped build the most industrial country in the world. We are therefore demanding of the white Christian churches and Jewish synagogues which are part and parcel of the system of capitalism, that they begin to pay reparations to black people in this country. We are demanding $500,000,000 from the Christian white churches and the Jewish synagogues. This total comes to fifteen dollars per nigger. This is a low estimate, for we maintain there are probably more than 30,000,000 black people in this country. Fifteen dollars a nigger is not a large sum of money, and we know that the churches and synagogues have a tremendous wealth and its membership, white America, has profited and still exploits black people. We are also not unaware that the exploitation of colored peoples around the world is aided and abetted by the white Christian churches and synagogues. This demand for $500,000,000 is not an idle resolution or empty words. Fifteen dollars for every black brother and sister in the United States is only the beginning of the reparations due us as people who have been exploited and degraded, brutalized, killed and persecuted. Underneath all of this exploitation, the racism of this country has produced a psychological effect upon us that we are beginning to shake off. We are no longer afraid to demand our full rights as a people in this decadent society.

We are demanding the $500,000,000 be spent in the following way:

1. We call for the establishment of a southern land bank to help our brothers and sisters who have to leave their land because of racist pressure, for people who want to establish cooperative farms, but who have no funds. We have seen too many farmers evicted from their homes because they have dared to defy the white racism of this country. We need money for land. We must fight for massive sums of money for this Southern Land Bank. We call for $200,000,000 to implement this program.
2. We call for the establishment of four major publishing and printing industries in the United States to be funded with ten million dollars each. These publishing houses are to be located in Detroit, Atlanta, Los Angeles, and New York. They will help to generate capital for further cooperative investments in the black com-

munity, provide jobs and an alternative to the white-dominated and controlled printing field.

3. We call for the establishment of four of the most advanced scientific and futuristic audio-visual networks to be located in Detroit, Chicago, Cleveland, and Washington, D.C. These television networks will provide an alternative to the racist propaganda that fills the current television networks. Each of these television networks will be funded by ten million dollars.

4. We call for a research skills center which will provide research on the problems of black people. This center must be funded with no less than 30 million dollars.

5. We call for the establishment of a training center for the teaching of skills in community organization, photography, movie making, television making and repair, radio building and repair, and all other skills needed in communication. The training center shall be funded with no less than ten million dollars.

6. We recognize the role of the National Welfare Rights Organization and we intend to work with them. We call for ten million dollars to assist in the organization of welfare recipients. We want to organize the welfare workers in this country so that they may demand more money from the government and better administration of the welfare system of this country.

7. We call for $20,000,000 to establish a National Black Labor Strike and Defense Fund. This is necessary for the protection of black workers and their families who are fighting racist working conditions in this country.

8. We call for the establishment of the International Black Appeal (IBA). This International Black-Appeal will be funded with no less than $20,000,000. The IBA is charged with producing more capital for the establishment of cooperative businesses in the United States and in Africa, our Motherland. The International Black Appeal is one of the most important demands that we are making for we know that it can generate and raise funds throughout the United States and help our African brother. The IBA is charged with three functions and shall be headed by James Forman: (a) Raising money for the program of the National Black Economic Development Conference. (b) The development of cooperatives in African countries and support of African Liberation movements. (c) Establishment of a Black Anti-Defamation League which will protect our African image.

9. We call for the establishment of a Black University to be funded with $130,000,000 to be located in the South. Negotiations are presently under way with a southern university.

10. We demand that IFCO allocate all unused funds in the planning budget to implement the demands of this conference.

In order to win our demands we are aware that we will have to have massive support, therefore:

1. We call upon all black people throughout the United States to consider themselves as members of the National Black Economic Development Conference and to act in unity to help force the racist white Christian churches and Jewish synagogues to implement these demands.

2. We call upon all the concerned people across the country to contact black workers, black women, black students and the black unemployed, community groups, welfare organizations, teachers organizations, church leaders and organizations, explaining how these demands are vital to the black community of the U.S. Pressure by whatever means necessary should be applied to the white power structure of the racist white Christian churches and Jewish synagogues. All black people should act boldly in confronting our white oppressors and demanding this modest reparation of fifteen dollars per black man.

3. Delegates and members of the National Black Economic Development Conference are urged to call press conferences in the cities and to attempt to get as many black organizations as possible to support the demands of the conference. The quick use of the press in the local areas will heighten the tension. These demands must be attempted to be won in a short period of time, although we are prepared for protracted and long range struggle.

4. We call for total disruption of selected church sponsored agencies operating anywhere in the U.S. and the world. Black workers, black women, black students and the black unemployed are encouraged to seize the offices, telephones, and printing apparatus of all church sponsored agencies and to hold these in trusteeship until our demands are met.

5. We call upon all delegates and members of the National Black Economic Development Conference to stage sit-in demonstrations at selected black and white churches. This is not to be interpreted as a continuation of the sit-in movement of the early sixties, but we know that active confrontation inside

white churches is possible and will strengthen the possibility of meeting our demands. Such confrontation can take the form of reading the Black Manifesto instead of a sermon or passing it out to church members. The principle of self-defense should be applied if attacked. On May 4, 1969, or a date thereafter, depending upon local conditions, we call upon black people to commence the disruption of the racist churches and synagogues throughout the United States.

6. We call upon IFCO to serve as a central staff to coordinate the mandate of the conference and to reproduce and distribute en masse literature, leaflets, news items, press releases and other material.

7. We call upon all delegates to find within the white community those forces which will work under the leadership of blacks to implement these demands by whatever means necessary. By taking such actions, white Americans will demonstrate concretely that they are willing to fight the white skin privilege and the white supremacy and racism which has forced us as black people to make these demands.

8. We call upon all Christians and Jews to practice patience, tolerance, understanding and nonviolence as they have encouraged, advised and demanded that we as black people should do throughout our entire enforced slavery in the United States. The true test of their faith and belief in the Cross and words of the prophets will certainly be put to a test as we seek legitimate and extremely modest reparations for our role in developing the industrial base of the Western world through our slave labor. But we are no longer slaves, we are men and women, proud of our African heritage, determined to have our dignity.

9. We are so proud of our African heritage and realize concretely that our struggle is not only to make revolution in the United States, but to protect our brothers and sisters in Africa and to help them rid themselves of racism, capitalism, and imperialism by whatever means necessary, including armed struggle. We are and must be willing to fight the defamation of our African image wherever it rears its ugly head. We are therefore charging the Steering Committee to create a Black Anti-Defamation League to be funded by money raised from the International Black Appeal.

10. We fully recognize that revolution in the United States and Africa, our Motherland, is more than a one dimensional operation. It will require the total integration of the political, economic, and military components and therefore, we call upon all our brothers and sisters who have acquired training and expertise in the fields of engineering, electronics, research, community organization, physics, biology, chemistry, mathematics, medicine, military science and warfare to assist the National Black Economic Development Conference in the implementation of its program.

11. To implement these demands: We must have a fearless leadership. We must have a leadership which is willing to battle the church establishment to implement these demands. To win our demands we will have to declare war on the white Christian churches and synagogues and this means we may have to fight the total government structure of this country. Let no one here think that these demands will be met by our mere stating them. For the sake of the churches and synagogues, we hope that they have the wisdom to understand that these demands are modest and reasonable. But if the white Christians and Jews are not willing to meet our demands through peace and good will, then we declare war and we are prepared to fight by whatever means necessary. . . .

The new black man wants to live and to live means that we must not become static or merely believe in self-defense. We must boldly go out and attack the white Western world at its power centers. The white Christian churches are another form of government in this country and they are used by the government of this country to exploit the people of Latin America, Asia and Africa, but the day is soon coming to an end. Therefore, brothers and sisters, the demands we make upon the white Christian churches and the Jewish synagogues are small demands. They represent fifteen dollars per black person in these United States. We can legitimately demand this from the church power structure. We must demand more from the United States government.

But to win our demands from the church which is linked up with the United States government, we must not forget that it will ultimately be by force and power that we will win.

We are not threatening the churches. We are saying that we know the churches came with the military might of the colonizers. Hence, if the churches in colonial territories were established by military might, we know deep within our hearts that we must be prepared to use force to get our demands. We are not saying that this is the road we want to take. It is not, but let us be very clear that we are not opposed to force and we are not opposed to violence. We were captured in Africa by violence. We were kept in bondage and political servitude and forced to work as slaves by the military machinery and the Christian churohes working hand in hand.

We recognize that in issuing this manifesto we must prepare for a long range educational campaign in all communities of this country.

Our objective in issuing this Manifesto is to force the white Christian church to begin the payment of reparations which are due to all black people, not only by the church but also by private business and the U.S. government. We see this focus on the Christian Church as an effort around which all black people can unite. Our demands are negotiable, but they cannot be minimized, they can only be increased and the church is asked to come up with larger sums of money than we are asking.

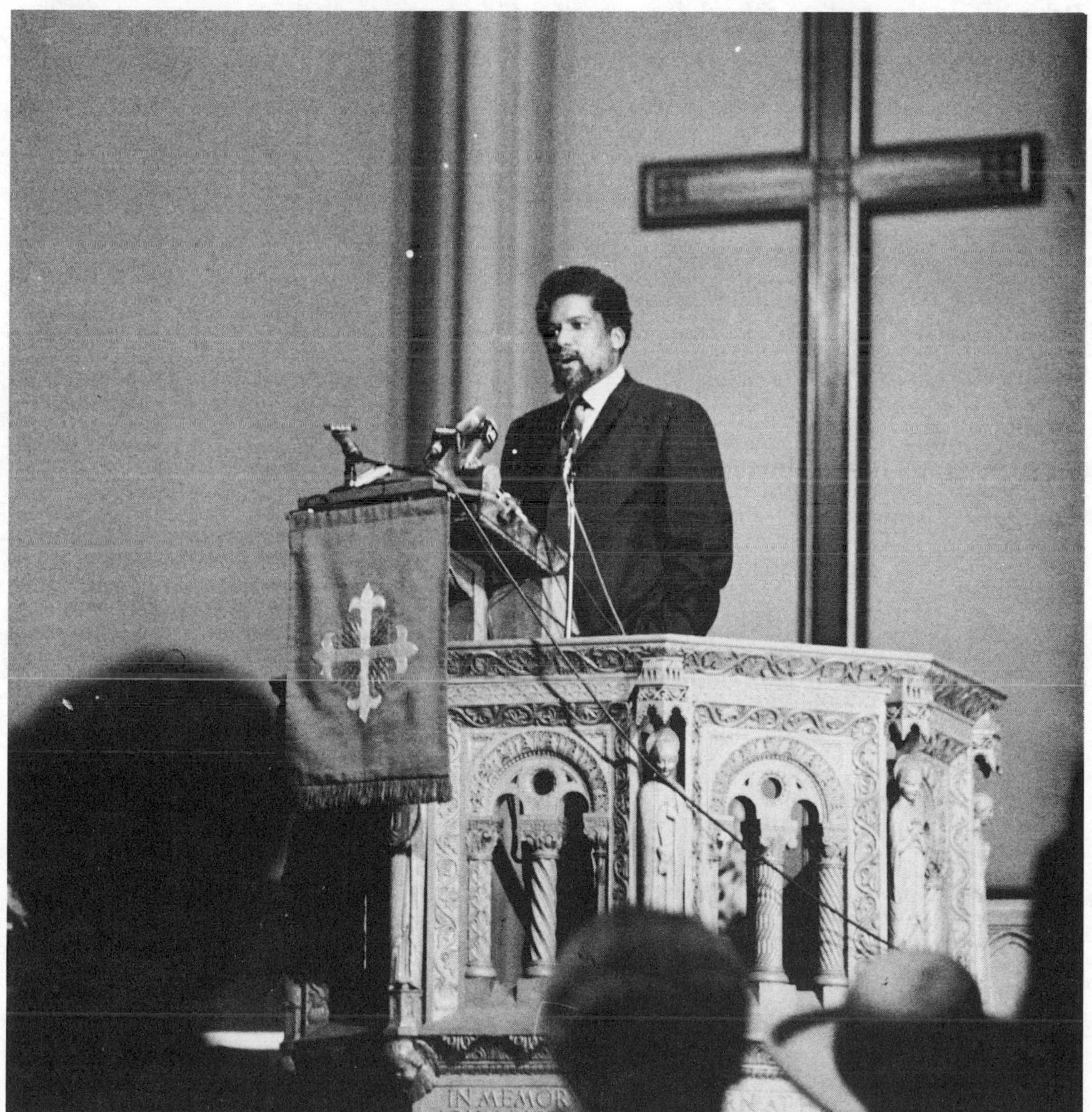

James Forman reads the Black Manifesto from the pulpit of St. George's Church.

THE NIXON DOCTRINE ON SCHOOLS, THE COURTS, SOCIETY & RACE: "THE COMPROMISE OF 1970"

On March 24, 1970, the Nixon Administration issued a carefully drafted comprehensive 8,000-word statement on the status of school desegregation in the United States. The president attempted to establish two philosophical and administrative priorities: one, to provide compensatory educational help to minority group children in de facto *segregated classrooms, two, to relieve the pressure on local districts to conform to* de jure *federal desegregation guidelines. The president also summarized the findings of various court rulings which have sought to untangle the complexities stemming from support for neighborhood school patterns in the North and freedom of choice plans in the South. His conclusion:* de facto *segregation does not violate the Constitution;* de jure *desegregation as practiced in the South does "in both Constitutional and human terms." The statement was attacked by most members of the black middle-class establishment as a retreat on school desegregation ("desegregation yes, integration no"), and a tacit endorsement of tax-exempt status for separate white "private" schools in the South. At the NAACP convention in July of 1970, critics of Nixon ticked off other grievances: Nixon's retreat on the use of federal registrars to enforce the Voting Rights Act of 1965, his emasculation of the cease-and-desist powers of the Equal Employment Opportunity Commission (EEOC), his willingness to sign defense contracts with textile companies not complying with desegregation guidelines, and his Supreme Court nominations. Although this statement does not explicitly contend with all these accusations, it does summarize Nixon's views on the principles for human advancement and the policies which he is prepared to back in order to guarantee black progress within the framework of American society. The document is printed in its virtual entirety as a statement of the President's intention to press for "a free and open society" in hiring, housing practices, and higher education.*

My purpose in this statement is to set forth in detail this Administration's policies on the subject of desegregation of America's elementary and secondary schools.

My specific objectives in this statement are:

¶To reaffirm my personal belief that the 1954 decision of the Supreme Court in Brown v. Board of Education was right in both constitutional and human terms.

¶To assess our progress in the 16 years since Brown and to point the way to continuing progress.

¶To clarify the present state of the law, as developed by the courts and the Congress, and the Administration policies guided by it.

¶To discuss some of the difficulties encountered by courts and communities as desegregation has accelerated in recent years, and to suggest approaches that can mitigate such problems as we complete the process of compliance with Brown.

¶To place the question of school desegregation in its larger context, as part of America's historic commitment to the achievement of a free and open society.

The Context

Progress toward school desegregation is part of two larger processes, each equally essential:

¶The improvement of educational opportunities for all of America's children.

¶The lowering of artificial racial barriers in all aspects of American life.

Only if we keep each of these considerations clearly in mind—and only if we recognize their separate natures—can we approach the question of school desegregation realistically.

It may be helpful to step back for a moment and to consider the problem of school desegregation in its larger context.

The school stands in a unique relationship to the community, to the family and to the individual students. It is a focal point of community life. It has a powerful impact on the future of all who attend.

It is a place not only of learning, but also of living—where a child's friendships center, where he learns to measure himself against others, to share, to compete, to cooperate—and it is the one institution above all others with which the parent shares the child. . . .

Overburdening the Schools

One of the mistakes of past policy has been to demand too much of our schools: They have been expected not only to educate, but also to accomplish a social transformation. Children in many instances have not been served, but used—in what all too often has proved a tragically futile effort to achieve in the schools the kind of a multiracial society which the adult community has failed to achieve for itself.

If we are to be realists, we must recognize that in a free society there are limits to the amount of government coercion that can reasonably be used; that in achieving desegregation we must proceed with the least possible disruption of the education of the nation's children; and that our children are highly sensitive to conflict, and highly vulnerable to lasting psychic injury.

Failing to recognize these factors, past policies have placed on the schools and the children too great a share of the burden of eliminating racial disparities throughout our society. A major part of this task falls to the schools. But they cannot do it all or even most of it by themselves.

Other institutions can share the burden of breaking down racial barriers, but only the schools can perform the task of education itself. If our schools fail to educate, then whatever they may achieve in integrating the races will turn out to be only a Pyrrhic victory. . . .

Policies and Enforcement: The Nixon Approach

It will be the purpose of this Administration to carry out the law fully and fairly. And where problems exist that are beyond the mandate of legal requirements, it will be our purpose to seek solutions that are both realistic and appropriate.

I have instructed the Attorney General, the Secretary of Health, Education and Welfare and other appropriate officials of the Government to be guided by these basic principles and policies:

¶Deliberate racial segregation of pupils by official action is unlawful, wherever it exists. In the words of the Supreme Court, it must be eliminated "root and branch"—and it must be eliminated at once.

¶Segregation of teachers must be eliminated. To this end, each school system in this nation, North and South, East and West, must move immediately, as the Supreme Court has ruled, toward a goal under which "in each school the ratio of white to Negro faculty members is substantially the same as it is throughout the system."

¶With respect to school facilities, school administrators throughout the nation, North and South, East and West, must move immediately, also in conformance with the Court's ruling, to assure that schools within individual school districts do not discriminate with respect to the quality of facilities or the quality of education delivered to the children within the district.

¶In devising local compliance plans primary weight should be given to the considered judgment of local school boards—provided they act in good faith and within constitutional limits.

¶The neighborhood school will be deemed the most appropriate base for such a system.

¶Transportation of pupils beyond normal geographic school zones for the purpose of achieving racial balance will not be required.

¶Federal advice and assistance will be made available on request, but Federal officials should not go beyond the requirements of law in attempting to impose their own judgment on the local school district.

Job Incentives

We have inaugurated new minority business enterprise programs—not only to help minority members get started in business themselves, but also, by developing more black and brown entrepreneurs, to demonstrate to young blacks, Mexican-Americans and others that they, too, can aspire to this same sort of upward economic mobility.

In our education programs, we have stressed the need for far greater diversity in offerings to match the diversity of individual needs—including more and better vocational and technical training, and a greater development of two-year community colleges.

Such approaches have been based essentially on faith in the individual—knowing that he sometimes needs help, but believing that in the long run he usually knows what is best for himself. . . .

We have overcome many problems in our 190 years as a nation. We can overcome this problem. We have managed to extend opportunity in other areas. We can extend it in this area. Just as other rights have been secured, so too can these rights be secured—and once again the nation will be better for having done so.

I am confident that we can preserve and improve our schools, carry out the mandate of our Constitution, and be true to our national conscience.

LIFT EVERY VOICE AND SING

Lift Every Voice and Sing *was written by the noted Negro poet and civil rights leader, James Weldon Johnson. It was originally intended for use in a program given by a group of Jacksonville, Florida schoolchildren to celebrate Lincoln's birthday. Inasmuch as its words tend to convey a sense of birthright and heritage, it is often referred to as the "Negro National Anthem," and sung at the opening of various public gatherings.*

Lift every voice and sing
Till earth and heaven ring,
Ring with the harmonies of Liberty;
Let our rejoicing rise
High as the listening skies,
Let it resound loud as the rolling sea.
Sing a song full of the faith that the dark past has taught us,
Sing a song full of the hope that the present has brought us,
Facing the rising sun of our new day begun
Let us march on till victory is won.

Stony the road we trod,
Bitter the chastening rod,
Felt in the days when hope unborn had died;
Yet with a steady beat,
Have not our weary feet
Come to the place for which our fathers sighed?
We have come over a way that with tears have been watered,
We have come, treading our path through the blood of the slaughtered,
Out from the gloomy past,
Till now we stand at last
Where the white gleam of our bright star is cast.

God of our weary years,
God of our silent tears,
Thou who has brought us thus far on the way;
Thou who has by Thy might
Led us into the light,
Keep us forever in the path, we pray.
Lest our feet stray from the places, Our God, where we met Thee,
Lest, our hearts drunk with the wine of the world, we forget Thee;
Shadowed beneath Thy hand,
May we forever stand.
True to our GOD,
True to our native land.

UNITED NATIONS PROCLAMATIONS

UNIVERSAL DECLARATION OF HUMAN RIGHTS

The Universal Declaration on Human Rights was drawn up in 1947 and 1948 by the Commission on Human Rights, headed by Mrs. Eleanor Roosevelt, widow of President Franklin D. Roosevelt. It was adopted at the Paris session of the UN General Assembly on December 10, 1948 without a dissenting vote, although there were eight abstentions. At the time of its adoption, it was widely regarded as a definitive statement of the basic rights and fundamental freedoms to which all men *are entitled.*

While the first two and the last three of the Declarations's 30 articles are general in character, the main body of the document covers personal, civil and political rights (Articles 3-21) as well as economic, social and cultural rights (Articles 22-27).

Preamble

Whereas **recognition of the inherent dignity and of the equal and inalienable rights of all members of the human family is the foundation of freedom, justice and peace in the world.**

Whereas **disregard and contempt for human rights have resulted in barbarous acts which have outraged the conscience of mankind, and the advent of a world in which human beings shall enjoy freedom of speech and belief and freedom from fear and want has been proclaimed as the highest aspiration of the common people,**

Whereas **it is essential, if man is not to be compelled to have recourse, as a last resort, to rebellion against tyranny and oppression, that human rights should be protected by the rule of law,**

Whereas **it is essential to promote the development of friendly relations between nations,**

Whereas **the peoples of the United Nations have in the Charter reaffirmed their faith in fundamental human rights, in the dignity and worth of the human person and in the equal rights of men and women and have determined to promote social progress and better standards of life in larger freedom,**

Whereas **Member States have pledged themselves to achieve, in co-operation with the United Nations, the promotion of universal respect for and observance of human rights and fundamental freedoms,**

Whereas **a common understanding of these rights and freedoms is of the greatest importance for the full realisation of this pledge,**

Now therefore

THE GENERAL ASSEMBLY proclaims *This Universal Declaration of Human Rights* as a common standard of achievement for all peoples and all nations, to the end that every individual and every organ of society, keeping this Declaration constantly in mind, shall strive by teaching and education to promote respect for these rights and freedoms and by progressive measures, national and international, to secure their universal and effective recognition and observance, both among the peoples of Member States themselves and among the peoples of territories under their jurisdiction.

Article 1. **All human beings are born free and equal in dignity and rights. They are endowed with reason and conscience and should act towards one another in a spirit of brotherhood.**

Article 2. **Everyone is entitled to all the rights and freedoms set forth in this Declaration, without distinction of any kind, such as race, colour, sex, language, religion, political or other opinion, national or social origin, property, birth or other status. Furthermore, no distinction shall be made on the basis of the political, jurisdictional or international status of the country or territory to which a person belongs, whether it be independent, trust, nonself-governing or under any other limitation of sovereignty.**

Article 3. **Everyone has the right to life, liberty and security of person.**

Article 4. **No one shall be held in slavery or servitude; slavery and the slave trade shall be prohibited in all their forms.**

Article 5. **No one shall be subjected to torture or to cruel, inhuman or degrading treatment or punishment.**

Article 6. **Everyone has the right to recognition everywhere as a person before the law.**

Article 7. **All are equal before the law and are entitled without any discrimination to equal protection of the law. All are entitled to equal protection against any discrimination in violation of this Declaration and against any incitement to such discrimination.**

Article 8. **Everyone has the right to an effective remedy by the competent national tribunals for acts violating the fundamental rights granted him by the constitution or by law.**

Article 9. No one shall be subjected to arbitrary arrest, detention or exile.

Article 10. Everyone is entitled in full equality to a fair and public hearing by an independent and impartial tribunal, in the determination of his rights and obligations and of any criminal charge against him.

Article 11. (1) Everyone charged with a penal offence has the right to be presumed innocent until proved guilty according to law in a public trial at which he has had all the guarantees necessary for his defence.
(2) No one shall be held guilty of any penal offence on account of any act or omission which did not constitute a penal offence, under national or international law, at the time when it was committed. Nor shall a heavier penalty be imposed than the one that was applicable at the time the penal offence was committed.

Article 12. No one shall be subjected to arbitrary interference with his privacy, family, home or correspondence, nor to attacks upon his honour and reputation. Everyone has the right to the protection of the law against such interference or attacks.

Article 13. (1) Everyone has the right to freedom of movement and residence within the borders of each state.
(2) Everyone has the right to leave any country, including his own, and to return to his country.

Article 14. (1) Everyone has the right to seek and to enjoy in other countries asylum from persecution.
(2) This right may not be invoked in the case of prosecutions genuinely arising from non-political crimes or from acts contrary to the purposes and principles of the United Nations.

Article 15. (1) Everyone has the right to a nationality.
(2) No one shall be arbitrarily deprived of his nationality nor denied the right to change his nationality.

Article 16. (1) Men and women of full age, without any limitation due to race, nationality or religion, have the right to marry and to found a family. They are entitled to equal rights as to marriage, during marriage and at its dissolution.
(2) Marriage shall be entered into only with the free and full consent of the intending spouses.
(3) The family is the natural and fundamental group unit of society and is entitled to protection by society and the State.

Article 17. (1) Everyone has the right to own property alone as well as in association with others.
(2) No one shall be arbitrarily deprived of his property.

Article 18. Everyone has the right to freedom of thought, conscience and religion; this right includes freedom to change his religion or belief, and freedom, either alone or in community with others and in public or private, to manifest his religion or belief in teaching, practice, worship and observance.

Article 19. Everyone has the right to freedom of opinion and expression; this right includes freedom to hold opinions without interference and to seek, receive and impart information and ideas through any media and regardless of frontiers.

Article 20. (1) Everyone has the right to freedom of peaceful assembly and association.
(2) No one may be compelled to belong to an association.

Article 21. (1) Everyone has the right to take part in the government of his country, directly or through freely chosen representatives.
(2) Everyone has the right of equal access to public service in his country.
(3) The will of the people shall be the basis of the authority of government; this will shall be expressed in periodic and genuine elections which shall be by universal and equal suffrage and shall be held by secret vote or by equivalent free voting procedures.

Article 22. Everyone, as a member of society, has the right to social security and is entitled to realisation, through national effort and international co-operation and in accordance with the organisation and resources of each State, of the economic, social and cultural rights indispensable for his dignity and the free development of his personality.

Article 23. (1) Everyone has the right to work, to free choice of employment, to just and favourable conditions of work and to protection against unemployment.
(2) Everyone, without any discrimination, has the right to equal pay for equal work.

(3) Everyone who works has the right to just and favourable remuneration insuring for himself and his family an existence worthy of human dignity, and supplemented, if necessary, by other means of social protection.
(4) Everyone has the right to form and to join trade unions for the protection of his interests.

Article 24. Everyone has the right to rest and leisure, including reasonable limitation of working hours and periodic holidays with pay.

Article 25. (1) Everyone has the right to a standard of living adequate for the health and well-being of himself and of his family, including food, clothing, housing and medical care and necessary social services, and the right to security in the event of unemployment, sickness, disability, widowhood, old age or other lack of livelihood in circumstances beyond his control.
(2) Motherhood and childhood are entitled to special care and assistance. All children, whether born in or out of wedlock, shall enjoy the same social protection.

Article 26. (1) Everyone has the right to education. Education shall be free, at least in the elementary and fundamental stages. Elementary education shall be compulsory. Technical and professional education shall be made generally available and higher education shall be equally accessible to all on the basis of merit.
(2) Education shall be directed to the full development of the human personality and to the strengthening of respect for human rights and fundamental freedoms. It shall promote understanding, tolerance and friendship among all nations, racial or religious groups, and shall further the activities of the United Nations for the maintenance of peace.
(3) Parents have a prior right to choose the kind of education that shall be given to their children.

Article 27. (1) Everyone has the right freely to participate in the cultural life of the community, to enjoy the arts and to share in scientific advancement and its benefits.
(2) Everyone has the right to the protection of the moral and material interests resulting from any scientific, literary or artistic production of which he is the author.

Article 28. Everyone is entitled to a social and international order in which the rights and freedoms set forth in this Declaration can be fully realised.

Article 29. (1) Everyone has duties to the community in which alone the free and full development of his personality is possible.
(2) In the exercise of his rights and freedoms, everyone shall be subject only to such limitations as are determined by law solely for the purpose of securing due recognition and respect for the rights and freedoms of others and of meeting the just requirements of morality, public order and the general welfare in a democratic society.
(3) These rights and freedoms may in no case be exercised contrary to the purposes and principles of the United Nations.

Article 30. Nothing in this Declaration may be interpreted as implying for any State, group or person any right to engage in any activity or to perform any act aimed at the destruction of any of the rights and freedoms set forth herein.

DECLARATION OF THE RIGHTS OF THE CHILD

The Declaration of the Rights of the Child was adopted on November 20, 1959 as an extension of the Universal Declaration of Human Rights. Its general objective is to create a climate in which the children of the world can enjoy a safe, happy and wholesome life.

The document, consisting of a preamble and 10 "principles," addresses itself not only to governments, but also to parents, voluntary organizations, and local authorities —encouraging them to recognize the rights of children, and to adopt appropriate legal and social measures for the safeguarding of these rights. Great care was taken by various UN agencies to formulate the principles in such a way that they would not conflict with the political, religious and ideological beliefs of any member nations.

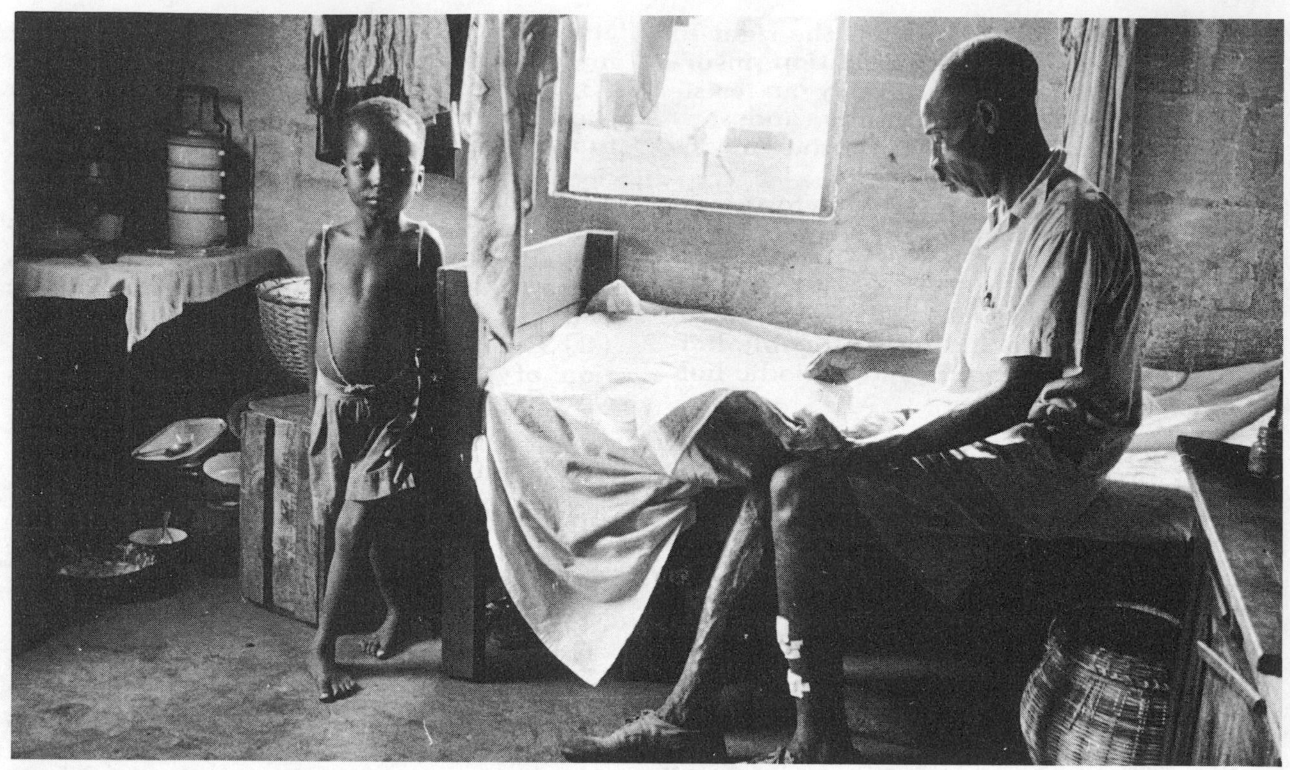

A boy from the Republic of Cameroun, West Africa.

Preamble

Whereas the peoples of the United Nations have, in the Charter, reaffirmed their faith in fundamental human rights, and in the dignity and worth of the human person, and have determined to promote social progress and better standards of life in larger freedom,

Whereas the United Nations has, in the Universal Declaration of Human Rights, proclaimed that everyone is entitled to all the rights and freedoms set forth therein, without distinction of any kind, such as race, color, sex, language, religion, political or other opinion, national or social origin, property, birth or other status,

Whereas the child, by reason of his physical and mental immaturity, needs special safeguards and care, including appropriate legal protection, before as well as after birth,

Whercas the need for such special safeguards has been stated in the Geneva Declaration of the Rights of the Child of 1924, and recognized in the Universal Declaration of Human Rights and in the statutes of specialized agencies and international organizations concerned with the welfare of children.

Whereas mankind owes to the child the best it has to give,

Now therefore,

The General Assembly

Proclaims this Declaration of the Rights of the Child to the end that he may have a happy childhood and enjoy for his own good and for the good of society the rights and freedoms herein set forth, and calls upon parents, upon men and women as individuals and upon voluntary organizations, local authorities and national Governments to recognize these rights and strive for their observance by legislative and other measures progressively taken in accordance with the following principles:

Principle 1

The child shall enjoy all the rights set forth in this Declaration. All children, without any exception whatsoever, shall be entitled to these rights, without distinction or discrimination on account of race, color, sex, language, religion, political or other opinion, national or social origin, property, birth or other status, whether of himself or of his family.

Principle 2

The child shall enjoy special protection, and shall be given opportunitites and facilities, by law and by other means, to enable him to develop physically, mentally, morally, spiritually and socially in a healthy and normal manner and in conditions of freedom and dignity. In the enactment of laws for this purpose the best interests of the child shall be the paramount consideration.

Principle 3

The child shall be entitled from his birth to a name and a nationality.

Principle 4

The child shall enjoy the benefits of social security. He shall be entitled to grow and develop in health; to this end special care and protection shall be provided both to him and to his mother, including adequate pre-natal and post-natal care. The child shall have the right to adequate nutrition, housing, recreation and medical services.

Principle 5

The child who is physically, mentally or socially handicapped shall be given the special treatment, education and care required by his particular condition.

Principle 6

The child, for the full and harmonious development of his personality, needs love and understanding. He shall, wherever possible, grow up in the care and under the responsibility of his parents, and in any case in an atmosphere of affection and of moral and material security; a child of tender years shall not, save in exceptional circumstances, be separated from his mother. Society and the public authorities shall have the duty to extend particular care to children without a family and to those without adequate means of support. Payment of State and other assistance towards the maintenance of children of large families is desirable.

Principle 7

The child is entitled to receive education, which shall be free and compulsory, at least in the elementary stages. He shall be given an education which will promote his general culture, and enable him on a basis of equal opportunity to develop his abilities, his individual judgment, and his sense of moral and social responsibility, and to become a useful member of society.

The best interest of the child shall be the guiding principle of those responsible for his education and guidance; that responsibility lies in the first place with his parents.

The child shall have full opportunity for play and recreation, which should be directed to the same purposes as education; society and the public authorities shall endeavor to promote the enjoyment of this right.

Principle 8

The child shall in all circumstances be among the first to receive protection and relief.

Principle 9

The child shall be protected against all forms of neglect, cruelty and exploitation. He shall not be the subject of traffic in any form.

The child shall not be admitted to employment before an appropriate minimum age; he shall in no case be caused or permitted to engage in any occupation or employment which would prejudice his health or education, or interfere with his physical, mental or moral development.

Principle 10

The child shall be protected from practices which may foster racial, religious and any other form of discrimination. He shall be brought up in a spirit of understanding, tolerance, friendship among peoples, peace and universal brotherhood and in the consciousness that his energy and talents should be devoted to the service of his fellow men.

BOOKER T·WASHINGTON
1856 1915
HE LIFTED THE VEIL OF IGNORANCE

HISTORIC LANDMARKS OF BLACK AMERICA

A review of the numerous landmarks, monuments, shrines and other points of interest across the United States of particular relevance to the American Negro

No more substantial testimony to the role of the Negro in the growth and development of America can be found than the numerous historical landmarks in various regions of the country which are associated with Negro Americana. Many of these—like the Alamo and Bunker Hill—are not conventionally known as sites involving chapters of Negro history.

ALABAMA

Florence: *Handy Heights Housing Development and Museum*

The Development and Museum is named for composer W. C. Handy, who was born in Florence in 1873. It includes a restored cabin in which are housed his piano, trumpet, and other mementoes.

Mobile: *Fort Gaines* (on Dauphin Island)

Site of the Battle of Mobile Bay (August 1864) during the Civil War. One of the key battles of the day was the engagement between Admiral David Farragut's flagship, the *Hartford,* and the Confederate ironclad, *Tennessee*. During the battle, black naval hero John Lawson manned his duty station despite serious injury, his role in keeping Union guns operative may well have saved the ship from destruction. For his valor, the Pennsylvania Negro was awarded the Medal of Honor. Black infantry units also participated in the capture of Fort Gaines and, later, the capture of Mobile itself. When nearby Fort Blakely fell, nine black regiments were included in the 1st Division of the federal force commanded by General John Hawkins.

Talladega: *Talladega College*

Home of the first college for Negroes in Alabama, Talladega was founded by the American Missionary Association as a primary school in 1867. Its Savery Library houses three fresco panels by Hale Woodruff (the celebrated Amistad Murals). Professor Woodruff studied abroad in France under the renowned Henry Ossawa Tanner, and also at the Herron Institute in Indianapolis.

Tuskegee: *Tuskegee Institute*

The Institute is a world-famous center for agricultural research and extension work. First opened on July 4, 1881 with a $2,000 appropriation from the Alabama State Legislature, it consisted of a single shanty, a student body of 30, and one teacher—Booker T. Washington. Tuskegee functioned originally as a normal school for the training of Negro teachers, the first of its kind established in the United States. Eventually it came to specialize in agricultural and manual training, areas which were to make both the school and Booker T. Washington famous.

In 1882, Washington moved the school to a 100-acre plantation, and began a self-help program which enabled students to finance their education. Most of the early buildings were built with the aid of student labor.

Next to Washington, the most famous person to be associated with the Institute was George Washington Carver, who became its director of agricultural research in 1896. Carver persuaded many Southern farmers to plant peanuts, sweet potatoes, and other crops instead of cotton, which was rapidly depleting the soil. Ultimately, Carver's research programs helped develop 300 derivative products from peanuts and 118 from sweet potatoes. At one point, he even succeeded in making synthetic marble from wood pulp.

Today, Tuskegee covers nearly 5,000 acres, and has more than 150 buildings. Notable places to visit there include: the Founder's Marker (the site of Washington's original shanty); the Oaks (Washington's home); the Booker T. Washington Monument, and the George Washington Carver Museum.

The Carver Museum houses the scientist's plant, mineral and bird collections, and includes exhibits of various products he developed, as well as a number of his paintings and research papers.

Tuskegee is also the home of the George Washington Carver Foundation, a research center founded by Carver in 1940.

ALASKA

Fairbanks: *Pioneers Home*

One of the few surviving Negro pioneers of Alaska is Mattie Crosby who first came

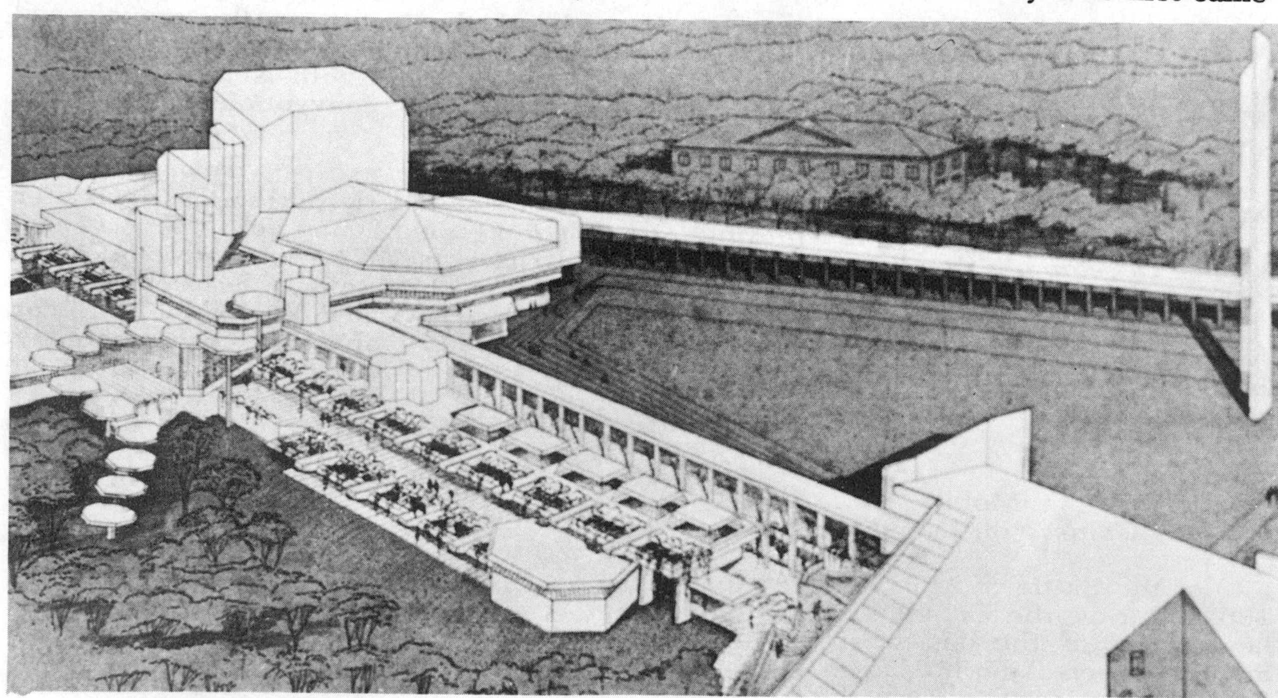

This two-million dollar cultural center will enhance the grounds of today's Tuskegee.

to the wilderness in 1900 with a Maine family that adopted her. Miss Crosby later opened a bathhouse, and became famous as one of Alaska's best cooks. Some Negroes came into the territory during the era of the Gold Rush, and others were occasionally seen on board ships which brought in supplies. Still, for nearly 17 years, Mattie Crosby lived in Fairbanks without meeting another Negro. In her advancing years, she wrote a book about her experiences, but it has unfortunately since been lost.

Mattie Crosby

ARIZONA

Apache:
Geronimo Monument

Geronimo was one of the last Apache chieftains to resist the oncoming hordes of white settlers and immigrants moving into the Southwest. Black cavalrymen finally escorted Geronimo and his renegades into exile at Fort Dickens, Florida and, later, returned with him to Fort Sill, where he died.

Bonita:
Old Fort Grant

Site of a fort at which black soldiers were housed during the Indian Wars. Two soldiers of the fort, Isaiah Mays and Benjamin Brown, received Congressional Medals of Honor while on duty at this station.

Fort Apache:
Old Fort Apache

Another fort at which black units served during the Indian Wars. The punitive expedition led by John Pershing in search of Pancho Villa originated at this point, the 10th Cavalry in the vanguard. This unit was stationed at the fort beginning in 1913, after having seen service in Cuba and the Philippines.

Fort Thomas:
Camp Thomas

This camp was a base of operations from which both black cavalry units operated in their mission to keep peace among the Apache tribes. One Negro, Sergeant William McBryar, won the Congressional Medal of Honor for demonstrating "coolness" and "bravery" under combat stress during the pursuit of a renegade Apache.

Phoenix:
State House

Among the eight murals at the State Capitol Building in Phoenix depicting vital episodes from Arizona's history is one portraying Estevanico, the Negro guide of Fray Marcos de Niza, the Franciscan Missionary whose search for the Seven Cities of Gold brought him into Arizona in 1539. Estevanico was killed at one of the seven Zuni pueblos after trying to escape.

San Carlos: *San Carlos Indian Reservation*

The Ninth and Tenth Cavalry, Negro regiments formed after the Civil War, were often sent out to combat the Cheyenne and Apache Indians in the American Southwest. The Indians called them *Buffalo Soldiers;* their own white officers referred to them as *The Brunettes.* Whatever their designation, however, they were considered to be among the best troops in the area. The first Negro officer assigned to the Tenth was Lieutenant Henry O. Flipper who, likewise, was the first Negro to graduate from West Point.

Negroes were among the troops under General Crook's command at the time of the surrender of the famed Apache chief Geronimo in 1876.

Today, the tribal council of the San Carlos Apaches meets regularly on the

Fort Apache, Arizona, in 1877. Black troops were quartered here after the Civil War.

site where the reservation of the Warm Springs Apaches was once found.

Sierra Vista:
Fort Huachuca

Fort Huachuca quartered troops of the 9th and 10th Cavalry during the Indian Wars. Elements of the 10th were stationed here in the first decade of the 20th century. During World War II, the men of the all-black 92nd Division trained here before being sent overseas to Africa and Europe.

Springerville:
Apache National Forest

Site, in the White Mountains, where troopers of the 10th Cavalry captured Mangas Coloradas on September 18, 1886. Coloradas was one of those fierce Apache chiefs who fought desperately for choice grazing lands for his people. Today the reservation at Springerville contains millions of acres of fertile land, the legacy of the tenacious resistance of the Apaches.

Tombstone: *John Swain (Slaughter) Grave in Boot Hill*

Born a slave in 1845, John Swain went to Tombstone in 1879 as a cowhand in the employ of John Slaughter, who was later to become sheriff of this town. Swain was an expert rider, and only one of several Negroes to work for Slaughter.

In 1884, Swain fought and lost a one-round boxing match with John L. Sullivan, then heavyweight champion of the world. He died just three months short of his 100th birthday, and was buried with honors by the citizens of Tombstone. A special tablet stands on the grave site, commemorating the close ties between the two men.

Tortilla Flat:
Battle of the Caves

Site, during 1872-1873, of General Crook's

campaign to wipe out Apache bands holed up in distant, and virtually inaccessible, mountain retreats. Black units approached the Indian hideout under cover of darkness, pinned down the enemy in their cave, and scored a notable victory. Few of the marauders escaped; several were killed by ricocheting bullets.

ARKANSAS

Camden: *Poison Spring State Park*

Site of an 1864 Civil War battle in which the 1st Kansas Colored Regiment suffered heavy casualties, some of which were apparently inflicted by Confederates on captured or wounded black soldiers. Negro troops, as they did at Fort Pillow, vowed to take no more rebel prisoners.

Helena: *The Battle of Helena*

Among the defenders of this Mississippi River port were members of the 2nd Infantry Regiment of African Descent. Black soldiers fought shoulder to shoulder with whites in repulsing a Confederate siege of the city in July 1863. The experience of one black unit stationed there—the 56th U.S. Colored Troops—is typical of many which confronted Negroes during the war. Disease was an even more potent enemy than combat. Only a handful of men lost their lives as a result of armed conflict, whereas literally hundreds fell victim to disease and poor medical treatment.

Little Rock: *Philander Smith College*

Opened in 1877 under the sponsorship of the Methodist Episcopal Church, Philander Smith (then known as Walder College) was renamed five years later after receiving a large donation which enabled the school to construct a permanent brick edifice.

Sheridan: *Jenkins Ferry State Park*

Two weeks after the Poison Spring engagement—on April 30, 1864, to be exact—the 1st and 2nd Kansas Colored Regiments saw action along the Sabine River, where they overran a Confederate battery, shouting, "Remember Poison Spring" and inflicting 150 casualties on the enemy.

CALIFORNIA

Arcadia: *Santa Anita Race Track*

Santa Anita Race Track is located on the former site of the E. J. "Lucky" Baldwin ranch, a spread at which John Fisher, a black man and former slave, was a prominent breeder and trainer. Fisher, a native of St. Louis, was at first reluctant to follow Baldwin to California out of fear of Indians, but was eventually persuaded to join him. He later became a foreman on the ranch.

Beckwourth: *Beckwourth Pass (U.S. Alt. 40, east of the junction with U.S. Route 395)*

Beckwourth Pass, which runs through the Sierra Nevada mountains, was discovered by James P. Beckwourth, one of a number of Negro traders and trappers dubbed *The Mountain Men* by many writers of American history.

Fond of telling a good yarn, Beckwourth not surprisingly added spice to his own life with a number of romantic legends, in which it is often difficult to separate fact from fantasy.

One such story has it that, toward the end of his life, he killed a man in an argument in Denver, and was held in custody for a time before being acquitted on a plea of self-defense. Beckwourth, who claimed to be a Crow chief, was subsequently welcomed by the tribe, which believed him to be a symbol of good fortune. When he talked of leaving, the Crow decided to keep their "talisman" with them forever by planning a sumptuous feast in his honor and then poisoning the stew.

A less embellished account of his end has it that he died on the trail two days after leaving Denver for a rendezvous with the Crow.

Beverly Hills: *Beverly-Wilshire Hotel*

Black architect Paul R. Williams designed this plush hotel, one of the most elegant in the area. Many stunning private residences of famous Hollywood stars have been designed by Williams, the Spingarn medalist for 1953.

Downieville:
The Pioneer Museum

Site of an 1849 gold strike involving a Scotch immigrant, William Downie, and 10 Negroes. One of the black adventurers was Waller Jackson, an Easterner who journeyed "'round the Horn" in 1849, and found his fortune with the rest of the prospecting party.

Folsom Lake:
"Negro Bar" Marker

Folsom Lake now covers the site of an old mining camp anonymously associated with black gold miners. Remains of these intrepid pioneers have been reburied at nearby Mormon Island Pioneer Cemetery.

Fremont Park:
Fremont Peak State Park

John C. Fremont—soldier of fortune, explorer, writer, politician—was a key figure in the development of California and in the war which was fought against Mexico to make this vast territory a part of the Union.

Fremont led four exploratory and mapping missions into California, and took along Negroes on two of them. John Dodson, a free Negro who was a servant of Fremont's father-in-law, Senator Thomas Hart Benton, accompanied the second of these expeditions, while Saunders Jackson, likewise a servant of Benton, volunteered for the fourth in order to raise the $1700 needed to buy his family's freedom.

After considerable hardship, the 'ill-fated fourth expedition ended with Fremont and his party finally arriving in California via a southern route. Once there, Fremont discovered that, in his absence, gold had been discovered on land he owned. Jackson was given permission to prospect for gold and, within a few days, had dug out nuggets valued at $1700. He then returned to Missouri, emancipated his family as planned, and disappeared from history.

Having become a millionaire, Fremont, whose political ideology was abolitionist, was to experience several ups and downs, both in military and in political affairs, during his later career. Ultimately, however, he became territorial governor of Arizona before his death in 1890.

Jim Beckwourth

Hollywood:
Grauman's Chinese Theater

In 1967, Sidney Poitier became the first black actor to record his footprints in the concrete of Grauman's Chinese Theater, a ritual which has become synonymous with stardom and success in Hollywood film circles.

Hornitos:
Gold Mining Camp

Home of Moses Rodgers, a successful and affluent black mine owner who was one of the finest engineers and metallurgists in the state. Rodgers was only one of several black miners who struck it rich in gold and quartz. One Negro, known to history only as Dick, reputedly amassed a fortune of more than $100,000, but lost it all on the Sacramento gaming tables and, in despair, blew his brains out.

Mokelumme Hill:
Gold Discovery Marker

Site of a legendary strike involving a black miner allegedly the butt of a white prank. According to the story, a befuddled Negro prospector asked his white colleagues where to dig and was told, with great fanfare, that a barren hillside in town was the most likely place to strike it rich. What took shape as an elaborate joke turned out, however, to be a startling prophecy, fulfilled inside of two days by a happy black prospector carrying a sack of gold. The butt of the joke had returned to thank his "friends" for their generous and abundant advice.

Oakland:
Oakland Art Museum

The museum has several pieces done by prominent black artists, including Sargent Johnson's *Forever Free* and lithographs by Grafton T. Brown, believed to be the first black artist active in the state.

Red Bluff:
Oak Hill Cemetery

Burial place of Aaron Coffey, only black man in the Society of California Pioneers. Coffey, descendant of an officer who fought under Jackson at New Orleans, came to California a slave in 1849. By day, he worked at his master's claim; by night, as a cobbler, accumulating money toward his $1,000 emancipation fee. Betrayed by his owner, he was forced to return to Missouri, where he was again sold. Coffey pleaded with his new master to allow him to return to California and earn the necessary money to free himself and his family, which he left behind as collateral. That mission accomplished, Coffey returned to Red Bluff, took up farming and settled down to a contented family life.

Sacramento:
St. Andrew's African Methodist Church

The first AME church in Califorina, organized in a private residence in 1850. Within four years, the congregation organized a school for black, Oriental and Indian children in the church basement.

San Francisco:
Leidesdorff Street

Named after William Alexander Leidesdorff, a wealthy and influential California pioneer of black and Danish ancestry and a native of the Danish West Indies. A merchant, Leidesdorff operated the first steamer to pass through the Golden Gate, was later appointed U.S. vice-consul, and ultimately became a civic and educational leader in San Francisco.

COLORADO

Breckenridge: *Barney Ford Hill*
(just southeast of city limits)

A fugitive slave who went to Colorado in 1860 in search of gold, Barney Ford had once operated a station in Chicago's Underground Railroad and been involved with the famed revolutionary, John Brown.

Ford found gold, but was cheated out of his claim by outlaws. He managed to get back to Denver, where rumors began to spread that he had buried a fortune in the hill which now bears his name.

Ford actually became a wealthy hotel owner and restauranteur (repeating the success he had originally had in Nicaragua) but, in spite of this, people persisted in believing his wealth was really derived from the hillside treasure-trove. The result was that, over the years, the hill became pockmarked with the diggings of those who refused to believe

Barney Ford

Ford's protestations and denials. Later in life, Ford was beleaguered by hoodlums and other riffraff who insisted on spying upon his every move in the hope that he would one day betray a vital clue to the whereabouts of the alleged treasure.

Central City: *"Aunt Clara" Brown Chair (Central City Opera House)*

This chair is a tribute to "Aunt Clara" Brown, believed to have been the first Negro resident of Colorado. "Aunt Clara" died in 1877 while in her 80's.

Born a slave in Virginia, "Aunt Clara" moved to Missouri where her husband and children were sold before she herself gained freedom through her master's last will and testament. From Missouri she headed for Kansas and then for the gold fields of Colorado, where she opened the territory's first laundry. From her earnings she soon began putting aside money for the purchase of her family.

Even though the Emancipation intervened and her immediate family was set free, she nonetheless returned to Missouri and brought back with her to Central City a group of 38 relatives and kin. She remained in the mining community for the rest of her life, nursing the sick and performing other charitable works.

She was buried with honors by the Colorado Pioneers Association, of which she was a member. Her chair was dedicated in 1932.

Denver: *Inter-Ocean Hotel, 16th and Market Streets*

The Inter-Ocean Hotel, once a showplace for millionaires and presidents, was built by Barney Ford, a Negro entrepreneur active during the gold rush days. (See first Colorado entry.)

Ford and his cohorts joined the fight over the organization of the Colorado territory and the question of statehood. Originally allowed to vote, they had seen this privilege abrogated by the territorial constitution and, as a result, sought to delay statehood for the territory until Negro voting rights were reinstated. Enlisting the aid of the famed Massachusetts abolitionist, Senator Charles Sumner, Ford urged President Andrew Johnson to veto the bill for statehood.

Ultimately, Johnson adopted this course of action and, as an ironic consequence, Colorado was unable to vote on the question of Johnson's impeachment. Had the territory become a state then, it is believed likely that the two provisional senators would have voted for impeachment, inasmuch as they were known to be vehemently anti-Johnson.

In Colorado, Ford was blamed for attempting to block statehood and for keeping Johnson in office. Once the 15th Amendment had been passed, however, Ford began to work vigorously on behalf of statehood. He supported the Republican state legislature and its representatives on the electoral commission which voted in the Hayes-Tilden election. Some claimed Ford was responsible for the deciding commission vote. In any event, the advent of Hayes to the presidency signaled the end of Reconstruction, and paved the way for a series of laws which soon deprived the Negro throughout the South of his precious and newly won voting right.

Ford retired and spent the remainder of his life in Denver where he died in December 1902. He is buried alongside his wife Julia in Denver's Riverside Cemetery.

Pueblo: *El Pueblo Museum, 905 S. Prairie Avenue*

The El Pueblo Museum houses a replica of the Gantt-Blackwell Fort which Jim Beckwourth, Negro explorer, scout and trader, claimed to have founded in 1842. The validity of the claim has not been established, inasmuch as Beckwourth is known to have had something of a reputation as a teller of tall tales.

CONNECTICUT

Groton Heights: *Fort Griswold State Park*

Freeman was the Negro orderly of the American commander, Colonel William Ledyard who was forced to surrender the fort to superior British forces. The British officer who accepted the surrender behaved ignobly, however. Ledyard was first induced to give up the sword and then run through with his own weapon, presumably in revenge for the death of a British officer at the hands of Freeman. Another Negro, Lambert Latham, avenged Ledyard's death by killing the treacherous British officer.

DELAWARE

Wilmington: *Asbury Methodist Episcopal Church*

This church, located at Third and Walnut Streets, was dedicated in 1789 by the distinguished orator Bishop Francis Asbury. Tradition has it that, on one occasion, a number of the town's leading citizens, many of whom were anxious to hear Asbury preach but considered Methodism beneath them socially, refused to enter the church, but stayed outside within hearing distance of the sermon. The listeners were impressed by the eloquence of the man they heard—not, as it turned out, the bishop, but his Negro servant Harry whose compelling testimony reached their ears and inspired their admiration. By 1805, however, Negroes had left this church, driven out by the decision of white worshippers to confine black members to the gallery. The Negroes who left formed their own church.

DISTRICT OF COLUMBIA

Association for the Study of Negro Life and History

The Association, located at 1538 Ninth St., N.W., was long the sole professional agency concerned with preserving the historical record of the Negro in American life. The organizing pioneer behind the Association was Carter Woodson, a scholar and lecturer who began publication of the *Journal of Negro History* in 1916. Ten years later, Woodson inaugurated observance of "Negro History Week," during which leaders of the black freedom struggle were appropriately honored, primarily in schools. Negro History Week is always celebrated in February, as close as possible to the birthdays of both Frederick Douglass and Abraham Lincoln. Woodson and his later colleague, Dr. Charles Wesley of Central State, collaborated on many historical studies.

Emancipation Statue: Lincoln Park

Former Negro slaves were responsible for financing and erecting the oldest memorial to Abraham Lincoln in the Washington, D.C. area.

After Lincoln's assassination in 1865, the first five dollars for the statue was donated by a Mrs. Charlotte Scott of Marietta, Ohio. Contributions were soon pouring in, whereupon Congress finally set aside appropriate grounds for Thomas Bell's statue of Lincoln breaking slavery's chains. The memorial was dedicated on April 14, 1876—the 11th anniversary of the assassination of the Great Emancipator.

Frederick Douglass Home, 1411 W. Street Southeast

"Cedar Hill," the 20-room colonial mansion in which Frederick Douglass lived for the last 13 years of his life, has been preserved as a monument to the great 19th-century abolitionist. In 1964, Secretary of the Interior Stewart Udall declared it a national shrine.

Credit for the restoration and preservation of the home belongs largely to the National Association of Colored Women's Clubs, which worked hand in hand with the Douglass Association.

Howard University

Howard University, founded in 1867, is the largest institution of higher learning established for the Negro in the immediate post-Civil War period.

Covering more than 50 acres on one of the highest elevations in the District of Columbia, the campus grounds and the physical plant are valued at more than 40 million dollars. Of particular interest is the famed Founders Library which contains more than 300,000 volumes and includes the Moorland Collection, one of the finest collections on Negro life and history in the United States.

FLORIDA

Daytona Beach: *Bethune-Cookman College*

One of the leading institutions in the South for the training of Negro teachers, *Bethune-Cookman College* was founded in 1904 by Mary McLeod Bethune on "faith and a dollar-and-a-half."

In her day, Mrs. Bethune, advisor to Presidents Franklin D. Roosevelt and Harry S. Truman, was one of the most powerful and influential Negroes in the United States.

Olustee: *Olustee Battlefield Historic Memorial*

Olustee was the site of a bloody Civil War

battle during which the unseasoned soldiers of the 8th U.S. Colored Troops lost more than 300 men, many of them untutored in the operation of their weapons and equipment. The veteran 54th Massachusetts, one of the two other black regiments serving among Union forces at the battle, fared better in the battle, checked the enemy, and held its position while it covered the retreat of the corps it had been sent in to rescue. Cited for valor in combat, Stephen A. Swails became the first Negro to be commissioned in the 54th. Federal troops retired to Jacksonville after the engagement at Olustee, remaining there until the end of the war.

GEORGIA

Atlanta: *Atlanta University System—Ebenezer Baptist Church South View Cemetery*

The campus of the *Atlanta University System* (consisting of Atlanta University, and Morris Brown, Clark, Morehouse and Spelman Colleges) is one of the most beautiful to be found anywhere in the South.

Ebenezer Baptist Church had as its associate pastor the Rev. Martin Luther King, Jr., the most celebrated spokesman for non-violent protest produced in America in the 20th century. It was from this church that Dr. King radiated outward through the rest of the South, organizing chapters of the Southern Christian Leadership Conference (SCLC), the civil rights coalition which he served as president. Funeral services for Dr. King were held in this church, and attended by a host of notables from all over the world. As millions watched on television, mourners lined up for miles behind the mule-drawn wagon that carried Dr. King from Ebenezer to Morehouse College, his alma mater. There, the eulogies were delivered, and more than 150,000 paid their last respects to a great and fearless American martyr.

Dr. King was laid to rest in *South View Cemetery*, where a marble crypt was inscribed with the words which he had used to conclude his famous speech delivered on the occasion of the 1963 March on Washington. The words, taken from an old slave song, are: "Free at last, free at last, thank God Almighty I'm free at last." South View was founded in 1886 by Negroes who balked at a prevailing policy which required that they be buried in the rear of the municipal cemetery.

Columbus: *"Blind Tom" Marker (U.S. 27A) Bragg Smith Marker*

The "Blind Tom" Marker refers visitors and pedestrians to the grave site of the famous black pianist, "Blind Tom" Bethune, son of a slave, but a remarkably gifted prodigy whose astonishing talent brought him into the salons of Europe, where royalty marvelled at his virtuoso performances. "Blind Tom" also toured his own country and excited the wonder and admiration of appreciative audiences everywhere.

The *Bragg Smith Marker,* located in the Columbus Colored Cemetery, marks the grave site and marble memorial built by the city in memory of Bragg Smith, who was killed while attempting to rescue the city engineer from a cave-in.

Savannah: *Rev. George Lisle Monument (First Bryan Baptist Church, 559 West Bryan Street)*

The *Rev. George Lisle Monument* is dedicated to the first American Negro Baptist missionary.

ILLINOIS

Chicago: *The Art Institute—the Historical Society—Milton L. Olive Park—Museum of African American History and Art—Provident Hospital and Training School—Underground Railway Marker—Victory Monument*

Among the nation's great art galleries, the *Art Institute* has works by Negro artists and sculptors, including Tanner's "The Two Disciples at the Tomb," Richard Hunt's "Hero Construction," and Marion Perkins "Man of Sorrows."

Among the treasures and exhibits of the *Chicago Historical Society* are many which relate to Negroes, including a replica of the cabin built by Jean Du Sable (see entry below) and numerous other artifacts relative to the days of slavery. John Jones (1811-1879), a successful businessman who settled in Chicago in 1845 and was Cook County Commissioner

Atlanta University held its first classes in abandoned railroad cars.

from 1871 to 1875, and his wife Mary are preserved for posterity by two Aaron Darling portraits. Other material explores the role played by black units from Illinois during campaigns of the Civil War.

The *Du Sable Marker* on the Michigan Avenue Bridge marks the site of the first building in the area that is now part of the city of Chicago. It was also the home of Jean Baptiste Pointe Du Sable, a Negro fur trapper and trader from Santo Domingo.

According to records in Cahokia, Illinois, Du Sable was married to a Potawatamie Indian in the year 1788. The earliest known reference to him appears in an army report by a British colonel in 1779, but there are several other descriptions of him and his home after that date. For instance, he is known to have owned a farm in Peoria, Illinois, as well as other property in St. Charles, Missouri, where his son eventually settled.

In 1796, Du Sable sold his 'Chicago' home, and went to live with his son in St. Charles, where he died in 1814.

The site of Du Sable's home is marked by a plaque on the northeast approach to the Michigan Avenue Bridge. Two other plaques exist—one in the Chicago Historical Society, the other in the lobby of Du Sable High School, at 49th and State Streets.

Milton L. Olive Park was dedicated by Chicago Mayor Richard Daley in honor of the first black soldier to be awarded a Congressional Medal of Honor during the Vietnam conflict. Olive died in action after exhibiting extraordinary heroism which saved the lives of several other soldiers exposed to a live grenade.

The Museum of African-American History and Art was founded recently by Mrs. Margaret Burroughs in an effort to "inspire Afro-American people by acquainting them with contributions other members of their race have made to society in the past." Of the many artifacts, including books and periodicals, relating to the Negro, perhaps the most distinctive is the powderhorn carried during the Revolutionary War by the Negro fifer Barzillai Lew.

Provident Hospital and Training School, 51st and Vincennes Avenue, is the first training school for Negro nurses in the United States. It was founded by Dr. Daniel Hale Williams, the renowned surgeon who performed the first successful operation on the human heart in 1893.

An *Underground Railway Marker*, which represents an in-transit point for slaves escaping into Canada, is located at 9955 South Beverly Avenue.

Victory Monument, at 35th Street and South Park Way, is a memorial statue by Leonard Crunelle honoring the Negro soldiers of Illinois who served in World War I.

Just opposite this statue is the Lake Meadows Shopping Center and Housing

Jean Baptiste Point du Sable (r.) and the fur trading settlement which became the city of Chicago.

Development. The Ida B. Wells Homes, named for the fiery civil rights advocate, can be found two blocks south of the development. The monument and tomb of Stephen A. Douglas, once the owner of much of the land in the area, is likewise located near 35th Street.

INDIANA

Bloomingdale: *Underground Railroad Marker (U.S. 41)*

This marker is only one of several once used to assist fugitive slaves brave enough to risk death by fleeing from the South and seeking freedom and safety in Canada. One of these, William Trail, liked Indiana so much he decided instead to stay on and go into farming. His efforts were met with success, and he became one of many prosperous farmers active in Union County, Indiana.

Fountain City: *Levi Coffin Home, North Main Street*

Levi Coffin, a Quaker abolitionist referred to as "The President of the Underground Railroad," used his own home as a way-station in which, from 1827 to 1847, he hid more than 300 slaves heading for Illinois, Michigan, or Canada.

Born in North Carolina in 1798, Coffin moved to Fountain City (then known as Newport) at the age of 28. From there he went to Ohio where he continued his activities, eventually helping over 3,000 slaves escape from the South. One of the founders of the Freedmen's Bureau (1865), he was still engaged in the resettlement of ex-slaves long after the Civil War had ended. Coffin died in Avondale, Ohio in 1877.

IOWA

Clinton: *Underground Railroad Station*

Before the Lafayette Hotel was built, the small house that once stood at Sixth Street South and South Second Street is known to have been a point of shelter and sustenance for Negro fugitives escaping from Missouri. Iowa was a free territory by virtue of both the Northwest Ordinance (1787) and the Missouri Compromise of 1820. Many Quakers who had come to the state before the Civil War took great pains to organize an efficient and effective Underground Railroad network.

Sioux City: *Pearl Street*

Once the city's main thoroughfare, Pearl Street is named for a Negro pioneer who arrived in the town by boat more than a century ago and achieved widespread popularity as a cook. Another Negro cook, Aunty Wooden by name, impressed many leading citizens with her speciality, an opossum dinner. Civil War veteran Henry Riding was another black pioneer who staked a claim to Iowa land, and had a successful career as a homesteader. He once prevented a railroad crew at gunpoint from laying track across his land, and forced the company to settle for $21,000 before granting them the right of access. Sioux City was a refuge for many slaves escaping from Missouri.

KANSAS

Beeler: *George Washington Carver Marker—Fort Scott*

Along route K-96 in Ness County, Kansas lies the plot of land once homesteaded by George Washington Carver, famed Negro agricultural scientist. He spent two years there before going to college in Iowa.

Fort Scott was the home of the First Kansas Colored Volunteers, a Negro unit organized by the Union Army in August 1862. The first such unit to go into combat during the Civil War, it beat back a superior Confederate force at the battle of Island Mount, Missouri on October 28, 1862.

Dodge City: *Fort Dodge*

Established in 1865, Fort Dodge was often used as a base of operations by the all-black 10th U.S. Cavalry, a unit which saw much action on the plains protecting settlers, pioneers and cattlemen from Indian uprisings, but which was equally active in Dodge City itself, a haven for gamblers, rustlers and even desperate killers. When a Negro named Taylor was murdered, the Fort Dodge commandant decided to take action against the town's criminal element. County government and a string of fearless sheriffs eventually quieted the town, reducing the major crime to less serious proportions. Many of the Negro cowboys active on the trail stopped at Dodge and many of them matched their white counterparts in let-

Slaves like these sought escape from the South via the Underground Railroad.

ting off steam and raising cain. Ben Hodges was not among these transients, partly because his game called for a more smooth operation. Hodges was fond of bilking ranchers by posing as a wealthy man and getting financial backing for supposedly reputable projects. Though he was eventually unmasked as an imposter, he was spared the rope or the bullet, and lived to a ripe old age, regaling youngsters with pioneer tales and eventually coming to be regarded as a revered and respectable old-timer.

Leavenworth: *Fort Leavenworth*

Fort Leavenworth was the first home of the 10th Cavalry, the all-black unit which not only participated in many important battles during the Indian wars, but also served with valor and distinction during the Spanish-American War. It was at Leavenworth that the Independent Kansas Colored Battery, a unit with several Negro officers, was recruited in 1864. Among its members was Captain H. Ford Douglass, son of the noted abolitionist Frederick Douglass. The younger Douglass joined the Illinois Volunteers as far back as 1862.

Nicodemus: *Nicodemus Colony*

Located along U.S. Route 24 two miles west of the Rooks-Graham County line, *Nicodemus Colony* is the last of three now-virtually-deserted colonies which were founded by the Exodusters—a group of Negro homesteaders active in Kansas during the 1870's. The name 'Nicodemus' was derived from a slave who, according to legend, foretold the coming of the Civil War.

Arriving in 1877, the first settlers lived in dugouts and burrows during the cold weather. From the outset, they were plagued by crop failures. Although never more than 500 in number, they managed nonetheless to create a real community—with teachers, ministers, civil servants, etc. The state of Kansas has commemorated this site with a historical marker located in a roadside park in Nicodemus.

Osawatomie: *John Brown Memorial State Park*

This state park, named in honor of the fiery insurrectionist, contains the cabin in which he lived during his brief sojourn in Kansas.

Wallace: *Fort Wallace*

Only a roadside marker and a cemetery are left as identifying marks of Fort Wallace, another of the military outposts used by the 10th Cavalry. One white officer who came to Fort Wallace as commandant of the 5th Cavalry after having refused a

Sodhouses like the one shown above were built by the first settlers of Nicodemus.

e BLOODY MASSACRE perpetrated in King-Street BOSTON on March 5th 1770 by a party of the 29th R
BUTCHER'S HALL
GR
CUSTOM HOUSE
Engrav'd Printed & Sold by PAUL REVERE BOSTON
ſton! ſee thy Sons deplore,
Walks beſmear'd with guiltleſs Gore.
leſs P—n and his ſavage Bands,
ous Rancour ſtretch their bloody Hands;
arbarians grinning o'er their Prey,
e Carnage, and enjoy the Day.
If ſcalding drops from Rage from Anguiſh Wrung
If ſpeechleſs Sorrows lab'ring for a Tongue,
Or if a weeping World can ought appeaſe
The plaintive Ghoſts of Victims ſuch as theſe;
The Patriot's copious Tears for each are ſhed,
A glorious Tribute which embalms the Dead.
But know FATE ſummons to that awful
Where JUSTICE ſtrips the Murd'rer of hi
Should venal C—ts the ſcandal of the
Snatch the relentleſs Villain from her
Keen Execrations on this Plate inſc
Shall reach a JUDGE who never can b
happy Sufferers were Meſs. SAML. GRAY, SAML. MAVERICK, JAMS. CALDWELL, CRISPUS ATTUCKS & PATK
Killed. Six wounded; two of them (CHRISTR. MONK & JOHN CLARK) Mortall

Paul Revere's broadside of the Boston Massacre, where Crispus Attucks fell.

regiment of Negro troopers changed his attitude in the field when Negro soldiers whom he fought alongside proved their mettle in battle against the Cheyenne. The black cavalrymen marched 230 miles in nine days, and killed 10 Cheyenne who had surrounded the escort party which was taking the major to his new regiment.

LOUISIANA

Baton Rouge: *Southern University*

Located in Baton Rouge since 1914, Southern University is the successor to an institute founded in New Orleans after the Civil War. The modern and well-financed plant now serves some 12,000 students on a breathtakingly landscaped site that includes a huge lake. The two university satellites now in existence are located in Shreveport and New Orleans.

New Orleans: *Chalmette National Historical Park—Louisiana State Museum*

Chalmette National Historical Park is the more precise site of what is usually recorded in history as the Battle of New Orleans, fought during the War of 1812. The battle pitted the motley forces of General Andrew Jackson against 5,400 seasoned English veterans of the Napoleonic campaigns fighting under Sir Edward Pakenham. About 200 of Jackson's soldiers were free Negroes commanded by Colonel Joseph Savary. These men, according to Jackson, manifested great bravery, "although they were poorly armed and sometimes forced to fight with empty guns used as clubs." After the first attack on December 23, 1814, Jackson withdrew his men to Chalmette, where he built a defensive breastwork which shielded his 4,000-man force. On Christmas Day, Pakenham arrived with his men, and sought immediately to engage Jackson's Creoles, Indians, Negroes, Kentuckians and pirates. The Americans repulsed two attacks before girding for the decisive engagement on January 8. Pakenham was felled in this last desperate charge, struck, according to Jackson, "from the bullet of a free man of color, who was a famous rifle shot and came from the Attakapas region of Louisiana." Among the hundreds of Negroes who had contributed to the victory was Jordan Noble, a 14-year-old drummer boy whose drum has been preserved at the Louisiana State Museum.

The Louisiana State Museum, 751 Charles Street, also contains a tablet inscribed to the memory of Norbert Rillieux, the New Orleans "quadroon libre" whose invention of the sugar evaporating pan revolutionized the sugar refining industry by reducing labor and costs to a bare minimum. Rillieux's father was a wealthy engineer and plantation owner; his mother was a slave.

Port Hudson: *Port Hudson Siege Marker*

The besieged city of Port Hudson was the scene of numerous acts of gallantry involving black troops from the 1st and Third Louisiana Native Guards—freedmen who were recruited in New Orleans by Union general Ben Butler. The city fell in July, but the bombardment began as far back as March of 1863. The New York *Times* wrote: ". . . official testimony settles the question that the Negro race can fight with great prowess. Those black soldiers had never before been in any severe engagement. They were comparatively raw troops, and were yet subjected to . . . the charging upon fortifications through the crash of belching batteries. The men, white or black, who will not flinch from that, will flinch from nothing. It is no longer possible to doubt the bravery and steadiness of the colored race. . . ." The great majority of the Negro units in the battle were led by Negro officers, including Captain Andre Cailloux who was given a state funeral after he fell on the battlefield. The funeral pageant was "the like of which" had never before been seen "in honor of a dead Negro."

MARYLAND

Annapolis: *Matthew Henson Plaque*

The *Matthew Henson Plaque* honors the memory of the only man to accompany Admiral Robert E. Peary on all of his polar expeditions. Henson was also the first man actually to reach the North Pole (April 6, 1909). Peary himself, barely able to walk, arrived there after Henson had taken a reading of his position and proudly planted the flag of the United States.

Matthew Henson

Baltimore: *Morgan State College*

Morgan State College has an interesting collection of artifacts on Benjamin Banneker, noted astronomer, compiler of almanacs and—together with L'Enfant—surveyor of the District of Columbia. It also houses a number of artifacts on Frederick Douglass and Matthew Henson.

Baltimore County: *Banneker Marker, Westchester Avenue at Westchester School*

This marker is a tribute to Benjamin Banneker, the Negro mathematician, astronomer and inventor who, in 1792, produced an almanac regarded as one of the most reliable of his day. His scientific knowledge, as well as the international renown that accrued to him, led to his assignment as a member of the surveying and planning team which helped lay out the nation's capital.

(Banneker's correspondence with President Thomas Jefferson can be seen at the Library of Congress.)

Rockville: *Uncle Tom's Cabin*

Site of the log cabin believed to be the birthplace of Josiah Henson, the escaped slave immortalized as Uncle Tom in Harriet Beecher Stowe's famous abolitionist study. Born in 1789, Henson was sold at auction at an early age, and transferred to many masters until he managed to escape in 1830. After setting up a community for fugitive slaves in Dawn, Canada, Henson frequently returned to the South to liberate others. Later a minister and mill owner, Henson journeyed to London in 1851, meeting the Archbishop of Canterbury who asked him from which university he had graduated. Henson replied cryptically: "The University of Adversity." Two years earlier, he had met Mrs. Stowe and given her the outline of his slave experiences which formed the basis for her celebrated story. In the introduction to Henson's *Autobiography,* published some years later, she acknowledged his story as the source of her own tale.

The Rev. Josiah T Henson

MASSACHUSETTS

Boston: *Crispus Attucks Monument—Shaw Monument—Bunker Hill Monument*

The *Crispus Attucks Monument,* located in the Boston Common, was dedicated in 1888 to honor the five victims of the Boston Massacre—Crispus Attucks, Samuel Maverick, James Caldwell, Samuel Gray, and Patrick Carr. The site of the Massacre is marked by a plaque on State Street, near the Old State House.

Attucks is believed by many historians to have been the same man who in 1750 was advertised as a runaway Negro slave from Framingham, Massachusetts. A stranger to Boston, he led a group which converged on a British garrison quartered in King Street to help enforce the Townshend Acts. One of the soldiers of the garrison panicked and fired, and Attucks was the first to fall. (Gray and Caldwell were also killed on the same spot. Maverick and Carr died later of wounds sustained during the clash. The British soldiers were later tried for murder and acquitted.)

The five men are buried in Granary Burying Ground, together with such famous Revolutionary War figures as John Adams and John Hancock, as well as Governor William Bradford of Plymouth Colony.

Executed by the famed sculptor Augustus Saint-Gaudens, the *Shaw Monument,* on Beacon Street facing the State House, is a group statue of Colonel Robert Gould Shaw and the 54th Massachusetts Volunteers, a Negro regiment which served in the Union Army. The regiment particularly distinguished itself in the battle for Fort Wagner during which Colonel Shaw was killed. Sergeant William H. Carney's valiant exploits during this battle later won him the Congressional Medal of Honor.

Standing in the Charlestown district of Boston, the *Bunker Hill Monument* commemorates the famous Revolutionary War battle, which—contrary to popular belief—was actually fought on Breed's Hill on June 17, 1775.

A number of Negroes fought alongside the colonists during the battle, including: Peter Salem, Salem Poor, Titus Coburn, Cato Howe, Alexander Ames, Seymour Burr, Pomp Fiske, and Prince Hall, founder of the Negro Masonic order.

The cornerstone for the monument was laid by the Marquis de Lafayette in 1825. A ceremony at which Daniel Webster was a featured speaker marked the completion of the monument in 1843.

The Crispus Attucks Monument

Cambridge: *Phillis Wheatley Folio*

During her celebrated trip to England in 1773, Phillis Wheatley, the first American Negro woman to write a book, was presented with a folio edition of John Milton's "Paradise Lost." It now resides in the library of Harvard University.

Miss Wheatley, who came to America in 1761 as a child of seven or eight, made rapid strides in mastering the English language and, by the time she was 14, had already completed her first poem. Always in delicate health, she died in Boston on December 5, 1784.

Central Village: *Memorial to Paul Cuffe*

Cuffe, son of a freedman, was born in 1759, became a prosperous merchant seaman, and resolved to use his wealth and position to campaign for the extension of civil rights for Negroes. On one occasion, Cuffe refused to pay his personal property tax on the grounds that he was being denied full citizenship rights. A court of law eventually upheld his action, whereupon he was granted the same privileges and immunities enjoyed by white citizens of the state. In 1815, Cuffe transported 38 Negroes to Sierra Leone in what was intended to become a systematic attempt at repatriating the black inhabitants of the United States. With the growth of abolitionist sentiment in the colonies, repatriation lost favor among both Negroes and whites as a means of solving the Negro question.

MICHIGAN

Battle Creek: *Sojourner Truth Grave*

The *Sojourner Truth Grave* in Oak Hill Cemetery marks the resting place of one of the most powerful abolitionist lecturers of the 19th century.

Sojourner settled in Battle Creek after the Civil War, but continued to travel on lecture tours until a few years before her death in 1883, at the approximate age of 85.

Cassopolis: *Underground Railroad Marker*

There is an *Underground Railroad Marker* located 2 1/2 miles east of Cassopolis on Route M-60.

Detroit: *Detroit Public Library—Douglass—Brown Marker*

The Azalia Hackley Memorial Collection is one of the major treasures available for public perusal at the Detroit Public Library, 5201 Woodward Avenue. Madame Hackley did pioneering work in the field of music, promoting Negro concert talent and seeking recognition for works done by Negro composers. Talented Negro musicians like Clarence Cameron White and Nathaniel Dett were among those who benefitted from scholarship aid provided by this tireless crusader. Included in her collection of artifacts, clippings and memorabilia are more than 600 books, sheet music for many popular songs, assorted photographs, and printed programs.

The *Douglass-Brown Marker,* on East Congress Street and St. Antoine, marks the site of the William Webb House, where fellow abolitionists John Brown and Frederick Douglass met in March of 1859 to map out the strategy which ultimately led to the abortive Harpers Ferry revolt. Douglass was strongly opposed to this course of action.

Marshall: *Crosswhite Boulder*

In Triangle Park, on Michigan Avenue and Mansion Street, stands *Crosswhite Boulder*—the site of the pitched battle fought in 1846 in defense of Adam Crosswhite, a fugitive slave who had fled from Kentucky. The Crosswhite case is said to have been instrumental in the enactment of the Fugitive Slave Law of 1850.

MINNESOTA

St. Paul: *Fort Snelling State Park*

Fort Snelling was that outpost in the Wisconsin Territory to which the slave later to become known as Dred Scott was transported from Illinois in 1836.

Scott met and married his wife Harriet at the fort, and also saw his first child born there. After having been taken to Missouri by his master, he filed suit for his freedom, and became a national figure as his case was tried, from 1847 to 1857, before numerous tribunals en route to the U.S. Supreme Court. Scott argued that he should be considered free by virtue of his having previously resided in Illinois and at Fort Snelling.

(See St. Louis, Missouri entry for discussion of Dred Scott decision.)

Dred Scott

Sojourner Truth

MISSISSIPPI

Natchez: *Natchez National Cemetery*

The Cemetery, located at 61 Cemetery Road, is the final resting of many Negro war dead, including landsman Wilson Brown, a Medal of Honor recipient during the Civil War. Brown and fellow seaman John Lawson received their medals for courage in action while serving aboard the *U.S.S. Hartford* in its Mobile Bay engagement of August 5, 1864. Another prominent Negro from Natchez, Hiram R. Revels, was the first Negro elected to the U.S. Senate. A Methodist minister, Revels recruited Negroes for the Union side during the war, and served as Chaplain of a Union regiment from Mississippi. He later became president of Alcorn A & M, and is buried in Holly Springs.

MISSOURI

Diamond: *Carver National Monument*

Located in a park, *Carver National Monument* commemorates the place where the great Negro scientist, George Washington Carver, was born and spent his early childhood.

Kidnapped when he was just six weeks old, Carver was eventually ransomed for a horse valued at $300. Raised in Missouri by the family of Moses Carver, his owner, he made his way through Minnesota, Kansas and Iowa before being 'discovered' by Booker T. Washington in 1896. That same year, Carver joined the faculty of Tuskegee Institute where he conducted most of the research for which he is famous.

The monument is the first created in honor of a Negro. It contains a statue of Carver as a boy, and encloses several trails leading to places of which he was particularly fond. The park also houses a visitors' center and a museum displaying many of his discoveries and personal belongings, as well as other artifacts of his day. It can be reached on U.S. Alt. 71, just west of Diamond.

Jefferson City: *Lincoln University*

More than $6,000 raised by the black fighting men of the 62nd and 65th U.S. Colored Infantry constituted the initial endowment for a 22-foot square room in which classes first began in 1866 at what is now Lincoln University in Jefferson City. Known then as Lincoln Institute, the school began receiving state aid to expand its teacher-training program in 1870. It became a state institution nine years later, and instituted college-level courses in 1887. It has been known as Lincoln University since 1921, and has had graduate school status since 1940. The more than 2,000 students now attending

The battlefield at Little Big Horn.

the school are often reminded that Lincoln was launched due to the generous philanthropy of ex-slaves, many of them illiterate, who fought for their freedom, and the freedom of succeeding generations.

St. Louis: *Old Courthouse (Jefferson National Expansion Memorial)*

It was in the *Old Courthouse* in 1847 that Dred Scott, the most famous fugitive slave of his day, first filed suit to gain his freedom.

For the next 10 years, the Dred Scott case was a burning political and social issue across the country. In 1857, it reached the Supreme Court. There, Chief Justice Roger Taney handed down the decision that slaves could not become free by escaping—or by being taken—into free territory, nor could they be considered American citizens.

Ironically, a few weeks after the decision was rendered, Scott was set free by his new owner, and died a year later.

MONTANA

Crow Agency: *Custer Battlefield National Monument—Reno-Benteen Battlefield National Monument*

These two monuments commemorate the famed Battle of the Little Big Horn, in which three batteries commanded by General George Custer were slaughtered on June 25, 1876 by a group of Indian tribes led by Chief Sitting Bull.

The first skirmish that day involved an advance party under the command of Major Marcus Reno. One of the first to fall was Isaiah Dorman, a Negro who had lived among the Sioux and was serving as an army interpreter. Dorman was known to the Indians as "Teat," or sometimes referred to as the "black white man."

According to one account, the dying Negro was found by Sitting Bull himself, who ordered that his body not be mutilated in any way.

Big Horn Station: *Fort Manuel Marker*

Captain William Clark and his party, including the lively and valuable slave York, camped at this site on July 26, 1806, a year before Manuel Lisa established Montana's first trading post. This site, too, was chosen by Major Andrew Henry as the Rocky Mountain Fur Company's first trading post. Leader of that expedition was Edward Rose, another of the famed Negro mountainmen and explorers active in the territory.

Fort Shaw: *Site of Fort Shaw*

This military outpost was founded in 1867 and named after Colonel Robert Gould Shaw, commandant of the heroic 54th Massachusetts who fell during his unit's spirited, valiant and unsuccessful charge against the breastworks of Fort Wagner during the Civil War. Fort Shaw was the home base of the 25th Infantry, one of the units sent into the wilderness to protect the territory's few pioneering settlers and indefatigable miners from Indian attacks.

Pompey's Pillar

This pillar, named for the Indian, Pomp, was discovered by Captain William Clark of the famed Lewis and Clark expedition. One of the members of Clark's group was a slave named York, a giant of a man who proved to be an invaluable asset to Clark—not only because of his prodigious strength and endurance, but also because he got along so well with the Indians, who were impressed with his dancing ability.

NEVADA

Reno: *The Jim Beckwourth Trail*

In the early days of pioneer settlement, the barren stretch of trail between Reno and the California line was the last obstacle to be overcome before passing through the gateway to the Golden West. The original trail was laid out by the loquacious and cantankerous Jim Beckwourth, one of the legendary mountain men whose exploits lend spice and sparkle to the Western saga. Beckwourth Pass helped put the city of Reno on the map, particularly after the railroad decided to put a station there and began selling acreage in the neighborhood. Reno was later the site of the famous Jim Jeffries-Jack Johnson heavyweight fight, won by the famed black champion who had bested Tommy Burns in Australia, in

Indians did not believe Lewis and Clark's slave York was black. They tried to rub off his color.

1908. Johnson held the crown for seven years, losing it to Jess Willard on a 26-round knockout.

NEW HAMPSHIRE

Jaffrey: *Amos Fortune Grave*

The *Amos Fortune Grave* is the resting place of an 18th-century Negro slave who purchased his freedom in 1770 at the age of 60, and went on to become one of the leading citizens of Jaffrey, his adopted hometown.

Nine years later, Fortune was able to buy freedom for his wife, Violet Baldwin, and his adopted daughter, Celyndia. In 1781, he moved to Jaffrey and set himself up as a tanner, employing both Negro and white apprentices. In 1795, six years before his death, Fortune founded the Jaffrey Social Library and, in his will, directed that money be left to the church and to the local school district.

The school fund begun by Fortune is still in existence, having grown from $233 to the present total of $1,600. Proceeds from the fund are used to provide annual prizes for high-school debating and oratorical contests.

Each year during July and August, the Amos Fortune Forum is held as a memorial to the Old Meeting House where the ex-slave attended church services. Both Fortune and his wife lie in the meeting-house burial ground.

Fortune's freedom papers and several receipt slips for the sale of his leather are on file at the Jaffrey Public Library. Similarly, the Fortune house and barn still stand intact.

NEW JERSEY

Newark: *The Newark Museum*

This museum, located at 43-49 Washington Street, owns the paintings of such famous Negro artists as Henry Ossawa Tanner ("The Good Shepherd"); Charles W. White ("Sojourner Truth and Booker T. Washington"), and Hale Woodruff ("Poor Man's Cotton"). Tanner was a student under Thomas Eakins and spent most of his life abroad. He excelled in religious subjects and sacred themes. White and Woodruff are among the most prominent black painters at work today.

NEW MEXICO

Columbus: *The Pancho Villa Expedition*

After one of his patented border raids had resulted in the burning of half of Columbus and the loss of many lives, Pancho Villa and his bandit army so aroused the ire of the U.S. government that it dispatched a punitive expedition into Mexico to track down Villa and eliminate him. "Black Jack" Pershing was in command of the 10th U.S. Cavalry during the strenuous journey. With only two days' rations in their knapsacks, the black troopers were forced to live off the land while in pursuit of the canny and fearless Mexican outlaw. The 10th engaged the Villistas at Carrizal, Mexico, and lost 10 men in a bloody skirmish. The expedition then returned to Fort Huachuca, its permanent base.

Lincoln: *Old Court House*

During the Lincoln County Cattle War of 1877-1878, Billy the Kid, the notorious outlaw, was held in custody at the *Old Court House*, now a frontier museum. Negro cowhands were involved on both sides of this struggle and, on one occasion, a group of Negro cavalrymen surrounded Billy the Kid during a particularly bloody battle. The outlaw, however, managed to escape the ambush. (Incidentally, it was a Negro trooper who delivered Governor Lew Wallace's proclamation declaring a cessation to hostilities and the granting of amnesty to all those involved.)

Zuni: *Zuni Pueblo*

Zuni Pueblo was discovered in 1539 by Estevanico, a Moorish slave who was one of the original party of Spanish explorers to land in Tampa Bay in 1528. After a succession of disasters, the party was ultimately reduced to four (including Estevanico) who, marooned on the Texas shore near Galveston, were soon captured and enslaved by Indians. After seven years in captivity, Estevanico and the others escaped to New Spain.

Having heard of the legend of the Seven Cities of Gold, reputed to be located in the Southwest, Estevanico signed on as an advance scout for an expedition led by a Father Marco. Often traveling ahead of the main party, Estevanico sent most of his messages back via friendly Indians. His last message—a giant cross emblematic of a major discovery—led the expedition to the *Zuni Pueblo* which Estevanico apparently thought was part of the legendary Seven Cities. By the time the expedition arrived, however, the suspicious Zuni had already put Estevanico to death.

Today, Estevanico is credited with the discovery of a territory which comprises the states of Arizona and New Mexico.

NEW YORK

Albany: *Emancipation Proclamation*

The New York State Library houses President Abraham Lincoln's original draft of the preliminary *Emancipation Proclamation* issued in September 1862. It was purchased by Gerritt Smith, a wealthy abolitionist and patron of the famed revolutionary, John Brown. The January 1, 1863 version of the proclamation resides in the National Archives of Washington D.C. The draft of this document was destroyed in the Chicago fire of 1871.

Auburn: *Harriet Tubman Home*

The *Harriet Tubman Home* stands as a monument to the woman who is believed to have led some 300 slaves to freedom via the Underground Railroad.

Miss Tubman settled in this home at the close of the Civil War—years after it had outlived its original function as a major way-station on the northbound freedom route of fugitive slaves. In 1953, the house was restored at a cost of $21,000. Born a slave in Maryland, Miss Tubman fled at the age of 25, only to return South at least 19 times to lead others to freedom. Rewards of up to $40,000 were offered for her capture, but she was never arrested, nor did she ever lose one of her passengers in transit. During the Civil War, she served as a spy for Union forces.

New York City:

African Methodist Episcopal Zion Church
Amsterdam News
Apollo Theatre
Booker T. Washington Plaque

Harriet Tubman

Calvary Baptist Church
Cornerstone Baptist Church
Franks Restaurant
Fraunces Tavern
Freedom National Bank
Hotel Theresa
Messiah Baptist
Schomburg Collection of Negro History and Literature
Sugar Hill

African Methodist Episcopal Zion Church: 151 West 136th Street

The *African Methodist Episcopal Zion* (AMEZ) Church was dedicated in 1801 on a plot of land located at Church and Leonard Streets in New York City. A year later, the trustees of the church signed an agreement with the General Conference of the Methodist Episcopal Church, thereby consenting to place themselves under the jurisdiction of the bishops from this latter church. The conference was also given the right to appoint a preacher for the Negro church. By 1820, however, the AMEZ Church had found this arrangement so unsatisfactory that it bolted from the General Conference. At this juncture, the leader of the Negro congregation was a former slave named Peter Williams. The first three ordained Negro ministers of the new church were Abraham Thompson, James Scott, and Thomas Miller, while the first exhorter (an unordained person authorized to preach) was William Miller. James Varick was the first bishop.

Amsterdam News: 2340 8th Avenue

The *Amsterdam News,* now New York City's largest Negro-owned newspaper as well as the largest weekly community paper in the U.S.A., was founded on December 4, 1909 in the home of James H. Anderson (132 West 65th Street). At that time only one of 50 Negro "news sheets" in the country, the *Amsterdam News* had a staff of 10, consisted of six printed pages, and sold for 2¢ a copy. Since then, the paper has been printed at several Harlem addresses.

Altogether, the *Amsterdam News* must be considered one of the most vital organs of information in any campaign to reach the Negro market in New York City.

New York City: *Apollo Theatre, 125th Street, between 7th and 8th Avenues*

The *Apollo Theatre* in Harlem, an entertainment mecca for all races, is one of the last great vaudeville houses in the United States. For 50 weeks of every year, the Apollo presents live entertainment—featuring rising young stars, as well as established Negro professionals who play there not so much for the financial reward as for the importance of exposure to a popular audience.

Bethel A.M.E. Church: 60 West 132nd Street

In the autumn of 1819, Bishop Richard Allen of Philadelphia dispatched William Lambert to New York City for the purpose of organizing an African Methodist Episcopal church there. Mother Bethel Church, the oldest and largest AME church in Manhattan, came into being both as a religious body and as a kind of protest organization.

Booker T. Washington Plaque

Booker T. Washington, educator and founder of Tuskegee Institute, is the only Negro honored by a plaque in the Hall of Fame, New York University.

Calvary Baptist Church: 111-10 New York Boulevard Jamaica 33, New York

Reverend Walter S. Pinn has been pastor of Calvary Baptist Church since 1946, at which time it was still housed in a tiny, one-story building with a seating capacity of only 100. Today, it is the largest Negro congregation on Long Island, and meets in a beautiful spacious structure which can seat some 2,000 persons. The new building contains several classrooms and meeting halls, a wedding chapel, and a modern kitchen. There are two Sunday services, supplemented by a 150-voice chorale under the direction of Mr. Samuel Daniels.

Cornerstone Baptist Church: Lewis and Madison Streets Brooklyn, New York

The Cornerstone Baptist Church, a congregation now boasting over 5,000 members, was founded on September 10, 1917 by eight faithful churchgoers assembled for communal worship in a single room of a private residence at 933 DeKalb Avenue, Brooklyn, New York. The church began to expand rapidly under the pastorship of Reverend T. W. Fentress who linked it in 1932 with the Unity Baptist Church.

Franks Restaurant: 312 West 125th Street

The largest Negro-owned restaurant in Harlem is *Franks,* run by the eminent East Coast restauranteur, Lloyd Von Blaine, and the equally well-known caterer, Selwyn Joseph. *Franks* has been *the* place for quality dining along Harlem's "main stem" for over 46 years.

Fraunces Tavern: Broad and Pearl Streets

One of the most famous landmarks in New York City, *Fraunces Tavern* was bought in 1762 from a wealthy Huguenot by Samuel Fraunces, a West Indian of Negro and French extraction. In those days, Fraunces called his establishment the *Queen's Head Tavern.* Before the Revolutionary War began, it served as a kind of meeting-place for numerous patriots already chafing under the tyranny of King George III.

On April 24, 1774, the Sons of Liberty and the Vigilance Committee met at the tavern to map out much of the strategy later used during the actual war. George Washington himself was a frequenter of the tavern, as were many of his senior officers. Washington's association with Fraunces continued for a number of years, with Fraunces eventually coming to be known as "Steward of the Household" in New York City. It was at *Fraunces Tavern*, in fact, that Washington took leave of his trusted officers in 1783 before retiring to Mount Vernon.

Much of the tavern's original furnishings and decor is still intact. The third floor—now a museum—contains several Revolutionary War artifacts while, on the fourth floor, one can find a historical library featuring paintings by John Ward Dunsmore. A restaurant, patronized by leading New York citizens, as well as by tourists from all over the country, is maintained on the ground floor.

Freedom National Bank: 275 West 125th Street

Freedom National Bank is Harlem's first Negro-chartered, Negro-run commercial bank. Founded in 1965, it already has 10,000 customers, and assets of over 10 million dollars—a figure which, by comparison with other banks maintaining branches in Harlem (Chase Manhattan, First National City, Manufacturers, Hanover, Chemical, and Bankers Trust), is small.

The most significant thing about this bank, however, is the fact that the Harlemite has come to refer to it as *his* bank, a symbolic phrase for residents of an area in which most fixed property and real estate continues to be controlled by white people. The chairman of the board of Freedom National is Jackie Robinson, former baseball great. The president is William R. Hudgins who has lived and worked in Harlem for the past 37 years.

(The first bank in Harlem—the Dunbar Bank—was founded by John D. Rockefeller in 1928, but folded 10 years later. In 1949, the Carver Federal Savings and Loan Association was established, with Hudgins serving as a member of the board. Today, Carver has two branches—one in Manhattan, the other in Brooklyn—and assets totalling some 30 million dollars.)

Hotel Theresa: 2090 7th Avenue (corner of 125th Street)

Built in 1913, the *Hotel Theresa* was once a luxury hotel serving white clientele from lower Manhattan and accommodating "white only" dinner patrons in its luxurious "Skyline Room." In 1936, a corporation headed by Love B. Woods tried to take over the hotel and transform it into a Negro business establishment. This move failed when Seidenberg Estates, the realtors, set a price on it beyond the reach of the group. Woods did eventually manage to purchase the hotel. (Its most publicized guest in recent years has been Cuban premier Fidel Castro.) Nowadays, the hotel has lost some of its original lustre.

Messiah Baptist Church: 866 Sutter Avenue Brooklyn, New York

Messiah Baptist Church has been in existence since March 1965, having been founded by its current pastor, Reverend Elijah Pope. Starting with a group of 15, the congregation has already grown to over 200. The dedicatory sermon was preached by Reverend Sandy F. Ray, pastor of Brooklyn's famous Cornerstone Baptist Church.

Reverend Pope has already organized several auxiliaries, as well as a Boy Scout troop and a street block association. The church is valued at $85,000.

Schomburg Collection of Negro Literature and History: 103 West 135th Street

The *Schomburg Collection of Negro Literature and History* is a library and archive of materials devoted to Negro life around the world.

This collection is built around the private library of Arthur A. Schomburg, a Puerto Rican of African descent. It contains books, pamphlets, manuscripts, photographs, art objects and recordings which cover virtually every aspect of Negro life—from ancient Africa to present-day Negro America.

Among the treasured items in the collection are:

1. The work of America's first Negro poet—Jupiter Hammon's Address to

the Negroes in the State of New York (1787).

2. Manuscript poems and early editions of the works of Phillis Wheatley.
3. Copies of the 1792 and 1793 Almanacs of Benjamin Banneker.
4. The scrapbook of Ira Aldridge, the Negro Shakespearean actor who achieved fame in Europe in the 19th century.
5. *Clotel*, the first novel by an American Negro (William Wells Brown).

Material in the Schomburg is not circulated, but can be used or viewed in the library. G. K. Hall and Co., 97 Oliver Street, Boston 10, Massachusetts has published a nine-volume edition of the "Dictionary Catalog of the Schomburg Collection of Negro Literature and History," priced at $605.00.

Sugar Hill

Sugar Hill is a handsome residential section in uptown Harlem. It is bordered on the west by Amsterdam Avenue; on the north by 160th Street; on the east by Colonial Park, and on the south by 145th Street. An area of tall apartment buildings and private homes, it is peopled largely by middle-class Negroes, sometimes referred to as the *black bourgeoisie*. Its only counterparts in the area of central Harlem are Riverton and Lenox Terrace.

North Elba: *John Brown's Grave*

Just six miles south of Lake Placid on Route 86A, *John Brown's Grave* is located on a farm he purchased after he had left Ohio. Brown lived there until he joined the free-soil fight in Kansas.

The farm was part of 100,000 acres set aside for both freedmen and slaves by Gerritt Smith, a wealthy abolitionist. Smith hoped to build an independent community peopled by ex-slaves who had learned farming and other trades. Brown joined Smith in the venture, but the idea failed to take hold and was eventually abandoned.

Ogdensburg: *Remington Art Memorial*

Artist/journalist Frederic Remington is easily the greatest visual chronicler of the saga and splendor of the Old West. Remington fashioned several durable portraits and sketches of black cavalrymen in action in the field, on bivouac, and even during ceremonial exercises. Remington was

The Schomburg Collection of Negro History and Literature is the best library in New York City for information on Negro life and culture.

also a correspondent during the Spanish-American War, and did a painting entitled "The Charge of the Rough Riders at San Juan Hill." The painting shows only one of the many Negroes who accompanied Teddy Roosevelt's men on their celebrated charge. The Ogdensburg Museum houses the Remington portrait in its permanent collection.

Rochester: *Frederick Douglass Monument*

New York Governor Theodore Roosevelt dedicated the *Frederick Douglass Monument* in 1899. The noted black abolitionist had helped organize all-black volunteer regiments during the Civil War, and saw two of his sons volunteer for duty.

Frederick Douglass

Ticonderoga: *Fort Ticonderoga*

Leading the Revolutionary War assault on the fort at Ticonderoga were Ethan Allen and his famed Green Mountain Boys, many of whom were Negroes, including Lemuel Haynes, Primus Black, and Epheram Blackman. After the American victory, some of the cannons were transported to Boston, where they were instrumental in providing heavy weapons support for General George Washington's thrust into, and capture of, the city.

NORTH CAROLINA

Milton: *The Yellow Tavern*

For more than 30 years, the Yellow Tavern was the workshop of Tom Day, one of the great black artisans and furniture makers of the Deep South prior to the Civil War. Day began making handwrought mahogany furniture in 1818 and, within five years, accumulated enough money to convert the old Yellow Tavern into a miniature factory. Both white apprentices and Negro slaves were taught this skilled trade under his coveted tutelage. Day's artistry was so revered by the citizens of Milton that they went to great pains to secure a special dispensation from a North Carolina law which made it illegal for any free Negro or mulatto to migrate into the state. The dispensation was needed because Day had married Acquilla Wilson in 1829, two years after the law took effect. The legislature actually went so far as to pass a law which exempted Day and his wife from the "fines and penalties of the Act of 1827." Day also found an ingenious way to integrate the Presbyterian church in Milton by offering to replace the worn-down mahogany pews on the main floor of the church—in return for the "privilege" of sitting in them, rather than in the gallery, during services. Day built the pews, but he confounded the parishioners by using maple instead of mahogany. The church, the pews, the Yellow Tavern and Tom Day's home and grave have all survived and are accessible to this day.

Raleigh: *John Chavis Memorial Park, E. Lenoir at Worth Street*

This park is named after John Chavis, a Negro educator and preacher who founded an interracial school in Raleigh which later numbered among its graduates several important public figures, including senators, congressmen and governors. As a result of the abortive Nat Turner slave rebellion in 1831, however, Negroes were barred from preaching in North Carolina, obliging Chavis to retire from the pulpit. He died in 1838.

OHIO

Akron: *John Brown Monument*

The *John Brown Monument* was built in honor of the fiery abolitionist whose ill-fated Harpers Ferry revolt led to his conviction for treason and execution by hanging in 1859.

Cincinnati: *Harriet Beecher Stowe Home*

The *Harriet Beecher Stowe Home* has been preserved as a memorial to the internationally known author of *Uncle Tom's Cabin.*

Dayton: *Paul Laurence Dunbar Home*

The *Paul Laurence Dunbar Home,* at 219 Summit Street in Dayton, has been preserved much as the poet left it at the time of his death in 1906, just prior to his 34th birthday. Along with his personal effects, several original manuscripts can be seen.

Dunbar, the first Negro poet after Phillis Wheatley to gain anything approaching a national reputation in the United States, was also the first to concentrate on dialect' poetry and exclusively Negro themes. His first collection of poetry, *Oak and Ivory,* was published before he was 20. By 1896, his book *Majors and Minors* had won critical favor in a Harper's Weekly review. Dunbar contracted tuberculosis in 1899, and was in failing health until his death on February 9, 1906.

Oberlin: *Oberlin College*

Before the Civil War, Oberlin was one of the centers of underground abolitionist planning and a haven for activists of every stamp and hue. On one occasion, 20 Oberlin villagers actually snatched away a black fugitive who was being returned to his Kentucky owner by Federal agents. Later, three of John Brown's raiding party at Harper's Ferry were identified as Negroes from Oberlin. After the war, Oberlin was able to devote more time to its stated mission: providing quality education to all regardless of race. Among the distinguished alumni of Oberlin was Blanche Kelso Bruce, who served a full term in the U.S. Senate (1875-1881). Another Oberlin graduate was Moses "Fleet" Walker who once played baseball with Toledo of the American Association, then recognized as a major league. Jackie Robinson was the first black player to play major-league baseball in the accepted modern sense of that term.

Put-in-Bay: *Battle of Lake Erie Memorial National Monument*

The memorial draws attention to the Battle of Lake Erie, fought during the War of 1812, and to the impatient and impetuous American sea captain who became immortal by virtue of his defeat of the British: Oliver Hazard Perry. Perry had at first criticized his superior, Commodore Isaac Chauncey, for sending him a motley lot of replacements, including Negroes. After the actual battle, however, these same men prompted him to revise his original estimate and praise the Negro seamen for being "absolutely insensible to danger."

Ripley: *John Rankin House Museum*

An Underground Railroad station prior to the Civil War, the *John Rankin House Museum* is believed to have been the haven of the fugitive slave on whose story the novelist Harriet Beecher Stowe based the flight incident in *Uncle Tom's Cabin.*

Upper Sandusky: *Wyandotte Indian Mission Church*

John Stewart, self-appointed missionary to the Wyandotte Indians, was of French, Negro and Indian stock. His missionary labors among this tribe began in 1816.

Harriet Beecher Stowe

He was assisted in this work by Jonathan Poynter, a Negro who had been raised by the Wyandottes and acted as Stewart's interpreter.

Stewart converted the Indians to Christianity with the help of a fine tenor voice which he used to good advantage in singing them the spirituals and hymns he had learned in Virginia. He died in 1823, one year before the construction of his church was completed.

When the Wyandottes signed the treaty which resulted in their move to Kansas, one of its conditions was that the church remain within the Methodist Episcopal Conference. In 1960, the latter listed the Stewart grave and the missionary church among the 10 official shrines of American Methodism.

OKLAHOMA

Lawton: *Fort Sill*

Units of the 10th Cavalry and the 24th Infantry were among those which served at Fort Sill in the aftermath of the Civil War. Like most black troopers in the territories, they did escort and patrol duty, but they were often called upon to round up cattle thieves and whiskey runners. It was to Fort Sill that the black cavalrymen of the 10th escorted the famed Apache chieftain, Geronimo. Geronimo spent his last days at the fort, and is buried in the Apache cemetery.

Ponca City: *101 Ranch (five miles south of Ponca City on U.S. Route 77)*

During the latter part of the 19th century, the *101 Ranch* was one of the largest and most famous in the West. In its prime, it employed several Negro cowhands, the most celebrated of whom was Bill Pickett.

The originator of the art of bulldogging or steer wrestling, Pickett also perfected a unique style unlike any used by current rodeo participants. He would leap from his horse, grab the steer around the neck or by the horns, and then sink his teeth into the animal's upper lip. In Mexico City, he once wrestled a fighting bull for a full six minutes to win a bet. In March 1932, though then in his 70's, Pickett was still active—the last of the original 101 hands. He died a month later, on April 21, 1932, after being kicked by a horse, and was buried on a knoll near the White Eagle Monument.

PENNSYLVANIA

Erie: *Harry T. Burleigh Birthplace Marker*

A friend of famed Czech composer Dvorak, and a composer/arranger in his own right, Harry T. Burleigh was born in 1866. Burleigh set to music many of the stirring poems of Walt Whitman, and arranged such unforgettable spirituals as "Deep River." He died in 1949.

Lower Merion Township (Montgomery County): *James A. Bland Grave*

In Montgomery County lies the grave of Negro composer James A. Bland who wrote "Carry Me Back to Old Virginny," now the state song of Virginia.

Philadelphia: *Mother Bethel African Methodist Episcopal Church, 419 S. Sixth Street— Negro Soldiers Monument, Lansdowne Drive, West Fairmount Park*

The *Mother Bethel African Methodist Episcopal (AME) Church* was the fourth church to be erected on the site where Richard Allen and Absalom Jones founded the Free African Society in 1787. This later grew into the AME, one of the largest Negro religious denominations in the United States.

Allen, the first Negro bishop, was born a slave, and became a minister and circuit rider after winning his freedom. In 1814, he and James Forten organized a force of 2,500 free Negroes to defend Philadelphia against the British. Sixteen years later, Allen organized the first Negro convention in Philadelphia, and was instrumental in getting the group to adopt a strong platform denouncing slavery and encouraging abolitionist activities. Allen died in 1831, and was buried in a basement vault at Mother Bethel's.

As for Forten, he had been born free in 1766 and, despite his youth, served aboard a Philadelphia privateer during the Revolutionary War. In 1800, he was one of the signers of a petition requesting Congress to alter the Fugitive Slave Act of 1793. Opposed to the idea of resettling slaves in Africa, Forten chaired an 1817 meeting held at Bethel to protest existing colonization schemes. In 1833, he put up

Bill Pickett of the 101 Ranch, Ponca City, Oklahoma.

the funds which William Lloyd Garrison needed to found *The Liberator*.

After his death, Forten's work was continued by his offspring who remained active in the abolitionist cause throughout the Civil War, and on behalf of the freedmen during Reconstruction. The Forten home was a meeting place for many of the leading figures in the movement.

The *Negro Soldiers Monument* was erected by the state of Pennsylvania in 1934 to pay tribute to her fallen Negro soldiers.

Valley Forge: ***Valley Forge State Park***

Negroes were among those who endured the winter hardships of Valley Forge with the bedraggled Continental Army of George Washington in 1777. One of the Negroes who died was Phillip Field, a New Yorker; among those who survived was Salem Poor, the very same Negro who had fought at Bunker Hill as a member of Colonel Frye's Massachusetts Regiment and been officially cited for having "behaved like an experienced officer, as well as an excellent soldier." The citation concluded as follows: ". . . in the person of this said Negro centers a brave and gallant soldier."

SOUTH CAROLINA

Fort Sumter: *Fort Sumter National Monument*

Site of the first shelling of the Civil War on April 12, 1861, Fort Sumter is an important site in Negro history due to the daring exploits of a black coastal pilot, Robert Smalls. On May 13, 1862, Smalls took control of the Confederate steamboat *Planter,* loading into it his family and a few other brave crewmen who endorsed his resourceful and cunning escape plan. Smalls sailed the ship past the Confederate checkpoints, imitating the captain at each vital juncture during which he was being observed from a distance. Once beyond the reach of Confederate shore batteries, Smalls hoisted the white flag of surrender, and delivered the ship into Union hands. Smalls was later elected to several terms as U.S. Congressman from South Carolina.

SOUTH DAKOTA

Deadwood: *Adams Memorial Museum*

Only one of the legendary claimants to the title of "Deadwood Dick" is a Negro, but he can back his assertion with a colorful and richly tapestried autobiography which takes the reader through his childhood in slavery, his early bronc-busting efforts and his fabled life as a range rider and Indian fighter in the old West. Nat Love claimed he won the title during a public competition held in Deadwood on the Fourth of July in 1876. The presence of other Negro cowboys, gambling house operators, and escort soldiers in the area during these years, as well as the convincing style of Love's narrative, lend a high degree of credibility to his adventurous tales although, like Jim Beckworth, he was probably given to moments of wanton exaggeration.

TENNESSEE

Henning: *Fort Pillow Marker*

Taken originally by Union forces in 1862, Fort Pillow was recaptured by Confederate troops under the command of the wily Nathan B. Forrest on April 12, 1864. The few Negro survivors of the engagement testified before the Federal Committee on the Conduct of the War, and documented several instances of massacre after their surrender. Southerners claimed the defenders had simply refused to surrender.

Memphis: *W. C. Handy Park—Tom Lee Memorial (foot of Beale Street on the river bank)*

The city of Memphis pays tribute to famed 'blues' composer W. C. Handy in the form of a park and a heroic bronze statue overlooking the very same Beale Street which he immortalized.

The statue shows Handy standing with

W. C. Handy: "Father of the Blues"

horn poised, about to play. Executed by Leone Tomassi of Italy, it was dedicated in 1960 at the close of a memorial campaign instituted by the city shortly after Handy's death in 1958. (Though born in Florence, Alabama, Handy lived most of his life in the Tennessee city.)

It was on the balcony of the Lorraine Hotel that Martin Luther King, Jr. was assassinated while emerging from a second-floor room, in the presence of a pair of his trusted advisers, Ralph Abernathy and Jesse Jackson. King died in the emergency room of St. Joseph's Hospital on April 4, 1968.

The 30-foot-high Tom Lee granite memorial was erected in 1954 to honor a Negro who, on May 8, 1925, saved the lives of 32 passengers aboard the *M. E. Norman*, an excursion boat which had capsized some 20 miles below Memphis near Cow Island. Alerted to the disaster, Lee pulled 32 people from the water onto his skiff. He was honored for his feat by the Memphis Engineers Club which provided him with money for the duration of his life. A fund was also raised to purchase him a home. After his death in 1952, a committee raised the money needed to erect the memorial.

Nashville: *Fisk University and Meharry Medical School*

Founded in 1866, *Fisk University* is today one of the most prestigious institutions of higher learning for Negroes in the United States. Much the same can be said of *Meharry Medical School*, one of the leading training centers for Negro doctors in the U. S. A.

TEXAS

San Antonio: *The Alamo*

Mystery shrouds the identity of all who fought at *The Alamo* in 1836, but evidence exists that there were some Negroes serving with the Texas troops defending this post. The most famous of them is known only as "Joe", the slave of Colonel W. B. Travis (a senior officer at the Alamo). After his release by the Mexican general Santa Anna, "Joe" reported the results of the battle to another contingent of Texas troops in what is believed to be the first known description of the Mexican assault.

It is also believed that "Joe" was later re-enslaved. According to a newspaper ad dated in 1837, a slave named "Joe" who had survived *The Alamo* had stolen a horse and run away from his master. No records exist to verify whether "Joe" or the horse were ever found.

UTAH

Fort Douglas: *The Old Fort*

Home of the 24th Infantry Regiment, a black unit which served in the trenches of San Juan Hill and later was utilized to combat the yellow fever epidemic at Siboney. Weakened and reduced in number because of the sickness, the men returned to a huge welcome in New York, but were barely able to get through the parade after their strenuous ordeal. More men died of yellow fever in Cuba than of combat wounds sustained in battle.

VIRGINIA

Fort Monroe

This was one of the few military posts not seized by the Confederacy at the outbreak of the Civil War and hence became a haven for fugitive Negroes escaping into Union lines. Known as "contraband" (the term was extended by Union General Ben Butler to cover runaways), these able-bodied Negroes were put to work building roads, erecting fortifications and as teamsters and foragers. Many eventually saw combat duty in the Army of the James after restrictions on enlistments were lifted.

Hampton: *Hampton Institute*

One of the earliest institutions of higher learning for Negroes in the United States, *Hampton Institute* was attended by the great Booker T. Washington before he went to Tuskegee. Washington also taught for a time at Hampton.

Richmond National Battlefield Park

The area around Richmond was the scene of several combat engagements involving black troops active in the Civil War. Among these engagements were Chaffin's Farm, New Market Heights, and Deep Bottom. General Butler found that the gallantry of these men merited special consideration, and so authorized the is-

Siege of the Alamo, March 6, 1836

suance of 200 medals which he presented personally to those outstanding soldiers who were recommended to his attention.

Rocky Mount: *Booker T. Washington National Monument*

The Burroughs plantation, on which Booker T. Washington was born a slave in 1856, can be found in a 200-acre park located in Rocky Mount.

WASHINGTON

Centralia: *George Washington Park*

The park is named after a liberated slave who escaped from slavery in Virginia when he was adopted by a white couple and taken to Missouri. He then left Missouri with a wagon train heading for the Pacific Northwest, settling on a homestead along the Chehalis River which was ultimately reached by the Northern Pacific Railroad. Washington subsequently laid out a town, setting aside acreage for parks, a cemetery, and churches. Soon, over 2,000 lots were in the hands of a thriving population which formed the nucleus of Centerville.

WEST VIRGINIA

Harpers Ferry: *Harpers Ferry National Monument*

Harpers Ferry derives its historical fame from the much-publicized anti-slavery raid conducted by John Brown and a party of 18 men (including five Negroes) from October 16-18, 1859. Brown hoped to set up a fortress and refuge for fugitive slaves which he could transform into an important way-station for escapees en route to Pennsylvania.

Brown lost two of his sons in the battle, and was himself seriously wounded. Later tried and convicted of treason, he was hanged at Charles Town on December 2, 1859.

Malden: *Booker T. Washington Monument*

This monument, erected in 1963, marks the site where the great Negro educator labored for several years in the salt works. At the time, Washington credited his employer, Mrs. Viola Ruffner, with having encouraged him to pursue a higher education at Hampton Institute.

John Brown's fort at Harpers Ferry.

WISCONSIN

Madison: *State Historical Society of Wisconsin*

The Wisconsin Historical Society has taken the impressive initiative of building up an archival collection of documents and other written materials relating to the modern-day civil rights struggle. Although it goes back only to 1960, archivists have already amassed the papers of more than 300 civil rights workers and agencies. The purpose of the collection is to create a repository of information for later historians and scholars who will seek to interpret the movement and extract its vital essence. Also included in the collection are broadsides of the Negro in the Civil War, and items pertaining to slavery.

Milton: *Milton House Museum*

The *Milton House Museum* (the oldest cement building in the United States) was once used as a hideaway for fugitive slaves escaping by means of the Underground Railroad.

Portage: *Silver Lake Cemetery*

Ansel Clark, "born a slave, died a respected citizen," settled in Wisconsin after the Civil War, during which he served as an impressed laborer in the Confederate cause and, as soon as he could escape, as a nurse in a Union hospital. There, he tended a Wisconsin resident who brought him home after the war to settle in Portage, where he became town constable and deputy sheriff. For 30 years, he worked in law enforcement, standing up to the town's rough characters and keeping them in line with "firmness and dignity." It was said, however, that he was such a gentle man with animals that his undertaker feared to crack the whip on the horses driving his hearse lest "Old Anse be out of that box and on my neck."

WYOMING

Fort Washakie Blockhouse

The blockhouse served as headquarters for both the 9th and 10th Cavalry regiments during their assorted campaigns on the Indian frontier. On one occasion, the 9th rescued a unit of infantry from Fort Steele which was being attacked by a Ute war party. The dug-in infantrymen, exhausted and low on provisions, were relieved to be reinforced by the black troopers who drove off the Indians and stayed at the site to start construction on what was to become Fort Duchesne.

CIVIL
RIGHTS

CIVIL RIGHTS ORGANIZATIONS & BLACK POWER ADVOCATES— PAST AND PRESENT LEADERSHIP

The Niagara Movement

The National Association for the Advancement of Colored People (NAACP)
- **Roy Wilkins**

The National Urban League
- **Whitney Young, Jr.**

The Congress of Racial Equality
- **Floyd McKissick**
- **Roy Innis**

The Southern Christian Leadership Conference (SCLC)
- **Rev. Martin Luther King, Jr.**
- **Ralph Abernathy**
- **Jesse Jackson**

The Student Nonviolent Coordinating Committee (SNCC)
- **Stokely Carmichael**
- **H. Rap Brown**

The Universal Negro Improvement Association (UNIA)
- **Marcus Garvey**

The Black Muslims
- **Elijah Muhammad**
- **Malcolm X**

The Black Panthers
- **Huey Newton**
- **Bobby Seale**

The civil rights cause in the 20th century has produced a number of organizations whose roles have varied with the historical forces of time and circumstance—particularly as they affect the black citizen of the United States. Since 1965, some civil rights leaders have persuasively argued that the movement has—for better or worse—turned away from a preoccupation with integration and opted instead for a brand of militancy which shows little regard for the opinions and sensibilities of white people. Two events in the 1960's are generally viewed as high-water marks in the ongoing crusade for black rights: the violent rush of Birmingham (1963) and the fiery orgy of Watts (1965). At Birmingham, white police turned their fury on nonviolent Negroes who had massed for a peaceful demonstration, and the civil rights movement claimed it had aroused the conscience of white America with unprecedented vigor. Two years later, in Los Angeles, Negroes did not expose themselves to brutal dogs and powerful hoses; instead, they took to the streets in spontaneous acts of violence which transformed the emphasis from rights and morality to self-sovereignty and power. There are, then, at this moment, two clearly identifiable and competing ideologies grappling for ascendancy within the kaleidoscopic world of the black American: one which stands for the cause of integration, the cause of Negroes; the other which affirms the black man's intrinsic right to choose alternatives other than integration, to wit, nationhood and separatism, if necessary.

THE NIAGARA MOVEMENT

The Niagara Movement was the first Negro protest organization in the 20th century. It was founded by a group of 29 Negro intellectuals—headed by W.E.B. DuBois, a professor at Atlanta University—who met from July 11-13, 1905 in Buffalo, New York.

The Niagara Movement represented a formal renunciation of the policy of accommodation which had been the keynote of Booker T. Washington's program for the Negro since his famed "Atlanta Compromise" address of 1895. Washington advocated manual and industrial training for the Negro as a means of gaining economic security, and preferred conciliation rather than agitation as a means of gaining social equality. "It is important and right," he said, "that all privileges of the law be ours, but it is vastly more important that we be prepared for the exercise of those privileges."

The Niagara Movement, on the other hand, maintained that it was even more important for Negroes to press for the immediate implementation of their civil rights. In the words of DuBois:

"We want full manhood suffrage and we want it now. . . .
We want the Constitution of the country enforced. . . .
We want our children educated . . . We are men! We will be treated as men. And we shall win!"

The organization held national conferences in 1906 and 1907 at Harper's Ferry and Boston, respectively, and initiated protest rallies in several American cities in 1908. Every aspect of the Negro's case was laid before the nation: voting rights; educational and economic opportunity; justice in the courts [the "separate but equal" doctrine of *Plessy* v. *Ferguson* (see page 46) was a particular bone of contention]; recognition in labor unions and in the military establishment; acceptance in the Christian church. Moreover, the leaders of the Niagara Movement appended certain duties to its list of basic grievances:

The duty to vote.
The duty to respect the rights of others.
The duty to work.
The duty to obey the laws.
The duty to be clean and orderly.
The duty to send our children to school.
The duty to respect ourselves, even as we respect others.

In 1909, the Niagara Movement was absorbed into the framework of the National Association for the Advancement of Colored People (NAACP), an organization founded on many of the same principles.

THE NATIONAL ASSOCIATION FOR THE ADVANCEMENT OF COLORED PEOPLE (NAACP)

As of 1970, the National Association for the Advancement of Colored People (NAACP) had 1751 branches in all 50 states of the Union and a local membership of 461,957, the great majority of them black. The organization's 1969 expenditures were 3.7 million dollars; its income for the same year, 3.9 million dollars.

The NAACP Board of Directors is a multiracial panel with nationwide representation. The executive secretary of the organization is Roy Wilkins, a Negro; its president, Kivie Kaplan, a white man. The head of the Legal Defense and Educational Fund is Jack Greenberg, also a white man.

The NAACP came into being on February 12, 1909, i.e., on the 100th anniversary of the birth of Abraham Lincoln. It was largely the brainchild of three people: William English Walling, a white Southerner who feared that racists would soon carry "the race war to the North"; Mary White Ovington, a wealthy young white woman who had attended the 1906 meeting of the Niagara group (see preceding) as a reporter for the New York *Evening Post* and had experience with conditions in the Negro ghettos of New York City; and Dr. Henry Moskowitz, a New York social worker. This trio proposed that a conference be called "for the discussion of present evils, the voicing of protests, and the renewal of the struggle for civil and political liberty."

The three-day conference (May 30-June 1) was followed by four meetings, the results of which were an increase in membership and the choice of an official name: The National Negro Committee. In 1910, the organization adopted its present name, and was incorporated in New York state. A year earlier, the Niagara movement and the NAACP had merged. By 1914, the association had already established some 50 branches throughout the country.

With the founding of the NAACP, the "Crisis" magazine, edited by W.E.B. DuBois, became its chief organ for propaganda and a major vehicle for the dissemination of educational and social programs. ("Crisis" is still being published on a monthly basis.)

Over the years, the NAACP has attempted to better the Negro's lot through "litigation, legislation and education." Perhaps its most significant judicial victory was won in 1954 when the historic *Brown* v. *Board of Education* case threw out the "separate but equal" doctrine established in *Plessy* v. *Ferguson*, thus opening the door for the elimination of segregation in public education.

The NAACP maintains a powerful Washington lobby which campaigns actively for new laws designed to protect and, where necessary, extend the rights of Negro citizens. The organization's chief regional offices are located in Atlanta, Dallas and San Francisco.

In recent years, the NAACP has shown a greater inclination to support the work of so-called "action groups" on the civil rights front. In many cases, it has organized and participated in selective buying campaigns, and joined in picketing businesses which refuse to accommodate or hire Negroes. At other times, it has provided legal aid and bail money—particularly for students engaged in "direct action" programs.

Despite its size and record, the NAACP has neither succeeded in truly representing the Negro masses, nor in making a mutually beneficial alliance with the labor movement. Consequently, it has tended to become a middle-class organization catering to the aspirations of relatively well-to-do Negroes and their white-liberal counterparts.

While other black organizations have tended in recent years to gravitate toward racial separatism, the NAACP has clung tenaciously to its goal of promoting racial integration. It has sought to improve the status of Negroes in many fields, includ[ing] jobs and schools, and has push[ed] doggedly and perseveringly for [civil] rights legislation.

THE CRISIS

A RECORD OF THE DARKER RACES

Volume One NOVEMBER, 1910 Number One

Edited by W. E. BURGHARDT DU BOIS, with the co-operation of Oswald Garrison Villard, J. Max Barber, Charles Edward Russell, Kelly Miller, W. S. Braithwaite and M. D. Maclean.

CONTENTS

PUBLISHED MONTHLY BY THE

National Association for the Advancement of Colored People

AT TWENTY VESEY STREET NEW YORK CITY

THE SPINGARN AWARD

The Spingarn Award, instituted in 1914 by J. E. Spingarn, Chairman of the Board of Directors of the NAACP, is a gold medal given annually by this organization for the "highest or noblest achievement by an American Negro." The medal is intended to publicize and reward the distinguished accomplishments of Negroes in all fields of endeavor, and to serve as an inspiration to Negro youth.

The nine-member Committee of Award, selected by the NAACP Board of Directors, is free to select the category of act or achievement which deserves the Spingarn accolade; it may choose a personality either on the basis of overall achievement, or for some outstanding work done in any one year. By the same token, it may also refuse to present any award, as was the case in 1938.

The medal is customarily presented at the annual convention of the NAACP. Nominations for the award may be submitted to the Secretary of the Committee of Award, 20 West 40th Street, New York City, and must be received before January 1 of each year.

WINNERS OF THE NAACP SPINGARN MEDAL

Year	*Winner*	*Category*
1915	Professor Ernest E. Just	Research in biology
1916	Major Charles Young	Services in Liberia
1917	Harry T. Burleigh	Excellence in creative music
1918	William Stanley Braithwaite	Achievement in literature
1919	Archibald H. Grimké	Service to race and country
1920	William E. B. DuBois	Founding Pan-African Congress
1921	Charles S. Gilpin	Performance in *The Emperor Jones*
1922	Mary B. Talbert	Service to Negro women Restoration of Frederick Douglass Home
1923	George Washington Carver	Research in agricultural chemistry
1924	Roland Hayes	Great singing artistry Solo performances with Boston Symphony Orchestra
1925	James Weldon Johnson	Achievements as author, diplomat, public servant
1926	Carter G. Woodson	Collecting and publishing Negro history in America
1927	Anthony Overton	Successful business career
1928	Charles W. Chesnutt	Pioneer literary work
1929	Mordecai Wyatt Johnson	Successful administration of Howard University
1930	Henry A. Hunt	Education of Negroes in Georgia
1931	Richard Berry Harrison	Portrayal of "De Lawd" in *The Green Pastures*
1932	Robert Russa Moton	Excellence as educator and author
1933	Max Yergan	Missionary work in South Africa
1934	William Taylor Burwell Williams	Contributions to Negro education
1935	Mrs. Mary McLeod Bethune	Contributions to Negro education
1936	John Hope	Leadership in education
1937	Walter White	Investigation of lynching Sponsorship of anti-lynching legislation
1938	NO AWARD GIVEN	
1939	Marian Anderson	Achievement in music
1940	Louis T. Wright	Contributions to music
1941	Richard Wright	Literary achievement
1942	A. Philip Randolph	Leadership in labor
1943	William H. Hastie	Distinguished career as jurist
1944	Charles R. Drew	Blood plasma research
1945	Paul Robeson	Achievement in theater and on conc[illegible] stage

1946	Thurgood Marshall	Contributions as lawyer before Supreme Court
1947	Dr. Percy L. Julian	Research in chemistry
1948	Channing H. Tobias	Role in defending fundamental American liberties
1949	Ralph J. Bunche	Distinguished scholarship in Myrdal study International statesmanship in the Middle East
1950	Charles Hamilton Houston	Leadership in the legal profession
1951	Mabel Keaton Staupers	Contribution to Negro nursing
1952	Harry T. Moore	Contributions to the "democratic ideal"
1953	Paul R. Williams	Contributions as a designer and architect
1954	Theodore K. Lawless	Research in dermatology
1955	Carl Murphy	Leadership role in employment, education, recreation
1956	Jack Roosevelt Robinson	Pioneer role in baseball
1957	Martin Luther King, Jr.	Leadership in Montgomery bus boycott
1958	Mrs. Daisy Bates and the Little Rock Nine	Upholding the ideals of American democracy
1959	Edward Kennedy (Duke) Ellington	Outstanding musical achievement
1960	Langston Hughes	"Poet laureate of the Negro race"
1961	Kenneth B. Clark	Research in psychology Organization of child development center
1962	Robert C. Weaver	Development of doctrine of "open occupancy" in housing
1963	Medgar Wiley Evers	Dedication to the "Fight for Freedom"
1964	Roy Wilkins	Contribution to "the advancement of the American people and the national purpose"
1965	Leontyne Price	"Outstanding soprano of our era"
1966	John H. Johnson	Pre-eminence in Negro publishing
1967	Edward W. Brooke	Distinguished career as a public servant; 1st Negro U. S. Senator in 20th century
1968	Sammy Davis, Jr.	"Superb and many-faceted talent," and meaningful civil rights participation
1969	Clarence Mitchell, Jr.	Director, Washington bureau, NAACP; pivotal role as civil rights lobbyist in promoting Civil Rights Act of 1968
1970	Jacob Lawrence	Eminence as Negro artist portraying Negro life and history on the American scene

ROY WILKINS

NAACP Executive Secretary

Roy Wilkins is executive secretary of the oldest, largest and probably the best-known civil rights organization in the United States—the National Association for the Advancement of Colored People (NAACP).

Born in St. Louis, Missouri on August 30, 1901, Wilkins was reared in the home of an aunt and uncle living in St. Paul, Minnesota. Though poor, he was able to ttend integrated schools in the city, and rew up in what might be termed a ra-lly mixed community.

Wilkins majored in sociology and minored in journalism while attending the University of Minnesota, and supported himself by doing a variety of odd jobs. He also served as night editor of the Minnesota *Daily* (the school paper), and edited a Negro weekly, the St. Paul *Appeal*. After receiving his B. A. in 1923, he joined the staff of the Kansas City *Call*, a leading Negro weekly. While in Missouri, Wilkins gained his first insight into segregation as an entrenched system, and resolved to broaden his activities in the NAACP, an organization which he had first joined while in college.

In 1931, Wilkins left the *Call* to serve under Walter White as assistant executive secretary of the NAACP. A year later, he substantiated charges of discrimination on a federally financed flood control project in Mississippi, and played an instrumental role in getting Congress to take action to curb its practice there.

In 1934, he joined a picket march in Washington, D. C., protesting the failure of the Attorney General to include lynching on the agenda of a national conference on crime. For his pains, he suffered the first arrest of his career. Beginning in this same year, Wilkins put his editorial talent to work for the NAACP, succeeding W. E. B. DuBois as editor of "Crisis" magazine. (He held this post for some 15 years.) In 1945, after having served as an advisor in the War Department, he acted as a consultant to the American delegation at the United Nations conference in San Francisco.

Wilkins was named acting executive secretary of the NAACP in 1949, the year Walter White took a year's leave of absence from the organization. At the same time, he functioned as Chairman of the National Emergency Civil Rights Mobilization, a pressure group which sent numerous lobbyists to Washington, D. C. to campaign for civil rights and fair employment legislation.

Wilkins assumed his present post in 1955 upon the death of Walter White. Since then, he has established himself as one of the most articulate spokesmen in the civil rights revolution. He has testified before Congressional hearings, conferred with the President, and written extensively for all manner of publications.

Although Wilkins and the organization he represents have become more militant in recent years, both he and the NAACP have nevertheless, not been immune from attacks by other more radical groups, such as the Black Muslims. However, he has not wavered in his determination to use all constitutional means at his disposal to help Negroes achieve the rights of full citizenship within the democratic framework of American society.

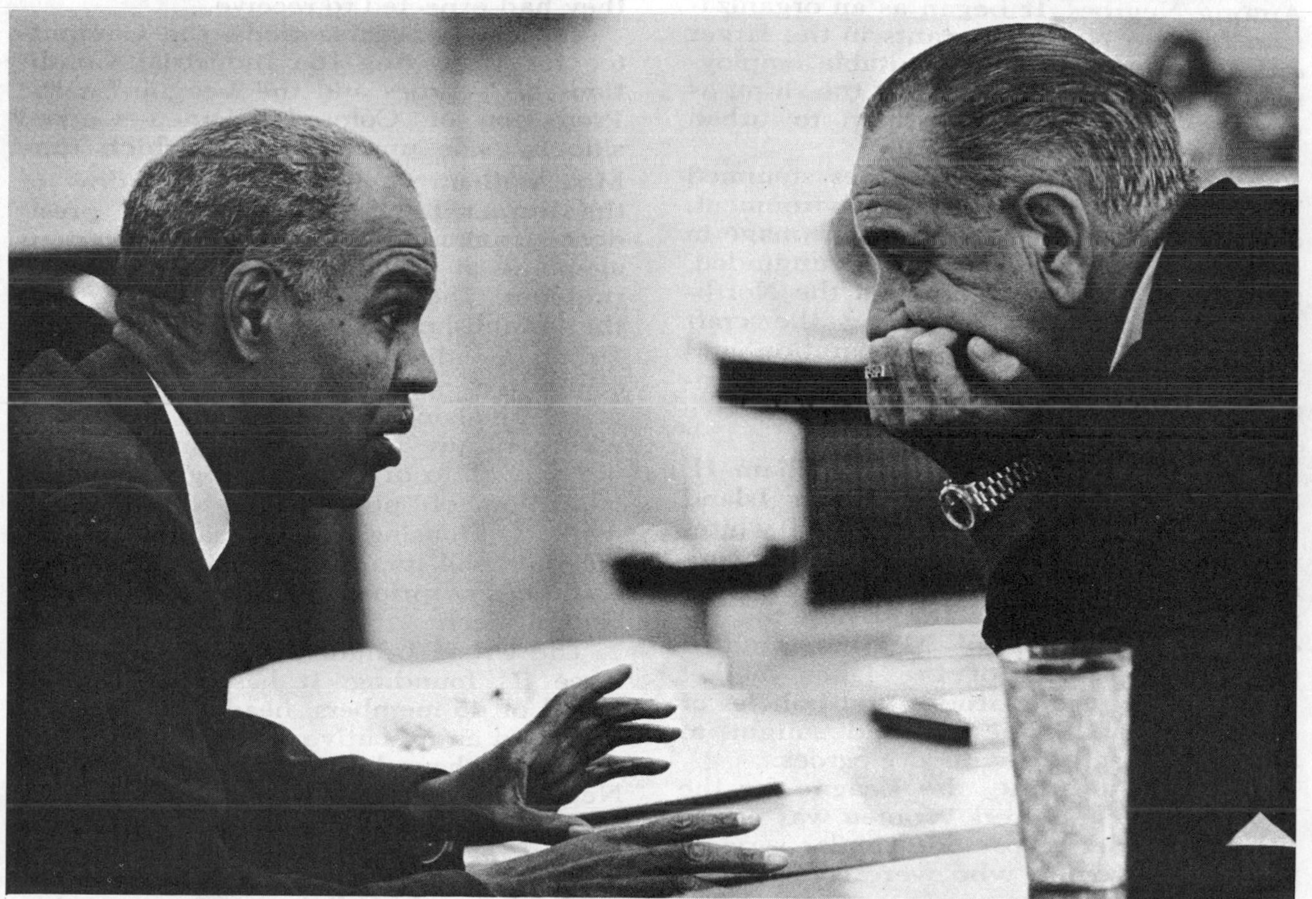

Roy Wilkins (left) gestures animatedly as he makes a point to President Johnson during a White House meeting.

Wilkins remains the Chairman of the Leadership Conference on Civil Rights, a group composed of some 100 national, civic, labor, fraternal and religious organizations. This Conference grew out of the 1950 FEPC mobilization and is conceded to be largely responsible for the enactment of most recent civil rights legislation.

A trustee of the Eleanor Roosevelt Foundation, The Kennedy Memorial Library Foundation and the Estes Kefauver Memorial Foundation, Wilkins is a member of the Board of Directors of the Riverdale Children's Association, the John LaFarge Institute and the Stockbridge School. He is a Director on the Board of "Peace with Freedom," an international organization working toward the goals described in its name.

Among the numerous awards already conferred on Wilkins are: the Anti-Defamation League's American Democratic Legacy Award, the Alpha Phi Alpha Fraternity's Medal of Honor, the Omega Phi Psi Fraternity's Outstanding Citizen Award, the American Jewish Congress' Civil Rights Award, and the Boy Scout's Scout of the Year Award. He has received the Outstanding Alumni Achievement Award of the University of Minnesota, and awards from the Japanese-American Citizens' League, the Unitarian Fellowship for Social Justice, B'nai B'rith Lodges, the Jewish War Veterans, the Postal Alliance, the National Medical Association, and the Eastern Star Lodge. He also holds the Russwurm Award of the National Newspaper Publishers Association. In 1964, NAACP honored him with its own Spingarn medal.

THE NATIONAL URBAN LEAGUE

The National Urban League, in existence since 1911, was originally known as the National League on Urban Conditions Among Negroes. It began as an organization to help Negro migrants in the larger cities of the North find suitable employment and make as smooth a transition as possible from rural Southern to urban Northern life.

Negro migrants to the cities stemmed largely from an agricultural environment, and had often lived in virtual peonage in the Black Belt. Unschooled and unguided, they faced the competition of the Northern labor markets, including the craft unions, with virtually no preparation, and without the protection of any governmental guidelines for their prospective employers.

In 1906, at the urging of William H. Baldwin, president of the Long Island Railroad, a group of Negroes and whites met for the purpose of studying the work needs of the Negro. This group, known as the Committee for Improving the Industrial Conditions of Negroes, studied the racial aspects of the labor market (particularly the attitudes and policies of employers and unions), and sought to find openings for qualified Negroes.

At the same time, the League for the Protection of Colored Women was established in order to provide similar services for Negro women who were coming into New York and Philadelphia from various parts of the South. These women often had no friends or relatives to meet and welcome them, and so fell prey to unscrupulous employment agencies which led them into jobs at wages far less than they had expected to receive.

These two organizations—the Committee for Improving the Industrial Conditions of Negroes and the League for the Protection of Colored. Women—worked side by side until 1910, at which time Mrs. William H. Baldwin, Jr., widow of the former Long Island Railroad president, summoned together the various agencies at work on the Negro urban problem. The result of this meeting was the establishment of the Committee on Urban Conditions among Negroes. The committee organized a nine-point program involving research into the exact nature of prevailing conditions, and set out as well to organize a program for the education of prospective Negro social workers. Housing, health, sanitation, recreation, self-improvement, job-assistance —all became primary areas for study and commitment.

The Urban League has been interracial since its founding. It has an executive board of 45 members, headed by a president and an executive secretary who, traditionally, have been a white man and a Negro. The League now describes itself as "a voluntary community service agency of civic, professional, business, labor and religious leaders . . . dedicated to the removal of all forms of segregation based on creed or color." It is currently headed by Whitney M. Young, Jr., formerly Dean of Atlanta University's School of Social Work. As executive director, Young is head of a staff of 1,000 paid professionals who are active in the 78 Urban League chapters located in most industrial cities with large Negro populations. An additional 6,000 volunteers carry out special assignments for the League's local branches.

The Urban League does not seek mass membership, and has only 50,000 members in its various affiliates. Funds are raised through business and industry, labor, foundations, government, local community chests, and individuals.

WHITNEY M. YOUNG, JR.
Executive Director,
National Urban League

Whitney M Young, Jr., Executive Director of the Urban League since 1961, was born in Lincoln Ridge, Kentucky, and received his B. S. degree at Kentucky State College in 1941. He later did graduate work at Massachusetts Institute of Technology, and earned an M.A. in social work from the University of Minnesota in 1947.

From 1954 to 1961, Young served as Dean of the Atlanta University School of Social Work. During the academic year 1960-1961, he was a visiting scholar at Harvard University under a Rockefeller Foundation grant.

A prominent lecturer and author of several articles which have appeared in professional journals, Young completed his first full-length book, *To Be Equal*, in 1964. A second, *Beyond Racism*, was published in 1969. On a regular basis, Young projects his philosophy and ideas in a syndicated column, entitled "To Be Equal." It is carried in more than 100 newspapers across the country.

Young is President of the National Association of Social Workers, and Past-President of the National Conference on Social Welfare. He holds membership in a number of professional associations, and serves on the boards and advisory committees of several important organizations and groups representing a variety of national interests and responsibilities. Among these are the Rockefeller Foundation, Urban Coalition, and Urban Institute. He has also served on seven Presidential Commissions of the Kennedy and Johnson administrations.

In 1969, Young was one of the 20 Americans selected by President Johnson to receive the "Medal of Freedom," the nation's highest civilian award.

CONGRESS OF RACIAL EQUALITY (CORE)

The organization of the Congress of Racial Equality (CORE) in 1942 heralded the presence of a new mood in the Negro community—one of open resistance and continuing confrontation with racial injustice in every corner of the United States. CORE recruited its early members from among students and other activists who were themselves dedicated to principles of what James Farmer once called "non-violent self-sacrifice," although admittedly within the context of "direct action."

CORE battlegrounds were many: a Chicago restaurant in 1943 where the sit-in is said to have been born; later, drug and department stores in St. Louis; theatres in Colombia, Missouri; registration drives in South Carolina and Louisiana and, ultimately in 1961, the celebrated Freedom Rides across the South. It was here that CORE achieved one of it's most noteworthy successes, helping in the desegregation of numerous interstate terminals and, in so doing, setting the stage for the subsequent Interstate Commerce Commission ruling which provided for the "non-racial" seating of all passengers in buses traveling between states.

CORE headquarters are located in New York City at 200 West 135th Street. The organization has a reputed membership of 70,000, serving in 96 affiliated and 50 unaffiliated chapters in 33 states, as well as in the District of Columbia.

Whitney M. Young, Jr., is seated at his desk behind a copy of his book, To Be Equal.
(COURTESY, NATIONAL URBAN LEAGUE)

In 1967, the CORE National Action Council approved a 15-point program which not only embodied the organization's policies and objectives for the coming decade, but set forth CORE's ideological and educational priorities. One CORE director, Robert Carson, went so far as to describe resettlement plans for ghetto residents similar to the Kibbutz patterns in evidence in modern Israel. At the same time, CORE vowed to stay active in ghetto politics, in labor union organization, and in dropout training. The points are enumerated below:

1. A total action program, promulgation of black power, particularly in the South.
2. The teaching of an African language —Swahili probably—in the ghettos.
3. A "country cousin" program to help welcome and settle into the ghettos rural blacks displaced from the farms.
4. The development of black arts and cultural centers in New York, along with the promotion of book, drama and craft workshops in the ghettos. This program might later be expanded to include the establishment of a black university.
5. The development of black city and county units. Young ghetto activists would be encouraged to move into underdeveloped black areas and build communities.
6. The cementing of international ties to Africa. CORE at present is planning an African tour as an incentive in a nationwide membership drive.
7. Continuation of present CORE projects in the target cities of Baltimore, Cleveland and Los Angeles.
8. A study of the feasibility of building or purchasing, in Harlem, a national CORE headquarters.
9. A program to raise funds in the ghetto to replace the drop in contributions from white liberals.
10. An international program to train blacks in skills needed by emerging African nations.
11. A project to develop a training school and a training staff.
12. The inauguration of continuing conferences on ghetto problems, including public schools, urban renewal and consumer education.
13. A program of economic cooperation for black people.
14. To study the feasibility of securing a chain of hotel management franchises which might be operated by ghetto residents.
15. To inaugurate an arts and cultural fair in Harlem.

Roy Innis (l.) succeeded Floyd McKissick as head of CORE.

ROY INNIS
National Director, Congress of Racial Equality (CORE)

Though some would say he looks menacing, those who have spoken to him quickly learn that Roy Innis is not a strident thunderer, but a fiercely independent and penetrating thinker. Innis has given CORE its most potent ideological push in the direction of black power and self-determination.

Born June 6, 1934 in St. Croix, Virgin Islands, Innis has lived in the United States since he was 12. He attended Stuyvesant High School, and went on to serve two years in the service, disguising his age as 18 though he was only 16. Back in civilian life, he majored in chemistry at City College, and did not originally plan to pursue a career in the racial movement.

By 1963, however, he was active in CORE circles, promoting the theme of economic competition and male assertiveness while downgrading the value of integration to blacks. Allies were few at this time, since the organization was multiracial in character and seemed to be irrevocably committed to integration. Patient and persuasive, however, Innis was elected chairman of Harlem CORE in 1965, and went on to become associate national director some three years later. By this time, he was effectively preaching the abandonment of the nonviolent philosophy in favor of a policy of self-defense.

On the economic front, he had founded the Harlem Commonwealth Council, an agency designed to create black-owned businesses and black-directed economic institutions in Harlem. To promote his ideas, he also took a plunge into journalism, serving with William Haddad as coeditor of the *Manhattan Tribune*, a weekly New York tabloid stressing the affairs of Harlem and the upper West Side. In print and in action, Innis has continued to stress black strength and black advancement over all other themes.

Innis is married to the former Doris Funneye of Georgetown, South Carolina, and the father of three children.

FLOYD B. McKISSICK
National Director, Congress of Racial Equality (CORE)

Floyd Bixler McKissick replaced James Farmer as head of the Congress of Racial Equality (CORE) on January 3, 1966.

Under his direction, CORE evolved from an interracial, desegregationist civil rights agency pledged to upholding nonviolence, to a militant and uncompromising advocate of the ideology of black power. Specifically, the CORE program McKissick sought to promote involved the preparation of Negroes for positions of political and economic responsibility in cities whose demographic trends indicated that black voters would achieve majority, or near-majority, status. McKissick directed his "cities project" under the aegis of the Metropolitan Applied Research Center, taking a leave of absence from CORE in September 1967. When he resigned in May of the following year, he was succeeded by Roy Innis, who had been acting director during his leave.

Born in Asheville, North Carolina on March 9, 1922, McKissick was reared with three sisters, two of whom have since become teachers, while the third is engaged in government work. He did his undergraduate work at Morehouse and North Carolina colleges, and later graduated from the University of North Carolina Law School.

During World War II, McKissick served in the European theater as a sergeant. After the war, he began legal practice in Durham, North Carolina, where he once represented his own daughter in her successful bid to gain admission to a previously all-white public school.

Despite the victory, later experience showed that "integration" itself only magnified the perils faced by many black children in and out of previously all-white classrooms. McKissick bitterly recalled how mercilessly his children had been taunted and harassed: "Patches cut out of their hair, pages torn out of books, water thrown on them in the dead of winter, ink down the front of their dresses"—a demoralizing array of constant and relentless pressures designed to crack their composure and destroy their will to learn. The adversity no doubt deepened McKissick's nascent radicalism and militant zeal.

As a lawyer, McKissick's most publicized efforts involved a segregated black local in the Tobacco Workers International, an AFL-CIO member. McKissick pressed to have black workers admitted to the skilled scale without loss of their seniority rating, contending with white workers who argued that they should enter the scale at the lowest rung. McKissick also successfully prosecuted thousands of sit-in cases throughout the South in the early 1960's.

It was at this time that the rupture widened between the older, established civil rights groups, dependent for their programming on a coalition of educated Negroes and affluent white liberals, and the younger, more rancorous black militants who turned their backs on most institutional white support. The militants argued that the civil rights groups did not appreciate the urgency of many problems affecting black urban majorities, particularly in the job area where technology often reduced people to useless ciphers.

When McKissick was elected national chairman of CORE in June 1963, he stepped to the convention podium and announced to the delegates: "The Negro people have dictated the course of the revolution. We shall proceed by carrying out the revolution." The emotional impact of McKissick's remarks was instantaneous. Direct action, rather than the coalition approach, was clearly in the ascendancy.

The high point in the fortunes of the coalition forces was reached, in McKissick's view, during the March on Washington. For all its apparent unity, the March was criticized by him as representing little more than a gigantic and impressive good will gesture between black and white Americans who were themselves exempt from the hardships plaguing the invisible black majority. The rumblings of discontent which McKissick and others like him detected beneath the surface of an alienated black America caused a wholesale reevaluation of the goals, techniques, and leadership of the movement. From that point on, civil rights organizations did not act in unison, but rather in conformity with the principles, ideology, and tactics which they themselves developed and espoused. Organizations such as CORE lent support only to those causes with which they could truly identify.

CORE, for example, disrupted the opening of the World's Fair in 1964, thereby alienating white liberal support even as it attempted to inspire black backing. On the other hand, CORE worked closely with Martin Luther King's Southern Christian Leadership Conference (SCLC) on the matter of voting registration in the South after the Johnson Administration passed the Voting Rights Act of 1965. Disillusionment reigned when the President seemed reluctant to send in hordes of federal registrars to prevent local officials from sabotaging the operation.

By 1966, McKissick was clearly identified as a man of action, a community organizer, and a figure of unmistakable "grass-roots" appeal. That year, he was elected to succeed James Farmer as national director. McKissick quickly linked CORE with an anti-Vietnam policy, declaring that the Johnson Administration was sending "black men . . . over to Vietnam" to die "for something that they don't have . . . here."

Domestically, McKissick steered CORE toward an endorsement of the black power ethic enunciated by Stokely Carmichael during the Meredith March Against Fear in Mississippi. Thereafter, McKissick was constantly pressed for a definition of the concept. In a 1966 interview, he stated it simply: "Black power . . . means putting power in black people's hands. We don't have any, and we want some. That is simply what it means."

A year later, the CORE convention struck the word "multi-racial" from its constitution, not, as the organization explained, to exclude white members, but to prevent them from assuming too much control of CORE's policies. Whites, in this view, would be most effective in educating their own community, rather than in controlling the fortunes of the black community. McKissick refused to support Martin Luther King's call for massive non violent civil disobedience in Northern cities, concentrating instead on programs aimed at increasing the political power and improving the economic position of the ghetto dweller. The difference in approach underlined the strength of McKissick's personal philosophy that a man cannot realize his destiny unless he develops a feeling that "he is somebody" and can relate to people "who express the same feeling."

CORE's mission, in McKissick's view, is to mount a "sustained effort" to make of America what he calls a place of "total equality," i.e. one where all men can "follow their dreams" without feeling that they are "frivolous and purposeless."

McKissick and his family live in the heart of Harlem.

Floyd McKissick

THE SOUTHERN CHRISTIAN LEADERSHIP CONFERENCE (SCLC)

The Southern Christian Leadership Conference (SCLC) is "a non-sectarian co-ordinating agency" for organizations and individuals engaged in non-violent protest in the major cities of the United States. SCLC seeks to gain for the Negro his "full citizenship rights," as well as "total integration" into the fabric of American life. It hopes to achieve this by utilizing the technique of "non-violent direct mass action," within the framework of a philosophy which espouses "the basic tenets of the Hebraic-Christian concept of satyagraha" (itself an Indian word translated as soul-force).

The organization, which has a distinct religious character, exhorts Negroes "to refuse to cooperate with evil" and "to accept Christian love in full knowledge of its power to defy evil." Further, it "calls upon them to understand that non-violence is not a symbol of weakness or cowardice."

The SCLC is interracial in character, and has supporters among people of all faiths, religions and creeds. It has its administrative headquarters in Atlanta, and maintains affiliates in 16 Southern and Border States. Its 33-member board is composed almost exclusively of Negro

...ers. The making and execution of ... policy is the responsibility of the Executive Board which represents the entire South.

Individuals hold membership in SCLC through such affiliated organizations as churches, fraternal orders and civic bodies. "Bona fide affiliates are restricted to the seventeen Southern states and the District of Columbia," but "supporting affiliates" are not under this geographical restriction.

Funds for the Conference are raised through the fees and pledges of affiliated organizations, through mass rallies and direct-mail appeals and, especially, through the personal appearances made by Dr. Martin Luther King and other conference leaders. Benefits featuring nationally known Negro and white entertainers are likewise a source of additional revenue.

SCLC has a full-time staff of more than 60 people, and an annual budget of over one million dollars.

MARTIN LUTHER KING, JR.

President, Southern Christian Leadership Conference (SCLC)

Any number of historic moments in the civil rights struggle of the last decade can be used to identify Martin Luther King, Jr.—prime mover of the Montgomery bus boycott (1956); keynote speaker at the March on Washington (1963); youngest Nobel Peace prize laureate (1964)—but it is as head of the Southern Christian Leadership Conference that he makes the day-to-day decisions underlying his entire civil rights program.

King was born Michael Luther King, Jr. in Atlanta on January 15, 1929—one of the three children of Martin Luther King, Sr., pastor of Ebenezer Baptist Church, and Alberta (Williams) King, a former schoolteacher. (He did not receive the name of "Martin" until he was about six years of age.)

After attending grammar school and high school locally, King enrolled in Morehouse College (also in Atlanta) in 1944, although he was at this time not inclined to enter the ministry. While there, he came under the influence of Dr. Benjamin Mays, a scholar whose manner and bearing convinced him that a religious career could have its intellectual satisfactions as well. After receiving his B. A. in 1948, King attended Crozer Theological Seminary in Chester, Pennsylvania, winning the Plafker Award as the outstanding student of the graduating class, and being awarded the J. Lewis Crozer Fellowship as well. King completed the course work for his doctorate in 1953, and was granted the actual degree two yea... later upon completion of his dissertati...

Married by then, King returned South, accepting the pastorate of the Dexter Avenue Baptist Church in Montgomery, Alabama. It was here that he made his first indelible mark on the civil rights movement by mobilizing the Negro community during a 382-day boycott of the city's bus lines. Working through the Montgomery Improvement Association, King overcame arrest and other violent harassment, including the bombing of his home. Ultimately, the U. S. Supreme Court declared the Alabama laws requiring bus segregation unconstitutional, with the result that Negroes were finally allowed to ride Montgomery buses on equal footing with whites.

At once a national hero and a civil rights figure of growing importance, King summoned together a number of Negro leaders in 1957, and laid the groundwork for the organization now known as the Southern Christian Leadership Conference (SCLC). Elected its president, he soon sought to assist other communities in the organization of protest campaigns against discrimination, and in voter-registration activities as well.

After completing his first book and making a trip to India, King returned to the United States in 1960 to become co-pastor, with his father, of Ebenezer Baptist Church.

Three years later, King's nonviolent tactics were put to their most severe test in Birmingham, Alabama during a mass protest for fair hiring practices, the establishment of a bi-racial committee, and the desegregation of department-store facilities. Police brutality used against the marchers dramatized the plight of the Negro to the nation at large with enormous impact. King himself was arrested, but his voice was not silenced as he is-

Martin Luther King, Jr. in a pensive moment.

sued his classic "Letter from a Birmingham Jail" to refute his critics.

Later that year, King was a principal speaker at the historic March on Washington (1963), where he delivered one of the most passionate addresses of his career. At the beginning of the next year, "Time" magazine saw fit to designate him as its *Man of the Year* for 1963. His greatest triumph came a few months later when he was named recipient of the 1964 Nobel Peace Prize.

Upon his return from Oslo, where he had gone to accept the award, King plunged himself almost immediately into a new battle, this time in Selma, Alabama, where he led a voter-registration campaign which culminated in the Selma-to-Montgomery Freedom March.

Thereafter, King brought his crusade to the North, settling in Chicago where he launched a slum-rehabilitation and open-housing program.

In the North, however, King soon discovered that young and angry Negroes (such as the ones in Watts who once replied "Martin Luther Who?" to a question about whether the civil rights leader would approve of their behavior) cared little for his pulpit oratory and even less for his solemn pleas for peaceful protest.

Their disenchantment was clearly one of the factors influencing his decision to rally behind a new cause and stake out a fresh battleground: the war in Vietnam. King himself antagonized many civil rights leaders by declaring the U.S. to be "the greatest purveyor of violence in the world." His clear aim was to fuse a new coalition of dissent based on equal support for the peace crusade and the civil rights movement.

The rift in the civil rights movement was immediate. The N.A.A.C.P. saw King's shift of emphasis as "a serious tactical mistake"; the Urban League warned the "limited resources" of the civil rights movement would be spread too thin in other domains; Bayard Rustin claimed black support of the peace movement would be negligible; Ralph Bunche felt King was undertaking an impossible mission in trying to bring the campaign for peace in step with the goals of the civil rights movement.

From the vantage point of history, King's timing could only be regarded as superb. In announcing his opposition to the war, and in characterizing it as a "tragic adventure" which was playing "havoc with the destiny of the entire world," King again forced the white middle class to concede that no movement could dramatically affect the course of government in the U. S. unless it involved deliberate and restrained aggressiveness, persistent dissent and even militant confrontation. These were precisely the ingredients of the civil rights struggle in the South in the early 1960's.

Speaking at the U.N., King again found words to prod the conscience of white America. "Let us save our national honor —stop the bombing. Let us save American lives and Vietnamese lives—stop the bombing. Let us take a single instantaneous step to the peace table—stop the bombing. Let our voices ring out across the land to say the American people are not vainglorious conquerors—stop the bombing."

As students, professors, intellectuals, clergymen and reformers of every stripe rushed into the movement (in a sense forcing fiery black militants like Stokely Carmichael and Floyd McKissick to surrender their control over anti-war polemics), King turned his attention to the domestic issue which, in his view, was directly related to the Vietnam struggle: the War on Poverty.

At one point, he called for a $4,000-a-year guaranteed family income, threatened national boycotts, and spoke of disrupting entire cities by non-violent "camp-ins." With this in mind, he began to draw up plans for a massive march of the poor on Washington, D. C. itself, envisioning a popular demonstration of unsurpassed intensity and magnitude designed to force Congress and, if necessary, the political parties to recognize and deal with the unseen and ignored masses of desperate and downtrodden Americans.

King's decision to interrupt these plans to lend his support to the Memphis sanitationmen's strike was based in part on his desire to discourage violence, as well as to focus national attention on the plight of the poor, unorganized workers of the city. The men were bargaining for little else beyond basic union representation and long-overdue salary considerations.

Though he was unable to eliminate the violence which had resulted in the summoning and subsequent departure of the National Guard, King stayed on in Memphis and was in the process of planning for a march which he vowed to carry out in defiance of a federal court injunction if necessary.

On the night of April 3, 1968, he told a church congregation: "Well I don't know what will happen now . . . But it really doesn't matter . . ." (At other times, musing over the possibility he might be killed, King had assured his colleagues that he had "the advantage over most people" because he had "conquered the fear of death.")

Death came for King on the balcony of the black-owned Lorraine Motel just off Beale Street on the evening of April 4. While standing outside with Jesse Jackson and Ralph Abernathy, a shot rang out. King fell over, struck in the neck by a rifle bullet which left him moribund. At 7:05 p.m., he was pronounced dead at St. Joseph's Hospital.

The assassination caused a wave of incredible violence in such major cities as Washington, D. C. (11 dead; 24 million dollars property damage, over 8,000 arrests, over 1,000 injuries); Chicago (nine dead, 11 million dollars property damage, nearly 3,000 arrests, 500 injured), and Baltimore (6 dead, 14 million dollars property damage, 5800 arrests, and 900 injured). Without restraint against looters, death tolls would have been even higher. Both grief and anger suffused the black community. The anger was assuredly all the more fanatic precisely because King had been so irretrievably dedicated to nonviolence.

RALPH D. ABERNATHY

President, Southern Christian Leadership Conference (SCLC)

Martin Luther King, Jr. had always made it clear that Ralph David Abernathy would be his successor in the event some catastrophe befell him. The mantle of leadership thus passed smoothly and dramatically onto the shoulders of Abernathy when his best friend and inspired colleague was murdered in April 1968. Abernathy's loyalty had long been tested; his experience had groomed him to seek "the promised land," even if "The Leader" were no longer with him.

Grandson of a slave, Abernathy was born on his father's farm in Linden, Alabama on March 11, 1926. His father, a stern man and a devout Christian, was a commanding figure in the community and a dominant force in the home as well. Abernathy had since reflected that "home, church, and school" were virtually the sole permissible ingredients of his childhood, although he has said that, as a child, he was always attracted to reading and studying, rather than to productive farm labor.

Abernathy served in the Army toward the close of World War II and, after his discharge, pursued training in mathematics at Alabama College in Montgomery, where he received a B.S. degree in 1950, two years after his ordination in the Baptist ministry.

Abernathy changed course in 1951 when he took an M.A. in sociology at Atlanta University. He first met Martin Luther King, Jr. at a church service in Atlanta, where the young King had just preached an impressive sermon. The pair later became close friends when they each pastored a Baptist church in Montgomery, King at the Dexter Avenue church and Abernathy at the First Baptist.

After the now-celebrated arrest of Mrs. Rosa Parks for refusing to give up her seat on a Montgomery city bus in 1955, King and Abernathy joined forces to organize a city-wide boycott of buses by Negroes. Although Abernathy had suggested the boycott initially, it was King who was quickly thrust into the limelight as its supervisor. Abernathy, recognizing the charisma of King and his leadership traits, willingly stepped aside in the interests of the cause, and because he considered his role to be one of offering strong support and backing to the leader, rather than risking divisive competition with him.

When victory was achieved in this early challenge to the municipal power structure, King and Abernathy at once sensed that, as of 1957, a new spirit of vigor and determination was spreading through black communities across the South. To mobilize this force and to channel it to its most constructive ends, the pair organized the Southern Christian Leadership Conference (SCLC) at a 1957 meeting held at the Ebenezer Church. King served as president; Abernathy, as secretary-treasurer.

The organization at once jumped into the vanguard of nonviolent resistance to segregation in the South, organizing sit-ins, leading voter-registration drives, and braving the assaults of fanatic white mobs and enraged police. King and Abernathy usually went to jail together, determined, as he says, to have "no hatred in our heart toward the jailer, and a stronger determination to tear down the system."

By 1961, Abernathy was such a key and trusted aide of King that he was obliged to relinquish his Montgomery pastorate and trade it in for an Atlanta church, the West Hunter Street Baptist. Over the next four years, the efficacy of nonviolence as a viable tactic in the struggle fell under increasing attack, with the result that King felt compelled to remind his staff that Abernathy, a follower steeped in the philosophy which had given the movement its initial impetus, was clearly in line to succeed him in the event of his death.

Over the next two years, the thrust of SCLC changed in the civil rights arena, as the organization became aware that the American economy was so structured that it invariably bypassed millions of urban blacks trapped in a bleak and seamy ghetto world with little hope of liberation through self-development. King then organized the Poor People's Campaign, a loose coalition of various ethnic groups equally victimized by poverty. Original plans called for a massive demonstration in March of 1968, but were postponed when the garbage collectors of Memphis staged a strike in quest of basic organizing rights and a living wage. King lent his support and prestige to the strike but it was to be his last gesture of protest. On the night of April 4, while standing on a motel balcony, King was felled by a sniper's bullet, even as Abernathy and other shocked members of his party stood at his side, helpless.

Abernathy quickly rallied the SCLC staff and thousands of supporters to the side of the garbage workers who won a settlement of their grievances in short order. Funds and contributions flooded the coffers of SCLC after King's assassination, thus making it possible for Abernathy to undertake the massive logistical task of bringing thousands of America's poor to the doorsteps of the nation's capital to plead their cause.

Abernathy, clad in denims and armed with carpenter's tools, presided over the quietly spectacular gesture of building a "new city of hope, Resurrection City, U.S.A." The city was a shantytown of A-frame plywood huts which dominated the Washington landscape for more than a month before police moved in to dismantle it. Abernathy resisted the gesture, and was thrown in jail for 20 days. Still, his presentation of the demands of the Poor People's Campaign to members of Congress stamped him as a bold new spokesman for the rights of the oppressed. Nonviolence would remain his theme, he avowed, but he intended to press for "the education of the oppressor," even if that education required wholesale "civil disobedience."

Abernathy and his wife and family (there are three children) continue to live in Atlanta where the SCLC leader has organized Operation Breadbasket and retained most of the civic, charitable, civil rights, and educational associations of his past. He has continued to appeal to poor people of all races, and has sought desperately to insure the allegiance of young activists disillusioned with nonviolence.

JESSE JACKSON
National Director, Operation Breadbasket (SCLC)

Jesse Jackson is possibly the most exciting and dynamic young black leader who has decided to work within the system while, at the same time, retaining the appearance, the ardor and the fervor of a black nationalist or revolutionary. Reared in the black ministry, Jackson has relied on the techniques of pulpit oratory to capture a huge and diverse following, but he has resisted efforts to be cast in the role of a "successor"—particularly to Martin Luther King. "You can be an orator or an organizer," he says. "I am an organizer."

Appointed by King in 1966 to head Operation Breadbasket, a selective buying and economic pressure campaign organized in Chicago by the Southern Christian Leadership Conference (SCLC), Jackson began mobilizing the black community by demanding to see the employment records of a local dairy operating in the South Side ghetto. When the dairy refused, word was issued from several church pulpits that neighborhood blacks should boycott the place.

The results were spectacular. Within three days, the dairy discovered 44 new or upgraded positions for the local black labor force. It took slightly longer—10 days in all—for a local grocery chain to hire 183 blacks in jobs ranging from department store managers to delivery boys. A second chain folded quickly under the pressure, went into bankruptcy, and condemned Jackson as "a liar and a phony."

The skirmishes over, Jackson and his cohorts went after more sturdy and stable targets, notably the A. & P. food store chain, which operated more than 40 markets in the Chicago black neighborhoods. Though A & P resistance was more tenacious, the eventual victory of the group after 16 weeks of steady pressure

Jesse Jackson

was more meaningful, if not more savory. Not only were 268 more blacks hired, but products appealing to black consumers were introduced into the stores for the first time—and on prominent display.

Neighborhood companies were then encouraged to utilize black banks and savings and loans associations to transact their financial affairs. The result: a rise in their assets from five million to 22 million dollars. Money flowed into, rather than out of, the ghetto.

Jackson has not confined his campaign to the white power structure, however. He is equally forceful in transmitting ripples of change to black areas where lethargy and hopelessness often abound. Thus, in Cleveland, the Breadbasket band once deliberately created a commotion at 5 a.m. in the morning on election day. No one could claim to have been too busy to vote for Carl Stokes before going to work.

The smooth, efficient organization of Breadbasket (it is now in 15 cities, all outside the South) has enabled Jackson to concentrate on another theme which is close to his heart: black pride. Every Saturday, Jackson presides over a mass meeting of black ministers, black businessmen, youth leaders, and other assorted fans to whom he sells pride and products in a 6,000-seat movie house on the South Side.

Despite his immense success and enormous appeal, he is singularly adept at avoiding entanglements by identifying alleged competitors for power. Nor will he readily condemn supposed fanatics, such as the Black Panthers, or reputed Uncle Toms involved with organizations like the NAACP. His skill lies in his ability to stress their accomplishments and their positive goals, rather than deride their failures or mistaken policies. He is also remarkably adept at persuading the power structure to respond to the needs of the people. This was dramatically demonstrated one year when he convinced the Illinois legislature to rescind a proposed 125 million dollar cutback in welfare funds.

Born poor in 1942 in Greenville, South Carolina, Jackson once worked with his stepfather cleaning an office owned by a then-unknown lawyer named Clement Haynsworth. At the age of six, he rushed innocently into a store looking for service, and found himself confronting the business end of a weapon and surrounded by silent black adults. Psychologically, the experience had as profound an impact as a bullet might have.

Jackson's own confidence stemmed from success as a high-school athlete. He later attended the University of Illinois on an athletic scholarship for a year, but quit in the face of the isolation which he experienced. At North Carolina A. & T., his athletic talents were equally in evidence, but the comfort of the surroundings helped him assume a leadership role in campus politics and on the academic scene.

A leader in Greensboro sit-in activities, Jackson became an activist in the summer of 1963 when he and hundreds of others were crammed into a bloc of cells designed to hold half their number. The Greensboro episode made civil rights work "a commitment for life," even as a later decision to study the ministry at Chicago Theological Seminary gave that commitment an operational framework. By 1965, Jackson had met King at the Selma March; three years later, he was one of King's most trusted lieutenants, the man who rushed to King's side on the motel balcony in Memphis and held the leader's head in his hands as life ebbed away.

Jackson is married and has three young children. He and his wife, a former co-ed at North Carolina A. & T., have worked together on various projects, including Breadbasket. Since beginning the program, Jackson has persuaded some 15 Chicago companies to upgrade or hire some 5,000 blacks. Significantly, the director of S.C.L.C.'s economic arm has not held out his hand to do so.

STUDENT NONVIOLENT COORDINATING COMMITTEE (SNCC)

The Student Nonviolent Coordinating Committee (SNCC) came into being on April 15, 1960. As its name implies, it is an organization for student groups engaged in "direct action" protest across the entire South. Snick has been effective in the desegregation of countless lunch counters and other Jim Crow facilities in several major cities. It has been a leading exponent of the sit-in tactic and the jail-in movement. (The latter involves refusal to pay fines, and an insistence to serve consequent jail sentences.)

Snick membership is drawn from students on both Negro and white college campuses across the country. The organization's headquarters are in Atlanta, also the home base of the SCLC.

Among the most ambitious projects undertaken by Snick has been the Mississippi summer program, in which more than 500 volunteers—many of them lawyers and law students—opened up a number of "Freedom Schools" designed to promote Negro voter registration (1964). Snick was joined in this work by a number of other civil rights groups and religious organizations, and eventually extended its program to Georgia, Arkansas and Alabama.

Snick was also one of the leading organizers of the Albany Movement (1962), during which a concerted effort was made to desegregate all public facilities in what many observers then described as a "completely closed" city.

By 1968, it was clear that the Student Nonviolent Coordinating Committee was losing much of its momentum to the Black Panthers, a group which had seized on the concept of a "black liberation struggle" pursuant to the Watts, Newark and Detroit riots.

According to a 1968 report carried in the New York *Times,* SNCC's Program Director Phil Hutchings announced that it was no longer possible for the organization to maintain its shaky alliance with the gun-toting Panthers. The SNCC staff was also informed that "Stokely Carmichael's relationship to the organization was terminated."

Before this, SNCC had enjoyed a period of encouraging growth during the early 1960's. Among its leadership elements was a broad coalition of white and black college students who sought to help register black voters, set up cooperatives, establish health clinics, and teach rural Negroes how to read and write.

After the 1964 Democratic convention, however, Carmichael tended increasingly to feel that the American system could not be turned around without being threatened by wholesale violence and disruption. Failure to seat the delegation of the SNCC-founded Mississippi Freedom Democratic Party (also known as the Lowndes County Freedom Organization or Black Panther Party) at the convention apparently sealed Carmichael's fate as an advocate of black power and supporter of urban-based guerrilla violence.

The Panthers to whom Carmichael moved represented what was believed to be the new thrust of the liberation movement. SNCC, however, depended heavily on the influx of middle-class black and white youths into what was essentially a civil rights movement. Once aggressive Northern ghetto youths roared into the picture, SNCC was left without a constituency.

By leaving the South, SNCC surrendered an essential base of support and a concrete program around which to organize. Never a large membership organization, it lost many of its remaining supporters to graduate study, anti-poverty work, teaching, law, etc.

SNCC did not recover its sense of direction or central focus once Carmichael departed. H. Rap Brown, formerly minister of justice in the old organization, renamed the new organization the Student National Coordinating Committee in the summer of 1969, at which time he indicated SNCC would retaliate violently if the situation so demanded.

Brown outlined plans for a new SNCC dimension, the creation of a Peoples Medical Center and a Peoples Sewing Center in Brooklyn. However, Brown's legal troubles made it virtually impossible for him to support these programs with any consistent leadership. As a result, SNCC became virtually defunct.

H. RAP BROWN
Chairman, Student Nonviolent Coordinating Committee (now Student National Coordinating Committee)

It is ironic that H. Rap Brown was once critical of a certain exiled black leader for leaving the country and so escaping the legal harassment and pressure to which he was subject for parole and bail violation. Though it cannot be said with certainty, it would seem, as of the vantage point of mid 1970 at least, that Brown had succumbed to the same fate—one would assume deliberately.

During 1968, the then 24-year-old Brown had several disastrous brushes with the law. Under indictment in Maryland, he was charged with inciting a riot by delivering a forceful harangue in the aftermath of which the black section of Cambridge was the scene of racial disturbances and an outbreak of arson. Meanwhile, he was awaiting the results of an appeal of a federal conviction in New Orleans for carrying a gun across state lines. In Richmond, Virginia, he was under bond for violating the conditions of his bail in New Orleans.

In short order, he made a trip to California to appear at two black power rallies, travelling at a time when he was supposed to be confined to his lawyer's custody in the Southern District of New York. Brown succeeded in getting some of his bail amounts lowered on appeal, but forfeited partial sums on others.

In at least one other encounter with police, Brown took refuge in the Cuban mission in New York while in possession of mysterious parcels whose contents were unknown, but which were suspected to contain weapons of some sort.

Brown disappeared in mid 1970 after being slated for trial in Maryland. Two of his friends were apparently murdered in the explosion of an automobile on March 9. Thereafter, Brown's lawyer, William Kunstler, protested that his client would probably not be safe even if he could be found.

H. Rap Brown, successor of Stokely Carmichael as head of SNCC, missing since early 1970.

STOKELY CARMICHAEL
Chairman, Student Nonviolent Coordinating Committee

Stokely Carmichael's meteoric rise to fame and an undisputed place in the gallery of prominent black leaders stems from several diverse and volatile events and associations. Foremost among these is his popularization of the dynamic phrase (Black Power), but not far behind are his creations in the South of the Lowndes County Freedom Organization (and his usage of the Black Panther symbol), his vigorous leadership of SNCC until 1967, his assumption of an important ministerial post among the urban Black Panthers until 1969, and his current emergence as a Pan-Africanist in exile in Guinea.

Born in Port-of-Spain, Trinidad in 1941, Carmichael is the son of Adolphus Carmichael, a carpenter, and Mabel F. or, as Carmichael refers to her, May Charles Carmichael. Carmichael's parents moved to the U.S. when young Stokely was only two, but the youngster remained in Trinidad with other family members until he reached the age of 11. White supremacy was drilled into Carmichael at school, and he resented it bitterly, although he at least experienced some form of identifiable black power in the civil service and constabulary of Trinidad.

In Harlem, Carmichael was jolted and disillusioned by the reverse world: one in which black and impotent seemed synonymous. Though the family managed to move to a white Bronx neighborhood, Carmichael soon became hooked into the patterns of gangs, booze and rootlessness which were destroying many of his peers.

Carmichael recovered while attending Bronx High School of Science, although he felt he was again straying into a dangerous world—one in which he associated with the well-meaning but often hopelessly artificial white liberal who adopted him as a mascot.

Rejecting this as well, Carmichael headed South in 1960, joining a "bunch of kids from CORE" who were picketing lunch counters and putting continuous pressure on the white power structure to relax or abolish its most blatant forms of prejudice in public accommodations.

Though offered scholarships to white universities, Carmichael opted for the black experience all the way, matriculating at Howard and continuing his regular jaunts into the South, where he was frequently arrested and brutalized. In 1964, after graduating from Howard, Carmichael joined "Snick" and led a task force into Lowndes County where Negro registration quickly jumped from only 70 to 2,600—more even than white totals.

Carmichael at once capitalized on the opportunity to organize the Lowndes County Freedom Organization, an independent political group disavowing any immediate affiliation with either of the major parties. By 1966, SNCC had changed its orientation from that of a peaceful, middle-class organization fostering integration to one in which black liberation and leadership were regarded as mandatory goals.

Within a few days after his election as head of "Snick," Carmichael joined the James Meredith Freedom March along Highway 50 in Mississippi, shouting the words "Black Power" to sharecroppers along the roadside and trumpeting them into the American consciousness with telling effect. Carmichael not only drove a wedge into the civil rights movement, but also emerged as the most dynamic spokesman on record for a concept which thrilled black audiences, stirred black militants and hypnotized virtually all of America because of its blinding relevance. From campus to campus, and from nation to nation, Carmichael delivered speech after controversial speech, boldly forging ahead of SNCC and emerging as a national spokesman for black aspirations around the world.

In short order, however, Carmichael opted for anonymity, resigning from SNCC because the organization did not agree with his militant and violent philosophy. By then, Carmichael's Black Panther symbol had captured the imagination of Oakland's Bobby Seale and Huey Newton, who incorporated the animal into their newly formed urban self-defense force. Carmichael joined the group, but plunged into an almost immediate feud with Eldridge Cleaver, minister of information for the party, over the issue of forming coalitions with white radicals. Carmichael rejected the idea, while Cleaver supported it.

In July 1969, Carmichael resigned, claiming that a premature alliance with such radicals would subvert the black movement. He also announced that he regarded himself as a Pan-Africanist whose mission it was to wage unrelenting warfare against "the white Western empire."

In 1968, Carmichael married Miriam Makeba, the South African singer, and moved with her to Conakry, Guinea, where, at last report, he was studying French at the Institute of Languages. A true internationalist, Carmichael is equally at home with Harlem talk, Southern sharecropper dialect, the King's English, and the melodious West Indian accents of his childhood.

One observer who interviewed him in recent years reflected on the visibility in his eyes of the grim Southern experiences which he had endured. Despite this, he had retained his humor, tenderness, and modesty. A powerful public orator, Carmichael is known in private as a friendly and charming man given to light and easy banter.

FORMER SNCC LEADERS

John Lewis, a 26-year-old Fisk University graduate, and James Forman, a former teacher in Chicago, headed Snick from 1964 to 1966. Both failed to win election in the latter year, with Lewis announcing his resignation from the organization as the result of policy clash with the new leadership. Deeply committed to nonviolence as a way of life, Lewis, a Baptist minister, "reportedly felt that Snick was becoming too militant—particularly in advocating a program of "black power" which would involve the exclusion of sympathetic and cooperative whites. Moreover, Lewis and other former frontline Snick leaders reacted favorably to what they termed the financial irresponsibility of the organization.

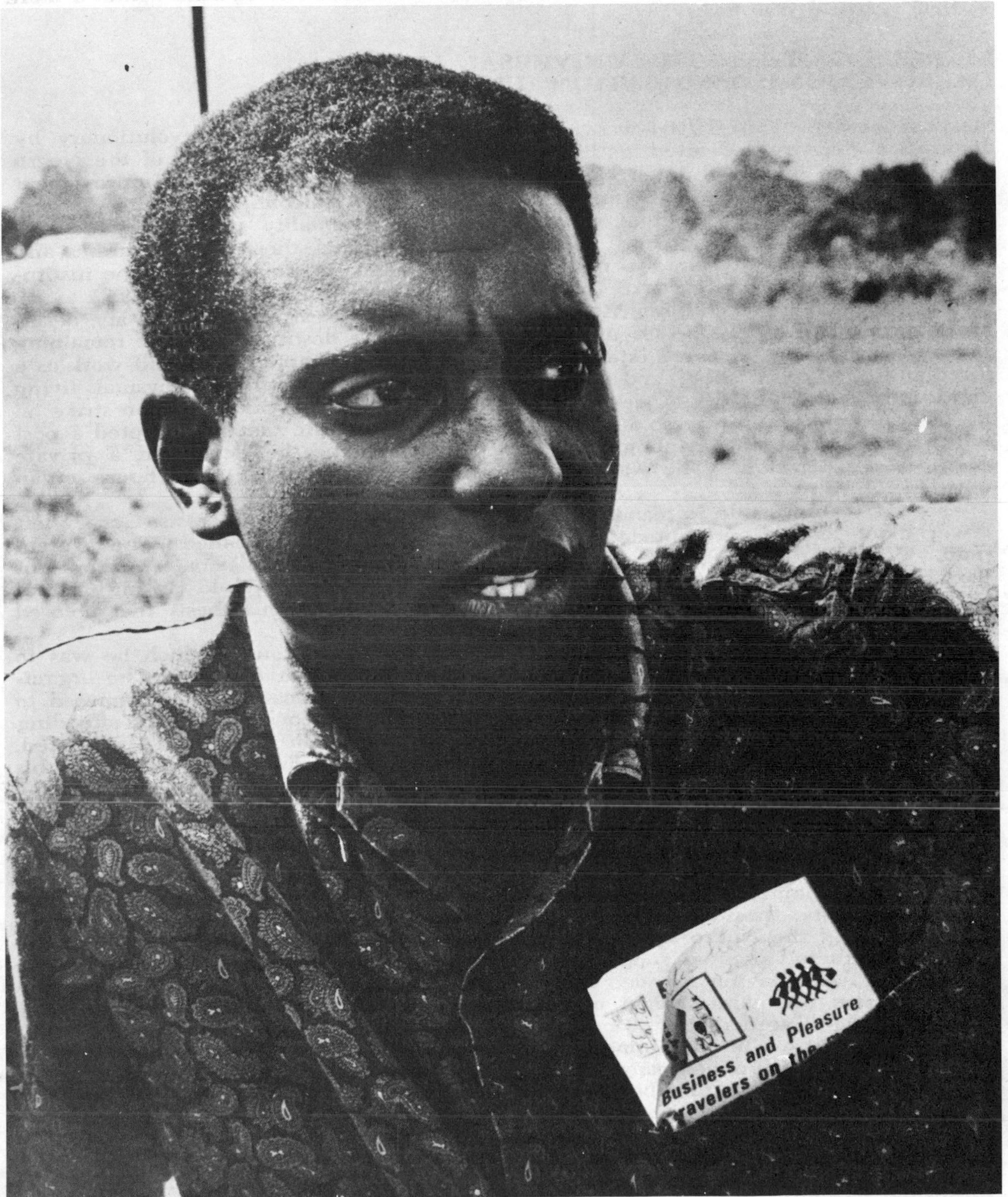

Stokely Carmichael, former head of SNCC, now resides in Guinea.

BLACK NATIONALIST ORGANIZATIONS

Like the civil rights organizations, black nationalist groups, another product of the Negro's position within American society, have developed programs designed to improve the Negro's lot, although they have tended to operate within a more radical political framework.

MARCUS GARVEY: THE UNIVERSAL NEGRO IMPROVEMENT ASSOCIATION (UNIA)

Marcus Garvey (1887-1940) was a West Indian by birth and a revolutionary by disposition. Garvey dedicated his life to what he called the "uplifting" of the Negro peoples of the world through the creation of the Universal Negro Improvement Association and the African Communities League. Like Malcolm X of a later generation, he believed that Negroes could never achieve equality unless they became independent—founding their own nations and governments, their own businesses and industrial enterprises, their own military establishments—in short, those same institutions by which other peoples of the world had risen to power.

The youngest of 11 children, Garvey was apprenticed to a printer at the age of 14. He moved to Kingston in 1903 after a severe hurricane destroyed the last remaining piece of land on his mother's estate. Once in the Jamaican capital, he found work as a foreman in a print shop, and soon became acquainted with the abysmal living conditions of the laboring classes. He participated in the first Printers' Union strike on the island, but came away so disillusioned by its total failure that he accepted a post with the Government Printing Office. At the same time, he developed a private political organization (The National Club), and began publishing a house organ entitled "Our Own."

Finding it impossible to maintain both his job and his outside interests, Garvey left government service and founded a more ambitious newspaper called "The Watchman." With funds failing, however, he found it necessary to leave Jamaica in hopes of earning enough money abroad to finance his projects at home. While visiting Central and South America, he amassed ample evidence to support his thesis that colored peoples everywhere were victims of discrimination.

Back again in Jamaica in 1911, he founded the organization to which he was to devote his life: the Universal Negro Improvement Association (UNIA). The organization did not immediately catch fire, inasmuch as many Jamaicans were opposed to the idea of an organized black majority, or else feared the consequences of offending the strongly entrenched, European-based power structure on the island. Undaunted, Garvey left for England in 1912 in search of additional financial backing for his schemes. While there, he worked for an Egyptian scholar, and learned much of the history of Africa—particularly with reference to the exploitation of black peoples by colonial powers. But his earnings were meager, and so in 1914, he returned to Jamaica, where he intensified his campaign to recruit supporters and spread his ideas, though with little immediate success.

In 1916, acquainted with the work of Booker T. Washington, he came to the United States, where he formulated what he called the "Back to Africa" program for the resettlement of the Negro in his ancestral homeland. In New York City particularly, his ideas attracted popular support, and his oratory convinced thousands to enroll in the UNIA. After having founded a newspaper ("The Negro World"), he toured the United States preaching Negro nationalism to popular audiences. In a matter of months, he had founded over 30 branches of the UNIA.

Garvey's most ambitious business venture during this period involved the founding of a Negro steamship company—"The Black Star Line." By encouraging the more than 1.5 million UNIA members to purchase shares in the company, he was able to acquire three vessels and put them into service between New York, Central America and the West Indies.

It was not long before he became embroiled in a dispute with the New York District Attorney's office, which threatened to sue him for criminal libel after he had published a highly critical article on the methods it had used in investigating his company. During this time, to complicate matters even further, an unsuccessful attempt was made on his life.

In 1920, Garvey and his followers convened a 31-day international conclave in Madison Square Garden in New York City, where they presented a policy statement on the "Back to Africa" program, and proclaimed a formal "Declaration of Rights" for Negroes all over the world. Following this, Garvey set himself the task of negotiating for the repatriation of Negroes in Liberia (West Africa). Rumors quickly began to circulate that Garvey's real intention was to seize power in Liberia and build a personal empire there. Liberia eventually withdrew all support from the venture, leaving Garvey stunned from the realization that he had actually been rebuffed by a black African nation.

With the Black Star Line in serious financial difficulties, Garvey soon found himself obliged to work doubly hard. Under his promotion, two new business organizations were set up—the African Communities League and the Negro Factories Corporation. He also tried to salvage his colonization scheme by sending a delegation to the League of Nations with instructions to appeal for the transfer to the UNIA of those African colonies taken from Germany during World War I.

Finally, in a last effort to save the Black Star Line from bankruptcy, Garvey went abroad where he somehow managed to raise the funds needed to save the venture. Upon his return, however, he found himself unable to re-enter the United States for more than five months. Taking advantage of this situation, some of Garvey's most trusted aides extorted large sums of money from the firm, accumulating such enormous debts that, by the time Garvey did finally manage to get back into the country, the UNIA was on the verge of complete financial ruin.

A host of ensuing legal entanglements, based on charges that Garvey had used the U. S. mails to defraud prospective investors, eventually led to his imprisonment in the Atlanta federal penitentiary for a term of five years. In 1927, his half-served sentence was commuted, and he was deported to Jamaica by order of President Calvin Coolidge.

Garvey left on a world tour the very next year, still stubbornly convinced that he could enlist the necessary support for his schemes. Upon his return to Jamaica, he organized still another international convention, at which various delegates reported on the deplorable conditions under which Negroes the world over were forced to live. Despite a groundswell of enthusiasm for his ideas, Garvey found himself plagued by an assortment of now-familiar financial woes, including payment of back salaries to members of his former New York staff. As a result of judgments against him, the assets of the Jamaica branch of the UNIA were almost totally depleted.

At this point, Garvey turned his energies to Jamaican politics, agitating in particular for the enforcement of already-existing British laws which were designed to protect the rights of plaintiffs against possible connivance between judges, lawyers and businessmen. For his pains, Garvey was convicted of libel and forced to serve a jail sentence of three months.

Upon his release from prison, Garvey ran unsuccessfully for a seat in the Legislative Council. In his campaign, he called for self-government in Jamaica, a minimum-wage law, land and judicial reform, the promotion of local industry, and the creation of both a national university and an opera house. Most of Garvey's followers, however, did not have the necessary voting qualifications, and he was thus soundly defeated at the polls.

Nevertheless, he continued to struggle for a political foothold in Jamaica and, ultimately, did manage to win a seat in a local council. By the mid 1930's, however, the Negro inhabitants of the island had found their economic and political position so improved that they paid less and less heed to Garvey's proposals.

In 1935, Garvey left for England where, in near obscurity, he died five years later in a cottage in West Kensington.

Critics of Garvey are quick to label him a pretentious crank, whereas his supporters are equally disposed to calling him an unqualified genius. From a more historically impartial viewpoint, however, he must be regarded as a kind of fanatic visionary—a utopian who undertook enormous and grandiose schemes, a man literally driven by the notion that the Negro's sole means for achieving a unique culture in the 20th century was through the foundation of a unified, separatist empire in Africa. Although his ideas, in their ultimate form, may have been rejected by most of the people of his day, it is clear that, since then, these very same ideas—in a different perspective—have had a favorable influence on the policies of many Negro leaders the world over.

Marcus Garvey

THE BLACK MUSLIMS

Although the Black Muslims are often regarded as members of a strictly religious organization, we have chosen to include them in our study of Negro protest groups. It is true that they are religious in the sense that they worship a supreme being ("There, is No God But Allah. Muhammad is His Apostle"), but their movement also has broad social implications, since it represents the antithetical position to the one taken by the white supremacists.

The preachments of Black Muslimism are basically puritanical. Followers are expected to give up tobacco and alcohol. (Women, in particular, are obliged to dress with extreme modesty. They must forego the use of lipstick and other ordinary cosmetics.)

Beyond this negative approach, however, there are also strong admonitions to pray often, and to improve personal habits of health and hygiene. Muslim "Fruit of Islam" bodyguards, for instance, are given vigorous training sessions in which they learn to ward off police dogs and other attackers. Muslim women are often given extensive domestic training, particularly in sewing. Muslim children are educated in sect-oriented grade schools, some of which have state accreditation, and learn the conventional subjects, although their ABC's are often supplemented by courses in the Arabic alphabet.

In short, Muslims belong to a nationwide and highly disciplined movement. Muslim society has all the appendages of the "conventional" world—everything from schools, stores, restaurants, police, temples (mosques), a newspaper (*Muhammad Speaks*), and a publishing arm. (Perhaps the most famous member of the Black Muslim sect is Cassius Clay, the world heavyweight champion, who, in recent years, has taken to fighting under the name of Muhammad Ali.)

After the assassination of Malcolm X, the Muslim organization was saddled with the reputation of being a fierce and fanatic hate group, fearlessly self-righteous and not at all hesitant to seek vengeance and retribution for alleged wrongdoing. Since then, however, the fiery rhetoric of Elijah Muhammad has cooled somewhat, and the Messenger has shown more sympathy for calculated moves designed to foster the organization's longstanding formula for black capitalism—"build black, buy black."

Thus, the black Islam nation has steadily become an entrenched fixture of the black ghetto, particularly in Chicago, headquarters for the cult. In 1968, the Muslims invested over four million dollars in the city's South Side ghetto, where it now owns a warehouse, apartment houses, two bakeries, a clothing store, two restaurants and two supermarkets.

Farming and food processing are among the other economic activities which have absorbed some two million dollars of Muslim capital. Muslim farms are as geographically dispersed as Cassopolis, Michigan; Albany, Georgia; and St. Clair County, Alabama. Residents of the last-named county reacted adversely to the news of Muslim entry into the county in 1970. The two real estate deals which enabled the Muslims to acquire the land were negotiated with diehard segregationists who confessed that they were motivated only by profit, and by a desire to introduce new industry to the county. Civil libertarians, though not in sympathy with the Muslims, moved to quash all legally sanctioned harassment of their bonafide purchase.

Most Muslim funds have traditionally been raised through tithing, but the group in recent years has sought to float large bank loans for other ambitious business and educational ventures, including the revitalization of the 47 schools operated by the sect across the U.S. Among them is the University of Islam in Washington.

Though they are indefatigably clannish, the Muslims are realistic enough to hire non-members for positions requiring special technical skills. Muslim standards are high. They believe in cleanliness, hard work, and segregation; they reject smoking, drinking, and adultery.

ELIJAH MUHAMMAD
Messenger of "Allah"

Elijah Muhammad, leader of the Black Muslim cult, is the son of a Baptist minister, and was born Elijah Poole in Sandersville, Georgia on October 7, 1897.

One of 13 children, Poole completed four grades of school before leaving home at the age of 16. In 1929, while in Detroit with his wife and two children, Poole claimed to have met "Allah on earth" (The Great Mahdi) and, from that time on, proclaimed himself Allah's "messenger." Espousing a doctrine which has since been labelled "black supremacy," Poole assumed the name Muhammad, dropping what he called his "slave-master name." He founded Temple No. 1 in Detroit in 1931.

Two years later, Muhammad was arrested by Detroit police for refusing to transfer his child from a Muslim school to a public school, and received a six-month probationary sentence. Forced to leave Detroit, Muhammad moved on to Chicago, where he was arrested by the FBI for draft-dodging during World War II.

Released in 1946, he again began to recruit a following in the Midwest. Organizing a community which attempted to shut itself off from all dependency on the "white world," Muhammad achieved noteworthy success in attracting several thousand followers, many from lower-income groups in disadvantaged urban areas. He set up a restaurant; a cleaning business; a barbershop; butcher, grocery and department stores, and even founded "Universities of Islam" in Chicago and Detroit.

Over the years, Muhammad has had a tendency to be wary of publicity, and has been extremely hesitant at revealing vital statistics about the size and extent of his following. In 1963, however, nationwide publicity was unavoidable in the wake of the resignation of Malcolm X—for many years Muhammad's right-hand man. Two years later, Malcolm X was shot to death in what many observers saw as a vendetta murder. Muhammad was forced to publicly disavow any involvement with the crime, although at least one of the men arrested was said to have been a Black Muslim enforcer.

MALCOLM X
Founder, Organization of African Unity

Malcolm X was one of the most fiery and controversial Negroes of the 20th century.

Elijah Muhammad being interviewed for a television documentary by Buzz Anderson of KQED.

Born Malcolm Little in Omaha on May 19, 1925, he was the son of a Baptist preacher who was an avid supporter of Marcus Garvey's United Negro Improvement Association. (See page 180.) At an early age, Malcolm moved to Lansing, Michigan with his parents, both of whom were tragically lost to him in childhood. (His father was run over by a streetcar, and his mother was committed to a mental institution.)

Leaving school after the eighth grade, Malcolm made his way to New York, working for a time as a waiter at Smalls Paradise in Harlem. Soon part of the seamy underworld life of the ghetto, Malcolm began selling marijuana; became a cocaine addict; turned to burglary, and was sentenced to a 10-year prison term in 1946.

While in prison, he became acquainted with the Black Muslim sect headed by Elijah Muhammad, and was quickly converted to its utopian and strongly racist point of view. Paroled from prison in 1952, he soon became an outspoken defender of Muslim doctrines, accepting the basic argument that evil was an inherent characteristic of the "white man's Christian world."

Unlike Muhammad, Malcolm sought considerable publicity, and made several provocative and inflammatory statements while addressing predominantly white civic groups and college campus audiences. Branding white people "devils," he spoke bitterly of a philosophy of vengeance and "an eye for an eye." When, in 1963, he characterized the Kennedy assassination as a case of "chickens coming home to roost," he was suspended from the Black Muslim movement by Elijah Muhammad, and soon formed his own protest group, the Organization of Afro-American Unity.

The group had built up only a small following at the time of Malcolm X's murder in 1965. He was buried as Al Hajj Malik al-Shabazz, the name he had taken in 1964 after making his holy pilgrimmage to Mecca. (See February 21, 1965 March of News entry for further details.)

The proximity of his death makes it difficult to offer an assessment of the role played by Malcolm X in the civil rights revolution. It is certain that he had a great emotional impact upon Negroes, a fact for which there is ample evidence not only in the statements made by many of his peers, but in the enormous turnout for his funeral. His appeal was not confined to the Negro masses, but had also spread to a whole host of militant young leaders who admired him for his uncompromising self-assertiveness, and his unwillingness to retreat in the face of hostility.

By 1970, it had become apparent that Malcolm X would be lionized, or even beatified, by those who sought as much to revere his memory as to promote their own distorted view of the true meaning of his ideology and striving. In practical terms, he was an advocate of self-help, self-defense, and education; as a philosopher and pedagogue, he succeeded in integrating history. religion and mythology to establish a framework for his ultimate belief in world brotherhood and in human justice. Faith, in his view, was a prelude to action; ideas were feckless without policy. At least three books published since his death effectively present his most enduring thoughts. They are his own classic *Autobiography*, a collection of *Speeches* given at Harvard, and *Malcolm X, The Man and His Times.*

Malcolm X, one of the most dynamic black leaders of his generation.

THE BLACK PANTHERS

Since its founding by Huey Newton and Bobby Seale in October 1966, the Black Panther Party has departed from the platform and tactics of all established civil rights organizations. It has condemned institutional structures which, in its view, have made American society corrupt; it has disavowed established channels of authority and operation which have either oppressed or overlooked significant portions of the black community; it has rejected "middle class values" because they contribute to callous indifference toward, or contempt for, the disinherited youth of the black ghetto. It is, therefore, a revolutionary organization that draws its support almost exclusively from rootless young blacks trapped in large urban slums.

It is to unemployed, undisciplined ghetto youth that the Panthers have held out the promise of a brighter future, or at least a safer one. The Panthers have imposed party discipline on many young males who are responsive to their militaristic regimen, their aggressive rhetoric, and their glorification of virile virtues. By insisting on the fundamental right of self-defense, the Panthers have sought to establish themselves as champions of the black poor against the police, whom they regard as agents of an insidious power clique. Police, on the other hand, feel threatened by the arrogance and intractability of the Panthers, and regard the party as a formidable and vicious nemesis.

Shooting incidents and other violent encounters between the police and the party have been numerous and costly. On April 6, 1968, for example, Panther national treasurer Bobby Hutton, 17, was killed in Oakland in a gun battle involving Panther Minister of Information Eldridge Cleaver. Cleaver, on parole at the time, was involved in the fracas, and has been a fugitive in exile since then. He and two white policemen were wounded during the shoot-out.

The violence reached a high point in December 1969 when Cook County plainclothesmen raided Panther headquarters in Chicago, searching for a cache of weapons. According to the police version, they forced open a barricaded door and were met instantly by shotgun fire and the challenge to shoot it out. At any rate, once order was restored, Illinois Panther Chairman, Fred Hampton, 21, and Mark Clark, also an Illinois party leader, both lay dead—Hampton in bed.

Police claimed that Hampton was firing his weapon from bed; the Panthers asserted that he had been sleeping. An investigator from the Afro-American Patrolmen's League reported that he found "no evidence that anyone had fired from inside the apartment," and doubted that the police would have escaped uninjured if a two-way gun battle had in fact been in progress.

Other clashes with police were reported in such major cities as Kansas City, Denver, Seattle, Salt Lake City, Los Angeles and San Francisco. Threats issued against the life of President Nixon in San Francisco resulted in the arrest of Dave Hilliard, party chief of staff, late in 1969. Twenty-one other Panthers were thrown into jail in New York that same year on charges of plotting to blow up department stores and other valuable commercial property. With party founder Huey Newton in prison until 1970, party chairman Bobby Seale sentenced to four years for contempt during the Chicago 7 trial, and Cleaver in exile, remaining party spokesmen claimed that police were systematically attempting to destroy the Panther leadership hierarchy. Black community leaders and politicians, civil rights moderates, and the American Civil Liberties Union (ACLU) tended to agree and demanded a probe of all Panther/police confrontations.

Charles Garry, the white San Francisco lawyer who has represented Seale and other jailed Panthers, claims that the death of Hampton and Clark brings to 28 the number of Panthers slain by police in the 1968-1969 period.

Police officials, the Justice Department and the FBI deny that such a vendetta is in progress, but they confess that law enforcement authorities "obviously keep an eye on" the Panthers. Granting the disruptive and abrasive nature of the group, it would not be surprising if that eye occasionally became bloodshot with rage and hysteria. Two such instances can be clearly documented: one in Brooklyn's Criminal Court building where off-duty policemen attacked members of the party in a gesture which the New York *Times* labelled "a mockery of the rule of law," another in Oakland when two white patrolmen who had been drinking while on duty unleashed a barrage of rifle fire into party headquarters.

What is particularly infuriating to police is the Panther rhetoric which lumps them all together as racially obnoxious "pigs." Panther literature is generously larded with such extremist references, and Panther propaganda clearly divides the world into two opposing camps. In the Panther view, the other side has already declared war, and so must be foiled by the very same weapons—including grenades and automatic rifles—upon which it continues to rely in times of crisis.

According to the Panthers, the training and preparation required to implement this objective instill in the young black a sense of real pride and full dignity. The realization that such pride may lead to unchecked and fanatic aggression is preferable to the risk that young black men will become racially disloyal and emotionally squeamish.

Despite their extremism, the Panthers have succeeded in effectively dramatizing the plight of the ghetto. None could quarrel with their free breakfast program that feeds some 10,000 needy black children every month, or with the free health clinics they have miraculously managed to set up in several cities on shoestring budgets.

Panther funds are derived mainly from sale of the organization's 25¢ newspaper (circulation is sometimes as high as 100,000), from speaking engagements and rallies on college campuses, from occasional cooperation with federal, state, or locally funded programs, and conceivably less reputable sources. Panther chapter and membership figures are generally not available since the organization guards closely against infiltrators, curiosity seekers, and travelling companions. Estimates put the number at between 500 and 2000 in some 40 chapters around the country. Both men and women are enrolled.

Though silence and loyalty are key virtues, and though inflammatory rhetoric is commonplace, Panther spokesmen have at times rendered clear and precise definitions of their ideology. In 1969, for instance, the National Commission on the Causes & Prevention of Violence was told: "We start with the basic (assumption) that black people in America are a colonized people in every sense of the term and that white America is an organized imperialist force holding black people in colonial bondage . . . (Violence) against the police and other agents . . . of authority is not crime, but heroism, not merely an unlawful act but a revolutionary gesture against an illegitimate goat."

Bobby Seale; co-founder of the Black Panther party.

BOBBY SEALE
Co-founder,
Black Panther Party

In 1966, there were but three Black Panthers: Huey Newton, Bobby Seale, and Bobby Hutton. Newton and Seale were summer youth workers for the Richmond, California poverty program; Hutton was only 15 and a high school dropout.

At 29, Seale, then foreman in a car wash, was in a position to carve out a satisfactory career in the poverty program, concentrating on "trades and technical skills, . . . a little black history . . ., and then cleaning lawns, repairing houses, chopping weeds."

When Seale took up residence at the North Oakland Service Center, his patience with such a program was wearing thin; it disintegrated completely one night when he led a group of black youths on a tour of Oakland's police headquarters and heard a white police lieutenant advise members of the party to turn in "people who burn down houses. Why don't you give us their names?"

Sensing then that he was involved in what he regarded as an insidious attempt to propagandize these youths and to distort their loyalties and sense of justice, Seale and Newton withdrew from such work, deciding instead to patrol the ghetto in their own fashion, "unified around the gun." Their objective: to monitor the movement of cops on the beat. The effort was designed to establish a mutual tolerance, Seale said, not to challenge the right of police to do their duty. It was also designed to show young Negroes that they had every right to demand respect and due process from police who patrolled their area.

Still, such a policy invariably involved more racial confrontation than programmatic performance. Seale and his cohorts succeeded in luring many youngsters away from the rootlessness and spiritual starvation of ghetto streets, but were unable to attract the kind of support from black intellectuals and professionals that might have complemented their emotionally resuscitating ideology.

By 1969, the cream of the Panther hierarchy—men like Huey Newton, Eldridge Cleaver, Fred Hampton, and Bobby Hutton—were either dead or in exile. Seale himself was in jail on charges stemming from the 1968 Chicago convention riots, and was one of 13 Panthers being held in custody for the alleged execution of suspected Panther informer, Alex Rackley.

Some encouragement stemmed from the party's attempts to enlist radical support in 1969 from such nationally known lawyers as Charles R. Garry of New York and William M. Kunstler of New York. That same year, the Panthers convoked a three-day conference during which some 3,500 young radicals from more than 300 organizations at least became exposed to Panther interpretations and Panther solutions.

Significant among the changes evident in the Panther positions was the group's emphasis on "people's" problems, rather than just those of the black ghetto. Seale spoke at the 1969 meeting, stressing "unity of the people" and pledging that Panthers would "not fight racism with more racism."

Both whites and blacks who listened sensed that Seale was shifting the emphasis away from the issue of race and committing the Panthers to the idea that class struggle was the deciding factor in American life.

"We will not fight capitalism with more capitalism—black capitalism. We will fight it with basic socialistic programs. We will not fight fire with fire. The best way to put out fire is with water."

Seale thus acknowledged the need to resort to propaganda, organization, and political activity as alternate tactics beyond arming the people and tutoring them in guerilla warfare. The question remains whether the Panthers will be consumed by the fiery confrontations of the past which may win them publicity, but so deplete their ranks that no one of any consequence is left to carry on their work.

HUEY NEWTON
Co-founder
Black Panther Party

Huey Newton, leader and founder of the Black Panther Party, was released from San Luis Obispo prison in 1970 after a California Court of Appeals reversed his 2-15 year manslaughter sentence in the October 1967 killing of an Oakland policeman. Panther lawyer Charles Garry first met Newton while the latter was recuperating from a serious stomach wound received during the gun battle. "With all of that," Garry recalls, "here was a man who was not afraid. This man is a natural born leader without any ego."

The youngest of seven children, Newton was born in Monroe, Louisiana on February 17, 1942. He attended Oakland City College, where he founded the Afro-American Society, and later studied at San Francisco Law School.

In 1966, Newton and Bobby Seale joined forces to establish the Black Panther Party for Self-Defense. The pair systematically set out to survey police practices in the ghetto, scouting through the area with cameras and loaded shotguns.

Newton and his partner almost immediately became the targets of sharp police resentment and uneasiness. The hostility came to a climax in the 1967 fracas during which Newton allegedly killed an Oakland officer. His eight-week trial was a *cause celebre* in which more than 2500 demonstrators surrounded the courthouse chanting Panther slogans and demanding his release. It was also one of the first public appearances of large numbers of the incipient Black Panther Party. Some 250 strong, they wore the berets and leather jackets which have since become a trademark in the public consciousness.

After his September 1968 conviction on a voluntary manslaughter charge, Newton was sent to the California Men's Colony, and placed in solitary confinement for his refusal to work in the mess hall. He agreed, however, to take a job in the institution's industrial training program.

His conviction was overturned by the California Court of Appeals on the grounds that the jury had not received proper instruction from the presiding judge. The Appeals court ruled that the judge should have instructed the jury to recognize Newton's defense as a complete one if it accepted his contention that he was unconscious at the time of the killing. Besides the "omitted instructions," the court cited several other prejudicial errors as grounds for overturning the conviction.

Newton, out on $50,000 bail, was slated for retrial on a manslaughter charge stemming from the shooting of the patrolman.

In September 1970, Newton spoke at the Temple University gymnasium in Philadelphia before an overflow crowd of 6,000. Newsmen, barred from the hall, heard the address over a campus radio station.

Newton listed some of the Panthers' aims as follows:

- Power to the people to determine their destiny
- Full employment and an end to capitalist exploitation
- Decent housing
- A true education
- Exemption from military service
- An end to police brutality, unfair jury trials, and confinement of political prisoners

"The people of the 18th century," Newton said, "have become the ruling class of the 20th century and the people of the 20th century are the descendants of the slaves and dispossessed of the 18th century. . . ."

"We will change this society," he continued. "It is up to the oppressor to decide whether this will be a peaceful change. We will use whatever means is necessary. We will have our manhood even if we have to level the earth."

WHITE LEAGUE
WHITE LINERS
K.K.K.
NEGROES SHOT IN COLD BLOOD AT HAMBURG.S.C
BLOOD
SOUTHERN RIOTS.
ONE WHITE.
SIX BLACKS
DECLARATION OF INDEPENDENCE 4th JULY 1776
CONSTITUTION OF THE U.S.
THE U.S. SHALL GUARANTEE TO EVERY STATE IN THIS UNION A REPUBLICAN FORM OF GOVERNMENT AND SHALL PROTECT EACH OF THEM AGAINST INVASION AGAINST DOMESTIC VIOLENCE.
NOR SHALL ANY STATE DEPRIVE ANY PERSON OF LIFE LIBERTY OR PROPERTY-NOR FROM EQUAL PROTECTION OF THE LAWS.
Th. Nast

THE LEGAL STATUS OF BLACK AMERICANS

U.S. Supreme Court
- **Due Process**
- **Education**
- **Forced Confessions**
- **Housing**
- **Jury Service**
- **Public Accommodations**
- **Recreation**
- **Transportation**
- **Voting**

Adverse U.S. Supreme Court Decisions

State Laws Governing Racial Intermarriage

State Anti-Discrimination Laws
- **Enforcement**
- **Total Population Affected**

Lynching

The Negro in The Judiciary

The legal transition of the Negro from the status of slave to the status of first-class American citizen has occupied the better part of the 19th and 20th centuries. Today, most of the principal instruments of justice are aligned in his favor as far as equal rights are concerned, although (as this section will show) there are still instances where national uniformity has not yet been achieved in the legal domain.

THE NEGRO AND THE SUPREME COURT

For the past 50 years, no other agency of the federal government has exercised a more profound influence on the progress of Negro civil liberties than the U. S. Supreme Court. In decision after decision, the Court has invalidated a host of legal barriers which have prevented the Negro from exercising those privileges associated with first-class citizenship in the United States. The following cases are presented here in digest form, having been arranged under a number of general categories into which they naturally fall.

DUE PROCESS

Moore v. Dempsey
261 U. S. 86 (February 19, 1923)
Justice Holmes delivered the opinion.

This case was an outgrowth of an Arkansas race riot, during which one white man was killed, and several people of both races were injured. Twelve Negroes were sentenced to death, and 67 to lengthy prison terms.

Negro witnesses appearing at the trial were whipped until they consented to testify against the accused. The all-white jury heard the case in the presence of a mob threatening violence if there were no convictions. The court-appointed counsel did not ask for a change of venue, and called no witnesses—not even the defendants themselves. The trial lasted 45 minutes, and the jury brought in a verdict of guilty after five minutes.

NAACP attorneys later applied for a writ of habeas corpus in the federal courts, a petition which was at first dismissed on demurrer. The U. S. Supreme Court ultimately ruled that the petition should be heard, and reversed the decision of the Arkansas District Court, with Justice Holmes stating in his opinion that ". . . counsel, jury and judge were swept to the fatal end by an irresistible wave of public passion. . . ."

United States v. *Adams, Bordenave and Mitchell*
319 U. S. 312 (May 24, 1943)

The three defendants in this case were convicted in a local U. S. court of the rape of a civilian while within the confines of Camp Claiborne, Louisiana. They were represented by a court-appointed lawyer, and sentenced to death.

The men then appealed to the NAACP for assistance, whereupon this organization applied for a writ of habeas corpus on the ground that the local court was without jurisdiction. The U. S. Court of Appeals for the Fifth Circuit was unable to decide the issue, and so certified the question to the U. S. Supreme Court.

This Court ruled that the lower court was without jurisdiction in the case, with the result that the men were subsequently released from the custody of civilian authorities, and returned to the Army for court-martial proceedings.

EDUCATION

State of Missouri, ex rel. Lloyd Gaines v. *University of Missouri*
305 U. S. 337 (December 12, 1938)
Chief Justice Hughes delivered the opinion.

After Lloyd Gaines, a Negro, had been refused admission to the law school of the State University of Missouri, he filed an action for mandamus on the grounds that his refusal constituted a denial of his rights under the 14th Amendment of the U. S. Constitution.

The University of Missouri defended its action by maintaining that Lincoln University (a predominantly Negro institution of higher learning) would eventually establish its own law school which Gaines could then attend and that, in the meantime, he could exercise the option of pursuing his studies outside the state on a scholarship. The Supreme Court of Missouri dismissed Gaines' petition for mandamus, and upheld the university's decision to reject his application.

The U. S. Supreme Court, however, reversed this decision, maintaining that the state of Missouri was obliged to provide equal facilities for Negroes or, in the absence of such facilities, to admit them to the existing facility.

Sipuel v. *University of Oklahoma*
332 U. S. 631 (January 12, 1948)

Ada Lois Sipuel, a Negro, was denied admission to the law school of the University of Oklahoma, and promptly appealed for legal assistance to the NAACP, which filed a petition in the

Oklahoma courts requesting an order directing her admission. The petition was denied on the grounds that the Gaines decision (see above) did not require a state with segregation laws to admit a Negro to its white schools. Further, the Oklahoma court maintained that the state itself was not obligated to set up a separate school unless first requested to do so by Negroes desiring a legal education. The decision was affirmed by the Supreme Court of Oklahoma.

The U. S. Supreme Court, however, reversed this decision, and held that the state was required to provide Negroes with equal educational opportunities as soon as it did so for whites.

Sweatt* v. *Painter
339 U. S. 629 (June 5, 1950)
Chief Justice Vinson delivered the opinion.

The Negro petitioner in this case was refused admission to the law school of the University of Texas on the grounds that substantially equivalent facilities were already available in another Texas school open to Negroes only.

The U. S. Supreme Court ruled that the petitioner be admitted to the University of Texas law school, since "in terms of number of the faculty, variety of courses and opportunity for specialization, size of the student body, scope of the library, availability of law review and similar activities, the University of Texas Law School is superior."

McLaurin* v. *Oklahoma State Regents for Higher Education
339 U. S. 637 (June 5, 1950)
Chief Justice Vinson delivered the opinion.

After having been admitted to the state university, G. W. McLaurin, a Negro, was required to occupy a special seat in the classroom, and a designated table in both the library and the cafeteria—all because of his race.

The U. S. Supreme Court declared unanimously that the Negro student must receive the same treatment at the hands of the state as other students, and could not be segregated.

Gray* v. *University of Tennessee
342 U. S. 517 (March 3, 1952)

This case was an outgrowth of the refusal of a three-judge court to act in the matter of enjoining the exclusion of Negroes from a state university. The lone district court judge to whom the matter had been referred ruled that the plaintiffs were entitled to relief, but did not enter an order.

A direct appeal was taken to the U. S. Supreme Court, and a petition for writ of mandamus was also filed. Pending this appeal, however, one of the plaintiffs was admitted to the university.

Brown* v. *Board of Education
347 U. S. 483 (May 17, 1954)
Chief Justice Warren delivered the opinion.

This case involved the practice of denying Negro children equal access to state public schools due to state laws requiring or permitting racial segregation. The U. S. Supreme Court unanimously held that segregation deprived the children of equal protection under the 14th Amendment to the U. S. Constitution. The "separate but equal" doctrine of *Plessy* v. *Ferguson* (see page 46) was said to have no place in the field of public education. After reargument a year later, the case was remanded (along with its four companion cases) to the District Court which was instructed to enter such orders as were necessary to insure the admission of all parties to public schools on a racially nondiscriminatory basis.

Hawkins* v. *Board of Control
347 U. S. 971 (May 24, 1954)

This case was an outgrowth of the Supreme Court of Florida ruling which denied a Negro the right to enter the University of Florida on the grounds that he had failed to show that the separate law school for Negroes was not substantively equal to the one for whites. The U. S. Supreme Court, on the other hand, granted a writ of certiorari, vacated the judgment and remanded the cause for consideration.

After two years, the Florida Supreme Court was still denying the petitioner the right to enter the University of Florida. By that time, however, it had appointed a commissioner to determine when in the future he could be admitted "without causing public mischief." This time, the U. S. Supreme Court ruled that the petitioner should be admitted to the school promptly, since there was no palpable reason for any delay.

Turead v. *Board of Supervisors*
347 U. S. 971 (May 24, 1954)

This case grew out of an interlocutory injunction requiring the admittance of Negroes to Louisiana State University. The State Court of Appeals reversed this action, declaring that it required the decision of a District Court of three judges. The U. S. Supreme Court—in a per curiam opinion—vacated this judgment, and remanded the cause for consideration.

Frazier v. *University of North Carolina*
350 U. S. 979 (March 5, 1956)

The U. S. Supreme Court—in a per curiam opinion—affirmed a district court judgment that Negroes may not be excluded from institutions of higher learning because of their race or color.

FORCED CONFESSIONS

Brown, Ellington and Shields v. *State of Mississippi*
297 U. S. 278 (February 17, 1936)
Chief Justice Hughes delivered the opinion.

An April 4, 1934, a few days after the murder of one Raymond Stewart, three Negroes were indicted for the crime. They were arraigned, tried, found guilty and sentenced to death.

The only evidence uncovered against them during the trial was the fact that they had confessed—admittedly after both force and physical torture had been applied. One had been hanged by a rope to a tree, severely beaten, and then permitted to return home after still refusing to "confess." A day or two later, he was again seized and whipped until he agreed to confess. At the time of the trial, the marks of violence were still visible on this victim's neck.

The conviction in this case was affirmed by the Supreme Court of Mississippi, but it was reversed by the U. S. Supreme Court which held that the rack and the torture chamber could not be used in place of, or as a prelude to, the witness stand.

Chambers v. *Florida*
309 U. S. 227 (February 12, 1940)
Justice Black delivered the opinion.

This case involved four Negroes convicted of murder in Pompano, Florida. After several appeals before the Florida Supreme Court, it was certified to the U. S. Supreme Court, which reversed the conviction on the grounds that the confessions used to convict the men had been extorted by force and violence.

Canty v. *Alabama*
309 U. S. 629 (March 11, 1940)

The U. S. Supreme Court—in a memorandum opinion—reversed without argument the decision of the Supreme Court of Alabama, which had upheld the conviction and sentence of Dave Canty for murder.

White v. *Texas*
309 U. S. 631 (March 25, 1940)

On the authority of the *Chambers* and *Canty* cases, the U. S. Supreme Court reversed the conviction and sentencing of Bob White which had been upheld by the Texas Court of Criminal Appeals.

Ward v. *State of Texas*
316 U. S. 547 (June 1, 1942)

This case involved William Ward, a Negro who, in 1939, was indicted in Texas for the murder of a white man. At his first trial, the jury was unable to agree on a verdict. At the second one, he was found guilty of murder (without malice), and sentenced to three years in the state penitentiary. The Texas Court of Criminal Appeals affirmed the lower court decision, but the case was then referred on a writ of certiorari to the U. S. Supreme Court which reversed the conviction on the grounds that Ward had originally been convicted as the result of a forced confession.

Lee v. *Mississippi*
332 U. S. 742 (January 19, 1948)
Justice Murphy delivered the opinion.

Albert Lee, a 17-year-old Negro, was indicted and convicted of assault with the intent to rape, his conviction having been based on a confession which had allegedly been coerced. The Mississippi Supreme Court affirmed the conviction, but the U. S. Supreme Court reversed it on the grounds that the confession had been coerced.

Watts v. *Indiana*
338 U. S. 49 (June 27, 1949)

The U. S. Supreme Court reversed the

conviction and death sentence of a Negro in a rape and murder case on the grounds that the confession had been coerced.

Reeves v. *Alabama*
348 U. S. 891 (December 6, 1954)

The defendant, sentenced to death for rape, attacked the conviction on the ground that it was based upon a coerced confession and that Negroes had been improperly excluded from service on the jury. The U. S. Supreme Court reversed the conviction in a per curiam decision which held that a conviction based on a coerced confession denied the due process stipulations of the 14th Amendment to the U. S. Constitution.

Fikes v. *Alabama*
352 U. S. 191 (January 14, 1957)
Chief Justice Warren delivered the opinion.
Sentenced to death for the crime of burglary with intent to rape, the defendant attacked the conviction on the grounds that it was based upon a coerced confession and because Negroes had been systematically excluded from service on the jury. The U. S. Supreme Court reversed the conviction on a number of grounds, including the fact that the prisoner was mentally retarded and had not had the assistance of counsel while being held incommunicado.

HOUSING (RIGHT OF SALE AND RESTRICTIVE COVENANTS)

Buchanan v. *Warley*
245 U. S. 60 (November 5, 1917)
Justice Day delivered the opinion.

The plaintiff Buchanan brought an action in this case for the performance of a sale of certain real estate in Louisville, Kentucky. The purchaser, Warley (a Negro), maintained that he would be unable to occupy the land since it was located within what was defined by a Louisville ordinance as a white block. (The ordinance prohibited whites from living in Negro districts, and vice versa.) Buchanan alleged that the ordinance was in conflict with the 14th Amendment to the U. S. Constitution.

The U. S. Supreme Court maintained that the ordinance was unconstitutional.

Harmon v. *Tyler*
273 U. S. 668 (March 14, 1927)

On the authority of *Buchanan* v. *Warley*, a similar New Orleans residential ordinance was upheld by the lower court, but reversed by the U. S. Supreme Court.

City of Richmond v. *Deans*
281 U. S. 704 (May 19, 1930)

The U. S. Supreme Court, again on the basis of *Buchanan* v. *Warley*, struck down the ruling of a lower court, and declared a Richmond residential segregation ordinance unconstitutional.

Shelley v. *Kraemer*
334 U. S. 1 (May 3, 1948)
Hurd v. *Hodge*
334 U. S. 26 (May 3, 1948)
Chief Justice Vinson delivered both opinions.

On August 11, 1945, the Negro petitioners Shelley received a warranty deed to a parcel of land which, unknown to them, was subject to a restrictive covenant barring its sale to Negroes. Suit was subsequently brought in the Circuit Court of St. Louis seeking to divest the Shelleys of title to the land. The Supreme Court of Missouri directed the trial court to strip the petitioners of said title.

The U. S. Supreme Court later reversed this decision, maintaining that restrictive covenants, though valid contracts, could not be enforced by state courts. In the *Hurd* v. *Hodge* case, involving a similar set of background circumstances, the U. S. Supreme Court ruling was made applicable to federal courts as well.

Barrows v. *Jackson*
346 U. S. 249 (June 15, 1953)

The U. S. Supreme Court in this case held it to be a violation of the equal protection and due process clauses of the 14th Amendment for a state court to award damages for the violation of a restrictive covenant.

JURY SERVICE

Hollins v. *Oklahoma*
295 U. S. 394 (May 13, 1935)

Charged with rape, the defendant in this case was convicted on December 29, 1931 at a trial held in the basement of the jail in Sapula, Oklahoma. Three days before the scheduled execution, the NAACP secured a stay and, later, a reversal of his conviction by the Supreme Court of Oklahoma.

The U. S. Supreme Court—in a memorandum opinion—affirmed the principle that the conviction of a Negro by a jury from which all Negroes had been excluded was a denial of the equal protection clause of the 14th Amendment to the U. S. Constitution.

Hale v. *Commonwealth of Kentucky*
303 U. S. 613 (April 11, 1938)

Charged with murder in McCracken County, Kentucky in 1936, Joe Hale moved to set aside the indictment on the grounds that the jury commissioners had systematically excluded Negroes from jury lists.

Hale established the fact that one out of every six residents of the county was Negro, and that there were at least 70 Negroes out of a total of 6,700 persons qualified for jury duty. Still, there had not been a Negro on jury duty for the period 1906-1936.

Hale's conviction and death sentence was upheld by the Court of Appeals of Kentucky, but both were struck down by the U. S. Supreme Court on the grounds that he had been denied equal protection of the laws.

Patton v. *Mississippi*
332 U. S. 463 (December 8, 1947)
Justice Black delivered the opinion.

This case involved Eddie Patton, a Negro who was indicted, tried and convicted of the murder of a white man in Mississippi. At his trial and as part of his appeal, Patton alleged that all qualified Negroes had been systematically excluded from jury service in Lauderdale County (the place of the trial) solely because of race. The state maintained that, since jury service was limited by statute to qualified voters, and since few Negroes were qualified to vote, such a procedure was valid in the eyes of the law.

The U. S. Supreme Court, however, reversed Patton's conviction on the grounds that such a jury plan, resulting in the almost automatic elimination of Negroes from jury service, constituted an infringement of his rights under the 14th Amendment.

Shepherd v. *Florida*
341 U. S. 50 (April 9, 1951)

The U. S. Supreme Court—in a per curiam opinion—reversed the conviction of a state court involving Negro defendants solely on the grounds that the method of selecting the grand jury discriminated against Negroes.

PUBLIC ACCOMMODATIONS

Katzenbach v. *McClung*
379 U. S. 802
Heart of Atlanta v. *United States*
379 U. S. 803
Both cases were decided on December 14, 1964; both opinions were delivered by Justice Clark.

In the former case, the Attorney General of the United States sued Ollie's Barbecue Restaurant in Birmingham, Alabama for its refusal to serve Negroes in its dining accommodations—in direct violation of Title II (the public accommodations clause) of the 1964 Civil Rights Act. The U. S. District Court, Northern District of Alabama, held that the Civil Rights Act could not be applied under the 14th Amendment to the U. S. Constitution, inasmuch as there was no "demonstrable connection" between food purchased in interstate commerce and sold in a restaurant, and the conclusion that discrimination in the restaurant would affect that commerce. The U. S. Supreme Court, however, reversed this view, holding that "the Civil Rights Act of 1964, as here applied, [is] plainly appropriate in the resolution of what . . (Congress has) . . . found to be a national commercial problem of the first magnitude. We find in it no violation of any express limitations of the Constitution and we therefore declare it valid."

Heart of Atlanta dealt with a Georgia motel which solicited patronage in national advertising, and had several out-of-state residents as guests from time to time. The motel had already instituted the practice of refusing to rent rooms to Negroes prior to the passage of the 1964 Civil Rights Act, and stated thereafter that it intended to continue this practice. The hotel owner filed suit, maintaining that the Civil Rights Act violated both the 5th and 13th Amendments. The United States countered with the argument that the refusal to accept Negroes interfered with interstate travel, and that Congressional power over interstate commerce was in no way a violation of either amendment. The U. S. Supreme Court upheld the right of Congressional regulation, stating that the power of Congress was not confined to the regulation of commerce among the states. "It extends to those activites intra-state which so affect interstate commerce or the exercise of the power of Congress over it as to make regulation of them appropriate means to the attainment of a legitimate end."

RECREATION

Rice v. *Arnold*
340 U. S. 848 (October 16, 1950)

This case involved the successful attempt to abolish segregation on a Miami (Florida) golf course owned and operated by the city. The U. S. Supreme Court granted a writ of certiorari, and vacated the judgment which authorized the segregated use of the course—in the light of the *McLaurin* and *Sweatt* decisions. (See education section above.)

Muir v. *Louisville Park Theatrical Association*
347 U. S. 971 (May 24, 1954)

Negroes in this case were refused admission to an amphitheater located in a Louisville city park leased and operated by a privately owned group not affiliated in any way with the city. The Kentucky Court of Appeals found no evidence of unlawful discrimination, but the U. S. Supreme Court—in a per curiam decision—vacated this judgment, and remanded the cause for consideration in the light of the prevailing legal climate, especially regarding previous segregation cases.

Mayor and City Council of Baltimore v. *Dawson*
350 U. S. 877 (November 7, 1955)

The U. S. Supreme Court—in a per curiam decision—granted a motion to affirm a judgment that the enforcement of racial segregation in public beaches and bathhouses maintained by public authorities was unconstitutional.

Holmes v. *Atlanta*
350 U. S. 859 (November 7, 1955)

This case involved a suit brought by Negroes for the integration of a city-owned and city-operated golf course in Atlanta. The segregated arrangements were sustained by the lower court, but vacated by the U. S. Supreme Court in a per curiam opinion which, among other decisions, cited *Brown* v. *Board of Education*.

TRANSPORTATION

Morgan v. *Commonwealth of Virginia*
328 U. S. 373 (June 3, 1946)
Justice Reed delivered the opinion.

Irene Morgan refused to move to the rear seat of a Greyhound bus which was travelling from Virginia to Washington, D. C., and was subsequently convicted in the lower Virginia courts for violating a state statute requiring segregation of the races on all public vehicles.

NAACP attorneys then carried the case through the Virginia courts and on to the U. S. Supreme Court, where it was decided that the Virginia statute could not apply to interstate passengers or motor vehicles engaged in such traffic. The ruling was of such a nature that it lent itself to application on railroads, in airplanes, etc.

Bob-Lo v. *Michigan*
333 U. S. 28 (February 2, 1948)
Justice Rutledge delivered the opinion.

In this case, the operator of a line of vessels used to transport patrons from Detroit, Michigan to an amusement park owned by the city on an island in Canadian waters was convicted of violating the Michigan Civil Rights Act for refusing passage to a Negro.

The U. S. Supreme Court upheld the application of the Michigan statute.

Flemming v. *South Carolina Electric and Gas Company*
351 U. S. 901 (April 18, 1956)

This case involved a suit brought by a Negro passenger against a bus company for damages due to the bus driver's having required her to change seats in accordance with South Carolina's segregation law. The trial judge dismissed the case on the grounds that the statute in question was valid, but the Court of Appeals reversed this decision, holding that the "separate but equal" doctrine was no longer valid. The U. S. Supreme Court—in a per curiam decision—upheld the Court of Appeals.

Gayle v. *Browder*
352 U. S. 114 (November 13, 1956)

This action challenged the constitutionality of state statutes and ordinances in effect in the city of Montgomery, Alabama, which required the segregation of whites and Negroes on public buses.

These statutes were first declared unconstitutional by the decision of a three-judge district court. The U. S. Supreme Court then granted a motion to affirm this judgment.

VOTING (REGISTRATION AND PRIMARIES)

Guinn v. *United States*
238 U. S. 347 (June 15, 1915)
Chief Justice White delivered the opinion.

By an amendment passed in 1910, the Constitution of Oklahoma restricted the franchise according to a "grandfather clause" which provided that no illiterate person could be registered to vote. The clause, however, granted an exemption for such a person provided he had lived in a foreign country prior to January 1, 1866; had been eligible to register prior to that date, or if his lineal ancestor was eligible at that time. Since no Negroes were eligible to vote in Oklahoma prior to 1866, the law disenfranchised all Negroes.

The U. S. Supreme Court held the "grandfather clause" invalid in Oklahoma, as well as in any other state where one was in effect.

Nixon v. *Herndon*
273 U. S. 536 (March 7, 1927)
Justice Holmes delivered the opinion.

By reason of a state statute providing that no Negro shall be "eligible to participate in a Democratic Party election held in the State of Texas," Dr. L. A. Nixon, a Negro, was refused the right to vote in a Texas primary election. Nixon filed suit against the election officials, and his case ultimately reached the U. S. Supreme Court on a writ of error. In his opinion, Justice Holmes said: ". . . it is too clear for extended argument that color cannot be made the basis of a statutory classification affecting the right set up in this case."

Nixon v. *Condon*
286 U. S. 73 (May 2, 1932)
Justice Cardozo delivered the opinion.

Pursuant to the decision in the above case, the Texas legislature passed a new statute, empowering the state Democratic committee to set up its own rules regarding the primary. The party promptly adopted a resolution stipulating that only white Democrats be allowed to participate in the primary. Dr. Nixon again filed suit, and his right to vote was again upheld by the U. S. Supreme Court.

Lane v. *Wilson*
307 U. S. 268 (May 22, 1939)
Justice Frankfurter delivered the opinion.

This case was an outgrowth of a decision by the state of Oklahoma to pass a statute which provided that all those who were already registered would remain qualified voters, but that all others would have to register within 12 days (from April 30-May 11, 1916), or be forever barred from the polls.

In 1934, I. W. Lane, a Negro, was refused registration on the basis of the above statute, and contended, as a result, that this statute was unconstitutional. The U. S. Supreme Court subsequently voted that the statute was in conflict with the 15th Amendment to the U. S. Constitution.

Smith v. *Allwright*
321 U. S. 649 (April 3, 1944)

Texas again changed its statutes (see the Nixon cases above) regarding the question of voting in primary elections, limiting the right of suffrage to white electors. In *Grovey* v. *Townsend*, the Supreme Court had upheld this action as not being unconstitutional but, pursuant to the case of Dr. Lonnie Smith of Houston, whose action for damages had been dismissed by the local federal court and by the Court of Appeals, the nation's highest tribunal overruled the *Grovey* v. *Townsend* dictum. "The United States is a constitutional democracy. Its organic law grants to all citizens a right to participate in the choice of elected officials without restriction by any state because of race."

Baker v. *Carr*
369 U. S. 186 (1962)

This case was brought by electors in several counties of the state of Tennessee who asserted that the 1901 legislative reapportionment statute was unconstitutional because, since then, the numbers of voters in the various districts had changed substantially. The plaintiffs requested the court either direct a reapportionment by mathematical application of the Tennessee constitutional formula to the 1960 census, or instruct the state to hold direct at-large elections. Although the district court dismissed the case on the grounds that it was a political question, the U.S. Supreme Court ruled that the case involved a basic Constitutional right within its jurisdiction. In effect, it declared that any state apportionment law that may deny equal protection is an issue which can be adjudicated in a federal court.

REQUIREMENTS FOR LEGISLATIVE MEMBERSHIP

Bond v. *Floyd* (1966)

This was the first of two crucial admissions cases involving other than the legal qualifications of an elected official to serve in a state legislature. Julian Bond, duly elected to the Georgia House of Representatives, was prevented from taking the oath of office constitutionally required of such representatives and thus excluded from membership in two successive sessions of the Georgia House. Grounds for his exclusion involved alleged statements he had either made or supported, in which U.S. policy in Vietnam, as well as the operation of the Selective Service laws, were attacked. Bond then sued in the U.S. District Court, Northern District of Georgia, on the grounds that the House action depriving him of his seat was unauthorized and a clear violation of his rights under the First Amendment. The District Court declared that it had jurisdiction to decide the Constitutionality of the case, that the Georgia House was authorized by state law to take such exclusionary action, and that the plaintiff's right to free speech was not violated. Bond's appeal, however, not only established that his statements did not constitute any incitement to violation of law, but reversed the lower court on the question of his right to freedom of expression as guaranteed by the First Amendment.

Powell v. *McCormack* (1969)

According to the Constitution, only three basic factors govern a man's eligibility to serve as a legislator in the U.S. House of Representatives: the proper age, the possession of U.S. citizenship, and the fulfillment of the state's residency requirement. When Congressman Adam Clayton Powell, Jr., was excluded from the 90th Congress on the grounds that he had misused public funds and defied the courts of his home state, the duly elected Congressman from the 18th Congressional District filed suit in federal court in an attempt to force the House to review only the necessary credentials for membership. The district court dismissed the first petition on the grounds that it lacked jurisdiction. By the time the case was finally heard before the U.S. Supreme Court, the 90th Congress had adjourned. Powell, however, was reelected and finally seated in the 91st Congress, a gesture which, in the view of the court, did not moot the case. The legal point on which the case hinged involved the distinction between "expulsion" and "exclusion." Despite the more than two-thirds majority required for expulsion, the Court ruled that the intent of the House was to "exclude," not to "expel." Many House members entertained severe doubts about their ability to expel a member for misconduct occurring during a prior session. The Court summation stated flatly that "the House was without power to exclude him from its membership."

ADVERSE U.S. SUPREME COURT DECISIONS

(*Scott* v. *Sandford*) (*Plessy* v. *Ferguson*)

In these two cases, the U. S. Supreme Court issued monumental decisions which adversely affected the legal progress of the Negro in the United States. The Dred Scott case denied the Negro all rights of citizenship in accordance with the U. S. Constitution, while the Plessy dictum not only institutionalized the concept of "separate but equal" facilities in public carriers, but also paved the way for the development of the "Jim Crow" system throughout the entire South.

* * *

Scott v. *Sandford*
(December Term, 1856)
Chief Justice Taney delivered the opinion.

In 1835, Dred Scott, born a slave in Virginia, became the property of John Emerson, an Army doctor, in the slave state of Missouri. From there, he was taken into the free state of Illinois and, later, to the free territory of Minnesota.

In 1847, Scott instituted suit in the Circuit Court of the County of St. Louis, Missouri, arguing that he should be given his freedom by virtue of his having resided on free soil. After nine years, his case was certified to the U. S. Supreme Court, where five of the nine justices, including Chief Justice Taney, were Southerners.

The Court considered three basic questions:

1. Was Scott a citizen of Missouri, and hence within the jurisdiction of the federal court there?
2. Did residence in a free area of the United States automatically entitle Scott to his freedom?
3. Was the Missouri Compromise (see page 89) constitutional?

In delivering his opinion, Chief Justice Taney declared that, by virtue of both the Declaration of Independence and the Constitution, Negroes could not be regarded as citizens of the United States. Moreover, the Court could not deprive slaveholders of their right to take slaves into any part of the Union, North or South. In effect, therefore, the Missouri Compromise, as well as other anti-slavery legislation, was declared to be unconstitutional.

". . . . if the Constitution recognizes the right of property of the master in a slave, and makes no distinction between that description of property and other property owned by a citizen, no tribunal, acting under the authority of the United States, whether it be legislative, executive, or judicial, has a right to draw such a distinction, or deny to it the benefit of the provisions and guarantees which have been provided for the protection of private property against the encroachments of the government. . . .

"Upon the whole, therefore, it is the judgment of this court, that it appears by the record before us that the plaintiff in error is not a citizen of Missouri, in the sense in which that word is used in the Constitution; and that the Circuit Court of the United States, for that reason, had no jurisdiction in the case, and could give no judgment in it."

Plessy v. *Ferguson* (1896)

Justice Brown delivered the opinion. The Plessy case was a test of the constitutionality of an 1890 Louisiana law providing for separate railway carriages for whites and Negroes.

"The information filed in the criminal District Court charged in substance that (Homer) Plessy, being a passenger between two stations within the state of Louisiana, was assigned by officers of the company to the coach used for the race to which he belonged, but he insisted upon going into a coach used by the race to which he did not belong."

In the majority opinion of the Court, "separate but equal" accommodations for Negroes constituted a "reasonable" use of state police power. Furthermore, it was said that the 14th Amendment "could not have been intended to abolish distinctions based on color, or to enforce social . . . . equality, or a co-mingling of the two races upon terms unsatisfactory to either."

Justice John Marshall Harlan delivered a dissenting opinion in this case which proved to be a prophetic one: ". . . . the judgment this day rendered will, in time, prove to be quite as pernicious as the decision made by this tribunal in the Dred Scott case. The thin disguise of equal accommodations for passengers in railroad coaches will not mislead anyone nor atone for the wrong this day done."

Civil Rights Cases (1883)

This group of civil rights cases was heard before the Supreme Court in an effort to determine the constitutionality of the 1875 Civil Rights Act, the first piece of national legislation which attempted to guarantee people of all races "full and equal enjoyment" of all public accommodations, including inns, public conveyances, theatres, and other places of amusement. The Court ruled, however, that the Act was unconstitutional inasmuch as it did not spring directly from the 13th and 14th Amendments to the Constitution. In the view of the Court, the 13th Amendment was concerned exclusively with the narrow confines of slavery and involuntary servitude. The 14th Amendment, by a comparable yardstick of interpretation, did not empower Congress to enact direct legislation to counteract the effect of state laws or policies. The effect of this ruling was to deprive the Negro of the very protections which the three post-war Freedom Amendments were designed to provide.

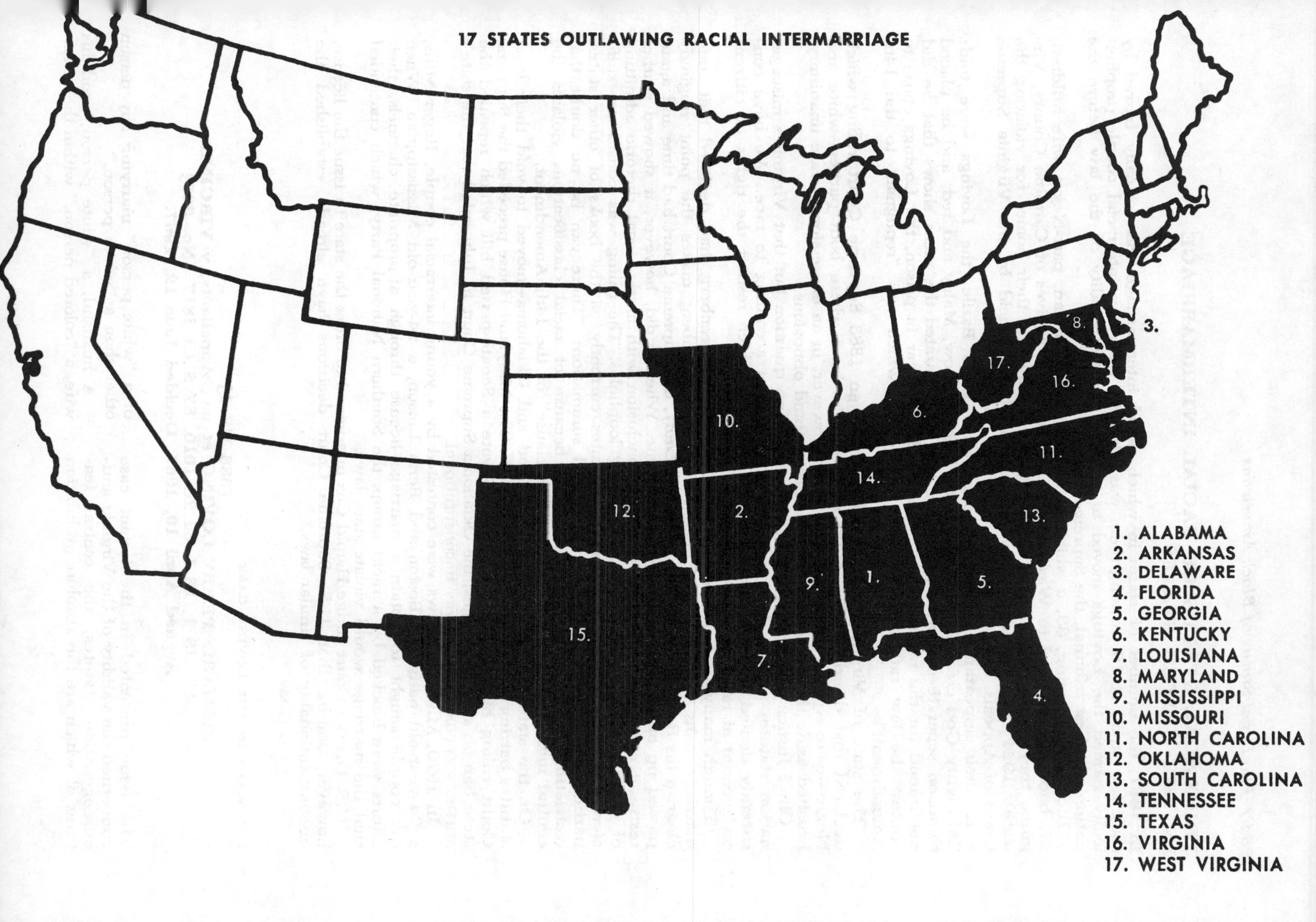
17 STATES OUTLAWING RACIAL INTERMARRIAGE
1. ALABAMA
2. ARKANSAS
3. DELAWARE
4. FLORIDA
5. GEORGIA
6. KENTUCKY
7. LOUISIANA
8. MARYLAND
9. MISSISSIPPI
10. MISSOURI
11. NORTH CAROLINA
12. OKLAHOMA
13. SOUTH CAROLINA
14. TENNESSEE
15. TEXAS
16. VIRGINIA
17. WEST VIRGINIA

THE LEGAL STATUS OF RACIAL INTERMARRIAGE IN THE UNITED STATES

In 1967, the number of states in which racial intermarriage was formally barred by state law stood at 16. Among them was Virginia, where an interracial couple prophetically named the Lovings moved to test the constitutionality of the law before the nation's highest tribunal, the Supreme Court.

Richard P. Loving, 33, a white man, and his part-Indian, part-Negro wife Mildred, 27, had been married in Washington, D.C. in 1958. Natives of Caroline County, Virginia, they were prosecuted as soon at they returned to their homes for violating the state's 1924 "racial integrity law" which had been upheld by the Virginia Supreme Court of Appeals.

In their appearance before Appeals Judge Leon Bazile, the Lovings were told: "Almighty God created the races white, black, yellow, Malay and red, and he placed them on separate continents. The fact that he separated the races shows that he did not intend for the races to mix." Sentenced to a year in prison, the Lovings chose to contest the law rather than accept a decision which was "repugnant to the 14th Amendment."

The state of Virginia based its defense on an 1883 Supreme Court ruling which declared that discrimination could not occur in cases where both parties—white and Negro—were equally punished. The Court, however, in an expression of rare unanimity, brushed aside this argument as both specious and obnoxious.

Chief Justice Warren wrote: "There can be no question but that Virginia's miscegenation statutes rest solely upon distinctions drawn according to race. We have consistently denied the constitutionality of measures which restrict the rights of citizens on account of race."

Though many lawyers, notably the LDF's Jack Greenberg, had declared that state marriage bans were patently unconstitutional (Greenberg makes the point ringingly clear in his *Race Relations and American Law*), the Supreme Court had time and again passed up opportunities to rule on the issue. When it did, however, it showed neither restraint nor a tendency to becloud its conclusion with murky legal rhetoric admitting of conflicting interpretations or disturbing loopholes. The ruling was considered sufficiently broad to void the remaining statutes currently on the books of other states, particularly in view of Warren's forceful summation: "There can be no doubt that restricting the freedom to marry solely because of racial classifications violates the central meaning of the equal protection clause" of the 14th Amendment.

On the state level, two states—Maryland and Oklahoma—moved to void their local statutes barring racial intermarriage in 1967. The Maryland House preceded the Supreme Court ruling by approving by a 97-25 vote a Senate-passed bill which repealed the state ban on such marriages; the Oklahoma Supreme Court in July ruled that the state's anti-miscegenation law was unconstitutional.

In 1970, Mississippi laws were contested by a young interracial couple, Roger Mills, a 24-year-old native of Boston and Berta Linson, a 24-year-old Mississippian. When the couple sought to obtain a marriage license through appropriate channels, their efforts were blocked by a racist group, the Southern National Party, which contended that the marriage would violate state laws.

U.S. District Court Judge Harold Cox intervened to order the state to issue the license, however, stating that U.S. Supreme Court decisions have already established the unconstitutionality of similar laws.

SUMMARY IN THE LOVING CASE

[388 US 1]
RICHARD PERRY LOVING et ux., Appellants, v VIRGINIA
388 US 1, 18 L ed 2d 1010, 87 S Ct 1817 [No. 395]
Argued April 10, 1967. Decided June 12, 1967.

The issue presented in the instant case concerned the validity of the Virginia anti-miscegenation statutes, the central features of which are the absolute prohibition of a "white person" marrying any person other than a "white person."

A husband, a "white person," and his wife, a "colored person," within the meanings given those terms by a Virginia statute, both residents of Virginia, were married in the District of Columbia, pursuant to its laws, and shortly thereafter returned to Virginia, where, upon their plea of guilty, they were sentenced, in a Virginia state court, to one year in jail for violating Virginia's ban on interracial marriages. Their motion to vacate the sentences on the ground of the unconstitutionality of these statutes was denied by the trial court. The Virginia Supreme Court of Appeals affirmed. (206 Va 924, 147 SE2d 78.)

On appeal, the Supreme Court of the United States reversed the conviction. In an opinion by WARREN, Ch. J., expressing the view of eight members of the court, it was held that the Virginia statutes violated both the equal protection and the due process clauses of the Fourteenth Amendment.

STEWART, J., concurred in the judgment on the ground that a state law making the criminality of an act depend upon the race of the actor is invalid.

HISTORICAL BACKGROUND

Marriage between a Negro and a white person was once forbidden by law in no less than 17 states, as indicated by the map on the opposite page.

After World War II, 14 states abolished their miscegenation statutes, i.e. Arizona, California, Colorado, Idaho, Indiana, Michigan, Montana, Nebraska, Nevada, North Dakota, Oregon, South Dakota, Utah and Wyoming. (Thus, prior to World War II, it was against the law for Negroes to marry whites in almost two-thirds of the nation.)

Following is a list of both the states where the ban once existed, as well as the penalties called for:

State	*Penalty*
Alabama	2-7 years imprisonment
Arkansas	1 year imprisonment and/or $250 fine
Delaware	$100 fine in default of which imprisonment for not more than 30 days
Florida	maximum 10 years imprisonment and/or maximum fine of $1,000
Georgia	1-2 years imprisonment
Kentucky	Fine of $500-$1,000 (if violation continues after conviction, 3-12 months imprisonment)
Louisiana	5 years imprisonment
Maryland	imprisonment from 18 months to 5 years
Mississippi	imprisonment up to 10 years
Missouri	2 years in state penitentiary; and/or fine of not less than $100, and/or imprisonment in county jail for not less than 3 months
North Carolina	imprisonment for 4 months-10 years
Oklahoma	imprisonment for 1-5 years; up to $500 fine
South Carolina	imprisonment for not less than 12 months, and/or fine of not less than $500
Tennessee	1-5 years imprisonment or, on recommendation of jury, fine and imprisonment in county jail
Texas	2-5 years imprisonment
Virginia	1-5 years imprisonment
West Virginia	fine not exceeding $100; jail no longer than one year

The full text of the appropriate state constitutional amendments and other statutes follows, with the states being named in alphabetical order.

ALABAMA

Constitution: Article 4, § 102

The legislature shall never pass any law to authorize or legalize marriage between any white person and a negro, or descendant of a negro.

Title 14, § 360-361

Sec. 360. Marriage, adultery, and fornication between white persons and negroes.

Sec. 361. Officer issuing license or performing marriage ceremony.

§ 360. (5001) (7421) (5096) (4018) (4189) (3602) (61) Marriage, adultery, and fornication between white persons and negroes.—If any white person and any negro, or the descendant of any negro intermarry, or live in adultery or fornication with each other, each of them shall, on conviction, be imprisoned in the penitentiary for not less than two nor more than seven years. (1927, p. 219.)

This section manifests a public policy to prevent race amalgamation and to safeguard the racial integrity of white and negro peoples. Dees v. Metts, 245 Ala. 370, 17 So. (2d) 137.

And does not violate 5th or 14th amendment.—See Jackson v. State, 37 Ala. App. 519, 72 So. (2d) 114; Rogers v. State, 37 Ala. App. 638, 73 So. (2d) 389.

The offense is a felony.—Under this section the offense of miscegenation, being punishable by imprisonment in penitentiary, is a felony. Williams v. State, 24 Ala. App. 262, 134 So. 34.

The punishment does not constitute an unconstitutional discrimination.—The fact that the punishment affixed to the offense of living in adultery or fornication, when committed by a white person and a negro together, is different from that affixed to that offense when committed by two white persons or two negroes, is not a discrimination in favor of or against either race, and is not violative of the 14th Amendment of the Federal Constitution. Pace v. State, 69 Ala. 231, 44 Am. Rep. 513.

Statute applies to person who is part Indian.—The contention that a person who is part Indian should be considered as of the Indian race, and therefore not subject to the operation of the miscegenation statute, is without merit. Agnew v. State, 36 Ala. App. 205, 54 So. (2d) 89.

The elements are the same as in adultery and fornication with exception of racial feature.—With the exception of the racial feature, the constituent elements of miscegenation are the same as in ordinary cases of adultery and fornication. As has been often explained, the statute is directed against a state or condition of cohabitation which the parties intend to continue so long as they may choose, as distinguished from a single or occasional act of illicit sexual intercourse.

Both defendants charged with miscegenation are equally guilty or equally innocent. Jackson v. State, 23 Ala. App. 555, 129 So. 306. But, under this section a defendant is not entitled to discharge on habeas corpus while serving sentence for miscegenation, on ground that codefendant received lesser punishment. State v. Ham, 24 Ala. App. 147, 133 So. 60.

But acquittal of one is not necessarily acquittal of other.—But acquittal of one of two defendants on charge of miscegenation committed by them jointly does not necessarily work an acquittal of the other defendant. Bailey v. State, 29 Ala. App. 161, 193 So. 871.

Nor does conviction of one necessarily justify conviction of the other.—Gore v. State, 58 Ala. 391, cited in Bailey v. State, 29 Ala. App. 161, 193 So. 871.

The race of each offender must be proven.—To sustain a conviction under this section the evidence must show adultery, fornication or marriage, between persons of the white and negro race. The race of each offender must be established; proof that one of them is negro without proving the other to be white is not sufficient. The appearance of defendant as a witness in a trial for miscegenation is sufficient to authorize the finding that she is of the negro race. Metcalf v. State, 16 Ala. App. 389, 78 So. 305.

In prosecution for miscegenation, under this section, prior to amendment by Acts 1927, p. 219, witness was held competent to testify that man was negro or white man if he knew type and was not testifying to mere conclusion, but when there was admixture of white and negro races, witness was not competent to testify to his conclusion that man was negro within third degree. Weaver v. State, 22 Ala. App. 469, 116 So. 893.

Proof that defendant's grandfather had kinky hair, which is one of determining characteristics of negro, and questions involving nose and other features of grandfather were properly admitted. Weaver v. State, 22 Ala. App. 469, 116 So. 893.

But proof of man's race may be made by his admissions, either verbally or by conduct in associating with negroes, attending negro churches, sending children to negro schools, and otherwise voluntarily living on terms of social equality with them. Weaver v. State, 22 Ala. App. 469, 116 So. 893.

Living together in adultery for a single day is sufficient, though no agreement to continue sexual intercourse is established. Linton v. State, 88 Ala. 216, 7 So. 261.

But evidence merely disclosing single act of intercourse without intention to continue illicit relations was insufficient to establish offense of miscegenation. Jackson v. State, 23 Ala. App. 555, 129 So. 306.

The conviction of miscegenation cannot be had on testimony of accomplice, unless corroborated by other evidence tending to connect defendant with offense. Jackson v. State, 23 Ala. App. 555, 129 So. 306.

Statutory marriage.—Where there was no evidence that defendants lived together in fornication or adultery, and state in prosecution for miscegenation, under this section, relied solely on statutory marriage for conviction, instruction that if jury believed evidence it could not convict defendant for living in adultery or fornication held not error.

Guilt of white man cannot be predicated on state of feeling between his wife and the other alleged particeps criminis.—Where defendant, a white man, and negro woman, who had been hired to attend the ill wife of defendant, were charged with miscegenation, testimony that upon the occasion of the moving of the negro woman into defendant's house the wife of defendant said in the woman's presence, "I don't want you to move her in," and that defendant said "I love her better than anything in the world and I have been going with her sixteen years," was inadmissible against defendant, since his guilt could not be predicated upon the state of feeling existing between his wife and the other alleged particeps criminis, and was inadmissible as "hearsay" as to the negro woman. Jordan v. State, 30 Ala. App. 313, 5 So. (2d) 110.

§ 361. (5002) (7422) (5097) (4019) (4190) (3603) (62) Officer issuing license or performing marriage ceremony.—Any probate judge who issues a license for the marriage of any persons who are prohibited by section 360 of this title, from intermarrying, knowing that they are within the provisions of that section; and any justice of the peace, minister of the gospel, or other person by law authorized to solemnize the rites of matrimony, who performs a marriage ceremony for such persons, knowing that they are within the provisions of such section, shall each, on conviction, be fined not less than one hundred nor more than one thousand dollars, and may also be imprisoned in the county jail, or sentenced to hard labor for the county for not more than six months.

This section is not unconstitutional as violative of the 14th Amendment to Federal Constitution. Green v. State, 58 Ala. 190, 29 Am. Rep. 739, overruling Burns v. State, 48 Ala. 195.

ARKANSAS

Statute 55-104: WHITES AND NEGROES OR MULATTOES FORBIDDEN TO MARRY

All marriages of white persons with negroes or mulattoes are declared to be illegal or void.

Statute 55-105: UNLAWFUL MARRIAGE PENALTY

Whoever shall contract marriage in fact, contrary to the prohibition of the third and fourth sections of this act, and whoever shall knowingly solemnize the same, shall be deemed guilty of a misdemeanor.

Statute 41-106: PENALTY FOR MISDEMEANOR WHEN NOT OTHERWISE PRESCRIBED

Every person who shall be convicted of any misdemeanor, the punishment of which is not defined in this or some other statute, shall be punished by imprisonment not exceeding one (1) year, or by fine not exceeding two hundred and fifty dollars ($250), or by fine and imprisonment.

DELAWARE

Del. Code Ann. Tit. 13, § 101, 102

a. A marriage is prohibited or void between . . .
   (2) A white person and a negro or mulatto.
b. Entering into a prohibited marriage; penalty.

The guilty party or parties to a marriage prohibited by section 101 of this title shall be fined $100, and in default of the payment of the fine shall be imprisoned not more than 30 days.

FLORIDA

Constitution, Art. 16, § 24: INTERMARRIAGE OF WHITE PERSONS AND NEGROES PROHIBITED

All marriages between a white person and a person of negro descent to the fourth generation, inclusive, are hereby forever prohibited.

Florida Stat. § 741.11: MARRIAGES BETWEEN WHITE AND NEGRO PERSONS PROHIBITED

It is unlawful for any white male person residing or being in this state to intermarry with any negro female person; and it is in like manner unlawful for any white female person residing or being in this state to intermarry with any negro male person; and every marriage formed or solemnized in contravention of the provisions of this section shall be utterly null and void, and the issue, if any, of such surreptitious marriage shall be regarded as bastard and incapable of having or receiving any estate, real, personal, or mixed, by inheritance.

Florida Stat. § 741.12: PENALTY FOR INTERMARRIAGE OF WHITE AND NEGRO PERSONS

If any white man shall intermarry with a negro, or if any white woman shall intermarry with a negro, either or both parties to such marriage shall be punished by imprisonment in the state prison not exceeding ten years, or by fine not exceeding one thousand dollars.

GEORGIA

Ga. Code Ann. § 53-106

It shall be unlawful for a white person to marry anyone except a white person. Any marriage in violation of this section shall be void.

53-9903. MISCEGENATION: PENALTY

Any person, white or colored, who shall marry or go through a marriage ceremony in violation of the provision of section 53-106 shall be guilty of a felony, and shall be punished by imprisonment in the penitentiary for not less than one year and not more than two years.

DEFINITIONS OF "WHITE PERSON" AND "PERSON OF COLOR"

53-312. The term "white person" shall include only persons of the white or caucasian race, who have no ascertainable trace of either Negro, African, West Indian, Asiatic Indian, Mongolian, Japanese, or Chinese blood in their veins. No person any one of whose ancestors has been duly registered with the State Bureau of Vital Statistics as a colored person or person of color, shall be deemed to be a white person.

KENTUCKY

402.020. OTHER PROHIBITED MARRIAGES

Marriage is prohibited and void:

1. With an idiot or lunatic;
2. Between a white person and a Negro or mulatto;
3. Where there is a husband or wife living from whom the person marrying has not been divorced;
4. When not solemnized or contracted in the presence of an authorized person or society;
5. When at the time of marriage the male is under sixteen or the female under fourteen years of age.

Ky. Rev. Stat. § 402.990. PENALTIES

(1) Any party to a marriage prohibited by KRS 402.010 or between a white person and a Negro or a mulatto shall be fined not less than five hundred nor more than five thousand dollars. If the parties continue after conviction to cohabit as man and wife, either or both of them shall be imprisoned in the penitentiary for not less than three nor more than twelve months.

(2) Any person who aids or abets the marriage of any feeble-minded person, or attempts to marry, or aids or abets any attempted marriage with, an idiot or lunatic shall be fined not less than fifty nor more than five hundred dollars.

(3) Any authorized person, with or without a license, who knowingly solemnizes a marriage prohibited by this chapter shall be fined not more than one thousand dollars or imprisoned not less than one month nor more than twelve months, or both.

(5) Any person who attempts to solemnize a marriage without a marriage license or without being authorized by the county court to solemnize marriages shall be fined not more than one thousand dollars or imprisoned for not less than one month nor more than twelve months, or both.

(6) Any unauthorized person who solemnizes a marriage under pretense of having authority, and any person who falsely personates the father, mother or guardian of an applicant in obtaining a license shall be imprisoned in the penitentiary for not more than three years.

(7) Any person who falsely and fraudulently represents or personates another, and in such assumed character marries that person, shall be imprisoned in the penitentiary for not less than one nor more than five years. Indictment under this subsection shall be found only upon complaint of the injured party and within two years after the commission of the offense.

(8) Any clerk who knowingly issues a marriage license to any persons prohibited by this chapter from marrying shall be fined not less than five hundred nor more than one thousand dollars, and removed from office by the judgment of the court in which he is convicted.

(10) If any deputy clerk or any person other than a county clerk knowingly issues a marriage license in violation of this chapter, but not for a prohibited marriage, he shall be fined not more than one thousand dollars, and if he knowingly issues a license for a marriage prohibited by this chapter he shall be fined not more than one thousand dollars or imprisoned not more than one year, or both.

(11) Any person who violates any of the provisions of KRS 402.090 shall be fined not less than ten nor more than one hundred dollars for each offense.

LOUISIANA

La. Civil Code, Art. 94. DIRECT RELATIVES—MISCEGENATION

Marriage between persons related to each other in the direct ascending or descending line is prohibited. This prohibition is not confined to legitimate children, it extends also to children born out of marriage. Marriage between white persons and persons of color is prohibited, and the celebration of all such marriages is forbidden and such celebration carries with it no effect and is null and void. [As amended, Acts 1894, No. 54.]

History. C. C. 1825, Art. 96, same as first two sentences, also Art. 95, prohibited marriages between free persons and slaves, and between free white persons and free persons of color; 1808, Art. 9, p. 24, same as Art. 96 of 1825 Code except for punctuation, also Art. 8, same in substance and meaning as Art. 95 of Effect on Children.

Children of a negress by a white man can not be legitimated by marriage, when both at the time of conception and at the time of marriage, marriage between whites and negroes was forbidden. Succession of Mingo, 143 La. 298, 78 So. 565.

1825 Code; C. N. 1804, Art. 161; Part., B 4, T 2, L 10.

Under Art. 113 party to marriage between negro and white person can not be released therefrom except by direct action of impeachment. Boyer v. Tassin, 9 La. Ann. 491.

Marriage between whites and colored is an absolute nullity, may be disregarded by either party, and neither can derive from it any of the consequences of a lawful marriage. Carter v. Veith, 139 La. 534, 71 So. 792.

This article does not apply to marriages contracted between whites and colored before adoption of amendment. Minor v. Young, 148 La. 610, 87 So. 472. See also Succession of Yoist, 132 La. 309, 61 So. 384.

La. Rev. Stat., Ch. 14 § 79. MISCEGENATION PENALTY

Miscegenation is the marriage or habitual cohabitation with knowledge of their differences in races; between a person of the Caucasian or white race and a person of the colored or negro race.

Whomever commits the crime of miscegenation shall be imprisoned with or without hard labor, for not more than five years.

MARYLAND

Md. Ann. Code Art. 27 § 398. MISCEGENATION

All marriages between a white person and a negro, or between a white person and a person of negro descent, to the third generation, inclusive, or between a white person and a member of the Malay race or between a negro and a member of the Malay race, or between a person of negro descent, to the third generation, inclusive, and a member of the Malay race, are forever prohibited, and shall be void; and any person violating the provisions of this section shall be deemed guilty of an infamous crime, and punished by imprisonment in the penitentiary not less than eighteen months nor more than ten years.

MISSISSIPPI

Constitution: Art. 14, § 263

The marriage of a white person with a negro or mulatto, or person who shall have one-eighth or more negro blood; shall be unlawful and void.

Title 4, § 459. UNLAWFUL MARRIAGES—BETWEEN WHITE PERSON AND NEGRO OR MONGOLIAN PROHIBITED

The marriage of a white person and a negro or mulatto or person who shall have one-eighth or more negro blood, or with a Mongolian or a person who shall have one-eighth or more of Mongolian blood, shall be unlawful and void; any party thereto, on conviction, shall be punished as for marriage within the degrees prohibited by the last two sections; and any attempt to evade this and the two preceding sections by marrying out of this state and returning to it shall be within them.

Title 11, § 2000. Adultery and fornication between kindred persons being within the degrees within which marriages are declared by law to be incestuous and void, or persons whose marriage is prohibited by law by reason of race or blood and which marriage is declared to be incestuous and void, who shall cohabit, or live together as husband and wife, or be guilty of a single act of adultery or fornication, upon conviction shall be punished by imprisonment in the penitentiary for a term not exceeding ten (10) years.

MISSOURI

Mo. Rev. Stat. § 451.020 CERTAIN MARRIAGES PROHIBITED—OFFICIAL ISSUING LICENSES TO CERTAIN PERSONS GUILTY OF MISDEMEANOR

All marriages between parents and children, including grandparents and grandchildren of every degree, between brothers and sisters of the half as well as the whole blood, between uncles and nieces, aunts and nephews, first cousins, white persons and negroes or white persons and Mongolians, and between persons either of whom is insane, mentally imbecile, feeble-minded or epileptic, are prohibited and declared absolutely void; and it shall be unlawful for any city, county or state official having authority to issue marriage licenses to issue such marriage licenses to the persons heretofore designated, and any such official who shall issue such licenses to the persons aforesaid knowing such persons to be within the prohibition of this section shall be deemed guilty of a misdemeanor; and this prohibition shall apply to persons born out of lawful wedlock as well as those in lawful wedlock. (R.S.1939, § 3361)

Former Revisions. 1929, § 2974; 1919, § 7299; 1909, § 8280; 1899, § 4312; 1889, § 6841.

Mo. Rev. Stat. 563.240. INTERMARRIAGE BETWEEN WHITE PERSONS AND NEGROES, PENALTY

No person having one-eighth part or more of Negro blood shall be permitted to marry any white person; nor shall any white person be permitted to marry any negro or person having one-eighth part or more of negro blood; and every person who shall knowingly marry in violation of the provisions of this section shall, upon conviction, be punished by imprisonment in the penitentiary for two years; or by a fine not less than one hundred dollars, or by imprisonment in the county jail not less than three months, or by both such fine and imprisonment, and the jury trying any such case may determine the proportion of negro blood in any party to such marriage from the appearance of such person.

NORTH CAROLINA

Constitution, Article XIV, § 8. INTERMARRIAGE OF WHITES AND NEGROES PROHIBITED

All marriages between a white person and a negro, or between a white person and a person of negro descent to the third generation, inclusive, are hereby forever prohibited.

N.C. Gen. Stat. § 51-3. WANT OF CAPACITY; VOID AND VOIDABLE MARRIAGES

All marriages between a white person and a negro or Indian, or between a white person and person of negro or Indian descent to the third generation, inclusive, or between a Cherokee Indian of Robeson County and a negro, or between a Cherokee Indian of Robeson County and a person of negro descent to the third generation, inclusive, or between any two persons nearer of kin than first cousins, or between a male person under sixteen years of age and any female, or between a female person under sixteen years of age and any male, or between persons either of whom has a husband or wife living at the time of such marriage, or between persons either of whom is at the time physically impotent, or is incapable of contracting from want of will or understanding, shall be void: Provided, double first cousins may not marry; and provided further, that no marriage followed by cohabitation and the birth of issue shall be declared void after the death of either of the parties for any of the causes stated in this section, except for that one of the parties was a white person and the other a negro or Indian, or of negro or Indian descent to the third generation, inclusive, and for bigamy; provided further, that no marriage by persons either of whom may be under sixteen years of age, and otherwise competent to marry, shall be declared void when the girl shall be pregnant, or when a child shall have been born to the parties unless such child at the time of the action to annul shall be dead. (R. C., c. 68, ss. 7, 8, 9;

1871-2, c. 193, s. 2; Code, s. 1810; 1887, c. 245; Rev., s. 2083; 1911, c. 215, s. 2; 1913, c. 123; 1917, c. 135; C. S., s. 2495; 1947, c. 383, s. 3; 1949, c. 1022.)

N.C. Gen. Stat. § 14-181

All marriages between a white person and a negro, or between a white person and a person of negro descent to the third generation inclusive, are forever prohibited, and shall be void. Any person violating this section shall be guilty of an infamous crime, and shall be punished by imprisonment in the county jail or State's prison for not less than four months nor more than 10 years, and may also be fined, in the discretion of the court.

OKLAHOMA

Okla. Stat., Tit. 43, § 12 MISCEGENATION PROHIBITED

The marriage of any person of African descent, as defined by the Constitution of this State, to any person not of African descent, or the marriage of any person not of African descent to any person of African descent, shall be unlawful, and is hereby prohibited within this State.

Okla. Stat., Tit. 43, § 13 PENALTY FOR MISCEGENATION

Any person who shall marry in violation of the preceding section shall be deemed guilty of a felony, and upon conviction thereof shall be fined in any sum not exceeding five hundred dollars, and imprisoned in the penitentiary not less than one nor more than five years.

SOUTH CAROLINA

Constitution, Art. 3, § 33. MARRIAGES OF WHITES AND NEGROES: SEXUAL INTERCOURSE

The marriage of (a) white person with a negro or mulatto, or (a) person who shall have one-eighth or more of negro blood, shall be unlawful and void.

S.C. Code, § 20-7. MISCEGENATION

It shall be unlawful (a) for any white man to intermarry with any woman of either the Indian or negro races or any mulatto, mestizo, or half-breed, (b) for any white woman to intermarry with any person other than a white man or (c) for any mulatto, half-breed, Indian, negro, or mestizo to intermarry with a white woman; and any such marriage or attempted marriage shall be utterly null and void and of no effect. Any person who shall violate any provision of this section shall be guilty of a misdemeanor and, upon conviction thereof, shall be punished by a fine of not less than five hundred dollars or imprisonment for not less than twelve months or both in the discretion of the court. . . .

Constitution, Article 11, § 14. INTERMARRIAGE BETWEEN WHITES AND NEGROES

The intermarriage of white persons with negroes, mulattoes, or persons of mixed blood, descended from a negro to the third generation inclusive or their living together as man and wife in this State is prohibited. The legislature shall enforce this section by appropriate legislation.

TENNESSEE

Tenn. Code Ann., § 36-402. WHITES AND NEGROES OR MULATTOES FORBIDDEN TO MARRY

The intermarriage of white persons with negroes, mulattoes, or persons of mixed blood descended from a negro, to the third generation inclusive, or their living together as man and wife in this state, is prohibited.

TEXAS

Tex. Rev. Civ. Stat. Art. 4607. CERTAIN INTERMARRIAGES PROHIBITED

It shall not be lawful for any person of Caucasian blood or their descendants to intermarry with Africans or the descendants of Africans. If any person shall violate any provision of this article, such marriage shall be null and void.

Art. 492. MISCEGENATION

If any white person and negro shall knowingly intermarry with each other in this State; or having so intermarried in or out of the State shall continue to live together as man and wife within this State, they shall be confined in the penitentiary not less than two nor more than five years.

Art. 493. "NEGRO" AND "WHITE" PERSON

The term "negro" includes also a person of mixed blood descended from Negro ancestry from the third generation inclusive, though one ancestor of each generation may have been a white person. Any person not included in the foregoing definition is deemed a white person within the meaning of this law.

VIRGINIA

Va. Code Ann. § 20-54. INTERMARRIAGE PROHIBITED; MEANING OF TERM "WHITE PERSONS".

It shall hereafter be unlawful for any white person in this State to marry any save a white person, or a person with no other admixture of blood than white and American Indian. For the purpose of this chapter, the term "white person" shall apply only to such person as has no trace whatever of any blood other than Caucasian; but persons who have one-sixteenth or less of the blood of the American Indian and have no other non-Caucasic blood shall be deemed to be white persons. All laws heretofore passed and now in effect regarding the intermarriage of white and colored persons shall apply to marriages prohibited by this chapter. (1924, p. 535; Michie Code 1942, § 5099a.)

Va. Code Ann. § 20-59. PUNISHMENT FOR INTERMARRIAGE

If any white person intermarry with a colored person, or any colored person intermarry with a white person, he shall be guilty of a felony and shall be punished by confinement in the penitentiary for not less than one nor more than five years. (Code 1919, §4546; 1932, p. 68.)

Violators are also liable to indictment for lewd and lascivious cohabitation.— The parties who violate the provisions of the sections prohibiting the intermarriage of a white with a colored person are liable to indictment for lewd and lascivious cohabitation. Kinney v. Com., 30 Gratt. (71 Va.) 858.

Applied in Keith v. Com., 165 Va. 705, 181 S. E. 283; Jones v. Com., 79 Va. 213.

WEST VIRGINIA

4697 (19). MISCEGENATION: PENALTIES

Any white person who shall intermarry with a negro shall be guilty of a misdemeanor, and, upon conviction thereof, shall be fined not exceeding one hundred dollars, and confined in jail not more than one year. Any person who shall knowingly perform the ceremony of marriage between a white person and a negro shall be guilty of a misdemeanor, and, upon conviction thereof, shall be fined not exceeding two hundred dollars.

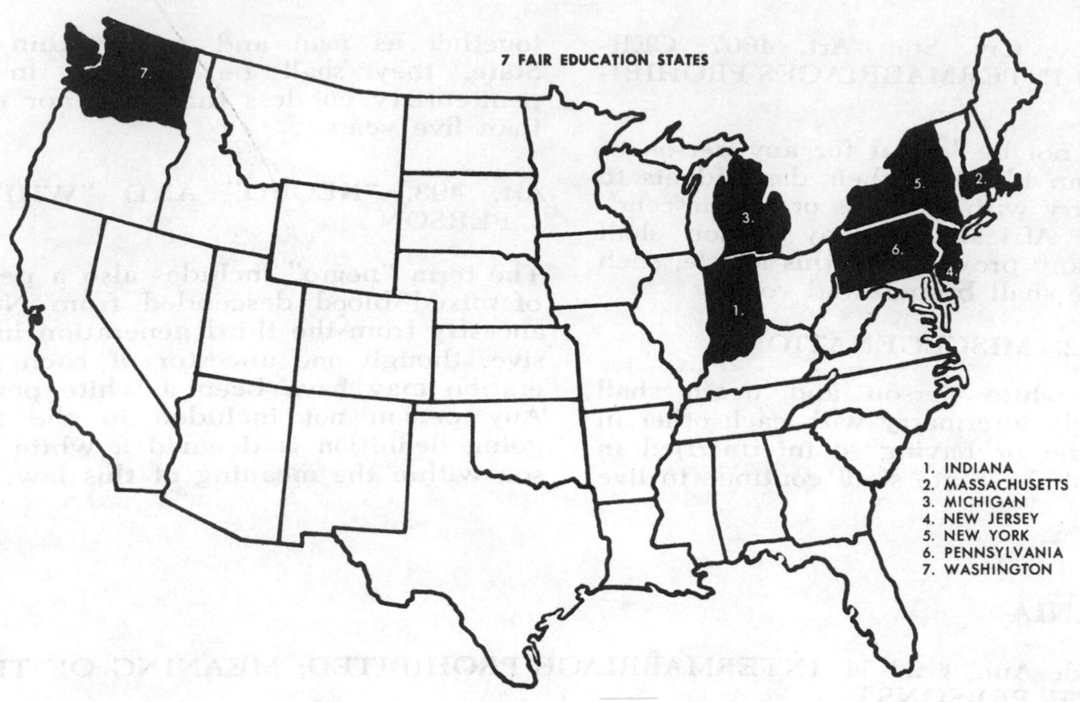
7 FAIR EDUCATION STATES
1. INDIANA
2. MASSACHUSETTS
3. MICHIGAN
4. NEW JERSEY
5. NEW YORK
6. PENNSYLVANIA
7. WASHINGTON

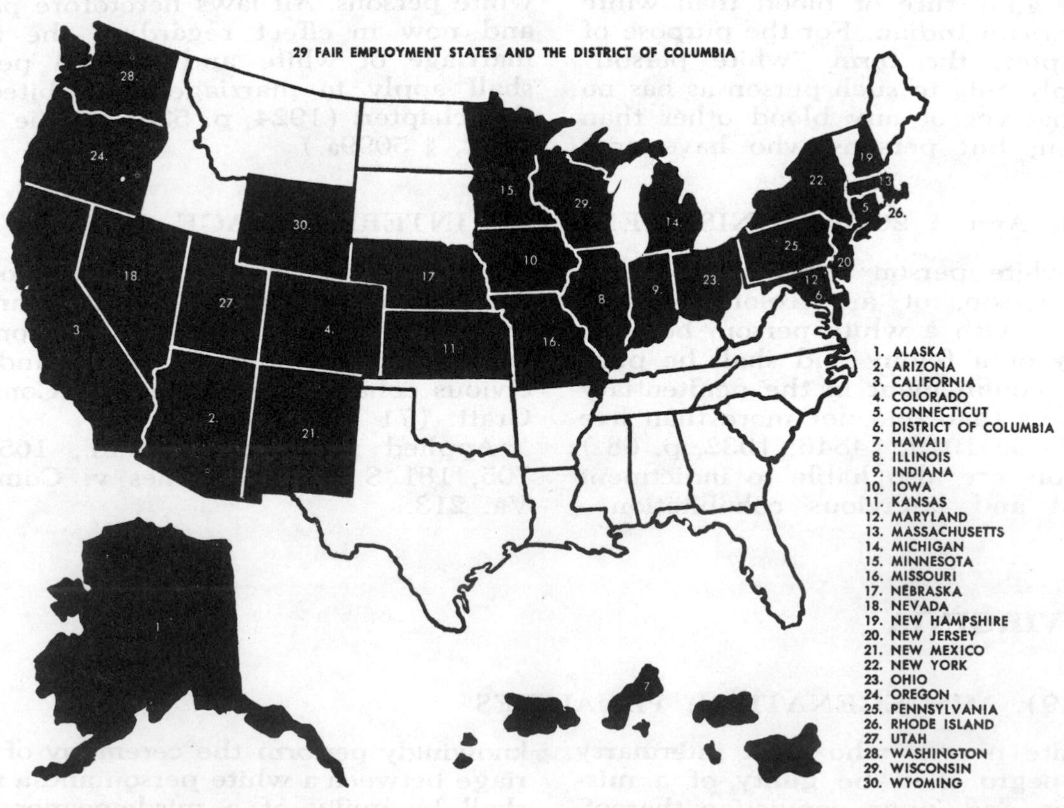
29 FAIR EMPLOYMENT STATES AND THE DISTRICT OF COLUMBIA
1. ALASKA
2. ARIZONA
3. CALIFORNIA
4. COLORADO
5. CONNECTICUT
6. DISTRICT OF COLUMBIA
7. HAWAII
8. ILLINOIS
9. INDIANA
10. IOWA
11. KANSAS
12. MARYLAND
13. MASSACHUSETTS
14. MICHIGAN
15. MINNESOTA
16. MISSOURI
17. NEBRASKA
18. NEVADA
19. NEW HAMPSHIRE
20. NEW JERSEY
21. NEW MEXICO
22. NEW YORK
23. OHIO
24. OREGON
25. PENNSYLVANIA
26. RHODE ISLAND
27. UTAH
28. WASHINGTON
29. WISCONSIN
30. WYOMING

STATE ANTI-DISCRIMINATION LAWS: 1964-1965

The major state anti-discrimination laws fall into four categories: education, employment, housing and public accommodations. Each year, more and more states enact or refine legislation designed to curb discrimination in these areas. In the 1962-1963 period, for example, 26 states adopted 49 new laws for this purpose. With the passage of the 1964 Civil Rights Act, a record number of states (31) were spurred to enact additional anti-discrimination legislation (67 laws) over the two-year period ending in 1965. The following legislative action was taken in the above-named categories:

Education: Massachusetts enacted a measure designed to eliminate racial imbalance in the state's public school system, threatening to withhold state funds unless demonstrable progress was made within a "reasonable" period of time. An amendment to an existing Indiana law called upon school officials to take affirmative action to effect "genuine" racial integration. California and Oklahoma added the study of Negro history to the curriculum as required courses. Oklahoma repealed its law providing for separate white and Negro schools.

Employment. Fair employment laws enforceable by administrative procedure were enacted by seven states: Arizona, Maryland, Nebraska, Nevada, New Hampshire, Utah, Wyoming, and the District of Columbia. A similar law requiring recourse to the courts was enacted in Montana. In Maine, violations of an existing law were made punishable by fines imposed by the courts after administrative complaints had been filed. Iowa, Kansas, and Missouri made revisions in their laws so as to bring them into closer conformity with the 1964 Civil Rights Act.

Housing. Five states—Indiana, Maine, Ohio, Rhode Island and Wisconsin—adopted their first fair housing laws, while Colorado, Connecticut, Massachusetts, New Hampshire, and New York acted to strengthen existing laws. In California, after a statewide referendum, Proposition 14 was adopted, and a clause nullifying the state's fair housing laws was added to the state constitution. (The constitutionality of this amendment is still pending in the courts.)

Public Accommodations. Arizona, Missouri, Nevada and Utah prohibited discrimination in places of public accommodation as of 1965. Eight other states—Connecticut, Iowa, Kansas, Maryland, Minnesota, Montana, New Hampshire, and New York—strengthened already-existing laws, most of which provide for administrative rather than judicial enforcement.

THE ENFORCEMENT OF ANTI-DISCRIMINATION LEGISLATION

As a whole, anti-discrimination legislation has sought to have an educative rather than a coercive effect on the public at large, shaping new attitudes toward racial bias rather than just establishing an overall pattern of judicial enforcement.

Various states—New York among them—have created so-called human rights commissions which seek first to enforce existing laws by conciliation and persuasion before initiating official legal investigations and hearings, at which witnesses are subpoenaed and testimony taken.

In recent years, there has been a growing tendency on the part of activist groups to advocate more stringent penalties against chronic violators of anti-discrimination legislation. Several states—notably Arizona, Nevada, Colorado, and Connecticut—have already shown a marked inclination to speed up the enforcement of such legislation.

THE TOTAL POPULATION AFFECTED BY ANTI-DISCRIMINATION LEGISLATION

Some 71.4% of the U. S. population is now covered by state laws prohibiting

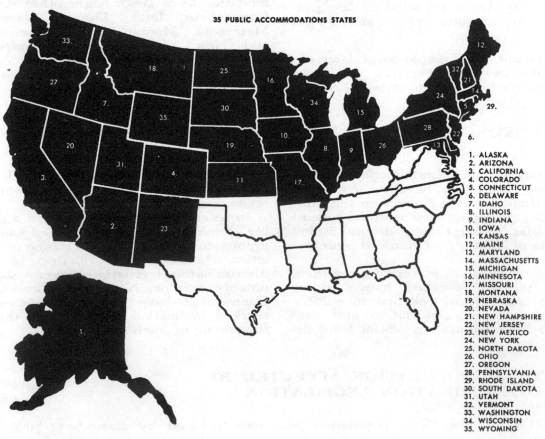

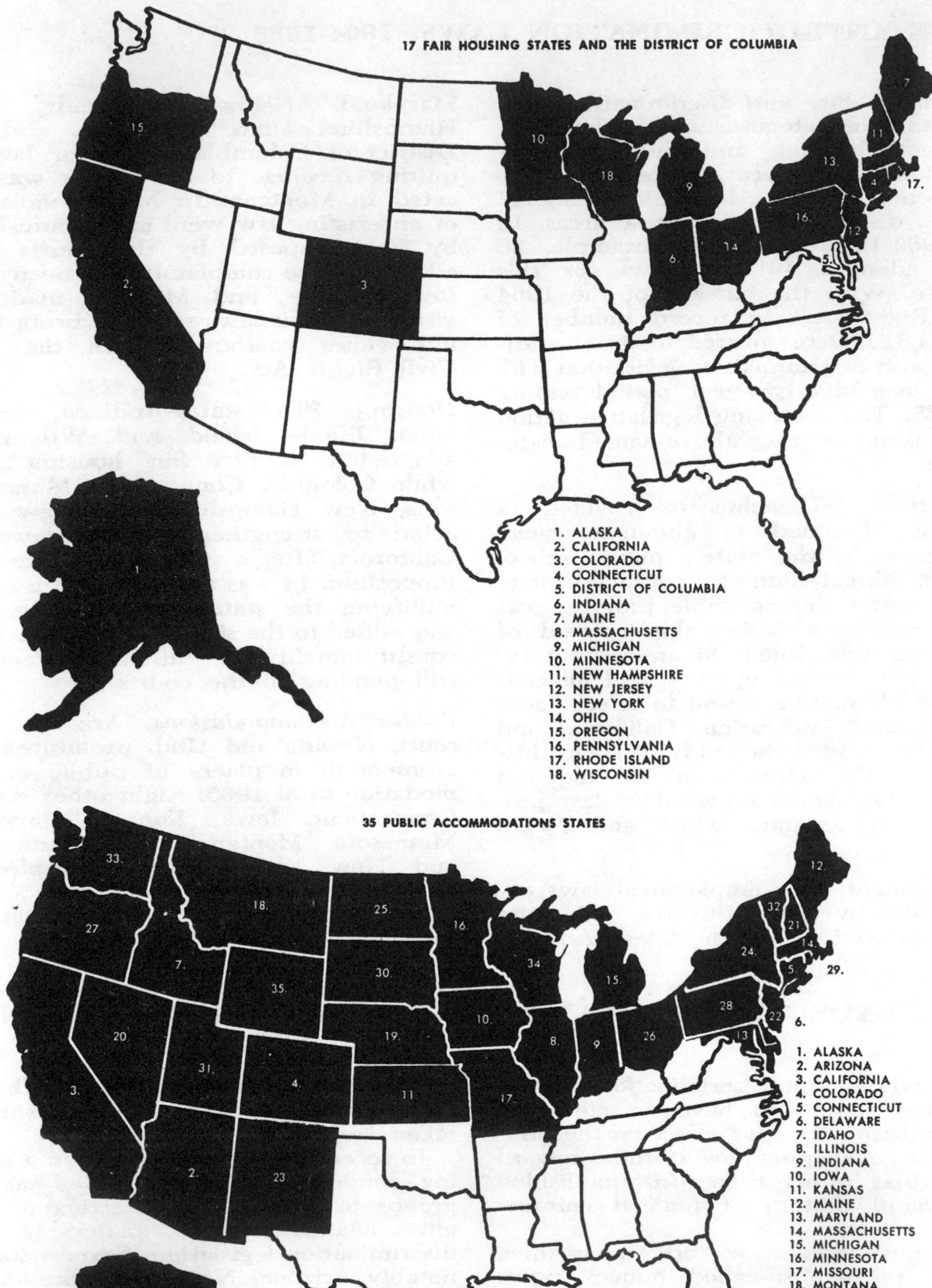
17 FAIR HOUSING STATES AND THE DISTRICT OF COLUMBIA
1. ALASKA
2. CALIFORNIA
3. COLORADO
4. CONNECTICUT
5. DISTRICT OF COLUMBIA
6. INDIANA
7. MAINE
8. MASSACHUSETTS
9. MICHIGAN
10. MINNESOTA
11. NEW HAMPSHIRE
12. NEW JERSEY
13. NEW YORK
14. OHIO
15. OREGON
16. PENNSYLVANIA
17. RHODE ISLAND
18. WISCONSIN
35 PUBLIC ACCOMMODATIONS STATES
1. ALASKA
2. ARIZONA
3. CALIFORNIA
4. COLORADO
5. CONNECTICUT
6. DELAWARE
7. IDAHO
8. ILLINOIS
9. INDIANA
10. IOWA
11. KANSAS
12. MAINE
13. MARYLAND
14. MASSACHUSETTS
15. MICHIGAN
16. MINNESOTA
17. MISSOURI
18. MONTANA
19. NEBRASKA
20. NEVADA
21. NEW HAMPSHIRE
22. NEW JERSEY
23. NEW MEXICO
24. NEW YORK
25. NORTH DAKOTA
26. OHIO
27. OREGON
28. PENNSYLVANIA
29. RHODE ISLAND
30. SOUTH DAKOTA
31. UTAH
32. VERMONT
33. WASHINGTON
34. WISCONSIN
35. WYOMING

discrimination in places of public accommodation; 71% by such laws in employment; 52.5% in housing, and 30.5% in fair education. For Negroes, the proportions range from 20.8% (fair education laws) to 45.3% (public accommodation laws). The reason for the lower average among Negroes is the fact that none of the states in the "Deep South" has enacted civil rights legislation.

The maps below show the states which now have fair employment, education, housing and public accommodation laws enforceable by administrative procedure.

LYNCHING

Lynching has not been an easy term to define. The following is a paraphrase of the definition which has been offered in most proposed federal anti-lynching legislation:

> Lynching is an act of mob violence which results in the death or maiming of a person or persons in the custody of a peace officer, or suspected of, charged with, or convicted of, a serious crime, often one punishable by death.

Other criteria for lynching were established in a conference arranged by F. D. Patterson at Tuskegee Institute in 1940. These include:

1. Legal evidence of a person's illegal death
2. Group participation in a killing under the pretext of service to justice, race or tradition

Since 1882, the trend in lynchings in the United States has gone downward, as an examination of the following tables provided through the courtesy of Tuskegee Institute will clearly show. In seven of the last 11 full years reported (Tuskegee information has been tabulated only as far as July 19, 1963), no lynchings have occurred, either among whites or Negroes.

LYNCHINGS BY STATES AND RACE 1882-1962*

State	*Whites*	*Negroes*	*Total*
Alabama	48	299	347
Arizona	31	0	31
Arkansas	58	226	284
California	41	2	43
Colorado	66	2	68
Delaware	0	1	1
Florida	25	257	282
Georgia	39	491	530
Idaho	20	0	20
Illinois	15	19	34
Indiana	33	14	47
Iowa	17	2	19
Kansas	35	19	54
Kentucky	63	142	205
Louisiana	56	335	391
Maryland	2	27	29
Michigan	7	1	8
Minnesota	5	4	9
Mississippi	40	538	578
Missouri	53	69	122
Montana	82	2	84
Nebraska	52	5	57
Nevada	6	0	6
New Jersey	0	1	1
New Mexico	33	3	36
New York	1	1	2
North Carolina	15	85	100
North Dakota	13	3	16
Ohio	10	16	26
Oklahoma	82	40	122
Oregon	20	1	21
Pennsylvania	2	6	8
South Carolina	4	156	160
South Dakota	27	0	27
Tennessee	47	204	251
Texas	141	352	493
Utah	6	2	8
Vermont	1	0	1
Virginia	17	83	100
Washington	25	1	26
West Virginia	20	28	48
Wisconsin	6	0	6
Wyoming	30	5	35
TOTAL	1,294	3,442	4,736

* No lynchings recorded as of July 19, 1963.

LYNCHINGS, WHITES AND NEGROES, 1882-1962

Year	*Whites*	*Negroes*	*Total*
1882	64	49	113
1883	77	53	130
1884	160	51	211
1885	110	74	184
1886	64	74	138
1887	50	70	120
1888	68	69	137
1889	76	94	170
1890	11	85	96
1891	71	113	184

Year	*Whites*	*Negroes*	*Total*
1892	69	161	230
1893	34	118	152
1894	58	134	192
1895	66	113	179
1896	45	78	123
1897	35	123	158
1898	19	101	120
1899	21	85	106
1900	9	106	115
1901	25	105	130
1902	7	85	92
1903	15	84	99
1904	7	76	83
1905	5	57	62
1906	3	62	65
1907	2	58	60
1908	8	89	97
1909	13	69	82
1910	9	67	76
1911	7	60	67
1912	2	61	63
1913	1	51	52
1914	4	51	55
1915	13	56	69
1916	4	50	54
1917	2	36	38
1918	4	60	64
1919	7	76	83
1920	8	53	61
1921	5	59	64
1922	6	51	57
1923	4	29	33
1924	0	16	16
1925	0	17	17
1926	7	23	30
1927	0	16	16
1928	1	10	11
1929	3	7	10
1930	1	20	21
1931	1	12	13
1932	2	6	8
1933	4	24	28
1934	0	15	15
1935	2	18	20
1936	0	8	8
1937	0	8	8
1938	0	6	6
1939	1	2	3
1940	1	4	5
1941	0	4	4
1942	0	6	6
1943	0	3	3
1944	0	2	2
1945	0	1	1
1946	0	6	6
1947	0	1	1
1948	1	1	2
1949	0	3	3
1950	1	1	2
1951	0	1	1
1952	0	0	0
1953	0	0	0
1954	0	0	0
1955	0	3	3
1956	0	0	0
1957	1	0	1
1958	0	0	0
1959	0	1	1
1960	0	0	0
1961	0	1	1
1962	0	0	0
TOTAL	1,294	3,442	4,736

CAUSES OF LYNCHINGS CLASSIFIED
1882-1962

Year	*Homicides*	*Felonious Assault*	*Rape*	*Attempted Rape*	*Robbery and Theft*	*Insult to White Persons*	*All Other Causes*
1882	54	0	33	0	16	0	10
1883	71	0	24	3	4	0	28
1884	62	0	36	0	10	0	103
1885	91	2	28	0	1	0	62
1886	70	1	32	0	8	0	27
1887	54	0	41	0	6	0	19
1888	62	0	31	0	3	4	37
1889	73	1	34	6	10	1	45
1890	35	0	31	2	5	0	23
1891	58	14	39	2	12	0	58
1892	93	3	49	12	15	1	57
1893	60	2	34	4	8	2	42

Year	Homicides	Felonious Assault	Rape	Attempted Rape	Robbery and Theft	Insult to White Persons	All Other Causes
1894	75	1	37	12	5	1	61
1895	68	0	34	13	7	0	57
1896	39	6	35	6	6	0	31
1897	67	2	26	9	14	2	38
1898	68	7	15	6	8	2	14
1899	43	2	17	9	7	1	27
1900	43	5	21	16	7	1	22
1901	51	7	17	8	10	0	37
1902	37	6	18	12	2	0	17
1903	50	7	15	8	0	1	18
1904	37	1	15	7	0	2	21
1905	32	3	11	7	2	0	7
1906	25	7	16	10	2	1	4
1907	16	7	12	12	4	1	8
1908	35	8	15	14	3	1	21
1909	46	5	14	5	3	4	5
1910	41	3	18	5	4	2	3
1911	36	3	6	7	3	4	8
1912	34	2	11	3	4	3	6
1913	25	4	7	3	1	1	11
1914	31	9	6	1	2	1	5
1915	27	9	11	6	9	3	4
1916	21	7	3	9	8	2	4
1917	7	3	7	6	1	6	8
1918	27	3	10	6	5	2	11
1919	29	8	9	10	1	7	19
1920	23	9	15	3	0	3	8
1921	19	8	16	3	0	3	15
1922	15	5	14	5	4	2	12
1923	5	5	6	1	1	2	13
1924	4	2	5	2	0	3	0
1925	8	1	4	2	0	1	1
1926	13	3	2	3	1	1	7
1927	7	2	2	3	0	0	2
1928	5	2	3	0	0	0	1
1929	1	3	3	0	0	2	1
1930	5	0	8	2	3	0	3
1931	5	3	0	5	0	0	0
1932	1	2	1	1	0	1	2
1933	8	4	3	3	1	1	8
1934	2	2	2	4	1	3	1
1935	8	1	3	3	0	1	4
1936	1	0	3	3	0	1	0
1937	4	2	1	0	1	0	0
1938	3	0	1	0	0	1	1
1939	2	0	0	0	0	0	1
1940	0	0	0	1	0	1	3
1941	0	0	0	1	1	0	2
1942	1	1	0	3	0	0	1
1943	1	0	0	0	0	1	1
1944	2	0	0	0	0	0	0
1945	0	0	0	1	0	0	0
1946	0	1	0	0	2	0	3
1947	1	0	0	0	0	0	0
1948	0	0	0	0	1	0	1
1949	0	0	0	0	0	0	3
1950	0	0	0	0	0	0	2

Year	Homicides	Felonious Assault	Rape	Attempted Rape	Robbery and Theft	Insult to White Persons	All Other Causes
1951	0	0	0	0	0	0	1
1952	0	0	0	0	0	0	0
1953	0	0	0	0	0	0	0
1954	0	0	0	0	0	0	0
1955	0	0	0	0	0	1	2
1956	0	0	0	0	0	0	0
1957	0	1	0	0	0	0	0
1958	0	0	0	0	0	0	0
1959	0	0	1	0	0	0	0
1960	0	0	0	0	0	0	0
1961	0	0	0	0	0	0	1
1962	0	0	0	0	0	0	0
TOTAL	1,937	205	911	288	232	85	1,078

COMPILED BY THE DEPARTMENT OF RECORDS AND RESEARCH
Tuskegee Institute, Alabama

THE NEGRO IN THE JUDICIARY

Inasmuch as Negroes have not always been able to regard the law as an impartial, justice-seeking force, it is not surprising that they do not have a long and extensive history in the legal profession. In some states in particular, the law tended to become an instrument of oppression, rather than a vehicle of redress. Before the Civil War, for example, the law constituted one of the forces which prevented the Negro's escape from slavery. Again, toward the end of Reconstruction, the laws of the South were clearly intended in part to institutionalize the practices of white supremacy.

Despite these obstacles, Negroes gradually began to enter the legal profession, albeit predominantly in the North, where they were given some degree of status, and the right to represent their clients on equal footing with their white counterparts. The formation of the National Association for the Advancement of Colored People (NAACP) played a vital role in broadening the legal horizons of both the Negro citizen and the prospective practitioner of law in the 20th century. By 1939, the year the NAACP Legal Defense and Educational Fund was incorporated, the Negro had ample reason to believe that the legal institutions of the nation were undergoing a profound metamorphosis—judging particularly from the large number of cases regularly being won by Negro petitioners before the United States Supreme Court. Most legal landmarks in the Negro's fight for constitutional privileges have been won with the assistance of the NAACP, many by a host of lawyers now active as federal judges in the courts of the United States.

Almost all Negro judges currently on the bench have received their appointments within the past decade. (Notable exceptions are Herman E. Moore of the U. S. District Court in the Virgin Islands, and William H. Hastie of the Third Circuit in Philadelphia.) Only one Negro has served as a member of the U. S. Supreme Court: Thurgood Marshall. Marshall's appointment to the Court in 1967 was among the most momentous decisions rendered during the Johnson Administration. Even before his confirmation, the former NAACP counsel and Solicitor General was subject to the irksome goading of Southern critics like South Carolina's Strom Thurmond who denounced Marshall's "activist" legal outlook as a judicial liability. Most U. S. Senators rallied to support the nomination, however, with the result that only 11 men voted against confirmation, while 69 favored it. Marshall spoke for himself and for the black man in general when he pledged "that I shall be ever mindful of my obligation to the Constitution and to the goal of equal justice under law." On October 2, 1967, in the presence of President Johnson, Marshall took the oath before the court's oldest member, Hugo Black. Reference to race was not part of the impressive words Marshall repeated in the five-minute ceremony: "I Thurgood Marshall, do solemnly swear that I will administer justice without respect to persons, and do equal right to the poor and to the rich, and that I will faithfully and impartially discharge and perform all the duties incumbent on me as Associate Justice of the United States according to the best of my abilities and understanding, agreeable to the Constitution and laws of the United States. So help me God."

Our section includes biographical sketches of the Negro federal judges currently on the bench, and makes mention of other important legal personnel active in related roles.

WILLIAM BENSON BRYANT
U.S. District Judge

William Benson Bryant was appointed U. S. District Judge for the District of Washington in 1965.

Born in Wetumpka, Alabama on September 18, 1911, Bryant received both his A. B. and LL. B. degrees from Howard University.

Before going on active military duty during World War II (he was honorably discharged with the rank of lieutenant-colonel), Bryant had served briefly with the Works Project Administration (WPA), and then with the Bureau of Intelligence in the Office of War Information.

In 1948, he opened a law office in Washington, D. C., practicing there until 1951 when he entered federal service as an assistant in the office of the U. S. Attorney for the District of Columbia. After three years, Bryant resigned from this post in order to become a member of a private law firm. He had already become a partner in this firm when President Lyndon B. Johnson announced his appointment to the federal bench.

WALTER ARTHUR GORDON
U.S. District Judge

Prior to his appointment in 1958 as a U. S. District Judge, Walter Gordon had served for three years as Governor of the Virgin Islands.

Gordon was born in Atlanta, Georgia, on October 10, 1894. In 1918, he was awarded his B. A. by the University of California at Berkeley and, four years later, won his J. D. from the same school.

After a number of years in private practice, Gordon became an attorney for the Golden State Insurance Company, and was promoted in 1944 to the position of administrative advisor.

His alma mater awarded him an honorary LL. D. in 1958.

WILLIAM H. HASTIE
U.S. Federal Judge, 3rd Circuit, Philadelphia

The first Negro federal judge in U. S. history (1949), William Hastie was also the first Negro governor of the Virgin Islands.

Hastie was born in Knoxville, Tennessee on November 17, 1904. First in his class and Phi Beta Kappa from Amherst in 1925, he received his LL. B. from Harvard University Law School five years later and almost immediately went into private practice.

In 1933, having been awarded a doctorate in juridical science by Harvard, he abandoned his own practice for an appointment as assistant solicitor of the U. S. Department of Labor. Secretary Harold Ickes was so impressed with his abilities that he urged President Franklin D. Roosevelt to name him judge of the District Court of the Virgin Islands. Two years later, however, Hastie resigned the judgeship to become a professor and, later, dean of the Howard University Law School.

Hastie left this administrative post in 1940 in order to accept the job of civilian aide and race relations advisor to Secretary of War Henry Stimson. Three years later, he resigned from this position in the wake of a decision by the Army to set up a segregated Air Corps Technical Training School in Missouri.

In 1943, Hastie was the recipient of the highly coveted NAACP Spingarn Medal.

A. LEON HIGGINBOTHAM
U.S. District Judge

A. Leon Higginbotham was appointed U. S. District Judge for the Eastern District of Pennsylvania in 1963. Just prior to this appointment, he had served on the Federal Trade Commission—the first Negro and the youngest person ever to hold the post of commissioner.

Higginbotham was born in Trenton, New Jersey in 1927. Originally an engineering student at Purdue University, he later enrolled at Antioch College as a liberal arts student, and then received his LL. B. in 1952 from Yale.

He was soon appointed assistant district attorney in Philadelphia; then joined a private law firm; and, later, was chosen by Pennsylvania's Governor David Lawrence to serve as a member of the Pennsylvania Human Rights Commission.

In 1959, he was elected president of the Philadelphia chapter of the NAACP and, four years later, was cited as "one of the 10 outstanding young men in America" by the U. S. Junior Chamber of Commerce.

THURGOOD MARSHALL
Associate Justice, U.S. Supreme Court

In July 1965, Thurgood Marshall was appointed to one of the most prestigious positions ever held by a Negro in the federal government—that of Solicitor General of the United States. Marshall assumed the task of acting as the government's chief legal spokesman in cases brought before the Supreme Court.

Marshall was born in Baltimore, Maryland on July 2, 1908. After receiving a B.A. degree from Lincoln University as a pre-dental student, he decided instead to become a lawyer and was admitted to Howard University's Law School, graduating in 1933 at the top of his class.

After five years of private practice in Baltimore, Marshall began what was to become a long and distinguished career with the NAACP—interrupted only briefly by an assignment as President John F. Kennedy's personal representative to the independence ceremonies of Sierra Leone.

In 1938, as national special counsel, he handled all cases involving questions of Negro constitutional rights. Then, in 1950, he was named director-counsel of the organization's 11-year-old Legal Defense and Educational Fund. In 1954, as part of an imposing team of lawyers, he played a key role in the now-historic Supreme Court decision on school desegregation. He also figured prominently in such important cases as *Sweatt* v. *Painter* (requiring the admission of a qualified Negro student to the law school of Texas University), and *Smith* v. *Allwright* (establishing the right of Texas Negroes to vote in Democratic primaries).

In 1961, Marshall sat on a federal bench as circuit judge for the Second Circuit. His outstanding achievements in the field of law led in 1946 to his winning the coveted Spingarn Medal, only one of the numerous citations he holds.

The climax of Marshall's legal and judicial career came in 1967 when he was nominated for a seat on the U.S. Supreme Court. At 59, the son of a sleeping-car porter and great grandson of a slave became the 96th man—and the first Negro—to sit among the nine Supreme Court justices.

WADE H. McCREE, JR.
U.S. District Judge

President John F. Kennedy named Wade McCree, Jr. U. S. District Judge for the Eastern District of Michigan in 1961. Prior to the appointment, McCree had been a judge in the Wayne County Circuit Court for some seven years.

A native of Des Moines, Iowa, McCree was born on July 3, 1920. Before entering World War II, where he served as a captain in the European theatre, he had already received his A. B. from Fisk University and an LL. B. from Harvard.

In 1952, after four years of private law practice, he was appointed Commissioner of the Michigan Workmen's Compensation Board.

IRVIN CHARLES MOLLISON
1898-1962
U.S. Customs Court Judge

Irvin Mollison was appointed judge of the U. S. Customs Court of New York City in 1945—the first Negro to hold this post. Prior to this presidential appointment, he had practiced law for more than 20 years in Chicago.

Mollison was born on December 24, 1898 in Vicksburg, Mississippi. In 1920, he graduated from the University of Chicago with a Ph. B. degree and, three years later, was awarded a J. D. from the same school. That same year, he was admitted to the Illinois bar.

Mollison died in 1962 after 17 years as a federal judge.

HERMAN EMMONS MOORE
U.S. District Judge

Herman Emmons Moore has been Judge of the U. S. District Court in the Virgin Islands since 1939.

Born on August 3, 1893, Moore left his hometown of Jackson, Mississippi to attend Howard University where he received his B. A. in 1914 and his LL. B. in 1917. Two years later, he was awarded an LL. M. by Boston University.

During the next 25 years, Moore ran his own law office, first in Boston and, later, in Chicago. He left private practice in 1934, and served for five years as assistant commissioner of the Illinois Commerce Commission.

JAMES BENTON PARSONS
U.S. District Judge

James Benton Parsons, chosen by President John F. Kennedy in 1961 and installed on the bench the following year, became the first Negro ever appointed a lifetime federal district judge within the continental United States (U. S. District Court for the Northern District of Illinois). Prior to this, he had been elected judge of the Superior Court of Cook County, Illinois, and had also held the office of Assistant U. S. Attorney.

A native of Kansas City, Missouri, Parsons was born on August 13, 1911. At first a student of music at the James Milliken University and Conservatory of Music, and, from 1938 to 1940, acting head of the Department of Music at Lincoln University, he attended summer sessions at Wisconsin University with an eye toward changing his major to political science. This plan was temporarily interrupted by four years of military service but, with the end of World War II, he pursued his graduate studies—this time at the University of Chicago. He ultimately received an M. A. in political science in 1946, and a Doctor of Laws Degree three years later.

After a brief stint as a teacher at the John Marshall School of Law, Parsons worked for two years as assistant corporation counsel for the City of Chicago, appearing often before the Illinois Appellate Court, as well as the State Supreme Court. He was then appointed to the U. S. Attorney's Office, serving there with distinction for nine years. During this period, he was particularly active with cases relating to juvenile delinquency and rehabilitation, as well as with those involving both civil rights and the selective service. For his success in prosecuting some 60 selective service violators, Parsons was presented with the first Selective Service System Certificate of Appreciation.

SCOVEL RICHARDSON
U.S. Customs Court Judge

In 1957, Scovel Richardson was named judge to the U. S. Customs Court for New York State, having previously acquired considerable legal experience both as a practicing lawyer and a professor of law.

Born in Nashville, Tennessee on February 4, 1912, Richardson obtained his B. A. and M. A. degrees from the University of Illinois and, in 1937, his LL. B. from Howard University.

With the exception of one year (1938) when he served as a private attorney in Chicago, and another year (1943) when he was a senior attorney for the Office of Price Administration (OPA), Richardson was associated with Lincoln University as a professor of law and dean of the law school. He left Lincoln in 1953 to accept an appointment from President Dwight D. Eisenhower to the U. S. Board of Parole, becoming its chairman the following year.

SPOTTSWOOD W. ROBINSON, III
U.S. District Judge

When Spottswood Robinson, III was appointed a judge of the U. S. District Court for the District of Columbia in 1963, he had already served in the legal field for many years—first as a private attorney, then as a faculty member and, ultimately, as dean of the Howard University School of Law.

Robinson was born in Richmond, Virginia on July 26, 1916. He received his B. A. at Virginia Union University, and his LL. B. from the Howard University Law School in 1939.

Judge Robinson was the Virginia representative of the NAACP Legal Defense and Educational Fund from 1948 to 1950, and later served for nine years as its southeast regional counsel. He was a member of the United States Commission on Civil Rights from 1961 to 1963.

THE BLACK AMERICAN AND THE VOTE

Civilian Population of Voting Age (1964)
24th Amendment to the U.S. Constitution

The evolution of suffrage as related to the American Negro has had a long and varied history—not only at the national level, but within the individual states as well. The ramifications of this story are not confined to the South, but find application in every corner of the country.

In colonial times, free Negroes first voted in the territory of South Carolina, but this short-lived privilege was withdrawn by the legislature in 1716, when the law stipulated that only white men professing Christianity were to be allowed to vote. Georgia (1761) and Virginia (1762) later imposed a color ban, but this did not alter the voting status of free Negroes in the other colonies.

At the close of the Revolutionary War, more than one million of the 3,250,000 people (excluding Indians) living in the United States were not yet free. These included 600,000 Negro slaves; 300,000 indentured servants, and 50,000 convicts. Of the more than two million free Americans, only 120,000 could meet the voting requirements established by individual states at that time. Generally, these requirements took into consideration the following factors: sex, age, residence, morality (character), property, religion, status of freedom, and race.

In the two decades immediately following the close of the Revolutionary War, most states imposed property and taxpaying requirements on prospective voters but, with the passage of time, other conditions were established as well. Convicts and mentally impaired persons were denied the right to vote, as were non-U. S. citizens, members of the military, paupers, and persons under guardianship.

Historically, the conception of the franchise which most framers of the Constitution had at the time they were deliberating this momentous document is most important in any consideration of the evolution of the franchise in the United States. Most of the delegates who met at Philadelphia in 1787 could agree on the two interrelated principles of the Declaration of Independence, to wit: that governments derived their just powers to rule from the consent of those they governed, and the corollary principle that sovereign power must, therefore, reside in the people. The question, however, of how many people would eventually be allowed to take an active part in this critical function of self-government was one on which the Founding Fathers could not express a uniform opinion.

The prevailing opinions generally fell into two categories: one embracing those men who were in favor of the creation of a strong central government by individual citizens entitled from the very outset to take part through the responsible exercise of the franchise; the other advocating the maintenance of a stable government brought to power by a select group of men whose rank and education made them suitable arbiters of the new nation's initial political course. The latter group feared "mob rule," and sought to make the extension of the franchise subject to a program of massive popular education. This outlook tended to prevail, however, and it was thus decided to extend to the states themselves the right to choose their own electorate.

By 1800, eight states had revised their constitutions and three new states had been admitted to the Union. New constitutions had been put into effect in Georgia and New Hampshire, both of which abandoned their property qualifications in favor of taxpaying requirements, and also inserted specific provisions limiting the the franchise to white males.

As appreciable numbers of Negroes gained their freedom (either by purchasing it themselves, or by being emancipated upon the death of their masters, as was the case with George Washington), the situation began to change rapidly. Between 1792 and 1838, for example, no less than nine states (generally those confined to the South and to Border areas) altered their constitutions so as to exclude Negroes. Moreover, Negroes were denied the ballot in every new state (except Maine) entering the Union between 1800 and 1861.

In New England, Negroes were not eliminated on racial grounds, although in New York they were obliged to meet certain property-owning and taxpaying requirements. (Even here, however, in 1821, with some 30,000 Negro voters in New York, members of the constitutional convention increased the freeholding requirement, and lengthened residency requirements for Negroes.)

At the beginning of the Civil War, free black men were permitted to vote on a par with their white counterparts in only five states: Maine, Massachusetts, New Hampshire, Rhode Island, and Vermont. In New York, they had hung on to the vote despite a gradual stiffening in the requirements demanded only of them.

The Civil War at once shattered the slowly evolving pattern of gradually elimi-

Electioneering to gain public office (circa 1870)

nating the Negro presence at the polls. Some four million Negro slaves were suddenly free, and instantly transformed into citizens possessing the right to vote. The Radical wing of the Republican party, led by Senator Charles Sumner of Massachusetts and Representative Thaddeus Stevens of Georgia, was committed to Negro enfranchisement, and to a strict and punitive program for the South as well.

The Reconstruction Act which divided the former Confederate states into military districts also called for new constitutional conventions elected by permanently enfranchised male delegates, regardless of race. Within three years, the right to vote has been legalized by the 15th Amendment to the U.S. Constitution, a measure which had its particular impact upon the South, but was not without application in the North.

The history of black suffrage during Reconstruction has, until recently, been written almost exclusively by white Southerners and other Northern apologists who often singled out black officeholders for alleged ignorance, incompetence, or unscrupulousness without applying comparable norms of judgment to white legislators. The fact is that the average white Southerner was already preconditioned to despise the black lawmaker—particularly the capable and conscientious one. "If there was one thing South Carolina feared more than bad Negro government," Dr. W. E. B. DuBois once wrote, "it was good Negro government."

It is certainly a historical fact that the harshness and excesses of the Reconstruction period were factors contributing to the creation of a strong backlash movement in the South. The backlash was evident in the growth of the Ku Klux Klan and other terrorist groups which sought to turn back the clock of Negro progress to an era in which white leadership was unchallengeable in the South.

The greatest force motivating the disenfranchisement of Negroes was the threat posed to the Southern Democratic party by the possibility of a political alliance between the Populist Party and the Republicans. In such an alliance, it was believed that the Negro would hold the balance of power — a fact which induced most Southern states to close ranks behind the concept of racial exclusion at the polls.

Thus, in 1890, the Mississippi state convention moved to disenfranchise the Negro. Five years later, South Carolina introduced such restrictive controls on Negro suffrage as the poll tax and the literacy test, and established a previous "criminal" record as sufficient grounds for disqualifying a prospective voter. In 1898, Louisiana passed what was known as the grandfather clause, a measure which debarred most Negro voters by basing eligibility on voter enrollment lists dating back to 1867. By 1910, such states as Virginia, Georgia, Alabama, North Carolina, and Oklahoma had accomplished the same end—each in its own fashion (Oklahoma by a grandfather clause similar to Louisiana's). By 1902, not a single Negro sat in either a state or federal legislature. Despite the Civil Rights Act of 1875 (see page 111), nearly all those institutions (state universities and public facilities, among others) that had been desegregated were now segregated again.

Hope Rekindled

The first signs of a significant groundswell and a rekindling of hope among Negroes on the issue of voting rights emerged at the beginning of the 20th century. From 1905 to 1908, W. E. B. DuBois fought hard for Negro suffrage, eventually winning the support of the Equal Suffrage League. DuBois was also instrumental in establishing the so-called Niagara Movement, which represented the first organizational effort on the part of the Negro to register his protest and to bring pressure to bear wherever it was needed. This movement was soon followed by the establishment in 1909 of the NAACP (see page 3), an organization made up of both Negroes and whites. Equally insistent on Negro suffrage, it contended in no uncertain terms that it was within *this* sphere that the Negro's best opportunity to protect *all* of his rights undoubtedly lay.

One of the first consequences of the pressure increasingly exerted by the NAACP was the Supreme Court decision in *Guinn* v. *U. S.* (1915) to outlaw the grandfather clause in Oklahoma. This case was followed by many others, among them *Nixon* v. *Herndon* (1927), which forbade the exclusion of Negroes from Democratic primaries. (The Democratic "white primary" device had by this time become the most effective method of disenfranchising Negroes. In effect, it ruled that the primary voter must be a party member, and then

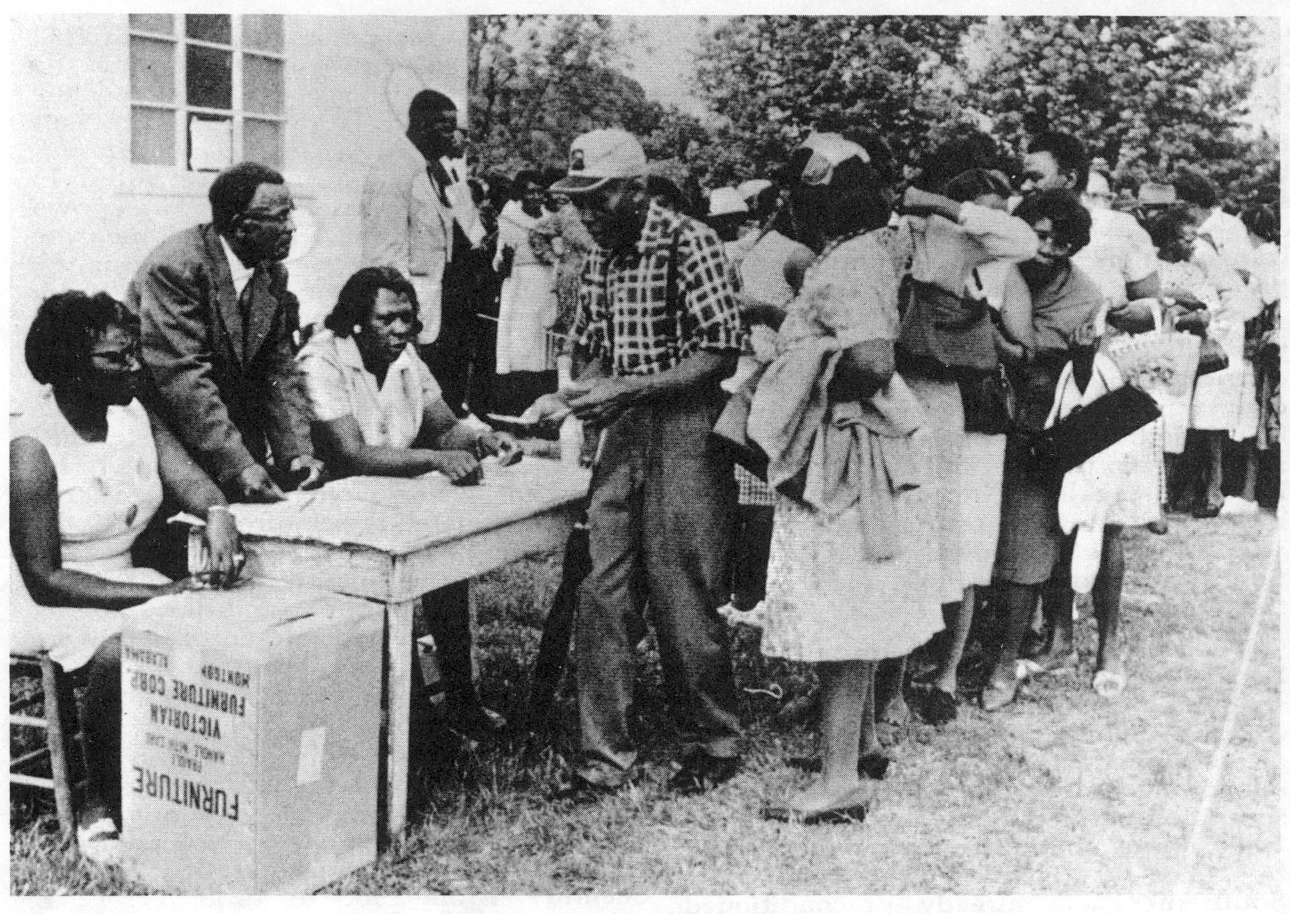

Black voters in Haynesville, Alabama file past makeshift polling place to cast ballots for seven mominees of the Lowndes County Freedom Organization in May 1966.

barred Negroes from membership in the Democratic party.) And, though some ground was being continually and inevitably lost (e.g. *Grovey* v. *Townsend* which gave a state convention the right to exclude the Negro by resolution), it was almost always regained—in this particular case by *Smith* v. *Allwright* which turned unswervingly to the 15th Amendment, again making all such exclusions in a primary election unconstitutional.

Negro Officeholders

The growing migration of Negroes to the major urban areas of the North also had a significant impact on the participation of the Negro in the elective process. Thus, in 1915, Oscar DePriest was elected Alderman from Chicago; in 1917, E. A. Johnson was elected to the New York State Assembly and, in 1934, Arthur B. Mitchell, a Democrat—and for that reason alone one of the key Negro officeholders of the 20th century —was returned to the Congress.

Since then, other Negroes have been elected to national office from various portions of the country, with the exception of the South. Where there has been an entrenched pattern of segregation at the polls, the Negro has had recourse to the courts to redress his grievances, often with considerable success. Moreover, during the 10-year period culminating in 1965, there were at least four important civil or voting rights bills, the last of which attempted to establish uniform methods of registration for all prospective voters. Beyond this, it has even been necessary to pass the 24th Amendment to the U. S. Constitution, abolishing the poll tax as a legitimate voting prerequisite.

Looking at the South in the decade 1960-1970, one detects a conspicuous trend toward the expansion of the black vote in such cosmopolitan centers as Atlanta, Memphis, Richmond, and Charlotte. Though the expansion was steady, it was not achieved without what seems to be the customary high price conventionally extracted from the black community and its white sympathizers. At least 16 people—nine of them in Mississippi alone—were murdered in connection with voter registration drives between 1946 and 1966. During the period 1948-1960, black voter registration in the South doubled to about 1.5 million; after passage of the Voting Rights Act of 1965, it climbed toward the three million mark, reaching it by the end of the decade. Even in Mississippi, black registration expanded dramatically from a low of 25,000 in 1965 to nearly 250,000 by the summer of 1966.

As of July 1970, black candidates were making several important bids for high elected office throughout the country. C. B. King (no relation to Martin Luther King, Jr.) was seeking the Democratic nomination for governor of Georgia; Rev. R. J. Hampton has similarly filed for the Republican nomination for governor in Arkansas. Earl Craig, Jr. is challenging former Vice President Hubert Humphrey for the Democratic-Farmer-Labor nomination for U. S. Senator in Minnesota. In Los Angeles, Mrs. Medgar Evers, a Democrat, is running for Congress against a white Republican opponent.

Changes in Congress may even affect such long-standing black representatives as William Dawson, who is expected to be succeeded by Ralph Metcalfe, the black winner of the Democratic primary in Dawson's district, and Adam Clayton Powell, the Harlem representative who may be ousted by Charles Rangel, also a black man. Black state senator Basil A. Paterson won the Democratic nomination for lieutenant governor in New York in June 1970. Elsewhere at the state level, SCLC official Hosea Williams is running for the post of Georgia Secretary of State, while Los Angeles lawyer James Flournoy is seeking the same position in California.

Voting analysts currently expect the numbers of black elected officials to triple in the South and double over the U. S. as a whole in the 1970's. Black leaders are already talking enthusiastically about electing mayors in such large cities as Baltimore, Philadelphia, Atlanta (where there is already a black vice mayor), Detroit, and Los Angeles (where black candidates have already come close to taking over City Hall).

The time seems at hand for black politicians and voters to join other American minorities in asserting their ethnic solidarity and gaining full political recognition in the governing councils of the nation. For most, black power is true participation in American institutions, not a strident clamoring for a separate identity and independent channels of operation. It is a simultaneous recognition of the existence of ethnic enclaves and the pervasiveness of American society.

The Metropolitan Applied Research Center compiled a list of black officeholders in 1970, producing a startling figure of nearly 600 black elected in the South (as compared with only 78 in 1965). The list showed 10 members of Congress, one state treasurer, 48 mayors, 575 other city officials, 362 school board members, 168 state legislators, 114 judges and magistrates, and 99 other law enforcement officers. Still, 1500 black elected officials represented only 3/10ths of one percent of the national total of over 500,000. A state-by-state breakdown:

BLACK ELECTED OFFICIALS IN UNITED STATES

	Members of U.S. Congress	*State Legislators*	*Mayors*	*Other City, County Officials*	*School-Board Members*	*Law-Enforcement Officials*	*Total*
Alabama	0	1	4	48	8	28	89
Alaska	0	0	0	0	1	0	1
Arizona	0	3	0	0	4	0	7
Arkansas	0	0	4	10	38	4	56
California	1	6	3	29	55	14	108

BLACK ELECTED OFFICIALS IN UNITED STATES

	Members of U.S. Congress	*State Legislators*	*Mayors*	*Other City, County Officials*	*School-Board Members*	*Law-Enforcement Officials*	*Total*
Colorado	0	3	0	2	1	1	7
Connecticut	0	5	0	25	11	5	46
Delaware	0	3	0	5	1	0	9
District of Columbia	0	0	0	0	8	0	8
Florida	0	1	2	32	1	2	38
Georgia	0	14	1	17	6	1	39
Hawaii	0	0	0	1	0	0	1
Idaho	0	0	0	0	0	0	0
Illinois	1	18	1	23	25	9	77
Indiana	0	3	1	13	11	3	31
Iowa	0	1	0	0	2	2	5
Kansas	0	3	1	1	1	0	6
Kentucky	0	3	1	23	6	8	41
Louisiana	0	1	3	34	8	20	66
Maine	0	0	0	0	0	0	0
Maryland	0	11	5	24	0	4	44
Massachusetts	1*	2	0	2	3	0	8
Michigan	2	13	2	49	32	12	110
Minnesota	0	1	0	1	4	2	8
Mississippi	0	1	3	54	5	21	84
Missouri	1	15	2	27	13	7	65
Montana	0	0	0	0	0	0	0
Nebraska	0	0	0	0	2	0	2
Nevada	0	1	0	1	0	1	3
New Hampshire	0	0	0	0	0	0	0
New Jersey	0	4	4	43	28	0	79
New Mexico	0	1	0	2	0	0	3
New York	2	12	0	16	71	20	121
North Carolina	0	1	5	48	13	1	68
North Dakota	0	0	0	0	0	0	0
Ohio	1	13	4	44	15	12	89
Oklahoma	0	5	2	10	19	0	36
Oregon	0	0	0	0	0	0	0
Pennsylvania	1	11	0	15	9	21	57
Rhode Island	0	1	0	1	0	0	2
South Carolina	0	0	2	32	4	4	42
South Dakota	0	0	0	0	0	0	0
Tennessee	0	8	0	9	4	18	39
Texas	0	3	1	15	11	0	30
Utah	0	0	0	0	0	0	0
Vermont	0	0	0	0	0	0	0
Virginia	0	3	0	36	0	6	45
Washington	0	1	0	1	0	2	4
West Virginia	0	0	0	0	1	0	1
Wisconsin	0	1	0	8	1	0	10
Wyoming	0	0	0	0	1	0	1
TOTALS	10	173	51	701	423	228	1,586

* U.S. Senator.
Source: Metropolitan Applied Research Center.

NEGRO VOTER REGISTRATION FOR SELECTIVE YEARS AND VOTING AGE POPULATIONS (VAP)*

STATE	*1952* No. Registered	*1952* % VAP Reg.	*1956* No. Registered	*1956* % VAP Reg.	*1960* No. Registered	*1960* % VAP Reg.
ALABAMA	25,224	4.9	53,366	10.3	73,272	15.2
ARKANSAS	61,413	26.4	69,677	30.0	72,604	37.6
FLORIDA	120,900	32.9	148,703	40.5	163,128	34.7
GEORGIA	144,835	23.3	163,389	26.2	180,000	29.3
LOUISIANA	120,000	24.9	161,410	33.5	156,938	30.4
MISSISSIPPI	20,000	4.0	20,000	4.0	22,000	5.2
N. CAROLINA	100,000	18.2	135,000	24.5	172,166	31.3
S. CAROLINA	80,000	20.5	99,890	25.6	58,122	15.7
TENNESSEE	85,000	26.6	90,000	28.2	185,000	58.9
TEXAS	181,916	31.2	214,000	36.7	226,818	34.9
VIRGINIA	69,326	16.4	82,603	19.5	100,100	23.8
TOTAL	1,008,614	21.3	1,238,038	26.2	1,410,148	28.2

* Source: Southern Regional Council

STATE	*Spring 1966* No. Registered	*Spring 1966* % VAP Reg.	*1950 CENSUS NEGRO VAP*	*1960 CENSUS NEGRO VAP*
ALABAMA	235,572	48.9	516,275	481,320
ARKANSAS	104,000	54.0	232,191	192,672
FLORIDA	288,069	60.2	366,797	470,306
GEORGIA	256,346	41.8	622,703	612,910
LOUISIANA	228,073	42.3	481,284	514,589
MISSISSIPPI	125,000	29.6	497,354	422,256
N. CAROLINA	269,328	48.9	549,741	550,929
S. CAROLINA	186,752	50.3	390,024	371,104
TENNESSEE	225,000	71.7	318,790	313,873
TEXAS	400,000	61.6	582,944	649,412
VIRGINIA	185,000	44.0	422,670	421,051
TOTAL	2,503,140	50.1	4,980,773	5,000,422

VOTER REGISTRATION IN THE SOUTH
Spring-Summer, 1970

State	*White VAP*	*Black VAP*	*Whites Registered*	*Blacks Registered*	*Percent White VAP Registered*	*Percent Black VAP Registered*
ALABAMA	1,353,058	481,320	1,300,000	308,000	96.1	64.0
ARKANSAS	850,643	192,626	683,000	138,000	80.3	71.6
FLORIDA	2,617,438	470,261	2,465,000	315,000	94.2	67.0
GEORGIA	1,797,062	612,910	1,610,000	390,000	89.6	63.6
LOUISIANA	1,289,216	514,589	1,137,000	318,000	88.2	61.8
MISSISSIPPI	748,266	422,256	650,000	285,000	86.9	67.5
N. CAROLINA	2,005,955	550,929	1,598,000	302,000	79.6	54.8
S. CAROLINA	895,147	371,873	656,000	213,000	73.3	57.3
TENNESSEE	1,779,018	313,873	1,570,000*	240,000*	88.3	76.5
TEXAS	4,884,765	649,512	3,599,000	550,000	73.7	84.7
VIRGINIA	1,876,167	436,720	1,472,000	265,000	78.4	60.7
TOTALS	20,096,735	5,016,100	16,740,000	3,324,000	83.3	66.3

VAP—Voting Age Population, 1960 Census.
*Corrects overestimate in 1969 summer-fall table.

Hiram Revels is sworn in as Senator from Mississippi, the first black man to occupy the office.

THE BLACK POLICYMAKER— PAST & PRESENT

The Federal Government
The U. S. Congress
Black State Representatives
Black State Senators
Black Mayors
Black Elected Officials
The United Nations

The role played by the Negro in the federal government has expanded dramatically in recent years, with Negroes experiencing a particularly significant upsurge in middle- and upper-level posts at the executive level. For the first time in our nation's history, Negroes are beginning to exercise authority and responsibility in positions which have nothing whatsoever to do with race.

For the Negro, this favorable trend stands in marked contrast to the time when members of his race were mainly clerks in various governmental agencies, notably in the postal service. In the pre-Roosevelt years, however, the financial security afforded the Negro by such minor federal posts often enabled him to send his children to colleges and universities which proved to be the fertile training ground for the leaders of a new generation.

During the Roosevelt years, Negro professionals were, as it were, moved up in the ranks, being induced to serve the government as "specialists" in Negro affairs, or as race relations "advisers." Ultimately, the most influential members of this cadre of Negro leaders formed what came to be known as the "Black Cabinet." Headed unofficially by Mary McLeod Bethune, the group was able to facilitate the entry of other young and energetic Negroes into government service, and also helped break down several established patterns of racial exclusion operative at various governmental levels.

Since then, particularly during the Kennedy and Johnson Administrations, prospects have broadened considerably for the Negro interested in a government career, and many Negroes have passed far beyond the "honorific" positions—i.e. those of racial or secondary importance only—to the more substantial, policymaking echelons of government service.

Numerous Negroes now occupy important sub-cabinet positions, and one—Robert Weaver—has become the first to be named to a presidential cabinet. Numerous Negroes serve as key members of the president's personal staff, in positions ranging from Associate Special Counsel to military and social aides. Others serve as U. S. ambassadors to foreign countries (not all of which inevitably are African), while still others serve in federal regulatory agencies like the Export-Import Bank, the National Labor Relations Board, and the Federal Reserve Board.

At the present time, there is only one Negro in the Senate, but prospects appear bright that Edward A. Brooke, once Republican Attorney General of the State of Massachusetts (then the highest state office held by a Negro), will become the standard bearer for a new breed of responsible political leaders. To date, Negro presidential and vice-presidential candidates have been confined to minority parties. (Clifton DeBerry ran for the nation's highest office on the Socialist Workers ticket in 1964, whereas James B. Ford ran for the vice-presidency three times—in 1932, 1936, and 1940.)

The scarcity of black officials in the federal government during the Nixon years is attributable in large measure to the obvious suspicions which greeted the President's election, particularly in view of the Southern and rural Midwestern strategy which brought him to power. Traditionally bastions of either anti-black or anti-urban sentiment, these conservative constituencies rarely attempt to cultivate abiding relationships with the black establishment. At the 1970 NAACP convention, overt criticism of the Nixon Administration reached a concerted pitch. It was as if most eligible black professionals were expressing rampant disillusionment with the identifiable working policies of the President. These included his reluctance to enforce court-ordered school integration, his unwillingness to rely heavily on Department of Justice registrars to enforce federally established voting guidelines, and his approval of legislation diluting the impact of the 1965 Voting Rights Act in the South. The two most prominent Nixon appointees are James Farmer of HEW and Dr. Jerome Holland, ambassador to Sweden.

Our review of the Negro in the federal government is necessarily a comprehensive one which attempts to take into account a representative cross-section of an imposing roster of important personalities. Additional data is supplied in a number of lists included at the close of this section.

SAMUEL CLIFFORD ADAMS, JR.
Overseas Director, Agency for International Development (AID)

On April 28, 1965, President Lyndon B. Johnson appointed Samuel Adams, Jr. Overseas Director of the Agency for International Development (AID), with administrative control over the U. S. mission to Morocco.

Born in Waco, Texas on August 15, 1920, Adams received his B. A. in sociology from Fisk University in 1940, and his M. A. from the same school in 1947. (Between degrees, Adams served as an Air Force cadet in Texas.)

In 1947, Adams also became a director of the Marion Cooperative Center of the American Missionary Association. Three years later, he served as a research assistant in the race relations division of the University of Chicago's School of Social Sciences.

Adams' official entry into government service came in August of 1954 when he was named acting chief in the education division of the U. S. Operations Mission to Vietnam. One year later, he was given a more important assignment in Cambodia, where he helped sponsor a program in advanced education. In 1958, after a year of post-doctoral study at the London School of Economics, Adams was given successive assignments in Nigeria and Mali. In both countries, his work was once again largely connected with educational projects. His return to the U. S. more or less coincided with his current assignment—the highest post he has yet achieved.

CLIFFORD ALEXANDER, JR.
Associate Special Counsel to the President

A native New Yorker, Clifford Alexander, Jr. was appointed President Lyndon B. Johnson's associate special counsel on August 25, 1965. He had previously served as the president's deputy special assistant.

Born in 1933, Alexander graduated from Harvard University, and then attended Yale's Law School where he was awarded an LL. B. At the age of 26, he became assistant district attorney of New York County and, two years later, executive director of the Hamilton-Grange Neighborhood Conservation District in Manhattanville. After four years at this job, Alexander moved to HARYOU in 1963 as an executive program director.

After leaving his post with the EEOC, where he was under constant pressure from Republican Senators like Everett Dirksen who accused him of bullying reluctant employers into complying with federal guidelines for minority employment, Alexander entered private law practice and became a Harvard overseer. His function at Harvard was comparable to the one he was empowered to exercise while in the federal government but, in this case, he was actually involved in working out details with craft unions which were obliged to offer and implement concrete proposals for improving minority group employment opportunities. At Harvard, the pact worked out by Alexander related to "two live buildings" and involved 300 workers, some one fifth of whom were black and Puerto Rican.

MARK BATTLE
Deputy Administrator, Neighborhood Youth Corps

Mark Battle has served as Deputy Administrator of the Neighborhood Youth Corps since May of 1965.

A native of New Jersey, Battle is a graduate of Bordentown High School and of the University of Rochester. He also holds an M.A. in Community Organization from Western Reserve University.

THEODORE MOODY BERRY
Director of the Community Action Program, Office of Economic Opportunity (OEO)

President Lyndon B. Johnson appointed Theodore Berry in 1965 to the post of Director of the Community Action Program within the Office of Economic Opportunity (OEO).

A native of Maysville, Kentucky, Berry received his B. A. from the University of Cincinnati, and his LL. B. from the same school in 1931. Almost immediately thereafter, Berry opened his own law office—devoting himself, with the passage of time, to civil, rather than criminal, cases.

In 1941, the poet Archibald MacLeish (who was then head of the Office of War Information) called him to Washington, D. C. to serve as Morale Officer. His role was primarily that of finding means to encourage and increase Negro participation in the war effort.

Back in Cincinnati in 1943, he took up his law practice again and, four years later, decided to enter the political arena as an independent candidate for the office of city councilman. Unsuccessful at first, he was later elected to this post in 1949. He held this office through two more campaigns, before being finally chosen as vice-mayor of Cincinnati. Though temporarily ousted in 1957 by political adversaries who saw in him a potential mayoralty threat, Berry was returned to office in 1963 with the help of Charles Taft, brother of the Ohio Senator Robert Taft.

ANDREW FELTON BRIMMER
Member, Federal Reserve Board

Andrew Brimmer, an eminent Negro economist and teacher, was named to the Federal Reserve Board in 1966 by President Lyndon B. Johnson.

Born in Newellton, Louisiana on September 13, 1926, Brimmer was awarded a Ph. D. in economics by Harvard University in 1957, having already done some of his graduate studies in India—both at the Delhi School of Economics and at the University of Bombay (1951-1952).

In 1955, after having spent a year at Harvard as a teaching fellow in economics, Brimmer joined the Federal Reserve Bank of New York as an economist—a post he surrendered in 1958 in order to become Assistant Professor of Economics at Michigan State University. In 1961, he joined the faculty of the Wharton School of Finance and Commerce, remaining there until his appointment to the position of Deputy Assistant Secretary of Commerce in May 1963.

His duties involved decisions relevant to the development of the American economy—duties which, under his later title as Assistant Secretary of Commerce, became broad enough to make him one of the key government spokesmen on such varied topics as balance of payments, tourist travel, and U. S. capital investment abroad. He was also in charge of the Bureau of Census and the Office of Business Economics, both of which provide valuable statistical data to the general public.

Aside from having taught at the University of California at Berkeley and at the City College of New York, Brimmer has published a number of books and monographs on his special field of interest, as well as several articles and reviews in some of the nation's leading economic journals. Perhaps his single most important project of 1964 was the research he contributed to the U. S. Supreme Court ruling on the constitutionality of the public accommodations sections of the Civil Rights Act.

Over the years, Brimmer has established himself as the most prominent black economist in the nation. It was natural, then, that he take an active stand pursuant to the Nixon Administration's stated policy of fostering black businesses and lending support to black entrepreneurs. Whereas many critics faulted Nixon for failing to provide a coordinated program of loans to would-be black entrepreneurs, Brimmer attacked the scheme on theoretical grounds, rather than for its organizational shortcomings. How, Brimmer asked, could most black businesses expect to be successful in the ghetto, where so much of the nation's black poor was concentrated? "Self-employment," Brimmer argued, ". . . offers a low and rather risky payoff." In his view, Negroes need more jobs as salaried managers and skilled craftsmen with major American companies, companies with the capital resources to command the attention of the national community.

LISLE C. CARTER, JR.
Assistant Secretary, Department of Health, Education and Welfare (HEW)

Lisle Carter was appointed Assistant Secretary of Health, Education and Welfare (HEW) by President Lyndon B. Johnson in 1966.

Born in New York City on November 18, 1925, Carter moved with his family to Barbados (British West Indies) and began his formal education there. On his return to New York in 1940, he enrolled at Cazenovia Seminary (Syracuse, New York) for one year of junior college before moving on to Dartmouth. In 1944, he received his B.A. in chemistry there and, after an interruption in his schooling caused by his induction into the Armed Forces, finally received an LL.B. from St. John's University School of Law in 1950.

From then until 1961, Carter combined his own law practice with the job of legal counsel for the National Urban League. Named Deputy Assistant Secretary in the Department of Health, Education, and Welfare, he led a departmental team in 1962 through an inspection of health and educational conditions in 11 African countries. Later, he helped conduct a comprehensive survey aimed at ending discrimination in federally assisted programs. Before accepting his present post, Carter was a top aide to Sargent Shriver, Director of the Office of Economic Opportunity (OEO).

ARTHUR A. CHAPIN
Special Assistant to the Secretary of Labor

Arthur Chapin has been associated with the Department of Labor since 1961 when he held the post of minority groups

Arthur Chapin

consultant in the Bureau of Employment Security.

Before accepting his federal assignment, Chapin had worked for many years at the state level as assistant to the president of the New Jersey CIO Council. Here, he was concerned with civil rights legislation and minimum wage and unemployment compensation. He also served as a member of the New Jersey Committee on Housing, and of the State Wage Panel for restaurant employees.

Since joining the Labor Department, Chapin has helped compile an annual *Directory of Negro College Graduates* which aids business and industry in finding competent and qualified personnel. The directory has enabled the Department to maintain close liaison with thousands of college graduates, as well as numerous employment agencies.

MERCER COOK
Ambassador to Niger; Ambassador to Senegal and Gambia

Dr. Mercer Cook, the first U. S. Ambassador to the Republic of Niger, is now Ambassador to the West African nations of Senegal and Gambia.

Born in Washington, D. C. in 1903, Dr. Cook lived across the street from Duke Ellington during his childhood, and attended the famed Dunbar High School in the nation's capital, numbering among his classmates William H. Hastie (now a federal judge); Sterling Brown (noted literary critic and author), and Charles Drew (a pioneer in the development of blood plasma).

After receiving his B. A. from Amherst in 1925, Dr. Cook did graduate work at the University of Paris, and later acquired both his M. A. and Ph.D. degrees from Brown University. From 1936 to 1943, he served on the faculty of Atlanta University. After a short stint in Haiti on an educational assignment, he returned to the United States to become professor of romance languages at Howard University, a post he held for the next 14 years.

Upon leaving Howard, Dr. Cook traveled widely, particularly in Africa. In 1963, he served briefly as an alternate delegate to the General Assembly of the United Nations.

Cook completed his diplomatic tour as ambassador to Senegal and Gambia in 1966. He returned to Howard University, where he became head of the Department of Romance Languages.

FREDERICK DOUGLASS
1817-1895
Abolitionist

One of a handful of names which immediately leaps to mind at the mention of the American Negro is that of Frederick Douglass, probably the foremost voice in the abolitionist movement of the 19th century.

Born in February of 1817 in Talbot County, Maryland, Douglass was sent to Baltimore as a house servant at the age of eight. He learned to read and write under the instruction of his mistress. At the death of her husband, Douglass was sent to the country as a field hand. In his early teens, he began to teach in a Sunday school which was forcibly shut down by hostile Southerners. Douglass himself was severely flogged for his resistance to slavery.

After making one unsuccessful attempt to escape, Douglass managed to make his way to New York disguised as a sailor. Once in the North, it was not long before he found his true calling—leader in the anti-slavery crusade. Taken on as an agent by the Massachusetts Anti-Slavery Society, he soon helped in the fight then taking place in Rhode Island against a new constitution aimed at disenfranchising the Negro.

As the years passed, Douglass became an increasingly familiar figure to abolitionists throughout the country. In 1845, after having published his *Narrative* at great personal risk (that of re-enslavement as a fugitive), he went to England, where he raised enough money, through lectures on slavery and women's rights, to buy his freedom. Upon his return to his native shores, he founded the famous newspaper, *The North Star*. Later, he was forced to flee to Canada when the governor of Virginia swore out a warrant for his arrest on charges that he had conspired with John Brown, leader of the Harpers Ferry revolt.

With the outbreak of the Civil War, Douglass—once again back in the United States—met with President Abraham Lincoln, and assisted him in recruiting what were to become the celebrated 54th and 55th Massachusetts Negro regiments.

In 1871, during the Reconstruction period, he was appointed to the territorial legislature of the District of Columbia; in

Frederick Douglass

1872, he served as one of the presidential electors-at-large for New York and, shortly thereafter, became secretary of the Santo Domingo Commission.

In 1877, after a short term as a police commissioner of the District of Columbia, he was appointed Marshal—a post he held until he was named Recorder of Deeds in 1881.

Eight years later, in return for his strong support of the presidential campaign of Benjamin Harrison, Douglass was appointed to the most important federal posts he was to hold—Minister Resident and Counsul General to the Republic of Haiti and, later, Chargé d'Affaires for Santo Domingo. However, when he saw his efforts being undermined by unscrupulous American businessmen interested solely in exploiting Haiti, he finally resigned his post in 1891.

Four years later, Frederick Douglass died at his home in Washington, D. C.

EDWARD RICHARD DUDLEY
Ambassador to Liberia

Appointed in 1948 by President Harry S. Truman, Edward R. Dudley was the first Negro to serve in Liberia with the rank of ambassador. (Many Negroes had previously held federal appointments in Liberia, but generally with the rank of minister.)

Born in South Boston, Virginia on March 11, 1891, Dudley was educated in the public schools of Roanoke, Virginia, and later earned his law degree at St. John's Law School. In 1942, he was named assistant attorney general for New York State, and soon accepted a position on the legal staff of the NAACP. From 1945 to 1947, he was legal counsel to the Governor of the Virgin Islands.

After serving in Liberia for five years, Dudley returned to the United States, and was named a justice in the Domestic Relations Court of New York City. At the request of New York's Mayor Robert Wagner, Dudley resigned from this court position in 1961 in order to become president of the Borough of Manhattan.

Dudley has since been appointed a judge in the Supreme Court of New York State.

ALFRED LEROY EDWARDS
Deputy Assistant Secretary of Agriculture

In 1963, President John F. Kennedy appointed Alfred Edwards Deputy Assistant Secretary of Agriculture. Edwards has become one of the key coordinators in the department's "Rural Renaissance" movement—a program aimed at reinvigorating those areas affected by a lack of real job opportunities, and the increasing migration of young people to the large cities.

Born on August 9, 1920 in Key West, Florida, Edwards received a B. A. from Livingstone College in 1948, an M. A. in Economics from the University of Michigan, and a Ph. D. from the University of Iowa in 1958.

Prior to becoming engaged in government service, Dr. Edwards was a faculty member of a number of leading universities. He also helped establish the University of Nigeria at Nsukka—arriving there with the first contingent of American teachers and administrators who were charged with the tremendous task of helping Nigeria organize and oversee the entire venture.

Essentially a social scientist, Dr. Edwards has tried to persuade qualified students to avail themselves of the many opportunities opening up in agriculture—a field which, he feels, has undeservedly been denied the status and importance currently due it.

JAMES FARMER
Assistant Secretary of Health, Education, and Welfare

One of the group that founded CORE in Chicago in 1942, James Farmer served as its national director until 1966. He was the first, and one of the few, prominent black government appointees in the Nixon Administration, accepting the post of Assistant Secretary of Health, Education, and Welfare (HEW) in 1969.

Born in Marshall, Texas on January 12, 1920, Farmer attended public schools throughout the South, and later earned his B. S. in chemistry from Wiley College. At first interested in medicine, he later enrolled in the School of Religion at Howard University with the intention of preparing for the Methodist ministry. Active in the Christian Youth Movement, and once vice-chairman of the National Council of Methodist Youth and the Christian Youth Council of America, Farmer received his Bachelor of Divinity degree in 1941, but refused ordination when confronted with the realization that he would have to practice in a segregated ministry.

In 1941, Farmer accepted a post as race relations secretary of the Fellowship of Reconciliation, a pacifist group. The following year, he and a group of University of Chicago students organized CORE, the first American Negro protest organization which utilized the techniques of nonviolence and passive resistance advocated by the Indian revolutionary, Mohandas K. Gandhi. In June 1943, CORE staged the first successful sit-in demonstration at a restaurant in the Chicago Loop. The organization soon supplemented this maneuver with what came to be known as the standing-line, which involved the persistent waiting in line by CORE groups at places of public accommodation where Negroes were being denied admission.

James Farmer

Throughout the 1950's, Farmer was active on a number of different fronts in the civil rights struggle. In 1958, he was one of a five-man delegation sent to 15 African countries by the International Confederation of Free Trade Unions. He also served as a radio and television commentator on programs sponsored by the United Auto Workers in Detroit, and functioned as program director for the NAACP while contributing several articles to the "Crisis" magazine.

In 1961, CORE introduced the Freedom Ride into the vocabulary and methodology of civil rights protest, dispatching a group of bus riders into the South for the purpose of testing whether terminal facilities there had been desegregated. Attacked in Alabama and later arrested in Mississippi, the Freedom Riders eventually succeeded in securing compliance with the Supreme Court decision of 1960 which had outlawed segregated bus terminals.

Farmer left CORE in 1966, phasing out his association with the organization as soon as he discerned what he deemed an irreversible trend toward separatism, and a lamentable tendency to restrict the activities of whites who had made a significant commitment to the goals of the organization. Originally, he was slated to head a nationwide literacy program sponsored by the Johnson Administration and funded with a $900,000 grant from the Office of Economic Opportunity (OEO). The project was cancelled, however, ostensibly because some urban politicians feared it would produce a black voter registration drive that would disrupt the voting patterns which kept them in power. Farmer later ran for Congress against Shirley Chisholm, but was defeated despite the fact that his name appeared on both the Liberal and the Republican line.

The Farmer appointment to the Nixon

team in 1969 created a furor in some black circles, but it was hailed by many students and leaders (among them, Whitney Young and Dr. Nathan Wright) as an important gesture and a constructive step to mend fences with the black community, which gave Nixon little support in the 1968 election.

Patricia Harris

PATRICIA ROBERTS HARRIS
Ambassador to Luxembourg

As ambassador to Luxembourg, Patricia Harris was the first Negro woman to hold this diplomatic rank in U.S. history.

Born in Mattoon, Illinois, Miss Harris attended elementary school in Chicago, and received her undergraduate degree from Howard University in 1945. After completing postgraduate work at the University of Chicago and at American University, she earned her doctorate in jurisprudence from George Washington University Law School in 1960.

Prior to her appointment, Miss Harris had worked for the YWCA in Chicago (1946-1949), and also served as executive director for Delta Sigma Theta in Washington, D. C. An attorney and professor before she entered politics, Miss Harris served under President John F. Kennedy as co-chairman of the National Women's Committee on Civil Rights, and was later named to the Commission on the Status of Puerto Rico.

A Phi Beta Kappa, she is also a member of numerous professional and civic organizations.

Miss Harris was made an alternate delegate to the U.N. in 1966.

After completing her tour of duty as ambassador to Luxembourg in 1967, she returned to the United States and became dean of the Howard University Law School. In 1970, she was named to the board of directors of Georgetown University, the youngest member in the school's history and only the second Negro to achieve that distinction.

ANDREW J. HATCHER
Associate Press Secretary

In 1960, President John F. Kennedy named Andrew Hatcher as his associate press secretary—thus making him the first major Negro appointee of the "New Frontier." Hatcher was the individual through whom many of the President's important news releases were made.

Born in Princeton, New Jersey in 1925, Hatcher attended Springfield College, graduating with a B. A. degree. During World War II, he served for three years in the Army as a second lieutenant and, after his discharge, took a job with the San Francisco *Sun-Reporter*.

In 1960, Hatcher campaigned ardently for Kennedy's election to the presidency. Hatcher resigned after the assassination of the President, and currently holds an executive position with a brewery company in New Jersey.

JEROME HOLLAND
U.S. Ambassador to Sweden

Easily one of President Nixon's shrewdest political appointments, Jerome Holland is an experienced educator whose diplomatic skills have already often come into play mediating between insistent student radicals and adamant campus authorities. Convivial, articulate, and persuasive, Holland is appropriately discreet and notably confident in his ability to add to the "backlog of cooperation and friendship" which he says characterize U.S.-Swedish relations. The estimate is perhaps a trifle optimistic in view of the Swedes' current policy of grantng asylum to U.S. deserters and aid to North Vietnam.

Born one of 13 children in Auburn, New York in 1916, Holland viewed education as the most obvious panacea against poverty, working his way through Cornell University with honor grades, and achieving stardom as an All-American end on the gridiron. (In 1965, he was elected to the Football Hall of Fame.)

Holder of a Ph.D. in sociology, Holland was president of Hampton Institute in Virginia for a full decade before accepting the Nixon assignment. At Hampton, he was a staunch advocate of integration, a firm believer in competitive capitalist economics, and a constant advocate of job training and education as the black man's best hope for liberation and advancement.

Holland's organizational memberships brand him as a tirelessly energetic moderate and a resourceful reformer. He has been, for example, a leading member of the Red Cross, the United Negro College Fund, and the Boy Scouts, and is chairman of the board of the Planned Parenthood-World Population Center of Greater New York.

Holland's wife Laura also has a strong academic background, including a master's in psychology from Radcliffe, and two years toward a doctorate. The Hollands have two teen-aged children, a daughter (Lucy) and a son (Joseph).

HOWARD JENKINS, JR.
Member, National Labor Relations Board (NLRB)

Howard Jenkins, Jr. was appointed by President John F. Kennedy in 1963 to a five-year term as a member of the National Labor Relations Board (NLRB)—the first Negro ever to serve with this federal government agency.

Born on June 16, 1915 in Denver, Colorado, Jenkins received his B. A. from the University of Denver in 1936 and, soon thereafter, became the first Negro to earn an LL. B. from the same institution. He was likewise the first Negro to be admitted to the Colorado bar.

After World War II (during which he had worked for the Office of Price Administration, the Denver War Labor Board, and the National Wage Stabilization Board), Jenkins taught labor and administrative law at Howard University for 10 years. In 1956, having completed a graduate program in law at New York University, he became an attorney for the Department of Labor. Over the years, he slowly climbed the rungs of this department's ladder, reaching the post of assistant commissioner in the Bureau of Labor Management Reports in 1962.

ROBERT W. KITCHEN
Director of the Office for International Training, Agency for International Development (AID)

Robert Kitchen, a native of Brunswick, Georgia, currently holds the post of Director of the Office for International Training within the Agency for International Development (AID). AID is the federal government agency which administers the American foreign aid program.

Kitchen attended Morehouse College in Atlanta from which he graduated in 1943 with a B. A. in economics. Three years later, he received an M. S. in business administration from Columbia University and, later, his Ph. D. from the same institution.

After four years' service as an associate professor at West Virginia State College, Kitchen entered government service in 1952. There, he worked with a number of foreign missions—first to Liberia, then to Pakistan and, in 1958, to Sudan. He also participated in many conferences throughout Europe, serving notably as a member of the Secretary of State's Advisory Committee on Africa.

This wide international background has served him well at his present AID post, where he not only supervises the agency's central office, but is responsible for planning and directing the training of recruits sent to the United States by scores of emerging nations from all over the world.

CLINTON EVERETT KNOX
Ambassador to Dahomey

Clinton Knox, a career foreign service officer with more than 20 years experience, was appointed U. S. Ambassador to Dahomey in 1964.

A native of New Bedford, Massachusetts, Knox acquired his Ph. D. from Harvard in 1940. Having taught at Morgan State College for eight years,

Knox joined the State Department at the close of World War II, doing research on Northern and Western Europe. In 1957, he was assigned to the NATO Defense College in Paris, and subsequently became first secretary in the U. S. mission to NATO. Knox was later counselor and deputy chief of mission in the U. S. Embassy in Tegucigalpa, Honduras.

E. FREDERIC MORROW
Administrative Assistant to the President

When President Eisenhower named E. Frederic Morrow as his administrative assistant in 1955, this represented the first time in U. S. history that a Negro held an executive position on a presidential staff.

Born in Hackensack, New Jersey in April 1909, Morrow graduated from Bowdoin College and later received an LL. B. from the Law School of Rutgers University. In the interim period, he had been business manager of "Opportunity," the official house organ of the National Urban League; Coordinator of Branches for the NAACP, and a major in the Armed Forces during World War II.

In 1952, after three years in the public affairs division of the Columbia Broadcasting System, he became part of Eisenhower's presidential campaign staff, and travelled some 100,000 miles all over the country on behalf of the Republican nominee. The following year, he became Advisor on Business Affairs to the Secretary of Commerce and was in close liaison with Congress on all legislation affecting his department.

After six years of service with President Eisenhower (1955-1961), Morrow left Washington and the new Democratic Administration to become vice president of the African-American Institute—the largest privately endowed foundation in the United States. Its main function is to improve American economic and cultural relations with the nations of Africa.

More recently, he has been appointed assistant vice president of the Bank of America, thus becoming one of the very few Negroes holding a major post in this section of the financial world.

JOHN HOWARD MORROW
Ambassador to Guinea

John Howard Morrow was appointed Ambassador to Guinea by President Dwight D. Eisenhower in 1959, and served in this post for the next two years.

A native of Hackensack, New Jersey, where he was born on February 10, 1910, Morrow received his B. A. from Rutgers and his M. A. and Ph. D. from the University of Pennsylvania. After some 25 years as a teacher, both on the high school and collegiate levels, Morrow was given his first political appointment in 1957 when President Eisenhower made him a member of the Commission on Government Security.

Since completing his assignment in Guinea, Morrow has served in several capacities: first as a member of the U. S. delegation to the U. N. General Assembly; then as vice chairman of a delegation on educational achievement which was posted off to Ethiopia; and, finally, as minister and permanent U. S. representative to UNESCO.

In 1963, he accepted a post with the Foreign Service Institute (Department of State, Washington, D. C.) which helps prepare promising candidates for careers overseas.

(Morrow's brother, E. Frederic, once served as an administrative aide to President Eisenhower in the White House.)

DR. SAMUEL NABRIT
Member, Atomic Energy Commission

Dr. Samuel Nabrit is the first Negro to serve on the Atomic Energy Commission, having been appointed to this post in 1966 by President Lyndon B. Johnson.

Born on February 21, 1905 in Macon, Georgia, Nabrit moved with his family to Augusta, where he attended Walker Baptist Institute. Active in sports, he edited the school newspaper, and graduated as class valedictorian. He continued his education at Morehouse, earning his B.A. in 1925. That same year, he began his teaching career at Atlanta University as a biology instructor. (He later became dean of the graduate school of arts and sciences.) In 1932, he won the distinction of being the first Negro to earn a Ph.D. from Brown University.

Dr. Nabrit taught at Columbia University in 1945, and then spent a year in Brussels doing research. In 1956, he was appointed to a post on the National Science Board by President Dwight D. Eisenhower and, during the Kennedy Administration, was made a special ambassador to Nigeria in West Africa.

His latest educational assignment has been as a marine biologist on the faculty of Texas Southern University, from which he has now taken a year's leave of absence. Dr. Nabrit is the brother of James M. Nabrit, Jr., the president of Howard University who was named an Ambassador to the United States delegation to the United Nations in 1965.

SAMUEL RILEY PIERCE
Assistant to the Undersecretary of Labor

A man who was later to have a broad background in education, in government as well as in private industry, Samuel Pierce served as assistant to the Undersecretary of Labor from 1955 to 1956.

Born in Glen Cove, New York on September 8, 1922, Pierce attended Cornell University where he received his B. A. in 1947 and his LL. B. in 1949. Three years later, he was awarded an LL. M. (in taxation) from New York University's School of Law.

From 1949 through 1955, he was first assistant district attorney for New York County and then assistant U. S. attorney for the Southern District of New York. Since 1958, Pierce has been a faculty member of the N. Y. U. Law School; served as a judge in the New York Court of General Sessions (1959-1961), and become a partner in a prominent New York law firm.

In 1964, he made news again—first, when he was named to the Board of Directors of U. S. Industries, Inc. and, some months later, as the first Negro to serve on the board of a major insurance company (Prudential).

Pierce is active in the NAACP and the New York chapter of CORE.

Pierce later became a professor at the New York University Law School, and was nominated in 1970 to succeed Paul W. Eggers as general counsel of the Treasury Department.

THOMAS E. POSEY
Chief of the Labor and Industry Division, Agency for International Development (AID)

Dr. Thomas Posey is chief of the Labor and Industry Division of the Office of International Training within the Agency for International Development (AID).

A native of Washington, D. C., Posey received his B. A. in economics, monetary theory and labor in 1923 from Syracuse University and, in 1926, his M. A. from the same school.

For the next 25 years, he taught economics at West Virginia State College, taking time out, with the aid of a Rosenwald fellowship, to acquire his Ph. D. in 1948 from the University of Wisconsin. During these many years, he was active in the political life of his state, serving as a member of the West Virginia State Planning Board, and as advisor to the West Virginia State Federation of Labor.

He also served as a consultant to the Fair Employment Practices Commission (1943); as Supervisory Industrial Economist with the Wage Stabilization Board (1951), and as an economic advisor for the Mutual Security Agency in Burma (1952).

From 1954 to 1960, Dr. Posey served on foreign missions to the Philippines and to Turkey, where his duties involved him primarily with questions of labor productivity and industrial relations. Upon completion of a three-year term as a U. S. delegate to the U. N. Conference in Geneva on the Application of Science and Technology for the Benefit of the Less-Developed Areas of the World, Dr. Posey returned to the United States where he assumed his present post with AID.

CARL ROWAN
Ambassador to Finland

Carl Rowan has held two major diplomatic and administrative posts in his lifetime: one as Ambassador to Finland (1963); the other as Director of the United States Information Agency (USIA).

Born in Ravenscroft, Tennessee on August 11, 1925, Rowan studied for a year at Tennessee A. & I. in Nashville and, at the age of 19, became one of the first 15 Negroes commissioned by the U. S. Navy during World War II. After the war, he received his B. A. from Oberlin College in Ohio, and later acquired an M. A. in journalism from the University of Minnesota.

Having established himself as a journalist and much-sought-after feature

Carl Rowan

writer, Rowan soon turned his energies to the writing of full-length books. His first, *South of Freedom*, was based on many of his personal experiences, and was followed by *The Pitiful and the Proud* (1956) and *Go South in Sorrow* (1957). Three years later, he wrote *Wait Till Next Year*, a biography of the famous Negro baseball player, Jackie Robinson.

Rowan returned to journalism after resigning from the USIA in July 1965. At present he writes a thrice-weekly column syndicated in 150 newspapers around the country. As he did in his Minneapolis *Tribune* days, Rowan covers more than just distinctly black stories. Only one in six columns is devoted to racial or civil rights topics.

ELLIOTT PERCIVAL SKINNER
Ambassador to Upper Volta

Dr. Elliott Percival Skinner was appointed by President Lyndon B. Johnson to succeed Thomas S. Estes as Ambassador to Upper Volta, thus becoming the seventh Negro to hold such a major appointment within the Johnson Administration (the others being Mercer Cook, Patricia Harris, Clinton Knox, Dr. James Nabrit, Hugh Smythe, and Franklin Williams).

An assistant professor of anthropology at New York University, Dr. Skinner was born in 1924 in Port-of-Spain, Trinidad (West Indies), and received his early education in that city. He later acquired his B.A. from N.Y.U., and both his M.A. and Ph.D. degrees from Columbia.

Skinner studied under a Whitney Fellowship in French West Africa from 1953 to 1955, and later continued his academic pursuits in French Guiana under a Ford Foundation Fellowship. A member of several professional associations, and an active participant in the work of the NAACP and the American Society of African Culture (AMSAC), Dr. Skinner has also authored or co-authored a number of books, including *An Analysis of the Political Organization of the African People* (1957); *Christianity and Islam Among the Mossi* (1958); *The Mossi of the Upper Volta* (1964), and *A Glorious Age in Africa* (1965).

HUGH H. SMYTHE
Ambassador to Syria

Ambassador to Syria since 1965, Hugh H. Smythe was formerly a special advisor to the Senate Foreign Relations Committee; a member of the U. S. delegation to the 16th U. N. General Assembly, and a State Department research consultant.

Born in Pittsburgh, Pennsylvania in 1914, Smythe was educated locally, and later received his B. A. and M. A. degrees from Virginia State College and Atlanta University, respectively. He also studied at Fisk and Chicago universities and, after World War II, won his Ph. D. in anthropology from Northwestern.

As a consequence of his ambassadorial appointment, Dr. Smythe was obliged to take a special leave of absence from Brooklyn College, where he was serving as a deputy chairman in the graduate division of the sociology department. His other governmental posts include: lecturer at the Foreign Service Institute of the State Department (1961-1963); trainer of Peace Corps volunteers (1962-1963), and U. S. advisor to the National Research Council of Thailand.

Late in 1964, Smythe became chief consultant to Youth in Action, an organization falling under the Anti-Poverty Program. A year later, he participated in an orientation program designed to train Fulbright grantees bound for Southeast Asia.

Dr. Smythe worked for a time with the NAACP as assistant director of the department of special research and, in 1951, spent two years as a visiting professor of sociology and anthropology at Yamaguchi National University in Japan.

Dr. Smythe and his wife, a New York City high school principal, collaborated on a study of Nigeria published in 1960 after the couple did extensive field work together in Africa.

HOBART TAYLOR, JR.
Director of the Export-Import Bank

Hobart Taylor, Jr. has been a director of the Export-Import Bank since 1965. In his government career, Taylor had previously served President Lyndon B. Johnson as an associate special counsel, and had also been executive vice chairman of the President's Committee on Equal Employment Opportunity.

Born in Texarkana, Texas, Taylor graduated from Prairie View College with a B. A., receiving his M. A. from Howard and his LL. B. from the University of Michigan. After a short period as a research assistant for the Chief Justice of Michigan's Supreme Court, he entered a Detroit law firm as a junior and, later, a full partner.

At his present post as one of a team of five directors, Taylor aids in financing and expediting the export and import of various commodities between the United States and foreign nations.

BOOKER TALIAFERRO WASHINGTON
1856-1915

Educator and statesman, Booker T. Washington was Frederick Douglass' successor as the foremost American Negro leader of his day. Unlike Douglass, Washington was never to hold official federal office, but he managed, nonetheless, to exert considerable influence upon several areas of public affairs—in particular, civil rights.

Washington was born a slave in Hale's Ford, Virginia, reportedly in April 1856. It is known that he entered Hampton Institute in 1872 and graduated four years later. After teaching for a short while, he continued his studies at Wayland Seminary in Washington, D.C.

Washington founded Tuskegee Institute in 1881, at the same time becoming its first president. Later, in addition to instituting a variety of programs for rural extension work there, he helped establish the National Negro Business League.

In sharp contrast to his famous predecessor, Washington was intent on setting forth a less militant and more conciliatory policy with respect to civil rights. Already in 1884, he emphasized the fact that "the best cause to pursue in regard to the civil rights bill in the South is to let it alone . . . and it will settle itself."

Some 11 years later, in his now-famous speech at the opening of the Cotton States Exposition, he expounded views that—by their very moderacy—were to turn most Negro intellectuals against him. It was even feared in certain quarters that the stand he was taking would only serve to encourage the foes of equal rights.

His central theme was that Negroes would best protect the rights vouchsafed them by the U. S. Constitution through their own economic and moral advancement; his major task, in this connection, was to win over to his moderate course diverse elements among Southern whites, without whose support the program he envisaged would have been impossible.

Booker T. Washington

In 1896, shortly after the election of President William McKinley, a movement was set in motion urging that Washington be named to a cabinet post, but Washington publicly withdrew himself from any possible consideration, preferring to work outside the political arena.

At the time of his death in 1915, Washington's philosophy had been largely discredited by more militant Negro groups working toward the achievement of their aims through protest organizations and other activist agencies. In the South, however, for all his stress on conciliation and cooperation, Washington still managed to play a major role in motivating Negroes to improve their economic and social lot through self-help programs and the development of skilled labor.

GEORGE LEON-PAUL WEAVER
Assistant Secretary of Labor for International Affairs

George Leon-Paul Weaver, a native of Pittsburgh, Pennsylvania, was named to the post of Assistant Secretary of Labor for International Affairs by President John F. Kennedy in 1961.

Born on May 18, 1912, Weaver attended Roosevelt University (at that time the YMCA School in Chicago), and the law school of Howard University.

Weaver has long been active in the labor movement, particularly in the areas of civil rights and international affairs. In 1941, for example, he joined the CIO as a member of the War Relief Committee and, within a year's time, was named assistant to the director of this organization's Civil Rights Committee. For the next 13 years, he continued to serve in both these capacities. In 1955 (the year of the AFL-CIO merger), he was appointed Executive Secretary of the new body's Civil Rights Committee.

Weaver was obliged to take occasional leaves of absence in order to handle a number of special government assignments with the International Confederation of Free Trade Unions, and with the National Security Resources Board. Traveling widely, he also was a member (during the mid 1950's) of various missions to the Far East and Southeast Asia. In 1957, he attended the conference of the International Labor Organization (ILO) and, after participating the following year for a second time, was chosen assistant to the president of the International Union of Electrical, Radio and Machine Workers. At present, Weaver serves as a permanent representative to the ILO and as chairman of the U. S. delegation to its annual conference.

Weaver has received, among many other honors, the Eleanor Roosevelt Key for outstanding service to the world community.

SAMUEL Z. WESTERFIELD
Deputy Assistant Secretary for Economic Affairs, Bureau of African Affairs, Department of State

Samuel Westerfield was named by President Lyndon B. Johnson in 1964 to the reactivated position of Deputy Assistant Secretary for Economic Affairs within the Bureau of African Affairs of the U. S. Department of State.

Born in Chicago in 1919, Westerfield received an A. B. in economics and political science from Howard University (1939), and later acquired both his M. A. and Ph. D. degrees in economics from Harvard. From 1940 to 1961, apart from a year spent as an economist with the War Labor Board and the United Auto Workers Union, he was actively engaged either in research projects or as a faculty member of such universities as Howard, West Virginia State, Lincoln, and Atlanta.

It was while holding the posts of professor of economics and dean of the school of business administration at the last of these institutions that Westerfield was appointed associate director of the debt analysis staff of the U. S. Treasury. He then became senior advisor to this department's Director of the Office of International Affairs, where he specialized in the economic problems facing the emerging nations of Africa and Latin America. While in this post, he served as a member of the U. S. delegation to the Inter-American Economic and Social Conference held in Mexico City in 1962.

CLIFTON R. WHARTON
Ambassador to Norway

Clifton Wharton's appointment as Ambassador to Norway in 1961 was the highlight of more than three decades as a foreign service officer of the United States government.

Born in Baltimore on May 11, 1899,

Wharton received his LL. B. from Boston University in 1920, the same year he was admitted to the Massachusetts bar. Three years later, he won his LL. M. from Boston University and, the following year, accepted a post as a law clerk in the Department of State.

Wharton entered the U. S. foreign service in 1925, functioning as third secretary to Monrovia, Liberia. Over the next three decades, he held such posts as consul at Tananarive (Malagasy Republic); consul and first secretary to Lisbon (Portugal), and Minister to Rumania (1958). In this last post, he became the first Negro diplomat to head a U. S. delegation to a European country.

Wharton resigned from his Norway post in 1964.

FRANKLIN H. WILLIAMS
Ambassador to the United Nations; Ambassador to Ghana

Franklin H. Williams has occupied two top-echelon diplomatic posts under the Johnson Administration, one as United States Representative to the Economic and Social Council of the United Nations (1964-1965) and, more recently, as U. S. Ambassador to Ghana, the post in which he now serves.

Born in 1917 in Flushing, New York, Williams was educated in the city's public school system, and later graduated from Lincoln University in Pennsylvania, and from Fordham University Law School. After serving briefly as an assistant to Thurgood Marshall, then special counsel for the NAACP, Williams was sent to the West Coast, where he helped restructure the organization's branch offices in nine states.

A member of the bar in New York and California, Williams has often appeared before the U. S. Supreme Court, particularly in a number of cases involving fundamental constitutional rights. He was once assistant to Sargent Shriver, Director of the Peace Corps.

HOWARD B. WOODS
Associate Director of the United States Information Agency (USIA)

Howard B. Woods was named Associate Director of the USIA in 1965, serving under Carl Rowan, who has since resigned from his post as head of this agency. Woods entered government service after a successful career in journalism, which included 16 years' experience as city editor and then executive editor of the *Argus*, one of the leading Negro newspapers in St. Louis, Missouri.

Born in Perry, Oklahoma on January 9, 1917, Woods began his journalistic apprenticeship at the age of 18, and worked for the next seven years with the St. Louis *Call*. In 1942, he acquired his first important journalistic post as St. Louis bureau chief of the Chicago *Defender*, a position he held through 1949.

His current position gives Woods considerable responsibility for USIA programs in the newly emerging countries of Africa, Asia, Latin America, and the Middle East.

SAMUEL F. YETTE
Special Assistant for Civil Rights, Office of Economic Opportunity (OEO)

Born in Harriman, Tennessee on July 2, 1929, Samuel Yette became Sargent Shriver's Special Assistant for Civil Rights within the Office of Economic Opportunity (OEO) in early 1965.

Primarily a journalist, Yette was aided in achieving this goal through his educational background. While studying at Tennessee A. & I. State University (from which he received his B. A. in 1951), Yette organized and then edited the first campus newspaper. The Korean War, in which he rose to the rank of first lieutenant, temporarily interrupted his academic pursuits but, in 1956, three years after his discharge from the Air Force, he was awarded an M. A. in journalism from the University of Indiana.

Early jobs, such as the setting up of the Tuskegee Information Bureau in Alabama, and the teaching of a course in journalism at Tuskegee itself, helped prepare him for his present job—spokesman for the federal government on the ultimate aims of the anti-poverty program. More important journalistic assignments have seen Yette work for "Life" magazine; as associate editor of "Ebony," and as staff journalist for the *Afro-American*.

BLACK POLICYMAKERS OF PAST ADMINISTRATIONS

Congressional Committees
Matthew, Eunice S.
Education Chief,
House Committee on
Education and Labor

Department of Justice
Branton, Wiley A.
Staff Assistant to the
Asst. Attorney General
for Civil Rights

District of Columbia
Duncan, Charles T.
First Assistant,
U. S. Attorney's Office,
District of Columbia

Duncan, John B.
Commissioner of the
District of Columbia

Edwards, G. Franklin
Board of National Capital
Transportation Agency

Moore, Luke
U. S. Marshal,
District of Columbia

Ridley, Peter
Recorder of Deeds

Waddy, Herbert E.
Assistant Postmaster

Washington, James
Chairman of D. C. Public
Utilities Commission

Washington, Walter E.
Executive Director,
National Capital
Housing Authority

Equal Employment Opportunity Commission
Jackson, Samuel C.
Member of Commission

Federal and District of Columbia Judges
Robinson, Aubrey E., Jr.
Associate Justice,
D. C. Juvenile Court

Waddy, Joseph C.
D. C. Domestic
Relations Court

Watson, James L.
U. S. Customs Court

Natl. Advisory Council, Office of Economic Opportunity
Johnson, John H.
Member of Council

Randolph, A. Philip
Member of Council

Young, Whitney M., Jr.
Member of Council

President's Committee on Equal Employment Opportunity
Dunnigan, Mrs. Alice
Education Consultant

Watson, Mrs. D'Jaris
Member of Committee

Wheeler, John
Member of Committee

President's Committee on Equality of Treatment in the Armed Forces
Sengstacke, John H.
Member of Committee

Young, Whitney M., Jr.
Member of Committee

President's Committee on Equal Opportunity in Housing
Jones, Theodore A.
Member of Committee

Sawyer, Roland
Member of Committee

Taylor, Miss Azie B.
Administrative Asst. to the
Executive Chairman

Sub-Cabinet
Carter, Chester
Deputy Chief of Protocol,
Department of State

Davenport, Roy K.
Dep. Undrsec., U.S. Army

Hope, John
Assistant Executive
Director for
Federal Employment,
Department of Labor

Scott, Christopher C.
Dep. Postmaster Gen. for
Transportation

Wilkins, Roger W.
Director, Community
Relations Service,
Dept. of Commerce

U. S. Attorneys
McCurdy, Merle M.
U.S. Atty., Northern Ohio

Poore, Cecil F.
U. S. Attorney, California

U.S. Comm., Civil Rights
Freeman, Mrs. Frankie M.
Member of Commission

Holman, Carl
Information Officer

Simmons, Samuel
Director,
State Advisory
Committees Division

White House
Cloud, Lieutenant
Commander Ben
Presidential Social Aide

Robinson, Major Hugh G.
Presidential Military Aide

Miscellaneous Agencies
Adams, Samuel C., Jr.
Overseas Director,
Agency for International
Development

Allen, Samuel
Assistant General Counsel,
U.S. Information Agency

Bailer, Kermit
Assistant Administrator,
Off. of Comm. Programs,
Housing and Home
Finance Agency

Bennett, L. Howard
Principal Asst. to the Dep.
Asst. Sec. (Civil Rights),
Department of Defense

Benson, Homer
Memb., U.S. Bd. of Parole

Bolen, David
Special Asst. to the Asst.
Sec. for African Affairs,
Department of State

Brice, Edward W.
Director,
Adult Education Branch,
Office of Education,
Department of Health,
Education and Welfare

Carter, George
Regional Director
for North Africa, Near
East, and South Asia,
The Peace Corps

Cowan, Mrs. Mary F.
Cultural Affairs Officer,
Department of State

Dent, Dr. Albert W.
Dept. of State Member,
Commission on
Presidential Scholars

Dixon, Henry
Special Assistant
to the Assistant
Postmaster General

Douglass, Joseph H.
Chief,
Off. of Interagcy. Liaison,
National Institute
of Mental Health

Flagg, Lewis S., III
Associate Solicitor,
Department of Interior

Fowler, William E.
Trial Attorney,
Criminal Division,
Department of Justice

Fox, Richard K.
Special Assistant
to the Dep. Undersec.,
Department of State

Franklin, Dr. John Hope
Bd. of For. Scholarships,
Bureau of Educational
and Cultural Affairs,
Department of State

Freeman, Robert T.
Associate Director
for Management,
Peace Corps

Granger, Shelton
Agency for
Internatl. Development
(Department of State)

Gregory, Francis
Assistant Director
for Manpwr. Dvlpmnt.,
Department of Labor

Harris, Laura
Executive Secretary,
Incentive Awards Prog.,
Department of Labor

Lightfoot, Mrs. Jean
Liaison Officer,
Bureau of Public Affairs,
Department of State

McGee, Henry
Regional Personnel Dir.,
Post Office Department

Mallory, Dr. Arenia
Manpower Development
Specialists,
Department of Labor

Mangum, Robert J.
Regional Director,
Office of Economic
Opportunity

Morrison, Oscar
International Relations
Officer,
Department of State

Noble, Dr. Jeanne
Member,
President's Task Force
on Poverty

Pitt, Mrs. Mildred
Equal Emplymnt. Officer,
Agency for
Internatl. Development,
Department of State

Prattis, Lawrence
Regional Counsel,
Housing and Home
Finance Agency

Proctor, Dr. Samuel D.
Associate Director
for Peace Corps
Volunteers

Roberts, Mrs. Anne M.
Deputy Regional
Administrator,
Housing and Home
Finance Agency

Rucker, Alvin C.
Labor Advisor to
Assistant Secretary for
African Affairs,
Department of State

Seabron, William
Assistant to
Director of Personnel,
Dept. of Agriculture

Shaw, Leslie
Postmaster, City of
Los Angeles

Shoecraft, Robert K.
Attorney General
of the Territory
of Guam

Sylvester, Edward
Deputy Administrator
for International
Affairs, Department
of Labor

Wallace, Leon
Assistant to
the Administrator,
Veterans Adm.

Wartman, Charles
Office of Civil Defense,
Department of Defense

Williams, Eddie N.
Protocol Officer,
Department of State

BLACK OFFICIALS IN THE NIXON ADMINISTRATION

The following list of prominent black officials currently serving in the Nixon Administration was furnished courtesy of White House aide Robert J. Brown. Many of the people included here are career foreign service personnel or civil service appointees whose period of service dates from the Kennedy and Johnson years. Some have been appointed under Nixon or upgraded during his Administration. Many are the subjects of fuller biographical entries found elsewhere in this volume.

Agency for International Development

Samuel C. Adams, Jr.
Assistant Administrator
Bureau of Africa

Herman S. Davis, Jr.
Deputy Director
Tunisia

Ullmont L. James
Deputy Director
Morocco

Vernon C. Johnson
Deputy Director
Nigeria

Nita H. Long
Director
Equal Employment
Opportunity

Charles J. Nelson
Director
Tanzania

William E. Reed
Deputy Director
Ethiopia

Harold D. Snell
Director
Kenya

BLACK OFFICIALS IN THE NIXON ADMINISTRATION—Cont.

Ambassadors and Embassy Staff

Clyde Ferguson
Ambassador to Uganda

Jerome Holland
Ambassador to Sweden

Clinton Knox
Ambassador to Haiti

Terence A. Todman
Ambassador to Chad

Samuel Z. Westerfield
Ambassador to Liberia

Clarence S. Wilson
American Embassy
Caracas, Venezuela

American Revolution Bicentennial Commission

Luther H. Foster
Member

Citizens Advisory Council on the Status of Women

Mary J. Klye
Member

Civil Service Commission

James Frazier
Director
Federal Equal
Employment Opportunity

James E. Johnson
Vice Chairman

Anthony W. Hudson
Member

Dept. of Agriculture

Betty Dotson
Confidential Assistant
to the Administrator
Food and Nutrition

Dr. Alfred Edwards
Dep. Assistant Secretary
for Rural Development
and Conservation

Arthur B. McCaw
Deputy Administrator
Food and Nutrition Serv.

William Seabron
Assistant to the Secretary

Department of Commerce

Richard Hurt
Public Information Office

John L. Jenkins
Assistant Director for
Community Services
Office of Minority
Business Enterprise

Lutrelle F. Parker
Examiner-in-Chief
Board of Appeals

Joe Scroggins, Jr.
Maritime Recruitment
Specialist

Jim Sexton
Division Director
Urban Program and
Commun. Organizations

Elizabeth Stone
Director
Independent Sector
Division
Minority Business
Enterprise

Abraham S. Venable
Director, Office of
Minority Business
Enterprise

Barber Walker
Attorney-Advisor EDA

Wilbert L. Whitsett
Attorney-Advisor
Office of the
General Counselor

Department of Defense

Howard E. Bennett
Principal Deputy to
Dep. Assistant Secretary

Brig. General
Daniel James, Jr.
Dep. Assistant Secretary
Public Affairs

Frank Render
Dep. Assistant Secretary
Civil Rights

Department of Health, Education and Welfare

Dr. Frank Bickles
Director, Natl. Center for
Family Planning Service
Health Services and
Mental Health
Administration

George T. Brooks
Deputy Director
Division of Research
Office of Deputy
Director for Science

Dr. Edward B. Cross
Asst. Surgeon General

James Farmer
Assistant Secretary
for Administration

Dr. William Green
Special Assistant to the
Commission for
Urban Education

Burton Lamkin
Associate Commissioner
for Libraries and
Educational Technology
Office of Education

Thomas E. Malone
Associate Director for
Extramural Programs
National Institute of
Dental Research

Constance Newman
Special Assistant to the
Assistant Secretary for
Planning and Research
Evaluation

Dr. Luther Robinson
First Assistant Physician
St. Elizabeth Hospital

Dr. Leonard Spearman
Director
Division of Student
Special Services
Office of Education

Leroy R. Swift
Special Assistant to
Director
Health Professions Bureau

Dr. Claudwell S. Thomas
Director, Natl. Center for
Family Planning Service
Health Services and
Mental Health
Administration

Stanley B. Thomas
Dep. Assistant Secretary

Department of Housing and Urban Development

T. M. Alexander
Assistant Commissioner
Home Mortgages

Carlos Campbell
Special Assistant to the
Assistant Secretary for
Metropolitan Dvlpmnt.

Theodore M. Daly, Jr.
Director, Equal Housing
Opportunity Division

Gilbert DeLorme
Special Assistant to the
Assistant Secretary for
Equal Opportunity

BLACK OFFICIALS IN THE NIXON ADMINISTRATION—Cont.

Napoleon P. Dotson
Director,
Assistant Programs Div.

Robert Grant
Special Assistant to the
Director of Int'l Affairs

Nathan A. Hicks, Jr.
Assistant Director
Equal Opportunity
Renewal and
Housing Assistance

William E. Hill
Director
Division of Equal
Housing Opportunity

Kenneth Holbert
Director
Office of Housing
Opportunity

Samuel W. Hudson, Jr.
Director
Housing Opportunity
Division

Melvin Humphrey
Deputy Director
Community Resources

Hubert M. Jackson
Atlanta Director
Assisted Programs Div.

Hugh D. Jackson
Senior Program Officer
Off. of Assisted Programs

Samuel C. Jackson
Assistant Secretary for
Metropolitan Dvlpmnt.

Clifton R. Jeffers
Assistant Regional
Administrator for
Equal Opportunity
San Francisco HUD Off.

Thomas O. Jenkins
Director
Contract Compliance
Division

Charles C. Johnson, Jr.
Administrator
Consumer Protection and
Environment Health
Service

Victor J. Labat
Special Assistant
Office for Civil Rights

Edward P. Lovett
Director
Special Projects Division
Housing Opportunity

Harold A. Odom
Fort Worth Director
Assisted Programs Div.

Mary D. Pinkard
Assistant Director
Assisted Programs
Model Cities and
Governmental Relations

William A. Ross
Director
Business Development
Division
Office of Contract
Compliance and
Employment Opportunity

Samuel J. Simmons
Assistant Secretary for
Equal Opportunity

Laura L. Spencer
Deputy Director
Office of
Housing Opportunity

Robert A. Thompson
Deputy Assistant to the
Reg. Administrator for
Eq. Opportunity, Atlanta

Richard T. Williams
Deputy Assistant
Reg. Administration for
Special Programs

Snowdon Williams
Director, Special Projects
Office of Planning
Programs and Evaluations
Office of Metropolitan
Division

James O. Wyatt
N.Y. Director
Housing Opportunity
Division

Dept. of the Interior

Melvin Evans
Governor, Virgin Islands

Benjamin L. Hunton
Co-ordinator
Interior Job Corps

John J. Scott
Supervisiory Attorney-
Adviser
Division of Territories
Wildlife and Claims

Joseph J. Simmons
Administrator
Oil Imports

Department of Justice

George Hall
Director,
Statistical Research
Law Enforcement
Assistance Administration

Benjamin Holman
Director
Community Relations

Donald W. Jones
Community Relations
Officer
Field Coordinator

Gerald Jones
Chief
Voting and Public
Accommodation Facilities

Oliver Lofton
Associate Director for
Program Direction
Community Relations
Services

L. Stanley Paige
Chief, Fraud Section
Civil Division

Department of Labor

John Blake
Deputy Manpower
Administrator

Arthur A. Fletcher
Assistant Secretary for
Wage and Labor Stand.

Elizabeth Koontz
Dir., Women's Bureau

John L. Wilks
Dep. Assistant Secretary

Department of State

Julia M. Cardoza
Junior Foreign Service
Officer

Johnnie Carson
Junior Foreign Service
Officer

William B. Carter
Dep. Assistant Secretary

Jacques Cook
Junior Foreign Service
Officer

Ruth Davis
Junior Foreign Service
Officer

Jake M. Dyels
Consular Officer

Joseph L. Fisher
Commercial Officer

BLACK OFFICIALS IN THE NIXON ADMINISTRATION—Cont.

Bernard Johns
Junior Foreign Service Officer

William B. Jones
Dep. Assistant Secretary
Bureau of Educational and Cultural Affairs

Ronald L. Kates
Junior Foreign Service Officer

Robert W. Kitchen
Special Adviser
Economic Development

Robert Lloyd
Junior Foreign Service Officer

James Myrick
Junior Foreign Service Officer

Lewis C. Smith
Administrative Officer

Barbara Watson
Administrator
Bureau of Security and Consular Affairs

Department of Transportation

Robert T. Adams
Economist
Highway Policy

Calvin D. Banks
Chief, Urban Programs

Wilbert E. Cantey
Systems Analyst
High Speed Ground Transportation

Benjamin F. L. Darden
Director
Aviation Policy

Elwood T. Driver
Special Assistant
Federal Highway Administration

William D. Fowler, Jr.
Hearing Examiner
National Transportation Safety Board

Alexander Gaither
Director of Civil Rights
Federal Highway Adminstration

George W. Haley
Chief Counsel
Urban Mass Transit Administration

William T. Hudson
Chief Coast Guard Civil Rights Office
Coast Guard Civil Rights Office

Joyce Mack
Assistant Director
Internatl. Co-operation

Robert L. Maxwell
Deputy Director
Systems Engineering

Alfred L. Sweeney
Assistant to the Director
Office of Information

Quentin S. Taylor
Director, Fed. Aviation Administration,
Civil Rights Office

Harold Thompson
Special Consultant to Secretary

James A. Washington, Jr.
General Counsel

Harold B. Williams
Director
Urban Mass Transp.
Civil Rights Office

Dept. of the Treasury

Samuel R. Pierce
General Counsel

District of Columbia Council

Jerry A. Moore
Member

Sterling Tucker
Vice Chairman

Equal Employment Opportunity Commission

William H. Brown III
Chairman

George Butler
Director
Technical Assistance Program Division
Office of Technical Assistance

Yvette Butler
Director of Administration

Julia Cooper
General Attorney

George Draper
Dep. Executive Director

Chester Gray
Regional Director, Cleveland

Stanley P. Herbert
General Counsel

Donald Hollowell
Reg. Director, Atlanta

Patricia Ann King
Special Assistant to the Chairman

Colston Lewis
Member

Elmer McLain
Reg. Director, Chicago

Andrew Muse
Director,
Office of Compliance

Monte Posey
Regional Director, New York

Chris Roggerson
Director, Educational Programs Division and Acting Director, Office of Technical Assistance

Delbert Spurlock
Member

General Services Administration

Jackie Batts
Equal Employment Opportunity Counselor

Calvin Brooks
Equal Employment Opportunity Counselor

Alfred Brothers
Equal Employment Opportunity Counselor

Robert Collins
Equal Employment Opportunity Counselor

Joseph Daniels
Executive Director for Equal Employment Opportunity

Elmer D. Jones
Deputy Commissioner (Communications)
Transportation and Communications

Curtis B. Kirkpatrick
Equal Employment Opportunity Counselor

Allie B. Latimer
Supervising Attorney
Advisor

BLACK OFFICIALS IN THE NIXON ADMINISTRATION—Cont.

Edward E. Mitchell
Deputy Assistant Administrator for Administration

Wayne Williams
Equal Employment Opportunity Counselor

Raymond Wilson
Confidential Assistant to the Administrator

Fletcher L. Yarbrough
Equal Employment Opportunity Counselor

National Highway Safety Commission

Dr. Basil Scott
Member

National Labor Relations Board

Howard Jenkins
Member

National Selective Service Appeals Board

Levi Jackson
Chairman

Office of Economic Opportunity

Robert Brown
Special Assistant
Office of Governmental Relations

Samuel Cornelius
Regional Director

Lois Hobson
Special Assistant to the Director of Program Development

Frank Kent
Director
Office of Civil Rights

Aster Kirk
Regional Director, Philadelphia

Earl Phillips
Director,
Community Development

Arthur J. Reid, Jr.
Deputy General Counsel

William Sharp
Director of Research
Office of Planning and Research

Peace Corps

Walter Carrington
Director, Africa

William Gaymon
Director, Nigeria

Joseph Kennedy
Dir., East Asia-Pacific

C. Payne Lucas
Director, Office of Voluntary Action

Calvin Raullerson
Director, Kenya

William Tutman
Deputy Director
Office of Voluntary Placement (OVP)

Edward White
Director
E. Caribbean (Barbados)

William T. White, Jr.
Chief, Private Resource Development and Special Programs

President's Commission on White House Fellows

Hobson R. Reynolds
Member

Small Business Administration & Council on Minority Enterprises

Berkeley Burrell
Vice Chairman

John H. Clay
Member

Connie Mack Higgins
Special Assistant to Administrator and Dir. of Equal Employment Opportunity

Rev. Arthur Marshall
Member

Arthur McZier
Assistant Administrator
Minority Enterprises

U.S. Advisory Committee for Internatl. Education and Cultural Affairs

Jewel LaFontant
Member

U.S. Information Agency

John E. Reinhardt
Asst. Director of USIA for East Asia and Pacific

U.S. Post Office

Emmett E. Cooper, Jr.
Director,
Postal Management

Clarence H. Featherson
Deputy Contract Compliance Officer

Ronald B. Lee
Assistant to Postmaster General

Charles H. Thomas
Director
Equal Employment Opportunity

Veterans Administration

George Holland
Director of Equal Employment Opportunity

Dr. Howard W. Kenney
Reg. Medical Director
VA Central Office
Washington, D.C.

Dr. Robert S. Wilson
Hospital Director
VA Hospital
Tuskegee, Alabama

The White House

Robert J. Brown
Special Assistant to the President

Lt. Col. V. C. Coffey
Military Aide to the President

Frank DeCosta
Assistant to the Vice President

Dr. Joseph Douglass
Chairman,
Executive Committee
White House Conference on Children and Youth

Adrian Dove
Analyst
Executive Office of the President
Bureau of the Budget

Harriet Elam
Aide to the President's Appointment Secretary

Carole Jones
Aide to Director of Communications

Thaddeus W. Ware
Staff Assistant to the President

THE U. S. CONGRESS

The role of the black elected official in the legislative branch of government expanded dramatically throughout the 1960's, culminating in the 1966 election of a black senator from Massachusetts, Edward W. Brooke, and the 1969 election of three black Congressmen (one a woman) from three different Northern states. Most black elected officials base their appeal to a broad, responsible, and involved middle section of the community, assuring the white electorate that they will not become mere tools of militant and revolutionary tacticians, even as they promise the black population to campaign vigorously and dynamically for the ample funds and trained manpower needed to reconstruct the nation's urban centers and rehabilitate their distressed inhabitants.

In the 1970 Congressional elections, of national significance was the fact that three new black Democrats were elected to represent constituencies in Chicago (the Sixth District), Oakland, and Baltimore. The winners were: George Collins, a Chicago alderman who defeated a Republican in a district that includes the heavily black West Side of Chicago and two white blue collar suburbs, Cicero and Berwyn; Roger V. Dellums, 34, a Berkeley, Calif. City Councilman who defeated Jeffery Cohelan (a five-time representative) in the primary, and then outran a Republican and a Peace and Freedom party candidate in a district that includes Berkeley and Oakland (Dellums spoke in defense of Black Panthers and student strikers), and Darren J. Mitchell, 48, a college professor who defeated a Republican in a district that includes parts of Baltimore city and county. In each case, the black candidates parlayed 40% black districts and white liberal coalitions into easy victory. Two other blacks elected to the House from black districts were: Ralph Metcalfe (he replaces William Dawson) and Charles B. Rangel (he replaces Adam Clayton Powell, Jr.). Among the prominent black losers were: Andrew Young of SCLC and Mrs. Medgar Evers, widow of the slain civil rights leader.

On the state level, the most stunning black victory came in California where Wilson Riles defeated Max Rafferty for the office of State Superintendent of Public Instruction. In Alabama, blacks swept all major elective offices in Greene County. Elsewhere, two black state legislators were elected in the state, the first since Reconstruction. In Alabama, blacks were elected sheriff in four counties; in Mississippi, five blacks won posts on county school boards.

Black victories at the polls reflected greater black solidarity, and more widespread support of black candidates by white liberals.

A. *During Reconstruction*

The first piece of legislation which affected what we might call the "post-Emancipation" American Negro—the Civil Rights Act of 1866—established the principle upon which his subsequent quest for equality before the law was based: CITIZENSHIP.

Emancipation, after all, succeeded only in granting the Negro his freedom. It did absolutely nothing to provide him with those credentials upon which a real identity is ultimately based: a sympathetic society, a decent home, a rewarding job, and a sense of dignity.

A century ago, white men in the South—indeed throughout the country—were not prepared to accept the Negro on such terms. They instituted and then refined various forms of discrimination, often embodying them in segregation ordinances and other suppressive statutes. Perhaps the most infamous of these were the "Black Codes," an organized system of vagrancy laws which levied fines against unemployed Negroes, prohibited their exercise of the franchise, and prevented them from socializing normally with white people.

At this juncture, the Republican party which controlled the Congress set in motion—for the first time in American history—plans to include the Negro in the governing councils of that nation to which he had been introduced in chains three centuries earlier. This phenomenon provided the Negro with the second stepping stone upon which his direct participation in American society must ultimately be reckoned: REPRESENTATION.

In 1865, Congress established the Freedmen's Bureau which resettled ex-slaves on abandoned lands and provided them with basic health and educational services. Two years later, the First Reconstruction Act stipulated that Negroes be given the right to vote. By 1870, the 14th and 15th amendments had even further broadened the Negro's right to discharge his duties as an American citizen.

Likewise, between 1870 and 1901, 22 Negroes—two Senators [from Mississippi] and 20 representatives [from South Carolina (8), North Carolina (4), Alabama (3), Florida (1), Georgia (1), Louisiana (1), Mississippi (1) and Virginia (1)]—were elected to serve in the Congress of the United States, thus tak-

Entered according to act of Congress in the year 1872 by Currier & Ives, in the Office of the Librarian of Congress at Washington.
ROBERT C. DE LARGE, M.C. of S.Carolina.
JEFFERSON H. LONG, M.C. of Georgia.
U.S. Senator H.R. REVELS, of Mississippi
BENJ. S. TURNER, M.C. of Alabama.
JOSIAH T. WALLS, M.C. of Florida.
JOSEPH H. RAINY, M.C. of S.Carolina.
R. BROWN ELLIOT, M.C. of S.Carolina.
THE FIRST COLORED SENATOR AND REPRESENTATIVES,
In the 41st. and 42nd. Congress of the United States.
NEW YORK, PUBLISHED BY CURRIER & IVES, 125 NASSAU STREET.

Black members of the Senate and House during Reconstruction

ing an active part—again for the first time in our nation's history—in the critical function of representative self-government.

It is not surprising that Negro legislators were usually forced to serve their constituents as relentless pleaders for civil rights. Such men were expected to become a special breed of miracle-worker, seeking, wherever possible, to establish free public schooling, to abolish debtors' punishments, to extend voting rights—in short, to deliver to the Negro a whole host of privileges and rights long taken for granted by the white majority.

Some Negro legislators were party hacks; some were misguided idealists; some were unprincipled scoundrels. Yet, on the whole, Negro Congressmen were eager and willing public servants. The majority of them were not motivated solely by self-interest and political opportunism, nor did they approach government with an overweening desire to seek revenge against their Southern oppressors.

The impact of these men upon American history has not been enormous, yet they cannot, for this reason, be regarded merely as historical peculiarities. They were products of their age, but they also made their imprint on that age. This fact alone warrants their recognition, and evokes the need for a review of their lives and accomplishments in this volume.

B. *During the 20th Century*

For the Negro legislator, the turn of the century was an ending, not a beginning. On January 29, 1901, George H. White stood in the Congressional chambers for the last time; by 1902, there was not even a single state legislature in the nation which could boast of a Negro member.

The next Negro was not elected to Congress until 27 years later. Oscar De Priest, the last of his race to be chosen before the onset of the Depression, was also the last Negro Republican to receive the backing of a predominantly Negro electorate. (Until President Franklin D. Roosevelt initiated his New Deal program, the Negro voter—when he was at all *able* to vote—was a Republican, i.e. a follower of the party of Abraham Lincoln.)

The massive shift in 1932 to the Democratic party was not only a result of the Depression, but was also a clear testimony to the success Roosevelt had achieved in convincing the Negro voter that, as president, he would be committing himself to principles of equality which would benefit all Americans, Negroes included. Moreover, Roosevelt was to launch a number of welfare programs which ultimately were to prove especially beneficial to Negroes in low-income brackets.

During the 1930's, Negroes were swept along on the crest of two interlocking migratory waves: from the South to the North, and from the country to the city. As a consequence, the political force latent in the compression of the Negro into the Northern urban ghetto began slowly to emerge in the person of a new kind of Negro politician.

In 1934, Arthur B. Mitchell of Illinois was the first of this new group to win election to Congress. He was followed by William L. Dawson who took the oath of office as representative of the First Congressional District of the same state on January 4, 1943. Two years later, Adam Clayton Powell, Jr.—the first Negro Congressman from the East—began his much-publicized career as "the man" from the 18th Congressional District of New York. In 1954, it was the turn of Charles Diggs from the Motor City of Detroit and, four years later, of Robert Nix from the Second District of Philadelphia. By 1963, still another major migratory trend had swelled the Negro population of California to a point where Augustus F. Hawkins was able to emerge as the representative of the 21st District of Los Angeles. Two years later, it was John Conyers of Michigan who, with labor union endorsement and the backing of the Negro district leadership, won a seat from Detroit's First Congressional District.

All this notwithstanding, the Negro legislator remained a racial protagonist. After Reconstruction, however, his role broadened to include the interests of several other minority groups. (Congressman Powell, for example, has the support of the substantial Puerto Rican electorate in his district.) But even beyond this, the Negro legislator increasingly sought to identify himself first as an American and, more incidentally, as a Negro. This became more particularly true as the Negro finally came to savor the fruits of first-class citizenship in his own country.

Today, the Negro legislator wishes to

reflect more than just his own heritage, or even the dominant interests of his own constituency. Admittedly, he is desirous of extending his role further in the Senate and, perhaps one day, even as far as the White House. Special interests aside, however, there is a new and further dimension being added to the saga of the Negro legislator in the 20th century.

Why, for instance, does an Adam Clayton Powell attend the Afro-Asian Conference in Bandung, Indonesia, or the independence celebration of Ghana in Africa? Why does a Charles Diggs investigate the complaints of American soldiers on military installations *all over the world?*

Such gestures can mean only one thing: that the Negro legislator is growing increasingly aware of the fact that his interests are not only inextricably bound up with those of emerging nations in other parts of the world, but that they will inevitably grow to be synonymous with those of the nation he more and more represents both at home *and* abroad—the United States of America.

The Supreme Court redistricting plan, carried out in accordance with the one-man, one-vote dictum, promises to bring about wholesale changes in the number of black representatives sent to Congress in the 1970's. Had the decision not precipitated such frequent squabbles at the state level, many of them necessitating court cases, it is reasonable to assume that the entry of more blacks into the political system would have been considerably hastened.

The three recently elected black members of the House—Louis Stokes of Ohio, William Clay of Missouri, and Shirley Chisholm of New York—all come from redrawn districts whose new composition phased out white Democratic leadership. Concurrent with the drawing of new district lines is the steady advance of black people into the heart of major U.S. cities. In 1950, blacks represented some 12% of the urban population; in 1960, the figure had risen to 17% and, in 1970, the total was at 20%.

Deputy Democratic National Committeeman Louis Martin expects the numbers of black officials to rise steeply during the 1970's. Martin predicts that, by 1974, there may be as many as 25 black Congressmen. Even though none of the present number are Southerners (Charles Evers lost his bid for a Congressional seat in 1968), many analysts are convinced that elected officials from the South will eventually come to outnumber those chosen in the North. One reason is that far more Negroes will be registered in these areas than in the North, where political repression and intimidation have never been as ruthlessly relentless as they have historically been throughout the South.

HIRAM RHOADES REVELS
U.S. Senator from Mississippi
(1870–1871)

Hiram Rhoades Revels, a native of North Carolina, is the first Negro to have served in the U.S. Senate. Revels was elected from his adopted state of Mississippi, and served for approximately one year, i.e. from February 1870 to March 1871.

Born in 1822 in Fayetteville County, Revels was educated in Indiana, and attended Knox College in Illinois. Ordained a minister in the African Methodist Church, he worked among Negro settlers in the Northwest Territory, and in the border states of Kentucky and Missouri before settling in Baltimore, Maryland. There, he served as a church pastor and school principal.

During the Civil War, Revels helped organize a pair of Negro regiments in Maryland and, in 1863, went to St. Louis to establish a freedmen school, and to carry on his work as a recruiter. For a year, he served as chaplain of a Mississippi regiment before accepting the post of provost marshall of Vicksburg. While in this part of the country, he was also active in organizing a number of Negro churches, particularly in Jackson, the state capital.

Revels settled in Natchez at the end of the war. In 1868, he joined the Methodist Episcopal Church, and was appointed alderman by the Union military governor of the state. Revels accepted this post with some trepidation, since he feared it would lead to a conflict of interests. Eventually, however, he won the respect of his constituents for his alert grasp of important state issues and, as such, found it advantageous to pursue a political career. He even supported legislation which would have restored voting and office-holding privileges to disfranchised Southerners.

Revels was named president of Alcorn University near Lorman, Mississippi after he had left politics for good. He devoted most of the remainder of his life to developing Alcorn as an institution of learning

Hiram Rhoades Revels

in which the Negro could place his trust. In 1876, he became editor of the *Southwestern Christian Advocate*, a religious journal.

Revels lived in Holly Springs during his last years, and remained active in religious work until his death on January 16, 1901. The former senator was survived by his wife, Phoebe, and two daughters.

BLANCHE K. BRUCE
U.S. Senator from Mississippi
(1875–1881)

Blanche K. Bruce, the only Negro to serve a full term in the United States Senate, was born a slave in Farmville, Prince Edward County on March 1, 1841. Bruce received his early formal education in Missouri, the state to which his parents had moved while he was still quite young. Bruce later studied at Oberlin College in Ohio.

In 1868, Bruce made Mississippi his permanent home by settling in the town of Floreyville. There he worked as a planter and eventually built up a considerable fortune in property.

In 1870, after having worked briefly as a teacher, Bruce entered politics and was elected Sergeant-at-Arms of the Mississippi Senate. A year later, he was named Assessor of Taxes in Bolivar County. In 1872, he served as sheriff of that county, and as a member of the Board of Levee Commissioners of the Mississippi.

Bruce was nominated for the U.S. Senate from Mississippi in February 1874. Once elected to the Senate, Bruce became an outspoken defender of the rights of minority groups, including those of the Chinese and the American Indian. Bruce also investigated alleged election frauds and worked for the improvement of navigation on the Mississippi in the hope of increasing interstate and foreign commerce. Like Revels, Bruce also supported legislation aimed at eliminating reprisals against those who had opposed Negro emancipation.

After Bruce completed his term in the Senate, he was named Register of the U.S. Treasury Department by President James A. Garfield. Bruce held this position until 1885. In 1889, President Benjamin Harrison appointed him Recorder of Deeds in Washington, D.C. Seven years later, President William McKinley reappointed him to his former Treasury Department post as Register.

Bruce died on March 17, 1898, and was survived by his widow, the former Josephine B. Wilson of Cleveland, Ohio. The Bruces had one child, a boy, Roscoe Conkling. He was named after a Senate colleague who had shown Bruce special kindness during his early days in the Senate chambers.

EDWARD W. BROOKE
U.S. Senator from Massachusetts
(1966-)

Edward W. Brooke is the first Negro to be elected to the U.S. Senate in the 20th century. A top vote getter and key figure within the Massachusetts Republican party, Brooke had been Attorney General of the state since 1962. He won election to the Senate over former Massachusetts governor Endicott Peabody on November 8, 1966.

Born into a middle-class Washington, D.C. environment, Brooke attended public schools locally, and went on to graduate from Howard University. Inducted into an all-Negro infantry unit during World War II, Brooke rose to the rank of captain, and was ultimately given a Bronze Star citation for his work in intelligence.

Returning to Massachusetts, Brooke attended the Boston University Law School, compiling an outstanding academic record and editing the law review in the process. After law school, he established himself as an attorney, and also served as chairman of the Boston Finance Commission.

Brooke was later nominated for the attorney general's office, encountering stiff opposition within his own party, but eventually winning both the Republican primary and the general election against his Democratic opponent.

Upon entering the national political scene, Brooke espoused the notion that the Great Society could not become a reality until it was preceded by the "Responsible Society." He called this a society in which "it's more profitable to work than not to work. You don't help a man by constantly giving him more handouts."

Brooke has also hastened to note that he is not merely "the first Negro this or the highest Negro that," but can likewise be described as "a Protestant in a Catholic state and a Republican in a Democratic state."

After his election, Brooke made a two-week fact-finding tour of Southeast Asia,

Sen. Edward W. Brooke (R.—Mass.)

seeking to determine first-hand whether he agreed with American policy there. Prior to his trip, he had argued that the U.S. "ought to take the first step toward creating a better climate for negotiations," possibly by ordering a bombing halt. Knowing that most black leaders had already expressed widespread disillusionment with the war and serious disagreement with President Johnson, Brooke seemed disposed at first to confirm these views.

Upon his return, however, he had this to say: ". . . those most familiar with the East Asian mentality are convinced that the enemy still waits, still aspires to victory through collapse of the American will. Let there be no doubt in the mind of Ho Chi Minh or anyone else that the American people will persevere in their fundamental support of the South Vietnamese." Since 1967, Brooke has tended to endorse most official expressions of U.S. foreign policy in Vietnam. (However, he is now on record as being a supporter of the Hatfield-McGovern amendment insuring U.S. withdrawal from Vietnam by 1971.)

As might be expected, though, matters of race rather than foreign affairs were almost unavoidably to become Brooke's area of expertise. Reluctant and subdued, Brooke proceeded carefully at first, waiting to be consulted by President Nixon and loyally accepting the latter's apparent indifference to his views. However, as pressure mounted from the established civil rights groups and impatient black militants to attack the Nixon policies, Brooke was roused into a more active role, speaking out against the Administration's vacillating school desegregation guidelines, its emasculation of the Voting Rights Act, its "firing" of HEW official Leon Panetta and, most significantly, the nominations to the Supreme Court of judicial conservatives Clement Haynsworth and G. Harrold Carswell.

The new Senator is married to the former Remigia Ferrari-Scacco, whom he met while stationed in Italy during World War II. He is the father of two daughters.

JOSEPH H. RAINEY
U.S. Congressman from South Carolina (1869-1879)

Joseph H. Rainey, the first Negro Congressman in the House of Representatives, was born on June 21, 1832 in Georgetown, South Carolina. Drafted to work on Confederate fortifications in Charleston harbor during the Civil War, Rainey eventually escaped to the West Indies. He did not return to his native state until the close of the war in 1865.

In 1868, Rainey was elected as a delegate to the state constitutional convention and came to occupy a seat in the State Senate. A year later, he was elected to the House of Representatives (the 41st Congress), remaining in office until 1879 (the 45th Congress).

Rainey's political ideology placed him on the side of those who were fighting for legislation to enforce the 14th Amendment (1868) and the Ku Klux Klan Act (1871). In his own right, he also presented some 10 petitions for a civil rights bill which would have guaranteed Negroes their full constitutional rights, as well as equal access to public accommodations. On one particular occasion, Rainey dramatized the latter issue by refusing to leave the dining room of a hotel in Suffolk, Virginia and by allowing himself to be forcibly ejected from the premises.

Rainey advocated passage of a bill to establish an American steamship line between the United States and Haiti. He also supported the rights of the Chinese minority in California, and became the first Negro to preside over the House of Representatives during a public debate—in this case, on a proposed bill to improve conditions on Indian reservations.

Rep. Joseph F. Rainey of South Carolina

Upon his retirement from politics, Rainey was appointed a special agent for the U.S. Treasury Department in Washington, D.C. He served until 1881, after which he pursued banking and brokerage interests there.

In 1886, he returned to Georgetown, where he died on August 1, 1887.

ROBERT C. DeLARGE
U.S. Congressman from South Carolina (1871-1873)

Robert C. DeLarge was born a slave on March 15, 1842 in Aiken, South Carolina. He received what was for his day and race an above-average education and, during Reconstruction, became a successful farmer. Turning to politics, he served two years in the state legislature before being elected to a seat in the U.S. Congress. The election, however, was marred by serious voting irregularities, and he was eventually obliged to take a leave of absence so as to investigate the original returns. During his absence, a Congressional Commission on Elections declared the seat vacant.

In 1873, his health failing, DeLarge was appointed a magistrate in the city of Charleston, a position he held until his death one year later.

ROBERT B. ELLIOTT
U.S. Congressman from South Carolina (1871-1875)

Robert B. Elliott was born in Boston, Massachusetts to West Indian parents on August 11, 1842. Much of his education was received abroad—first in the grammar schools of Jamaica; later in High Holborn Academy (London), and finally at Eton from which he graduated with honors. While in England, he also studied for the law.

Upon his return to the United States, Elliott became an editor with the *Charleston Leader*, was elected to the South Carolina Constitutional Convention and, in 1868, won a seat in the lower house of the state legislature.

Subsequently, he was elected to the 42nd U.S. Congress. After serving two terms, he retired to New Orleans where he practiced as a lawyer until his death on August 9, 1884.

ALONZO J. RANSIER
U.S. Congressman from South Carolina (1873-1875)

Born free in Charleston, South Carolina on January 3, 1834, Alonzo J. Ransier received a rudimentary education and, during his youth, worked as a shipping clerk. After serving as Registrar of Elections in 1865, Ransier attended South Carolina's first Republican convention the following year, and was commissioned to dispatch a memorandum to the U.S. Congress seeking federal protection for Negro citizens. While in Washington, D.C., he joined the "Outside Congress," a powerful lobbying group.

In 1868, Ransier participated again in the South Carolina convention as a presidential elector and as chairman of the State Executive Committee. Two years later, he was elected to the lieutenant-governorship of South Carolina, amassing a 33,000-vote plurality.

Ransier was elected to the House of Representatives in 1873. The early bills he introduced were of little consequence, but he eventually became a key figure in the controversy over a "full and complete" civil rights bill. In addition, he advocated the extension of the presidential term to a period of six years, voted for the national tariff and against a salary increase for federal officials. He also sought funds for the improvement of Charleston harbor.

Ransier failed to gain his party's nomination for a second term, whereupon he returned to Charleston, and eventually became a day laborer for the city government. He died on August 17, 1882.

RICHARD H. CAIN
U.S. Congressman from South Carolina (1873-1875; 1877-1879)

Richard Harvey Cain was born on April 12, 1825 in Greenbriar County, Virginia of free parents. While still young, he moved northwards to Ohio and, like many Negroes of his day, found work on the steamboats servicing the nation's major waterways.

At the age of 16, Cain was converted to the Methodist faith and, three years later, was preaching in Missouri for the Methodist Episcopal Church. Soon disillusioned, he returned to Ohio where he joined the African Methodist Episcopal (AME) Church, and was given a congregation in Iowa.

With the close of the Civil War, Cain, who had not only served as a minister, but also helped publish a newspaper known as *The Missionary Record*, was chosen as a member of the South Carolina Constitutional Convention of 1868, and was elected State Senator. Subsequently, he served South Carolina in the U.S. Congress, where he established a reputation for clean politics.

On his retirement from public life in 1880, Cain was named AME bishop of the Louisiana and Texas conference, and became president of Paul Quinn College in Waco, Texas. He died in 1887.

ROBERT SMALLS
U.S. Congressman from South Carolina (1875-1879; 1881-1887)

Robert Smalls of South Carolina served a longer period in Congress than any other Negro Reconstruction Congressman.

Born a slave to Lydia and Robert Smalls in Beaufort, South Carolina on April 5, 1839, Smalls received a limited education before moving on to Charleston with the family of his owner. In 1856, while working at a variety of odd jobs—waiter, hack driver and rigger—Smalls met a young woman, Hannah, whom he was permitted to marry.

Despite the privileges ostensibly accorded him, Small chafed under the oppression of slavery and, with the outbreak of the Civil War, immediately took advantage of the opportunity to become a member of the crew of the *Planter*, a dispatch and transport steamer flying the Confederate flag.

On the morning of May 13, 1862, Smalls smuggled his wife and three children on board, assumed command of the vessel, and sailed it into the hands of the Union squadron blockading Charleston harbor. Singlehanded, he was thus responsible not only for the freedom of his own family, but also for that of the 12 Negro crewmen.

His daring exploit led President Abraham Lincoln to name him a pilot in the Union Navy. He was also awarded a large sum of money for what constituted the delivery of war booty, and was accorded a hero's status in the eyes of the Union forces.

In December 1863, during the siege of Charleston, Smalls took command of the

Planter and sailed it to safety—a feat for which he was promoted to captain. The only Negro to hold such a rank during the Civil War, Smalls relinquished his post in 1866, the same year his vessel was officially taken out of service.

By this time, politics loomed invitingly for an ambitious young man of Smalls' background. Regarded as a moderate, he soon won widespread support and was elected to the South Carolina State Senate, serving there from 1868 to 1870. In 1875, he began a period of Congressional service which was interrupted only by his defeat in the 1878 election. Smalls attributed his defeat to vote-counting irregularities at the polls; however, it is possible that an accusation made a year earlier to the effect that he had accepted a $5,000 bribe while a state senator had diminished his popularity. (Convicted at first, Smalls was eventually fully exonerated by Governor William Dunlap Simpson of South Carolina.)

After having been re-elected in 1880, Smalls was succeeded in Congress by another Negro, Thomas E. Miller. Remaining active in public life, Smalls became one of six Negro members of the State Constitutional Convention of 1895, and later served as duty collector for the port of Beaufort.

An outstanding Congressman, Smalls consistently supported a wide variety of progressive legislation, such as a bill to provide equal accommodations for Negroes in interstate travel, as well as an amendment designed to safeguard the rights of children born of interracial marriages.

Beyond politics, Smalls showed an active interest in military affairs, serving from 1865 to 1877 as an officer in the South Carolina State Militia, where he rose to the rank of major-general.

Seven years after the death of his first wife, Smalls was married to Annie E. Wigg on April 9, 1890. He died on February 22, 1916.

THOMAS E. MILLER
U.S. Congressman from South Carolina (1889-1891)

Born in Ferebeeville, South Carolina on June 17, 1849, Thomas Ezekiel Miller attended public schools (first in Charleston, then in Hudson, New York) before graduating from Lincoln University. Having studied for the law and then passed the bar in 1875, he set up private practice in Beaufort.

Soon, however, he began to turn an eye to politics, and held a number of local offices before being elected State Senator in 1880. After an unsuccessful campaign for the lieutenant-governorship, Miller was elected for one term to the U.S. House of Representatives. In 1895, after having been chosen a member of the South Carolina Constitutional Convention, he left politics altogether and became president of the State Colored College of Orangeburg, South Carolina, the first such institution for the higher education of the Negro in the state.

He died at his Charleston home just before his 89th birthday.

GEORGE WASHINGTON MURRAY
U.S. Congressman from South Carolina (1893-1897)

Long an advocate of free silver and a supporter of stronger federal election laws, George Washington Murray was the lone Negro representative in the 53rd U.S. Congress.

Born a slave in Rembert, South Carolina on September 22, 1853, Murray was left an orphan at Emancipation. Nonetheless, he managed to acquire a substantial education, highlighted by his completion of two years of study at South Carolina University.

A teacher for some 14 years, Murray showed little interest in politics until he was chosen Republican party chairman for Sumter County in 1888. President Benjamin Harrison subsequently appointed him Customs Inspector for the port of Charleston. In 1893, he narrowly won a seat in Congress in a disputed election.

An exponent of industrial education, Murray sought to use his office in the promotion of better schooling opportunities for Negroes in the South. He also induced Congress to print a list of those inventions which had been patented by Negroes, neglecting to mention the fact that eight of these were for his own agricultural implements.

In 1895, Murray was given a leave of absence from his Congressional duties for business and health reasons. A year later, he was returned to the 54th Congress, this time by a margin of 2,000 votes.

Murray's political aspirations were dashed when he led a faction of dissident

Negroes in what proved to be an unsuccessful breakaway from the Republican ranks. Returning to Sumter County in 1897, he began a new career in real estate. He died in Chicago on April 21, 1926.

JOHN A. HYMAN
U.S. Congressman from North Carolina
(1875-1877)

The first Negro to represent the state of North Carolina in the U.S. Congress was John A. Hyman.

Born a slave on July 23, 1840 near Warrenton, North Carolina, Hyman was sold and sent to Alabama where he was forced to remain until the end of the Civil War.

In 1868, Hyman, who was self-educated, made his first entry into politics by participating in the Constitutional Convention of North Carolina. Soon thereafter, he was selected to the state legislature and served there for six years. In 1875, he won a seat in Congress, but was not re-elected. He remained in Washington, D.C. in a minor post with the Revenue Service until his death on September 14, 1891.

JAMES E. O'HARA
U.S. Congressman from North Carolina
(1883-1887)

Born in New York City on February 26, 1844, James E. O'Hara first came to public office as an engrossing clerk for the North Carolina constitutional convention. He then served a single term in the state legislature before going on to study law at Howard University. Admitted to the bar in 1873, he became one of six Negro delegates to the state constitutional convention two years later.

O'Hara first ran for Congress in 1878, but the seat was awarded to his adversary, William Hodges Kitchin. In 1882, however, he was successful—winning by a substantial majority.

Like most other Negro Reconstruction Congressmen, O'Hara placed the civil rights issue in the forefront of his legislative program. One bill, in which he proposed to secure for Negroes equal access to public dining facilities, was shelved, but he did manage to attach a rider to an interstate commerce bill, thereby sponsoring an amendment which guaranteed to all citizens equal accommodations. He also appended an anti-discrimination clause to the Pension Appropriation Bill. In 1884, O'Hara was renominated for his Congressional post and won by a margin of 6,700 votes. During this term, he again associated himself with programs seeking to render equal justice before the law to all citizens.

That O'Hara lost in his bid for a third term was largely due to party dissension and the resurgence of the Democratic vote. Withdrawing from politics, he practiced law in New Bern, North Carolina, where he died on September 15, 1905.

HENRY P. CHEATHAM
U.S. Congressman from North Carolina
(1889-1893)

Henry Plummer Cheatham was born in Henderson, North Carolina on December 27, 1857. He won his B.A. and M.A. degrees from Shaw University, and later studied for the law, although he did not practice this profession.

Cheatham first entered public life as Register of Deeds for Vance County, North Carolina, serving in this post from 1884 to 1888. Thereafter, he was principal of the State Normal School at Plymouth, which was later incorporated into Elizabeth City State Teachers College.

In 1888, Cheatham ran successfully as a Republican candidate for the Second Congressional District of North Carolina. He won re-election in 1890, but was defeated in his try for a third term.

Henry P. Cheatham

In 1901, Cheatham returned to North Carolina, settling in Oxford where he became superintendent of a Negro orphan asylum. He helped raise money for this institution, and served its interests unstintingly until his death on November 29, 1935.

GEORGE H. WHITE
U.S. Congressman from North Carolina
(1897-1901)

The last Negro Congressman in the aftermath of Reconstruction, George H. White was born in Rosedale, North Carolina on December 18, 1852. After graduating from Howard University in 1877, he taught school in his native state and studied law. Licensed in 1879 to practice in all state courts, he proved to be a brilliant lawyer, winning several cases against the best of his white colleagues.

In 1880, White entered politics—first as a member of the North Carolina House of Representatives and, four years later, as state senator. At the end of his two-year term, he was chosen state solicitor for the Second Judicial District.

While in Congress, White championed the cause of Negro constitutional liberties, and was particularly outspoken in denouncing lynching and mob law. White left Congress in 1901, and was the last Negro to serve in the House until Oscar De Priest was elected from Illinois in 1928.

Once out of politics, White turned his energies to the establishment of an all-Negro residential community—eventually known as Whitesboro after its founder—near Cape May in New Jersey. He later retired to law practice in Philadelphia where he died on December 28, 1918.

BENJAMIN S. TURNER
U.S. Congressman from Alabama
(1871-1873)

Born a slave on March 17, 1825 in Halifax, North Carolina, Benjamin S. Turner was taken at an early age to Alabama where he was emancipated and then given the rudiments of a private education. As a young man, he served as tax collector of Dallas County and councilman in Salem before becoming a prosperous livery stable owner.

In September of 1870, having manifested a growing interest in politics, he was unanimously nominated by the Republican party for the Congressional seat from the 1st District of Selma, Alabama.

During his term of office, Turner introduced several bills onto the House floor, none of which was enacted, however. Although renominated in 1872, Turner was the victim of a split within his own party, which led to his defeat and eventual abandonment of politics.

Turner returned to his home in Alabama and resumed his former business activities. He died on March 1, 1894.

JAMES T. RAPIER
U.S. Congressman from Alabama
(1873-1875)

Active in both the fields of politics and of labor, James T. Rapier was born in Florence, Alabama on November 13, 1837. Rapier's father, a successful planter, engaged a private tutor to educate his son, who later studied at Montreal College in Canada, at the University of Glasgow in Scotland, and at Franklin College in Nashville, Tennessee. Although reputedly trained as a lawyer, he never practiced this profession.

Shortly after the Civil War, Rapier (by then a successful cotton planter in his own right) became involved in state politics, although he was defeated the first time he ran for office as a candidate for Secretary of State in 1870.

Rapier was later sent to Montgomery as one of an enterprising group of reformers who sought to rewrite the state constitution so as to include provisions for universal suffrage and free public schooling. Instrumental in the organization of Alabama's first Republican party, he served as its vice-president before turning his attention to the field of labor. Urging urban workers and rural sharecroppers to organize, Rapier was a key force in setting up Alabama's first Negro labor convention, which he himself served as chairman.

Having spawned a vigorous labor movement in his home state, Rapier next concentrated on establishing a newspaper through which he could develop a platform voicing his strongly libertarian sentiments. To this end, he served as editor and publisher of the *Montgomery Sentinel*, which not only strengthened the solidarity of the Negro community, but also created a greater rapport between the two races in Alabama.

Rapier was first nominated as a Congressional candidate at the Republican party convention of 1872. He won election by some 3,000 votes, and went to Washington, D.C. where he worked for the passage of such progressive legislation as the Civil Rights Act of 1875.

Rapier's Congressional career came to a close with the rapid rise of the Ku Klux Klan and the ascension to power of a Democratic bloc which eventually came to control Alabama's politics.

In 1879, he represented his state at the World's Fair in Paris and later served as United States Revenue Officer to Alabama. He died in Montgomery on May 31, 1882.

JEREMIAH HARALSON
U.S. Congressman from Alabama
(1875-1877)

At one time considered the most influential Negro in the state of Alabama, Jeremiah Haralson was elected to the 44th Congress, serving in office from 1875 to 1877.

Born a slave in Muscogee County, Georgia on April 1, 1846, Haralson was basically self-educated. After Emancipation, he moved to Alabama where, in 1868, he was defeated in his first attempt to win a Congressional seat.

Once in office, Haralson introduced several bills, but none was passed. In addition to this, he was accused of fraud, and was forced to submit to a runoff election which he won, however, with a safe majority.

An ardent defender of the principal of amnesty, Haralson encountered widespread opposition from Alabama party regulars who accused him of trying to maintain too close a relationship with Jefferson Davis, the former president of the Confederate States of America. Among his chief opponents was James T. Rapier, the Negro Congressman whom he succeeded.

Defeated in the 1878 and 1884 elections, Haralson spent his last days in Colorado where he was killed in a hunting mishap.

JOSIAH T. WALLS
U.S. Congressman from Florida
(1871-1877)

The only Negro Congressman from the state of Florida, Josiah T. Walls was born free in Winchester, Virginia on December 30, 1842. He received his early education in his adopted state and was a successful farmer when the Civil War broke out.

Drafted into the Confederate Army, he served in an artillery battery until he was taken prisoner by Union forces during a battle fought at Yorktown. He soon joined the Northern army and, by the end of hostilities, had risen to the rank of sergeant-major.

Walls then returned to Florida and to farming, but it was not long before he entered politics and served a term as a member of the Florida legislature.

Elected to the U.S. Congress in 1871, he represented the state during the next five years, although his tenure was interrupted because of a contested election and the opposition of the governor.

As a Congressman, Walls was in favor of granting military support to insurgent Cubans in their revolt against Spain, which had not only introduced African slaves on the island's sugar and tobacco plantations, but had also treated the original Indian inhabitants with great brutality. (Cuba was eventually granted independence in 1898, and became a U.S. protectorate in 1902.)

His Congressional career ended, Walls returned to private life as a planter, although he kept in contact with politics through his staunch advocacy of Rutherford B. Hayes for the presidency. When a severe frost one year almost ruined him financially, he accepted the post of superintendent of a farm on the campus of Tallahassee State College, remaining there until his death on May 5, 1905.

JEFFERSON F. LONG
U.S. Congressman from Georgia
(1869-1871)

The only Negro from the state of Georgia ever to serve in Congress, Jefferson Franklin Long was born a slave on March 3, 1836 near Knoxville, Georgia. Primarily self-educated, he moved to Macon at an early age. There, he found work with a merchant tailor and eventually saved enough money to open a similar shop of his own.

At the close of the Civil War, Long showed an interest in politics and rapidly rose to a position of influence within the local Republican party structure. He won his party's Congressional nomination in 1869, and was elected to the 41st Congress where he campaigned vigorously against the spread of lynch law in Georgia. He also fought hard for enforcement of the 15th Amendment, for universal suffrage in the District of Columbia, and for several other bills in the national interest.

Long retired at the end of his term in March 1871, returning to Macon where he devoted the last decades of his life to his prosperous tailoring business. He did attend the Southern Republican Convention in Chattanooga in 1874, and also served as a delegate to the Republican National Convention of 1880.

He died in Macon on February 4, 1900.

CHARLES E. NASH
U.S. Congressman from Louisiana (1875-1877)

Born May 23, 1844 in Opelousas, Louisiana, Charles Edmund Nash grew up to become the only Negro ever to represent the state of Louisiana in the U.S. House of Representatives.

Having had the chance for only a limited education, he earned his living as a bricklayer until his enlistment in the Union Army in 1863. A member of the famed *Chasseurs d'Afrique*, Nash lost a leg during the storming of Fort Blakely. After his discharge as a sergeant-major, he was named U.S. Inspector of Customs for his native state.

Elected to the 44th Congress, Nash returned to Louisiana in 1876 at the end of his first term but, though renominated, failed in his bid for re-election. He thereupon permanently withdrew from the political arena, and became postmaster of a small Louisiana town. Soon after his retirement from this post, he moved to New Orleans where he died on June 21, 1913.

JOHN R. LYNCH
U.S. Congressman from Mississippi (1873-1877; 1881-1883)

The first Negro to preside over a national convention of the Republican party, Mississippi Congressman John R. Lynch was elected to the House of Representatives on three separate occasions—in 1873, 1875 and 1881.

Born a slave in Concordia Parish, Louisiana on September 10, 1847, Lynch attended evening classes in Natchez, Mississippi, acquiring a sound education. In 1869, he was named a justice of the peace for Adams County. That same year, he was elected to the Mississippi State Legislature where he ultimately served as Speaker of the House.

From 1871 to 1889, a period which encompassed his Congressional service, Lynch was chairman of the Executive Committee of the Republican party. On three occasions, he was a delegate to that party's national convention. Understandably, therefore, the party paid him a unique tribute by allowing him to preside over its presidential nominating convention in 1884.

In 1889, Lynch served under Benjamin Harrison as Fourth Auditor of the United States Treasury, but declined this same appointment when it was offered him four years later by Grover Cleveland. In 1896, he campaigned vigorously on behalf of presidential candidate William McKinley who showed his gratitude by naming him U.S. Paymaster during the Spanish-American War.

Lynch retired to private law practice in 1911, the same year in which he married Mrs. Cora E. Williamson of Chicago. (His first wife, Emma W. Somerville, whom he married in 1884, had died.)

During his later years, he wrote two books: *The Facts of the Reconstruction* and *Some Historical Errors of James Ford Rhodes*. He died in Chicago on November 2, 1939.

JOHN MERCER LANGSTON
U.S. Congressman from Virginia (1889-1891)

John Mercer Langston, U.S. Congressman from Virginia, was born in Louisa County, Virginia on December 14, 1829 of Negro, Indian and English ancestry.

Upon the death of his father Ralph Quarles, an estate owner, young Langston was emancipated and sent to Ohio, where he was given over to the care of a friend of his father. Langston spent his childhood there, attending private school in Cincinnati before graduating from Oberlin College in 1849. Four years later, after getting his degree from the theological department of Oberlin, he took up the study of law and was admitted to the Ohio bar in 1854, the same year as that of his marriage to Carolina M. Wall.

Langston began his practice in Brownhelm, Ohio. He was chosen in 1855 to serve as clerk of this township by the Liberty Party. During the Civil War, he served as a recruiting agent for Negro servicemen, helping to raise such famed regiments as the 54th and 55th Massachusetts, and the 5th Ohio.

After the war, Langston served as inspector-general of the Freedmen's Bureau and, from 1869 to 1876, as dean and vice president of the newly incorporated Howard University. In 1877, he was named Minister Resident to Haiti and Chargé d'Affaires to Santo Domingo, remaining in diplomatic and consular service until 1885.

Soon after his return to the United States and to his law practice, he was named president of the Virginia Normal and Collegiate Institute. In 1888, he won election to Congress from Virginia, but was not seated for two years until certain vote-counting irregularities had been thoroughly investigated.

Defeated in his bid for a second term, Langston nonetheless remained interested in politics. In 1894, he wrote an autobiography, *From the Virginia Plantation to the National Capital.* (Eleven years earlier, he had already published a volume of his speeches, *Freedom and Citizenship.*)

Langston died on November 15, 1897.

OSCAR DE PRIEST
U.S. Congressman from Illinois
(1929-1934)

Oscar De Priest was not only the first Negro to win a seat in the U.S. House of Representatives in the 20th century, but also the first to be elected from a Northern state. His election was in part attributable to the large-scale migration of Negroes to urban areas in the North in the wake of the Great Depression.

Born to Alexander R. and Mary (Karsner) De Priest on March 9, 1871 in Florence, Alabama, De Priest moved to Kansas with his family at the age of six. His formal education there consisted of business and bookkeeping classes which he completed before running away to Dayton, Ohio with two white friends. By the year 1889, he had reached Chicago and become a painter and master decorator.

Shortly after marrying Jessie Williams on February 28, 1898, De Priest sought a career in politics. Having already amassed a fortune in real estate and the stock market, he finally won Republican backing in 1904 in what proved to be a successful bid for the office of Cook County Commissioner. He was re-elected to this post in 1906.

Although he was chosen as an alternate delegate to the Republican convention of 1908, De Priest saw his political ambitions largely thwarted until 1915, at which time he became Chicago's first Negro alderman. During the 1920's, he aligned himself with a number of conflicting interests, some of which cut across party lines. In 1928, he was a candidate for the post of Republican committeeman for the Third Ward, and a prospective delegate to the Republican National Convention. A supporter of Martin B. Madden for Congress, De Priest saw a prime opportunity materialize for himself with the sudden death of Madden after his election. This enabled De Priest to wage a successful campaign for the vacant seat.

The unofficial spokesman for the 11 million Negroes in the United States during this period, De Priest faced a formidable challenge, particularly since the country was undergoing a profound political and economic transformation during the Depression years. Though sincerely desirous of improving the Negro's lot, he found himself in a difficult partisan position and obliged to shift his support from Republican to Democratic candidates on the local level. On the national level, he usually voted with his party. In 1934, he was defeated by Arthur Mitchell, the first Negro Democrat elected to serve in a U.S. Congress.

De Priest remained active in public life, serving from 1943 to 1947 as alderman of the Third Ward in Chicago. His final withdrawal from politics came about after a sharp dispute with his own party. A member of the Presbyterian Church and of the Grand Lodge of Elks, De Priest returned to his real estate business in Chicago, where he died on May 12, 1951.

ARTHUR W. MITCHELL
U.S. Congressman from Illinois
(1934-1942)

The 1934 victory of Arthur W. Mitchell, the first Negro Democrat ever elected to serve in Congress, was emblematic of the first major shift in Negro voting sentiment in the United States since the days of Reconstruction. Conversely, Oscar De Priest, the man whom he defeated, was the last Negro Republican to serve in the House. (Since then, there have been six other Negro Democrats in the lower chamber of the legislature.)

Born to slave parents in 1883 in Chambers County, Alabama, Mitchell was educated at Tuskegee Institute, and at Columbia and Harvard Universities. By 1929, he had founded Armstrong Agricultural School in West Butler, Alabama, and become a wealthy landowner and a lawyer with a thriving practice in Washington, D.C. When he left the nation's capital that year, it was with the avowed purpose of entering politics and becoming a representative from Illinois.

Mitchell won Democratic approval only after Harry Baker (who had defeated him in the primary) died suddenly, leaving the nomination vacant.

Aided by the overwhelming national sentiment for the Democratic party during this period, he unseated the Republican incumbent De Priest by the slender margin of some 3,000 votes.

An effective lobbyist for civil rights legislation, Mitchell dedicated himself in Congress to exposing the injustices perpetrated on the Negro, and sought to enlist the support of his white colleagues on both sides of the aisle.

However, his most significant victory on behalf of civil rights came, not in the legislative chamber, but in the courts. In 1937, Mitchell had brought suit against the Chicago and Rock Island Railroad after having been forced to leave his first-class accommodations en route to Hot Springs, Arkansas, and sit in a "Jim Crow" car. He argued his own case before the Supreme Court in 1941, and won a decision which declared "Jim Crow" practices illegal.

A year later, Mitchell retired from Congress and settled on his estate near Petersburg, Virginia. He lives there now with his second wife Clara. His first wife, Annie Harris, and his only son, Arthur, Jr. are both buried on the estate.

WILLIAM L. DAWSON
U.S. Congressman from Illinois
(1943-)

William L. Dawson represented the First Congressional District of Illinois, and was in office longer than any other Negro currently in Congress.

A native of Albany, Georgia where he was born on April 26, 1886, Dawson received his early education locally and later graduated *magna cum laude* from Fisk University in Nashville, Tennessee. Interested at first in law, Dawson studied at Kent College before joining the U.S. Expeditionary Forces in 1917 as an officer. He saw combat with the 365th Infantry in the famous Argonne offensive, and was wounded and gassed while on the front lines.

At the end of the war, Dawson went back to law, completing his studies at Northwestern University and opening up a practice in Illinois. After nine years as an attorney, he tried his hand at politics, running unsuccessfully as a Republican candidate for Congress in 1928. A year later, while serving as Republican State Committeeman in the First Congressional District, he was called upon to manage Judge John H. Lyle's mayoralty campaign.

Congressman William L. Dawson

Dawson's first political success came in 1935, when he was elected alderman. While serving on the City Council, he crossed party lines and became an avid supporter of President Franklin D. Roosevelt. In 1940, Dawson was elected Democratic committeeman from the Second Ward, and thus given an official seat in the governing councils of his party. Two years later, he won a seat in the House of Representatives (78th Congress).

In 1944, Dawson was appointed Assistant Chairman of the Democratic National Committee, and soon became the first Negro to be elected as its Vice Chairman. He campaigned on behalf of President Harry S. Truman, whose surprise victory over Thomas E. Dewey was later attributed, at least in part, to the support of the Negro electorate. He was thus able to see to it that, for the first time, Negroes were invited in more than token numbers to the Inaugural Ball, a practice which has since been taken for granted.

Dawson has occupied a number of key Congressional posts. During the 81st Congress, he was Chairman of the House Committee on Expenditures in the Executive Departments, and later became Chairman of the Committee on Government Operations—considered to be among the most important on Capitol Hill.

Investigations by the Dawson committee have resulted in substantial government savings of direct benefit to the American taxpayer. Since 1957, the committee has been engaged in an annual survey of U.S. property holdings abroad, and in processing all bills which deal with budgetary matters other than those concerning appropriations.

Married to the former Miss Nellie Brown for over 40 years, Dawson is the father of two children, William and Barbara Ann. He is a member of several social and fraternal organizations, and the holder of several honorary academic degrees.

ADAM CLAYTON POWELL, JR.
U.S. Congressman from New York (1945-)

Congressman from New York's 18th District, Chairman of the House Committee on Education and Labor, and pastor of the world's largest congregation at Harlem's Abyssinian Baptist Church, Adam Clayton Powell was once the most controversial Negro politician in the United States.

Born in 1908 to Mattie Fletcher and Adam Clayton Powell, Sr., Adam, Jr. was bred in New York City, and attended high school there before entering Colgate University.

The young Powell launched his career as a crusader for reform during the depth of the Depression. He forced several large corporations to drop their unofficial bans on employing Negroes, while, at the same time, directing a kitchen and relief operation which fed, clothed and provided fuel for thousands of Harlem's needy and destitute.

Congressman Adam Clayton Powell, Jr.

In 1930, he organized a demonstration which was instrumental in persuading the officials of Harlem Hospital to integrate their medical and nursing staffs. He also helped many Negroes find employment along Harlem's "main stem," 125th Street, and campaigned against the city's bus lines which were discriminating against Negro drivers and mechanics.

When Powell, Sr. retired from Abyssinian in 1937, his son, who had already served as manager and assistant pastor there, was named his successor. Within a year, the new pastor was commended for his outstanding work by Shaw University, which awarded him an honorary doctor of divinity.

In 1939, Powell served as chairman of the Coordinating Committee on Employment, which organized a picket line before the executive offices of the World's Fair in the Empire State Building and eventually succeeded in getting employment for hundreds of Negroes out at the Fair. In addition, Powell sought to provide better hospital services for Negroes, to improve conditions in Harlem tenements, and to better the job potential of the community's citizens. At one point, too, he turned his attention to the problem of higher education, protesting that the city's college faculties were not integrated.

Powell won a seat on the New York City Council in 1941 with the third highest number of votes ever cast for a candidate in municipal elections. In 1942, he turned to journalism for a second time (he had already been on the staff of the New York *Evening Post* in 1934), and published and edited the weekly *People's Voice* which he called "the largest Negro tabloid in the world."

In 1945, Powell went to Washington, D.C. as the sole Congressional representative of a community of 300,000, 89% of whom were Negro. Identified almost at once as "Mr. Civil Rights," he encountered a whole host of discriminatory procedures. To begin with, he could not rent a room in downtown Washington, nor could he attend a movie in which his famed wife Hazel Scott had been starred. Within Congress itself, he was not authorized to use such communal facilities as dining rooms, steam baths, showers and barber shops. Powell met these rebuffs head on by making use of all such facilities, and by insisting that his entire staff follow his lead.

As a freshman legislator, Powell was a firm believer in the importance of being 'radical.' He engaged in several fiery debates with arch-segregationists, fought hard for the abolition of discriminatory practices at U.S. military installations around the world, and sought—through the controversial Powell amendment—to deny federal funds to any project where discrimination existed. (This amendment eventually became part of the Flanagan School Lunch Bill, making Powell the first Negro Congressman since Reconstruction to have legislation passed by both houses.)

Powell likewise sponsored legislation advocating federal aid to education, a minimum-wage scale, and greater benefits for the hard-core unemployed. He lost no time in drawing attention to certain long-overlooked discriminatory practices on Capitol Hill itself, and in effecting their immediate elimination. It was Powell who first demanded that a Negro journalist be allowed to sit in the Senate and House press galleries. It was Powell who introduced the first Jim Crow transportation legislation, as well as the first bill to prohibit segregation in the Armed Forces. And it was Powell again who finally forced Congress to recognize the existence of discrimination in such organizations as the Daughters of the American Revolution (DAR). In fact, at one point in his career, the *Congressional Record* reported that the House Committee on Education and Labor had processed more important legislation than any other major committee.

In 1960, Powell, as senior member of this committee, became its chairman. Since then, he has had a hand in the development and passage of such significant legislation as the Minimum Wage Bill of 1961, the Manpower Development and Training Act, the Anti-Poverty Bill, the Juvenile Delinquency Act, the Vocational Educational Act, and the National Defense Education Act. (In all, the Powell committee has helped pass 48 laws involving a total outlay of 14 billion dollars.)

During his career in Congress, Powell has attended several conferences abroad as a spokesman for the United States. These include the Afro-Asian Conference in Bandung (1955) and the independence celebration of Ghana (1957).

He is particularly proud of the fact that he was the first Northerner, regardless of race, to endorse Lyndon B. Johnson for the presidency. In 1964, he claimed to have covered more than 12,000 miles for the Johnson-Humphrey ticket at his own expense. That same year, he also amassed the largest plurality he had ever obtained in a Congressional election.

In 1967, the controversies and irregularities surrounding Powell's Congressional career finally led to censure in the House and a vote to exclude him from his seat in the 90th Congress. The House based its decision on the allegation that he had misused public funds and was in contempt on the New York courts due to a lengthy and involved defamation case which had resulted in a trial for civil and criminal contempt. Despite his exclusion, Powell was readmitted to the 91st Congress in 1968. In mid 1969, the Supreme Court ruled that the House had violated the Constitution by excluding Powell from membership, but left open the questions of his loss of 22 years seniority and the Chairmanship of the powerful Education and Labor Committee. Also unresolved were the $25,000 fine levied against him, and the matter of back pay.

In 1970, at primary time, it appeared that Harlem's voters had rejected Powell's erratic and self-indulgent behavior, naming State Assemblyman Charles Rangel to run on the Democratic slate for the House seat which Powell has held since 1944. Powell, however, filed to run for the seat as an independent.

CHARLES C. DIGGS
U.S. Congressman from Michigan
(1954-)

The senior Negro representative from Michigan, Charles C. Diggs is a native of Detroit, where he was born on December 2, 1922. Diggs was educated locally, and already showed great promise in high school where he excelled as a debater and compiled an outstanding academic record.

Enrolled thereafter at the University of Michigan, he won the university's oratorical championship during his second year there. In 1942, he transferred to Fisk University in Nashville, Tennessee before being drafted into the Air Force. During the following two years, he attended a number of service schools, and was ultimately commissioned as a second lieutenant and assigned as an administrative officer to Tuskegee Army Air Field in Alabama. He remained there until he was honorably discharged on June 1, 1945.

Back in Detroit, Diggs enrolled at the Wayne State University School of Mortuary Science. At the same time, he was radio commentator on a program cosponsored by the House of Diggs, the family business which has come to be the largest funeral home in Michigan.

Diggs began his political career in 1951 when he was elected to the State Senate. Compiling a fine legislative record, particularly in the area of civil rights and in business and labor relations as well, Diggs won the admiration of several key figures in the Democratic party and, by 1953, was in a position to campaign for a seat on the Detroit Common Council. He did not win, but his political star was fast on the rise, nonetheless.

In the August 1954 primary, having defeated the favored incumbent, Diggs became the Democratic candidate for Congress from the 13th District. After his election, he quickly familiarized himself with life on Capitol Hill. By identifying himself with the problems of the Southern Negro, he soon came to be known as 'Mississippi's Congressman-at-large.' An avid supporter of voter-registration programs and an ever-vigilant watchdog on the lookout for discrimination in federally financed programs throughout the South, Diggs led a fact-finding group on a tour of Selma, Alabama in February of 1965, interviewing both residents and officials, and publicizing his findings for the benefit of appropriate governmental agencies. Diggs has also been particularly effective in promoting equal treatment in the Armed Forces. By means of committee reports, he has often brought the legitimate grievances of Negro servicemen to the attention of the Secretary of Defense, and persuaded him to rectify prevailing patterns of *de facto* discrimination on military installations.

Congressman Charles C. Diggs receives a commendation from a Washington, D.C. Boy Scout.

ROBERT N. C. NIX
U.S. Congressman from Pennsylvania (1958-)

Born in Orangeburg, South Carolina on August 9, 1905, Robert Nix is the son of Sylvia and Nelson Nix. After attending a private elementary school in Harlem and Townsend Harris Hall High School (a prep school for CCNY with exceptionally high academic requirements), he went on to Lincoln University where he was a "straight A" student, and the University of Pennsylvania Law School.

Having passed his bar examination, Nix was allowed to practice in all the courts of Pennsylvania, as well as in the U.S. District and Circuit Courts. Specifically, he was a special deputy attorney general for Pennsylvania (Escheats Division of the State Department of Revenue) from 1934 to 1936 and, from 1958 to 1960, served in a similar post under Governor David Lawrence.

After gaining much valuable experience in Philadelphia ward politics, Nix was elected in 1958 to fill the unexpired term of Congressman Earl Chudoff, and thus became the 26th Negro Congressman in United States history. Since then, he has served on the Foreign Affairs, Post Office and Civil Service committees, and as chairman of the Mexico-United States Interparliamentary Group.

A long-time liberal, Nix was one of the first Congressmen to speak out in support of the Montgomery bus boycott, and has continued to support the civil rights movement in all of its major phases. He was regarded by Speaker of the House Sam Rayburn, Jr. as one of the most brilliant men he had ever known.

Nix, married to the former Ethel Lanier of Washington, D.C., and the father of one son, resides in Philadelphia, where he is a member of numerous professional and civic organizations.

AUGUSTUS F. HAWKINS
U.S. Congressman from California
(1963-)

Augustus Hawkins was born in Shreveport, Louisiana on August 31, 1907, and moved to California at the age of 12. He went to high school there, and pursued higher education at the University of California and at the University of Southern California.

Hawkins' professional career was begun in Los Angeles County in the field of juvenile delinquency and its prevention. In 1934, having been elected to the State Assembly, he authored a successful bill setting up a coordinating agency so as to deal in a more effective manner with one of the major problems of our day, juvenile crime.

For the next 30 years, before being elected Democratic representative to Congress from the 21st District, Hawkins was an ardent supporter of legislation in the fields of civil rights, labor relations, health, welfare and housing. Nothing bears more striking witness to this fact than the more than 300 laws on the California statute books which either bear his name or acknowledge his co-authorship.

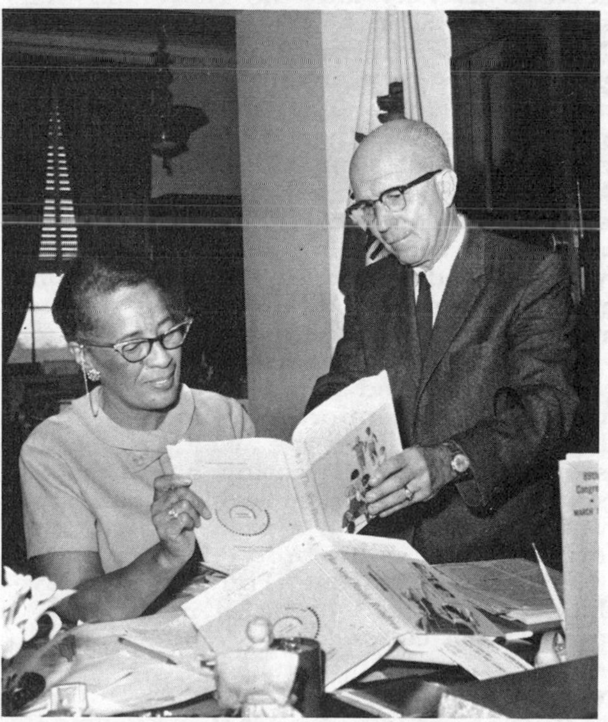

Congressman Augustus F. Hawkins examines a new textbook with a member of his staff.

In private life, Hawkins has been engaged in the insurance and automobile appliance business, as well as in real estate. He is a Mason, and an active member of many civic, church and social groups in his state.

JOHN CONYERS, JR.
U.S. Congressman from Michigan
(1965-)

Congressman John Conyers is the first Negro to serve on the House Judiciary Committee.

Conyers is a native of Detroit, Michigan, where he was born on May 16, 1929. He received his B.A. and LL.B. degrees from Wayne State University, and served his political apprenticeship for three years as legislative assistant to Congressman John Dingell.

Before his election to Congress, Conyers was a referee for the Michigan Workmen's Compensation Department, and senior partner in the firm of Conyers, Bell and Townsend. Active in union affairs, he was general counsel for the Trade Union Leadership Council; a member of Local 900 of the United Auto Workers (UAW), and of Local 42 of the AFL-CIO. He also belonged to the Committee on Political Education in Michigan's 15th Congressional District.

In 1963, President John F. Kennedy appointed Conyers to the National Lawyers Committee for Civil Rights Under Law, an organization designed to foster greater racial tolerance in the legal field. Conyers later served as a member of the Committee to Assist Southern Lawyers (CASL), and represented a number of clients who had been arrested in connection with alleged voter-registration irregularities throughout the South.

Conyers encountered far greater difficulty in gaining the Democratic nomination in Michigan's First Congressional District than in defeating his eventual Republican opponent, Robert Blackwell. Conyers won the primary election by a mere 45 votes, but, aided by his father, a trade unionist, and a group of dedicated volunteers, he then proceeded to trounce Blackwell, emerging with 138,000 votes, or 84% of the total cast. (He also had the highest plurality—113,000—in the state, and the seventh highest of anyone returned to Congress.)

Conyers was co-sponsor of the Johnson Administration's Medicare program, and a strong supporter of the 1965 Voting Rights Bill.

LOUIS STOKES
U.S. Congressman from Ohio
(1969-)

The older brother of Cleveland's mayor-elect Carl Stokes, Congressman Louis Stokes skillfully engineered his 1968 victory by welding together a successful coalition embracing both the ghetto poor and the affluent suburbanite in the redrawn 21st Ohio Congressional District (Cleveland's East Side, Garfield Heights, and Newburgh Heights). Showing a commendable understanding of the conditions and fragilities of both worlds brought Stokes some 86,000 votes as compared with only 31,000 for his black Republican opponent, Charles Lucas.

Both Stokes and Lucas had been allies after 1965, the year the Ohio legislature divided the 21st District in such a way that black voting strength was largely emasculated. Under such an arrangement, it would have been virtually impossible for a black Congressional candidate to develop a stronghold and capture a House seat. Lucas then brought suit before the U.S. Supreme Court protesting the gerrymander, and was joined by Stokes in arguing the case. The merits of their argument were so convincing that the Court readily instructed the legislature to shelve its original plan, whereupon the Ohioans hatched a new redistricting setup in which the black electorate formed 65% of the voting total. The victory severed the temporary alliance between Stokes and Lucas, inasmuch as both were anxious to campaign for the opening.

Louis Stokes on Capitol Hill

A native of Cleveland, Stokes endured poverty as a child, although he was always enterprising and energetic. He is still remembered by many in the Outhwaite homes as the shoe-shine boy who cheerfully prowled the project, taking in extra money to help his widowed mother, Mrs. Louise Stokes, and his younger brother, Carl. Stokes did other odd jobs too—everything from peddling newspapers to selling clothes in the local Army-Navy store.

Stokes enlisted in the Army after finishing high school and used the GI Bill to finance higher education at Western Reserve University and the Cleveland-Marshall Law School. He later joined the NAACP as a crusading lawyer whose prominence in anti-discrimination lawsuits won him popular favor among the ghetto poor. Whether it was a civil rights marcher protesting discrimination, a housewife seeking action from an unresponsive school board, or even a black nationalist contending with police, Stokes was on hand to defend the Constitutional rights of arrested blacks, often without remuneration.

Congenial and experienced, Stokes has always impressed people with his ability to circulate comfortably among strait-laced businessmen as well as casual, street-wise billiard parlor habitues. His smooth style and personable manner are undeniable assets to a man who can now expect to act as his brother's alter ego on the Washington scene. The voice of Cleveland, and indeed of cities in general, is a heartbeat closer to the White House.

WILLIAM CLAY
U.S. Congressman from Missouri
(1969-)

Youthful, ambitious, and intense—Con-

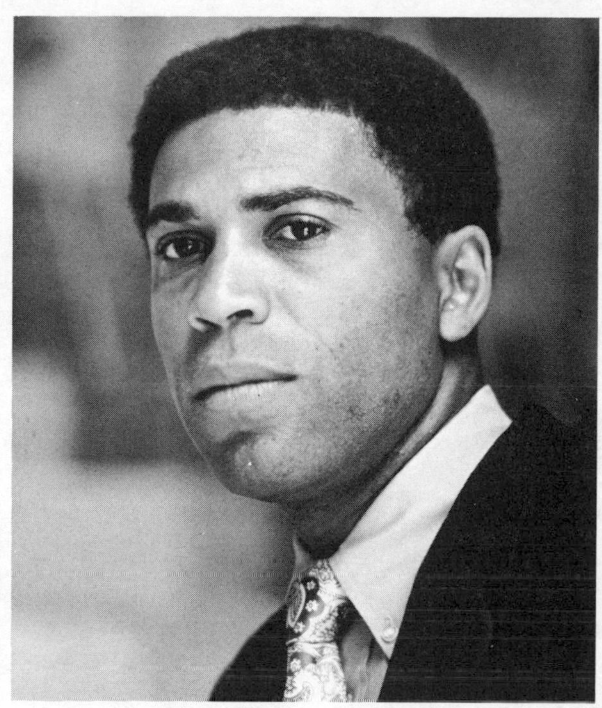

Rep. William Clay

gressman-elect William Clay is the first black man to represent the state of Missouri in the U.S. Congress. Nearly two-thirds of the 120,000 people who voted in St. Louis' First Congressional District selected Clay over his black Republican opponent, Curtis Crawford, a turncoat Democrat who actually ran a "law and order" campaign and advocated cuts in federal expenditures. It was a program, in Clay's words, "that any white racist would run on."

Rather than seeking to assume a moderate position, Clay surveyed the scene, decided he didn't really need white votes to gain victory (55% of the registered voters in the district are black, 10% less than the district's black population), and so unhesitatingly assumed the label and stance of a "civil rights activist." His literature, his campaign oratory, and his lapel buttons all carried this self-imposed description.

Born in 1931 in the lower end of what is now St. Louis' First District, Clay was educated locally, and later took a degree in political science at St. Louis University, where he was one of four blacks in a class of 1100. After serving in the Army until 1955, Clay became active in a host of civil rights organizations, including the NAACP Youth Council and CORE. During this time, he worked as a cardiographic aide, bus driver, and insurance agent, but his heart had already surrendered to politics, at least judging from the number of demonstrations and picket lines he had joined.

In 1959, and again in 1963, Clay was elected alderman of the predominantly black 26th Ward. During his first term, he served nearly four months of a nine-month jail sentence for disruptive demonstrations at a local bank. Meanwhile, on the outside, the number of white collar jobs held by blacks in St. Louis banks began a steady ascent from a low of 16 to a high of 700. In 1964, Clay stepped down from his alderman's post to run for election as Ward Committeeman, winning handily and being reelected in 1968.

Clay's election platform in 1969 included a number of progressive, even radical, planks. For one thing, he advocated that all penal institutions make provisions for the creation of facilities in which married prisoners could set up house with their spouses for the duration of their sentences. For another, he branded most testing procedures and diploma requirements, as well as references to arrest records and to periods of unemployment as unnecessary obstacles complicating the path of a prospective employee. In his view, a demonstrated willingness to work and an acceptance of responsibility should be the major criteria determining one's selection for a job. All other "irrelevant" factors should be eliminated.

Clay's last job before being elected to Congress was as race relations coordinator for Steamfitters Union Local 562. Subjected to considerable criticism from other St. Louis blacks who labelled the union a racist body, Clay pointed out that dramatic changes in the hiring practices of the union since he had joined it in 1966 were responsible for the employment of 30 black steamfitters in St. Louis—30 more than the union had previously put to work. Still, Clay conceded that the high-paying job had led him to reduce his active involvement with the civil rights struggle to some degree.

In assuming his new office on the banks of the Potomac, however, Clay plans to pick up the tempo in this area, to speak aggressively, and even possibly to pattern himself after his Harlem idol, Adam Clayton Powell. "We've been too quiet since Powell left," says Clay. "He had a kind of genius that's needed." Looking back, Powell too was elected to Congress in his late 30's. Could the coincidence possibly be an omen for Clay's career?

Shirley Chisholm, the first black woman to serve in the House

SHIRLEY CHISHOLM
U.S. Congresswoman from New York (1969-)

Charisma, spunk, determination — these are words that are frequently used to characterize the manner and personality of the first black woman to occupy a seat in the U.S. House of Representatives: Mrs. Shirley Chisholm. Since her opponent James Farmer was also a Negro, sex and political affiliation were far more important factors influencing the outcome of the 1968 election than race. Farmer allegedly sought to create a whisper campaign around the theme that black women had already exercised far too much influence on the fate of black communities and on the development of black self-assertiveness, but the issue, if it had any relevance at all, did not succeed in swaying much public opinion. Members of the newly created predominantly black and Puerto Rican 12th Congressional District chose the dynamic Mrs. Chisholm over Farmer by a more than 3-1 margin.

Mrs. Chisholm originally entered public life only in response to local pleas for an honest and conscientious public servant in the New York State Assembly. While there, she sponsored the SEEK program which offers qualified students from minority groups the opportunity to obtain college-level training even if they do not yet have high-school diplomas. She also introduced legislation to establish publicly supported day-care centers and to extend unemployment insurance to domestic workers.

Her decision to run for higher office was based in part on the continued appeals of the common people of her district, the people who had known her since she was a child, the people who trusted her and with whom she identified, the people whose problems she knew because she had chosen to remain in Bedford-Stuyvesant, rather than moving on to more affluent surroundings.

Once she had defeated State Senator William C. Thompson, the hand-picked black candidate endorsed for the post by powerful Democratic county boss, Stanley Steingut, she felt she had learned the ropes and weathered the infighting of intra-party politics. Thereafter, she regarded herself as largely unbeatable, even though former CORE National Chairman James Farmer, a figure of national prominence, was her announced foe. Farmer, however, was unknown to the people of the district, and was quickly labelled a carpetbagger whose Republican-Liberal affiliations stamped him as a candidate with rich backing, stuffy airs, and an inappropriate style.

Born Shirley St. Hill in 1926, Representative Chisholm is descended from West Indian immigrant laborers (her mother was a seamstress from Barbados and her father, a native of British Guiana, worked in a burlap factory). One of three sisters, she was sent to Barbados at the age of three to live with other immediate family members while her parents struggled to save money for the girls' education. At age 11, Shirley returned to Brooklyn, attending grade school and high school before earning a scholarship to pursue higher education. A graduate of both Brooklyn College and Columbia University, holder of a masters in elementary education, Mrs. Chisholm worked as a nursery school teacher, director of a daycare center, and consultant for the New York Department of Social Services before entering public life as a state representative in Albany.

After her election, Mrs. Chisholm indicated her early preference for committee assignments which would reflect her interests and areas of expertise (education, labor management, and inner-city conditions in general), and take advantage of her experience in the social services. When saddled with a committee assignment in the area of agriculture, she not only openly balked at the idea, but complained outspokenly of the gross misuse of her talents. Other committees in which she expressed interest were the Foreign Relations Committee (she feels strongly that the emergence of both the African and the Afro-American are inextricably linked) and the Postal and Civil Service Committee (she believes that black people have made an unusually high human investment in this area without reaping some of the more obvious rewards available to those who climb into upper-level management).

Mrs. Chisholm is a tough, tenacious crusader whose belief in organization is almost as strong as her faith in the good will and basic decency of black people. Her efforts on their behalf dictate a practical and result-oriented philosophy which focuses on self-determination through the meaningful participation in the economic life of the nation. In her view, this means that black people need sound vocational education, access to higher learning, and sensible business counseling, advice, and guidance.

Though sympathetic with the goals of militants, she feels that they are often undisciplined and incapable of executing real change in a structured environment serving large numbers of people. She is, however, equally critical of the shallow thinking that produces appeals to law and order without placing equal emphasis on the theme of justice in American society.

Congressman-elect Charles Rangel of New York

CHARLES RANGEL
U.S. Congressman from New York
(1970-)

Harlem-born Charles Rangel vaulted into the national spotlight in 1970 when he defeated the seemingly invincible Adam Clayton Powell in the latter's bid for yet another Democratic nomination in New York's 18th Congressional District. Rangel's upset victory stirred hopes among black leaders that a grass-roots political movement generated from within Harlem, rather than stemming from beyond the community, might result in the grooming of an energetic, capable, and untainted successor to the volatile and unpredictable Powell, whose personal foibles and uneven record no longer inspire the admiration they once commanded.

Born June 11, 1930, Rangel attended Harlem elementary and secondary schools before volunteering to serve in the U.S. Army during the Korean war. While stationed in Korea with the 2nd Infantry, he saw heavy combat and received such distinguished decorations as the Purple Heart, the Bronze Star Medal for Valor, as well as U.S. and Korean Presidential citations. Discharged honorably as a staff sergeant, Rangel returned to Harlem, intent on finishing high school (DeWitt Clinton in 1953) and taking advantage of the G.I. Bill to study at New York University's School of Commerce, from which he graduated in 1957. The recipient of a scholarship, Rangel then attended St. John's Law School, graduating in 1960.

After being admitted to the bar, Rangel earned a key appointment as Assistant U.S. Attorney in the Southern District of New York in 1961. For the next five years, he acquired legal experience in a variety of roles—as Legal Counsel to the New York City Housing and Redevelopment Board, as Legal Assistant to Judge James L. Watson, as Associate Counsel to the Speaker of the N.Y. State Assembly, and as General Counsel to the National Advisory Commission on Selective Service.

Rangel first came to occupy elective office in 1966, when he was chosen to represent the 72nd District, Central Harlem, in the State Assembly. Since then, he has served as a member of, and secretary to, the New York State Commission on Revision of the Penal Law and Criminal Code.

Rangel has kept abreast of community affairs and leadership patterns by joining various civil rights and civic groups, including the NAACP, CORE, the Harlem Self-Help Project, the United Block Association, and the Narcotic Law Enforcment Association. He is also a member of the 369th Veterans Association.

BLACK STATE SENATORS AND REPRESENTATIVES*

Arizona
Cloves Campbell, Sen.
Mrs. E. Maynard, Rep.
Leon Thompson, Rep.

California
Mrs. Yvonne Brathwaite, Rep.
Willie L. Brown, Jr., Rep.
Mervyn M. Dymally, Sen.
Bill Greene, Rep.
John J. Miller, Rep.
Leon Ralph, Rep.

Colorado
George Brown, Sen.
Paul L. Hamilton, Rep.
Jerome C. Rose, Rep.

Connecticut
Boce W. Barlow, Jr., Sen.
Otha N. Brown, Jr., Rep. (Maj. Leader)
Leonard G. Frazier, Rep.
Lorenzo Morgan, Rep.
Bruce L. Morris, Rep.

Delaware
Charles E. Butcher, Rep.
Oliver Fonville, Rep.
H. Holloway, Sr., Sen.

Florida
Joe Lang Kershaw, Rep.

Georgia
Wm. H. Alexander, Rep.
Julian Bond, Rep.
Benjamin D. Brown, Rep.
Julius C. Daugherty, Rep.
James E. Dean, Rep.
Richard A. Dent, Rep.
Clarence G. Ezzard, Rep.
Mrs. Grace T. Hamilton, Rep.
Bobby L. Hill, Rep.
John Hood, Rep.
Leroy Johnson, Sen.
E. J. Shepherd, Rep.
A. W. Thompson, Rep.
Horace T. Ward, Sen.

Illinois
L. A. H. Caldwell, Rep.
James Y. Carter, Rep.
Charles Chew, Jr., Rep.
Otis G. Collins, Rep.

BLACK STATE SENATORS AND REPRESENTATIVES* cont'd

Corneal A. Davis, Rep.
Raymond W. Ewell, Rep.
J. Horace Gardner, Rep.
Elwood Graham, Rep.
Kenneth Hall, Rep.
James E. McLendon, Rep.
R. H. Newhouse, Sen.
Cecil A. Partee, Sen.
Isaac R. Sims, Rep.
Fred J. Smith, Sen.
Genoa Washington, Rep.
Harold Washington, Rep.

Indiana
Mrs. H. B. Conn, Rep.
Ray P. Crowe, Rep.
Choice Edward, Rep.

Iowa
A. June Franklin, Rep.

Kansas
James P. Davis, Rep.
Clarence C. Love, Rep.
Billy Q. McCray, Rep.

Kentucky
Georgia M. Davis, State Senator
Mae Street Kidd, Rep.
Hughes McGill, Rep.

Louisiana
Ernest N. Morial, Rep.

Maryland
Floyd B. Adams, Del.
Dr. Aris T. Allen, Del.
Troy Brailey, Del.
Joseph A. Chester, Del.
Isaiah Dixon, Jr., Del.
Calvin A. Douglas, Del.
Mrs. Lena K. Lee, Del.
C. Mitchell III, Sen.
Lloyal Randolph, Del.
Mrs. Verda F. Welcome, Sen.

Massachusetts
F. W. Holgate, Rep.
George A. Johnson, Rep.

Michigan
James Bradley, Rep.
Basil Brown, Sen.
Arthur Cartwright, Sen.
James Del Rio, Rep.
George H. Edwards, Rep.
Daisy Elliott, Rep.
Rosetta Ferguson, Rep.
D. S. Holmes, Jr., Rep.
Raymond W. Hood, Rep.
Matthew McNeeley, Rep. (Assoc. Speaker)
Nelis J. Saunders, Rep.
Jackie Vaughn II, Rep.
Coleman A. Young, Sen.

Mississippi
Robert G. Clark, Rep.

Missouri
Johnny S. Aidens, Rep.
J. B. Banks, Rep.
Mrs. D. L. Calloway, Rep.
Russell Goward, Rep.
Harold L. Holliday, Rep.
Raymond Howard, Sen.
Herman A. Johnson, Rep.
Leon J. Jordan, Rep.
T. D. McNeal, Sen.
Leroy Malcolm, Rep.
Franklin Payne, Rep.
Nathaniel J. Rivers, Rep.
Henry C. Ross, Rep.
James T. Troupe, Rep.
Fred Williams, Rep.

Nevada
W. Wilson, Rep.

New Jersey
Frank Conwell, Rep.
Ronald Owens, Rep.
G. C. Richardson, Rep.
S. Howard Woodson, Jr., Rep.

New Mexico
Lenton Malry, Rep.

New York
Guy Brewer, Rep.
Arthur O. Eve, Rep.
Thomas R. Fortune, Rep.
Joseph L. Galiber, Sen.
Hulan E. Jack, Rep.
Mark T. Southall, Rep.
Edward Stevenson, Rep.
Waldaba Stewart, Sen.
Samuel D. Wright, Rep.

North Carolina
Henry E. Frye, Rep.

Ohio
David D. Albritton, Rep.
John W. E. Bowen, Sen.
William F. Bowen, Rep.
Philip M. DeLaine, Rep.
Phale D. Hale, Rep.
Thomas E. Hill, Rep.
M. Morris Jackson, Sen.
Troy Lee James, Rep.
Calvin C. Johnson, Sen.
Casey Jones, Rep.
C. J. McLin, Jr., Rep.
William Mallory, Rep.
Larry G. Smith, Rep.

Oklahoma
Mrs. Hannah D. Atkins, Rep.
A. B. Hill, Jr., Rep.
Rev. Ben H. Hill, Rep.
A. Visanio Johnson, Rep.
E. Melvin Porter, Sen.

Pennsylvania
Sarah A. Anderson, Rep.
Herbert Arlene, Sen.
James D. Barber, Rep.
Freeman Hankins, Rep.
K. Leroy Irvis, Rep. (Maj. Leader)
Joel J. Johnson, Rep.
Theodore Johnson, Rep.
Paul M. Lawson, Rep.
Mitchell W. Melton, Rep.
Ulysses Shelton, Rep.
Earl Vann, Rep.

Rhode Island
Peter J. Coelho, Rep.

Tennessee
M. G. Blakemore, Rep.
Robert J. Booker, Rep.
Alvin King, Rep.
Harold M. Love, Rep.
Ira H. Murphy, Rep.
J. O. Patterson, Jr., Sen. & Councilman
James I. Taylor, Rep.
A. N. Williams, Jr., Sen.

Texas
Curtis M. Graves, Rep.
Zan Wesley Holmes, Jr., Rep.
Miss Barbara Jordan, Sen.

Virginia
William Ferguson Reid, House of Delegates
Dr. William P. Robinson, House of Delegates
Lawrence D. Wilder, Sen.

Washington
George Fleming, Rep.

Wisconsin
Lloyd Barbee, Rep.

BLACK MAYORS

The 1960's saw black mayors begin to forge new and prophetic roles as custodians of municipal power. Some had previously won figurehead posts in cities run by professional managers; some, like Robert C. Henry of Springfield, Ohio, and Floyd McCree of Flint, Michigan were not popularly elected mayors, but came to occupy their posts by virtue of local ordinances entitling them to the office. Henry, for example, was elected one of the three city commissioners in 1965, and named mayor because he had amassed the highest vote total among the trio. McCree was named to the post of mayor of Flint by the City Commission.

The most important mayors, however, gained leverage in cities with large black populations by actively and aggressively affirming their faith in the traditional elective process. Men like Carl Stokes, Richard Hatcher and Kenneth Gibson presumed that the possession of political power was a necessary prerequisite to the creation of constructive programs which would be responsive to the needs of their constituents.

It is one thing to acquire power and quite another to administer it, however. Mayor Hatcher, for example, has found that people tend to expect more from a black man in office, assuming at times that he can achieve miraculous results in such long-term problem areas as inadequate housing and poor recreational facilities. Though there is assuredly a change of atmosphere when a black man takes office, and though most black mayors have been able to attract considerable contributions from the federal government, from local business coalitions, and from wealthy foundations, none has been able to effect a comprehensive solution for problems of urban blight and community tension. Such a goal is clearly beyond their limited resources.

The Old Guard has been a constant thorn in the side of Hatcher and many party regulars have never really supported him; Stokes, on the other hand, has had trouble with the Cleveland police department which has accused him of unjust favoritism and of undue meddling in their affairs; Gibson, no doubt, will find that ethnic pressures and rivalries, as well as pockets of municipal corruption, will militate against his capacity to govern; Washington has been irritated by Congressional unwillingness to afford him sufficient flexibility in the dispensation of the monies to which he has access.

Despite the noteworthy success stories for black mayors which have captured national headlines in recent years, there have also been conspicuous failures for black aspirants—notably in Detroit and Los Angeles. The Detroit case was far less venomous than the Los Angeles debacle, however.

In the Motor City, the election pitted Wayne County auditor Richard Austin, a black man, against white Wayne County Sheriff Roman Gribbs. Austin defeated Gribbs in the primary by 129,941 votes to 105,460, roughly 38% of the total votes cast. By law, a runoff was called for, and both men proceeded to publicize their respective records in their areas of specialty. Austin took credit for maintaining fiscal responsibility with county finances, and Gribbs stood on his record of having cleaned up corruption in the county sheriff's office.

Both men avoided inflaming afresh the scars of racial tension left over from the 1967 riot; each stressed his own specific programs and his solid record. Fears for a confrontation between black militants and white police were rife, however, particularly with the obvious presence of Austin's pigmentation and Gribbs' badge. Though it did not occur, and the election was a squeaker, Austin lost by some 7,000 votes out of more than half a million cast.

Even before the results were in, Austin and Gribbs pledged joint cooperation "in the interest of unity and brotherhood." Despite the friendly gestures exchanged by the two political foes, the ingredients of the outcome were clear: Austin's isolated and overwhelming black vote was not enough to offset Gribbs' support among liberals, conservatives, and moderates—all of them white.

The tenuous nature of the coalition which has placed the leading black urban mayors in office was nowhere more clearly demonstrated than in the 1969 Los Angeles mayoralty election in which incumbent Sam Yorty defeated black councilman Thomas Bradley. In the April primary, Yorty was badly drubbed by Bradley, who captured 42% of the vote (293,753) to Yorty's 26% (183,334). (In all, Yorty opponents tallied 74% of the total vote.)

A retired police lieutenant and a lawyer by profession, Bradley counted on his support from a coalition of conscience," organizing a constituency which included the black and Mexican-American communities, white liberal Democrats and Republicans, and other independents dissatisfied with Yorty's lacklustre record and mediocre leadership. Bradley disavowed violence, stating that his goal was "to make that which unites us . . . stronger than that which keeps us apart." Yorty, on the other hand, realized that his sole hope for success lay in an ability to arouse the apprehensions of a largely conservative constituency, including many white- and blue-collar workers who feared the consequences of racial and radical unrest.

Thus, the hordes of outspoken youth workers who flocked to Bradley's side were more than counterbalanced by the silent numbers who marshalled their strength among small homeowners and police sympathizers. Yorty associated Bradley with militant organizations like the Panthers and US, claimed that the increasingly assertive Mexican-American population had declared their allegiance to him, and maintained that police morale was being seriously undermined, particularly in the wake of Police Chief Thomas Reddin's sudden resignation. (A sample Yorty statement: "In Los Angeles, you don't have the mayor fighting with the police department, as they are in Cleveland, where they elected a Negro mayor.")

Through no fault of his own, Bradley became labelled as the tool of power-hungry black militants, even possibly Communist revolutionaries preparing the city for renewed violence. Soft-keyed and subdued, Bradley appealed to the centrist attitudes typical of upper middle-class audiences. Yorty, on the other hand, aroused fears among white families that their children would not be "safe" if Bradley came to power, and suggested that critics of America "love it or leave it."

The heavy turnout (840,000 of the 1.1 million eligible voters) clearly influenced the election in Yorty's favor, enabling him to register a decisive 53.3% to 46.7% victory. (Blacks constituted only 18% of the registered voters.) The victory confounded the pollsters who had predicted a Bradley victory by anywhere from five to 17 percentage points. Though Bradley accused Yorty of making a "blatant appeal to racial prejudice," he nevertheless appealed for calm and counselled his supporters to cooperate with the victorious administration. His dignified approach and his moderate stance may have won him many admirers, but the disappointments he endured no doubt further alienated an already skeptical and embittered black community. The alienation was clearly fuel for black militant and separatist theoreticians; those who counselled cautious trust of many sober and enlightened whites found themselves unable to deliver the reasonable victory they were counting on to insure their own credibility and strengthen their own appeal.

The same tensions, then, are present in all U.S. cities in which black mayors are currently in office. Those like Stokes and Hatcher who have squeaked to victory have either been able to reduce incidents of ghetto violence, moderate the demands of militants, reinforce popular faith by pointing to tangible progress and sensible legislation, or consolidate a power base which relies on a coalition of the black masses, the white intellectuals, and loyalist labor forces. Even while Austin was losing by 7,000 votes in Detroit, the victim of defection from some part of the coalition, Stokes was winning re-election by less than 4,000 votes, the beneficiary of the momentary cohesiveness of the very same coalition.

A final roundup shows that there are some 50 black mayors in the United States. Many of these, however, govern small hamlets in all-black or predominantly black areas and, as such, are not directly associated with the urban crisis. In large cities, demographic patterns will determine the political prospects of other possible black aspirants, including Detroit's Austin who has not as yet indicated any intention to run again in 1972. In Atlanta, although blacks will not constitute a majority until the 1980's, black Vice Mayor Maynard Jackson, Jr. seems a likely candidate for City Hall in 1973. Other cities expected to achieve black majorities by the 1970's are New Orleans, Baltimore and Jacksonville; by the 1980's, Oakland, Philadelphia and Chicago should follow suit. As these population shifts occur, the politics of transition will be strengthened, and black office seekers will multiply accordingly.

Our section concludes with biographical sketches of the black mayors who have struggled to the top.

CHARLES EVERS
Mayor, Fayette, Mississippi
(1969-)

The first black mayor of a Mississippi town since Reconstruction, Charles Evers is undoubtedly the most active, abrasive, and ambitious political force in the state of Mississippi. Despite the fact that his brother Medgar, former state NAACP Field Secretary, was murdered in 1963 for precisely the kind of activity which he himself has now undertaken, Charles Evers has moved fearlessly, shrewdly and steadfastly to press for public denunciation of serious criminal acts like the 1964 lynching of the three civil rights workers, to effect policies of reconciliation with Mississippi moderates, and to warn and cajole them into respecting the political rights of black majorities.

Born in Decatur, Mississippi in 1923, Evers grew up in a relatively prosperous setting. His family operated a funeral home and a lumber contracting business. Close to his brother Medgar from childhood, Evers joined the Army after completing 11 grades of schooling, serving in the Pacific until his discharge in 1946. He then finished high school in Newton, and went on to attend Alcorn A. & M., a Negro college in Lorman, on an athletic scholarship. Majoring in social studies, he earned a teacher's degree upon graduation in 1950, but he decided instead to take over the family's business interests — funeral parlor, hotel, restaurant, taxicab service, and gas station—in Philadelphia, a small town north of Decatur.

In 1957, Evers decided to examine life in the Northern urban ghetto, moving to Chicago, where he taught physical education and worked at a variety of jobs until he was able to open his own cocktail lounge and nightclub. He then branched out into real estate, and was enjoying marked success when the tragedy that was to change his life struck: the assassination of his brother.

Evers at once remembered the boyhood pact which dictated that one brother would always continue the other's work should tragedy befall either of them. Returning at once to Mississippi, Evers lost no time petitioning the NAACP leadership to allow him to take over his brother's vacant post.

Evers next ventured into local politics, where his support was solid, and his persistence more likely to pay off. His election as mayor of Fayette, Mississippi in June 1969 did not bring him a powerful political office, but it did give him a suitable base for gaining the type of experience that will serve him well in the future. Fayette is the county seat of poverty-ridden Jefferson County, a shantytown badly in need of paved streets and other municipal services, not to mention a measure of industrial activity which will break the welfare cycle so well entrenched among the lethargic populace.

Evers' campaign slogan was perhaps the first crushing blow to the town's complacency and apathy. "Don't vote for a black man," it said. "Or a white man. Just a good man." After the election, Evers made an impressive pledge to the white citizens of the racially mixed community of 1,700. "We're not going to allow our power to abuse you or mistreat you like you've mistreated us. We're going to show you what love and working together can do."

Charles Evers at victory headquarters

KENNETH GIBSON
Mayor, Newark
(1970-)

"We must begin to reconcile the community . . . come together to show America that determined people can reverse the trend of decay in our city and other cities across the country."

These words were spoken in triumph June 16, 1970, on a historic night in Newark, New Jersey when a 38-year-old engineer, Kenneth Gibson, became the first black mayor of a major Eastern city. The election campaign, culminating only that morning, had been riddled with charges and countercharges of racism and criminal neglect, causing virtually the entire city to feel a sense of jittery apprehension as the polls opened. Clearly, one of the factors in Gibson's favor was Mayor Addonizio's indictment on federal charges of corruption, his alleged involvement in scandalous kickback operations with city contracts, and reputed income tax evasion.

As the racial implications of the election became more and more intense with each passing day, support from what might be described as more obviously beneficial sources poured in for Gibson. Campaign contributions from such popular black entertainers as Bill Cosby lightened the financial burden, even as dramatic statements by men like Harry Belafonte appealed to sentiments of black solidarity.

"Ken Gibson is the property of black people around the world," Belafonte said. "His destiny . . . is our destiny."

The large black turnout for the May 12 primary had brought Gibson a dramatic step closer to the victory which had eluded him in the 1966 campaign, when he was active for only six weeks. It had taken him four more years to consolidate his support, and the evidence was unmistakable in the more than 2-1 majority he piled up over Addonizio. Despite his impressive victory (37,895 to 18,212), Gibson did not pull the absolute majority required for election, polling 43% of the vote.

In the succeeding months, it became apparent that Addonizio would step up his activity among white voters who had bolted to support other white candidates. Crucial to the ultimate result would be the 12,000 people who had supported John P. Caulfield, a disgruntled official in the Addonizio administration. Voters like this, it appeared, stayed with Gibson.

Pandemonium broke loose among Gibson supporters when it was announced, in unofficial returns, that he had amassed almost 55,000 votes to Addonizio's 43,000. Though his primary victory vote margin had been sharply cut, Gibson still had 54% of the total.

Acceptance of challenge and a cool temperament were perhaps the major ingredients in the Gibson victory. Born in Enterprise, Alabama in 1932, Gibson migrated to Newark with his parents at the age of eight. Ghetto life closed in on the Gibsons fast, but it did not deter them from matching their wits and drive to succeed against the adverse conditions they first faced in a one-room apartment. Gibson's father took a job as a butcher, while his mother worked as a seamstress.

Gibson and his brother Harold grew up on the streets of Newark's heavily black South Ward, where his parents still live. The streets of Newark were safe in those days, Gibson remembers, and black youths released their energies in such outdoor activities as track meets and other athletic contests. Gibson first met Leroi Jones on the streets of Newark, but the two pursued different careers as they grew older.

Gibson managed to graduate from Central High School, but he was strapped for money and unable to continue on to college. As a result, he drifted for a time into various kinds of factory work. He was finally able to enroll as a night student at the Newark College of Engineering. His studies there were interrupted by such things as another job in the New Jersey State Highway Department, a two-year hitch in the Army, and his happy marriage.

Gibson ultimately graduated with a degree in civil engineering, and was placed on the municipal payroll by Addonizio himself in an effort to consolidate his previous support in the black community.

Working at the grass-roots level, however, Gibson was busily engaged in culti-

Mayor Kenneth Gibson of Newark

vating closer ties with this same constituency through his active contact with the YMCA and the YWCA, and through useful memberships in the Urban League and the NAACP.

It was clear, after the furor of the election died down, that Gibson's victory formula was comparable to the one which all other black big-city mayors had relied on. Gibson had become associated with civil rights causes and job opportunity programs which called upon business and industrial firms in the city to cooperate. His low-keyed overtures and his understated campaign rhetoric solidified his support among the middle-class professionals who stayed on his team and helped put him over. Black support was virtually unanimous.

RICHARD HATCHER
Mayor, Gary
(1967-)

"Richard Hatcher is running for his life," the New York *Times* ad said. "And yours. And the life of every American saddened and sickened by the mounting violence in this country. . . . Many of us *say* we're for peace and unity. Now is the time to put our money where our mouth is."

The situation for Richard Hatcher in 1967 was a desperate one. The Lake County Democratic Committee had withheld its financial support, and this was more than enough to offset the money contributed by the AFL-CIO Central Labor Council, and by the regional offices of the steelworkers and the autoworkers unions.

On August 24, 1967, Hatcher placed a $7,000 ad in the New York *Times* and an $860 ad in the Gary *Post-Tribune*. That left him with only $14 in promotional money for his mayorality campaign in Gary.

The prelude to the 1967 election was a startling reversal of the Democratic party politics which had governed the life of Gary for more than a generation. Gary's black and white population were split along strict racial lines, with the Latin population regarded as the potential holders of the key votes which might ensure a Republican victory.

Hatcher had defeated two white candidates, including the incumbent, in the party's May primary. In normal times, this would have been tantamount to victory in Gary. As it was, Hatcher nosed out Joseph B. Radigan in the hotly contested election by an official count of 39,330 to 37,941.

Mayor Richard Hatcher of Gary

The election was conducted in an atmosphere heavy with the threat of violence, voter intimidation, alleged fraud, charges of militancy, and claims of Communist involvement. County Democratic head John Krupa claimed that Hatcher had "leftwingers in his camp," that he had once said "American fliers ought to be treated as war criminals if they are captured in North Vietnam," and that he refused to denounce "Stokely Carmichael and people like that by name."

Hatcher countered by asserting that the so-called "leftwing" support had been present in the Democratic camp in previous elections without generating comparable charges. He denied he had spoken against American fliers in Vietnam and protested that Vietnam was a national, not a local, issue. Moreover, Hatcher felt that his statement denouncing violence implicitly contained the necessary repudiation of all who advocated violence.

Hatcher's election victory as a Reformer placed him in the awkard position of fencing with complaints stemming from white diehards who refused to support any job, housing or neighborhood programs which would promote any measure of integration and from black citizens equally appalled by his alleged failure to create instant jobs for all.

Whatever optimism was generated in the city was attributable to the calibre of Hatcher's appointments (many men took assignments with the Hatcher team at considerable personal financial sacrifice), and to prospects for successful appeals to the federal government for extensive aid in combatting Gary's more acute problems, particularly slum conditions.

Hatcher also succeeded in raising the morale of the Police Department by making it clear that its long-dormant enforcement role was to be revitalized. He then enlisted the support of various concerned business groups in his bid to crack down on Gary's crime, graft and vice. This strategy strengthened his support in white professional and Jewish areas, and gave him some added strength in middle European ethnic areas as well.

Born the 12th of 13 children in 1923, Hatcher is a native of rural Georgia. He made his way through college on an athletic scholarship, working part-time on tables and benefitting from the assistance rendered by his surviving brothers and sisters. After graduation, Hatcher entered Valparaiso University Law School, working full-time at a nearby state mental hospital. Hatcher moved to Gary in 1959 to practice law, deciding instead to make a dash at the mayor's seat after being voted president of the city council in 1963.

Mayor Howard N. Lee of Chapel Hill

HOWARD NATHANIEL LEE
(Mayor, Charlotte, N.C.)

Howard Nathaniel Lee was once described in a "third world magazine" as a "black mountainman" from North Carolina. Born one of seven children on July 28, 1934, Lee graduated from Bruce St. High School as "Best All Around Student," and went on to college at Clark and Fort Valley State, graduating in 1959. After serving a tour of duty in Korea, Lee became a juvenile probation officer under the auspices of the Juvenile Domestic Relations Court in Savannah. Later, he did graduate work at the University of North Carolina, receiving his master's in 1966. He then became, successively, Director of Youth Services and Director of Employee Relations at Duke University.

Lee thus becomes the first black mayor to be elected in a predominantly Southern white community. His election is all the more remarkable by virtue of the fact that only 10% of the voting population of the town is black. Lee's success, however, stemmed from the town's disenchantment with the prior administration's laggard record in public transportation, recreation, city planning, and housing. Like any black mayor, Lee understands that his most challenging task may well be to evolve a formula for dealing with the two factions out to "slaughter" him: the white racists and the black militants.

JAMES HOWELL McGEE
Mayor of Dayton, Ohio

Dayton's black mayor James Howell McGee no longer allows himself to be stung by the familiar rebuke offered by black militants that "he does not take a stand on issues" involving the city's black population. Shrewd and unruffled now that he is in the driver's seat (Dayton is the fourth largest city in the nation to have a black mayor), McGee prefers instead to remind people of his justly deserved reputation as "that militant lawyer," earned while he crusaded, as an NAACP lawyer, to integrate the public accommodations of the city.

One of seven children, McGee was born on November 8, 1918 in Berryburg, Virginia. Raised in Steubenville, Ohio, McGee began working as a floor sweeper in the downtown business district of the city at age 12, but he did not allow adversity to deter him from pursuing higher education, first at Wilberforce and, later, after his Army discharge, at Ohio State's law school.

After struggling for several years to make a living in his profession, McGee began to file legal actions in cases then regarded as revolutionary, particularly one pursuant to the 1954 Supreme Court decision declaring separate public schools unconstitutional. McGee filed one of the first tests cases in the North involving *de facto* segregation.

Over the years, McGee built up a considerable following in Dayton's predominantly black West Side wards. This strategy ultimately paid off in November 1969 when he was elected one of the four city-wide commissioners who govern the Ohio city of 250,000 (including 70,000 blacks).

When McGee's predecessor resigned for health reasons in May 1970, a deadlock developed over his successor. Two commissioners dropped out of the running, however, whereupon McGee was chosen to head the government.

CARL STOKES
Mayor, Cleveland (1967-)

Carl Stokes was the first of what has now become a well-established roster of important black political figures occupying positions of prestige and influence in municipal government across the United States. Elected mayor of Cleveland on November 13, 1967, Stokes approached the grassroots change that was taking place in American life with a skillful measure of political savvy and understanding. Though his city, like so many in urban America, possessed a large and assertive ethnic bloc of black voters eager for change, Stokes counted on a moderate and reasonable platform to amass the necessary white votes required to insure victory. His strategy: to show the whites he "did not have horns." His re-election in 1969 was based on his continuing ability to satisfy this portion of the electorate, as well as his untiring efforts to promote meaningful change and orderly advancement among the inner-city inhabitants of Cleveland.

Stokes' early career was erratic, and marked by sudden shifts of fortune and outlook. Born in the poor central ghetto of Cleveland, Stokes lost his father at the age of two, and was raised by his mother, Louise, and his older brother, Louis. Education held little appeal for the young Stokes, with the result that, at the age of 17, he dropped out of East Technical High School, and went to work in a foundry for a year before joining the Army.

After completing his overseas hitch, Stokes followed the advice of a buddy, earned his high school diploma, and then attended, successively, West Virginia State College and Western Reserve University, majoring, at the latter institution, in psychology. Dissatisfied again with academic life, Stokes joined the state liquor

Carl Stokes, winner of a squeaker for re-election, poses jubilantly with his wife.

authority as an armed agent, experiencing first-hand the trials of enforcing the law on wayward and uncooperative saloon operators. After three years, he was again persuaded to return to school, this time returning to the University of Minnesota, where he completed his studies for a B.S. degree in law in 1954. His resolution to pursue law led him to take an LL.B. at Cleveland-Marshall Law School in 1956. A year later, he won admission to the Ohio bar and began practice in Cleveland, where he had already been named a probation officer for the Cleveland Municipal Court. In 1958, he was appointed assistant city prosecutor under Ralph S. Locher. During this period, Stokes expanded his activities on the civil rights front, becoming an executive member of the Cleveland NAACP and an active participant in the affairs of the Community Council of Mt. Pleasant.

Stokes left the city administration in 1962 to form a business partnership with his brother, Louis, by then a lawyer in his own right. Stokes' entry into politics was an instant success, as he became the first black Democrat to win a seat in the Ohio General Assembly. From the outset, Stokes sought to establish himself as a moderate, voting readily, during his three consecutive terms, for civil rights and welfare bills, but also backing legislation designed to authorize the governor to use National Guard troops in the event serious rioting menaced a city.

The strong anti-black bias demonstrated by white officials like the City's Police Chief, Richard Wagner, stirred ethnic tensions in the city and gave many aroused civil rights leaders a legitimate platform to demand clear action from the incumbent mayor, Ralph Locher. Locher's indecision alienated responsible white middle-class voters, as well as much of the black community, only then beginning to respond to concerted appeals to increase its political awareness and assess its potential strength. Locher, dependent on machine support and the backing of organized labor, was clearly a lacklustre candidate unable to win considerable backing from either the Johnson Administration or the Democratic National Committee. At the election, he emerged the winner by the barest of majorities, some 2,000 votes in all.

Since his election, Stokes has gained a reputation as a skillful and hard-working administrator. He has managed to quell some disturbances in the ghetto, although he has certainly not conquered all the problems implicit in its existence. As anticipated, he had been an understanding, sympathetic, and resourceful public servant in the area of racial unrest.

WALTER E. WASHINGTON
District Commissioner, Washington, D.C. (1967-)

In his position as commissioner of the District of Columbia, Walter E. Washington has all of the responsibilities to which the chief executive of a large city falls heir when he takes office. Washington was named to the post in 1967 under President Lyndon B. Johnson's reorganization plan for the District of Columbia, a plan which called for replacement of the three-man governing board with a single official

The great-grandson of a slave, Washington was born in Dawson, Georgia on April 15, 1915. He attended public schools in Jamestown, New York, and graduated from Howard University in 1938 with a B.A. in public administration and sociology. He later did graduate work at American University.

Washington began 25 years of service with the National Capital Housing Authority (NCHA) in 1941. Attending law school at night, he obtained his LL.B. degree in 1948, and was admitted to the bar. After 20 years with the NCHA, Washington was promoted to the post of executive director. His period of service was distinguished by his persistent attention to the personal and social aspects of the D.C. housing crisis. He was known for his willingness to meet the people in their own communities and his insistence on making the rounds personally to gather as much first-hand information as he could.

In 1966, Washington accepted a bid from New York's Mayor John Lindsay to serve as chairman of the New York City Housing Authority. In the course of almost a year's service, Washington increased the number of day-care centers in the city, expanded the operation of credit unions, and broadened the availability of job and financial counseling. In the summer of 1967, an elaborate recreation program organized by Washington was a smashing success, with 400,000 people participating in a variety of events, including sporting contests, amateur dramatics, and floral competitions.

The appointment of Washington as commissioner of D.C. brought with it a sizeable cut in salary, but restored the housing official to a city by now ingrained in his bones. Serving under Washington in the current organizational setup are an assistant commissioner and a nine-man city council (with a black majority of five).

Washington quickly set out to mend fences with groups protesting cuts in antipoverty funds, and streamlined several departments which were operating sluggishly or inefficiently. Still, he has had to win Congressional approval of his budgets, and has found the going tough whenever he seeks to persuade Congress to allow him a certain measure of flexibility in the disposal of those funds.

The year 1968 was clearly a test of the mettle and savvy of the man. The assassination of Dr. King led to serious rioting in the nation's capital, but Washington acted skillfully to reduce tension by enforcing a curfew, banning the sale of firearms and liquor, and centralizing welfare services to aid riot victims. Washington then girded to receive the vanguard of Poor People's marchers, meeting with leaders of the campaign, extending his cordial cooperation, and helping to insure its relatively peaceful termination.

THE NEGRO IN THE UNITED NATIONS

The basic blueprint for what was to become the United Nations was first drawn up at Dumbarton Oaks in Washington, D. C. in 1944. It was thought then that the five leading powers (the United States, Russia, Great Britain, China and France) should be permanently united as members of a single body which would dedicate itself to the preservation of world peace.

In 1945, the delegates of 50 nations assembled in San Francisco for the purpose of drawing up a charter which would embody the preliminary agreements reached at Dumbarton Oaks. Ratification of this charter by the "Big Five" in October of the same year paved the way for the establishment of the most comprehensive international organization in the history of mankind—the United Nations.

For the American Negro (as indeed for Negroes in other parts of the world), the United Nations immediately became a symbol of mankind's highest aspirations to create a world order based on principles of liberty and justice. Called upon to offer concrete evidence of its preparedness to adhere to these same principles, the United States soon began to assign a number of qualified Negroes to serve on its delegations —even as a host of other nations dispatched men and women of all races and creeds to represent them in the world body.

ROBERT L. BROKENBURR
Alternate Delegate to the United Nations

For many years a lawyer, twice State Senator from Indiana, and several times at different levels within the Indiana court system, Robert L. Brokenburr served as an alternate delegate to the U.N. General Assembly from 1955 to 1956.

A native of Phoebus, Virginia, Brokenburr was born on November 16, 1886. Educated initially in his hometown, he later attended Hampton Institute in Hampton, Virginia, receiving his B. A. in 1906. He completed his law studies at Howard in 1909.

RALPH J. BUNCHE
U. N. Undersecretary for Special Political Affairs

The first American Negro to win the Nobel Peace Prize, Ralph Bunche is an internationally acclaimed statesman whose record of achievement places him among the most significant American diplomats of the 20th century. Bunche received the coveted award in 1950 for his role in effecting a cease-fire in the Arab-Israeli dispute which threatened to engulf the entire Middle East in armed conflict.

Born in Detroit on August 7, 1904, Bunche graduated from UCLA in 1927 *summa cum laude* and with Phi Beta Kappa honors. A year later, he received his M. A. in government from Harvard. Soon thereafter, he was named head of the Department of Political Science at Howard University, remaining there until 1932 at which time he was able to resume work toward his doctorate from Harvard. (He later studied at Northwestern University; the London School of Economics, and Capetown University.)

Before World War II broke out, Bunche did field work with the Swedish sociologist, Gunnar Myrdal, author of the widely acclaimed *An American Dilemma*. During the war itself, he served initially as Senior Social Analyst for the Office of the Coordinator of Information in African and Far Eastern Affairs, and was then reassigned to the African section of the Office of Strategic Services. In 1942, he helped draw up the territories and trusteeships sections ultimately earmarked for inclusion in the United Nations charter.

But the single event which brought the name of Ralph Bunche into the international limelight occurred soon after his appointment in 1948 as chief assistant to Count Folke Bernadotte, U. N. mediator in the Palestine crisis. With the latter's assassination, Bunche was faced with the great challenge of somehow continuing cease-fire talks between Egypt and Israel. After six weeks of intensive negotiations, Bunche worked out the now-famous "Four Armistice Agreements," which effected an immediate cessation of the hostilities between the two combatants. Once the actual cease-fire was signed, Bunche received numerous letters and telegrams from many of the leading heads of state the world over, and was later accorded a hero's welcome upon his return to the United States.

In 1955, Dr. Bunche was appointed U.N. Undersecretary for Special Political Affairs, the highest post currently held in the world body by an American Negro. Over the past decade, he has carried out a number of special assignments in such trouble spots as the Suez, the Congo, Kashmir and Cyprus.

ARCHIBALD J. CAREY
Alternate Delegate to the United Nations

Archibald Carey served as an alternate delegate to the United Nations from 1953 to 1956.

A native of Chicago and a graduate of John Marshall Law School, Carey presided for 19 years (1930-1949) as pastor of the Woodlawn A.M.E. Church in that city. Twice elected alderman from Chicago's Third Ward, Carey was on the Chicago city council for eight years, and later became an avid presidential supporter of Dwight D. Eisenhower, from whom he received his U.N. appointment. During the Eisenhower Administration, he was vice chairman of the President's Committee on Government Employment Policy.

WILLIAM T. COLEMAN, JR.
Alternate Delegate to the United Nations

Philadelphia-born William T. Coleman, Jr. brought to his position as alternate delegate to the 24th Session of the United Nations a distinguished legal and judicial record and more than a decade of continuing service to such prestigious political officials as Presidents Eisenhower and Kennedy, and former Pennsylvania governor, William Scranton.

A graduate of the University of Pennsylvania and Harvard Law School, Coleman embarked on his professional career by acting as law secretary to Circuit Court Judge Herbert F. Goodrich and Associate Supreme Court Justice Felix Frankfurter, serving under each man for one year. He later joined the law firm of Dillworth, Paxson, Kalish, Kohn and Levy, becoming a partner in 1956. By then, he was already serving as Special Counsel for the City of Philadelphia for Transit Matters. In 1965, he was retained by Governor Scranton to represent the Commonwealth of Pennsylvania in litigation to remove racial restrictions at Girard College. At the time of his appointment, he was active as trial and appellate lawyer in federal and state courts in business, corporate, liability insurance and natural gas litigation.

WILLIAM H. DEAN
1910–1952
Chief of the African Unit, Division of Economic Stability and Development

William H. Dean was appointed chief of the African unit in the Division of Economic Stability and Development in 1949, and served in this capacity until his death.

Born in Lynchburg, Virginia on July 6, 1910, Dean graduated from Bowdoin College in Maine in 1930, and later attended Harvard on a fellowship. He received both his M. A. and Ph. D. degrees from this university in 1932 and 1938, respectively.

During the 1940's, Dean devoted his energies to a number of important posts in government, notably as a consultant to the National Resources Planning Board (1940-1942), and as a member of several technical missions to such places as Haiti, Libya and the Virgin Islands (1944-1949). He also taught for a time at Atlanta University and City College of New York.

Dean committed suicide on January 9, 1952.

ZELMA GEORGE
Alternate Delegate to the United Nations

Zelma George was appointed an alternate delegate to the 15th General Assembly of the United Nations in 1960.

Born in Hearne, Texas, Dr. George moved to Kansas with her family at an early age, and later studied voice at the American Conservatory of Music in Chicago. She received an undergraduate degree from the University of Chicago, and earned her doctorate in sociology from New York University.

Miss George worked for a time as a probation officer for a juvenile court and then as Dean of Women at Tennessee State College. In 1955, she was appointed to the Defense Advisory Committee on Women in the Services and, four years later, under the auspices of the State Department, completed a three-month assignment in Southeast Asia, culminating in her attendance at the Pan Pacific and Southeast Asia Women's Assembly which took place in Singapore.

CHARLES H. MAHONEY
1886–1966
Delegate to the United Nations

Charles H. Mahoney is the first Negro to become a *permanent* member of a United States delegation to the United Nations.

Born in Decatur, Michigan on March 29, 1886, Mahoney later received his B. A. from Fisk University, and his LL. B. from the University of Michigan. An attorney for some 30 years, Mahoney was active in a number of civic and business enterprises in Michigan.

During his five-year UN tour (1954-1959), Mahoney was an important member of several committees, and also served on the Panel for Inquiry and Conciliation.

Mahoney died in Detroit on January 29, 1966.

CARMEL CARRINGTON MARR
Legal Advisor to the U. S. Mission to the United Nations

An experienced lawyer in her own right —particularly in matters pertaining to international law—Carmel Carrington Marr was appointed to her post as legal advisor to the United States Mission to the United Nations in 1953.

Apart from her specific duties, she is in close and constant contact with missions from other parts of the world, and has served on a number of key committees of the U. N. General Assembly.

A native New Yorker, Miss Marr is a graduate of Hunter College, and holds an LL. B. degree from Columbia University.

FRANK MONTERO
Advisor to the U. S. Mission to the United Nations

Frank Montero received his appointment as advisor to the U. S. Mission to the U. N. in 1962 after having served for almost 15 years as the assistant executive director of the National Urban League.

In addition to acting for a time as a special assistant to the late Adlai Stevenson, he has represented the United States at the independence celebrations of Niger, Kenya and Zanzibar, and as senior advisor on economic and social affairs for many of the specialized committees in the U. N. proper.

Born in New York City in 1912, Montero is a graduate of Howard University (1934), and holds graduate degrees from Columbia University (social administration) and New York University (public administration).

JAMES M. NABRIT, JR.
Ambassador to the United Nations

With his appointment on August 25, 1965 as an ambassador to the U. N., James M. Nabrit, Jr. became the highest-ranking American to serve on any U. S. delegation to the world body.

Born in Atlanta, Georgia on September 4, 1900, Nabrit received his early education in his home state, and later earned his B. A. from Morehouse. Drawn to the law at an early age, Nabrit set up his own practice in Houston, Texas in 1930, three years after having received his LL.B. from Northwestern University.

At once a specialist in civil rights, Nabrit participated in a number of historic cases tried before the Supreme Court, including one of the five cases connected with the monumental *Brown v. Board of Education* decision which outlawed segregation in U. S. public schooling.

During World War II, Nabrit was on both the Selective Service and Price Control Board. In 1954, he served as legal advisor to the Governor of the Virgin Islands and, later, was twice a delegate to the annual International Labor Conference held in Geneva, Switzerland.

Nabrit will return to Howard at the end of his U. N. assignment.

EDITH SAMPSON
Alternate Delegate to the United Nations

The first Negro woman to be named to the United Nations, Edith Sampson served in this body from 1950 until 1953, first as an appointee of President Harry S. Truman and later during a portion of the Eisenhower Administration.

A native of Pittsburgh, Pennsylvania, Miss Sampson acquired a Bachelor of

Mrs. Edith Sampson presents a Booker T. Washington memorial coin to Nasrollah Entezan of Iran. Watching is Benjamin Cohen of the U.N. Departments of Public Information.

Laws degree from the John Marshall Law School in Chicago in 1925 and, two years later, became the first woman to receive a Master of Laws from Loyola University.

A member of the Illinois bar since 1927, she was admitted to practice before the Supreme Court in 1934. During the 1930's, she maintained her own private practice, specializing particularly in domestic relations and in criminal law.

After her U.N. appointment, Miss Sampson traveled around the world, often as a lecturer under State Department auspices. She was elected Associate Judge of the Municipal Court of Chicago in 1962.

CHANNING H. TOBIAS
1882–1961
Alternate Delegate to the United Nations

U. S. Alternate Delegate to the United Nations from 1951 to 1952, Channing H. Tobias functioned in a number of roles during his lifetime: as an ordained minister of the Colored Methodist Episcopal Church; as a professor of Bible literature at Paine College; as senior secretary of the YMCA (Colored Men's Division), and as chairman of the board of directors of the NAACP.

Born in 1882 in Augusta, Georgia, Tobias attended Paine College where he received his B.A., and later studied at Drew Theological Seminary and at the University of Pennsylvania. During World War II, he was a member of numerous civil rights and governmental advisory committees and, in 1946, was named director of the Phelps-Stokes Fund, a foundation devoted to the improvement of educational opportunities for Negroes.

A Spingarn medalist and holder of numerous other citations, Tobias in 1950 became the first Negro to receive an honorary degree from New York University.

He died on November 5, 1961.

Negro Population, by States

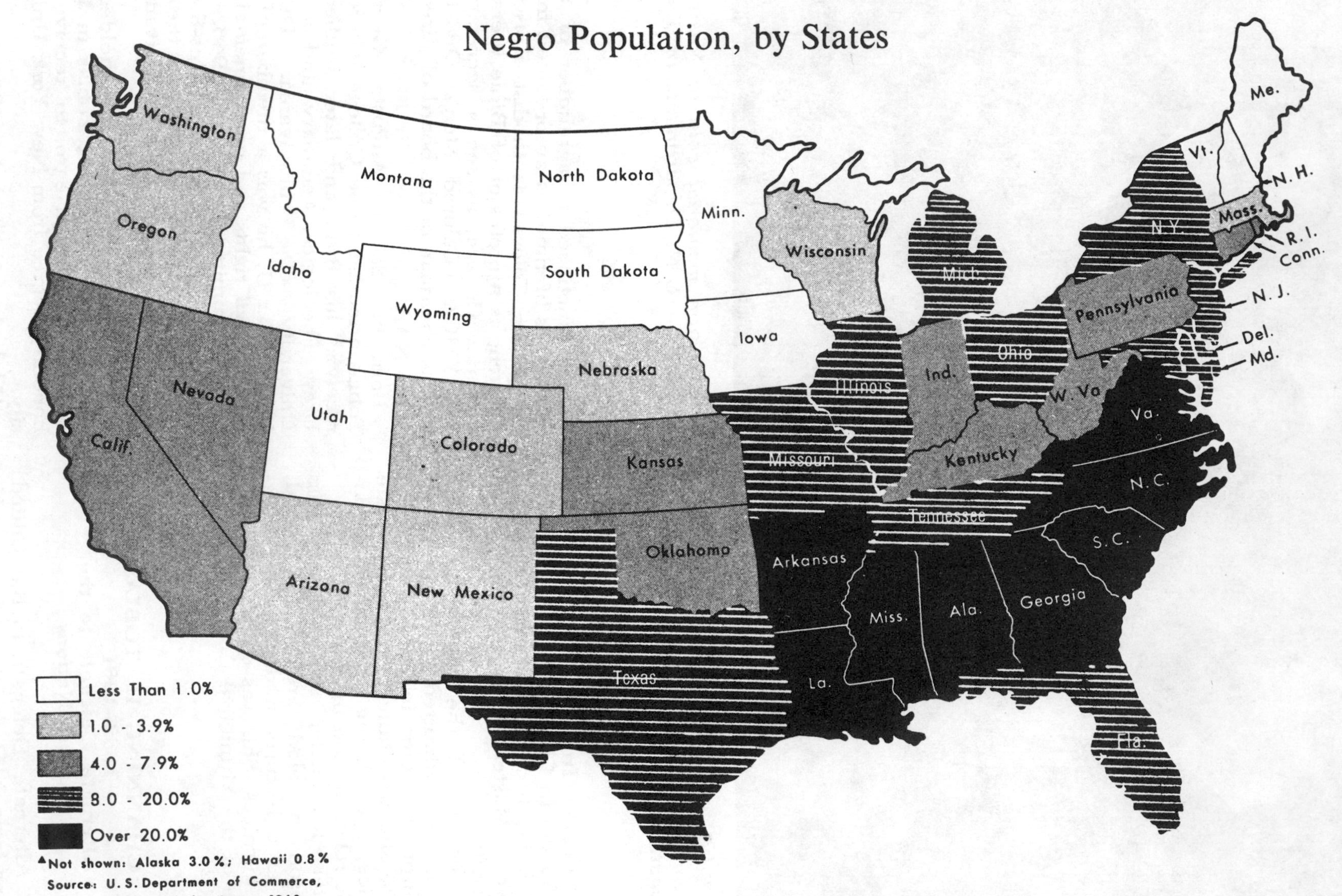

GROWTH AND DISTRIBUTION OF THE BLACK POPULATION

At least three definitions of the term "Negro" exist in the United States today: the legal, the social, and the census.

Legal definitions of the term Negro vary from one state to the next and, even within certain states themselves, additional distinctions are made to regulate racial intermarriages.

Defined socially, the Negro is anyone with a *known* trace of Negro blood, regardless of when that trace was acquired. Community knowledge and physical visibility are the two criteria upon which the social definition is based. In other words, exceptions can occur only when an individual with an unknown or undetected trace of Negro blood is able to "pass" as other than Negro, or be assimilated into an other-than-Negro community.

The U. S. Bureau of Census does not recognize the term Negro as such, choosing instead—for purposes of enumeration rather than contrast—to divide racial data into "white" and "nonwhite." Nonwhite includes Negroes, American Indians, Chinese, Japanese, Filipinos, Hindus, and "others." Anyone with even the slightest trace of Negro ancestry is automatically classified as nonwhite by the Census Bureau.*

* N.B. Most nonwhites are Negroes (the percentage varying from 96% in the 1950 census to 93% in the 1960 census). Geographically, nonwhites who are not Negroes are concentrated in two areas: the Pacific states (where there are many Chinese and Japanese), and Oklahoma and the Rocky Mountain states (where there are many American Indians). In many cases, the data in this volume was amassed on the basis of white and nonwhite statistics obtained from federal government sources. For practical purposes, in any one listing, nine out of 10 nonwhites can be regarded as Negroes. Thus, for example, a figure of 100,000 nonwhites would be one dealing with 90,000 Negroes. In conclusion, the editors of this volume have not chosen to concern themselves with any of the numerous and arbitrary usages of the term Negro, nor have they attempted in any way to define, for example, the African or West Indian Negro.

Population in Colonial America

The beginnings of America's black population can be traced back to the year 1619, when 20 blacks were landed at Jamestown, Virginia — the vanguard, as it were, of the slaves who were to be imported (legally or otherwise) into the United States before the outbreak of the Civil War. Some degree of conflict exists among historians as to whether the date of 1619 is accurate, some believing it was 1620, while others insist on 1618; consensus accepts 1619 as the most probable date.

Although no doubt exists as to the fact that a Dutch man of war brought the first black slaves to be purchased by the British colonies, into the new world, questions exist as to whether they were actually landed in Virginia from that ship. Some historians believe that they were landed in Bermuda, purchased there by a Captain Argall of the British merchant ship, "The Treasurer," and subsequently landed in Virginia, having been transported there by the British vessel.

A third dispute noted by historians is the number of black people who involuntarily participated in the momentous and consequential transaction; some argue the number as being 14, although consensus again states that it was 20.

According to the census of February 16, 1624, there were 22 blacks in the entire colony; 11 were at Floradieu Hundred; three were in James City; one was on James Island; one on the plantation opposite James City; four at Warisquosyak; and two were at Elizabeth City.

Twenty-four years later, in the year 1648, there was a black slave population of 300. Until the year 1662 slavery existed without any legal sanction; statutory laws enacted in that year not only legalized the importation and utilization of slaves but decreed, as well, that all children born of slaves were to be themselves slaves for life.

Table 1

GROWTH OF SLAVERY IN THE COLONIES (1630–1780)

	1630	*1640*	*1650*	*1660*	*1670*	*1680*	*1690*	*1700*
North	10	427	880	1,162	1,125	1,895	3,340	5,206
South	50	170	720	1,758	3,410	5,076	13,389	22,611
Total	60	597	1,600	2,920	4,535	6,971	16,729	27,817

	1710	*1720*	*1730*	*1740*	*1750*	*1760*	*1770*	*1780*
North	8,303	14,091	17,323	23,958	30,222	40,033	48,460	56,796
South	36,563	54,748	73,698	126,066	206,198	285,773	411,362	518,624
Total	44,866	68,839	91,021	150,024	236,420	325,806	459,822	575,420

Table 2

GROWTH OF SLAVE AND FREEDMAN POPULATION (1790–1860)

	1790	*1800*	*1810*	*1820*
Slave	697,624	893,602	1,191,362	1,538,022
Free	59,557	108,435	186,446	233,634
Total	757,181	1,002,037	1,377,808	1,771,656

	1830	*1840*	*1850*	*1860*
Slave	2,009,043	2,487,355	3,204,313	3,953,760
Free	319,599	386,293	434,495	488,070
Total	2,328,642	2,873,648	3,638,808	4,441,830

In the 1680's, the colonies were beginning to flourish and conditions were the most prosperous since their inception. The agrarian society demanded greater manpower to increase productivity, and this manpower was supplied by additional slave labor, adding to even higher levels of profit. By the year 1690, 70 years after the first importation of black slaves, there were 16,729 people at forced labor in the American colonies. Slavery had taken a firm hold on the economic life of the Southern colonies, and the importation of slaves, with enormous profits for all involved in the trade (except for the enslaved) increased rapidly. In 1700 there were 27,817 slaves in the colonies and, 10 years later, in the year 1710, this population had virtually doubled.

Table 3

NEGRO POPULATION GROWTH AND DISTRIBUTION (1790-1970)

Year	*Total Population*	*Negro Population*	*Percent*
1790	3,929,214	757,181	19.3
1800	5,308,483	1,002,037	18.9
1810	7,239,881	1,377,808	19.0
1820	9,638,453	1,771,656	18.4
1830	12,866,020	2,328,642	18.1
1840	17,169,453	2,873,648	16.1
1850	23,191,876	3,638,808	15.7
1860	31,443,790	4,441,830	14.1
1870	39,818,449	4,880,009	12.7
1880	50,155,783	6,580,793	13.0
1890	62,947,714	7,488,676	11.0
1900	75,994,775	8,833,994	11.6
1910	93,402,151	9,827,763	10.7
1920	105,710,620	10,463,131	9.9
1930	122,775,046	11,891,143	9.7
1940	131,669,275	12,865,518	9.8
1950	150,697,361	15,042,286	10.0
1960	179,323,175	18,871,831	10.5
1966	194,100,000	21,300,000	11.0
1967	196,100,000	21,700,000	11.0
1968	198,200,000	22,000,000	11.0
1969	199,800,000	22,300,000	11.0
1970 est.	204,000,000	22,500,000	11.0

First United States Census of 1790

The first official census of the new government of the United States was taken in 1790, and 757,181 black people were counted. Not all were slaves. Although black freedmen had existed in the colonies for some time, there was no indication as to how extensive this population was. The 1790 census showed that roughly 9% or some 59,557 blacks had managed to acquire freedom, and this group was beginning to become an important factor in the society in general. By the year 1790, most Middle and Eastern states had enacted legislation providing for gradual emancipation. These states included Pennsylvania, Massachusetts, Connecticut, Rhode Island, New York, New Jersey and the new Northwest Territory.

The census of 1790 gave the slave population as follows:

Slave Population — Census of 1790

Connecticut	2,759
Delaware	8,887
Georgia	29,264
Kentucky	11,830
Maryland	103,036
New Hampshire	158
New Jersey	11,423
New York	21,324
North Carolina	100,572
Pennsylvania	3,737
Rhode Island	952
South Carolina	107,094
Vermont	17
Virginia	293,427
Ohio Territory	3,417

Despite the new laws of many states, slavery continued to flourish, and even subsequent international laws against the importation of slaves failed to halt the trade which continued almost to the time of the Civil War. By 1860, there were almost four million black slaves in the United States, 90% of whom were located in the South. The freedmen population, most of whom were in the North, numbered just short of half a million.

Chart 1

IN THE DECADES 1940-1970, ALMOST FOUR MILLION BLACKS HAVE LEFT THE SOUTH.

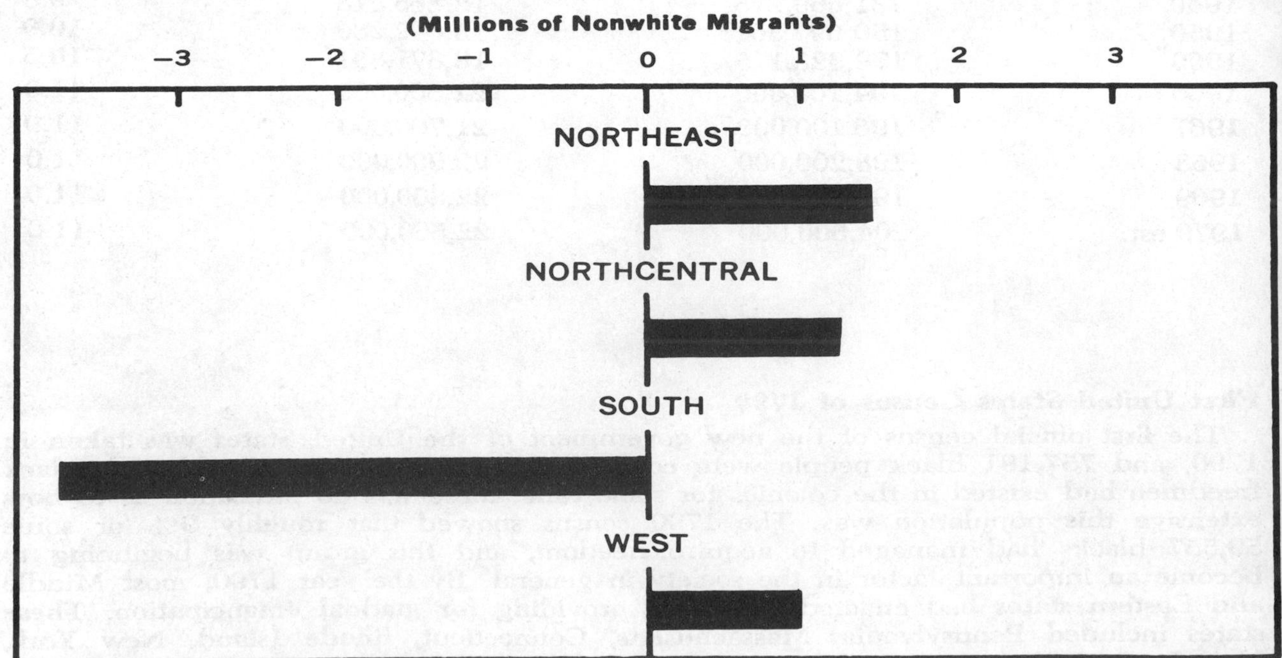

The first exodus from the South occurred in the period 1879-1881 when some 60,000 blacks moved into Kansas. This spontaneous movement was made under the most difficult of circumstances by riverboat, railroad, deteriorated wagons and on foot. The in-migration to Kansas created situations that strained the state, and several cities became refugee camps. The motivational force behind this initial thrust to new lands was the need for social and economic freedom and the avoidance of political abuse. One of the towns created by this exodus was Nicodemus, which still exists today as a small all-black community on the plains of Kansas.

Migration to the Cities

From 1790 to 1900, about 90% of all blacks resided in the South. Even after the Civil War, the rural character of the black population remained virtually intact, although there was some movement into new agricultural areas in Louisiana and Texas. The first large northward migration of Negroes occurred between 1910 and 1920, resulting in a drop of the Southern Negro population from 89% to 85%. By 1940, this figure had been reduced to 77%. Since then almost 4 million blacks have migrated northward, most of them being absorbed in the Northeast and North Central regions of the country. As of 1970 the percent of blacks in the South dropped to approximately 52%.

Statistics for the black population have become more detailed since the Civil War. Earlier census reports reflected greater detail for whites than for Negroes. In 1790, the number of slaves was ascertained without distinction of sex or age. Slavery, emancipation, freedom, racial progress, are the most prominent facts in the history of the black population.

The First Census (1790) showed two-fifths of the total Negro population of the country was resident in Virginia with a black population of 305,493. Other states reporting Negro populations in excess of 100,000 were: Maryland, 111,079; North Carolina, 105,547; South Carolina, 108,895. The fifth largest Negro population was that of Georgia, 29,662, while the sixth largest was that of New York, 25,978.

The Vicksburg Wharf from which many blacks departed West in the Exodus of 1879-1881.

From 1790-1850, the black population more than doubled. Earlier increase was in part attributable to importation of slaves during 1790-1808. In 1790, the black population of the United States was 757,181, with 239 Negroes per thousand of the white population. During the period of 90 years (1790-1880), the center of the Negro population moved from a point in Dinwiddie County, Va., to a point 443 miles southwest, located in Walker County, northwestern Georgia. The center of population is defined as the point to which the population in the aggregate is nearest—the point at which the population could assemble by travelling in the aggregate the least number of miles, assuming each individual could travel in a direct line from his place of residence to the point.

In 1860, 46.5% of the slave population was located in the South Atlantic states. Of the free colored population, 46.2% was in the North and 44.6% in the South. The proportion in the East and West—4.4 and 3.9% respectively—was much smaller than the proportion of slaves in these regions.

The census of 1910 provides varied information on the Negro population. In 1910, the Negro population of the South numbered 9,827,763, and amounted to 89%, or approxi-

A newspaper editorial cartoon of the 1880's showing blacks heading west and Chinese heading east to escape racial persecution.

mately nine-tenths of the total Negro population in the country. The Southern white population was 20,547,420, or one-fourth of the total white population. The South contained the mass of the Negro population while the majority of the white population was in the North and West. In the North, for instance, the Negro population numbered 1,027,674, and in the West, 50,662, the white populations for these two sections being respectively 54,640,209 and 6,544,328.

Chart 2

ALTHOUGH MILLIONS OF BLACKS HAVE LEFT THE SOUTH, 52% OF THE NATION'S BLACK POPULATION STILL RESIDES THERE.

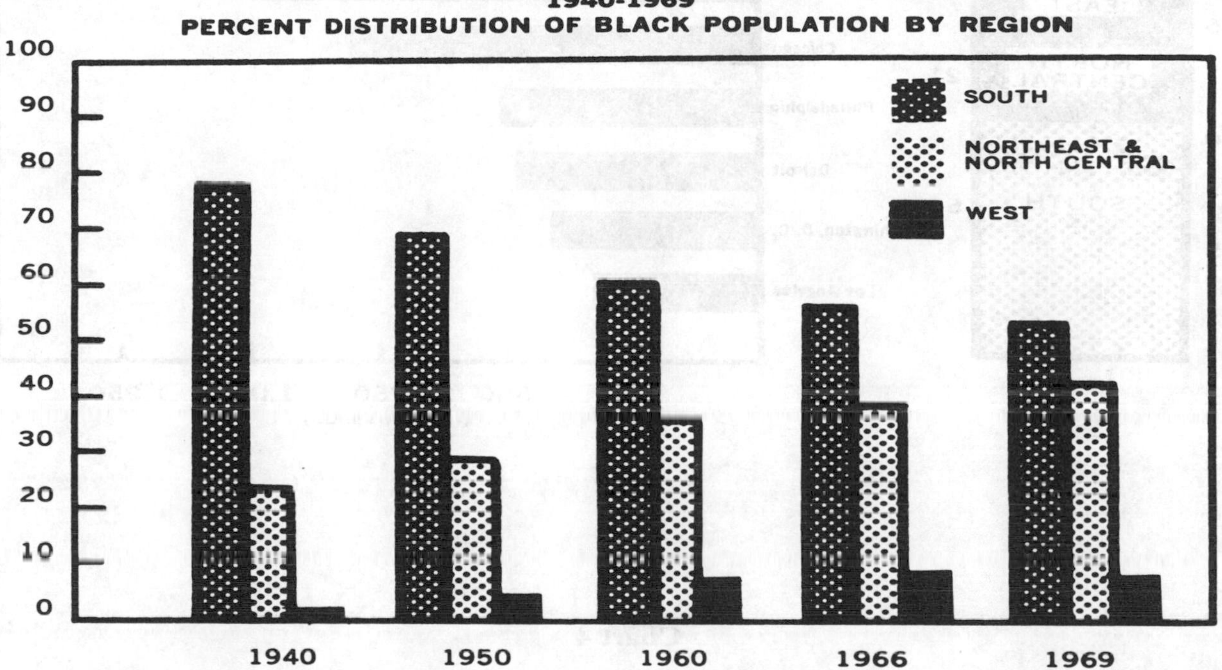

Since the beginning of the 20th century, the percentage of blacks in the total population has remained relatively stable, dropping in the period, 1900-1930 from 11.6% to 9.7% (the latter figure representing the lowest figure ever recorded in U. S. history), but rising in the period 1930-1970 from 9.7% to 11%.

In 1910, the first signs of the urbanization of America's black population began to appear. By this date, some 27% of them were in the cities. While in the South the black population was virtually all rural, in the North and West almost 80% of blacks lived in cities. The first substantial northward migration of blacks occurred between 1910 and 1920, resulting in the first significant change in the Southern black population as it was reduced from 90 to 85% during that period.

Patterns of Urban Concentration

The most dramatic change in the black population between 1940 and 1970 has not been in terms of numbers or percent of the total U. S. population but rather in location—away from the South and into the urban areas of the North and West. In 1940 over 77% of the black population was in the South. As of 1970 this figure had dropped just below the 52% level. During the 1950's blacks were leaving the South at a rate of some 146,000 people a year, and although the pace slackened during the 1960's the annual out-migration rate was roughly 88,000 people per year.

As of 1970 most of the nation's blacks who still lived on farms or in rural areas were to be found in the South. Nevertheless, even in the South, almost three out of five blacks lived in urban centers. In the nation as a whole 75% of the black population reside in urban areas. The heaviest urban concentrations are in the North and West where approximately 97% of the black population of the area reside in urban centers.

Chart 3

THE PREVIOUS SHARP OUT-MIGRATION OF BLACKS FROM THE SOUTH APPEARS TO NOW BE SLOWING. IN THE 1950's THE ANNUAL RATE OF OUT-MIGRATION WAS 146,000 WHILE IN THE 1960's IT WAS 88,000.

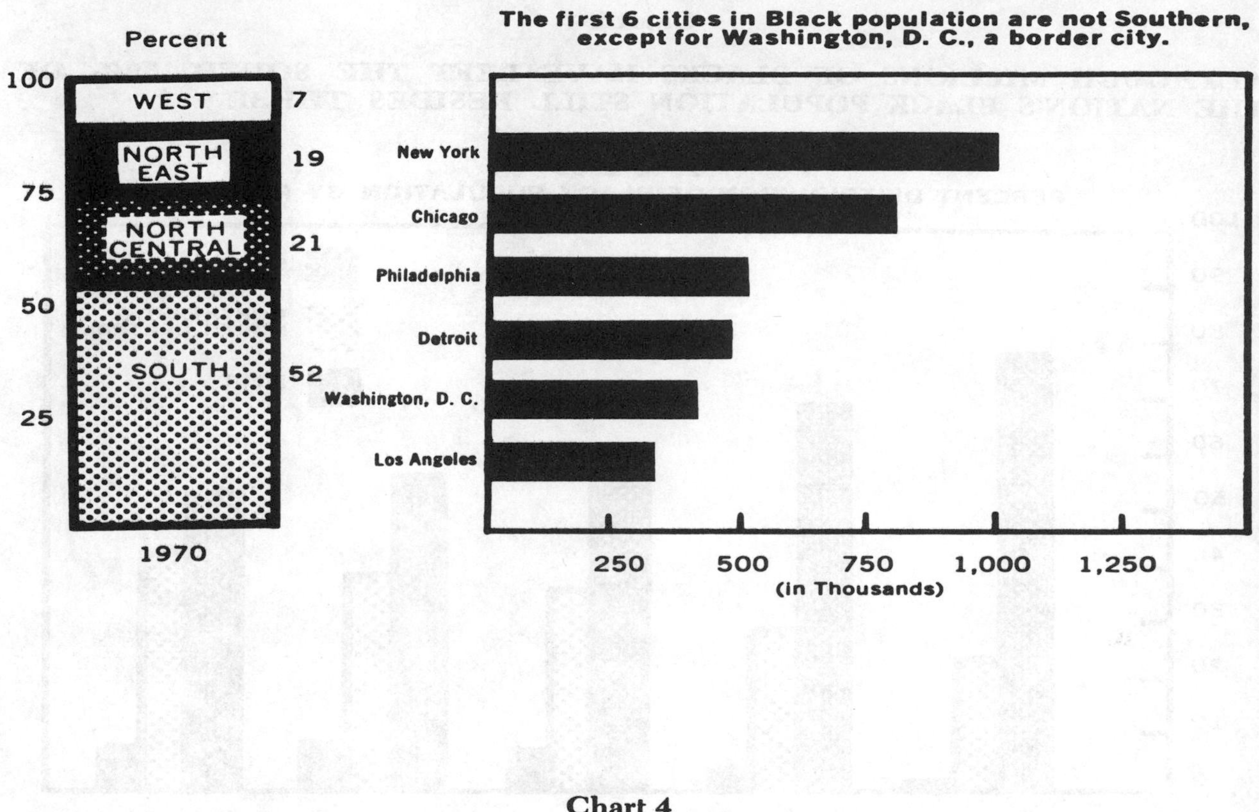

Chart 4

BLACKS WITH GREATER EDUCATIONAL ATTAINMENT ARE MORE INCLINED TO MIGRATE THAN THOSE WITH LESS EDUCATION.

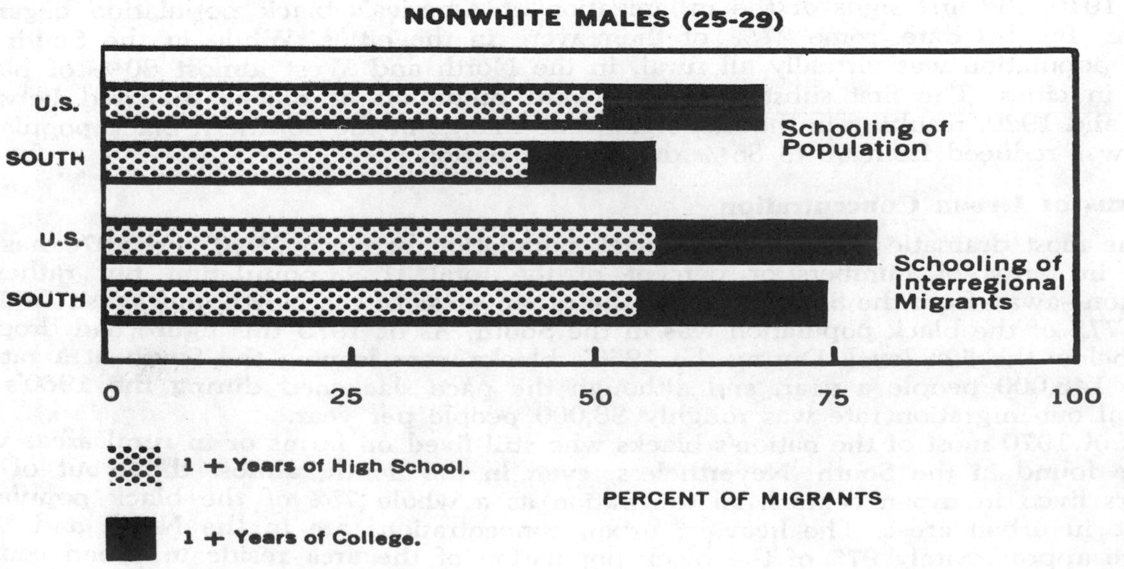

PERCENTAGE OF NEGRO AND WHITE POPULATION LIVING IN URBAN AREAS, BY REGION, CONTERMINOUS UNITED STATES, 1910–60

Table 4

Year	*United States*		*South*		*North and West*	
	Negro	*White*	*Negro*	*White*	*Negro*	*White*
1910	27.4	48.7	21.2	23.2	77.5	57.3
1920	35.4	53.3	27.0	28.5	84.3	61.6
1930	43.7	57.6	31.7	35.0	88.1	65.5
1940	48.6	59.0	36.5	36.8	89.1	67.4
1950	62.4	64.3	47.7	48.9	93.5	70.1
1960	73.2	69.6	58.4	58.6	95.3	73.7

SOURCES:

1920–40: *Sixteenth Census of the United States: 1940 Population, Vol. II, Characteristics of the Population*, Pts. 1–7, tables 4, 5, for each State (U.S. Bureau of the Census).

1950: *Census of Population, 1950, Vol. II, Characteristics of the Population*, Pt. 1, United States Summary, table 145 (U.S. Bureau of the Census).

1960: *Census of Population, Detailed Characteristics, United States Summary*, Final Report PC(1) 1D, tables 158, 233; 1910: *Abstract of the Thirteenth Census* (1910), table 28, p. 103 (U.S. Bureau of the Census).

Chart 5

IMMIGRANTS (CHIEFLY FROM THE SOUTH) CONSTITUTE ONE OUT OF EVERY TWO NONWHITES IN NORTHERN AND WESTERN CITIES OF GREATEST NEGRO POPULATION.

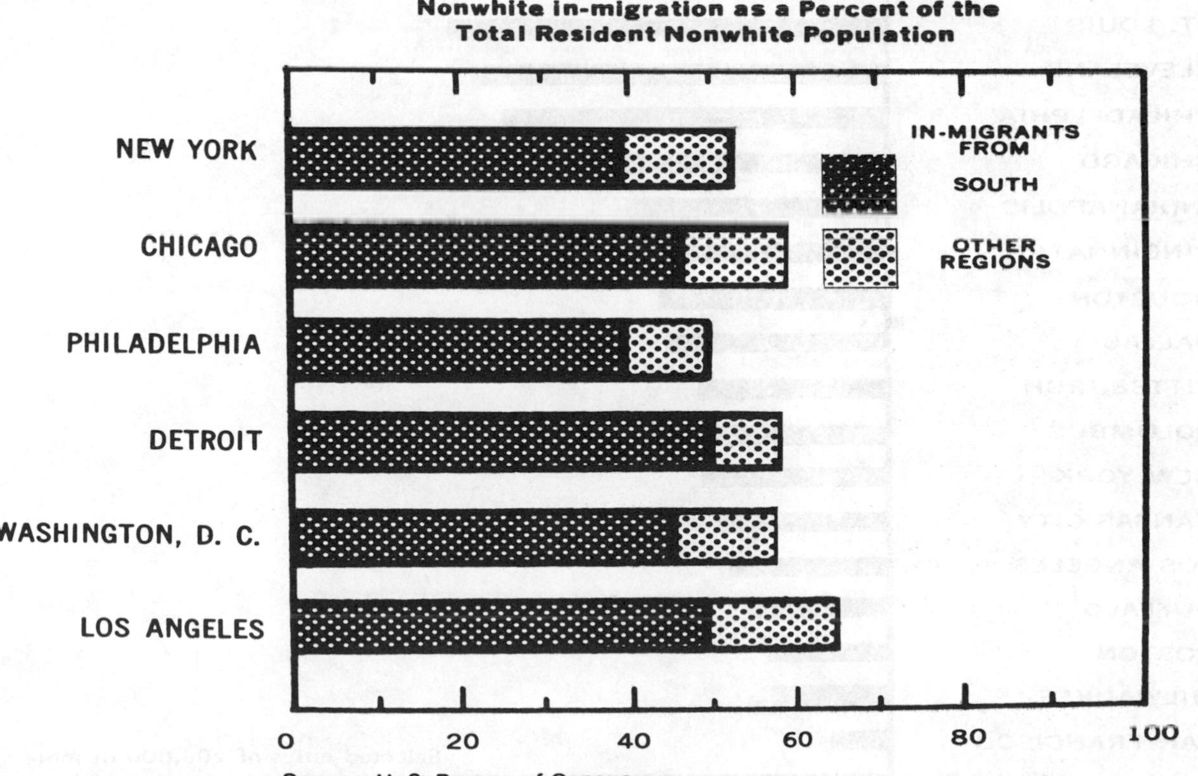

Source: U. S. Bureau of Census.

Population growth in the metropolitan areas had taken place at a much more rapid pace than that of the nation as a whole.

The largest population increase in the metropolitan areas has occurred primarily in the suburbs as whites move from the central cities. The black population in the central cities increased by 2.6 million persons in the 1960-1970 decade while the white population in the central cities showed a decline of 2.1 million.

As of 1970, 55% of all blacks in the nation live in the central cities. Virtually the entire rural black population is in the South, while some 97% of the black population in the North and West is located in the cities. Whites in the metropolitan area live predominantly outside the central cities and three-fourths of the white population live in the suburbs.

Blacks today (1970) constitute 21% of the total population of central cities in metropolitan areas; in 1950 this figure was 12%. The proportion of blacks in the suburban population has remained about the same since 1950.

Chart 6

THE 24 CITIES OF THE UNITED STATES WHICH HAVE BLACK POPULATIONS OVER 9%.

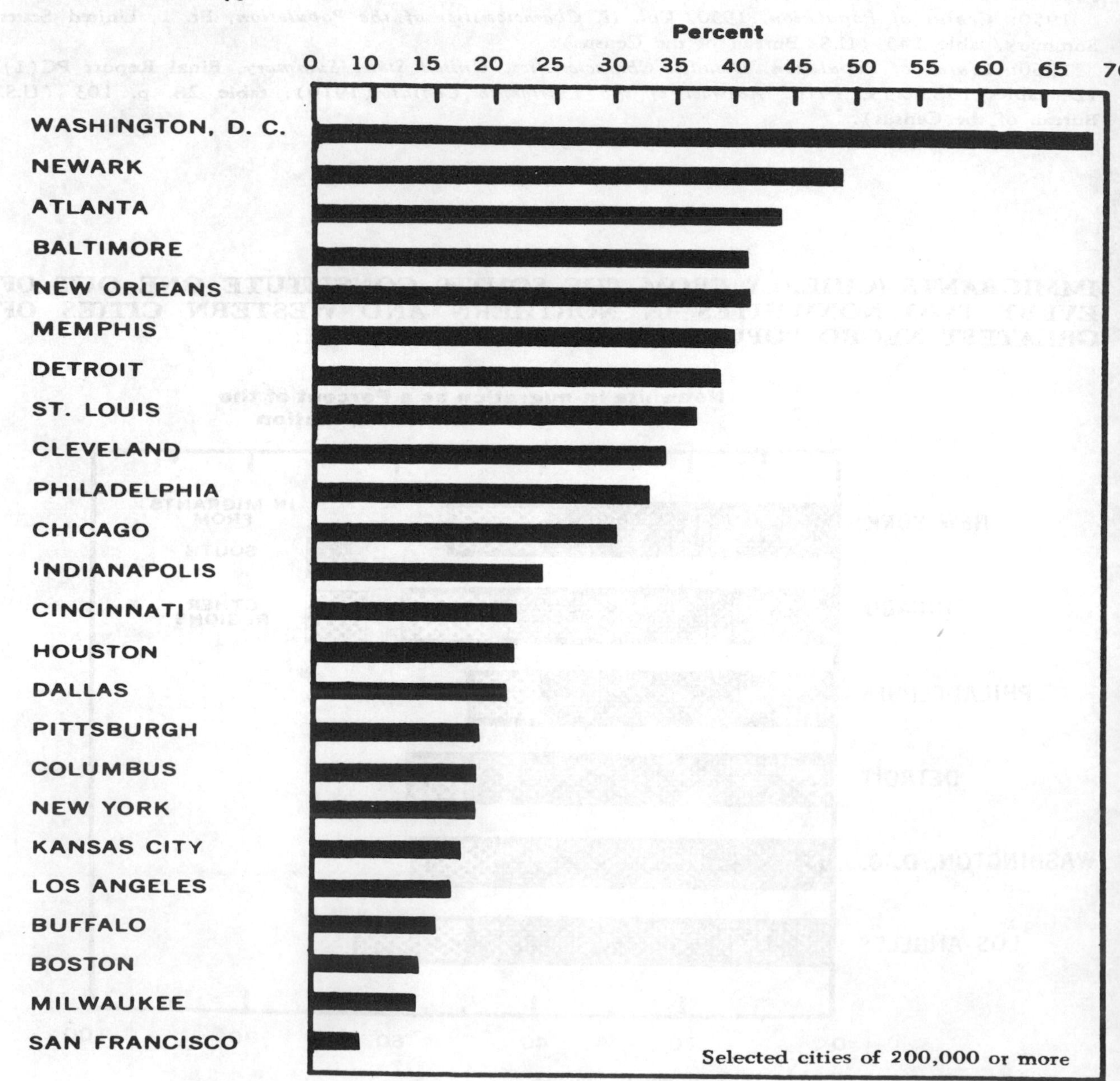

In 1960 the total black population of the United States was 18,800,000. As of 1970 the population was estimated to be 22,300,000 for an increase of some 3,500,000 persons. Of the total black population approximately 11,600,000 reside in the South; 4,600,000 reside in the North Central area; 4,300,000 live in the Northeast while the remainder, or 1,560,000 people are located in the West.

During the 1960-1970 decade more than three-fourths of the total growth of the black population occurred in the central cities of metropolitan areas. This ten year interval has seen an increase in central cities population by some 2,600,000. The majority of this increase was due primarily to an increase in births over deaths, however, about one-third of the total, or some 800,000, was due to in-migration from rural areas of the South.

Like immigrant groups in general, Negroes in the cities show distinct patterns of concentration. They are particularly numerous in those areas which are known as Standard Metropolitan Statistical Areas (SMSAs)—sometimes called Central City. As of 1960, for instance, the six cities with the largest Negro populations had some 20% of all Negroes in the United States. (With the exception of Washington, D. C., all were in the North.) In the largest cities, increasing Negro migration has been accompanied by the large-scale exodus of whites into suburban areas. In the more moderate SMSA areas, the trend of opposing migration is not so steep. In the smallest SMSAs, both white and Negro migration has continued to increase.

In all cases, however, the problem is not the number or proportion of Negroes, but their economic and "spatial" status. In most large cities, the population density per square mile is particularly high. (Color is the only common characteristic of these pockets of Negro residence. Range of income, education, etc. vary considerably.)

Although there is a rising trend in the proportion of pre-school Negro children, especially in the cities, a distinct possibility exists that Negro fertility rates may fall below white fertility rates in areas of heavy Negro concentration. This is thought to be dependent upon increased economic expansion, as well as governmental commitments to educational, employment and housing programs.

Chart 7

WHILE THE SOUTH HAS SHOWN A DRAMATIC SHIFT TOWARD URBANIZATION, THE PATTERNS OF MOVEMENT TO THE CITIES HAVE BEEN THE SAME FOR BOTH BLACK AND WHITE.

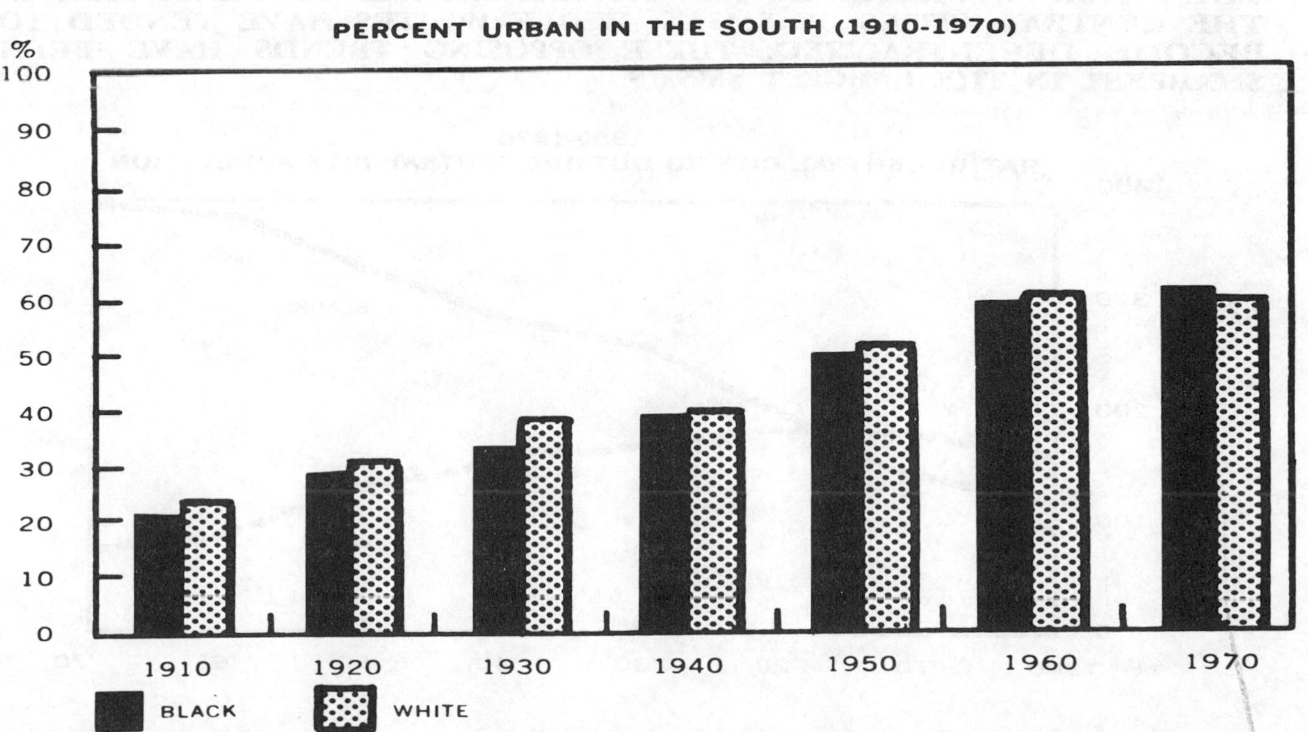

Chart 8

BLACKS HAVE TENDED TO MOVE INTO THOSE SECTIONS OF THE NATION WHERE HIGHER-STATUS AND BETTER-PAYING JOBS ARE AVAILABLE.

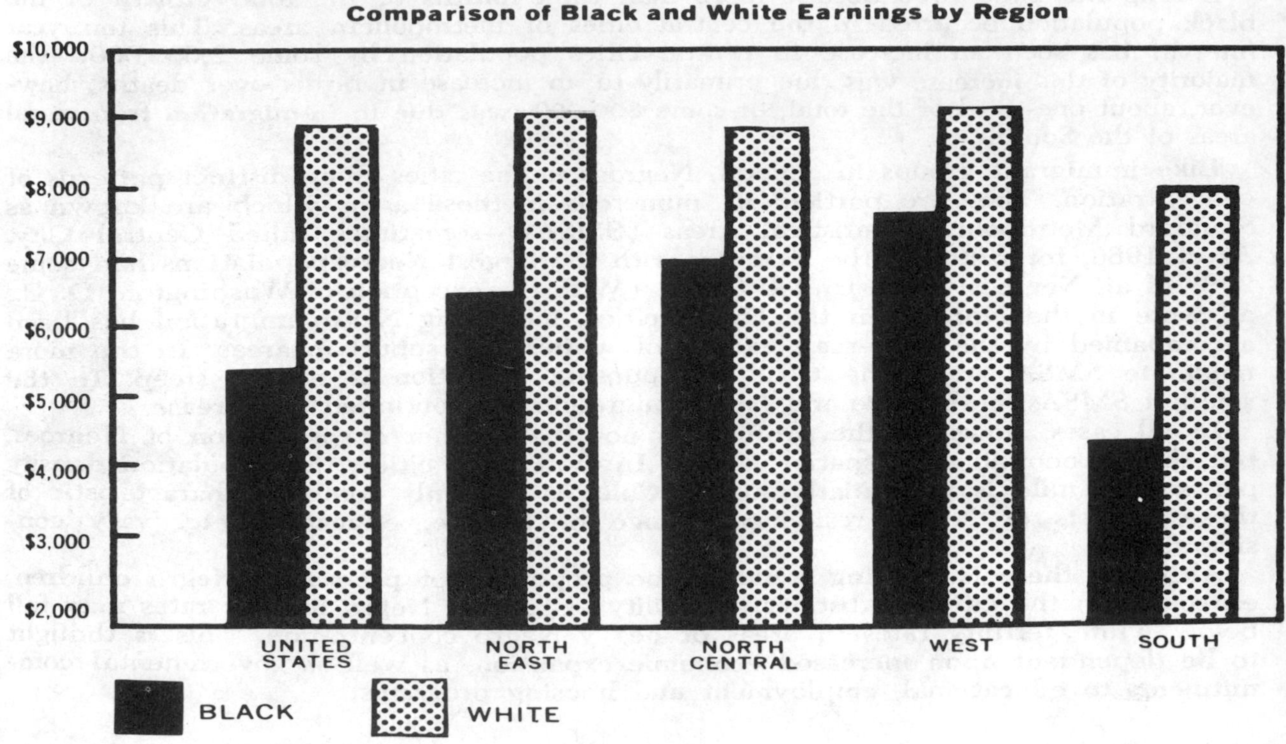

Chart 9

THE BLACK POPULATON OF THE U. S. HAS BECOME CONCENTRATED IN THE CENTRAL CITIES OF SMSA'S, WHILE WHITES HAVE TENDED TO BECOME DECENTRALIZED. THESE OPPOSING TRENDS HAVE BEEN SHARPEST IN THE LARGEST SMSA'S.

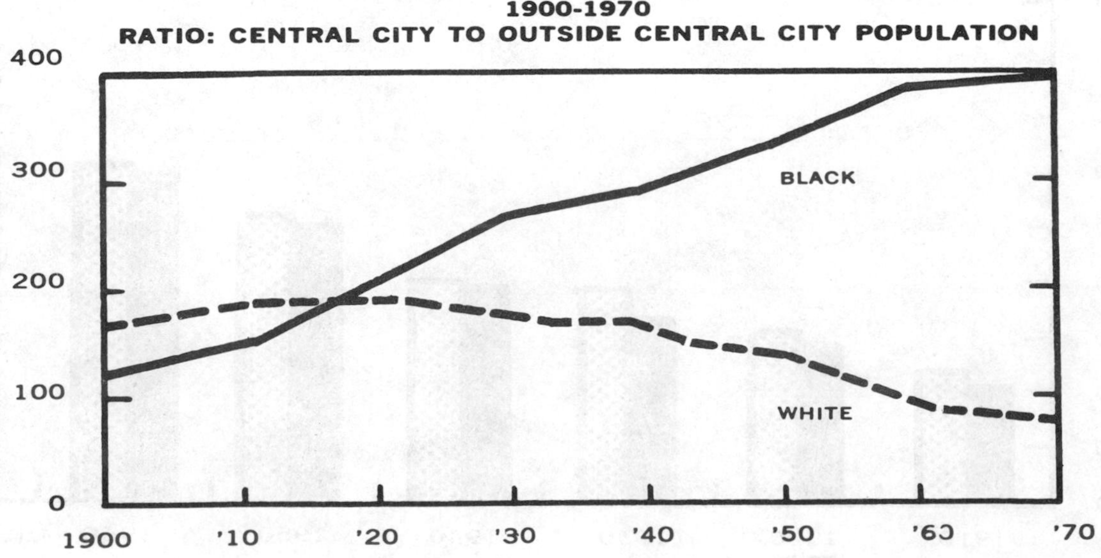

Chart 10

IN THE NORTH AND WEST, THE MAJOR CONCENTRATION OF THE BLACK POPULATION HAS ALWAYS BEEN IN THE CITIES.

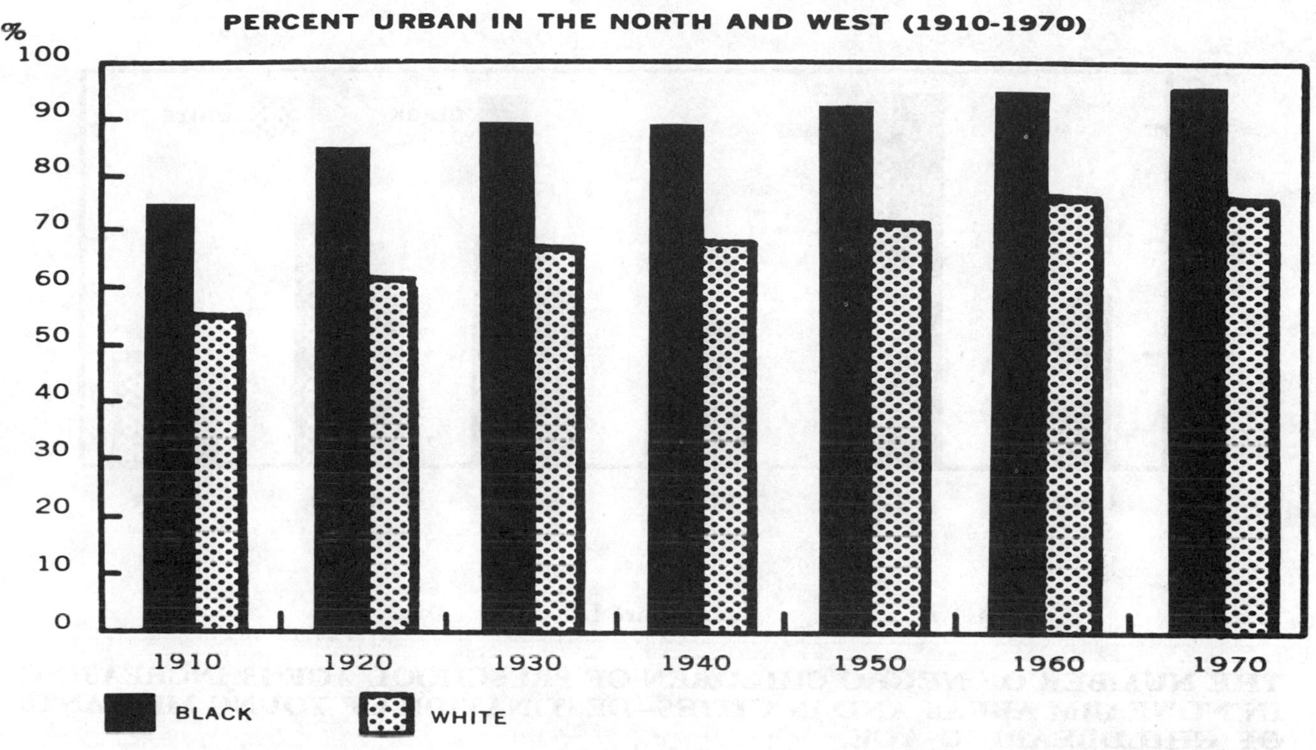

Chart 11

THE MOVEMENT OF BLACKS INTO THE CITIES THROUGHOUT THE U. S. CONTINUES AT A RAPID PACE WHILE WHITES ARE STILL LEAVING THE CITIES FOR THE SUBURBS.

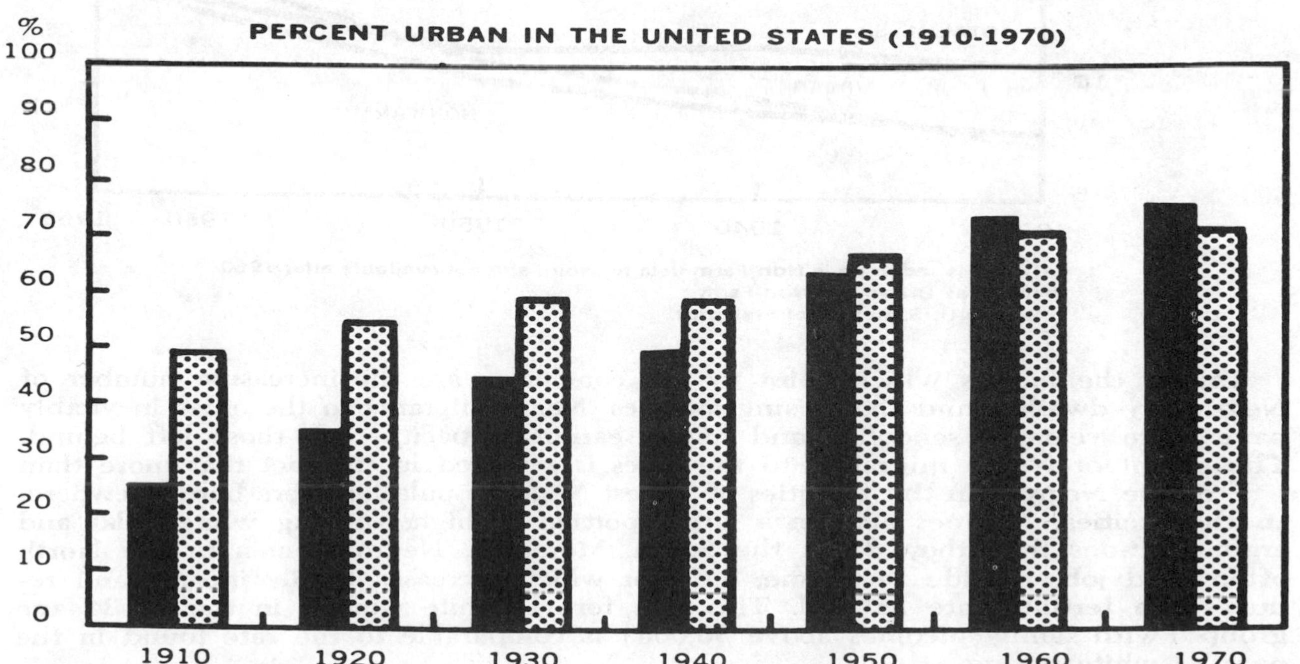

Chart 12

ON THE AVERAGE, THE BLACK POPULATION IS SLIGHTLY YOUNGER THAN THE WHITE POPULATION.

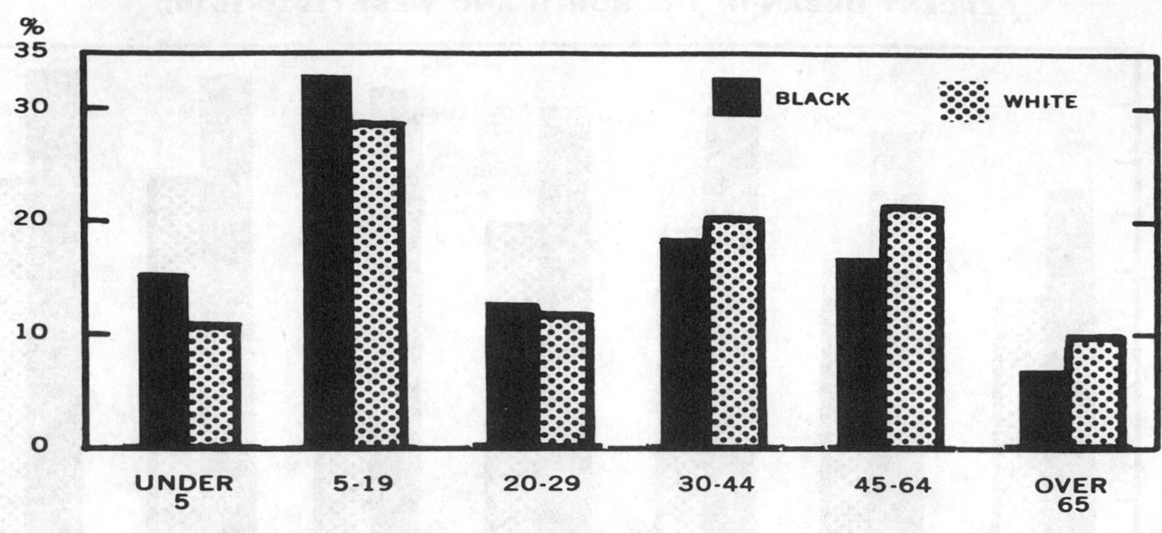

Chart 13

THE NUMBER OF NEGRO CHILDREN OF PRESCHOOL AGE IS INCREASING IN NONFARM AREAS AND IN CITIES—DESTINATION OF YOUNG MIGRANTS OF CHILDBEARING AGE.

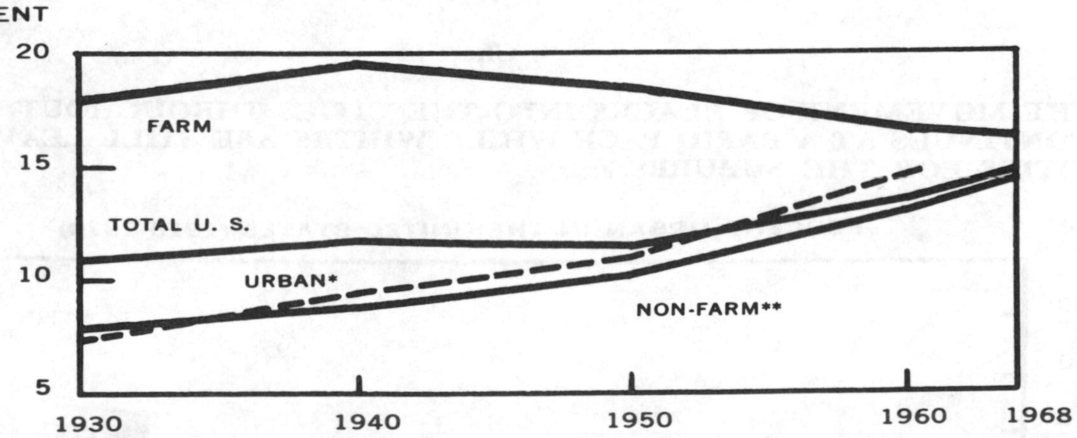

*Urban is included in Non-Farm data for Non-Farm not available after 1960
**Includes Urban and Non-Farm
Source U. S. Bureau of Statistics.

Among the factors which point to this conclusion are the increasing number of Negro city dwellers and their rising incomes. Negro migrants to the cities inevitably have more years of schooling and higher earning capacity than those left behind. The extent of Negro migration to the cities is reflected in the fact that more than lf of the Negroes in the six cities of largest Negro population were born elsewhere. in these cities, Negroes acquire a larger portion of higher-paying white-collar and craft positions than they do in the South. Moreover, Negro women in the North often hold jobs outside the home, a factor which increases family income and reduces the fertility rate as well. This rate for nonwhite women in the 25–34 age group (with family incomes above $6,000) is comparable to the rate found in the parallel white setting.

Chart 14

AT MAJOR CHILD-BEARING AGES,* THE NONWHITE TO WHITE FERTILITY RATIO DECREASES WITH INCREASING INCOME, AND TENDS TO BE LOWEST IN CITIES.

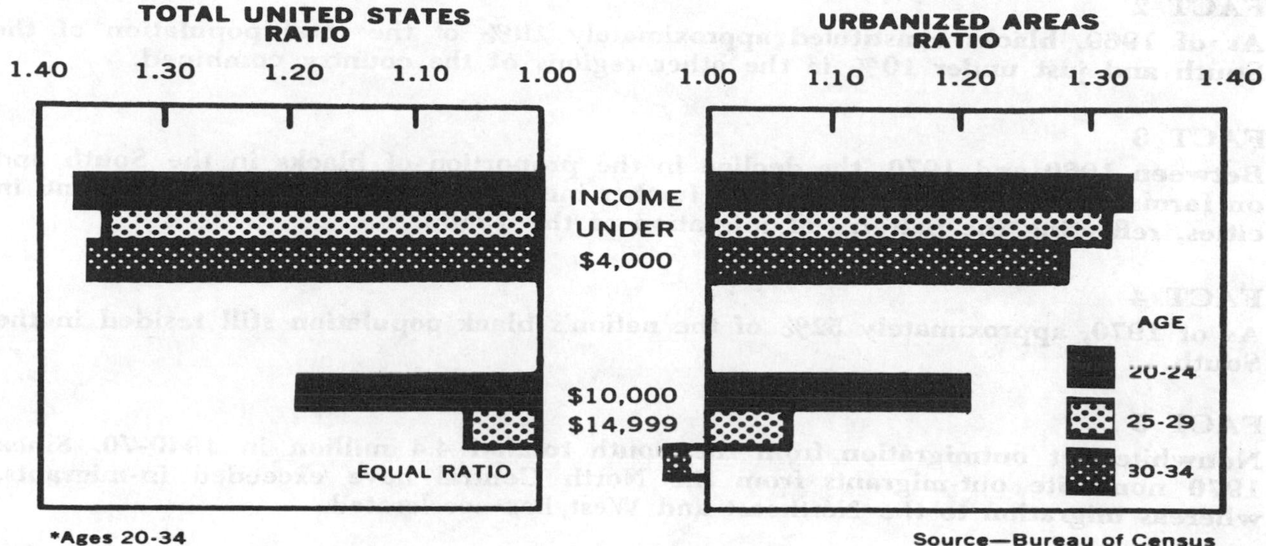

*Ages 20-34

Source—Bureau of Census

**Number of Nonwhite to White children ever born per 1,000 mothers.

Chart 15

FOR THE PERIOD 1900-1970, THE BLACK POPULATION HAS REMAINED AT A FAIRLY CONSTANT 10 TO 11% OF THE TOTAL U. S. POPULATION.

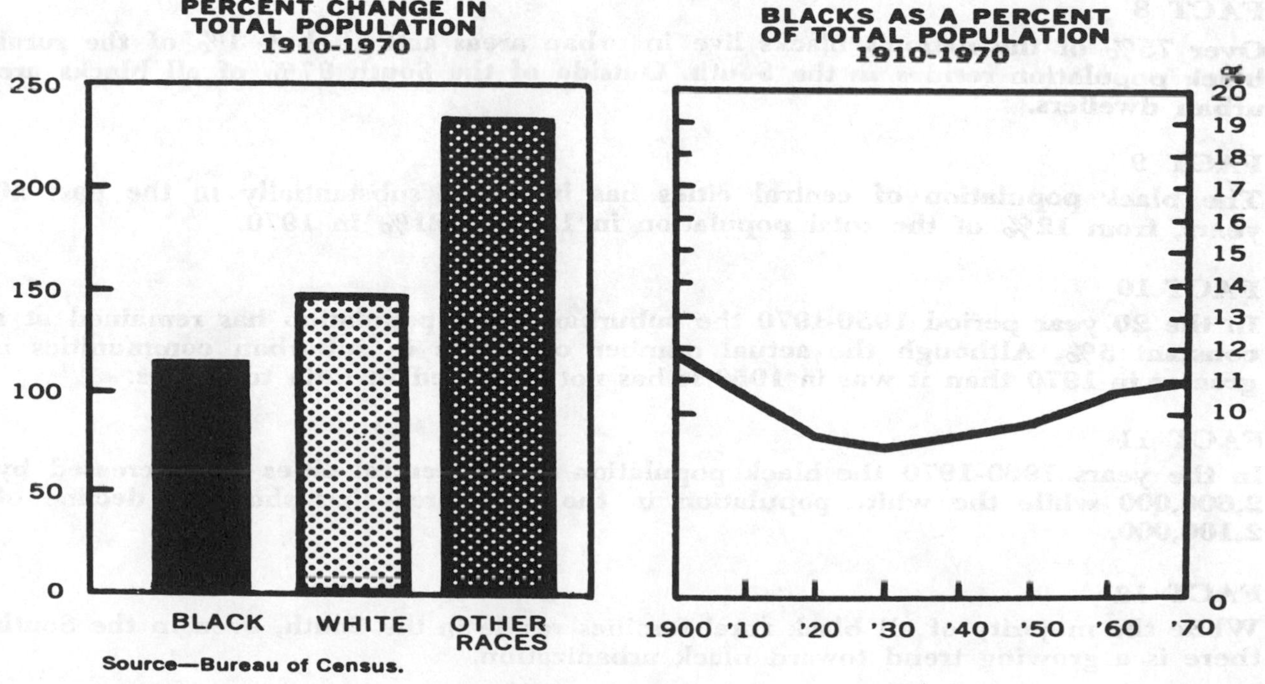

Source—Bureau of Census.

SELECTED POPULATION FACTS

FACT 1
During the period 1900-1970 the black population of the nation remained at a fairly constant 10 to 11% of the total population.

FACT 2
As of 1969, blacks constituted approximately 19% of the total population of the South and just under 10% in the other regions of the country combined.

FACT 3
Between 1960 and 1970, the decline in the proportion of blacks in the South and on farms continued, and there was a further increase in the West and North, and in cities, reflecting the patterns of migration of the 1950's.

FACT 4
As of 1970, approximately 52% of the nation's black population still resided in the South.

FACT 5
Nonwhite net outmigration from the South totaled 4.4 million in 1940-70. Since 1970 nonwhite out-migrants from the North Central have exceeded in-migrants, whereas migration to the Northeast and West has accelerated.

FACT 6
The average annual out-migration of blacks from the South has declined over the past ten years (1960-1970) and is currently 88,000 per year. In the 10 years preceding (1950-1960) the rate was 146,000 per year.

FACT 7
In the North and West, Negroes have been highly urban throughout this century, and continue to be substantially more urban than the white population. In the South, however, urbanization has proceeded at about the same pace among Negroes and whites.

FACT 8
Over 75% of the nation's blacks live in urban areas and all but 3% of the rural black population resides in the South. Outside of the South 97% of all blacks are urban dwellers.

FACT 9
The black population of central cities has increased substantially in the past 20 years, from 12% of the total population in 1950 to 21% in 1970.

FACT 10
In the 20 year period 1950-1970 the suburban black population has remained at a constant 5%. Although the actual number of blacks in suburban communities is greater in 1970 than it was in 1950 it has not increased in ratio to whites.

FACT 11
In the years 1960-1970 the black population in the central cities has increased by 2,600,000 while the white population in the same areas has shown a decline of 2,100,000.

FACT 12
While the majority of all black rural families reside in the South, even in the South there is a growing trend toward black urbanization.

FACT 13
Almost 97% of all blacks who live outside of the South reside in central cities of the metropolitan areas.

FACT 14
Outside of the South and since the 1910 census, the major concentration of the black population has always been in cities.

FACT 15
In the largest Northern and Western cities one out of every two black inhabitants is from the South.

FACT 16
The only major city of the nation which has a predominantly black population is Washington, D. C. In Newark, New Jersey, the black and white populations are about equally divided.

FACT 17
The black population is considerably younger than the white population; the median age of blacks is 21 years of age, while for whites it is 29 years of age.

FACT 18
While the number of blacks in the suburbs is higher than ever before, the proportion or ratio of blacks to whites has remained stable since 1950.

FACT 19
Of the small proportion of Negroes who lived in the West in 1970 (less than 10 percent), eight in 10 were in California, chiefly in the large cities.

FACT 20
Since the turn of the century, the proportion of Negroes has risen from two to seven percent of the Northern population, but declined steadily from almost ⅓ to about ⅕ in the South, largely through migration. While the proportion of Negroes almost doubled in the cities and declined on farms, it remained relatively stable in rural nonfarm places.

FACT 21
About the same proportion of Negroes as whites lived in SMSA's in 1960; however, the ratio of the population in central cities to the population outside tripled among Negroes between 1900 and 1960, whereas it decreased by nearly half among whites.

FACT 22
Well over half of the increase in Negro population between 1950 and 1960 was in the central cities of SMSA's in the North—the only areas which lost white population during the decade.

FACT 23
The concentration of Negroes in central cities of SMSA's and the whites' exodus to the outside have been greatest since 1900 in the larger SMSA's. The shift among Negroes from outside to inside the central city has been least sharp, however, in the smallest SMSA's (up to 250,000 population), where whites as well as Negroes were living chiefly in central cities in 1960.

FACT 24
Almost all of the 1960-70 Negro increase in the five SMSA's of largest Negro population (all of which are outside the South) was in the central city.

FACT 25

The distribution of the population by age, 1960-70, and 1930-70, shows more of an increase in the proportion of Negroes under five than among whites of this age. Since 1950, the increase was entirely in urban and rural nonfarm areas. The proportion of Negroes in other age groups declined, except among the elderly whose ratio increased slightly, chiefly in rural areas. The white population has shown similar trends, but with somewhat greater increases in the percent of elderly.

FACT 26

The proportion of Negro children under five in the total population of that age increased most in the cities from 1930-70, the destination of Negro migrants who tend to be young and of childbearing age.

FACT 27

The number of nonwhite migrants leaving the South has accelerated in recent years, especially to the West and North Central regions. Substantial numbers are migrating to the West from Northern states.

FACT 28

Nonwhite net outmigration from the South totaled three million in 1940-60, and another 880,000 in 1960-70. Since 1960, nonwhite out-migrants from the North Central exceeded in-migrants, whereas migration to the Northeast and West has accelerated.

FACT 29

Negroes born in the West or the Northeast and North Central regions are far more likely to remain there than those born in the South.

FACT 30

About one-half of the Negro residents in the 10 cities of the North and West that led in Negro population in 1960 were not born there. Of this group, most were born in the South.

FACT 31

Negroes were about 19 percent of the total population in the South, but less than 11% in other regions in 1970.

POPULATION TABLES

Table 5

Negroes as a Percent of Total Population by Location, Inside and Outside Metropolitan Areas, and by Size of Metropolitan Area, 1950, 1960, and 1969

Region	Percent Negro 1950	1960	1969
United States	10	11	11
Metropolitan areas[1]	9	11	12
Central cities	12	17	21
Central cities in metropolitan areas of—			
1,000,000 or more	13	19	26
250,000 to 1,000,000	12	15	18
Under 250,000	12	12	12
Suburbs	5	5	5
Outside metropolitan areas	11	10	9

[1]Population of the 212 SMSA's as defined in 1960.

Source: U.S. Department of Commerce, Bureau of the Census.

Table 6

Percent of All Negroes in Selected Cities Living in Census Tracts Grouped According to Proportion Negro in 1960 and 1964-1968

Region	Year	All census tracts	75 percent or more Negro	50 to 74 percent Negro	25 to 49 percent Negro	Less than 25 percent Negro
Cleveland, Ohio	1960	100	72	16	8	4
	1965	100	80	12	4	4
Memphis, Tenn.	1960	100	65	26	5	4
	1967	100	78	14	4	4
Phoenix, Ariz.	1960	100	19	36	24	21
	1965	100	18	23	42	17
Buffalo, N. Y.	1960	100	35	47	6	12
	1966	100	69	10	13	8
Louisville, Ky.	1960	100	57	13	17	13
	1964	100	67	13	10	10
New Haven, Conn.	1960	100	—	33	19	48
	1967	100	16	19	27	38
Rochester, N. Y.	1960	100	8	43	17	32
	1964	100	16	45	24	15
Sacramento, Calif.	1960	100	9	—	14	77
	1964	100	8	14	28	50
Des Moines, Iowa	1960	100	—	28	31	41
	1966	100	—	42	19	39
Providence, R. I.	1960	100	—	23	2	75
	1965	100	—	16	46	38
Shreveport, La.	1960	100	79	10	7	4
	1966	100	90	—	6	4
Evansville, Ind.	1960	100	34	27	9	30
	1966	100	59	14	—	27
Little Rock, Ark.	1960	100	33	33	19	15
	1964	100	41	18	22	19
Raleigh, N. C.	1960	100	86	—	7	7
	1966	100	88	4	2	6
Trenton, N. J.	1960	100	26	9	48	17
	1968	100	24	55	13	8

— Represents zero.

NOTE.—Selected cities of 100,000 or more in which a special census was taken in any of the years 1964-1968. Ranked according to total population at latest census.

Source: U.S. Department of Commerce, Bureau of the Census.

Table 7

Population of the United States, by Metropolitan-Nonmetropolitan Residence, 1960, 1964, and 1969

Region and color	Numbers in thousands			Percent change		Average annual percent change	
	1960	1964	1969	1950–60	1960–69	1950–60	1960–69
Negro	18,793	20,514	22,331	25.5	18.8	2.3	2.0
Metropolitan areas	12,168	13,970	15,594	46.2	28.2	3.8	2.8
In central cities	9,687	11,282	12,317	50.4	27.1	4.1	2.7
Outside central cities	2,481	2,688	3,278	31.6	32.1	2.7	3.2
Nonmetropolitan areas	6,625	6,541	6,736	−0.3	1.7	(Z)	0.2
White	158,051	167,146	175,311	17.6	10.9	1.6	1.2
Metropolitan areas	99,740	106,406	111,736	24.3	12.0	2.2	1.3
In central cities	47,463	47,632	45,348	4.7	−4.5	0.5	−0.5
Outside central cities	52,277	58,774	66,387	49.8	27.0	4.0	2.7
Nonmetropolitan areas	58,311	60,735	63,577	7.6	9.0	0.7	1.0

Source: U.S. Department of Commerce, Bureau of the Census.

Table 8

Percent Distribution of the Negro Population, by Region, 1940, 1950, 1960, 1966, and 1969

Region	Year				
	1940[1]	1950[1]	1960	1966	1969
United States	100	100	100	100	100
South	77	68	60	55	52
North	22	28	34	37	41
Northeast	11	13	16	17	19
North Central	11	15	18	20	21
West	1	4	6	8	7

[1] Data exclude Alaska and Hawaii.
Source: U.S. Department of Commerce, Bureau of the Census.

Table 9

Negroes as a Percent of the Total Population in the United States and Each Region, 1940, 1950, 1960, and 1969

Region	Percent of total population			
	1940[1]	1950[1]	1960	1969
United States	10	10	11	11
South	24	22	21	19
North	4	5	7	9
Northeast	4	5	7	9
North Central	4	5	7	8
West	1	3	4	5

[1] Data exclude Alaska and Hawaii.
Source: U.S. Department of Commerce, Bureau of the Census.

Table 10

Percent Distribution of Population by Location, Inside and Outside Metropolitan Areas, 1950, 1960, and 1969

Region	Percent and color					
	Negro			White		
	1950	1960	1969[1]	1950	1960	1969[1]
United States	100	100	100	100	100	100
Metropolitan areas	56	65	70	60	63	64
Central cities	43	52	55	34	30	26
Suburbs	13	13	15	26	33	38
Outside metropolitan areas	44	35	30	40	37	36

[1] Based on 5-quarter average centered on January 1969.
Source: U.S. Department of Commerce, Bureau of the Census.

Table 11

Proportion of Negroes in Each of the 30 Largest Cities, 1950, 1960, and Estimated 1967

Region	1950	1960	1967 (Estimate)[1]
New York, N. Y.	10	14	19
Chicago, Ill.	14	23	30
Los Angeles, Calif.	9	14	18
Philadelphia, Pa.	18	26	33
Detroit, Mich.	16	29	39
Baltimore, Md.	24	35	41
Houston, Tex.	21	23	22
Cleveland, Ohio	16	29	34
Washington, D.C.	35	54	69
St. Louis, Mo.	18	29	37
Milwaukee, Wis.	3	8	14
San Francisco, Calif.	6	10	14
Boston, Mass.	5	9	15
Dallas, Tex.	13	19	22
New Orleans, La.	32	37	41
Pittsburgh, Pa.	12	17	21
San Antonio, Tex.	7	7	8
San Diego, Calif.	5	6	7
Seattle, Wash.	3	5	7
Buffalo, N.Y.	6	13	17
Cincinnati, Ohio	16	22	24
Memphis, Tenn.	37	37	40
Denver, Colo.	4	6	9
Atlanta, Ga.	37	38	44
Minneapolis, Minn.	1	2	4
Indianapolis, Ind.	15	21	24
Kansas City, Mo.	12	18	22
Columbus, Ohio	12	16	19
Phoenix, Ariz.	5	5	5
Newark, N.J.	17	34	49

[1] Except for Cleveland, Buffalo, Memphis, and Phoenix, for which a special census has been made in recent years, these are very rough estimates computed on the basis of the change in relative proportions of Negro births and deaths since 1960.

Source: U.S. Department of Commerce, Bureau of the Census.

Table 12

Negro Population and Estimated Net Out-Migration of Negro and Other Races from the South, 1940-1969
(In thousands)

	1940	1950	1960	1969[1]
Negro population in the South	9,905	10,222	11,312	11,630
	1940–50	1950–60	1960–69	
Average annual net out-migration from the South of Negroes and other races	159.7	145.7	88.3	

[1] Excludes Armed Forces living in barracks and similar types of quarters.

Source: U.S. Department of Commerce, Bureau of the Census.

Table 13

Population by Age and Sex, 1969
(In thousands. Five-quarter average centered on January 1969)

Age and Sex	Negro	White	Percent Negro	Percent White
MALE				
All ages	10,660	85,189	100	100
Under 14 years	3,987	23,954	37	28
Under 5 years	1,435	7,665	13	9
5 to 13 years	2,552	16,289	24	19
14 to 15 years	510	3,411	5	4
16 to 19 years	869	6,065	8	7
20 to 24 years	766	5,863	7	7
25 to 34 years	1,189	10,393	11	12
35 to 44 years	1,065	10,155	10	12
45 to 64 years	1,658	17,788	16	21
65 years and over	618	7,560	6	9
Median age	19.8	28.2	(X)	(X)
FEMALE				
All ages	11,671	90,123	100	100
Under 14 years	3,964	22,944	34	25
Under 5 years	1,427	7,342	12	8
5 to 13 years	2,537	15,602	22	17
14 to 15 years	498	3,309	4	4
16 to 19 years	924	6,146	8	7
20 to 24 years	916	6,981	8	8
25 to 34 years	1,359	10,717	12	12
35 to 44 years	1,279	10,526	11	12
45 to 64 years	1,936	19,280	17	21
65 years and over	794	10,218	7	11
Median age	22.4	30.3	(X)	(X)

X—Not applicable.
Source: U.S. Department of Commerce, Bureau of the Census.

Table 14

NEGRO POPULATION AND PERCENT NEGRO BY STATES, 1910, 1960 AND 1970

Region	*Negro Population* 1910	1960	1970	*Percent Negro* 1910	1960	1970
NORTH	1,027,674	6,474,536	8,913,687	1.8	6.7	8.4
New England	66,306	243,363	388,398	1.0	2.3	3.0
Maine	1,363	3,318	2,800	0.2	0.3	0.3
New Hampshire	564	1,903	2,505	0.1	0.3	0.3
Vermont	1,621	519	761	0.5	0.1	0.2
Massachusetts	38,055	111,842	175,817	1.1	2.2	3.1
Rhode Island	9,529	18,332	25,338	1.8	2.1	2.7
Connecticut	15,174	107,449	181,177	1.4	4.2	6.0
Middle Atlantic	417,870	2,785,136	3,953,739	2.2	8.2	11.0
New York	134,191	1,417,511	2,166,933	1.5	8.4	12.0
New Jersey	89,760	514,875	770,292	3.5	8.5	11.0
Pennsylvania	193,919	852,750	1,016,514	2.5	7.5	9.0
East North Central	300,836	2,884,969	3,872,905	1.6	8.0	10.0
Ohio	111,452	786,097	970,477	2.3	8.1	9.0

Table 14–Continued

Region	Negro Population 1910	1960	1970	Percent Negro 1910	1960	1970
Indiana	60,320	269,275	357,464	0.9	2.2	7.0
Illinois	109,049	1,037,470	1,425,674	0.5	1.9	13.0
Michigan	17,115	717,581	991,066	0.9	0.6	11.0
Wisconsin	2,900	74,546	128,224	0.2	0.1	3.0
West North Central	**242,662**	**561,068**	**698,645**	**5.6**	**2.1**	**4.0**
Minnesota	7,084	22,263	34,868	0.2	0.3	0.9
Iowa	14,973	25,354	32,596	0.2	0.7	1.2
Missouri	157,452	390,853	480,172	10.0	4.8	10.0
North Dakota	617	777	2,494	—*	0.1	0.4
South Dakota	817	1,114	1,627	—*	0.1	0.2
Nebraska	7,689	29,262	39,911	0.3	0.6	2.7
Kansas	54,030	91,445	106,977	0.6	3.2	4.8
SOUTH	**8,749,427**	**11,311,607**	**12,064,258**	**36.8**	**29.8**	**19.0**
South Atlantic	**4,112,488**	**5,844,565**	**6,423,710**	**38.4**	**33.7**	**21.0**
Delaware	31,181	60,688	78,276	19.3	15.4	14.0
Maryland	232,250	518,410	701,341	24.9	17.9	18.0
District of Columbia	94,446	411,737	537,712	19.1	28.5	71.0
Virginia	671,096	816,258	865,388	34.4	32.6	18.6
West Virginia	64,173	89,378	73,931	—	5.3	4.0
North Carolina	697,843	1,116,021	1,137,664	36.4	31.6	22.0
South Carolina	835,843	829,291	789,041	58.6	55.2	30.0
Georgia	1,176,987	1,122,596	1,190,779	44.1	45.1	26.0
Florida	308,669	880,186	1,049,578	44.6	41.0	15.0
East South Central	**2,652,513**	**2,698,839**	**2,597,005**	**34.7**	**31.5**	**20.1**
Kentucky	261,656	215,949	241,292	20.4	11.4	7.5
Tennessee	473,088	586,876	631,696	25.5	21.7	16.0
Alabama	908,282	980,271	908,247	45.4	42.5	26.0
Mississippi	1,009,487	915,743	815,770	55.3	56.2	37.0
West South Central	**1,984,426**	**2,768,203**	**3,043,543**	**36.9**	**22.6**	**16.0**
Arkansas	442,801	388,787	357,225	25.6	28.1	19.0
Louisiana	713,874	1,039,207	1,088,734	49.5	43.1	30.0
Oklahoma	137,612	153,084	177,907	—	8.3	7.0
Texas	690,049	1,187,125	1,419,677	30.3	17.7	13.0
WEST	**50,662**	**1,085,688**	**1,694,655**	**0.7**	**0.7**	**4.9**
Mountain	**21,467**	**123,242**	**180,382**	**0.1**	**0.8**	**2.0**
Montana	1,834	1,467	1,995	—	0.5	0.3
Idaho	651	1,502	2,130	—	0.2	0.3
Wyoming	2,235	2,183	2,568	—	1.5	0.8
Colorado	11,453	39,992	66,411	0.1	1.4	3.0
New Mexico	1,628	17,063	19,555	0.1	0.5	2.0
Arizona	2,009	43,403	53,344	—	1.0	3.0
Utah	1,144	4,148	6,617	0.2	0.3	0.6
Nevada	513	13,484	27,762	0.7	0.6	6.0
Pacific	**29,195**	**962,446**	**1,514,243**	**1.0**	**0.7**	**6.0**
Washington	6,058	48,738	71,308	0.3	0.5	2.0
Oregon	1,492	18,133	26,308	0.2	0.2	1.0
California	21,645	883,861	1,400,143	1.1	0.9	7.0
Alaska	—	6,771	8,911	—	—	3.0
Hawaii	—	4,943	7,753	—	—	1.0
U.S. TOTAL	**9,827,763**	**18,871,831**	**22,672,520**	**14.1**	**10.7**	**11.0**

* Dakota Territory.

SOURCE: 1860 and 1910 from U.S. Bureau of the Census, *Negroes in the United States, 1920–32,* Chapter II, Table 12 and Chapter III, Table 4; 1960 from U.S. Bureau of the Census, *U.S. Census of Population: 1960, General Population Characteristics, U.S. Summary,* Final Report PC(1)–1B, Table 56.

Table 15

Cities With 100,000 Inhabitants or More in 1960—Population, 1910 to 1960, and Area, 1960

[Increase from census to census includes that due to annexation of territory as well as to direct growth. "Cities" refers to political subdivisions which are incorporated as cities, boroughs, towns, or villages with the exception that towns are not recognized as incorporated places in New England States, New York, and Wisconsin. Land area figures generally supplied by city engineers and reviewed for reasonableness by Bureau of the Census]

City	1910	1930	1950	1960						
				Population					Land area (sq. mi.)	Population per square mile
				Rank order	Total	Nonwhite				
						Number	Percent			
Akron, Ohio	69,067	255,040	274,605	45	290,351	37,894	13.1		54	5,387
Albany, N.Y	100,253	127,412	134,995	93	129,726	10,972	8.5		19	6,828
Albuquerque, N. Mex	11,020	26,570	96,815	59	201,189	5,925	2.9		56	3,580
Allentown, Pa	51,913	92,563	106,756	116	108,347	847	0.8		18	6,156
Amarillo, Tex	9,957	43,132	74,246	88	137,969	8,029	5.8		55	2,518
Anaheim, Calif	2,628	10,995	13,556	123	104,184	712	0.7		25	4,201
Atlanta, Ga	154,839	270,366	331,314	24	487,455	186,820	38.3		128	3,802
Austin, Tex	29,860	53,120	132,459	67	186,545	24,739	13.3		49	3,776
Baltimore, Md	558,485	804,874	949,708	6	939,024	328,416	35.0		79	11,886
Baton Rouge, La	14,897	30,729	125,629	80	152,419	45,603	29.9		31	4,917
Beaumont, Tex	20,640	57,732	94,014	102	119,175	35,004	29.4		71	1,683
Berkeley, Calif	40,434	82,109	113,805	114	111,268	29,187	26.2		10	11,471
Birmingham, Ala	132,685	259,678	326,037	36	340,887	135,267	39.7		75	4,576
Boston, Mass	670,585	781,188	801,444	13	697,197	68,493	9.8		48	14,586
Bridgeport, Conn	102,054	146,716	158,709	79	156,748	15,565	9.9		15	10,381
Buffalo, N.Y	423,715	573,076	580,132	20	532,759	73,388	13.8		39	13,522
Cambridge, Mass	104,839	113,643	120,740	119	107,716	6,787	6.3		6	17,098
Camden, N.J	94,538	118,700	124,555	103	117,159	27,892	23.8		9	13,476
Canton, Ohio	50,217	104,906	116,912	109	113,631	11,147	9.8		14	7,946
Charlotte, N.C	34,014	82,675	134,042	58	201,564	56,471	28.0		65	3,111
Chattanooga, Tenn	44,604	119,798	131,041	92	130,009	43,226	33.2		37	3,542
Chicago, Ill	2,185,283	3,376,438	3,620,962	2	3,550,404	837,656	23.6		224	15,836
Cincinnati, Ohio	363,591	451,160	503,998	21	502,550	109,682	21.8		77	6,501
Cleveland, Ohio	560,663	900,429	914,808	8	876,050	253,108	28.9		81	10,789
Columbus, Ga	20,554	43,131	79,611	104	116,779	31,547	27.0		26	4,423
Columbus, Ohio	181,511	290,564	375,901	28	471,316	78,305	16.6		89	5,296
Corpus Christi, Tex	8,222	27,741	108,287	74	167,690	9,327	5.6		38	4,436
Dallas, Tex	92,104	260,475	434,462	14	679,684	131,211	19.3		280	2,428
Dayton, Ohio	116,577	200,982	243,872	49	262,332	57,547	21.9		34	7,808
Dearborn, Mich	911	50,358	94,994	110	112,007	144	0.1		25	4,427
Denver, Colo	213,381	287,861	415,786	23	493,887	35,261	7.1		71	6,956
Des Moines, Iowa	86,368	142,559	177,965	55	208,982	10,558	5.1		65	3,240
Detroit, Mich	465,766	1,568,662	1,849,568	5	1,670,144	487,174	29.2		140	11,964
Duluth, Minn	78,466	101,463	104,511	122	106,884	1,125	1.1		63	1,707
Elizabeth, N.J	73,409	114,589	112,817	120	107,698	11,880	11.0		12	9,205
El Paso, Tex	39,279	102,421	130,485	46	276,687	7,424	2.7		115	2,414
Erie, Pa	66,525	115,967	130,803	87	138,440	6,745	4.9		19	7,364
Evansville, Ind	69,647	102,249	128,636	86	141,543	9,389	6.6		32	4,423
Flint, Mich	38,550	156,492	163,143	61	196,940	34,812	17.7		30	6,587
Fort Wayne, Ind	63,933	114,946	133,607	78	161,776	11,989	7.4		37	4,396
Fort Worth, Tex	73,312	163,447	278,778	34	356,268	56,922	16.0		141	2,536
Fresno, Calif	24,892	52,513	91,669	90	133,929	13,123	9.8		29	4,683
Gary, Ind	16,802	100,426	133,911	70	178,320	69,340	38.9		42	4,287
Glendale, Calif	2,746	62,736	95,702	101	119,442	574	0.5		29	4,077
Grand Rapids, Mich	112,571	168,592	176,515	71	177,313	14,778	8.3		24	7,267
Greensboro, N.C	15,895	53,569	74,389	100	119,574	31,130	26.0		49	2,460
Hammond, Ind	20,925	64,560	87,594	112	111,698	2,586	2.3		24	4,753
Hartford, Conn	98,915	164,072	177,397	77	162,178	25,151	15.5		17	9,321
Honolulu, Hawaii	52,183	137,582	248,034	43	294,194	213,920	72.7		84	3,506
Houston, Tex	78,800	292,352	596,163	7	938,219	217,672	23.2		328	2,860
Indianapolis, Ind	233,650	364,161	427,173	26	476,258	98,684	20.7		71	6,689
Jackson, Miss	21,262	48,282	98,271	84	144,422	51,629	35.7		47	3,106
Jacksonville, Fla	57,699	129,549	204,517	60	201,030	82,744	41.2		30	6,657
Jersey City, N.J	267,779	316,715	299,017	47	276,101	37,274	13.5		13	21,239
Kansas City, Kans	82,331	121,857	129,553	98	121,901	28,327	23.2		41	3,002
Kansas City, Mo	248,381	399,746	456,622	27	475,539	84,191	17.7		130	3,664
Knoxville, Tenn	36,346	105,802	124,769	111	111,827	20,886	18.7		25	4,403
Lansing, Mich	31,229	78,397	92,129	118	107,807	6,993	6.5		21	5,085
Lincoln, Nebr	43,973	75,933	98,884	95	128,521	2,400	1.9		25	5,060
Little Rock, Ark	45,941	81,679	102,213	117	107,813	25,352	23.5		28	3,810
Long Beach, Calif	17,809	142,032	250,767	35	344,168	14,769	4.3		46	7,498
Los Angeles, Calif	319,198	1,238,048	1,970,358	3	2,479,015	417,207	16.8		455	5,451
Louisville, Ky	223,928	307,745	369,129	31	390,639	70,449	18.0		57	6,841
Lubbock, Tex	1,938	20,520	71,747	94	128,691	10,427	8.1		75	1,716
Madison, Wis	25,531	57,899	96,056	[1] 96	126,706	2,388	1.9		36	3,549
Memphis, Tenn	131,105	253,143	396,000	22	497,524	184,725	37.1		128	3,881
Miami, Fla	5,471	110,637	249,276	44	291,688	65,800	22.6		34	8,529
Milwaukee, Wis	373,857	578,249	637,392	11	741,324	65,752	8.9		91	8,137

See footnotes at end of table.

Table 16

CITIES WITH 100,000 INHABITANTS OR MORE IN 1960—POPULATION, 1910 TO 1960, AND AREA, 1960—Continued

CITY	1910	1930	1950	1960						
				Population				Land area (sq. mi.)	Population per square mile
				Rank order	Total	Nonwhite			
						Number	Per-cent		
Minneapolis, Minn	301,408	464,356	521,718	25	482,872	15,594	3.2	57	8,546
Mobile, Ala	51,521	68,202	129,009	62	194,856	(NA)	(NA)	112	1,735
Montgomery, Ala	38,136	66,079	106,525	89	134,393	47,432	35.3	32	4,226
Nashville, Tenn	110,364	153,866	174,307	73	170,874	64,830	37.9	29	5,892
New Bedford, Mass	96,652	112,597	109,189	125	102,477	3,333	3.3	19	5,365
New Haven, Conn	133,605	162,655	164,443	81	152,048	22,665	14.9	18	8,494
New Orleans, La	339,075	458,762	570,445	15	627,525	234,931	37.4	199	3,157
New York, N.Y. [2]	4,766,883	6,930,446	7,891,957	1	7,781,984	1,141,322	14.7	315	24,697
Bronx Borough	430,980	1,265,258	1,451,277	(X)	1,424,815	168,531	11.8	43	32,830
Brooklyn Borough	1,634,351	2,560,401	2,738,175	(X)	2,627,319	381,460	14.5	76	34,525
Manhattan Borough	2,331,542	1,867,312	1,960,101	(X)	1,698,281	426,459	25.1	22	76,156
Queens Borough	284,041	1,079,129	1,550,849	(X)	1,809,578	154,619	8.5	113	16,014
Richmond Borough	85,969	158,346	191,555	(X)	221,991	10,253	4.6	60	36,814
Newark, N.J	347,469	442,337	438,776	30	405,220	139,331	34.4	24	17,170
Newport News, Va	20,205	34,417	42,358	108	113,662	39,060	34.4	75	1,515
Niagara Falls, N.Y	30,445	75,460	90,872	126	102,394	7,664	7.5	14	7,585
Norfolk, Va	67,452	129,710	213,513	41	[3] 305,872	80,621	26.4	50	6,117
Oakland, Calif	150,174	284,063	384,575	33	367,548	97,025	26.4	53	6,935
Oklahoma City, Okla	64,205	185,389	243,504	37	324,253	42,282	13.0	322	1,009
Omaha, Nebr. [4]	124,096	214,006	251,117	42	301,598	26,268	8.7	51	5,891
Pasadena, Calif	30,291	76,086	104,577	105	116,507	17,967	15.4	23	5,151
Paterson, N.J	125,600	138,513	139,336	85	143,663	21,353	14.9	8	17,103
Peoria, Ill	66,950	104,969	111,856	124	103,162	9,776	9.5	15	6,787
Philadelphia, Pa	1,549,008	1,950,961	2,071,605	4	2,002,512	535,033	26.7	127	15,743
Phoenix, Ariz	11,134	48,118	106,818	29	439,170	25,651	5.8	187	2,343
Pittsburgh, Pa	533,905	669,817	676,806	16	604,332	101,739	16.8	54	11,171
Portland, Oreg	207,214	301,815	373,628	32	372,676	20,919	5.6	67	5,546
Portsmouth, Va	33,190	45,704	80,039	106	114,773	39,681	34.6	18	8,043
Providence, R.I	224,326	252,981	248,674	56	207,498	11,973	5.8	18	11,592
Richmond, Va	127,628	182,929	230,310	52	219,958	92,331	42.0	37	5,945
Rochester, N.Y	218,149	328,132	332,488	38	318,611	24,228	7.6	36	8,753
Rockford, Ill	45,401	85,864	92,927	[1] 96	126,706	5,450	4.3	26	4,873
Sacramento, Calif	44,696	93,750	137,572	63	191,667	24,296	12.7	45	4,250
St. Louis, Mo	687,029	821,960	856,796	10	750,026	216,022	28.8	61	12,296
St. Paul, Minn	214,744	271,606	311,349	40	313,411	9,317	3.0	52	6,004
St. Petersburg, Fla	4,127	40,425	96,738	69	181,298	24,188	13.3	54	3,357
Salt Lake City, Utah	92,777	140,267	182,121	65	189,454	3,975	2.1	56	3,377
San Antonio, Tex	96,614	231,542	408,442	17	587,718	43,221	7.4	101	3,662
San Diego, Calif	39,578	147,995	334,387	18	573,224	44,712	7.8	192	2,979
San Francisco, Calif	416,912	634,394	775,357	12	740,316	135,913	18.4	45	16,599
San Jose, Calif	28,946	57,651	95,280	57	204,196	6,793	3.3	55	3,747
Santa Ana, Calif	8,429	30,322	45,533	130	100,350	2,681	2.7	21	4,711
Savannah, Ga	65,064	85,024	119,638	82	149,245	53,258	35.7	42	3,596
Scranton, Pa	129,867	143,433	125,536	113	111,443	763	0.7	25	4,405
Seattle, Wash	237,194	365,583	467,591	19	557,087	46,528	8.4	89	6,295
Shreveport, La	28,015	76,655	127,206	76	164,372	56,719	34.5	36	4,566
South Bend, Ind	53,684	104,193	115,911	91	132,445	13,169	9.9	24	5,565
Spokane, Wash	104,402	115,514	161,721	68	181,608	4,508	2.5	43	4,223
Springfield, Mass	88,926	149,900	162,399	72	174,463	13,361	7.7	33	5,271
Syracuse, N.Y	137,249	209,326	220,583	53	216,038	12,281	5.7	25	8,642
Tacoma, Wash	83,743	106,817	143,673	83	147,979	7,873	5.3	48	3,115
Tampa, Fla	37,782	101,161	124,681	48	274,970	46,456	16.9	85	3,235
Toledo, Ohio	168,497	290,718	303,616	39	318,003	40,423	12.7	48	6,598
Topeka, Kans	43,684	64,120	78,791	100	119,484	9,797	8.2	36	3,310
Torrance, Calif	[5]	7,271	22,241	128	100,991	1,398	1.4	20	5,050
Trenton, N.J	96,815	123,356	128,009	107	114,167	25,852	22.6	7	15,428
Tucson, Ariz	13,193	32,506	45,454	54	212,892	9,278	4.4	71	3,003
Tulsa, Okla	18,182	141,258	182,740	50	261,685	26,065	10.0	48	5,475
Utica, N.Y	74,419	101,740	101,531	129	100,410	3,193	3.2	17	5,906
Washington, D.C	331,069	486,869	802,178	9	763,956	418,693	54.8	61	12,442
Waterbury, Conn	73,141	99,902	104,477	121	107,130	7,221	6.7	28	3,882
Wichita, Kans	52,450	111,110	168,279	51	254,698	21,159	8.3	52	4,907
Wichita Falls, Tex	8,200	43,690	68,042	127	101,724	8,551	8.4	37	2,727
Winston-Salem, N.C	22,700	75,274	87,811	115	111,135	41,240	37.1	31	3,573
Worcester, Mass	145,986	195,311	203,486	66	186,587	2,307	1.2	37	5,043
Yonkers, N.Y	79,803	134,646	152,798	64	190,634	8,052	4.2	18	10,417
Youngstown, Ohio	79,066	170,002	168,330	75	166,689	31,905	19.1	33	5,021

NA Not available. X Not applicable.

[1] The cities of Madison, Wis., and Rockford, Ill., share the same rank of 96. In order to have the lowest rank equal to the number of cities presented, the number 97 is omitted.

[2] Population shown is for New York City as now constituted.

[3] Revised population figure for Norfolk is 304,869.

[4] Omaha and South Omaha cities consolidated between 1910 and 1920. Combined population, 1910: 150,355.

[5] Not incorporated in 1910.

Source: Dept. of Commerce, Bureau of the Census; *U.S. Census of Population: 1960*, Vol. I.

The emerging middle class. Richard Wilson, principal of Tarboro High School, Camden County, Georgia, and his family.

THE CURRENT STATUS OF THE BLACK FAMILY

Analysis of The Moynihan Report
The Muslim View
The Black Panther View
Economic Polarization
Income and Family Stability
Selected Facts
Selected Tables

Considerable evidence exists to support the thesis that the black family is in fact being split into two distinct and largely non-interacting groups: the stable middle class group and the unstable lower class group. In recent years, the emergence of a successful middle class group demonstrated the axiom that family disorganization diminishes to a considerable extent as economic pressures are relieved. There appears to be a direct relationship between marriage stability and income since 90% of all black families above the $7,000 income level remain intact. At the lower income levels, almost 30% of the black families in America have been victimized by either separation or divorce. Close to 40% of all black children are from broken homes, and 90% of these children are from families with incomes below $3,000.

Until very recently, the Black Family as a topic was confined to a coterie of academicians in the social sciences and occasionally discussed in sociology classes at the universities. The Black Family has now become the center of heated controversy on the city, state, and federal level of the American political scene and within the black community itself.

The controversy, in the main, has been sparked by three occurrences:

- The Moynihan Report of 1965 which contended that there is powerfully persuasive evidence "that the Negro family in the urban ghettos is crumbling."
- Wider acceptance among Negroes of the view, advanced by such militant groups as the Black Muslims, that black men have been enfeebled by a tendency for women to dominate Negro families.
- A growing belief among Negroes in lower income and politically militant groups, that prosperous and prestigious Negro families were accumulating more power and, increasingly, drawing aloof from the plight of less affluent Negroes.

Analysis of The Moynihan Report

In effect, the Moynihan Report contended that low income, urban Negro families were so unstable that equal opportunity legislation could do little to free them from "the cycle of poverty and disadvantage." Three centuries of oppression plus rapid urbanization had left the mass of black families incapable of shaping progeny who could function effectively and responsibly within the American system. Only a small middle class group had managed to save itself. By contrast, noted the report, "The white family has achieved a high degree of stability and is maintaining that stability."

In support of its position, The Moynihan Report cited statistics from the early 1960s to the effect that, compared with white families, Negro families were more likely to be dependent on welfare assistance, to have women with absentee husbands, daughters who bear illegitimate children, high rates of crime, delinquency and narcotics use and low standards of education and performance in mental tests. (See section on income and expenditures for data on earnings, welfare, and medical care.)

Black groups and white supporters took less issue with the report's statistics than with its interpretations and use of them. Critics of the report sensed that it blamed unstable black families, rather than white oppression for the Negroes' failure to progress. The high rates of illegitimacy among Negroes, contended one critic of the report, were due to the fact that a white woman can better afford a divorce, has greater access to medical care and advice, is more able to arrange for an abortion and if she has a baby, better able to con-

Chart 16

DURING THE YEARS 1950-1969 THERE HAS BEEN A SUBSTANTIAL INCREASE IN BLACK FAMILIES HEADED BY FEMALES.

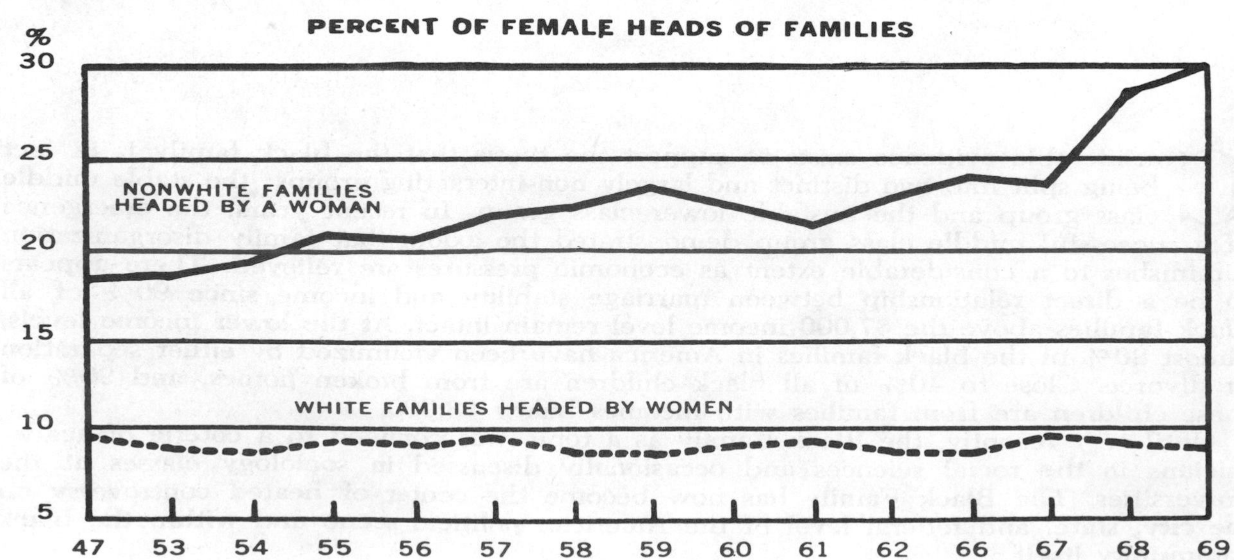

ceal it or arrange for adoption. In addition, economic factors often make it impossible for a black couple to marry when they have conceived a child illegitimately. And America's welfare laws, which severely restrict aid to families with able-bodied men, discourage marriage and encourage separation.

Pointing to the increase in the white divorce rate, Moynihan's critics also took issue with the contention that white families are stable or worthy of emulating. William Ryan, a mental health consultant to the Massachusetts Committee on Children and Youth, replied that: "Inspected by a narrow framework, the Negro family does look as if it's falling apart when compared to the white family, but, by the same token, the urban family looks as if it's falling apart when compared with the farm family, and the modern family looks as if it's falling apart when compared with the family of our grandfathers."*

* "Crisis," published by The National Association for the Advancement of Colored People, Dec. 1965.

The battle over the integrity and the acuity of the Moynihan Report raged into the 1970's as proposed welfare legislation was geared to providing incentives for low-income black families to stay together and obtain employment. (See section on income and expenditures.)

The Muslim View

While politicians and professors argued the merits of the Moynihan Report in their cloak rooms and colleges, the Negro family was gaining increasing attention from new, radical movements on ghetto street corners, first from the Black Muslims and later from the Black Panthers.

Throughout the 20th century, black leadership had resided almost entirely with a loose, middle-class alliance of clergymen, lawyers, moderate labor leaders and academic men who believed in waging a courteous fight that appealed primarily to the conscience of whites. This middle-class leadership had been challenged from time

Most black families in the Central Cities live in ghettos similar to this one in New York City.

to time by such race-conscious, unconventional men as Marcus Garvey, but it had never met with much open or implicit recognition from whites. The dominant, moderate black leaders believed strongly that a good appearance should be presented to whites, that black linen shouldn't be washed in public. As a result, the internal class and family structures of the Negro community received little attention from established civil rights groups. Even E. Franklin Frazier's masterpiece on the Negro family evoked little response in powerful Negro and white circles.

With the passage of the Civil Rights Act of 1964 and the riots that followed almost immediately, moderate black organizations were challenged by radical working class oriented groups that stressed such conventional family values as discipline, masculinity, frugality, integrity, abstinence, pride, and work.

The first such group to appear in strength was the Black Muslims. Though the Muslims declared Moynihan to be a white devil, they clearly shared many of his critical opinions, most crucially a view that efforts to help blacks should focus on ghetto homes as well as on the houses of Congress. The Muslims handed down a series of rules about diet, dress, and decorum that in effect told the men to be responsible and the women to get in line. Muslim women dress decorously in white, are usually segregated from men at Muslim services and urged to serve men and the cause rather than assert leadership.

Muslim leader Malcolm X repeatedly charged that the "white devil" exercised his oppression by undermining the Negro family . . . with narcotics and implicit approval of sexual promiscuity. Unlike the liberals of his day, Malcolm did not regard promiscuity and narcotics so much a result of oppression as a weapon of repression. A sound, felicitous family structure was crucial in the war against whites. Muslims also urged followers to avoid friendships with whites, particularly interracial marriages and sexual relationships. The latter position was one on which moderate black groups maintained official silence. Muslims stress the value of dark skin, a position much in contrast to the values observed earlier by Frazier, whereby a light-skinned wife was felt to enhance the status of a dark-skinned man.

Chart 17

DURING THE PAST NINETEEN YEARS (1950-1969) THERE HAS BEEN A SUBSTANTIAL INCREASE IN THE BREAKUP OF HUSBAND AND WIFE HEADED FAMILIES AMONG BLACKS.

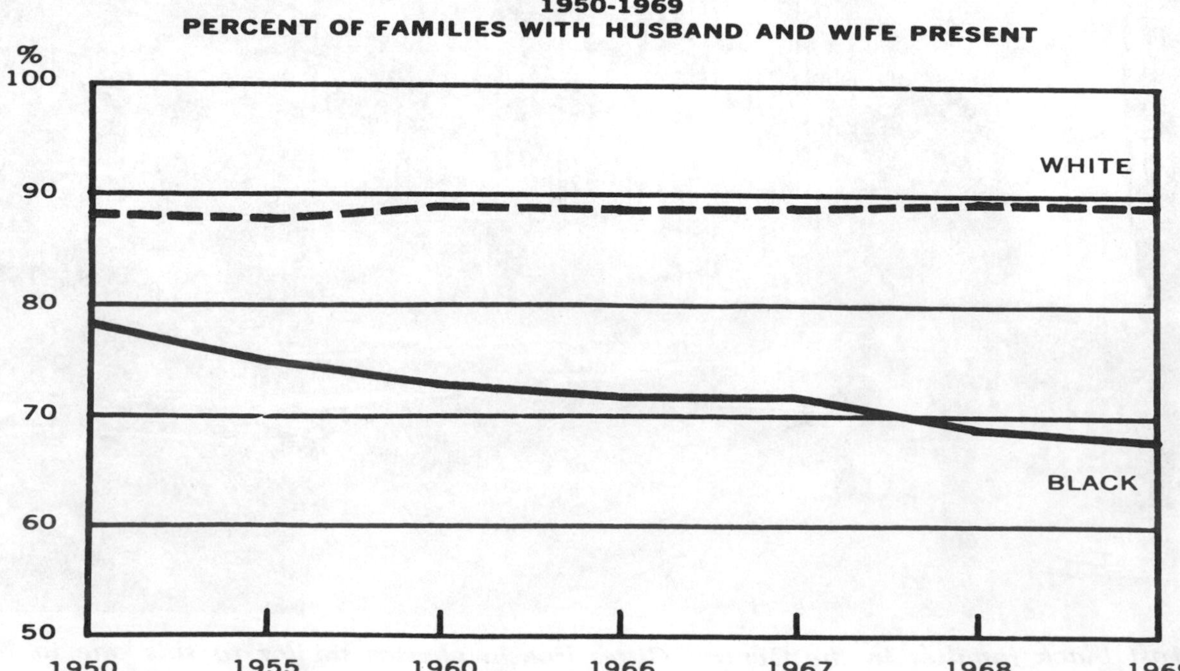

The Black Panther View

The Black Panthers, a more conventional revolutionary movement that nods in the direction of Asian Communism and Middle Eastern Socialism, also demands that its men display leadership and set examples of masculine responsibility and brotherhood in their families and communities. "Shooting" narcotics or stealing from one another are grounds for immediate dismissal, though smoking marijuana off duty is apparently permitted.

The Panthers, Muslims and other radical black groups, such as CORE, have underscored the differences which exist between black families of varying economic means and social background. Class divisions within the black community go back to slavery, to the high degrees of prestige accruing to house slaves, the children of white slave holders and Negro women, and to Negroes who obtained their freedom prior to the Civil War. As in most social groups, these class differences have survived and been strengthened by the accumulation of capital, marriage within the leadership, and reinforcements in the form of the educated children of self-made men.

Economic Polarization

Prominent Negroes, such as Andrew Brimmer, have expressed concern that black family income is becoming polarized, that earnings of affluent Negroes are growing at a faster rate than the earnings of the poor. While this is true, polarization of black family income, and the growth of the black middle class, is similar to the pattern of developments among whites, though increasing numbers of black professionals and white collar workers are earning middle class incomes and projecting middle class values. (See quantile table in income and earnings chapter.) Significantly, older middle class Negro families have long been thought to put a higher premium on such traditional virtues as stability and thrift than white middle class families.

Chart 18

AT THE HIGHER INCOME LEVELS ABOUT NINE TENTHS OF NEGRO FAMILIES ARE HEADED BY MEN.

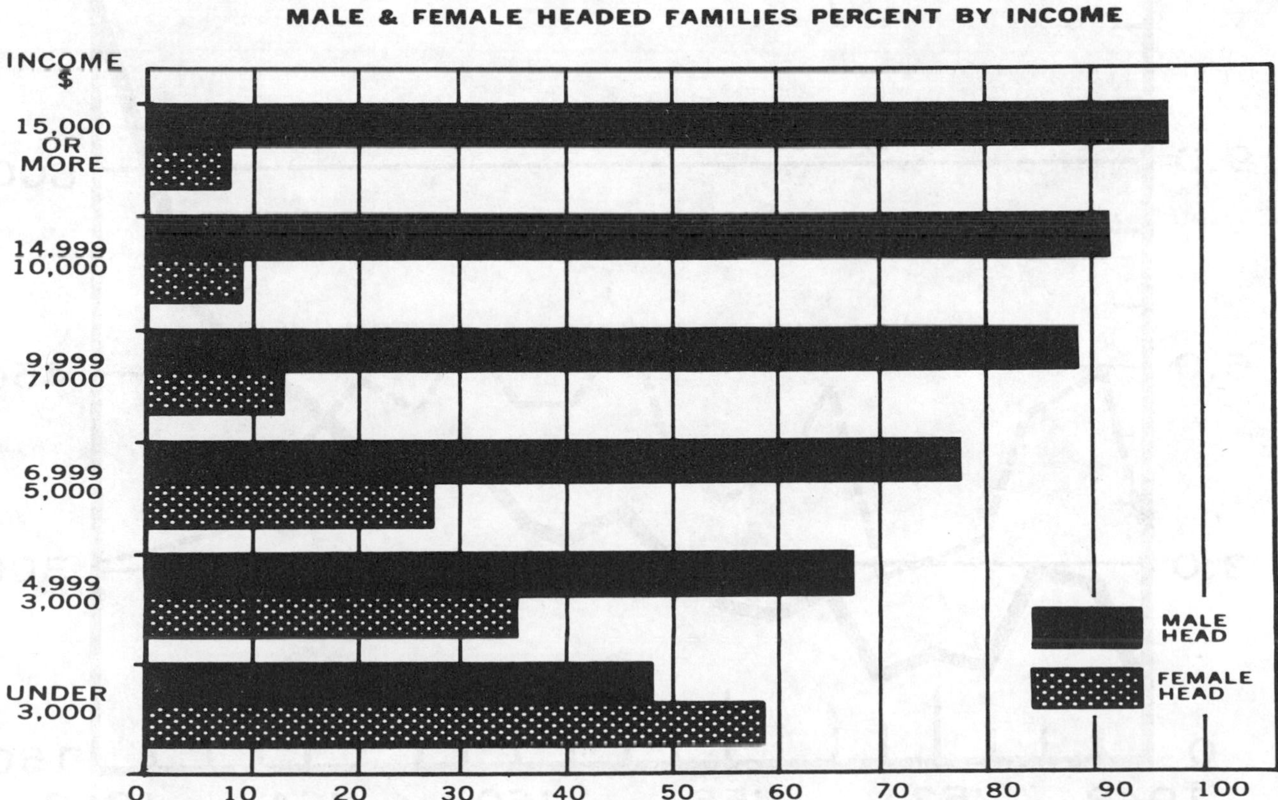

Income and Family Stability

On the other hand, the instability characteristic of poor Negro families is a most serious social problem. Historically, this phenomenon can be traced to the slave experience, during which the traditional role of men as protectors of women and children was obliterated. Even after slavery, the Negro family was restricted and oppressed, and former slaves, reared in a menial agricultural environment, were largely illiterate and unskilled.

The proportion of female-headed families of Negro and other races has apparently increased during the 1960's, leaving about 70 percent of all families of Negro and other races headed by a man with a wife present. 90 percent of white families are headed by a man with a wife present.

The percentage of divorce, on the other hand, is greater among white female heads of families than among Negro heads. Statistics indicate that one-half of Negro female heads of families are separated or divorced as compared with about one-third of white female heads. The percent of Negro female heads separated from the husbands is three times as great as that for whites.

There is indication too that a higher percentage of married women of nonwhite races are separated from their husbands. At incomes below $3,000, half of Negro

Chart 19

AID TO FAMILIES WITH DEPENDENT CHILDREN HAS INCREASED APPRECIABLY DESPITE SHARP DROPS IN UNEMPLOYMENT DURING THE 1960-1969 PERIOD. THE RISE IS APPARENTLY DUE TO PREVIOUSLY UNREALISTIC STATE STANDARDS FOR AID AND AN INCREASED AWARENESS AMONG THE NEEDY AS TO HOW TO INITIATE A CLAIM.

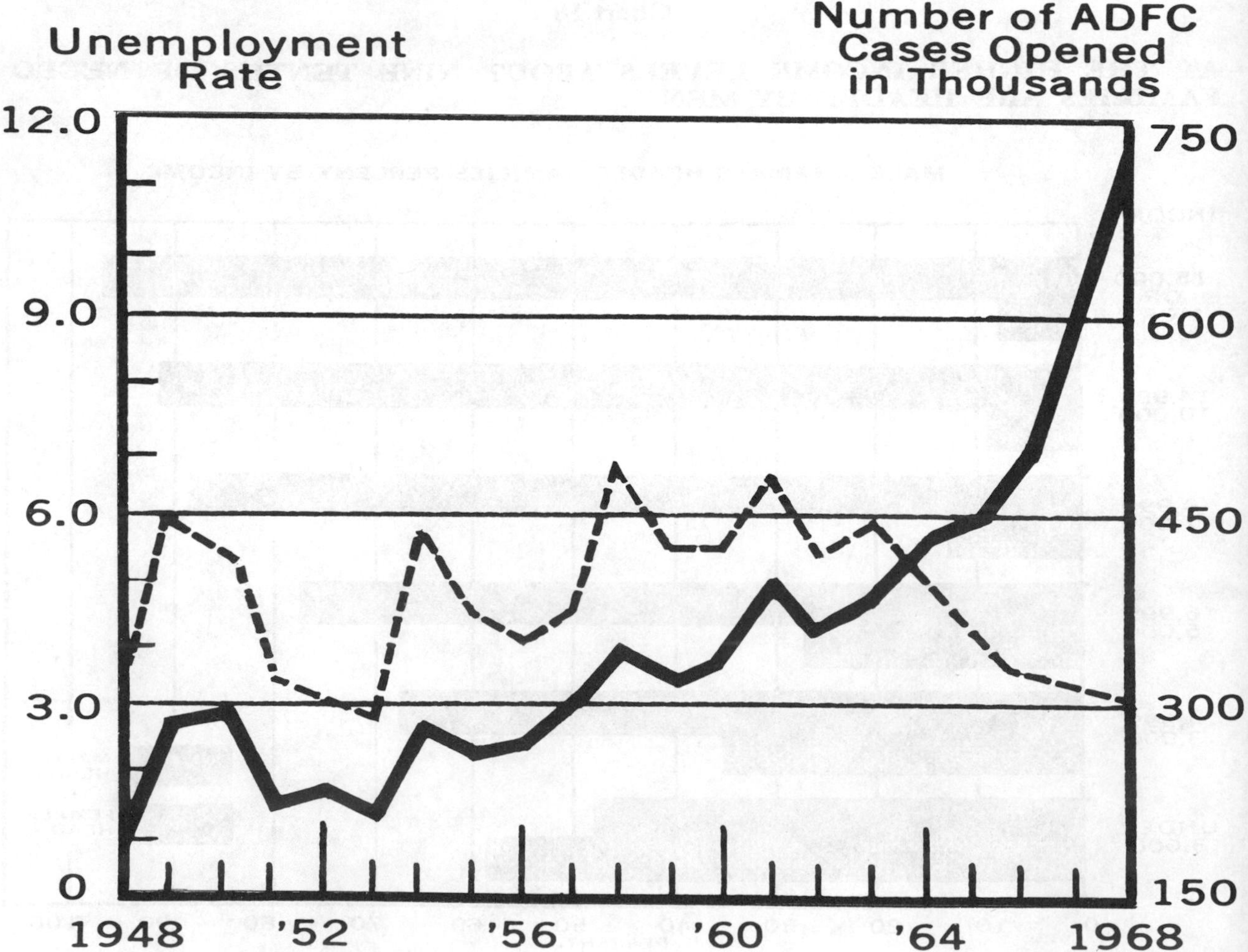

families remain headed by a male. Among white families at the same economic level three-fourths are headed by males. At the higher income levels, about nine-tenths of the Negro families are headed by men.

Among nonwhite races about 70 percent of children of family heads live with both parents. About 90 percent of children of white family heads live with both parents. At family income levels $7,000 and above, about 90 percent of Negro children are living with both parents. At the other end of the economic scale, only about one-fourth of Negro children in families with incomes below $3,000 are living with both parents. Significantly, working Negro women who are college graduates and who live with their husbands earn more than white women in the same group.

Reproductivity & Health

Fertility rates for all races have decreased sharply since 1961, but the fertility rate for Negro and other races remains greater than that of whites. With regard to illegitimate births however, the relative increase since 1960 has been much greater for whites than for nonwhites. In general the ratio of illegitimate births to all live births is higher for nonwhites than for whites: 29 percent for the former as compared with 5 percent for the latter. In general, Negro women have higher fertility than white women. The frequency of childlessness and one-child families among women above age 30 is greater among Negroes than among whites, but this is more than counterbalanced by the higher

Chart 20

THE ILLEGITIMATE BIRTH RATE FOR BLACKS IS 6 TIMES GREATER THAN THAT FOR WHITES (27% VERSUS 5%). THE RELATIVE INCREASE FOR WHITES, HOWEVER, INCREASED OVER 100% IN THE YEARS 1960-1967 WHILE THE INCREASE FOR BLACKS DURING THE SAME PERIOD WAS 7%.

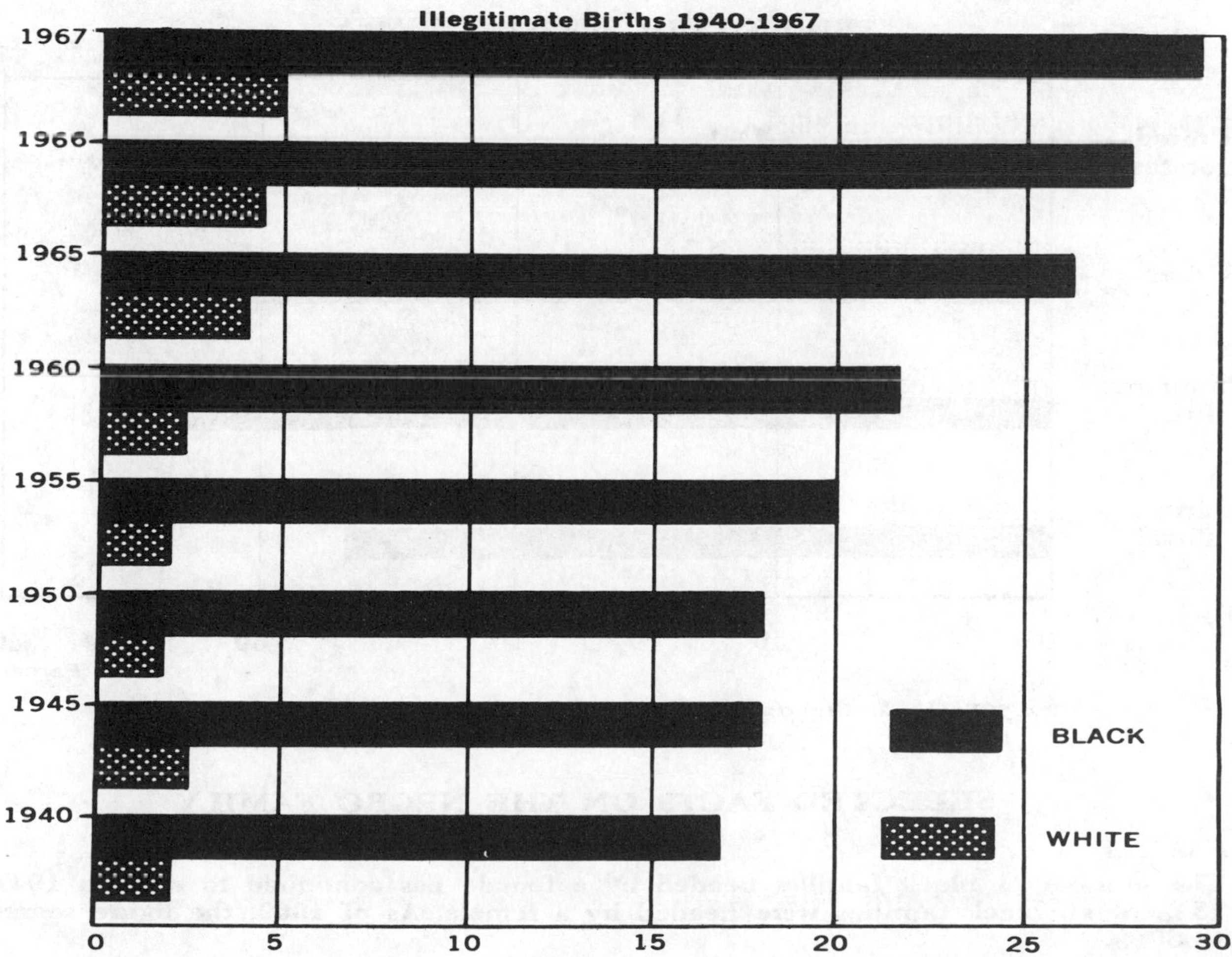

proportion of Negro women with five children or more. Roughly two-thirds of white women above age 30 have 2 to 4 children, while less than one-half of the Negro women above age 30 fall in this category.

Among Negroes, fertility has long been higher in the South than in the remainder of the country. This is due largely to the fact that in the South only about half the Negro population lives in metropolitan areas whereas in the remainder of the country, the figure is over 90 percent. There is a strong inverse relation between education and fertility among both whites and Negroes. However, the relation is more pronounced among Negroes. It is also clear that Negro women both in the labor force and not in the labor force have higher fertility than their white counterparts.

Between 1950 and 1965, there were increases in fertility among Negro women and white women in most age groups in the childbearing span. Among Negro women in the 30 to 39 age group, the increase was about one child per woman. In 1969, both Negro women and white women in the 20 to 29 age group had borne fewer children than women 20 to 29 in 1960. (These data suggest that women of both groups now in their twenties will have smaller families than the women who are now in their thirties.)

The life expectancy is still longer for whites than for nonwhites in all age groups in the prime working years. Infant and maternal mortality rates have dropped sharply during the past two and one-half decades. However, the mortality rate for mothers of Negro and other races is still about three times the white rate. Infant mortality rates for nonwhites are also much higher than for whites.

In terms of health care, nonwhites are somewhat less likely to have the treatment of a physician or a dentist than are whites. Among certain income groups, however, they are more likely than whites to receive care in hospital clinics.

Chart 21

PRODUCTS OF BROKEN HOMES

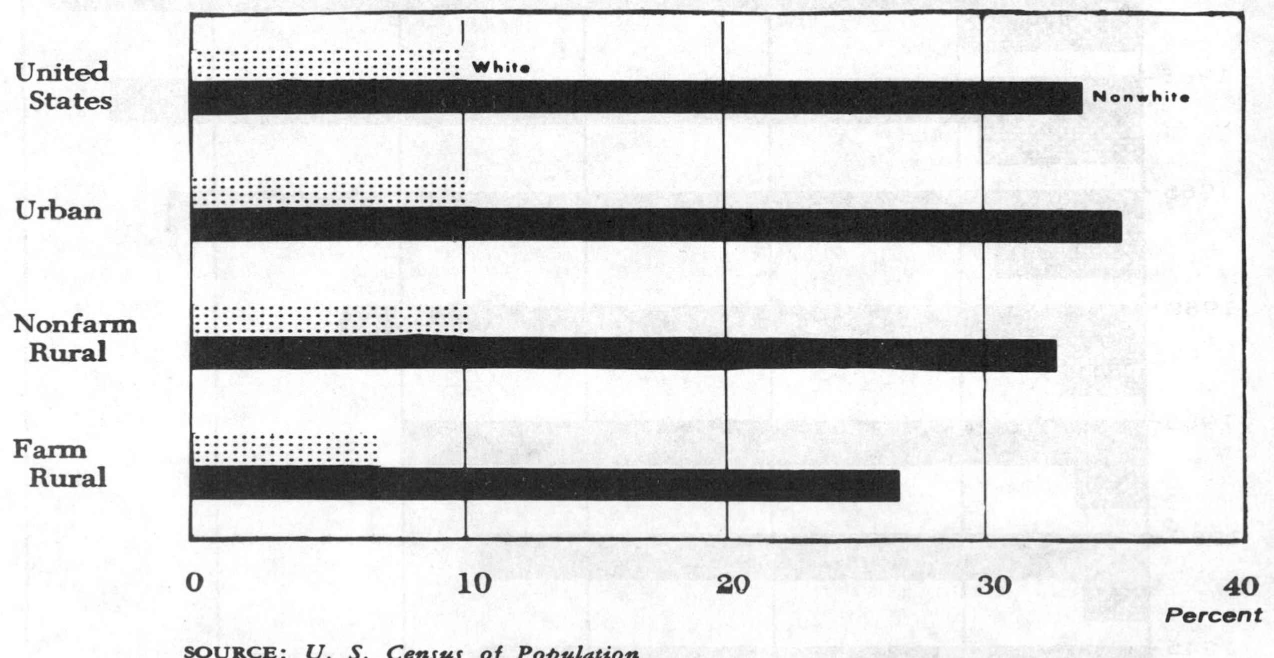

SOURCE: *U. S. Census of Population*

SELECTED FACTS ON THE NEGRO FAMILY

FACT 1

The number of black families headed by a female has continued to rise. In 1947, 18% of all black families were headed by a female. As of 1969, the figure soared to 30%.

FACT 2

Seventy percent of all black families have a husband and wife present, compared to 90% for white families.

FACT 3

The percent of husband and wife separation and/or divorce for blacks is three times as great as for whites.

FACT 4

There appears to be a direct relationship between marriage stability and income since 90% of all black families above the $7,000 income level remain intact.

FACT 5

Close to 40% of all black children come from broken homes, and 90% of these children are from families with incomes below $3,000.

FACT 6

Most black as well as white children receiving AFDC aid in 1969 were legitimate.

FACT 7

The preponderance of female heads of families, both black and white, is in urban areas.

FACT 8

Black families average more members than white families at every age level and with each type of family composition.

FACT 9

The fertility rates for both black and white women between the ages of 15 and 44 have sharply decreased.

FACT 10

At all ages blacks have a higher birth rate than whites.

FACT 11

Fertility rates tend to decline with increased educational attainment.

FACT 12

The ratio of illegitimate births to all live births is far greater among blacks than whites. Approximately 29% of all births among blacks are illegitimate while for whites it is 5%.

FACT 13

Nonwhite mothers average more children than white mothers, but the difference is greatest at fifth and later births, for which the birth-rate decline in recent years has been greater among nonwhite than white mothers.

FACT 14

The nonwhite-white gap in birth rates is greatest in the youngest and oldest age groups, although, at all ages, nonwhites have a higher birth rate than whites.

FACT 15

Fertility and the ratio of nonwhite/white fertility fall with rising income, and are usually least in urban areas. In 1960, for the income group $10,000–$14,999 in urbanized areas, the fertility of nonwhite mothers approximated that of white mothers.

FAMILY TABLES

Table 17

Composition of Families, 1950, 1955, 1960, and 1966-1969
(Percent)

Year	Husband-wife		Other male head		Female head[1]	
	Negro and other races	White	Negro and other races	White	Negro and other races	White
1950 . . .	77.7	88.0	4.7	3.5	17.6	8.5
1955 . . .	75.3	87.9	4.0	3.0	20.7	9.0
1960 . . .	73.6	88.7	4.0	2.6	22.4	8.7
1966 . . .	72.7	88.8	3.7	2.3	23.7	8.9
1967 . . .	72.6	88.7	3.9	2.1	23.6	9.1
1968 . . .	69.1	88.9	4.5	2.2	26.4	8.9
1969 . . .	68.7	88.8	3.9	2.3	27.3	8.9

[1]Female heads of families include widowed and single women, women whose husbands are in the armed services or otherwise away from home involuntarily, as well as those separated from their husbands through divorce or marital discord.

Source: U.S. Department of Commerce, Bureau of the Census.

Table 18

Percent of Ever-Married Women Not Living With Their Husbands Because of Marital Discord, 1950-1969

	Separated[1]		Divorced	
	Negro and other races	White	Negro and other races	White
1950	11	2	3	3
1951	9	(NA)	3	(NA)
1952	10	1	3	3
1953	8	2	4	3
1954	14	1	4	3
1955	12	2	3	3
1956	11	2	4	3
1957	10	1	4	3
1958	12	2	3	3
1959	14	2	4	3
1960	11	2	5	3
1961	11	2	5	3
1962	11	2	5	3
1963	11	2	6	3
1964	12	2	5	4
1965	12	2	5	4
1966	11	2	5	4
1967	11	2	5	4
1968	12	2	6	4
1969	12	2	6	5

NA Not available.

[1]Excludes separations for reasons such as spouse being in Armed Forces, employed and temporarily living considerable distance from home, or inmate of institution.

Source: U.S. Department of Commerce, Bureau of the Census.

Table 19

Marital Status of Female Heads of Families, 1969
(Percent distribution)

Status	Negro	White
Total	100	100
Single (never married)	14	10
Separated or divorced	50	35
Separated	37	12
Divorced	13	23
Married, husband absent	6	8
In Armed Forces	2	3
Other reasons	4	5
Widowed	31	48

Source: U.S. Department of Commerce, Bureau of the Census.

Table 20

Families by Sex of Head, by Income Group, 1968
(Percent)

Income	Negro			White		
	Total	Female	Male	Total	Female	Male
All families	100	29	72	100	9	91
Under $3,000	100	56	44	100	27	73
$3,000 to $4,999	100	36	64	100	17	83
$5,000 to $6,999	100	22	78	100	12	88
$7,000 to $9,999	100	11	89	100	6	93
$10,000 to $14,999	100	9	91	100	4	96
$15,000 and over	100	7	93	100	3	98

Source: U.S. Department of Commerce, Bureau of the Census.

Table 21

Percent of Children of Family Heads Living with Both Parents, by Family Income, 1969

Income	Negro	White
Under $3,000	27	49
$3,000 to $4,999	55	75
$5,000 to $6,999	78	88
$7,000 to $9,999	90	95
$10,000 to $14,999	88	97
$15,000 and over	87	98

NOTE—Unmarried children under 18 years old living in families.
Source: U.S. Department of Commerce, Bureau of the Census.

Table 22

Percent of Children of Family Heads Living With Both Parents, 1960-1969

	Negro and other races	White
1960	75	92
1961	76	92
1962	73	92
1963	70	92
1964	71	92
1965	71	91
1966	71	91
1967	73	92
1968	69	92
1969	69	92

NOTE—Unmarried children under 18 years old living in families.
Source: U.S. Department of Commerce, Bureau of the Census.

Table 23

Children Ever Born to All Women 35 to 44 Years Old, by Specified Characteristics of Women, 1969

Region	Negro		White	
	Children ever born per woman	Replacement index[1]	Children ever born per woman	Replacement index[1]
United States	3.6	175	2.9	142
Regions:				
South	4.0	191	2.9	138
Remainder of United States	3.3	160	3.0	143
Residence:				
Metropolitan	3.3	162	2.8	137
In central cities	3.3	159	2.7	131
Outside central cities	3.6	172	2.9	140
Nonmetropolitan	4.5	216	3.1	151
Education:				
Elementary, 0 to 8 years	4.5	215	3.6	172
High school, 1 to 4 years	3.5	107	2.9	139
College, 1 year or more	2.3	113	2.6	128
Labor force status:				
Labor force	3.2	153	2.6	125
Not in labor force	4.3	208	3.2	157

[1]Index of 100 denotes that the women will have exactly the number of children ever born by age 45 needed for replacement of the women. Negro women 35 to 44 years old have completed approximately 96 percent of their eventual lifetime childbearing and white women of this group have completed approximately 97 percent of their eventual lifetime childbearing.

NOTE—"All Women" includes those ever married and never married.
Source: U.S. Department of Commerce, Bureau of the Census.

Table 24

Children Ever Born by Age and Marital Status of Woman, 1969

Age Group	Percent distribution of women ever married by children ever born: Total	0-1	2-4	5 and over	Children ever born: Per woman[1]	Per ever married woman
Negro						
15 to 44 years	100	33	42	25	2.0	3.1
15 to 19 years	100	73	27	(Z)	0.1	1.1
20 to 24 years	100	48	47	5	1.0	1.8
25 to 29 years	100	29	51	20	2.3	2.8
30 to 34 years	100	26	43	32	3.1	3.5
35 to 39 years	100	22	38	40	3.7	4.0
40 to 44 years	100	31	37	32	3.5	3.6
White						
15 to 44 years	100	33	56	11	1.7	2.4
15 to 19 years	100	91	9	(Z)	0.1	0.6
20 to 24 years	100	71	28	(Z)	0.7	1.0
25 to 29 years	100	34	62	4	1.8	2.0
30 to 34 years	100	18	69	13	2.7	2.9
35 to 39 years	100	17	64	19	3.0	3.1
40 to 44 years	100	18	64	18	2.9	3.0

Z Represents zero or rounds to zero.
[1]Including single women.
Source: U.S. Department of Commerce, Bureau of the Census.

Table 25

Fertility Rates, 1955-1967

Year	(Live births per 1,000 women age 15 to 44) Negro and other races	White
1955	155	114
1956	161	116
1957	163	118
1958	161	115
1959	162	114
1960	154	113
1961	154	112
1962[1]	149	108
1963[1]	145	104
1964	142	100
1965	134	91
1966	126	86
1967	120	83

[1]Excludes data for New Jersey.
NOTE—Births 1955-59 adjusted for under-registration of births.
Source: U.S. Department of Health, Education, and Welfare.

Table 26

Illegitimate Births, 1940-1967

Year	Number (thousands)		Percent illegitimate of all live births	
	Negro and other races	White	Negro and other races	White
1940	49	40	16.8	2.0
1945	61	56	17.9	2.4
1950	88	54	18.0	1.8
1955	119	64	20.2	1.9
1960	142	83	21.6	2.3
1965	168	124	26.3	4.0
1966	170	133	27.7	4.4
1967	176	142	29.4	4.9

Source: U.S. Department of Health, Education, and Welfare.

Table 27

Estimated Illegitimacy Rates by Age of Mother, 1940, 1950, 1960, 1965 and 1967

Age Group	(Rates per 1,000 unmarried women in specified group)				
	1940	1950	1960[1]	1965[1]	1967[2]
Negro and other races					
15 to 44 years[3]	35.6	71.2	98.3	97.6	89.5
15 to 19 years	42.5	68.5	76.5	75.8	80.2
20 to 24 years	46.1	105.4	166.5	152.6	128.2
25 to 29 years	32.5	94.2	171.8	164.7	118.4
30 to 34 years	23.4	63.5	104.0	137.8	97.2
35 to 39 years	13.2	31.3	35.6	39.0	28.9
40 to 44 years	[4]5.0	[4]8.7			
White					
15 to 44 years[3]	3.6	6.1	9.2	11.6	12.5
15 to 19 years	3.3	5.1	6.6	7.9	9.0
20 to 24 years	5.7	10.0	18.2	22.1	23.1
25 to 29 years	4.0	8.7	18.2	24.3	22.7
30 to 34 years	2.5	5.9	10.8	16.6	14.0
35 to 39 years	1.7	3.2	[5]3.9	[5]4.9	[5]4.7
40 to 44 years	[4]0.7	[4]0.9			

[1]Based on a 50 percent sample of births.

[2]Based on a 20 to 50 percent sample of births.

[3]Rates computed by relating total illegitimate births regardless of age of mother to unmarried women 15 to 44 years old.

[4]Rates computed by relating illegitimate births to mothers aged 40 and over to unmarried women 40 to 44 years old.

[5]Rates computed by relating illegitimate births to mothers aged 35 and over to unmarried women 35 to 44 years old.

Source: U.S. Department of Health, Education, and Welfare.

Table 28

Children Ever Born by Age of Woman, 1940-1969

Age Group	Children ever born per woman				
	1940	1950	1960	1965	1969
NEGRO					
15 to 19 years.........	0.1	0.2	0.2	0.2	0.1
20 to 24 years.........	0.8	1.0	1.3	1.2	1.0
25 to 29 years.........	1.4	1.7	2.4	2.6	2.3
30 to 34 years.........	1.9	2.0	2.9	3.4	3.1
35 to 39 years.........	2.5	2.3	2.9	3.5	3.7
40 to 44 years.........	2.9	2.5	2.8	3.1	3.5
WHITE					
15 to 19 years.........	0.0	0.1	0.1	0.1	0.1
20 to 24 years.........	0.5	0.7	1.0	0.9	0.6
25 to 29 years.........	1.0	1.4	2.0	2.1	1.8
30 to 34 years.........	1.6	1.8	2.4	2.7	2.7
35 to 39 years.........	2.1	2.0	2.5	2.8	3.0
40 to 44 years.........	2.5	2.1	2.4	2.7	2.9

Source: U.S. Department of Commerce, Bureau of the Census.

BY
WELDIN
MUSKEGO

THE BLACK WORKER IN THE LABOR MOVEMENT

A Study of Trade Unionism As It Has Affected the Black Worker
Prominent Black Trade Unionists
The Black in Agriculture

The historical position of the Negro within the labor movement cannot be accurately delineated without some reference to the crucial forces which helped shape the movement itself in the 19th century: the Industrial Revolution and the consequent growth of the cities; the influx of European immigrants (1820–1860), and the emancipation of the nation's slaves (1863).

The mad scramble for jobs created by the Industrial Revolution produced intense rivalry and competition between native-born whites and foreign-born whites for available jobs. In the early years of the craft or trade union movement, both these groups joined forces in propagating policies of racial exclusion—already part of the prevailing social climate of the United States. By the eve of the Civil War, many labor unions had formed nationally federated associations which incorporated these basic social attitudes as a matter of course.

After the war, Negro workers were encouraged by organizations like the National Labor Union (the first national federation of trade unions) to form their own counterpart unions within the framework of white-dominated federations. (In this way, the Colored National Labor Union came into being as an arm of the Republican party, falling into decline, however, with the panic of 1873 and the end of Reconstruction in 1877.)

For a brief period, the Noble Order of the Knights of Labor did attempt to maintain a labor organization which would include male and female, skilled and unskilled, and white and Negro workers. Organized in 1869, the Order grew rapidly until 1886, at which time it was in a position to boast of some 60,000 Negroes among its more than 700,000 members. That year, however, May Day demonstrations in Chicago* and the Haymarket bombing caused both press and public alike to equate it with destructive anarchism, and to brand it a social menace. Despite the fact that it too had denounced the bombings, the Order itself was never able to recover from the bad publicity it received, nor did it manage to live down the ominous nickname with which it was tagged—the "Black International."

For the first three decades of the 20th century, organized labor as a whole reflected the dominant attitude of American society toward the Negro population, i.e., one of prejudice and hostility. In so doing, the trade union movement at times seemed impotent to deal effectively with the 'divide-and-conquer' attitudes of the employer class. New York City Councilman Paul O'Dwyer, for example, recalls how shipowners and stevedore contractors along the Brooklyn waterfront exploited ethnic rivalries in the creation of segregated locals, e.g. the Irish local, the Polish local, several Italian locals, and the Negro local. (Nowadays, all Brooklyn longshoremen's locals are joined together so that employers can no longer pit one group against the other.)

Attempts to End Discrimination

At various intervals throughout the history of the labor movement, several attempts have been made to end discrimination and segregation among the working class. The tradition begun by the Knights of Labor was continued by the militant members of the I.W.W., (or the "wobblies" as they were known) who went so far as to organize the underpaid and unskilled lumber workers in the South regardless of race. "Big Bill" Haywood, a leader of the I.W.W., refused to countenance segregated meetings of the white and Negro workers in Louisiana even when joint meetings were prohibited by state law.

At its inception, the American Federation of Labor included as part of its credo the statement that "working people must unite and organize, irrespective of creed, color, sex, nationality or politics." For all its good intentions, the AFL found it impossible for the first quarter of the century to implement policies which counteracted the racist attitudes prevalent within its ranks. Thus, it organized Negroes into separate locals, or affiliated them with central unions whenever they were refused admission on the basis of color.

During the whole dark chapter covering the period from the turn of the 20th century to the 1930's, enlightened Negro leadership, despite the rebuffs which Negroes themselves had suffered, continued to recognize the importance of the labor movement to all American workers and its potential usefulness to the Negro people.

"I carry on the title page of this magazine the union label," wrote W.E.B. DuBois in the "Crisis" magazine (1918), "and yet I know, and everyone of my Negro readers knows, that the very fact that this label is there is an advertisement that no Negro's hand is engaged in the printing of this magazine." DuBois added:

> "Collective bargaining has undoubtedly raised modern labor from something like chattel slavery to the threshold of industrial freedom and in this advance of labor white and black have shared."

Progressivism in the CIO

With the Roosevelt era and the passage of the Wagner Act, some enlightened leaders within the ranks of the AFL began to reject the discriminatory policies of the majority of the International Union leaders. It became obvious to others that, if the international unions continued to exclude Negroes, employers would have little trouble in recruiting strikebreakers from the excluded class. Under the rising pressure of Negro protest, a number of AFL leaders launched a series of organizing campaigns in the mass-production industries, and ultimately formed the Congress of Industrial Organizations (CIO).

The resulting AFL-CIO rivalry ultimately caused a schism in the ranks of labor—one which led the CIO to concern itself primarily with the organization of the steel, auto, mining, packinghouse, and rubber industries, all of which employed large numbers of Negroes. It has been said that no other CIO leader better understood "the importance of equalitarian racial policies for successful unionism than John L. Lewis of the United Mine Workers." In this union, the common economic and occupational hard-

* Labor's major quest at the time was the eight-hour working day.

ships endured by all minimized—although they did not totally eliminate—racial differences among members, even those in the South. Lewis' pioneering policies in this area were soon followed by such men as Philip Murray, president of the steel workers, and by Walter Reuther, head of the auto workers. CIO policies ultimately prompted Thurgood Marshall to declare that "the program (of this organization) has become a Bill of Rights for Negro labor in America."

These new unions broke sharply with traditional racial practices. Segregationist constitutions and by-laws were erased. Locals admitted Negroes and, in a few cases, integrated seniority lines. Negroes were elected to executive positions within locals. Some new unions gave priority to lifting wage scales for low-paying jobs, most of which were filled by Negroes, and to training and upgrading "underemployed" Negro workers. One such union was the Transport Workers Union in New York which negotiated substantial wage increases for change clerks and saw to the promotion of Negro workers to skilled well-paying white collar positions.

Unfortunately, such achievements were rare. exceptions that proved the rule of discrimination throughout America's labor movement, especially in craft locals (e.g. cooks and electricians) and hall-oriented locals (e.g. seafarers and lumber and sawmill workers). In the South, the Negro's position in unions was actually weakened when, in reaction to the 1954 Supreme Court desegregation decision, segregationist groups formed alliances with union locals.

Far from being conducted in an aura of secrecy, the cooperation of Southern segregationists and union leaders was widely publicized. In many localities, notices were advertised in local papers stating that the White Citizens Council or the Ku Klux Klan would be holding a meeting in a union hall.

In 1960, six years after the desegregation decision, the NAACP charged that the "Ku Klux Klan and White Citizen Council Forces, especially in Alabama, have moved into many local unions and made them, in effect, virtual extensions of segregationist organizations." Such union-segregationist alliances were apparent to Southern Negroes who were understandably more concerned with the situation in their locality than with pro civil rights declarations from national union headquarters. As a result, Southern Negroes often voted in a bloc, in NLRB elections, against union certification. In some cases, Negro votes defeated major organizational campaigns. One such election, still discussed in union circles, was held at the South Wire Company, Carrollton, Georgia, where 45 Negro workers out of several hundred are believed to have voted en masse against certification of the International Brotherhood of Electrical Workers. The union lost by 8 votes. At the Savannah River Atomic Energy Project in Aiken, South Carolina, 600 Negro workers out of 3,100 tipped an election against certification of 17 metal trades unions.

Willard Townsend (center, holding fedora) pioneer black union organizer

The Merger

It is against this background of erratic progress and racist reaction that the AFL and CIO merged in late 1955. The elimination of racism within unions was announced as a major goal of the new giant union. Its constitution pledged that the AFL-CIO would encourage all workingmen "without regard to race, creed, color or national origin or ancestry to share equally in the benefits of union organization." A Civil Rights Committee was established to achieve these goals.

This pledge was, of course, applauded by civil rights and liberal organizations. But, five years later, in a report on racism within organized labor, the NAACP charged that "the national labor organization has failed to eliminate the broad pattern of racial discrimination and segregation"—and that—"efforts to eliminate discriminatory practices within trade unions have been piecemeal and inadequate and usually the result of protest . . ."

There was considerable evidence to support these charges. Despite the exemplary declarations accompanying the merger, the AFL-CIO shortly thereafter admitted two unions, the Brotherhood of Locomotive Firemen and the Brotherhood of Railroad Trainmen, at a time when they had racist clauses in their constitutions.

The AFL-CIO also ignored defiance of state anti-discrimination orders by segregated locals. In April 1957, the New York State Commission against Discrimination ordered the merger of the all-white George N. Harrison Lodge and the all-black Friendship Lodges of the Brotherhood of Railway and Steamship Clerks. The white union disobeyed the order and the lodges remained segregated for several years.

The AFL-CIO also refrained from pressure or comment when member unions went to court to defend exclusion of Negroes. In 1958, after elimination of a "caucasian only" clause from its constitution, the Brotherhood of Locomotive Firemen and Enginemen successfully defended continued exclusion of Negroes in a suit brought by Negro firemen in a Cincinnati Federal Court.

Leading Negro trade unionists were openly disappointed with the progress of blacks. They observed that the AFL-CIO could expel unions for corruption or Communist ties, but not for violating civil rights laws and policies.

A. Philip Randolph, President of the Brotherhood of Sleeping Car Porters, conceded that the AFL-CIO civil rights program was a "step forward," but complained about the failure of the national union to impose sanctions against unions that excluded Negroes.

The NAACP charged that the Civil Rights Committee had very little power, that its chairman was not a member of the 79-man executive board and that the two Negroes who were board members, Randolph and Willard S. Townsend, president of the United Transport Service Employees, did not provide adequate policy-making representation for Negroes within the national union's upper councils.

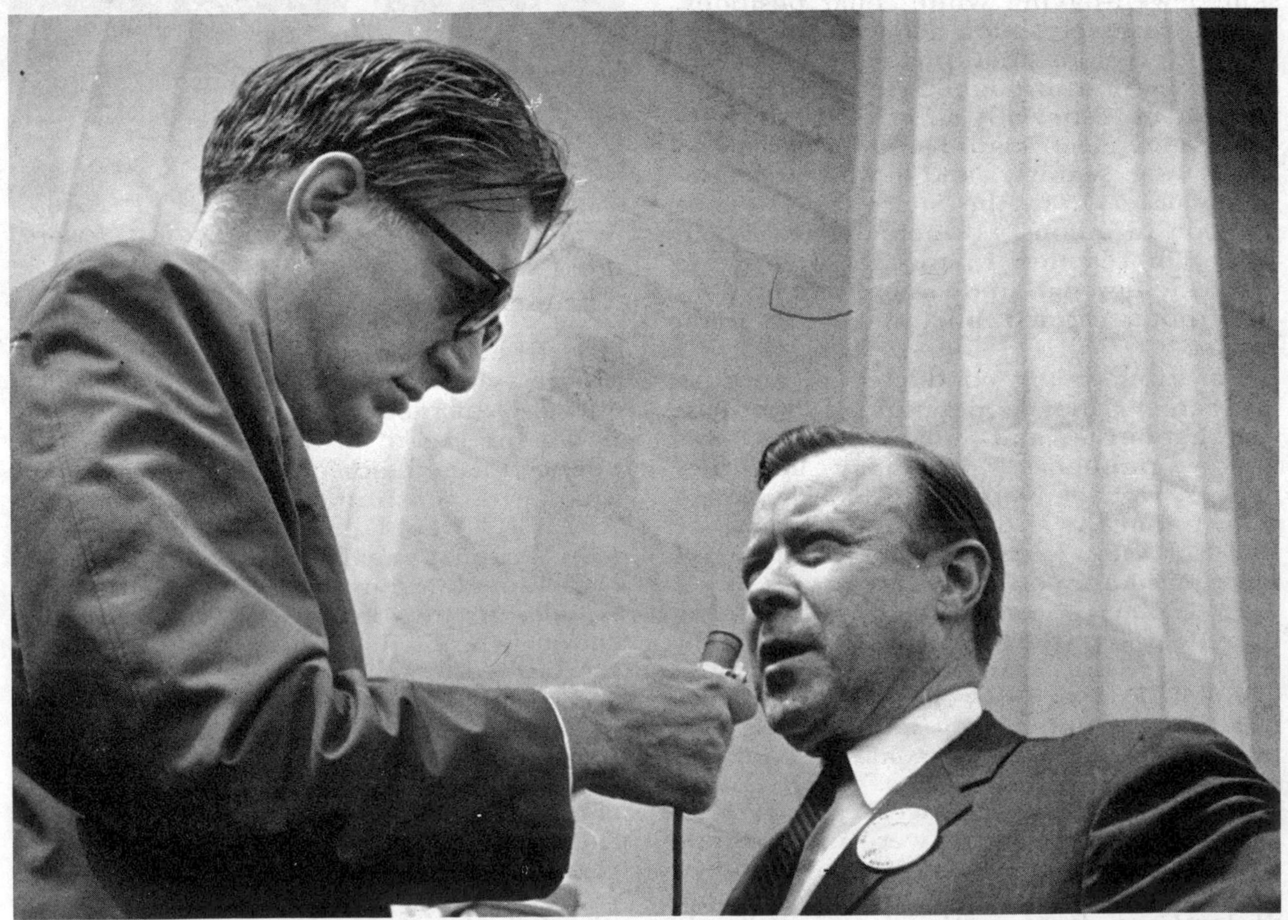

Walter Reuther, head of the Auto Workers union, interviewed during the 1963 March on Washington.

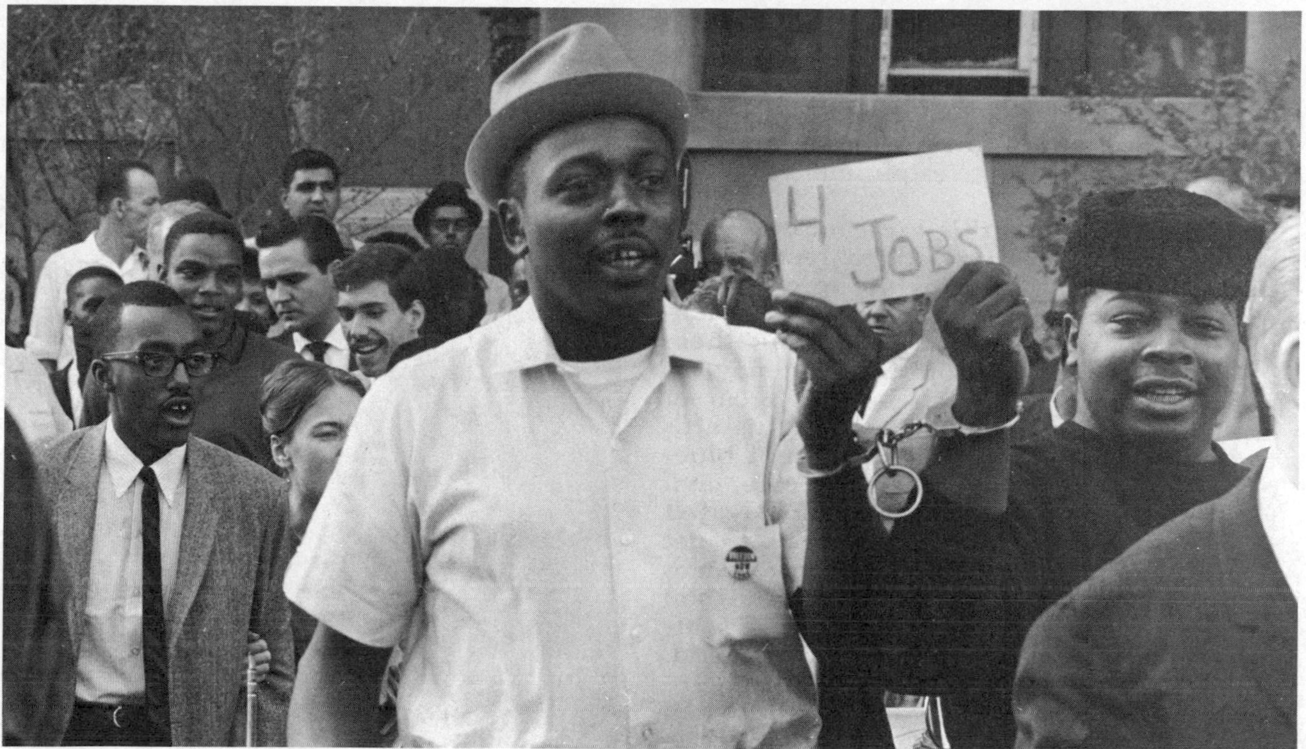

Job equality in trade unions which practice black exclusion has been a major target of protest groups throughout the country.

The infighting between Negro and union leaders intensified in the late 1950's. The NAACP brought a number of suits under state fair employment practice laws to force admission of Negroes to unions. Activists attacked labor's historic Gods. In a scathing article in *Commentary Magazine*, Herbert Hill, labor director of the NAACP, charged, with some telling evidence to support him, that Samuel Gompers, after struggling with some early idealism, became a racist who despised Negroes and hated Asians. Hill also charged that the East St. Louis and Chicago Negro pogroms of 1917 and 1919 were incited and executed by white unions who feared the use of Negro strike breakers, and that Gompers defended the rioters in a debate with Theodore Roosevelt.

For its part, the AFL-CIO promised it would try to eliminate discrimination from "within the house of labor." George Meany, president of the AFL-CIO, stated that discrimination only survived in the labor movement as "bootleg product, sneaked in by subterfuge."

Meany added that those "that practice discrimination know that its days are numbered." But other leaders of the federation argued that it could not compel locals to adhere to the national union's egalitarian policies.

The Civil Rights Alliance

Paradoxically, while Negro and union leaders were fighting one another over union racial practices, they were cooperating in support of state and federal civil rights legislation.

This anomaly becomes less curious when one reviews the American political scene of the 1950's and the ideology and hangups of Negro and union leaders.

Negroes and union leaders were in part forced into an alliance because the only strong and consistent political support for each group stemmed from liberal Democrats.

Liberal Democrats favored civil rights legislation and such traditional union objectives as increases in the minimum wage and unemployment compensation, while Republicans and Southern Democrats generally opposed pro-labor and civil rights measures.

Republicans and Southern Democrats had achieved enactment of the Taft Hartley Act, which proscribed the closed shop and increased the government's authority to prevent and end strikes. This same political alliance also combined to prevent cloture of filibusters against civil rights legislation.

Tensions between Negro and labor leaders were also diminished by the fact that Negro progress within labor unions was not really a major aim of civil rights leaders. The civil rights movement of the 50's and early 60's was far more intense about integration in schools, housing, transportation and restaurants than in unions.

The reasons for this are complex. Civil rights leadership tended to rest in the hands of black and white professional men—lawyers, ministers, journalists, teachers. There was a tendency among these people, perhaps a snobbish tendency, to despise blue collar work both as a career and as a political issue. Perhaps this attitude was related to an association of blue-collar labor with slavery. At any rate, civil rights leaders of that time obviously felt it far more important for Negroes to get degrees from colleges, houses in suburbs and jobs in corporate suites than to soil their hands on railway engines or scaffolds, no matter how well such work paid.

Also, the immediate objectives of Negro leaders tended to be legalistic rather than economic. The thrust was for new legislation and constitutional interpretations that would provide legal sanction for equality and integration and would eventually, it was assumed, lead to good economic progress.

George Meany

It was not until Malcolm X, a criminal who embraced Muslimism while in prison and went on to become a charismatic modern-day black leader, achieved notoriety that a "working man" was to obtain any renewed following among the post-war Negro generation.

Thus, though Negroes were bitter about union exclusion, Negro leaders tended to take it easy on unions—in order to sustain their political alliance with unions and because civil rights advocates were really not all that interested in manual labor, skilled or unskilled.

The AFL-CIO leadership, however, was interested in Negroes. The union leadership was not happy about its many surrenders and silences to segregationist affiliates. Many important unions were losing strength in the 50's, both in terms of real numbers and comparative bargaining strength with employers.

Malcolm X

Automation in the coal mines and the weak competitive position of coal vis-a-vis other forms of power forced the United Mine Workers to accept massive layoffs and the closing of marginal pits. Organization in service industries was disappointingly slow, partly because of union racist policies. Corporations were acquiring bargaining strength via mergers and internal expansion. And the prospect of Negroes again appearing in large numbers as scabs haunted labor leaders who had come up through the ranks to union leadership and who had long and clear memories of the days when Negro strike breakers received police protection in the mines of the Rocky Mountains and on the rails in Pennsylvania.

Also, a tinge of working-class socialist idealism survived, and still survives, amidst the guild exclusiveness and suburban conservatism of the labor movement. Labor leaders find it easier to think of solidarity in terms of economic class than race, and of progress in terms of social legislation rather than political reaction.

This idealism was tempered by the McCarthyite red scare of the early 1950's and genuine concern about Communist infiltration of unions. Walter Reuther had been a particular target of "witch hunters." But union leaders still did not like bigotry or the subjugation of the Negro working man.

Thus it was that the 50's ended, on an eccentric note. Individual unions and locals were coolly excluding qualified Negroes from good jobs and apprenticeships while union and Negro leaders were cooperating in attempts to achieve legislation that would, hopefully, guarantee Negroes the right to live, learn, vote and work with whites, and on the same terms as whites.

The 1960's—From Cooperation to Conflict

The 60's saw vast and violent changes within both the Negro and labor movements, with the two groups tending to pull in opposite directions. Negroes became more radical and assertive, labor more sluggish and cautious, with the end result that by 1970 the AFL-CIO and selected discriminatory unions were the prime targets of militant and moderate Negro groups.

Negro activity during the 1960's can be traced in terms of its changing targets and ways of exerting pressure.

From 1960 to 1964, the major objective remained civil rights legislation. The main target was Congress and the Kennedy and Johnson administrations. Pressure, however, was exerted more aggressively than during the 50's, as Negroes increasingly resorted to sit-ins, marches and other forms of direct, non-violent confrontation.

From 1964 until spring 1968, the period of ghetto riots, the objective was immediate improvement of living conditions. The main target was the "business establishment," which Negro leaders of varying militancy felt had the financial and political muscle to effect rapid change.

From spring 1968 to the end of the decade, the period of conservatism and "law and order," the major objectives were economic progress, recognition of black ability and uniqueness and protection of legislation and constitutional gains made since World War II. The main targets were labor unions which segregated or otherwise demeaned blacks.

While Negroes were becoming more radical in the 60's, the labor movement, as a whole, was becoming more conservative. As workers prospered, they moved to the suburbs or better urban residential areas where they lost interest in social reform, and saw Negroes as a threat to their new-found middle-class status. Resistance to integration in unions, and other changes, became so firm by 1970 that A. H. Raskin, assistant editor and labor specialist of the New York *Times* was to describe labor as "a static force in a chaotic society."

"A movement born as a voice of dissent," continued Raskin, "has become a mainstay of the status quo in a period when even the staidest institutions—educational, corporate, governmental—have felt obliged to take a look at all their most cherished precepts and scrap those made obsolete by changing technology and mores."

The New York hospital strike where service workers, predominantly black and economically exploited, demanded a living wage.

1960-1964: The Alliance Succeeds

Negro-union relations entered the sixties with the same combination of conflict and cooperation that existed in the 1950's.

At the community level tensions intensified as Negroes increasingly demonstrated against exclusion by craft unions and formed black caucuses within industrial unions.

At the policy-making level, both groups supported civil rights and pro-labor legislation and John F. Kennedy for president. Without an overwhelming Negro and labor vote, Kennedy would have been soundly defeated by Richard Nixon who lost narrowly and only after some questionable vote counts in Chicago.

Cooperation at the policy-making level reached its high water mark during the "1,000 days" of Kennedy and the first year or so of the Johnson administration.

President John F. Kennedy

Kennedy had promised strong civil rights legislation during his campaign, but by 1963 was clearly pessimistic of his chances of steering a strong bill through Congress. He was especially cynical about Congress' interest in enacting an equal employment opportunities requirement.

Labor historians credit George Meany with the eventual passage of equal opportunities provisions. Notes Raskin: "The AFL-CIO itself was chiefly responsible for the inclusion of the equal employment opportunities requirement in the Civil Rights Act of 1964. When the original omnibus bill was drawn up in 1963, President Kennedy and Attorney General Robert F. Kennedy were both convinced that it would have trouble enough getting through Congress without a provision forbidding job discrimination by employers or unions. Their view would have prevailed if George Meany had not insisted that such a clause was essential. His insistence grew out of the difficulty the AFL-CIO had had in getting recalcitrant local unions, especially those in the construction crafts, to comply with the federation's own constitutional ban on Jim Crow unions. . . . Through every phase of the long fight that followed on Capitol Hill, the AFL-CIO was a mainstay of the coalition that lobbied for a strong anti-bias law."

A number of individual unions were also strong supporters of the Civil Rights Act. Walter Reuther, then an AFL-CIO vice-president, was conspicuous in the 1963 March on Washington, as were the heads and memberships of other unions with large quantities of Negro members. Negro labor leaders A. Philip Randolph and Cleveland Robinson were key organizers of the March.

During this period, Negroes were progressing in such integration-minded service-trades unions as the State, County and Municipal Employees and District 65 of the Retail, Wholesalers, Department Store Union. But in most unions, they were progressing slowly or not at all. Blacks were still excluded from the lucrative referral construction unions. And, in large industrial unions, such as the steelworkers, Negroes were usually consigned to menial jobs and deprivable seniority lines.

Action in States

Despite cooperation on civil rights legislation, Negroes did press unions during the 1960-64 period. Negro groups urged states which had anti-discrimination laws to enforce them against discriminatory unions. However, little was achieved with state Fair Employment Practice Commissions. Although many states have FEP laws, their miniscule staffs and budgets confined the Commissions to slow case-by-case conciliation, where investigation of bias and enforcement of the laws was necessary to effect any real change in the job status of minorities.

However, Negro militancy was soon to provoke more forceful action by state FEP commissions. In 1963, mass demonstrations in Philadelphia halted construction of a large municipal building and of a school which was being built in a Negro neighborhood without use of Negro skilled labor. In July, pickets similarly halted construction in Harlem. The result of this action and ensuing FEPC hearings were a series of orders in New York and Pennsylvania prohibiting discrimination by the unions. Although these FEPC rulings did not result in large-scale use of skilled Negro labor, they did set a pattern for the Negro demonstrations and governmental action against discrimination in craft unions that was to occur at the end of the sixties.

Negro and civil rights groups also sought redress, though with only modest success, through such other public agencies as the courts, National Labor Relations Board, Department of Defense, etc. The unions generally resisted integrationist pressures. AFL-CIO officials continued to protest that the national union lacked authority to interfere with locals. Negro labor leaders, such as A. Philip Randolph, chastised the national union and its Civil Rights Division for their indifferent progress in effecting integration.

In 1960, Randolph and Cleveland Robinson, an executive of District 65 of the Retail Wholesale Department Store Union, formed the Negro American Labor Council. The objective was to establish a pressure group within labor for its 1.5 million Negro members. Although the NALC was to become more a local than national force, it did further the cause of Negroes in the United Auto Workers, and was a spur to black caucus activity in the late 60's. By the late 60's, black caucuses were to achieve a pronounced influence within many unions, particularly the UAW. In some cases, the caucuses were to renounce ties with parent unions and become the core of separate "breakaway" unions.

Cleveland Robinson was to become the head of an integrated breakaway union, the National Council of Distributive Workers, a group of some 40,000 workers who in 1969 withdrew from the RWSDU. District 65 of the RWSDU joined the National Council.

1964-1968: The Alliance Collapses

The union-civil rights alliance, strained at the best of times, disintegrated with the passage of civil rights legislation and the urban ghetto riots of 1964-1968.

However, Negro attention was focused elsewhere. Though Negroes continued to challenge discrimination in unions, the main targets of their fury were the police, and white ghetto merchants.Their main sources of hope were the government and large corporations, whom Negroes hoped would invest money and wield influence to erase employment, health and housing problems.

Coretta King at hospital workers rally in Charleston, S. C. in 1969.

White leaders who were seeking progress also displayed little interest in unions. For example, the National Advisory Commission on Civil Disorders (The Kerner Commission) was critical of unions and recommended steps to assure Negroes access to skilled jobs, but obviously regarded exclusion from unions as a lesser matter on the Negroes' imposing list of grievances.

The government's response to the riots was to emphasize employment and training of poor Negroes. The main responsibility for this was assigned to business. The Johnson administration set up the JOBS Program to subsidize recruiting and training of "hard core" ghetto residents and major corporations formed the National Alliance of Business to guide business in these activities. Unions were merely asked to cooperate and in many instances were granted the right to veto training programs which they felt threatened to glut a labor market. This veto power was, in effect, a continuation of a privilege unions had acquired over Department of Labor training programs earlier in the 60's.

The reaction of unions to JOBS and NAB was erratic. The AFL-CIO pledged support to recruitment and training efforts. Support was forthcoming from many unions, particularly service industry unions with large numbers of minority-group members. Others were quick to exercise their vetoes.

Such opposition to training programs aroused the ire of Negroes and other minorities. In 1968, a group of Negro and Puerto Rican teenagers in New York armed themselves with cherry cream pies to protect government sewing machines that were being removed, they felt, at the insistence of the International Ladies Garment Workers Union. In August 1963, the ILGWU had declared federally sponsored training of apparel workers to be "a waste of funds" and "detrimental to the health and stability of our industry."

The New York Teachers Strike

Perhaps the most significant labor dispute of the sixties occurred in 1968, when local 6 of the United Federation of Teachers struck against the New York City Board of Education. This strike achieved more than increases in wages and fringe benefits for teachers. It also gained the union control of important segments of public policy.

The UFT strike was directed at the city's intention to decentralize its public schools and hand control to community school boards. Such a program was underway in three experimental school districts, notably the Negro Bedford Stuyvesant section of Brooklyn. The local school board there exhibited a strong distaste for some white teachers who allegedly had little interest in, or aptitude for, motivating black students. It proceeded to dismiss a number of them and to react sluggishly on behalf of other white teachers who were being harassed in classrooms. Union leader Albert Shanker called a strike which kept over 1,000,000 children out of school for two months. The central issue was the school board's power to hire and fire teachers. Underlying issues were alleged black anti-Semitism and the questionable conscientiousness of many whites who teach in black neighborhoods. The strike was not resolved until the local school board's authority was greatly diminished.

The union maintained that it was necessary to use the strike weapon to lessen the impact of radical new policies on public employees. Negroes contended that the strike was essentially a veto over policies designed to help blacks help themselves. AFL-CIO officials tended to support the UFT.

Reuther Bolts

The AFL-CIO suffered a major defection from its ranks in 1966 when Walter Reuther, after failing to impose reforms or oust Meany as head of the union, withdrew his United Auto Workers and formed the American Labor Alliance with the Teamsters. Though both the Teamsters and the UAW had uneven race-relations records, their Negro members did fare relatively well. The ALA was subsequently to take pro-Negro positions on a number of issues and disputes.

During the 1964-68 period, the AFL-CIO did take some positive steps on behalf of minorities. The union supported the grape boycott on behalf of the Mexican and Filipino grape pickers in California. Discriminatory by-laws and agreements were virtually erased from union constitutions and contracts. Negro leaders were quick to point out that such legalistic moves were rarely followed by integration and that discrimination was now illegal anyway, but elimination of these provisions did at least erase a major humiliation for Negroes.

The AFL-CIO also supported the Negro sanitation worker demonstrations in Memphis.

It was in Memphis, during the course of these labor demonstrations, that Martin Luther King was assassinated. This assassination not only ended the life of a moderate and cohering Negro leader, but brought to a close the period of urban riots. National Guard and Army troops were quickly dispatched to Kansas City, Missouri, Chicago and Washington to control the violence which followed King's death. This action was in sharp contrast to policy during earlier disturbances in Watts, Detroit and Newark where authorities hesitated to use force.

The nation generally supported this prompt use of the military to halt violence in the cities, and exhibited a rising interest in "law and order."

In a backlash to the riots, the segregationist ideas of Alabama Governor George Wallace were to receive a significant measure of support from union members in the North as well as the South.

1968-1970: Black Power Focuses on Unions

A number of ideological and practical factors served to divide Negroes and unions during the final years of the sixties and to induce Negroes to focus "black power" efforts on organized labor.

In the face of white backlash, unions tended to increase their resistance to integration. They maintained that this was necessary to prevent a massive defection by union voters from the Democratic Party to George Wallace. After the 1968 Presidential election union leaders claimed, though not for publication, that Wallace's vote in Northern cities, which generally ranged from 5 to 10%, would have been much larger if the unions had not stressed the low wages earned by workers in Wallace's home state of Alabama.

Whatever the case, there can be no doubt that Wallace aroused substantial support from Northern blue collar whites and by 1970 loomed as a potent force in the 1972 election. To Negroes, however, the blue-collar shift to the right cleared the air. The white urban laborer, regarded at best as an uncertain ally, now seemed an outright racist.

Negroes and the AFL-CIO were also divided by varying positions on the Vietnam war. The AFL-CIO strongly supported President Johnson's positions in Vietnam while Negroes, though fighting there in large numbers, tended to regard it as a racist war which was absorbing money needed to improve Negro conditions in the United States.

The civil rights movement had also shifted strongly from its legal-legislative orientation to one of economic improvement. To be sure, court cases were abundant and many of them referred to the older issues of school and housing integration. But an increasing number were directed toward economic improvement, toward erasing bias by employers and unions.

Economic efforts tended to concentrate on improving the Negro position as entrepreneurs, corporate executives, unskilled workers and skilled workers.

The place of skilled workers was soon to become the top issue on the list of grievances.

Progress as executives and "black capitalists," desirable though it was, was largely confined to Negroes with advanced educations. This could do little to help the mass of Negroes.

Also, achievement as capitalists and executives and the hiring and training of unorganized hard-core workers rested pretty much in the hands of business. Negroes did not want to take on business for a number of reasons. Since the country was in the midst of a conservative trend, it was thought that business would be a strong foe. And the record of many leading businesses in hiring and advancing Negroes was fairly good.

Many unions, however, especially the referral unions which had the power to hire and fire skilled workers, continued to exclude Negroes in the face of protestations by union leaders, the "persuasion" efforts of federal agencies, and the orders of courts and state anti-discrimination agencies.

The Construction Unions

Negroes also had good reason to expect sympathy from business in any reasoned attack they made on exclusive skill unions. Of these, the construction unions were the most logical target. By creating conditions of artificial scarcity through restrictive apprentice programs and journeymen certifications, construction unions had achieved astronomical pay scales. Union plumbers in Philadelphia, for example, negotiated an annual minimum wage of $19,400. Such wages contributed to inflationary pay raises throughout the economy. The addition of Negro construction workers could reduce the scarcity and give blacks a piece of some well-paid action.

The construction unions—the electricians, carpenters, plumbers, etc. — were also a likely target because the nation was in dire need of new houses and offices and lacked the skilled manpower to build them. It was estimated in 1965 that 1,000,000 skilled construction men would have to be added to the labor force by 1975. But the Depression-conscious construction unions worked effectively to minimize entrants into the field.

Also, there were a number of provisions in federal and local law to require acceptance of Negroes on government-supported construction projects. As Herbert Hill of the NAACP remarked to the Senate Judiciary Committee in October 1969, the public share of the current dollar value of construction rose from 17% in 1947 to 34% in 1967. The government is very much in the construction business. And the construction industry is very dependent on government funds.

Police scuffle with demonstrators of the Black Construction Coalition at the construction site of the new Pittsburgh sports stadium.

The new emphasis on black history, by reminding Negroes that they were able craftsmen during slavery, may also have contributed to their decision to assault the skilled trades.

It should be said for the unions that economic gain has been more a factor than racial bias in their exclusionist policies. By limiting the supply of officially qualified workers, they have strengthened their wage demands and buttressed their position against the ever-present ogre of a recession.

The AFL-CIO replied to Negro charges by repeating their assertion that national headquarters lacked the power to interfere with local unions, that Negroes often failed to pass journeymen and apprenticeship qualification tests and that under an AFL-CIO "Apprentice Outreach" program, the unions had trained 3,862 nonwhites in construction trades in two years.

The black groups replied that the tests were often rigged against Negroes and that 3,862 was a meaningless quantity in an industry that had 3½ million union members.

Pittsburgh, Chicago and the "Philadelphia Plan"

As already noted, Negroes had demonstrated in large numbers at construction sites during the early sixties. These earlier demonstrations were to pale before those which Negro groups undertook in 1969 in Chicago, Pittsburgh, and other cities.

In the summer of 1969, the "Pittsburgh Black Construction Coalition," an amalgam of skilled laborers and civil rights groups, blocked entrances to major construction projects for three days. The workers counter-demonstrated, some of them carrying "Wallace in '72" placards. The police were called upon to prevent violence.

In Chicago, also in the summer of 1969, the "Chicago Coalition for United Community Action," a group of about 60 minority-group organizations ranging from the Southern Christian Leadership Conference to street gangs, halted work for several days on construction jobs valued at $100 million. The Coalition demanded 10,000 jobs for minorities and the easing of qualification requirements for minorities.

The Chicago & Cook County Building & Construction Trades Council, in a plan endorsed by George Meany, promised in January 1970 to "endeavor to obtain employment for 1,000 qualified journeymen" to be supplied by the Coalition, to accept workers of uncertain skills for 30-day probationary periods and to expand information, recruiting and training programs. In February, the "agreement" awaited ratification by the unions and Coalition.

In response to rising pressure on construction unions, Secretary of Labor George Shultz, in 1969, advanced the Philadelphia Plan, a program which would require builders to display a "good faith effort" toward hiring representative quotas of Negroes to skilled jobs on all federally supported construction. The quotas would approximate the percentage of Negroes resident in each city included in the plan.

George Meany, a number of Southern senators and the U. S. Comptroller General opposed the Philadelphia Plan, some of them on the grounds that quotas are illegal under the Civil Rights Act of 1964. But Attorney General Mitchell, who wielded considerable power in the government, declared the Plan to be legal and Shultz stood by it. Negro groups tended to support it, though they criticized the enforcement provisions as being too weak. At the start of 1970, the government was proceeding with the Philadelphia Plan and leaking word to the press that it would soon be expanded to 20 other cities.

The Charleston Hospital Strike

Important as they are, the construction unions serve only a skilled minority of American workers. A large majority of American workers are not highly skilled or even industrial, but are employed in service jobs, a great many of which are menial, low paying and not unionized. Negroes are "over-represented" in low-end service trades.

Thus, the Charleston College Hospital Strike of 1969 assumes special significance. The strike, conducted by Local 1199 of the RDSWU, was cited by *Business Week* magazine as "a successful union-Negro alliance in which a fight for economic betterment is fused with a fight for racial dignity." The strike was provoked by the hospital's dismissal of 12 Negro workers. The union won recognition and reinstatement of the workers.

The strike also betrayed some of the conflict commonplace between unions that have varying orientations to Negro workers. The AFL-CIO supported the strike, but some black union leaders charged that support from the national union was reluctant, tardy and motivated solely by fear that Local 1199 would withdraw from the RDSWU, as Cleveland Robinson's distributive workers had done. A large number of Negro labor militants also claim that support from Walter Reuther's ALA was more generous and sincere than that of the AFL-CIO.

Nevertheless, the fact remains that the AFL-CIO did support the Charleston strikers and that, for all its internal bickering, organized labor was united on behalf of a group of low-paid Negro service workers.

Encouraged by their success in Charleston, 1199 branched out to organize hospital and nursing homes in the East and Midwest. In the fall of 1969, it organized the Johns Hopkins Hospital in Baltimore and achieved more modest successes in Pennsylvania.

Local 1199 relies heavily on civil rights activists and their persistent community-disruption methods in its organizing campaigns. Mrs. Martin Luther King Jr. was a vocal supporter of the Charleston strike and in 1969 was named honorary chairman of the National Union of Hospital and Nursing Home Employees, the title under which Local 1199 expanded its efforts. The group enlisted the aid of local black and student leaders wherever it could and staged dramatic demonstrations that harvested publicity and thwarted public services. In Charleston, the state police were called out to maintain order as pro-union demonstrations impeded hospital service, reduced the city's tourist and retail revenue and produced 1,000 arrests. In Pittsburgh, 1199 staged a sit-in at the headquarters of the Mellon National because a hospital trustee had an office there and the bank was a symbol of the "establishment."

In its readiness to frustrate public services on behalf of its aims, Local 1199 was something of a black power counterpart to the United Federation of Teachers in New York. In 1970, about 75% of the union's members were Negroes.

By March 1970, about 10% of America's hospital and nursing and psychiatric home employees were unionized. The vast majority were in Local 1199 or the larger, more moderate Service Employees Union.

Economic Progress and Representation

In historic terms, the Negro's standard of living has improved over the years. Unionization has contributed to this rise. However, the Negro's living standard has increased at a slower rate than that of whites. As a result, the ratio of Negro income to white income has consistently declined.

As of 1969, two Negro labor leaders, A. Philip Randolph and Frederick O'Neal, who is president of Actors Equity Association, held positions on the AFL-CIO executive board.

Of greater importance, Negroes have been attaining executive positions in "internationals" and locals. As noted, Cleveland Robinson is president of the integrated National Council of Distributive Workers.

The Outlook

By 1970, black activity against and within unions promised to cause more cracks in the "house of labor." The AFL-CIO convention in February 1970 promised to continue civil rights efforts. Blacks expressed scepticism about the promises and the NAACP charged that the AFL-CIO Civil Rights Division was propounding segregation in unions with legalistic delays similar to those used by Southerners fighting school desegregation.

Business cutbacks in 1969, following the administration's efforts to curb inflation, threatened to undermine hard-core training programs. Hard-core recruits, lacking union seniority, were the first to be laid off when the auto and steel industries cut back production in 1969. Increasing automation also threatened Negro industrial union members who lacked seniority.

In early 1970, the administration, expressing fear about inflationary wage settlements and strikes that crippled public service facilities, hinted that it might soon seek legislation allowing "public representatives" to participate in union-management negotiations. This contributed to a widespread feeling that the government would become more and more involved in union affairs and find it easier to influence union policy in a number of areas.

On the whole, the prospects for Negroes in the labor movement were brighter at the start of the 1970's than ever before. The outlook was for slow progress and mounting legal and extra-legal pressure on unions that continued policies of discrimination.

Cleveland Robinson (extreme right), President, American Negro Labor Council.

MINORITY GROUP MEMBERSHIP IN REFERRAL LOCAL UNIONS, AS REPORTED IN 1967

International Union/Trade	*Membership in Referral Units* Total	Negro	% Negro	SSA*	% SSA*
ALL UNIONS NOT IN BUILDING TRADES	770,123	92,095	12.0	71,735	9.3
Bakery & Conf. Workers	14,881	1,699	11.2	2,030	13.6
Bookbinders	20,289	1,350	6.6	1,693	8.3
Building Serv. Empl.	29,089	8,290	28.4	2,306	7.9
Distillery Workers	13,098	1,646	12.5	368	2.8
Hotel & Restaurant Employees	139,616	18,093	12.9	18,362	13.1
Lithographers & Photoengravers	20,153	281	1.3	264	1.3
Masters, Mates, & Pilots	6,765	21	0.3	177	2.6
Meat Cutters	42,892	3,644	8.4	4,013	9.3
Musicians	12,487	805	6.4	184	1.4
Office Employees	7,393	1,061	14.3	582	7.8
Patternmakers	7,751	5	0.1	55	0.7
Printing Pressmen	21,710	962	4.4	1,383	6.3
Retail Clerks	17,497	1,127	6.4	641	3.6
Seafarers	9,274	141	1.5	580	6.2
Shoe Workers	6,580	480	7.2	2,247	34.1
Stage & Motion Picture Operators	22,756	672	2.9	1,202	5.3
Teamsters	213,632	20,573	9.6	11,984	5.6
Other Non-Building Trade Unions	164,260	31,245	19.0	23,664	14.4

**Spanish Surnamed American.*
SOURCE: *Equal Employment Opportunity Commission, Local Union Report EEO-3.*

MINORITY GROUP MEMBERSHIP IN REFERRAL LOCAL UNIONS, AS REPORTED IN 1967

International Union/Trade	*Membership in Referral Units* Total	Negro	% Negro	SSA*	% SSA*
ALL UNIONS	2,028,052	198,358	9.7	127,797	6.3
ALL BUILDING TRADES UNIONS	1,257,929	106,263	8.4	56,062	4.5
Asbestos Workers	6,104	61	0.9	75	1.2
Boilermakers	23,946	934	3.9	917	3.8
Bricklayers	34,069	3,300	9.6	733	2.1
Carpenters	315,538	5,284	1.6	8,692	2.7
Electrical Workers	133,904	915	0.6	2,490	1.8
Elevator Constructors	6,728	33	0.4	89	1.3
Operating Engineers	103,677	4,200	4.0	1,450	1.4
Iron Workers	70,273	1,197	1.7	2,406	3.4
Laborers	266,243	81,457	30.5	26,350	9.8
Lathers	4,660	177	3.7	147	3.1

Marble, Slate & Stone Polishers	4,355	387	8.8	699	16.0
Painters	66,714	2,498	3.7	4,502	6.7
Plasterers	28,182	3,947	14.0	3,568	12.6
Plumbers	147,862	320	0.2	2,038	1.4
Roofers	10,807	1,461	13.5	357	3.3
Sheet Metal Workers	34,867	92	0.2	1,543	4.4

*Spanish Surnamed American.
SOURCE: *Equal Employment Opportunity Commission, Local Union Report EEO-3.*

THE NEGRO IN AGRICULTURE

Centuries of toil on the cotton and tobacco plantations of the South have no doubt contributed to the almost universal disenchantment of the rural Negro with farming as a possible career. The federal government is presently engaged in a far-reaching "Rural Renaissance" program designed to reverse the trend of urban migration among Negro farm youth.

Little has occurred in recent years to reverse the ongoing trend of the Negro's diminishing role in U. S. agriculture. More and more, the Negro has come to abandon the farm, migrating to the cities in search of greater economic opportunity and a more diversified life.

The vast majority of Negro farmers in the United States today are in the tobacco and cotton country of eastern North and South Carolina, and in the Cotton Belt lying 50 miles north, and 75 miles south, of Memphis, Tennessee. In the North and West, the largest number of Negro farmers are to be found in Michigan (Cass and Berien counties), Ohio, and California.

The growth of cotton and the westward expansion of the United States are the two historical factors which have largely determined the Negro's role in U. S. agriculture since his introduction into the South more than three centuries ago. The Louisiana Purchase (1803) and the doctrine of Manifest Destiny (i.e. the inevitable expansion of the United States) instilled in most Southerners the belief that cotton would remain king as long as fertile land could be acquired by moving westward. By 1850, some 2.8 million slaves lived within the confines of the Cotton Kingdom, working on farms and plantations. Of these, some 1.8 million were engaged in the cultivation of cotton, with the remainder being used to raise tobacco, rice and sugar cane.

Emancipation did not radically alter the Negro's role in agriculture, particularly since it did not afford him the opportunity to participate in the great post-war homesteading movement which accompanied the continued westward settlement of the country.

The next significant development in the history of the Negro farmer was the introduction of the tenant system in the South. Under this system, the Negro was assigned to work a particular piece of land with the stipulation that he receive a portion of the crop as wages (sharecropping). Tenants were furnished with necessary living supplies over a period of one year under a simple credit system. In return for supplies and equipment, they mortgaged their share of the crops, and repaid their debts at harvest time. However, exorbitant interest rates and high-priced goods often left the Negro with little chance to extend himself beyond survival. In addition, most rural Negroes remained illiterate and, as such, were disadvantaged by a host of accounting malpractices.

Apart from this gloomy picture, it is important to remember that agricultural education experienced its first real flowering after the Civil War. Hampton Normal and Agricultural Institute was opened at Hampton, Virginia in 1868 and, within a decade had graduated Booker T. Washington who, in turn, founded Tuskegee (1881). Within the next two decades, the work of Tuskegee's George Washington Carver had revolutionized the growth of soybeans and peanuts throughout the South, and helped diversify the economy of the entire region.

After the turn of the century, however, rice farming in the South Atlantic states fell into decline, as did agriculture engaged in by most Negroes in the border areas. World War I ushered in a tremendous industrial boom in the United States, leading to an even sharper drop in the number of Negro farmers, most of whom sought factory work in the cities.

Then, too, the boll weevil scourge all but crippled the cotton crop, causing further financial losses in the Negro farm community. Many Negro owners were once again forced into tenancy, a system which became even more solidly entrenched than it had been during the post-Civil War years.

The Depression of the 1930's brought extreme hardship to both white and Negro farmers. In 1934, however, the federal government began to take a hand in reorganizing the nation's agricultural system by providing cheap credit for farmers and by helping them become landowners. This was done by purchasing heavily indebted plantations which were subdivided into smaller farms suitable for one family. Many such plots were sold to former Negro tenants. In addition, the government put into effect certain crop acreage controls and a system of price supports designed to stabilize the market value of a variety of produce.

Since the Depression, the number of Negro farm operators has continued to drop drastically. In 1964 (not shown in the table below), the total number was estimated at only 180,000. As of 1965, only 3% of all employed Negro men were farm operators, with an additional 8% engaged as farm laborers.

Other data of interest from the Department of Commerce Census of Agriculture:

- About 45% of non-white farmers in the South were tenant farmers in 1964.
- The average size of Southern farms operated by non-whites in 1964 was 56.6 acres.
- Two thirds of the non-white operated farms in the South are less than 50 acres. In 1964, some 70% of these farms sold less than $2,500 in farm products. 55% of the operators of these farms reported greater income from off-the-farm than farm sources.

The poverty of Southern Negro farmers has affected the entire country, especially since World War II. Negro emigrants from Southern farms have swollen ghettoes in northern and western cities, while most who have remained in the South require public assistance.

Thousands of Negro farm emigrants have become migrant farm laborers throughout the country. Their living and work conditions are usually squalid and low. Despite some improvements in a few states, migratory farm laborers have had little effective statutory protection or labor union support. Thus, the unionized efforts of the California grape pickers are important to Negroes, even though the great majority of these workers are of Mexican and Philippine extraction.

BLACK FARM OPERATORS IN THE UNITED STATES (1900-1964)

Area	*1964*	*1959*	*1950*	*1940*	*1930*	*1920*	*1900*
United States	**184,004**	**272,541**	**559,980**	**681,790**	**882,850**	**925,708**	**746,715**
Northeast	3,032	590	1,002	1,432	1,021	1,469	1,761
North Central		4,259	6,700	7,466	10,083	7,911	12,255
South	180,418	267,008	551,469	672,214	870,936	915,595	732,362
West	554	678	809	678	812	735	337
Selected States							
Missouri		1,684	3,214	3,686	5,844	2,824	4,950
Maryland		2,132	3,595	4,049	5,264	6,208	5,842
Virginia		15,629	28,527	35,062	39,598	47,690	44,795
North Carolina		41,023	69,029	57,428	74,636	74,849	53,996
South Carolina		30,953	61,255	61,204	77,331	109,005	85,381
Georgia		20,163	50,352	59,127	86,787	130,176	82,822
Florida		3,664	7,473	9,731	11,010	12,954	13,521
Kentucky		3,327	4,882	5,546	9,104	12,624	11,227
Tennessee		15,018	24,044	27,972	35,123	38,181	33,883
Alabama		29,206	57,205	73,338	93,795	95,200	94,069
Mississippi		55,174	122,709	159,256	182,578	161,001	128,351
Arkansas		14,654	40,810	57,011	79,556	72,275	46,978
Louisiana		17,686	40,599	59,556	73,734	62,036	58,096
Oklahoma		2,633	5,910	8,987	15,172	13,403	6,353
Texas		15,432	34,389	52,648	85,940	78,597	65,472

During the past three years, the federal government has taken some steps to ease the privations of Negro farmers and tenants. Redress has been granted under the Fair Labor Standards Act. In 1968, a federal judge in Clarksdale, Mississippi, upheld a Department of Labor order that a white Delta farmer pay $50,000 in back wages to 200 Negro employees, who had been required to pay the farm owner $70 a month in rent for dwellings the Labor Department valued at $5.

In 1967, a national minimum farm wage of $1.00 took effect. This rose to $1.30 per hour in 1969.

THE NEGRO AMERICAN LABOR COUNCIL

The Negro American Labor Council (NALC) was formed in May of 1960, approximately a year after more than 75 Negro trade union leaders had met in New York to consider the need for creating a national organization especially dedicated to the interests of Negro trade unionists.

The organization sees as its major objective the establishment of a national clearing house through which the problems common to the 1.5 million Negro trade union members may be aired and clarified. Moreover, the NALC desires to strengthen lines of communication between Negro trade unions across the country, as well as within specific Negro communities. It is not, in the eyes of A. Philip Randolph, a splinter group at odds with the basic policies of the AFL-CIO.

Dedicated to the furtherance of the total trade union movement, the NALC seeks "the democratic welfare of all members regardless of race, creed, or color." Working closely with the trade union movement in the consideration of problems common to Negro workers, it is "independent of the control or domination of any union or segment of the labor movement."

Originally headed by Randolph, who served as chairman of the organization's National Steering Committee, the NALC is now being directed by Cleveland Robinson.

PROMINENT NEGRO TRADE UNIONISTS

A. PHILIP RANDOLPH
President, International Brotherhood of Sleeping Car Porters

Regarded as the "elder statesman" among civil rights leaders, A. Philip Randolph was for many years head of the Brotherhood of Sleeping Car Porters and, later in his career, also served as president of the Negro American Labor Council.

Born in Crescent City, Florida in 1889, Randolph was at first attracted to a writing career, and served for a time as an editor of the "Messenger," a journal of opinion, also contributing articles to "Opportunity" magazine. In 1925, he organized the Brotherhood of Sleeping Car Porters, eventually to become the strongest Negro labor union, and later became the first Negro vice-president of the AFL-CIO.

During World War II, Randolph threatened to stage a march on the nation's capital in protest against discriminatory practices in the defense establishment, and eventually helped persuade President Franklin D. Roosevelt to issue an executive order eliminating such practices. Later, he was an effective lobbyist for the establishment of a fair employment practices committee.

Randolph was one of the major forces behind the 1963 March on Washington. Three years later, he stepped down from his post with the Negro American Labor Council, where he was succeeded by Cleveland Robinson.

At the AFL-CIO convention of 1967, Randolph, who had long been a critic of the national union's civil rights progress, altered his position and strongly defended the civil rights efforts of the union and its Civil Rights Division. In 1970 he was semi-retired and living in Florida.

A Philip Randolph has for many years been regarded as the "elder statesman" of Negro leaders.

CLEVELAND ROBINSON
President, Negro American Labor Council (NALC)

The president of the Negro American Labor Council (NALC) since May of 1966, Cleveland Robinson is a native of Jamaica, West Indies. A U.S. citizen by naturalization, Robinson joined District 65 of the Retail Wholesale and Department Store Union (RWDSU) in 1946, serving first as a shop steward and then as a trainee organizer.

In 1952, Robinson, who is nearly blind, was elected Secretary-Treasurer of this local and, almost simultaneously, chosen as international vice president and executive board member of the International Union of the RDSWU. After serving in many responsible positions in District 65 of this union, Robinson, in May 1969, led the District's 25,000 workers in a breakaway from the parent union and the AFL-CIO. He was elected president of the new union, the National Council of Distributive Workers. Robinson thus became America's first Negro president of a multiracial union. Ten other locals joined the new union. About half of its new membership is black.

In August of 1963, Robinson played a key role in coordinating the March on Washington by serving as chairman of the administrative committee in charge of this historic event. Later that year, he was appointed to the New York City Commission on Human Rights, a post to which he was again named in December of 1965.

One of the founders of the NALC, Robinson held the post of National Vice President and assistant to A. Philip Randolph until the latter's resignation in 1966.

Active in the civil rights cause, Robinson holds a life membership in the NAACP; is a member of the Urban League, and an Executive Board and Steering Committee member of the American Committee on Africa. He also belongs to the Research Committee of the Southern Christian Leadership Conference (SCLC).

He is regional representative of the Southern Christian Leadership Conference and a member of the New York City Commission on Human Rights.

BAYARD RUSTIN
Executive Director,
A. Philip Randolph Institute

Bayard Rustin could easily be identified with any number of civil rights organizations, pacifist groups, massive popular demonstrations, etc., but it is through his 30-year association with A. Philip Randolph, and his present directorship of the A. Philip Randolph Institute, that he is able to give shape to his most abiding and progressive ideas on labor management and economic planning.

As executive director of the Institute since its inception in 1964, Rustin has worked unstintingly to develop and promote sound radical programs designed to cure the economic and social ills of the country. Though he does not totally discount the value of federally sponsored poverty programs and other schemes for insuring every American family a guaranteed annual income, he feels nonetheless that real progress can only occur in the wake of a government decision to mobilize all employable persons and assign to them the basic task of improving their environment: rebuilding ghetto neighborhoods, ghetto schools and ghetto hospitals at public expense.

Tax money allocated for this objective would not only provide decent income for the unemployed, but generate real growth in a sector of the nation which traditionally cannot produce the taxes needed to finance its progress, and so becomes dependent on regular public assistance. In Rustin's view, it is the nation's incredible distortion of public priorities that has led to the bloodbaths of the inner city, the wholesale carnage, destruction, and looting, the ascendancy of the riot mentality, and the burning tempers of disillusioned and explosive youth. Poverty money can only relieve such conditions for a time; it cannot, by definition, assuage the anger because it does not reach the heart of the problem.

Rustin defines the problem as the onslaught of a technology that fails to take into account basic human needs, that displaces unskilled and semi-skilled laborers without concern for their welfare or economic adaptability, thus indirectly causing social fragmentation, urban decay, family disintegration, and loss of hope. The solution he advocates calls for the orderly seizure of political power by responsible groups able to agree on the defects and to map strategy for their elimination. The groups which, in his view, engineered such impressive movements as the March on Washington, the passage of the 1964 Civil Rights Act, and the Johnson landslide, must increase their power base, stimulate greater support for their ideology of social reconstruction, and force government to respond to the needs of predominantly urban constituencies. The four identifiable groups present in Rustin's sturdy coalition are: the black community, white liberals, religious parties, and labor unions.

Rustin, in other words, advocates the growth and strengthening of those organizations and agencies identified with the non-Communist political left. He feels black separatism and guerrilla warfare rhetoric are not only suicidal, but also criminally destructive and self-defeating. Inevitably, he argues, they play into the hands of reactionary groups able to capitalize on internecine squabbling and disruptive fragmentation.

Rustin's philosophy has not been conceived in Olympian aloofness. More than just a theoretician, he has been arrested 23 times in the cause of peace and civil rights, and has demonstrated time and again his willingness to take to the streets in defense of his beliefs and in promotion of his ideology.

Born in West Chester, Pennsylvania in March 1910, Rustin was raised by his grandparents, though he was particularly influenced by his grandmother, a devout Quaker. At school, he was an honor student and star athlete, experiencing his first real anger at discrimination when he was refused restaurant service in Pennsylvania while on tour with the football team.

After graduation, he studied literature and history at Cheyney State and Wilberforce Colleges, but his most serious interests already lay in politics. In 1936, Rustin joined the Young Communist League, becoming an organizer two years later. Rustin earned an irregular livelihood in New York singing at the old Cafe Society with such notables as Josh White and Leadbelly.

Realizing the error of his ways, Rustin left the Party by 1941, joining instead the Fellowship of Reconciliation, a nonviolent anti-war group. That same year, he became a youth organizer for A. Philip Randolph's projected March on Washington to demand better job opportunities for Negroes in the defense industry. During World War II, Rustin was imprisoned as a conscientious objector, serving some 2½ years behind bars. Released in 1945, he immediately joined the Indian independence movement, and was again jailed for demonstrating before the British Embassy.

In 1947, Rustin participated in a historic "journey of reconciliation," an event now popularly known as a Freedom Ride. The experience brought with it another jail term, but enabled Rustin to expose chain gang abuses in North Carolina which were subsequently abolished. By this time, Rustin was not only identified with the Congress of Racial Equality (CORE), the organization which had pioneered in the Freedom Ride movement, but also with A. Philip Randolph's Committee Against Discrimination in the Armed Forces.

Until 1955, Rustin was preoccupied with various peace conventions, efforts to restrict nuclear armaments, and movements toward African independence. That year, he joined Martin Luther King's Southern Christian Leadership Conference (SCLC), again in an organizational capacity as King's Special Assistant. In 1963, he was named chief logistics expert and organizational coordinator of the March on Washington.

In the latter part of the '60's, Rustin was increasingly hard pressed to maintain support for the non-violent philosophy to which he had dedicated his life. His charismatic appeal, relentless logic, and debating effectiveness carried him through crisis after crisis, however. Nonviolence, he argued, was not outdated; it was a necessary and inexorable plan called for by the Negro's condition in the U. S. Guerrilla warfare and armed insurrection, Rustin explained, required friendly border sanctuaries, a steady source of arms and equipment, and the support of the majority of a country's inhabitants.

Still, Rustin was equally appalled by the ignorance and shallowness of government groups who failed to respond to the legitimate appeals of young blacks for better education, increased job opportunity, improved housing, and general medical care. When Negroes finally went on a rampage in Watts in 1965, Rustin, as he had done previously in Harlem in 1964, braved jeers and insults in a desperate attempt to explain the hopelessness of violence and to restore order, but was hooted down by angry militants and the uncontrollable mob.

In response to the difficulty, Rustin set his sights on the enunciation of a broad platform of economic proposals geared primarily to advance the poor and the underprivileged of all races. The general solution involved the acquisition of political power by such groups and a rapid refashioning of the nation's economic priorities.

By taking over the Randolph Institute, Rustin came to occupy a post where his considerable intellectual abilities and rare organizational talents could be combined to create a clearinghouse of information on the viable alternatives to senseless violence and Communist demagoguery.

WILLARD S. TOWNSEND
1895-1957
President, United Transport Service Employees of America

Willard Townsend, whose union included railroad, bus and airline red caps, Pullman laundry and repair-shop workers, and dining-car employees, was born in Cincinnati, Ohio on December 4, 1895.

Having graduated from the Walnut Hills High School in 1912, he took his first job as a red cap for the Cincinnati Union Terminal Company, and later became a dining car waiter for the Chesapeake and Ohio Railroad.

Returning from service after World War I, Townsend went to Chicago as a dining car waiter for the Sante Fe Railroad. Later, he enrolled at the University of Toronto in Canada, embarking upon pre-med studies. After two years, however, he transferred to the Royal Academy of Science and took a degree in chemistry.

By 1932, he was again back in Chicago working as a red cap with the Chicago Western Railroad. Four years later, Chicago red caps organized a local within the American Federation of Labor (AFL), electing Townsend vice-president and, later, president. In 1937, a number of organized groups of red caps met in Chicago to form the International Brotherhood of Red Caps (IBRC). Townsend was also elected president of the new organization.

In 1940, the IBRC changed its name to the United Transport Service Employees of America (UTSEA), and broadened its jurisdiction to include other railway service employees. Again, Townsend remained in the top executive position with the new organization.

In 1942, the UTSEA voted to affiliate itself with the Congress of Industrial Organizations (CIO), whereupon Townsend was placed on the General Executive Board of the CIO. When this group merged with the AFL, Townsend was named a vice-president of the new organization.

Townsend died in 1957.

GE
EMPLOY
ON
STR
For Bett
and Job
Local 492

EMPLOYMENT, UNEMPLOYMENT AND THE CIVILIAN LABOR FORCE

The day-to-day economic realities of the American Negro play a significant role in determining the pace of his integration into the total fabric of American life. The dignity of his labor, his ability to command an equal wage for that labor, and his opportunity to advance according to the full scope of his talent—all these are key factors underlying his quest for social and political equality.

Major problems facing the black labor force as it enters the 1970s are:

- Unemployment. The official rate of black unemployment continues to be double that of whites, and the actual rate probably higher.
- Underemployment. Despite some progress, blacks remain concentrated in menial jobs, and scarce in professional and skilled occupations.

- Poor education. Although the percentage of blacks graduating from high school and college has increased, blacks still lack the training and the credentials to keep apace of the economy's accelerating emphasis on professionalism and technology.
- Demography. The population of blacks in large cities continues to grow at a time when an increasing number of urban-based industries are moving to suburbs and small cities.
- Cutbacks in job programs. Allocations for a number of government and business job programs were cut in 1969 and 1970, as the government and businesses struggled with inflation and the recession.

Review of the 1960s: A Changing Focus

Betterment of the job situation for blacks aroused increasing attention throughout the 1960s and by the end of the decade was the principal aim of public officials and businessmen interested in relaxing racial tensions.

The growing concern about black unemployment and underemployment reflected a significant change in America's approach to racial problems. In the early sixties, efforts to ease the burdens of blacks were based on the ideal of integration and directed toward a variety of issues—housing, education, welfare, and constitutional justice as much as employment. Response to the integration ideal peaked with the passage of the Civil Rights Act in 1964 and thereafter subsided before the shock waves from ghetto riots and the sudden intensity of black nationalism. Following the violent urban disturbances in the summer of 1967, the nation's "establishment" decided that it was urgent to get blacks "off the streets and into jobs." Integration was downgraded as an unworkable liberal theory that benefited only a minute proportion of blacks. Racial peace and racial justice, it was decided, depended on obtaining jobs for the "hard core," the black

Chart 22

UNEMPLOYMENT AMONG BLACKS OUTSIDE THE SOUTH HAS PERSISTED AT CATASTROPHIC LEVELS SINCE THE FIRST STATISTICS WERE GATHERED IN 1930.

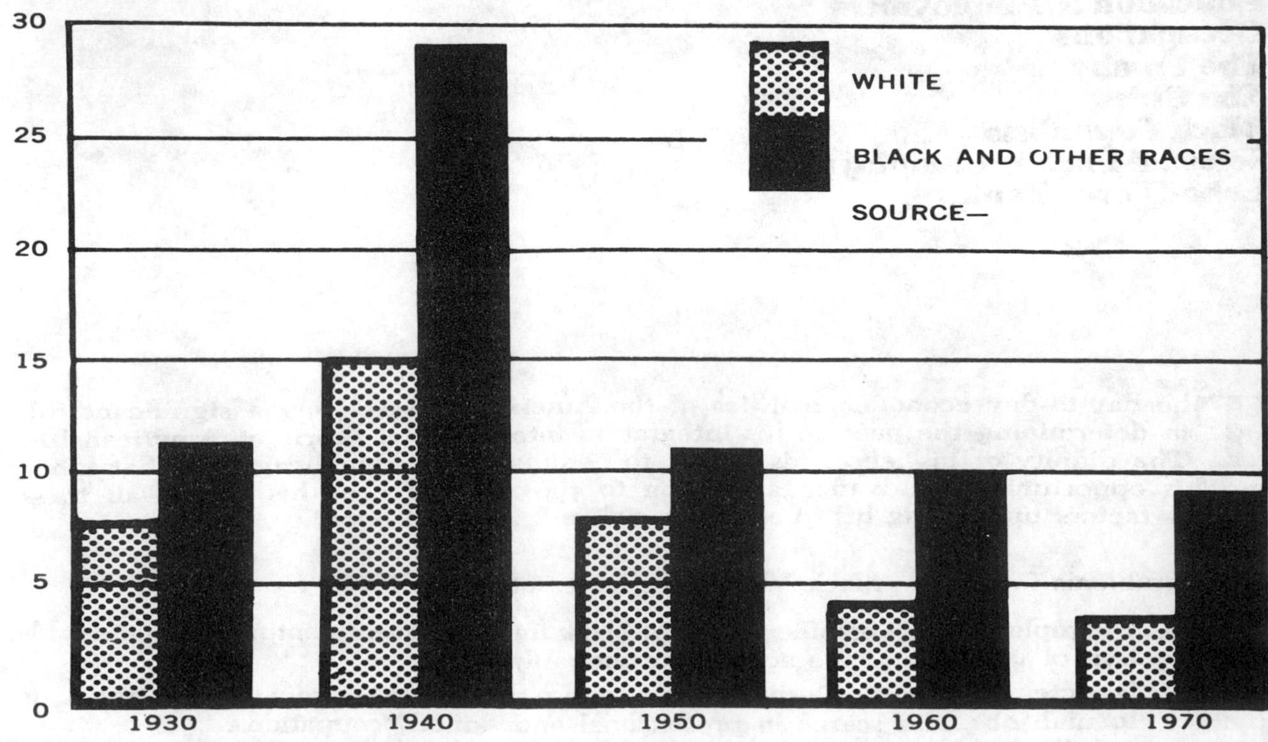

Chart 23

WHILE MORE BLACKS ARE EMPLOYED THAN EVER BEFORE, IT IS ONLY AS A RESULT OF AN OVERALL INCREASE IN POPULATION. THE RATE OF UNEMPLOYMENT FOR BLACKS IS TWICE THAT OF WHITES AND HAS REMAINED FAIRLY CONSTANT IN THIS RATIO SINCE 1954.

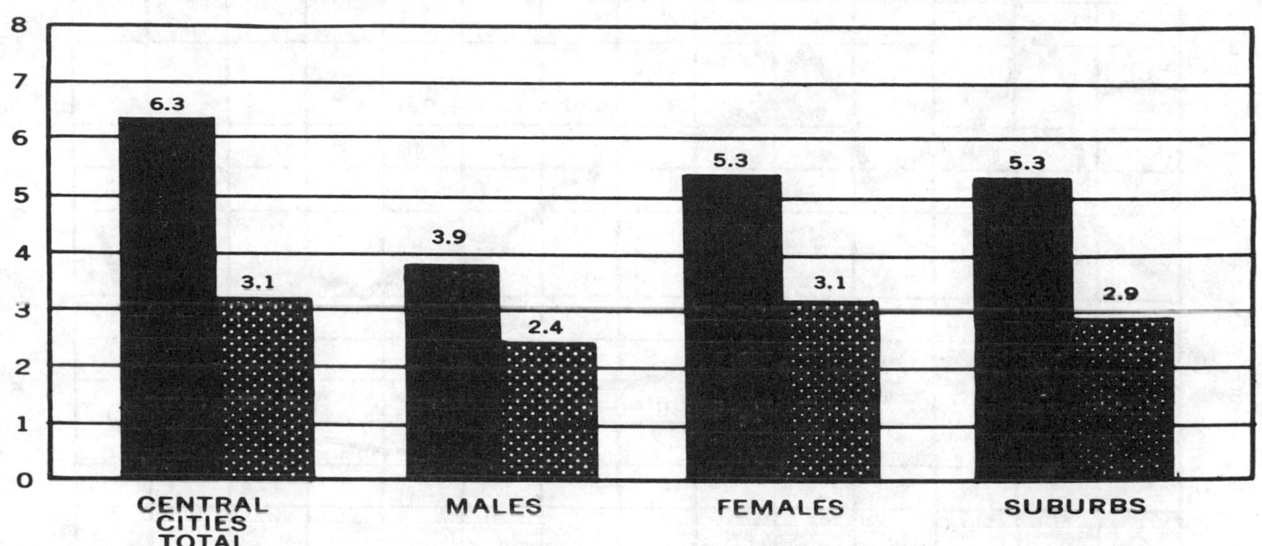

SOURCE: U. S. Dept. of Labor.

who was abandoned, despised and unemployed in squalid neighborhoods in large cities. Actually, as the Kerner Report was to reveal, employed blacks were as prone to riot as the unemployed. Nevertheless, the emphasis turned to "jobs."

As a result, there are now scores of federally assisted manpower programs and thousands of diverse, publicly supported training and placement ventures on the state and local levels. In addition, a number of urban-based service industries such as banks and public utilities have, on their own, intensified efforts to recruit and train black and Spanish-speaking employees.

The government programs provide businesses with incentives to employ people whose abilities and job motivation are unproven. The incentives take the form of subsidies to businesses for on-the-job training and referrals of prospective employees who have been located and trained at public expense.

These programs reflect a change of approach to employers — a change from pressure to blandishment by public officials charged with the responsibility of bettering the black employment situation. Earlier efforts to rectify the employment status of blacks relied largely on legal and monetary pressure. Employers who discriminated against blacks were threatened with court action or denial of government contracts. Although these avenues of redress are still used, the emphasis now is on aiding the employer who agrees to hire blacks who are regarded as underqualified for available jobs.

Legislation

Efforts to reduce job discrimination against minorities first became conspicuous after World War II, when a number of states adopted fair employment practice legislation. As is noted in the labor union section of *The Negro Almanac*, these programs were largely ineffectual. Funds were insufficient for adequate investigation and follow-up. Penalties were mild and rarely invoked. And the thrust of state fair employment commissions was toward easing the way of individuals into professional jobs rather than pressing employers and unions to hire and promote people in meaningful numbers.

The EEOC

There was little significant fair employment legislation on the federal level until the Civil Rights Act of 1964. Title 7 of this Act prohibits discrimination on the part of employers and unions who have more than 25 employees or members and

Chart 24

THE UNEMPLOYMENT RATIO BETWEEN BLACKS AND WHITES HAS REMAINED FAIRLY CONSTANT AT ABOUT 2 TO 1.

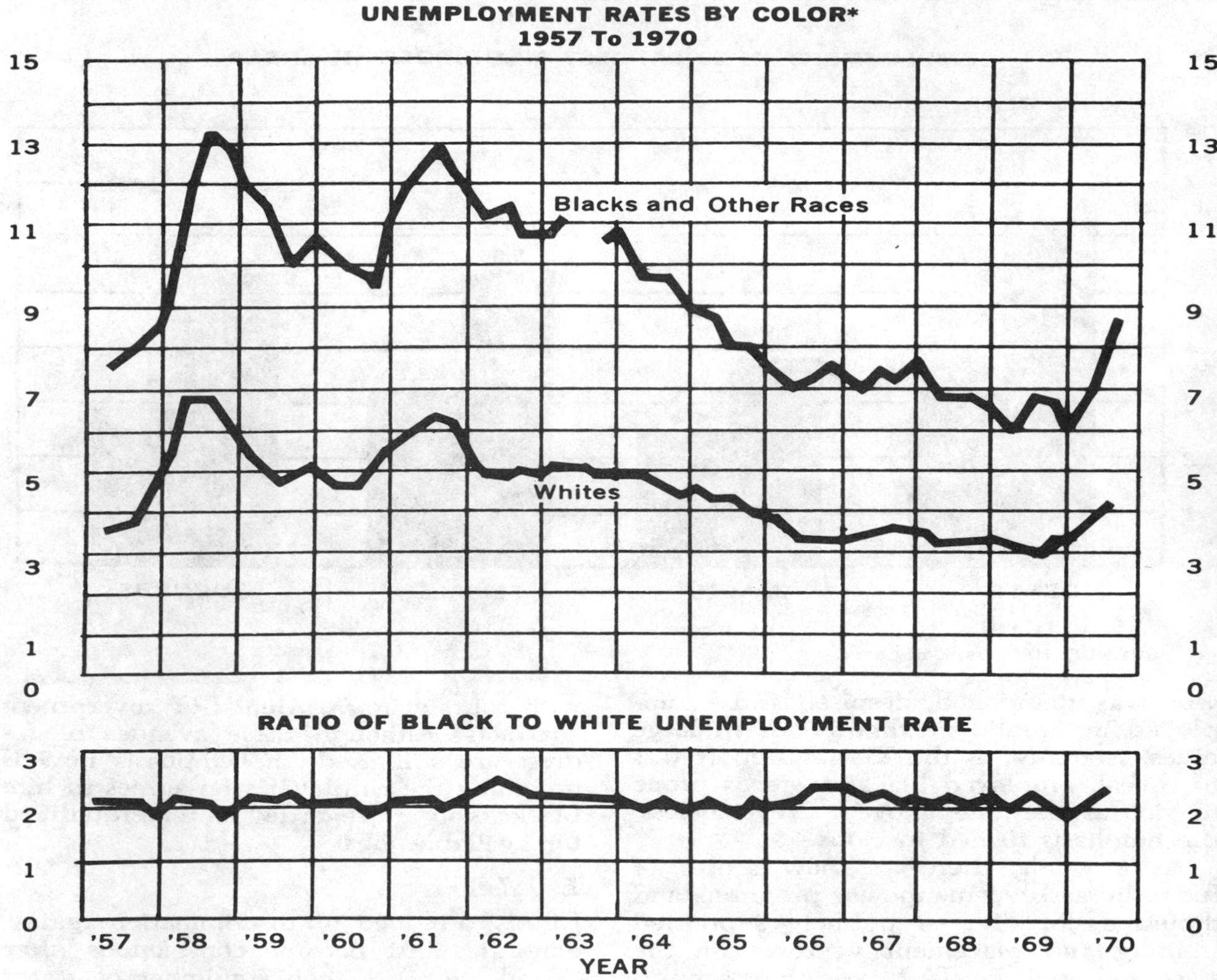

*Seasonally adjusted quarterly figures.

who are involved in interstate commerce. Title 7 also established the Equal Employment Opportunities Commission to mediate disputes and identify patterns of deliberate and systematic discrimination. The EEOC can refer discrimination cases to the Attorney General, who, in turn, can bring them before a three judge federal court. The EEOC is also empowered to refer cases of discrimination to the Office of Federal Contract Compliance which can press businesses dealing with the government to adhere to fair employment practices.

In 1970, as the Nixon Administration entered its second year, moderate and militant black groups intensified criticism of its equal employment activities. They charged the administration with weakening EEOC by underfinancing it and undercutting Congressional moves that would grant it cease and desist powers. And they charged the administration with failing to use the equal employment enforcement powers available to it through such means as the Office of Federal Contract Compliance and the Model Cities Bill of 1966. Criticism of the Philadelphia Plan (see Labor Union chapter) was milder, but this, too, Negro leaders regarded as insufficient. They also felt the administration was economizing too stringently on manpower programs.

The government replied that it was intent on making manpower programs more efficient (see section on Manpower Programs), that it was maintaining most existing manpower programs, and was adding zest to the Public Service Careers Program and the Work Incentive Program. (See Guide to Federally Assisted Manpower Programs.) Administration supporters added that inflation necessitated some streamlining of manpower activities and made it difficult for the private sector to participate as fully as it would like.

EEOC reported that in fiscal 1968 it completed 3,500 investigations and 640 conciliations which benefited 29,000 persons, 70% of whom were blacks. EEOC also claims that its 1967 hearings of discrimination in the textile industry, together with favorable economic conditions, led to significant black employment increases in the Carolinas. However, the textile industry hired few black white collar workers, less than 1 in 40 between 1966 and 1968, though half its new workers were black. EEOC has also held active investigations of the drug and media industries, the latter a source of embarrassment to liberal publications and broadcast stations that advocated fair employment but did not always practice it. In 1969 the motion picture industry was negotiating with EEOC to reach a settlement that would avoid a lawsuit by the Department of Justice.

Chart 25

LABOR FORCE PARTICIPATION RATES HAVE REMAINED RELATIVELY STABLE FOR WHITES, BUT HAVE STEADILY DECLINED FOR BLACKS SINCE THE KOREAN WAR.

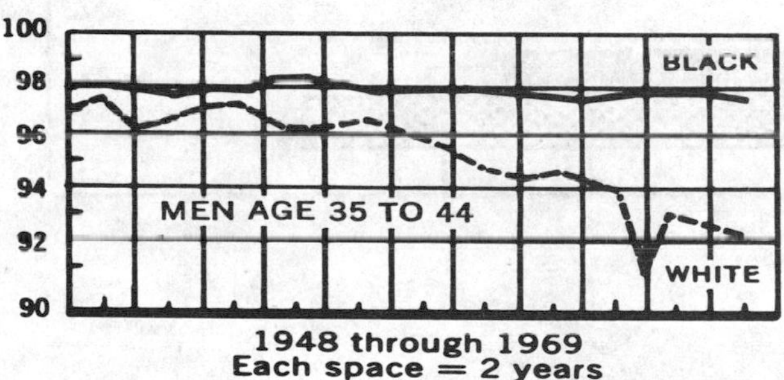

1948 through 1969
Each space = 2 years

Manpower Programs

The Manpower Development & Training Act of 1962 was the first of many important legislative measures that were to serve as a wide base for federal support and activity in job training and placement. The Concentrated Employment Program, the

Chart 26

FOR MEN OVER THE AGE OF 65 THERE HAS BEEN A SHARP DECLINE FOR ALL ETHNIC GROUPS IN LABOR FORCE PARTICIPATION.

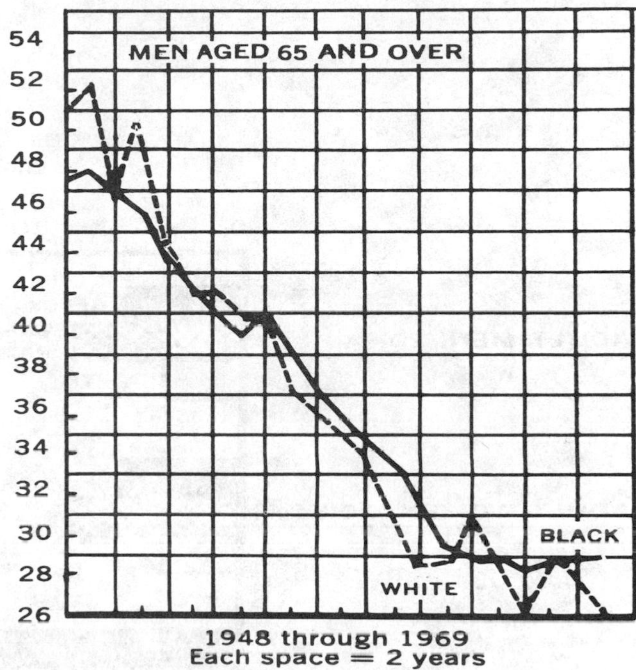

1948 through 1969
Each space = 2 years

Chart 27

IN THE 55-64 AGE GROUP THERE HAS BEEN A GREATER DECLINE IN THE LABOR FORCE PARTICIPATION RATE AMONG BLACKS SINCE THE KOREAN WAR.

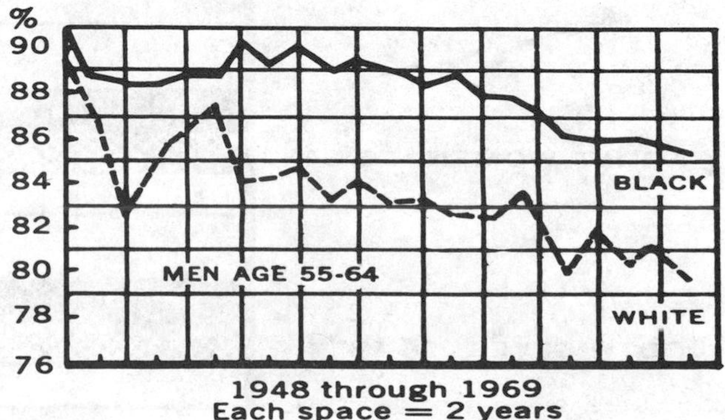

1948 through 1969
Each space = 2 years

Chart 28

THE JOBLESS RATE FOR BLACKS IN RATIO TO WHITES HAS STEADILY DECLINED IN THE NEW YORK CITY AREA. OF THE 20 OTHER MAJOR CITIES IN THE NATION, ONLY WASHINGTON, D. C. AND SAN FRANCISCO-OAKLAND HAVE BETTER RATIOS. THE PUERTO RICAN JOBLESS RATE CONTINUES TO BE HIGHEST OF THE THREE MAJOR ETHNIC GROUPS IN THE NEW YORK CITY AREA.

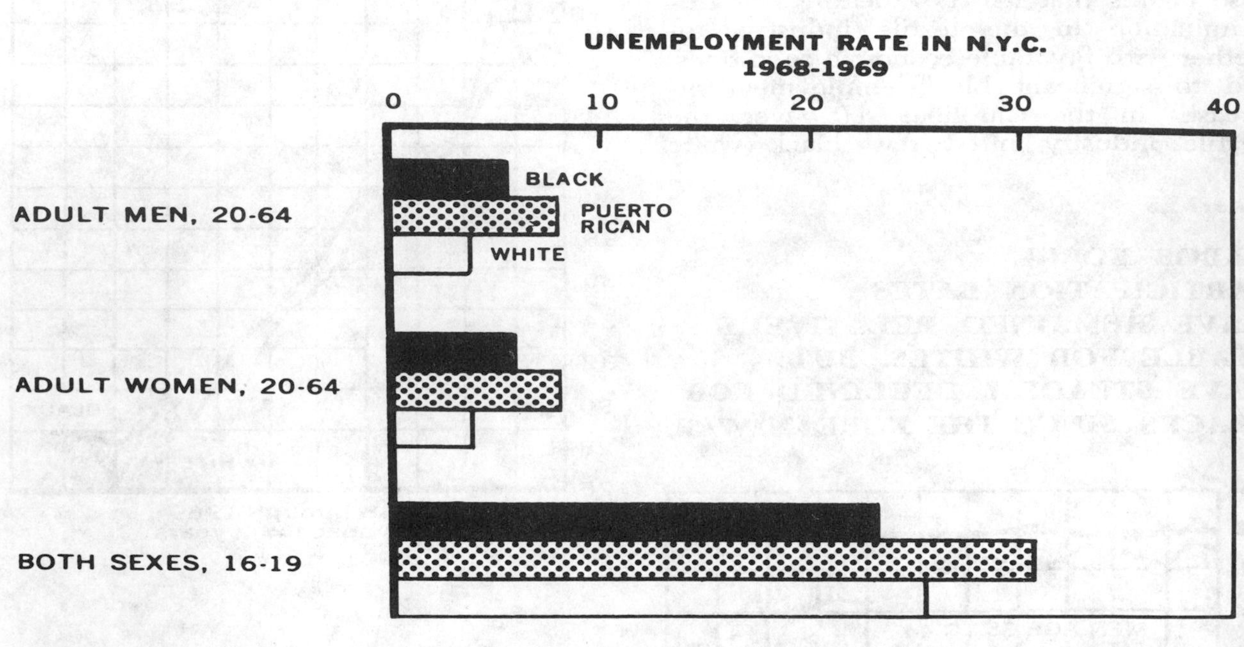

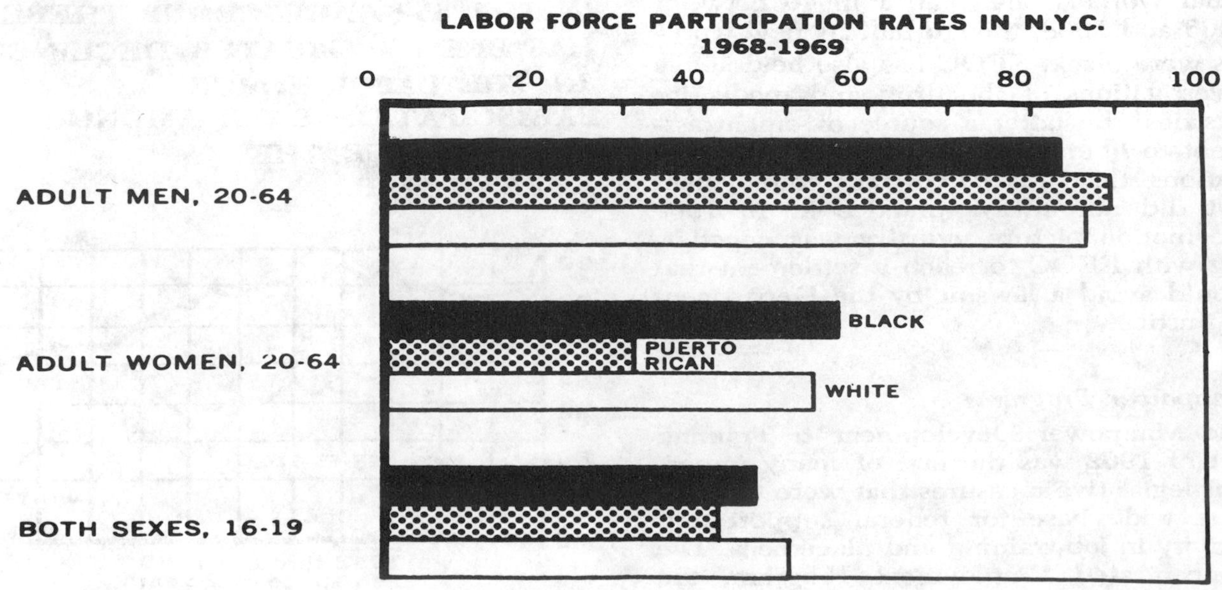

Job Corps, the Work Incentive Program for Welfare Clients and other "manpower" acts followed. The Manpower Report of the President, which was submitted to Congress in March 1970, states that enrollments in federally assisted work and training programs rose from 278,000 in fiscal 1964 to nearly 1,800,000 in fiscal 1969. The administration's budget requests for 1970 anticipated an enrollment of about 2 million Negro participation in these programs ranges from 21 to 78% (see Table 85).

The role of private industry in job programs was enlarged with the JOBS (Job Opportunities in the Business Sector) Program launched in 1967 after the summer riots. "JOBS," a joint venture of the Department of Labor and the National Alliance of Businessmen, is based on commitments of business leaders to hire hundreds of thousands of "disadvantaged" persons. Businesses can call on the Department of Labor for training funds and facilities. JOBS reports that 170,000 persons were hired under its auspices in 1969, and that 78% of these were Negroes. The President's manpower report states that by January 1970 a total of 300,000 disadvantaged people were hired as a result of independent company efforts through JOBS and 80,000 as a result of Department of Labor JOBS contracts. Some three out of four hired from the federally financed activities of JOBS were Negroes, one of eight was Spanish-American.

"Project Transition" is another cooperative government-private sector employment venture of importance to blacks. Administered by the Department of Defense, "Transition" facilitates on-the-job training, vocational guidance and job placement for men about to leave the armed forces. Some 100,000 Negro servicemen were discharged in 1969.

Though many thousands of blacks have attained employment through special government and business efforts, the positive impact of this manpower activity can be overestimated. Much of the hiring efforts materialized in industries and occupations where a severe labor shortage necessitated special employment efforts anyway. This was particularly true in service industries

Chart 29

THE UNEMPLOYMENT RATE FOR YOUNG BLACKS 16 TO 19 YEARS OF AGE IS MORE THAN DOUBLE THAT OF THEIR WHITE COUNTERPARTS.

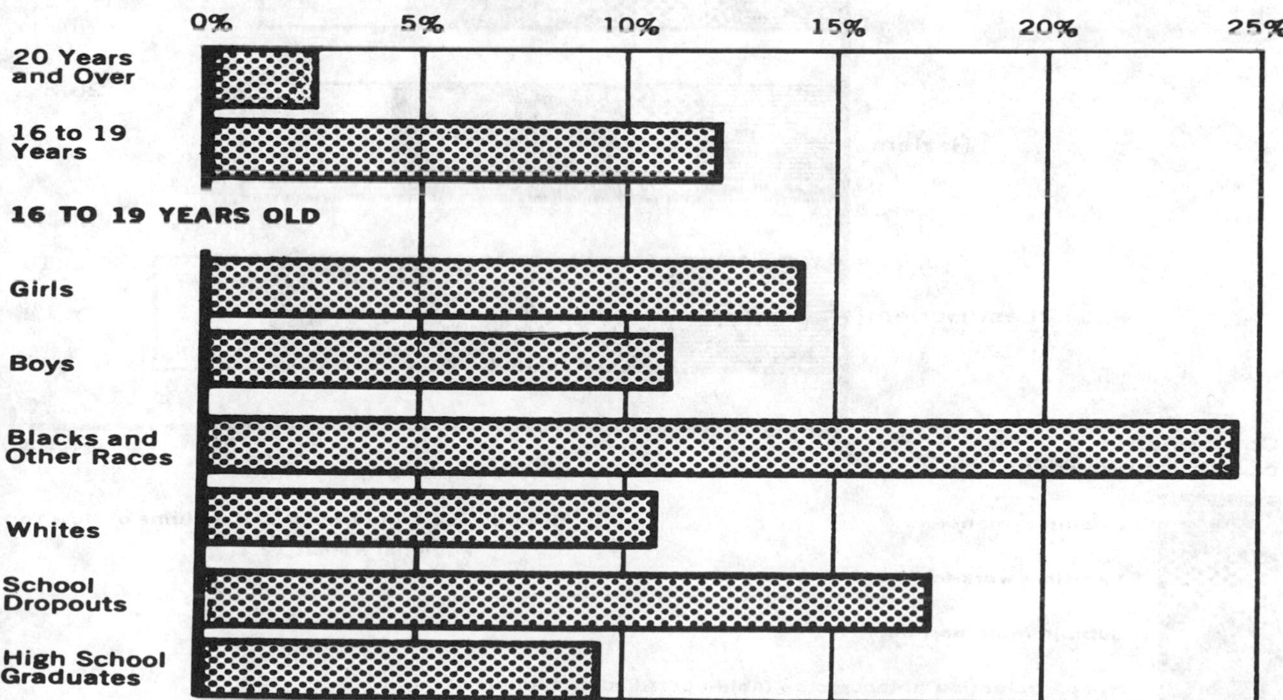

Note: Data relate to 1969 averages except for dropouts and graduates which relate to October 1968.
Source: Department of Labor.

and clerical occupations.

Also, the "hard core" classification was often applied, overzealously, to blacks with established and reputable work records.

In addition, the job retention of "hard core" employees was often very brief. Many "hard core" trainees, who were listed officially as "served" by training and placement programs, left the job or were dismissed after short periods of employment. And many Negroes of proven competence and motivation were discharged during the recession and defense cutbacks of 1969 and 1970 because they lacked seniority.

Reliable overall statistics on job retention of manpower trainees are not available. It is significant though that retention has varied extensively from company to company, that some companies kept few trainees for as long as six months, while others retained as many as 80% and actually had better retention rates among hard-core Nogroes than among whites and Negroes hired through conventional channels. Such disparate retention figures indicate that hard-core workers will respond to competent training and a sincere and intelligent employer.

White backlash, inflation and recession have threatened the future of manpower programs. Public support of programs designed to help Negroes started to decline in 1968, and in 1970 business enthusiasm for job programs was dampened by a cooling economy and rising costs of doing business.

The manpower programs are also threatened by their own abundance and com-

Chart 30

IT HAS BECOME INCREASINGLY CLEAR THAT PRESENT UNEMPLOYMENT DATA DO NOT ADEQUATELY DESCRIBE THE LABOR FORCE PARTICIPATION OF MINORITY GROUPS SINCE LARGE GROUPS OF SUCH INDIVIDUALS ARE EITHER SUB-EMPLOYED OR NOT REFLECTED IN UNEMPLOYMENT STATISTICS. THIS MAY WELL INDICATE THAT THE UNEMPLOYMENT RATES AMONG MINORITIES MAY BE FAR MORE EXTENSIVE THAN PRESENTLY THOUGHT.

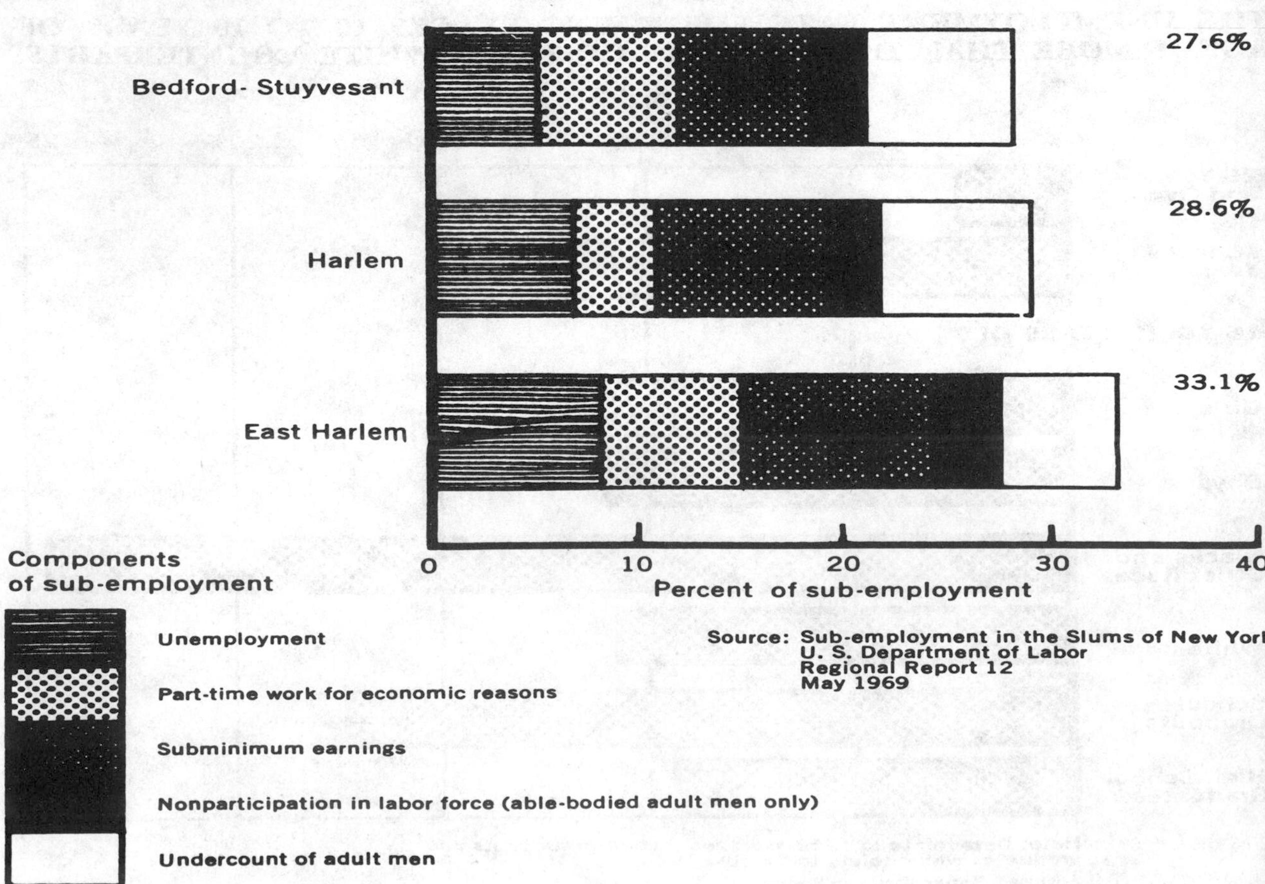

Chart 31

BLACKS IN THE LABOR FORCE WILL INCREASE THREE MILLION BY THE YEAR 1980 AND WILL ENTER THE LABOR FORCE OVER THE 1970-1980 DECADE AT A GREATER PERCENTAGE RATE THAN WILL WHITES.

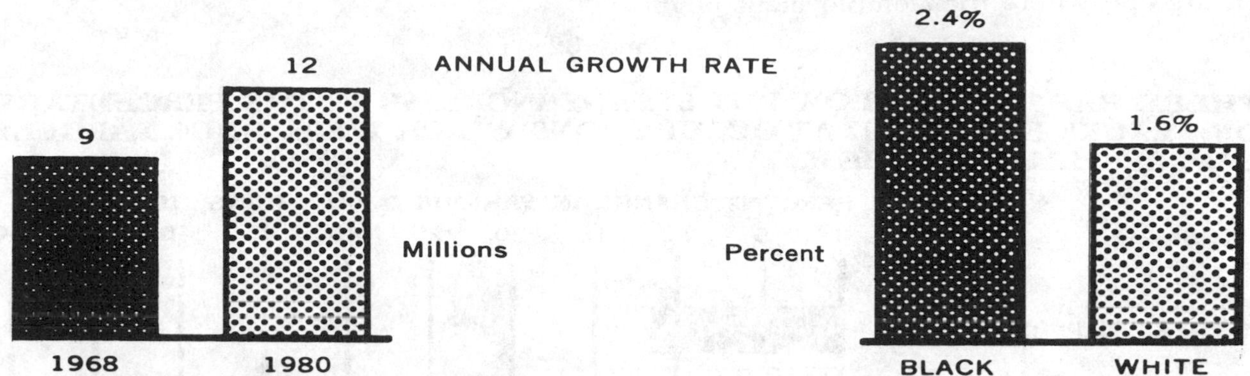

plexity. Many businesses did not seek federal aid simply because of red tape and difficulties in evaluating it. And response to job programs from Negroes was often tepid. One major problem was lack of sufficient child day-care facilities to permit women who headed families to obtain full-time employment. Another problem was welfare statutes and regulations which discouraged family heads from seeking work.

Concerned about the fragmentation and complexity of manpower programs, the Nixon Administration has proposed a Manpower Training Act which would pass more authority to state and local governments. Under the program, each state governor would appoint a manpower planning council to assess needs and integrate plans of various agencies. The Secretary of Labor would provide guidelines and national priorities, review and approve state plans and with the concurrence of the Secretary of Health, Education, and Welfare, evaluate state and area systems.

Supporters of the plan declare it would be more responsive to local needs and disentangle the federal manpower bureaucracy.

Opponents claim it would encourage discrimination against Negroes and subject manpower training to political pressure groups more interested in the needs of middle income groups than the poor.

CURRENT HIGHLIGHTS

Employment

Another indication that the manpower programs have fallen short of their objectives was the fact that black employment gains during the sixties barely managed to stay apace of the progress achieved by whites.

The Negro unemployment rate remained double that of whites throughout most of the 1960s and, despite some progress, the quality of jobs held by blacks remained markedly inferior.

Because of a very strong economy, unemployment rates for both whites and Negroes declined sharply during the sixties. Unemployment of "Negroes and Other Races"* dropped from 10.2% for 1960 to 6.5% for 1969, the white rate from 4.9 to 3.2%. The ratio of Negro to white unemployment was about 2.0 throughout the 1960s, reaching a high point of 2.2 as recently as 1967 and falling to 1.9 in the winter of 1969-70. However, black unemployment increased ominously in the spring of 1970. From March to April 1970 black unemployment leaped from a seasonally adjusted 7.1 to 8.7%, while white unemployment rose slightly, from 4.1 to 4.3%. At the end of June 1970, the rates were 8.8% for Negroes, 4.2% for whites. The sharp rise in black unemployment indicated that job programs have done little to assure them stable employment.

* In 1969, the government switched its "non-white" classification to "Negroes and Other Races." Negroes have long comprised 92% of this group, Asians, Eskimos, and American Indians the other 8%. For the sake of brevity we will refer to this group simply as "Negroes." Spanish-American groups, such as Mexicans and Puerto Ricans, are classified as "whites" in official reports, unless otherwise noted.

Official figures probably understate Negro unemployment. The Department of Labor itself has conceded this likelihood. In cities, large numbers of unemployed blacks are too far outside the labor market frame to be included in official data. They have never had conventional employment, applied for unemployment insurance, been counted in a census or otherwise appeared on a scene where their employment plight might be recorded. In a regional report issued in May 1969, the Department of Labor estimated that the "undercount" of adult men in three New York City slums amounted to about 7% of the workforce (Chart 12). The Labor Department has also reported that the 1960 census missed 3% of the population and that 38% of this total were Negroes.

Chart 32

THERE HAS BEEN A SLOW BUT STEADY INCREASE IN THE PERCENTAGE OF BLACKS EMPLOYED AT OCCUPATIONS WHICH WERE ONCE LARGELY INACCESSIBLE TO THEM.

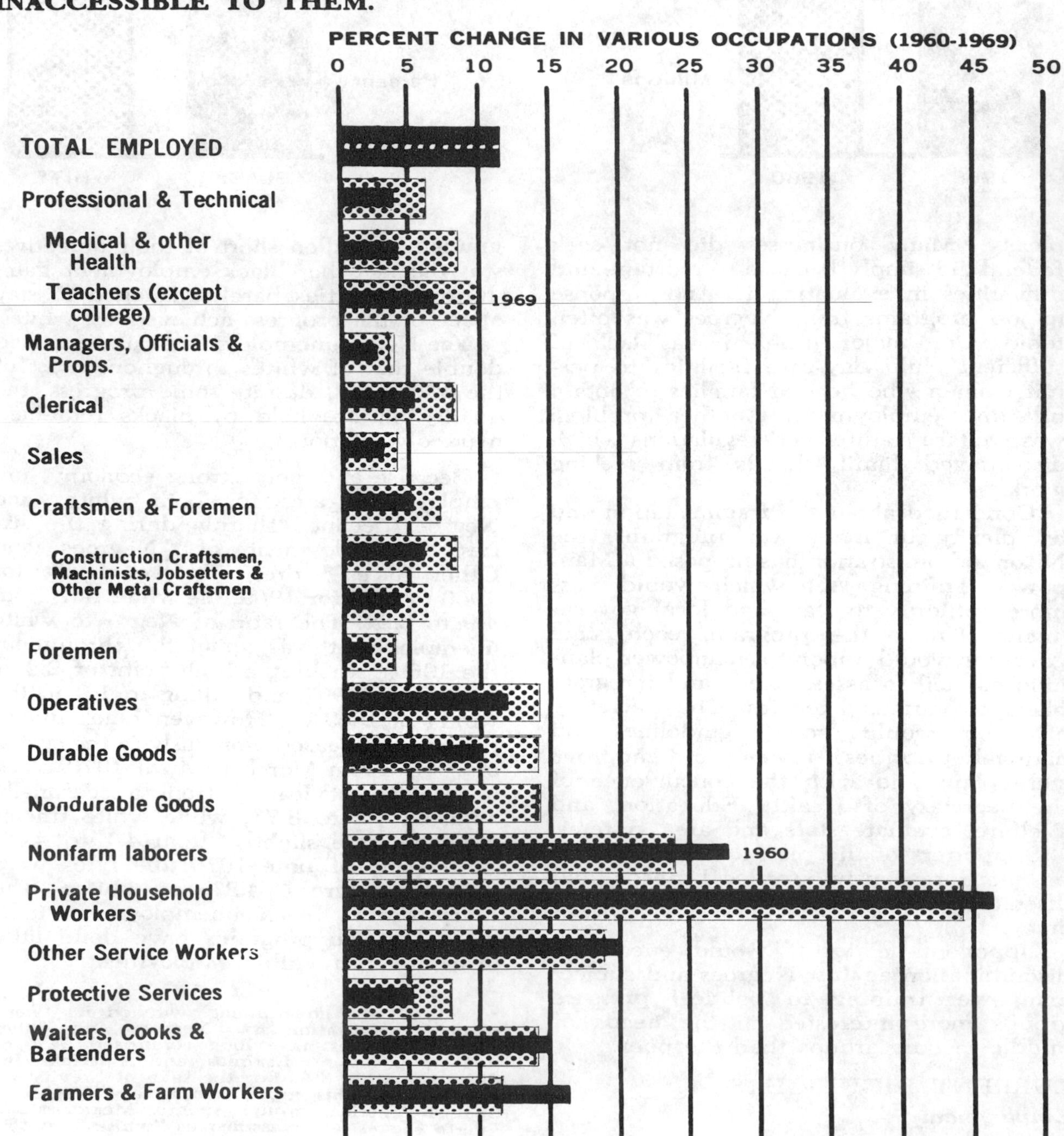

Occupations

Blacks have been moving into higher level jobs. Between 1960 and 1969, Negro employment in white collar, crafts and operative occupations increased 67% compared with 22% for whites. In 1969, there were one million more Negroes employed in these occupations than in labor and service jobs. Meanwhile, Negro employment declined in low-paying private household and farm work.

Negro gains in professional and technical occupations were most pronounced near the end of the sixties. The number of black workers in such occupations increased 8% between 1968 and 1969 compared with 4% for whites. The increase for blacks in clerical occupations was 12% compared with 4% for whites. The number of black craftsmen and foremen rose 8% compared with 1.3% for whites.

Blacks are also faring better in federal employment. Between June 1965 and November 1967, the number of blacks with federal jobs increased 26%, nearly double the rate of increase for whites. By the end of 1968, 16% of federal workers were blacks, a rise from 13.5% in June 1965.

However, blacks are still underrepresented, and often scarcely represented at all, in the more lucrative and prestigious occupations. There are, still, few Negro managers, officials, proprietors, salesmen, lawyers and doctors. The imposing percentage increases on government tables and charts usually reflect a small base and gains in such low echelon professional fields as nursing, grade-school teaching, and civil service jobs rather than large numerical increases in executive or administrative positions. And, Negroes remain underrepresented as foremen and in crafts jobs.

Blacks have also progressed slowly in the executive ranks of service industries where they comprise a large proportion of the rank-and-file. This is especially true in retailing where blacks are heavily employed as sales and stock workers. In 1968, the Negro Retail Advisory Group of New York estimated that there were only 12 Negroes in the United States who were full fledged buyers for major retail companies.* Black executives were similarly rare in major advertising, publishing, broadcast, banking, investment and insurance companies. Blacks have made some progress in these fields since 1968, but it is not substantial. Somewhat better progress has been achieved in the computer field and among a limited number of manufacturing corporations.

In recent years, Negro occupational progress has been retarded by some social and business trends that are only indirectly related to racism.

In better paying technical fields, hiring emphasis has increasingly stressed advanced college training and specific job experience, attributes a limited number of Negroes have had the resources or contacts to acquire.

In middle and junior corporate executive positions, hiring emphasis has tended increasingly to stress social orientation more than personal ability. This is a result of efforts during the 1960s to standardize and systematize the occupational functions of corporate personnel. Corporate jobs have tended to become more routine. It has become easier for a man of average ability to do a "good" job. As a result, corporations are less interested in talented young men who might make a unique contribution and more interested in merely competent young people who "fit in." Thus, a Negro may be bypassed for a young white of lesser ability, but whose education, background, and credentials promise an "organization man" style and orientation.

The Family

The most dramatic Negro employment gains of the 1960s were achieved by adult men. From 1961 to 1969, total employment of black men increased 16% compared to 9% for white men. The unemployment rate for black men over twenty dropped 6% more than the unemployment rate for white men over twenty. The drop in unemployment was most marked among Negro men who head stable families.

The unemployment rate for black women over twenty declined 5% more than the rate for white women over twenty between 1961 and 1969. A larger percentage of black women than white women participate in the labor force, 50% to 42% for women over 16. However, during the sixties, the participation of white women accelerated at a greater rate, up 5% from 1961 compared with a 1½% increase for black women. White participation increases were most pronounced among women over 35, a large proportion of whom are returning to the job market or working for the first time. However, the participation rate of black women over 25 remains much higher than that of white women.

Negro unemployment during the sixties was most severe among teenagers. In 1969,

* "Crisis '68!," Number 3, July 1968, published by the National Retail Merchants Association.

21% of Negro boys between sixteen and nineteen and 28% of Negro girls were unemployed. The gap in unemployment between Negro and white youth increased during the 1960's, despite the attention of job placement and training programs directed to Negro youth.

The Cities

Negro unemployment is intense in the poverty areas of big cities, but in some cities, New York for one, it is more severe among Spanish speaking minorities. However in June 1969, the unemployment rate of blacks in Los Angeles' poverty areas was 15.2, compared with about 6.1% for Mexican Americans. Unemployment among black teenagers in Los Angeles was 45%. Negro unemployment in central cities in 1969 was 6.2 compared with 3.2% for whites. Teenage unemployment in central cities was 26.1% for Negroes, 9.8% for whites.

In 1969, Negro unemployment figures in 15 large central cities were highest in Detroit and Los Angeles-Long Beach, lowest in Washington, D. C. and San Francisco-Oakland.

In America's twenty largest standard metropolitan statistical areas (SMSA's), Negro unemployment is lowest in northeastern states, highest in north-central and western states.

Black Capitalism

Following the riots of 1967, increasing attention was devoted to Negroes who wished to own businesses. The "black capitalism" idea formed a major part of the Republican presidential campaign in 1968 and obtained some support from militant black groups which felt black capitalism a step toward racial pride and self-sufficiency. A number of interracial advisory groups were established and various federally assisted programs were promulgated, most conspicuously through the Small Business Administration and the

Chart 33

THE GAP BETWEEN NEGRO AND WHITE PARTICIPATION IN THE LABOR FORCE IS EXPECTED TO NARROW DURING THE 1970's FOR BOTH SEXES.

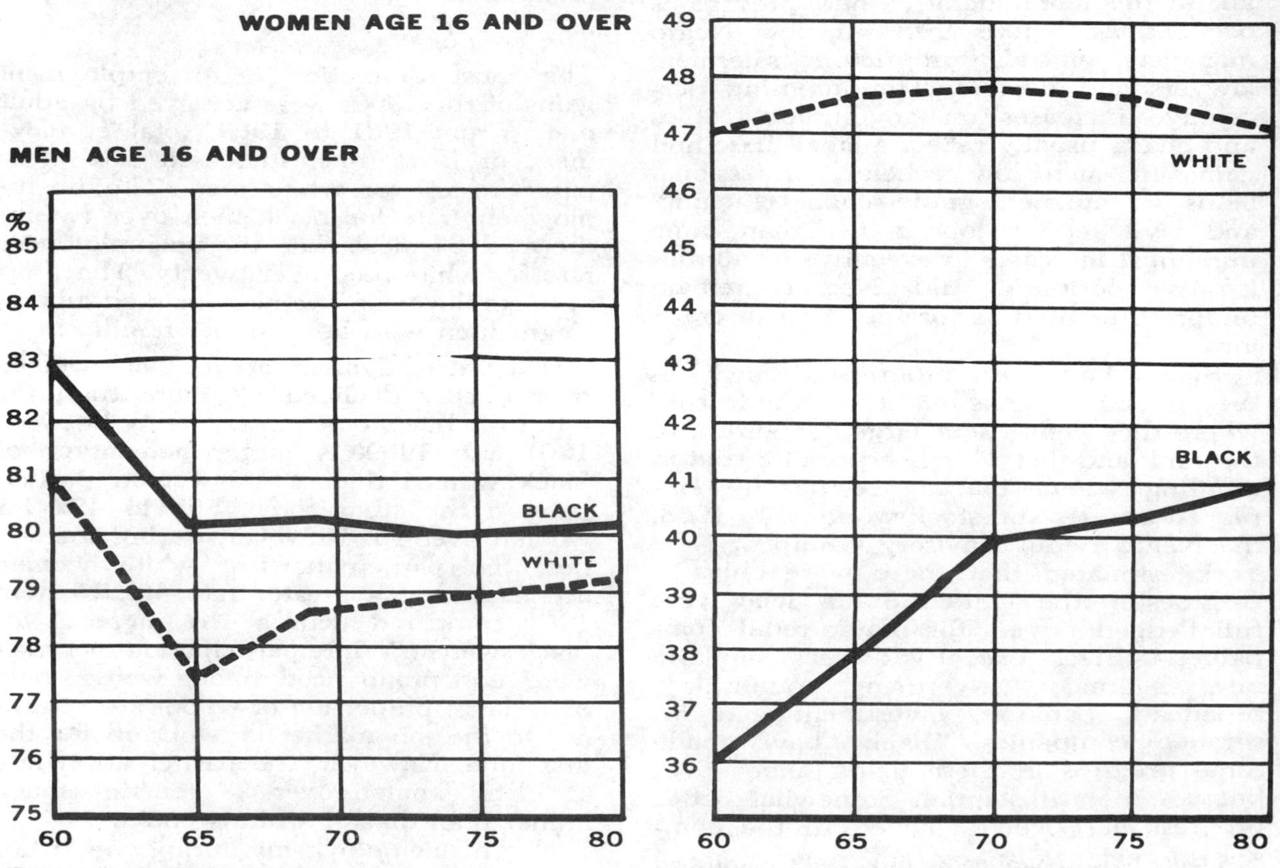

Source: U. S. Dept. of Labor.

Source: U. S. Dept. of Labor.

Chart 34

ALTHOUGH BLACKS ARE NOW EMPLOYED AT OCCUPATIONS FROM WHICH THEY WERE ONCE EXCLUDED THEY ARE STILL UNDERREPRESENTED OR SCARCELY REPRESENTED AT ALL IN THE MORE PRESTIGIOUS OCCUPATIONS.

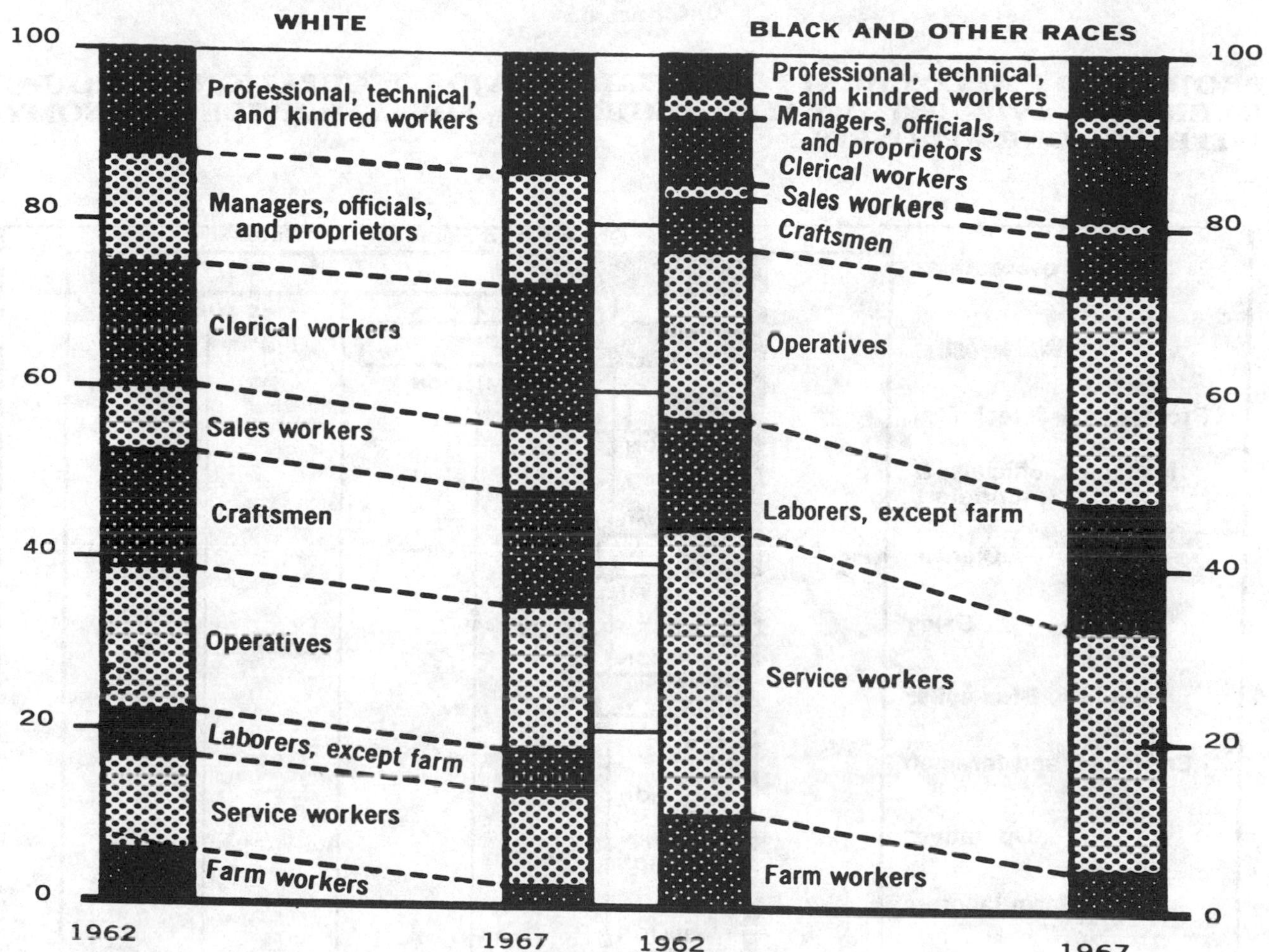

Department of Commerce.

Progress has been very slow. Black capitalism has not become part of the American scene. The preponderance of retail and manufacturing businesses in Negro neighborhoods are still owned by whites. Blacks have done somewhat better in small, general service businesses catering to whites, such as short-haul trucking and construction sub-contracting. Negro owned banks and savings and loan companies have started to appear, and the number of Negro advertising firms has increased, in response to a demand for specialists in Negro marketing.

Black capitalism has been retarded mainly by the reluctance of lending institutions to finance loans for Negroes who lack entrepreneurial experience. High interest rates, and the recession of early 1970, discouraged investment by white businesses. One program, Project Enterprise, launched by the Department of Commerce in 1969 to garner financial support for minorities businessmen from private sources attracted only $1 million of its $500 million goal by June 1970.

On the positive side, the Department of Commerce's Economic Development Administration did allocate $4.4 million to support minority business enterprises during the first four months of 1970. Some of the money went for administrative expenses of local black capitalism organizations, some to support specific Negro entrepreneurial efforts. And, government agencies have been making conscious efforts to award contracts to minority business firms. The Commerce Department's Office of Minority Business Enterprise, which attempts to direct government contracts to minority businesses, reported in March, 1970, that in the preceding six months it had secured 95 sub-contracts worth $27.3 million for minority-owned companies.

Chart 35

PROJECTED EMPLOYMENT POTENTIAL IN MAJOR OCCUPATIONAL GROUPS OVER THE 1970-1980 DECADE (PROJECTED FOR A SERVICE ECONOMY WITH 3% UNEMPLOYED).

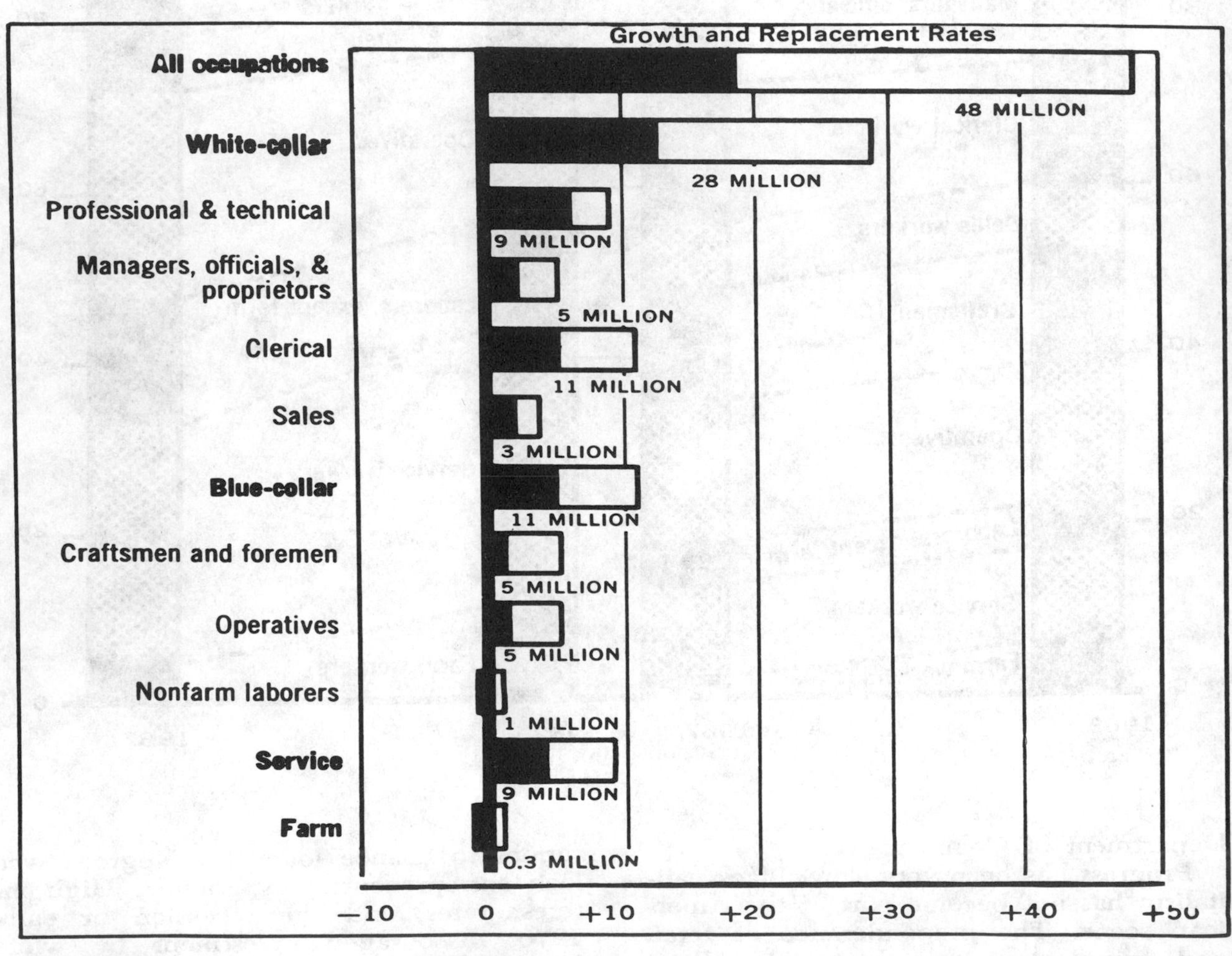

Chart 36

PROJECTIONS FOR THE 1970-1980 DECADE INDICATE A MORE THAN 100% INCREASE IN JOB AVAILABILITY. JOB OPPORTUNITIES FOR BLACKS SHOULD INCREASE SUBSTANTIALLY AS A GREATER PORTION OF THE POPULATON WILL BE NEEDED TO FILL ALL OCCUPATIONAL CATEGORIES.

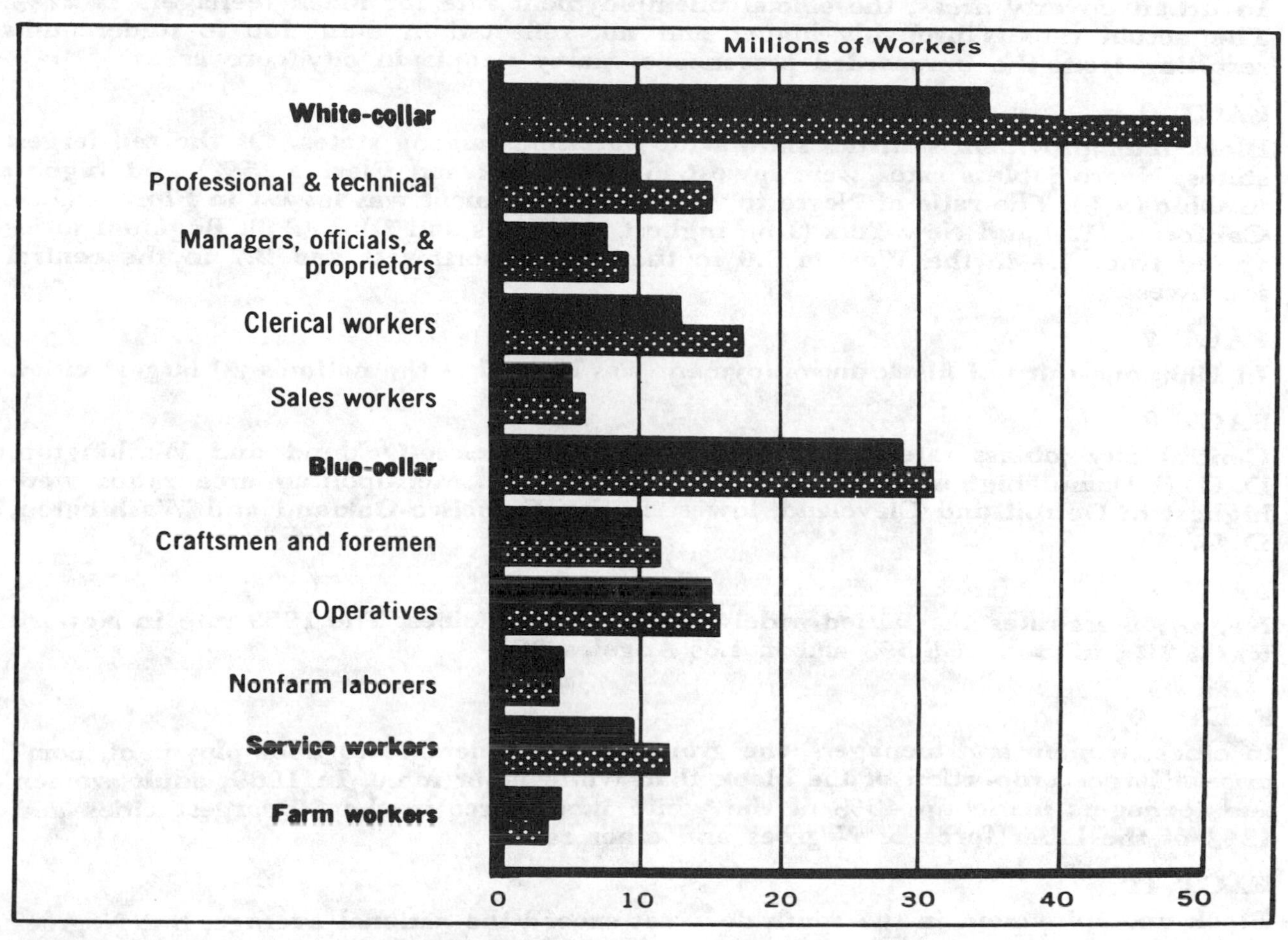

SELECTED FACTS ON THE LABOR FORCE

FACT 1

Black men are less likely to be in the labor force than white men, black women more likely than white women. Black men were about as likely to be in the labor force as white men until the late 1960s when Negro rates started to decline.

FACT 2

Employment of Negroes increased by about 215,000 in 1969, a 2½% gain, approximately equal to the gain in white employment. Almost two-thirds of the increase in Negro employment was among adult black women and about one-fourth among adult black men. (Manpower Report of the President—1970)

FACT 3

The Department of Labor expects the Negro labor force to grow at a greater rate than the white force. Negroes are expected to increase 12% between 1960 and 1980, whites to increase 8%. The participation rate of black men is expected to grow at nearly double the white male rate.

FACT 4

In April 1970, the unemployment rate of Negroes 14 and 15 years old was four times that of the unemployment rate for whites of the same age: 33% for Negroes, 8% for whites.

FACT 5

In urban poverty areas, the official unemployment rate for black teenagers is 27%. The actual rate is probably higher and not reflected in data due to undercounts resulting from the unrecorded presence of many people in city core areas.

FACT 6

Black unemployment statistics show wide variations among states. Of the ten largest states, Negro jobless rates were lowest in New York and Florida (5%) and highest in Ohio (8%). The ratio of Negro to white unemployment was lowest in Florida (1.5), California (1.5) and New York (1.6); highest in Illinois and Ohio (2.6). Regional ratios varied from 1.4 in the West to 3.0 in the central northwest and 2.7 in the central southwest.

FACT 7

In 1969 one-third of black unemployment was located in the nation's 20 largest cities.

FACT 8

Central city jobless rates were lowest in San Francisco-Oakland and Washington, D. C. (1.1) and highest in Houston and Dallas (3.1). Metropolitan area ratios were highest in Detroit and Cleveland, lowest in San Francisco-Oakland and Washington, D. C.

FACT 9

Negro jobless rates also varied widely in major "riot" cities. The 1969 rate in Newark was 4.2%, in Detroit 8.5% and in Los Angeles 8%.

FACT 10

In cities, women and teenagers, the groups most vulnerable to unemployment, comprise a larger proportion of the black than white labor force. In 1968, adult women and teenagers made up 43% of the white labor force in the 20 largest cities and 48% of the labor force of Negroes and other races.

FACT 11

Black unemployment in the South does not exceed the national average, but Negroes there often have to settle for part-time work. In 1969, 7½% of Negroes in the South were engaged in part-time work for economic reasons. This was more than twice the rate of part-time work in the other three regions. The main reason is that many Southern blacks are confined to household and farm labor where work is often not available on a full-time basis.

FACT 12

In the South, 1 of every 4 Negro family heads who worked full time throughout 1968 earned too little to bring his family income above the poverty line. The comparable figure in the northeast and north central states was one out of 20, and in the West 1 out of 30. (President's Manpower Report—1970)

FACT 13

About two-thirds of black women workers in Atlanta are in service occupations, mostly private household work. Most of the white women working in Atlanta had white collar or operative jobs.

FACT 14

In urban poverty areas containing black and Spanish-American workers, the unemployment rate of blacks tends to be higher than the Mexican rate and lower than the Puerto Rican rate.

FACT 15

The ratio of Puerto Rican to Negro unemployment in New York in 1969 was greatest among women over twenty (1.7) and lowest among teenagers (1.1). In Los Angeles, the rate of teenage unemployment among blacks was nearly three times that of Mexican teenagers (45.5% and 15.8%). The unemployment rate among Puerto Rican men 25 to 54 years old was twice that of Negro men in the same age group in 1970.

FACT 16

Despite the fact that Puerto Ricans fared more poorly than blacks in New York, and Mexicans better than blacks in Houston and Los Angeles, the proportion of Puerto Ricans unemployed in New York at some time between July 1968 and June 1969 was lower than the proportion of Mexicans unemployed at various periods during the same year in Houston and Los Angeles.

FACT 17

In 1968 the unemployment rate for American Indians living on reservations was more than 6 times that of Negroes; 40% compared with 6.7%. In 1962 the unemployment rate of reservation Indians was 49%. Two-thirds of the 650,000 Indians in the United States live on reservations.

FACT 18

The percentage of Negro college graduates living in metropolitan areas and central cities did not increase between 1960 and 1968, remaining at 5%, but the percentage of white college graduates rose from 14 to 18%. The percentage of Negro college graduates living in the suburbs, where Negroes comprise only 5% of the total population, increased from 4 to 9%.

FACT 19

Four out of every five Negro college graduates were in professional and managerial occupations in 1969. However, the proportion of Negro college graduates is only half that of whites and the data provide no information on the grades of position held by Negroes and whites of the same age and education. (The President's Manpower Report—1970)

FACT 20

Mexican-Americans generally fare better than blacks in obtaining skilled and white collar jobs in Texas and California (Table 51 and other data), but Puerto Ricans fare no better than Negroes in New York. Mexican-Americans in Texas are comparatively well represented in white collar jobs in retailing, food and apparel industries.

FACT 21

Barriers to employment of blacks in civil service jobs are greater among uniform policemen and firemen than in any other sector of state and local government. Reports of discriminatory treatment in work assignments, promotions and personal relationships are also more frequent in these than in any other area of government studied. (The President's Manpower Report—1970)

FACT 22

Almost half the white men located in central cities worked in white collar occupations in 1968, compared with only one-fifth of Negro men.

FACT 23

The ratio of Negro to white unemployment has actually increased during the past twenty years. It was 1.6 in 1949, rose to a high of 2.3 in 1956 and was about 2.0 in the spring of 1970.

FACT 24

More than three-fifths of the increase in Negro employment between 1961 and 1969 was in professional white collar and skilled occupations. However, the proportion of Negroes in professional, managerial and technical occupations is only about ⅓ that of whites and the number of Negroes in corporate executive positions remains minute.

FACT 25

The percentage of Negro foremen doubled between 1960 and 1969, but Negroes still comprise only 4% of the total.

FACT 26

Negro employment in the lowest paying occupations, household and farm work, declined substantially between 1961 and 1969. Many household workers moved into service industries where employment increased 150,000 in 1969. (President's Manpower Report—1970)

FACT 27

Negroes are twice as likely as whites to be unemployed and more than twice as likely to be among the long-term unemployed (15 weeks or more).

FACT 28

Black women resident in central cities have achieved greater progress than white women. Between 1960 and 1968, the proportion of white women engaged in white collar work remained at 68% while the proportion of Negro women increased from 21 to 34%. Most of this increase took place in clerical and sales jobs.

FACT 29

In 1968, 79% of Negro female family heads had at least one child, 59% had two or more children. Only half of the white female family heads had at least one child and only 29% had two or more.

FACT 30

The reasons for unemployment tend to be similar among whites and blacks, but very different between men and women. Both white and black men tend to be unemployed because they lost their last job. Women tend to be listed as unemployed because they are entering or reentering the labor force.

FACT 31

The greatest future need for professional workers is anticipated in the computer industry. Requirements for systems analysts and programmers are expected to rise over 100% between 1968 and 1980. Thus far, Negroes have made only moderate progress in these occupations. Nursing and school teacher positions—areas in which Negroes have progressed well—are expected to rise about 65% and 10% respectively between 1968 and 1980.

FACT 32

The percentage of Negroes enrolled in MDTA sponsored institutional training programs declined substantially between 1968 and 1969, but increased slightly in on-the-job training.

FACT 33

On the average, workers hired from federally financed JOBS programs had completed 10.3 years of school, had been unemployed for 23 weeks during the year before their enrollment, and had an annual income of $2,400. Half were under 27 years of age, only 4% were over 45.

FACT 34

On-the-job training and institutional training appear to help people who drop out as well as the "completers." The Department of Labor reports that earnings of Negro noncompleters in on-the-job training increased 124% between 1958 and 1968, compared with a 147% rise for "complëters."

FACT 35

The black labor force in New York has been swelled by a relatively unnoticed phenomena, the immigration of blacks from Haiti, Jamaica, the Bahamas, the Dominican Republic and other West Indian countries. Immigration from the West Indies in the 1960s totaled some 2.3 million, the large proportion of whom were blacks. A large proportion of these immigrants settled in New York City, substantial but lesser numbers in other northeastern cities and in Miami.

FACT 36

There were no substantial differences in unemployment between rioters and the noninvolved in the Detroit and Newark riots, but self-reported rioters were more likely to be only intermittently employed. Underemployment was more an issue than unemployment. In Newark, only 29% of the rioters but 44% of the non-involved thought their present job to be appropriate for them and 68% of the rioters compared with 56% of the noninvolved thought it would be impossible to get the kind of job they wanted. (The Kerner Report)

FACT 37

Arrestees in the Detroit riot were more likely to be employed than people who reported that they did not participate in the disturbances. (The Kerner Report)

EMPLOYMENT TABLES

Table 32

Unemployment Rates, 1949-1969

(Annual averages for 1949 to 1968; January-November averages for 1969)

Year	Percent unemployed		Ratio
	Negro and other races	White	Negro and other races to white
1949	8.9	5.6	1.6
1950	9.0	4.9	1.8
1951	5.3	3.1	1.7
1952	5.4	2.8	1.9
1953	4.5	2.7	1.7
1954	9.9	5.0	2.0
1955	8.7	3.9	2.2
1956	8.3	3.6	2.3
1957	7.9	3.8	2.1
1958	12.6	6.1	2.1
1959	10.7	4.8	2.2
1960	10.2	4.9	2.1
1961	12.4	6.0	2.1
1962	10.9	4.9	2.2
1963	10.8	5.0	2.2
1964	9.6	4.6	2.1
1965	8.1	4.1	2.0
1966	7.3	3.3	2.2
1967	7.4	3.4	2.2
1968	6.7	3.2	2.1
1969	6.5	3.2	2.0

NOTE.—The unemployment rate is the percent unemployed in the civilian labor force.
Source: U.S. Department of Labor, Bureau of Labor Statistics.

Table 33

Unemployment rates in the 20 largest SMSA's by color, annual averages, 1968-69

SMSA	All persons				Negro and other races[1]			
	1969		1968 rate	Error on 1968–69 change[3]	1969		1968 rate	Error on 1968–69 change[3]
	Rate	Range[2]			Rate	Range[2]		
Total	3.4	—	3.4	—	5.9	—	6.4	—
Baltimore	3.5	3.0–4.0	3.4	.7	6.1	4.5–7.7	6.1	2.3
Boston	2.8	2.4–3.2	2.5	.5	[4]	[4]	[4]	[4]
Buffalo	3.7	3.1–4.3	4.0	.8	[4]	[4]	[4]	[4]
Chicago	3.0	2.7–3.3	3.0	.4	6.2	5.1–7.3	7.6	1.7
Cincinnati	2.7	2.1–3.3	2.9	.9	[4]	[4]	[4]	[4]
Cleveland	3.1	2.6–3.6	3.5	.7	7.2	5.0–9.4	8.3	3.3
Dallas	2.2	1.7–2.7	2.3	.7	5.3	2.3–8.3	[4]	[4]
Detroit	4.1	3.7–4.5	3.8	.5	7.9	6.5–9.3	7.5	1.9
Houston	3.2	2.6–3.8	3.3	.8	6.7	4.0–9.4	5.7	3.5
Los Angeles-Long Beach	4.8	4.5–5.1	4.7	.4	7.9	6.3–9.5	8.5	2.3
Milwaukee	2.3	1.9–2.7	2.9	.6	[4]	[4]	[4]	[4]
Minneapolis-St. Paul	2.3	1.8–2.8	2.4	.7	[4]	[4]	[4]	[4]
Newark	2.7	2.4–3.0	4.1	.6	4.2	3.0–5.4	9.1	2.9
New York	3.2	3.0–3.4	3.0	.3	4.6	3.6–5.6	3.9	1.3
Paterson-Clifton-Passaic	3.6	2.9–4.3	2.6	.9	[4]	[4]	[4]	[4]
Philadelphia	2.9	2.6–3.2	3.2	.4	5.6	4.5–6.7	6.0	1.6
Pittsburgh	4.1	3.7–4.5	4.4	.6	7.4	5.2–9.6	11.9	4.0
San Francisco-Oakland	4.5	4.1–4.9	4.8	.6	5.6	4.3–6.9	7.9	2.2
St. Louis	3.5	3.1–3.9	3.1	.6	7.5	5.9–9.1	6.9	2.2
Washington	2.6	2.2–3.0	2.7	.6	3.0	1.8–4.2	4.4	2.2

[1] This designation includes all races other than white.

[2] In 90 cases out of 100, on the average, the unemployment rate for a complete census would fall within the indicated ranges.

[3] Year-to-year changes in the unemployment rate cannot be considered statistically significant unless they exceed figures shown in this column.

[4] Data not published where unemployment estimate is less than 5,000 or civilian labor force estimate is less than 50,000.

Table 34

Unemployment rates in selected central cities by color, annual averages, 1968-69

Central city	All persons				Negro and other races[1]			
	1969		1968 rate	Error on 1968–69 change[3]	1969		1968 rate	Error on 1968–69 change[3]
	Rate	Range[2]			Rate	Range[2]		
Baltimore	4.5	3.8–5.2	5.0	1.1	6.4	4.7–8.1	6.5	2.4
Chicago	3.4	3.1–3.7	3.8	.4	5.9	4.9–6.9	7.4	1.6
Cleveland	5.1	4.2–6.0	5.4	1.3	7.7	5.2–10.2	9.2	3.9
Dallas	2.5	1.9–3.1	2.6	.9	5.6	2.4–8.8	[4]	[4]
Detroit	5.5	4.8–6.2	5.1	1.0	8.5	6.6–10.4	7.3	2.5
Houston	3.3	2.7–3.9	3.4	.8	6.6	3.9–9.3	5.8	3.6
Los Angeles-Long Beach	5.4	5.0–5.8	5.4	.6	8.0	6.2–9.8	8.6	2.6
Milwaukee	2.2	1.8–2.6	3.7	.8	[4]	[4]	[4]	[4]
Minneapolis-St. Paul	2.4	1.8–3.0	3.1	1.0	[4]	[4]	[4]	[4]
New York	3.6	3.4–3.8	3.1	.3	4.7	3.7–5.7	4.0	1.3
Philadelphia	3.6	3.2–4.0	3.9	.6	6.5	4.9–8.1	6.1	2.2
San Francisco-Oakland	4.8	4.2–5.4	6.2	1.0	4.7	3.4–6.0	6.6	2.2
St. Louis	4.9	4.1–5.7	4.9	1.2	7.5	5.4–9.6	7.0	2.9
Washington, D. C.	3.0	2.1–3.9	3.8	1.4	3.1	1.6–4.6	4.5	3.1

[1] This designation includes all races other than white.

[2] In 90 cases out of 100, on the average, the unemployment rate from a complete census would fall within the indicated ranges.

[3] Year-to-year changes in the unemployment rate cannot be considered statistically significant unless they exceed figures shown in this column.

[4] Data not published where unemployment estimate is less than 5,000 or civilian labor force estimate is less than 50,000.

Table 35

Extent of Employment and Unemployment of Men, Women, and Teenagers in Poverty Neighborhoods of Six Large Cities Combined, July 1968-June 1969

Employment status	Employed & unemployed by color, sex and age					
	Adult men		Adult women		Teenagers	
	Negro	White	Negro	White	Negro	White
Total civilian labor force (thousands)	168.5	79.8	168.4	48.9	46.8	15.1
Percent of total[1]	100	100	100	100	100	100
Worked full time all year (50–52 weeks)	70	71	50	51	12	15
Worked full time part year (less than 50 weeks)	23	21	30	33	46	44
Worked part time	5	6	16	13	31	34
Unemployed at any time during the year[2]	20	18	17	16	49	38

[1] Percents total more than 100 because of overlap between those who were unemployed at any time during the year and other categories.

[2] Employment and unemployment were not confined strictly to the time period July 1968-June 1969. Depending on the actual week of interview, "at any time during the year" could extend as far back as late 1967.

NOTE.—Six large cities: Atlanta, Chicago, Detroit, Houston, Los Angeles and New York City
Source: U.S. Department of Labor, Bureau of Labor Statistics.

Table 36

Self-Employment by Industry, 1969
(January-November averages)

Industrial group	Number (thousands)		Percent distribution	
	Negro and other races	White	Negro and other races	White
Total	387	6,782	100	100
Agriculture	94	1,818	24	27
Mining	—	15	—	—
Construction	36	653	9	10
Manufacturing	10	256	3	4
Durable goods	9	156	2	2
Nondurable goods	1	100	—	1
Transportation	23	162	6	2
Trade	78	1,575	20	23
Finance, insurance, and real estate	7	254	2	4
Private household	6	23	2	—
Other service	135	2,026	35	30

— Represents zero or rounds to zero.
Source: U.S. Department of Labor, Bureau of Labor Statistics.

Table 37

Labor Force Participation Rates by Age and Sex, 1969
(Includes Armed Forces. January-November averages)

Age	Men		Women	
	Negro and other races	White	Negro and other races	White
Total, 16 years and over	78	81	50	42
16 and 17 years	39	50	25	35
18 and 19 years	67	70	46	55
20 to 24 years	88	87	59	57
25 to 34 years	95	97	58	42

Source: U.S. Department of Labor, Bureau of Labor Statistics.

Table 38

Labor Force Participation Rates by Age and Sex, 1969
(Includes Armed Forces. January-November averages)

Age	Men		Women	
	Negro and other races	White	Negro and other races	White
35 to 44 years	93	98	59	49
45 to 54 years	89	95	61	53
55 to 64 years	78	84	48	43
65 years and over	26	27	12	10

Source: U.S. Department of Labor, Bureau of Labor Statistics.

Table 39

Number of Employed and Unemployed Persons, 1960-1969
(In millions. Annual averages for 1960 to 1968; January-November averages for 1969)

Year	Employed		Unemployed	
	Negro and other races	White	Negro and other races	White
1960	6.9	58.9	.8	3.1
1961	6.8	58.9	1.0	3.7
1962	7.0	59.7	.9	3.1
1963	7.1	60.6	.9	3.2
1964	7.4	61.9	.8	3.0
1965	7.6	63.4	.7	2.7
1966	7.9	65.0	.6	2.3
1967	8.0	66.4	.6	2.3
1968	8.2	67.8	.6	2.2
1969	8.4	69.5	.6	2.3
Change 1960–1969:				
Number	+1.5	+10.6	−.2	−.8
Percent	+21	+18	−27	−27

Table 40

Unemployment and Long Term Unemployment, 1969
(Numbers in thousands. January-November average)

Employment status	Total	Negro and other races	White	Percent Negro and other races
Total civilian labor force...	80,671	8,948	71,723	11
Unemployed................	2,849	579	2,271	20
Percent of labor force.......	3.5	6.5	3.2	(X)
Long term unemployed[1].......	377	78	299	21
Percent of labor force.......	0.5	0.9	0.4	(X)

X—Not applicable.
[1] Unemployed for at least 3½ consecutive months, 15 weeks or more.
Source: U.S. Department of Labor, Bureau of Labor Statistics.

Table 41

Employment by Occupation, 1969, and Net Change, 1960-1969
(Annual averages for 1960; January-November averages for 1969)

Occupation Group	Employed, 1969		Change, 1960 to 1969: Number		Change, 1960 to 1969: Percent	
	Negro and other races	White	Negro and other races	White	Negro and other races	White
Total............	8,369	69,452	1,442	10,602	21	18
Professional and technical...........	692	10,031	361	2,893	109	41
Managers, officials, and proprietors......	254	7,721	76	832	43	12
Clerical...............	1,078	12,282	575	3,023	114	33
Sales.................	163	4,488	62	365	61	9
Craftsmen and foremen..	704	9,485	289	1,346	70	17
Operatives............	1,998	12,379	584	1,843	41	17
Service workers, except private household....	1,525	6,371	311	1,535	26	32
Private household workers.............	712	900	−270	−91	−28	−9
Nonfarm laborers......	876	2,809	−75	207	−8	8
Farmers and farm workers............	366	2,986	−475	−1,349	−56	−31

Source: U.S. Department of Labor, Bureau of Labor Statistics.

Table 42

Employment by Broad Occupational Groups, 1960 and 1966-1969

Year	Total		White-collar workers craftsmen, and operatives		All other workers	
	Negro and other races	White	Negro and other races	White	Negro and other races	White
Number (millions):						
1960	6.9	58.9	2.9	46.1	4.0	12.8
1966	7.9	65.0	4.0	52.5	3.9	12.6
1967	8.0	66.4	4.3	53.6	3.7	12.7
1968	8.2	67.8	4.6	54.9	3.6	12.8
1969	8.4	69.5	4.9	56.4	3.5	13.1
Change, 1960–69:						
Number (millions)	+1.4	+10.6	+2.0	+10.3	−.5	+.3
Percent	+21	+18	+67	+22	−13	+.2

NOTE—The 1966, 1967, and 1968 data pertain to persons 16 years of age and over, while in 1960 the age cutoff was 14 years. The 1960 figures shown here are estimated figures for the employed population 16 years and over. Data shown in this table are annual averages except 1969 for which January-November averages are shown.

Source: U.S. Department of Labor, Bureau of Labor Statistics.

Table 43
SELECTED DATA ON RIOT PARTICIPANTS AND NON PARTICIPANTS IN NEWARK AND DETROIT, 1967

Key: R—Rioter
NI—Not Involved

Selected characteristics	Newark		Detroit	
	R.	N.I.	R.	N.I.
Percent unemployed	30	19	30	32
Unemployed a month or more during preceding year	61	43		
Arrestees who were unemployed			22	
Occupational Level				
Unskilled	50	40		
Skilled or semi-skilled	50	60		
Perceived Job Outlook				
Present Job About Right	29	44		
Should have More Pay and Responsibility	71	56		
Perceived Job Obstacles				
Lack of Training	18	41		
Lack of Experience	13	9		
Discrimination	69	50		

Source: *Compiled from The Report of the National Advisory Commission on Civil Disorders.*

Table 44

Percent Distribution of Employment by Occupation and Sex, 1969
(January-November averages)

Occupational Group	Color and Sex			
	Negro and other races		White	
	Male	Female	Male	Female
Total employed (thousands)	4,768	3,601	44,075	25,377
Percent	100	100	100	100
Professional, technical, and managerial	11	12	29	19
Clerical and sales	9	22	13	44
Craftsmen and foremen	14	1	21	1
Operatives	28	18	19	15
Service workers, exc. household	13	25	6	15
Private houschold workers	—	20	—	3
Nonfarm laborers	18	1	6	—
Farmers and farm workers	7	2	6	2

— Represents zero or rounds to zero.
X Not applicable.
Source: U.S. Department of Labor, Bureau of Labor Statistics.

Table 45

Negro and Other Races as a Percent of All Workers in Selected Occupations, 1060 and 1069
(Annual averages for 1960 and January-November averages for 1969)

Occupational Group	Percent Non-white	
	1960	1969
Total, employed	11	11
Professional and technical	4	6
Medical and other health	4	8
Teachers, except college	7	10
Managers, officials, and proprietors	2	3
Clerical	5	8
Sales	3	4
Craftsmen and foremen	5	7
Construction craftsmen	6	8
Machinists, jobsetters, and other metal craftsmen	4	6
Foremen	2	4
Operatives	12	14
Durable goods	10	14
Nondurable goods	9	14
Nonfarm laborers	27	24
Private household workers	46	44
Other service workers	20	19
Protective services	5	8
Waiters, cooks, and bartenders	15	14
Farmers and farm workers	16	11

Source: U.S. Department of Labor, Bureau of Labor Statistics.

Table 46

Unemployed Teenagers and Percent Still in School, 1963 and 1966-1969
(Annual averages for 1963 to 1968; January-November averages for 1969)

Year	Unemployment rate		Number (thousands)		Percent still in school	
	Negro and other races	White	Negro and other races	White	Negro and other races	White
1963	30.4	15.5	176	708	22	34
1966	25.4	11.2	185	651	28	39
1967	26.5	11.0	204	635	30	37
1968	25.0	11.0	195	644	30	38
1969	24.4	10.8	196	667	27	37

(All columns under the heading "Unemployed".)

NOTE—"Teenagers" include those 16 to 19 years old. Students are also counted as unemployed if they want a job and have been actively looking for work during the 4-week period prior to interview in the monthly survey of the labor force.

Source: U.S. Department of Labor, Bureau of Labor Statistics.

Table 47

Percentage of Negroes in Part Time Work for Economic Reasons—1969 by Region

	Percent unemployed	Percent working part time for economic reasons
Total	6.4	5.1
North	5.5	2.6
North Central	6.8	2.9
South	6.4	7.5
West	6.8	3.1

Source: Manpower Report of the President.

Table 48

Unemployment Rates by Sex and Age, 1967-1969
(Annual averages for 1967 and 1968; January-November averages for 1969)

Age group and sex	Negro and other races 1967	1968	1969	White 1967	1968	1969
Total	7.4	6.7	6.5	3.4	3.2	3.2
Adult men	4.3	3.9	3.7	2.1	2.0	1.9
Adult women	7.1	6.3	6.0	3.8	3.4	3.4
Teenagers[1]	26.5	25.0	24.4	11.0	11.0	10.8

[1]"Teenagers" include persons 16 to 19 years old.

Source: U.S. Department of Labor, Bureau of Labor Statistics.

Table 49

Employment Status of Female Family Heads, March 1968
(Numbers in thousands)

	Negro and other races	White
Total families with female head	1,384	4,054
In labor force	692	2,112
Percent of total	50	52
Unemployed	36	77
Percent of labor force	5.2	3.6
Not in labor force	692	1,942

Source: U.S. Department of Labor, Bureau of Labor Statistics.

Table 50

Women With Children Under 6 Years Old, by Labor Force Participation, Employment, and Unemployment, March 1969
(Numbers in thousands. Consists of wives, husband present; and widowed, divorced, and separated women)

	Negro and other races	White
All women with children under 6	1,666	12,217
Percent in labor force	45	28
Employed	662	3,270
Unemployed	88	203
Percent unemployed	11.7	5.8

Source: U.S. Department of Labor, Bureau of Labor Statistics.

Table 51

Men and Women, 20 Years Old and Over, by Reason for Unemployment, 1969
(January-November averages)

Status	Men		Women	
	Negro and other races	White	Negro and other races	White
Percent distribution:				
Total unemployed	100	100	100	100
Lost last job	60	56	33	33
Left last job	14	18	16	18
Reentered labor force	22	23	43	45
Never worked before	5	3	7	5
Unemployment rate:[1]				
Total unemployment rate	3.7	1.9	6.0	3.4
Job loser rate	2.2	1.1	2.0	1.1
Job leaver rate	0.5	0.3	1.0	0.6
Reentrant rate	0.8	0.4	2.6	1.6
New entrant rate	0.2	0.1	0.4	0.2

[1] Unemployment rates are calculated as a percent of the civilian labor force.
Source: U.S. Department of Labor, Bureau of Labor Statistics.

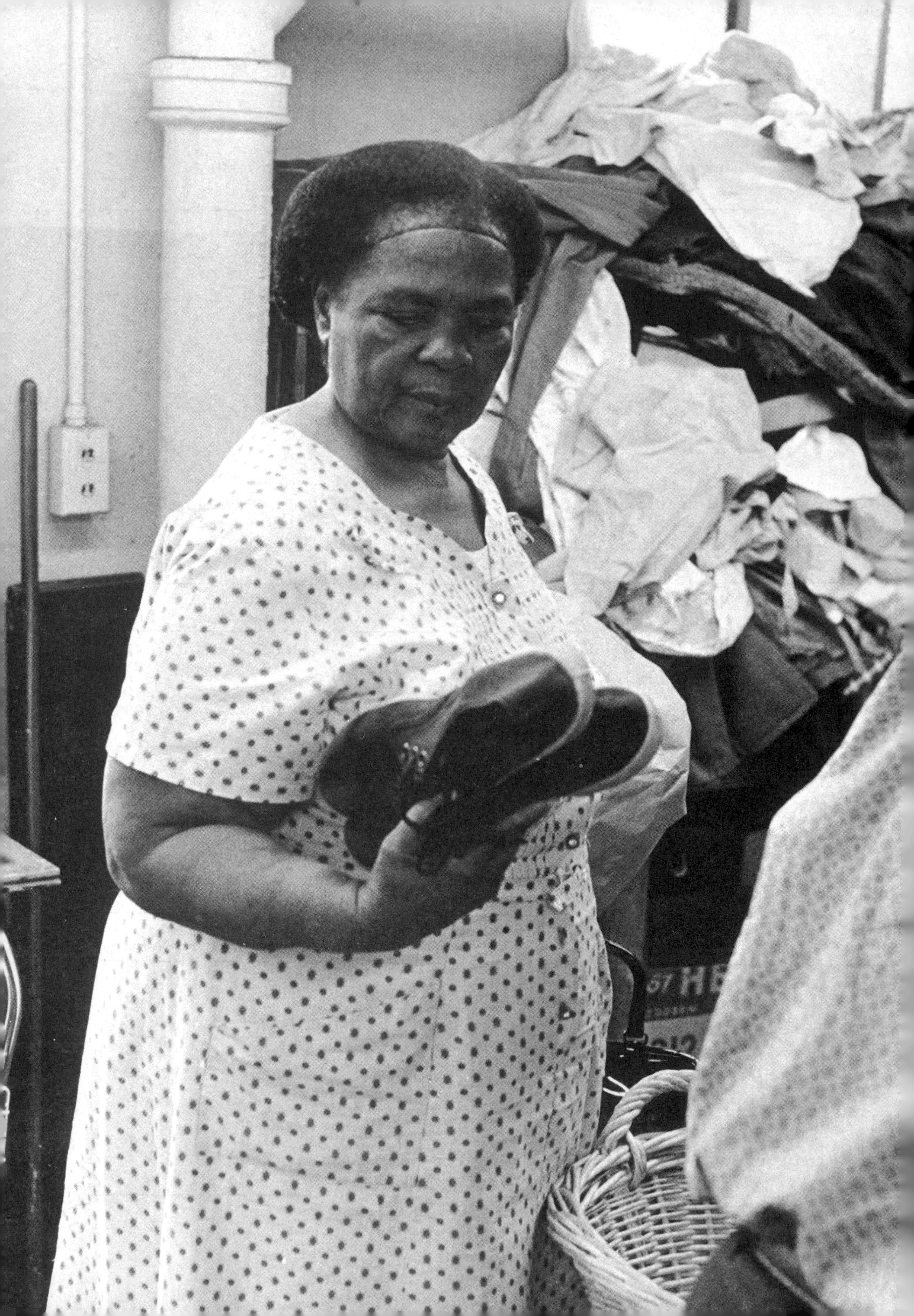

INCOME, EARNINGS, INCIDENCE OF POVERTY AND EXPENDITURE PATTERNS

The most significant facts concerning black income, earnings and consumer expenditure patterns continue to indicate substantive and, at times, widening gaps between the white and the black population. Although the median earning power of the black family rose over $1800 in the period 1960-1968, it still did not keep pace with the $2100 increase registered by the typical white family surveyed during this period. As the 1970's approach, the ratio of poor black citizens to poor white citizens is increasing, a fact which puts added caseload pressures on the already overburdened welfare system. The black consumer continues to pay more money for shoddier goods and unreliable services. Though black prospects are improving in many labor unions and in the retail field, the economic status of the black population is still subject to the larger economic picture. A weak and sluggish national economy will continue to drain the meager resources of the black community.

Income and Poverty

The earnings of blacks rose significantly and at an accelerating pace during the 1960's, but white increases were greater. In 1968, the median family income for blacks was $5,590, a rise of about $1,800 over the median family income of $3,794 in 1960, computed in terms of "constant" 1968 dollars. However, the median income of white families rose nearly $2,100 during the same period, from $6,857 to $8,437. Median white income exceeded Negro income by $3,063 in 1960 and by $3,346 in 1968.

The continuing gap between white and black living conditions is reflected in other indicators. The proportion of Negroes residing in substandard and decrepit housing remains very much higher. Whites are far more likely to own new cars, dishwashers, color television sets and other modern appliances. Whites make more visits to doctors' offices while a large proportion of Negroes continue to attend clinics. And, the ratio of Negroes to whites with incomes below poverty levels has been rising.*

The number of persons living below poverty levels has declined in the United States—from 22% of the population in 1959 to 13% in 1968. The number of blacks living below poverty levels dropped from 11 million in 1959 to 8 million in 1968. However, the Negro poverty rate declined more slowly than that of whites. The Negro to white poverty ratio increased during the 1960s—from 3.1 in 1959 to 3.6 in 1968. In 1968, about one-tenth of the white population and one-third of the Negro population were below the poverty level.

Disturbing as they are, these figures do not adequately reflect the Negroes' continuing plight. The migration of blacks from the South to urban areas throughout the country brought many of them out of poverty classifications only in an official

* A number of labels and norms are used to define income of limited means. The most common are "poverty," "low income" and "low-cost budget." In 1959 the poverty standard index, as established by the Social Security Administration, was $2,943 for a nonfarm family of four. In 1968 it was $3,531, the $600 increase representing a rise in the cost of living. Farm poverty levels are 85% of nonfarm levels. "Low income" levels are 25% above "poverty levels." The low income cutoff in 1968 was $4,444 for a nonfarm family of four. The "low-cost budget" was established to portray the income that a family with a fully employed head can exist on. In 1969 the low-cost budget for an urban family of four was about $6,600. Poverty standards do not account for regional differences in the cost of living. The cost of living in the South is 8 to 10% lower than in the rest of the country.

Chart 37

MOST OF THE GAINS MADE BY BLACK FAMILIES OVER THE LAST TWO DECADES, 1947-1968, HAVE BEEN AT THE HIGHER INCOME LEVELS. YET ONLY 32% OF ALL BLACK FAMILIES ARE ABOVE THE $8,000 FIGURE, COMPARED TO 58% OF ALL WHITE FAMILIES.

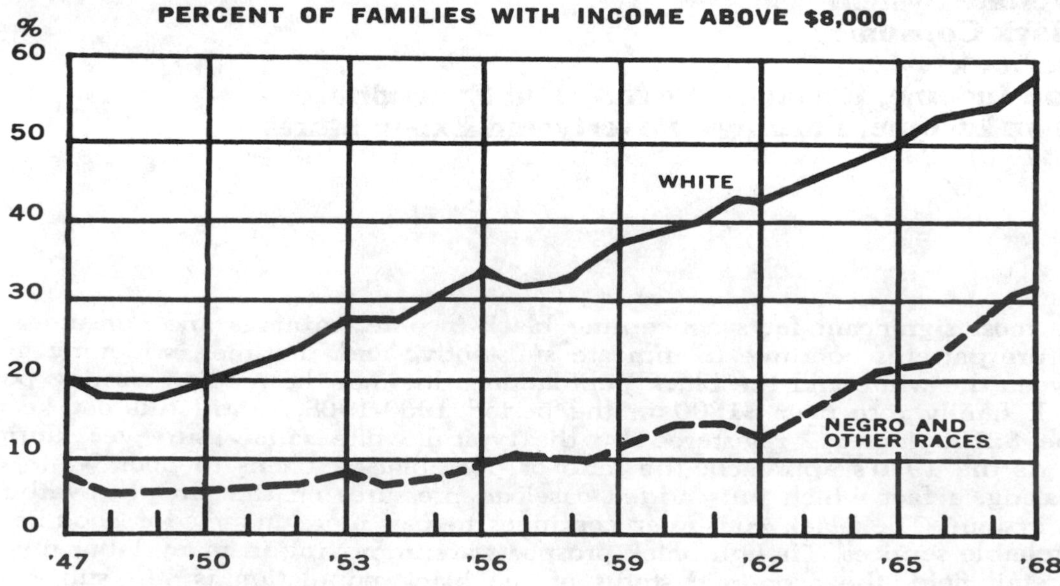

Chart 38

THE MEDIAN FAMILY INCOME FOR BLACK FAMILIES IN 1968 WAS $5,590 WHILE FOR WHITE FAMILIES IT WAS $8,937. IN 1947, THE DOLLAR GAP WAS $2,500; IN 1968, IT HAD RISEN TO $3,300.

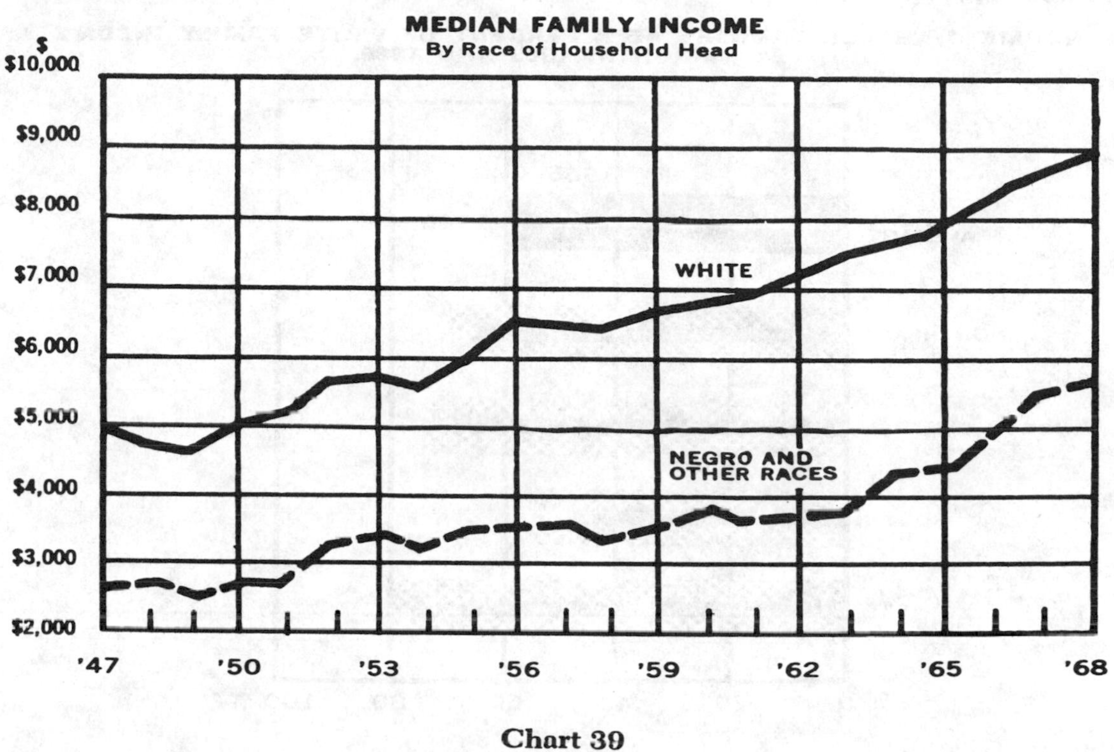

Chart 39

IN 1968, THE MEDIAN INCOME OF BLACK FAMILIES WAS 35% LESS THAN THE MEDIAN INCOME OF WHITE FAMILIES.

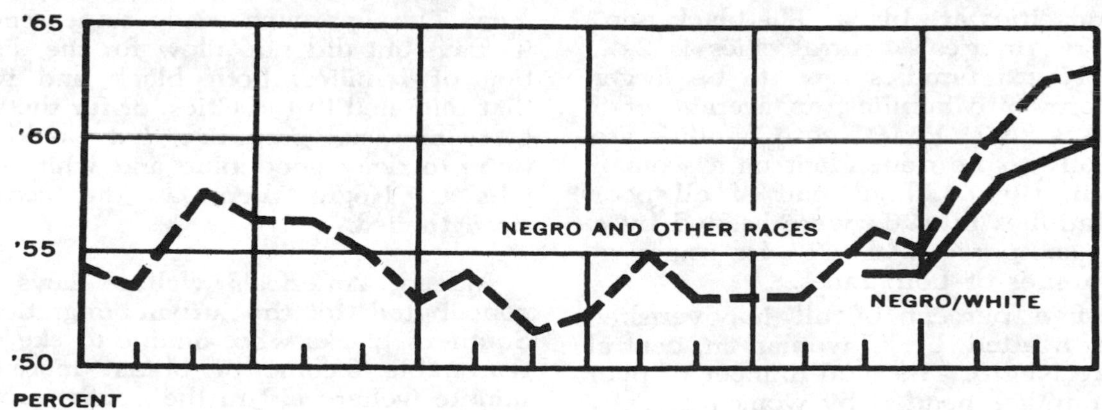

sense. Living costs are lower in the South than in the North, a fact not reflected in poverty indexes, and many impoverished blacks in urban areas are not recorded in statistics.

Poverty declined in small towns and rural areas faster than in cities between 1959 and 1968. In 1968 the poverty distribution was about equal between urban and nonurban areas, having dropped 45% in nonurban parts of the United States and about 25% in cities. In 1968, 25% of poor white and 42% of poor Negroes lived in cities.

In both urban and nonurban areas, the percentage drop of whites classified as

Chart 40

THE MEDIAN INCOME FOR BLACK FAMILIES RESIDING IN THE SOUTH IS SUBSTANTIALLY LOWER THAN IN ANY OTHER SECTION OF THE COUNTRY.

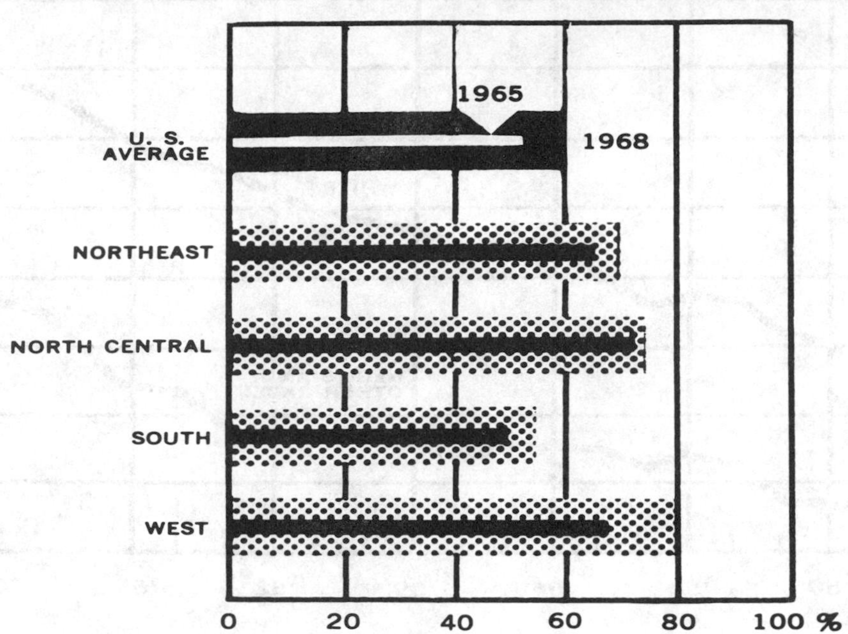

poor was greater than the percentage drop of poor Negroes.

The extent of Negro poverty in cities is underscored by the fact that 42.3% of impoverished urban families of both races in central cities are black. The black population in America's central cities is 21%.

Poor Negro families tend to be larger than poor white families, an average of 5 members to 3.7. Poor Negro families are more likely to be dependent on a woman to sustain them. About half of all poor Negro families in 1968 were headed by a woman, compared with 41% for impoverished families of both races.

Fifty-five percent of all impoverished families headed by a woman in central cities are Negro. The total number of poor Negro families headed by women actually increased between 1959 and 1968, despite the fact that the number of impoverished Negroes dropped more than 3 million.

The Welfare System

The rise in the number of welfare families headed by women is, in large part, a result of America's welfare system in which federal aid to state and local governments excludes help for families which contain an able-bodied man. The system dates back to the Depression years of the 1930s when the government wished mothers to stay at home with the children and leave the scant number of available jobs for men. This approach made some sense in its day, but did not allow for the disruption of families, both black and white, that migrated to the cities, or for the durability of racial prejudice that would continue to deny good blue and white collar jobs to Negro men, as the economy strengthened.

Indeed, America's welfare laws have contributed to the urban migration of Southern blacks who, unable to eke out a reasonable income or obtain more than minute welfare aid in the South, continue to move to richer northern and western states which are more politically and financially able to supplement federal welfare assistance. Over 90% of America's welfare payments are made through programs that are federally funded. State and local governments contribute about 45% of the costs with each state setting the level of grants for its residents. In fiscal 1967, monthly payments per recipient ranged from $9.30 in Mississippi to $62.55 in New York. States sometimes neglect to implement federal regulations. In 1970 the Department of Health, Education & Welfare threatened California, Indiana and Nebraska with curtailment of welfare support for failing to comply with federal requirements for cost of living increases.

The logical result of denying aid to families with men is that men desert their families. Often, the desertion is merely pretended. Ghetto folklore is full of stories about husbands "disappearing" into a neighbor's apartment until a welfare investigator's visit is completed, and then returning. But, much more often, the welfare rules have impelled the destruction of families by passing effective family leadership to women and inducing men to believe that their families are better off without them. In 1968, only 18% of the families encompassed by the federally supported Aid to Families With Dependent Children Program, the largest welfare program in effect, had fathers at home. Two-thirds of these men were incapacitated. Support for families with able-bodied men comes almost entirely from state and local general assistance funds, which are usually insufficient and, at the time of writing, in danger of being cut by financially burdened state governments. Federal support for families with disabled men is usually dependent on certification by a state doctor, a bureaucratic encounter many Negroes avoid.

In addition to disrupting families and encouraging migration to cities, the welfare program has intensified the dependency of the poor by sharply reducing the amount of aid available to welfare families in which members do work.

The Depression-oriented welfare system did hold up fairly well until the 1960s, the AFDC caseload generally rising and falling along with the unemployment rate. But, between 1963 and 1969, with unemployment dropping sharply, the number of AFDC recipients zoomed from 3.9 million to 6.6 million. Much of this increase has been attributed officially to black women between the ages of 15 and 24 who, ac-

Chart 41

THE PROPORTION OF BLACK FAMILIES AT BOTH THE UPPER AND LOWER ECHELONS OF INCOME IS DISPROPORTIONATE IN RELATION TO WHITE FAMILIES.

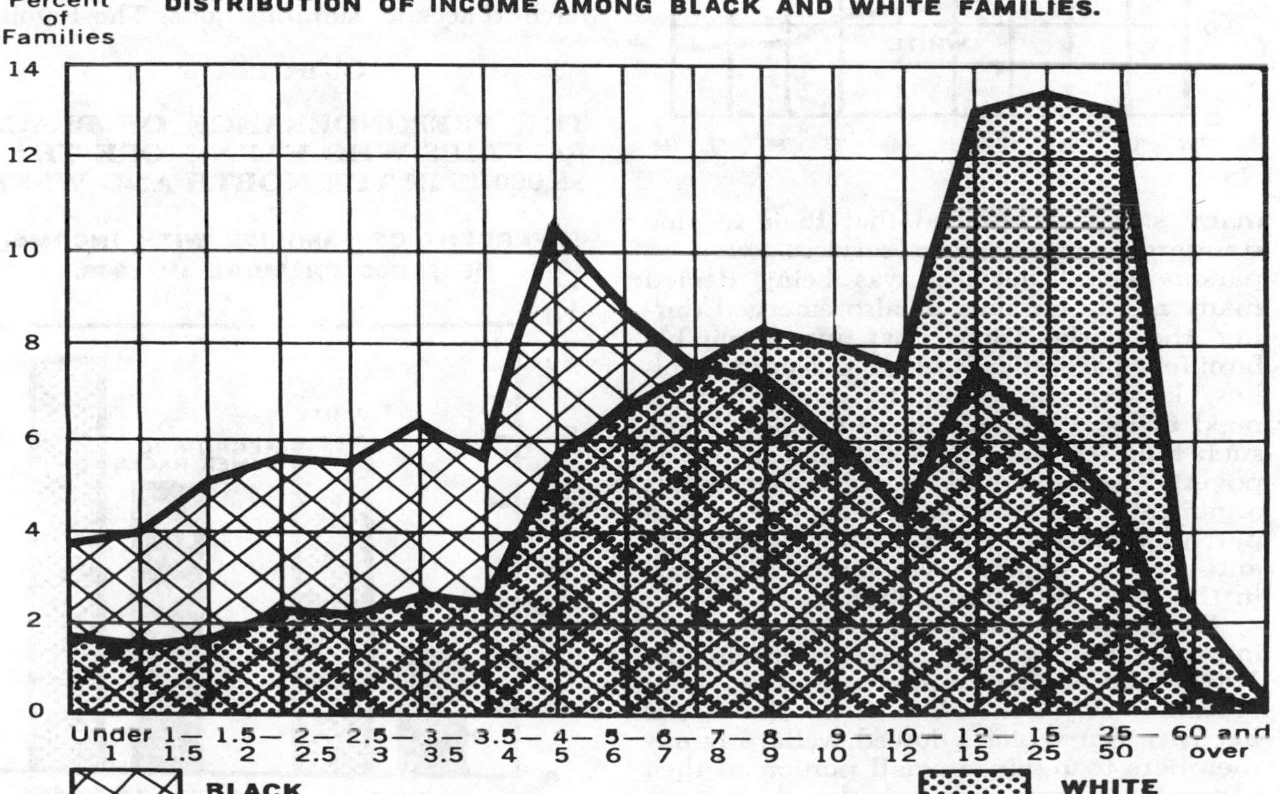

cording to the President's Manpower Report, produce 40% of America's illegitimate births. This factor, as much as "Womens Lib" contributed to the enactment, in 1970, of New York State's permissive abortion law.

The increase in AFDC caseloads also reflects insufficiencies of welfare programs that were not recognized until the Kennedy Administration launched its "war on poverty" in the early 1960s. At this time,

Chart 42

MORE THAN ONE IN FOUR BLACK FAMILIES WERE POOR IN 1968 COMPARED WITH LESS THAN ONE IN 12 FOR WHITE FAMILIES.

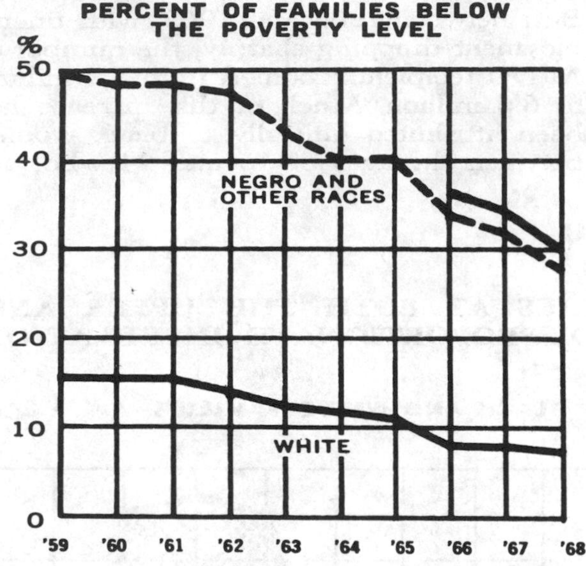

many states recognized that their income standards and welfare services were so parsimonious that aid was being denied many needy families. It also emerged during the early 1960s that many eligible families, particularly eligible Negro families, lacked the savvy to establish their need in local welfare bureaucracies. Many such families were guided to assistance by poverty workers and local welfare rights organizations that were activated and partly financed by federally supported anti-poverty agencies which were instituted in the early and mid-sixties.

There were some legislative efforts to improve the welfare system during the 1960s and a few minor successes, most conspicuously amendments to the Social Security Act which allowed welfare family members to retain a small portion of their earnings if they were employed. But for the most part, welfare reform has foundered on opposition from an unsympathetic Congress and confusion among reformers as to whether the "welfare mess" should be remedied by a guaranteed minimum income, a reverse income tax, children's allowances, stronger work incentives or simply massive infusions of money.

Leaders of anti-poverty efforts in the Kennedy and Johnson Administrations sought to bypass the problems at the government level by encouraging political organization of the poor. As noted, this did contribute to an increase in the number of families receiving welfare, but the black militancy, monetary corruption and bureaucratic confusion found in local anti-poverty agencies aroused influential opposition. By the end of the sixties federal support of local organizational efforts was waning.

In 1969 the Nixon Administration presented a Basic Family Assistance Program to Congress which guarantees $1,600 annually to a family of four and provides assistance up to $3,920 for families in which people earn outside income. It also provides for the sale of food stamps that could increase spending power up to $870 a year. All adult aid recipients except mothers of preschool age children would have to register with their state employment services for employment, training, and other manpower services and would have to accept "suitable" jobs. The Family

Chart 43

THE PREPONDERANCE OF BLACK FAMILIES WHO EARN MORE THAN $8,000 IS IN THE NORTH AND WEST.

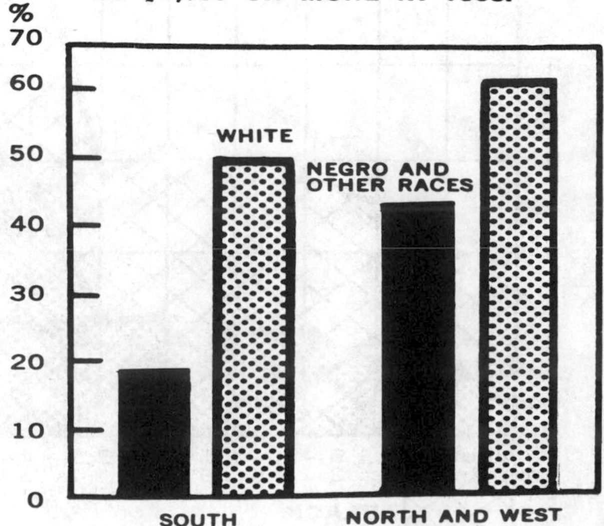

Assistance Plan would aid about 5 million families plus unattached individuals, totaling 25 million people.

The bill passed the House of Representatives by a comfortable margin in April 1970, but in July was encountering heavy and effective opposition in the Senate. Much of the bill's problems were attributed to white backlash and the preoccupation of liberals with the more fashionable issues of Vietnam and ecology.

Opponents claimed variously that the Family Assistance Plan was too expensive, insufficient and would require aid recipients to accept demeaning and low-income jobs. Supporters conceded flaws, but contended that the plan was at least a start out of the poverty-welfare morass and would reduce welfare and unemployment insurance costs.

Chart 44

THE NUMBER OF BLACK FAMILIES WITH INCOME OVER $10,000 HAS RISEN SUBSTANTIALLY IN THE METROPOLITAN AREAS, ALTHOUGH NOT IN PROPORTION TO WHITE FAMILIES.

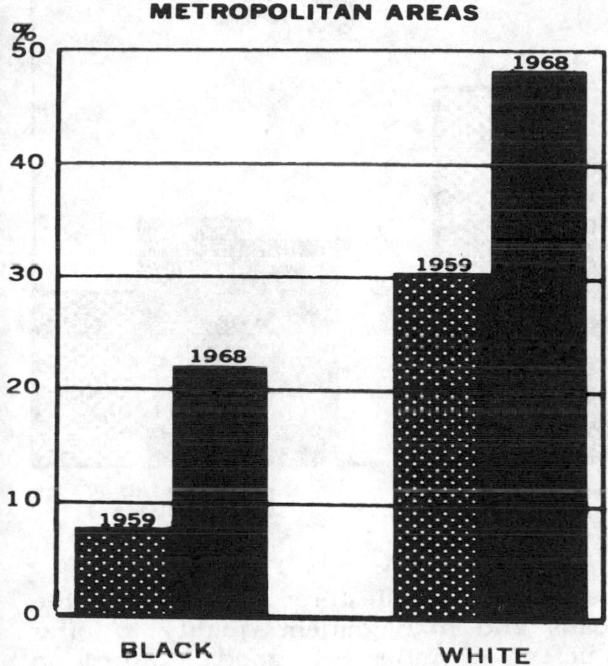

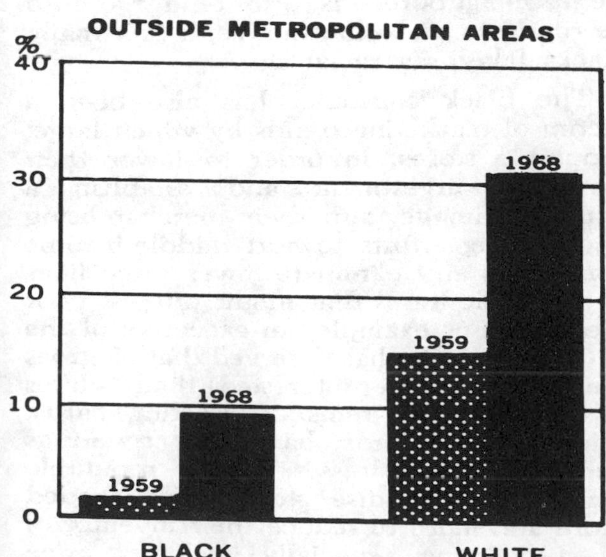

The Negro Consumer

The Negro consumer is courted and derided, exploited and succored. He is the direct victim of white bigotry and contempt and the indirect victim of depersonalizing marketing trends that cast him as an unnecessary customer. The ghetto consumer issue has been almost as explosive as the issue of "police brutality" and has rent the civil rights movement by evoking antagonism of Negroes toward Jews, many of whom operate retail stores and services in black neighborhoods.

A number of reports in the sixties established the fact that in Negro and Spanish ghettos retail prices are higher and services poorer than in downtown and middle-class neighborhoods. The situation is particularly serious in such cities as Detroit and Los Angeles where Negro neighborhoods are remote from downtown areas and public transportation is poor. The practical effect has been to increase the cost of living in Negro neighborhoods and thereby reduce their income.

Significant problems encountered by Negro consumers, especially in large cities, are:

- Higher prices. Merchants in ghettos often have an effective monopoly which enables them to obtain very high mark-up. In partial defense, they must invariably survive higher costs of doing business due to higher than average rates of credit default, insurance and theft in poor neighborhoods and the limited buying power of small businesses.
- High credit costs. Credit and service charges in Negro neighborhoods are often exorbitant and credit contracts and procedures so complicated as to minimize the chances of comprehension or redress for consumers who suffer from them. This is especially true of jewelry, furniture and appliance stores, and of purchases made from door to door salesmen. The Truth in Lending Act, enacted in 1969, does limit garnishees of wages and require some credit information,

Chart 45

APPROXIMATELY 50% OF ALL FAMILIES LIVING IN POVERTY AREAS HAD INCOMES OF $6000 OR LESS IN 1969. IN GENERAL, PUERTO RICAN FAMILIES IN POVERTY AREAS FARED LESS WELL THAN OTHER ETHNIC GROUPS, WHILE BLACK FAMILIES IN POVERTY AREAS TENDED TO EARN SLIGHTLY BETTER INCOMES THAN WHITES IN SIMILAR ENVIRONMENTS. THE INCIDENCE OF HIGHER BLACK EARNINGS IN POVERTY AREAS MAY BE DUE TO LACK OF MOBILITY IN HOUSING SELECTION AS INCOME RISES.

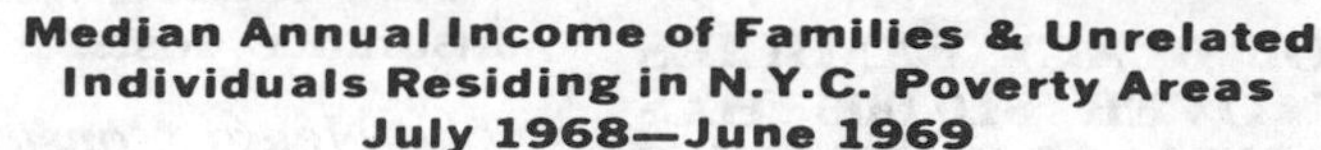

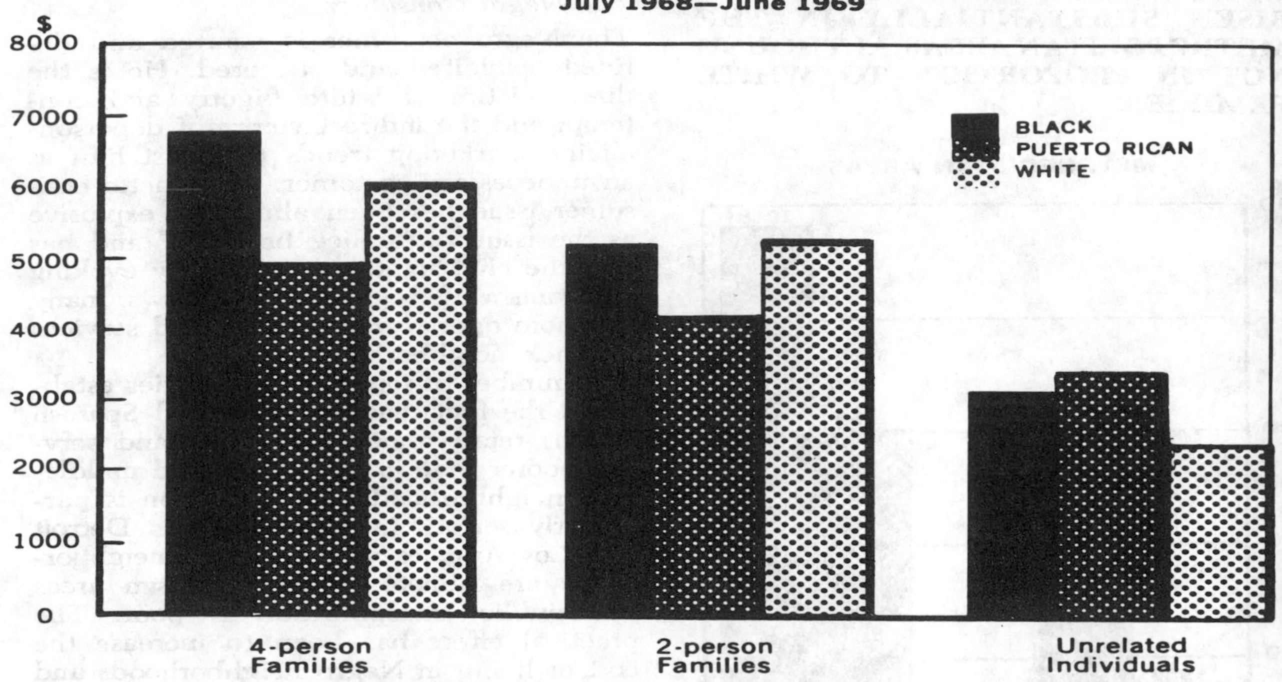

but the problem has not lessened much. Welfare rights organizations have tried to obtain credit for Negroes in large reputable stores, but with small success in terms of the number of people granted credit and the limits placed on the amount they can charge. The credit limit is rarely more than $50 and poor Negroes must usually obtain credit authorization every time they wish to charge a purchase.

Poor Service. Stores tend to close earlier in Negro neighborhoods, especially supermarkets. This lessens the shopping alternatives for ghetto residents who work. Increasingly in recent years, stores and repair services have refused to deliver and make service calls in Negro neighborhoods.

Assortments of merchandise are also smaller in Negro than in other neighborhoods. This is partly due to the fact that large stores have hesitated to locate in ghettos and small stores usually lack the means and management quality to offer sufficient varieties of goods. Stores in Negro neighborhoods also tend more to be rundown and unattractive, a fact many blacks take as a racial slur.

The black consumer has also been a victim of marketing trends by which large, reputable stores, in order to lower their inventory investment and establish a "quality" image, aim their merchandising and pricing efforts toward middle-income consumers and eliminate lower price lines and specific items that might interest poor Negroes. For example, an executive of the J. C. Penney Co. has observed that Negroes tend to be more interested than whites in buying such items as greeting cards, phonograph records, hard floor coverings and large-sized dresses. Large, reputable general merchandise stores have tended more and more to reduce their inventories of such items, especially in lower price lines. This forces Negroes to buy, at greater expense, in local ghetto stores. However, large stores have been stocking some new items produced and priced for lower-middle income Negroes. The trend is most apparent in cosmetics.

Other factors have the effect of decreasing the income of poor blacks by raising the cost of living. Fire and burglary insurance are very difficult to obtain in Negro neighborhoods and Negroes must usually pay more than whites for life and auto insurance. Rents are higher, 20 to 45% more for a single room, according to Commissioner Mary Gardiner Jones of the Federal Trade Commission. Housing services are inferior. The Negro must often weatherproof his windows, repair broken fixtures and paint his rented dwelling at his own expense. And with a few outstanding exceptions achieved by poverty workers, good medical and legal service are very costly and sometimes impossible to obtain.

Negroes of better income groups also find the cost of living higher. Mortgages invariably cost Negroes more, as do other bank loans. Negroes of all income groups must usually go to high interest savings and loan associations to borrow money or even go to racketeer loan sharks.

Efforts of Negro groups, such as Southern Christian Leadership Conference and the Students Non-Violent Coordinating Committee, to combat the high prices and credit denial of large retailers have achieved modest success. Efforts to strengthen local code enforcement against exploitive practices have largely failed, as have efforts to obtain consistent help from local business groups such as Chambers of Commerce and Better Business Bureaus. The jurisdiction and budget of the Federal Trade Commission are sparse.

Pending consumer legislation, while of potential value to poor Negroes, is oriented primarily to the middle class. This is the case with class action lawsuit proposals which would enable consumers to join forces to sue manufacturers of defective products, and of legislation that would guarantee consumers a measure of protection from credit checking bureaus and services.

The Outlook

At the start of the 1970s the long range earnings prospects for Negroes were clouded by an uncertain economy, white backlash, slowness to achieve welfare reform,

Chart 46

IN TERMS OF ACTUAL DOLLAR INCOME PER INDIVIDUAL WORKER, THE WHITE FROM POVERTY AREAS EARNS SUBSTANTIALLY MORE THAN THE BLACK.

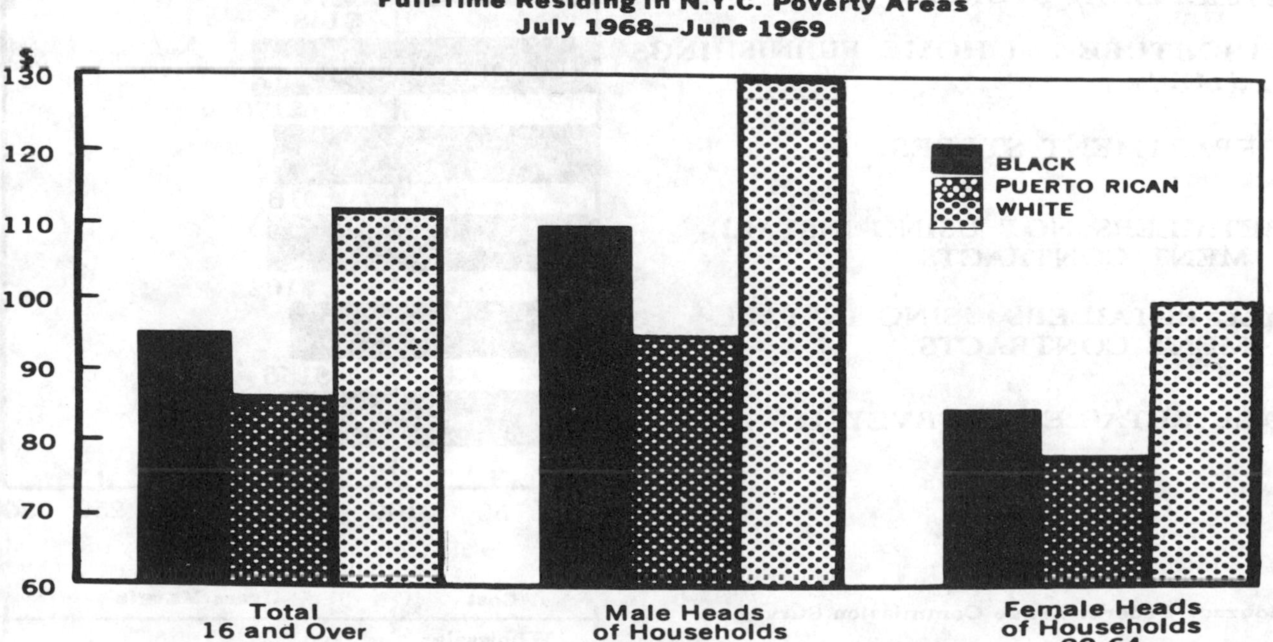

and the survival of exclusionary policies in many unions and businesses.

However, some favorable trends were apparent.

Union organization of low paid service workers was progressing in some major cities. Substantial wage increases were obtained for hospital workers, most of whom are members of minority groups. Substantial increases were also achieved in some retail stores in which Negroes fill most of the stock and receiving jobs and many sales positions. Continued success in these industries would do much to raise the living standards of low income Negroes.

As noted in the employment chapter of *The Negro Almanac*, black representation is increasing in better paid white collar and professional jobs, though progress is slow. Limited progress is also apparent in better paying skilled work.

The political and demographic needs of the country call for expansion of the work force in such well-paid occupational areas as construction, medicine, and computer programming. Though resistance to Negroes persists in these and similar fields, the demand for more workers plus a measure of pressure from various federal and

Chart 47

MERCHANDISE IN LOW INCOME AREAS HAS AN AVERAGE MARKUP BY THE GENERAL MARKET RETAILERS OF 60%.

AVERAGE SELLING PRICE, ASSUMING $100 WHOLESALE COST, BY TYPE OF RETAILER DISTRICT OF COLUMBIA, 1966

Type of Retailer

LOW-INCOME MARKET RETAILERS

GENERAL MARKET RETAILERS

APPLIANCE, RADIO and TELEVISION STORES

FURNITURE and HOME FURNISHINGS STORES

DEPARTMENT STORES

RETAILERS NOT USING INSTALLMENT CONTRACTS

ALL RETAILERS USING INSTALLMENT CONTRACTS

ALL RETAILERS SURVEYED

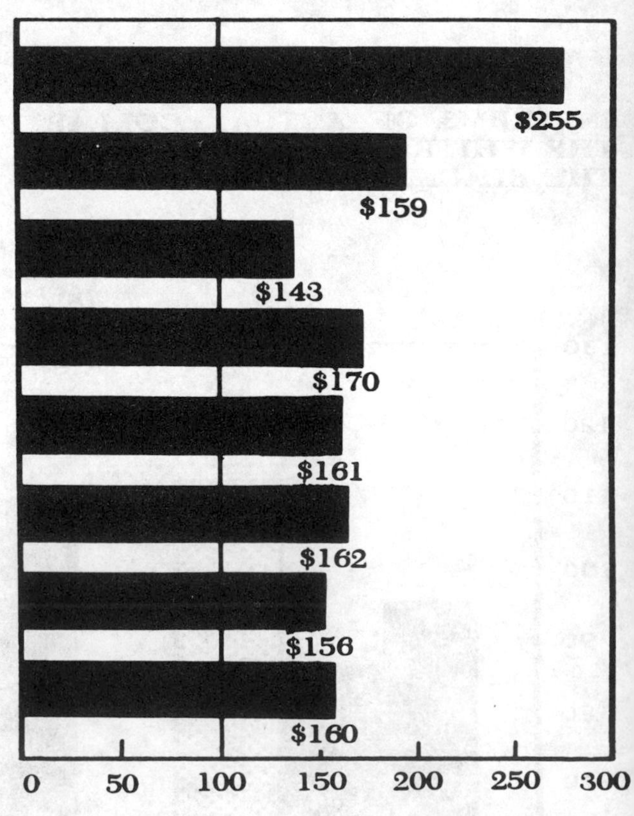

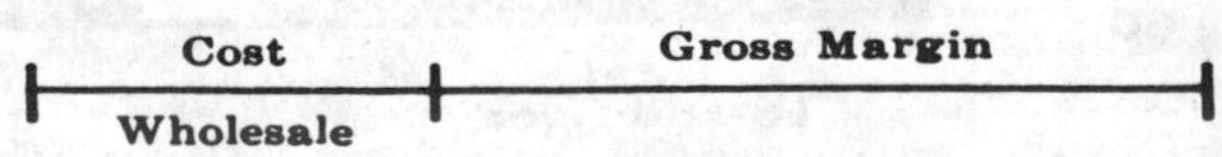

Source: Federal Trade Commission Survey.

Chart 48

THE HOUSING SITUATION FOR NONWHITES HAS SHOWN LITTLE IMPROVEMENT OVER THE 1960-1970 DECADE AND IS FAR MORE LIKELY TO BE SUBSTANDARD THAN THE HOUSEHOLDS OF WHITES.

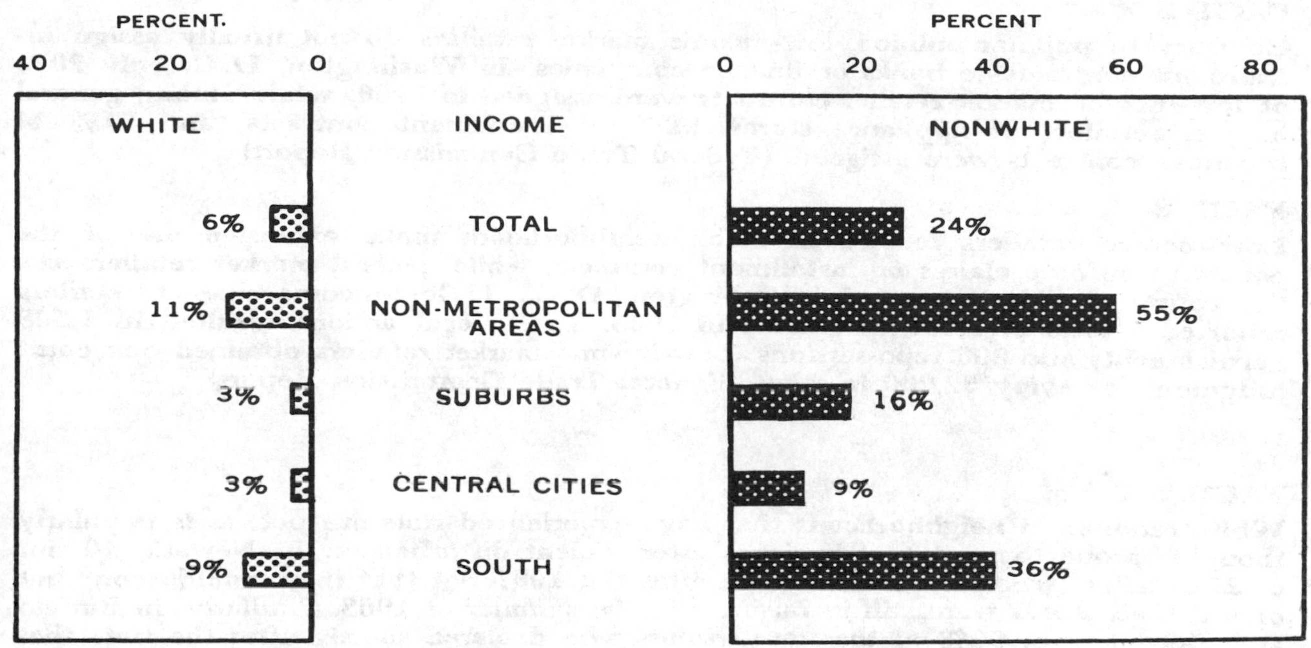

SOURCE—Department of Health Ed. & Welfare.

state agencies should increase the numbers of Negroes performing such work.

On the negative side, Negroes will have to contend with increasing competition for better paying jobs from white women who are entering the labor force in large numbers, and with rising educational and credential demands in white collar, scientific, technical and professional fields.

Above all else, the most important influences will be the strength of the economy and the energy with which corporations and federal and state governments pursue their equal opportunity commitments.

FACTS ON INCOME, EARNINGS, POVERTY AND EXPENDITURES

FACT 1

Retail mark-up in poor neighborhoods tends to be higher in functional than in recreational household items. It is especially high for sewing machines. (FTC Survey of Washington, D. C.)

FACT 2

Low-income market retailers of furniture and appliances get nearly twice the mark-up of general market retailers in virtually every large American city. In Washington, D. C., furniture and appliance retailers in low-income areas paid an average of $37.80 for every $100 of retail sales in 1966, while general market retailers paid $64.50. (Federal Trade Commission survey)

FACT 3

Clothing stores in poor neighborhoods are less likely to offer credit than clothing stores in high-income areas. In Atlanta, in 1966 100% of stores in high-income areas offered credit while less than half in low income areas offered credit.

FACT 4

In 1966, appliances that retailed on the average for $255 in Washington, D. C. low-income market stores retailed at an average of only $159 in general market stores. The people paying the higher prices were mostly black low-income laborers and welfare and Social Security recipients. (A Federal Trade Commission Study)

FACT 5

Contrary to popular opinion, low-income market retailers do not usually assign installment contracts to banks or finance companies. In Washington, D. C. only 20% of low-income market retailer contracts were assigned in 1966, while among general market retailers of appliance stores, 98% of installment contracts, and 57% of furniture contracts were assigned. (Federal Trade Commission Report)

FACT 6

Low-income retailers located in black neighborhoods make extensive use of the courts to enforce claims on installment contracts, while general market retailers use the courts as a last resort. In Washington, D. C., 11 low-income market retailers reported a total of 2,690 judgments in 1966. These legal actions resulted in 1,568 garnishments and 306 repossessions. Low-income market retailers obtained one court judgment for every $2,200 in sales. (Federal Trade Commission Report)

FACT 7

White retailers in neighborhoods that have experienced riots are not, as is popularly thought, prone to go out of business after violent disturbances. In Newark, 20 out of 21 retailers who declared a month after the 1967 riot that they would soon shut or sell their stores were still in business in the summer of 1968. Similarly, in Buffalo and Detroit, over 90% of the store owners who declared shortly after the riots that they would close, did not do so. (Survey by *The Negro Almanac* in 1967 and 1968)

FACT 8

Negro owners and proprietors of ghetto stores tend to be much younger than white owners and proprietors. In New York and Newark in 1969, 83% of white ghetto merchants who were surveyed said they were over 50 years of age and 41% over 60, while 72% of black owners and proprietors reported they were under 50, and 43% under 40. (Survey by *The Negro Almanac*)

FACT 9

The gap in median annual earnings between female white and black workers declined from $1,200 per year to $800 between 1959 and 1967. However, the gap between white and black men increased from $700 to $800.

FACT 10

In most occupation groups, the earnings of black women in central cities with year-round work equaled those of white women. But the earnings of black men were consistently lower than those of white men in similar occupation groups.

FACT 11

The percent of black to white family income has risen markedly since 1964, from 54% to 60%.

FACT 12

Families of other races as a group earn more than Negroes and about as much as whites. The "other races" category encompasses about 8% of the "Negro and Other Races" classification.

FACT 13

Regionally, Negroes' income is greatest in the West where the median in 1968 was $7,506 or 80% of the white median. The lowest income was in the South, a median of $4,270 and only 54% of the white median.

FACT 14

The median dollar gap between white and Negro family income has increased since World War II, from $2,400 in 1947 to $3,400 in 1968, in terms of 1968 dollars. However, the percent of Negro families earning less than $3,000 in 1968 dollars dropped from 60% to 23%.

FACT 15

During the 1960's, white income growth exceeded black growth in four of the five income level quantiles. Negro growth was slightly greater in the second highest quantile, but even in this group the level for Negroes in 1968 ($8,283) was lower than the white level in 1959 ($8,801). In the upper fifth, the white increase has been substantially greater than the Negro increase.

FACT 16

The proportion of black families earning over $8,000 in terms of 1968 dollars increased from 6 to 32% between 1947 and 1968, while white families earning over $8,000 rose from 20 to 58%, 1½ times the Negro increase. However, since 1962 the Negro increase has been more rapid.

FACT 17

The disparity between Negro and white family incomes tends to increase with age. The disparity is greatest in the 55 to 64 age group, least in the 14 to 24 age group.

FACT 18

Black families in which husbands and wives live together are tending more and more to approach the earning capacities of white "husband-wife" families. This is especially true of Negro husband-wife families in which the husband is under 34 years old. However, Negroes in the "all family" group still lag far behind whites in the same group.

FACT 19

In 1968 the median income of black families with three earners was about the same as the median income of white families with only one earner: 57% of black families had more than one earner, compared with 53% for whites.

FACT 20

Black women compared to black men earn a little more than white women compared to white men.

FACT 21

The median income of black high school graduates is considerably lower than the median income for whites who have completed only 8 years of elementary school. And the median income of Negroes who have completed one year of college is considerably lower than the median income of whites who have only completed high school.

FACT 22

The percentage of black families below the poverty level has been declining steadily, but in 1968 it was still three and one-half times that of white families below the poverty level; 29% and 8%. In the suburbs, the incidence of poverty among Negroes is nearly five times that of whites (28% and 6%).

FACT 23

Nearly one-fifth of black families living in metropolitan areas in 1967 had incomes exceeding $10,000, three times the proportion in 1959. However, more than two-fifths of whites in metropolitan areas had incomes of $10,000 or more.

FACT 24

The most dramatic income gains for blacks, in terms of percentage statistics, has occurred in the lowest fifth of their income groups, in which the median income between 1959 and 1968 more than doubled in terms of 1968 dollars. However, in 1968 the median income of the lowest fifth of whites was 80% greater than this income for Negroes.

FACT 25

The dollar difference between whites and blacks in the highest fifth income group was also greater in 1968 than in 1959. The median white income rose from $13,031 to $19,341, the Negro highest fifth from $8,483 to $13,000.

FACT 26

In March 1969, some two-thirds of white and black poor family heads were in farm, service, laborer or semiskilled blue collar jobs.

FACT 27

In 1969, half of all families in the United States that were headed by domestic service workers had incomes below the poverty level. Forty-four percent of America's domestic service workers were black, even though Negroes comprised only 11% of the population.

FACT 28

In 1968, only 54% of black families compared with 68% of white families were headed by a full-time year-round worker. Eleven percent of black and 3% of white families with full-time year-round workers earn less than poverty minimums. Only 8% of black families in central cities headed by full-time year-round workers were poor.

FACT 29

Nearly half of all poor black family heads in 1969 had completed less than 8 years of school.

FACT 30

Half of all black families in the South earn below "low income" levels. Eighty percent of impoverished Negro families with full-time year-round workers were located in the South in 1968. One-fourth of Negro families in the South with full-time year-round workers earned below the poverty level, compared with one in 18 in the Northeast, one in 22 in the North Central and one in 35 in the West.

FACT 31

Sixty-one percent of all black families living on farms outside metropolitan areas, even those headed by year-round full-time workers, were below the poverty level in 1968.

FACT 32

Forty-five percent of all poor black families live in the cities and 23% of all black city families were poor in 1968.

FACT 33

The incidence of poverty among black families was almost double that of Mexican Americans in Houston and Los Angeles. But poverty among Puerto Ricans is greater than that of Negroes in New York City.

FACT 34

The incidence of poverty among unrelated individuals in large metropolitan areas tends to be nearly equal among Negroes and whites, but poverty in families is much greater among blacks.

FACT 35

In Atlanta, black families comprise about four-fifths of the families in the poverty districts and are three times as likely to be poor as white families in the same area. Much of this is attributable to concentration of Atlanta Negro women in private household work.

FACT 36

The ratio of Negro to white families with annual incomes under $3,000 living in urban poverty areas is less than 1.0 in Los Angeles and New York, 1.1 in Detroit and 1.4 in Atlanta, 1.8 in Houston. However, the ratio of Negro to white families

becomes greater in the $3,000 to $5,000 group. The median income of blacks is higher than that of white non-Spanish families in poverty areas of New York and Los Angeles.

FACT 37

In 1968, 27% of all black families compared with 43% of poor Negro families, resided outside metropolitan areas. The proportion of poor black families in the suburbs was about the same as in central cities.

FACT 38

The proportion of white and Negro persons over 65 who are poor increased between 1959 and 1968. In 1968 about 14% of poor people over 65 and 34% under 65 were blacks.

FACT 39

Less than half of America's poor received welfare assistance in 1968. About 48% of the Negro poor and 32% of the white poor received welfare.

FACT 40

Nearly one-fourth of the housing units in which blacks lived in 1968 failed to meet specified criteria, that is they lacked an essential plumbing facility or were dilapidated. In 1960, 44% of the housing units in which Negroes lived were substandard or dilapidated. The figures for whites: 6% in 1968, 13% in 1960.

FACT 41

The decrease in substandard housing has been greatest in cities. The drop from 1960 to 1968 in metropolitan areas has been 49% for Negroes and 52% for whites. Outside metropolitan areas the substandard housing was much greater for whites than Negroes, 48% for whites, 18% for Negroes. However, these statistics do not include the large numbers of dwellings in low income areas that were abandoned and left vacant during the 1960's.

FACT 42

A greater proportion of whites own major household appliances than Negroes. In 1969, one-third of America's white households had at least one color television set compared with one-eighth of black households. One-sixth of white households had a dishwasher, compared with only one in thirty black households.

FACT 43

A much larger proportion of whites own cars than blacks. In 1969, 52% of white households owned one car compared with 40% of Negro households. Thirty-one percent of white households owned two or more cars compared with 13% Negro. White-owned cars were also newer, 23% were less than two years old compared with 11% for Negroes.

FACT 44

Whites are by far the greatest consumers of health care in doctor's offices, while blacks attend clinics in greater numbers. More than half the whites in the $7,000 to $10,000 income bracket attend a dentist at least once a year, compared with only a third of Negroes. About three-fourths of whites in this income group visit a doctor in his office compared with less than two-thirds of the Negroes. Twenty-two percent of the Negroes visited a hospital clinic compared with only 7% of the white population.

FACT 45

The percentage of Negroes visiting doctors' offices drops as income levels drop, but white office visits do not.

FACT 46

At incomes below $3,000, 44% of black families and 73% of white families are headed by a man. As black family incomes grow, they are more likely to be headed by a man, but a higher proportion of white than Negro families are led by a man at all income levels.

FACT 47

A greater percentage of white than black children live with both parents, but the differences decrease as income rises. In families with annual incomes below $3,000, about one-fourth of black children of family heads live with their parents compared with one-half of white children. But in the $7,000 to $10,000 group, 90% of black children and 95% of white children live with both parents.

FACT 48

Between 1959 and 1967 median family income increased 22% in the suburbs, only 16% in central cities. In 1967 the median income of city dwellers was 83% that of suburban families, compared with 88% in 1959. The percentage of blacks living in the suburbs has increased in number but not percentage.

FACT 49

The proportion of blacks among all poor families with female heads under the age of 65 increased from 30% in 1959 to 43% in 1968. There was a reduction of 54% in the number of poor Negro families headed by a man.

FACT 50

About 53% of black families with five or more members under 18 years of age were below the poverty standard in 1968.

FACT 51

Poor black families tend to be more impoverished than poor white families. The median impoverished white family was $910 below the poverty level in 1968, the median Negro $1,260 below.

FACT 52

Almost $10 billion would have been required to raise poor families of both races to the poverty level in 1968, $4 billion less than in 1959.

FACT 53

About three-fifths of the self-reported rioters in Newark belonged to families earning more than $5,000 a year and nearly half of the self-reported Detroit rioters were individuals who reported earnings of over $5,000 a year. Nearly one-third of the self-reported Detroit rioters indicated that they earned $7,500 or more per year.

INCOME, EARNINGS, POVERTY & EXPENDITURES TABLES

Table 52

Median Income of Central City Families, by Number of Earners (1967 dollars)

Year and Color	All families	No earners	One earner	Two earners	Three or more earners
1967					
Total	$7,813	$2,476	$6,810	$9,054	$12,454
White	8,294	2,615	7,285	9,543	12,891
Negro	5,623	2,144	4,199	7,225	9,507
Percent of white	68	82	58	76	74
1959					
Total	$6,719	$1,923	$5,872	$8,104	$11,308
White	7,159	2,083	6,255	8,467	12,332
Negro	4,397	1,427	3,500	5,711	7,460
Percent of white	61	69	56	67	60

Table 53

Median Income of Negro Male and Female Workers, by Region, 1968

Region	Median income of Negro workers		Ratio: Female to male income	
	Male	Female	Negro	White
All wage and salary workers[1]	$4,733	$2,454	.52	.48
Year-round full-time workers[2]	5,370	3,561	.66	.58
Northeast	5,900	3,945	.67	.61
North Central	6,856	4,096	.60	.55
South	4,167	2,884	.69	.59
West	7,517	4,547	.60	.59

[1] With wage and salary income, including full and part-time workers.
[2] Refers to total income.
Source: U.S. Department of Commerce, Bureau of the Census.

Table 54

Median Family Income in Poverty Areas of Six Large Cities, July 1968-June 1969

Color	City					
	Atlanta	Chicago	Detroit	Houston	Los Angeles	New York City
Negro and other races	$4,700	$7,000	$6,200	$4,700	$5,800	$5,700
White	$6,200	(B)	$6,300	$6,000	$6,600	$5,300
Negro and other races as a percent of white	76	(NA)	98	78	88	108

B—Base 2,000 or less.
NA—Not available.
Source: U.S. Department of Labor, Bureau of Labor Statistics.

Table 55

Number and Percent of Persons Below the Poverty Level and of Persons Receiving Welfare, 1968
(In millions)

Group	Color	
	Negro and other races	White
Total population	24.5	175.6
Below poverty level	8.0	17.4
Percent of total population	33	10
Receiving welfare	3.8	5.6
Percent of total population	16	3

Source: U.S. Department of Commerce, Bureau of the Census; U.S. Department of Health, Education, and Welfare.

Table 56

Median Earnings in 1967 of White and Negro Year-Round Workers in Central Cities Currently Employed in Selected Occupation Groups

Sex and Occupation Group	Median earnings in 1967		Negro median earnings as a percent of white		Year-round workers as a percent of all workers in group	
	White	Negro	1967	1959	White	Negro
MALE						
Professional and managerial workers	$9,542	$6,208	65	(B)	86	87
Clerical and sales workers	6,878	5,515	80	82	78	84
Craftsmen and foremen	7,545	5,962	79	75	80	76
Operatives	6,475	5,414	84	79	72	75
Nonfarm laborers	5,355	4,492	84	77	63	62
Service workers, exc. private household	5,536	4,159	75	67	75	69
FEMALE						
Professional and managerial workers	$5,910	$6,209	105	(B)	69	66
Clerical and sales workers	4,312	4,425	103	99	68	59
Operatives	3,590	3,296	92	85	61	66
Private household workers	880	1,410	160	100	26	62
All other service workers	3,061	2,905	95	85	54	59

B—Base less than 75,000.
Source: U.S. Department of Labor, Bureau of Labor Statistics.

Table 57

Influence of Number of Earners on Family Income, 1968

Family Characteristic	All families	No earners	One earner	Two earners	Three earners	Four earners or more
Negro:						
Percent	100	10	33	41	10	6
Median income	$5,359	$2,288	$4,151	$7,181	$7,891	$9,360
White:						
Percent	100	8	39	39	10	4
Median income	$8,936	$2,940	$7,724	$10,000	$12,658	$14,566
Negro median income as a percent of white	60	78	54	72	62	64

Source: U.S. Department of Commerce, Bureau of the Census.

Table 58

Percent of Families with High Income
(1967 dollars)

Color and Region	$10,000 and over		$15,000 and over	
	1967	1959	1967	1959
Metropolitan areas	40	26	15	9
White	42	28	16	9
Negro	18	7	5	1
Central cities	33	23	12	7
White	37	27	13	9
Negro	18	7	5	1
In metropolitan areas of 1,000,000 or more	34	27	13	8
White	39	30	15	10
Negro	20	10	6	2
In metropolitan areas under 1,000,000	33	21	11	6
White	35	23	12	7
Negro	15	4	4	4
Suburban rings	45	29	17	10
White	46	30	18	10
Negro	19	8	6	1

Source: U.S. Department of Commerce.

Table 59

Median Family Income in 1968, and Negro Family Income. 1965-1968, as a Percent of White, by Region

Region	Median family income, 1968		Negro income as a percent of white			
	Negro	White	1965	1966	1967	1968
United States	$5,359	$8,936	54	58	59	60
Northeast	6,460	9,318	64	68	66	69
North Central	6,910	9,259	74	74	78	75
South	4,278	7,963	49	50	54	54
West	7,506	9,462	69	72	74	80

Source: U.S. Department of Commerce, Bureau of the Census.

Table 60

Median Income of Men 25 to 54 Years Old, by Educational Attainment, 1968

Educational Attainment		Median income, 1968		Negro income as a percent of white
		Negro	White	
Elementary:	Total	$3,900	$5,844	67
	Less than 8 years	3,558	5,131	69
	8 years	4,499	6,452	70
High school:	Total	5,580	7,852	71
	1 to 3 years	5,255	7,229	73
	4 years	5,801	8,154	71
College:	1 or more years	7,481	10,149	74

Source: U.S. Department of Commerce, Bureau of the Census.

Table 61

Median Income of Negro Families as a Percent of White, by Type of Family and Age of Family Head, 1968

Family Characteristics	All families	Husband-wife families
All ages	60	72
14 to 24 years	70	88
25 to 34 years	62	78
35 to 44 years	59	72
45 to 54 years	62	70
55 to 64 years	57	59
65 years and over	65	63

Source: U.S. Department of Commerce, Bureau of the Census.

Table 62

Median Income of Families of Negro and Other Races as a Percent of White Family Income, 1950-1968

Years 1950–1968	Negro and other races	Negro
1950	54	(NA)
1951	53	(NA)
1952	57	(NA)
1953	56	(NA)
1954	56	(NA)
1955	55	(NA)
1956	53	(NA)
1957	54	(NA)
1958	51	(NA)
1959	52	(NA)
1960	55	(NA)
1961	53	(NA)
1962	53	(NA)
1963	53	(NA)
1964	56	54
1965	55	54
1966	60	58
1967	62	59
1968	63	60

NA—Not available. The ratio of Negro to white median family income first became available from this survey in 1964.

Source: U.S. Department of Commerce, Bureau of the Census.

Table 63

Percent of Families with Income of $8,000 or More, 1947-1968

(Adjusted for price changes, in 1968 dollars. An $8,000 income in 1968 was equivalent in purchasing power to about $5,100 in 1947)

Year and Region	Percent	
	Negro and other races	White
United States:		
1947	6	20
1948	4	18
1949	4	18
1950	4	20
1951	4	21
1952	5	23
1953	8	26
1954	7	26
1955	8	30
1956	9	34
1957	10	32
1958	10	33
1959	12	37
1960	15	39
1961	15	41
1962	14	42
1963	17	45
1964	20	47
1965	21	50
1966	25	53
1967	29	55
1968	32	58
South:		
1966	14	44
1967	17	48
1968	19	50
North and West:		
1966	36	56
1967	40	58
1968	43	61

Source: U.S. Department of Commerce, Bureau of the Census.

Table 64

Distribution of Families by Income in 1947, 1960, and 1968
(In 1968 dollars)

Family Income	Negro and other races			White		
	1947	1960	1968	1947	1960	1968
Number of families (in millions)	3,717	4,333	5,075	34,120	41,123	45,440
Percent	100	100	100	100	100	100
Under $3,000	60	41	23	23	16	9
$3,000 to $4,999	23	23	22	28	16	11
$5,000 to $6,999	9	16	17	23	21	14
$7,000 to $9,999	5	13	18	15	26	24
$10,000 to $14,999	3	6	15	11	17	26
$15,000 and over		2	6		7	16
Median income	$2,514	$3,794	$5,590	$4,916	$6,857	$8,937
Net change, 1947–1968:						
Number	(X)	(X)	$3,076	(X)	(X)	$4,020
Percent	(X)	(X)	122.4	(X)	(X)	81.8

X Not applicable.
Source: U.S. Department of Commerce, Bureau of the Census.

Table 65

Comparison of Reported Wholesale and Retail Prices for Best-Selling Products, Low-Income Market and General Market Retailers

Products	Wholesale Cost		Retail Price[1]	
	Low-Income Market Retailer	General Market Retailer	Low-Income Market Retailer	General Market Retailer
Television sets:				
Motorola portable	$109.00	$109.50	$219.95	$129.95
Philco portable	108.75	106.32	199.95	129.95
Olympic portable	90.00[2]	85.00	249.95	129.95
Admiral portable	94.00	91.77	249.95	129.99
Radio: Emerson	16.50	16.74	39.95	25.00
Stereo: Zenith	32.99	32.99	99.95	36.99
Automatic washers:				
Norge	144.95	140.00	299.95	155.00
General Electric	183.50	160.40	339.95	219.95
Dryers:				
Norge	80.00	87.00	249.95	102.45
General Electric	206.90	205.00	369.95	237.76
Admiral	112.00	115.97	299.95	149.95
Vacuum Cleaners:				
Hoover upright	39.95	39.95	79.95	59.95
Hoover canister	26.25	24.55	49.95	28.79

[1] Retail prices are cash and do not include separately imposed finance charges.
[2] Reported as approximately wholesale cost.
Source: Federal Trade Commission Survey.

Table 66

Net Profit After Taxes as a Percent of Sales and Rates of Return After Taxes for District of Columbia Retailers Surveyed, 1966

Type of Retailers	Percent	
	Net Profit after Taxes as a Percent of Sales	Percent of Rate Return after Taxes on Stockholders Equity
Low-income Market Retailers	4.7	10.1
General Market Retailers:		
Appliance, radio, and television stores	2.1	20.3
Furniture and Home-furnishings stores	3.9	17.6
Department Stores	4.6	13.0

Source: Federal Trade Commission Survey.

Table 67

Classification of Types of Alleged Deceptive Practices Involved in District of Columbia Consumer Protection Complaints and Investigations

Type of Practice	Number of Matters Involved	Percent of Total Matters[1]
Bait-and-Switch Advertising	28	41.2
False and Misleading Statements Concerning Nature of Products and Services Offered	20	29.4
False and Misleading Statements Concerning Guarantee	12	17.6
Misrepresenting Nature of Business	11	16.2
Low-Balling Tactics in the Sale of Services (similar to Bait-and-Switch)	8	11.8
Failure to Reveal that Installment Contracts would be Sold to Finance Company or Other Third Party	8	11.8
Failure to Furnish Free Merchandise or Services when Offered	8	11.8
Failure to Reveal Full Amount of Purchase Price and Financing Charges	7	10.3
Deceptive Pricing and Misrepresentation of Regular Prices as Reduced Prices	6	8.8
Failure to Disclose Segregated Housing Policy	6	8.8
Using Fake Drawings, Contests, Telephone Surveys and Scholarships for Promotional Purposes	5	7.3
Used Merchandise Sold as New	5	7.3
Fictitious Wholesale Price Lists	3	4.4
Refusal to Give Itemized Bills	3	4.4
Failure to Disclose Terms Regarding Refund of Deposits	3	4.4

[1] This is based upon a total of 68 cases. Supplementing the data by complaints approved by the Commission (circulated date) would not change the types of practices involved in the pilot program, only the frequency with which they have been involved in outstanding complaints. The number of "matters" referred to in the preceding column exceeds the 98 cases involved in this program because of the fact that many of the practices listed were involved in more than one case.

Source: Federal Trade Commission Survey.

Table 68

Percent of Occupied Housing Not Meeting Specified Criteria, by Location, 1960 and 1968

Region	Percent			
	Negro and other races		White	
	1960	1968	1960	1968
United States	44	24	13	6
Metropolitan areas:				
Central cities	25	9	8	3
Suburbs	43	16	7	3
Nonmetropolitan areas	77	55	23	11

Source: U.S. Department of Commerce, Bureau of the Census.

Table 69

Percent of Households Owning Selected Durables, July 1967 and July 1969

Item	Percent			
	Negro		White	
	1967	1969	1967	1969
Automobiles:				
One	41.6	40.3	53.5	51.8
Two or more	10.3	12.6	28.8	30.9
One or more recent model automobiles[1]	10.0	11.0	23.2	23.4
Household durables:				
Black and white TV	83.9	81.9	85.8	77.5
Color TV	6.5	12.4	18.7	33.5
Dishwasher	4.0	3.5	15.0	17.4

[1] In 1967 a 1966 or 1967 model; in 1969 a 1968 or 1969 model.
Source: U.S. Department of Commerce, Bureau of the Census.

Table 70

Value of Installment Contracts as a Per Cent of Sales, District of Columbia Retailers, 1966

Type of Retailer	Number of companies	Net Sales ($000)	Installment Contracts: Value ($000)	% of Total	As % of Net Sales
Total	65	$150,970	$45,251	100.0	30.0
Low-income market retailers	18	7,874	7,296	16.1	92.7
General market retailers	47	143,096	37,955	83.9	26.5
Appliance, radio and television	22	25,089	8,466	18.7	33.7
Furniture and home furnishings	22	26,643	10,608	23.5	39.8
Department stores	3	91,364	18,881	41.7	20.6

Source: FTC Survey.

Table 71

Average Gross Margins of District of Columbia Retailers on Best-Selling Items of Appliances and Furniture, 1966

Merchandise Items	Average per cent gross margin of:			
	Low-Income Market Retailers	General Market Retailers		
		Appliance Stores	Furniture Stores	Department Stores
Television sets	46.4	23.7	28.4	25.2
Carpets	50.0	—	37.5	33.2
Refrigerators	50.6	24.5	24.9	34.6
Washing machines	51.0	25.0	32.3	35.3
Stereo-phonographs	52.7	33.0	36.5	34.7
Freezers	53.7	24.8	—	33.7
Dryers	53.9	25.7	28.4	37.7
Furniture	56.2	—	47.5	50.4
Vacuum Cleaners	57.9	26.3	30.2	36.4
Radios	60.0	23.4	38.0	27.9
Sewing Machines	66.3	49.0	—	42.7

[1] Appliance and furniture stores have been classified on the basis of their principal merchandise lines. Furniture stores carry appliances as a substantial secondary merchandise line, and for this reason average gross margins of appliances sold by furniture stores are included in this table.

Federal Trade Commission Survey.

Table 72

Net Sales and Gross Margins of District of Columbia Retailers, 1966

Type of Retailer	Number of companies	Net Sales		Gross Margin[1]	
		Value ($00)	Percent of Total	Value ($00)	As Percent of Sales
Low-income market retailers	18	$7,874	5.2	$4,790	60.8
General Market retailers	47	143,096	94.8	52,988	37.0
Appliance, radio, and TV	22	25,098	16.6	7,586	30.2
Furniture and home-furnishings	22	26,643	17.7	10,979	41.2
Department Stores	3	91,364	60.5	34,423	37.7
Total, Retailers using Installment Contracts	65	150,970	100.0	57,778	38.3
Retailers not using Installment Contracts	31	74,842		26,902	35.9
Total, All Retailers Surveyed	96	225,812		84,680	37.5

[1] Gross margins reported by different types of retailers may not be strictly comparable. One low-income retailer included finance charges and one general market appliance retailer included service charges in their net sales. Adjustments were made in these instances but other retailers in the sample may have included such charges in their net sales and not reported their inclusion. To the extent that finance, service and other charges might have been included in net sales and no corresponding adjustment made in cost of goods sold, gross margins for these retailers would be slightly overstated. However, every effort was made to calculate gross margins in this study net of finance and other charges.

Federal Trade Commission Survey.

Table 73

Average "Retail Prices" of District of Columbia Retailers on Best-Selling Items of Appliances and Furniture in 1966, Assuming Wholesale Cost of $100 for Each Item[1]

Merchandise Items	Average "retail price" assuming $100 wholesale cost of:			
	Low-Income Market Retailers	General Market Retailers		
		Appliance Stores[2]	Furniture Stores[2]	Department Stores
Television sets	$187	$131	$140	$134
Carpet	200	—	160	150
Refrigerator	202	132	133	153
Washing machine	204	133	148	155
Stereo-phonograph	211	149	157	153
Freezer	216	133	—	151
Dryer	217	135	138	160
Furniture	228	—	190	202
Vacuum Cleaner	237	136	143	157
Radio	250	130	161	139
Sewing Machine	297	196	—	174

[1] These are cash prices and do not reflect separately imposed finance charges.

[2] Appliance and furniture stores have been classified on the basis of their principal merchandise lines. Furniture stores carry appliances as a substantial secondary merchandise line, and for this reason average "retail prices" of appliances sold by furniture stores are included in this table.

Source: Federal Trade Commission Survey.

N. Y.

FEDERAL EMPLOYMENT AND GOVERNMENT ASSISTANCE PROGRAMS

During the 1960's, the federal government increasingly played a direct role in helping to effect the economic rehabilitation and well being of black Americans. It did this as a manager and subsidizer of special programs for the disadvantaged and as a civil service employer.

The number of Negroes participating in federally aided job programs multiplied at least five-fold between 1964 and 1969 as funds allocated annually to the "war on poverty" rose from $400 million to $2.2 billion.

Negro increases in civil service employment were less dramatic. Between 1965 and 1967, the number of Negroes in full-time civil service employment rose from 309,000 to 391,000. However, this pattern did not persist and the number of federally employed Negroes had dipped to 389,000 by November 1969. Between 1967 and 1969, the number of Spanish surnamed workers increased from 69,000 to 74,000.

In 1969, Negroes comprised about 15% of the total federal workforce, compared with 13.5% in 1965. The Post Office and Defense Departments each account for about one-third of all Negroes in the federal civil service. The greatest gains between 1965 and 1969 were achieved in the Post Office, 45,000 and the Defense Department, 25,000. Lesser but substantial gains were also achieved in the Department of Health, Education & Welfare.

The percentage of Negroes in better paying civil service jobs also increased, but blacks remain concentrated in lower paying classifications. Negroes occupy nearly 25% of full-time civil service jobs paying less than $7,000 annually, but only 8% of jobs paying between $7,000 and $12,000 per year and only 2% of jobs paying over $12,000.

The Public Service Careers Program, launched in 1970, is intended to place disadvantaged persons in public service agencies and to finance upgrading activities. It emphasizes the selection and on the job training of people whose education would normally be insufficient to qualify them for civil service positions.

By the end of 1970, PSCP remained largely in its pilot phase.

Chart 49

PERCENTAGE INCREASE OR DECREASE IN THE NUMBER OF MINORITY AND NON-MINORITY EMPLOYEES BETWEEN NOVEMBER 1967 AND NOVEMBER 1969 BY GRADE GROUPING.

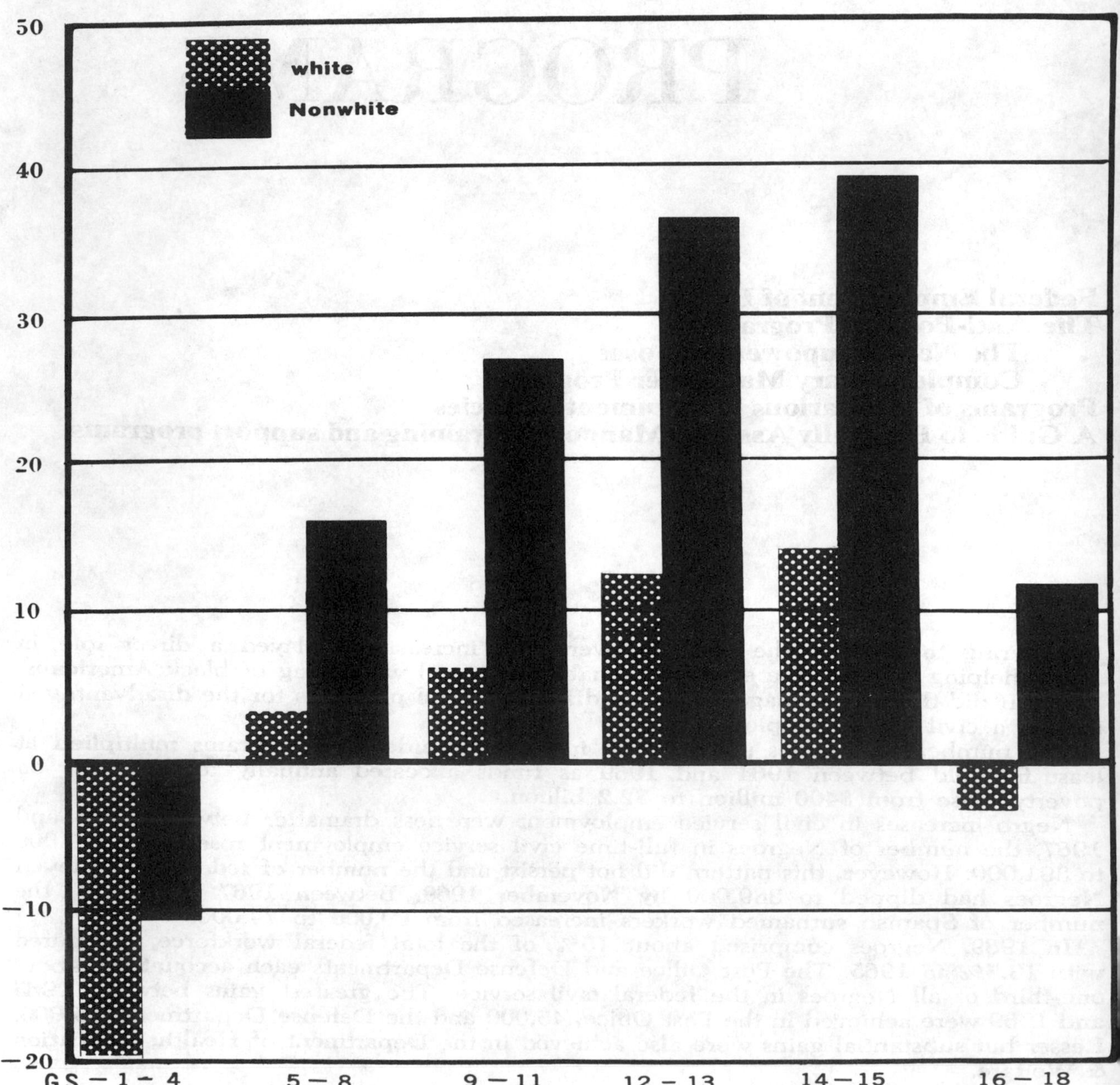

ANTI-POVERTY PROGRAM. The anti-poverty program, propounded by President Kennedy shortly before his assassination and a major feature of the Johnson Administration, encountered serious opposition from the Nixon Administration and the 91st Congress. By the end of 1970, its future was far from propitious.

The "War on Poverty" of the sixties differed from the "New Deal" of the thirties in two crucial respects. Through the Office of Economic Opportunity it encouraged and trained the poor to organize politically, to become a pressure group in their own right; secondly, it directed the bulk of its activity toward the training, education and utilization of youth, with the intention of reducing the high unemployment rate and riot potential of Negroes in their teens and early twenties.

The War on Poverty has increased the economic and political strength of poor Americans. No overall official figures for minorities have been released, but *The Negro Almanac* estimates that in fiscal 1969 some 800,000 Negroes were enrolled in federally assisted manpower programs. Total enrollment in these programs was about 1,800,000. The Neighborhood Youth Corps, alone, enrolled nearly 1 million Negroes between its inception in 1965 and 1970.

However, despite such imposing statistics, the War on Poverty has obviously fallen far short of its goals. Statistics tell part of the story. Today, there are still 8 million Americans living in sub-standard housing; there are still some 1,500 Americans who die

The War on Poverty was designed to aid poor people living in dire circumstances.

every year from diseases caused by malnutrition; there are still some 7 million Americans subsisting on free government surpluses and over 30 million Americans, one-third of them Negroes, subsisting below government established poverty levels.

Major reasons the Poverty Program has had great problems are:

- Lessening fear of riots, following widespread use of Army and National Guard units to quell disturbances after the assassination of Martin Luther King in 1968.
- The conservative trend in American politics, manifested in 1968 when President Nixon and Governor Wallace of Alabama received nearly 3/5ths of the presidential vote.
- Fear of whites toward the militancy of black-conscious groups organized under OEO's Community Action Program.
- Corruption within some local agencies of the poverty program. In New York, several hundred thousand dollars in government funds were embezzled by groups of poverty officials and workers.
- The decline in the economy as a whole in late 1969.
- Failure of job training programs to provide skilled and semi skilled workers in sufficient quantities and the resistance of some craft unions to skilled Negroes.

In 1969, the Nixon Administration maintained a distant, non-committal position toward the anti-poverty program. Funds were not cut, but were not increased to compensate for inflation. President Nixon moved the Job Corps and Operation Head Start from the Office of Economic Opportunity, partly in response to fears that OEO had attained too much power, partly to give these programs the institutional protection of more established departments. The Administration expressed approval of Head Start and declared its intention to extend its services to the first year in the lives of poverty area children.

As 1970 drew to a close, pressures for drastic cuts in the Poverty Program were strong, as the cost of living continued to rise and politicians increasingly paid ritualistic respect to "law and order" and to "blue collar" white workers. However, the midterm elections of 1970 indicated that the administration's "southern strategy" was unproductive. And it was possible that the administration would strengthen jobs programs to stem the rise in unemployment, which neared 6% in October.

The New Manpower Proposal

The Nixon Administration is presently concerned with efforts to simplify and coordinate the manpower programs, stating that there is too much fragmentation and complexity to the current operation and that the federal government cannot effectively operate the diverse functions which are required to meet the individual community needs across the country. Key features of the proposed new Manpower Act are:

Individual Services. Persons 16 years of age or older who are unemployed, underemployed, or in a low-income status would be eligible for a variety of services—basic education, literacy and communications skill training, testing and work evaluation, preapprenticeship and occupational training, prevocational training, supportive health services, child day care, and relocation assistance, as needed. Others could participate if the Secretary of Labor found that this would improve utilization of the Nation's manpower resources. Each participant would have an employability development plan tailored to his needs.

State Authority and Responsibility. Each State would be required to establish a comprehensive manpower agency, in order to secure administrative control over the manpower funds to be spent in the State (as discussed below under *State Apportionment*). The comprehensive agency would include the following State agencies: The employment service; the unemployment compensation agency; and all agencies responsible for the administration of programs authorized by the act and of any other State-supported manpower programs. Vocational education and rehabilitation agencies could be included when requested by the State, as could other related agencies. An existing "lead" agency experienced in administering manpower programs could be designated by the Governor by agreement with the Secretary to administer a portion of the State's share of funds, pending the development of a comprehensive agency.

Each State would be required to establish a manpower planning organization with broad representation as another condition for obtaining administrative control over funds. Specifically, this organization would include representatives of: (1) State agencies for manpower training, employment, apprenticeship, general and vocational education, vocational rehabilitation, welfare, industrial development, labor, economic opportunity, and human resources; (2) local manpower training and employment programs; (3) typical client groups; and (4) the general public. Each year, the State planning organization would submit consolidated State plans, looking ahead several years, for approval by the Department of Labor and by the Department of Health, Education, and Welfare for areas traditionally under that Department's jurisdiction.

Each Governor would designate prime sponsors to administer manpower programs in major metropolitan and other appropriate areas—either the elected executive of the central city or an organization chosen by the elected heads of local governments representing 75 percent of the area's population. Local prime sponsors would prepare area plans for inclusion in State plans.

Three-Stage Decentralization. A single, flexible grant, instead of the many separate grants-in-aid now available, would be turned over to each State to administer—in steps, as specified conditions are met:

- 25 percent when the State names a "lead" agency and develops an approved manpower plan;
- 66⅔ percent when the State adds a comprehensive manpower agency to operate the unified programs and fulfills other requirements;
- 100 percent when a State meets objective standards of exemplary performance.

When a State does not meet the conditions set by the act for receiving a single grant, or is in only partial compliance, the Federal government would arrange directly for the operation of all or part of the programs in that State.

Allowance and Wages. The basic allowance to manpower trainees would be a percentage of average weekly pay in jobs covered by the State's unemployment compensation law — 40 percent in fiscal 1971, 45 percent in 1972, and 50 percent from 1973 onward. Family allowances would be $5 per dependent per week (up to a maximum of six dependents). Welfare recipients would continue to receive benefits, plus an extra incentive payment of $30 per month while in training.

Upon successful completion of an authorized training course lasting at least 15 weeks, trainees would receive a lump-sum incentive payment of twice their weekly allowance.

Work-experience trainees would be paid at least the Federal minimum wage; in employer-compensated on-the-job training, they would be paid the applicable minimum wage or the prevailing wage, whichever is higher.

State Apportionment. The Secretary of Labor would apportion among the States at least 75 percent of the basic appropriation. This apportionment would be in accordance with criteria to be published by the Secretary, with a guaranteed minimum "pass-through" to metropolitan areas. States and areas would have to provide $1 in cash or in kind for each $9 in Federal funds, unless this matching requirement is waived by the Secretary in special circumstances.

Another 5 percent of Federal funds would go into an incentive pool for States or local areas making "supplementary" efforts; that is, already carrying out exemplary programs and prepared to allocate new State funds for manpower activity. Here, the matching requirement is one State to each two Federal dollars.

Complementary Manpower Programs. Manpower research and experimental and demonstration programs would be authorized, along with comprehensive labor market information open to private as well as government users. Also provided for are a new manpower utilization program designed to ease labor shortages; program evaluation; staff training; and technical assistance. Twenty percent of the basic appropriation would be reserved for the Secretary of Labor to finance these activities, national projects, and Federal administration.

A computerized job bank to match jobs and workers would be established in each State, or on a regional basis for sparsely populated States. The job banks would have to be compatible; the Department of Labor would operate interstate phases of the total system.

Economic Stabilizer Feature. During any fiscal year in which national unemployment reaches 4.5 percent for 3 consecutive months, an additional sum equal to 10 percent of the amount appropriated would be triggered for use in manpower programs. If unemployment again dropped below 4.5 percent during that year, any triggered funds remaining would be returned to the Treasury.

Advisory Bodies. The National Manpower Advisory Committee would be reconstituted and a new Intergovernmental Advisory Council on Manpower, composed of representative Governors and local elected officials, would be established to advise the Secretary on Federal-State-local relations under this act.

Effect on Other Legislation. The Manpower Development and Training Act and title V-A of the Economic Opportunity Act (authorizing work experience and training) would be repealed. The activities authorized by this legislation, together with those provided for by title I-B of the EOA, would be incorporated in the MTA. Title I-A of the EOA would be transferred to the MTA – placing the Job Corps under the Department of Labor, where it now is by the delegation from the Office of Economic Opportunity. A new EOA title I-B would authorize an OEO program of research and experimental and demonstration activities on the employment and employment-related problems of the poor.

The following is a review of a number of the major OEO-sponsored programs in operation today:

COMMUNITY ACTION. The Community Action Program (CAP) is the "business corporation" of the poverty program. It operates a number of local projects in conjunction with the residents of depressed areas strictly for members of those groups caught up in the "poverty cycle." In practice, this means that residents of poor neighborhoods usually occupy 30% of the seats on city anti-poverty boards. The fundamental reasoning behind this system is that the poor can help themselves most effectively by mobilizing their potential political strength. Over 15 million needy Americans, including Indians from 118 tribes on 48 federal reservations, had participated in community action since the program's inception.

HEAD START. Project Head Start is designed to reach children of pre-school age who usually require additional training and assistance in order to begin on an even par with children from less disadvantaged backgrounds. Launched with a budget of only 17 million dollars and a target of 100,000 children, it has proved to be the poverty program's most striking success. In the summer of 1965, nearly 560,000 pupils in some 2,400 communities attended classes which, on the average, ultimately helped boost IQs eight to ten points within an encouragingly short period of time. HEAD START also offered children complete medical checkups, thus insuring against the sustained development of many undetected physical disabilities. (In Boston alone, for example, one-third of the children tested were found to have major physical ailments or mental problems requiring clinical treatment. Four out of five had serious tooth decay. On a nationwide level, fully 100,000 such children needed glasses.) In fiscal year 1970, Project Head Start intended to provide comprehensive services to one-half million low-income children at a cost of 326 million dollars. Through 1969, and since its inception, Project Head Start has serviced 3,321,243 children. Head Start has demonstrated that children of preschool age can learn more, faster, and at an earlier age than previously thought.

NEIGHBORHOOD YOUTH CORPS. The Neighborhood Youth Corps, established in 1964 under the Economic Opportunity Act, has three main components—an in-school program designed to provide paid jobs for youth inclined to drop out of school and thus encourage their continued school enrollment; a summer program with similar objectives; and an out-of-school program for those who have already left school and need work experience and remedial education to compete in the job market. The NYC has enrolled more than 2 million youth since its inception.

The in-school program, which served 134,000 youth in 843 projects in fiscal 1969, has displayed a mixed picture of failure and success, according to evaluations and research studies conducted by and for the Department of Labor.

Preparation for employment is given through skill training and work-experience which help enrollees acquire the work habits and attitudes necessary for holding a job. Project staff attempts to locate jobs for enrollees after they leave the program or assist them in going on to higher education or entering other training programs. Enrollees are encouraged to stay in school not only by the financial assistance provided but also through cultural enrichment activities and personal and vocational counseling.

In fiscal 1969 there were 591 out-of-school projects enrolling 120,000 young people who, on the average, were 18 years old, had completed 10 grades of school, and had

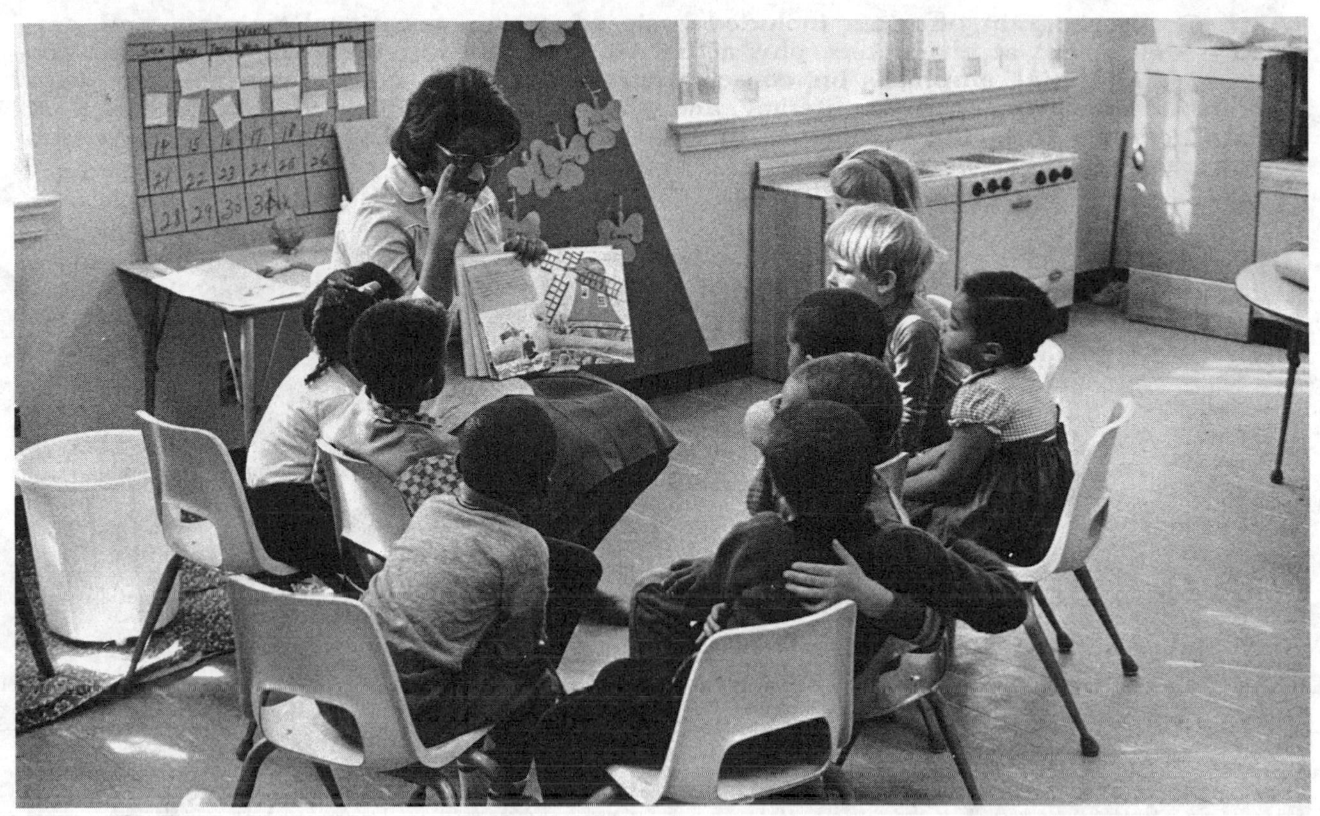

A Project Head-Start classroom.

dropped out of school at least a year prior to NYC enrollment. Under the new program design, out-of-school youth aged 18 and older will be channeled into other programs, including JOBS and the Job Corps. Focusing on 16- and 17-year-olds, the new NYC out-of-school program will provide intensive prevocational training with both academic and occupational content. This training will last at least a year, compared with an average of less than 6 months under the old program design. Upon reaching 18, most of the youth should be ready to compete in the open job market. If they are not, they will be directed to opportunities for further education and training. The goal of encouraging return to school has not been abandoned, but it is recognized that for many dropouts repeated failure in school in the past makes their return highly improbable.

JOB CORPS. The Job Corps, which was established in 1965, had the specific purpose of removing disadvantaged youth from home or community environments so deprived or so disruptive as to prevent their rehabilitation. Certain presumptions, in addition to that of need for new surroundings, guided the original program: That shifting youth from urban ghettos to rural settings would be rehabilitative; that intensive supportive services like basic education, "life skills" preparation, and activities to promote physical development and offer recreation experience were as important to these youth as skill training; and that each center should be substantially self-sufficient.

Immediately before restructuring of the Job Corps early in 1969, 82 rural conservation centers for young men were operating, with an average enrollment of 150. Of these, 75 were run by the Departments of Agriculture or the Interior, two by States, and five by the Commonwealth of Puerto Rico. There were six large centers for young men, five of which were operated by private companies (average enrollment 1,800). Although denoted as urban, these centers were some miles from cities, usually on abandoned military bases. The 17 urban centers for young women (with an average enrollment of about 500) were run mainly by private firms. Both a large men's center and a women's center were operated by a nonprofit educational foundation sponsored by the State of Texas; one women's center by the University of Oregon; and two women's centers by private, nonprofit organizations.

Job Corps program offerings included basic education, vocational training, and personal development at all centers, plus actual work experience, primarily at conservation centers. The initial emphasis on conservation work at the conservation centers later diminished in favor of more literacy and skill training, similar to that provided at "urban" centers from the beginning. In 1970 some 47,000 individuals will receive Job Corps training.

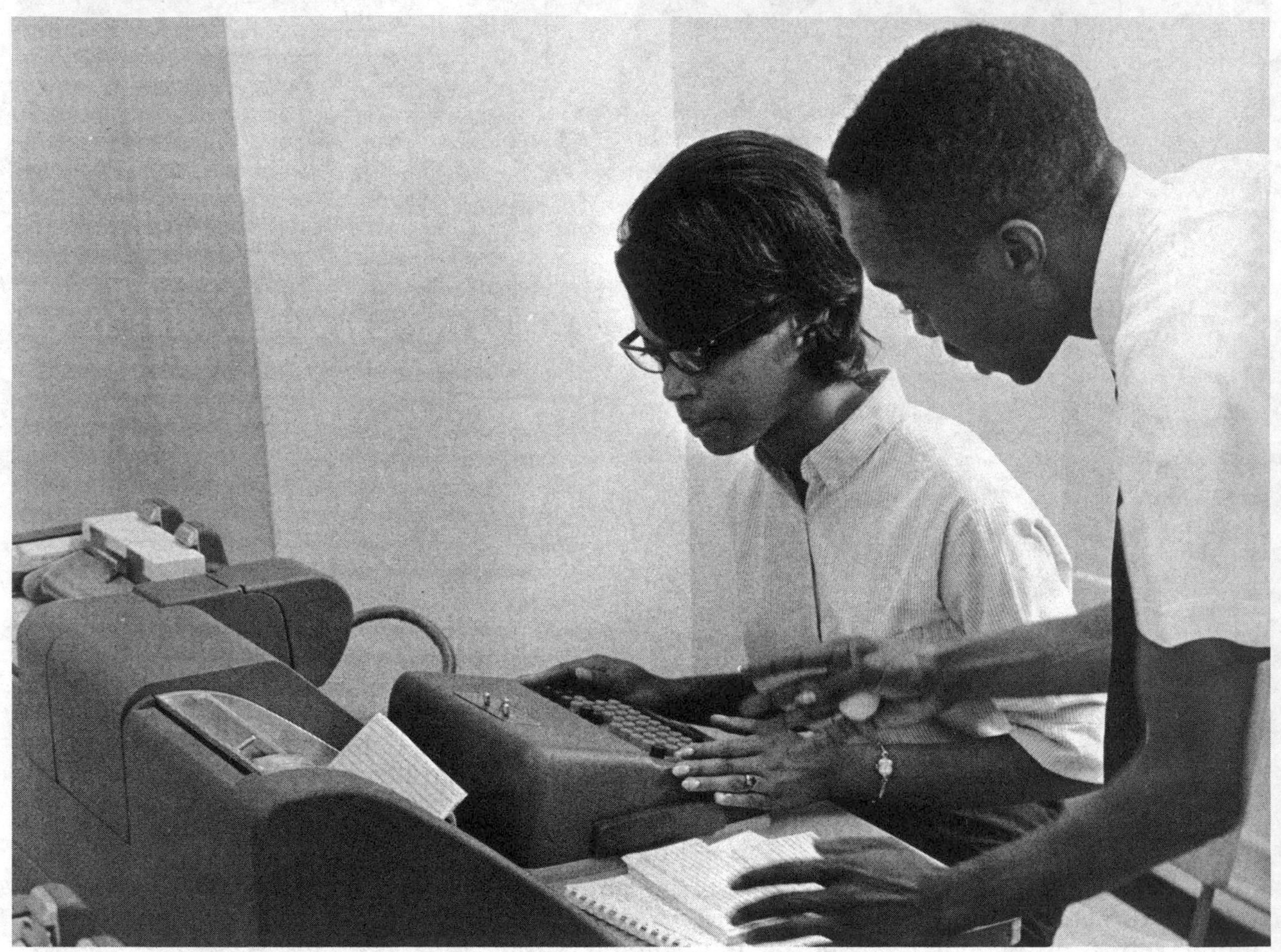

A key punch operator and her Job Corps instructor.

WORK INCENTIVE PROGRAM. The Work Incentive Program (WIN), established by the 1967 amendments to the Social Security Act, has in its brief history provided a foundation for the much larger program of family assistance that would be authorized by the Administration's proposed Family Assistance Act.

The goal of the WIN Program is economic independence for all employable persons aged 16 or over in families now receiving Aid to Families with Dependent Children (AFDC). WIN projects first enrolled clients, nearly 6,000 of them, in October 1968. By the end of fiscal 1969, the level of enrollments rose to 62,000, as 38 States and the Trust Territories participated in the program. Operations are beginning in the remaining States during fiscal 1970. Enrollments are expected to reach 150,000 by the end of fiscal 1971, making WIN one of the largest manpower programs. Nevertheless, it will be several years before WIN, or any successor program, can enroll the entire target population—the estimated 1.1 million adults on welfare rolls for whom jobs and job training are possible avenues to self-sufficiency.

The WIN Program is administered by the Department of Labor, through State employment security agencies. Local welfare agencies refer clients to employment service offices for interviewing, testing, counseling, and placement in jobs, job training, or special work experience, depending on their degree of job readiness. Stress is on helping clients to obtain meaningful jobs as rapidly as possible—at not less than the minimum wage or the prevailing wage, whichever is higher. Another possible alternative, for those least ready for training or jobs in the regular economy, is special work projects run by public or private nonprofit organizations, but so far such projects have been set up in only one State. All WIN enrollees receive their welfare benefits plus some training incentive payments. Welfare agencies continue to supply supportive medical and social services, including child day-care services.

A significant feature of the WIN Program has been the development and implementation, during its first year of operation, of the "team concept" of providing services, in accordance with an individual employability plan for each enrollee. Staff members are organized into a team, usually composed of a counselor, a manpower specialist, a work-training specialist, a coach, and a clerk-stenographer. Team members, each contributing his special knowledge and experience, work with the trainee to develop an employability plan, specifying the training and other services he will need to attain a job he both wants and is capable of performing.

VISTA. **Volunteers in Service to America, also known as the "domestic Peace Corps," recruits, selects, trains and channels the skills and concerns of more than 5,000 Volunteers a year into constructive projects which directly help relieve poverty in urban slums, rural areas, migrant camps and Indian reservations. It provides volunteer manpower to assist low-income citizens and communities striving to help themselves.**

Established under the Economic Opportunity Act of 1964, VISTA was designed to give individual Americans an opportunity to serve their country by joining the nation's effort in alleviating poverty.

As of 1970 an average of 4700 Volunteers will serve in more than 1,000 urban and rural communities in 49 states, the District of Columbia, Puerto Rico and the flag territories.

Any resident of the United States 18 years of age or older may apply. Married couples may serve together, if both are accepted. Volunteers may work with projects in any of the 50 states, the District of Columbia or the U.S. Territories. Volunteers are trained for six weeks—two weeks at one of 10 regional training centers and four weeks on the project under a supervisor. Volunteers are assigned to local, public and private agencies which have requested them. Sponsors include community action agencies, settlement houses, Indian Tribal Councils, Migrant Councils, State Economic Opportunity Offices, city governments, church groups, universities, the Urban Coalition and the Urban League.

Volunteers serve for a year, and may extend their service for a second year. They receive a living allowance, based on their basic needs and the area in which they serve. They also receive a $50 a month stipend, put aside for them and paid at the conclusion of their service.

All Volunteers are rated on the basis of an application. An increased effort is being made to recruit volunteers with professional and technical skills—educators, architect/planners, lawyers, business schools graduates, and health specialists.

Community Volunteers are recruited to work in the communities where they reside in order to combine their "inside leadership" with the "outside" skills of other Volunteers.

In the coming year Volunteers will be concentrated on programs in six areas of service—health, education and manpower, economic development, housing, community planning and social services.

The VISTA program received $32 million in funds for Fiscal Year 1969 and had 5,032 Volunteers in service at the close of the year. VISTA's budget for Fiscal Year 1970 is $35 million.

PUBLIC SERVICE CAREERS PROGRAM. The Public Service Careers (PSC) Program provides jobs in government service agencies for disadvantaged workers and also assists in upgrading employees in dead end, low-paid positions. The program operates within merit principles of personnel selection. Its aim is to overcome both the institutional barriers and the educational and other deficiencies which restrict the employment of disadvantaged people in the rapidly growing public sector.

The more than 80,000 units of State and local government in the United States had some 9 million employees in 1969 and may well employ over 11 million by 1975. These diverse government units use workers in a wide variety of occupations, some calling for highly specialized skills, others requiring little preparation. Examples of occupations for which disadvantaged persons can readily be trained include mail clerk, guard, switchboard operator, messenger, and payroll clerk.

To help meet growing manpower requirements and, at the same time, open permanent jobs for the disadvantaged, the PSC Program will pay part of the costs of on-the-job training and intensive supportive services for disadvantaged workers hired by public agencies. It will also help to finance upgrading activities. The fiscal 1970 appropriations bill includes $47 million for the PSC Program; this would fund about 26,000 enrollment opportunities.

The first PSC projects will be pilot or experimental in nature. They will use innovative techniques and will be designed to test program concepts. As experience is gained with these early projects, those which prove successful will be expanded and replicated in other parts of the country.

The PSC Program has four plans, or categories. The concept of "hire now, train later" is central to the first category, *employment and upgrading in State and local governments.* Disadvantaged workers will be hired for existing entry jobs. Their salaries and fringe benefits will be paid from the agency's regularly budgeted funds, while PSC funds will cover the extra costs involved in removing the barriers to employment of disadvantaged people. The barriers to be attacked include inadequate education; lack of occupational skills and of orientation to the world of work; problems with respect to health, transportation, and child care; and institutional barriers such as outmoded job structures and inadequate recruitment and training systems. Not only adults but also disadvantaged youth aged 17 or over may be hired under this plan.

The upgrading phase of the program will be restricted to agencies that have an entry project. This upgrading component is designed to help agency personnel staff in restructuring and modernizing their merit systems in order to facilitate employee advancement. Emphasis will be on the underutilized, low-income employee—the worker whose advancement has been hindered by artificial or only partly justified requirements.

Under the second option, *employment and upgrading in Federal grant-in-aid programs,* the Department of Labor will negotiate agreements with other Federal agencies to build arrangements for PSC projects into their grant-in-aid programs.

New Careers in human service, the third PSC component, will incorporate existing New Careers projects authorized under the Economic Opportunity Act.

Entry employment and upgrading in the Federal service, the fourth PSC component, is still in the developmental stage. It will focus primarily on expansion of the Civil Service Commission's new Worker-Trainee Supplement to the register of persons eligible for maintenance and service worker jobs.

UPWARD BOUND. This is an educational program which seeks to motivate non-college-bound high school students from low-income families to further their education at accredited academic institutions. Begun on a national basis in June 1966, UPWARD BOUND programs were supported by the Office of Economic Opportunity for the first year at 215 colleges, universities, and residential secondary schools. These academic institutions in 47 States, the Virgin Islands, Puerto Rico, and Guam, in turn committed themselves to serve 20,000 youngsters, most of whom had completed the 10th and 11th grades.

By 1968, approximately 300 institutions were participating in the program, in every State in the country, serving 26,000 students – many of whom were returning after previous enrollment in UPWARD BOUND.

The typical UPWARD BOUND program was offered by an educational institution combining secondary school and college teachers as faculty, making use of the physical facilities of a college campus for the students, and utilizing the experience and energies of college and university students as tutors.

Almost all UPWARD BOUND students were residents on college, university, and secondary school campuses for 6 to 8 weeks in the summer. During the academic year the UPWARD BOUND institutions continued to meet the students through classes on Saturdays, tutorial sessions during the week, and periodic cultural enrichment programs. In administering these programs, academic institutions have used a wide variety of teaching techniques.

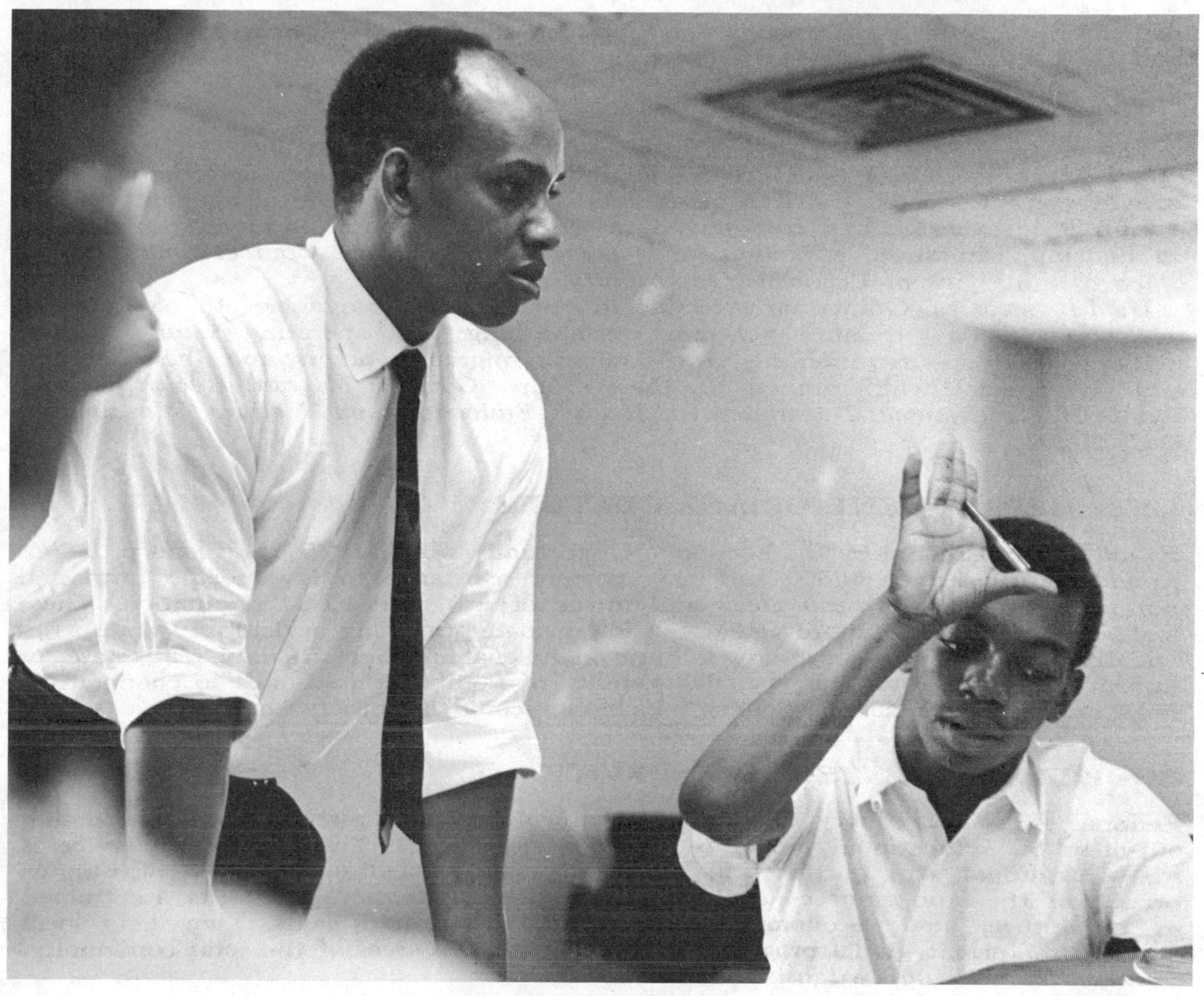

A classroom scene in Project Upward Bound at Columbia University.

Work Study. Originally a program administered by the Office of Economic Opportunity, Work Study (now under HEW) stimulates and promotes part-time employment for college and university students from low-income families. Participating institutions provide students with on-campus and off-campus employment for no more than 15 hours per week while classes are in session.

Adult Basic Education. The Adult Basic Education Program (also under HEW) provides for the elementary-level education of hard-core poor adults 18 and over. It is directed at the 11.5 million persons in the United States with less than a sixth-grade reading and writing level. The program also helps train teachers and develop instructional materials. Funds are granted to state educational agencies on the basis of the proportionate number of the adults in the state who fall into the above category. During the program's first year, the federal government contributed 90% of the funds, with the states supplying 10%. Thereafter, each source financed half the program.

Work Experience. This program provides constructive work-experience and training for unemployed heads of families with dependent children, and other needy persons. It is designed to provide thousands of Americans now on the welfare rolls with the experience and job training needed to secure gainful employment. Adult basic education, vocational instruction, medical care and social services for participants and their families are typical features of the program.

MIGRANTS

OEO Assistance. OEO assistance for migrant agricultural workers and their families provides grants, loans, and loan guarantees to assist state and local agencies, private nonprofit institutions, and cooperatives in setting up programs to meet special needs in housing, sanitation, education, and day care of children. *Contact your regional office of the Office of Economic Opportunity.*

Health Services. Grants are available to state and other agencies to pay part of the cost of (a) training personnel, establishing and operating family clinics, without residence requirements, for domestic migrant workers and their families and (b) special health projects for these groups. *Contact: Migrant Health Section, Public Health Service, Department of Health, Education, and Welfare, Washington, D.C. 20201.*

U. S. DEPARTMENT OF AGRICULTURE

Rural Loans. Created by the Economic Opportunity Act of 1965, rural loan programs provide loans up to $2500 and management assistance to low-income farm and non-farm families in rural areas and towns of less than 5,500 population. These loans are for making improvements on low-income-producing agricultural enterprises and for strengthening cooperatives. Farm loans enable farmers to buy real estate, or improve the operation and financial stability of family farms. Loans to cooperatives help small farmers buy machinery which they could not otherwise afford.

COOPERATIVE EXTENSION SERVICE

Federal, state, and county governments share in financing, planning, and conducting out-of-school educational programs to serve local needs. The Extension Service is the educational arm of the U.S. Department of Agriculture and the off-campus branch of the land-grant colleges and universities. Extension specialists are trained in agriculture, home economics, youth work, and related fields. They help local citizens organize regional programs to develop the resources of the total community. *Contact: Your county extension agent.*

SMALL BUSINESS ADMINISTRATION

Small Business Loans. This program provides loans of up to $15,000 for persons desirous of going into a new business, or expanding an existing business. It is especially designed for people who are unable to meet the credit requirements of other loan programs. Loans are generally made for retail or service enterprises, and are available only in areas served by a Small Business Development Center.

FOOD DISTRIBUTION

Special Milk Program. This program encourages consumption of fluid milk in public and private nonprofit schools, nursery schools, and so forth. State education agencies generally administer the program under agreements with the Department of Agriculture. The Food Distribution Division of the Department makes the payments directly to nonprofit private schools and child-care institutions in the states in which the program is not administered by the state agency. *Contact: Your state education agency or Food Distribution Division, Agricultural Marketing Service, Department of Agriculture, Washington, D.C.*

School Lunch Program. Grants are made to state education agencies for distribution to both public and nonprofit private schools participating in the lunch program. Participating schools must agree to make lunches available free or at a reduced cost for needy children. *Contact: Your state education agency or Food Distribution Division, Agricultural Marketing Service, Department of Agriculture, Washington, D.C.*

Commodity Distribution Program. To encourage consumption of agricultural products, commodities are donated to public and private agencies for distribution to low-income groups. Agreements are made between the Secretary of Agriculture and state agencies, which act as distributing agents. The Federal government pays costs to the point of delivery to the state-designated agency. The state, or local government, determines which institutions, families, or individuals are eligible, provides local storage and transportation, and handles local distribution. *Contact: Your state education agency or Food Distribution Division, Agricultural Marketing Service, Department of Agriculture, Washington, D.C.*

NATIONAL SCIENCE FOUNDATION

National Science Foundation Act of 1950 (P.L. 81-507). This Act supports programs aimed at improving scientific education through special institutes for teachers, curriculum planning, and projects to modernize materials of instruction. Secondary school and college students of high ability can participate in projects to secure added scientific experience. *Additional information may be obtained from the National Science Foundation, Washington, D.C. 20550.*

A GUIDE TO FEDERALLY ASSISTED MANPOWER TRAINING AND SUPPORT PROGRAMS[1]

Program title and date started	Legislative authorization (source of funds)	Administering agencies	Services provided and groups served[2]	Persons served in fiscal 1969[3]
Adult Basic Education (ABE), 1964.	Adult Basic Education Act of 1966. (Initially, Economic Opportunity Act of 1964.)	Department of Health, Education, and Welfare, Office of Education (through grants to State and local educational systems).	Provides basic education in classroom setting for persons 16 years of age and older, with less than eighth-grade achievement.	Estimated 523,000 enrollments.
Apprenticeship, 1937.	National Apprenticeship Act of 1937.	Department of Labor, Bureau of Apprenticeship and Training.	Encourages and assists employers and unions in developing apprenticeship programs for youth, including the unemployed and disadvantaged and inmates of correctional institutions.	Estimated 250,000 registered apprentices. June 1969.
Community Action Program (CAP), late 1964.	Economic Opportunity Act of 1964 (title II).	Office of Economic Opportunity.	Provides human resource development services, including manpower and related services and adult basic education, for persons below the poverty level (18 years of age and over for basic education).	108,000 enrollments in training and job placements; estimated 350,000 additional persons furnished manpower-related services.
Concentrated Employment Program (CEP), May 1967.	Economic Opportunity Act of 1964 and Manpower Development and Training Act of 1962.	Department of Labor. (Local prime sponsors are usually Community Action Agencies.)	Provides a coordinated program of manpower and supportive services for hard-core unemployed youth and adults in selected areas where they are concentrated.	127,000 first-time enrollments.
Employment Assistance for Indians, 1952.	Adult Vocational Training Act for Indians of 1956 and appropriations legislation of 1921.	Department of Interior, Bureau of Indian Affairs.	Provides vocational, apprenticeship, and on-the-job training and job placement assistance for Indians 18 years of age and over residing on or near reservations.	11,300 family units.
Federal-State employment service system, 1933.	Wagner-Peyser Act of 1933 and Social Security Act of 1935.	Department of Labor.	Recruits, tests, refers to training, and places job applicants; enhances the employability of disadvantaged persons; provides job market information. Serves entire labor force but focuses on the unemployed.	9,963,000 job applications.

See footnotes at end of table.

GUIDE TO FEDERALLY ASSISTED MANPOWER TRAINING AND SUPPORT PROGRAMS[1] – Continued

Program title and date started	Legislative authorization (source of funds)	Administering agencies	Services provided and groups served[2]	Persons served in fiscal 1969[3]
Job Corps, January 1965.	Economic Opportunity Act of 1964 (title IA).	Office of Economic Opportunity until delegated to Department of Labor, July 1, 1969.	Assists low-income disadvantaged youth 16 to 21 years of age, who require a change of environment to profit from training, to become more responsible, employable, and productive citizens through a residential program of intensive education, skill training, and related services.	53,000 first-time enrollments.
Job Opportunities in the Business Sector (JOBS), March 1968.	Manpower Development and Training Act of 1962 (title II) and Economic Opportunity Act of 1964 (title IB).	Cooperative arrangement between Department of Labor and National Alliance of Businessmen (NAB).	Encourages private industry to hire, train, retain, and upgrade hard-core unemployed and underemployed 18 years of age and over. Initially limited to major metropolitan areas but expanding to nationwide basis in fiscal 1970.	51,200 hired under contract with the Department of Labor; 119,200 noncontract hires.
MDTA institutional training, August 1962.	Manpower Development and Training Act of 1962 (title II).	Department of Labor; Department of Health, Education, and Welfare.	Provides occupational training or retraining in a classroom setting for unemployed and underemployed persons 16 years of age and over, at least two-thirds of them disadvantaged. Eligible persons receive training, subsistence, and transportation allowances.	135,000 first-time enrollments.
MDTA on-the-job training (OJT), August 1962.	Manpower Development and Training Act of 1962 (title II).	Department of Labor; Department of Health, Education, and Welfare, when projects include related classroom instruction.	Provides instruction combined with supervised work at the jobsite, under contracts with public and private employers, for unemployed and underemployed persons 16 years of age and over, at least two-thirds of them disadvantaged. Preference given to persons at least 18 years of age.	85,000 first-time enrollments.
MDTA part-time and other-than-skill training, last half of 1967.	Manpower Development and Training Act (title II) as amended in 1966.	Department of Labor; Department of Health, Education, and Welfare.	Provides upgrade training and training in job-related requirements, such as communication skills, work habits, and interpersonal relations for underemployed persons 16 years of age and over.	Included in MDTA institutional enrollments.
MDTA training for inmates of correctional institutions (pilot program), August 1968.	Manpower Development and Training Act (title II) as amended in 1966.	Department of Labor; Department of Health, Education, and Welfare.	Provides training, related supportive services, job placement assistance (including bonding), and followup for inmates of local, State, and Federal correctional institutions whose scheduled release follows completion of training by no more than 6 months. Some projects provide incentive and dependents' allowances.	Included in MDTA institutional enrollments (approximately 3,000).
MDTA training in redevelopment areas, 1961.	Manpower Development and Training Act (title II) as amended in 1965. (Initially Area Redevelopment Act of 1961.)	Department of Labor; Department of Health, Education, and Welfare; Department of Commerce.	Provides classroom and on-the-job training, associated with area economic development, for unemployed and underemployed residents of redevelopment areas designated by the Economic Development Administration.	Included in MDTA institutional and OJT enrollments (approximately 17,000).

See footnotes at end of table.

A GUIDE TO FEDERALLY ASSISTED MANPOWER TRAINING AND SUPPORT PROGRAMS[1] — Continued

Program title and date started	Legislative authorization (source of funds)	Administering agencies	Services provided and groups served[2]	Persons served in fiscal 1969[3]
Model Cities, 1966.	Demonstration Cities and Metropolitan Development Act of 1966 (title I).	Department of Housing and Urban Development. (Services also supplied by other agencies, principally Department of Health, Education, and Welfare; Office of Economic Opportunity; and Department of Labor.)	Improves the environment and general welfare of residents of designated urban poverty areas having a high incidence of disadvantaged persons. Usually includes manpower services.	Program largely in planning phase in fiscal 1969.
Neighborhood Youth Corps (NYC): in-school, summer, and out-of-school programs, January 1965.	Economic Opportunity Act of 1964 (title IB).	Department of Labor.	Encourages disadvantaged youth of high school age (14 to 21) to continue in or return to school by providing paid work experience. Emphasis shifting to job preparation, especially in out-of-school program. New design for out-of-school program limited to 16- and 17-year-old dropouts.	504,100 total first-time enrollments: 84,300 in-school; 345,300 summer; 74,500 out-of-school.
New Careers, first half of 1967. (To be absorbed by Public Service Careers Program during fiscal 1970.)	Economic Opportunity Act of 1964 (title IB) as amended in 1966.	Department of Labor.	Prepares disadvantaged adults and out-of-school youth for careers in human service fields (e.g., health and education) through work experience, education, and training.	3,800 first-time enrollments.
Operation Mainstream, December 1965.	Economic Opportunity Act of 1964 (title IB) as amended in 1965.	Department of Labor.	Provides counseling, basic education, and work experience for chronically unemployed adults in newly created jobs in community betterment and beautification, mainly in rural areas.	11,300 first-time enrollments.
Project 100,000, October 1966.	Military Service Acts.	Department of Defense.	Qualifies men with low academic achievement or remediable physical defects for military service who would not have been accepted except for lowering of entrance requirements.	103,000 served.
Public Service Careers (PSC), early in 1970.	Economic Opportunity Act of 1964 (title IB) as amended in 1966 and Manpower Development and Training Act of 1962 (title II).	Department of Labor.	Secures, within merit principles, permanent employment in public service agencies of disadvantaged, unemployed youth and adults and stimulates upgrading of current employees, thereby meeting public sector manpower needs.	New program in fiscal 1970; 27,800 training opportunities budgeted.
Special Impact, first half of 1968.	Economic Opportunity Act of 1964 (title ID) as amended in 1966 and 1967.	Office of Economic Opportunity. (Delegated to Department of Labor prior to July 1969.)	Provides manpower training as a component of economic and community development for poor and unemployed persons in selected urban poverty areas.	2,700 first-time enrollments.

A GUIDE TO FEDERALLY ASSISTED MANPOWER TRAINING AND SUPPORT PROGRAMS[1] — Continued

Program title and date started	Legislative authorization (source of funds)	Administering agencies	Services provided and groups served[2]	Persons served in fiscal 1969[3]
Transition, January 1968.	National Defense Act of 1916.	Department of Defense with cooperating agencies: Department of Labor (MDTA); Department of Commerce; Department of Justice; Civil Service Commission; Post Office Department; Veterans Administration.	Provides counseling, basic education, skill training, and placement assistance in civilian employment for enlisted personnel with approximately 6 months of active duty remaining. Priority given those with job handicaps. Participation voluntary.	66,600 trained; 302,000 counseled.
Vocational Education, 1917.	Smith-Hughes Act of 1917 (substantially amended in 1946) and Vocational Education Act of 1963 (substantially amended in 1968).	Department of Health, Education, and Welfare, Office of Education (through grants to State school systems).	Provides vocational training, primarily in a classroom setting, full or part time, for youth and adults, in or out of regular public schools. New emphasis on the poor and disadvantaged.	Estimated 8,034,000 enrollments: secondary schools, 4,344,000; post-secondary schools, 693,000; adults, 2,997,000.
Vocational Rehabilitation, 1920.	Vocational Rehabilitation Act of 1920 (substantially amended in 1943, 1954, 1965, and 1968).	Department of Health, Education, and Welfare.	Provides intensive rehabilitation services to enable youth and adults who are physically or mentally handicapped to obtain jobs commensurate with their maximum capabilities.	781,000 persons served; 241,400 persons rehabilitated.
Work Incentive (WIN), first half of 1968. (Replaced Work-Experience and Training Program under the EOA, title V, which operated from 1965 into fiscal 1969.)	Social Security Act of 1935 (title IVC) as amended in 1967.	Department of Labor. (Department of Health, Education, and Welfare is responsible for referral of enrollees and for furnishing social services during enrollment.)	Provides work, training, child care, and related services designed to move into productive employment employable persons on rolls of the Aid to Families with Dependent Children (AFDC) and AFDC—Unemployed Parents programs.	80,600 first-time enrollments.

[1] Includes primarily those Federal programs aimed at assisting the unemployed and the poor to obtain satisfactory employment. Some programs have additional objectives such as community betterment or meeting manpower demands in shortage occupations. Omits income maintenance programs such as unemployment insurance and workmen's compensation.

[2] "Disadvantaged" means poor, not having suitable employment, and either (1) a school dropout, (2) a member of a minority, (3) under 22 years of age, (4) 45 years of age or over, or (5) handicapped.

[3] The intent of this column is to show the general magnitudes of programs. Some entries are based on enrollment records; others are estimates.

FEDERAL EMPLOYMENT AND ASSISTANCE PROGRAMS TABLES

Table 74

Distribution of All Minority Groups Combined, by Pay Category As of November 30, 1967 and 1969

Pay System	1967 Number	1967 Percent	1969 Number	1969 Percent	Percent Change
All Pay Systems	496,672	100.0	500,536	100.0	0.8
General Schedule and Similar	173,951	35.0	181,726	36.3	4.5
Wage Systems	166,506	33.5	152,967	30.6	−8.1
Postal Field Service	151,602	30.5	158,945	31.8	4.8
All Other	4,613	0.9	6,898	1.4	49.5

Table 75

Percentage Distribution of Minority Groups Within Pay Category, As of November 30, 1969

Pay System	All Employment	Minority Group Status: Total	Negro	Spanish Surnamed	American Indian	Oriental	All Other
All Pay Systems	100.0	19.2	15.0	2.8	0.6	0.8	80.8
General Schedule and Similar	100.0	14.1	10.7	1.8	0.8	0.8	85.9
Wage Systems	100.0	27.6	19.7	5.7	1.0	1.2	72.4
Postal Field Service	100.0	22.7	19.5	2.5	0.2	0.6	77.3
All Other	100.0	11.9	9.8	1.2	0.3	0.7	88.1

Table 76

Increase (or Decrease) in the Number of Minority and Non-Minority Employees Between November 1967 and November 1969, By Grade Grouping

Grade Groupings	Non-Minority Number	Non-Minority Percent Change	Minorities Number	Minorities Percent Change
GS- 1—GS- 4	−48,286	−17.44	−9,635	−10.35
GS- 5—GS- 8	9,602	3.24	8,788	16.76
GS- 9—GS-11	19,157	6.93	5,423	27.06
GS-12—GS-13	22,279	12.26	2,468	36.42
GS-14—GS-15	8,719	14.78	721	48.42
GS-16—GS-18	−183	−3.39	10	11.49

Table 77

Percentage of Employees in Specified Grade Groupings, By Minority Group Status, As of November 1967 and November 1969

Grade Groupings	Non-Minority		Minority Groups			
			All		Negro	
	1969	1967	1969	1967	1969	1967
Total, All Grades	85.9	86.3	14.1	13.7	10.7	10.5
GS- 1—GS- 4	73.2	74.8	26.8	25.2	21.6	20.5
GS- 5—GS- 8	83.3	85.0	16.7	15.0	13.0	11.6
GS- 9—GS-11	92.1	93.2	7.9	6.8	5.1	4.3
GS-12—GS-13	95.7	96.4	4.3	3.6	2.5	2.1
GS-14—GS-15	96.8	97.5	3.2	2.5	1.5	1.2
GS-16—GS-18	98.2	98.4	1.8	1.6	1.2	1.2

Table 78

Percentage of Minority and Non-Minority Employees by Salary Groupings Under Wage Systems As of November 1967 and November 1969

Salary Groupings	Non-Minority		Minority Groups			
			All		Negro	
	1969	1967	1969	1967	1969	1967
Total, All	72.4	72.1	27.6	27.9	19.7	20.4
Up Thru $5,499	44.7	50.1	55.3	49.9	45.2	40.5
$ 5,500 Thru $6,999	59.1	70.6	40.9	29.4	31.9	20.8
$ 7,000 Thru $7,999	75.5	83.6	24.5	16.4	15.6	10.5
$ 8,000 Thru $8,999	82.5	90.1	17.5	9.9	10.4	5.4
$ 9,000 Thru $9,999	86.3	94.0	13.7	6.0	8.2	2.9
$10,000 Thru $13,999	91.9	96.1	8.1	3.9	4.2	1.3
$14,000 Thru $17,999	92.2	97.6	7.8	2.4	3.9	0.5
$18,000 And Over	96.2	97.8	3.8	2.2	2.1	...

Table 79

Increase (or Decrease) from November 1967-1969 in the Number of Minority and Non-Minority Employees By Salary Groupings Under Wage Systems

Salary Groupings	Non-Minority		Minorities	
	Number	Percent Change	Number	Percent Change
Up Thru $5,499	−47,474	−68.88	−42,186	−61.37
$ 5,500 Thru $ 6,999	−73,050	−45.28	−6,158	−9.16
$ 7,000 Thru $ 7,999	−16,928	−13.77	10,167	42.02
$ 8,000 Thru $ 8,999	55,347	144.85	15,539	370.11
$ 9,000 Thru $ 9,999	18,500	72.92	5,366	330.22
$10,000 Thru $13,999	32,185	256.60	3,435	670.90
$14,000 Thru $17,999	2,057	277.60	219	1,216.67
$18,000 And Over	698	775.56	29	1,450.00

Table 80

1969 Minority Group Study
All Agency Summary
Full-time employment as of November 30, 1969

Pay system	Total Full-time employees	Negro		Spanish surnamed		American Indian		Oriental		All other employees	
	Number	Number	Pct.	Number	Pct.	Number	Pct.	Number	Pct.	Number	Pct.
TOTAL WAGE SYSTEMS	554,443	109,356	19.7	31,778	5.7	5,392	1.0	6,441	1.2	401,476	72.4
Up thru $4,999	20,484	11,605	56.7	1,777	8.7	133	.6	357	1.7	6,612	32.3
$ 5,000–$ 5,499	27,528	10,100	36.7	2,088	7.6	329	1.2	170	.6	14,841	53.9
$ 5,500–$ 5,999	37,657	14,524	38.6	3,136	8.3	596	1.6	343	.9	19,058	50.6
$ 6,000–$ 6,499	51,992	16,379	31.5	2,971	5.7	581	1.1	585	1.1	31,176	60.5
$ 6,500–$ 6,999	59,678	16,780	28.1	3,773	6.3	741	1.2	627	1.1	37,757	63.3
$ 7,000–$ 7,999	140,355	21,896	15.6	9,665	6.9	1,398	1.0	1,406	1.0	105,990	75.5
$ 8,000–$ 8,999	113,357	11,755	10.4	5,706	5.0	898	.8	1,442	1.3	93,556	82.5
$ 9,000–$ 9,999	50,863	4,150	8.2	1,743	3.4	303	.6	795	1.6	43,872	86.3
$10,000–$11,999	38,554	1,696	4.4	750	1.9	233	.6	564	1.5	35,311	91.6
$12,000–$13,999	10,121	337	3.3	122	1.2	122	1.2	123	1.2	9,417	93.0
$14,000–$15,999	2,046	61	3.0	30	1.5	46	2.2	20	1.0	1,889	92.3
$16,000–$17,999	989	56	5.7	9	.9	11	1.1	4	.4	909	91.9
$18,000–$19,999	495	8	1.6	4	.8	—	—	2	.4	481	97.2
$20,000–$21,999	210	3	1.4	4	1.9	—	—	3	1.4	200	95.2
$22,000–$23,999	78	4	5.1	—	—	—	—	—	—	74	94.9
$24,000–$25,999	10	—	—	—	—	1	10.0	—	—	9	90.0
$26,000–$27,999	4	—	—	—	—	—	—	—	—	4	100.0
$28,000–$29,999	4	1	25.0	—	—	—	—	—	—	3	75.0
$30,000 and over	18	1	5.6	—	—	—	—	—	—	17	94.4

Table 81

1969 Minority Group Study
All Agency Summary
Full-time employment as of November 30, 1969

Pay system	Total Full-time employees	Negro		Spanish surnamed		American Indian		Oriental		All other employees	
	Number	Number	Pct.	Number	Pct.	Number	Pct.	Number	Pct.	Number	Pct.
TOTAL ALL PAY SYSTEMS	2,601,639	389,251	15.0	73,619	2.8	16,478	.6	21,188	.8	2,101,103	80.8
TOTAL GENERAL SCHEDULE OR SIMILAR	1,289,114	137,919	10.7	23,681	1.8	9,752	.8	10,374	.8	1,107,388	85.9
GS- 1 thru 4	312,047	67,252	21.6	9,180	2.9	5,051	1.6	1,993	.6	228,571	73.2
GS- 5 thru 8	367,410	47,838	13.0	7,855	2.1	2,616	.7	2,927	.8	306,174	83.3
GS- 9 thru 11	321,140	16,318	5.1	4,548	1.4	1,465	.5	3,131	1.0	295,678	92.1
GS-12 thru 13	213,261	5,370	2.5	1,618	.8	473	.2	1,784	.8	204,016	95.7
GS-14 thru 15	69,937	1,078	1.5	466	.7	140	.2	526	.8	67,727	96.8
GS-16 thru 18	5,319	63	1.2	14	.3	7	.1	13	.2	5,222	98.2
TOTAL WAGE SYSTEMS	554,443	109,356	19.7	31,778	5.7	5,392	1.0	6,441	1.2	401,476	72.4
Up thru $5,499	48,012	21,705	45.2	3,865	8.1	462	1.0	527	1.1	21,453	44.7
$ 5,500 thru $ 6,999	149,327	47,683	31.9	9,880	6.6	1,918	1.3	1,555	1.0	88,291	59.1
$ 7,000 thru $ 7,999	140,355	21,896	15.6	9,665	6.9	1,398	1.0	1,406	1.0	105,990	75.5
$ 8,000 thru $ 8,999	113,357	11,755	10.4	5,706	5.0	898	.8	1,442	1.3	93,556	82.5
$ 9,000 thru $ 9,999	50,863	4,150	8.2	1,743	3.4	303	.6	795	1.6	43,872	86.3
$10,000 thru $13,999	48,675	2,033	4.2	872	1.8	355	.7	687	1.4	44,728	91.9
$14,000 thru $17,999	3,035	117	3.9	39	1.3	57	1.9	24	.8	2,798	92.2
$18,000 and over	819	17	2.1	8	1.0	1	.1	5	.6	788	06.2

* Includes 4th class postmasters and rural carriers.

Table 82

1969 Minority Group Study
All Agency Summary Continued
Full-time employment as of November 30, 1969

Pay system	Total Full-time employees	Negro		Spanish surnamed		American Indian		Oriental		All other employees	
	Number	Number	Pct.	Number	Pct.	Number	Pct.	Number	Pct.	Number	Pct.
TOTAL POSTAL FIELD SERVICE	700,304	136,322	19.5	17,494	2.5	1,182	.2	3,947	.6	541,359	77.3
PFS- 1 thru 5*	595,654	124,173	20.8	15,847	2.7	992	.2	3,312	.6	451,330	75.8
PFS- 6 thru 9	84,311	11,343	13.5	1,485	1.8	165	.2	575	.7	70,743	83.9
PFS-10 thru 12	15,359	623	4.1	127	.8	22	.1	44	.3	14,543	94.7
PFS-13 thru 16	4,509	170	3.8	33	.7	3	.1	15	.3	4,288	95.1
PFS-17 thru 19	432	11	2.5	2	.5	—	—	1	.2	418	96.8
PFS-20 thru 21	39	2	5.1	—	—	—	—	—	—	37	94.9
TOTAL OTHER PAY SYSTEMS	57,778	5,654	9.8	666	1.2	152	.3	426	.7	50,880	88.1
Up thru $6,499	11,792	2,782	23.6	177	1.5	95	.8	50	.4	8,688	73.7
$ 6,500 thru $ 9,999	18,488	2,053	11.1	246	1.3	35	.2	190	1.0	15,964	86.3
$10,000 thru $13,999	11,809	496	4.2	112	.9	12	.1	85	.7	11,104	94.0
$14,000 thru $17,999	6,063	141	2.3	49	.8	5	.1	48	.8	5,820	96.0
$18,000 thru $25,999	5,935	132	2.2	61	1.0	1	—	39	.7	5,702	96.1
$26,000 and over	3,691	50	1.4	21	.6	4	.1	14	.4	3,602	97.6

* Includes 4th class postmasters and rural carriers.

Table 83

Characteristics of Enrollees in Federally Assisted Work and Training Programs, Fiscal Year 1969

Program	Percent of all enrollees						
	Women	Negro[1]	Age		Years of school completed		On public assistance[2]
			Under 22 years	45 years and over	8 or less	9 to 11	
Manpower Development and Training Act							
Institutional training	44	40	38	10	19	39	13
On-the-job training	35	35	36	10	17	35	5
Neighborhood Youth Corps							
In school	47	47	100	-------	20	79	30
Out of school	54	48	97	-------	27	69	32
Operation Mainstream	18	21	2	58	60	24	17
New Careers	70	61	8	12	10	40	35
Concentrated Employment Program	42	65	37	11	26	44	13
Job Opportunities in the Business Sector [3]	29	78	48	4	14	53	10
Work Incentive Program	60	40	16	10	31	41	100
Job Corps [4]	28	58	100	-------	38	50	27

[1] Substantially all the remaining enrollees were white, except in Operation Mainstream, JOBS, and Job Corps. In these programs, 10 to 12 percent were American Indians, Eskimos, or Orientals.

[2] The definition of "public assistance" used in these figures varies somewhat among programs (e.g., it may or may not include receipt of food stamps and "in kind" benefits). In the NYC program, it may relate to enrollees' families, as well as enrollees themselves.

[3] Includes only those enrollees in the JOBS Program who were hired by employers under contracts with the Department of Labor.

[4] Data relate to calendar year 1968.

Table 84

First-Time Enrollments[1] in Federally Assisted Work and Training Programs, Fiscal Years 1964, 1968–71

[Thousands]

Program	Fiscal years				
	1964	1968[2]	1969	1970 (estimated)	1971 (projected)
Total	278	1, 514	1, 761	1, 953	2, 126
Manpower Development and Training Act					
Institutional training	69	140	135	148	152
On-the-job training	9	101	85	81	30
Neighborhood Youth Corps		467	504	482	486
Concentrated Employment Program		54	127	152	155
Job Opportunities in the Business Sector[3]		6	51	75	173
Work Incentive Program			81	133	180
Job Corps		65	53	47	49
Vocational Rehabilitation	179	330	368	432	452
Other programs[4]	21	351	357	403	449

[1] Estimated number of new enrollees during the fiscal year, generally larger than the number of training or work opportunities programed because turnover or short-term training results in more than one individual using an enrolment opportunity. Persons served by more than one program are counted only once.

[2] Minor differences between certain of these figures and comparable data in append x table F-1 result from similar small differences in definition.

[3] Includes only those enrollees in the JOBS Program who were hired by employers under contracts with the Department of Labor.

[4] Includes a wide variety of programs, some quite small; e.g., Operation Mainstream, New Careers, Foster Grandparents, the Veterans Administration's on-the-job training and vocational rehabilitation programs, and the Transition Program and Project 100,000 of the Department of Defense. Data for some of these programs are estimated.

Source: Bureau of the Budget, "Special Analysis of Federal Manpower Programs."

Table 85

Enrollments in Manpower Programs at End of Month for Selected Months, 1968–70

[Thousands]

Program	1968			1969				1970
	April	July	October	January	April	July	October	January[1]
Total[2]	355. 3	534. 6	306. 1	380. 7	433. 6	678. 4	409. 2	426. 6
Manpower Development and Training Act								
Institutional training	60. 4	54. 0	48. 7	54. 5	56. 7	45. 8	38. 6	45. 8
On-the-job training	38. 9	40. 0	43. 3	37. 1	36. 9	38. 3	38. 4	39. 6
Neighborhood Youth Corps								
In school and summer	131. 9	330. 9	95. 5	99. 9	101. 6	356. 4	96. 1	103. 9
Out of school	57. 6	43. 6	43. 5	45. 7	47. 5	37. 1	31. 3	32. 1
Operation Mainstream	9. 0	10. 1	10. 0	8. 1	10. 2	10. 9	12. 8	12. 3
New Careers	3. 8	3. 5	3. 2	3. 3	3. 4	3. 4	3. 7	3. 8
Concentrated Employment Program	19. 8	18. 7	20. 6	50. 8	70. 5	76. 7	68. 6	54. 9
Job Opportunities in the Business Sector[3]				14. 0	20. 4	27. 9	33. 7	37. 0
Work Incentive Program			6. 2	33. 8	56. 2	62. 7	67. 0	77. 7
Job Corps	32. 5	32. 2	33. 1	32. 9	29. 8	18. 4	18. 9	19. 5

[1] Preliminary.

[2] Includes only programs administered by the Department of Labor. Persons enrolled in Special Impact programs, not shown separately, are included in the totals.

[3] Includes only those enrollees in the JOBS Program who were hired by employers under contracts with the Department of Labor.

Note: Detail may not add to totals due to rounding.

PERSPECTIVES ON BLACK EDUCATION

Education Prior to 1861
Educational Efforts of the Civil War Period
Education Since the Civil War
Chronology of Education
Scholarships, Loans and Awards
Elementary and Secondary Education Act
Selected Programs for Disadvantaged Children under ESEA
Higher Education Act
Vocational Education
Civil Rights Institutes
National Defense Education Act
Handicapped
Patterns of Segregation in U.S. Public Schools
Professional Education
Predominantly Black Institutions, Colleges and Universities in the U.S.
Education Tables
Education Films

The dramatic expansion of educational facilities across the country in the post-World War II decades has had a great impact on the scope of the Negro's educational horizons. Nevertheless, as in most other areas, the Negro at all levels of the educational system is still required to contend with difficulties and hardships often unknown to his white counterpart. The great gains which Negroes have made in the 20th century in the midst of enormous and, at times, encouraging change suggest—rather than confirm—the achievement of equality. Though the prospects for continuing breakthroughs cannot be dimmed regardless of which President holds office, this is not to say that black students are no longer subject to grave indignities and severe difficulties. Pockets of segregation are still identifiable despite legislative, judicial, and administrative efforts to break them down; black studies programs, though a viable entity, distress too many white educators and inflame too many black radicals to become conventional educational experiences.

EDUCATION PRIOR TO 1861

Many Africans who came to the English colonies in 1619 as indentured servants were previous residents of West Africa, which had had a brilliant cultural and educational history before slavery. The West African Empire of Ghana, which became the Empire of Mali, was mentioned by Arab sources in 800 A.D. Timbuktu and Gao were prominent cultural centers of the Moslem world for 300 years. A school system was established in the 6th century by Emperor Askia Mohammed Toure, ruler of Songhay from 1493 to 1512. Black students and others in the Moslem world looked to the University of Sankore at Timbuktu as a major institution of higher learning. Accomplished scholars taught law, history, medicine, and literature, including the works of Plato and Aristotle.

Early supporters of the Negro in the United States were masters who desired to increase the economic efficiency of their labor supply, sympathetic persons who wished to help the oppressed, and zealous missionaries who taught slaves English so that they might learn the principles of the Christian religion. The Church of England which founded the Society for the Propagation of the Gospel in Foreign Parts was instrumental in teaching reading, prayers, and catechism to blacks and Indians of the colonies. Other religious groups such as the Quakers advocated the education of the Negro. Two patterns of education emerged: 1) Instruction by religious groups and 2) Emphasis on occupational training.

The young slave Frederick Douglas being taught to read by his owner, Mrs. Auld of Baltimore

Anthony Benezet, opponent of slavery and a teacher of black youth in colonial America.

Early Negro education met great difficulties. Alexander Garden, Commissioner of North and South Carolina and the Bahamas, wrote of insuperable educational problems relating to age, race, and language, and suggested in 1740 that only those born in the colonies and under the age of 10 be educated. South Carolina, for instance, received most of her slaves directly from Africa during the 18th century. Over 100,000 black people were imported directly to South Carolina and Georgia prior to 1808. Charleston served as a direct point of landing by ships sailing from Africa. Many masters observed that slaves could be more useful if they acquainted themselves with the language and customs of the colonies rather than African customs and speech.

In spite of statutes which prohibited education of Negroes, progress was made in urban areas. The growth of the American city made possible the contact of blacks with many people, affording an opportunity to embrace Western civilization. Many slaves became mechanics, clerks, overseers. Mulattoes, protected from the rigors of the slave codes, helped their fellow blacks read, write, and improve themselves. Urban Negroes had further advantage in their opportunity to attend well-regulated Sunday schools which, though cloaked with the purpose of instructing blacks in the Christian religion, permitted, in many cases, the teaching of reading and writing.

Free Negroes in Charlestown and other metropolitan areas established societies and organizations devoted to the cause of Negro education. One of the earliest was the Brown Fellowship Society organized in 1790 which had as its purpose the construction and maintenance of schools for Negro children. Others established in Charlestown were the Humane and Friendly Society (1802), the Minors Moralist (1803), and the Unity and Friendship Society. Benevolent societies of free Negroes advanced the cause of education until 1830-1835 when stringent laws were passed by state legislatures limiting Negro education because of slave uprisings by Denmark Vesey and Nat Turner.

The Principles of the Rights of Man, which preceded the Revolution of 1776, affected the thinking of many Americans, white and black. As early as 1787, Prince Hall, a free black and Boston property owner, petitioned the city to establish schools for black children equal in quality to those for whites. The increase in free black people in the North and South provided pressure for more Negro education. In 1829, Congressmen and Washington citizens founded the African Education Society with the avowed object of giving Negroes academic, mechanical, and agricultural skills. Whites feared that slaves would read the literature of the French and Haitian revolutions and writings of abolitionists. Prudence Crandall met mob resistance in trying to integrate her Canterbury, Connecticut girls' school. In spite of discouragements, black schools continued to function. In 1842, a school for Negro and Indian boys was opened in Ohio by Augustus Wattles of the American Anti-Slavery Society and Samuel Emlen, a Quaker.

Although general education for Negroes had been forbidden in the South and limited in the North, many schools had been established by 1861 (see Chronology).

EDUCATIONAL EFFORTS OF THE CIVIL WAR PERIOD

The Civil War successfully removed legal prohibitions against the education of the Negro and freed some 4,000,000 persons. As Union armies penetrated the South, blacks looked to the federal government for help, refuge, and education. In May 1863, the War Department established a Bureau of Colored Troops with schools devoted to the training of commanders of black regiments. The idea of using the army as a training school for freedmen was voiced by Representative John Hickman of Pennsylvania. Declaring that the rebellion would not have broken out if poor whites and colored people of the South had been better educated, he introduced a bill on January 27, 1863, to increase the number of colored regiments to 300. Although Congress defeated the proposal, the idea that the army could serve as a potential school for Negroes gained many supporters. Congress later declared that proceeds from rebel property were to be used to establish a system of education in the South provided that education taught that liberty was the fundamental principle of the government of the United States, and that education was available to all persons without regard to race, sex, or color.

The African Methodist Episcopal Zion Church school for black children in Charleston, South Carolina in 1866.

Lincoln was well aware of his educational responsibilities towards blacks. As a member of the House of Representatives, he declared on January 10, 1849, that Negroes should be apprenticed and educated in the District of Columbia. Later, on August 5, 1863, he expressed his concern to General Nathaniel Banks in Louisiana that provision be made for the education of young blacks. The Proclamation of Amnesty and Reconstruction provided that states must include provisions to provide education for freedmen in order to be restored to the Union. Lincoln further showed his interest in the education of Negroes by signing a bill on June 25, 1864, providing schools for Negro children in the District of Columbia.

Many opposed the education of blacks. In April 1860, Jefferson Davis declared that he was opposed to the use of tax money to put Negro and white children on the same level. Southerners feared genuine education for poorer people, black or white. Davis declared that colored people had already been educated by means of 1) regular and systematic work 2) language and 3) the religion of a civilized country. On March 18, 1863, Secretary of War Stanton appointed an American Freedman's Inquiry Commission to investigate the conditions of the black population. Robert Dale Owen of Indiana, Colonel James McKay of New York, and Samuel Howe of Massachusetts traveled along the Eastern seaboard and reported that black refugees were very concerned about schools for their children and religious instruction for themselves. In Alexandria, Virginia, one of the first acts of freed Negroes was to establish schools at their own expense. Many declared, however, that they still wished the presence and teaching of educated whites.

Four stages mark the attitude of the federal government toward the Negro during the first two years of the Civil War: 1) The Negro was ignored 2) The Negro was declared contraband 3) The Second Confiscation Act provided that the Army could receive Negroes and take them from their masters 4) Emancipation Proclamation and Federal Guardianship.

Congress was concerned that an immense Negro population without education could not know how to use freedom wisely. With Union victories, the aid of Northern philanthropy was sought to provide funds for experiments in mass education of freedmen. General Frederick Augustus Mitchel, Commander of the Department of the South, epitomized the feeling of the times when he said to a Negro congregation, "There is a new time coming for you colored people, a better day is dawning for you oppressed and downtrodden blacks. If now you are unwilling to help yourselves, nobody will be

At the close of the Civil War informal education by the army took place to inform black people of their new status.

willing to help you. I believe the good God will lift you up to a higher level than you have yet occupied, so that you and your children may become educated and industrious citizens."

Hundreds of schools were founded in colored regiments, contraband camps, towns, and plantations. That a public school system for Negroes appeared in the South prior to the establishment of the Freedman's Bureau and with little available money is one of the wonders of American history.

An important experiment in black education took place in the Sea Islands located between Charleston and Savannah on the Atlantic seaboard. This includes St. Helena, Port Royal, Morgan, Paris, Ladies and Phillips Islands. Lesser islands including Folly, James, and others in Georgia are known collectively as "Port Royal." Possession of these islands by General Thomas W. Sherman was accomplished in November of 1861 when contraband camps were established at Hilton Head, South Carolina. Classes for pupils six to 15 years of age were organized in Beaufort, the largest town in the area, by the Reverend Peck of Massachusetts and Reverend French of New York. Black teachers supervised educational activities, but were hampered by lack of funds and supplies. General Sherman divided the territory into districts and asked Congress for help in meeting administrative and educational problems of the black population. Congress failed to act, but sympathetic attention was received from relief societies in Philadelphia, New York, and Boston.

The first was known as the Educational Commission and later became the New England Freedmen's Aid Society, organized in Boston on February 7, 1862. Its object was the intellectual improvement of persons released from slavery and the promotion of education among the blacks. Supporters included Edward Everett Hale, Samuel Cabot, Charles Barnard, William Lloyd Garrison and William Cullen Bryant. New York City organized the National Freedmens Relief Association on February 20, 1862. This was followed by the Port Royal Relief Committee, later known as the Pennsylvania Freedmens Relief Association, founded in Philadelphia on March 3, 1862. Many societies confederated in 1863 to form the United States Commission for the Relief of the National Freedmen which, in 1865, became the American Freedmans Aid Union.

General Saxton in the Department of the South was instrumental in helping Negroes advance themselves. He declared that black children showed as much aptitude and learning as the average of children in the North and were eager to learn to read and write. Numerous and orderly schools were established in which classes were often held with teachers dispensing clothing and food from their own pocket. Cotton barns, sheds, tents, were utilized. School farms were organized and the profits used for educational purposes. Desks were often boards thrown across chairs. Yellow fever and smallpox caused hardship and even death among pupils and teachers alike. By March 1863, Port Royal had 30 schools with 40 teachers and an enrollment of over 3,000 children from eight to 12 years of age. Hillards *Second Primary Reader* and Wilsons *Second Reader* were among the 36,000 books sent by Northern agencies to the South.

The Port Royal experiment was important in that it 1) Destroyed the myth of the ineducability of the Negro and 2) demonstrated the necessity that the Negro be fully integrated into American society.

Elsewhere, in North Carolina and Virginia, General Benjamin Butler encouraged the construction of school houses and school farms and laid the foundations of a labor and educational system in the area. By March 1865, school attendance for 5-14 year olds was made compulsory. General Ulysses Grant and Chaplain John Eaton in the Department of Tennessee and the State of Arkansas allowed teachers from relief societies to assume a multiplicity of duties. Schools for Negroes were prohibited by municipal law in Memphis. By 1865, however, 51 schools with 105 teachers and 7360 pupils were engaged in carrying out a humane educational policy. The Department of the Gulf under the direction of General Nathaniel Banks created Boards of Education with the power to levy school taxes to defray educational expenses for the contrabands of Louisiana. School commenced at 8:45 and ended at 2:30, with teachers receiving a remuneration of 65 dollars per month. Negro soldiers had their own schools which were supervised by black officers and chaplains.

Statistics show that, by the summer of 1865, South Carolina had 10,000 pupils, 48 schools, 76 teachers, of whom 24 were black. Additional data includes Georgia with 3,603 pupils, 69 schools, 69 teachers of whom 43 were black; Florida with 1,900 pupils, 30 schools, and 19 teachers, Arkansas with 10 schools, 19 teachers, 1,393 pupils; Mississippi with 31 schools, 50 teachers, and 3,396 pupils; Western Tennessee with 56 teachers, 4,095 pupils and Alabama with 13 schools, 30 teachers, and 1,620 pupils.

EDUCATION SINCE THE CIVIL WAR

The Congress on July 16, 1865, passed a bill which made education an authorized function of the Bureau of Refugees, Freedmen, and Abandoned Lands (Freedmen's Bureau which came into existence on March 3, 1865). General Oliver Otis Howard was appointed Commissioner of the Bureau and announced his intention of furthering Negro education by working with benevolent societies in dispensing aid. Later, Howard University was named in honor of this commissioner who, with John M. Langston, a black lawyer graduate of Oberlin College and Inspector-General of schools, worked to establish educational facilities for Negroes. The influence of the Bureau declined after 1870 and ceased in 1874.

A decade after the Civil War, the character of the educational program for Negroes had changed. This was due to the following: 1) State education authorities began to take over administration of schools 2) disagreement on the question of segregation of the races, and 3) controversy as to whether schools should be purely educational or parochial. Churches withdrew support from national organizations and established denominational societies. This proved helpful to blacks in that many permanent institutions which later became senior colleges were established. Lack of general public support led to the establishment of private funds such as the Peabody and John F. Slater Funds (see Chronology). Cooperation between philanthropic organizations and denominational societies made possible the growth of higher education for Negroes, especially in the South.

Successful efforts to establish educational institutions were those that made no attempt at integration. The Supreme Court declared in 1883 that the Fourteenth Amendment enjoined states, not individuals, from discrimination. The decision of 1896 holding that separate and equal facilities for Negroes was constitutional provoked controversy for many years. In 1899, the Court ruled that Richmond County, Georgia, could operate white schools, although there were no schools for black children. It was not until 1954 that the doctrine of "separate but equal" was declared unconstitutional, thus ending the legality of segregated facilities.

Not all black Americans had sought integration. Booker T. Washington, speaking to the Atlanta Exposition in 1895, gained white support by arguing that education would enable blacks to maintain a separate society while advancing the progress of the nation as a whole. On the other hand, William Edward Burghardt Dubois a founder of the NAACP, demanded total equality, declaring that Negro schools were generally inferior

"UNION IS STRENGTH."

DEATH TO US,
FUN FOR THEM.
PUBLIC SCHOOL
POLITICAL INFLUENCE
ROMAN CATHOLIC
ROMAN CATHOLIC NAVY
DIPLOMATIC
ACADEMY FOR THE
COLLEGIE
HONEST VOTES
FRAUDULENT VOTES
JUSTICE
$000000
THE RICH AND POORMANS TAXES $1000
STATE MONEY
TAX LEVY FOR SCHOOLS

DISTRIBUTION OF THE SECTARIAN FUND.

SECTARIAN BITTERNESS.

to white ones.

Between 1900 and 1930, black teachers earned $100-$400 per year, compared with $200-$900 for their white counterparts. Segregated schools were not providing education equal to that of white schools. It was not until the Depression that federal interest in black education increased. The Civilian Conservation Corps, the National Youth Administration, and the Works Progress Administration helped educate many Negroes. Mary McLeod Bethune, who helped create Bethune-Cookman College in Florida, directed the National Youth Administration's Division of Negro Affairs. More than 600,000 black students participated in educational activities. 60,000 Negroes gained occupational skills in work-study programs. 200,000 Negroes were trained by the Civilian Conservation Corps for employment in forestry and related fields. Federal projects enabled black artists to pursue their vocation. Well-known WPA artists included Langston Hughes, Charles Wright, Ralph Ellison, and Richard Wright.

By 1970, progress was apparent. But the ultimate aim of excellent and nonsegregated education for all the schools in the United States had not been achieved. The National Guard was continually used to control public defiance of attempts to desegregate schools. Southern states enacted 145 laws between 1954 and 1958 to protect segregation. New Rochelle, New York, was ordered to integrate its schools which had been segregated by pattern of attendance areas. Berkeley, California effected an integrated school plan. Dr. Harvey Scribner, a white educator and former Superintendent of Schools for Teaneck, New Jersey, sought educational change and innovation by creating a central integrated sixth grade school which was successfully put into operation in an all-white suburb. Elsewhere, integration was met with sit-ins, demonstrations, and boycotts, though in a number of places it was put into effect quietly and successfully. Black mothers demonstrated in Chicago, New York, and elsewhere in the nation against poor educational conditions and de facto segregation. In New York, Intermediate School 201 became a center of controversy concerning integration, local responsibility, and quality education. Community control became a rallying cry and black people tried to gain control of the educational institutions which affected them.

The federal government advanced the cause of the Negro by initiating legislation such as Title I of the Elementary and Secondary Education Act of 1965 and Title IV of the Civil Rights Act of 1964, outlawing discrimination in the use of federal funds for educational projects. Title IV made funds available for institutions engaged in desegregation. New problems for black people arose. Between May and September, 1965, over 660 black teachers were displaced for reasons relating to integration. By 1966, 5,000 black teachers had been adversely affected.

Shifts in housing patterns imposed *de facto* resegregation. *De facto* segregation results from residential housing patterns and does not violate the constitution. By contrast, *de jure* segregation arises by law or by the deliberate act of school officials and is unconstitutional. In 1955 (*Briggs* v. *Elliott*) a District Court held that the Constitution does not require integration. It merely forbids the use of governmental power to enforce segregation. In 1966, another court pointed out that this doctrine had been used to justify techniques for perpetuating school segregation. In 1969, the Fourth Circuit Court of Appeals invalidated the *Briggs* v. *Elliott* dictum. Thus, in 1970, a California state court ordered the Los Angeles school board to establish a virtually uniform racial balance throughout its 711-square-mile district with 775,000 children in 561 schools.

President Nixon declared in March, 1970, that there is a constitutional mandate that dual school systems and other forms of *de jure* segregation be totally eliminated. School boards were requested to act in good faith and formulate plans of desegregation which best suited their needs. To obtain the benefits of integration without depriving the child of his neighborhood school, it was suggested that a portion of a child's educational activities be shared with children from other schools. Many experts considered integration a vital aid to educating the disadvantaged. James S. Coleman, author of the 1966 study on educational equality, called for massive programs to aid blacks in the 1970's.

Among the new educational ideas which have been advocated are: after-school schools and "voucher systems" in which parents, black and white, can "buy" the kind of education they choose in a "market" that would generate the establishment of a variety of innovative schools. Integration and availability of educational opportunity for black and white is the ultimate goal.

School districts implementing voluntary desegregation plans are presently making

Culturally disadvantaged children are able to get a "Head Start" through the federal government's program of the same name.

significant and effective progress in providing an equal educational opportunity. In 1968, 23.4 percent of the Negro students in the nation's public elementary and secondary schools attended schools of predominantly white (non-minority) enrollment, with 61 percent isolated in 95 through 100 percent minority schools.

In 1968, there were 55 school districts which submitted acceptable plans under Title VI, which called for desegregation in the 1968-69 school year. Of the 35,815 Negro students in these districts, 31,089, or 86.8 percent attended schools of predominantly white enrollment. This compared with the 23.4 percent desegregation figure nationally, the 18.4 percent figure for 11 Southern states, and the 10.5 percent figure for the five Southern states of Alabama, Georgia, Louisiana, Mississippi and South Carolina.

In 1969, the indicated volume of desegregation in formerly dual school system states accelerated significantly, with more than 200 Title VI plans calling for complete desegregation in the 1969-70 school year accepted, and over 100 calling for substantial desegregation steps in the same year. The average student population in these districts was considerably higher than in 1968. Early results show that, among 20 districts in Florida which submitted plans for 1969, the desegregation rate climbed from 45.1 percent in 1968 to 63.5 percent in 1970. In Georgia, the desegregation rate among 31 districts climbed from 26.7 percent in 1968 to 59.7 percent in 1970. Similarly, in Mississippi, among 14 districts reporting, the rate climbed from 31.7 percent to 69.1 percent.

Although desegregation ratios have improved in former dual system states, stark ethnic isolation in schools continues. When white non-minority enrollment patterns are compared with minorities, data shows that 21 percent of the non-minority students are in 50 percent or more minority schools, while 16.5 percent are in 100 percent white schools. Some 65.6 percent are in 95 through 100 percent white schools. In a regional study of Negro segregation, there is a great variation in the number of Negroes attending 100 percent minority schools, from six heavily industrial Northern states, where 15.4 percent of the Negroes attended 100 percent minority schools, to six Border states and the District of Columbia, where 25.2 percent of the Negroes attended 100 percent minority schools, to five deep Southern states, where 81.9 percent of the Negroes attended 100 percent minority schools.

The years 1969-1970 saw the percentage of blacks in white schools double. Black school board members, superintendents, and county officials will continue to grow. The notion that effective steps can be taken through education to bring American society together remains the greatest challenge of the time.

CHRONOLOGY OF NEGRO EDUCATION

1634 *French Catholics are instrumental in providing instruction for laborers in Louisiana.*

The French and Spanish had liberal attitudes toward slaves. Many were respected for their worth and given privileges as freemen. Estevanico, an enlightened slave sent by Niza, the Spanish adventurer, to explore Arizona, was a favored servant of this class. French Jesuits, among them missionary Paul LeJeune, promote educational opportunities for Negroes.

1685 *Virginia laws prohibiting slaves from attending Quaker meetings for the purposes of instruction are denounced by the Reverend Morgan Goodwyn in a sermon preached in Westminster Abbey, London.*

1695 *Reverend Samuel Thomas of Goose Creek Parish, South Carolina, instructs Negroes in reading and writing. Enlisting community support, he is able to educate many blacks in his parish.*

1700 *Monthly meeting for Negroes established by William Penn.*

Penn advocated the emancipation of slaves that they might have every opportunity for improvement. Many colonists were teaching slaves and free Negroes.

1701 *Chief Justice Sewall of Massachusetts publishes anti-slavery pamphlet,* Selling of Joseph.

The Sewall pamphlet represented the first direct attack on slavery in New England. One of the few Puritans to espouse the Negro cause, he urged emancipation and education. Earlier, Cotton Mather and other Massachusetts Puritans made efforts to organize black people when they founded the Society of Negroes in 1693. Later, in 1717, Mather began an evening school for Indians and Negroes.

1701 *Organization by the Church of England of the Society for the Propagation of the Gospel in Foreign Parts for the purpose of converting and educating Negro slaves.*

Although merchants and other vested interests pressured religious groups in America to sanction slavery, the churches endorsed policies of Christianization which proved to be the first great step in providing educational opportunity for the Negro. Dr. Thomas Bray was sent to Maryland by the Bishop of London in 1696, and exerted a profound influence in the conversion and education of Negroes.

1704 *Founding of catechizing school at Trinity Church in New York City under the direction of Elias Neau.*

Instruction was given regularly at this church until 1712, when blame for a local slave uprising was attributed by some masters to Neau's work. While enrollment was temporarily curtailed, instruction continued until the middle of the century despite Neau's death in 1722.

1724 *A document encouraging the Christian education of Indian, Negro & mulatto children is circulated in Virginia.*

The document stated that slaves should be educated and that baptized children who understood the Christian religion should receive exemption from taxes until the age of 18.

1728 *Nathaniel Piggott announces that he is opening a school for "instruction of Negroes in reading, catechizing, and writing."*

The Penn School for black children on St. Helena Island, South Carolina, established and operated by the Quakers soon after the Civil War.

1738 *Moravians establish a mission exclusively for Negroes.*
A mission for Negroes was established by the Moravian brethren at Bethlehem, Pennsylvania. A painting of a group of their converts prior to 1747 shows, among others, two Negroes, Johannes of South Carolina and Jupiter of New York.

1743 *School for Negro youths opens in Charlestown, South Carolina.*
Mr. Garden's school for training Negro youths opened in Charlestown, South Carolina on September 12, 1743. Supported almost entirely by the people of Charlestown, the school exerted a profound influence throughout the province. Individual missionaries saw an earnest desire among Negro parents to have their children instructed. Fifty-five children were taught during the day and 15 adults in the evening. Mr. Bray died on September 27, 1756.

1745 *French* Code Noire *makes it incumbent upon masters to enlighten their slaves in order that they might grasp the principles of Christianity.*

1747 *Presbyterians begin religious instruction of Negroes in Virginia.*
In 1740, Hugh Bryan, a wealthy Presbyterian, showed interest in the education of blacks and, by 1755, was operating a school for slaves.

1749 *Reverend Thomas Bacon preaches four sermons in Talbot County, Maryland, declaring that, next to one's children, slaves enjoyed certain rights, including the right to knowledge and enlightenment.*

1750 *Anthony Benezet opens an evening school for Philadelphia Negroes in his home.*
Quakers made the most conscientious efforts to fight slavery and educate Negroes, permitting them to attend Quaker meetings in the face of great opposition. After teaching Negroes in his home for 20 years, Benezet opened a free school for them in Philadelphia under Moses Patterson. Upon Benezet's death, money he left was used for the continuation of the school, known thereafter as Benezet House. Benezet, a French Protestant persecuted on account of his religion, had moved from France to England and, later, to Philadelphia. He declared that he had "found among Negroes, a variety of talents as amongst a like number of whites." Besides fighting for the amelioration of the condition of blacks, he published some of America's first textbooks, and urged religious equality.

1751 ***Society for the Propagation of the Gospel sends Joseph Ottolenghi to convert and educate Negroes in Georgia.***

Ottolenghi, a convert from Judaism and a native of Italy, arrived in Georgia in July 1751. He "promised to spare no pains to improve the young children" and asked God's blessings on his educational efforts which included reading and religious instruction to Negroes. He became so successful and influential in the colonies that he was later elected a member of the Georgia Assembly and remained a member till 1765.

1773 ***Benjamin Rush advocates abolition of slave trade and right of Negroes to be educated.***

In *An Address to the Inhabitants of the British Settlements of America upon Slavekeeping*, Benjamin Rush showed himself to be a staunch supporter of the rights of Negroes, and urged their education. Rush, a Philadelphia physician of Quaker parentage, was in contact with the most enlightened men of his time, and by persuasive argument, advanced the Negro cause.

1774 ***Benjamin Franklin opens school for Negroes.***

While students of government were exposing the inconsistency of slaveholding among a people contending for political liberty, and men like Samuel Webster, James Swan and Samuel Hopkins attacked slavery on economic grounds, Benjamin Franklin, Jonathan Boucher, and Dr. Rush were devising plans to educate slaves for freedom. Benjamin Franklin associated with friends of colored people and was made president of the Abolition Society of Philadelphia which in 1774 founded a successful colored school.

1777 ***New Jersey begins educating Negro children. By 1801, schools are in operation in Salem, Burlington, and Trenton.***

New York African Free School No. 2

Negro women took the initiative in attending schools established by the Freedmen's Bureau. When these schools were burned down they were quickly rebuilt.

1787 *New York African Free School established by the Manumission society.*
Beginning with 40 students, it encountered opposition, but grew when New York required masters to teach the children of slaves to read Scripture. By 1820, more than 500 Negro children were enrolled.

1788 *New Jersey passes an Act making the teaching of slaves to read compulsory under a penalty of five pounds.*

1791 *Thomas Jefferson writes letter to Benjamin Banneker, Negro mathematician and astronomer.*
Jefferson declared that he wished to see blacks improve their condition and stated that lack of progress was due to the degraded condition of the black man in Africa and America. Writing the Declaration of Independence, he had in mind the rights of blacks as well as whites, and declared that Negroes had a natural right to education and freedom. He advocated training of slaves in industrial and agricultural schools to equip them for a higher station in life.

1798 *School for Negro children established in home of Primus . Hall, prominent Boston Negro.*

1794 *American Convention of Abolition Societies expresses hope that freedmen would participate in the battle for civil rights as fast as they gained their education.*

1800-1830 *Development of individual schools for Negroes by churches, slaveholders, and free Negroes.*
Despite legal restrictions in the South, Negroes did receive some education from their masters and in small clandestine private schools. In the North, however, Negroes benefitted from the general trend to establish and improve schools in the new nation. In 1820, for example, the city of Boston opened an elementary school for Negroes. In the District of Columbia, George Bell, Nicholas Franklin, and Moses Liverpool, former slaves, built the first schoolhouse for Negroes in 1807. Unsuccessful, it opened again in 1818 under the direction of the *Resolute Beneficial Society*, an association of free people of color. Catholics vied with Quakers in admitting Negroes to parochial schools.

During these years, a few Negroes were beginning to attend institutions of higher learning. (In 1826, Edward A. Jones graduated from Amherst and John Russwurm received his degree from Bowdoin. They were the first two Negro college graduates in the United States.)

In Philadelphia (1804), free people of color organized a school with John Trumbull as teacher. At this time, African Episcopalians founded a school at their church. Eleven of the 16 schools in Philadelphia in 1822 were taught by teachers of African descent. In 1830, one fourth of the 1200 colored children in the schools of that city paid for their instruction, whereas in 1825 only 250 students were in attendance.

1830–1860 *Curtailment of educational opportunities for Negroes due to rising fear of the increasing power of slaves.*

This was precipitated by the fear aroused in the white population after the slave insurrection led by Nat Turner in Virginia in 1831. "Black Codes" were then enacted in several states to keep the Negro "in his place" by denying him access to educational facilities of any kind.

1831 *Vocational education for Negro youth proposed by Negro convention.*

The First Annual Negro Convention was held in Philadelphia June 6-11, 1831. Delegates attended from New York, Pennsylvania, Delaware, Maryland, and Virginia. The idea was suggested by Samuel Cornish in 1827 and taken up by the Rev. S. S. Jocelyn, an anti-slavery white minister from New Haven. Vocational education for Negro youth was discussed at this

An 1874 drawing called "school's out-hurrah!" in an article on Negro schools in Harpers Magazine.

and ensuing conferences held in Philadelphia, New York, and Rochester. The conference declared that colleges and high schools were needed where youth could be instructed in the manual labor system and the arts of civilized life. Money was raised for a school in New Haven, but the citizens objected and declared that "the founding of colleges for colored people was a dangerous undertaking."

1834 *Prudence Crandall imprisoned and mobbed at Canterbury, Connecticut.*

Reaction to the education of Negroes was apparent when Prudence Crandall, a young Quaker who had established a boarding school at Canterbury, tried to enroll Sarah Harris, a colored girl at her institution. When whites objected, she advertised for young women of color. Imprisonment and violence resulted.

1840 *Negroes attend school with whites in Wilmington, Delaware.*

1842 *School for Negro and Indian boys opens in Ohio.*

Augustus Wattles, agent of American anti-slavery society, and Samuel Emlen, New Jersey philanthropist, open *Emlen Institute for Negro and Indian Boys,* in Mercer County, Ohio. The school specialized in the teaching of agricultural and skilled crafts.

1848 *Negro industrial training school opens in Philadelphia at the House of Industry.*

By 1851, Sarah Luciana was teaching 70 youths at the training school and at the Sheppard School, another industrial institution. Other schools in

Noon at the primary school for freedmen at Vicksburg, Mississippi

operation were the Corn Street Unclassified School (1849), the Holmesburg Unclassified School (1854), and the Home for Colored Children (1859). By this date there were 1031 pupils in the colored public schools of Philadelphia; 748 in the charity schools; 211 in the benevolent schools; 331 in private schools. In all, 2,321 were in attendance, whereas ten years earlier there were only 1643. Besides supporting these institutions, the colored people of Philadelphia maintained many small schools and organized a system of lyceums and debating clubs, one of which had a library of 1400 volumes.

1849 ***Roberts* v. *City of Boston***

Robert Morris, a prominent black lawyer, and Charles Sumner argue that segregation hurts white and black children alike. The suit was filed in Boston by Benjamin F. Roberts on behalf of his daughter, Sarah, who had applied under the Equal Education Act of 1845 to attend a white school closer to her home. The court ruled against Sumner and a local ordinance providing for the separate education of the races was upheld. During the next six years, however, public opinion persuaded the Massachusetts legislature to repudiate the court. This was accomplished in 1855 by a law which forbade distinction of race, color, or religion for purposes of admission into the public schools of Massachusetts.

1852 ***Students in the North become converted to the doctrine of equality in education through the efforts of President C. B. Storrs of Western Reserve College, Hudson, Ohio.***

By this date, colored students had attended the Institute at Easton, Pennsylvania; the Normal School of Albany, New York; Bowdoin College, Brunswick, Maine; Rutland College, Vermont; Jefferson College, Pennsylvania; Athens College, Athens, Ohio; Franklin College, New Athens, Ohio; Hanover College, near Madison, Indiana. Negroes had taken courses at: the Medical School of New York; the Castleton Medical School in Vermont, the Berkshire Medical School in Pittsfield, Massachusetts; the Rush Medical School in Chicago; the Eclectic Medical School in Philadelphia; the Homeopathic College of Cleveland, and the Medical School of Harvard University. Black preachers had been educated at the Theological Seminary in Gettysburg, Pennsylvania, the Dartmouth Theological School and the Theological Seminary of Charlestown, South Carolina.

Vocational schools were abundant. Statistics of 1850 and 1860 show that there was an increase in the number of black mechanics, especially in Philadelphia, Cincinnati, Columbus, the Western Reserve, and Canada. But this was probably due to the decreasing prejudice of the local white mechanics toward Negro artisans fleeing from the South rather than to formal industrial training.

1855 *Massachusetts legislature enacts law providing that no distinction be made on account of race, color, or religion, in admitting scholars to public schools.*

1864 *Civil War sees mass education of Negroes.*

The Christian Commission sponsors 50 teachers who taught blacks in the Union Army. Chaplains also teach colored troops. By war's end, 20,000 soldiers have been taught to read.

1865 *Founding of the Freedman's Bureau under General Oliver O. Howard.*

The Bureau is created by Congress on March 3, 1865, to cooperate with benevolent and religious societies in the establishment of schools for Negroes. John Mercer Langston, black lawyer, and Inspector-General of Schools in the Bureau, reports in August 1869, the existence of many good schools for colored people. By 1870, the Freedmen's Bureau operates over 2600 schools in the South with 3300 teachers educating 150,000 students. Four thousand schools were in operation prior to the abolition of the Bureau.

1865–1871 *Establishment of several predominantly Negro institutions of higher learning.*

During these years, a number of important Negro institutions of learning were founded, including Virginia Union and Shaw University (1865); Fisk University and Lincoln Institute (1866); Talladega College, Augusta (Georgia) Institute, Biddle University, Howard University, and Scotia Seminary (1867); Tougaloo College (1869), and Alcorn College and Benedict College (1871). Many of these colleges have changed their names since they were originally founded.

Classrooms like these were typical of early colleges affiliated with the United Negro College Fund.

1867 *Establishment of the Peabody Fund*

The two million dollar Peabody Fund is established for promotion and encouragement of intellectual, moral, and industrial education among the young of the more destitute portions of the Southern and Southwestern states.

1872 *Alcorn College becomes the first Negro land-grant college.*

This was made possible under the Morrill Act of 1862 which provided federal land-grant funds for higher education. It was the Morrill Act of 1890, however, which provided that funds for Negro education be distributed on a "just and equitable basis." Such legislation, however, also served to strengthen the doctrine of "separate but equal," with the result that the 17 Southern states maintained colleges which came to be known as "Negro land-grant colleges."

1897 *Founding in Washington, D. C. of the American Negro Academy*

Organized on March 5, 1897, by the Rev. Alexander Crummell, Negro theologian and educator, the Academy has five stated objectives: 1) Defense of the Negro against vicious assaults 2) Publication of scholarly work 3) Fostering higher education among Negroes 4) Formulation of intellectual tastes 5) Promotion of Literature, Science, and Art.

Crummell's father was a prince and son of a West African Tribal Chief (Temne tribe). Crummell himself first conceived the idea of an American Negro Academy when a student at Cambridge University, England. The Academy was the first body in America to bring Negro scholars from all over the world together. The general purpose of the organization was to foster scholarship and culture in the Negro race and encourage budding Negro genius. In March 1897, the year of McKinley's inauguration, celebrated scholars and writers of the Negro race assembled in the Lincoln Memorial Church, and organized into a brotherhood of scholars. In attendance was Dunbar, the poet; DuBois, the sociologist; Scarborough, the Greek scholar; Miller, the mathematician; Grimke, the theologian; Cromwell, the historian, and many other noted educators. At Crummell's death on September 12, 1908, W. E. Burghardt DuBois was elected President and stated that those with higher education must take responsibility for uplifting the Negro race. Many brilliant papers were published which are still today the best discussion on Negro Suffrage and Southern Disfranchisement.

1900 *The New York legislature, under the governorship of Theodore Roosevelt, passes an act providing that no one should be denied admittance to any public school on account of race, color, or previous condition of servitude.*

1902 *Founding of the General Education Board, supported by John D. Rockefeller.*

Funds from this organization aided Negro education materially in such categories as endowment, scholarships, teacher-training, and industrial education.

1908 *Founding of the Anna T. Jeanes Fund.*

The Jeanes Fund sponsored the Jeanes Teacher Program to improve the quality of instruction in rural Negro schools.

1908 *Berea College* v. *Kentucky*

Kentucky law had made segregation mandatory. At issue was whether a private college had the right to teach blacks and whites together. The Supreme Court ruled, on technical grounds, against the college.

1913 *Founding of the Julius Rosenwald Fund.*

The Rosenwald Fund provided grants for constructing schools. By 1932, more than 5,000 school buildings in 883 counties of 15 states had been built under Rosenwald sponsorship.

1932 *Publication of the Journal of Negro Education.*

This organ, published at Howard University, has done much to improve educational opportunities for Negroes, and to democratize education in general.

1954 ***Brown v. Board of Education.***
This decision by the U. S. Supreme Court eliminated segregation in all public schools. It was based upon the theory that "the segregation of children in public schools solely on the basis of race, even though the physical facilities and other tangible factors may be equal, deprives children of the minority group of equal educational facilities." (For fuller coverage of this case, see "review" section, p. 22, and Supreme Court section, page 189.)

1957 *Little Rock Crisis.*
After a federal court ordered desegregation in Little Rock, Arkansas, Governor Orval Faubus called out the Arkansas National Guard to prevent nine Negro students from entering Central High School. As a result of this, President Dwight D. Eisenhower dispatched U. S. troops to Little Rock to enforce the court order, and ultimately federalized the Arkansas National Guard as well.

1961 *New Rochelle: The Lincoln School Case.*
In this case, Federal District Court Judge Irving A. Kaufman ruled that the New Rochelle Board of Education had deliberately created and maintained Lincoln as a racially segregated school. Judge Kaufman ordered the Board to present a plan to desegregate the predominantly Negro school at all levels. This case marked the first court decision against "de facto" segregation in the North.

1964 *Passage of the Civil Rights Act.*
This act placed further legal restrictions on discrimination in education.

1965 *Passage of the Elementary and Secondary School Education Act.*
This act provides funds under Title I for promoting racial integration in the public schools of the United States.

1966 *Federal judge orders Lowndes County school districts to desegregate.*
Federal District Court Judge Frank M. Johnson, Jr. directs the Lowndes County, Alabama school board to install a sweeping desegregation order. All grades are ordered desegregated within two years. A free choice transfer system to any school is to be effected and all Negro teachers integrated.

1966 *Teaching profession continues to appeal to black students despite emphasis on the need to diversify careers.*
Secretary of Labor Willard Wirtz declares that two-thirds of all Negro college students are preparing to teach and that many of these students should be preparing for careers other than in education in order to fill positions that are finally becoming available to Negro applicants.

1966 *The Kennedy plan for urban ghettos.*
Senator Robert F. Kennedy calls for eradication of huge central city ghettos and criticizes the deliberate location of public housing in ghettos. To help desegregate schools, he urges a program for boarding children in the suburbs.

1966 *The Chester school case*
The Court of Common Pleas of Dauphin County decides the Chester school case. The court upholds the order by the Pennsylvania Human Relations Commission that the Chester school board stop assigning Negro teachers and clerks only to all-Negro schools, and that the board cease refusing to assign white teachers to a predominantly Negro school. The court rejects two contentions: 1) That it has authority to act against de-facto segregation 2) That the school board has engaged in extensive gerrymandering.

1966 *The Tometz case against the Waukegan school board*
State Circuit Court Judge Philip W. Yaeger of Illinois rejects a Waukegan school board motion to dismiss the Tometz case filed against it by a group of Negro parents. The suit, which charged gerrymandering, is the first court test of the Armstrong Act of 1963.

1966 *Detroit suburb agrees to integrated textbooks.*
The school board of Inkster, Michigan, a Detroit suburb, signs a contract with Local 1068 of the American Federation of Teachers agreeing that effective education must be integrated education. Only integrated textbooks are to be used in reading and social studies classes.

1966 *Prince Edward County school board guilty of contempt*
The U.S. Circuit Court of Appeals for the Fourth Circuit finds the Prince Edward County, Virginia school board guilty of contempt of court for illegally distributing state funds to be used for tuition in private schools so as to avoid desegregation.

1966 *Desegregation of Plaquemine Parish, Louisiana*
The public schools of Plaquemine Parish, Louisiana are ordered by a federal district court to desegregate six of 12 grades through a free choice plan.

1966 *Integration in Fayette, Mississippi*
In Fayette, Mississippi, 13 Negro children are enrolled in two formerly all-white schools as a result of an agreement between the school board and the state NAACP headed by Charles Evers.

1966 *Integration question raised at I.S. 201 in Harlem.*
A community movement in East Harlem calls upon the school board to integrate the new intermediate school I.S. 201 or place its management under effective community control.

1967 *Civil Rights Commission releases important study.*
The U.S. Commission on Civil Rights releases its study, *Racial Isolation in the Public Schools* made in response to a November 1965 request by President Johnson.

1967 *The Girard College case*
Girard College in Philadelphia does not have to admit Negroes under the state's Public Accommodations Act, according to a ruling by the U.S. Court of Appeals for the Third Circuit. This part of the opinion thus reverses an earlier ruling by Federal District Court Judge Joseph S. Lord III.

1967 *Court of Appeals declares Southern states obliged to foster integration.*
The United States Court of Appeals for the Fifth Circuit endorses an earlier ruling that six Southern states have an affirmative responsibility to integrate their public schools. In April, the U.S. Supreme Court declines to delay the implementation of the Court of Appeals' order. A motion by the states to bring about a full-scale Supreme Court review of the order is pending. A federal court strikes down an Alabama law against the HEW desegregation guidelines as a violation of the Constitutional supremacy of Congressional legislation.

1967 *Final ruling on the Tometz case by the Illinois Supreme Court.*
The Illinois Supreme Court holds unconstitutional the Armstrong law and thus reverses the earlier Tometz ruling. The statute, enacted in 1963, required school boards to redistrict attendance boundaries periodically to reduce segregation and prevent further segregation. The state high court finds the law to be arbitrary and unreasonable and in violation of the equal protection clause of the Fourteenth Amendment.

1967 *Supreme Court upholds Court of Appeals ruling in Oklahoma City Dowell case*
The U.S. Supreme Court refuses to review a Tenth Circuit Court of Appeals decision in the Oklahoma City Dowell case, thus leaving intact a District Court order of September 5, 1965. The 1965 order called for sweeping changes in school organization; the attendance areas of various schools were to be merged so as to promote desegregation; a child in a racial majority would be permitted to transfer to a school in which he was in a racial minority; faculties were to be desegregated by 1970 so that the racial composition in each school approximated the system-wide composition (plus or minus a ten percent tolerance).

1968 *Racial imbalance in Massachusetts, the District of Columbia, and Lansing*
The Massachusetts racial imbalance law withstands attack before the U.S. Supreme Court. The statute which requires a school board to take action whenever a school's enrollment exceeds 50 percent nonwhite is unsuccessfully challenged as unconstitutional by Boston school authorities. The Supreme Court rules that the suit failed to raise a substantial federal question. In the District of Columbia, the Board of Education reports on plans to effectuate the court's ruling in *Hobson* v. *Hansen.* Plans are submitted to the court regarding the reduction of racially imbalanced student bodies and faculties; measures include attendance boundary changes and busing. New teachers are being assigned to achieve racial balance. Discussions are being held with suburban school officials about attendance of District students in schools outside the city. The Ingham County Circuit Court rules that the Lansing school board can change attendance boundaries to bring about racial balance.

1968 *Rise in population of black students recorded at predominantly white colleges*
Between 1963 and 1967, the percentage of Negro students in predominantly white colleges and universities increases from 0.4 percent to 1.6 percent, according to the North Carolina Board of Higher Education.

1968 *"One man, one vote" applied to school board elections*
The U.S. Supreme Court holds that the "one man, one vote" rule must be applied to elections of school boards and other local agencies. "Units with general governmental powers over an entire geographic area," ruled the court, "must not be apportioned among single-member districts of substantially unequal population."

1968 *The Supreme Court rules on "open enrollment" or "freedom of choice."*
The Supreme Court rules unanimously that "freedom of choice" desegregation plans (called "open enrollment" in the North) must promise significant progress before being approved. Desegregation plans that result in no substantial change of segregation will be rejected. School boards are given the affirmative responsibility of finding realistic plans. The Supreme Court explicitly limits its ruling to Southern and border states that had permitted legal segregation before 1954.

1968 *The Tometz case: a final ruling*
The State Supreme Court reverses its earlier ruling in the Tometz case. At issue was the 1963 Illinois Armstrong Act which requires school districts to change or revise school attendance areas to prevent or eliminate segregation. In its 1967 ruling the court invalidated the law, holding that race could not properly be a consideration in attendance area revision. Now, however, it determines that the "issue here is whether the constitution permits, rather than prohibits, voluntary state action aimed toward reducing and eventually eliminating *de facto* school segregation. The Armstrong Act was thereupon found to be constitutional . . ."

1968 *Deliberate segregation unearthed in South Holland*
Legal proceedings continue in the federal complaint of deliberate segregation against School District No. 151 in South Holland, Illinois. In a deposition, Superintendent Charles B. Watts states he was present when a school board member acknowledged that race was taken into account in locating the site of two schools. Federal attorneys introduce evidence showing that a white school board member had been allowed to enroll his children in a white school although he lived nearer a Negro school. The next year the school board rejects the effort of four Negro parents to enroll their children in a white school.

1968 *Central issues at Ocean Hill-Brownsville in New York*
The right of an experimental school district—Ocean Hill Brownsville Demonstration School District—to transfer or dismiss teachers becomes the central issue in a continuing confrontation between the United Federation of

The Ocean Hill Brownsville demonstration School District.

Teachers and Negro parents constituting the majority of the district's governing board.

1968 *The Girard case: a final ruling*
In May, the U.S. Supreme Court refuses to review a lower court ruling that ends a 120-year-old practice of exclusion of Negro boys from Girard College, a free boarding school in Philadelphia. Four weeks later, numerous Negro mothers bring their youngsters to register for entrance in September.

1968 *U.S. Circuit Court of Appeals declines to rule on "freedom of choice."*
The fifth U.S. Circuit Court of Appeals refuses to strike down 42 freedom of choice plans in four Southern states. It orders federal district courts in the states to determine by November 4th how effective the plans were. The court defines an effective plan as one that produces integration of faculties, staff, facilities, transportation, and school activities along with integration of students.

1968 *U.S. Justice Department intervenes against Ku Klux Klan*
The U.S. Department of Justice files suit against a Ku Klux Klan chapter in Crenshaw County, Alabama, charging interference with a court-ordered "free choice desegregation plan." The Klan, according to Federal complaint, intimidated Negro parents into withdrawing their children from white schools.

1968 *Busing begins in South Holland, Illinois*
Federal court-ordered desegregation takes effect in South Holland, Illinois without incident in September. Nine-tenths of the white enrollment as of June re-entered the desegregated schools. About 800 pupils equally divided between Negro and white were bused daily.

1968 ***Federal panel in Illinois refuses to rule on per-pupil expenditure disparities between school districts.***
A three-man federal court panel in Illinois refuses to rule unconstitutional large per-pupil expenditure disparities between school districts in the state. One suburb spent $1,283 per high school student, another $919. Plaintiffs contended state laws permitting such disparities violated the equal protection clause of the Fourteenth Amendment. Without doubt, ruled the panel, the educational potential of each child should be cultivated to the utmost and the poorer districts should have more funds, but the allocation of public revenues is a basic policy decision, more appropriately handled by a legislature than a court.

1969 *Integration pressure applied to Los Angeles school district*
Lawsuit filed in Los Angeles Superior Court asking that the Inglewood Unified School District be ordered to eliminate *de facto* segregation in school district number 17. The board allegedly refuses even to adopt a policy statement committing the district to integration.

1969 *Move to bar erection of de facto segregated high school in Muncie, Indiana*
Black citizens file suit in federal court, Muncie, Indiana, to bar construction of a high school in an all-white area. The suit charges that the resulting exclusion of black children from the new facility would be in violation of their Constitutional rights to equal educational opportunities.

1969 *Desegregation of Mt. Vernon elementary schools*
The State Supreme Court of New York upholds a state order to desegregate the Mt. Vernon elementary schools.

1969 *Pennsylvania directed to achieve greater integration of schools of higher learning*
Pennsylvania is directed by H.E.W. to desegregate its public colleges and universities. Pennsylvania, H.E.W. charged, "is operating a system of higher education that is segregated on a statewide basis." The state's only predominantly black school, Cheyney State, contains 85 percent Negroes, which amount to more than four and one-half times the number of blacks in all the other 13 state colleges combined.

SCHOLARSHIPS FOR BLACK STUDENTS

The importance of scholarships for Negroes becomes evident when one considers the rising cost of a college education in the United States, and the fact that education often provides the sole basis for the advancement of the Negro in our highly complex and industrialized society. The inverse relationship that exists between high college costs and low family incomes among Negroes makes urgent the need for financial aid to students in predominantly Negro colleges.

This need is being met by an increasing number of scholarships, work-study programs, and loans. Scholarships are generally obtained from the following principal sources: colleges and universities; corporate philanthropy; religious groups; and federal, state, and local government agencies.

Below is a list of scholarship programs which are granted predominantly to Negro students. A guide which includes scholarships available to *all* students is published by the Scholarship Information Center of the University of North Carolina YMCA-YWCA, and can be ordered at 25¢ per copy (plus 5¢ postage) from the University of North Carolina YMCA-YWCA Human Relations Committee, Chapel Hill, North Carolina 27514. The annotated items which open this section are followed by a less detailed, but more comprehensive, listing of additional scholarship and loan sources. These have been provided courtesy of the United Negro College Fund, Research Division, W. L. Spearman, Director.

NATIONAL ACHIEVEMENT SCHOLARSHIP PROGRAM FOR OUTSTANDING NEGRO STUDENTS. *Eligibility:* High school seniors. *Where valid:* Anywhere. *Restrictions:* None. *Value:* Two hundred four-year $1,000-$6,000 scholarships. *How to apply:* Through high school principal or write to: National Achievement Scholarship Program, 990 Grove Street, Evanston, Illinois 60201. *Basis of award:* Need and scholarship. *Deadline:* Apply very early. By December 10 of year *before* entry into college.

NATIONAL SCHOLARSHIP SERVICE AND FUND FOR NEGRO STUDENTS (SUPPLEMENTARY SCHOLARSHIP FUND). *Eligibility:* High school seniors. *Where valid:* Any regionally accredited, degree-granting, INTERRACIAL institution at which campus facilities are extended equally without regard to race. *Restrictions:* Must have been counseled by organization. *Value:* Unspecified number, up to $600 per year. Renewable—TWICE ONLY. *How to apply:* WRITE EARLY IN JUNIOR YEAR TO: NSSFNS, 6 East 82nd Street, New York, New York 10028. *Basis of awards:* NEED, scholastic record, extra-curricular activities, staff interviews, SAT tests. *Deadline:* Early in senior year for final applications.

NORTH CAROLINA COLLEGE AT DURHAM $1,000 STUDENT SCHOLARSHIPS. *Eligibility:* High school graduating seniors. *Where valid:* North Carolina College only. *Restrictions:* SAT score of at least 1000. *Value:* Several $1,000 grants available. Renewable. *How to apply:* Chairman of Committee on Financial Assistance to Students, North Carolina College at Durham, Box 601 Durham, North Carolina. *Basis of awards:* SAT score of 1000 and good high school records. *Deadline:* May 1.

HERBERT LEHMAN EDUCATION FUND. For Negroes at recently desegregated colleges in the Deep South. Apply Herbert Lehman Education Fund, 10 Columbus Circle, Suite 2040, New York 19, New York.

MARTIN DE PORRES FOUNDATION. For Philadelphia Catholics planning to attend nearby Catholic colleges. Apply M. H. McCloskey III, Martin De Porres Foundation, 2050 Suburban Station Building, Philadelphia 3, Pennsylvania.

MINORITY GROUPS SCHOLARSHIP PROGRAM (Endowed by Rockefeller Fund). *Eligibility:* High school senior. *Where valid:* Any of 7 specified colleges or universities. *Restrictions:* Must be member of minority group (Negro, Mexican, Oriental in the United States). *Value:* Determined by individual college. *How to apply:* Admissions Office of particular member college. *Basis of award:* Exceptional academic drive, leadership potential, financial need. *Deadline:* Unannounced.

POLYTECHNIC INSTITUTE OF BROOKLYN, NEW YORK. *Eligibility:* High school seniors. *Where valid:* Polytechnic Institute of Brooklyn, New York. *Restrictions:* None. Priority given to southern Negroes. For students interested in electrical engineering. *Value:* Remedial course work in summer if needed. Full tuition and maintenance for three or more students. *How to apply:* Have principal write to Polytechnic Institute requesting information. *Basis of award:* Need and scholarship. Interest in electrical engineering. *Deadline:* None.

ELEANOR ROOSEVELT SCHOLARSHIP PROGRAM. For students who have been actively involved in the civil rights movement. Apply CORE Scholarship, Education and Defense Fund, Inc., 150 Nassau Street, New York 10038. The CORE Fund grants scholarships of up to $1,500 to cover tuition and living costs for a period of one year. Scholarships are awarded twice a year—in the spring and fall.

ALFRED P. SLOAN FOUNDATION. *Eligibility:* High school seniors (½), high school juniors (½). *Where valid:* Ten major Negro colleges and universities. *Restrictions:* Male students only. *Value:* For juniors: Two summers remedial instruction at listed schools (Dillard University, New Orleans; and Morehouse College, Atlanta). Will be granted scholarship for four years on completion of courses. For seniors: four-year grants to any of 10 schools. About 60 in number. *How to apply:* For juniors: United Negro College Fund, 22 East 54th Street, New York, New York 10022. For seniors: Apply to listed colleges. *Basis of awards:* Need. *Deadline:* Ideally in spring.

RALPH E. SMITH FREEDOM SCHOLARSHIPS. *Eligibility:* High

school seniors. *Where valid:* Macalester College, St. Paul, Minnesota. *Restrictions:* Three white and three Negro awards yearly. *Value:* Four-year scholarships, maximum value $2,000 yearly. *How to apply:* Make application to Macalester and request consideration for Ralph E. Smith Freedom Scholarships. *Basis of awards:* 1) leadership, 2) scholarship, 3) desire to work toward humanitarian goals in the tradition of the American way of life. *Deadline:* March 1.

TEXAS SOUTHERN UNIVERSITY SCHOOL OF BUSINESS, HOUSTON, TEXAS SCHOLARSHIPS. *Eligibility:* High school senior. *Where valid:* Texas Southern University only. *Restrictions:* None, interest in business career. *Value:* Fifteen four-year full payment grants. *How to apply:* Have guidance counselor write to Texas Southern University. *Basis of awards:* Recommendations of principal and high school counselor, results of CEB and American College Testing Program examinations. *Deadline:* March 31.

UNITED NEGRO COLLEGE FUND. *Eligibility:* High school seniors and college undergraduates. *Where valid:* Any of 33 listed Southern Negro colleges and universities. *Restriction:* None. *Value:* The Fund grants money to the listed schools who then make the funds available to entering students. (In 1965, the goal was over $5,000,000.) *How to apply:* Apply to the Director of Admissions at the college or university listed. *Basis of award:* Set by each college or university. Need is certainly taken into consideration. *Deadline:* Unspecified.

JOHN HAY WHITNEY FUND. The "Opportunity Fellowships" of this fund are open to citizens from a number of diverse racial and cultural backgrounds, including Negroes. Candidates under 35 are given decided preference. Awards range to a maximum of $3,000, and are governed by the need of the candidate, as well as the nature of the program he desires to undertake. They are limited to a full year of serious graduate study. For further information (or applications), write the John Hay Whitney Foundation, 111 West 50th Street, New York 10020.

OTHER SCHOLARSHIPS

COOPERATIVE COLLEGE DEVELOPMENT PROGRAM. Established with the assistance of the Alfred P. Sloan Foundation in 1965, the Cooperative Development Program extends its services to 23 Southern Negro colleges and universities. The program assists member colleges in making presentations to industry, government, private foundations and other potential sources of funds.

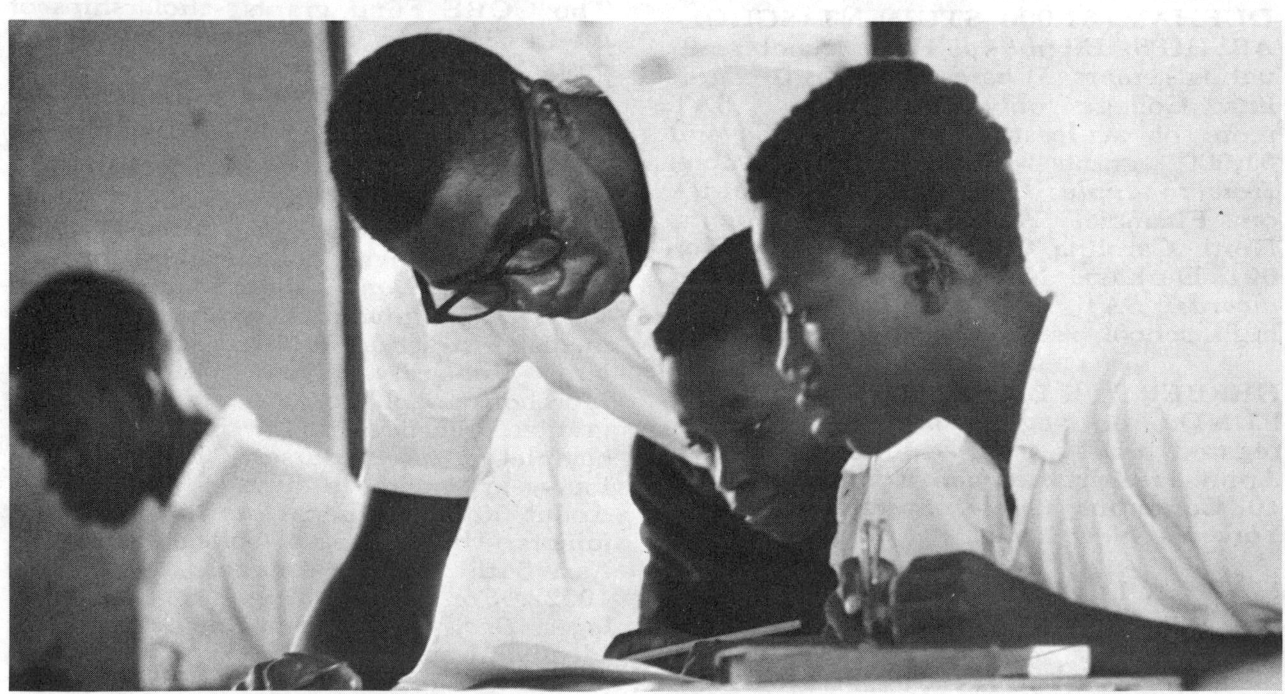

More black youths are attending, and completing, high school than ever before.

LEVER BROTHERS. This organization provides 51 renewable $500 scholarships (one in each state and the District of Columbia) for study in the pharmaceutical field. Through the National Merit Program, Lever Brothers also contributes to graduate fellowships for Negroes who wish to pursue a career in management.

For more information, contact state pharmaceutical associations or Public Relations Department, Lever Brothers, 390 Park Avenue, New York, New York.

NATIONAL MERIT SCHOLARSHIP CORPORATION. Established by the Ford Foundation and the Carnegie Foundation of New York in 1955, the National Merit Scholarship Corporation awards about 1,600 scholarships each year to high school students who qualify both on the National Merit Scholarship Qualifying Test, given in the spring, and the Scholastic Aptitude Test, given in the autumn, and who then pass the third and final phase of competition, where the criteria are outstanding grades, extra-curricular activities, and leadership qualities. Winners receive up to $1,500 per year, depending on financial need, and may enroll in the school of their choice. For information, write Mr. Edward Smith, Executive Vice President, National Merit Scholarship Corporation, 990 Grove Street, Evanston, Illinois.

PULITZER FREE SCHOLARSHIP COMMITTEE. This committee awards 10 four-year scholarships at $250 per year to male New York high school students. In addition, it awards graduate fellowships to a number of institutions participating in the program. For more information, contact Pulitzer Free Scholarship Committee, 105 Low Library, Columbia University, New York, N. Y.

RADIO CORPORATION OF AMERICA. The institutions (white and Negro) participating in the Radio Corporation of America program offer 34 undergraduate scholarships at $800 per year in various fields. In addition, RCA awards 11 fellowships for graduate study in electrical engineering, physics, electronics, dramatic arts and journalism. The stipend is $2,100, with a supplementary $900 to a married graduate student with dependent children. An additional $500 may be made available for summer work.

GENERAL SCHOLARSHIP AID

Alco Foundation Scholarship Fund
Pittsburgh, Pennsylvania

Alpha Chi Rho Educational Foundation, Inc.
225 Lafayette Street
New York, New York 10012

American Baptist Convention
152 Madison Avenue
New York, New York
Conditions: Student must attend Baptist college.

American Machine and Foundry Company
261 Madison Avenue
New York, New York 10016

American Schools & Colleges Association
30 Rockefeller Plaza
New York, New York 10020
Conditions and Limits: 1200 scholarships to New York and New Jersey graduates. Candidates must have worked during high school and shown scholastic and essay-writing ability.

ASARCO Foundation
120 Broadway
New York, New York

George F. Baker Trust
2 Wall Street
New York, New York 10005

Bell Foundation, Inc.
Buffalo, New York
Conditions and Limits: (2) tuition scholarships (Erie County Technical Institute and Niagara University)

Boy's Club of America
771 First Avenue
New York, New York 10017
Conditions and Limits: Those interested in Boy's Club career

Campe (Ed. Lee & Jean) Foundation
U. S. Trust Company of New York
New York, New York 10005

Celanese Corp. of America
522 Fifth Avenue
New York, New York 10036

College Scholarship Service (CEEB)
Princeton, New Jersey
Booklet: Sponsored scholarship programs using College Board Service.

Cook (Wm. J.) Fund Scholarships
Chicago Community Trust
10 South La Salle Street
Chicago, Illinois 60603

Cornell Club of Buffalo
92 Pearl Street
Buffalo, New York
Conditions: for students wishing to attend Cornell

Dedombrowski (G. Louise Robinson) Charitable Trust
Simpson, Tatcher, Baetlett
120 Broadway
New York, New York 10005

The Dillon Fund
c/o Sherman and Sterling
20 Exchange Place
New York, New York 10005

Dolan Foundation
Edward Joy Company
905 Canal Street
Syracuse 3, New York

Education Funds, Inc.
10 Dorrance Street
Providence 3, Rhode Island
Up to $2,500 per year
Renewable: any educational expenses; no tests

Elks National Foundation Scholarship Plan
Chairman
Elks National Foundation
16 Court Street
Boston, Mass.
(142) High school seniors in upper five per cent of their class.
$700 to $1,500 annually

Field Foundation, Inc.
250 Park Avenue
New York, New York 10017

Fischbach Foundation, Inc.
454 Madison Avenue
New York, New York 10022

Foresight Foundation, Inc.
30 East 71st Street
New York, New York 10021

Friedman Foundation, Inc.
250 West 57th Street
New York, New York 10017

The Fund for Theological Education, Inc.
163 Nassau Street
Princeton, New Jersey 08540

General Motors College Scholarship Plan
General Motors Corporation
General Motors Building
Detroit 2, Michigan
(350) High school seniors
Up to $2,000 annually

Generoso Pope Scholarship Awards
Columbus Citizens Committee, Inc.
136 West 52nd Street
New York, New York

Grant (Ulysses S.) Scholarship Foundation
New Haven, Connecticut

Green Foundation
167-10 Hillside Avenue
Jamaica 32, New York

Greenspan (The Henry) Foundation
469 Seventh Avenue
New York, New York 10018

Hirsch Memorial Foundation, Inc.
350 Fifth Avenue
New York, New York

Honig (Ely) Memorial Scholarship Fund
Angelo Fabrics Company, Inc.
1407 Broadway
New York, New York
Fashion Industry

Insurance Federation of New York
116 Nassau Street
New York, New York 10038
Essay Contest determines winner of scholarship.

International Supreme Council of World Masons
1775 West Forest Avenue
Detroit, Michigan

Interracial Scholarship Committee of Greater Hartford
Hartford Foundation for Public Giving
621 Farmington
Hartford 5, Connecticut
Conditions: Hartford residents.

J. R. S. Foundation, Inc.
530 Fifth Avenue
New York, New York 10036

Jephson Educational Trust
c/o Chase Manhattan Plaza
New York, New York 10005

Jones (W. Alton) Foundation, Inc.
70 Pine Street
New York, New York 10005

Kiwanis Club of New York
Hotel Lexington
New York, New York 10017

Knights of Columbus Scholarships
New York State Council
486 Park Avenue
Yonkers, New York

Knights Templar Educational Foundation
Committee
Division of New York
71 West 23rd Street, Room 1527
New York, New York 10010

Levy (Adele R.) Fund, Inc.
100 Park Avenue
New York, New York 10017

Levy (Jacob) Foundation, Inc.
1440 Broadway
New York, New York

Littauer Foundation, Inc.
345 East 46th Street
New York, New York 10017

Lutheran Scholarships
National Lutheran Council
50 Madison Avenue
New York, New York 10010
Graduate Students in Social Work

Wheat Ridge Foundation
Scholarship Office
2590 Devon, East
Des Plaines, Illinois
Conditions: Lutheran students preparing careers in Lutheran Welfare Service

Marcus Foundation, Inc.
1410 Broadway
New York, New York 10018

Mazer (The Abraham) Family Fund
477 Madison Avenue
New York, New York 10022

McCormack Foundation
5 Broadway
New York, New York 10004

McGregor Fund
2486 First National Building
Detroit 26, Michigan

McMillin Foundation, Inc.
435 East 52nd Street
New York, New York

Mercy College
Detroit, Michigan

Muehlstein Foundation, Inc.
60 East 42nd Street
New York, New York 10017

National Council of Boy Scouts of America
New Brunswick, New Jersey 08903
A summary of colleges and universities that offer scholarships for boy scouts

National Honor Society Scholarships
1201 Sixteenth Street, N.W.
Washington, D. C.
Conditions: (225) High school seniors who are National Honor Society members. $500 to $5,000 for four years.

National Merit Scholarships
National Merit Scholarship Corporation
1580 Sherman Avenue
Evanston, Illinois
Conditions: (750) High school seniors in upper five per cent of their class. $100 to full tuition for four years.

National Methodist Scholarships
Department of Student Loans &
Scholarships
P. O. Box 871
Nashville, Tennessee 37202
Conditions: Outstanding Methodist students in Methodist colleges

National Presbyterian College Scholarships
Office of Education Loan for Scholarships
Board of Christian Education
United Presbyterian Church in the U.S.A.
425 Witherspoon Building
Philadelphia, Pennsylvania 19187
Conditions: Up to $1,000 to qualified members of Presbyterian church enrolled in Presbyterian colleges.

National Restaurant Association
Educational Director
1530 North Lakeshore Drive
Chicago, Illinois 60610
Conditions: (5) Scholarships at $1,000 each to persons entering the field of Food Service Administration

National Scholarship Fellowship Program
of YMCA
Program of YMCA Personnel Services
National Council of YMCA
291 Broadway
New York, New York 10007
Conditions: Full time graduate professional study to prepare for YMCA work.

New York City — Board of Higher
Education
Superintendent of Schools
110 Livingston Street
Brooklyn, New York

New York State Funeral Directors
Association
369 Lexington Avenue
New York, New York 10017

New York State Regents College
Scholarship
State Education Department
Regents Exam and Scholarship Center
Albany 1, New York
(17,000) High school seniors who are residents of New York State
$250 to $750 annually

Jessie Smith Noyes Foundation
205 East 42nd Street
New York, New York 10017
Conditions: Undergraduates with the exception of freshmen
Range from $500 to $1,500 with 2 per cent interest after graduation.

Azalia P. Oberg Foundation, Inc
Thomas & Thomas
504 Broadway, Room 1016
Gary, Indiana

P.E.O. Educational Fund
Executive Office
Mt. Pleasant, Iowa
Conditions: Women students

Proctor and Gamble Company
Scholarship Program
P. O. Box 599
Cincinnati, Ohio
Conditions: Full tuition plus allowance for books, fees, supplies renewable up to four years. No restrictions.

Revlon Foundation, Inc.
666 Fifth Avenue
New York, New York 10019

Henry Warren Roth Educational Fund
Henry Warren Roth
University of Pittsburgh
Pittsburgh, Pennsylvania
Conditions: All undergraduates; range from $500 to $1,500 maximum 4 per cent interest after graduation

Rothschild Fund, Inc.
470 Park Avenue, South
New York, New York 10016

Royal A. & Mildred D. Eddy Student Loan Fund
Eddy Student Loan Fund
Thomas & Thomas
504 Broadway, Room 1016
Gary, Indiana
$1,500 annually
Conditions: no restrictions other than financial need; no tests; no deadline.

S & H Foundation National Scholarship Program
Educational Testing Service
Princeton, New Jersey
Conditions: High School seniors
Up to $1,000 renewable for four years

Sandy Hill Foundation
27 Allen Street
Hudson Falls, New York
Scholarship Foundation, Inc.
120 East End Avenue
New York, New York

Scott Fund, Inc.
Five Quaker Center
Scarsdale, New York

Schepp Leopold Foundation
551 Fifth Avenue
New York, New York 10017

Sloan (Alfred P.) Foundation
630 Fifth Avenue
New York, New York 10020
Conditions: (150) Scholarships awarded to juniors and seniors in participating schools. Range from $200 to $2,400

Society of Exploration Geophysicist
Scholarship Committee
Shell Building
Tulsa, Oklahoma 74119
Conditions: Scholarships for persons interested in a career in geophysicist.

Social Research Foundation, Inc.
345 Park Avenue
New York, New York 10022

Henry Strong Educational Foundation
50 South LaSalle Street
Chicago, Illinois

Student Opportunity Scholarships
475 Riverside Drive, Room 1140
New York, New York 10027

Telluride Association
Ithaca, New York
Conditions: Students to attend Cornell

Tiffany Foundation
1083 Fifth Avenue
New York, New York 10028

Vocational Advisory Service
23 East 26th Street
New York, New York 10010

Weisberg Foundation, Inc.
29 Cooper Road
Scarsdale, New York

Western Golf Association
Golf, Illinois
Conditions: Four year scholarships to qualified caddies

Westinghouse Science Talent Search
Westinghouse Electric Corporation
East Pittsburgh, Pennsylvania
Conditions: (40) High school seniors in top 10 per cent of their class. $250 to $7,500 for four years.

White Scholarship Fund
73 Main Street
Cooperstown, New York

Woike Foundation, Inc.
1775 Broadway
New York, New York 10019

Woodrow Wilson National Fellowship Foundation
Box 642
Princeton, New Jersey
Conditions: (1000) Fellowships for first year graduate students interested in college teaching careers.

BUSINESS AND INDUSTRY

SCHOLARSHIP SOURCES*

Association of American Railroads
59 East Van Buren Street
Chicago, Illinois

Atlantic Refining Company
260 South Broad Street
Philadelphia, Pennsylvania

Boston Insurance Company
87 Kilby Street
Boston, Massachusetts

Brown and Sharpe Manufacturing Company
Providence, Rhode Island

Bryant Chucking Grinder Company
Springfield, Vermont

Buckeye Pipe Line Company
30 Broad Street
New York, New York

Bulova Watch Company, Inc.
Bulova Park
Flushing, New York

Chance Vought Aircraft, Inc.
P. O. Box 5907
Dallas, Texas

Chicago Title & Trust Foundation
Chicago, Illinois

Chubb Foundation
90 John Street
New York, New York 10038

Climax Molybdenum Company
Langeloth, Pennsylvania

Cummins Engine Company, Inc.
Columbus, Indiana

Fairchild Aircraft Division
Hagerstown, Maryland

* Courtesy, United Negro College Fund

Firestone Tire & Rubber Company
1200 Firestone Parkway
Akron, Ohio

Fisher Scientific Company
717 Forbes Street
Pittsburgh, Pennsylvania

Food Fair Stores, Inc.
2223 East Allegheny Avenue
Philadelphia, Pennsylvania

Ford Motor Company
Central Building
American Road
Dearborn, Michigan

Fruehauf Trailer Company
c/o Frank Strick Foundation
1335 Glenbrook Road
Huntingdon Valley, Pennsylvania

General Dynamics Corporation
445 Park Avenue
New York, New York

General Electric Company
Schenectady, New York

General Motors Corporation
3044 West Grand Boulevard
Detroit, Michigan

Goodbody & Company
115 Broadway
New York, New York

Goodrich, B. F. Company
Akron, Ohio

Greenfield Tap & Die Corporation
Greenfield, Massachusetts

Gruman Engineering Company
Bethpage, New York

Greenwall, Susan Foundation
Holmdel, New Jersey

Gulf Oil Company
Pittsburgh, Pennsylvania

Handcraft Company, Inc.
Princeton, Wiscônsin

Handy & Harman
82 Fulton Street
New York, New York

Hood Dairy Foundation
500 Rutherford Avenue
Boston, Massachusetts

Hunt, C. Howard Pen Company
7th & State Streets
Camden, New Jersey

Imperial Coal Company
Johnstown, Pennsylvania

Inland Steel Company
38 South Dearborn Street
Chicago, Illinois

International Business Machines
Corporation
590 Madison Avenue
New York, New York

Joanna Cotton Mills
Joanna, South Carolina

Johnstown Coal and Coke Company
Johnstown, Pennsylvania

Jones & Laughlin Steel Corporation
3 Gateway Center Pittsburgh, Penna.

Joy Manufacturing Company
Henry W. Oliver Building
Pittsburgh, Pennsylvania

Katz Underwear Company
Honesdale, Pennsylvania

Luria Engineering Company
1745 Eaton Avenue
Bethlehem, Pennsylvania

Mayer, Oscar & Company
Madison, Wisconsin

McCormick & Company
414 Light Street
Baltimore, Maryland

Mead Corporation
Dayton, Ohio

Merck & Company, Inc.
Rahway, New Jersey

National Starch Products Company
270 Madison Avenue
New York, New York

Niles-Bement-Pond Company
West Hartford, Connecticut

Norfolk & Western Railway Company
Roanoke, Virginia

North American Aviation, Inc.
International Airport
Los Angeles, California

Northern Illinois Gas Company
c/o National Merit Scholarship
Corporation
1580 Sherman Avenue
Evanston, Illinois

Ohio Boxboard Company
Rittman, Ohio

Ohio Oil Company
539 South Main Street
Findlay, Ohio

Ohmite Manufacturing Company
Skokie, Illinois

Outboard Marine Corporation
Evinrude Motors
Milwaukee, Wisconsin

Pan American Petroleum Corporation
c/o National Merit Scholarship
Corporation
1580 Sherman Avenue
Evanston, Illinois

Paragon Oil Company
2100 Hunters Point Avenue
Long Island City, New York

Pennsylvania Power & Light Company
901 Hamilton Street
Allentown, Pennsylvania

Pennsylvania Railroad
1617 Pennsylvania Boulevard
Philadelphia, Pennsylvania

Pennsylvania Salt Manufacturing Co.
Three Penn Center
Philadelphia, Pennsylvania

Phelps Dodge Corporation
300 Park Avenue
New York, New York

Philip Morris Inc.
100 Park Avenue
New York, New York

Philips Petroleum Company
Adams Boulevard
Bartlesville, Oklahoma

Pitney-Bowes, Inc.
Walnut & Pacific
Stanford, Connecticut

Pittsburgh Plate Glass Company
632 Fort Duquesne Boulevard
Pittsburgh, Pennsylvania

Pratt & Whitney Company, Inc.
Charter Oak Boulevard
West Hartford, Connecticut

Public Service Electric & Gas Company
Newark, New Jersey

Pullman Company
11024 South Michigan Avenue
Chicago, Illinois

Purolator Products, Inc.
970 New Brunswick Avenue
Rahway, New Jersey

Riegel Paper Corporation
Box 170, Grand Central Station
New York, New York

Riegel Textile Corporation
Box 170, Grand Central Station
New York, New York

Riverside Memorial Chapel
180 West 76th Street
New York, New York

Rockefeller Center, Inc.
50 Rockefeller Plaza
New York, New York

Santa Fe Foundation, Inc.
Chicago, Illinois

Schlumberger Well Surveying
Corporation
P. O. Box 2175
Houston, Texas

Schmidt, Christian
3965 Germantown Avenue
Philadelphia, Pennsylvania

Shatterproof Glass Corporation
c/o William B. Chase Foundation
4815 Cabot Avenue
Detroit, Michigan

Standard Oil Company of Indiana
910 South Michigan Avenue
Chicago, Illinois

Standard Oil Company of New Jersey
30 Rockefeller Plaza
New York, New York

Standard Oil Company of Ohio
c/o Foundation of Independent Colleges
4554 Starret Road
Columbus, Ohio

Superior Tube Company
Norristown, Pennsylvania

Time-Life
Time & Life Building
New York, New York

UARCO, Inc.
141 West Jackson Boulevard
Chicago, Illinois

United Aircraft Corporation
East Hartford, Connecticut

United States Industries, Inc.
250 Park Avenue
New York, New York

Van Raalte Company
417 Fifth Avenue
New York, New York

Victor Adding Machine Company
3900 N. Rockwell Street
Chicago, Illinois

Visking Corporation
6733 West 65th Street
Chicago, Illinois

West Chemical Products, Inc.
(Marcuse Fund)
c/o National Merit Scholarships Corp.
1580 Sherman Avenue
Evanston, Illinois

Western Union Telegram Company
60 Hudson Street
New York, New York

William Manufacturing Company
Gallia & Murray Streets
Portsmouth, Ohio

Wings Shirt Company, Inc.
4 West 33rd Street
New York, New York

Young & Rubicam, Inc.
285 Madison Avenue
New York, New York

FEDERAL FINANCIAL AID

Division of Student Financial Aid
U. S. Office of Education
Washington, D. C. 20202
(Request publication OE-55001-65)
Conditions: Loans may not exceed $1,000 per year or $5,000 for all years to any student.

National Defense Education Act of 1958:
Students Loans for High Education—
Title II
Conditions: For the college where student is enrolled or has been accepted.

ARCHITECTURE AND ENGINEERING

The American Institute of Architects
110 Pearl Street
Buffalo 2, New York
Conditions: (1) Scholarship for student interested in architecture as a career.

The Cooper Union (For the Advance of
Science and Art)
Director of Admissions

The Cooper Union
Cooper Square
New York, New York 10003
Conditions: Scholarships valued at $1,500 to $2,000 per year. Competitive—scholar ships in Art, Architecture, Engineering and Science.

Antioch-Niagara Frontier Council
116 Hartwell Road
Buffalo 16, New York
Conditions: (2) Scholarships, from $400 to $800 in Engineering.

Director
Polytechnic Institute of Brooklyn
Brooklyn, New York
Conditions: Students wishing to graduate in electrical engineering, especially those from Southern Negro high schools. All tuition and maintenance costs.

Union Carbide Education Fund
270 Park Avenue
New York, New York 10017
Conditions: Engineering scholarships at 35 engineering colleges and universities.

JOURNALISM AND DRAMA

The Newspaper Fund
P. O. Box 300
Princeton, New Jersey 08540
Conditions: List of nearly $700,000 in scholarships offered by schools and departments of Journalism.

William Randolph Hearst Foundation
3rd and Market Streets, Suite 1018
San Francisco, California 94103
Conditions: Grants for study to undergraduate journalism students range from $75 to $100 each month.

Abbott (George) Educational Foundation, Inc.
630 Fifth Avenue
New York, New York 10020
Conditions: Students with talent in dramatic playwriting willing to attend the University of Rochester

MEDICAL AND ALLIED PROFESSIONS

American Dental Association
Council of Dental Education
222 East Superior
Chicago, Illinois 60611
or
American Association of Dental Schools
840 North Lakeshore Drive
Chicago, Illinois 60611
American Medical Association
Education & Research Foundation
535 North Dearborn Street
Chicago, Illinois 60610
Conditions: Loans: Students admitted to approved medical schools.

Association of American Medical Colleges
2530 Ridge Avenue
Evanston, Illinois
Conditions: Brochure: For sources of financial aid to medical students.

Bergen Foundation
6536 Sunset Boulevard
Hollywood 28, California
Conditions: Loans: Nurses Training.

Beta Chi Inc.
1211 Leeds Street
Utica, New York
Conditions: One scholarship of $500 for a girl to attend any accredited hospital school of nursing.

Bureau of State Services (Community Health)
U. S. Department of Health, Education, and Welfare
Washington, D. C. 20201
(Request publication 1154)
Conditions: Person enrolled or accepted for enrollment as full-time students in an accredited school of nursing having a loan fund under the Act. Students may borrow up to $1,000 an academic year.

Bureau of State Services (Community Health)
U. S. Department of Health, Education, and Welfare
Washington, D. C. 20201
(Request publication 1347)
Conditions: Persons enrolled or accepted as full-time students in a school which has a loan fund under the Act.
Establishes student loans funds, for students pursuing a degree in medicine, dentistry, optometry, or osteopathy.
May obtain loans of up to $2,000 a year.

COSTEP
Surgeon General
U. S. Public Health Service
Washington, D. C.
Att: Office of Personnel
Conditions: For juniors and seniors in health related fields and students in programs of engineering and science.

The Health Profession Educational Assistance Act of 1963:
The Health Professions Student Loan Program—PTA.
Conditions: Institution where student is enrolled or has been accepted.

National Institute of Health
Division of Research Grants
U. S. Public Health Service
Bethesda, Maryland 20014

Conditions: Undergraduate and graduate training grants.

Navy Nurse's Corps Candidate Program
Nearest U. S. Navy Recruiting Station
Conditions: Open to students for Junior and Senior years in an accredited college or nursing school.
Provide for tuition, salary and/or allowance benefits.

Nurse Training Act of 1964:
Nursing Student Loan Program
Conditions: Institution where student is enrolled or has been accepted.

National League for Nursing
10 Columbus Circle
New York, New York 10019
Conditions: Scholarships for persons interested in Nursing.

Reyngolds Foundation, Inc.
Polikoff & Clarehen
11 West 42nd Street
New York, New York 10036
Conditions: Students of Medical and Social Sciences

The Surgeon General
Department of Army
Washington, D. C. 20315
Conditions: Scholarships for Dietetic Therapeutics fields under the Army.

VETERANS

AMVETS National Foundation
P. O. Box 6038
Mid-City Station
Washington 5, D. C.
Conditions: Children whose fathers are deceased or totally disabled as a result of military service.
$2,000 total for four years.

War Orphans Education Program
Local Veterans Administration Office
Conditions: Children of servicemen who died in U. S. Armed Forces; must be between ages 18-23.
$110 monthly.

MISCELLANEOUS PROFESSIONS

The Kroger Company
1014 Vine Street
Cincinnati, Ohio
Areas: Freshman scholarships for students majoring in Agricultural and Home Economics at land grant colleges in the Mid-West and South.

Sears, Roebuck Foundation
Apply to Dean of land Grant College in home State.
Areas: Scholarships for male agricultural students and female home economics students.

The Ralston Purina Fellowships
Ralston Purina Company
Education Department
St. Louis, Missouri 63102
Areas: Scholarships for training in Animal Husbandry.

Allstate Foundation
10 Columbus Circle
New York, New York 10009
Areas: Scholarships for Driver Education to high school teachers.

National Board of Civil Air Patrol
Civil Air Patrol
Ellington Air Force Base
Texas
Areas: Undergraduate and graduate scholarships awarded to Civil Air Patrol members.

Institute of Food Technology
176 West Adam Street
Chicago, Illinois 60603
Areas: Scholarships range from $300 to $1000.
Scholarships for the field of Food Technology or Food Science

Council of Hotel, Restaurant, and Institutional Education
Statler-Hall
Ithaca, New York 14858
Areas: Summary of financial aid available to students pursuing courses of study leading to a career in hotel, restaurant, and institutional work.

Abraham & Strauss Scholarships
Areas: Executive scholarships annually for students to combine on-the-job training and studies in retailing at Adelphi College, City College, Hofstra College, Long Island University, and New York University.

National Commission for Social Work Careers
345 East 46th Street
New York, New York 10017
Areas: Handbook of graduate scholarships in the field of social work.

Public Inquiry Branch
U.S. Department of Health, Education & Welfare
Washington, D. C. 20201
Areas: Undergraduate college students and graduate students training for teach-

ing. Provides for scholarships of up to $800 to $1,000 based on need and academic standing in high school.

FINANCIAL AID FOR SPANISH SPEAKING STUDENTS

ASPIRA Agency Scholarships
137 West 72nd Street
New York, New York

Barnard College
New York, N.Y. 10027
(2) Scholarships (Spanish Speaking)

Barnard College
New York, N.Y. 10027
(1) Scholarship — Girl

Board of Home Missions
287 Fourth Avenue
New York, New York
(4) Scholarships

Mercy College
Detroit, Michigan
Catholic Puerto Rican Students

Miami University
Oxford, Ohio
Conversational Classes.

New York Puerto Rican Scholarship Fund, Inc.
250 Church Street
New York, New York
Competitive

St. Lawrence University
Canton, New York

St. Mary of the Woods College
St. Mary of the Woods, Indiana

Southern Illinois University
Cardonale, Illinois

University of Arizona
Tucson, Arizona
(10) Scholarships of $360 each.

University of Chattanooga
Chattanooga, Tennessee
Scholarships available in return for help in conversational classes.

University of New Mexico
Albuquerque, New Mexico
Scholarship and stipend for tuition, board and room

STUDENT COUNSELING SERVICES

College Admission Assistance Center
41 East 65th Street
New York, New York
($20.00 Service Fee)

College and Career Consultants
YWCA
New York, New York

National Scholarship Service and Fund for Negro Students
6 East 82nd Street
New York, New York

New York City Board of Education
Bureau of Guidance
110 Livingston Street
Brooklyn, New York

GENERAL LOANS

Beans Foundation
2 Broadway
New York, New York 10004
Grants and Loans: students attending colleges and universities

Central Scholarship Bureau, Inc.
819 W. Monument Street
Baltimore 1, Maryland
Limit: $750

Insured Tuition Plan
38 Newbury Street
Boston 16, Massachusetts
Loans: no restriction on school location

ADDITIONAL SOURCES OF FINANCIAL AID

Catholic Scholarships for Negroes, Inc.
Mrs. Roger L. Putnam
224 Union Street
Springfield, Mass. 01105

The Fund for Theological Education, Inc.
163 Nassau Street
Princeton, New Jersey 08540

Howard University Foreign Service Grant
Howard University
Washington, D. C.

Minority Groups Scholarship Program
Write to:
Antioch College, Yellow Springs, Ohio
Carleton College, Northfield, Minn.
Grinnell College, Grinnell, Iowa
Oberlin College, Oberlin, Ohio
Occidental College, Los Angeles, Calif.
Reed College, Portland, Oregon
Swarthmore College, Swarthmore, Pa.

Polytechnic Institute of Brooklyn, N.Y.
Electrical Engineering (Priority given to Southern Negroes for remedial courses.)

Ralph L. Smith
Freedom Scholarships
Macalester College
St. Paul, Minnesota

Student Opportunity Scholarships
Room 1140
475 Riverside Drive
New York, New York 10027

Texas Southern University School of Business
Houston, Texas

Home Guidance Counselor
Catholic Scholarships for Negroes
254 Union Street
Springfield, Mass.

Elks National Foundation
Chairman Scholarship Awards
16 Court Street
Boston, Mass.

Field Foundation Inc.
250 Park Avenue
New York, New York 10017

International Supreme Council of World Masons
2775 W. Forest Avenue
Detroit, Michigan

Alfred P. Sloan Foundation
630 Fifth Avenue
New York, New York 10020

The Dillon Fund
c/o Shearman & Sterling
20 Exchange Place
New York, New York 10005

American Baptist Convention (In order to attend Baptist College)
152 Madison Avenue
New York, N. Y.

George F. Baker Trust
2 Wall Street
New York, New York 10005

Jephson Educational Trust
c/o Chase Manhattan Bank
1 Chase Manhattan Plaza
New York, New York 10005

McGregor Fund
2486 First National Building
Detroit, Michigan

Chemistry class at one of the predominantly black colleges.

National Scholarship Service & Fund for Negro Students
6 East 82nd Street
New York, New York 10028

Omega Psi Phi Fraternity
3104 13th Street, N.W.
Washington, D. C.

Rockefeller Foundation Scholarship Aid
Duke University, Durham, North Carolina
Emory University, Atlanta, Georgia
Tulane University, New Orleans, La.
Vanderbilt University, Nashville, Tenn.
For disadvantaged graduates of Southern high schools. Tuition varies.

Rockefeller Foundation Scholarship Aid for Negro Students
Antioch College, Yellow Springs, Ohio
Carleton College, Northfield, Minnesota
Grinnell College, Grinnell, Iowa
Oberlin College, Oberlin, Ohio
Occidental College, Los Angeles, Calif.
Reed College, Portland, Oregon
Swarthmore College, Swarthmore, Penna.
High School Juniors — Tuition for four years.

The Eleanor Roosevelt Scholarship Program
CORE Scholarship Education & Defense Fund, Inc.
150 Nassau Street, Room 312
New York, New York 10038
Students who have actively involved in efforts to eliminate racial prejudice and discrimination and to secure legal rights for persons of all races. Up to $2,000 annually.

Roosevelt University
3430 S. Michigan Avenue
Chicago, Illinois
Negro and Indian students wishing to study in the college of Business Administration. $1,500 a year.

St. Mary's College
Notre Dame, Indiana
(1) Scholarship for Negro girl, competitive

Ralph L. Smith Freedom Scholarships
Macalester College
St. Paul, Minnesota

Texas Southern University
Houston, Texas
(107) High School Juniors
Tuition and fees for four years
Texas Southern University School of Business
Home Guidance Counselor
Houston, Texas

John Hay Whitney Foundation
11 West 50th Street
New York, New York 10020
Graduate work in the Creative Arts — Minority group solicit.
Range from $1,000 to $3,000 a year.

ELEMENTARY AND SECONDARY EDUCATION ACT

The passage of the Elementary and Secondary Education Act of 1965 served notice of the intention of the federal government to assume direct responsibility for providing all children—particularly the disadvantaged—with quality education. The five key provisions of the act can be summarized as follows:

TITLE I. *Opportunity for the Disadvantaged*

This title provides funds to school districts under state plans approved by the U. S. Office of Education. During the first year of the program, Congress appropriated 775 million dollars to individual states and school districts. Each local public school is eligible to receive half the average current school expenditure per child in the state, multiplied by the number of school-age children in the district whose families earn less than $2,000 annually.

Funds may be used to benefit both public and nonpublic school children through such arrangements as dual enrollment, educational media centers, mobile education services and equipment, and educational radio and television. They may also be used for broadened health programs, school breakfasts, guidance and counseling, in-service teacher training, additional teaching personnel, curriculum development, preschool training, and special audio-visual

aids and other equipment.

Title I funds are in the form of 100% grants to state educational agencies which then allocate money to school districts according to a formula established by Congress.

TITLE II. *School Library and Instructional Resources*

Under Title II, Congress has authorized 100 million dollars for school library aid. Funds may be used to purchase textbooks, library books, periodicals, documents, tapes, records, physical facilities, equipment, and for administration and financing. (Under present estimates, Title II funds are expected to add about $2 per pupil annually for *each* of the nation's 47 million school children.) Funds are allocated under state plans on the basis of public and nonpublic elementary and secondary school populations.

Administrative plans under this title require the approval of the U. S. Office of Education. They must spell out criteria for fund use and provide assurance that materials will be available on an equitable basis *for all children.* Materials are loaned to private school pupils, and remain the property of the designated public agency.

Since the needs and requirements of each state vary, uniform plans are not mandatory.

TITLE III. *Supplementary Educational Centers*

This title is designed to help local school districts relate research to practice through the support of supplementary centers and services. These must seek to improve the quality of education by providing services *not now available* to the children within a given community, such as psychological testing, audiovisual aids, radio and television, programmed materials, etc.

Congress appropriated 75 million dollars for Title III supplementary centers for fiscal 1966. Services are available to public and nonpublic pupils on a non-sectarian basis.

TITLE IV. *Educational Research*

Under this title, Congress has appropriated 100 million dollars over a five-year period in an effort to improve the depth of U. S. educational research. The money is being used to construct and equip national and regional research facilities, including educational laboratories. These laboratories are regionally based, and work in such areas as basic research, curriculum development and teacher training.

TITLE V. *Strengthening State Education Agencies*

Under this title, Congress has appropriated 17 million dollars for the first year of a five-year program designed to strengthen state education departments. (Title V provides unmatched federal grants for the first two years, and then calls for matching state grants of from 33 to 50% of the federal total.)

Two kinds of grants—basic and experimental—are authorized under this title. Eighty-five per cent of the funds must be used for basic administrative improvements, with the remainder earmarked for experimental projects. Provision has also been made under Title V for the exchange of personnel between the U. S. Office of Education and state education departments in order to establish a better understanding of programs and problems.

SELECTED PROGRAMS FOR EDUCATIONALLY DISADVANTAGED CHILDREN UNDER THE ELEMENTARY AND SECONDARY EDUCATION ACT (1965)

Educational personnel:

- Inservice training for teachers.
- Additional teaching personnel to reduce class size.
- Teacher aids and instructional secretaries.
- Supervisory personnel and full-time specialists for improvement of instruction and to provide related pupil services.
- Team tutoring.
- Provide trained, paid leaders for science youth clubs and educational clubs.
- Exchange programs for teachers and inservice teacher training.
- College-based institute for training teachers in special skills.
- Employment of consultants for improvement of program.
- Program to train teacher aids.

Curriculums:

- Supplementary instructional materials.
- Curriculum materials center for disadvantaged children.
- Classes for talented elementary students.
- Special classes for disturbed and socially maladjusted children.
- Preschool training programs.
- Remedial programs—especially reading and mathematics.
- Education in family living and home management.
- Enrichment programs such as story hours for grades 1, 2, and 3 on Saturday mornings and during summer.
- Ungraded primary grades.
- Programmed instruction.
- English programs for non-English-speaking children.
- Special audiovisuals for disadvantaged.

Related educational services:

- Program for the early identification and prevention of dropouts.
- Increased guidance services.
- Guidance programs for pupils and families.
- School-job coordinators.
- Home and school visitors and/or social workers.
- Early identification of gifted among disadvantaged.
- Area guidance centers.

Financial and other assistance to individuals:

- Supplemental health and food services.
- School health psychiatric, and psychological services.
- Provision of clothing, shoes, and books where necessary.
- Financial assistance to needy high school pupils.

Equipment:

Special laboratories.

School plant improvements—elementary school science laboratories, libraries, kitchens, and cafeterias.

Equip elementary classrooms for television and radio instruction.

Purchase of musical recordings of classical nature, and recordings of poems and addresses.

Mobile learning centers.

Educational camps.

College coaching classes.

Expansion of recreation to include physical education, health, and hygiene.

Arts and crafts programs during summer vacation.

Summer school and day camp.

Summer programs for development of language skills growing out of activities.

Community centers for organized recreation, hobbies, and special interests.

Full-day summer school.

Shop and library facilities available after regular school hours.

Informal play group program with young children.

Sports and other activities designed to improve physical fitness and develop sportsmanship.

Vocational or occupational:

Occupational training classes.

Work experience programs.

On-the-job training for high school students.

Program for unemployed, out-of-school youth, between the ages of 16 and 21.

Extended operation of youth organizations—future farmers, business leaders, homemakers, nurses, etc.

A group of Negro youngsters watches attentively as an elementary school teacher guides them through their reading lessons.

Libraries and cultural enrichment:
- Field trips for cultural and educational development.
- Expansion of libraries in major disciplines.
- Scheduling of concerts, dramas, and lectures; mobile art exhibits and libraries.
- Saturday morning special opportunity classes.
- Bookmobiles—home oriented.

Miscellaneous:
- Afterschool study centers.
- Preschool pupil transportation.
- Pupil exchange programs (semester, year, summer).
- Residential schools in demonstration areas.

THE HIGHER EDUCATION ACT

The Higher Education Act of 1965 seeks to "strengthen the educational resources of our colleges and universities and to provide financial assistance for students in post-secondary and higher education." In short, this act seeks to take advantage of the skills and knowledge of the university by, in effect, putting the university to work toward solving the problems of the community. The first five titles of the act may be summarized as follows:

TITLE I. *Community Service and Continuing Education Programs*

Title I authorizes the appropriation of 25 million dollars in fiscal 1966 for community service and continuing education programs. The programs, set up by the states, place special emphasis on solving problems in urban and suburban areas. Each participating state has chosen an existing agency or institution to carry out this title. This agency, through a federally approved plan, has established guidelines for giving federal funds to qualifying colleges and universities.

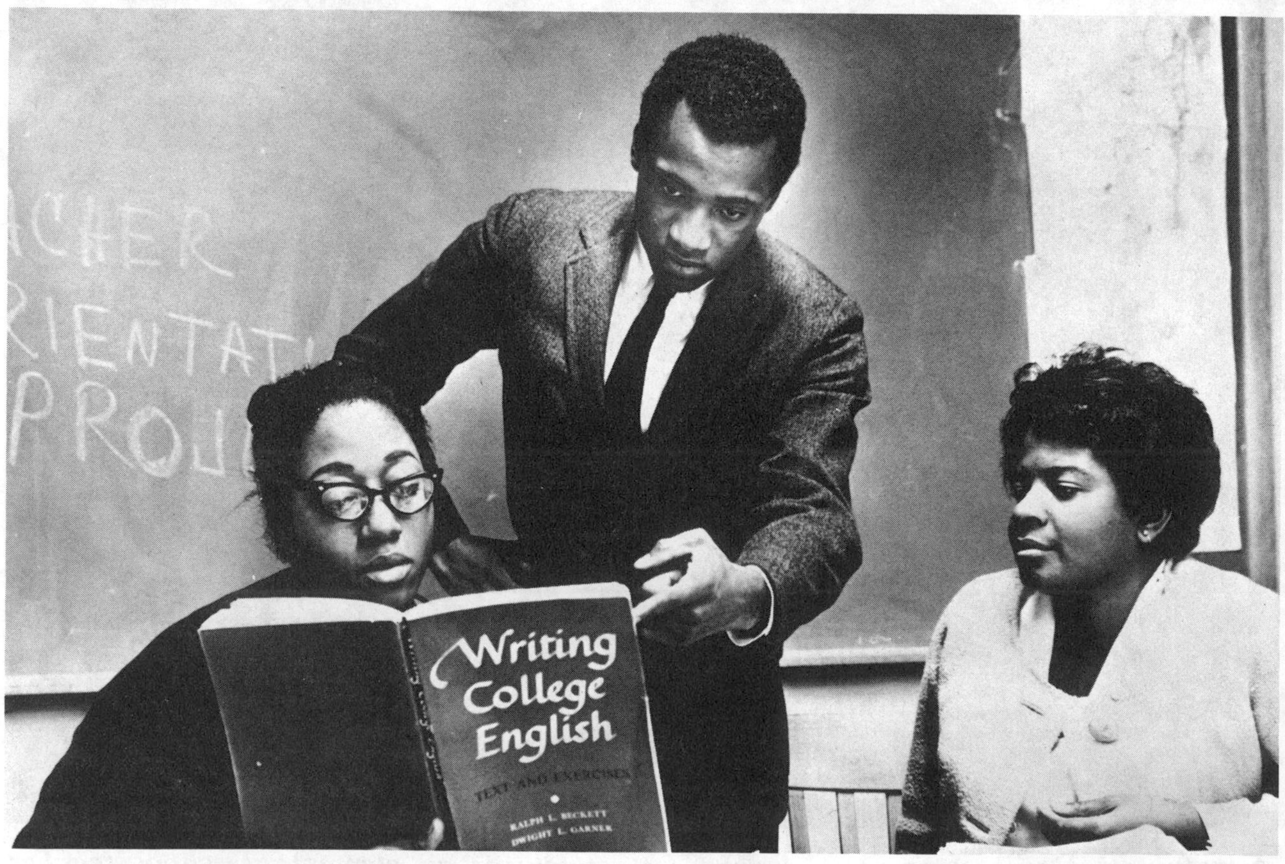

TITLE II. *College Library Assistance and Library Training and Research*

Title II provides grants to colleges and universities for library materials such as books, periodicals, documents, magnetic tapes and phonograph records. These grants sometimes double and triple the funds available for library development in small and poorly supported colleges.

TITLE III. *Strengthening Developing Institutions*

Under this title, 55 million dollars has been provided to carry out cooperative programs and set up national teaching fellowships for developing institutions. Seventy-eight per cent of the money goes to four-year colleges; the remaining 22% to two-year colleges.

To be eligible, institutions must meet the following requirements:

1. Admit as regular students only high school students, or the equivalent.
2. Award a bachelor's degree, or provide a two-year program creditable toward such a degree, or a two-year technical program.
3. Be accredited, or be making reasonable progress toward reaching this status.

TITLE IV. *Student Assistance*

Title IV establishes educational opportunity grants, and provides federally subsidized student loans. Seventy million dollars has been authorized for these grants in the 1966–1967 school year. Colleges themselves administer the grants, select the eligible students, and decide on the size of individual grants.

TITLE V. *Teacher Programs*

Title V is aimed at improving the calibre and increasing the number of America's teachers, with a view toward thus increasing the educational opportunity offered America's elementary and secondary school children. It also establishes the National Teacher Corps (NTC), providing fellowships for graduate study. Members of the NTC are often used to visit impoverished school districts, and supplement the teaching force there.

Library facilities in the Negro colleges have been greatly expanded through funds made available by the Higher Education Act.

THE HIGHER EDUCATION AMENDMENTS OF 1968

Amendments to the Higher Education Act constitute the most comprehensive aid-to-education package to take effect since the Elementary and Secondary Education Act of 1965. These amendments not only extend through 1971 such key legislation as the National Defense Education Act and the Higher Education Act, but also create six new higher education programs, including Special Services for Disadvantaged Students, Cooperative Education and Education for the Public Service. As a whole, the amendments broaden the search for talented and ambitious youths from the pre-school to the Ph.D. level. The five amendments can be summarized as follows:

TITLE I: *Student Assistance*

Student assistance has several features which can be characterized under a number of appropriate headings. The Educational Opportunity Grant Program increases maximum student grants from $800 to $1,000 a year. The federal government is still paying interest charges on loans to borrowers in college or in their deferment period. The College Work-Study Program allows students to work more than 15 hours per week during the summer, with 80% of salary being paid by the federal government. Under Cooperative Education, grants are authorized to plan and develop programs which alternate full-time study with full-time employment. The National Defense Student Loan Program permits teachers in low-income schools to cancel up to 100% of their loans.

TITLE II: *Amendments to Other Provisions of The Higher Education Act*

Other amendments to HEA offer assistance to college libraries, to junior colleges, to state educational authorities recruiting teachers and teacher aides, sharing faculty, and improving graduate programs. The Law School Clinical Experience Program (title 9) will pay up to 90% of the cost of establishing clinical experience projects at accredited law schools.

TITLE III: *Amendments to Provisions of the National Defense Education Act*

The NDEA amendments include those which provide 7,500 new fellowships per year, offer short-term training sessions for guidance counselors and extend, without change, language development.

TITLE IV: *Amendments to the Higher Education Facilities Act*

New legislation appended to the HEFA authorizes Federal interest grants to help cover the cost of non-Federal financing of construction, and makes student health facilities eligible for building funds. These apply to both graduate and undergraduate facilities.

TITLE V: *Miscellaneous Amendments*

The HEA amendments extend the life of Section 12 of the National Foundation on the Arts and Humanities Act and the International Education Act of 1966. These amendments also specify instances in which Federal assistance can be cut off, to wit: when a student is convicted of a serious crime involving force or seizure of a campus facility which denies the majority access to the institution.

VOCATIONAL EDUCATION

Vocational Education Act (P.L. 88-210). Funds are available for state vocational education programs for persons in high school, for persons who have completed or left high school, for persons who are unemployed or underemployed, and for persons who have academic, socioeconomic, or other handicaps that prevent them from succeeding in regular vocational education programs. Residential vocational schools, work-study programs, teacher-training, and research programs are included in the provisions of this Act. School systems interested in knowing more about this resource should contact their state education agency. *Additional information may be obtained from the Division of Vocational and Technical Education, Bureau of Adult and Vocational Education, Office of Education, Washington, D.C. 20202.*

Aid to technical and vocational education. (This was formerly NDEA, Title VIII, P.L. 85-864, as amended by P.L. 88-210.) Grants are available to states for the development of area vocational education programs in scientific or technological fields. These programs are designed to train persons for employment as highly skilled technicians in recognized occupations requiring scientific knowledge in fields necessary for the national defense. Provision can be made for retraining and refresher courses for adults in such fields as electronics and industrial chemistry. School systems interested in knowing more about this resource should contact their state education agency. *Additional information may be obtained from the Division of Vocational and Technical Education, Bureau of Adult and Vocational Education, Office of Education, Washington, D.C. 20202.*

CIVIL RIGHTS INSTITUTES

Civil Rights Act of 1964, Title IV (P.L. 88-352). Title IV provides funds to colleges and universities to conduct institutes for school personnel, grants to the school boards for in-service training and the employment of advisory specialists, and technical assistance, including consultants, to enable schools to deal more effectively with educational problems caused by desegregation. *Further information may be obtained from the Equal Educational Opportunities Program, Office of Education, Washington, D.C. 20202.*

NATIONAL DEFENSE EDUCATION ACT

Loans to Students in Institutions of Higher Learning, Title II (P.L. 85-864, as amended by P.L. 88-665). Undergraduate and graduate students at American colleges and universities may obtain loans under this Title to pursue their higher education. Students receiving loans who become full-time teachers in public or other nonprofit elementary or secondary schools or institutions of higher education may have up to 50 percent of their loans canceled. *Additional information may be obtained from the Director, Division of Student Financial Aid, Bureau of Higher Education Programs, Office of Education, Washington, D.C. 20202.*

Grants to Strengthen Subject Areas, Title III (P.L. 85-864, as amended by P.L. 88-665). Matching grants to states are available for the purpose of strengthening education in elementary and secondary schools in the critical subjects of science, mathematics, history, civics, geography, modern foreign language, English, and reading. This is accomplished through Federal grants and loans for the acquisition of laboratory and other special equipment and through Federal grants for state programs of supervisory and related services in those subjects. School systems interested in knowing more about this resource should contact their state education agency. *Additional information may be obtained from the Division of Program Operations, Bureau of Elementary and Secondary Education, Office of Education, Washington, D.C. 20202.*

Guidance, Counseling, and Testing, Title V (P.L. 85-864, as amended by P.L. 88-665). State education agencies may receive matching grants under this Title to establish and maintain elementary and secondary school programs of testing, guidance, and counseling. These programs are designed for the early identification of students with outstanding aptitude. School systems interested in knowing more about this resource should contact their state education agency. *Additional information may be obtained from Division of Program Operations, Bureau of Elementary and Secondary Education, Office of Education, Washington, D.C. 20202.*

Institutes for Advanced Study, Title XI (P.L. 88-665). Funds are available to institutions of higher education to conduct institutes for advanced study in order to improve the qualifications of individuals engaged in the teaching of disadvantaged youth. Short-term or regular session institutes may be held; usually summer programs predominate. The law defines such youth as those who are "culturally, economically, socially, and educationally handicapped." An institute may focus on teachers whose students are rural, urban, migrant, Indian, non-English speaking, and so forth. *Additional information may be obtained from the Division of Educational Personnel Training, Bureau of Elementary and Secondary Education, Office of Education, Washington, D.C. 20202.*

HANDICAPPED

Captioned Films for the Deaf (P.L. 85-505, as amended by P.L. 87-715). Under this Act a service of films is available to provide cultural and educational experiences and to promote educational advancement for the deaf. The Act also supports research in the use and production of these films and for training persons in this area. *Additional information may be obtained from Director, Captioned Films for the Deaf Branch, Division of Research Training and Dissemination, Bureau of Research, Office of Education, Washington, D.C. 20202.*

National Technical Institute for the Deaf (P.L. 89-36). The National Technical Institute for the Deaf will provide a residential vocational school for post-secondary training of deaf youth for employment in high-skill jobs. *Additional information may be obtained from Phillip Des Marias, Office of the Secretary, Department of Health, Education, and Welfare, Washington, D.C. 20201.*

PATTERNS OF SEGREGATION IN U.S. PUBLIC SCHOOLS

The great majority of American children attend schools that are largely segregated—that is, where almost all of their fellow students are of the same racial background as they are. Among minority groups, Negroes are by far the most segregated. Taking all groups, however, white children are most segregated. Almost 80 percent of all white pupils in 1st grade and 12th grade attend schools that are from 90 to 100 percent white. And 97 percent at grade 1, and 99 percent at grade 12, attend schools that are 50 percent or more white.

For Negro pupils, segregation is more nearly complete in the South (as it is for whites also), but it is extensive also in all the other regions where the Negro population is concentrated: the urban North, Midwest, and West.

More than 65 percent of all Negro pupils in the first grade attend schools that are between 90 and 100 percent Negro. And 87 percent at grade 1, and 66 percent at grade 12, attend schools that are 50 percent or more Negro. In the South most students attend schools that are 100 percent white or Negro.

The same pattern of segregation holds, though not quite so strongly, for the teachers of Negro and white students. For the nation as a whole, the average Negro elementary pupil attends a school in which 65 percent of the teachers are Negro; the average white elementary pupil attends a school in which 97 percent of the teachers are white. White teachers are more predominant at the secondary level, where the corresponding figures are 59 and 97 percent. The racial matching of teachers is most pronounced in the South, where by tradition it has been complete. On a nationwide basis, in cases where the races of pupils and teachers are not matched, the trend is all in one direction: white teachers teach Negro children but Negro teachers seldom teach white children; just as, in the schools, integration consists primarily of a minority of Negro pupils in predominantly white schools but almost never of a few whites in largely Negro schools.

In its desegregation decision of 1954, the Supreme Court held that separate schools for Negro and white children are inherently unequal. When measured by that yardstick, American public education remains largely unequal in most regions of the country, including all those where Negroes form any significant proportion of the population.

At latest report, the federal government had set the autumn of 1967 as the deadline for integration at all grade levels of public schools seeking to qualify for federal funds. The Department of Health, Education and Welfare (HEW) had gone so far as to issue a statement declaring an end to the era of "paper compliance."*

In the first week of 1970, then-Secretary of Health, Education and Welfare Robert Finch announced that school districts implementing voluntary desegregation plans were making "significant and effective progress" in providing equal educational opportunity. It was difficult to reconcile this report with the 23.4% nationwide figure of black students enrolled in predominantly white public elementary and secondary schools. Some 61% of black students were shown to be isolated in 95-100% minority schools. Some 43.3 million students were represented by the ethnic data collected by the HEW Office for Civil Rights.

In 1968, 55 school districts submitted acceptable plans under Title VI. Of the 35,815 black students in these districts, 31,089 (86.8%) attended schools of predominantly white enrollment. This compared with the 23.4% desegregation figure nationally, the 18.4% figure for 11 Southern states, and the 10.5% figure for Alabama, Georgia, Louisiana, Mississippi and

South Carolina, i.e., the Deep South. In 1969, more than 200 Title VI "acceptable" plans called for complete desegregation in the year 1969-1970, and over 100 called for "substantial desegregation."

Leon Panetta, former Director of the Office for Civil Rights, interpreted the data as follows: "With the aid of thousands of cooperating state and local school officials who submitted raw data, we can see a stark portrayal of ethnic isolation in schools. Whether a child is isolated with his own or other minorities, he is still likely to suffer educationally as a result of this segregation, according to numerous education studies."

In a regional study of black segregation, for example, it was shown that there is a great variation in the number of Negroes attending 100 percent minority schools, from six heavily industrial Northern states, where 15.4% of the Negroes attended 100% minority schools, to six Border states and the District of Columbia, where 25.2% of the Negroes attended 100% minority schools, to five deep Southern states, where 81.9% of the Negroes attended 100% minority schools. (This last figure is based on 431 districts in five states out of 4,477 districts in 17 Southern and Border states.)

SOUTHERN SCHOOL DESEGREGATION*

State	*Districts Reporting*	*Total Enrollment*	*Black Enrollment*	*Black Students in Integrated Schools*	*Percent-age*
Alabama	89	588,639	204,365	15,039	7.4
Arkansas	173	376,470	94,791	22,048	23.3
Florida	57	1,160,644	282,226	67,961	24.1
Georgia	144	883,287	268,044	38,196	14.2
Louisiana	50	774,140	299,152	26,354	8.8
Mississippi	100	398,725	193,602	13,839	7.1
North Carolina	143	1,120,602	330,449	92,028	27.8
South Carolina	76	486,509	196,203	29,198	14.9
Tennessee	120	843,525	140,287	34,098	24.3
Texas	501	2,264,881	306,648	119,259	38.9
Virginia	115	992,047	236,023	60,587	25.7
Total	1,568	9,889,469	2,551,790	518,607	20.3

* The latest available data reflects 1968 figures, and was supplied by the Office for Civil Rights.

NEGRO PROFESSIONAL EDUCATION

Over the past two decades, the percentage of Negroes who have completed four or more years of college has been rising slowly and steadily. Nonetheless, the relatively small proportion of Negroes in professional and related occupations is traceable as much to their limited education as it is to the pressure of discrimination in employment. (As of 1969 close to 7% of the black population in the age group 25 to 34 years of age were in professional or related occupations compared to about 16% of whites in related occupations.)

The major resource for training Negroes at the college level has long been the predominantly Negro colleges and universities, most of which are located in the South. Public Negro colleges have existed for more than a century. Most of them were founded in the decades following the Civil War between 1867 and 1900 to provide an education for newly freed slaves. The colleges are located in 19 states, most of them Southern and border states. The oldest is Cheyney State College in Pennsylvania founded in 1837 and the only one predating the Civil War. The youngest is Mississippi Valley State College founded in 1950. Sixteen of the colleges were founded in the 19th century as land grant colleges or later given this status to conform with federal requirements that benefits of land grant programs be available to both Negro and whites. A majority of the colleges were founded as state colleges, often with significant Negro leadership. Elizabeth City State University, for example, was created in 1891 by a bill introduced into the North Carolina legislature by Hugh Cale, a Negro legislator from Pasquotank County. In 1871, when Alcorn A & M College was officially opened for Mississippi's black citizens, Hiram R. Revels, the first Negro elected to the U.S. Senate resigned his seat to become the college's first president. Alcorn originated as Oakland College, a school for the education of white males.

Thirteen of the colleges were initially organized under private auspices, generally with gifts from both Negro and white individuals and groups. The soldiers and officers of the 62cnd U.S. Colored Infantry gave $5,000 to provide funds for Lincoln University's incorporation in Missouri and are credited with the college's founding and eventual financing. Fort Valley State College was established in 1895 by leading local white and Negro citizens and was generously supported by gifts from Miss Anna T. Jeanes of Philadelphia. Albany State College in Georgia was begun as the Albany Bible and Manual Training Institute, receiving financial support from the Hazard family of Newport, Rhode Island, as well as from concerned local philanthropists. Financial problems led some private colleges to seek state support, and they became public institutions. There remain about 70 private Negro colleges in the nation today.

Public Negro colleges currently enroll 93,470 students and are growing rapidly. Their 1968-1969 enrollment was 7.7 percent higher than their 1967-1968 enrollment, and more than double their 1956 enrollment. In fact, it is anticipated that 34 public Negro colleges will have an enrollment of 100,000 in 1970.

Public Negro Colleges enroll approximately three-fifths of all students in predominantly Negro colleges. Nationally, they enroll about one-third of all black students in higher education today.

The average enrollment at public Negro colleges is 2749 students. There are, however, wide variations in size. Southern University in Louisiana is the largest institution, enrolling 9978 students. Maryland State College is the smallest, enrolling 717. Six of the 34 colleges enroll more than 4000 students while two enroll fewer than 1000.

Students come from all parts of the country and from abroad. Most are from Southern and border states with 89 percent living in the state in which their college is located. The remaining ten percent represent every state except Alaska. New York and New Jersey alone contribute about one-fifth out of state students at public Negro colleges. Men account for 40 percent of the enrollment; women, 54 percent. About 3% of the undergraduate students and 13% of the graduate students are white. Some 85% of the students attend full time ranging from 15% of the graduate students to 92.7% of the freshmen.

Public Negro Colleges award approximately 10,000 bachelors and 1400 masters degrees annually. At the masters level, education accounts for 81.6 percent of all degrees. Mathematics and science fields account for ten percent.

Outstanding alumni of Kentucky State College include Whitney Young, Executive Director of the National Urban League, Mrs. Ersa Poston, President of the New York State

Civil Service Commission and Harvey C. Russell, Vice President of PepsiCo Inc. Opera singer Leontyne Price is an alumnus of Central State University. Russell Frye, the first Negro elected to the North Carolina State Legislature since Reconstruction, is a graduate of North Carolina A & T State University. Miss Barbara Jordan, a member of the Texas State Senate, is a graduate of Texas Southern University.

Chart 50

BLACK STUDENTS IN HIGHER EDUCATION TODAY

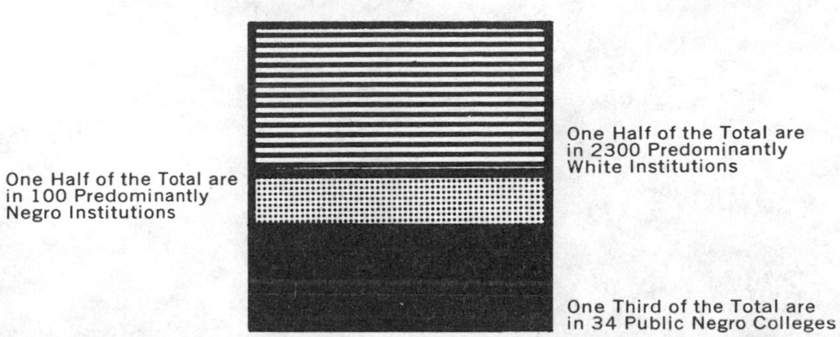

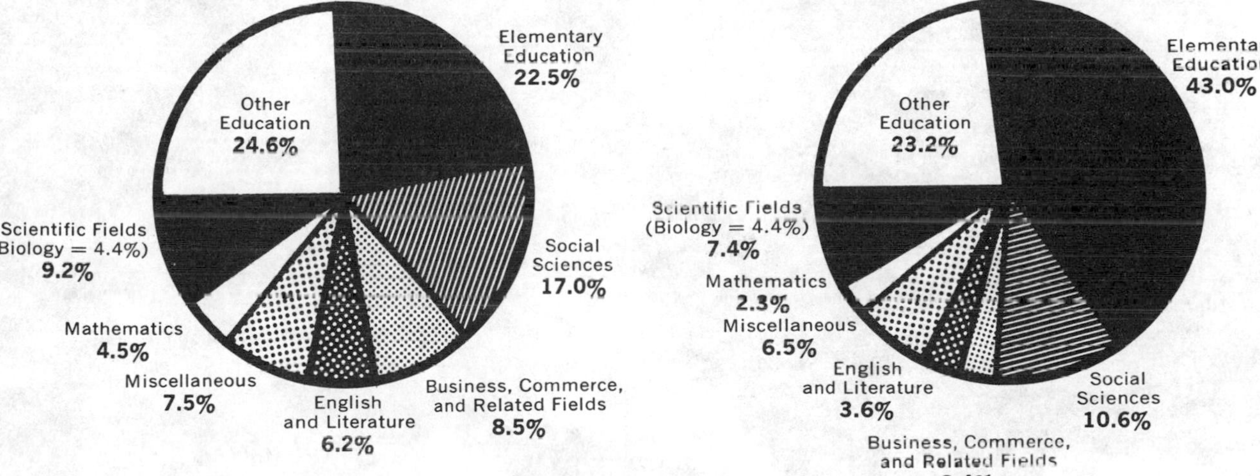

Source: U.S. Office of Education

The combined physical plants of 34 public Negro colleges are worth an estimated $442.3 million. Their libraries hold a total of 3.4 million books and about 100,000 reels of microfilm. In addition to 163,000 books in its own library, Texas Southern can also make available to its students and staff the collection of 27 other Texas and Louisiana college libraries through a teletype inter-library loan program.

As of 1970, 5,000 full time faculty members were teaching at the 34 colleges. About 27% hold Ph.D. degrees. Major white institutions threaten to siphon off many outstanding faculty members at public Negro colleges.

The 1970's will see black enrollments gain at white institutions due to migration of Negroes to North and West, gains in desegregation of Southern Colleges, and vigorous recruiting of black students by Northern schools. Current trends indicate that Negro colleges will lose black students to white institutions faster than they will gain white students from them. Fewer than 5% of students in previously all black colleges are white and the percentage is expected to increase slowly. Morehouse College in Atlanta, for example, has less than twelve white students. Although one of the four Phi Beta Kappa institutions in Georgia which leads all other four year colleges in the state in alumni who have received Ph.D. degrees, Morehouse is bypassed by whites who avoid the adjustment involved in attending a Negro institution in the South.

PREDOMINANTLY NEGRO INSTITUTIONS, COLLEGES AND UNIVERSITIES IN THE UNITED STATES

Institution, Accreditation and Date of Founding	*Enrollment*	*Type*	*Control*	*President*
ALABAMA				
Alabama A. & M. (S) 1875 **Normal 35762**	1,222	Coed	State	R. D. Morrison
	Liberal arts and general program, teacher-preparatory and and terminal-occupational training. Master's and/or second professional degree.			
Alabama State 1874 **915 S. Jackson** **Montgomery 36101**	2,082	Coed	State	Levi Watkins
	Liberal arts and general program. Teacher-preparatory training. Master's and/or second professional degree.			
Daniel Payne Jr. College (S) 1880 **6415 Washington Blvd.** **Birmingham 35212**	312	Coed	Ame	Howard D. Gregg
	Two-year college with a three-year professional school.			
Miles College 1907 **Birmingham 35064**	816	Coed	Cme	L. H. Pitts
	Liberal arts and general program. Teacher-preparatory training. Bachelor's and/or first professional degree.			
Oakwood College (S) 1896 **Huntsville 35806**	410	Coed	Sda	Frank Hale, Jr.
	Liberal arts program, A.B. and B.S. degrees.			
Selma University 1878 **150 Lapsley St., Selma**	224	Coed	Mbc	J. H. Owens
	Junior college and school of religion operated by the Alabama State Baptist Convention.			
Stillman College (S) 1876 **3601 15th Street** **Tuscaloosa**	522	Coed	Pc	Harold N. Stinson
	Liberal arts and general program. Teacher-preparatory training. Bachelor's and/or first professional degree.			
Talladega College (S) 1867 **Talladega 35160**	413	Coed	Ucc	Herman H. Long
	Liberal arts and general program. Teacher-preparatory training. Bachelor's and/or first professional degree.			
Tuskegee Institute (S) 1881 **Tuskegee 36088**	2,182	Coed	Pr	L. H. Foster
	Liberal arts and general program. Several professional schools. Master's and/or second professional degree.			
ARKANSAS				
Arkansas Agr., Mech. & Normal College (C) 1873 **N. Cedar Street** **Pine Bluff 71601**	2,490	Coed	State	Lawrence A. Davis
	Liberal arts and general program. Terminal-occupational training. Bachelor's and/or first professional degree.			
Philander Smith College (C) 1868 **812 West 13th Street** **Little Rock 72203**	614	Coed	Mc	Walter R. Hazzard
	Liberal arts and general program. Teacher-preparatory and terminal-occupational training. Bachelor's and/or first professional degree.			
Shorter College 1886 **604 Locust Street** **Little Rock 72114**	216	Coed	Ame	H. Solomon Hill
	Two-year college with a three-year professional school. Liberal arts and general program. Bachelor's and/or first professional degree.			
DELAWARE				
Delaware State (M) 1891 **Dover 19901**	788	Coed	State	Luna Isaac Mishoe
	Liberal arts and general program. Teacher-preparatory training. Bachelor's and/or first professional degree.			
DISTRICT OF COLUMBIA				
District of Columbia (M) 1851 **11th & Harvard, N.W.** **Washington, D.C. 20009**	2,205	Coed	Dg	Paul O. Carr
	Teacher-preparatory training. Bachelor's and/or first professional degree.			

PREDOMINANTLY NEGRO INSTITUTIONS, COLLEGES AND UNIVERSITIES IN THE UNITED STATES—(Continued)

Institution, Accreditation and Date of Founding	*Enrollment*	*Type*	*Control*	*President*
Howard University (M) 1867 2400 6th Street, N.W. Washington, D.C. 20001	6,517	Coed	Fg	James Cheek
	Liberal arts and general program. Several professional schools. Ph.D. and equivalent degrees.			
FLORIDA				
Bethune-Cookman College (S) 1904 640 Second Avenue Daytona Beach, Florida 32015	867	Coed	Mc	Richard V. Moore
	Liberal arts and general program. Teacher-preparatory and terminal occupational training. Bachelor's and/or first professional degree.			
Edward Waters College 1886 1658 Kings Road Jacksonville, Florida 32209	740	Coed	Cg	William B. Stewart
	Liberal arts and general program. Terminal-occupational training leading to the bachelor's and/or first professional degree.			
Florida A. & M. University (S) 1887 Tallahassee So. Blvd. Tallahassee, Florida 32307	2,884	Coed	State	Benjamin L. Perry, Jr.
	Liberal arts and general program. Several professional schools. Master's and/or second professional degree.			
Florida Memorial College (S) 1892 St. Augustine 32084	377	Coed	Abc	R. W. Puryear
	Liberal arts and general program. Teacher-preparatory training. Bachelor's and/or first professional degree.			
Gibbs Jr. College (S) 1957 9th Avenue & 34th Street St. Petersburg 33733	762	Coed	State	Michael M. Bennett
	Liberal arts and general program. Terminal-occupational training. Two-year college-level curriculum. No degrees.			
Hampton Jr. College 1958 1214 N.W. 16th Avenue Ocala 32670	375	Coed	State	William H. Jackson
	Liberal arts and general program. Teacher-preparatory and terminal-occupational training. No degrees.			
Johnson Jr. College 1962 P. O. Box 297 Leesburg 32748	282	B	Cg	P. E. Williams
	Liberal arts and general program. Terminal-occupational training. No degrees.			
Lincoln Jr. College 1960 1001 North 17th Street Fort Pierce 33451	122	Coed	State	Leroy C. Floyd
	Liberal arts and general program. Terminal-occupational training. No degrees.			
Roosevelt Jr. College (S) 1958 1235 15th Street West Palm Beach 33401	183	Coed	State, Cg	Britton G. Sayles
	Liberal arts and general program. Teacher-preparatory and terminal-occupational training. No degrees.			
Rosenwald Jr. College 1958 1100 Bay Avenue Panama City 32401	113	Coed	Cg	C. C. Washington
	Liberal arts and general program. Teacher-preparatory and terminal-occupational training. No degrees.			
Volusia County Community College 1958 Daytona Beach 32015	412	Coed	State	J. Griffen Green
	Liberal arts and general program. Teacher-preparatory and terminal-occupational training. No degrees.			
Washington Jr. College 1949 N. Miller & 34th Street Pensacola 32503	307	Coed	State, Cg	G. T. Wiggins
	Liberal arts and general program. Teacher-preparatory and terminal-occupational training. No degrees.			

PREDOMINANTLY NEGRO INSTITUTIONS, COLLEGES AND UNIVERSITIES IN THE UNITED STATES—(Continued)

Institution, Accreditation and Date of Founding	*Enrollment*	*Type*	*Control*	*President*
GEORGIA				
Albany State College (S) 1903 Albany 31705	1,036	Coed	State	Thomas Miller Jenkins
	Liberal arts and general program. Teacher-preparatory and terminal-occupational training. Bachelor's and/or first professional degree.			
Atlanta University (S) 1865 223 Chestnut Street Atlanta 30314	841	Coed	Pr	Thomas D. Jarrett
	Liberal arts and general program. Several professional schools. Ph.D. and equivalent degrees.			
Clark College* (S) 1869 240 Chestnut Street Atlanta 30314	800	Coed	Mc	Vivian W. Henderson
	Liberal arts and general program. Teacher-preparatory training. Bachelor's and/or first professional degree.			
Interdenominational* Theological Center (S) 1957 671 Beckwith Street Atlanta 30314	124	Coed	Pr	Oswald P. Bronson
	Professional school offering master's and/or second professional degree.			
Morehouse College* (S) 1867 223 Chestnut Street Atlanta 30314	883	M	Pr	Hugh M. Gloster
	Liberal arts and general program. Bachelor's and/or first professional degree.			
Morris Brown College* (S) 1881 643 Hunter Street Atlanta 30314	928	Coed	Ame	John A. Middleton
	Liberal arts and general program. Teacher-preparatory training. Bachelor's and/or first professional degree.			
Spelman College* (S) 1881 350 Leonard Street Atlanta 30314	726	W	Pr	Albert E. Manley
	Liberal arts and general program. Teacher-preparatory training. Bachelor's and/or first professional degree.			
Fort Valley State College (S) 1895 S. Macon Street Macon 31030	1,401	Coed	State	Waldo W. E. Blanchet
	Liberal arts and general program. Teacher-preparatory training. Bachelor's and/or first professional degree.			
Paine College (S) 1883 1235 15th Street Augusta 30901	371	Coed	Mc	Eugene C. Calhoun
	Liberal arts and general program. Teacher-preparatory training. Bachelor's and/or first professional degree.			
Savannah State College (S) 1891 State C. Branch Savannah 31400	1,390	Coed	State	Howard Jordan
	Liberal arts and general program. Teacher-preparatory training. Bachelor's and/or first professional degree.			
KENTUCKY				
Kentucky State College (S) 1886 Frankfort 40601	813	Coed	State	Carl M. Hill
	Liberal arts and general program. Teacher-preparatory training. Bachelor's and/or first professional degree.			
LOUISIANA				
Dillard University 1869 2601 Gentilly Blvd. New Orleans 70122	882	Coed	Ucc	Broadus N. Butler
	Liberal arts and general program. Teacher-preparatory training. Bachelor's and/or first professional degree.			
Grambling College (S) 1901 Grambling 71245	3,225	Coed	State	R. W. E. Jones
	Liberal arts and general program. Teacher-preparatory training. Bachelor's and/or first professional degree.			

PREDOMINANTLY NEGRO INSTITUTIONS, COLLEGES AND UNIVERSITIES IN THE UNITED STATES—(Continued)

Institution, Accreditation and Date of Founding	*Enrollment*	*Type*	*Control*	*President*	
Southern University (S) 1881 Baton Rouge 70813	6,326	Coed	State	G. Leon Netterville (Acting)	Liberal arts and general program. Several professional schools. Master's and/or second professional degree.
Xavier University (S) 1925 Palmetto & Pine Streets New Orleans 70125	779	Coed	Rc	Norman C. Francis	Liberal arts and general program. Several professional schools. Master's and/or second professional degree.
MARYLAND					
Bowie State College (M) 1867 Jericho Park, Bowie 20715	406	Coed	State	Samuel L. Myers	Liberal arts and general program. Teacher-preparatory training. Bachelor's and/or first professional degree.
Coppin State College (M) 1900 2500 W. North Avenue Baltimore 21216	377	Coed	State	Parlett L. Moore	Teacher-preparatory program. Bachelor's and/or first professional degree.
MISSISSIPPI					
Alcorn A. & M. (S) 1871 Rural Station Lorman 39096	1,491	Coed	State	J. D. Boyd	Liberal arts and general program. Teacher-preparatory and terminal-occupational training. Bachelor's and/or first professional degree.
Maryland State College (M) 1886 Princess Anne 21853	544	Coed	State	John T. Williams	Liberal arts and general program. Teacher-preparatory and terminal-occupational training. Bachelor's and/or first professional degree.
Morgan State College (M) 1867 Hillen Road Baltimore 21212	2,420	Coed	State	Martin D. Jenkins	Liberal arts and general program. Teacher-preparatory and terminal-occupational training. Master's and/or second professional degree.
Coahoma Jr. College 1949 R. I. Box 616 Clarksdale 38614	517	Coed	State	B. F. McLavrin	Professional and teacher-preparatory training. No degrees.
Jackson State College (S) 1877 1325 Lynch Street Jackson 39217	1,687	Coed	State	John A. Peoples, Jr.	Liberal arts and general program. Teacher-preparatory training. Master's and/or second professional degree.
J. P. Campbell College 1500 W. Lynch Street Jackson 39203	*College temporarily closed*			Robert M. Stevens	Liberal arts and general program. Terminal-occupational training. No degrees.
Mary Holmes Jr. College 1892 P. O. Box 336 West Point 39773	450	Coed	Up	D. I. Horn, Jr.	Liberal arts and general program. Teacher-preparatory and terminal-occupational training. No degrees.
Mississippi Industrial College 1905 N. Memphis Street Holly Springs 38635	488	Coed	Cme	E. E. Rankin	Liberal arts and general program. Teacher-preparatory training. Bachelor's and/or first professional degree.
Natchez Jr. College 1885 1010 Ext. N. Union Natchez 39120	250	Coed	Pr	J. R. Buck	Liberal arts and general program. No degrees.
Okolona College Okolona 38860	153	Coed	Pec	A. P. Wilburn	Liberal arts and general program. Teacher-preparatory and terminal-occupational training. No degrees.

PREDOMINANTLY NEGRO INSTITUTIONS, COLLEGES AND UNIVERSITIES IN THE UNITED STATES—(Continued)

Institution, Accreditation and Date of Founding	*Enrollment*	*Type*	*Control*	*President*
Piney Woods County Life School 1910 Piney Woods 39148	122	Coed	Pr	Laurence C. Jones
	Teacher-preparatory training. No degrees.			
Prentiss Normal & Industrial Institute 1907 Prentiss 39474	227	Coed	Pr	Mrs. J. E. Robinson
	Liberal arts and general program. Terminal-occupational training. No degrees.			
Rust College 1866 Rust College Holly Springs 38635	566	Coed	Mc	W. A. McMillan
	Liberal arts and general program. Teacher-preparatory training. Bachelor's and/or first professional degree.			
Saints Jr. College 1918 P. O. Box 419 Lexington 39095	375	Coed	Cc	Arenia C. Mallory
	Liberal arts and general program. Terminal-occupational training. No degrees.			
T. J. Harris Jr. College 1956 3951 12th Street Meridian 39304	215	Coed	Mg	W. A. Reed, Jr.
	Liberal arts and general program. Terminal-occupational training. No degrees.			
Tougaloo College (S) 1869 Tougaloo 39174	521	Coed	Ucc	G. A. Owens
	Liberal arts and general program. Teacher-preparatory training. Bachelor's and/or first professional degree.			
Utica Jr. College 1903 Utica 39175	446	Coed	Dg	Walter Washington
	Liberal arts and general program. Terminal-occupational training. No degrees.			
MISSOURI				
Lincoln University (C) 1866 Jefferson City 65102	1,624	Coed	State	Earl E. Dawson
	Liberal arts and general program. Teacher-preparatory training. Master's and/or second professional degree.			
NORTH CAROLINA				
A. & T. College of North Carolina (S) 1891 312 N. Dudley Street Greensboro 27411	3,005	Coed	State	Lewis D. Dowdy
	Liberal arts and general program. Several professional schools. Master's and/or second professional degree.			
Barber-Scotia College (S) 1867 Concord 28025	315	Coed	Up	Jerome Gresham
	Liberal arts and general program. Teacher-preparatory training. Bachelor's and/or first professional degree.			
Bennett College (S) 1873 Washington Street Greensboro 27402	594	W	Mc	Isaac H. Miller
	Liberal arts and general program. Teacher-preparatory training. Bachelor's and/or first professional degree.			
Elizabeth City State College (S) 1891 Elizabeth City 27909	837	Coed	State	Marion D. Thorpe
	Liberal arts and general program. Teacher-preparatory and terminal-occupational training. Bachelor's and/or first professional degree.			
Fayetteville State College (S) 1887 Fayetteville 28301	1,098	Coed	State	Rudolph Jones
	Teacher-preparatory training. Bachelor's and/or first professional degree.			
Johnson C. Smith University (S) 1867 100 Beattiesford Charlotte 28208	1,050	Coed	Up	Lionel H. Newsom
	Liberal arts and general program. Several professional schools grant bachelor's and/or first professional degree.			

PREDOMINANTLY NEGRO INSTITUTIONS, COLLEGES AND UNIVERSITIES IN THE UNITED STATES—(Continued)

Institution, Accreditation and Date of Founding	*Enrollment*	*Type*	*Control*	*President*
Livingstone College (S) 1879 701 W. Monroe Street Salisbury 28144	698	Coed	Amez	F. George Shipman
	Liberal arts and general program. Several professional schools grant bachelor's and/or first professional degree.			
North Carolina College at Durham (S) 1910 Fayetteville Street Durham 27707	2,762	Coed	State	Albert N. Whiting
	Liberal arts and general program. Several professional schools grant the Ph.D. and equivalent degrees.			
St. Augustine's College (S) 1867 Oakwood Avenue Raleigh 27602	1,062	Coed	Pec	Prezell R. Robinson
	Liberal arts and general program. Teacher-preparatory training. Bachelor's and/or first professional degree.			
Shaw University (S) 1865 118 E. South Street Raleigh 27602	680	Coed	Nbc	King V. Cheek, Jr.
	Liberal arts and general program. Teacher-preparatory training. Bachelor's and/or first professional degree.			
Winston-Salem State College (S) 1892 Winston-Salem 27100	1,045	Coed	State	K. R. Williams
	Professional and teacher-preparatory training. Bachelor's and/or first professional degree.			
OHIO				
Central State University (C) 1887 Wilberforce 45384	2,400	Coed	State	Herman Branson
	Liberal arts and general program. Teacher-preparatory and terminal-occupational training. Master's and/or second professional degree.			
Wilberforce University (C) 1856 Wilberforce 45384	410	Coed	Ame	Rembert E. Stokes
	Liberal arts and general program. Several professional schools grant bachelor's and/or first professional degree.			
OKLAHOMA				
Langston University (C) 1897 Langston 73050	717	Coed	State	William H. Hale
	Liberal arts and general program. Teacher-preparatory and terminal-occupational training. Bachelor's and/or first professional degree.			
PENNSYLVANIA				
Cheyney State College (M) 1837 Chester and Creek Roads Cheyney 19319	1,190	Coed	State	Wade Wilson
	Liberal arts and general program. Teacher-preparatory training. Bachelor's and/or first professional degree.			
Lincoln University (M) 1854 Lincoln University Oxford 19352	466	Coed	Pr	Marvin Wachman
	Liberal arts and general program. Teacher-preparatory training. Bachelor's and/or first professional degree.			
SOUTH CAROLINA				
Allen University 1870 1530 Harden Street Columbia 29204	734	Coed	Ame	J. W. Hairston
	Liberal arts and general program. Teacher-preparatory training. Bachelor's and/or first professional degree.			
Benedict College (S) 1870 Taylor at Harden Columbia	1,061	Coed	Abc	Benjamin F. Payton
	Liberal arts and general program. Several professional schools grant bachelor's and/or first professional degree.			

PREDOMINANTLY NEGRO INSTITUTIONS, COLLEGES AND UNIVERSITIES IN THE UNITED STATES—(Continued)

Institution, Accreditation and Date of Founding	*Enrollment*	*Type*	*Control*	*President*
Claflin College (S) 1869 College Avenue Orangeburg 29115	411	Coed	Mc	H. V. Manning
	Liberal arts and general program. Teacher-preparatory training. Bachelor's and/or first professional degree.			
Friendship Jr. College 1891 Allen Street Rock Hill 29732	26	Coed	Abc	J. H. Goudlock
	Liberal arts and general program. Pre-professional and terminal-occupational training. No degrees.			
Mather Jr. College (State) 1954 Ribaut Road Beaufort 29903	55	Coed	Abc	E. I. Anderson
	General education program for students planning to transfer to baccalaureate colleges. Terminal-occupational training.			
Morris College 1908 N. Main Street Sumter 29150	465	Coed	Sbc	O. R. Reuben
	Liberal arts and general program. Teacher-preparatory training. Bachelor's and/or first professional degree.			
South Carolina State College (S) 1896 Orangeburg 29115	2,351	Coed	State	M. Maceo Nance, Jr.
	Liberal arts and general program. Several professional schools grant master's and/or second professional degree.			
Voorhees College (S) 1897 Denmark 29042	251	Coed	Pec	John F. Potts
	Liberal arts and general program. Terminal-occupational training. No degrees.			
TENNESSEE				
Fisk University (S) 1866 17th Avenue N. Nashville 37203	926	Coed	Pr	James R. Lawson
	Liberal arts and general program. Teacher-preparatory and terminal-occupational training. Master's and/or second professional degree.			
Knoxville College (S) 1875 901 College Street Knoxville 37921	803	Coed	Up	Robert L. Owens, III
	Liberal arts and general program. Teacher-preparatory training. Bachelor's and/or first professional degree.			
Lane College (S) 1882 501 Lane Avenue Jackson 38301	578	Coed	Cme	C. A. Kirkendoll
	Liberal arts and general program. Teacher-preparatory training. Bachelor's and/or first professional degree.			
Le Moyne College (S) 1870 807 Walker Street Memphis 38106	555	Coed	Ucc	Hollis F. Price
	Liberal arts and general program. Teacher-preparatory training. Bachelor's and/or first professional degree.			
Meharry Medical College 1876 1005 18th Avenue N. Nashville 37208	342	Coed	Mc	Lloyd C. Elam
	Professional training in medicine leading to bachelor's and/or first professional degree.			
Morristown College (S) 1923 Morristown 37814	164	Coed	Mc	Elmer P. Gibson
	Liberal arts and general program. Teacher-preparatory and terminal-occupational training. No degrees.			
Owen College (S) 1954 370 So. Orleans Memphis 38102	318	Coed	Gar	Charles L. Dinkins
	Liberal arts and general program. Terminal-occupational training. No degrees.			

PREDOMINANTLY NEGRO INSTITUTIONS, COLLEGES AND UNIVERSITIES IN THE UNITED STATES—(Continued)

Institution, Accreditation and Date of Founding	*Enrollment*	*Type*	*Control*	*President*
Tennessee Agr. & Indus. State University (S) 1912 35th & Centennial Nashville 37203	3,759	Coed	State	Walter S. Davis
	Liberal arts and general program. Several professional schools grant master's and/or second professional degree.			
TEXAS				
Bishop College (S) 1880 Dallas 75241	940	Coed	Abc	M. K. Curry, Jr.
	Liberal arts and general program. Teacher-preparatory training. Bachelor's and/or first professional degree.			
Butler College 1905 Bellwood Road, Tyler	100	Coed	Sbc	M. J. Smith
	Liberal arts and general program. Theological training and teacher education. Bachelor's and/or first professional degree.			
Huston-Tillotson College (S) 1877 1820 East 11th Street Austin 78702	637	Coed	Mc	John Q. Taylor King
	Liberal arts and general program. Teacher-preparatory training. Bachelor's and/or first professional degree.			
Jarvis Christian College 1912 U. S. Highway 80 Hawkins 75765	618	Coed	Pr	J. O. Perpener
	Liberal arts and general program. Teacher-preparatory and terminal-occupational training. Bachelor's and/or first professional degree.			
Paul Quinn College 1872 1620 Elm Street Waco 76703	292	Coed	Ame	L. H. McCloney
	Liberal arts and general program. Teacher-preparatory and terminal-occupational training. Bachelor's and/or first professional degree.			
Prairie View A. & M. (S) 1876 Prairie View 77455	3,702	Coed	State	A. I. Thomas
	Liberal arts and general program. Teacher-preparatory and terminal-occupational training. Master's and/or second professional degree.			
St. Philip's College (S) 1898 2111 Nevada Avenue San Antonio 78203	776	Coed	Dg	Wayland P. Moody
	Liberal arts and general program. Terminal-occupational training. No degrees.			
Southwestern Christian College 1950 P. O. Box 10 Terrell 75160	77	B	Cc	A. V. Isbell
	Theological training. No degrees.			
Texas College 1894 2404 Grand N. Tyler 75703	483	Coed	Dc	Allen C. Hancock
	Liberal arts and general program. Teacher-preparatory training. Bachelor's and/or first professional degree.			
Texas Southern University (S) 1947 3201 Wheeler Street Houston 77004	4,037	Coed	State	Granville M. Sawyer
	Liberal arts and general program. Several professional schools grant master's and/or second professional degree.			
Tyler Jr. College (S) 1926 1400 Henderson Tyler 75701	2,252	Coed	State	H. E. Jenkins
	Liberal arts and general program. Terminal-occupational training. No degrees.			
Wiley College (S) 1873 711 Rosborough Spr. Marshall 75670	545	Coed	Mc	T. W. Cole, Sr.
	Liberal arts and general program. Teacher-preparatory training. Bachelor's and/or first professional degree.			

PREDOMINANTLY NEGRO INSTITUTIONS, COLLEGES AND UNIVERSITIES IN THE UNITED STATES—(Continued)

Institution, Accreditation and Date of Founding	*Enrollment*	*Type*	*Control*	*President*
VIRGINIA				
Hampton Institute (S) 1868	1,725	Coed	Pr	Jerome H. Holland
E. Queen Street Hampton 23368	Liberal arts and general program. Teacher-preparatory and terminal-occupational training. Master's and/or second professional degree.			
St. Paul's College (S) 1888	616	B	Pec	E. H. McClenney
Lawrenceville 23868	Liberal arts and general program. Teacher-preparatory training. Bachelor's and/or first professional degree.			
Virginia State College (S) 1882	4,717	Coed	State	Robert P. Daniel
Petersburg 23806	Liberal arts and general program. Teacher-preparatory and terminal-occupational training. Bachelor's and/or first professional degree.			
Virginia Theological Seminary and College 1888	110	Coed	Pr	M. C. Southerland
Lynchburg 24501	Liberal arts and general program. Teacher-preparatory training. Bachelor's and/or first professional degree.			
Virginia Union University (S) 1865	1,203	Coed	Abc	Alix James (Acting)
1500 N. Lombardy Richmond 23220	Professional training leading to bachelor's and/or first professional degree.			
WEST VIRGINIA				
Bluefield State College (C) 1895	816	Coed	State	L. B. Allen
218 Rock Street Bluefield 24703	Liberal arts and general program. Teacher-preparatory and terminal-occupational training. Bachelor's and/or first professional degree.			
West Virginia State College (C) 1891	2,487	Coed	State	W. J. L. Wallace
Institute 25112	Liberal arts and general program. Teacher-preparatory and terminal-occupational training. Bachelor's and/or first professional degree.			

*Part of Atlanta University complex.

Key to Control Symbols: Abc—American Baptist Convention; Ame—African Methodist Episcopal Church; Amez—African Methodist Episcopal Zion Church; Cc—Church of Christ; Cg—County government; Cme—Christian Methodist Episcopal Church; Dc—Disciples of Christ; Dg—District government; Fg—Federal government; Gar—General Association of Regular Baptist Churches; Mbc—Mennonite Brethren Churches of North America; Mc—Moravian Church in America; Nbc—National Baptist Convention, U.S.A.; Pc—Presbyterian Church in the U.S.; Pec—Protestant Episcopal Church; Pr—Private organization; Rc—Roman Catholic; Sbc—Southern Baptist Convention; Sda—General Conference Seventh Day Adventists; Ucc—United Church of Christ; Up—United Presbyterian Church in the U.S.A.

Key to Accreditation Symbols: C—North Central Association of Colleges and Secondary Schools; M—Middle States Association of Colleges and Secondary Schools; S—Southern Association of Colleges and Secondary Schools.

EDUCATIONAL FILMS WITH BLACK THEMES

The following list was compiled under the direction of Wendell Wray, Director, North Manhattan Project, Countee Cullen branch of the New York Public Library, and William Sloan, librarian of the NYPL's film division. Their kind permission makes possible its reproduction here. The films are ideal for classroom or community use.

AN AFRICAN COMMUNITY: THE MASAI color 17 minutes
Illustrates the dependence of the nomadic Masai of East Africa on the land, their adaptation to their environment, their tribal interdependence and the roles of men, women and of different age groups. A good pictorial record; the commentary is superficial. Produced by Frank Gardonyi and Clifford Janoff, 1969.
Bailey-Film Associates

AFRICAN GIRL – MALOBI color 11 minutes
Presents the experiences of Malobi, a ten year old girl of the Ibo tribe of Nigeria. There are scenes of the tribe building homes in the traditional way, her grandfather carving furniture, and Malobi attending school. Directed by Michael Hagopian. 1960.
Atlantis Productions

AFRICAN VILLAGE LIFE (Series title):

ANNUAL FESTIVAL OF THE DEAD color 14 minutes
Follows the annual ceremony of the Dogon tribe of Mali, Africa, near the Niger River in the interesting and unusual festival they hold for those who have died during the year. Produced by Julien. Bryan. 1968.

DAILY LIFE OF THE BOZO color 15 minutes
Exciting photography, without narration, but with effects and music recorded on the spot, offers an honest picture of the daily life of the Bozo tribe in Mali, Africa near the Niger River. Photography by Hermann Schlenker. Produced by Julien Bryan. 1967.

FISHING ON THE NIGER RIVER color 17 minutes
A careful depiction of fishing on the Niger River by members of the Bozo Tribe of Mali, in Africa. Natural sounds of the people at work provide the background; no narration. Photography by Hermann Schlenker. Produced by Julien Bryan. 1967.

HERDING CATTLE color 7 minutes
Records the activities of the Peul Tribe of Mali, Africa, as the men and young boys skillfully lead a herd of cattle across the Niger River. Sound background is recorded on the spot. Photography by Hermann Schlenker. Produced by Julien Bryan. 1967.
International Film Foundation

ANANSI THE SPIDER color 10 minutes
A folk tale from the Ashanti tribe retold in delightful abstract animation using African designs and brilliant colors to account for a troublesome spider and the origin of the moon. By Gerald McDermott. 1969.
Landmark Educational Media, Inc.

BLACK PANTHERS color 26 minutes
Journalistic record of Oakland, California Black Panthers. Discussions by Huey Newton, Bill Brandt, Bobby Seale, Stokely Carmichael, and Mrs. Eldridge Cleaver. By Agnes Varda. 1969.
Grove Press

BLACK POWER color 15 minutes
Juxtaposition of widely varying opinions and comments by Malcolm X, Eldridge Cleaver, Floyd McKissick, Martin Luther King, and others as they view the problems and prospects of the black movement generally and the concept of black power specifically. 1969.
Reaction Films

THE BLUES color 21 minutes
Shows the music and some of the environment of several country-blues singers including Sleepy John Estes, Memphis Willie B., and J. D. Short. A low budget film in which the visuals are not synchronized with the sound. Produced by noted blues authority Samuel X. Charters. 1963.
Brandon

DISCOVERING THE MUSIC OF AFRICA color 22 minutes
A master drummer of Ghana demonstrates various African instruments and describes their uses. Traditional dances are also seen. A studio-made film with excessively artificial lighting. Informative, but not outstanding cinematically. Produced by Bernard Wilets.
Bailey-Film Associates

FAMILY OF GHANA 30 minutes
A somewhat dated, but still moving documentary of the people who live on the coast of Ghana and make their living from the sea. Conflict between the old ways and the new is represented between the father and his son. Produced by the National Film Board of Canada. Directed by Julian Biggs. National Film Board of Canada. 1958.
McGraw-Hill

FIRST WORLD FESTIVAL OF NEGRO ARTS color 20 minutes
Pictures scenes of the first World Festival of Negro Arts held at Dakar in 1966, showing music, dance, sculpture, painting and the reciprocal influences of Negro art and culture in relation to the modern Western World. A pedestrian presentation of an important subject. U. S. release. 1969.
Contemporary/McGraw-Hill

THE GAME 17 minutes
Negro and Puerto Rican teenagers act out their lives in a series of games which depict their situations in a New York City ghetto. A powerful and moving film. Produced by Roberta Hodes in association with Mobilization for Youth. 1967.
Grove Press

HARLEM WEDNESDAY color 10 minutes
Paintings and sketches by American artist Gregorio Prestopino are colorfully arranged and backed with a vibrant jazz score by Benny Carter to evoke the activities and mood of a Wednesday in Harlem. Directed by John Hubley and Faith Elliot. 1959.
Brandon

HERITAGE IN BLACK color 27 minutes
Panorama of the history and contributions of black people to the United States from the Revolution to present times. c1969.
Encyclopaedia Britannica

HISTORY OF THE NEGRO IN AMERICA (Series title):

PART 1. 1619-1860: OUT OF SLAVERY 17 minutes
The development of the slave trade and the growth of slavery from the ancient world to colonial times and on through the Revolution is depicted in stills, prints, and drawing. Narrated by James Earl Jones. 1965.

PART 2. 1861-1877: CIVIL WAR AND RECONSTRUCTION 20 minutes
Traces the causes and effects of two critical periods in U. S. history, the Civil War and Reconstruction, and indicates how the Emancipation Proclamation, Thirteenth, Fourteenth, and Fifteenth amendments sought to protect and preserve the Negro's newly won freedom. Made from still pictures. 1965.

PART 3. 1877-TODAY: FREEDOM MOVEMENT 20 minutes
Portrays the post-Reconstruction flight of the Negro, the problems of segregation, Negro heroism in World War I and II, and the advances made in the area of civil rights since 1950; uses stills, prints, drawings, and film footage. Narrated by James Earl Jones. 1965.
McGraw-Hill

HISTORY OF THE NEGRO PEOPLE (Series title):

PART 1. HERITAGE OF THE NEGRO 30 minutes
Explores the heritage of the Negro by examining the civilization and achievements of ancient Africa and their significance to the American Negro today. Produced by NET. 1965.

PART 2. NEGRO AND THE SOUTH 30 minutes
Interviews Negroes (a teacher, a mechanic, and a minister), and whites (a mayor, a sheriff, and a judge) of Mississippi, to depict the "Southern way of life." Produced by NET. 1965.

PART 3. SLAVERY 30 minutes
Based on actual testimony of former slaves, tells of the tragic and sometimes humorous experiences of life in the Old South and depicts the liberation of slaves by the Yankee troops. Uses Negro spirituals to help tell the story. Produced by NET. 1965.

PART 4. BRAZIL: THE VANISHING NEGRO 30 minutes
Depicts the interracial experiences of the Negro in Brazil and stresses that they differ markedly from the experiences of North American Negroes. Produced by NET. 1965.

PART 5. FREE AT LAST 30 minutes
Uses dramatic readings from the works of Frederick Douglass, Booker T. Washington, W. E. DuBois, and Marcus Garvey to trace the history of the American Negro from emancipation to the end of World War II. Produced by NET. 1965.

PART 6. OMOWALE – THE CHILD RETURNS HOME 30 minutes
Pictures author John Williams, a Mississippi-born Negro, on an odyssey to Africa to explore his ancestral roots and the relationship of the American Negro to Africa and the Africans. Produced by NET. 1965.

PART 7. NEW MOOD 30 minutes
Reviews the civil rights struggle of the past decade and traces the impact of the new Negro militancy on both white and Negro Americans. Produced by NET. 1965.

PART 8. OUR COUNTRY, TOO 30 minutes
Explores the inner world of the American Negro: his values, attitudes, and impressions of life through interviews at such places as an African rite in Harlem, a Negro debutante ball, the office of a Negro newspaper, and a Negro-owned radio station. Produced by NET. 1965.

PART 9. FUTURE AND THE NEGRO 75 minutes
Presents a panel discussion on the subject of the Negro's future. Discusses the economic plight of the Negro in the United States and in the Negro nations and emphasizes the racism felt to be deeply ingrained in people throughout the world. Produced by NET. 1965.
Indiana University

HOUSE ON CEDAR HILL 17 minutes

Events in the life of Frederick Douglass, the runaway slave who became an editor, orator, and statesman, are presented with skill and sensitivity, through historical documents, period drawings, photographs, and mementos found in the Douglass House in Washington, D. C. Written and directed by Carlton Moss. 1953.
Contemporary/McGraw-Hill

THE HURDLER color 16 minutes
Biographical account of Dr. Charles Drew, the research physician who discovered the value of blood plasma in transfusions and set up the first Blood Bank in the United States during World War II. The forced comparison between a hurdler and Drew's life lessens the effectiveness of the film for some audiences. Narrated by Ossie Davis. 1969.
New York Times/Arno Press

I HAVE A DREAM 35 minutes

The biography of Martin Luther King made from newsreel footage of the civil rights movement during the 1950's and 1960's. Reveals his dedication to the movement and to the principles of nonviolence.
Bailey-Film Associates

IN THE COMPANY OF MEN 52 minutes

Documents the role playing and sensitivity training of hardcore unemployed blacks and white foremen—techniques implemented to establish communication between these two groups in a large General Motors assembly plant in Georgia. A film by William Greaves. 1969.
William Greaves

J.T. color 51 minutes

Just before Christmas, a lonely Harlem boy steals a radio and hides in an abandoned building. There he finds a sick cat which he nurtures back to health and develops a sense of responsibility in the process. Presented on CBS Children's Hour; stereotyped characterizations may bother some adults. Written by Jane Wagner; directed by Robert Young; produced for CBS-TV. 1969.
Carousel Films

JACKIE ROBINSON 26 minutes

A graphic biography of the life of the famous ball player, the first Negro to play in the major leagues. From the television program *Biography*; produced by David Wolper. 1965.
Sterling

LAY MY BURDEN DOWN 60 minutes

An important document on the economic and educational plight of the Negro tenant farmers of the southern United States. Directed by Jack Willis for National Educational Television. 1966.
Indiana University

MALCOLM X: STRUGGLE FOR FREEDOM 22 minutes

Filmed during his trip to Europe and Africa, just three months before his assassination in the United States, Malcolm X discusses racial and other social ills of our age. Directed by Lebert Bethune. 1964.
Grove Press

MARTIN LUTHER KING: THE MAN AND THE MARCH 83 minutes

A documentary of the late Martin Luther King, Jr.'s "Poor People's March." Shows Dr. King conferring with aides, speaking at rallies and traveling as he solicits support for and develops the operational details of the March. Indicates the methods used by his aides to create interest and support on a local level and with other ethnic groups. Produced by Public Broadcast Laboratory of NET. 1968.
Indiana University

MARTIN LUTHER KING, JR.: A MAN OF PEACE 30 minutes

The film centers on Dr. King receiving the Nobel Peace Prize and his work in the Southern Christian Leadership Conference. King explains his philosophy of achieving racial equality through the use of nonviolence. Provides a look at the man, the minister, the father and the leader of the civil rights movement. Produced by Walter Schwimmer, Inc. 1964.
Journal Films

MARTIN LUTHER KING, JR.: FROM MONTGOMERY TO MEMPHIS 27 minutes

Excellent use of newsreel footage to cover the major events in Martin Luther King's civil rights struggles from the Montgomery bus boycotts through Memphis.
Bailey-Film Associates

MEMORY OF JOHN EARL 6 minutes

A black teenager refuses to submit to rude treatment by a white storekeeper and is chased and threatened with a gun by some Rednecks. Powerful recreation of an actual incident in the life of the young filmmaker, John McFadden. Produced 1968?
Youth Film Distribution Center

MY CHILDHOOD 51 minutes

A distinctive two-part film: part one is on Hubert Humphrey; part two, which may be used separately, is on the early years of James Baldwin. Brilliantly directed by Arthur Barron. Produced by Metromedia Television. 1964.
Benchmark Films

THE NEGRO AND THE AMERICAN PROMISE 60 minutes

Dr. Martin Luther King, Jr., Malcolm X, Dr. Kenneth Clark and James Baldwin discuss their motivations, doctrines, methods, goals and place in the American Negro's movement for social and racial equality.
Indiana University

NO VIETNAMESE EVER CALLED ME NIGGER 68 minutes

Three black G.I.'s discuss their experiences in Vietnam, the racism that exists in the armed forces and their dissatisfaction with life in the U. S. upon their return. This is intercut with scenes of a Black Anti-Vietnam War protest march. By David Loeb Weiss. 1969.
Bob Maurice Paradigm

NOW IS THE TIME 36 minutes

Chronicles the history of the American Negro and his emergence from the slave state over 300 years ago to 1968 where he now demands his rights and equal status, by combining the sounds and rhythms of the violence of race riots with folk, rock, and hymnal music and the works of Langston Hughes, Countee Cullen, James Baldwin, Malcolm X and Stokely Carmichael. Produced by WCAU-TV, Philadelphia. 1967.
Carousel Films

OF BLACK AMERICA (Series title):

BLACK HISTORY: LOST, STOLEN OR STRAYED color 2 films 27 minutes each

Bill Cosby reviews the achievement of Negroes which our history books have omitted and shows how Negroes have been denied recognition of their contributions to American culture. Produced by CBS News. 1968.

BLACK WORLD color 2 films 26 minutes each

A world-wide panel discussion in which Mike Wallace interviews prominent Negroes. of many countries to reveal their social and cultural problems and their reactions to current racial and political problems. Produced by CBS News. 1968.

PORTRAIT IN BLACK AND WHITE 2 films 27 minutes each

By means of a public opinion poll, the film explores the attitudes of blacks and whites toward each other, and the misconceptions and prejudices of each group. Produced by CBS News. 1968.

THE HERITAGE OF SLAVERY color 2 films 26 minutes each

Traces the history of the Emancipation and explains the freed slave and his descendants; also shows the debilitating effect of slavery on the nation's social and economic life. Produced by CBS News. 1968.

THE BLACK SOLDIER 25 minutes

Surveys the black American's participation in U. S. wars, from the Revolution to the Vietnamese conflict. Produced by CBS News. 1968.

PRUDENCE CRANDALL **50 minutes**
Depicts the life of 19th-century New England schoolteacher Prudence Crandall who tried to open an integrated girls' school against legal and social opposition. One of the Profiles in Courage television series. For older children. Produced by Robert Saudek Associates. 1964.
Robert Saudek

RAFER JOHNSON STORY **55 minutes**
Relates the story of Olympic decathlon champion Rafer Johnson, his early life, and his eventual triumph as one of the most honored athletes in the world. Produced by David Wolper Productions. 1964.
Sterling

SIT IN **54 minutes**
A highly dramatic news analysis of the sit in movement as it occurred in Nashville at the beginning of the sixties. The very objectivity of the film confirms the courage of the students in the face of intransigence. An NBC White Paper produced by Al Wasserman. Narrated by Chet Huntley. 1961.
McGraw-Hill

SOME OF MY BEST FRIENDS ARE WHITE **30 minutes**
A provocative examination of America's racial problem as discussed from the point of view of the middle-class Negro involving his acceptance by society and the future of his children growing up in white suburbia. A BBC-TV production. Produced by Michael Latham. 1967.
Robeck

STILL A BROTHER: INSIDE THE NEGRO MIDDLE CLASS **90 minutes**
Documents the economic, social and personal life of America's Negro middle-class, now constituting approximately 25% of the Negro population. Through conversations with prominent Negroes and a study of various trends in behavior, examines the conflict between the middle-class Negro's personal aspirations and his commitment to the general black movement. Narrated by Ossie Davis. Produced by William Greaves and William Branch. 1967.
McGraw-Hill

TROUBLEMAKERS **54 minutes**
A moving cinéma vérité account of an unsuccessful attempt by the Students for a Democratic Society and the people of a Newark, New Jersey ghetto neighborhood to improve the living conditions of the community. Made by Robert Machover and Norman Fruchter. 1966.
Blue Van Films

A TIME FOR BURNING **58 minutes**
Cinéma vérité account of a young minister's attempt, and failure, to lead his congregation to taking one small step towards integration and inter-group relations in his church in Omaha. Made by William Jersey and Barbara Connell, for the Lutheran Film Associates. 1966.
Contemporary/McGraw-Hill

THE WEAPONS OF GORDON PARKS **color** **28 minutes**
The story of the internationally known Negro Life magazine photographer seen at work, in his home, with his family, and on the streets of Harlem, as part of his past life is recreated. An inspiring and moving photographic essay. Directed by Warren Forma. 1967.
Contemporary/McGraw-Hill

WHAT HARVEST FOR THE REAPER? **59 minutes**
A documentary which describes how a group of black farmworkers, recruited in Arkansas to work on farms in Long Island, get trapped in a system that keeps them perpetually in debt. Growers and processors are interviewed and the labor camps and working conditions are shown. Produced by NET. 1968.
Indiana University

A STATISTICAL INTERPRETATION OF THE CURRENT STATUS OF BLACK EDUCATION, WITH TABLES

During the decade 1960-1970 there was a substantial increase in the number of black students attending school on every level from pre-school through college. In 1968 some 19% of black pre-school children were enrolled in Head Start programs; eight years earlier, few, if any, black children were enrolled in public pre-school programs.

Although there is still a substantial segment of the black population who have not completed high school, more and more black youths are joining the ranks of high school graduates. Still, some 42% of all blacks, male and female, in the 20-21 age group in the year 1969 had not finished high school. This figure is some 10% lower than it was in 1960. Since 30 years ago, only 9% of the high-school-aged black population completed a high school education.

The percentage of young people of all races attending schools has been on the rise and, with the exception of the college-age population, the numbers of blacks to whites in attendance seem fairly proportionate.

College enrollment for both blacks and whites is on the increase. As of 1969 21% of all blacks in the age group 20-21 had received at least one year of college education. For whites in the same bracket the figure was 40%. Although blacks are disproportionately represented in colleges the ratio between black and white attendance has been on a slow but steady decline. Between the years 1964 and 1968 the enrollment of black students in colleges rose 85%. This increase is reflected in general in colleges throughout the country with the exception of the South.

There appears to be a trend among whites to attend parochial or other private schools. Some 14% of all white youngsters attended such schools. On the other hand about 97% of all blacks attended the public schools. For both groups, black and white, there is a definite increase in private school enrollment as family income increases.

Chart 51

THE LEVEL OF EDUCATIONAL ATTAINMENT REACHED BY BLACK YOUNG ADULTS IS MARKEDLY ON THE RISE.

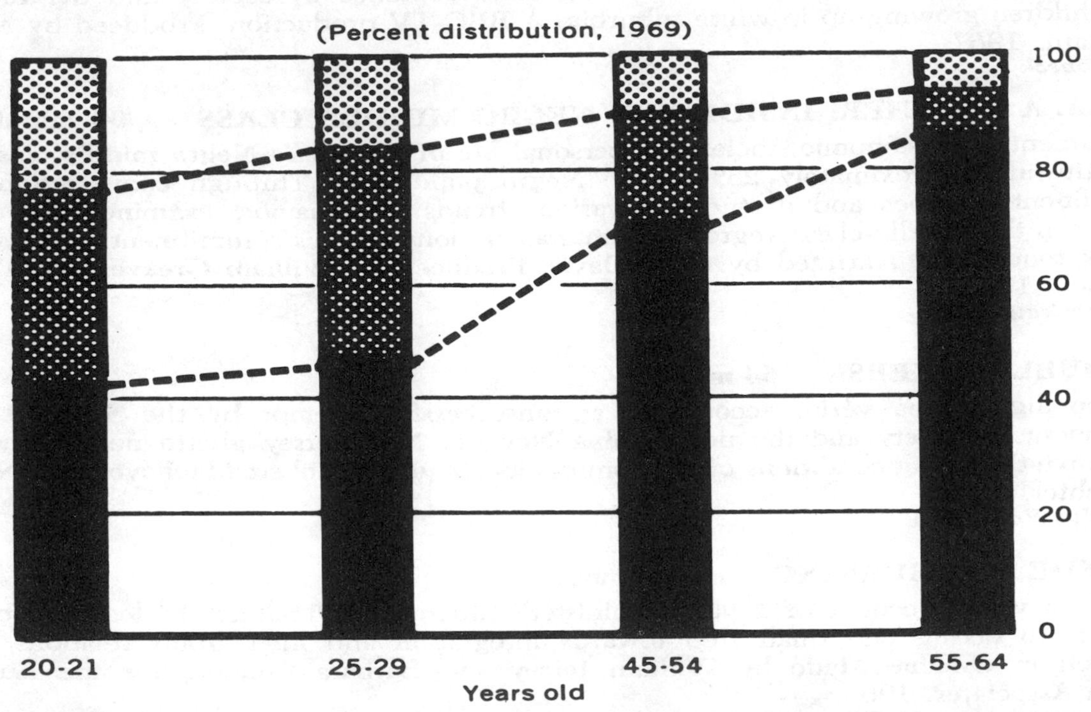

Chart 52

THE PERCENT OF BLACKS COMPLETING COLLEGE HAS MORE THAN DOUBLED OVER THE LAST DECADE BUT IS DISPROPORTIONATE TO THAT OF WHITE GRADUATES.

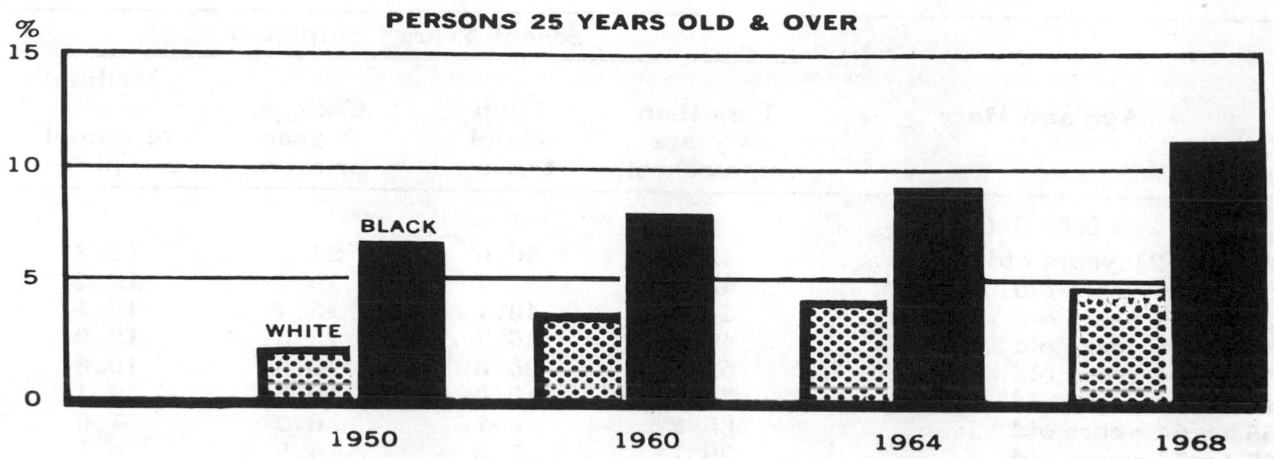

EDUCATION TABLES.

Table 86

Negro College Students Enrolled in 1964 and 1968, by Type of Institution
(Numbers in thousands)

Enrollment and type of institution	1964 (Fall)	1968 (Fall)	Change, 1964–68 Number	Change, 1964–68 Percent
Total enrollment	4,643	6,801	2,158	46
Total Negro enrollment	234	434	200	85
Percent of total enrollment	5	6	(X)	(X)
Enrollment in predominantly Negro colleges	120	156	36	30
Percent of all Negroes in college	51	36	(X)	(X)
Enrollment in other colleges	114	278	164	144
Percent of all Negroes in college	49	64	(X)	(X)

X Not applicable.
Source: U.S. Department of Labor, Bureau of Labor Statistics; U.S. Department of Commerce, Bureau of the Census; U.S. Department of Health, Education and Welfare, Office of Education.

Table 87

Percent Distribution by Years of School Completed for Persons 20 Years Old and Over, by Age, 1969

Age and Race	Less than 4 years high school	High school, 4 years	College, 1 year or more	Median years of school completed
NEGRO				
20 and 21 years old	42.1	36.6	21.2	12.2
22 to 24 years old	43.9	37.1	19.1	12.2
25 to 29 years old	44.3	40.1	15.7	12.1
30 to 34 years old	49.8	36.7	13.5	12.0
35 to 44 years old	62.8	26.8	10.5	10.6
45 to 54 years old	70.8	18.9	10.3	9.1
55 to 64 years old	85.2	8.7	6.2	7.6
65 to 74 years old	89.7	5.5	4.9	6.1
75 years old and over	92.4	4.1	3.5	5.2
WHITE				
20 and 21 years old	18.1	41.6	40.1	12.8
22 to 24 years old	19.6	44.8	35.7	12.7
25 to 29 years old	23.0	44.8	32.1	12.6
30 to 34 years old	27.3	44.9	27.6	12.5
35 to 44 years old	33.9	41.0	25.1	12.4
45 to 54 years old	40.7	39.3	20.0	12.2
55 to 64 years old	55.2	27.5	17.3	10.9
65 to 74 years old	67.6	18.9	13.4	8.9
75 years old and over	75.1	13.8	11.1	8.5

Source: U.S. Department of Commerce, Bureau of the Census.

Table 88

Percent Enrolled in School, by Age, 1960, 1966, and 1968

Age	Negro			White		
	1960[1]	1966	1968	1960	1966	1968
3 and 4 years	—	[1]14	19	—	12	15
5 years	51	65	69	66	71	78
6 to 15 years	98	99	99	99	99	99
16 and 17 years	77	85	86	83	89	91
18 and 19 years	35	38	45	39	48	51
20 to 24 years	8	8	12	14	21	22

— Represents zero.
[1]Negro and other races.
Source: U.S. Department of Commerce, Bureau of the Census.

Table 89

Percent of Pupils Enrolled in Grades 1 to 8, in Public, Parochial and Other Private Schools, by Family Income, 1968

	Negro		White	
	Public	Parochial and other private	Public	Parochial and other private
Total (thousands)	4,569	147	24,628	4,053
Percent				
Total	97	3	86	14
Under $3,000	100	—	92	8
$3,000 to $4,999	98	2	92	8
$5,000 to $7,499	96	4	88	12
$7,500 to $9,999	95	5	85	15
$10,000 to $14,999	88	12	83	17
$15,000 and over	86	14	79	21

— Represents zero or rounds to zero.
Source: U.S. Department of Commerce, Bureau of the Census.

Table 90

Percent of Population 25 to 34 Years Old Who Completed 4 Years of College or More, by Sex, 1960, 1966, and 1969

Year	Completion of 4 years of college or more					
	Negro			White		
	Total	Male	Female	Total	Male	Female
1960	4.3	3.9	4.6	11.7	15.7	7.8
1966	5.7	5.2	6.1	14.6	18.9	10.4
1969	6.6	7.6	5.6	16.2	20.2	12.3

Source: U.S. Department of Commerce, Bureau of the Census.

Table 91

Percent of Persons 25 to 29 Years Old Who Completed 4 Years of High School or More, by Sex, 1960 and 1966 to 1969

Year	Male		Female	
	Negro	White	Negro	White
1960	[1]36	63	[1]41	65
1966	49	73	47	74
1967	52	74	55	75
1968	58	76	54	75
1969	60	78	52	77

[1]1960 data for Negro and other races.
Source: U.S. Department of Commerce, Bureau of the Census.

Black troopers of the 10th Cavalry charge up San Juan Hill in support of the RoughRiders.

BLACK SERVICEMEN AND THE MILITARY ESTABLISHMENT

The Nation's Wars—
A Chronology of Military Events
Black Congressional Medal of Honor Winners
Black Graduates of the U.S. Military Academy
Black Graduates of the U.S. Naval Academy
Black Cadets Enrolled at the Service Academies (1971-1974)
Military Heroes

The experience of settling America, and the burden of defending it, have been shared by the men of many continents. Black men, too, have been among those who built the nation, forged its destiny in peace, and defended its interests in war. They began serving America long before the nation had come into being, and they have fought long and honorably in every major American conflict. As in other areas of American life, the black man in the military establishment has been subject to discriminatory treatment and second-class status. In the Revolutionary War, he achieved parity with the white patriot only because conditions were too desperate to impose artificial barriers between men in the field; in the War of 1812, he excelled on land and sea when emergency conditions required his involvement; during the Civil War, he was a pawn until his importance was recognized by both sides, and he was thrust into the heat of battle, often without adequate preparation and with the added risk of being slaughtered by a vengeful enemy. The black soldier fought in isolation on America's last frontier at the close of the 19th century, but he developed a great sense of camaraderie with white counterparts of the same hardy and robust breed. Even in Cuba during the Spanish-American War, much of this mutual respect for each other's combat prowess was in evidence between the four black regiments and Teddy Roosevelt's "Rough Riders." In both world wars, however, a cumbersome and often insensitive military bureaucracy imposed conditions which created class divisions between the men and so contributed

to the systematic demoralization cf most black forces. Blacks, in other words, fought to fight alongside white men, but were summarily rejected—often on the uninformed grounds that they possessed no military tradition worthy of recognition. With the coming of integration in 1948, black men widened their role in combat and support functions, often exhibiting a sense of pride in personal excellence and sometimes cultivating a framework of exclusivity. Today, both trends are in evidence: the constant policing by the military itself of placement and promotion opportunities, and the dynamic drive by young black men to express their manhood even before considering questions of involvement with whites. Whatever the merits of these policies and attitudes, one thing remains indisputable: black men have served with valor and distinction in all of America's wars, and come away with a substantial share of its major citations and decorations.

THE REVOLUTIONARY WAR (1775-1781)

American Negroes fought in most major battles of the Revolutionary War including, among others, Lexington and Concord, Bunker Hill, Trenton, Long Island, Savannah, Valley Forge, and Yorktown. In the most serious pre-war clash between the Americans and the British, the Boston Massacre of 1770, one of the five colonists who fell was a runaway slave Crispus Attucks. Attucks was in the vanguard of marchers protesting the general presence of British "occupation" forces in Boston, and a specific incident involving the alleged beating of an unruly youth by a British "lobster-back."

After war broke out in 1775, General George Washington at first moved to bar all Negro enlistments in the Continental Army, but was forced to modify his stand as soon as the British governor of Virginia, Lord Dunmore, promised to free all Negroes who would desert their masters and fight for the British Crown. Washington then recommended that free Negroes be allowed to enlist in the Continental Army, although many of the 5,000 who

Many black crewmen served in the Revolutionary Navy, alongside such well-known heroes as John Paul Jones and Stephen Decatur.

eventually saw combat were in reality slaves who passed muster because of the difficulty recruiters encountered in meeting their monthly quotas.

Negroes served in a variety of capacities — as spies, as pilots, as infantrymen, and as laborers, cooks and teamsters. Some were with the Minutemen at Lexington & Concord; others wintered with Washington at Valley Forge, and crossed the Delaware with him enroute to surprising the Hessians quartered at Trenton. Two Negroes — Peter Salem and Salem Poor — were singled out for gallantry at the Battle of Bunker Hill in 1775. Lemuel Haynes, a minister, served at Lexington and with the Ticonderoga expedition. All told, between 8,000 and 10,000 Negroes served in the colonial armies of the Revolution. Statistics are available for some states, including Massachusetts (572 Negroes); Virginia (250 Negroes); Rhode Island (one all-black battalion and hundreds of other Negroes scattered through "white" regiments); Connecticut (49 Negroes in the 2nd Company, Third Regiment); New Hampshire (almost every Negro of military age); Maryland (780 Negroes in one regiment, others in mixed ranks); New York (two battalions of Negroes as of 1780); New Jersey and Pennsylvania (mixed battalions).

Negroes serving in the Revolutionary Navy were, for example, pilots in the colonial navy of John Paul Jones, or aboard the *Royal Lewis* with Stephen Decatur.

THE WAR OF 1812

On a June morning in 1807, the British man-of-war *Leopard* attacked the U. S. Navy's *Chesapeake*, killing three men and wounding 18 others in a skirmish outside Norfolk harbor. British officers then boarded the *Chesapeake*, and threw irons on four alleged Royal Navy deserters, among them three black seamen — Daniel Martin, William Ware and John Strachan. Impressment of U. S. seamen was one of the issues which culminated in the War of 1812, a conflict which was waged primarily at sea and saw its most celebrated battle—the Battle of New Orleans—fought after a peace treaty had been signed in Ghent, Belgium.

The most famous naval figure associated with the war is Oliver Hazard Perry who requested reinforcements for a projected battle at Lake Erie in 1813, and was appalled when his immediate superior, Commodore Isaac Chauncey, sent him a parcel of "blacks, soldiers, and boys." The word used to describe the reinforcements: "motley."

Peter Salem shooting the British Major Pitcairn at the Battle of Bunker Hill.

Blacks served with Andrew Jackson at the Battle of New Orleans.

Chauncey, in his turn, was irritated at his subordinate's sharp criticism, though his reply is subdued and philosophical: "I have yet to learn that the color of the skin or the cut and trimmings of the coat can affect a man's qualifications or usefulness. I have fifty blacks on board this ship and many of them are my best men; and these people you call soldiers have been to sea from two to seventeen years; and I presume you will find them as good and useful as any men on board your vessel."

Perry changed his appraisal once the "motley" brigade proved itself under fire. They seemed, in his words, "absolutely insensible to danger," despite the far-from-ideal circumstances under which they had served. The lack of fresh water, for example, had been particularly critical on board ship, impairing the health of many and causing widespread discomfort.

Nathaniel Shaler of the schooner *Governor Tompkins* registered similar approval of the combat prowess of one of his crew members during a subsequent sea engagement. One man, according to Shaler, "ought to be registered in the book of fame, and remembered with reverence as long as bravery is considered a virtue. He was a black man, by the name of John Johnson. A twenty-four-pound shot struck him in the hip, and took away all the lower part of his body. In this state, the poor brave fellow lay on the deck, and several times exclaimed to his shipmates: 'Fire away, my boys; no haul a color down. The other was also a black man, by the name of John Davis, and was struck in much the same way. He fell near me, and several times requested to be thrown overboard, saying he was only in the way of others.

"When America has such tars, she has little to fear from the tyrants of the ocean."

The most famous land battle of the war found Old Hickory Andrew Jackson so hard pressed for troops that he was forced to issue a call for black recruits in a letter to Louisiana governor Claiborne. Jackson declared: "They must be either for us, or against us. Distrust them and you make them your enemies, place confidence in them, and you engage them by every dear and honorable tie to the interest of the country, who extends to them equal rights and privileges with white men." His address to the "Free Colored Inhabitants" of Louisiana is far more exalted in tone. "As sons of freedom, you are now called upon to defend our most inestimable blessing. As Americans, your country looks with confidence to her adopted children for a valorous support, as a faithful return for the advantages enjoyed under her mild and equitable government. As fathers, husbands and brothers, you are summoned to rally around the standard of the eagle, to defend all which is dear in existence . . .

"To every noble-hearted, generous freeman of color, volunteering to serve during the present contest with Great Britain, and no longer, there will be paid the same bounty in money and lands, now received by the white soldiers of the United States, viz. one hundred and twenty-four dollars in money, and one hundred and sixty acres of land . . .

"Due regard will be paid to the feelings of freemen and soldiers. You will not, by being associated with white men in the same corps, be exposed to improper comparisons or unjust sarcasm. As a distinct, independent battalion or regiment, pursuing the path of glory, you will, undivided, receive the applause and gratitude of your countrymen."

Given the era, "feelings" could hardly be expected to hold much weight among brusque frontiersmen of the Jackson breed. Still, they had been brought up by the general himself, apparently out of regard for a code of chivalry which had some relevance among Southern gentlemen. Such chivalry, however, was not the pri-

Black "deserters" impressed by the British from the U.S. Navy's Chesapeake.

Blacks saw naval service during the War of 1812, particularly during the battles of Lake Erie and Lake Champlain (above).

mary concern when it came to the matter of the men's pay which was held up by some subordinate. Outraged, Jackson quickly ordered that the men be paid — whether they were "white, black, or tea."

Applause and gratitude held little appeal for the average Southerner who had participated in the glorious victory over the British. After all, what value could there be in according to the black man a share of the triumph? Surely, it might cause him to feel a dangerous sense of importance even as it dramatized his undeniable competency with combat weapons in a critical situation. Thus, the annual New Orleans parade commemorating the event afforded Negroes little opportunity to feel that they had played a part in this significant chapter of American military history. Ironically, the next time black drummer boy Jordan B. Noble marched through the streets of town was in 1862—the year Union troops took possession of New Orleans.

Noble had wanted to stay in service, but he was declared ineligible in the aftermath of an 1820 General Order which stated: "No Negro or Mulatto will be received as a recruit of the Army."

THE CIVIL WAR (1861-1865)

The Crispus Attucks incident (the Boston Massacre), the *Chesapeake-Leopard* debacle, the John Brown Raid — all have a common denominator as skirmishes which portended the arrival of full-scale war in these United States.

By 1859, slavery had so aroused the indignation of black and white activists (compromises had kept the agitation in check, but the Dred Scott decision of 1857 had added fuel to the flames of the cause) that there seemed little chance to avoid an armed showdown over the issue. White abolitionist John Brown was never one to wait for a battle, however. Crucial to his strategy was the element of surprise and the prospect of guerrilla warfare. On October 16, 1859, Brown and a band of 21 men—five of them black—seized the arsenal at Harpers Ferry, and held it for a few precious hours until federal troops commanded by Robert E. Lee forced him to flight. Brown's capture did not appease the outraged South which interpreted the very gesture as symptomatic of the North's alleged willingness to attempt the forcible overthrow of slavery. Relatively few abolitionists would ever publicly advocate such a posture, however, since they realized that the more explicit they became, the more they increased the risk of publicizing the struggle as a racial, rather than a sectional, one.

Those hanged alongside Brown at Charlestown in December 1859 included: Dangerfield Newby, a runaway slave; John A. Copeland, a North Carolinian; Sheridan Leary, a harness maker and a freedman, and Shields Green, a sailor from South Carolina. (Black Green died alongside White Brown.) One of the five, Osborne Perry Anderson, escaped death, only to write his memoirs and eventually to serve in the Union Army.

Once the South determined to bring the issue to the battlefield, it was not, as is often implied, an appreciably weaker foe than the North. In arms and material, yes, but not in the coherence of its cause and the passion of its defenders. The South knew at once what the stakes were; the North was, conversely, ambiguous and equivocal.

None realized the indecisiveness of the North better than Lincoln, a man whose demonstrated moral aversion to slavery should suffice to prove the efficacy of his intentions. It is well to remember, however, that Lincoln came to abolition by guarded stages, not in one grand uninterrupted movement. Originally, he had argued containment of slavery, i.e., prevention of its spread to the Western territories. For those touched by its blight, he proposed resettlement in Africa, mainly out of a genuine realization that little real hope existed for a reconciliation of the races in the South. Compensation of the slaveowner was an unsavory part of this proposed course of action, a gesture embraced by Lincoln mainly in keeping with his stated objective of "preserving the Union."

Political considerations aside, however, there was clearly little resolve cementing the fighting men of the North in their approach to the war. Lincoln issued an initial order calling for 75,000 volunteers—whites only. Black frontiersman Jacob Dodson came forward with an offer to raise 300 black volunteers to defend Washington, D. C. Over 100 Wilberforce students followed suit by attempting to join Union forces. These and all other gestures of black support were rejected for political reasons.

As in the Revolutionary War, however, military concerns soon became the overriding issue. The South could put the black man to use tilling the soil and performing other functionary labors which freed the white gentry to fight the war. The North had no such readymade class to provide a similarly needed service.

Negroes themselves held the answer. Would they remain loyal to their immediate oppressors, those who, however benevolent, owned them outright, or would they seek refuge in another territory which might potentially alter their condition? For obvious reasons, the risk was worth taking. The black tide of humanity soon flowing into Union lines volunteered to do teamster work, to build roads and fortifications, to forage for units in the field, to load weapons, to serve as personal valets—whatever was needed to guarantee *de facto* freedom. By the summer of 1861, Lincoln had gone so far as to instruct Union commanders not to return such fugitive slaves to their place of origin. Pressure was already mounting to plug up all the military loopholes that were making victory dubious.

In 1862, one of the "contraband" (this was the name applied to black refugees entering Union lines, a name usually applied to materiel) brought in a Confederate gunboat he had sailed out of Charlestown harbor at dawn's early light. Robert Smalls was declared a hero, and declared himself and his family free men. There was compensation, too, for the singular deed of valor in the form of prize booty from the U. S. Senate.

Elsewhere, some white generals sought to obtain a clear directive from Washington, D. C. on the possible use of black fighting men. "Black Dave" Hunter raised the First South Carolina Volunteers, but was unable to requisition the necessary equipment and uniforms to incorporate the group properly. Jim Lane of Kansas, an abolitionist and Free Soiler who later became a U. S. senator, cut through the mass of red tape by organizing the First and Second Regiments of Kansas Colored Volunteers. Being frontier soldiers, they were perhaps less preoccupied with the formal regalia of their station. They had two brief and successful skirmishes with the enemy—one at Clay County, Mississippi, the other at the Osage River in Bates County, Missouri. "They fought like tigers," said one Confederate observer. Still another Union commander was comparatively quick to realize the virtues of "Africa." The word "Africa" is extracted from General Ben Butler's own quote in which he professed willingness to "call on

A Union Officer instructs black recruits in the use of the minie rifle.

Africa to intervene," and confidence that he would not "call in vain." The First Regiment Louisiana Native Guards were mustered into the U. S. Army on September 27, 1862. They fought under the impressive name *Chasseurs D'Afrique*.

By January 1, 1863, it was clear that the nation was at a historic crossroads. The Union was torn asunder, its armies unable to bring the rebellious South to heel. It would be presumptuous to claim that the Emancipation Proclamation changed all of this; but it would be equally foolish to see no connection between the Union victory and the freedom promised slaves by the document. Lincoln's edict not only pronounced the dread word "freedom," but also paved the way for black participation in the conflict — not as support units, but as fighting men.

Three years, the recruiting order stated, not three months as Lincoln's first summons had dictated. By the summer of 1863, Mayor George Stearns of Meford, Massachusetts, reported, somewhat obtusely, that "colored men" were beginning "to understand they gain nothing by standing off but if they would gain their rights and secure protection at the hands of government they must rally at its call." The implication that Negroes were hanging back, waiting for whites to get the job done, is not only insulting, it is woefully inaccurate. Dodson and the Wilberforce students were among those who knew otherwise.

Word from Massachusetts read as follows:

"Massachusetts now welcomes you to arms as her soldiers. She has but a small colored population from which to recruit. She has full leave of the General Government to send one regiment to the war, and she has undertaken to do it. Go quickly and help fill up this first colored regiment from the North. I am authorized to assure you that you will receive the same wages, the same rations, the same equipment, the same protection, the same treatment, and the same bounty secured to white soldiers . . ."

Thus, the 54th and the 55th took the banner of the U. S. Army, and marched into South Carolina to face the entrenched legions of Fort Wagner in July 1863. Even after the Union batteries had pummeled the fort in an effort to soften it up for an infantry attack, it was virtually unscathed and ready for the onslaught. "Forward, Fifty-Fourth! For God and Governor Andrew," regimental commander Robert Gould Shaw bellowed to his men. The

This black regiment was attacked by "rebels and bloodhounds" in South Carolina.

A black regiment in action during the Civil War, Harpers 1863.

men charged into withering barrages of small-arms fire, held ranks, and reached the outer parapet before Shaw fell. A few feet away lay black standard bearer William H. Carney, Company C, shot several times. Carney managed to drag himself to safety, the colors always held aloft. Miraculously, he got back, but over 1500 of his comrades didn't. His regiment alone lost more men than all the Confederate forces combined.

Battles in which black casualties were high were numerous throughout the war. At Port Hudson, Louisiana, in May 1863, 600 men were left dead on the battlefield after what amounted to near suicidal charges against the enemy. The First and Third Louisiana Negro Regiments, raised in New Orleans, were the primary units involved in the engagement. Of them, General Nathanael Banks said:

"The highest commendation is bestowed upon them by all officers in command . . . (The) history of this day proves conclusively . . . that the Government will find in this class of troops effective supporters and defenders."

Elsewhere up the Mississippi, at Milliken's Bend, the 9th Louisiana, the 11th Louisiana and the 1st Mississippi were attacked by Confederate troops further spurred by the knowledge that their adversaries were black troops. Untrained troops who relied on instinct to survive, they prevented the Confederates from realizing their objective, and once again proved what one eyewitness put into words. "Tauntingly it has been said that Negroes won't fight. Who says it . . . when the Battle of Milliken's Bend finds its place among the heroic deeds of this war? . . . (The) freed slaves will fight."

They fought, too, at the Battle of Olustee in Florida where, according to one press report, "the first North Carolina and the Fifty-fourth Massachusetts . . . did admirably. The first North Carolina held the positions it was placed in with great tenacity, and inflicted heavy losses on the enemy . . . The Fifty-fourth sustained the reputation they had gained at Fort Wagner, and bore themselves like soldiers throughout the battle."

Perhaps it was combat fatigue that triggered the upsurge of a new issue: equal pay for equal risks. The black units which had been recruited on the basis of Union slogans promising "the same wages" as all other campaigners had begun to protest shortly after the Fort Wagner struggle.

Their pleas had been reasonable and subdued; their arguments logical and persuasive. ". . . (Are) we soldiers," they asked, "or are we laborers? We have done a soldiers duty. Why can't we have a soldiers pay?"

Among their supporters were such prominent Bostonians as Oliver Wendell Holmes and Charles Eliot Norton, and such capable field commanders as General Ben Butler who was appalled at the logic of

month as a clothing allowance when "the colored man fills an equal space in the ranks while he lives, and an equal grave when he falls." It was not until 1864 that the Army Appropriation Act finally succeeded in obliterating the invidious racial distinction which institutionalized separate pay ledgers.

This was the year of one of the most infamous and demoralizing combat episodes of the war, the brutal Fort Pillow Massacre. The few black survivors of the bloody affair were unanimous in their condemnation of the fighting practices of Confederate forces. Their butchery not only increased Union casualties at the close of the day, but bore ugly testimony to the hysteria and hatred gripping certain elements of the Confederacy. Only desperate men could have clubbed wounded soldiers, burned them alive, or impaled them on buildings and trees. Hospital patients were sabred to death in their beds; women and children were slain without quarter by men either gone berserk or so furious with rage that hardly a shred of reason or compassion prevailed. Though the massacre was condemned after an official inquiry, no concrete measures were taken to impose a severe penalty on the officers who had somehow permitted, or even justified, the bloodshed.

Another key battle of the war in which black soldiers were subjected to undue pressure and risk occurred at the Crater near Petersburg, Virginia, in the summer of 1864. The military objective of the battle was to destroy a small fort protecting Confederate lines. Union General Ambrose Burnside ordered his men to dig a tunnel under the fort, lay explosive mines in the excavation, and blow up the obstruction. The strategy then called for an assault wave to engage the enemy. Black troops, originally singled out to lead the attack, were withdrawn in an eleventh-hour gesture by General Grant himself. After mines were detonated, leaving a gigantic crater in the middle of the battlefield, three white divisions made a rush at the enemy, but they were unable to reach his lines and forced to seek refuge in the crater itself. Exposed and immobilized, they were virtual sitting ducks for Confederate sharpshooters.

Black reserve troops were immediately summoned to the rescue, but were soon slowed down in their spirited advance by demoralized white troops. Still, they formed a tiny beachhead at the crest of the crater, hanging on tenaciously until they too were forced to retreat. By this time, however, they found themselves lodged between white Union and white Confederate forces. The results of this impasse were disastrous. Panic-stricken Union troops fired wildly into the ranks of their black comrades, even as well-disciplined Confederate forces took full advantage of the desperate plight of the black troops. A Union colonel reported:

> "The bravest (white troops) lost heart and men who distrusted Negroes vented their feelings freely. Some colored men . . . found a worse fate than death in the charge . . . (Some) white men bayoneted blacks who fell back into the crater."

The Battle of Nashville, fought in December 1864, was one of the few engagements in which the coordinated efforts of both black and white troops resulted in the effective repulsion of Confederate forces. Union General James B. Steedman explained:

> "All, white and black, nobly did their duty as soldiers and evinced cheerfulness and resolution, such as I have never seen excelled in any campaign of the war in which I have borne a part."

Overall, the extent of black participation in the war can be tabulated with reasonable accuracy, both in terms of the kinds of units in which they were enrolled and the geographical distribution of such troops. Besides the 186,000 combat troops, there were more than 200,000 members of so-called service units. Of the combat troops, nearly 100,000 were mustered into service through the federal government, with the remainder being raised through state levy. Regionally, there were some 34,000 soldiers from the New York-New England area, including Pennsylvania and New Jersey. An additional 12,000 came from the West, including its territories. Over 45,000 came from the Border States, which Lincoln had feared he would lose and whose loyalty and manpower proved to be valuable adjuncts to the Union victory. Over 93,000 were raised in the rebellious states of the South, which might have done well to utilize black manpower, had it been possible.

Organizationally, black units were subdivided into 120 combat infantry regiments (close to 100,000 men); seven cavalry regiments (over 7,000 men); 12 heavy artillery regiments (over 12,000 men), and 10 companies of light artillery with over 1,300 men. Statistically, these men saw combat in more than 200 battles classified either as full-scale engagements or minor skirmishes.

Not all black participants in the war served with Union forces. Indeed, as hostilities ground to a close, the South searched desperately for some last-ditch measure to stave off defeat. In agonizing frustration, some Southern authorities entertained the notion of arming slaves, rationalizing this proposed policy by claiming that many Negroes would still regard the South as their homeland, and so fight to save it from "foreign" encroachment, while others would follow their masters out of fear or personal loyalty.

On at least one occasion, the South gave at least momentary consideration to a formal proposal to recruit slaves. The proposal was made by General Pat Cleburne, an Irish supporter of the Confederacy, who broached the subject at a meeting of senior officers in 1864. Since every slave, in Cleburne's view, was a potential free man, he constituted an ever-present source of rebellion within the Confederacy itself, as well as an instant collaborator with Union troops. What had been a source of Southern strength at the outset of the war was now "one of our chief sources of weakness." Cleburne proposed that the South turn slavery from weakness to strength again, by boldly and resolutely promising freedom to all slaves who would enlist.

His proposal was signed by three other generals and a handful of lower-echelon officers from his own command, but the high command listened in stunned silence. "I will not attempt to describe my feelings," one Confederate officer later wrote, "on being confronted with a proposal so startling in its character, so revolting to Southern sentiment, Southern pride and Southern honor . . . If this thing is once openly proposed to the Army, the total disintegration of that Army will follow in a fortnight."

Dejectedly, General Cleburne put away

Black contrabands enjoy a moment of leisure in in a Union camp during a lull in the fighting.

his proposal. The war ground on, as before. On the very day of Lee's surrender to Grant at Appomattox, black Union troops were still under fire on other battlegrounds, serving under such commanders as General Birney and General Sherman. Negro soldiers were complemented by some 200,000 Negro civilians employed by the Union Army as laborers, cooks, teamsters, and in other support functions.

All told, one out of every four Union navy men—29,511 in all—was black. They fulfilled any variety of roles, on vessels engaged in coastal blockades and in pursuit craft activity, hunting down enemy privateers and gun runners. Black river and harbor pilots were among the best operating in the states. Others served as gunners, loaders, coal heavers, stewards and firemen. On the docks, black men were equally active as laborers unloading supplies and other equipment. Negroes served aboard the *Kearsage* when she destroyed the *Alabama*, aboard the *Monitor* in its famed engagement with the *Merrimac*, and aboard Farragut's flagship in the Battle of Mobile Bay.

Four black sailors won Congressional Medals of Honor for valor in combat conditions. (For full explanation, see list of winners elsewhere in this section.)

THE CONFEDERATE "EXPERIMENT"

No definitive record exists to determine just how many black soldiers fought on the side of the Confederacy during the Civil War. Most who were readied for combat, however, were freedmen rather than slaves. The latter were generally engaged in construction work on roads, fortifications, and canals. They were also regarded as the "Army of the Soil," workers whose primary function it was to tend and harvest the crops which helped feed an army in the field.

The largest of the black units was the First Louisiana Volunteer Regiment, also known as the Native Guards and consisting of nearly 1,000 men. The volunteers had answered Governor Moore's call to arms, issued on March 21, 1862:

"The Governor and Commander-in-Chief, relying implicitly upon the loyalty of the free colored people of this city and state . . . calls upon them to maintain their organizations and be prepared for such orders as may be transmitted to them."

There were at the time in New Orleans some 13,000 or so free Negroes, many of them direct descendants of men who had fought with Andrew Jackson during the War of 1812. Many were educated men of

Black troops storm the battlements of Fort Wagner, 1863.

The Volunteer's Return (Die Heimkehr des Freiwillingen), *painted in 1867 by Frank Buchser.*

property, even slaveowners themselves, who felt that emancipation and a Union victory would only bring an end to their privileged status.

There may have been no more than 150 soldiers in the 15 other black militia units serving throughout the country. This figure remains dubious, however. It is based on the muster roll of a Mississippi militia unit with 12 black infantrymen. Many more are known to have served in the defense of Richmond toward the close of the war, and presumably were also present in numbers greater than 12 in the First South Carolina Volunteer Regiment. One black officer, a Colonel Gregg (regiment unknown), surrendered his life on the battlefield of Fredericksburg.

The fate of the First Louisiana Militia remains shrouded in mystery, however. There is no report of their having followed regular Confederate troops out of the city when it was evacuated following the triumphant entry of the Union forces in the spring of 1862. Four months later, in August to be exact, General Ben Butler reorganized the Native Guards and recruited them for the Federal side.

An 1862 issue of Harpers' *Magazine* provides full insight into the scope of black activity during the war:

"The works before Charleston, commenced late in 1860, were mainly thrown up by large gangs of negroes (sic) from the plantations, and by free negroes (sic) of Charleston, of whom 150 in a single day offered their services to the Governor of South Carolina. In April the Lynchburg *Republican* proposed 'three cheers for the patriotic free Negroes of Lynchburg,' of whom seventy had 'tendered their services to the governor to act in whatever capacity may be assigned them in defense of the state.' It was triumphantly announced that all the fortifications required for the harbor of Norfolk could be erected by the voluntary labor of negroes (sic). In June the Legislature of Tennessee passed an act authorizing the governor to receive into the military service of the state all male free persons of color between the ages of fifteen and fifty;' and if a sufficient number did not volunteer they were to be impressed. The Southern newspapers of 1861 were full of accounts of colored volunteers. One told of a grand display, held November 23 at New Orleans, where 28,000 troops were reviewed, among whom was a 'regiment composed of 1400 free colored men.' The works at Manassas Junction were mainly thrown up by the slaves of the neighboring planters. In February, 1862, the Virginia House of Delegates passed a bill ordering the enlistment of free colored persons for six months. On the 10th of March Mr. Foote declared in the Confederate Congress that, when Nashville was surrendered, 1000 or 1500 slaves had been called out and employed on the fortifications. In November, Governor Brown, of Georgia, called for slaves to complete the fortifications of Savannah; if these were not voluntarily tendered a levy would be made upon every planter in the state of one slave out of five, which would give a working force of 15,000. Subsequent to this time still more stringent measures were taken to bring negroes (sic) into the Confederate service."

It was not until July 17, 1862 that Congress authorized President Lincoln to employ "persons of African descent" in the naval and military service of the United States. On August 15, 1862, President Davis bitterly denounced "two at least of the generals of the United States" for exciting servile insurrection, and ". . . arming and training slaves for warfare against their masters, citizens of the Confederacy." Clearly however, from the evidence at least, it was a case of the pot calling the kettle black.

By the spring of 1865, the Confederates, poised upon the abyss of defeat, again broached the subject of arming slaves. Again Harpers *Magazine* reported the particulars with unfailing accuracy:

"In September, 1864, the Governor of Louisiana urged upon the Secretary of War that the time had come to put into the army every able-bodied negro (sic) as a soldier. 'I would,' he said, 'free all able to bear arms, and put them into the field at once.' In his message in November Mr. Davis discussed the question. It was to be viewed, he said, 'solely in the light of policy and our domestic economy.' Late in February, 1865, Lee strongly urged the employment of negroes (sic) as soldiers. 'I think,' he said, 'the measure not only important, but necessary. I do not think our white population can supply the necessities of a long war. I think those who are employed should be freed. It would not be just or wise to require them to remain as slaves.' An impressment or draft he thought would not bring out the best class; he would rather call upon those who were willing to come, with the consent of their owners."

An Act of Congress was ultimately passed (the margin of victory was a lone vote) which empowered the Confederacy to experiment with the idea of using slaves on a limited scale and granting them freedom for their efforts. Critics regarded the motion as an admission of despair to foreign observers, an abandonment of the very principles for which the Confederacy was ostensibly fighting. a gesture which would further demoralize their own white forces, and a decision which would remove too much needed black manpower from the fields. Though the matter remained academic, the. stipulations of the enactment are intriguing and revealing:

1. Pay and rations the same for both white and black troops.
2. **A quota from each state "not exceeding 300,000 troops . . . to be raised . . . irrespective of color."**
3. **Eligibility for no more than 25% of** the male slaves of any state.
4. "Nothing in this act shall be construed to authorize a change in the relation (between master and slave)."

A drawing of black Confederate pickets as seen through a field glass by a Union officer, Harpers 1864.

The last-named condition was, of course, logically impossible, the desperately incongruous act of a faltering enemy seeking vainly to preserve its ebbing life by arming its natural enemy.

LIST OF CIVIL WAR BATTLES ENGAGED IN BY THE UNITED STATES COLORED TROOPS (USCT)

Amite River
Appomattox Court House
Arkansas River
Ash Bayou
Ashepoo River
Ashwood Landing
Athens
Barrancas
Bayou Bidell
Bayou Boeuf
Bayou Macon
Bayou St. Lewis
Bayou Tensas
Bayou Tunica
Bermuda Hundreds
Berwick
Big Creek
Big River
Big Springs
Black Creek
Black River
Boggs' Mill
Boyd's Station
Boykin's Mills
Bradford Spring
Brawley Fork
Brice's Cross Roads
Brigsen Creek
Brush Creek
Bryant's Plantation
Cabin Creek
Cabin Point
Camden
Cedar Keys
Chapin's Farm
Charleston
Chattanooga
City Point
Clarkesville
Clinton
Coleman's Plantation
Columbia
Concordia Bayou
Cow Creek
Cox's Bridge
Dallas
Dalton
Darbytown Road
David's Bend
Decatur
Deep Bottom
Deveraux Neck
Drewry's Bluff
Dutch Gap
East Pascagoula
Eastport
Fair Oaks
Federal Point
Fillmore
Floyd
Fort Adams
Fort Anderson
Fort Blakeley
Fort Brady
Fort Burnham
Fort Donelson
Fort Gaines
Fort Gibson
Fort Jones
Fort Pillow
Fort Pocahontas
Fort Smith
Fort Taylor
Fort Wagner
Franklin
Ghent
Glasgow
Goodrich's Landing
Grand Gulf
Gregory's Farm
Haines' Bluff
Hall Island
Harrodsburg
Hatcher's Run
Helena
Henderson
Holly Springs
Honey Hill
Hopkinsville
Horse Head Creek
Indian Bay
Indian Town
Indian Village
Island Mound
Island No. 76
Issequena County
Jackson
Jacksonville
James Island
Jenkin's Ferry
John's Island
Johnsonville
Jones' Bridge
Joy's Ford
Lake Providence
Laurence
Little Rock
Liverpool Heights
Madison Station
Magnolia
Marengo
Mariana
Marion
Marion County
McKay's Point
Meffleton Lodge
Memphis
Milliken's Bend
Milltown Bluff
Mitchell's Creek
Morganzia
Moscow Station
Mound Plantation
Mount Pleasant Landing
Mud Creek
Murfreesboro
Nashville
Natchez
Natural Bridge
New Kent Court House
New Market Heights
Olustee
Owensboro
Pass Manchal
Palmetto Ranch
Petersburg
Pierson's Farm
Pine Barren Creek
Pine Barren Ford
Pine Bluff
Plymouth
Point Lookout
Point of Rocks
Point Pleasant
Poison Springs
Port Hudson
Powhatan
Prairie d'Anne
Pulaski
Raleigh
Rector's Farm
Richland
Richmond
Ripley
Roache's Plantation
Rolling Fork
Roseville Creek
Ross Landing
Sabine River
Salkehatchie
Saltville
Sand Mountain
Sandy Swamp
Scottsboro
Sherwood
Shipwith's Landing
Simpsonville
Smithfield
South Tunnel
Spanish Fort
St. John's River
St. Stephens
Steamer *Alliance*
Steamer *Chippewa*
Steamer *City Bolle*
Steamer *Lotus*
Suffolk

Sugar Loaf Hill
Sulphur Branch
Swift Creek
Taylorsville
Timber Hill
Town Creek
Township
Trestle
Tupelo
Vicksburg
Vidalia
Wallace Ferry
Warsaw
Waterford
Waterloo
Waterproof
White Oak Road
White River
Williamsburg
Wilmington
Wilson's Landing, Wharf
Yazoo City
Yazoo Expedition

Mustered-out black volunteers meet their loved ones in Little Rock, Arkansas.

INDIAN WARS ON THE FRONTIER

At the close of the Civil War, several USCT regiments remained on active duty for a time, but Congress later authorized the creation of only. two regular regiments of cavalry (the 9th and the 10th) and two of infantry (the 24th and the 25th). Known to the Indians as "Buffalo Soldiers," they served on isolated posts located in Texas and the Southwest—building roads, stringing telegraph wire, escorting groups crossing Indian territory, and scouting hostile tribes as well. During this period, 12 Negroes won Congressional Medals of Honor for bravery in combat. (See Negro Congressional Medal of Honor section for names and units.)

The first action between black troopers and Indians came 40 miles east of Fort Hays, Kansas in September 1867 when 40 troopers on duty protecting workers of the Kansas Pacific Railroad engaged 300 Cheyenne; the last action of black troopers and Indians was likewise the last Indian fight between the U.S. Army and the Indian on this continent and took place on January 9, 1918 between Troop E of the 10th Cavalry and a well-armed band of Yaqui Indians 25 miles west of Nogales, Mexico in Bear Valley, Arizona. Between these years the black soldiers on the American frontier played important roles in General Phillip Sheridan's campaign against the Cheyennes and Arapahoes and in subduing the Apache uprisings of the Southwest against Victorio, Mangus Colorado and Geronimo.

The most famous Indian uprising punctuating those years occurred at the Little Big Horn in the Dakota Territory between June 25th and 26th, 1876. This is one of history's most frightfully memorable battles, largely because it resulted in the extermination of three whole U.S. battalions, led by Colonel George Armstrong Custer, at the hands of Sioux and Cheyenne Indians. It is not generally known that a black cavalryman by the name of Isaiah Dorman fought and fell at the Little Big Horn.

Originally an interpreter and scout, Dorman was an escaped slave who made his way into Indian territory and lived there for some years before taking an Indian wife. The "black white man," as the Indians called him, was trusted by them even though he worked for the white man. It would seem that he enjoyed the role of intermediary between the U.S. government (represented by the cavalry) and the Sioux nation (represented by an explosive mixture of volatile young chiefs and their more reluctant elders).

While reconnoitering the area through which Custer had decided to ride, Dorman detected various signs of a hostile Indian presence. His warnings were communicated to Custer, who paid as little heed to them as he paid to his War Department orders to avoid an armed confrontation. He led his men—Dorman among them—right into the trap the Indians had laid.

Dorman was one of those who fell. He was found on the battlefield by a bevy of Sioux women whose custom it was to circulate among the wounded, and strip them of arms and valuables. He was not scalped, according to one version of the story, because Sitting Bull himself intervened once he had learned his old friend was among the day's victims. Seeing that it was too late to save him, the chief then requested that he be spared from the customary ritual of mutilation designed, in Indian eyes, to prevent the victim from passing into the spirit world as a "whole man."

Although battles such as these tend to etch themselves into the public consciousness, it is well to remember that the glamorous or adventurous aspects of frontier

A weary black trooper refreshes himself on the trail.

life were generally far outweighed by the prosaic and uneventful routine of garrison or escort duty.

No chronicler of the West has captured the authentic flavor of life in these regiments more dramatically than author/illustrator Frederic Remington. In much of his writing, Remington recreates the up-front aura of the 10th Cavalry—not a stately, majestic, spruced-up lot of men suited for parades and other ceremonial gestures, but a rough-and-ready detail of "old soldiers who know what it is all about, this soldiering." The all-black 10th, Remington tells us, "never had a 'soft detail since it was organized," and was composed exclusively of "good horses and hardy men, divested of military fuss." Remington respected men such as these, for he knew that it was they who were best equipped to grapple with the rigors of the frontier and to subdue "the great strange stretches of the high plains." The soldiers "in the colored regiments" were all veterans with several years of frontier life behind them, men who could never be replaced, men whose like would "never come again." The artist admired the obvious physical equipment of the black cavalrymen—fellows who were "great chested, broad shouldered (and) bull-necked," ideally built to contend with the rigors of the strenuous life.

The sociological significance of the passing of the frontier may have been lost on the men themselves, but was of primary concern to the artist himself. Remington not only correctly identified the signs of encroaching civilization, but captured its essential flavor with noteworthy sensitivity, and unmistakable sympathy for the meritorious service of the Army regular.

A black trooper scans the horizon for signs of Indian warriors.

> "The country through which we were then operating was a howling wilderness; it is now traversed by railroads and covered with villages and farms. Children at play unwittingly trample the grass over the graves of soldiers who gave their lives that they might live and thrive, and communities throughout the West generally send representatives to Congress, some of whom, in the peace and plenty of their comfortable homes, fail to recognize, in Washington, the hardships, privations, and sacrifice of life suffered by the army, before their prosperity could be possible or the lives of their constituents assured.
>
> "In this the simple duty of soldiers was performed, and no credit is claimed, but should not the record of past deeds such as these, accompanied by the prosperity that has followed, at least guarantee a more generous feeling for the army by all citizens, more especially by those who are called upon to support it?"

THE SPANISH-AMERICAN WAR (1898)

It was the jingoistic Spanish-American War which roused the nation to reconsider the status of its black frontier regiments. The diary of a black sergeant of the 25th Infantry, Frank Pullen, suggests the hardships which the unit had undergone at its duty stations in Minnesota and, later, the Dakotas, and Montana:

> "This gallant regiment of colored soldiers served eighteen years in that climate, where, in winter, which lasts five months or more, the temperature falls as low as 55 degrees below zero, and in summer

rises to over 100 degrees in the shade and where mosquitoes rival the Jersey breed."

Considering the isolation, drudgery, and discomfort the troops had undergone, it is not surprising that they reacted with unvarnished enthusiasm when news reached them that they were to embark for Cuba to avenge the sinking of the *Maine*.

Despite the ostensible importance of their patriotic mission, the men were at times subjected to considerable harassment and to humiliating affronts. They were jeered at whistle stops in Southern towns; they were not only given separate quarters on government transport ships, but officially forbidden to socialize in any manner with white troops while enroute to their destinations; they ate in separate sections of the mess hall, which they entered only after white troops were all seated; they took their morning coffee alone after their white counterparts were finished.

Despite these indignities, black soldiers fought spiritedly and with great determination during the brief encounter. One white Southerner who saw them in action commented: ". . . of all the men I saw fighting, there were none to beat the 10th Cavalry and the colored infantry, and I don't mind saying so." Rough Rider Frank Knox, a cohort of Theodore Roosevelt's, promised that many of the black cavalrymen who had rushed up San Juan Hill would "live in my memory forever."

Roosevelt, on the other hand, recalled incidents in which black troopers had allegedly shown a tendency to "drift to the rear." In a magazine article, he described his stalwart intercession at crucial points to prevent mass desertions, but neglected to take into account the possibility that orders from actual battle zones may have governed the men's behavior. As it turned out, Sergeant Preston Holliday of the 10th Cavalry later explained that black soldiers were often ordered to the rear to remove casualties, or to stock up on rations, water, and other supplies. Other white Rough Riders backed the sergeant, although they did not command the same audience which Roosevelt addressed.

As in other wars, conflicting white opinions concerning the calibre of black troops determined, to a large degree, their overall deployment and combat effectiveness. Individual heroes like Private T. C. Butler of the 25th Infantry and Sergeant Major Edward L. Baker of the 10th Cavalry (as

The Hotchkiss battery in action at Las Guasimas

Sergeant Horace W. Bivins

well as six other Medal of Honor winners) distinguished themselves in combat at El Cavey, Santiago and San Juan Hill, but the mass of black men who tried desperately to participate in the conflict were either discouraged, delayed, or rejected.

In the South, National Guard units did not accept black volunteers; elsewhere volunteer regiments found the War Department in Washington, D. C. sluggish in responding to their pleas for active involvement. Among the state militias which were eventually raised pursuant to Congressional authorization were: the 9th Ohio (a unit commanded by former West Pointer Charles Young); the 3rd Alabama Infantry; the 3rd North Carolina Infantry; the 6th Virginia; the 23rd Kansas; the 8th Illinois, two infantry companies from Indiana and Company L of the 6th Massachusetts (otherwise an all-white regiment).

Officer promotions during the war were scanty, although some black men were advanced on the basis of combat heroism. In most cases, however, few command positions were meted out to black officers at the head of regimental-sized units. There was also a distinct reluctance on the part of American authorities to utilize black troops as part of the overall occupying force on the island after hostilities ended.

Significantly, some black critics of the war pointed to it as little more than an exercise in American imperialism, and saw black involvement in it as a double tragedy. In the view of historian Kelly Miller, blacks were in the awkward position of being subject to a form of domination at home which they themselves imposed on people fighting for liberation in Cuba and the Philippines.

WORLD WAR I: 1917-1918

When the United States declared war on Germany on April 6, 1917, the call went out for thousands of black volunteers to help supply the war zones in France and Germany. Segregated in the draft and in a lone officer's training camp, and allowed at first to volunteer only as laborers in the Army and as servants in the Navy, Negroes were assigned to the American Expeditionary Force, serving as stevedores, road builders, wood choppers, railroad hands, mechanics, gravediggers—in short, as cogs in the war machinery.

Black combat troops were organized into two divisions (the 92nd and the 93rd), each composed of four regiments. The 92nd consisted of the 365th-368th regiments, and the 93rd was made up of the 369th-372nd regiments. The most famous of the regiments was unquestionably the "Fighting 369th," an outgrowth of the

Sergeant Frank W. Pullen

Sergeant of the colors, World War I

old Eighth Illinois and a contingent well stocked with New Yorkers. This unit landed at Brest, France in the spring of 1918, went into action in the Champagne sector, and remained on the front lines for 191 consecutive days without losing a trench, retreating an inch, or surrendering a prisoner. The unit was awarded the Croix de Guerre by the appreciative French.

Two members of the 369th showed particular valor in combat, and became the most celebrated black heroes of the war. Privates Henry Johnson, an Albany, New York, Redcap, and Trenton, New Jersey, resident Needham Roberts, while on forward observer duty, were suddenly overrun by a sizable band of German infiltrators. Though wounded, Roberts held the enemy at bay for a time by lobbing hand grenades into their midst. Low on supplies and losing strength, Roberts was soon overwhelmed by the Germans and in the process of being dragged off to German lines. Johnson then rushed the enemy with a bolo knife, creating such a diversion and inflicting so many casualities that he managed singlehandedly to disperse the invaders. The next morning, four German bodies were found, and unit commander William Hayward praised the "two brave Colored boys" who had fought "like tigers at bay." The French added their approval by nominating the men for the nation's highest military honor, The Croix de Guerre.

The other three black regiments were also brigaded with the French. The 370th saw action north of the Oise-Aisne canal; the 371st and the 372nd Regiments helped defend the Meuse-Argonne front and earned the Croix de Guerre (with Palm) for their efforts.

The 92nd Division, left under American command, fared badly in comparison to its sister unit—largely because of familiar taunts by Southern commanders that the troops were badly motivated, cowardly and a detriment to overall morale. As a result, the unit saw little action at the front.

Such behind-the-scenes harangues between the U.S. military officials were not disclosed until CRISIS correspondent W. E. B. DuBois uncovered a blatantly discriminatory document which explored the "official" U.S. position on the use and status of black troops.

During World War I, Negro soldiers fought at Bois d'Havza and at Minaucourt, and participated in the attack at Maison-en-Champagne, which brought them to the Rhine River in Germany.

Young black officer candidates were not aware of these disturbing policies when they pleaded so earnestly with Washington Congressmen for the creation of a training camp. The Des Moines, Iowa camp which finally came into existence graduated hundreds of junior officers, among them Charles Houston, later dean of Howard University's Law School. Howard's experiences in France led him to exclaim: "There (is) no sense of dying in a world ruled by them. German prisoners were kinder than our white American comrades."

After the famous parade up Fifth Avenue which marked the triumphant return of the 369th to Harlem, Dr. DuBois served notice on America that returning black servicemen meant to realize full equality under the law as first-class citizens:

> "We stand again to look America squarely in the face. It lynches . . . it disfranchises . . . it insults us . . . We return fighting. Make way for Democracy! We saved it in France, and by the great Jehovah, we will save it in the U.S.A."

Homecoming is the same in all wars. These black troops are returning from overseas duty during World War I.

WORLD WAR II: 1941-1945

World War II blasted its way onto the American scene on the infamous morning of December 7, 1941, when Japanese fighters flew over Pearl Harbor and rained a hail of bombs and bullets on the slumbering U.S. naval base there. Among the battle vessels sunk or reduced to helpless hulks was the *U.S.S. Arizona,* the ship on which black messman Dorie Miller was routinely going about his duties collecting laundry when the ear-splitting sounds of battle sirens and exploding shells rent the air. Miller rushed up on deck, and instantly hauled his wounded captain to safety. Moments later, he sprung into action behind an anti-aircraft gun he had never been trained to operate. Firing calmly and accurately, he brought down four Zero fighter planes before the cry to abandon ship was heeded by all survivors.

On May 7, 1942, messman Dorie Miller was cited for bravery by Fleet Admiral Chester Nimitz, who decorated him with a Silver Star and so acknowledged the nation's debt to a black man of "extraordinary courage." The medal did not bring with it an instant promotion, or a transfer to a line of duty which might have been more in keeping with Miller's demonstrated aptitudes or preferences. After returning from a trip back to Harlem, where he drummed up support for U.S. war bonds, Miller was assigned to the *Liscome Bay* which went down in the Pacific on November 25, 1944 with no survivors.

Troops of the 92nd Division, an all-black unit, file past a destroyed tank in Italy, World War II.

There seems little doubt that the treatment accorded black servicemen was a contributing factor to the severe disillusionment gripping elements of the black community with the announcement of war. Dr. DuBois, for example, sensed instantly that Negroes would continue to face the double burden of defending a nation abroad even as that nation, by virtue of its domestic policies, had not yet assured all of its citizens equal protection under the Constitution. Both Bayard Rustin and Elijah Muhammad were conscientious objectors during the war, Rustin on pacifist grounds and Muhammad in consequence of his religious separatism. (Muhammad was indicted for pro-Japanese sympathies in 1942.)

Black airman Sergeant Conway Waddy

Still, most black civilians rallied to the side of the nation, endorsed the war effort, and sought to make a vital contribution to it. In the case of air cadet Yancy Williams, that endorsement involved a fearless insistence on the right of prospective black airmen to join the Air Force as fighter pilots, not merely ground jockeys or maintenance personnel. Williams, a Howard graduate, threatened a lawsuit, whereupon the Air Force quickly succumbed to the pressure of adverse publicity and opened its Jim Crow training facility at Tuskegee Institute.

The Navy, however, was equally lax in withdrawing the restrictions under which black sailors were forced to serve until pressure from the White House overturned existing policies of apathy and neglect. By the summer of 1942, some trainees in segregated camps and schools were receiving instructions as gunner's mates, petty officers, quartermasters and coxswains. Despite these gestures, by 1945, the Navy was still operating under a de-facto quota system which kept some 19 out of every 20 black seamen in the messman's branch.

The bread-and-butter branch of the military complex remained the Army, however. Here, by the end of 1942, it was apparent that there was widespread reluctance to utilize black combat forces abroad. One unit of black engineers had been sent to Liberia to prepare landing strips for anticipated combat missions over North Africa, but War Plans Chief Dwight D. Eisenhower was frankly doubtful that large blocs of Negro troops could be indiscriminately assigned to overseas duty in Europe. In the Pacific theatre, Generals Douglas MacArthur and Millard F. Harmon responded more to manpower needs than to an anticipated maze of social roadblocks and circumspect pressures. "Please disabuse yourself," wrote MacArthur to Washington, "of any idea that I might return these troops after your decision to dispatch them."

Black troops of the 93rd Division later fought at Bougainville and the Treasury Islands, and joined MacArthur in a historic moment of triumph and national glory when the Philippines were retaken in October 1944. By then, black marines had helped win the Battle of Saipan, and black engineers had pitched in to build the "Burma Road" on the Asian mainland. Black aviation engineers had built runways and landing strips in New Caledonia, the point of origin for the Air Force escort bombers who struck the Japanese in the crucial Battle of the Coral Sea, fought in 1942.

The 92nd also saw combat overseas, although its record was by far the most controversial of all black fighting units. General Benjamin O. Davis, the Army's first black general, joined the unit overseas in Italy, where he shot a propaganda film entitled *Teamwork* in an effort to prepare the American public for the advent of black combat troops on the European firing line. Great Britain's crusty and indomitable leader Winston Churchill was also on hand to offer words of encouragement. In his wake emerged dozens of

Captain Hugh Mulzac

white correspondents scripting the occasion and acquiescing readily in the temptation to compose hyperbole. Perhaps the most transparent public relations episode was the "battlefield promotion" invented by General Mark Clark to demonstrate the vital combat role already being played by the 92nd when it had not in fact taken its positions on the Gothic Line. General Clark rashly promoted 1st Lieutenant Charles F. Gandy of Washington, D.C., as a gesture to allay black criticism of the promotion policies in effect for black officers. Clark simply plucked off the captain's bars of one of his white staff members, and placed them on the shoulders of a man he had designated, clairvoyantly so it seemed, as one who ought to be made visible.

Other problems of morale, level of training, and competence were simply overlooked by the high command of the 92nd. There were some initial combat successes, largely against light resistance along Highway 12 enroute to the foothills of the Apennines. Once in the mountains, however, the 92nd faltered badly. Some ran; some hesitated; some advanced sluggishly and without any combat crispness and determination. Still, there were contingents which engaged the enemy aggressively and fought earnestly to capture key objectives. Mass frustration, mismanagement, and confusion keynoted the experience as a whole, however. Lieutenant Colonel Marcus Ray, a black officer, conceded he was "heartsick," but was emphatic in denying the 92nd was "a complete failure as a combat unit."

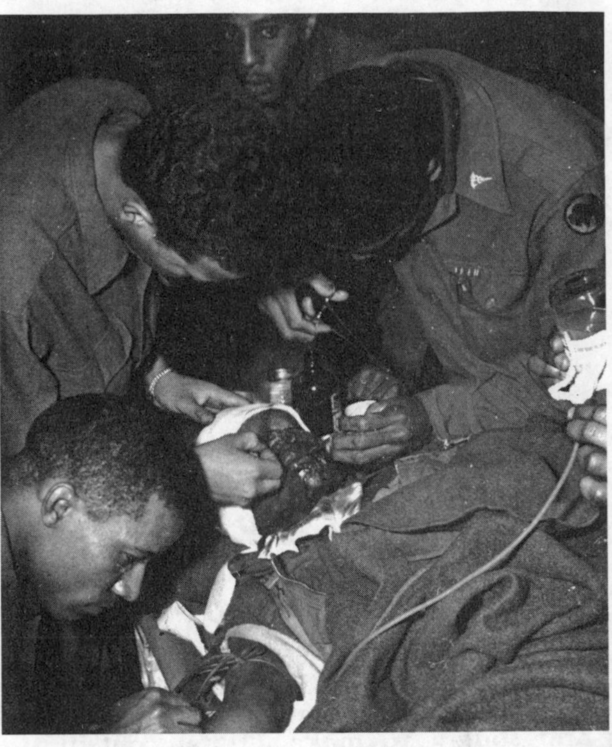

Medics and a wounded black infantryman

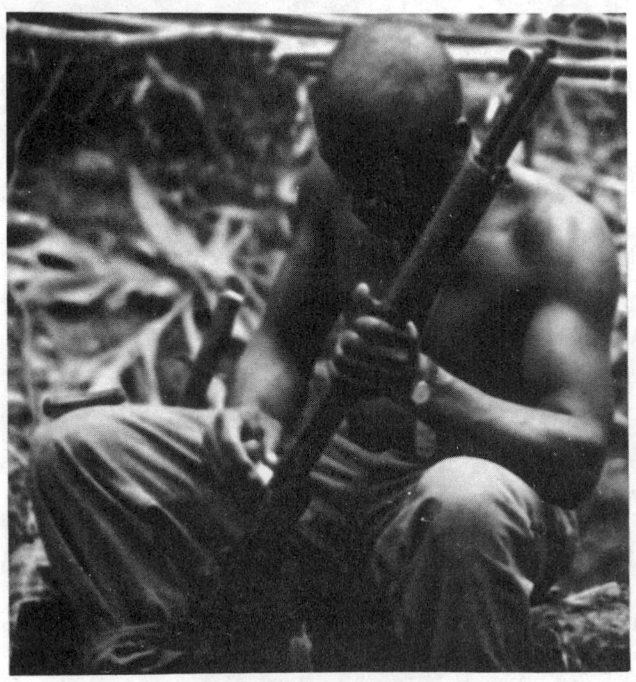

A black rifleman, World War II

Other black units performed many missions without any stigma of controversy. General Eisenhower, watching a black battalion scurry up the. beach at Normandy, commended the troops for carrying out their mission "with courage and determination." General George S. Patton found the all-black 761st Tank Battalion worthy of fighting in his select company. "I would never have asked for you,'" he told the men bluntly, "if you weren't good." The men were good enough to be on hand for the German capitulation in Austria.

At the Battle of the Bulge, Germany's last-ditch attempt to drive a wedge into Allied lines, black troops were called into action on an emergency basis to help withstand a ferocious Nazi assault. General Lanham commented that he had "'never seen soldiers who have performed better in combat." Again, neither proficiency nor praise were sufficient to override rigid patterns of segregation. The "heroes" were returned to their all-black units as soon as the crisis passed.

The 99th Pursuit Squadron remains the most glamorous black unit associated with World War II. Commanded by Colonel Benjamin O. Davis, this unit had flown over 500 combat missions and more than 3,000 sorties against the Germans by the summer of 1944. After being attached to the 332nd Fighter Group, the record of the unit grew even more impressive. By the spring of 1945, it boasted of nearly 1,600 combat missions and over 15,000 sorties; it had downed Messerschmitts in the air and on the ground, and terrorized enemy shipping as well in the role of the roving marauder.

Neither the Navy nor the Marines could boast of such an accomplished unit. The Merchant Marine, on the other hand, had recruited some 24,000 black members, most of whom had had ample opportunity to win their spurs in a relatively unencumbered and desegregated environment. Eighteen Liberty ships were actually named for black men, including the S.S. *Frederick Douglass* and the S.S. *Robert L. Vann.*

Pressure mounted in the wake of World War II to continue to break down the most onerous patterns of racial segregation and to assure Negroes—both in and out of service—the opportunity to make professional progress commensurate with their ability.

Negroes could point to impressive statistics as a testimonial to their unflagging commitment to the war effort. Three million had registered for service; 700,000 had served in the Army, 165,000 in the Navy, 5,000 in the Coast Guard, 17,000 in the Marines, and 4,000 in the WAVES and WACS.

Despite the record, recognition was not forthcoming until pressure was applied. In June 1948, A. Philip Randolph made extensive preparations to urge Negroes to resist induction into a segregated Armed Forces. His League for Nonviolent Civil Disobedience Against Military Segregation threatened to cause heavy embarrassment to the Truman Administration. After studying the situation carefully, President Truman decided not only to issue Executive Order 9981 barring segregation in the Armed Forces, but also to appoint a blue-ribbon panel to study equality of treatment and opportunity throughout the Armed Forces. The resulting group, the Fahy Committee, still found considerable evidence of unconscionable manipulation in the training patterns of black enlisted men, but reported that segregation was largely a thing of the past in the Army, Navy, Marines, and Air Force. Remnants of all-black units were to surface one last time before being officially doomed to oblivion: in the Korean War.

KOREA

On June 25, 1950, North Korean forces, armed with Soviet weapons, ripped across the 38th parallel, driving hard for the Republic of Korea (ROK) capital at Seoul. Seventeen days after the Korean bombshell burst, the men of the 24th Infantry Regiment, a unit which, for all of its 81 years, had been composed entirely of black combatants, landed in Korea from Japan. The 24th entered the grim fighting against an enemy which had all but routed the ROK army, and forced them into one strategic retreat after another. It was a somber beginning. Then, on July 22, 1950, the New York *Times* reported that the important railhead city of Yech'on had been recaptured by *American soldiers; American soldiers of the 24th Infantry; black American soldiers of the 24th Infantry.* And the New York *Daily News* headlined: "Negroes Gain 1st Korea Victory." Thus, remnants of an all-black unit were credited with the first victory for U.N. forces in Korea.

Despite this initial success, terrible controversy surrounded the performance of many black fighting units during the War. As in other wars, criticism of black units was sometimes unduly harsh. In January 1951, NAACP counsel Thurgood Marshall was dispatched to Japan to investigate the conditions surrounding court-martial proceeding involving 32 convicted Negroes accused of violating the 75th Article of War. Of the 32, half had been given death or life imprisonment, and the remainder anywhere from 10 to 50 years. After examining the trial records, Marshall found that several of the deliberations which had resulted in the conferral of life sentences had lasted less than an hour. Four life sentences had been issued in a space ranging from 42 to 50 minutes, hardly time for the observance of court formalities and the presentation of adequate arguments.

Later interviews with the prisoners uncovered other germane facts. One soldier had actually been in an Army hospital at the time he was accused of being absent without leave; another had falsified his age in order to enlist, and was not yet 18 at the time of his conviction; four others were found guilty of cowardice even though they were doing mess duty behind the battle lines at the time of their alleged disappearance. Five other men had been placed on trial in the aftermath of a confused withdrawal during which they had become separated from their unit. An examination of the trial testimony showed thta the captain who testified against them had given three different versions of what happened on the night in question. Despite these discrepancies, the captain was promoted to major, and the five men were all convicted of being AWOL. In all, 32 black GIs had been sentenced to imprisonment for criminal behavior as opposed to only two whites. Moreover, many of the convicted blacks, though accused of the same offense as the convicted whites, had been given far stiffer penalties.

From Japan, Marshall went on to Korea, where he conducted many interviews with infantrymen who claimed that their officers frequently berated them and made no effort whatsoever to disguise their contempt for "nigger troops." Marshall concluded his investigation by maintaining that the frequency of such episodes not only contributed to the high rate of casualties, but also encouraged the practice of scapegoating, i.e., the habit of blaming Negro troops for every conceivable combat snafu.

Marshall's findings offered convincing proof that many Negroes were being accused by, and tried before, officers who held them in the kind of prejudicial contempt which made legal justice a virtual impossibility. The NAACP marshalled enough evidence to reverse many of the courts-martial entirely and to lighten sentences in the majority of other cases. It also succeeded in drawing renewed attention to the numerous instances of combat heroism involving Negroes.

Two black infantrymen received Congressional Medals of Honor, both of them awarded posthumously. Private William H. Thompson, one of the designees, had manned a machine-gun nest singlehanded, and remained at his post until his buddies withdrew to safety. Sergeant Cornelius H. Charlton, the other medal winner, had led three valiant attacks up an enemy-held hill and, though wounded, somehow continued to fire until the enemy emplacement under attack was destroyed.

Private Edward O. Cleaborn was honored by an official ceremony in his home town of Memphis, Tennessee, for covering the withdrawal of his comrades, including wounded buddies, while under fire on a ridge near the town of Kuri. Cleaborn's

Three Mustang fighter pilots in Korea.

parents, presented with the Distinguished Service Cross, were told how their son had wiped out the Communist machine-gun crews threatening Company A of the 24th. He had mowed down enemy infiltrators which had outflanked the platoon, staying at his post and pumping his weapon until it grew hot enough to burn his hand. Everyone had made it back . . . except Private Cleaborn.

Lieutenant Harry Sutton was so conspicuous in fighting off a Communist breakthrough at Hungnam beachhead in December 1950, that the ridge he and his black infantry platoon had defended came to be known as "Sutton's Ridge." Sutton was later killed by Communist machine-gun fire while fighting in the Suwon sector, and thus never got to wear his Silver Star back home.

Among the black heroes who survived the rigors of combat were Lieutenant Ellison Wynn, acting commander of Company B, 9th Infantry Regiment. When dawn broke after a night attack, Lieutenant Wynn, out of ammunition, threw rocks and C-ration cans at scores of charging Chinese troops attempting to overrun his position near the Yalu River. Wynn was thus able to cover the retreat of 34 men, losing only four.

Sergeant Arthur Dudley, holder of a Distinguished Service Cross, was known to his war-weary senior officers on the line as "the best damn squad leader in Korea." The head of an international and interracial squad consisting of three KATUSAs (Koreans attached to the U.S. Army), and four Americans (one of them black), Dudley personally accounted for 53 enemy dead while under fire with the 19th Regiment. He had received his DSC for heroism displayed at the Battle of Ch'angyong, near the Naktong River, early in August 1950.

By the end of the Korean War, deactivation and reorganization had proceeded throughout the various military echelons. All black infantry units were discontinued, their men redistributed elsewhere. The 9th and 10th Cavalries were reconstituted as the all-black 509th and 510th Tank Battalions, and white replacements soon filtered into them. Statistics showed that only 88 all-black concentrations were still identifiable within the Army's structure, and full 95% of black personnel were serving in integrated units. These included units stationed in Alaska and Australia, along with the Orient. Only in Europe and the United States did a few pockets of segregation remain.

VIETNAM

During the brief period of cease fire which intervened between the end of the Korean War and the intensification of the conflict in Vietnam, the Kennedy Administration proceeded energetically with a program designed to ferret out the remaining vestiges of discrimination in the Armed Forces. President Kennedy, speaking through his Secretary of Defense, Robert McNamara, impressed upon the military establishment the need for fostering friendship and equal opportunity for black servicemen, both on and off base. By 1965, however, it was apparent that the nation was no longer on a peacetime footing: statistics released by the Department of Defense showed that almost 15% of the infantrymen serving in Vietnam were black. Added to these were 5.1% of the Navy, 8.9% of the Marine Corps, and 8.3% of the Air Force. The grand total: 9.3% of the Armed Forces.

The figures, and the war itself, generated tremendous controversy in the black community. In 1965, Malcolm X claimed that the U.S. government was "causing American soldiers to be murdered every day, for no reason at all." Two years later, Martin Luther King, Jr., reminded the American public that "the Negro" had always managed to become a "100% citizen in warfare," but was always reduced to a "50% citizen on American soil." The most famous defector from the ranks was heavyweight champion Muhammad Ali, who declared himself a conscientious objector on religious grounds as a Black Muslim. Ali was convicted of violating the Selective Service Act, and stripped of his championship as well.

Still, most young blacks were willing to answer the draft board's call when it came. Pfc. Milton Olive, 19, of Chicago, was typical of the young black men who risked, and sometimes lost, their lives in arduous battle far from the familiar sounds of home. Olive was blown to bits by an exploding grenade on which he had fallen to save the lives of his comrades, and posthumously awarded the Congressional Medal of Honor. By mid-1969, nine other Negroes had joined Olive as recipients of the medal. They were: Captain Riley L. Pitts, 1st Lieutenant Ruppert L. Sargent, Sergeant Rodney M. Davis, Sergeant Matthew Leonard, Sergeant Donald R. Long, SP5 Lawrence Joel, SP5 Clarence E. Sasser, SP5 Dwight H. Johnson, and Pfc. James Anderson, Jr.

Like Olive, many perished in combat.

For Sergeant Davis, the end came in Quahg Nam on September 6, 1968 when, like Olive, he threw himself on a live grenade to protect his comrades.

Those black men stationed in Vietnam are represented in hazardous combat zones, and in a variety of other support functions. Thus, one finds them patrolling the Mekong Delta, advising the South Vietnamese Army at Pleiku, repairing jet planes on aircraft carriers in the Gulf or Tonkin (or flying them over Hanoi), joining the gruelling sieges (as at the Citadel of Hue after the Tet Lunar New Year offensive) or the bloody fights (as at Hill 875, Dakto), wading across the treacherous rice paddies and slashing through the barely penetrable bamboo thickets. Black men in the ranks are unloading ships, digging latrines, driving trucks, servicing warplanes, and walking mountain ranges, even as black desk men and strategists are planning battles, practicing international law and running press centers, to name but a few of their diversified assignments.

According to New York *Times* reporter Thomas Johnson, officers in the Military Assistance Command say that the 173rd Airborne Brigade, a crack outfit with heavy black representation, is "the best performing unit in Vietnam." In elite combat units like these, one out of every four combat troops is a black man; elsewhere in Vietnam's battle zones, the ratio drops to one out of every five men apt to see action. This same ratio prevails among the Army's front-line supervisors (ranging in rank from Sfc to Master Sergeant).

Until General Davis retired (he became Cleveland's Public Safety Director), two of the 1,342 admirals and generals in the U.S. military establishment were black. General Davis was last assigned to deputy command of MacDill Air Force Base in Florida after serving as full commander of the 13th Air Force in the Philippines and, prior to that, in a Korean headquarters assignment. The other is Lieutenant General Frederic E. Davison, appointed Brigadier General in July 1968, and named deputy commanding officer of the 199th Infantry Brigade in Vietnam. He was the highest ranked of 35 black senior officers in the U.S. Army at the time of his promotion.

By 1969, it had become apparent that many young black combat troops were beginning to exhibit the same trends toward racial separatism that had characterized the behavior of white troops. Experience quickly showed that such efforts at racial elitism, spawned no doubt by the constancy of rejection on the part of white troops, constituted a dangerous menace to the peace and well being of all concerned. The primary cause of the difficulty was the unwillingness of the average white GI to accept black troops; the more obvious manifestation of the problem was reflected in the black GI's contempt for his intransigent white counterpart.

At Fort Bragg, North Carolina, in the summer of 1969, for instance, racial unrest flared into a full-fledged brawl when 35 black troops at an enlisted men's club squared off with a squad of about 25 white MP's. The club was described as a voluntarily segregated meeting place for black soldiers who, like their white counterparts, had opted for exclusivity in their after-hours leisure and recreation. Such a withdrawal, thought to be harmless enough on the surface, allowed young men to lock up their assorted complaints, nourish their private rages and magnify their gnawing grievances and suspicions. Though the Bragg incident had no tragic outcome, it afforded unmistakeable evidence that a base camp could be transformed into gangland turf as soon as two militantly uncompromising factions found an explosive issue around which to rally.

The violence which erupted at the Marine base in Kaneohe, Hawaii, bore some similarities to the Bragg fisticuffs, although the rumble on the island cen-

Lt.Col. Frank Petersen, first black Marine aviator.

tered on more readily discernible discriminatory trends, such as inequities in military discipline and punishment, as well as unjust favoritism involving promotions. The black-power salute rendered by a group of black leathernecks brought the series of provocations to a flash point, resulting in a donnybrook which left 16 injured and three hospitalized.

A black infantryman on a search-and-destroy mission in Vietnam.

At Camp LeJeune, North Carolina, one white Marine died in the aftermath of an interracial brawl whose origins were not immediately apparent. Even before the incident, however, an Ad Hoc Committee on Equal Treatment and Opportunity had outlined some of the more deliberate practices which could lead to racial confrontations, including *de facto* segregation in housing, bars and barber shops. Still, the Committee had not proceeded beyond the warning-and-advice stage by the time the tragedy struck.

The Marine Corps responded, several weeks later, with a directive which restated the integration policies of the Corps, ordered all officers and men to observe them, and added a pair of human touches which might have been amusing if the situation had not become so serious:

a) Afro haircuts, with certain minimal modifications, would henceforth be allowed and

b) Black-power salutes would be permitted so long as they were intended as greetings between "brothers" and not in defiance of the Corps.

The Army quickly realized that orders regarding haircuts and ghetto salutes were not substantive enough measures to prevent further outbreaks. This was communicated to Washington officials who began to formulate a preliminary blueprint for easing the conflicts and preventing their escalation. Structural reform was clearly required, and the Department of Defense offered concrete proposals to clear the air and improve the racial climate within the military establishment. Implicit in its formula was the assumption that the Armed Services could not merely quarantine the problems of the civilian community with a stern and inflexible mandate. Instead, the Armed Services would have to face up to every vestige of bias which both raw recruits and seasoned commanders had inherited from civilian life. Such defects would have to be dissected in special indoctrination courses and mandatory biracial councils on such problems as housing, recreation, officer-soldier relationships and promotion opportunities.

With such vigorous and affirmative action, the Armed Services sought to overcome the failures which rank-and-file violence underscored and recover its acknowledged position as a stalwart leader in the fight to achieve integration in American life.

STATISTICS ON NEGRO COMMISSIONED OFFICERS

Number and percent in parentheses of Negro personnel in each rank

Rank: Army, Air Force, Marine	Rank: Navy	ARMY	NAVY	AIR FORCE	MARINE
Gen.	Adm.	0(0)	0(0)	1(0.2)	0(0)
Col.	Capt.	9(0.2)	4(.0007)	29(0.4)	0(0)
Lt. Col.	Comm.	172(1.3)	23(.0003)	175(1.0)	3(0.2)
Maj.	Lt. Comm.	788(4.5)	86(.005)	504(1.8)	12(0.3)
Capt.	Lieut.	1,580(5.2)	133(.007)	1,098(2.4)	90(1.4)
1st Lieut.	Lieut. j.g.	541(3.5)	87(.005)	345(1.6)	90(1.4)
2d Lieut.	Ensign	555(2.8)	112(.015)	188(1.7)	82(2.0)
Total officers and percentages		3,645(3.6)	445(.007)	2,355(1.7)	277(1.2)

1970 DATA FOR ALL SERVICES. ALL FIGURES ARE COMPLETE AND WORLD-WIDE IN SCOPE.

STATISTICS ON NEGRO ENLISTED PERSONNEL

Number and percent (in parentheses) of Negro personnel in each grade

Grade	ARMY	NAVY	AIR FORCE	MARINE
E9	162(3.7)	42(1.3)	188(2.8)	28(2.4)
E8	980(7.1)	178(2.0)	545(4.0)	220(5.4)
E7	3,884(9.8)	1,077(3.0)	2,769(5.9)	927(10.0)
E6	13,063(15.5)	3,518(5.0)	8,539(9.6)	2,099(13.4)
E5	27,241(18.4)	6,107(6.5)	21,476(14.1)	3,596(11.0)
E4	25,632(14.6)	7,276(5.9)	17,056(9.6)	3,325(8.2)
E3	28,524(14.9)	10,478(6.6)	16,643(10.8)	5,171(10.6)
E2	12,490(13.4)	7,057(6.0)	6,683(12.7)	6,313(13.3)
E1	21,325(10.1)	1,230(4.4)	1,621(15.0)	5,431(15.9)
Total Men and Percent	133,311(13.9)	36,963(5.8)	75,520(10.7)	27,110(11.6)

1970 DATA FOR ALL SERVICES. ALL FIGURES ARE WORLD-WIDE AND COMPLETE IN SCOPE.

BLACK SERVICEMEN ON ACTIVE DUTY IN VIETNAM

	1967			1968			June 1968		
	Total	*Black*	*%*	*Total*	*Black*	*%*	*Total*	*Black*	*%*
Army	242,043	30,603	(12.6)	337,234	37,456	(11.1)	383,660	44,867	(11.7)
Navy	57,840	3,108	(5.4)	69,336	3,228	(4.7)	75,499	3,609	(4.1)
Marine Corps	67,601	5,461	(8.0)	78,374	6,462	(8.2)	85,857	8,657	(10.1)
Air Force	52,006	5,379	(10.3)	83,188	8,758	(10.5)	84,713	8,883	(10.5)
Total	419,490	44,551	(10.6)	568,132	55,904	(9.8)	629,729	66,016	(10.5)

BLACK SERVICEMEN ON ACTIVE DUTY AROUND THE WORLD

	Officers	*Enlisted Men*	*Totals*
Army	5,694 (3.4%)	167,956 (12.0%)	173,650 (11.1%)
Navy	365 (0.4)	31,820 (4.7)	32,185 (4.2)
Marine Corps	197 (0.8)	31,276 (11.1)	31,473 (10.2)
Air Force	2,441 (1.7)	78,149 (10.3)	80,590 (8.9)
Total	8,697 (2.1%)	309,201 (9.9%)	317,898 (9.0%)

DISTRIBUTION OF NEGROES BY PERCENTAGE WITHIN EACH SERVICE

	Officers	*Enlisted*	*As of*
Army	2.17	13.1	30 June 1970
Navy	0.67	5.58	30 June 1970
Air Force	1.7	11.0	31 March 1970
Marine Corps	1.3	11.6	30 June 1970

A CHRONOLOGY OF MILITARY EVENTS: FROM SEGREGATION TO INTEGRATION (1770-1954)

March 5, 1770 *Crispus Attucks,* "a mulatto fellow, about 27 years of age . . . 6 feet 2 inches high, short, curled hair, his knees nearer together than common," is the first to fall in the "Boston Massacre."

May 20, 1775 The *Hancock and Warren Committee* decides to use free Negroes in the conflict, but rejects slaves.

June 17, 1775 *Peter Salem,* a former slave in Framington, Massachusetts, becomes a hero of the day at *Bunker Hill* by shooting British *Major Pitcairn,* the officer who had ordered the British to fire on the Minutemen at *Lexington.*

July 9, 1775 *George Washington* directs colonial recruiters not to enlist "any deserter from the ministerial army, nor any stroller, Negro or vagabond or person suspected of being an enemy to the liberty of America."

November 7, 1775 The British Colonial Governor of Virginia, *John Murray, Earl of Dunmore,* seeks to recruit Negroes for the loyalist cause. His recruits become known as *"Dunmore's Ethiopian Regiment."*

January 16, 1776 The Continental Congress accepts a December 30, 1775 proposal from Washington for the enlistment of free Negroes. During the war approximately 5,000 Negroes serve in the Colonial Army.

December 25, 1776 Negroes *Prince Whipple* and *Oliver Cromwell* cross the Delaware with Washington. By this time more Negroes are serving among white units than fighing in separate units. Many are "substitutes" for whites. One separate unit distinguishes itself: men from Massachusetts who proudly call themselves "The Bucks of America."

Black troops fought alongside white comrades at Bunker Hill.

August 29, 1778 *"The Battle of Rhode Island."* An all-Negro regiment from Connecticut "distinguishes itself by deeds of desperate valor" against German mercenaries fighting for the British.

July 15, 1779 *Pompey Lamb,* posing as a vegetable vender, aids materially in the capture of Stony Point by *General Anthony Wayne.* Spies and saboteurs like Lamb were active in many roles and on many fronts during the war.

June 22, 1807 The American man-of-war *Chesapeake* is captured by the British frigate *Leopard* in one of the key skirmishes that led to the War of 1812. Negro sailors are among those impressed aboard the British vessel.

September 12, 1813 Captain (later Commodore) *Oliver Hazard Perry* wins a decisive victory against the British in the *Battle of Lake Erie.* The Commander reverses earlier criticisms regarding the possible effectiveness of Negro sailors.

September 21, 1814 *General Andrew Jackson* calls upon all Negro citizens to enlist in the defense of New Orleans.

December 23-24, 1814 The *Battle of Chalmette Plains* or the *Battle of New Orleans.*

Negro troops hold a strategic position in Jackson's defense force and contribute materially to the crushing defeat of the British.

After the black troops and others have some trouble collecting their pay, *Jackson* angrily writes: "It is not enough for you to receive my orders for the payment of the necessary muster roll without inquiring whether the troops are white, black or tea."

May 13, 1846 Few Negroes see combat during the *Mexican War.* It is largely a war supported by the South and West and thus chiefly a white man's affair. Negroes who do participate go mostly as personal servants.

June 28, 1861 The Tennessee Legislature authorizes the enlistment of free Negroes between 15 and 50 years of age. Many Southern Negroes work on fortifications and, through their labor on plantations, help feed the bulk of the Confederate force. There are occasional all-Negro units in the early years of the War, but almost every Confederate regiment has its share of Negroes who accompany white masters into battle and occasionally see action.

August 6, 1861 The *Confiscation Act* declares that property used in direct or indirect acts against the Union are lawful prizes of war. Slaves which fit this category are considered free.

May 9, 1862 *General David "Black Dave" Hunter,* holding captured South Carolina territory, begins to enlist Negroes. This is the first organized attempt to use Negro manpower for combat duty in the War. By August, however, military pressures force Hunter to disband his *"First South Carolina Volunteers."*

July 16, 1862 Congress authorizes the enlistment of Negroes "for the purpose of constructing entrenchments, of performing camp service, or any war service for which they may be found competent." *The Enlistment Act,* signed the next day, provides that whites with the rank of private should receive $13 a month and $3.50 for clothing, but Negroes of the same rank are to receive $7 and $3 respectively. Pay is not equalized until 1864.

October 28, 1862 The *First Kansas Colored Volunteers,* the first official all-Negro unit in the Civil War, fights a victorious skirmish at Island Mound, Missouri.

January 1, 1863 President *Abraham Lincoln* formally issues the *Emancipation Proclamation.*

January 13, 1863 *The First Kansas Colored Volunteers* are formally mustered.

May 22, 1863 The *Bureau of Colored Troops* is established by the War Department. Union Negro troops are organized into 165 regiments of light and heavy artillery, cavalry, infantry and engineers. They are called "United States Colored Troops."

May 27, 1863 During the attack on *Port Hudson*, the ***First Louisiana Native Guards*** fight valiantly, despite heavy losses. ***Captain Andre Cailloux*** distinguishes himself with a heroic death at the head of his men.

October 2, 1863 *Dr. A. T Angusta* is appointed surgeon of the 17*th* Regiment, U.S. Colored Volunteers. He is said to be the first commissioned Negro medical officer.

March 13, 1865 A Negro enlistment bill is passed in the South. The action, originally initiated in 1864, comes too late to affect the outcome of the war.

April 9, 1865 Surrender at Appomattox.

July 28, 1866 The 9th and 10th all-Negro Cavalry Regiments are formed under provisions of an Act of Congress. The 38th, 39th, 40th and 41st Infantry Regiments are also formed.

March 3, 1869 A consolidation of the 38th and 41st makes the 24th all-Negro Infantry Regiment. A consolidation of the 39th and 40th makes the 25th all-Negro Infantry Regiment. The four regiments, mostly staffed by white officers, patrol the plains and participate in the opening of the Western frontier in the late 19th century.

June 15, 1877 *Henry O. Flipper* is the first Negro to graduate from West Point. Other Negro graduates follow in 1887 (John H. Alexander) and 1889 (Charles Young). A fourth *B. O. Davis, Jr.*, completed his training at the Point in 1936.

August 13, 1906 One man is killed and several are wounded in Brownsville, Texas after racial disturbances involving black infantry men of the 25th. When the men of the 25th refuse to identify those who participated in the violence, *President Theodore Roosevelt* takes extreme action and dishonorably discharges three whole companies. The Senate, in 1908, upholds his action in the *"Brownsville Affair."*

February 28, 1917 War with Germany.

A black choral group celebrates their safe return, World War I.

March 25, 1917 The District of Columbia National Guard is called up to help protect the nation's capital; black units are included, reluctantly.

May 1, 1917 The *Central Committee of Negro College Men* is set up at *Howard University* to prove the willingness of Negroes to fight.

May 12, 1917 Negro leaders succeed in getting a Negro officer's training base at Des Moines, Iowa. The camp opens on June 15.

May 18, 1917 Passage of a Selective Service Act greatly increases Negro participation in the Expeditionary Force.

July 5, 1917 *Registration Day.* Some 700,000 Negroes register for the draft.

October 5, 1917 Secretary of War *Newton D. Baker* announces the appointment of *Emmett J. Scott,* Secretary to *Booker T. Washington,* as Special Assistant to the Secretary of War serving as "confidential adviser in matters affecting the interests of the 10 million Negroes of the United States and the part they play in connection with the present war." Scott remains in the position until June 1919.

October 24, 1917 Formation of the *92nd Division,* an all-Negro outfit.

December 27, 1917 The *369th Infantry Regiment* of the 93rd arrives in Brest, the first Negro unit overseas. After training, they move up to the fighting front in April of 1918. Fighting with the French they create an enviable record. In 191 days of front line action, the regiment never loses a man, a trench or a foot of ground. Soon the 369th is known to the Germans as the "Hell Fighters."

March 28, 1917 *"The Bulletin #35 Incident." General C. L. Ballou,* commander of the *92nd Division,* in response to discrimination against a Negro NCO at a theater in Kansas orders "all colored members . . . [to] refrain from going where their presence will be resented . . . The sergeant is guilty of the greater wrong in doing anything, *no matter how legally correct.*"

May 15, 1918 "The Battle of *Henry Johnson.*" When rifle fire fails to stop advancing Germans and his fellow sentry, *Needham Roberts,* has been captured, Henry Johnson attacks the enemy with his bolo knife, freeing his friend and forcing the Germans into retreat. Both he and Roberts receive the highest French military award, the *Croix de Guerre*—the first Americans of the War to do so.

August 7, 1918 A document is circulated among the French entitled *"Secret Information Concerning Black-American Troops."* It describes the necessity for separating Negroes and whites. The *92nd Division,* at the front, finds itself confronted with German propaganda aimed at undermining Negro loyalty to a country which enjoins them to fight for rights abroad they still do not have at home.

September 26, 1918 The *368th Infantry Regiment* of the 92nd begins a mission against the enemy which ends in confusion and disorder. Despite honorable records of the majority of Negro units, this incident is offered by many in the military and the white press as proving Negro inability to survive combat pressure. Secretary of War *Baker* later makes the following statement: "The circumstances disclosed by a detailed study of the situation do not justify the highly colored accounts which have been given of the troops in the action, and they afford no basis at all for any of the general assumptions with regard to the action of colored troops in this battle and elsewhere in France."

February 17, 1919 The famed 369th marches up 5th Avenue to Harlem through cheering crowds. The celebration over, most Negro units are quickly disbanded except for the four permanent regiments. Finally, as Negroes and whites fresh from the service compete for jobs, increased racial friction occurs. By year's end, some 25 race riots have breached the peace.

July 12, 1923 A War Department directive provides for use of Negroes in emergencies—and then only on a limited scale. The letter adds: "No Negro troops are to be mobilized in the state of Texas." Military policy becomes even more specific in 1938 with the recommendation that Negroes be accepted in proportion to the general population—at that time about 9% of the total.

September 11, 1939 *West Virginia State College* is granted the right to establish the first Negro Civilian Pilot Training Program approved in peacetime.

September 16, 1940 Congress passes the *Selective Training and Service Act* containing the following antidiscrimination clause: "In the selection and training of men under this Act, and in the interpretation and execution of the provisions of this Act, there shall be no discrimination against any person on account of race or color." The 10% quota system is not regarded as discriminatory.

September 27, 1940 With U.S. entry into the war more and more probable, President *Franklin D. Roosevelt* receives a delegation of three Negroes: Walter White, A. Philip Randolph and T. Arnold Hill, concerning utilization of Negro manpower in the war effort.

October 9, 1940 With *Roosevelt's* initials, Assistant Secretary of War, *Robert Patterson* issues a memo declaring the initial policy on the use of Negro troops: segregation as usual. ". . . It has been proven satisfactory over a long period of years and to make changes would produce situations destructive to the morale and detrimental to the preparations for national defense."

October 25, 1940 *Colonel B. O. Davis, Sr.*, veteran of the *Spanish American War*, becomes the first Negro General Officer.

November 1, 1940 The Office of the Civilian Aide to the Secretary of War in matters of Negro rights is established with *William H. Hastie,* Dean of Howard University Law School. This is a position similar to the one occupied by *Emmett Scott* during World War I. Hastie holds the office until February 1943. *Colonel Campbell Johnson,* Negro head of Reserve Officer Training at Howard University is made special aide to draft director *Lewis B. Hershey*.

February 10, 1941 The first all-Negro officered regular Army Infantry Regiment (366th) is activated.

March 21,1941 A *99th Fighter Squadron* of Negro aviators is activated.

May 1, 1941 The first Negro Signal Unit (275th Cons. Co.) is activated.

June 1, 1941 The first Negro Tank Battalion (758th)is activated.

July 1, 1941 Integrated Officers' Candidate Schools open, the first major step toward an integrated Army.

July 19, 1941 Inaugural ceremonies are held at Tuskegee Institute, beginning Negro air training, which culminates in the 99th Squadron.

July 25, 1941 *President Roosevelt* issues *Executive Order #8802* forming the FEPC.

December 7, 1941 The Japanese attack Pearl Harbor. Negro mess steward *Dorie Miller* mans a machine gun during the attack and downs 4 Japanese fighters, winning a Navy Cross.

February 6, 1942 The first Negro military police battalion (730th) is activated.

March 7, 1942 First Negro pilots complete training and are commissioned into the Air Corps. Included among them is West Point graduate *B. O. Davis, Jr.*, son of the Army's first black general.

March 24, 1942 The first Negro numbered Station Hospital (25th) is activated.

April 7, 1942 Secretary of Navy *Frank Knox* initiates a policy calling for acceptance of Negroes in the general service in the Navy and Reserves of the Marine and Coast Guard.

April 14, 1942 The first Negro officer is commissioned into the Coast Guard: Ensign *Joseph C. Jenkins,* a graduate of the Coast Guard Academy.

May 15, 1942 The *93rd Infantry Division* is activated.

June 1, 1942 The Marine Corps begins the enlistment of Negroes at the Marine

Training Center, Camp Lejeune, North Carolina. The Navy, too, begins to accept Negroes in positions other than the stewards branch.

July 20, 1942 With the formation of the Women's Army Auxiliary Corps (WAC), Negro women are accepted with whites.

August 24, 1942 *Colonel B. O. Davis, Jr.*, takes command of the newly formed 99th Squadron.

Major Charity Adams reviews her troops during World War II.

October 13, 1942 The *332nd all-Negro Fighter Group* is activated, joining the 99th.

October 15, 1942 The *92nd Division* is activated.

December 5, 1942 *Executive Order #9279* requires all services to accept recruits through the Selective Service System. The order portends a greater percentage of Negroes in service.

February 19, 1943 *Truman K. Gibson, Jr.*, succeeds *William H. Hastie* as Civilian Aide. Gibson, Assistant since November 1940, officially becomes Civilian Aide in September 1943, and stays in the position until November of 1945.

February 28, 1943 The Navy makes a decision to induct Negroes into all branches of the service according to their percentage of the total population, 10%. The announcement is made next month.

April 24, 1943 The 99th arrives in North Africa at Oued N'ja, is moved to Fardjourna and attached to the *33rd Fighter Group*.

June 1, 1943 The third Negro air unit, the *477th Bomb Group*, is activated.

June 20, 1943 Race tension explodes in the most serious race riot of the war in Detroit. The cause is largely black exclusion from the huge military efforts which are lucrative to civilian defense workers.

July 2, 1943 Negro pilots see action over Italy, and down their first aircraft.

January 3, 1944 The 332nd enters the European theater.

January 27, 1944 The 99th distinguishes itself over the Anzio-Nettuno Beachhead. Eight confirmed hits are scored. The Negro air units, especially the 99th, go on to establish an outstanding combat record. Numerous Negro pilots will win the Distinguished Flying Cross by the end of the war.

February 23, 1944 The Navy Department announces that two anti-submarine vessels being commissioned will be manned by all-Negro crews. The two all-Negro vessels, the *U.S.S. Mason* and the *PC-1264*, will only have one Negro officer aboard between them.

May 20, 1944 Secretary of the Navy *Forrestal* orders all Naval vessels to be integrated. A group of 25 pre-selected ships are thoroughly briefed before the Negroes arrive in August.

June 6, 1944 *D-Day*. The 320th Negro Anti-aircraft Barrage Balloon Battalion helps with the landing.

July 3, 1944 The 99th is attached to the 332nd.

July 8, 1944 In an attempt to partially remedy the cause of most racial incidents still breaking out in service, the War Department forbids racial discrimination in recreation and transportation facilities on all Army stations. Serious riots occur at Fort Bragg, Camp Robinson, Camp Davis, Camp Lee and Fort Dix.

August 9, 1944 The *"Port Chicago Mutiny"*: After an ammunition explosion at the docks near San Francisco on July 17, Negro stevedores, some of them with advanced technical training, refuse to return to work. They are then brought to trial and sentenced to 8-15 years hard labor. *Thurgood Marshall* appeals the case and wins an acquittal in January of 1946.

October 19, 1944 Negro women are notified they will be admitted into the WAVES. The first are sworn in on November 13 and the first WAVE officers graduate from training at Smith College on December 21.

December 26, 1944 The Germans strike back at the Allies, creating a bulge in the broad advancing force. A directive is issued by Lt. Gen. John C. H. Lee for Negro volunteers to be integrated by platoons into the white units fighting in the area. The move succeeds, but does not usher in a new policy.

January 31, 1945 The "Bulge" is neutralized. Most officials still refuse to recognize the Bulge Experiment as any kind of precedent, but rather simply as a successful special case.

February 7, 1945 During a planned attack on the German Gothic Line on the *Cinquale Canal*, elements of the all-Negro *92nd Division* reportedly fall back in a disordered retreat and are accused of "melting away" in the face of enemy resistance. "Failure" is again trotted out as proof of the Negro's inability to endure combat pressure. Segregation continues to evade exposure as the real culprit.

March 8, 1945 The first Negro nurse is sworn in the Navy Nurse Corps in New York City. She is Miss *Phyllis Mae Dailey*.

March 24, 1945 The 332nd stages a raid over Berlin and later receives a Distinguished Unit Citation for its bravery.

April 13, 1945 The Navy lifts all restrictions on the number and type of auxiliary vessels to which Negro personnel can be assigned.

May 8, 1945 *V-E Day*.

July 23, 1945 An urgent appeal goes out "to qualified women to join with the two Negro commissioned officers and the 54 enlisted WAVES in playing an active part in a speedy victory."

August 25, 1945 Reviewing the Bulge Experiment, General *George C. Marshall* agrees that the results of the integrated force should be regarded as a special case and not lead to premature judgments.

September 2, 1945 *V-J Day*.

October 4, 1945 Secretary of War *Robert P. Patterson* sets up the *Gillem Board* to study the use of Negro manpower in the armed forces.

October 17, 1945 The 332nd returns triumphantly to the U.S.

January 2, 1946 *Lt. Col. Marcus H. Ray,* fresh from the Italian campaign, becomes Civilian Aide, a post he holds until July 1947.

February 27, 1946 Secretary of the Navy *James V. Forrestal* announces: "Effective immediately, all restrictions governing the types of assignments for which Negro Navy personnel are eligible are hereby lifted. Henceforth, they shall be eligible for all types of assignments in all ratings in all activities and all ships of the Naval Service."

March 4, 1946 The Gillem report calls for the continuation of the 10% quotas and is released as *War Department Circular 124* on April 27, 1946.

June 23, 1946 The first group of 31 Negro officers are integrated into the Regular Army.

December 5, 1946 *Executive Order #9808* establishing the ***President's Commission on Civil Rights.***

March 15, 1947 Ensign *John W. Lee* is the first Negro officer to be transferred into the Regular Navy.

October 29, 1947 The Office of Civilian Aide is transferred to the Office of the Secretary of Defense. *James C. Evans* officially begins his duties in this post in January 1948.

February 2, 1948 *President Truman* issues a Civil Rights message to Congress which states: "During the recent war and in the years since its close we have made much progress toward equality of opportunity in our armed services without regard to race, color, religion or national origin. I have instructed the Secretary of Defense to take steps to have the remaining instances in the armed services eliminated as rapidly as possible. The personnel policies and practices of all the services in this regard will be made consistent."

February 12, 1948 The first Negro nurse is integrated into the Regular Army Nurse Corps.

April 1, 1948 The *New York Times* announces that *A. Philip Randolph* has formed a Committee Against Jim Crow in the Military Service and Training. The group threatens mass civil disobedience and Negro boycott of the draft.

June 9, 1948 The first doctor is integrated into the Regular *Army Medical Corps.*

June 23, 1948 The *Republican Party* platform states "We are opposed to the idea of racial segregation in the armed forces of the United States."

July 1, 1948 ROTC units are established at Morgan State University, Florida A&M and Southern University, all predominantly black schools.

July 15, 1948 The *Democratic Party* platform states: "We call upon the Congress to support our President (to guarantee) the right of equal treatment in the service and defense of our nation."

July 17, 1948 *A. Philip Randolph* impresses upon *President Truman* the "bipartisan mandate to end military segregation."

July 25, 1948 Training centers for Negroes and whites are established at Fort Riley, Kansas and Fort Ord, California.

July 26, 1948 *President Truman* issues *Executive Order #9981,* setting up a Committee to Study Equality of Treatment and Opportunity in the Armed Services *(The Fahy Committee).*

October 23, 1948 The Navy commissions and assigns to duty its first Negro aviator, *Ensign Jessie Brown.*

April 6, 1949 Secretary of Defense *Louis Johnson* directs the Secretaries of the Army, Navy and Air Force to examine their personnel practices in line with *Executive Order #9981.*

April 28, 1949 Now under the Defense Department the title Civilian Aide is changed to Civilian Assistant to the Secretary of Defense. *James C. Evans* still occupies the position.

June 1, 1949 The *332nd Fighter Wing* is deactivated at *Lockbourne Air Force Base* and integrated into the Regular Air Force throughout the world. Integration seems to proceed more smoothly within the military, than with the civilian community.

June 3, 1949 *Wesley A. Brown* of Washington, D. C. graduates from the U.S. Naval Academy, the first Negro in its history.

June 7, 1949 The Secretary of Defense approves of the Department of Navy's policies under *Executive Order #9981.*

June 23, 1949 Secretary of the Navy *Francis Matthews* declares: "It is the policy of the Navy Department that there shall be equality of treatment and opportunity for all persons in the Navy and Marine Corps without regard to race, color, religion or national origin."

September 30, 1949 A non-discriminatory job policy adopted by Army. All school courses opened to Negroes.

October 1, 1949 New Army Secretary *Gordon Gray* issues orders abolishing Negro quotas.

January 16, 1950 The Department of the Army promulgates Special Regulations Nos. 600-629-1, *"Utilization of Negro Manpower"* and declares its new policy: Negroes with special skills will be "assigned to any . . . unit without regard for race or color."

March 27, 1950 Quotas in Army enlistments are officially abolished.

May 22, 1950 The Report of the President's Committee on Equality of Treatment and Opportunity in the Armed Services *(Fahy Committee), "Freedom to Serve,"* is issued.

June 25, 1950 The outbreak of the *Korean War.*

July 20, 1950 The first United States victory in Korea is won by the all-Negro *24th Infantry Regiment.*

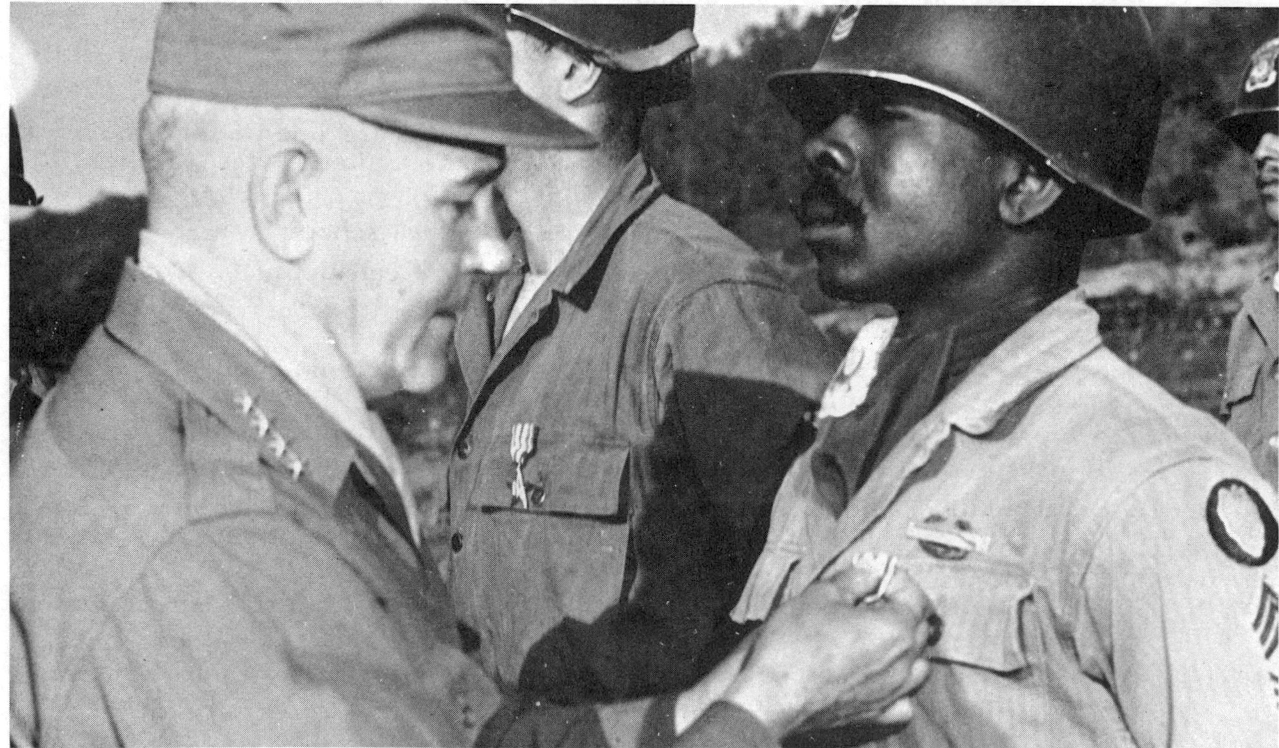

Jonathan Wilingham of the 24th U.S. Infantry is presented the Silver Star for action in Korea by Gen. U. Lawton Collins.

The Second Infantry saw service near the Chongchon River in Korea.

October 20, 1950 The *9th and 10th Cavalry* are converted into the 509th and 510th Negro Tank Battalions and integrated with white units on March 7, 1953 and December 31, 1952 respectively. The 25th Infantry is broken into smaller units and integrated with white units during early 1951 and 1952.

June 21, 1951 In Korea, the first Negro since the *Spanish American War* is posthumously awarded the Medal of Honor.

July 21, 1951 The Army makes its first cautious press release concerning its integration plans. They announce that the *24th Infantry Regiment* will be broken up and that plans are underway to integrate the *Far Eastern Command.*

July 26, 1951 The Department of the Army announces plans for the complete racial integration of the Far Eastern Command. Integration has, however, already existed to a greater or lesser extent for some time in Korea.

October 1, 1951 The *24th Infantry Regiment* is deactivated and its personnel is integrated into white units. Much of the 24th is already spread out among white units in Korea.

November 1, 1951 The *Draft Form of Project Clear* (3 volumes) "Utilization of Negro Manpower in the Army" is issued. It clearly shows that an integrated force is effective, even much more effective than a segregated service.

April 1, 1952 Plans for racial integration throughout the Army's *European Command* are announced. Meanwhile, the Air Force has been at work and now announces complete integration of its personnel.

August 20, 1953 Secretary of the Navy *Robert Anderson* directs the elimination of segregation in all facilities at Naval shore installations.

January 12, 1954 The Secretary of Defense *Charles Wilson* announces that "the operation of all school facilities located on military installations shall be conducted without segregation on the basis of race or color."

May 17, 1954 The Supreme Court hands down its historic decision on the unconstitutionality of school segregation. The armed forces has already moved to break down segregationist practices.

June 11, 1954 The Secretary of Defense provides a program "to familiarize contracting officers" with the Department's policies on discrimination. On paper, at least, integration is finally a general policy within the military establishment.

NEGRO CONGRESSIONAL MEDAL OF HONOR WINNERS*

In view of the absence of racial identification of many military records dating from the Civil War, it is difficult to determine how many Negro servicemen have been awarded the Medal of Honor. By pinpointing a number of segregated units in which Negroes served until World War II, however, the editors of this volume have been able to verify the names of 46 Negroes who have won this coveted award since it was instituted during the Civil War. The Department of Defense is at present compiling a definitive list of all Negro CMH recipients. According to the preliminary information gathered by this agency, 38 Negro soldiers have won the Medal: 16 in the Civil War; 14 in the Indian Wars; five in the Spanish-American War; two during the Korean Conflict, and one so far in Vietnam. Of the eight winners in the Navy, five were honored for their exploits during the Civil War; one for a feat of peacetime bravery (1872), and two in the Spanish-American War.

Pending further research, the following list is offered to our readers, along with biographical data where available.

ARMY MEDAL OF HONOR WINNERS IN THE CIVIL WAR

1863

Sergeant William H. Carney, Company C, 54th Massachusetts Colored Infantry

Born in New Bedford, Massachusetts, Carney was the first Negro to win the Congressional Medal of Honor. He was cited for valor on June 18, 1863 during the Battle of Fort Wagner, South Carolina, in which he carried the colors, and led a charge to the parapet after the standard bearer had been felled by rifle fire. During this battle, Carney was twice severely wounded. His medal was issued on May 23, 1900.

1864

(The following 13 men won their awards for valor during the Battle of New Market Heights on September 29, 1864. With the exception of Sergeant James H. Harris, all were awarded their citations on April 6, 1865.)

Private William H. Barnes, Company C, 38th U. S. Colored Troops; born St. Mary's County, Maryland.

First Sergeant Powhatan Beaty, Company G, 5th U. S. Colored Troops; born Richmond, Virginia.

First Sergeant James H. Bronson, Company D, 5th U. S. Colored Troops; born Indiana County, Pennsylvania.

Sergeant-Major Christian A. Fleetwood, 4th U. S. Colored Troops, born Baltimore, Maryland.

Private James Gardiner, Company I, U. S. Colored Troops; born Gloucester, Virginia.

Sergeant James H. Harris, Company B, 38th U. S. Colored Troops; born St. Mary's County, Maryland.

Sergeant Alfred B. Hilton, Company H, 4th U. S. Colored Troops; Harford County, Maryland.

Sergeant-Major Milton M. Holland, 5th U. S. Colored Troops; born Austin, Texas.

Corporal Miles James, Company B, 36th U. S. Colored Troops; born Princess Anne County, Virginia.

First Sergeant Alexander Kelly, Company F, 6th U. S. Colored Troops; born Pennsylvania.

First Sergeant Robert Pinn, Company I, 5th U. S. Colored Troops; born Stark County, Ohio.

First Sergeant Edward Radcliff, Company C, 38th U. S. Colored Troops; born James County, Virginia.

Private Charles Veal, Company D, 4th U. S. Colored Troops; born Portsmouth, Virginia.

* Some of the current literature on the Negro in the military establishment of the United States lists the name of Glaine Stokes, 24th Infantry, as a Medal of Honor winner during the Korean War. However, *Medal of Honor Recipients: 1863-1963*, a publication prepared for the Subcommittee on Veterans Affairs in 1964, does not include the name of Stokes in its "official" roster of CMH winners. The *Negro Handbook: 1946-1947* (New York: Current Books) lists Corporal Clinton Greaves and Sergeant George Jordan (9th Cavalry) twice, thus accounting for 14 names in the Indian campaigns. In this list, the names of Sergeant Benjamin Brown and Corporal Isaiah Mays are missing. The Handbook also erroneously includes Clement Dees of the *U.S.S. Pontoosuc*, omitting John Lawson and James Mifflin (Battle of Mobile Bay).

Sergeant-Major Thomas Hawkins, 6th U. S. Colored Troops
Born in Cincinnati, Ohio, Hawkins was cited for valor in the Battle of Deep Bottom, Virginia on July 21, 1864. He was credited with the rescue of his regimental colors from the enemy. His medal was issued on February 8, 1870.

Sergeant Decatur Dorsey, Company B, 39th U. S. Colored Troops
Born in Howard County, Maryland, Dorsey was cited for valor in the Battle of Petersburg, Virginia on July 30, 1864. When his regiment was driven back to Union lines, he carried the colors, and rallied the men in his unit. His medal was issued on November 8, 1865.

INDIAN WARS 1870-1890

Sergeant Emanuel Stance, Troop F, 9th U. S. Cavalry
Born in Carroll County, Louisiana, Stance was cited for valor in the Battle of Kickapoo Springs, Texas. An outstanding Indian scout, he was awarded his medal on June 28, 1870.

Corporal Clinton Greaves, Troop C, 9th U. S. Cavalry
Born in Madison County, Virginia, Greaves was cited for valor in the Battle of Florida Mountain, New Mexico on June 24, 1877. His medal was issued on June 26, 1879.

Sergeant Thomas Boyne, Troop C, 9th U. S. Cavalry
Born in Prince George County, Maryland, Boyne was cited for bravery in action during two New Mexico battles in 1879. His medal was issued on January 6, 1882.

Sergeant John Denny, Troop B, 9th U. S. Cavalry
Born in Big Flats, New York, Denny was cited for removing a wounded comrade to a place of safety while under heavy fire in Las Animas Canyon, Mexico on September 18, 1879. His medal was issued on November 27, 1894.

Sergeant Henry Johnson, Troop D, 9th U. S. Cavalry
Born in Boynton, Virginia, Johnson was cited for valor in the Battle of Milk River, Colorado on October 25, 1879. While under heavy fire, he fought his way to a creek to bring water to the wounded. His medal was issued on September 22, 1890.

Sergeant George Jordan, Troop K, 9th U. S. Cavalry
Born in Williamson County, Tennessee Jordan was cited for bravery in two battles: one at Fort Tulersu, New Mexico on May 14, 1880; the other at Carrizo Canyon, New Mexico on August 12, 1881.

Sergeant Thomas Shaw, Troop K, 9th U. S. Cavalry
Born in Covington, Kentucky, Shaw was cited for valor in Carrizo Canyon, New Mexico on August 12, 1881. He forced the enemy back after holding his ground in a dangerous position. His medal was issued in December 1890.

First Sergeant Moses Williams, Troop I, 9th U. S. Cavalry
Born in Carroll County, Pennsylvania, Williams was cited for valor in the Battle of Cuchillo Negro Mountains, New Mexico on August 16, 1881. His medal was issued on November 12, 1896.

Private Augustus Walley, Troop I, 9th U. S. Cavalry
Born in Reisterstown, Maryland, Walley was cited for bravery in action in the Battle of Cuchillo Negro Mountains, New Mexico on August 16, 1881. His medal was issued on October 1, 1890.

Sergeant Brent Woods, Troop B, 9th U. S. Cavalry
Born in Pulaski, Kentucky, Woods was cited for valor in New Mexico on August 19, 1881. His medal was issued on July 12, 1894.

Sergeant Benjamin Brown, Company C, 24th Infantry Regiment
Born in Virginia, Brown won his award during an attempted robbery in Arizona on May 11, 1889. His medal was issued on February 19, 1890.

Corporal Isaiah Mays, Company B, 24th Infantry Regiment
Born in Carter's Bridge, Virginia, Mays was cited for gallantry during an attempted robbery in Arizona on May 11, 1889. Like Brown, he was awarded his medal on February 19, 1890.

Corporal William O. Wilson, Troop I, 9th U. S. Cavalry
Born in Hagerstown, Maryland, Wilson was cited for bravery in the Sioux campaign of 1890. His medal was issued on September 17, 1891.

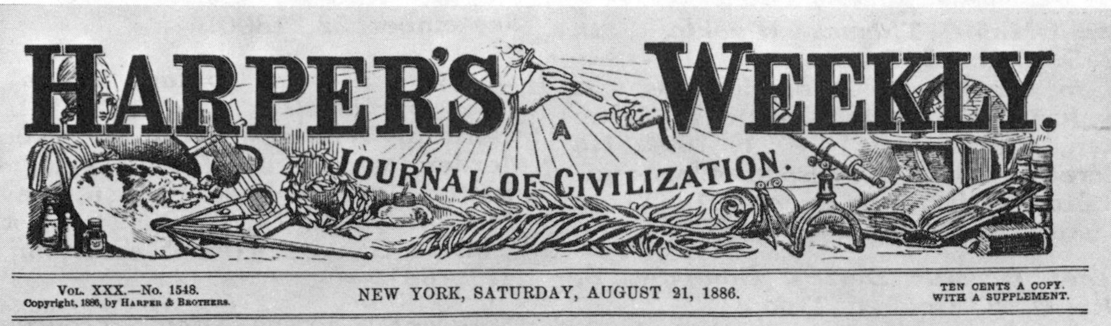

HARPER'S WEEKLY.

A JOURNAL OF CIVILIZATION.

Vol. XXX.—No. 1548.
Copyright, 1886, by Harper & Brothers.

NEW YORK, SATURDAY, AUGUST 21, 1886.

TEN CENTS A COPY.
WITH A SUPPLEMENT.

SOLDIERING IN THE SOUTHWEST—THE RESCUE OF CORPORAL SCOTT.—Drawn by Frederic Remington.—[See Page 535.]

Soldiering in the Southwest—the rescue of Corporal Scott. Black troopers were often awarded the Medal of Honor for valorous deeds such as these.

Sergeant William McBryar, Troop K, 10th U. S. Cavalry
Born in Elizabeth, North Carolina, McBryar was cited for bravery in an engagement against Apache Indians in Arizona on March 7, 1890. His medal was issued on May 15, 1890.

SPANISH-AMERICAN WAR 1898

(The first four men on this list were cited for bravery at Tayabacoa, Cuba. They received their medals on June 23, 1899.)

Private Dennis Bell, Troop H, 10th U. S. Cavalry; born Washington, D. C.

Private Fitz Lee, Troop M, 10th U. S. Cavalry; born Dinwiddie County, Virginia.

Private William H. Thompkins, Troop G, 10th U. S. Cavalry; born Paterson, New Jersey.

Private George Wanton, Troop M, 10th U. S. Cavalry; born Paterson, New Jersey.

Sergeant-Major Edward L. Baker, 10th U. S. Cavalry
Born in Laramie County, Wyoming, Baker was cited for bravery in the under-fire rescue operation of a wounded comrade in Santiago, Cuba on July 1, 1898. His medal was issued on July 3, 1902.

KOREAN WAR 1950-1953

Pfc. William Thompson, Company M, 24th Infantry
Born in Brooklyn, New York, Thompson was the first Negro to win the CMH since the Spanish-American War. He lost his life on August 6, 1950 after fighting off the enemy singlehanded during a withdrawal operation. The medal was awarded in June 1951.

Sergeant Cornelius Charlton, Company C, 24th Infantry
Born in the Bronx, New York, Charlton was the second Negro to win the Congressional Medal of Honor in Korea. On June 2, 1951, he was killed while leading a platoon attack on a Communist-held ridge. The medal was awarded on February 12, 1952.

Pfc. Milton L. Olive.

VIETNAM 1966-

Pfc. Milton L. Olive III, Company B, 503rd Infantry, 173rd Airborne Brigade
While participating in a search and destroy operation in the vicinity of Phu Coung on October 22, 1965, Pfc. Milton Olive saved the lives of his fellow soldiers by falling on a live grenade, and absorbing the shock of its blast with his body. Olive was cited for conspicuous gallantry by the President of the United States at the White House on Thursday, April 21, 1966, at which time the Medal was awarded posthumously to his parents.

Born in Chicago, Illinois on November 7, 1946, Olive attended parochial school in his native city, and later went to Saints Junior College High School for three years. He took basic combat training at Fort Knox, Kentucky, and also attended a number of service schools. During his service tour, he won the Combat Infantryman Badge; the Armed Forces Expeditionary Medal, and the Purple Heart with an Oak Leaf Cluster.

Olive died a few weeks before his 19th birthday.

Pfc. James Anderson, Jr., Company F, 2nd Battalion, 3rd Marine Division

Like Pfc. Olive before him, James Anderson, Jr. reacted instantaneously to danger "with complete disregard for his own personal safety," grabbing a live grenade thrown into the midst of his platoon, pulling it to his chest and curling around it as it exploded. The shock was so great that other Marines received shrapnel wounds from the fragmentation. Anderson was killed instantly. The highly decorated soldier (he had won the Purple Heart and several service medals) was a native of Los Angeles, California, where he was born January 22, 1947.

Sergeant First Class Webster Anderson, Battery A, 2nd Battalion, 320th Artillery, 101st Airborne Division

Complete disregard for his personal safety and the ability to function in an exemplary fashion while under fire earmarked Sergeant Anderson for the Medal of Honor, presented him by President Nixon at the White House on November 24, 1969. Anderson, a native of Winnsboro, South Carolina, entered the U.S. Army on September 11, 1953.

Sergeant First Class Eugene Ashley, Jr. Company C, 5th Special Forces Group (Airborne), 1st Special Forces

Ashley, a native of Wilmington, North Carolina where he was born October 12, 1931, was killed in action during an attempted rescue operation at Camp Lang Vei in Vietnam. Ashley lost his life while being carried from the summit of the hill from which he and his men had dislodged the enemy. He was killed by an artillery shell.

Pfc. Oscar P. Austin, Company E, 2nd Battalion, 1st Marine Division

On February 23, 1969, Pfc. Oscar P. Austin threw himself on an enemy grenade to protect an injured Marine, and later was mortally wounded when he lunged in front of a fallen comrade who was exposed to enemy rifle fire. Austin was cited for "inspiring initiative and selfless devotion to duty." A native of Nacogdoches, Texas, Austin was born January 15, 1948. He completed high school in Phoenix, Arizona, and joined the Marine Corps in April 1968. Austin had won other medals, including the Purple Heart, before being designated a Medal of Honor winner.

Sergeant Rodney M. Davis, Company B, 1st Battalion, 1st Marine Division

During a heavy battle in Quang Nam Province (Republic of Vietnam), Sergeant Rodney M. Davis and his platoon were pinned down by mortars, heavy automatic and small arms fire. Unable to withstand the enemy assault, the Marines were lodged in a trench and in danger of being overrun by the enemy. A grenade lobbed in from close range landed in the trench, threatening the lives of the entire unit. Sergeant Davis "instantly" threw himself upon it in what was described as "a final valiant act of complete self-sacrifice." Davis died September 6, 1967. Born in Macon, Georgia in 1942, he had enlisted in the Corps on August 31, 1961.

Pfc. Robert H. Jenkins, Company C, 3rd Reconnaissance Battalion, 3rd Marine Division

Pfc. Robert H. Jenkins was killed in action on the morning of March 5, 1969 while occupying a defense position south of the DMZ. Jenkins and his comrade constituted a two-man fighting emplacement manning a machine-gun. When a North Vietnamese grenade was thrown into their midst, Jenkins seized his comrade, shielding him from the full impact of the explosion. He died later of injuries sustained on the scene. Born June 1, 1948, Jenkins was a graduate of Central Academy High School in Palatka, Florida. He enlisted in the Marines in 1968.

Specialist Six Lawrence Joel, HQ & HQ Company, 1st Battalion (Airborne), 503rd Infantry, 173rd Airborne Brigade

One of the earlier winners of the Medal of Honor, Specialist Joel was cited for "gallantry and intrepidity at the risk of his life above and beyond the call of duty" while serving as a medical aidman in a combat operation on November 8, 1965. Despite his own wounds, Joel left his cover to minister to several fallen comrades, giving them plasma, pain killers and other necessary medication while under a continuous barrage. Joel, a native of Winston-Salem, North Carolina, was born February 22, 1928.

Pfc. Ralph H. Johnson, Company A, 1st Reconnaissance Battalion, 1st Marine Division

As part of a 15-man reconnaissance patrol deep in enemy territory, Pfc. Ralph H. Johnson was manning an observation post on Hill 146 when a heavily-armed, platoon-sized Vietnamese force attacked his position. A grenade tossed into the three-man fighting hole occupied by Johnson and two comrades threatened the lives of all until Johnson flung himself on the device, and absorbed its shattering fragments. Johnson was killed in action on March 5, 1968, less than a year after he had enlisted in the Regular Marine Corps. Johnson was a native of Charleston, South Carolina, where he was born January 11, 1949.

Specialist Five Dwight Hal Johnson, Company B, 1st Battalion, 69th Armor, 4th Infantry Division

Climbing fearlessly out of his disabled tank, Johnson, armed only with a .45 caliber pistol, engaged the heavily armed enemy and killed several North Vietnamese. After running out of ammunition, he returned to his tank, where he grabbed a submachine gun before braving yet another enemy barrage. Johnson also rescued comrades, and killed several North Vietnamese at close range. A native of Detroit, Michigan, Johnson is a graduate of Northwestern High School. He was born May 7, 1947.

Private First Class Garfield M. Langhorn, Troop C, 7th Squadron (Airmobile), 17th Cavalry, 1st Aviation Brigade

A radio operator, Langhorn lost his life after falling on a grenade thrown into the midst of a group of wounded men he was helping rescue during a helicopter mission. Born in 1948 in Cumberland, Virginia, Langhorn attended Riverdale High School before being inducted into service in 1968.

Platoon Sergeant Matthew Leonard, Company B, 1st Battalion, 16th Infantry, 1st Infantry Division

Sergeant Leonard was awarded the Medal of Honor in 1967 for "conspicuous gallantry and intrepidity in action" during combat operations near Suoi Da in Vietnam. Surviving numerous assaults and several gunshot wounds, Leonard showed remarkable "fighting spirit" and qualities of "heroic leadership." Leonard is a native of Eutaw, Alabama, and was born on November 26, 1929.

Sergeant Donald Russell Long, Troop C, 1st Squadron, 4th Cavalry, 1st Infantry Division

Sergeant Long was killed in action during an attack on his troop by a Viet Cong regiment on June 30, 1966. Long abandoned the relative safety of his armored personnel carrier and exposed himself to withering enemy fire while carrying the wounded to evacuation helicopters. He was killed by an exploding grenade whose shock he absorbed with his body. Born August 27, 1939, Long was a native of Blackfork, Ohio

Captain Riley Leroy Pitts, Company C, 2nd Battalion, 27th Infantry, 25th Infantry Division

Captain Pitts died in Vietnam on October 31, 1967 after leading an airmobile assault in the vicinity of Ap Dong, Vietnam. The captain risked his life when a grenade which he had lobbed against the entrenched enemy rebounded off the dense jungle foliage and threatened to explode in the midst of his men. Pitts fell on the grenade but, miraculously, it failed to explode. He was later mortally wounded during an exchange of gunfire with the enemy. Captain Pitts, a native of Fallis, Oklahoma, was born October 15, 1937.

Lieutenant Colonel Charles Calvin Rogers, 1st Battalion, 5th Artillery, 1st Infantry Division

Rogers is the highest-ranking black officer to have received the Medal of Honor while on active duty in Vietnam. Rogers served in the embattled country from November 1967 to November 1968, and was cited for exceptional gallantry while on duty with the 1st Infantry Division. Despite several wounds, Colonel Rogers rallied the beleaguered men of a fire support base which was in danger of being overrun by a numerically superior enemy, and prevented it from being captured. Rogers' citation singled out his "relentless spirit of aggressiveness, conspicuous gallantry and intrepidity in action."

First Lieutenant Ruppert L. Sargent, HQ & HQ Company, 3rd Battalion, 60th Infantry, 9th Infantry Division

Lieutenant Sargent died in action on March 15, 1967.

Specialist Five Clarence Eugene Sasser, HQ & HQ Company, 3rd Battalion, 60th Infantry, 9th Infantry Division.

Medical aidman Clarence E. Sasser was awarded the Medal of Honor in recognition of his heroic efforts, under fire, on behalf of wounded comrades stranded in an exposed rice paddy. Sasser himself was wounded, but stayed at his post for several hours tending others. Born September 12, 1947 in Chenango, Texas, Sasser is a graduate of Marshal High School in Angleton, Texas.

Staff Sergeant Chester Sims, Company D, 2nd Battalion (Airborne), 501st Infantry, 101st Airborne Division

Squad leader Sims distinguished himself in action on February 21, 1968 while his company was engaged in a furious assault of a heavily fortified enemy position. While advancing his unit, Sims heard the unmistakable noise of a concealed booby trap and unhesitatingly hurled himself on the device, absorbing its shock with his body. Vice President Agnew presented the medal posthumously at the White House on December 21, 1969. Sims, a native of Port Saint Joe, Florida, was born June 18, 1942.

First Lieutenant John E. Warren, Jr., Company C, 2nd Battalion (Mechanized), 22nd Infantry, 25th Infantry Division
The bravery of Lieutenant Warren cost him his life in Vietnam on January 14, 1969. Warren and his men were moving through a rubber plantation to join a friendly unit when they were set upon by a well-fortified enemy. The lieutenant maneuvered his men to within six feet of the enemy bunker, at which point a hostile grenade was thrown into their midst. Warren fell on the grenade and saved three others. A native of Brooklyn, New York, Lieutenant Warren was born November 16, 1946.

NAVY MEDAL OF HONOR WINNERS IN THE CIVIL WAR

Robert Blake, U.S.S. Marblehead
While on board the *U.S.S. Marblehead* off Legareville in the Stono River on December 25, 1863, Blake was instrumental in getting the enemy to abandon its position. His medal was awarded on April 16, 1864.

John Lawson, loader aboard the *Hartford* (flagship of Rear Admiral David Farragut)

James Mifflin, loader aboard the *Brooklyn*

Both these men showed "marked courage" during the Battle of Mobile Bay on August 5, 1864, and won Congressional Medals of Honor. Wounded in the leg, Lawson refused to go below for first-aid, remaining at his duty station for the duration of the battle.

Joachim Pease, Seaman, U.S.S. Kearsage
Born on Long Island, New York, Pease served as a seaman on board the *U.S.S. Kearsage*, acting as loader of the ship's number two gun. His medal was awarded on December 31, 1864.

John Lawson received the Congressional Medal of Honor during the Battle of Mobile Bay.

Aaron Anderson, Landsman, U.S.S. Wyandank
Anderson was cited for his valor at Mattox Creek on March 17, 1865. His medal was awarded on June 22, 1865.

SPANISH-AMERICAN WAR 1898

Daniel Atkins, ship's cook, U.S.S. Cushing
Born in 1867 in Brunswick, Virginia, Atkins was cited for gallant conduct on February 11, 1898. He attempted to save the life of Ensign Joseph C. Breckinridge who had fallen overboard at sea. His medal was awarded on May 20, 1898.

Robert Penn, Fireman First Class, U.S.S. Iowa
Born October 10, 1872 in City Point, Virginia, Penn was cited for valor while on board the *U.S.S. Iowa* off Santiago, Cuba on July 20, 1898. His medal was awarded on December 14, 1898.

(One Congressional Medal of Honor was awarded during peacetime—to *Joseph B. Noil*, a seaman aboard the *U.S.S. Powhatan*. Born in 1841 in Nova Scotia, Noil was cited for saving boatswain J. C. Walton from drowning on December 26, 1872. His medal was awarded on May 20, 1898.)

Lt. Henry O. Flipper, the first black graduate of West Point

NEGRO GRADUATES OF THE U.S. MILITARY ACADEMY (1877-1970)

(Courtesy, Lt. Patrick H. Dionne, IO, West Point)

Name	*Class*	*Branch/Service*
* Flipper, Henry O.	1877	Cavalry
* Alexander, John H.	1887	Cavalry
* Young, Charles D.	1889	Cavalry
**** Davis, Benjamin O., Jr.	1936	USAF
**** Fowler, James D. (1)	1941	Infantry
* Tresville, Robert B., Jr.	1943	USAF
Davenport, Clarence M.	1943	Artillery
**** Francis, Henry M.	1944	Artillery

Davis, Ernest J., Jr.	1945	USAF
**** Rivers, Mark E., Jr.	1945	USAF
* McCoy, Andrew A., Jr.	1946	USAF
Howard, Edward B.	1949	Signal Corps
Smith, Charles L.	1949	Artillery
** Carlisle, David K.	1950	CE
** Green, Robert W.	1950	CE
* Brown, Norman J.	1951	Armor
Wainer, Douglas F.	1951	Signal Corps
Robinson, Roscoe, Jr.	1951	Infantry
** Woodson, William B.	1951	Artillery
Young, James R., Jr.	1951	USAF
** Corprew, Gerald	1953	Signal Corps
Hughes, Bernard C.	1953	CE
Worthy, Clifford	1953	Artillery
** Lee, Ronald B.	1954	Signal Corps
** Turner, LeRoy C.	1954	Infantry
Robinson, Hugh G.	1954	CE
Hamilton, John M., Jr.	1955	Infantry
** Olive, Lewis C., Jr.	1955	USAF
** Cassells, Cyrus C., Jr.	1955	USAF
Batchman, Gilbert R.	1955	Infantry
Brown, John M.	1955	Infantry
Blunt, Roger R.	1956	CE
Bradley, Martin G.	1957	USAF
McCullom, Cornell, Jr.	1957	Signal Corps
** Brunner, Ronald S.	1958	Artillery
Baugh, Raymond C.	1959	Signal Corps
Kelley, Wilbourne A., III	1959	CE
Dorsey, Ira	1960	Artillery
Brown, Reginald J.	1961	Infantry
Quinn, Kenneth L.	1961	Signal Corps
Gorden, Fred A.	1962	Artillery
Banks, Edgar, Jr.	1963	Artillery
Jackson, David S.	1963	Artillery
Ivy, William L.	1963	USAF
Handcox, Robert C.	1963	Infantry
Miller, Warren F., Jr.	1964	Artillery
† Ramsay, David L.	1964	USAF
Hester, Arthur C.	1965	Armor
Anderson, Joseph B.	1965	Infantry
Jenkins, Harold A., Jr.	1965	Infantry
Conley, James S.	1965	Artillery
# Cox, Ronald E.	1966	Armor
Davis, Thomas B., III	1966	Infantry
† Ramsay, Robert B.	1966	USAF
Fowler, James D., Jr.	1967	Artillery
Whaley, Bobby G.	1967	Infantry
Martin, John T., III	1968	Field Artillery
Garcia, Victor	1968	Signal Corps
Jordan, Larry R.	1968	Armor
Flowers, Ernest, Jr.	1968	Field Artillery
Rorie, Wilson L., Jr.	1968	Infantry
Outlaw, LeRoy B.	1968	Field Artillery
Howard, James T.	1968	Med. Service Corps
Tildon, Ralph B.	1968	Infantry
Robinson, Benny L.	1968	Infantry
Copeland, Rene G.	1969	Armor
Tabela, Francis E.	1969	Infantry
Hackett, Jerome R.	1969	Signal Corps
Cooper, Cornelius M., Jr.	1969	Field Artillery
Groves, Sheridon H.	1969	Armor
Williams, Michael M.	1969	Infantry
Minor, James A., Jr.	1969	Infantry

† Steele, Michael F.	1969	Infantry
Cousar, Robert J., Jr.	1970	Signal Corps
Thomas, Kenneth L.	1970	USAF
Reid, Trevor A.	1970	Infantry
Morgan, Roderick H.	1970	Infantry
Robinson, Bruce E.	1970	Infantry
† Steele, Gary R.	1970	Infantry
Mason, Robert E.	1970	Air Def. Artillery
Price, Willie J.	1970	Infantry
(81)		

† Brothers
* Deceased
** Resigned
*** Graduated but not commissioned (none)
**** Retired
# Name changed from "Hobart R. E. Cox" to "Ronald E. Cox"

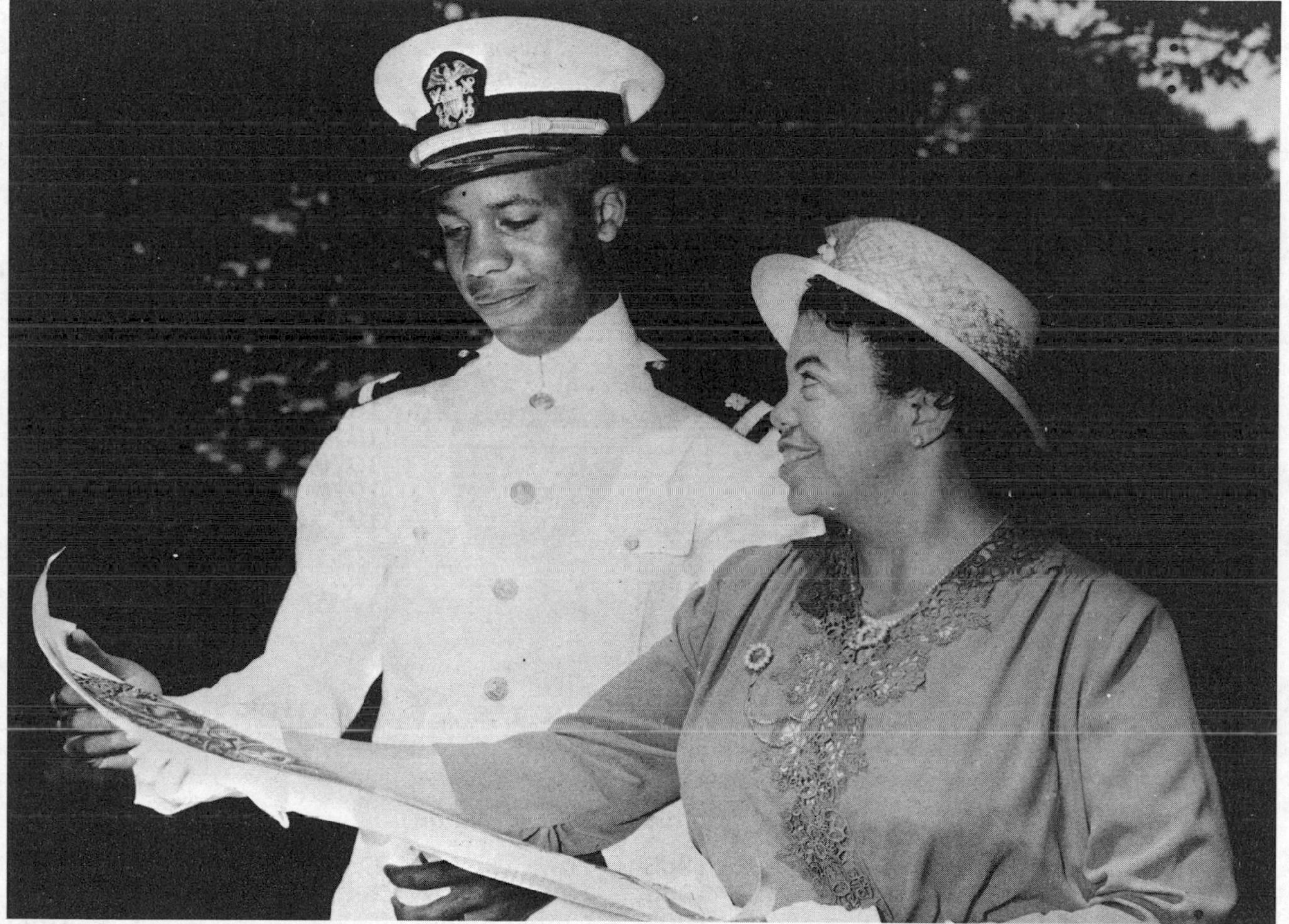

Wesley A. Brown, who in 1949 became the first black to graduate from the U.S. Naval Academy.

NEGRO GRADUATES OF THE U. S. NAVAL ACADEMY (1949-1970)

Name	*Class*	*Branch*
Brown, Wesley A	1949	USN
Chambers, Lawrence	1952	USN
Taylor, Reeves	1953	USN
***Raiford, John	1954	USN
Gregg, Lucius P., Jr	1955	USAF
Sechrest, Edward	1956	USN

Bauduit, Harold S	1956	USAF
Jamison, Vencin	1957	USN
Slaughter, Kent W	1957	USAF
*Fennell, George M	1958	USN
Bruce, Malvin D	1959	USN
Bush, William S., III	1959	USN
Clark, Maurice E	1959	USN
Powell, William E., Jr	1959	USN
Byrd, Willie C	1961	USN
Johnson, Mack, Jr	1961	USN
Shelton, John A	1961	USN
Jackson, John Thomas	1962	USAF
McCray, Donald	1962	USN
Newton, Robert Chester	1963	USN
Jones, William Charles	1964	USMC
McDonald, James Edward, Jr.	1964	USMC
Prout, Patrick Michael	1964	USMC
Thomas, Benjamin Francis	1964	USN
Carter, Stanley Jerome, Jr.	1965	USN
Grayson, Floyd Fred	1965	USN
Reason, Joseph Paul	1965	USN
Huey, Calvin Windell	1967	USN
Tzomes, Chancellor A.	1967	USN
Bolden, Charles F., Jr.	1968	USN
Clark, William Stanton, Jr.	1968	USN
Lucas, Robert Gillem	1968	USN
Simmons, David Franklin	1968	USN
Carr, Emerson Frank	1969	USN
Jones, Frederick Eugene	1969	USN
Freeman, Joseph Bertram	1970	USMC
Greene, Everett Lewis	1970	USN
Henry, Bruce Alan	1970	USMC
Roberts, Michael Charles	1970	USN
Watson, Anthony John	1970	USN
Williams, Leo V.	1970	USMC

*Deceased.
**Resigned.
***Graduated but not commissioned.

NEGRO GRADUATES OF THE U.S.A.F. ACADEMY

(1964-1970)

Name	*Class*
Bush, Charles V	1963
Payne, Isaac S., IV	1963
Sims, Roger	1963
Gregory, Frederick	1964
Beamon, Arthur L	1965
Thomas, Charles	1965
Plummer, Bentley V	1965
Wiley, Fletcher H	1965
Cunningham, Thomas L.	1967
Ecung, Maurice C.	1968
Gibson, Samuel B.	1968
Groves, Weldon K., Jr.	1968
Marshall, Marion A.	1968
Moore, Frank M.	1968
Thompson, James E.	1968
Capron, Charles M.	1969
Hopper, John D., Jr.	1969
Howland, Walter T.	1969
Love, James E.	1969
Spooner, Richard E.	1969
Williams, Thurmond	1969
Little, Kenneth H.	1969
Stevenson, Kenneth E., Jr.	1969
Arnold, Harry	1970
Battles, Dorsey	1970
Bowie, Harold V.	1970
Bryant, Robert S.	1970
Elliott, Norman	1970
Jones, Reuben D.	1970
Keys, George R.	1970
Mohr, Dean	1970

NEGRO CADETS ENROLLED AT THE SERVICE ACADEMIES (1971-1974)

U.S. Military Academy

Name	*Class*	*Name*	*Class*
Burns, Cornelious	1971	Rowe, Dennis W.	1973
Freeman, Robert E.	1971	Sayles, Andre H.	1973
James, Kevin T.	1971	Simpson, Ernest L.	1973
Plummer, William W., III	1971	Spellman, Seth W.	1973
Anderson, Edgar L.	1972	Sutton, Lloyd L.	1973
Bonner, Brian A.	1972	Topping, Gary E.	1973
Brice, David L.	1972	Twitty, Theophlise L.	1973
Dedmond, Tony L.	1972	Anderson, Gary J.	1974
Edwards, Joseph R.	1972	Banks, Allan A.	1974
Mension, Danny S.	1972	Best, Marshall	1974
Robinson, Lenwood, Jr.	1972	Braxton, Maceo	1974
Squire, Percy	1972	Bryant, Albert	1974
Adams, Jesse B.	1973	Chachere, Ernest G.	1974
Allen, Ollie W., II	1973	Craig, Gregory L.	1974
Baker, James L.	1973	Edwards, William F.	1974
Bell, Richard, Jr.	1973	Elmore, Terry E.	1974
Bivens, Courtland C., III	1973	Ferguson, Lawrence H.	1974
Bonner, Garland C.	1973	Fowler, David L.	1974
Broussard, Bernard	1973	Gibbs, Edward L.	1974
Christian, James L.	1973	Harris, Mickey E.	1974
Christopher, Clyde J.	1973	Helton, Dwight A.	1974
Coats, Charles S., Jr.	1973	Holmes, Keith B.	1974
Colbert, Malcolm N., II	1973	Hughes, Samuel J., III	1974
Coleman, Frederick D.	1973	Hunter, Joseph	1974
Crisp, William I.	1973	Ivery, Reginald L.	1974
Crumpler, Arthur B.	1973	Jones, Harvey D., Jr.	1974
Demerson, Elijah B. } twins	1973	King, Jimmie D.	1974
Demerson, Elisha L. } twins	1973	Lewis, Kevin M.	1974
Edwards, Lawrence D.	1973	Lynch, Myron C.	1974
Farquhar, Ralph R.	1973	Mallory, Phillip L.	1974
Ferguson, Mercer E.	1973	Mayson, William A., Jr.	1974
Fountain, Foster F., III	1973	McCullough, William H.	1974
Gaines, Michael B.	1973	McDuffie, Ernest L.	1974
Get, Donald	1973	Morris, Frank S.	1974
Greene, Reginald D.	1973	Morrison, James M.	1974
Harris, Henry	1973	Ramsey, Harold G.	1974
Hedgebeth, Lesie J.	1973	Reede, James W.	1974
Jenkins, Gil S.	1973	Reid, Ronny E.	1974
Johnson, Edward C., Jr.	1973	Sample, Allen L.	1974
Jones, William H.	1973	Scruggs, Stephen B.	1974
Lewis, Brett H.	1973	Spaulding, Milton C.	1974
Martin, Edwin L.	1973	Stuart, Eugene N.	1974
Moore, William L.	1973	Taylor, Theodore R.	1974
Perry, William H.	1973	Topping, Gerald W.	1974
Stacy S. Poullard	1973	Wallace, Michael D.	1974
		Wheeler, Clayton R.	1974

* Deceased
** Resigned
*** Graduated but not commissioned (none)
**** Retired

(1) His son, James D. Fowler, Jr., was graduated from the USMA in 1967; and a second son, David L. Fowler entered as a cadet in 1970 with the Class of 1974.

U.S. Naval Academy

Name	*Class*	*Name*	*Class*
Collier, Charles M.	1971	Burnette, Edwin A.	1972
Porter, John F.	1971	Coleman, Alfred B.	1972
Shuffer, George M., III	1971	Crump, Walter L., Jr.	1972

Name	Class
Files, Clifton E.	1972
Jones, Nelson M.	1972
Keaser, Lloyd W.	1972
Lovely, Eugene	1972
Mason, Matthew T.	1972
McMillan, Julius A.	1972
Rucks, Charles H.	1972
Smith, Earl M.	1972
Smith, Earl M.	1972
Staton, Ronald B.	1972
Tindall, Julius S.	1972
Young, Ernest C.	1972
Borders, Henry A.	1973
Bryant, Gregory B.	1973
Calhoun, Larry W.	1973
Caliman, Kerry H.	1973
Campbell, James H.	1973
Evans, William G.	1973
Faust, Homer L.	1973
Harvey, Collins	1973
Jackson, James E.	1973
Jones, Larry W.	1973
Kennard, Wayne M.	1973
Martin, Kenneth D.	1973
Samuels, Richard G.	1973
Shockley, Rodney L.	1973
Watts, Robert D.	1973
Casey, Ronald L.	1974
Clayton, Larry E.	1974
Corpin, Owen D.	1974
Dunn, Kenneth D.	1974
Gilford, Michael R.	1974
Harris, William M.	1974
Johnston, Jeffrey P.	1974
Jolly, Ernest L.	1974
Kirk, Forrest L.	1974
Martin, G. L.	1974
Martin, Stephen D.	1974
Minor, Thomas E.	1974
Montgomery, Donald	1974
Rasin, Steven E.	1974
Robinson, Charles	1974
Tate, John D.	1974
Walls, Gordon S.	1974
Washington, Leroy L.	1974
Williams, Anthony B.	1974
Williams, Raymond B.	1974

U.S. Air Force Academy

Name	Class
Banks, Reginald I.	1971
Edmondson, William E.	1971
Jennings, Ernest R.	1971
Martin, Curtis J.	1971
Randall, Robert J.	1971
Rogers, Robert P.	1971
Sprott, Robert E.	1971
Watson, Orrin S.	1971
White, Leon G.	1971
Wimberly, Bruce	1971
Arrington, Ronald M.	1972
Bassa, Paul, Jr.	1972
Brown, Ralph B., Jr.	1972
Charlton, Thomas J.	1972
Harrison, Booker	1972
Hawkins, Robert A.	1972
Henderson, Clyde R.	1972
Jones, Raymond J.	1972
McDonald, Michael	1972
Meredith, Keith S.	1972
Nelson, Michael V.	1972
Parks, Reginald D.	1972
Rhaney, Mahlon C., Jr.	1972
Ross, Joseph D., Jr.	1972
Rucker, Raymond I., Jr.	1972
Slade, John B., Jr.	1972
Abraham, Robert E.	1973
Baker, Richard A.	1973
Bolton, Robert M.	1973
Butler, Ernest E., Jr.	1973
Childress, Charlie, Jr.	1973
Dunn, Arthur L., Jr.	1973
Gilbert, Robert L.	1973
Harrison, Herbert A.	1973
Hodges, Rudnaldo	1973
Kyle, Frank M.	1973
Lewis, Gerald E.	1973
Minter, Oscar J., 3d	1973
Mitchell, David L.	1973
Mitchell, Joseph R., Jr.	1973
Mitchell, Orderia F.	1973
Price, Lloyd C., Jr.	1973
Rattley, Elliott A., Jr.	1973
Richardson, Donald L.	1973
Battles, George T.	1974
Berry, William	1974
Blake, David G.	1974
Brown, George L.	1974
Bryant, Frederic B., Jr.	1974
Caldwell, Richmond H., Jr.	1974
Collins, Dennis F.	1974
Crenshaw, Ronald L.	1974
Fitzhugh, Fred, Jr.	1974
Hairston, Carlton P.	1974
Hawkins, Warren R., Jr.	1974
Jackson, Marcus	1974
Jones, Gregory Duane Hogan	1974
Lockette, Emory W., Jr.	1974
Matlock, Earl W.	1974
McAlpen, Sherman E.	1974
Murphy, Franklin	1974
Ponder, William L., Jr.	1974
Robinson, Neal T.	1974
Smith, Clarence D., Jr.	1974

Name	*Class*
Tarleton, Gadson J., III	1974
Thomas, Dirk C.	1974
Timberlake, Marion, Jr.	1974
Tinney, Alvin F., Jr.	1974
Walker, Philip E.	1974
Watson, Ronald W.	1974
Webb, Lance C.	1974
White, Emmett, Jr.	1974

MILITARY HEROES

LIEUT. GEN. BENJAMIN O. DAVIS, JR. 1912-

Described by a former instructor as "the closest thing to a model cadet I ever saw," General Benjamin O. Davis rose to become the highest-ranking black military man in U. S. history.

Born in Washington in 1912, Davis was educated in Alabama (his father taught military science at Tuskegee) and, later, in Cleveland, where he graduated as president of his class with one of the highest scholastic averages in the city.

Davis attended Western Reserve University and the University of Chicago before accepting an appointment to the U. S. Military Academy in 1932. Davis survived the silent treatment as a cadet, and graduated 35th in his class of 276.

After serving in the infantry for five years, he transferred to the Army Air Corps in 1941, and was among the first six black air cadets to graduate from the Advanced Army Flying School in 1942.

As commander of the 99th Fighter Squadron (and later commander of the all-black 332nd Fighter Group) Davis flew 60 missions in 224 combat hours during World War II, winning several medals, including the Silver Star.

Davis became a lieutenant general in 1965, and closed out his career as deputy commander of the U. S. Strike Command at McDill Air Force Base in Tampa, Florida. In civilian life, Davis worked briefly in the administration of Cleveland's black mayor Carl Stokes, but resigned after a policy dispute.

LIEUT. HENRY O. FLIPPER 1877-1940

The first black officer to graduate from West Point and the first to be assigned to a command position in a black unit after the Civil War, Henry O. Flipper was the victim of a controversial court-martial proceeding which cut short the career of one of the most promising black military men to wear the uniform of an American soldier.

Flipper was not defeated by the debacle, however. He went on, as a civilian, to become a notable figure on the American frontier—as a mining engineer and consultant and, later, as a translator of Spanish land grants.

Flipper tried on many occasions to vindicate himself, befriending such prominent Washington officials as Senator A. B. Fall of New Mexico. When Fall became Secretary of the Interior, Flipper became his assistant until the infamous Teapot Dome affair severed their relationship.

Flipper returned to Atlanta at the close of his mining career, living with his brother, an AME bishop, until his death in 1940. His quest—to remove the stain of "conduct unbecoming an officer and a gentleman" — remained unfulfilled to his dying day, partly because certain records which might shed light on the situation are not yet open for public scrutiny.

Lt. Gen. Benjamin O. Davis, Jr.

BRIG. GEN. DANIEL JAMES
1920-

Deputy Assistant Secretary of Defense (Public Affairs) since March 31, 1970, Brig. Gen. Daniel "Chappie" James came to his most recent assignment after serving as commander of the 7272nd Flying Training Wing at Wheelus Air Force Base in Libya.

Born February 11, 1920 in Pensacola, Florida, James graduated from Washington High School in 1937 and attended Tuskegee Institute until 1942, the year he completed civilian pilot training under the government-sponsored Civilian Pilot Training Program.

By 1945, James had received his commission as a second lieutenant in the Army Air Corps. He then completed fighter pilot training in Michigan and served six years with various fighter units stationed in the U. S.

During the Korean War, James flew 101 combat missions in F-51 and F-80 aircraft. After the war, he served in various staff assignments until 1957, the year he graduated from the Air Command and Staff College at Maxwell Air Force Base, Alabama. In 1966, James became Deputy Commander for Operations of the 8th Tactical Fighter Wing, stationed in Thailand.

General "Chappie" James

A recipient of numerous awards and combat decorations, General James is widely known for speeches on Americanism and patriotism. One citation he received reads in part: "fighter pilot with a magnificent record . . . and eloquent spokesman for the American Dream we so rarely achieve."

HENRY JOHNSON
1897–1929
World War I hero

A member of the 15th National Guard of New York which became the 369th Infantry, Henry Johnson was probably the most famous Negro soldier to have fought in World War I.

The 369th itself was the first group of Negro combat troops to arrive in Europe. After a summer of training, the group saw action at Champagne, and fought its way to the Rhine River in Germany, receiving the Croix de Guerre from the French government. Johnson and another soldier (Needham Roberts) were the first Americans to receive this French medal for individual heroism in combat.

During a night skirmish, Johnson fought off an entire German patrol singlehanded, rescuing his wounded comrade from almost certain capture in the process. He personally accounted for four dead, a host of wounded, and a virtual stockpile of abandoned equipment. Wounded himself, he lost a shin bone and had several broken bones in one of his feet.

Johnson was cited by the French as a "magnificent example of courage and energy." He was later promoted to sergeant.

DORIE MILLER
1919–1943
Hero of Pearl Harbor

A messman aboard the *U.S.S. Arizona*, Dorie Miller had his first taste of combat at Pearl Harbor on December 7, 1941, when he manned a machinegun and brought down four Japanese planes.

Born on a farm near Waco, Texas in 1919, Miller was the son of a sharecropper, and grew up to become star fullback on the Moore High School football team in his native city. At 19, he enlisted in the U.S. Navy, and was nearing the end of his first hitch at the time of the Pearl Harbor attack.

For his heroism, Miller was awarded the Navy Cross, which was conferred by Admiral Chester W. Nimitz, the commander in chief of the Pacific Fleet.

He remained a messman during the hostilities, serving aboard the aircraft carrier *Liscome Bay* and being promoted to Mess Attendant Third Class. He was killed in action in the South Pacific in December of 1943. Miller was commended for "distinguished devotion to duty, extreme courage, and disregard of his personal safety during attack."

(Miller was one of several "noncombatant" Negroes who distinguished themselves for heroism during combat. Others included: Leonard Roy Harmon of the U.S.S. *San Francisco*; William Pinckney of the U.S.S. *Enterprise*, and Elbert H. Oliver of the U.S.S. *Intrepid*. Harmon and Pinckney were awarded the Navy Cross; Oliver, the Silver Star.)

Lt. Charles D. Young, class of 1889

COLONEL CHARLES YOUNG
1864–1922
Highest-ranking Negro officer in World War I

Charles Young saw his first major combat during the Spanish American War, less than 10 years after he had become the third Negro to have graduated from the U.S. military academy at West Point.

Born on March 12, 1864 in Mayslick, Kentucky, Young moved to Ripley, Ohio with his parents at an early age. Having finished high school, he taught for a time until winning an appointment to West Point in 1884. Upon graduation, Young was commissioned a second lieutenant in the 10th Cavalry, an all-Negro unit. In 1894, he became a military instructor at Wilberforce University in Ohio and, with the outbreak of the Spanish American War, was reassigned to the 9th Ohio Regiment which was transferred to Cuba.

After the war, Young served in the Philippines and in Haiti, and also in the Mexican campaign of 1915, when he commanded a squadron of the 10th Cavalry which rescued a group of ambushed white soldiers near Parral, Mexico. Declared physically unfit for service overseas in World War I, Young rode on horseback from his home in Xenia, Ohio to Washington, D.C. where, to no avail, he protested the decision of the War Department to retire him from active duty.

Five days before the Armistice, however, Young was ordered to Camp Grant in Illinois to take charge of trainees. Sent to Liberia after completing this assignment, Young helped organize the army there.

He died in 1922 of a fever contracted while he was on furlough in Nigeria, and was buried with full military honors at Arlington National Cemetery in Virginia.

Tommie Smith (center) and John Carlos (right) give the Black Power salute at the 1968 Olympics in Mexico City.

THE BLACK AMATEUR & PROFESSIONAL ATHLETE

The Sports Scene: **Baseball—Boxing**
Basketball—Football
Track and Field
Tennis—Wrestling
Golf—Horse Racing

Outstanding Black Athletes

Sports is an area in which the Negro's preeminence has already captured worldwide attention. Negro amateur and professional athletes have reached stardom in virtually all the major sports engaged in by Americans and, in so doing, have created vast audiences of dedicated fans both at home and abroad. In the last decade, however, sports has become increasingly politicized, with the result that rival camps have emerged in which certain black athletes have demonstrated occasionally virulent contempt for the amateur system. In their view, they are often expected to express support for a way of life which subjects them to subtle forms of humiliation and second-class treatment. Young radicals such as these threatened to boycott the 1968 Olympic games, and certainly disrupted them by rendering the black power salute from the victory stand. The gesture conveyed their sense of racial solidarity, rather than a feeling of identifying with their national origins.

BASEBALL

In the 20 years which have elapsed since Jackie Robinson broke the color barrier in major league baseball, Negro stars have become almost too numerous to catalogue. There is hardly a single position in the game at which at least one Negro star has not excelled: as pitcher (Don Newcombe); catcher (Roy Campanella and Elston Howard); infielder (Maury Wills, holder of the stolen-base record which once belonged to the immortal Ty Cobb), and outfielder (Willie Mays, already the leading right-handed home run hitter of all time).

Many of the early stars of the game played out their careers before 1969. This applies to such stalwart players as Dan Bankhead and Joe Black, Brooklyn Dodger pitchers; Monty Irvin and Hank Thompson of the New York Giants Sam Jethroe of the Boston Braves; Luke Easter and Harry "Suitcase" Simpson of the Cleveland Indians, and a number of others.

1969-1970

Our section provides a roster of black and Latin major leaguers for the 1969 and 1970 seasons, accompanied by a brief review of outstanding performances for that year.

NATIONAL LEAGUE

The top black baseball star in the major leagues in 1969 was Willie McCovey of the San Francisco Giants, voted the league's Most Valuable Player on the merits of leading the league with 45 home runs and 126 runs-batted-in in addition to compiling a .320 batting average. Other black players making large contributions to their teams were Pittsburgh's Roberto Clemente (91 rbi's, .345 batting average); Cleon Jones of the world champion New York Mets (75 rbi's, .342); Matty Alou, Pittsburgh (231 hits, .331); Tony Perez, Cincinnati (37 hrs., 123 rbi's); and the Dodgers' Willie Davis (.311 batting average in addition to compiling a 31 game hitting-streak, longest in the major leagues). The top black moundsmen were San Francisco's Juan Marichal (21-11 won-lost record and a league-leading 2.10 Earned Run Average) and St. Louis' Bob Gibson (20-13, 2.17 ERA and 268 strikeouts).

In 1970, four of the top five NL hitters (400 or more at-bats) were black. These included the league batting champ Rico Carty of the Atlanta Braves (.366 batting average); Pittsburgh's Roberto Clemente (.352) and Manny Sanguillen (.327); and Billy Williams of the Chicago Cubs (.322, 42 home runs, 129 runs-batted-in). Other black athletes showing strength at the plate were Tony Perez (.317, 40 hrs., 129 rbi's) and Bob Tolan (.316, 80 rbi's, a league-leading 57 stolen bases) of the National League champion Cincinnati Reds; the Braves' Orlando Cepeda (34 hrs., 112 rbi's) and Hank Aaron (38 hrs., 118 rbi's); San Diego's Clarence Gaston (.318, 29 hrs., 92 rbi's); and the San Francisco Giants' slugging Willie McCovey (39 hrs., 126 rbi's).

The top black hurler was the Cardinals' Bob Gibson. He won the National League's Cy Young Award (awarded annually to the league's best pitcher) on the merits of a 23-7 won-lost record and 273 strikeouts. Joining Gibson as a 20-game winner was the mainstay of the Chicago Cubs' pitching staff, Ferguson Jenkins. He compiled a 22-16 won-lost record while striking out 274 batters.

1970 ROSTER

NATIONAL LEAGUE, EASTERN DIVISION

St. Louis Cardinals

S. Guzman—p
Richie Allen—if
Lou Brock—of
Jose Cardenal—of
Vic Davalillo—of
Bob Gibson—p
Leron Lee—of
Julian Javier—if
M. Ramirez—if
Cookie Rojas—if
Mike Torrez—p

New York Mets

Tommie Agee—of
Donn Clendenon—if
Joe Foy—if
Cleon Jones—of
Ken Singleton—of

Chicago Cubs

Ernie Banks—of
Willie Smith—p
Cleo James—if
Billy Williams—of

Montreal Expos

Angel Hermosa—if
Jose Herrera—of
Mack Jones—of
Coco Laboy—if
A. Phillips—of

Pittsburgh Pirates

Matty Alou—of
Roberto Clemente—of
Dock Ellis—p
John Jeter—of
J. Martinez—if
Al Oliver—if
Jose Pagan—if
Dave Ricketts—c
Manny Sanguillen—c
Willie Stargell—of
Bob Veale—p

Philadelphia Phillies

John Briggs—of
G. Jackson—p
R. Joseph—if
Byron Browne—of
Larry Hisle—of
Tony Taylor—if

NATIONAL LEAGUE, WESTERN DIVISION

San Francisco Giants

Bobby Bonds—of
Tito Fuentes—if
Juan Marichal—p
Willie Mays—of
Willie McCovey—if

Atlanta Braves

Hank Aaron—of
Tommie Aaron—if
Rico Carty—of
Orlando Cepeda—if
Ralph Garr—of
Gil Garrido—if
Tony Gonzalez—of
Sonny Jackson—if
Hal King—c
Felix Milan—if

Cincinnati Reds

Angel Bravo—of
Dave Concepcion—if
Lee May—if
Tony Perez—if
Wayne Simpson—p
Bob Tolan—of
Hal McRae—of

Los Angeles Dodgers

Alvin McBean—p
Willie Crawford—of
Willie Davis—of
Manny Mota—of
Jose Pena—p
Maury Wills—if

Houston Astros

Jesus Alou—of
Tommy Davis—of
Leon McFadden—if
Joe Morgan—if
M. Martinez—if
John Mayberry—if
Bob Watson—c
Don Wilson—p
Jim Wynn—of

San Diego Padres

Ollie Brown—of
Nate Colbert—if
Clarence Gaston—of
Jerry Morales—of
Ivan Murrell—of
Ramon Webster—if

The incomparable Willie Mays

AMERICAN LEAGUE

Top black batsmen in the American League in 1969 were Minnesota's Rod Carew (league-leading .332 batting average) and Tony Oliva, (24 hrs., 101 rbi's, .309); Frank Robinson of the American League Champion Baltimore Orioles (32 hrs., 100 rbi's, and a .308 batting average); Boston's Reggie Smith (25 hrs., 93 rbi's, .309); and Reggie Jackson, Oakland (47 hrs., 118 rbi's). The top black pitcher was Oakland's John Odom (15-6, 2.94 ERA).

In 1970, Alex Johnson of the California Angels won the AL batting title with a .329 batting average. Not far behind him was the Twins' Tony Oliva (.325, 204 hits, 107 rbi's). Other black batsmen making their presence known were Frank Robinson of the world champion Baltimore Orioles (.306, 25 hrs., 79 rbi's); Boston's Reggie Smith (.303, 22 hrs., 74 rbi's); Tommy Harper of the Milwaukee Brewers (.296, 31 hrs., 82 rbi's); and the Yankees' Roy White (.296, 22 hrs., 94 rbi's).

Among the league's top pitchers was Baltimore's Mike Cuellar with a 24-8 won-lost record.

1970 ROSTER

AMERICAN LEAGUE, EASTERN DIVISION

Baltimore Orioles

Paul Blair—of
Chico Salmon—if
Frank Robinson—of
Curtell Motton—of
Dave May—of
Mike Cuellar—p
Marcelino Lopez—p
Elrod Hendricks—c
Don Buford—of

Washington Senators

Hank Allen—if
Ed Stroud—of
Paul Casanova—c
Lee Maye—of
Dave Nelson—if
John Roseboro—c

Boston Red Sox

George Scott—if
Reggie Smith—of
Luis Alvarado—if

New York Yankees

Jerry Kenney—if
Bill Robinson—of
Roy White—of
Ron Woods—of
Horace Clark—if

Detroit Tigers

Gates Brown—of
Ike Brown—if
Willie Horton—of
Elliott Maddox—if
Earl Wilson—p

Cleveland Indians

Ted Ford—of
Vada Pinson—of
Chuck Hinton—of
Roy Foster—of

WESTERN DIVISION

Minnesota Twins

Rod Carew—if
Leo Cardenas—if
Tom Hall—p
Jim Holt—of
Minnie Mendoza—if
Tony Oliva—of
Luis Tiant—p
Cesar Tovar—of

Oakland Athletics

Felipe Alou—of
Al Downing—p
Jim Grant—p
Reggie Jackson—of
John Odom—p
Diego Segui—p
Jose Tartabull—of

Kansas City Royals

Luis Alcaraz—if
J. Hernandez—if
Pat Kelly—of
Bob Oliver—if
Amos Otis—of
E. Rodriguez—c
George Spriggs—of

California Angels

Sandy Alomar—if
Joe Azcue—c
Jim Hicks—of
Alex Johnson—of
Rudy May—p

Chicago White Sox

C. Bradford—of
John Matias—of
Carlos May—of
Tom McGraw—if
Walt Williams—of

Milwaukee Brewers

Tommie Harper—if
Ted Savage—of
Sandy Valdespino—of

NEGRO BATTING CHAMPIONS (NATIONAL LEAGUE)

Player	*Year*	*Average*
Jackie Robinson, Brooklyn Dodgers	1949	.342
Willie Mays, New York Giants	1954	.345
Hank Aaron, Milwaukee Braves	1956	.328

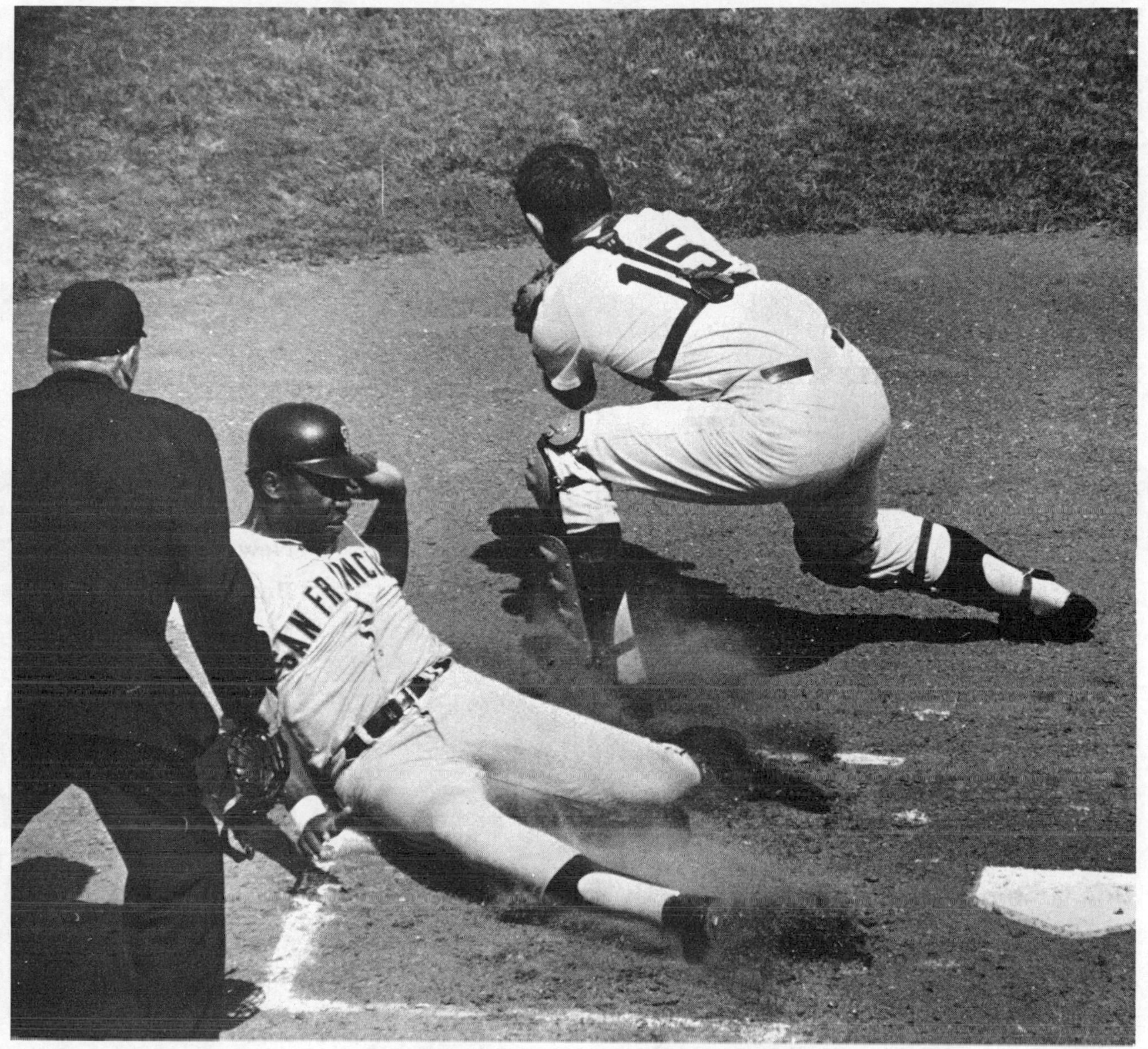

Willie McCovey, 1969 National League homerun champion

Hank Aaron, Milwaukee Braves	1959	.355
Roberto Clemente,* Pittsburgh Pirates	1961	.351
Tommy Davis, Los Angeles Dodgers	1962	.346
Tommy Davis, Los Angeles Dodgers	1963	.326
Roberto Clemente,* Pittsburgh Pirates	1964	.339
Roberto Clemente,* Pittsburgh Pirates	1965	.329
Matty Alou,* Pittsburgh Pirates	1966	.342
Roberto Clemente, Pittsburgh Pirates*	1967	.357
Rico Carty, Atlanta Braves	1970	.366

* Denotes Latin player.

NEGRO BATTING CHAMPIONS (AMERICAN LEAGUE)

Player	Year	Average
Tony Oliva,* Minnesota Twins	1964	.323
Tony Oliva,* Minnesota Twins	1965	.321
Frank Robinson, Baltimore Orioles	1966	.316
Rod Carew, Minnesota Twins*	1969	.332
Alex Johnson, California Angels	1970	.329

NEGRO MOST VALUABLE PLAYER AWARDS (NATIONAL LEAGUE)

Player	Year	Team
Jackie Robinson	1949	Brooklyn Dodgers
Roy Campanella	1951, 1953, 1955	Brooklyn Dodgers
Willie Mays	1954	New York Giants
Don Newcombe	1956	Brooklyn Dodgers
Hank Aaron	1957	Milwaukee Braves
Ernie Banks	1958, 1959	Chicago Cubs
Maury Wills	1962	Los Angeles Dodgers
Willie Mays	1965	San Francisco Giants
Roberto Clemente	1966	Pittsburgh Pirates
Orlando Cepeda*	1967	St Louis Cardinals
Bob Gibson	1968	St Louis Cardinals
Willie McCovey	1969	San Francisco Giants

NEGRO MOST VALUABLE PLAYER AWARDS (AMERICAN LEAGUE)

Player	Year	Team
Elston Howard	1963	New York Yankees
Zoilo Versalles*	1965	Minnesota Twins
Frank Robinson	1966	Baltimore Orioles

NEGRO HOME RUN CHAMPIONS (NATIONAL LEAGUE)

Player	Total	Year
Willie Mays, New York Giants	51	1955
Hank Aaron, Milwaukee Braves	44	1957
Ernie Banks, Chicago Cubs	47	1958

* Denotes Latin player.

Player	*Total*	*Year*
Ernie Banks, Chicago Cubs	41	1960
Orlando Cepeda,* San Francisco Giants	46	1961
Willie Mays, San Francisco Giants	49	1962
Willie McCovey, San Francisco Giants	44	1963
Hank Aaron, Milwaukee Braves	44	1963
Willie Mays, San Francisco Giants	47	1964
Willie Mays, San Francisco Giants	52	1965
Hank Aaron, Atlanta Braves	44	1966
Hank Aaron, Atlanta	39	1967
Willie McCovey, San Francisco Giants	36	1968
Willie McCovey, San Francisco Giants	45	1969

NEGRO HOME RUN CHAMPIONS (AMERICAN LEAGUE)

Player	*Total*	*Year*
Larry Doby, Cleveland Indians	32	1952
Larry Doby, Cleveland Indians	32	1954
Frank Robinson, Baltimore Orioles	49	1966

* Denotes Latin player.

Jackie Robinson slides home in a game against the Chicago Cubs. One of the game's great second basemen, Robinson was the first Negro to break the color barrier in the majors.

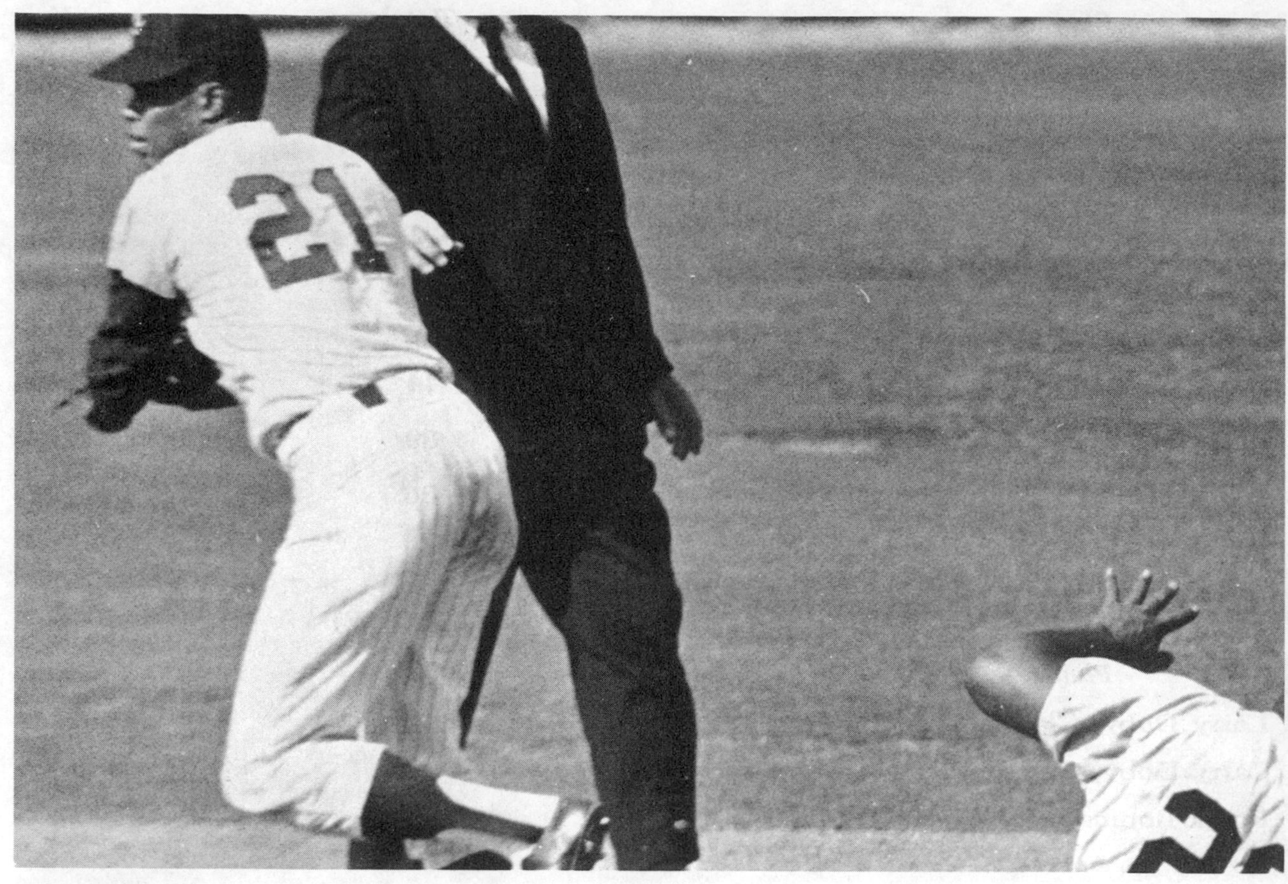

Rod Carew (21), 1969 American League batting champion, starting a double play

NEGRO RUNS-BATTED-IN LEADERS (NATIONAL LEAGUE)

Player	*Team*	*Year*	*Total*
Monte Irvin	New York Giants	1951	121
Hank Aaron	Milwaukee Braves	1957	126
Ernie Banks	Chicago Cubs	1958	129
Ernie Banks	Chicago Cubs	1959	143
Hank Aaron	Milwaukee Braves	1960	126
Orlando Cepeda	San Francisco Giants	1961	142
Tommy Davis	Los Angeles Dodgers	1962	153
Hank Aaron	Milwaukee Braves	1963	130
Hank Aaron	Atlanta Braves	1966	127
Orlando Cepeda	St. Louis Cardinals	1967	111
Willie McCovey	San Francisco Giants	1968	105
Willie McCovey	San Francisco Giants	1969	126

NEGRO RUNS-BATTED-IN LEADERS (AMERICAN LEAGUE)

Player	*Team*	*Year*	*Total*
Larry Doby	Cleveland Indians	1954	126
Frank Robinson	Baltimore Orioles	1966	122

BOXING

The Negro prize fighter has been active in America for well over two centuries. In fact, the first American heavyweight contender was himself a Negro, Tom Molineaux, a Virginia slave. Molineaux lost two championship fights against the English titleholder, Tom Crib, in 1810 and again in 1811.

With the advent of the 20th century, the Negro boxer came to occupy a place of ever-growing importance in American ring annals—in particular after Jack Johnson (see page 653), regarded by many as the greatest fighter of all time, won the heavy weight championship of the world in 1908.

By the 1930's, Negroes were challenging for supremacy in other divisions as well. Henry Armstrong (see page 647) had become featherweight, lightweight and welterweight champion of the world—the first and only fighter to hold three titles at once. Joe Louis (see page 655) had already been world heavyweight champion for almost 10 years when Ray Robinson (see page 660) took the welterweight crown at the end of 1946. Robinson moved up to the middleweight championship in the 1950's, and came close to taking the light-heavyweight title from Joe Maxim, losing only after wilting in the heat at Yankee Stadium in 1952.

Throughout most of this era, (in fact, for all but five years since 1937) Negroes have retained the heavyweight championship of the world. Although there have been many champions in all divisions, we are listing the records of only the heavyweight titleholders, along with those of Henry Armstrong and Ray Robinson, two of the greatest Negro champions in other divisions. (These records are reprinted here through the courtesy of Nat Fleischer and "Ring" magazine.)

Olympic heavyweight boxing champion George Foreman delivers the victory salute at the 1968 Games. Foreman is now a professional.

NEGRO BOXING CHAMPIONS (ALL DIVISIONS)

Heavyweight

Name	*Years Held*
Jack Johnson	1908-1915
Joe Louis	1937-1949
Ezzard Charles	1949-1951
Jersey Joe Walcott	1951-1952
Floyd Patterson	1956-1959; 1960-1962
Sonny Liston	1962-1964
Cassius Clay (Muhammad Ali)	1964-
Joe Frazier	1970-

Light Heavyweight

Name	*Years Held*
Battling Siki	1922-1923
John Henry Lewis	1935-1939
Archie Moore	1952-1961
Harold Johnson	1961-1963
Jose Torres	1965-1966
Dick Tiger	1966-1968
Bob Foster	1968-

Middleweight

Name	*Years Held*
Tiger Flowers	1926
Gorilla Jones	1931-1932
Sugar Ray Robinson	1951; 1951-1952; 1955-1957; 1957; 1958-1960
Randy Turpin	1951
Dick Tiger	1962-1963; 1965-1966
Emile Griffith	1966-

Welterweight

Name	*Years Held*
Joe Walcott	1901-1904; 1904-1906
Young Jack Thompson	1931
Henry Armstrong	1938-1940
Sugar Ray Robinson	1946-1951
Johnny Bratton	1951
Kid Gavilan	1951-1954
Johnny Saxton	1954-1955; 1956
Virgil Akins	1958
Benny Kid Paret	1960-1961;
Emile Griffith	1963-1966
Curtis Cokes	1966-1969
Jose Napoles	1969-

Lightweight

Name	*Years Held*
Joe Gans	1901-1908
Henry Armstrong	1938-1939
Beau Jack	1942-1944 (New York)
Bob Montgomery	1944-1947 (New York)
Ike Williams	1945-1947 (NBA); 1947-1951
Jimmy Carter	1951-1952; 1952-1954; 1954-1955
Wallace Bud Smith	1955-1956
Joe Brown	1956-1962

Featherweight

Name	*Years Held*
George Dixon	1890-1899
Kid Chocolate	1932-1934 (New York)
Henry Armstrong	1937-1938
Chalky Wright	1941-1942
Sandy Saddler	1948-1949; 1950-1957
Hogan Kid Bassey	1957-1959
Davey Moore	1959-1963

Bantamweight

Name	*Years Held*
George Dixon	1890-1892
Panama Al Brown	1929-1935
George Pace	1940
Harold Dade	1947

TITLE BOUTS OF NEGRO CHAMPIONS

HENRY ARMSTRONG

(Fought early in career as Melody Jackson). Won 58 out of 62 amateur bouts.

Date / Opponent	Result	Rd.
October 29, 1937		
Petey Sarron, New York City	KO	6
May 31, 1938		
Barney Ross, L.I. City, N.Y.	W	15
August 17, 1938		
Lou Ambers, New York City	W	15
November 25, 1938		
*Ceferino Garcia, N.Y.C.	W	15
December 5, 1938		
*Al Manfredo, Cleveland	KO	3
(Armstrong relinquished Featherweight Championship)		
*Welterweight Title Bout.		
August 22, 1939		
Lou Ambers, New York City	L	15
December 11, 1939		
Jimmy Garrison, Cleveland	KO	7
October 4, 1940		
Fritzie Zivic, New York City	L	15
January 17, 1941		
Fritzie Zivic, N.Y.C.	KO by	12

MUHAMMAD ALI

February 25, 1964
Sonny Liston, Miami Beach KO 7
May 25, 1965
Sonny Liston, Lewiston, Me. KO 1
November 22, 1965
Floyd Patterson, Las Vegas KO 12
March 29, 1966
George Chuvalo, Toronto W 15
May 21, 1966
Henry Cooper, London KO 6
August 6, 1966
Brian London, London KO 3
September 10, 1966
Karl Mildenberger, Frankfurt KO 12
November 14, 1966
Cleveland Williams, Houston KO 3
March 8, 1971
Joe Frazier, N.Y.C. L 15
(Loses in Title Bid)

JOE FRAZIER

Born January 12, 1944, Philadelphia, Pa.
Weight 200 lbs., Height 5 ft., 11 in.

March 4, 1968
Manuel Ramos, New York TKO 2
(Wins Portion of Title)
December 1, 1968
Oscar Bonavena, Philadelphia W 15
(Retains Title)
June 23, 1969
Jerry Quarry, New York TKO 7
(Retains Title)
February 16, 1970
Jimmy Ellis, New York TKO 5
(Wins Undisputed Official Title)

March 8, 1971
Muhammad Ali, N.Y.C. W 15
(Retains Title)

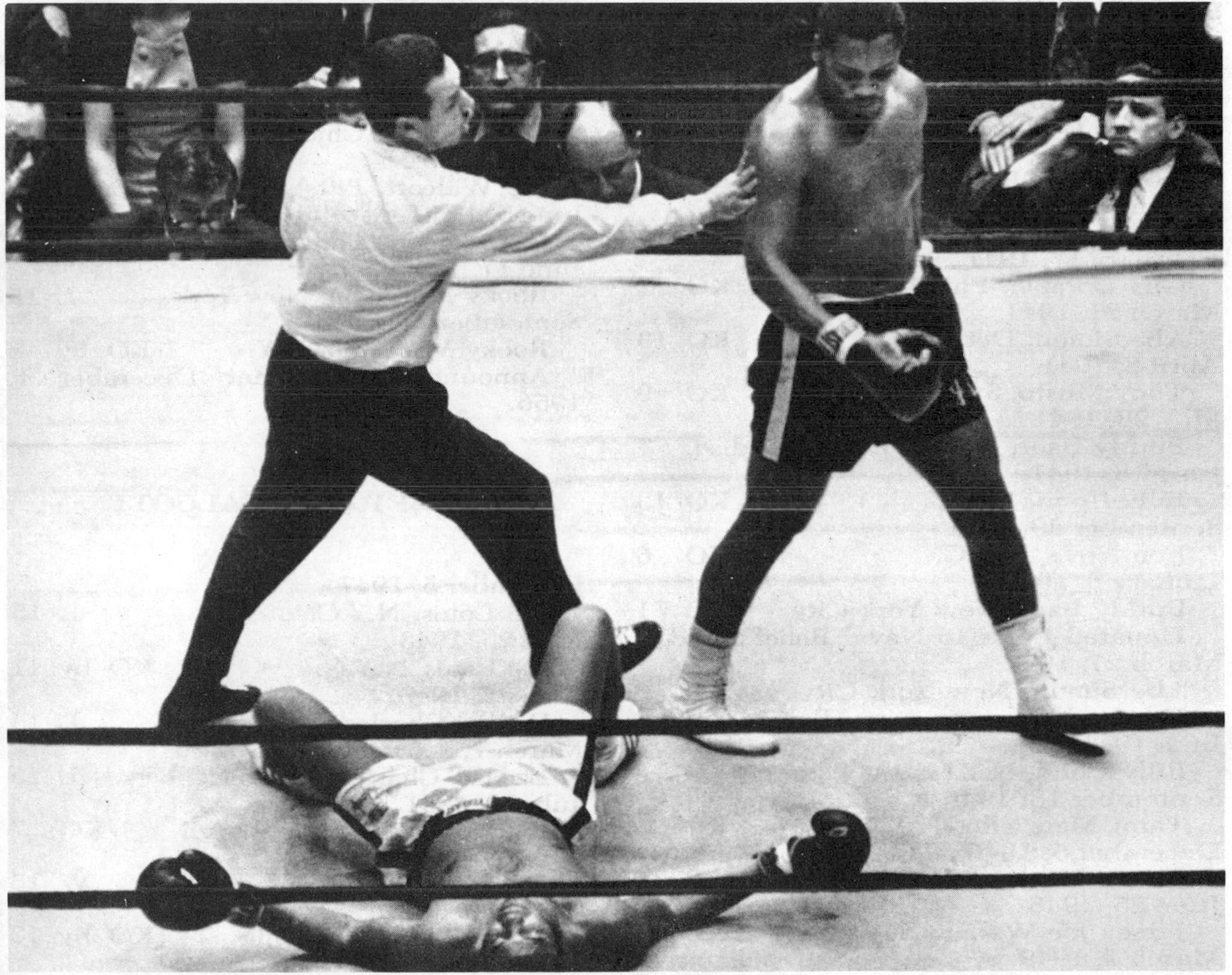

Joe Frazier (l.) looms over Jimmy Ellis after flooring him during a successful 1970 title defense.

JOE LOUIS

June 22, 1937
James J. Braddock, Chicago KO 8
(Won the Heavyweight Championship of the World)
August 30, 1937
Tommy Farr, N.Y.C. W 15
February 23, 1938
Nathan Mann, N.Y.C. KO 3
April 1, 1938
Harry Thomas, Chicago KO 5
June 22, 1938
Max Schmeling, N.Y.C. KO 1
January 25, 1939
John Henry Lewis, N.Y.C. KO 1
April 17, 1939
Jack Roper, Los Angeles KO 1
June 28, 1939
Tony Galento, N.Y.C. KO 4
September 20, 1939
Bob Pastor, Detroit KO 11
February 9, 1940
Arturo Godoy, N.Y.C. W 15
March 29, 1940
Johnny Paychek, N.Y.C. KO 2
June 20, 1940
Arturo Godoy, N.Y.C. KO 8
December 16, 1940
Al McCoy, Boston KO 6
January 31, 1941
Red Burman, N.Y.C. KO 5
February 17, 1941
Gus Dorazio, Philadelphia KO 2
March 21, 1941
Abe Simon, Detroit KO 13
April 8, 1941
Tony Musto, St. Louis KO 9
May 23, 1941
Buddy Baer, Wash., D.C. W disq. 7
June 18, 1941
Billy Conn, N.Y.C. KO 13
September 29, 1941
Lou Nova, N.Y.C. KO 6
January 9, 1942
Buddy Baer, New York City KO 1
(Donated Purse to Naval Relief Fund)
March 27, 1942
Abe Simon, New York City KO 6
(Donated Purse to Army Relief Fund)
June 19, 1946
Billy Conn, N.Y.C. KO 8
September 18, 1946
Tami Mauriello, N.Y.C. KO 1
December 5, 1946
Jersey Joe Walcott, N.Y.C. W 15
June 25, 1948
Jersey Joe Walcott, New York KO 11
March 1, 1949
Louis announced his retirement as undefeated world heavyweight champion.
September 27, 1950
Ezzard Charles, New York L 15

TB	KO	WD	WF	D	LD
71	54	13	1	0	1

LF	KOBY	ND	NC
0	2	0	0

Elected to Boxing Hall of Fame 1954.

EZZARD CHARLES

June 22, 1949
Joe Walcott, Chicago W 15
August 10, 1949
Gus Lesnevich, New York KO 7
October 14, 1949
Pat Valentino, San Francisco KO 8
August 15, 1950
Freddy Beshore, Buffalo KO 14
September 27, 1950
Joe Louis, New York W 15
December 5, 1950
Nick Barone, Cincinnati KO 11
January 12, 1951
Lee Oma, New York KO 10
March 7, 1951
Joe Walcott, Detroit W 15
May 30, 1951
Joey Maxim, Chicago W 15
July 18, 1951
Joe Walcott, Pittsburgh KO by 7
June 5, 1952
Joe Walcott, Philadelphia L 15
June 17, 1954
Rocky Marciano, New York L 15
September 17, 1954
Rocky Marciano, N.Y. KO by 8
Announced retirement December 1, 1956.

JERSEY JOE WALCOTT

December 5, 1947
Joe Louis, N.Y.C. L 15
June 25, 1948
Joe Louis, N.Y.C. KO by 11
June 22, 1949
Ezzard Charles, Chicago L 15
March 7, 1951
Ezzard Charles, Detroit L 15
July 18, 1951
Ezzard Charles, Pittsburgh KO 7
June 5, 1952
Ezzard Charles, Philadelphia W 15
September 23, 1952
Rocky Marciano, Phila. KO by 13
May 15, 1953
Rocky Marciano, Chicago KO by 1
Retired to become a parole officer and a referee.

THE NEGRO IN PROFESSIONAL FOOTBALL

The great black fullback Jim Brown may have rewritten most of the professional record book, but he is far from being the only black man to excel in the game. As of 1968, there were 275 black men playing professional football. In fact, there are more black men playing professional football than any other paying sport in America.

Black men were prominent in professional football from 1919 to 1933, an era roughly spanning the playing careers of Fritz Pollard (Akron Indians) and Joe Lillard of the Chicago Cardinals. Thereafter, they disappeared until 1946, at which time the Los Angeles Rams signed Kenny Washington and Woody Strode. That same year, the Cleveland Browns (then in the All-American Conference) signed Bill Willis and Marion Motley. Motley went on to become one of the great pro fullbacks in the history of the game. Other great backs of this era included Claude "Buddy" Young (New York Yankees); Joe Perry (San Francisco 49ers); and "Tank" Younger (Los Angeles Rams).

In the late fifties-early sixties the premier black performers were offensive stars Lenny Moore (Baltimore Colts) and all-time great Jimmy Brown (Cleveland Browns). Jim Parker, of the Baltimore Colts, received all-star acclaim not only at offensive guard but also at offensive tackle. Terrorizing opponents on defense were top stars Emlen Tunnell (New York Giants); Jim ("Big Daddy") Lipscomb of the Baltimore Colts and Pittsburgh Steelers, and Detroit's Dick (Night Train) Lane.

The late sixties were marked by the retirements of stars Moore and Brown and the emergence of black performers at positions that have traditionally been restricted to white ballplayers. The most notable of these performers are Willie Lanier, all-star middle linebacker of the Kansas City Chiefs (winners of the 1970 Super Bowl); and quarterbacks Jimmy Harris (Buffalo Bills); Marlin Briscoe (Denver Broncos-Buffalo Bills); and Eldridge Dickey (Oakland Raiders). Other black stars performing brilliantly during this period were Brown's successor at Cleveland, Leroy Kelly; the Bears' all-everything, Gale Sayers; wide receivers Charley Taylor (Washington Redskins); Bob Hayes, the former Olympic sprint champion, (Dallas Cowboys); and Art Powell (New York Titans-Oakland Raiders-Buffalo Bills). Top offensive linemen were Bob Brown, considered by many to be the top offensive lineman in the game, (Philadelphia Eagles-Los Angeles Rams); Charlie Cowan (Los Angeles Rams); the Cardinal's Bob Reynolds and Ernie McMillan; Gene Upshaw (Oakland Raiders); Sherman Plunkett (New York Jets); John Thomas (San Francisco 49ers); John Wooten (Cleveland Browns-Washington Redskins); and Rosey Brown, of New York Giant fame.

Top defensive performers, and there were many, included linemen Deacon Jones (L. A. Rams); Rosey Grier (N. Y. Giants-L. A. Rams); Roger Brown (Detroit Lions-L. A. Rams); Lamar Lundy (L. A. Rams); Minnesota's Carl Eller, Alan Page and Jim Marshall; Ernie Ladd (San Diego Chargers-Kansas City Chiefs); Verlon Biggs (New York Jets); Rich Jackson (Denver Broncos); Buck Buchanan (Kansas City Chiefs); and Aaron Brown, also of the Chiefs. Two of the top linebackers, and they are rated on par with any in the game, are, in addition to the Chiefs' Lanier, Dave Robinson (Green Bay Packers) and George Webster (Houston Oilers). Heading the list of top personnel in the defensive secondary is Detroit's Len Barney. Other stalwarts in their teams' pass defenses are Herb Adderly, Bob Jeter, and Willie Wood, all of the Green Bay Packers. The list also includes Mel Renfro (Dallas Cowboys); Carl Lockhart (N. Y. Giants); Jim Johnson and Kermit Alexander, both of the San Francisco 49ers; Erich Barnes (most recently of the Cleveland Browns); Rosey Taylor (Chicago Bears); Johnny Sample (Baltimore Colts-Washington Redskins-Pittsburgh Steelers-New York Jets); Butch Byrd (Buffalo Bills); and a pair of Oakland Raiders, Willie Brown and Dave Grayson.

In 1970 several black stars continued to dominate the game in the newly aligned conferences. There were as yet no star quarterbacks on any of the teams, but the backfields, the lines, and the defensive secondaries of all teams had ample, if not overwhelming, black representation. Players like Ron Johnson of the Giants, George Nock of the Jets, Paul Warfield of the Dolphins — and numerous others — either made their marks for the first time, or starred with teams other than those on which they originally played.

NEGRO PROFESSIONAL FOOTBALL PLAYERS: 1969-70

NFL

Green Bay Packers

Herb Adderly—DB
Lionel Aldridge—DE
Bob Brown—DE
Willie Davis—DE
Marv Fleming—TE
Claudis James—RB
Bob Jeter—DB
Dave Robinson—LB
Elijah Pitts—RB
John Rowser—DB
Ben Wilson—FB
Travis Williams—RB
Willie Wood—DB

Baltimore Colts

Roy Hilton—DE
Lenny Lyles—DB
John Mackey—TE
Willie Richardson—SE
Bubba Smith—DE
Charlie Stukes—DB
Bob Grant—LB
Timmy Brown—RB
John Williams—OT
Ocie Austin—DB

Los Angeles Rams

Dick Bass—RB
Roger Brown—DT
Bernie Casey—FL
Charlie Cowan—OT
Irv Cross—DB
Willie Ellison—B
Deacon Jones—DE
Lamar Lundy—DE
Jim Stiger—RB
Willie Tucker—FL
Clancy Williams—DB

Dallas Cowboys

Phil Clark—DB
Dick Daniels—DB
Cornell Green—DB
Bob Hayes—SE
Mike Johnson—DB
Don Perkins—RB
Jethro Pugh—DE
Mel Renfro—DB
Les Shy—RB
Willie Townes—DT
R. Wright—E
Pettis Norman—TE
D. McDaniels—E

Detroit Lions

Len Barney—DB
Bill Cottrell—C
Mel Farr—RB
Jerry Rush—DE
B. Thompson—DB
Tom Vaughn—DB
Bill Triplett—RB
E. McCullough—FL
John Baker—DE
C. Sanders—TE

Minnesota Vikings

Carl Eller—DE
Clint Jones—RB
E. Mackbee—DB
Jim Marshall—DE
Alan Page—DT
Gene Washington—SE
Oscar Reed—RB
Charley West—DB

Philadelphia Eagles

Bob Brown—OT
Ben Hawkins—FL
Lane Howell—OT
Israel Lang—RB
Al Nelson—DB
Jim Nettles—DB
Nate Ramsey—DB
Harold Wells—LB
Alvin Haymond—DB
Harry Wilson—RB

St. Louis Cardinals

Charlie Bryant—RB
W. Crenshaw—RB
Fred Herson—DE
Ernie McMillan—OT
Bob Reynolds—OT
Johnny Roland—RB
Roy Shivers—RB
Sam Silas—DT
B. Williams—DB
Sid Edwards—RB
Lonnie Sanders—DB
Bob Atkins—DB
Brady Keys—DB
Ernie Clark—LB
M. Lane—RB

Atlanta Falcons

Lee Calland—DB
Ken Reaves—DB
Jerry Simmons—FL
C. Humphrey—DE
C. Dabney—DT
Bill Harris—RB

Cleveland Browns

Erich Barnes—DB
Ben Davis—DB
Ernie Green—RB
C. Harraway—RB
Mike Howell—DB
Carl Ward—DB
Paul Warfield—SE
Walter Johnson—DT
Leroy Kelly—RB
Eppie Barney—FL

New Orleans Saints

John Douglas—DB
John Gilliam—RB
Jim Hester—TE
Don McCall—RB
E. Wheelwright—RB
Jerry Jones—DT
E. Kimbrough—DB

Chicago Bears

Frank Cornish—DT
Curtis Gentry—DB
Dick Gordon—SE
B. McRae—DB
Bob Pickens—OT
Gale Sayers—RB
George Seals—OG
Rosey Taylor—DB
Joe Taylor—DB
Willie Holman—DE
Gary Lyle—RB
Cecil Turner—FL

New York Giants

Homer Jones—SE
Carl Lockhart—DB
Freeman White—TE
Willie Young—OT
Henry Davis—LB
Jim Holifield—DB
McKinley Boston—DE
Ronnie Blye—RB
Willie Williams—DB

Washington Redskins

Gerald Allen—RB
Rickie Harris—DB
Bobby Mitchell—RB
Brig Owens—B
S. Musgrove—DT
Jim Snowden—OT
Charley Taylor—SE
A. D. Whitfield—RB
John Wooten—OG

San Francisco 49ers

K. Alexander—DB

C. Johnson—DT
Jim Johnson—DB
Roland Lakes—DT
Gary Lewis—RB
Mel Phillips—DB
Al Randolph—DB
John Thomas—OG
Bill Tucker—RB

Pittsburgh Steelers

Bill Asbury—RB
John Brown—OT
Bob Wade—RB
Sam Davis—OG
Chuck Hinton—DT
Roy Jefferson—SE
Ben McGee—DE
Ray May—LB
Don Shy—DB
Marv Woodson—DB

AFL

Kansas City Chiefs

Bobby Bell—LB
Aaron Brown—DE
Buck Buchanan—DT
Mike Garrett—RB
Willie Lanier—LB
Curtis McClinton—RB
Willie Mitchell—DB
Gloster Richardson—FL
Noland Smith—FL
Otis Taylor—SE
Goldie Sellers—DB
Al Dotson—DT
Frank Pitts—SE
E. Thomas—DB

Miami Dolphins

Sam Price—RB
Jim Warren—DB
Willie West—DB
D. Westmoreland—DB
F. Woodson—G
M. Lamb—DB

Oakland Raiders

Willie Brown—DB
Clem Daniels—RB
Hewritt Dixon—RB
Dave Grayson—DB
Ike Lassiter—DE
Carleton Oats—DE
Gene Upshaw—OG
Warren Wells—SE
L. Williams—DB
Eldridge Dickey—QB
Arthur Shell—OT

San Diego Chargers

Jim Beauchamp—DB
Leslie Duncan—DB
Gene Foster—RB
Willie Frazier—SE
Kenny Graham—DB
Bob Howard—DB
Brad Hubbert—RB
Houston Ridge—DT
R. Washington—DT
Larry Little—T
Jim Tolbert—DB

New York Jets

Verlon Biggs—DE
Emerson Boozer—RB
Cornell Gordon—DB
Randy Beverly—DB
Johnny Sample—DB
Matt Snell—RB
Jeff Richardson—DT
Earl Christy—RB
Billy Joe—RB

Boston Patriots

Houston Antwine—DT
John Charles—DB
Larry Garron—RB
Jim Hurd—DT
L. Mitchell—DB
Jim Nance—RB
Karl Singer—G
Don Webb—DB
Mel Witt—DE
Willie Porter—RB
Gene Thomas—RB
Aaron Marsh—SE
Daryl Johnson—DB
R. C. Gamble—RB
T. Funches—DE

Houston Oilers

George Allen—OT
Sid Blanks—RB
G. Boyette—LB
W. Campbell—RB
Larry Carwell—DB
Miller Farr—DB
Charlie Frazier—SE
W. K. Hicks—DB
Roy Hopkins—RB
Ken Houston—DB
Alvin Reed—TE
Pete Barnes—LB
Zeke Moore—DB
Willie Parker—DT
George Webster—LB
Lionel Taylor—SE
Elvin Bethea—DG

Denver Broncos

Eric Crabtree—OE
Al Denson—TE
Rich Jackson—DE
Floyd Little—RB
Jimmy Jones—OE
Garrett Ford—RB
Marlin Briscoe—QB
Drake Garrett—DB
Charlie Greer—DB
W. Highsmith—C

Cincinnati Bengals

Warren McVea—RB
Al Beauchamp—LB
Andre White—SE
Tom Smiley—RB
Estes Banks—RB
Ernie Wright—T
Monk Williams—FL
W. L. Jones—DE
S. T. Saffold—SE
Fletcher Smith—DB

Buffalo Bills

Butch Byrd—DB
E. Dubenion—FL
B. Edgerson—DB
John Pitts—FL
Tom Day—DE
Haven Moses—FL
Max Anderson—RB
Ben Gregory—RB

*** Key to abbreviation:**
DB = defensive back; TE = tight end; SE = split end; RB = running back; LB = line backer; FB = fullback; OT = offensive tackle; FL = flanker; DT = defensive tackle; DE = defensive end; G = guard; C = center.

NEGRO NFL RUSHING LEADERS

Year	*Player and Team*	*Yards*
1957	Jim Brown, Cleveland	942
1958	Jim Brown, Cleveland	1527
1959	Jim Brown, Cleveland	1329
1960	Jim Brown, Cleveland	1257
1961	Jim Brown, Cleveland	1408
1963	Jim Brown, Cleveland	1863*
1964	Jim Brown, Cleveland	1446
1965	Jim Brown, Cleveland	1544
1966	Gale Sayers, Chicago	1331
1967	Leroy Kelly, Cleveland	1205
1968	Leroy Kelly, Cleveland	1239

NEGRO NFL SCORING LEADERS

Year	*Player and Team*	*Points Scored*
1958	Jim Brown, Cleveland	108
1964	Lenny Moore, Baltimore	120
1965	Gale Sayers, Chicago	132
1968	Leroy Kelly, Cleveland	120

* NFL record

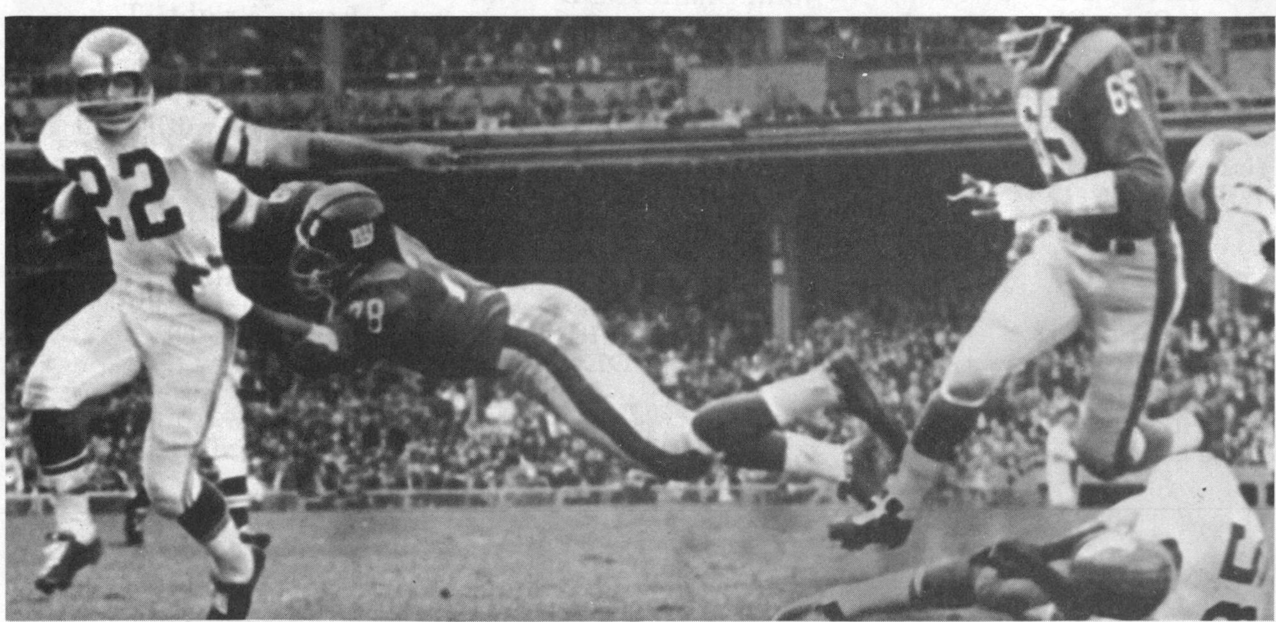

Speedster Timmy Brown (l.) was once one of the chief running threats of the Philadelphia Eagle attack. Here, he is about to be brought down by Lane Howell of the New York Giants.

NEGRO NFL RECEIVING LEADERS

Year	*Player and Team*	*No. Caught*
1962	Bobby Mitchell, Washington	72
1966	Charley Taylor, Washington	72
1967	Charley Taylor, Washington	70
1968	Clifton McNeil, San Francisco	71

THE NEGRO IN PROFESSIONAL BASKETBALL

The first black man to play professional basketball in the National Basketball Association (NBA) was Chuck Cooper, a 6′6″ forward who was signed by the Boston Celtics in 1950, and remained with the team for the next six years. Former Harlem Globetrotter star Nat "Sweetwater" Clifton joined the pro ranks the same year as Cooper, playing with the New York Knickerbockers.

Within the decade, many of the top players in both leagues were black men. Boston had Bill Russell, K. C. Jones, and Sam Jones. New York could boast of Ray Felix and Willie Naulls. Minneapolis

Dick Barnett of the New York Knickerbockers shooting over the head of Wilt Chamberlain in the 1970 championship playoffs won by the Knicks.

looked to Elgin Baylor as one of its mainstays. By 1964, most teams had five or six Negroes each, many of them occupying star status, including the incomparable Wilt Chamberlain, holder of almost all of professional basketball's scoring records, and Oscar Robertson, at 6'5" regarded as the best "small" man in the game.

The coming of the late sixties was accompanied by a rash of new and highly talented black ballplayers. Heading the list was Lew Alcindor, three-time All-American at UCLA. In addition to leading his team to three NCAA titles, Alcindor was twice chosen as the top collegiate player. After completion of his collegiate career, Alcindor signed a contract with the Milwaukee Bucks of the NBA calling for 1.4 million dollars.

In his first season (1969-70) Alcindor led the Bucks to a second-place finish in the NBA's tough Eastern Division. Other black ballplayers competing for headlines were San Diego's Elvin Hayes, third all-time college scorer and winner of the NBA scoring title in just his rookie year (1968-69); defensive genius Walt Frazier of the New York Knicks along with teammate Willis Reed (NBA MVP for the 1969-70 season); Wes Unseld, NBA MVP in 1968-69, his rookie season, for leading Baltimore to the Eastern Division title; Earl Monroe, Unseld's teammate in the backcourt; and last, but by no means least, the great Connie Hawkins, who after years of being banned from competing in the NBA was finally given his chance in 1969-70, playing for the Phoenix Suns.

Most basketball experts agree that at least four black men belong with greatest players yet produced in the game: Wilt Chamberlain, Bill Russell, Elgin Baylor, and Oscar Robertson.

NEGRO SCORING LEADERS IN THE NBA

Year	*Player and Team*	*Points Scored*	*Average*
1959	Wilt Chamberlain, Philadelphia Warriors	2707	29.2
1960	Wilt Chamberlain, Philadelphia Warriors	3033	37.6
1961	Wilt Chamberlain, Philadelphia Warriors	4029	38.4
1962	Wilt Chamberlain, San Francisco Warriors	3586	50.4
1963	Wilt Chamberlain, San Francisco Warriors	2948	44.8
1964	Wilt Chamberlain, Philadelphia 76ers	2534	36.9
1965	Wilt Chamberlain, Philadelphia 76ers	2649	33.5
1967	Dave Bing, Detroit	2142	27.1
1968	Elvin Hayes, San Diego	2327	28.4

NEGRO REBOUNDING LEADERS IN THE NBA

Player and Team	*Year*	*Rebounds*
Maurice Stokes, Rochester	56-57	1256
Bill Russell, Boston	57-58	1564
Bill Russell, Boston	58-59	1612
Wilt Chamberlain, Philadelphia	59-60	1941
Wilt Chamberlain, Philadelphia	60-61	2149
Wilt Chamberlain, Philadelphia	61-62	2052
Wilt Chamberlain, San Francisco	62-63	1946

Bill Russell, Boston	63-64	1930
Bill Russell, Boston	64-65	1878
Wilt Chamberlain, Philadelphia	65-66	1943
Wilt Chamberlain, Philadelphia	66-67	1957
Wilt Chamberlain, Philadelphia	67-68	1952
Wilt Chamberlain; Los Angeles	68-69	1712

NEGRO ASSIST LEADERS IN THE NBA

Player and Team	*Year*	*Assists*
Oscar Robertson, Cincinnati	60-61	690
Oscar Robertson, Cincinnati	61-62	899
Guy Rodgers, San Francisco	62-63	825
Oscar Robertson, Cincinnati	63-64	868
Oscar Robertson, Cincinnati	64-65	861
Oscar Robertson, Cincinnati	65-66	847
Guy Rodgers, Chicago	66-67	908
Wilt Chamberlain, Philadelphia	67-68	702
Oscar Robertson, Cincinnati	68-69	772

THE NEGRO IN TRACK AND FIELD

The number of Negro stars produced in track and field is such that the compilation of a roster of stars quickly becomes something approaching a herculean task. In view of this fact, we have decided instead to provide a number of lists containing the names of Negro World, Olympic and American record holders. (Biographies of Jesse Owens, Rafer Johnson and Wilma Rudolph are available on pages *656*, *654*, and *660* respectively.)

AMERICAN TRACK AND FIELD RECORDS HELD BY NEGRO WOMEN

Holder	*Distance or Event*	*Time, Height or Distance*	*Year*
Wilma Rudolph	100-Meter Dash	11.2	1961
Wilma Rudolph	200-Meter Dash	22.9	1960
Rosie Bonds	80-Meter Low Hurdles	10.8	1964
Mildred McDaniel	Running High Jump	5′ 9½″	1956
Willye White	Running Broad Jump	21′ 6″	1964
Earlene Brown	Four-Kilogram Shot Put	54′ 9″	1960
Earlene Brown	Discus Throw	176′ 10½″	1960

Wilma Rudolph displays the three gold medals she won in the 1960 Olympics.

WORLD TRACK AND FIELD RECORDS HELD BY AMERICAN NEGROES

Athlete	Distance or Event	Time or Distance	Year
Bob Hayes	100 Yards	9.1	1963
Jim Hines	100 Yards	9.1	1967
Charlie Greene	100 Yards	9.1	1967
John Carlos	100 Yards	9.1	1969
Tommie Smith	220 Yds. (turn)	20.0	1966
Tommie Smith	220 Yds. (strgh. way)	19.5	1966
Curtis Mills	440 Yards	44.7	1969
Charlie Greene	100 Meters	9.9	1968
Jim Hines	100 Meters	9.9	1968
Ronnie Ray Smith	100 Meters	9.9	1968

Tommie Smith	200 Meters (turn)	19.8	1968
Tommie Smith	200 Meters (strgh. way)	19.5	1966
Lee Evans	400 Meters	43.8	1968
Charlie Greene Mel Pender Ronnie Ray Smith Jim Hines	400 Meter Relay	38.2	1968
Earl McCullough O. J. Simpson Lennox Miller Lee Evans	440 Yard Relay	38.6	1967
Tommie Smith Lee Evans	800 Meter Relay	1:22.1	1967
Tommie Smith Vince Matthews	880 Yard Relay	1:22.1	1967
Ron Freeman Larry James Lee Evans	1,600 Meter Relay	2:56.1	1968
Lennox Yearwood Kent Bernard Edwin Roberts Wendell Mottley	1 Mile Relay	3:02.8	1966
Lee Calhoun	120 Yd. High Hurdles	13.2	1960
Earl McCullough	120 Yd. High Hurdles	13.2	1967
Erv Hall	120 Yd. High Hurdles	13.2	1969
Willie Davenport	120 Yd. High Hurdles	13.2	1969
Lee Calhoun	110 Met. High Hurdles	13.2	1960
Earl McCullough	110 Met. High Hurdles	13.2	1967
Willie Davenport	110 Met. High Hurdles	13.2	1909
Bob Beamon	Long Jump	29′ 2¼″	1968
Otis Davis (team member)	1600-Meter Relay (each runner does 400 meters)	3.02.2	1960
Wilma Rudolph	100-Meter Run	11.2	1961
Wilma Rudolph	200-Meter Run	22.9	1960
Willye White Ernestine Pollards Vivian Brown Wilma Rudolph	400-Meter Relay (each runner does 100 meters)	44.3	1961

TRACK AND FIELD ACHIEVEMENTS OF NEGRO U.S. OLYMPIC TEAM MEMBERS*

Athlete	*Distance or Event*	*Result & Winning Times, Distances*	*Place and Year*
George C. Poag	200-Meter Hurdles	Third	St. Louis, 1904
George C. Poag	400-Meter Hurdles	Third	St. Louis, 1904
J. B. Taylor (*member of team*)	1600-Meter Relay (*Each runner does 400 meters.*)	First—3.29.4	London, 1908
Dehart Hubbard	Running Broad Jump	First—24′ 5⅛″	Paris, 1924
Edward Gourdin	Running Broad Jump	Second—23′ 10⅞″	Paris, 1924
Eddie Tolan	100-Meter Dash	First—10.3 (*Olympic and world record*)	Los Angeles, 1932
Ralph Metcalfe	100-Meter Dash	Second—10.3	Los Angeles, 1932

* Arranged by year from 1904 to 1964.

Eddie Tolan	200-Meter Dash	First—21.2	Los Angeles, 1932
Ralph Metcalfe	200-Meter Dash	Third—21.5	Los Angeles, 1932
Edward Gordon	Running Broad Jump	First—25′ ¾″	Los Angeles, 1932
Jesse Owens	100-Meter Dash	First—10.3 (*Ties Olympic and world record*)	Berlin, 1936
Ralph Metcalfe	100-Meter Dash	Second—10.4	Berlin, 1936
Jesse Owens	200-Meter Dash	First—20.7 (*Olympic record*)	Berlin, 1936
Matthew Robinson	200-Meter Dash	Second—21.1	Berlin, 1936
Archie Williams	400-Meter Run	First—46.5	Berlin, 1936
James DuValle	400-Meter Run	Second—46.8	Berlin, 1936
John Woodruff	800-Meter Run	First—1.52.9	Berlin, 1936
Fritz Pollard, Jr.	110-Meter Hurdles	Third—14.4	Berlin, 1936
Cornelius Johnson	High Jump	First—6′ 8″ (*Olympic record*)	Berlin, 1936
Jesse Owens	Running Broad Jump	First—26′ 5-5/16″ (*Olympic and world record*)	Berlin, 1936
Jesse Owens Ralph Metcalfe (*members of team*)	400-Meter Relay (*Each runner does 100 meters.*)	First—39.8 (*World record*)	Berlin, 1936
Harrison Dillard	100-Meter Dash	First—10.3	London, 1948
Norwood Ewell	100-Meter Dash	Second—10.4	London, 1948
Norwood Ewell	200-Meter Dash	First—21.1	London, 1948
Mal Whitfield	400-Meter Run	Third—46.9	London, 1948
Willie Steele	Running Broad Jump	First—25′ 8-1/16″	London, 1948
Herbert Douglass	Running Broad Jump	Third—24′ 9″	London, 1948
Lorenzo Wright	Running Broad Jump	Fourth—24′ 9″	London, 1948
Harrison Dillard Norwood Ewell Lorenzo Wright (*members of team*)	400-Meter Relay (*Each runner does 100 meters.*)	First—40.6	London, 1948
Mal Whitfield (*member of team*)	1600-Meter Relay (*Each runner does 400 meters.*)	First—3.10.4	London, 1948
Audrey Patterson	Women's 200-Meter Dash	Third—25.2	London, 1948
Alice Coachman	Women's High Jump	First—5′ 6¼″	London, 1948
Andrew Stanfield	200-Meter Dash	First—20.7	Helsinki, 1952
James Gathers	200-Meter Dash	Third—20.8	Helsinki, 1952
Ollie Matson	400-Meter Run	Third—46.8	Helsinki, 1952
Mal Whitfield	400-Meter Run	Sixth—47.8	Helsinki, 1952
Mal Whitfield	800-Meter Run	First—1.49.2 (*Olympic record*)	Helsinki, 1952
Reginald Pearman	800-Meter Run	Sixth	Helsinki, 1952
Harrison Dillard	110-Meter Hurdles	First—13.7 (*Olympic record*)	Helsinki, 1952
Jerome Biffle	Running Broad Jump	First—24′ 10″	Helsinki, 1952
Meredith Gourdine	Running Broad Jump	Second—24′ 8-7/16″	Helsinki, 1952
Harrison Dillard Andrew Stanfield (*members of team*)	400-Meter Relay (*Each runner does 100 meters.*)	First—40.1	Helsinki, 1952
Ollie Matson Mal Whitfield (*members of team*)	1600-Meter Relay (*Each runner does 400 meters.*)	Second—3.04.1	Helsinki, 1952
Bill Miller	Javelin	Second—237′ 8¾″	Helsinki, 1952

Milton Campbell	Decathlon	Second—6,975 points	Helsinki, 1952
Mae Faggs	Women's 100-Meter Dash	Sixth	Helsinki, 1952
Catherine Hardy Mae Faggs Barbara Jones (*members of team*)	Women's 400-Meter Relay (*Each runner does 100 meters.*)	First—45.9 (*Olympic and world record*)	Helsinki, 1952
Andrew Stanfield	200-Meter Dash	Second--20.7	Melbourne, 1956
Charles Jenkins	400-Meter Run	First—46.7	Melbourne, 1956
Lou Jones	400-Meter Run	Fifth—48.1	Melbourne, 1956
Arnold Sowell	800-Meter Run	Fourth—1.48.3	Melbourne, 1956
Lee Calhoun	110-Meter Hurdles	First—13.5	Melbourne, 1956
Josh Culbreath	400-Meter Hurdles	Third	Melbourne, 1956
Charles Dumas	High Jump	First—6′ 11¼″ (*Olympic record*)	Melbourne, 1956
Gregory Bell	Running Broad Jump	First—25′ 8¼″	Melbourne, 1956
Ira Murchison (*member of team*)	400-Meter Relay (*Each runner does 100 meters.*)	First—39.5 (*Olympic record*)	Melbourne, 1956
Lou Jones Charles Jenkins (*members of team*)	1600-Meter Relay (*Each runner does 400 meters.*)	First—3.04.8	Melbourne, 1956
Milton Campbell	Decathlon	First—7,937 points	Melbourne, 1956
Rafer Johnson	Decathlon	Second—	Melbourne, 1956

Rafer Johnson competes in the 100-meter dash during the decathlon event which he won at the 1956 Olympics in Melbourne.

Athlete	*Distance or Event*	*Result & Winning Times, Distances*	*Place and Year*
		7,587 points	
Mildred McDaniel	Women's High Jump	First—5′ 9¼″ (*Olympic and world record*)	Melbourne, 1956
Willye White	Women's Running Broad Jump	Second—19′ 11¾″	Melbourne, 1956
Mae Faggs Margaret Matthews Isabelle Daniels Wilma Rudolph (*members of team*)	Women's 400-Meter Relay (*Each runner does 100 meters.*)	Third—45.4	Melbourne, 1956
Les Carney	200-Meter Dash	Second—20.6	Rome, 1960
Lee Calhoun	110-Meter Hurdles	First—13.8	Rome, 1960
Willie May	110-Meter Hurdles	Second—13.8	Rome, 1960
Hayes Jones	110-Meter Hurdles	Third—14.0	Rome, 1960
John Thomas	High Jump	First—7′ ¼″	Rome, 1960
Ralph Boston	Running Broad Jump	First—26′ 7¾″ (*Olympic record*)	Rome, 1960
Irv Roberson	Running Broad Jump	Second—26′ 7⅜″	Rome, 1960
Ira Davis	Hop, Step and Jump	Fourth—53′ 11″	Rome, 1960
Otis Davis (*member of team*)	1600-Meter Relay (*Each runner does 400 meters.*)	First—3.02.2	Rome, 1960
Rafer Johnson	Decathlon	First—8,392 points (*Olympic record*)	Rome, 1960
Wilma Rudolph	Women's 100-Meter Dash	First—11.0 (*Olympic record*)	Rome, 1960
Wilma Rudolph	Women's 200-Meter Dash	First—24.0	Rome, 1960

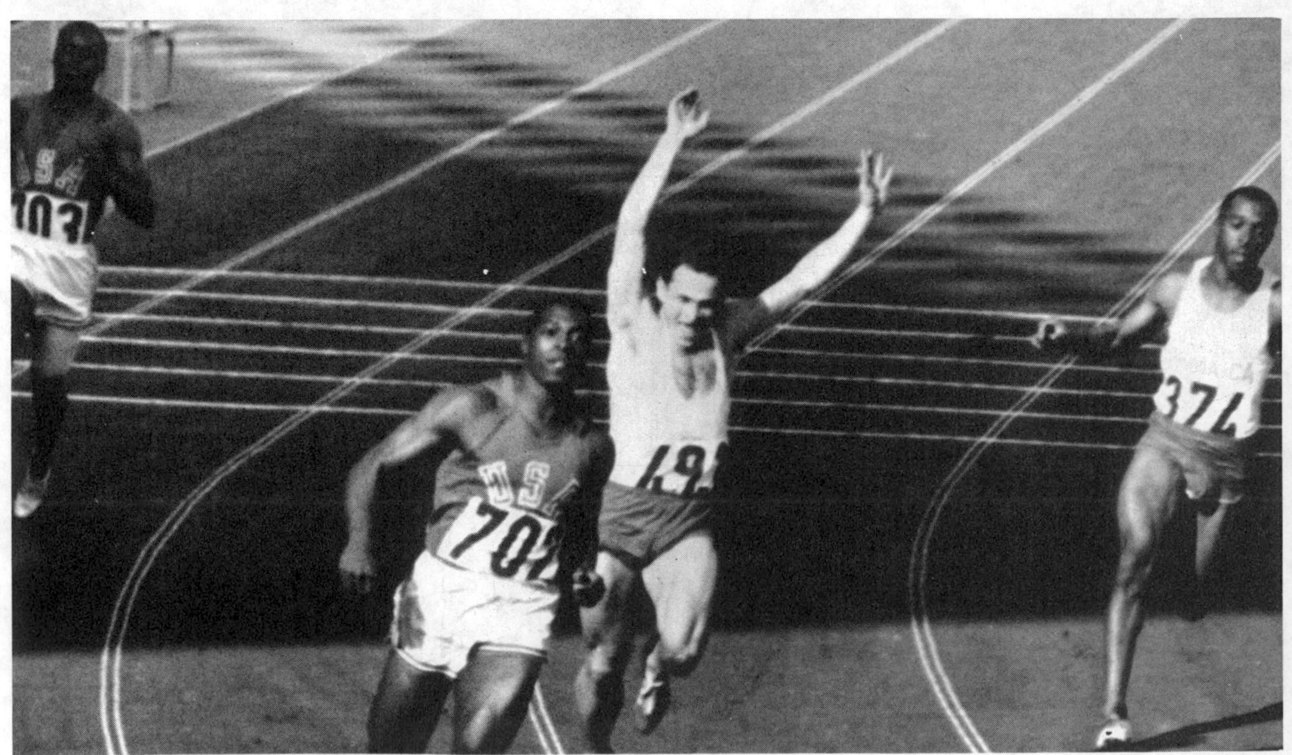

Bob Hayes races to victory in the 100-meter semi-finals at Tokyo. His time was 9.9.

Athlete	Distance or Event	Result & Winning Times, Distances	Place and Year
Earlene Brown	Women's Shotput	Third—53′ 10⅜″	Rome, 1960
Martha Judson Lucinda Williams Barbara Jones Wilma Rudolph (*members of team*)	Women's 400-Meter Relay (*Each runner does 100 meters.*)	First—44.5 (*Olympic and world record*)	Rome, 1960
Robert Hayes	100-Meter Dash	First—9.9 (*World record disallowed—aiding wind*)	Tokyo, 1964
Mel Pender	100-Meter Dash	Seventh—10.4	Tokyo, 1964
Henry Carr	200-Meter Dash	First—20.3	Tokyo, 1964
Paul Drayton	200-Meter Dash	Second—20.5	Tokyo, 1964
Ulis Williams	400-Meter Run	Fifth—46.0	Tokyo, 1964
Hayes Jones	110-Meter Hurdles	First—13.6	Tokyo, 1964
Paul Drayton Robert Hayes (*members of team*)	400-Meter Relay (*Each runner does 100 meters.*)	First—39.0 (*Olympic and world record*)	Tokyo, 1964
John Thomas	High Jump	Second— 7′ 1¾″	Tokyo, 1964
John Rambo	High Jump	Third—7′ 1″	Tokyo, 1964
Ralph Boston	Running Broad Jump	Second—26′ 4″	Tokyo, 1964
Ira Davis	Hop, Step and Jump	Fifth—52′ 1¾″	Tokyo, 1964
Wyomia Tyus	Women's 100-Meter Dash	First—11.4	Tokyo, 1964
Edith McGuire	Women's 100-Meter Dash	Second—11.4	Tokyo, 1964
Marilyn White	Women's 100-Meter Dash	Third—11.6	Tokyo, 1964
Rosie Bonds	Women's 80-Meter Hurdles	Eighth—10.8	Tokyo, 1964
Willye White Wyomia Tyus Marilyn White Edith McGuire (*members of team*)	Women's 400-Meter Relay (*Each runner does 100 meters.*)	Second—43.9	Tokyo, 1964
Eleanor Montgomery	Women's High Jump	Eighth—5′ 7¾″	Tokyo, 1964
Willye White	Women's Running Broad Jump	Twelfth—19′ 8¾″	Tokyo, 1964
Earlene Brown	Women's Shotput	Twelfth—48′ 6¾″	Tokyo, 1964

BLACK WINNERS AT THE 1968 OLYMPICS*

Athlete	Distance or Event	Time or Distance	Place
Jim Hines	100 Meter Dash	9.9	Mexico City, Mexico
Tommie Smith	200 Meter Dash	19.8	Mexico City, Mexico
Lee Evans	400 Meter Dash	43.8	Mexico City, Mexico
Willie Davenport	110 Meter Hurdles	13.3	Mexico City, Mexico
Charlie Greene Melvin Pender Ronnie Ray Smith Jim Hines	400 Meter Relay	38.2	Mexico City, Mexico
Vincent Matthews	1,600 Meter Relay	2:56.1	Mexico City, Mexico

(restricted to gold medal winners)

Athlete	Distance or Event	Time or Distance	Place
Ron Freeman			
Larry James			
Lee Evans			
Bob Beamon	Long Jump	29 2¼″	Mexico City, Mexico
Wyomia Tyus	Women's 100 Meters	11.0	Mexico City, Mexico
Madeline Manning	Women's 800 Meters	2:00.9	Mexico City, Mexico

THE BLACK GOLFER

In the late '60's, golfers Lee Elder and Pete Brown began to challenge Charlie Sifford as the most successful black pro playing on the PGA circuit. Sifford was the first black golfer to win admission to the Professional Golfers Association. His most successful money-winning year was in 1967 when he earned $57,000, largely on the heels of a spectacular triumph in the Hartford Open. This occurred a full 10 years after he had become the first black man to capture a nationwide tournament, the Long Beach Open in which he defeated Eric Monti in a sudden-death playoff. Sifford slipped to $33,000 in 1968, the year Lee Elder made a rush at top prize money in the American Classic at Akron, Ohio. Playing against one of the all-time greats, Jack Nicklaus, Elder finished the regulation eight under par, at 280. A sudden death playoff, carried on nationwide television, pitted him against Nicklaus, whom he played stroke for stroke until the fifth hole, at which point Elder missed a putt and had to settle for a little over $12,000, rather than first-prize money of $25,000. Still, by year's end, Elder finished the tour with earnings of more than $31,000.

Another up-and-coming black golfer, Pete Brown, was the third leading black money winner in 1968 with some $8,300. Brown came from nowhere three years later to capture the San Diego Open, winning $30,000 in a sudden-death playoff against Britain's Tony Jacklin.

The top woman golfer, at least judging from her numerous national titles over the past decade, is Ethel Funches, who won the 1968 championship at Lanston Golf Course in Washington, D.C. Althea Gibson, the former tennis great, tried golfing for a while, but performed indifferently, winning only $2,700 in 1968.

Pete Brown, winner of the 1970 Andy Williams San Diego Open, embraced by his wife

THE NEGRO IN HORSE RACING

From the time of the first running of the Kentucky Derby in 1875 until 1911, the last year a black jockey (Jess Conley) rode in the event, black riders were featured performers in the gala pageantry which surrounded the annual Churchill Downs classic. No less than 11 black jockeys have won a total of 15 Kentucky Derbies in the history of the event. The race was every bit as glamorous and thrilling in its early days at it is now; audiences were as tense and as animated; the clubhouse, the grandstand, the lawns, the flower beds, the track itself were all meticulously and irreproachably prepared for the rush of excitement that was to grip thousands of onlookers for the race's few, but unforgettable, moments. The stable scene was dominated not only by black jockeys, but by black trainers, exercise riders, grooms and stable boys—a whole cadre of skilled black racetrack people without whom the glorious and magical atmosphere of uproarious and suspenseful competition would never have developed. These were men more preoccupied with the attraction of sport than with the blandishments of money. They cherished the moment; they loved the horses; victory inspired them, even as defeat crushed them. Two great black jockeys towered over their contemporaries: Isaac Murphy (the Colored Archer), and Jimmy Winkfield.

Except for Murphy (three-time winner of the Derby) and Winkfield (twice winner of the same racing classic), few of the early black jockeys who once dominated the riding end of the sport are known to the public. One of the reasons is that jockeys were not generally identified in the programs of the early days. Another is that, as the sport was transformed into a big business with staggeringly lucrative purses for owners and high annual income for jockeys, black aspirants were gradually phased into the more menial aspects of turf life, shunted aside by a base professionalism which completely undercut their long and distinguished association with the sport.

Winkfield might possibly have competed with Murphy for top honors as the leading black jockey of all time, but the wiry little Kentuckian left the United States to ride in Europe, where he won such prominent races as the Polish Derby, the Grand Prix de Baden, the Emperor's Purse, the Moscow Derby and the Russian Derby. At the time of the Russian Revolution, he was reportedly making $100,000 a year, but was forced to flee to France in the wake of the upheaval. Winkfield continued to race on the Continent, winning several important races in France, Italy, and Spain. In 1930, after amassing a total of 2,600 winners on tracks all over the globe, Winkfield re-

In recent years, few black jockeys have been found at the major race tracks. Before the turn of the century, however, most racehorses were ridden by black jockeys.

tired, built a stable near Paris, and bred a string of successful racehorses until he was driven out by the Nazis in World War Two. In 1953, Winkfield returned to Maisons-Lafitte, and was able to remodel his stable and remain in business.

Winkfield was not the first black man to win the derby. That feat was accomplished by Oliver Lewis who rode his mount (Aristides) to victory in the first running of the event in 1875, during which 14 of the 15 starters in the race were ridden by black mounts.

In recent years, the best-known black jockey has been Bob McCurdy, a native of Atlantic City. McCurdy posted over 100 victories in 1963, and earned over $60,000 at his profession. He also won the jockey championship at the Garden State Park meet with 27 wins. He is the first black man to ride at Tropical Park, Florida. Interviewed regarding the potential for black jockeys in the business today, McCurdy claims "the sport is wide open for Negroes now." Those who have seen him ride like his style and his attitude. One trainer feels it is all a matter of "good home training." McCurdy will succeed, says George Howell, "because he has had a good upbringing."

Still, as late as 1967, the New York *Times* wrote: "In recent years, Negro jockeys, could be counted on the fingers of one hand."

BLACK WINNERS OF THE KENTUCKY DERBY (1875-1895)

Jockey	*Mount*	*Year*
Oliver Lewis	Aristides	1875
Billy Walker	Baden Baden	1877
Barrett Lewis	Fonso	1880
Babe Hurd	Apollo	1882
Isaac Murphy	Buchanan	1884
Erskine Henderson	Joe Cotton	1885
Isaac Lewis	Montrose	1887
Isaac Murphy	Riley	1890
Isaac Murphy	Kingman	1891
Alonzo Clayton	Azra	1892
James Perkins	Halma	1895

THE BLACK TENNIS PLAYER

The most outstanding black tennis stars have been Arthur Ashe and Althea Gibson. Miss Gibson, winner of both the Wimbledon and U.S. championships in 1957 and 1958 while in her early 30's, was the first black athlete to win a major tennis title. At that time, Arthur Ashe was a teenager who was playing in the semi-finals of the under-15 division of the National Junior Championships, which he won in 1960 and 1961. Ashe's most successful year on the court was in 1968 when, as a member of the U.S. Davis Cup Team, he guided the United States to its first championship in five years. Ashe won every match in the Cup preliminaries, showing particularly impressive form against Premjit Lall and Ramathan Krishnan of India. The U.S. thus qualified to play Australia, and Ashe, despite an ailing elbow, won the opening match against Ray Ruffels in four sets. He did not play again until the final match, by which time the U.S. had already clinched the crown. (Ashe lost the final to Bill Bowery, 2-6, 6-3, 11-9, 8-6).

Even more impressive was Ashe's sensational showing in the U.S. Open Tournament, a competition featuring the world's best players, regardless of professional or amateur standing. Ashe, an amateur, defeated Tom Okker of Holland in a gruelling five-set match, thus earning his rightful plaudits as the world's top amateur player. Ashe won other tournaments that year, including the U.S. amateur title. He then finished his active tour with the Army, and joined the Urban League as a community organizer.

There has been a long tradition of "Negro" tennis much the same as has existed in baseball. One black player, Jimmie McDaniel, once played U.S. Singles champion Don Budge, and was easily defeated by him, although inexperience and lack of opportunity to play in championship competition were clearly factors influencing the outcome. The first Negro to play in the U.S. Lawn Tennis Singles Championships, Dr. Reginald S. Weir, did not appear until 1948.

THE NEGRO IN WRESTLING

Relatively few Negroes have claimed world championships in professional wrestling, but this sport is not without its Negro participants. Jack Claybourne, one of the earlier successful Negro pro wrestlers, did lay claim to the Negro world's heavyweight title by pinning Rufus Jones in 1943. Seven years later, Don Blackman was reported to be the only Negro to hold a world's wrestling title, that of light-heavyweight champion. Woody Strode, the football star turned Hollywood actor, was also active for a time as a wrestler, as were Bobo Brazil, Shag Thomas, Frank James and "Black Panther" Mitchell. Negro women also perform in this sport from time to time.

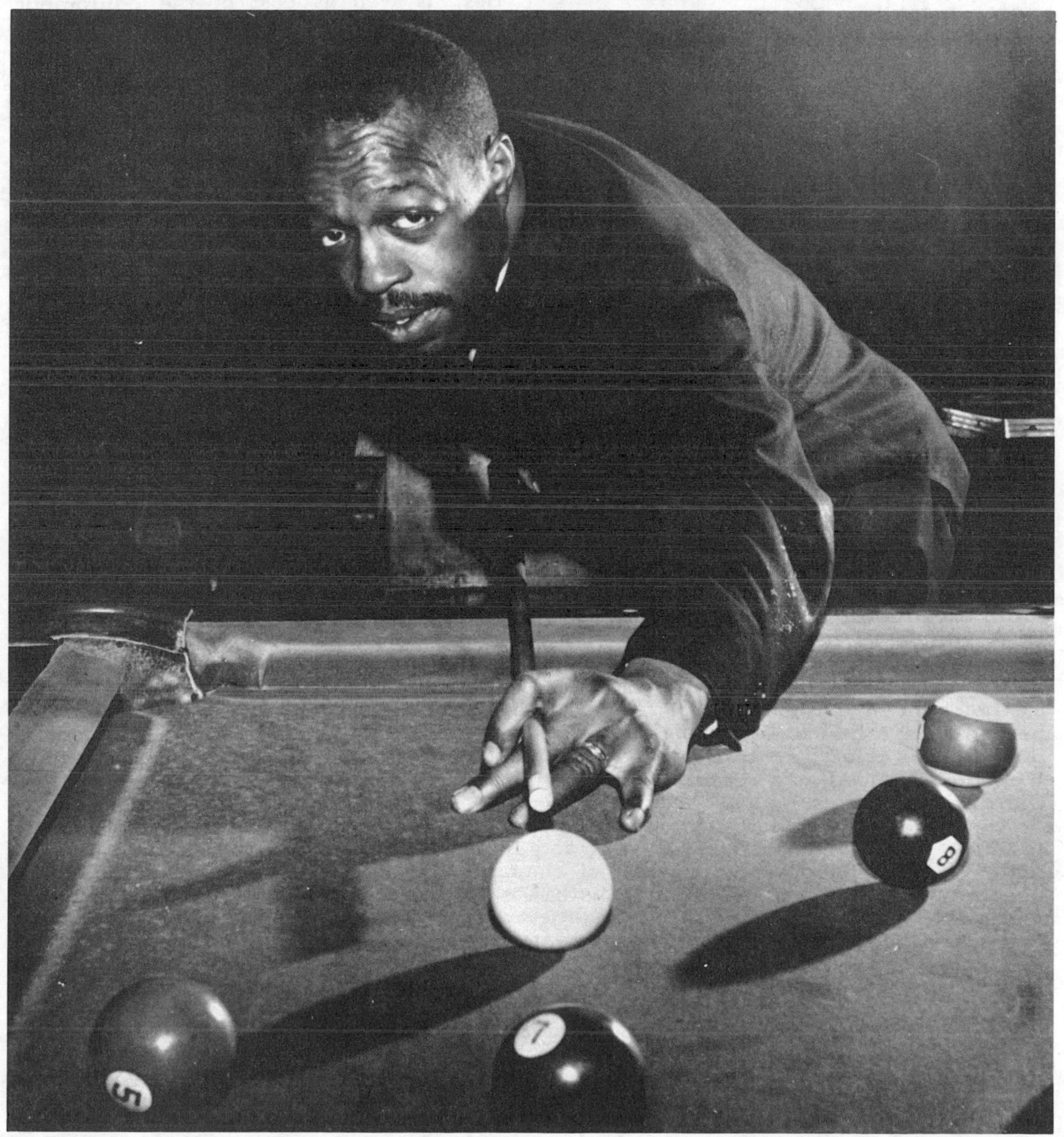

Cicero Murphy, the best of the black billiard performers

MISCELLANEOUS SPORTS

Other competitive sports which deserve some mention include swimming and bowling, although Negroes have not achieved any great prominence in either of these.

A National Negro Bowling Association was established in Detroit in 1939, two years before the first Negro bowling alley was opened in Cleveland. By the early 1960's, J. Wilbert Sims had won for himself a solid reputation as a topflight Negro bowler, but his performance could not be matched by too many other Negro bowlers. Clearly, "separate competition" has contributed in part to the Negro's "separate development" in this sport.

Swimming exhibits a similar pattern, inasmuch as it has been difficult for Negroes to find suitable recreational facilities in which to develop their skills. Lack of good coaching, the difficulty in finding standard-sized pools nearby, and the consequent inability to develop a systematic method of training are all related factors which must be taken into account in any attempted evaluation of the Negro's performance in swimming.

Hockey is another sport in which Negroes have not yet come to the fore. At the present time, there are no Negroes on any of the six teams in the National Hockey League, despite the fact that some Negroes have managed to play minor league hockey. Again, access to the facilities, as well as cost of the equipment, must be cited as contributory factors for the Negro's non-participation.

Only one Negro, Cicero Murphy, has ever competed for the world's billiards championship. Murphy defeated his first rival in the 1965 playoffs by a 150-32 count, and lost to his second opponent, 150-105. Now in his early 30's, he seems destined to win permanent rating among the world's best in this sport.

Negroes are notably absent in any large numbers from a host of other sports which are conventionally associated with higher-income groups, including boating, big-game hunting, fishing and, in some cases, even camping.

Outstanding Black Athletes

It is possible to discuss the sports specialties of the American Negro largely in terms of two causes: economics, and the desire for individual recognition. In those sports which are generally fostered in more affluent circles—such as golf, tennis, or even swimming—the Negro has not produced many outstanding performers. (There are some exceptions, of course, like Althea Gibson and Arthur Ashe in tennis, as well as PGA golf pro Charlie Sifford, but they are admittedly few and far between at the moment.) Conversely, in sports such as boxing, basketball and track which in varying degrees are accessible even to the poorest ghetto child, the Negro has made progress to the point of dominance. The Negro engaging in these sports has often found that his feats have had to be prodigious in order for him to gain the kind of attention he desires. (As related to track, this—along with the harsh nutritional facts of life—may well be advanced as a reason for his having chosen the more glamorous sprints over the distance events.)

Apart from the underlying causes for the Negro's performance in sports, however, the fact remains that he has a vital and impressive history in this area of human endeavor—one filled with long lists of champions and record holders. Negro "stars" become too numerous to catalog, with the result that we are compelled, in this section, to include only those personalities who must be rated "superstars"* in their respective fields. They are household names to the widest public, and must stand as being representative of the hundreds of other performers whom it is impossible to include. In addition, they are almost all 20th-century figures.

Since we are concerning ourselves with contemporary athletes, it is perhaps important to pause momentarily and give some attention to the place of the American Negro in organized sports from a historical point of view. In earliest days, although no records were kept, it is safe to assume that Negroes indulged in the conventional athletic activities native to the society in which they lived. It is significant, however, that the first sport in which they are known to have come to the fore was in boxing.

In 1777, a British officer took back to England with him one Bill Richmond, a Negro who became the first famous American prizefighter. In the early 1800's, Tom

Molineaux, an ex-slave who had earned his freedom by defeating the champion of a neighboring plantation, proclaimed himself America's first heavyweight champion, although he was twice beaten by the English champion, Tom Crib.

In more modern times, Negroes were systematically excluded from many other sports, although they were able to participate by subterfuge or by forming their own counterpart leagues. In 1887, for example, Moses Fleetwood was a catcher for the Toledo team (then considered to be in the major leagues) but, after that, those Negroes who did play claimed to be Indians, Cubans, or Mexicans. (John McGraw of the New York Giants once tried to employ a Negro player named Grant by maintaining that he was really an Indian but, when the Giants played in Baltimore, the city's Negro sports public showed up in such droves that the rest of the league soon pressured the Giants into dismissing Grant.)

When Jackie Robinson finally broke the color barrier in 1947, the pattern was followed in other major sports. In professional football, for instance, a recent survey indicated that there were 140 players in the National Football League and 80 in the American Football League. In professional basketball, the Negro role is also significant, with Negroes accounting for from 30 to 40% of the players on most teams. Negro participation in hockey, horse racing and wrestling continues to be minimal, although there are some Negroes represented in these sports as well.

* Satchel Paige is included, although he reached his peak as a player while in Negro baseball. The Globetrotters, a star team, also receive mention here.

The hard-hitting Cleon Jones of the New York Mets

Year	*Total*
1954	13
1955	27
1956	26
1957	44
1958	30
1959	39
1960	40
1961	34
1962	45
1963	44
1964	24
1965	32
1966	44
1967	39
1968	29
1969	44
Total	554

*Aaron passed the 3,000-hit total in 1970.

LEW ALCINDOR
Basketball

Ferdinand Lewis Alcindor, Jr., 7′ 1½″ tall, was easily the most sought-after high school basketball player during the 1960's, particularly after he established a New York City record of 2,067 points and 2,002 rebounds in leading Power Memorial High School to three straight schoolboy championships. Power won 95 and lost only six during Alcindor's years with the team; 71 of these victories were consecutive.

Taller than Wilt Chamberlain at the time of his entrance to UCLA, Alcindor combined his height with cat-like moves and a deft shooting touch to lead UCLA to three consecutive NCAA Championships. Twice, as a sophomore and a senior, he was chosen the top collegiate player in the country. He finished his career at UCLA as the ninth all-time collegiate scorer, accumulating 2,325 points in 88 games for an average of 26.4 points per game. After leading UCLA to its third consecutive NCAA title Alcindor signed a contract with the Milwaukee Bucks of the NBA calling for 1.4 million dollars.

In his rookie season, 1969-70, he wasted little time showing any doubters that he was worth every penny of it by leading the Bucks, a recently established expansion club, to a second place finish in the Eastern Division, only a few games behind the division winners — the New York Knickerbockers. Alcindor won personal acclaim for his outstanding play in the 1970 NBA All-Star game, combining with the Knicks' Willis Reed to lead the East to victory.

Lew Alcindor who almost singlehandedly has brought the Milwaukee Bucks into championship contention

HENRY ARMSTRONG
Boxer

The only fighter ever to hold three titles at one time is Henry Armstrong, who accomplished this feat on August 17, 1938, when he added the lightweight championship to the featherweight and welterweight titles which he had won earlier.

Armstrong was born on December 12, 1912 in St. Louis, and orphaned five years later. One of 13 children, he managed not only to get an elementary education, but to graduate from Vashon High School as well.

In 1929, while fighting under the name of Melody Jackson, he was knocked out in his professional debut in Pittsburgh. Within two weeks, however, he had won his first fight and, for the next eight years, he learned his trade from coast to coast, fighting all comers until he was finally given a shot at the featherweight title on October 29, 1937. Armstrong defeated Petey Sarron, knocking out a champion who had never before been off his feet.

Less than a year later, on May 31, 1938, Armstrong picked up his second title with a decision over welterweight champion Barney Ross. Less than three months later, he completed the triple crown with a decision over lightweight champion Lou Ambers.

ARTHUR ASHE
Tennis

Arthur Ashe is the world's leading black amateur tennis player. In a sport traditionally closed to blacks because of its private-club setting and the financial cost involved, Ashe has risen to a late sixties rating as the No. 1 amateur tennis player in America.

Born in 1943 in Richmond, Virginia, Ashe learned the game at the Richmond Racket Club, which had been formed by local black enthusiasts. Dr. R. W. Johnson, who had served as an advisor and benefactor to Althea Gibson, also sponsored Ashe's tennis career, spending thousands of dollars and a great deal of time with him.

Arthur Ashe ranks among the best tennis players in the world

By 1958, Ashe had reached the semi-finals in the under-15 division of the National Junior Championships. In 1960 and 1961, he won the Junior Indoors Singles title. Even before he finished high school, he was already ranked 28th in the country.

In 1961, Ashe entered UCLA on a tennis scholarship. Since then, on the way to winning the U. S. Amateur Tennis Championship and the U. S. Open Tennis Championship, in addition to becoming the first black man ever named to a Davis Cup Team, Ashe has beaten most of the world's top players. Tennis great Pancho Gonzales says: "He has the fastest service since mine." Harry Hopman, the coach of the Australian Davis Cup Team, regards Ashe as "the most promising player in the world today, and the biggest single threat to our . . . supremacy."

Ashe is also the author of the book, *Advantage Ashe*.

ELGIN BAYLOR
Basketball

The owner of a National Basketball Association team once made a serious offer to trade his entire team for Elgin Baylor of the Lakers . . . and was quickly turned down! The Laker star is rated among the top three or four players in professional basketball today, his proneness to injury notwithstanding.

Born in 1936 in Washington, D.C., Baylor first became an All-American while attending Spingarn High School. He and R. C. Owens (later a professional football star) then joined forces to lead the College of Idaho to a 23-4 record.

Later, Baylor enrolled at Seattle University. Over the next two years, he became an All-American as the team won 45 out of 54 games, losing to Kentucky in the 1958 NCAA finals.

In 1959, Baylor made a sensational professional debut. (He was the first rookie to be named Most Valuable Player in the All-Star Game.) That same year, he was named to the All-League team, and set a scoring record of 64 points in a single game.

Slowed down by calcium deposits in his knees, Baylor has still maintained his status as a "superstar," having been chosen All-League in every season in which he has not been incapacitated.

His coach, Fred Schaus, calls him "the greatest player, inch for inch, who ever played this game."

JIMMY BROWN
Football

Jimmy Brown was the greatest offensive back in the history of football and, in the view of many observers, the greatest all-round athlete since the legendary Jim Thorpe.

Brown was born February 17, 1936 on St. Simon Island, Georgia, and moved to Manhasset, Long Island at the age of seven. At Manhasset High School, he became an outstanding competitor in baseball, football, track and field, basketball, and lacrosse. At graduation, he had a choice of 42 college scholarships, as well as professional offers from both the New York Yankees and the Boston Braves.

Brown chose Syracuse University, where his athletic prowess gained him national recognition. An All-American performer in both football and lacrosse, he turned down the opportunity to compete in the decathlon at the 1956 Olympics because it would have conflicted with his football schedule. When he graduated from Syracuse in 1957, he spurned a three-year $150,000 offer to

Jim Brown

become a professional fighter.

Brown's 1957 entry into professional football with the Cleveland Browns was emblematic of the manner in which he would dominate the game in the decade to come. He led the league in rushing; paced Cleveland to a division championship; and was unanimously named "Rookie of the Year."

Thereafter, Brown broke rushing and scoring records in both single season and lifetime totals, and he was All-League fullback virtually every season. He was also voted "Football Back of the Decade" for 1950-1960.

Brown announced his retirement in the summer of 1966, deciding to devote his time to a budding movie career, and to the improvement of black business. In little more than three years following his retirement from professional football, he has made eight films; Rio Conchos; The Dirty Dozen; Ice Station Zebra; Year of the Cricket; The Split; The Riot; and 100 Rifles. In addition to his movie-making activities, he is president and founder of the Negro Industrial and Economic Union, and organization that arranges financing for black businessmen and provides business expertise.

ROY CAMPANELLA
Baseball

The only Negro baseball star to be named Most Valuable Player on three separate occasions is Roy Campanella, who won this coveted title in 1951, 1953, and 1955.

Campanella, the second Negro in modern times to establish himself in the major leagues, was born in Philadelphia in 1921, and began playing semi-pro baseball 15 years later with the Bacharach Giants. In time, he became part of the hectic life of Negro professional baseball—touring the states in buses with the Baltimore Elites during the summer, and playing Latin American ball in winter.

In 1945, Campanella turned down the opportunity to become the first Negro in the major leagues when he mistakenly understood Branch Rickey's offer to be a contract with a rumored Negro team in Brooklyn. A few days later, he learned from Jackie Robinson that the offer had involved the possibility of playing with the Brooklyn Dodgers of the National League.

In 1946, Campanella was signed by the Dodgers and, along with pitcher Don Newcombe, assigned to their Nashua, New Hampshire team. Two years later, Branch Rickey delayed Campanella's debut with the Dodgers by deciding instead to break the color barrier of the American Association, specifically at St. Paul.

Before the year was out, however, Campanella was brought up to Brooklyn. Over the next eight years, the Dodger star played with five National League pennant winners, and one world championship team.

In January of 1958, his career as a player was ended by an automobile accident which left him paralyzed, and confined to a wheel chair. Today, he remains active in the game as a sports commentator.

WILT CHAMBERLAIN
Basketball

Wilt Chamberlain is certainly the greatest offensive player in the history of basketball. He has led the league in scoring since 1959, and also holds the single-game record of 100 points—a feat achieved against the New York Knickerbockers on March 2, 1962.

Chamberlain was born in Philadelphia on August 21, 1936. By the time he entered high school, he was already 6′ 11″, two inches short of his present height.

Unlike most men this tall, Chamberlain is strong, graceful, and extremely agile. He has run a 47-second quarter-mile, put a 16-pound shot 55 feet, and high-jumped 6 feet 10 inches. When he graduated from high school, he had his choice of 77 major colleges, and 125 smaller ones. He chose Kansas University, but left after his junior year with two years of All-American honors behind him. He then played with the Harlem Globetrotters before joining the Philadelphia Warriors of the NBA in 1959.

In his rookie season, with 14 games left, Chamberlain had already broken the existing full-season scoring and rebounding records in the league. Before the year was out, he had set eight new NBA records.

He has continued to dominate the sport with the Philadelphia 76ers, and with the Los Angeles Lakers, leading the lastnamed team to a division championship in 1970.

Wilt Chamberlain (right) is fouled by Willis Reed of the New York Knickerbockers while attempting a tap-in. Chamberlain has led the league in scoring since 1959, and is certainly the greatest offensive player the game has yet produced.

NBA ALL-TIME RECORDS HELD BY WILT CHAMBERLAIN
(as of the start of the 69-70 season)

Most Points Scored in One Game:
Wilt Chamberlain, 100
Philadelphia vs. New York
March 2, 1962

Most Points Scored in One Season:
Wilt Chamberlain, 4,029
1961-62

Most Field Goals Attempted in One Game:
Wilt Chamberlain, 63
Philadelphia vs. New York
March 2, 1962

Most Field Goals Made in One Game:
Wilt Chamberlain, 36
Philadelphia vs. New York
March 2, 1962

Most Free Throws Attempted in One

Game:
Wilt Chamberlain, 34
Philadelphia vs. St. Louis
February 22, 1962

Most Free Throws Made in One Game:
Wilt Chamberlain, 28
Philadelphia vs. New York
March 2, 1962

Most Rebounds in One Game:
Wilt Chamberlain, 55
Philadelphia vs. Boston
November 24, 1960

Highest Scoring Average, Season:
Wilt Chamberlain, 50.4
1961-62

Highest Scoring Average, Career:
Wilt Chamberlain, 34.4

Most Points, Career:
Wilt Chamberlain, 27,098

Most Field Goals Attempted, Career:
Wilt Chamberlain, 20,716

Most Field Goals Made, Career:
Wilt Chamberlain, 10,962

Highest Field Goal Percentage, Career:
Wilt Chamberlain, .529

Most Free Throws Attempted, Career:
Wilt Chamberlain, 10,053

LEE ELDER
Golf

Lee Elder picked up golf as a 15-year-old caddie in Dallas. After his father's death during W.W. II Elder moved his mother to Los Angeles, where he met and travelled with the famed black golfer, Ted Rhodes. While learning from Rhodes he was drafted by the Army where he was allowed to sharpen his skills as captain of the golf team at Fort Lewis, Washington. In 1960, after his discharge, he taught at the Langston Golf Course. In 1962 he debuted as a pro winning the United Golf Association (a black organization) National Title. He debuted in the PGA in November, 1967 in the Cajun Classic of New Orleans, finishing one stroke out of the money. Prior to his participation on the PGA tour Elder had done 17 years on the Negro tour (participating in close to 50 tournaments). In 30 tournaments as a PGA rookie (1968), Elder earned $38,000 (40th on PGA list of money-winners). He gained the respect of many by his brilliant play in losing to Jack Nicklaus in the "sudden death" playoff of the American Golf Classic in Akron, Ohio in 1968. As the 1969 PGA tour progressed, Elder was being tabbed as the leading PGA sophomore.

ALTHEA GIBSON
Tennis

Negro participation in the world of tennis is so rare that Althea Gibson's rise to the top is truly one of America's more remarkable success stories. In a sport which is traditionally developed on the more affluent "private club" circuit, she became the most accomplished female player in the world after learning to play "paddle tennis" on a play street in Harlem.

Born in Silver, South Carolina on August 25, 1927, Miss Gibson was raised in Harlem. After her "paddle tennis" days, she entered and won the Department of Parks Manhattan Girls' Tennis Championship. In 1942, she began to receive professional coaching at the interracial Cosmopolitan Tennis Club and, a year later, won the New York State Negro Girls Singles Title. In 1945 and 1946, she won the National Negro Girls Singles championship and, in 1948, began a decade of domination of the same title in the Women's Division.

A year later, Miss Gibson entered Florida A. & M., where she played tennis and basketball for the next four years. In 1950, she was runner-up for the National Indoor Championship and, that same year, became the first Negro to play at Forest Hills.

The following year, she became the first Negro to play at Wimbledon. In 1957, she won the Wimbledon singles crown, and teamed with Darlene Hard to win the doubles championship as well. When she returned to New York, she was greeted by a ticker-tape parade in recognition of her position as the best woman tennis player in the world.

Since then, Miss Gibson has engaged in public relations work with a bakery firm, married, and begun what promises to become a successful career as a professional golfer.

HARLEM GLOBETROTTERS
Basketball

The most widely known Negro team in the world is the Harlem Globetrotters, whose comic brand of basketball has captivated audiences in virtually every corner of the globe.

The original Globetrotters, formed in the 1927-1928 basketball season by Abe Saperstein, travelled to local engagements by automobile. The present-day Globetrotters are really three separate troupes playing simultaneously in different parts of the world under the name "Harlem Globetrotters."

The Globetrotters have become more an entertainment package than an athletic team, playing against familiar opponents who travel with them and follow the script. But the athletic ability of the group has always been there when needed. Such stars as Sweetwater Clifton and Wilt Chamberlain went from the Globetrotters to stardom in the National Basketball Association. Other stars have included Reece "Goose" Tatum, and dribbling sensation Marcus Haynes.

The current lead clown is Meadowlark Lemon.

BOB HAYES
Track, Football

"The world's fastest human" — sprint champion Bob Hayes is currently one of professional football's most dazzling performers as a split end and flanker back for the Dallas Cowboys of the National Football League.

Hayes still holds the world record for the 100-yard dash, 9.1 seconds. At the 1964 Olympics in Tokyo, Hayes came away with two gold medals for victories in the 100 meter dash and 400 meter relay.

Born on December 20, 1942 in Jacksonville, Florida, Hayes played football at high school, and later attended all-black Florida A. & M. He first captured the national track spotlight in 1961 by equal-

The Harlem Globetrotters have astounded basketball fans the world over with their amazing feats of ballhandling wizardry.

Jack Johnson

ling the then world record of 9.3 seconds for the 100-yard dash. Two years later, he set the current record for this distance at the National AAU championships in St. Louis, Missouri.

After finishing college, Hayes signed to play football with the Dallas Cowboys. In 14 games with the team, he caught 46 passes for 1,003 yards and 12 touchdowns. Right up through the late-sixties Hayes was one of the big reasons for the Cowboys' dominance of the NFL's Eastern Division.

JACK JOHNSON
1878-1946
Boxer

Jack Johnson, the first Negro heavyweight champion, won the crown from Tommy Burns in Sydney, Australia on December 26, 1908. Nat Fleischer, the editor of "Ring" magazine and a foremost boxing authority, has said: "After years devoted to the study of heavyweight fighters, I have no hesitation in naming Jack Johnson as the greatest of them all. He possessed every asset."

Johnson was born in Galveston, Texas in 1878, the son of a school janitor. He was so tiny as a boy that he was nicknamed "Li'l Arthur," a name that stuck with him throughout his career. As a young man, he hoboed around the country, making his way to Chicago, Boston, and New York, and learning the fighting trade by working out with veteran professionals whenever he could. When he finally got his chance at the title, he had already been fighting for nine years and had lost only three of some 100 bouts.

With his victory over Burns, Johnson became the center of a bitter racial controversy, as the American public clamored for the former white champion, Jim Jeffries, to come out of retirement and recapture the crown. When the two fought on July 4, 1910 in Reno, Nevada, Johnson knocked Jeffries out in the 14th round.

In 1913, Johnson left the United States because of legal entanglements. Two years later, he defended his title against Jess Willard in Havana, Cuba and was knocked out in the 26th round.

In 1946, Johnson died in an automobile crash in North Carolina.

RAFER JOHNSON
Track and field

Rafer Johnson holds the Olympic record (set in 1960) for points scored in the decathlon, considered to be the toughest test of all-around athletic ability in the world of sports.

The decathlon consists of 10 events (Greek: deka = 10, athlos = contest) designed to test strength, speed, and agility under the most gruelling of conditions. The events are as follows: the 100-meter dash; the broad jump; the shot put; the high jump; the 400-meter run; the 110-meter hurdles; the discus throw; the pole vault; the javelin toss, and the 1500-meter run. Only an athlete with a considerable combination of athletic skills and endurance can compete in such a formidable event.

Johnson was born in Hillsboro, Texas on August 18, 1935, and competed in his first decathlon in 1954 while attending U.C.L.A., where he was president of the student body.

In spite of a knee injury in the 1956 Olympics at Melbourne, Australia, Johnson competed in the event, and finished second to Milt Campbell, another American Negro who was the first of his race to win an Olympic decathlon.

Competing in Moscow in 1958, Johnson shattered the world record with a

"The Brown Bomber"

total of 8,302 points. Two years later, at the Olympics in Rome, Johnson won the decathlon gold medal with another record-breaking performance, amassing 8,392 points to gain recognition as "the greatest all-around athlete in the world."

JOE LOUIS
Boxer

Joe Louis held the heavyweight championship longer than anyone else (11 years, eight months, and seven days), and defended it more often than any other heavyweight champion. His 25 title fights were more than the combined total of the eight champions who preceded him.

Born in a sharecropper's shack in Chambers County, Alabama in 1914, Louis moved to Detroit as a small boy. Taking up boxing later as an amateur, he won 50 out of 59 bouts (43 by knockout) before turning professional in 1934. He quickly gained a reputation in the Midwest and, in 1935, came East to meet Primo Carnera, the former champion who was then staging a comeback. Louis knocked out Carnera in six rounds, and earned his nickname, "The Brown Bomber."

After knocking out ex-champion Max Baer, Louis suffered his lone pre-championship defeat at the hands of Max Schmeling, the German titleholder who knocked him out in the 12th round. Less than a month later, Louis knocked out another former champion, Jack Sharkey, in three rounds. After defeating a number of other challengers, he was given a title fight with Jim Braddock on June 22, 1937. He stopped Braddock in the eighth round, and began the long championship reign that was to see him defending his crown as often as six times in six months (1941), and battering Schmeling to the canvas in one round in their 1938 return bout.

One of Louis's greatest fights was his 1941 come-from-behind 13th-round-knockout of Billy Conn. After winning a disputed decision over Joe Walcott in 1947, Louis knocked out the Jersey challenger six months later, and then went into retirement.

His later comeback attempts against the likes of Ezzard Charles and Rocky Marciano were unsuccessful.

WILLIE MAYS
Baseball

In his 18 seasons with the Giants, Willie Mays has hit 600 home runs (only the second man to hit 600 or more homers), a feat that in itself should be enough to guarantee his admission to the Hall of Fame. A great hitter, Mays has also been called the game's finest defensive outfielder.

Born in Fairfield, Alabama on May 6, 1931, Mays made his professional debut on July 4, 1948 with the Birmingham Black Barons. He was signed by the Giants in 1950, and reached the major leagues in 1951—in time to become the National League's Rookie of the Year with 20 home runs, 68 rbi's, and the sensational fielding which contributed to his team's pennant victory.

After two years in the Army, Mays returned to head the Giants to the World Championship in 1954, gaining recognition as the league's Most Valuable Player for his 41 homers, 110 rbi's and .345 batting average.

After the Giants moved to San Francisco, Mays continued his phenomenal home run hitting, and led his team to a 1962 pennant. A year later, "Sport" magazine named him "the greatest player of the decade." He won the MVP award again in 1965, after hitting 52 home runs and batting .317.

Today Mays is not only the greatest right-handed home run hitter of all-time but also one of only seven ballplayers to have hit four home runs in one game. In addition to that he was the only black member of the living all-time baseball team selected in 1969 by the Baseball Writer's Association of America.

Year	*Total*	*Year*	*Total*
1951	20	1961	40
1952	4	1962	49
1953	—	1963	38
1954	41	1964	47
1955	51	1965	52
1956	36	1966	37
1957	35	1967	22
1958	29	1968	23
1959	34	1969	13
1960	29	Total	600

*Mays passed the 3,000-hit total in 1970.

JESSE OWENS
Track and field

The track and field records which Jesse Owens once set have all been eclipsed in the quarter century since he established them, but his reputation as one of the first great athletes with the combined talents of sprinter, low hurdler, and broad jumper has hardly diminished with the passing of time.

Born on September 12, 1913 in Danville, Alabama, Owens moved to Ohio at an early age. The name "Jesse" derived from the way a teacher pronounced his initials, "J.C." In 1932, while attending East Technical High School in Cleveland, Owens gained national fame with a 10.3 clocking in the 100-meter dash.

Two years later, Owens entered Ohio State University and, for the next four years, made track history, becoming universally known as "The Ebony Antelope." While competing in the Big Ten Championships at Ann Arbor, Michigan on May 25, 1935, Owens had what has been called "the greatest single day in the history of man's athletic achievements." In the space of about 70 minutes, he tied the world record for the 100-yard dash, and surpassed the world record for five other events, including the broad jump, the 220-yard low hurdles, and the 220-yard dash.

In 1936, at the Berlin Olympics, Owens won four gold medals, at that time the most universally acclaimed feat in the history of the games. When Adolf Hitler refused to present him medals he had won in the various competitions, Owens' fame became even more widespread as a result of the publicity.

SATCHEL PAIGE
Baseball

Long before Jackie Robinson broke the color barrier of "organized baseball," Satchel Paige was a name well-known to the general sports public. As the outstanding performer in "Negro baseball," Paige had become a legendary figure whose infrequent encounters with major league players (he defeated Dizzy Dean in a 1-0 game in 1933 and, four years later, was called "the best pitcher I ever faced" by Joe Dimaggio) added considerable laurels to his athletic reputation.

Paige was born in Mobile, Alabama in September 1904, and began playing semipro ball while working as an iceman and porter. In the mid 1920's, he became a professional with the Birmingham Black Barons and, later, while playing at Chattanooga, acquired the nickname "Satchel" because of his "Satchel-sized feet."

Satchel Paige follows through on his delivery.

For the next two decades, Paige compiled a phenomenal record. In 1933, he won 31 games and lost four. The following year, he pitched for a Brunswick, North Dakota team which reportedly took 104 out of 105 games, with Paige himself starting a total of 29 games over a one-month span. Along with Josh Gibson and other black stars, Paige also dominated winter ball in Latin America during the 1930's.

In 1942, Paige led the Kansas City Monarchs to victory in the Negro World Series, and four years later, helped them to the pennant by allowing only two runs in 93 innings, a performance which included a skein of 64 straight scoreless innings.

In 1948, when he was brought up to the major leagues, Paige was well past his prime, but he still was able to contribute six victories in Cleveland's pennant drive. Four years later, while pitching for the St. Louis Browns, he was named to the American League All-Star squad.

Up until the 1969 baseball season Paige was primarily active on the barnstorming circuit with the Harlem Globetrotters and a host of other exhibition teams. It was in 1969 that the Atlanta Braves, in an attempt to make Paige eligible for baseball's pension plan, signed him to a one-year contract as coach.

WILLIS REED
Basketball

Although his personal achievements do not yet place him in the company of the game's all-time greats, Willis Reed, in the 1970 basketball season at least, proved to be a remarkable performer whose steady play, clutch shooting, defensive agility, and near indestructibility led the New York Knickerbockers to their first championship in 24 years.

Reed not only captured rave notices from opposing centers who admired his shooting prowess and jarring "picks," but capped the Knicks' most successful season in two decades by winning three Most Valuable Player Awards: one for the regular season, one for the All-Star game, and one for the sudden-death playoffs as well. Particularly memorable was his astonishing comeback after being injured in the fifth game of the playoffs against the Los Angeles Lakers, a game which New York miraculously won to assume a 3–2 lead

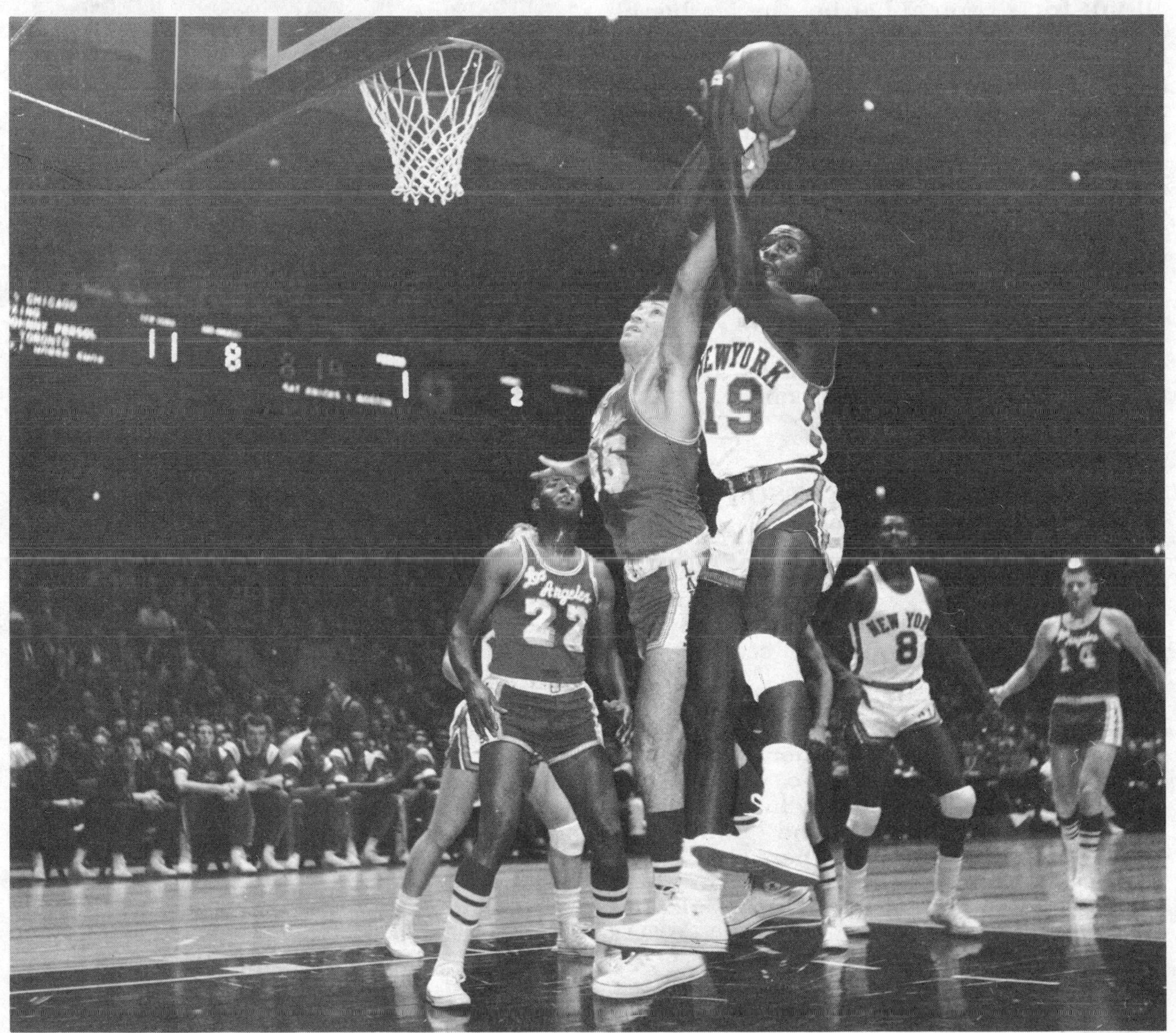

Willis Reed led the New York Knickerbockers to the 1970 NBA Championship.

in the best of seven series. The Lakers, with Wilt Chamberlain dominating the sixth game, evened the series at three games apiece by a lopsided 135-113 score, thus demonstrating that Reed alone was capable of controlling the giant and legendary cager.

In the seventh game, Reed took the floor, his mobility seriously impaired by his injured leg and hip. By scoring the first two baskets of the game, he not only gave his team a tremendous psychological lift, but also triggered cheers of delirium from the rabid New York sports fans. The Knicks not only won the game handily but, in the process, established themselves as one of those incredible teams whose attributes and assets will be debated and glorified in decades to come.

At 6-9 and 240 pounds, Reed is not at all tall for a center. During the season, he managed 13.9 rebounds per game (6th best in the league) and 21.7 points per game, by no means phenomenal statistics. Still, he anchored the defense of the best team in the NBA, was a fine shooter and an intense competitor, and left no doubt in anyone's mind that he was the bellwether of a phenomenal Knick quintet.

A native of Louisiana, Reed spent his boyhood picking cotton around his hometown of Bernice, where he was born in 1943. He attended Grambling College, where he was discovered by Red Holzman, now coach of the Knicks, but then employed as their chief scout.

"Big O" (Oscar Robertson) is regarded as the best "little man" in the game today.

OSCAR ROBERTSON
Basketball

Standing 6′ 5″, Oscar Robertson is often regarded as the best "small man" in professional basketball—particularly in view of his outstanding scoring and playmaking ability.

Born on November 29, 1938 in Charlotte, Tennessee, Robertson is the great-grandson of Marshall Collier, an ex-slave who died in 1954 at the age of 116, allegedly the oldest person in the United States at that time. The Robertsons moved to Indianapolis when Oscar was three. As soon as he and his brothers were old enough, they began playing basketball at the local YMCA. (Oscar's oldest brother, Bailey, later played briefly for the Harlem Globetrotters.)

At Crispus Attucks High School, Robertson led his team to an unbeaten season (the first in Indiana history); a 45-game winning streak, and two consecutive state championships. He was All-State for three years, broke numerous individual scoring records, and was named a high school All-American. In addition to starring on the baseball and track teams, Robertson also was a member of the National Honor Society.

At the University of Cincinnati, Robertson became the nation's leading scorer as a sophomore, then went on to set 14 major collegiate records while leading his team to 89 wins in 98 games.

As a professional with the Cincinnati Royals, he has been the game's leading backcourt scorer. In 1965, he was third in the league in scoring behind Wilt Chamberlain and Jerry West, but had the highest number of free throws, 665.

Going into the 1969-70 season Robertson ranked as the leader in career assists with 7,173. In other career categories his ranking is as follows: points (fourth, 20,261); average points per game (second, 29.7); field goals made (fourth, 7,056); field goal percentage (fifth, .486); free throws made (third, 6,129) and free throw percentage (second, .841).

FRANK ROBINSON
Baseball

Frank Robinson's sparkling play with the Baltimore Orioles during the 1966 baseball season has enhanced his reputation as one of the top Negro stars of the past decade. While in the National League, Robinson had been denied some of the recognition he deserved by having to play in the shadow of such greats as Willie Mays and Henry Aaron.

Born in Beaumont, Texas in 1936, Robinson moved with his family to Oakland, California at the age of five. During his teens, he was a football and baseball star at McClyronds High School (which also produced Bill Russell, Vada Pinson, and Curt Flood). After graduation in 1953, he signed with the Cincinnati Reds.

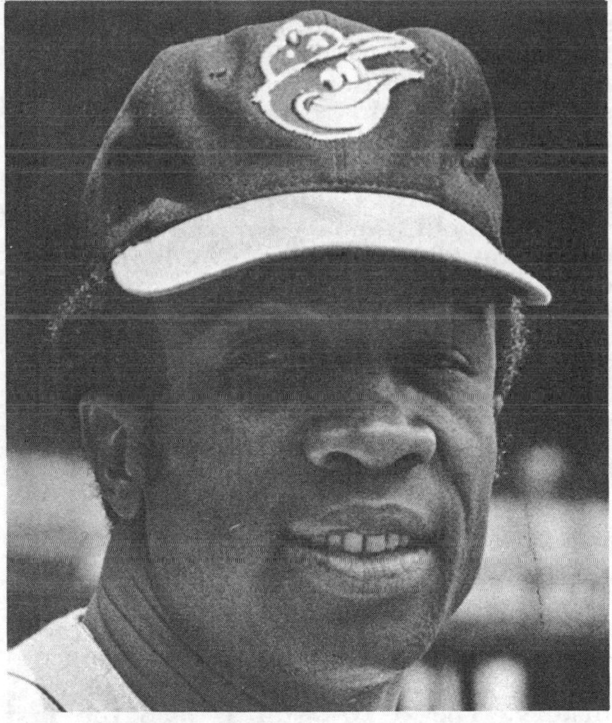

Frank Robinson.

In his first year of professional ball, Robinson batted .348 and led Ogden, Utah to the Pioneer League pennant. The following year, he batted .336 in the Sally League.

In 1956, he made a smash debut in the major leagues, hitting 38 homers and winning Rookie of the Year honors. Over the next eight years, he hit 259 homers and had 800 RBI's, an outstanding record, but one which was often underpublicized.

In 1961, Robinson was named Most Valuable Player for leading Cincinnati to the National League pennant.

Five years later, Robinson won the American League's Triple Crown. In the 1966 World Series, he was one of the key players in leading the Baltimore Orioles to a four-game sweep of the Los Angeles Dodgers. As a result, he was named the outstanding player in the Series.

JACKIE ROBINSON
Baseball

Jackie Robinson's pioneer efforts in breaking the color barrier in organized baseball not only opened the door for other Negro players, but for Negro athletes in all major American sports.

Robinson's importance, however, can never be limited to the "sociological feat" which he performed. It was solely on the basis of his playing baseball that he was named, on July 3, 1962, to the Hall of Fame in Cooperstown, New York.

Born in Cairo, Georgia on January 31, 1919, Robinson was raised in Pasadena, California. At U.C.L.A., he gained All-American honorable mention as a halfback, but left college in his junior year to play professional football for the Los Angeles Bulldogs. After serving as an Army lieutenant during World War II, Robinson returned to civilian life with the hope of becoming a physical education coach. To achieve this, he felt he had to make a name for himself and, for this reason, decided to spend a few seasons in Negro baseball.

In 1945, while he was playing with the Kansas City Monarchs, Branch Rickey of the Brooklyn Dodgers assigned him to the Montreal Royals, the team's top farm club, where he was to be groomed for a career in the majors.

On April 10, 1947, the Dodgers announced that they had purchased Robinson's contract and, the following day, he began his major league career. When he retired in 1956, he had compiled an outstanding record as a hitter, fielder, and base-stealer.

He had won the National League's Most Valuable Player award in 1949, and played on six National League pennant winners, as well as one world championship team.

"SUGAR RAY" ROBINSON
Boxer

Ray Robinson is often labelled the greatest fighter "pound-for-pound" in the history of boxing.

Born Walker Smith in Detroit on May 3, 1921, he took the name Robinson from the certificate of an amateur boxer whose identity enabled him to meet the age requirement for getting a match in Michigan. The "Sugar" came from his having been dubbed "the sweetest fighter."

As a 10-year-old boy, Robinson had watched a Detroit neighbor, Joe Louis, train for an amateur boxing career. When Robinson moved to New York two years later, he began to spend most of his time at local gyms in preparation for his own amateur career.

After winning all 89 of his amateur bouts and the 1939 Golden Gloves featherweight championship as well, he turned professional in 1940 at Madison Square Garden, fighting for the first time on a card headlined by the Fritzie Zivic-Henry Armstrong fight. (Armstrong, Robinson's idol, lost the fight.) A year later, Robinson himself decisioned Zivic, and, three months after that, knocked him out.

After several years of being "the uncrowned king of the welterweights," Robinson beat Tommy Bell in an elimination title bout in December 1946. He successfully defended the title for five years and, on February 14, 1951, took the middleweight crown from Jake LaMotta.

In July 1951, he lost the title to Randy Turpin, only to win it back two months later. Retiring for a time, Robinson subsequently fought a series of exciting battles with Carl "Bobo" Olson, Carmen Basilio, and Gene Fullmer before retiring permanently with six victories in title bouts to his credit—more than any other fighter in history.

WILMA RUDOLPH
Track and field

Wilma Rudolph is the only American woman runner ever to win three gold medals in the Olympic Games. Her performance is all the more remarkable in light of the fact that she was unable to walk properly until she was eight years old.

Born on June 23, 1940 in St. Bethlehem, Tennessee, she soon moved with the family to Clarksville, the town in which she grew up. At an early age, she survived an attack of double pneumonia and scarlet fever, but was left with the use of her right leg only. Through daily leg massages administered in turn by different members of her family, she progressed to the point where, at the age of eight, she was able to walk only with the aid of a special left shoe. Three years later, however, she discarded the shoe, and began joining her brother in backyard basketball games.

At Burt High School in Clarksville, Miss Rudolph broke the state basketball record for girls while a sophomore. As a sprinter, she was undefeated in all her high school track meets.

In 1957, she enrolled at Tennessee State University, and began to set her sights for the Olympics in Rome three years later. In the interim, she gained national recognition in collegiate meets, setting the world record for 200-meters in July 1960.

In the Olympics, she earned the title of the "World's Fastest Woman" by winning gold medals for the 100-meter dash; the 200-meter dash (Olympic record); and for anchoring the 400-meter relay (world record). She was named by the Associated Press as the U. S. Female Athlete of the Year for 1960, and also won United Press Athlete of the Year honors.

BILL RUSSELL
Basketball

Bill Russell is regarded as the finest defensive basketball player in the game's history. The 6′ 10″ star is also the first Negro to coach and play for a National Basketball Association team—in both cases the Boston Celtics.

Russell was born on February 12, 1934 in Monroe, Louisiana. The family moved to Detroit when he was nine. Two years later, after his mother died, they continued on to Oakland. There, at McClyronds High School (the starting point for numerous Negro professional athletes), Russell proved to be an awkward but determined baseball player who eventually received a scholarship to the nearby University of San Francisco.

In college, Russell came into his own, in his sophomore year becoming the most publicized athlete on the West Coast. Over the next two years, his fame spread across the nation as he led his team to 60 consecutive victories (a collegiate record) and two straight NCAA titles.

The Celtics had never won the title before Russell's arrival, but since his specialties (blocking shots, rebounding outstandingly) have been added to their attack, they have become the most successful team in the history of professional sports, winning the world championship eight years in a row. Russell himself has been named Most Valuable Player on four separate occasions.

After the 1968-69 season, having led the Celtics to their eleventh NBA crown, Russell retired as both coach and player. The move had its impact on the team, for the next season (1969-70) the Celtics failed to make the playoffs for the first time in a good many years. Having retired, Russell can be proud of having been named the NBA's Most Valuable Player no less than four times. In addition he is the NBA leader in career minutes (40,726) and career rebounds (21,721).

GALE SAYERS
Football

With the retirement of Jimmy Brown, football's greatest offensive weapon is now Gale Sayers of the Chicago Bears. In 1965, the 200-pound 22-year-old Sayers combined great speed and agility with explosive power to capture Rookie of the Year Honors in the National Football League in what was surely the most remarkable debut in professional football. Not only did Sayers win the scoring title but, in the process, he also broke the league scoring record with 22 touchdowns (including six in one game).

Sayers was born in Wichita, Kansas and moved to Omaha, Nebraska in 1952. At the University of Kansas, he earned All-American honors and received $50,000 for signing with the Bears.

A dazzling runner from scrimmage, he is also adept at punt and kickoff returns, and has pass-catching and pass-throwing ability. In 1966, having set the scoring standard the previous year, Sayers led the league in rushing with 1,231 yards. In 1968, in route to one of his best years ever, Sayers suffered a crippling knee injury. During the off-season there was much speculation as to whether Sayers would ever be able to play again. In the 1969 season, Sayers not only played but led the league in rushing as well.

Gale Sayers of the Chicago Bears is one of the most dazzling backs in the NFL.

CHARLES SIFFORD
Golf

Charlie Sifford started caddying at the age of nine in his hometown of Charlotte, N.C. As a 13-year-old Sifford won a Charlotte tournament for caddies. In the late '30s he moved to Philly where it was somewhat easier for a black golfer to gain access to a golf course.

From 1947-1953 Sifford worked between matches as private golf instructor and sometime chauffeur and valet to singer Billy Eckstine, who later offered Sifford the financial support he needed to keep playing golf. From 1953 on he won the Negro National Title six times. In the late fifties Charlie got to play in a few tournaments on the PGA tour. In 1967 on the tour Sifford earned $57,000. In 1968 he added $33,000 more from competing on the tour. In 1968 he won the first PGA tournament of the year, the Los Angeles Open, copping the $20,000 first prize. The victory was his second major one (he had earned $20,000 in 1967 while winning the Hartford Open).

Eldridge Cleaver: the most dynamic and virile black writer of the decade.

BLACK WRITERS, SCHOLARS AND POETS

The Slave Experience
The Genteel Tradition
The Harlem Renaissance
Old and New Voices of Black Protest
Black Self-Concept
Outstanding Literary Figures

Negro literature in America has been inextricably linked with the complex racial realities which have surrounded the Negro writer. With few exceptions, the major literary efforts of the American Negro have stemmed—directly or indirectly—from the existential facts-of-life for the Negro in "White America." Although a handful of novelists like Frank Yerby and Willard Motley have derived their material from experiences in what might be termed the "white world," the work of the overwhelming majority of serious Negro writers is continually rooted in some form of racial consciousness.

Much of the early literature produced by American Negroes (as with Phillis Wheatley, for example) was merely imitative of the general literature of the time, its racial facet being the attempt to exhibit the writer's intrinsic effort as sufficient refutation of the belief that the Negro was an inherently inferior creature. Other early works were little more than pious tracts written to assure the masters that the servants wanted nothing more than to serve in religious humility, as in the case of Jupiter Hammon. In contrast to these, however, there was also a long succession of autobiographical narratives by ex-slaves who chose to attack the existing system in an attempt to force "White America" to look into the human face of "Negro America."

From the post-Reconstruction period to the decade of the 1920's, much of American Negro literature was an attempt to show the general public that "Negro America" could be every bit as respectably middle-class in its outlook and ideals as "White America." (If much of "Negro America" was unable to afford the creature comforts of such an environment, it could still produce literary commentaries which would at least show a people happily laughing at their assigned lot.)

It was in the 1920's that Negro literature made a sharp change of direction, removing itself once and for all from both its polite and strait-laced conventions and its grinning, dancing, ingratiating manner. With the emergence of the "Harlem School" came a sense of racial pride which expressed itself in earthy, realistic terms—the protests of both the Negro and white establishments notwithstanding.

The literature of the American Negro which is being written today—true to the tradition begun in the 1920's—has, nevertheless, not yet been able to resolve a fundamental dilemma underlying its very substance: Is the Negro writer limiting himself by dealing with strictly racial themes, or does his best chance to achieve artistic stature depend on his using the material which he feels most deeply—not to produce parochial propaganda pieces, but to help illuminate the universal human condition?

At present, black literature is enjoying an increasing and sustained interest on college campuses across the nation. In conjunction with Black Studies Programs as well as apart from them, the works of black authors are receiving a long overdue critical attention. Most publishing companies are beginning to recognize the advantage of bringing to print works dealing with the black experience in America and around the world. WCBS-TV has been presenting an on-going series dealing with the poetry, short stories, novels, essays and plays of black authors in a program called *Black Letters*, co-hosted by Dr. Roscoe C. Brown, Jr., and Dr. Frank Miceli. All across the nation the electronic media have included blacks in all areas of production, altering the image of the black man as he begins to re-define himself.

The writers reviewed in this section have been included for their historical and/or aesthetic importance. In this limited space, the list can be only minimally representative, although it will hopefully serve as a vital springboard for developing a greater understanding of the contributions made by the American Negro writer—both to the mainstream and to the tributaries of the American literary experience.

JAMES BALDWIN
Novelist, Essayist

James Baldwin is easily the most widely quoted Negro writer of the past decade.

Born on August 2, 1924 in New York City, Baldwin turned to writing after an early career as a boy preacher in Harlem's storefront churches. He attended Frederick Douglass Junior High School in Harlem and later graduated from De Witt Clinton High School, where he was editor of the school magazine. Three years later, he won a Eugene Saxton Fellowship which enabled him to write full-time.

Baldwin's first novel, *Go Tell It on the Mountain*, was published in 1953, and received good critical notices, although it did not become a best-seller. Two years later, his first collection of essays, *Notes of a Native Son*, again won favorable critical acclaim without reaching a wide general audience. This was followed in 1956 by the publication of his second novel, *Giovanni's Room*, set in Paris. Ironically, it was his second collection of essays, *Nobody Knows My Name*, which brought him into the literary spotlight, and established him as a major voice in American literature.

In 1962, *Another Country*, Baldwin's third novel, was a critical and commercial success. A year later, he wrote *The Fire Next Time*, an immediate best-seller and already regarded as one of the most brilliant essays written in the history of Negro protest.

Since then, two of Baldwin's plays—*Blues for Mister Charlie* and *The Amen Corner*—have been produced on the New York stage, where they achieved modest success.

His latest novel, *Tell Me How Long The Train's Been Gone*, was published in 1968. Baldwin himself regards it as his first "grown-up novel," but it has generated little enthusiasm among critics on the literarv scene.

Eldridge Cleaver is among those who have interpreted the Baldwin phenomenon, after having been initially impressed by the vigor and passion of the Harlemite's work. In Cleaver's view, Baldwin's writing is tainted by a basic flaw: "total hatred of the blacks." Part of Cleaver's criticism stems no doubt from Baldwin's own repudiation of his mentor, Richard Wright. In tone and content, however, Cleaver's critique is analytical, rather than being petty or chauvinistic. It attempts to proceed from evidence presented in Baldwin's work, placing it in a societal context beyond that originally attributed to it by other less perceptive critics.

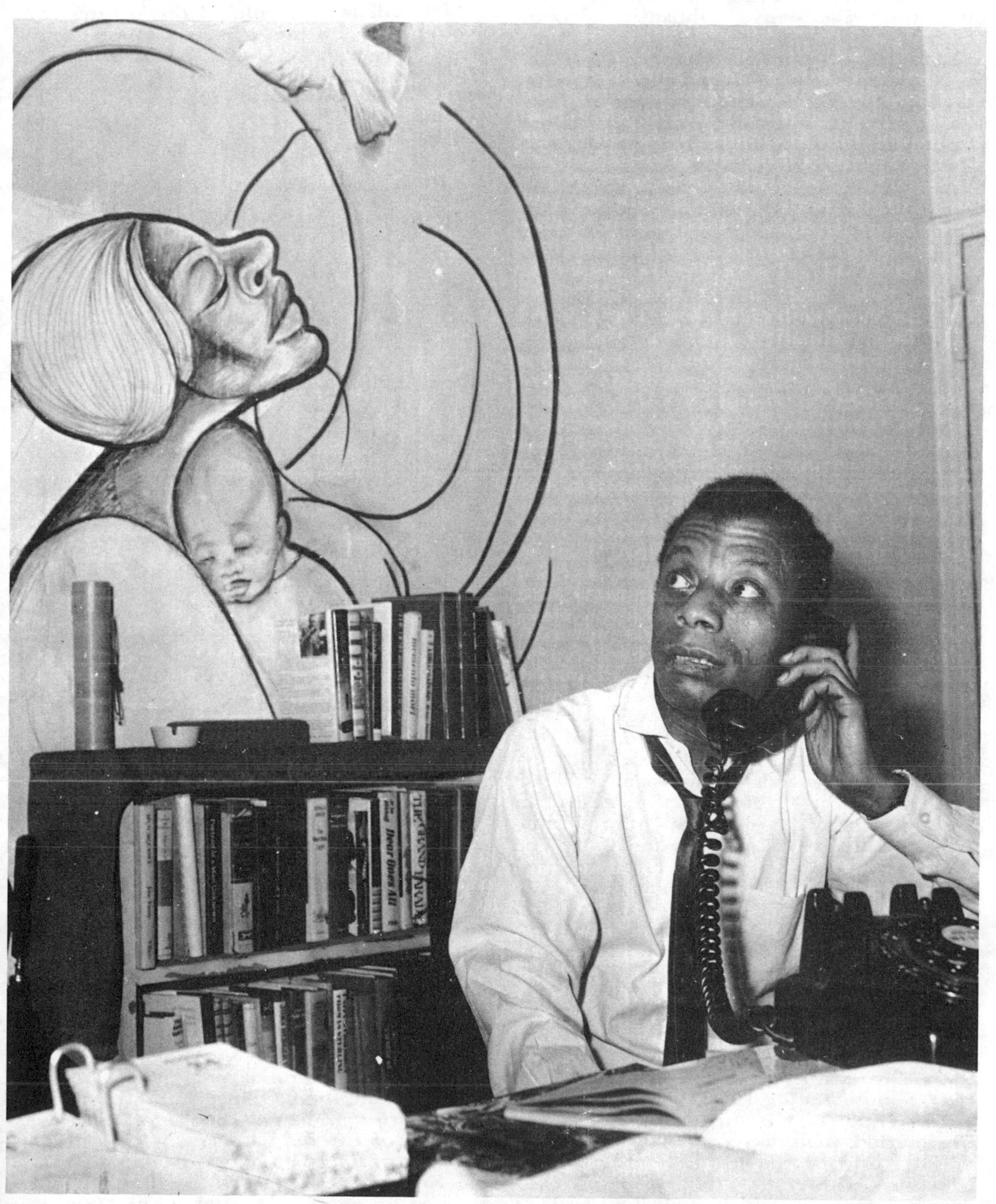

James Baldwin in his New York apartment

LERONE BENNETT, JR.
Historian

Lerone Bennett, Jr. is often referred to as the "resident historian" of the Johnson Publishing Company, publishers of both "Ebony" and "Jet."

Bennett was born on October 17, 1928 in Clarksdale, Mississippi, and was educated in the public school system of Jackson, where he worked on his high school paper and edited the local Negro weekly, *The Mississippi Enterprise.*

At Morehouse College in Atlanta, he was editor of the student newspaper and, after graduation, became a reporter and, later, city editor of the *Atlanta Daily World.*

Bennett joined Johnson in 1953 and worked as associate editor of "Jet" and "Ebony" before being named the latter's first senior editor in 1960.

His books include: *Before the Mayflower* (1962), *The Negro Mood and Other Essays* (1964), *What Manner of Man* (a biography of Martin Luther King published in 1964), *Confrontation: Black and White* (1965), *Black Power, U.S.A., the Human Side of Reconstruction 1867-1877* (1967), and *Pioneers in Protest* (1968).

In 1969 he published a revised and enlarged edition of *Before the Mayflower.*

ARNA BONTEMPS
Poet, novelist, dramatist

Arna Bontemps has been one of the most productive Negro writers of the 20th century.

Born in Alexandria, Louisiana in 1902 and raised in California, Bontemps received his B. A. degree from Pacific Union College in Angwin in 1923. The very next year, his poetry first appeared in print in "Crisis" magazine, the NAACP periodical edited by Dr. W. E. B. DuBois. Two years later, *Golgotha is a Mountain* won the Alexander Pushkin Award and, in 1927, *Nocturne at Bethesda* achieved first honors in the "Crisis" poetry contest.

At this point in his career, Bontemps decided to try his hand at prose and, over the next decade, produced such novels as *God Sends Sunday* (1931) and *Drums at Dusk* (1939). His historical books for this period include *We Have Tomorrow* (1945) and *Story of the Negro* (1948). Likewise of literary merit are such children's books as *Sad-Faced Boy* (1937) and *Slappy Hooper* (1946).

Bontemps has also engaged in a teaching career, and once served as the chief librarian at Fisk University in Nashville, Tennessee. He is now Director of University Relations there.

In 1968, he completed the editing of a volume of children's poetry. His most recent publications have been, *Anyplace But Here* (published in 1966 in collaboration with Jack Conroy), *Black Thunder* (1968), and *Great Slave Narratives* (1969).

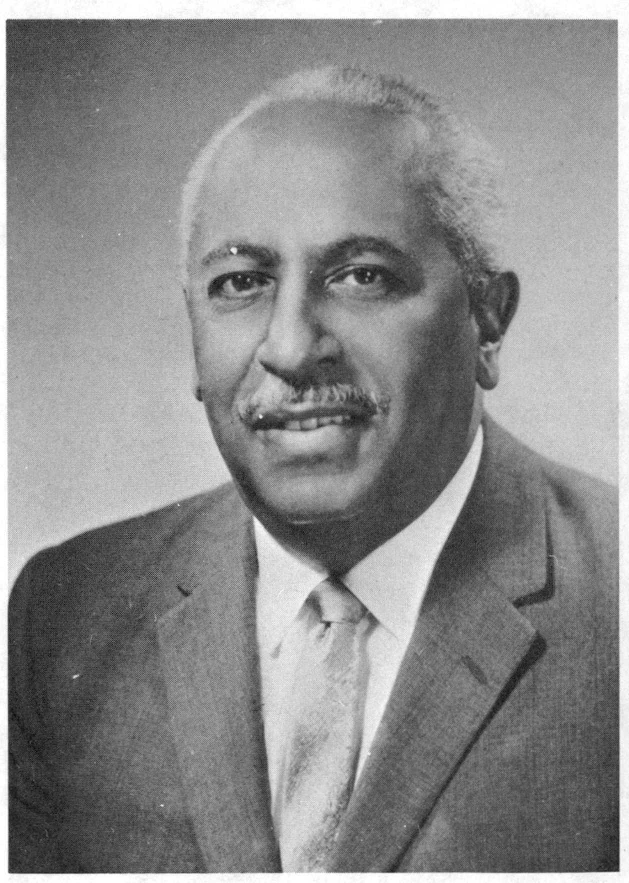

Arna Bontemps

WILLIAM STANLEY BRAITHWAITE
1878–1962
Poet, critic

In the early part of his career, it was not generally known that William Stanley Braithwaite was a Negro, although his name was familiar to many readers through his book reviews for the *Boston Transcript* and such books of poetry as *Lyrics of Life and Love* (1904) and *The House of Falling Leaves* (1908).

From 1913 to 1929, Braithwaite published an annual "Anthology of Magazine Verse" which brought before the public many of the works of such noted American poets as Edgar Lee Masters, Vachel Lindsay and Carl Sandburg long before they were ever published in book form.

Braithwaite's other books include *The Book of Elizabethan Verse* (1906), *The Book of Georgian Verse* (1908), *The Book of Restoration Verse* (1909), and *Selected Poems* (1948).

The recipient of the NAACP's Spingarn Medal in 1918, Braithwaite spent most of his later years in education, serving notably as professor of creative literature at Atlanta University.

He died on June 8, 1962.

BENJAMIN BRAWLEY
1882–1939
Literary historian

Although he wrote a number of poems and short stories during his lifetime, the major portion of Benjamin Brawley's work was in the field of literary and social history.

Brawley was born in 1882 in Columbia, South Carolina and educated at Morehouse College, the University of Chicago, and Harvard. He later taught at Morehouse, Shaw, and Howard.

His books include *A Short History of English Drama* (1921); *A New Survey of English Literature* (1925); *The Negro Genius* (1937), and *Negro Builders and Heroes* (1937). The latter was written two years before his death.

GWENDOLYN BROOKS
Poet

Gwendolyn Brooks is the only Negro ever to have won a Pulitizer prize. She received this prestigious award in 1950 for *Annie Allen*, a volume of her poetry which had been published a year earlier.

Miss Brooks was born in Topeka, Kansas on June 7, 1917. She moved to Chicago at an early age, and was educated there, graduating from Wilson Junior College in 1936.

She had her first taste of the more sordid aspects of ghetto life during her first job as secretary to a "spiritual advisor" who sold "love drops." Although unfamiliar with these conditions from her native environment, she was nonetheless alert enough to realize that they could offer her much in the way of unique material for her writing.

Gwendolyn Brooks

In 1945, she completed a book of poems, *A Street in Bronzeville*, and was selected by "Mademoiselle" as one of the year's 10 most outstanding American women. She was made a fellow of the American Academy of Arts and Letters in 1946, and received Guggenheim Fellowships for 1946 and 1947.

In 1949, she won the Eunice Tietjen Prize for Poetry in the annual competition sponsored by "Poetry" magazine.

Her other books include a collection of children's poems, *Bronzeville Boys and Girls* (1956); a novel, *Maud Martha* (1953), and two books of poetry, *The Bean Eaters* (1960) and *Selected Poems* (1963).

Her poems and stories have also been published in magazines and the anthologies *Soon, One Morning*, and *Beyond the Angry Black*.

CLAUDE BROWN
Author

Claude Brown's claim to literary fame rests exclusively on his best-selling autobiography *Manchild in the Promised Land* which was published in 1965 when its author was 28.

The book is the story of Brown's life in Harlem and, in the process, becomes a highly realistic documentary of life in the ghetto. It tells of Brown's escapades with the Harlem Buccaneers, a "bopping gang," and of his later involvement with

Claude Brown

the Forty Thieves, an elite stealing division of this same gang.

After attending the Wiltwyck School for emotionally disturbed and deprived boys, Brown returned to New York, was later sent to Warwick Reform School three times, and eventually made his way downtown to a small loft apartment near Greenwich Village. Changing his style of life, Brown finished high school, and went on to graduate from Howard University in 1965. By this time, he had announced that his political ambition was to unseat Harlem representative Adam Clayton Powell.

Brown began work on his book in 1963, submitting a manuscript of some 1,500 pages which was eventually cut and reworked into the finished product over a two-year period. Despite the success of his first work, Brown is not planning to do another book, preferring law (he is currently attending Rutgers University) and politics as future careers.

STERLING BROWN
Poet, critic

In the period immediately following the "Harlem Renaissance," Sterling Brown received favorable attention for *Southern Road,* a volume of poetry published in 1932. In contrast to the urban environment of the Harlem school of poets, Brown drew on the rural South for his material.

Born in Washington, D. C. in 1901, Brown was educated at Williams College and at Harvard. Except for brief periods during which he has served as visiting lecturer at the New School for Social Research, at Vassar, and at the University of Minnesota, he has spent his entire teaching career at Howard University.

In 1937, Brown received a Guggenheim Fellowship and, the following year, published two works: *The Negro in American Fiction,* and *Negro Poetry and Drama.*

WILLIAM WELLS BROWN
1815–1884
Novelist, dramatist

William Wells Brown was the first American Negro to publish a novel, the first to publish a drama, and the first to publish a travel book.

Born a slave in 1815 in Lexington, Kentucky and taken to St. Louis as a young boy, Brown worked for a time in the offices of the St. Louis *Times,* and then took a job on a riverboat in service on the Mississippi. In 1834, Brown fled to Canada, taking his name from a friendly Quaker whom he met there. While working as a steward on Lake Erie ships, he educated himself and became well known as a public speaker. In 1849, he went to England and Paris to attend the Peace Congress, remaining abroad for the next five years.

His first published work was the *Narrative of William H. Brown,* which went into three editions within only eight months' time. A year later, a collection of his poems was published under the title *The Anti-Slavery Harp* and, in 1852, his travel book *Three Years in Europe* appeared in London.

Brown's *Clotel, or the President's Daughter*, a melodramatic novel about miscegenation, was first published in London in 1853. As the first novel by an American Negro (it subsequently went through two revisions), its historical importance transcends its aesthetic shortcomings.

Brown's other books include the first Negro drama *The Escape, or a Leap for Freedom* (1858); *The Black Man: His Antecedents, His Genius, and His*

THE NEGRO

IN THE

AMERICAN REBELLION

His Heroism and his Fidelity

BY

WILLIAM WELLS BROWN

AUTHOR OF "SKETCHES OF PLACES AND PEOPLE ABROAD," "THE BLACK MAN," ETC

BOSTON

LEE & SHEPARD, 149 WASHINGTON STREET

1867

The original title page of Brown's classic war study on the black fighting man.

Achievements (1863); *The Negro in the American Rebellion: His Heroism and Fidelity* (1867), and *The Rising Son* (1874).

Brown died in 1884.

ED BULLINS
Dramatist, Essayist, Poet

Ed Bullins is a writer of drama, and one of the founders of the Black Arts/West in the Fillmore District of San Francisco. He patterned this experiment after the Black Arts Repertory Theater School in Harlem, New York, which was founded and directed by LeRoi Jones, and is active in analyzing the black experience in America.

The main themes of Ed Bullins are: the violence and tragedy of drug abuse, and the oppressive life-style of the ghetto. He presents his material in a realistic and naturalistic style. In productions from 1965 to 1968 he wrote *The Rally, How Do You Do, Goin'a Buffalo, Clara's Old Man, The Electronic Nigger,* and *In The Wine Time.*

He has been a most creative member of Black Arts Alliance, working with LeRoi Jones in producing films on the West Coast. Bullins has published stories, plays, essays and poetry in such diverse magazines as *Contact, Nexus, Wild Day, Soulbook, Ante, Illuminations, S. F. Oracle* and *Negro Digest.*

At present, Bullins is connected with the New Lafayette Theater in Harlem where he is a resident playwright.

PHILIP BUTCHER
Essayist, Scholar

Philip Butcher was born in Washington, D. C. in 1918. He attended Howard University where he received an A.B. in 1942 and an M.A. in 1947. He pursued his education at Columbia University where he was awarded a Ph.D. in 1956.

After serving in the United States Army during World War II, he received fellowships from the General Education Board (1948), and also from the John Hay Whitney Foundation (1951).

The works of Philip Butcher can be found in *Opportunity, Phylon, Journal of Negro History, CLA Journal, Shakespeare Quarterly* and *The American Literary Realism.* His essays present vital analyses of, and key insight into, the works of major American writers. The subject matter of his doctoral dissertation was *George W. Cable: The Northampton Years.* He made available to his profession scholarly materials previously unknown to literary critics.

Presently Butcher is a professor of English at Morgan State College in Baltimore, Maryland.

CHARLES WADDELL CHESNUTT
1858–1932
Novelist

Charles Waddell Chesnutt was the first Negro writer to work in the area of the "problem" novel, dealing with the race question from the Negro's point of view.

Born in Cleveland, Ohio in 1858, Chesnutt moved to North Carolina with his family at the age of eight. Largely self-educated, he was admitted to the Ohio bar in 1887, the same year in which his first story "The Gophered Grapevine" was published in the "Atlantic Monthly." This was followed in 1899 by two collections of his stories—"The Conjure Woman" and "The Wife of His Youth."

His first novel *The House Behind the Cedars* (1900) dealt with a young girl's attempt to "pass" for white. A year later, *The Marrow of Tradition* examined the violence of the post-Reconstruction period. His final novel *The Colonel's Dream* was published in 1905 and typified Chesnutt's basically ingratiating approach to his art, one which the writers of the "Harlem School" were later to reject, without reservation.

ELDRIDGE CLEAVER
Author

Known primarily as a revolutionary social critic although he has been Minister of Information for the Black Panther party and was nominated in 1968 as the presidential candidate of the Peace and Freedom Party, Eldridge Cleaver is a product of both the black ghetto and the California penal system. His most famous work, *Soul on Ice,* is a collection of impassioned love letters and brilliant essays probing the depths and conundrums of the modern black psyche.

The thesis of the book may be somewhat familiar, but the hip eloquence and imagery of Cleaver's writing easily affords it a new dimension. The black man, Cleaver argues, has been so systematically castrated that his consequent loss of masculinity makes it impossible for him to assume his rightful status as an heir to, and participant in, the intellectual and social life of the Western world. The white liberal enemies Cleaver excoriates have also been singled out before, just as other wrathful black polemicists have preceded him in pouring forth their raw and abrasive hatred. Nevertheless, Cleaver's fiery, grating moods and evocative imagery stamp him as a unique literary stylist, and a genuine new revolutionary voice in the black world.

Born in 1935 in Wabbeseka, Arkansas (near Little Rock), Cleaver was convicted of possessing marijuana at age 18 and, in 1954, began a 12-year cycle of assorted prison terms at Soledad, Folsom, and San Quentin. While in prison, he obtained a diploma from Bay View High School, was converted to the Black Muslim faith (he was an ardent follower of Malcolm X), and began writing for the first time in earnest.

After his release from prison, he became a staff writer for *Ramparts* magazine and a much-publicized lecturer on college campuses, where he sought to inspire and motivate black students, particularly those with ghetto backgrounds. He was once invited to address a group of Berkeley students as a black studies lecturer, a move roundly opposed by California governor Ronald Reagan. The course Social Analysis 139X was never conducted regularly.

In 1969, Cleaver left the United States secretly, fleeing a prison sentence which had been imposed on him for violating parole and for alleged involvement in a shoot-out with Oakland police. He was found by a Reuters correspondent in Havana, ostensibly working on a sequel to *Soul on Ice*. Later that year, however, he emerged in Moscow, where he granted an interview which confirmed his connection with the "international proletarian movement." Critical of both the Soviet Union and Red China for pursuing "narrow interests," Cleaver contended that "big Communist countries" should invest in the future by pooling their arsenals, supplying more generous arms supplies to fledgling liberation movements, and facing up to the imperialism of the United States.

At this juncture, it developed that Cleaver, his wife, and young son were residing in Algeria. The author/revolutionary did not disclose why he had left Cuba, although he made it clear that he could presumably return at will since he was free to circulate through most Communist countries, armed only with a driver's license and a copy of his FBI wanted poster.

Cleaver maintains that his ties with the Black Panthers have not been severed by exile. In his view, revolution is international business, and converts must be cultivated everywhere. He and Stokely Carmichael appear to be at odds over this point; the latter has reportedly been critical of joint alliances between white and black radicals.

JOSEPH SEAMON COTTER, SR.
1861–?
Poet

Though he did not, in his youth, attend school past the third grade, Joseph Seamon Cotter, Sr. achieved distinction during his lifetime as a poet—primarily in the dialect idiom. Cotter's earliest work, *A Rhyming* (1895), was followed in later years by the prize-winning "Tragedy of Pete" which was awarded an *Opportunity* Prize during the Harlem Renaissance. His *Collected Poems* appeared in 1938.

Born at Bardstown, Kentucky, Cotter worked in various odd jobs during his youth, and became a schoolteacher in Louisville after he returned to his schooling at the age of 22. His poetry reflects more than 50 years experience as a teacher, and is a dynamic mixture of the storytelling art, the young man's thirst for racial leadership, and the tutor at work. His dialect poetry is mindful of Dunbar at his best, although Cotter tends to be more racially critical than his more famous poet.

* * *

JOSEPH SEAMON COTTER, JR.
1895-1919
Poet

Young Joseph Seamon Cotter, Jr. followed in his father's footsteps as a poet, although he enjoyed the benefit of collegiate training at Fisk University in Nashville. Sickly, Cotter was forced to abandon the school in his second year after contracting tuberculosis. His most distinguished work, *The Band of Gideon*, a thin volume of only 30 pages, was published in 1918, shortly before his death.

COUNTEE CULLEN
1903–1946
Poet

Countee Cullen was one of the leading figures in the "Harlem Renaissance."

Born Countee Porter on May 30, 1903 in Baltimore, he was orphaned at an early age, and adopted by Reverend Frederick Cullen, pastor of New York's Salem Methodist Church. At New York University, Cullen won Phi Beta Kappa honors, and was awarded the Witter Bynner Poetry Prize. In 1925, while still a student at N. Y. U., Cullen completed *Color*, a volume of poetry which received the Harmon Foundation's first gold medal for literature two years later.

In 1926, he earned his M. A. at Harvard and, a year later, finished both *The Ballad of the Brown Girl* and *Copper Sun*. This was followed, in 1929, by *The Black Christ*, written during a two-year sojourn in France on a Guggenheim Fellowship.

Countee Cullen

Upon his return to New York City, Cullen began a teaching career in the public school system. During this period, he also produced a novel, *One Way to Heaven* (1932); *The Medea and Other Poems* (1935); *The Lost Zoo* (1940), and *My Nine Lives and How I Lost Them* (1942).

In 1947, a year after his death, Cullen's own selections of his best work were collected in a volume published under the title *On These I Stand*.

ARTHUR P. DAVIS
Essayist, Scholar

Arthur P. Davis was born in Hampton, Virginia, in 1904. He achieved his Ph.D. from Columbia University in 1942. He has served as a college professor at North Carolina College (1927-1928) and at Virginia Union (1929-1944).

Davis is most noted for co-editing *The Negro Caravan* (1941) with Sterling A. Brown and Ulysses Lee. He published a book, based on his doctoral dissertation, called *Issac Watts: His Life and Works* (1943).

He is interested in, and is a foremost critic of, Negro literature. Many of his essays can be found in *Phylon*, *Common Ground*, and *Opportunity*. His most famous essays have been definitive analyses of works by Phyllis Wheatley, Langston Hughes, Countee Cullen, and the writers of The Harlem Renaissance.

He is presently teaching literature at Howard University where he has been a professor since 1944.

MARTIN R. DELANEY
1812-1885
Essayist, Author

Most of Martin R. Delaney's writing busied itself with what is perhaps the most pervasive theme in all of black literature: the search for identity and self-realization. Delaney, a native of Charlestown, Virginia, was widely read and travelled, and developed in his lifetime a dynamic and expressive black power ethic.

One of Delaney's first serious ventures was to trace his lineage with scientific accuracy to the African chieftains whom he believed were his actual forefathers. Delaney pursued formal education with resolve and vigor once his parents had escaped from Virginia to western Pennsylvania. He eventually studied medicine at Harvard University Medical School and, while a practicing physician in Pittsburgh, was instrumental in putting down a cholera epidemic which had erupted there.

Prior to the outbreak of the Civil War, Delaney led an investigation into the Niger Valley in West Africa, later publishing an official report of his explorations in a study which contained specific recommendations for black repatriation. During the war itself, Delaney served as a medical officer, and rose to the rank of major. Reconstruction found him active in politics, albeit unsuccessfully.

Retirement enabled him to prepare his most ambitious work, *Principles of Ethnology* (1879). His best-known work, however, remains a political tract entitled *The Condition, Elevation, Emigration and Destiny of the Colored People of the United States, Politically Considered* (1852).

Delaney died in Xenia, Ohio, home of Wilberforce University.

Major Martin R. Delaney

OWEN DODSON
1914-
Dramatist, Poet

Poet/dramatist Owen Dodson's most ambitious work revolves about the Father Divine legend and is, with deliberately punnish intent, entitled *The Divine Comedy*. First produced at the Yale University Theatre in 1938, the play is thought to be the first serious full-length effort designed to exploit the dramatic possibilities inherent in the uncannily popular and pseudo-mysterious cult of Father Divine.

A native of Brooklyn, Dodson attended Bates College and went on to earn a Master of Fine Arts degree from Yale. His alma mater also presented another of Dodson's major dramatic efforts, *The Garden of Time*. Success in university theatre led to the play's later appearances at predominantly black universities throughout the South, but did not materialize in a Broadway production. There was, however, at this time, little opportunity for other than stereotyped commercial portrayals of black themes along the Great White Way.

Dodson later went into teaching at the Atlanta University complex, although he was commissioned to write a play on the Amistad Mutiny, a shipboard slave uprising in the 1840's. His traditional and experimental verse was published in several quarterlies and anthologies.

W. E. B. DUBOIS
1868–1963
Author, historian

An outstanding critic, editor, scholar, author and civil rights leader, William Edward Burghardt DuBois is certainly among the most prominent and influential Negro leaders of the 20th century.

Born in Great Barrington, Massachusetts on February 23, 1868, DuBois received a bachelor's degree from Fisk University, and went on to win a second bachelor's, as well as a Ph. D., from Harvard. He was for a time professor of Latin and Greek at Wilberforce and the University of Pennsylvania, and also served as a professor of economics and history at Atlanta University.

One of the founders of the National Association for the Advancement of Colored People (NAACP) in 1909, DuBois served as that organization's director of publications and editor of "Crisis" magazine until 1934. In 1944, he returned from Atlanta University to become head of the NAACP's special research department, a post he held until 1948. Dr. DuBois emigrated to Africa in 1961 and became editor-in-chief of the Encyclopedia Africana, an enormous publishing venture which had been planned by Kwame Nkrumah, since then deposed as president of Ghana. DuBois died in Ghana in 1963 at the age of 95.

His numerous books include *The Suppression of the Slave Trade* (1896); *The Philadelphia Negro* (1899); *The Souls of Black Folk* (1903); *John Brown* (1909); *Quest of the Silver Fleece* (1911); *The Negro* (1915); *Darkwater* (1920); *The Gift of Black Folk* (1924); *Dark Princess* (1928); *Black Folk; Then and Now* (1939); *Dusk of Dawn* (1940); *Color and Democracy* (1945); *The World and Africa* (1947); *In Battle for Peace* (1952), and a trilogy, *Black Flame* (1957-1961).

It is this enormous literary output on such a wide variety of themes which offers the most convincing testimony to DuBois' lifetime position that it was vitally necessary for the Negro to cultivate his own aesthetic and cultural values even as he made valuable strides toward social emancipation. In this, he was opposed by Booker T. Washington who felt that the Negro should concentrate on developing technical and mechanical skills before all else.

In 1961, at age 93, DuBois joined the Communist Party. He died two years later.

It was DuBois' affiliation with the Communist Party that prompted a spirited protest against the plan to erect a memorial in his hometown in 1969. Though DuBois was a lifelong radical, he functioned within the pale of society as an American during his most productive years.

W. E. B. DuBois

PAUL LAURENCE DUNBAR
1872–1906
Poet

The first Negro poet to gain a national reputation in the United States, Paul Laurence Dunbar was also the first to use Negro dialect within the formal structure of his work.

Born of former slaves in 1872 in Dayton, Ohio, Dunbar went to work as an elevator operator after graduating from high school. His first book of poetry *Oak and Ivy* was privately printed in 1893, and was followed by *Majors and Minors* which appeared two years later. Neither book was an immediate sensation, but there were enough favorable reviews in such magazines as "Harper's" to encourage Dunbar in the pursuit of a full-fledged literary career. In 1896, Dunbar completed *Lyrics of a Lowly Life*, the single work upon which his subsequent reputation was irrevocably established.

Before his untimely death in 1906, Dunbar had become the dominant presence in the world of American Negro poetry. His later works included *Lyrics of Love and Laughter* (1903); *Lyrics of Sunshine and Shadow* (1905), and *Complete Poems*, published posthumously in 1913.

This last work contains not only the dialect poems which were his trademark, but many poems in conventional English as well. The book has enjoyed such enormous popularity that it has, to this day, never gone out of print.

RALPH ELLISON
Novelist, essayist

Ralph Ellison's critical and artistic reputation rests largely on a single masterpiece, his first and only novel, *Invisible Man*. Acclaimed by virtually all who have read it, the novel was given the National Book Award for fiction in 1952. It had been five years in the making, and its success heralded the emergence of a major writing talent, one separate and distinct from Richard Wright, who had been Ellison's mentor long before *Invisible Man* was published.

Ellison was born in Oklahoma City, Oklahoma on March 1, 1914, and came to New York City in the late 1930's after having studied music at Tuskegee Institute for three years. At first interested in

Ralph Ellison

sculpture, he turned to writing after coming under the influence of T. S. Eliot's poetry, and as a direct consequence of his friendship with Richard Wright.

In 1955, the American Academy of Arts and Letters awarded Ellison the Prix de Rome which enabled him to live and write in Italy for a time. Since then, he has lectured at New York University and at Bennington College, and has been writer-in-residence at Rutgers University.

His last published work was *Shadow and Act*, a book of essays which appeared in 1964.

MARI EVANS
Poet

A poet who arose in the early 1960's, Mari Evans is noted for her ability to jolt her readers with the beauty of blackness.

Born in Toledo, Ohio, she studied at the University of Toledo. In 1963 her poetry was published in *Phylon, Negro Digest* and *Dialog*. Two years later she was awarded a John Hay Whitney Fellowship.

One of her most well known works is probably "The Alarm Clock," which deals with the rude awakening of the black American to the white "Establishment." It captures and summarizes the scene of the sixties in the United States.

Miss Evans is presently employed as the producer-director of "The Black Experience," a half-hour series aired weekly in Indianapolis on WTTV-Channel 4.

JESSIE FAUSET
Novelist

Jessie Fauset is one of the last mainstays of the so-called "traditional school" of Negro literature. Written in a genteel style, her novels deal primarily with middle-class Negroes, and are in sharp contrast to the work produced by the young writers of the "Harlem School" who sought to capture the stark realism of life in the Negro ghetto.

As an editor of "Crisis," Miss Fauset often championed the works of the young writers, even though their direction ran counter to her own. She herself was the most prolific of the Negro Renaissance novelists, publishing four books over a 10-year span: *There Is Confusion* (1924); *Plum Bun* (1928); *The Chinaberry Tree* (1931), and *Comedy American Style* (1933).

In later years, Miss Fauset was a teacher in the New York City public school system.

RUDOLPH FISHER
1897-1934
Novelist, Short Story Writer

Rudolph Fisher was born May 9, 1897 in Washington, D. C. and raised in Providence, Rhode Island. He attended Brown University and Howard Medical School. Fisher came to New York to study biology at Columbia University's College of Physicians and Surgeons, and then went on to specialize in roentgenology.

"The City of Refuge," Fisher's first short story, was written while he was still in medical school and depicted Harlem life during the 1920's. It was subsequently reprinted in the anthology *The Best Short Stories of 1925*.

Fisher's two novels, *The Walls of Jericho* (1928) and *The Conjure Man Dies* (1932) never became as popular as his short stories. Other short stories by Fisher are "Ringtail," "High Yaller," "The Promised Land," and "Miss Cynthie."

CHARLOTTE FORTEN
1837-1914
Author, Poet

A member of the distinguished Forten family (her grandfather James served in the Revolutionary War), Charlotte Forten attended school in Salem, Massachusetts, winning early honors for her poetry while at Higginson Grammar School. (She was unable to obtain an education in her native city of Philadelphia because of race.)

Her education prepared her for a career in teaching, which she pursued until the Civil War when she served as an agent with the Freedmen's Aid Society at Port Royal, St. Helena Island, off South Carolina.

Her best-known writing was a series of articles entitled *Glimpses of New England*, which was published in the *National Anti-Slavery Standard*. Other articles on life in the Sea Islands were printed in *Atlantic Monthly*, a publication which gave her widespread circulation.

Though her work is by no means lasting literature, it is important for the exposure Miss Forten gave to racial prejudice in antebellum New England in a middle-class atmosphere, and for her equally relevant characterization of the Sea Islands, which would otherwise be virtually unknown to American readers.

JOHN HOPE FRANKLIN
Historian

Negro history has had no more scholarly spokesman in the last two decades than John Hope Franklin, whose classic analysis of American history and the Negro's place in it, *From Slavery to Freedom* (1947), is ranked in the company of the most authoritative studies of the period.

A native of Rentiesville, Oklahoma, Franklin graduated from Fisk University in 1935, and later received his M.A. and Ph.D. degrees from Harvard. Since then, he has taught at Howard, at Alabama State Teachers College, and at Harvard, and has received Rosenwald and Guggenheim Fellowships for research in his chosen field.

In addition to having written numerous articles in such periodicals as the "American Historical Review," the "Journal of Negro History," the "Journal of Southern History," and the "Journal of Modern History," Franklin has an impressive list of full-length book credits, including *The Free Negro in North Carolina, 1790-1860* (1943); *The Civil War, Diary of James Ayers* (1947); *Reconstruction After the*

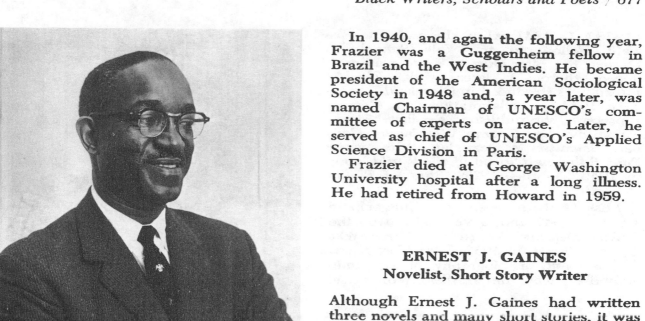

John Hope Franklin

Civil War (1961), *The Emancipation Proclamation* (1963), *The Negro in Twentieth Century America* (1967), and *Color and Race* (1968).

Franklin is currently a professor in the History Department at the University of Chicago.

E. FRANKLIN FRAZIER
18 -962
Historian, ociologist

Onc e chairman of oward University's so iology departmentE. Franklin Frazier i s best remembered or his controversial book *Black Bourgeoie* in which he expounded the theo that the Negro middle class was olating itself from the problems of rginal or poverty-stricken Negroes.

Born in Baltimo in 1894, Frazier graduated from Hvard in 1916, and received his Ph.D. om the University of Chicago in 1931. Three years later, he began a 25-year riod of service in the sociology departmt of Howard, interrupting his tenurthere on occasion to teach at Co University, New York University r centers of higher learning.

In 1940, and again the following year, Frazier was a Guggenheim fellow in Brazil and the West Indies. He became president of the American Sociological Society in 1948 and, a year later, was named Chairman of UNESCO's committee of experts on race. Later, he served as chief of UNESCO's Applied Science Division in Paris.

Frazier died at George Washington University hospital after a long illness. He had retired from Howard in 1959.

ERNEST J. GAINES
Novelist, Short Story Writer

Although Ernest J. Gaines had written three novels and many short stories, it was not until the publication of *Bloodline* in 1968 that he began to receive considerable attention.

Gaines was born in 1933 on a plantation in Louisiana. He moved to California in 1949 where he did his undergraduate study at San Francisco State College. The year after graduating college, 1958, he received the Wallace Stegner Fellowship in creative writing. The following year he was awarded the Joseph Henry Jackson Literary Award.

His first novel to be published was *Catherine Carmier* (1964). Other novels by Gaines are *Of Love And Dust* (1967) and *Barren Summer* (completed in 1963).

SHIRLEY GRAHAM
Biographical historian

Shirley Graham has brought to her work as a biographical historian a writing style which was refined by more than a decade of activity as a dramatist.

Born on November 11, 1904 in Indianapolis, Indiana, Miss Graham received her A. B. degree in 1934 at Oberlin College, and her M. A. from the same institution a year later. While at Oberlin, she wrote and composed her first musical play, *Tom-Tom,* which was produced in 1932. She then studied music composition at the Sorbonne, and later taught at Morgan State and Tennessee State universities.

During a short stint with the Chicago Federal Theatre, she directed, designed and composed for *Little Black Sambo* (1937) and created *The Swing Mikado*

(1938). In 1941, while she was a Rosenwald Fellow at the Yale School of Drama, her play *Dust to Earth* was produced there. A later work, *Elijah's Raven*, was produced in Cleveland.

In 1944, in collaboration with George Lipscomb, she published her first historical study, *Dr. George Washington Carver, Scientist*. A year later, she wrote *Paul Robeson, Citizen of the World*, and, in 1949, completed *The Story of Phillis Wheatley*.

Miss Graham received a Guggenheim grant in 1947 and, a year later, won the Julian Messner Award for *There Was Once A Slave*. In 1950, *Your Most Humble Servant*, a biography of Benjamin Banneker, won the Anisfield Wolf prize.

JUPITER HAMMON
1720?–1800?
Poet

The first Negro to be published in America was Jupiter Hammon, whose "An Evening Thought, Salvation by Christ, with Penitential Cries" appeared in 1761. Hammon was a slave belonging to a Mr. Lloyd of Long Island, New York.

Due to his fondness for preaching, the major portion of Hammon's poetry is religious in tone, and is usually dismissed by critics as being of little aesthetic value because of its pious platitudes, faulty syntax, and forced rhymes. Hammon's best-known work, however, is a prose piece, "An Address to the Negroes of the State of New York," delivered before the African Society of New York City on September 24, 1786. This speech was published the following year and went into three editions.

LORRAINE HANSBERRY
1930–1965
Dramatist

The artistic reputation of Lorraine Hansberry rests largely on the success of her first play *A Raisin in the Sun* which was awarded the New York Drama Critics Circle Award for the year 1959. (Miss Hansberry is the first Negro playwright to win this award.)

Born in Chicago on May 19, 1930, Miss Hansberry became interested in the theatre while still in high school, but decided to study art instead—first at Chicago's Art Institute, then at the University of Wisconsin and, finally, in Guadalajara, Mexico.

Lorraine Hansberry

She wrote *Raisin* while living in New York's Greenwich Village, having conceived it originally after reacting distastefully to what she called "a whole body of material about Negroes. Cardboard characters. Cute dialect bits. Or hip-swinging musicals from exotic scores." It opened on Broadway on March 11, 1959—at a time when it was generally held that all plays dealing with N[illegible] "death" at the box-office. [illegible]duced, direc[illegible]ted and acted by Negroe[illegible] it was later [illegible] made into a successful movie starring Si[illegible]dney Poitier.

Her final play *The Sign in Sidn[illegible] Brustein's Windo*[illegible] dealt with ". . . the Western intellectu[illegible] poised in hesitation before the flam[illegible] of involvement." Shortly after its B[illegible]adway opening, Miss Hansberry succum[illegible]ed to cancer on January 12, 1965 in N[illegible] York City.

FRANCES E[illegible]W. HARPER
1825[illegible]1911
[illegible]et

Frances Ellen Wat[illegible]s Harper was born in 1825 in Baltimore[illegible] free parents, and orphaned a few year[illegible]er. She attended a school for free Negroes conducted by her uncle, William Watkins, interrupting her formal education at the age of 13 to find employment as a nursemaid.

While she was still in her teens, her early poetry and prose were published in a volume called *Autumn Leaves*. Her biggest commercial success came in Philadelphia in 1854, when she published *Poems on Miscellaneous Subjects*, which sold 10,000 copies in its first five years.

Her next work *Moses, A Story of the Nile* appeared in 1869. Four years later, she completed *Sketches of Southern Life* which is notable for its attempt to recreate the speech of American Negroes while avoiding dialect.

MIDDLETON A. "SPIKE" HARRIS
Historian

Born and schooled in New York City, Middleton A. Harris is not a historian in the strictly formal and narrow academic confines of that term. He is, rather, a collector, a researcher—even a "detective," to use the word with which "Spike" Harris is most often associated.

Harris' early formal education began at P.S. 9 in Brooklyn and continued through Brooklyn's Manual Training High School and the Manhattan Textile High School. He later attended Howard University, graduating with a degree in sociology.

After college Harris became a social worker, directing numerous youth groups before joining the City of New York as a parole officer. During World War II, "Spike" served as social director for the American Red Cross in the South Pacific.

Curiosity about his own family beginnings started Harris on his lifelong quest for his own origins and for the largely buried elements of black history. Like Joel Rogers, Harris realized the history of his people was dispersed, and would require intensive research. Thus, he wrote letters to government officials, conducted investigations of records in local Court Houses, nd relentlessly followed every lead. Over e years, Harris was thus able to accumute a vast personal collection of memoralia, mementos, tokens, souvenirs, and versified keepsakes germane to the history of the Negro.

Harris' personal library of rare books, aphics, audio-visual materials, and duplies of governmental records relative to history of the black American provides esource for eager students and a treasure trove for accomplished scholars. As President of Negro History Associates, Harris has successfully assumed responsibility for generating interest in what he calls the "lost pages of our national history." He has already dedicated four historical plaques in Manhattan which pertain to episodes involving black contributions or achievements.

Harris is also the author of a unique guidebook of Manhattan Island as seen from the vantage point of a black observer. The book is called *A Negro History Tour of Manhattan* and contains several startling, revealing and intriguing facts and incidents.

Middleton A. "Spike" Harris

ROBERT E. HAYDEN
1913-
Poet

Poet Robert E. Hayden, a graduate of Wayne University, found little outlet for the superior poetry which he was able to produce during the Depression years, and so was forced to content himself with a less-than-desirable post as chief researcher on Negro history and folklore for the Federal Writers Project in 1936.

Undaunted, he later went on to do advanced work in English, play production, and creative writing at the University of Michigan and, while there, won the Jule and Avery Hopwood Prize for poetry. Hayden also completed radio scripts, and a finished version of a play about the Underground Railroad, *Go Down Moses.*

His first book of poems, *Heart-Shape in the Dust,* was published in 1940, shortly before he assumed the music and drama critic function for the *Michigan Chronicle.*

CHESTER HIMES
Novelist

Chester Himes began his career as a writer of popular material, and later moved to biting works of fiction, often double-edged with satiric humor.

Born in Jefferson City, Missouri in 1909, Himes was educated at Ohio State University, and now lives in France.

In 1945, he completed his first novel *If He Hollers Let Him Go,* the story of a Negro working in a defense plant. His second book *The Lonely Crusade* (1947) was set in similar surroundings.

Since then, Himes has written many other books: *Third Generation* (1954); *Cotton Comes to Harlem* (1965), and *Pinktoes* (1965). His later work has often been praised by James Baldwin, but it has not as yet received a wide readership.

A scene from the screen version of the Himes novel, Cotton Comes to Harlem.

GEORGE MOSES HORTON
1797–1883?
Poet

George Moses Horton was born in slavery on the plantation of William Horton in North Carolina. While working as a janitor at the University of North Carolina, Horton wrote light verse for some students in exchange for spending money.

Some of his early poems were printed in the newspapers of Raleigh and Boston. When Horton published his first book of poems in 1829, he entitled it *The Hope of Liberty* in the belief that profits from its sales would be sufficient to pay for his freedom. His hopes did not materialize, however, with the result that he remained a slave until the coming of Emancipation.

In 1865, he published *Naked Genius*, a poem containing many bitter lines about his former condition which are in sharp contrast to the conformist verse of earlier Negro poets.

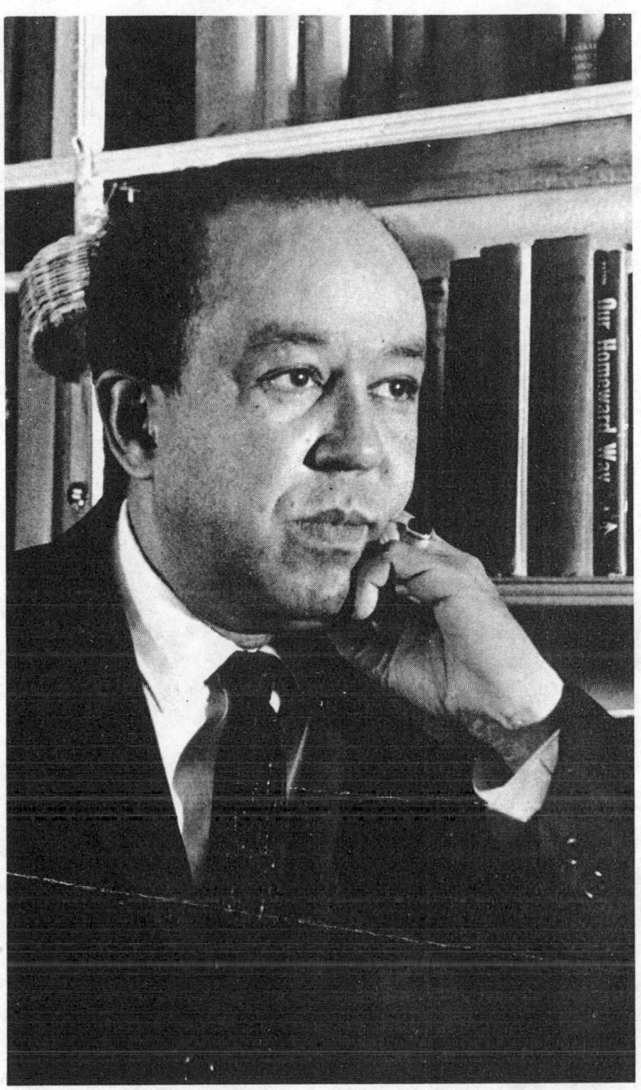

Langston Hughes

LANGSTON HUGHES
1902-1967
Poet

Few would quarrel with Langston Hughes' unofficial designation as the "Negro poet laureate" of our day. An established poet and critic, Hughes belongs in the ranks of the major American writers of the 20th century.

Born in Joplin, Missouri on February 1, 1902, Hughes moved to Cleveland at the age of 14. Having graduated from Central High School, he spent a year in Mexico before studying for a time at Columbia University. After roaming the world as a seaman and writing some poetry as well, Hughes returned to the United States, winning the Witter Bynner Prize for undergraduate poetry while attending Lincoln University, later his alma mater (1928). Two years later, he received the Harmon Award and, in 1935, with the help of a Guggenheim Fellowship, traveled to Russia and Spain.

The long and distinguished list of Hughes' prose works includes: *Not Without Laughter* (1930), a collection of short stories, and *The Big Sea* (1940), his autobiography. To this must be added such collections of poetry as *The Weary Blues* (1926); *The Dream Keeper* (1932); *Shakespeare in Harlem* (1942); *Fields of Wonder* (1947), and *One Way Ticket* (1947).

Hughes was also an accomplished song lyricist, librettist, and newspaper columnist. Through his newspaper columns, he created Jesse B. Simple, a Harlem character who saw life on the musical stage in *Simply Heavenly*.

Throughout the 1960's Hughes edited several anthologies in an attempt to popularize and expose black authors and their works. Some of these are: *An African Treasury* (1960), *Poems From Black Africa* (1963), *New Negro Poets: U.S.A.* (1964), and *The Best Short Stories by Negro Writers* (1967). Published after his death was *The Panther and the Lash; Poems Of Our Times* (1969).

In tone and spirit, Hughes remained a poet with a twist of gray humor. Sadness, rather than anger, seemed his primary emotion.

Tomorrow

We have tomorrow
Bright before us
Like a flame,
Yesterday
A night-gone thing,
A sundown-name,
And dawn—today
Broad arch above
The road we came.
We march!

Langston Hughes
To the Freie
Akademie der Künste
in appreciation and
gratitude, Hamburg,
October 1, 1964

A rare handwritten version of a Langston Hughes poem.

ZORA NEALE HURSTON
1903–1960
Novelist

Once placed "in the front rank, not only of Negro writers, but all American writers" for her mastery of folklore, Zora Neale Hurston was born and raised in an all-Negro town in Florida (Eatonville), an experience that left a deep imprint on her later literary efforts.

After traveling North as a maid with a Gilbert and Sullivan Company, she acquired her education at Morgan State, Howard, and Columbia. While at Howard, under Alain Locke's influence, she became a figure in the Negro Renaissance, publishing short stories in "Opportunity" and serving with Langston Hughes and Wallace Thurman on the editorial board of "Fire."

In 1934, *Jonah's Gourd Vine* was published after her return to Florida. Her more important novel *Their Eyes Were Watching God* appeared three years later, and was followed in 1948 by *Seraph on the Suwanee*. Her other works range from books of folklore to plays and librettos, and include her autobiography.

Toward the end of her life, Miss Hurston was a drama instructor at the North Carolina College for Negroes in Durham, North Carolina. She died in obscurity and poverty on January 28, 1960.

FENTON JOHNSON
1888–1958
Poet

Fenton Johnson was born in Chicago in 1888, and received his formal education there, first in the public school system and, later, at the University of Chicago. In 1914, Johnson completed his first volume of poetry, *A Little Dreaming*, followed in 1916 by *Visions of the Dusk* and *Songs of the Soil*. Johnson's prose works include *Tales of Darkest America* (1920), and a book of short stories.

His last published work, *WPA Poems*, appeared posthumously, Johnson having died in 1958.

GEORGIA DOUGLAS JOHNSON
1886–1966
Poet

Georgia Douglas Johnson was born on September 10, 1886 in Atlanta, Georgia, and educated at Atlanta University and at the Oberlin Conservatory in Ohio.

Her initial interest was in musical composition, but gradually she turned her creative energies more and more toward the writing of lyric poetry. After teaching school in Alabama, she moved to Washington, D. C. with her husband who had been appointed as Recorder of Deeds by President William Howard Taft. While in the nation's capital, she too engaged in government work while completing such books as *The Heart of Woman* (1918); *Bronze* (1922), and *An Autumn Love Cycle* (1928).

JAMES WELDON JOHNSON
1871–1938
Poet, lyricist, critic

Like W. E. B. DuBois, Negro intellectual James Weldon Johnson played a number of vital roles in the earlier phase of the civil rights movement of the 20th century—as poet, teacher, critic, diplomat, and NAACP executive secretary. Johnson is perhaps most often popularly remembered as the lyricist for *Lift Every Voice and Sing*, the poem which is often referred to as the "Negro National Anthem."

Born on June 17, 1871 in Jacksonville, Florida, Johnson was educated at Atlanta and Columbia universities. His career included service as a school principal; a lawyer; and a diplomat (U. S. Consul at Puerto Cabello, Venezuela and, later, in Nicaragua). From 1916 to 1930, he was one of the key policy makers of the National Association for the Advancement of Colored People (NAACP), eventually serving as the organization's Executive Secretary.

In his early days, Johnson's fame rested largely on his work as a lyricist for popular songs but, in 1917, he completed his first book of poetry, *Fifty Years and Other Poems*. Five years later, he followed this with *The Book of American Negro Poetry* and, in 1927, established his literary reputation with *God's Trombones*, a collection of seven folk sermons in verse. Over the years, this work has been performed countless times, both on stage and on television.

In 1930, Johnson finished *St. Peter Relates an Incident of the Resurrection* and, three years later, his lengthy autobiography, *Along This Way*.

Johnson died in 1938 following an automobile accident in Maine.

Leroi Jones

LEROI JONES
Poet, dramatist

LeRoi Jones has come to the forefront of American literature in the 1960's as both poet and playwright.

Born October 30, 1934 in Newark, N.J., the son of a postal superintendent father and social worker mother, Jones was a scholarship student at the Newark branch of Rutgers University before transferring to Howard.

After military service with the Air Force, Jones returned to civilian life as a teacher and writer, publishing his first book, *Preface to a Twenty-Volume Suicide Note,* in 1961. His poetry and fiction won him a John Hay Whitney Fellowship for that year.

In 1964, his play *The Dutchman* opened in New York, and he was widely acclaimed as one of the most promising of the new crop of American playwrights. Dutchman received the Obie Award as the best off-Broadway play for the 1963-1964 season. The shocking honesty of Jones' treatment of racial conflict in this and in later plays has become the hallmark of his work. In 1965, *The Slave* and *The Toilet*—plays widely divergent in style and approach—were also produced off-Broadway.

Jones' books include *Blues People* (1963); *The Dead Lecturer* (1964), *The System of Dante's Hell* (1966), *Home* (1966), *Tales* (1967), and *Black Music* (1967). He is also the co-editor of an anthology of Afro-American writing called *Black Fire* published in 1968.

WILLIAM MELVIN KELLEY
Novelist

William Melvin Kelley is considered by many critics to be among the most promising American novelists of the 1960's.

In 1962, his first novel *A Different Drummer* was widely acclaimed for its provocative theme and imaginative development. (The story concerns the mass exodus of the Negro inhabitants of an imaginary Southern state.)

Born in New York City in 1937, Kelley is a graduate of the Fieldston School and of Harvard, where he studied under Archibald MacLeish and John Hawkes. He has won the Dana Reed Literary Prize, and the Rosenthal Foundation Award of the National Institute of Arts and Letters.

John O. Killens

In 1964, a collection of his stories appeared under the title *Dancers on the Shore.* The following year his second novel was published, *A Drop of Patience*. His most recent novel, *Dem,* a surrealistic fantasy, was published in 1967.

JOHN OLIVER KILLENS
Novelist

John Oliver Killens is considered by many critics to be one of the most articulate novelists of the past decade.

His first novel *Youngblood* (1954) dealt with life in a Southern Negro family, a theme which Killens knew well, having been born into just such an environment in Macon, Georgia in 1916.

Interested at first in a legal career, Killens studied at the Terrell Law School, at Columbia, and at New York University. From 1936 to 1942—and again in 1946 after completing his military service—Killens worked with the National Labor Relations Board in Washington, D. C.

After serving for a time as head of the Harlem Writers' Workshop, Killens saw his second novel *And Then We Heard the Thunder* published in 1963. Prior to that, he had written the script for *Odds Against Tomorrow,* a film which starred Harry Belafonte in 1959.

Killens' most recent book, *Black Man's Burden,* appeared in 1965.

JULIUS LESTER
Essayist and Critic

Julius Lester has recently been propelled to the forefront of the black militant movement by his many outspoken views in his essays and on his radio program.

Lester is the author of *Look Out, Whitey! Black Power's Goin' Get Your Mama, To Be A Slave,* and *Revolutionary Notes* (1969). *To Be A Slave* (1968) was the 1968 Newbery Medal runner-up. His various writings have appeared in *The Village Voice, The Guardian, The Movement, Broadsides, Liberator,* and *Sing Out.* On WBAI, the Pacifica Foundation station in New York City, Lester's program has presented views by black people who are attempting to define what it means to be black in America. In addition to all this, Lester has made two records for Vanguard Records. His reviews have appeared frequently in the pages of the New York *Times.*

Julius Lester

ALAIN LEROY LOCKE
1886–1954
Critic

Alain Leroy Locke shares the spotlight—along with Benjamin Brawley and Sterling Brown—as a leading critic and chronicler of the "Harlem Renaissance."

Locke was born in Philadelphia on September 3, 1886 and educated at Harvard and, as a Rhodes scholar, at Oxford. He served for many years as chairman of the philosophy department at Howard University, but his main contribution to American culture lies in his efforts to make the general public aware of the Negro's aesthetic achievements—from the art and artifacts of Africa to the poetry and novels of the American writer.

In 1925, Locke completed *The New Negro,* a volume which sought to define the aims of the Negro artists then in the full flush of the "Harlem Renaissance." Consisting of the representative work of a number of young Negro writers, this anthology served notice of the existence of a new literary self-image for the Negro, founded partly on an uncompromising demand for equal rights. Traceable in part to the challenge posed by Dr. W. E. B. DuBois to the "conciliatory" policies of Booker T. Washington, this new intellectual trend was given even ticipation in World War I.

Locke's championing of the new writers who had outgrown what he called "the pathetic over-compensation of a group inferiority complex," helped promote a number of outstanding literary works written by Negroes during the post-war period.

Locke died in 1954 while in the midst of collecting material for what he hoped would be his greatest contribution to American letters. This work, later completed by Margaret Just Butcher, is entitled *The Negro in American Culture* (1956).

RAYFORD W. LOGAN
1897-
Historian

A prolific writer, historian Rayford W. Logan is a native of Washington, D. C., where he received a public school education prior to attending Harvard and Williams College.

During World War I, Logan served abroad with the 372nd Infantry of the segregated 93rd Division, a unit which was brigaded with French troops overseas. After the war, Logan went into teaching, first at Virginia Union University, then at Atlanta University, and lastly at Howard. While there, he became an assistant to Carter Woodson in the Washington-based Association for the Study of Negro Life and History.

While in this capacity, he contributed numerous articles to a gigantic variety of scholarly and popular periodicals, edited

The Attitude of the Southern White Press Toward Negro Suffrage, 1932-1940 (1940), and wrote a study entitled *The Diplomatic Relations of the United States with Haiti, 1776-1891* (1941). He has written numerous other books since then, including *The Negro in the United States* (1957), and *The Betrayal of the Negro from Rutherford B. Hayes to Woodrow Wilson* (1965).

PAULE MARSHALL
Novelist, Short Story Writer

Paule Marshall is one of the most critically acclaimed Negro novelists of the day.

She was born in Brooklyn, New York in 1929 and graduated from Brooklyn College as a member of Phi Beta Kappa. She spent much time in Barbados (the birthplace of her parents) where she wrote her first novel *Brown Girl, Brownstones* (1959), which deals with the theme of the dislocation which one experiences in moving from the tropics of Barbados to the cruel reality of a home in Brooklyn, New York.

She is also the author of *Soul Clap Hands and Sing* (1961), which is a collection of short stories dealing with the locales of Brazil, Barbados, British Guiana and Brooklyn. Her most recent literary effort has been a novel entitled *The Chosen Place, The Timeless People* (1969). It has achieved an extraordinary recognition in the field of popular fiction.

JULIAN MAYFIELD
Novelist, Essayist, Editor

Julian Mayfield was born in Greer, South Carolina, in 1928. At the age of 10 he moved with his family to Washington, D. C. Upon completing his high school education he served in the United States Army in the Pacific area. At the conclusion of World War II he resumed his studies at Lincoln University in Pennsylvania. As with many other creative artists he was employed in a myriad of odd unrewarding jobs. He acted in the Broadway play *Lost in the Stars.*

He spent many years in both Africa and Europe. Much of his work can be found in the *Puerto Rico World Journal, The African Review* in Accra, *Commentary, The New Republic,* and *The Nation.*

His novels include *The Hit* (1957), *The Long Night* (1958), and *The Grand Parade* (1961). His works have been translated into French, Japanese, Czech, and German. He is presently working on a book about Ghana, and is a teaching fellow at Cornell University.

CLAUDE McKAY
1890–1948
Poet

Claude McKay is generally regarded as the herald of the "Harlem Renaissance" period.

Born the son of a farmer in Jamaica (then British West Indies), on September 15, 1890, McKay began his writing career early in life. Two books of his poems—*Songs of Jamaica* and *Constab Ballads*—were published just after he had turned 20. In both of them, he made extensive use of the Jamaican dialect known as *patois.*

In 1913, McKay came to America to study agriculture at Tuskegee Institute and at Kansas State University, but his interest in poetry soon induced him to move to New York City, where he began to publish his work in small literary magazines.

McKay then made a trip abroad, visiting England for a time. While there, he completed a collection of lyrics entitled *Spring in New Hampshire.* When he returned to the United States, he became associate editor of "The Liberator" under Max Eastman. In 1922, he completed *Harlem Shadows,* a landmark work during the "Harlem Renaissance" period.

McKay then turned to the writing of such novels as *Home to Harlem* (1928) and *Banjo* (1929), and traveled extensively abroad before returning to the United States, where he died on May 22, 1948. His final work—*Selected Poems*—was published posthumously in 1953.

During World War II, when Winston Churchill addressed a joint session of the U. S. Congress in an effort to enlist American aid in the battle against Nazi-ism, the climax of his oration was his quotation of the famous line *If We Must Die,* which is taken from a stirring poem originally written by McKay to assail lynchings and mob violence in the South.

KELLY MILLER
1863-1939
Historian

A native of Winnsboro, South Carolina, historian Kelly Miller was associated with

Howard University for most of his academic life, serving in such varied capacities as professor of mathematics, professor of sociology, dean of the College of Arts & Sciences, and dean of the Junior College.

An avid lecturer and pamphleteer, Miller was educated at Howard and Johns Hopkins, and immediately entered academic life, although he produced many historical writings regarded as controversial for their time.

Among them were *Race Adjustment* (1908), *Out of the House of Bondage* (1914), and *The Everlasting Stain* (1924). He was also the author of an important *History of the World War and the Important Part Taken by the Negroes* (1919).

LOFTEN MITCHELL
Dramatist

Raised in the Harlem of the 1930's, Loften Mitchell first began to write as a child, creating scripts for backyard shows he and his brother put on. After completing junior high school, he decided to enroll at New York Textile High because he had been promised a job on the school newspaper there. However, he soon realized that he needed the training of an academic high school and, with the help of one of his teachers, transferred to DeWitt Clinton.

Graduating with honors, Mitchell found a job as an elevator operator and a delivery boy in order to support himself while he studied playwriting at night at the City College of New York. However, he longed to devote all his time to his art, and was finally able to do so when he met a professor from Talladega College in Alabama who helped him win a scholarship to study there. He graduated with honors in 1943, having won an award for the best play written by a student.

With two years of service in the Navy behind him, Mitchell enrolled as a graduate student at Columbia University in New York. After a year's full study there, he accepted a job with the Department of Welfare as a social investigator, and continued to go to school at night. During this time, he wrote one of his first successful plays, *Blood in the Night*, and, in 1957, wrote *A Land Beyond the River* which had a long run at an off-Broadway theater.

The following year, he won a Guggenheim award, which enabled him to return to Columbia and write for a year. Since then, he has continued to write articles for several magazines and newspapers, and has written a new play *Star in the Morning* which is the story of Bert Williams, famous Negro entertainer.

Loften Mitchell

In 1967 Mitchell published a study entitled *Black Drama*, the story of the American Negro in the theatre.

WILLARD MOTLEY
1912–1965
Novelist

Because most of his work dealt with poor whites on Chicago's West Side, it was not generally known that Willard Motley was a Negro.

Born in a middle-class Chicago neighborhood on July 14, 1912, Motley wrote his first book *Knock on Any Door* in 1947. One of the first naturalistic novels to deal with the problem of juvenile delinquency, it enjoyed enormous commercial success before being made into a Hollywood film starring Humphrey Bogart.

In 1951, Motley completed *We Fished All Night*, an attempt to describe the impact of World War II on three young Chicagoans. Seven years later, a sequel to his first novel was published under the title *Let No Man Write My Epitaph*, also made into a movie.

Motley died of gangrene in Mexico City on March 4, 1965, a year before his last novel, *Let Noon Be Fair*, was published.

WILLIAM C. NELL
1816-1874
Historian, Journalist

The most important contribution of William C. Nell to American military history is easily his *The Colored Patriots of the American Revolution* (1855), a highly factual and yet vividly descriptive account of the role played by Negroes in the "Wars of 1776 and 1812."

Though he had little formal education, Nell struggled impressively to improve his condition, and eventually came to be a close friend of William Lloyd Garrison, with whom he was closely associated in the publication of *The Liberator*. Other abolitionists associated with Garrison encouraged Nell in his writing, and two of them — Wendell Phillips and Harriet Beecher Stowe—contributed introductions to his historical writing.

Nell not only documented rare and underpublicized events of the Revolutionary War and the War of 1812, but also painstakingly sifted his sources to separate fact from hearsay. His account of the Boston Massacre is particularly revealing and helpful in understanding the full implication of the event—both when it happened and generations later.

DANIEL A. PAYNE
1811-1893
Historian, Educator

Though he was a bishop of the African Methodist Episcopal Church, Daniel Payne is perhaps best remembered for his remarkable efforts on behalf of black self-help and other improvement projects. Education and expansion of the Negro church were the two activities which occupied most of his professional career, although he found time late in life to record his experiences in a number of valuable publications.

Born in Charleston, South Carolina, Payne was educated at the school of the Miner's Moralist Society in his native city and later at the Gettysburg Lutheran Seminary. Payne ran a private school for Negroes in ante bellum Charleston until 1835—the year a state law against schools for Negro children was passed. Forced to close down, he moved to Philadelphia where he established a similar operation.

During the Civil War, after urging President Lincoln to sign a bill emancipating slaves in the District of Columbia, Payne urged the AME church to purchase Wilberforce Payne served as president of the school for some 16 years.

In retirement, Payne turned to writing. His most important full-length work is *The History of the A.M.E. Church* (1891).

Rev. Daniel A. Payne

ANN PETRY
Novelist, short story writer, critic

Ann Petry was born in 1911 in Saybrook, Connecticut, where her father was a druggist. After graduating from the College of Pharmacy at the University of Connecticut, she went to New York where she found employment as a social worker and newspaper reporter, studying creative writing at night.

Her early short stories appeared in "Crisis" and "Phylon." In 1946, after having received a Houghton Mifflin fellowship, she completed her first novel, *The Street*. This was followed by *Country Place* (1947) which is considered by many critics to be the most successful portrayal of "white life" as seen through the eyes of a Negro.

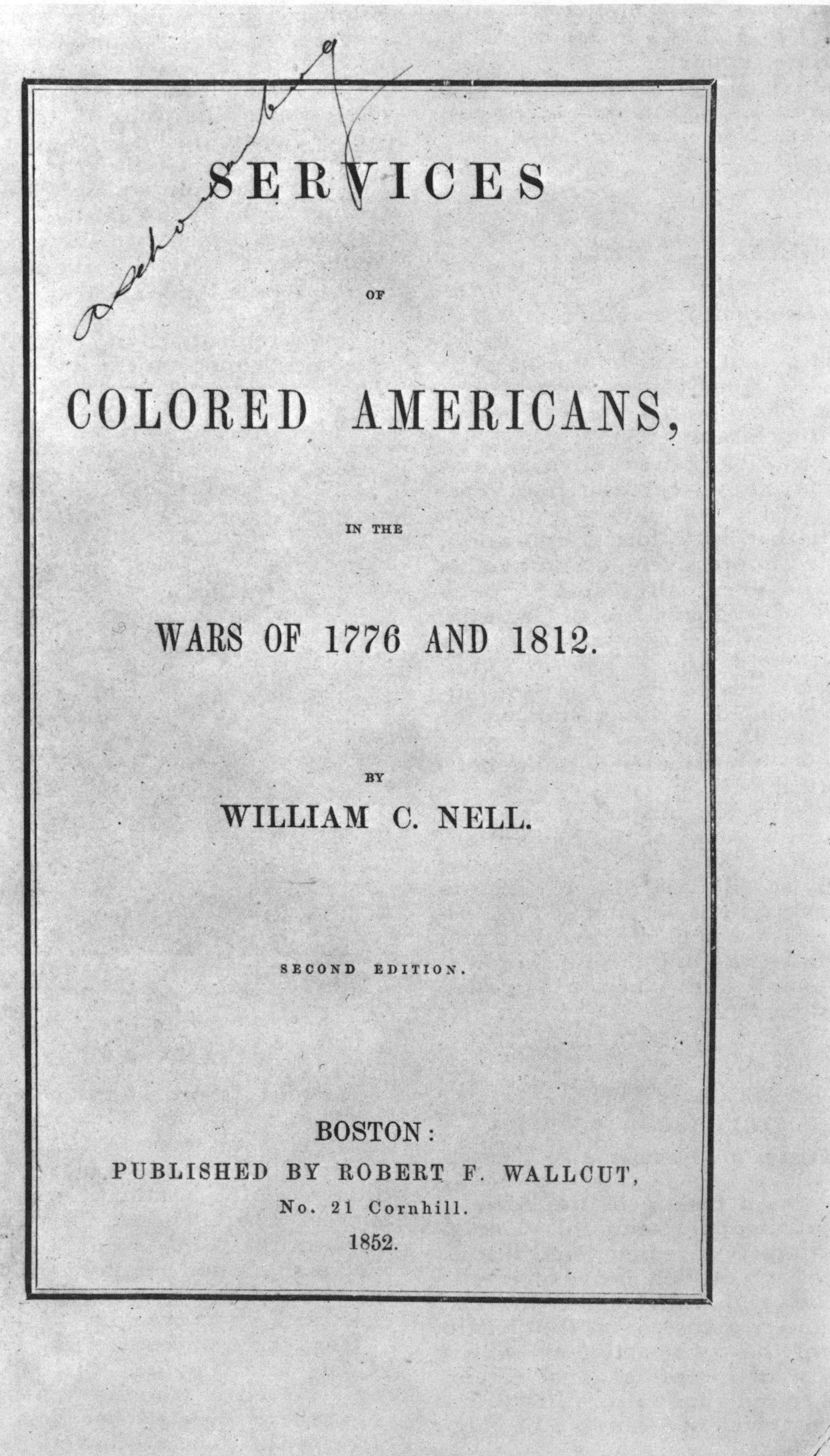

SERVICES

OF

COLORED AMERICANS,

IN THE

WARS OF 1776 AND 1812.

BY

WILLIAM C. NELL.

SECOND EDITION.

BOSTON:
PUBLISHED BY ROBERT F. WALLCUT,
No. 21 Cornhill.
1852.

A rare title page of William C. Nell's military study, autographed by Arthur Schomburg himself.

BENJAMIN QUARLES
Historian

A specialist in military history, Benjamin Quarles has done extensive research in both the Revolutionary War and the Civil War, and has produced two full-length books dealing with the Negro's role in both these conflicts.

Born in Boston, Massachusetts and educated in the public schools there, Quarles has also studied at Shaw University in North Carolina and at the University of Wisconsin. He has taught for several years at Dillard University in New Orleans, and served as an associate editor of the "Journal of Negro History."

The recipient of Rosenwald Fellowships and the University of Wisconsin President Adams Fellowship in Modern History, Quarles has completed a number of books on Negro history and life, including full-length studies of Frederick Douglass and Abraham Lincoln.

Among the titles to his credit are: *Frederick Douglass* (1948), *Lincoln and the Negro* (1962), *The Negro in the Civil War* (1953), *The Negro in the American Revolution* (1961) and *The Negro in the Making of America* (1964).

J. SAUNDERS REDDING
Critic

J. Saunders Redding has written a number of perceptive appraisals of Negro literature, and has completed a novel, an autobiography, and several volumes of history as well.

Born in Wilmington, Delaware, Redding received his undergraduate and graduate degrees from Brown University where he won Phi Beta Kappa honors. In 1942, he received the Mayflower Award for the best book by a resident of North Carolina. Three years later, a Guggenheim Fellowship enabled him to take a leave from his teaching position at Hampton Institute in Virginia.

Redding's books include *To Make A Poet Black* (1939); *No Day of Triumph* (1942); *Stranger and Alone* (1950); *They Came In Chains* (1950); *On Being Negro in America* (1951); *An American in India* (1955), and *The Lonesome Road* (1958).

In recent years, Redding has assumed several prominent and important educational and consulting assignments. His reviews on black historical, cultural and scholarly themes have often appeared in *The New York Times*.

JOEL A. ROGERS
1880-1966
Historian

For more than 50 years, Joel A. Rogers was one of the foremost Negro historians in the United States.

Born in Jamaica, West Indies in 1880, Rogers came to the United States in 1906, and became an American citizen in 1917.

Originally a journalist, he covered Haile Selassie's coronation as Emperor of Ethiopia in 1930 and, five years later, became the first Negro war correspondent in U. S. history by reporting the Italo-Ethiopian War for the Pittsburgh *Courier*.

Rogers was a member of the American Geographical Society and the Academy of Political Science. He was the author of numerous newspaper and magazine articles and wrote an illustrated feature ("Your History") for the Pittsburgh *Courier*. His books included: *Superman to Man* (1917); *As Nature Leads* (1919); *World's Greatest Men of African Descent* (1931); *Real Facts About Ethiopia* (1935); *Sex and Race* (1940-1944), and *World's Great Men of Color* (1947).

Although the work of Joel Rogers has at times been challenged for the accuracy of its documentation and interpretation, it is nonetheless impressive when one considers that Rogers was conducting much of his research at a time when Negro historians were virtually non-existent in the United States.

Rogers continued to work on a number of manuscripts until his death in New York City in January 1966.

DAVID RUGGLES
?-1849
Author

David Ruggles could be included in any anthology as a publisher, pamphleteer, anti-slavery agitator, or simply a writer. The truth is that he probably gained his most lasting fame because he aided Frederick Douglass' escape from slavery, but he is easily worthy of recognition in his own right.

Described as a Jack-of-all-trades, Ruggles seems to have been a self-educated activist who was involved with the ministry, opened a reading room in New

York *exclusively* for Negroes, served as Secretary of the Committee of Vigilance of New York, ran a magazine, deluged the press with anti-slavery letters, and somehow found time to be proprietor of a spa.

His two books are both polemical in tone, and somewhat effusive, but give considerable evidence of the man's unbounded enthusiasm and debating excellence. They are: *The "Extinguisher" Extinguished, or David M. Reese, M.D., Used Up* (1834), and *An Antidote for a Poisonous Combination Recently Prepared by a "Citizen of New York," alias Dr. Reese.*

NATHAN ALEXANDER SCOTT, JR.
Critic, Essayist

Relatively unknown as a Negro, Nathan A. Scott, Jr. is a critic of modern literature who has written extensively on the relationships between the literary and religious imagination.

Born in Cleveland in 1925, Scott attended the University of Michigan and the Union Theological Seminary in New York. He received his Ph.D. from Columbia University at the age of 24. Presently he is Chairman of the Theology and Literature Field of the Divinity School at the University of Chicago.

Scott's essays are noted for their length, diversity and quality. His works have appeared frequently in journals such as *Review of Metaphysics,* and *Christian Century,* as well as *Saturday Review* and *The Kenyon Review.*

In addition to his teaching, lecturing, and essays, Scott has written seven books: *Rehearsals of Discomposure: Alienation and Reconciliation in Modern Literature* (1952), *Modern Literature and the Religious Frontier* (1958), *Albert Camus* (1962), *Reinhold Niebuhr* (1963), *Samuel Beckett* (1965), *The Broken Center: Studies in the Theological Horizon of Modern Literature* (1966), and *Craters of the Spirit: Studies in the Modern Novel* (1968).

GEORGE SCHUYLER
1895-
Journalist, Author

Primarily a journalist although he also wrote fiction and sketches, George Schuyler was born in Providence, Rhode Island in 1895. Educated in the Syracuse public schools, Schuyler served as a first lieutenant in World War I, and returned to civilian life as a newspaperman for such publications as The Pittsburgh *Courier, Crisis, Opportunity* and *The Nation.*

Schuyler graduated into fiction as his style matured, publishing a novel *Black No More* (1931), and a slave account entitled *Slaves, Today: A Story of Liberia.* Other sketches and short stories appeared in Harlem publications which highlighted the work of black writers before the onset of the Depression. Schuyler drew heavily from his military experience (he was in the U. S. Army from 1912-1920), and from various odd jobs to create the setting and mood for his various vignettes.

WILLIAM STILL
1821-1902
Journalist, Editor

William Grant Still was the 19th century's foremost chronicler of the *Underground Railroad,* having compiled numerous case histories involving fugitive slaves involved in 1,001 situations and disguises. Perhaps the most harrowing and revealing escapade involved an encounter with a man who turned out to be his brother—an escapee from Alabama. That episode strengthened Still's resolve to keep records on as many slaves as possible. Still kept these records from 1850 to 1860 and, in 1872, compiled a thick volume entitled *Underground Railroad Records.*

Still himself was born free, only because his parents had escaped separately from Maryland's Eastern shore to New Jersey. The young man was frequently involved in forwarding Negro passengers to safety in Canada, and also aided survivors of the Harper's Ferry debacle to escape from Virginia. In 1861, Still organized a social, civil and statistical clearinghouse to collect and preserve historical materials relating to the Negro. Some 20 years later, he founded the first YMCA branch for Negroes. He engaged in civil rights and welfare work until his death.

ELLEN TARRY
Author

Ellen Tarry's service as the "Story Lady" of Friendship House, a Catholic community center in Harlem, brought her into close contact with the actual person who served as the model for "Hezekiah Horton," the character she created in the book of the same name. This same character appears in *The Runaway Elephant,* which was enthusiastically received by both critics and public alike after its publication in 1950.

The Runaway Elephant was illustrated by cartoonist Oliver Harrington whose "Bootsie" is one of the best-known cartoon characters in the Negro press.

Born in 1906 in Birmingham, Alabama, Miss Tarry was educated in a Southern convent school and converted to Catholicism. Later a journalist in the South and in New York, she began her work in Harlem in 1929, becoming associated with Catherine De Hueck, founder of Friendship House, and going on to establish a similar institution in Chicago. During World War II, she served as a staff member of the National Catholic Community Service.

Her books include *Katherine Drexel* (1958), and *Martin de Porres* (1963). Her autobiography *The Third Door* was published in 1955.

LUCY TERRY
(Dates of birth and death unknown)
Poet

Lucy Terry is generally considered to be the first Negro poet in America. In a ballad which she called "Bars Fight," she recreated an Indian massacre which occurred in Deersfield, Massachusetts in 1746 during King George's War. (Although of little poetic value, "Bars Fight" has been hailed by some historians as the most authentic account of the massacre.)

A semi-literate slave in the household of Ensign Ebenezer Wells, she was married to a freedman named Prince. The Prince house served as a center for young people who gathered to listen to their hostess' story-telling.

HOWARD THURMAN
1899-
Author

Almost all of Howard Thurman's considerable writing has centered on religious themes, and been printed in such publications as *Christian Century, The World Tomorrow, The Southern Workman, Christendom, The Journal of Religion,* and *Religion and Life.*

Born in Florida and educated at the Florida Baptist Academy (later Florida Normal Institute), Thurman later received collegiate training at Morehouse and Rochester Theological Seminary, the Oberlin Divinity School and Haverford. In 1935, Thurman led a "pilgrimage of friendship" of students of religion to colleges in Burma, India and Ceylon. Later, he was pastor and religious advisor at Oberlin, Morehouse and Howard. He was also professor of Christian theology at Howard.

WALLACE THURMAN
1902-1934
Novelist, Playwright

Death claimed Wallace Thurman not long after he had produced two of his major works, a play *Harlem* (1929), and a novel *The Blacker the Berry,* published the same year. His other major literary effort was *Infants of the Spring,* published in 1932.

Born in Salt Lake City and educated at the University of Southern California (USC), Thurman served on the editorial staffs of *The Messenger* and of Macaulay Publishing Company. He was also involved in a pair of short-lived magazine ventures, entitled *Fire* and *Harlem,* respectively.

MELVIN B. TOLSON
1900-1966
Poet

In the words of poet Karl Shapiro, Melvin B. Tolson is "a great poet (who) has been living in our midst for decades, and is almost totally unknown, even by literati (and) poets." Tolson has only recently begun to achieve a greater degree of recognition after many years of poetic endeavor.

Educated at Fisk, Lincoln and Columbia universities, Tolson has been a contributor to many newspapers, and to publications such as "Arts Quarterly" and "American Poets." The recipient of several prizes from state and local organizations, he has also won the National Poetry Contest sponsored by the American Negro Exposition in Chicago for his poem "Dark Symphony." In 1952,

"Poetry" magazine presented him with the Bess Hokin Award for a poem called "F+OE."

To date, his best-known work is probably "Libretto for the Republic of Liberia." Another of his narrative poems —"Harlem Gallery"—was published in 1965.

JEAN TOOMER
1894-1967
Novelist

Jean Toomer's *Cane,* published in 1923, has been called one of the three best novels ever written by an American Negro, in company with Richard Wright's *Native Son* and Ralph Ellison's *Invisible Man*. According to Yale critic Robert Bone, it is "by far the most impressive product of the Negro Renaissance."

A mixture of poems and sketches, *Cane* was written during that period in which most Negro writers were reacting against earlier "polite" forms by creating works marked by literary realism. Toomer even went beyond this realm to the threshold of symbol and myth, using a "mystical" approach which is much more akin to the contemporary mood than it was to the prevailing spirit of his own day.

Born in Washington, D. C. in 1894, Toomer was educated for law at the University of Wisconsin and City College of New York before he turned to writing. His transcendental bent is said to have stemmed in part from his early study under Gurdjieff, the Russian mystic.

Cane sold only 500 copies on publication, and is still little-known.

GUSTAVUS VASSA
1754–1801?
Author

Gustavus Vassa was born in 1754 in Benin in Southern Nigeria. At the age of 11, he was kidnapped and shipped to the United States as a slave. His masters included a Virginia plantation owner, a British officer, and a Philadelphia merchant from whom he eventually purchased his freedom.

Vassa then settled in England where he worked diligently for the elimination of slavery. He even went so far as to present a petition to Parliament calling for its abolition.

His autobiography *The Interesting Narrative of the Life of Oloudah Equiano, or Gustavus Vassa* was published in London in 1789 and went through five editions in the next five years. It is regarded as a highly informative account of the evils of slavery as it affected both master and slave.

Vassa died around 1801.

DAVID WALKER
1785-1830
Pamphleteer

David Walker is something of a mystery, both as a literary figure and as a man. His fame rests exclusively on a small but explosive pamphlet which circulated clandestinely through the ante-bellum South and "rumored" slave uprisings as the only possible solution to the black problem. The full title of Walker's work was: *Walker's Appeal in Four Articles Together With A Preamble to the Colored Citizens of the World, But in Particular and Very Expressly to Those of the United States (1829).*

Born of a free mother and a slave father, Walker left his native North Carolina while in his teens, and settled in Boston, where he earned a living as a dealer in old clothes. After his *Appeal* was published, it is known that his life was threatened, but he steadfastly refused to flee to Canada and seek anonymity. Instead, he vowed to fight on, and died, shortly thereafter, in circumstances which led many abolitionists to believe that he had been murdered. The Negroes of Boston believed him a true martyr to their cause.

MARGARET WALKER
Poet

Margaret Walker was born on July 7, 1915 in Birmingham, Alabama, and received her early education in Alabama, Louisiana, and Mississippi. She earned her B. A. from Northwestern University, and her M. A. from the University of Iowa (1940).

In 1942, Miss Walker completed *For My People* and, two years later, was awarded a Rosenwald Fellowship for creative writing. She has taught English and literature at Livingstone College in

GUSTAVUS VASSA,

OR

Olaudah Equiano.

A NATIVE AFRICAN FROM THE COAST OF GUINEA

who after being freed from American Slavery, made voyages to Europe, the West Indies, &c. and accompanied an Expedition to explore a North West passage. He was a worthy, pious, and enlightened Negro, and published his own Narrative dedicated to the British Parliament.

North Carolina, at West Virginia State College, and at Jackson State College in Mississippi. Her most recent publication appeared in 1966 and is entitled *Jubilee.*

ERIC WALROND
1898-1966
Essayist, Short Story Writer

Eric Walrond was born in Georgetown, British Guiana. He came to Harlem in 1918, and studied at Columbia University and The City College of New York, while he held several odd jobs. He received the position of Associate Editor of *The Negro World* in 1923.

Two years later he wrote an essay entitled "On Being Black" which was published in *The New Republic* and brought him a measure of attention from the literary world.

Tropic Death, his first and only book, was published in 1926. It is a collection of stories depicting the contrast between the natural beauty of the American tropics and the poverty, disease, and death of its inhabitants.

SAMUEL RINGGOLD WARD
1817-1864
Author

Primarily a serious orator, although his writing was larded with much humor and satire, Samuel Ringgold Ward published only one full-length book in his lifetime, *The Autobiography of a Fugitive Slave* (1855).

An escapee from slavery, Ward was raised in New York, where he was sufficiently educated to teach school and become a preacher. He soon extended his involvements to include the anti-slavery cause, and was eventually forced to flee to Canada because of his fiery speechmaking on behalf of fugitive slave Jerry McHenry. Though lost to the cause in the U. S., Ward remained an active lecturer in Canada and England. He died during the Civil War in Jamaica.

CHARLES WESLEY
Historian

Charles H. Wesley, president since 1942 of Central State College (known for many years as Wilberforce), is still one of the major American Negro historians writing in the United States.

Born on December 2, 1891 in Louisville, Kentucky, Wesley studied at Fisk, Howard, Harvard, Yale, Columbia, and the Guilde International in Paris. Among his many awards were scholarships from Yale (1913) and Harvard (1920-1921), as well as a Guggenheim Fellowship (1930-1931).

Before assuming his present position, Wesley served as professor and dean of Howard. He is the author of such works as *Negro Labor in the United States, 1850-1925: A Study in American Economic History* (1927); *Richard Allen, Apostle of Freedom* (1935); *The Collapse of the Confederacy* (1938); and *The Negro in the Americas* (1940).

His most recent works include: *Neglected History* (1965), *The Collapse of the Confederacy* (1968), *In Freedom's Footsteps* (1968), and *The Quest For Equality* (1968).

PHILLIS WHEATLEY
1753?–1794
Poet

Born in Senegal (c. 1753), Phillis Wheatley was brought to the United States as a slave, and received her name from Mrs. Susannah Wheatley, the wife of the Boston tailor who had bought Phillis.

Miss Wheatley received her early education in the household of her master. Her interest in writing stemmed from her reading of the Bible and the classics under the guidance of the Wheatleys' daughter, Mary.

In 1770, her first poem was printed under the title *A Poem by Phillis, A Negro Girl on the Death of Reverend George Whitefield.* After a trip to England for health reasons, she returned to the United States and was married. She published *Liberty and Peace* in 1794, shortly before her death.

Although George Washington was among her admirers (she had once sent him a tributary poem which he graciously acknowledged), her poetry is considered important today largely because of its historical role in the growth of American Negro literature. In its style and thematic preoccupations, Miss Wheatley's poetry reflects Anglo-Saxon models, rather than her African heritage. It is nevertheless, a typical example of the verse manufactured in a territory — the British colonies — not yet divorced from its maternal origins.

Phillis Wheatley

WALTER WHITE
1893-
Journalist

Walter White, who could have passed for white, chose instead to identify with his black ancestry, and ultimately came to be the most ardent protagonist in the fight to stamp out lynching in America, particularly after World War I. His most famous work was *Rope and Faggot: A Biography of Judge Lynch* (1929).

Born in Atlanta and educated in that Georgia city as well as in New York, White worked as secretary of the National Association for the Advancement of Colored People (NAACP). He completed his important study after two years as a Guggenheim Fellow. This work stood alongside two earlier novels, *Fire in the Flint* (1924) and *Flight* (1926). White's other work appeared in the leading periodicals of the day, including *Harper's, Nation* and *New Republic*. White was awarded a Spingarn Medal in 1937 in recognition of his tireless efforts on behalf of all black Americans.

GEORGE WASHINGTON WILLIAMS
1849-1891
Historian

George Washington Williams was unquestionably the greatest black historian of the 19th century, and can still lay claim to being the writer of a pair of definitive works on at least two aspects of the black experience, The Civil War and the period stretching from the Jamestown landing to the end of Reconstruction. Williams' major works are: *The History of the Negro Race in America from 1619-1880* and *A History of the Negro Troops in the War of the Rebellion* (1888).

A native of Bedford Spring, Pennsylvania, Williams enlisted in the Union Army at the age of 14, served through the war, and went on to become a lieutenant-colonel in the Mexican army. After the fall of Maximillian, he moved out West, serving in several Indian campaigns on the frontier. Later, he attended Howard University and Newton Theological Seminary. the latter after he had decided on a career in the ministry. His career eventually reached into the journalism field (he conducted two newspapers), into law (he practiced in Ohio), and into politics (he served in the Ohio state legislature and as minister to Haiti). Williams

George Washington Williams

subsequently became interested in the Congo and entered the service of the Belgian government. He died in England while still in the service of Leopold II, the Belgian King.

JOHN A. WILLIAMS
Novelist

John A. Williams was born in 1925 in Syracuse. Educated locally, he also took both his undergraduate and graduate degrees at Syracuse University.

His first novel *The Angry Ones* was published in 1960, and was followed, within a year, by a second offering entitled *Night Song*. In 1962, Williams wrote the text for *Africa: Her History, Lands and People*.

That same year, he won the Roman Fellowship of the American Academy in Rome, the unanimous choice of the jury here. The award, however, was rescinded by officials in Rome in an unprecedented action which caused considerable controversy.

To date, Williams has also written two other books: *Sissie* (1963) and *This Is My Country Too* (1965).

To date Williams has also written four other books: *Sissie* (1963), *This Is My Country Too* (1965), *Beyond the Angry Black* (1966), and *The Man Who Cried I Am* (1967).

In 1970, Williams published a controversial work in which he lamented the alleged "failure" of Dr. Martin Luther King, Jr. The book, *The King God Didn't Save*, professed to be an objective appraisal of the life and work of the slain civil rights leader. It sought, therefore, not only to catalog his victories, but also to expose his weaknesses and the probable liabilities of his close association with the "white power" structure. Though Williams pays tribute to the man King might have become, he insists upon seeing him as a man corrupted by the illusion of power.

CARTER WOODSON
1875-1950
Historian

Carter Woodson was for many years the lone voice of any consequence in American Negro historiography.

Born on December 19, 1875 in New Canton, Virginia, Woodson received his education at Berea College, the University of Chicago, Harvard and the Sorbonne in Paris.

In 1921, Woodson organized Associated Publishers in order to produce textbooks and other supplementary material on the Negro which, at the time, was not readily accepted by most commercial publishers. A year later, he retired from academic life in order to devote full time to research as Director of the Association for the Study of Negro Life and History and as editor of the "Journal of Negro History." (Woodson had taught at the elementary and high school level, and served as Dean of the School of Liberal Arts of Howard University.) He also traveled extensively in Europe, Asia and Egypt.

Many of Woodson's books have become the foundations upon which more contemporary historians have based their own research. These include *The Education of the Negro Prior to 1861* (1915); *A Century of Negro Migration* (1918); *The Negro in Our History* (1922), and *The Rural Negro* (1930).

Woodson died in Washington, D. C. on April 3, 1950.

RICHARD WRIGHT
1908–1960
Novelist

The work of Richard Wright is still used as the yardstick by which all Negro novelists in America are measured. It was Wright who, in the 1940's, set the standard for a whole generation of prose writers, including Ralph Ellison and James Baldwin.

Born on a plantation near Natchez, Mississippi on September 9, 1908, Richard Wright drew on his personal experience to dramatize to a nationwide audience the issue of racial injustice and its brutalizing effects. In 1938, under the auspices of the WPA Illinois Writers Project, Wright published *Uncle Tom's Children*, a collection of four novels based on his Mississippi boyhood memories. The book won an award for the best work of fiction by a WPA writer, and Wright received a Guggenheim Fellowship.

Two years later, *Native Son*, a novel of Chicago's Negro ghetto, further enhanced Wright's reputation. A Book-of-the-Month Club choice, it was later a successful Broadway production under Orson Welles' direction, and was filmed in South America with Wright himself in the role of Bigger Thomas.

Richard Wright

In 1945, Wright's largely autobiographical *Black Boy* was again selected by the Book-of-the-Month Club, and went on to become a second best seller.

Wright later moved to Paris where he continued to write both fiction and non-fiction, including *The Outsider* (1953); *Black Power* (1954); *The Color Curtain* (1956); *The Long Dream* (1958), and *Lawd Today* (1963). The last of these was published posthumously, Wright having died on November 28, 1960.

FRANK YERBY
Novelist

Frank Yerby has been the most commercially successful Negro writer in America for more than 20 years. He has published 19 novels which have sold more than 20 million copies, and earned for their author a gross amount in excess of 10 million dollars.

Born in Augusta, Georgia in 1916, Yerby studied at Fisk University and the University of Chicago, and taught briefly at Florida A. & M. and Southern University before moving to Detroit in 1942 to work in a wartime assembly plant.

His early work often dealt with significant social issues such as race. In 1944, for example, "Harper's" published his short story "Health Card," which won a special O. Henry award. Later, after studiously researching the ingredients of popular fiction, Yerby turned his talent to the creation of swashbuckling costume novels which were an immediate success.

In 1949, he published *The Foxes of Harrow*, soon to become a bestseller and a successful movie as well. His commercial successes then became an annual occurrence: *The Vixens* (1947); *The Golden Hawk* (1948); *Pride's Castle* (1949); *Floodtide* (1950); *A Woman Called Fancy* (1951); and *The Saracen Blade* (1952).

Yerby has lived in Europe since 1952. His two most recent books—*The Old Gods Laugh* and *An Odor of Sanctity*—are departures from the "costume motif," and he has himself expressed a desire to create literature of greater substance.

OTHER NEGRO LITERARY FIGURES

Name	*Place of Birth*	*Dates of Birth and Death*
George Leonard Allen	Lumberton, N.C.	1905-1935
Samuel Allen	Columbus, Ohio	1917-
Russell Atkins	Cleveland, Ohio	1926-
William Attaway	———	1912-
Gwendolyn B. Bennett	Giddings, Texas	1902-
Horace Julian Bond	Atlanta, Ga.	1940-
Jonathan Brooks	Lexington, Miss.	1904-1945
William Browne	New York City	
James E. Campbell	Pomeroy, Ohio	1860-1905
Catherine Cater	———	1917-
Marcus B. Christian	———	1900-
Leslie M. Collins	Alexandria, La.	1914-
Waring Cuney	Washington, D.C.	1906-
Margaret Danner	Pryorsburg, Ky.	
Frank Marshall Davis	Arkansas City, Kan.	1905-
Clarissa Scott Delaney	Tuskegee Institute, Ala.	1901-1927
Alfred A. Duckett	New York City	1918-
James A. Emanuel	———	1921-
Julia Fields	Alabama	1938-
Yvonne Gregory	———	1919-
Angelina W. Grimké	Boston, Mass.	1880-1958
Donald Jeffrey Hayes	Raleigh, N.C.	1904-
Leslie Pinckney Hill	Lynchburg, Va.	1880-
Carl W. Hines, Jr.	Wilson, N.C.	1940-
M. Carl Holman	Minter City, Miss.	1919-
Frank Horne	New York City	1899-
Ted Joans	Cairo, Ill.	1928-
Helene Johnson	Boston, Mass.	1907-
Bruce McM. Wright	———	1918-
Clarence Major	Atlanta, Ga.	1936-

Pauli Murray	Baltimore, Md.	1910-
Effie Lee Newsome	Wilberforce, Ohio	1885-
Gloria C. Oden	———	1923-
Myron O'Higgins	Chicago, Ill.	1918-
Roi Ottley	———	1906-1960
Oliver Pitcher	Massachusetts	1923-
Dudley Randall	Michigan	1914-
Conrad Kent Rivers	Atlantic Cty, N.J.	1933-
Anne Spencer	Lynchburg, Va.	1882-
James Vaughn	Xenia, Ohio	1929-
Charles Enoch Wheeler	Augusta, Ga.	1909-
James M. Whitfield	Boston, Mass.	1830-1870
Lucy Ariel Williams	Mobile, Ala.	1905-

The outspoken and talented Dana Chandler with one of his provocative self-descriptive works.

THE BLACK ARTIST

African Antecedents
"Negro" Painting
The Last Decade: Art or Polemics?

The role of the Negro in the fine arts in America has been one of discovery and rediscovery. Cut off from his African artistic heritage, and often forced to believe that the fine arts lay outside his province, the American Negro underwent his early period of development as an artist independent of an ancestral foundation.

In Africa, manual arts such as woodcarving, bone-carving, and metal-work had reached great heights during the Middle Ages but, in America, these same arts were largely lost to the Negro. The slave artisan, for instance, was limited in his work to the creation of practical implements, tools, and household equipment. In the wrought-iron industry, he was able to display some of his artistic facility, but never on a par with the representative material created by his predecessors.

Negro Painting

The first American Negro painter was probably Scipio Morehead, who is known as an allegorical landscapist by virtue of a dedicatory poem written by Phillis Wheatley some time before 1773. What little Negro painting there was in the Revolutionary era was largely imitative of the far from memorable work of most American artists. With the exception of a few outstanding colonial painters, America produced no really great painters until the decade of the 1870's when Whistler and Homer emerged.

In his "apprenticeship period" (1865-1890), the Negro artist was not far behind the general level of the age. In his "journeyman period" (1890-1914), he gained a greater degree of international attention, but he did not begin to realize his true potential until the coming of the Negro Renaissance in the 1920's. The pseudo-classical imitations and the stilted, overly formal approach once typical of him gave way in this decade to an abundant use of subject matter close at hand—Negro historical themes, domestic scenes, and symbolism filled with the vitality and thrust of the "New Negro." Then, too, the greatness of African art was re-discovered, not only by the Negro artist, but by a number of white artists (among them, Picasso), and by the art-loving public as well.

At the present time, there are no boundaries to the creative vistas of the American Negro artist. The forms which his work takes range from primitive simplicity to

sophisticated complexity; the subject matter, from personal evocations, to Negro thematic statements, to the most avant-garde abstractions. It seems likely that the American Negro's achievements in the fine arts will one day—if, indeed, they have not already done so—rival those of his musical heritage.

The Last Decade: Art or Polemics?

The search for a black identity and the expression of black militancy were the two most pervasive and explosive themes which characterized black art in the 1960's. The potent emotions welling up in several black artists could not always be contained on canvas, channeled into familiar forms, or even exhibited in traditional settings. Art literally often took to the streets of the ghetto to meet with, appeal to, indeed in many cases simply to celebrate the people.

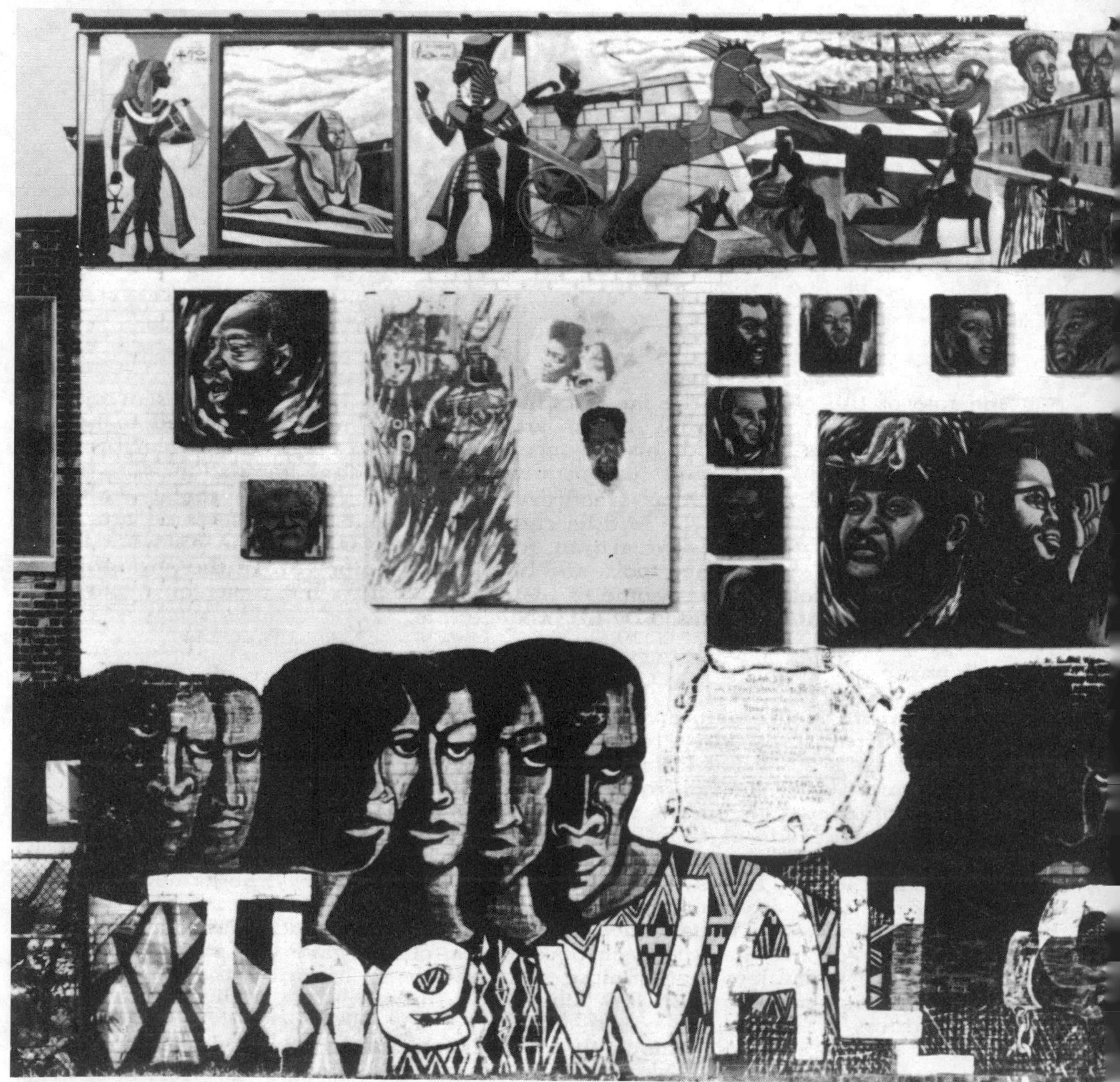

The New Black Art—Detroits Wall of Dignity.

Many artists joined their own vital energies and spiritual visions with the raw grit and seething rage of black revolutionaries. Together, they often accused America of terrible and vicious indifference, including complicity in murder. (Dana Chandler, for example, shot real bullets through his canvas memorializing slain Black Panther Fred Hampton.) Don McIlvane chose an old Chicago wall to dramatize the pained recognition of his people to the lynching of a black man. Yet, for all its omnious qualities, its scowling, glowering indignation, its billboard-sized acclamation of the menacing will to resist and the ravenous determination to be liberated, the mural professes to portray the irreversibly inevitable progress of the black man, despite the degradation to which he has been subjected.

Chapters of black history and giants of the black past are equally massive on Detroit's Wall of Dignity and Chicago's Wall of Respect. In Boston's Orchard Park, black art adorns the walls of a local handball court, celebrating black contributions to the dance,

theatre, and music. The public nature of such art is unashamedly propagandistic; it seeks in all its manifestations to rivet the white viewer's attention to the nature and condition of the black man but, even more importantly, it seeks to arouse the black man and his offspring to a burning awareness of his situation, his prospects, and his achievements.

Young black artists like Malcolm Bailey, Melvin Edwards and David Hammons create works which proudly demonstrate an abiding preoccupation with social themes and an aroused social consciousness. Other artists, however, seek to separate their art from their social involvement—to find personal refuge, as it were, in the ability to create beautiful forms, striking objects, or lavish and bizarre color patterns. Sculptor Richard Hunt, for example, is fascinated by junked automobiles and their mangled parts; once out of his "studio," however, he is equally serious about campaigning for low-cost housing in his neighborhood.

Daniel Johnson, on the other hand, is not at all defensive about the total absence of black roots in his work. In his view, the question of blackness is not only "frivolous," but has "nothing to do with the consciousness of people who attempt to make art." Men like Johnson, however, are clearly more concerned with their status as artists than with their reputations as polemicists. It is they who will be attentive to the collecting trends manifested by the nation's leading museums. Though the figures are by no means inspiring, they do reflect the first glimmering hopes of representation. New York's Metropolitan, for example, has 10 black artists in its permanent collection; the National Collection of Fine Arts has 11; the Museum of Modern Art and the Whitney account for another 27.

Enrollments at art schools show a sizeable increase in black students; the fellowship picture is also improving, what with the National Endowment for the Arts now reporting that 25 of its 186 grants are held by blacks. The Whitney Foundation has awarded 32 of 74 Opportunity Fellowships to blacks; since 1952, some 35 blacks have received Fulbright scholarships in the arts.

Withal, black artists are demanding no more than formal exposure and the opportunity to break through the facade of formal custom which has prevented them from even attempting to become creative individuals. This achieved, the art world may finally be able to boast of parity between its black and white members.

CHARLES ALSTON
Painter

It is the mural art of painter Charles Alston that has established his reputation and insured his fame as a black American artist of standing and importance.

Born in North Carolina in 1907, Alston studied at Columbia University in New

was later awarded several fellowships and grants to launch his painting career.

Alston's most notable paintings and sculpture are in such collections as those of IBM and the Detroit Museum. His murals depicting the history of medicine adorn the facade of Harlem Hospital in New York. Alston is a member of the National Society of Mural Painters.

ROBERT BANNISTER
1828-1901
Painter

Robert Bannister was the first Negro to win acclaim as an important American regional painter.

Born in Nova Scotia in 1828, Bannister studied in Boston and then moved to Providence, where he remained until his death in 1901.

In 1867, a newspaper claim that "the Negro seems to have an appreciation of art, while manifestly unable to produce it," so fired his resolve to succeed in America without the benefit of patronage that he turned down numerous offers to study abroad.

Some of his better-known landscapes include: "Sabin Point, Narragansett Bay" and "After the Storm."

RICHMOND BARTHÉ
Sculptor

Richmond Barthé, whose honors and awards have continued to accumulate for the past 40 years, is probably the best-known Negro sculptor living in the United States today.

Born in 1901 in Bay St. Louis, Mississippi, Barthé was educated at the Art Institute in Chicago from 1924 to 1928. His first love was painting, but it was

Example of the work of Richmond Barthe "Stevedore"

through his experiments with sculpture that he began initially to gain critical attention in 1927.

His first commisssions were busts of Henry Ossawa Tanner and Toussaint L'Ouverture. The acclaim resulting from them led to a one-man show in Chicago, and a Rosenwald Fellowship for study in New York City.

Barthé's work has been exhibited at several major American museums, including the Metropolitan in New York City. In 1946, he received the first commission given to a Negro for a bust slated for inclusion in New York University's Hall of Fame. A year later, he was one of a committee of 15 artists chosen to help modernize the sculpture prevalent in the Catholic churches of the United States.

Barthé's work has given the Negro face and form a prominent place in the world of sculpture. He is the only Negro sculptor who holds membership in the National Academy of Arts and Letters.

ROMARE BEARDEN
Painter

The foremost collagist among American Negro artists today is Romare Bearden who, in recent years, has come to specialize in photomontages, or what he calls "projections."

Bearden was born in Charlotte, North Carolina in 1914, and raised in Pittsburgh and New York. He is a graduate of N.Y.U., and has studied under George Grosz at the Art Students League. His early paintings belong to the school of "social realism" but, since World War II, his work has become more abstract, often expressing the universal themes of suffering and loneliness through the use of Christ-figures and bullfighters. His "projections" are haunting montages of his early memories and current Negro aspirations—an attempt to "redefine the image of man in terms of the Negro experience I know best." These include: "Street Corner," "He is Arisen," "The Street," and "The Burial."

JOHN BIGGERS
Painter

John Biggers has been a leading figure in "social realism" as a painter, sculptor, printmaker, and teacher, and an outstanding "surrealistic" muralist as well.

Born in Gastonia, North Carolina in 1924, Biggers has derived much of his subject matter from the contributions made by American Negroes to the development of the country.

While teaching at Texas Southern University, Biggers has become a significant influence on several young Negro painters. His works include: "Cradle," "Mother and Child," and "The Contribution of Negro Women to American Life and Education."

WILLIAM CARTER
Painter

Muralist William Carter was one of the leading black painters active during the early 1940's, a comparatively productive period for black artists in the annals of American art.

Born in Missouri in 1909, Carter received his education at the Art Institute of Chicago and the University of Illinois. Though he is primarily known as a muralist, Carter is equally adept on canvas.

Charles Alston's mural on the black participation in the exploration and colonization of California.

CALIFORNIA REPUBL

DANA CHANDLER
Painter

Dana Chandler is one of the most visible, outspoken and provocative black painters on the American scene today. Chandler's huge, colorful Black Power murals are spotted throughout the ghetto area of Boston, a constant reminder of the resolve and determination manifested by the new breed of young black urban dwellers—proud and even scornful.

"All this stuff whites are buying," Chandler says, "tells the black man a lot about where the white community is at, namely, nowhere."

Chandler's easel works are bold and simple. One, *The Golden Prison*, shows a black man with a yellow and red-striped flag "because America has been yellow and cowardly in dealing with the black man." Another, *Freddie Hampton's Door* shows a bullet-splintered door replete with a stamp of U.S. government approval. Others celebrate Bobby Seale and Martin Luther King, Jr.

Born in Lynn, Massachusetts in 1941, Chandler received his B.S. from the Massachusetts College of Art in 1967. Since his graduation, he has lectured widely on black art, had one-man shows at Boston College, Rhode Island School of Design and other comparable schools. He is presently Director of the Model Cities Consortium Art Program at the National Center of Afro-American Artists in Boston.

ERNEST CRICHLOW
Painter

The Negro child has never been more effectively employed as subject matter than in the work of Ernest Crichlow. Although adolescence and motherhood are often recurring themes in Crichlow, it is through his portrayal of the touching simplicity of children that he has made his most memorable contribution as a painter.

Crichlow was born in 1914 in New York City, and received art instruction at New York University and the Art Students League. He has illustrated such books as *Two Is A Team* (1945); *Corrie and the Yankee* (1959), and *Enter In* (1959). His paintings include: "The Domestic," "Lend Me Your Hand," and "Young Mother."

AARON DOUGLAS
Painter

The leading painter of the "Negro Renaissance" was Aaron Douglas, who served as the prototype for the Alain Locke study which describes the emerging artist of the 1920's: *The New Negro*.

In 1927, Douglas illustrated James Weldon Johnson's book *God's Trombones: Seven Negro Sermons in Verse*. The angular figures and mystical light patterns which made these illustrations so striking were to appear with even greater impact in Douglas later murals.

Douglas was born in Topeka, Kansas in 1899, and received his A. B. in Fine Arts at the University of Kansas in 1923. The recipient of numerous study grants, Douglas continued his artistic apprenticeship in New York City and in Paris. In 1938, he traveled through the South and in Haiti on a Rosenwald Grant.

Douglas' murals are mainly scenes of the historical life or cultural background of the American Negro, and can be seen in such places as the Fisk University Library, Bennett College, and the Countee Cullen branch of the public library in New York City.

He has illustrated a number of books, including *Caroling Dusk* by Countee Cullen, *Plays of Negro Life* by Alain Locke, and *Not Without Laughter* by Langston Hughes.

ROBERT DUNCANSON
1873-1910
Painter

The history of studio art began for the American Negro with the work of Robert Duncanson, who was born in New York, and educated in Canada.

Duncanson was a literary romantic, a devotee of Tennyson and Scott, and his spiritual identity was more British than American. An early painting—"The Trial of Shakespeare"—led the Freedmen's Aid Society of Cincinnati to finance Duncanson's study in Scotland in 1840.

On his return to the United States, Duncanson became one of the leading painters in Cincinnati, producing such landscapes as "Blue Hole, Flood Waters, Little Miami River" (1851). His only known painting of a Negro subject is a portrait of Bishop Daniel Payne and his family done in 1848.

Duncanson died in Detroit in 1871.

META VAUX WARRICK FULLER
Sculptor

Meta Vaux Warrick Fuller has been a productive and well-received Negro sculptor for most of the 20th century.

Born in 1877 in Philadelphia, she was educated at the School of Industrial Art and the Pennsylvania Academy. Her interest in sculpture led to her studying with Charles Grafly, and then with Rodin at the Academie Colarossi in Paris.

In 1903 and again in 1904, her group entitled "The Wretched" (considered by most experts to be her masterpiece) was exhibited at the Paris Salon. In 1910, most of her works were destroyed by fire, but her subsequent efforts were exhibited by the Harmon Foundation and the Boston Art Club, among others.

Today, her work can be found in the Cleveland Museum and the Schomburg Collection of Negro History and Literature, located in New York City.

An Alice Gafford still life.

ALICE GAFFORD
Painter

Mrs. Alice Gafford is among the pioneer black artists who have worked in the Los Angeles area for several generations.

Born in Kansas in 1886, Mrs. Gafford studied at the Otis Art Institute, at UCLA, and with private tutors. Mrs. Gafford is a member of several local art associations, and has exhibited her work all over the United States. It is today represented in several private collections.

SAM GILLIAM
Painter

Mississippi-born Sam Gilliam produces hanging canvasses which are laced with pure color pigments rather than shades or tones. The artist bunches these pigments in wierd configurations on drooping, drape-like canvasses, giving the effect, in the words of TIME *Magazine*, of "clothes drying on a line." His canvasses are said to be "like nobody else's, black or white."

Born in Tupelo in 1933, Gilliam took

***The bold and brilliant** Sam Gilliam.*

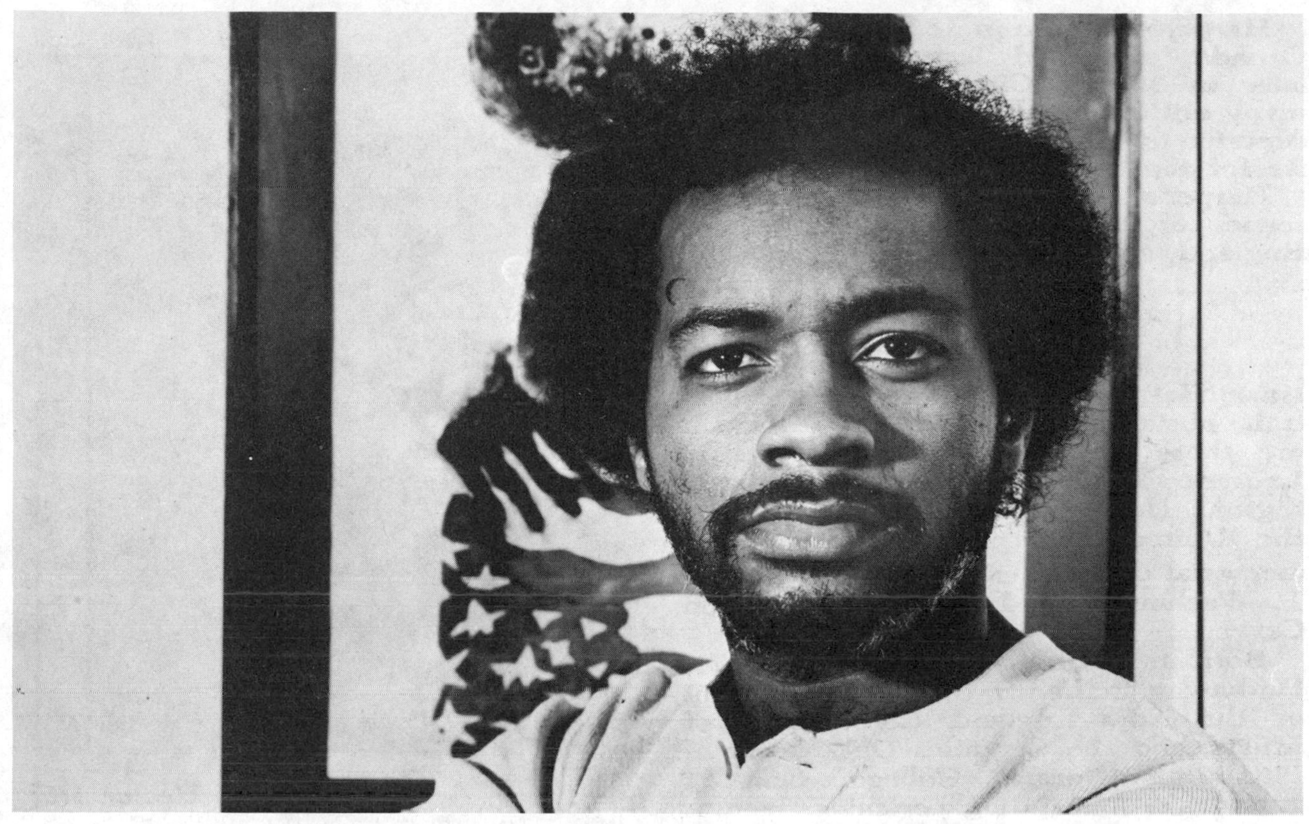

David Hammons —his paintings speak against oppression.

his M.A. from the University of Louisville, and was awarded a National Endowment of Humanities and Arts Grant in 1966. Since then, he has had one-man shows at the Washington Gallery of Modern Art, Jefferson Place Gallery and Adams-Morgan Gallery in Washington, D. C.

Gilliam has also been represented in several group exhibitions, including the First World Festival of Negro Arts in Dakar, Senegal (1966), "The Negro in American Art" at UCLA (1967), and the Whitney Museum's American Art Annual (1969).

The artist is currently a teacher at the Maryland Institute of Art in Baltimore.

ROSE GREEN
Painter

Youthful Rose Green is in the process of establishing herself nationally, although she has exhibited most of her work in the East.

Miss Green was awarded first prize in a Tuskegee Institute Annual Exhibit, and has won several prizes at Atlanta University.

DAVID HAMMONS
Painter

Born in Springfield, Illinois, the youngest of 10 children in a family on welfare, 26-year-old David Hammons passed the home of Abraham Lincoln every day on his way to school and somehow derived from this experience an abiding preoccupation with the American flag, a recurrent theme or motif in his art.

"I do use the flag for some kind of shock value," Hammons admits. "I don't know whether it's the black skin against the bright colors or the irony of the flag being held by an oppressed people."

Hammon's black identity is thus a strong and obvious feature of his work. He is now a resident of Los Angeles.

WILLIAM HARPER
1873-1910
Painter

William Harper was a protege of Henry Ossawa Tanner and, along with him, came to be regarded as one of the two significant American Negro painters of the 19th century.

Harper was born in 1873 near Cayuga, Canada, and died less than 37 years later in Mexico City, at a time when many critics already considered his work superior to Tanner's, and of great promise for the development of Negro art.

Harper's many landscapes include scenes of Brittany, Provence, Southern England, and Mexico.

ISAAC HATHAWAY
Sculptor, ceramist

Isaac Hathaway's major works are portrait busts, the most famous of which are those of Frederick Douglass, Paul Laurence Dunbar, and Booker T. Washington. He was also commissioned by the United States Mint to design the memorial coins issued in honor of Booker T. Washington and George Washington Carver.

Born in Lexington, Kentucky in 1871, Hathaway studied in the Art Department of the New England Conservatory of Music, and the Ceramics Department of Pittsburgh Normal College. One of America's outstanding ceramists, he was for many years head of the Ceramics Department at Alabama State Teachers College in Montgomery.

Hathaway, still living, is now retired in Alabama.

HECTOR HILL
1934-1963
Painter

Hector Hill's approach to art was mirrored in his simple dictum to "take a wider look around."

Born in New York City in 1934, Hill was a graduate of Music and Art High School and, later, (while in the Air Force) studied at San Bernardino Valley College in California. After having served in the Korean War, Hill attended sketch seminars at the Louvre Museum in Paris, and continued his formal studies at the Brooklyn Museum Art School (1957-1958).

Hill had one of his earliest showings at the Marino Gallery in 1958 and, three years later, began to be featured at the First Assembly District Democratic Club; the Market Place Gallery and the Ligoa Duncan Gallery. His work was also shown at a number of art fairs.

Hill used concepts of color and form associated with both old and modern masters of art, and worked in both the figurative and abstract mediums. He spent the summer of 1963 in Cuba with a group of students, and died there in a swimming mishap.

A self-portrait of Hector Hill

RICHARD HUNT
Painter

Painter Richard Hunt was born in Chicago in 1935, and began his formal career after studying at the School of the Art Institute of Chicago, where he received a number of awards.

After graduating in 1957, Hunt was given the James Nelson Raymond Traveling Fellowship. He later taught at the School of the Art Institute of Chicago and at the University of Illinois. From 1962 to 1963, he pursued his craft while under a Guggenheim Fellowship.

Hunt has had several one-man shows and been included in major exhibits throughout the United States. His work can also be seen in, among others, the permanent collections of the Museum of Modern Art and the Cleveland Museum of Art.

MAY HOWARD JACKSON
1877-1931
Sculptor

Executing busts of famous people remained the forte of May Howard Jackson during her entire artistic career although, as of 1914, she became more preoccupied with the production of Negro thematic sculpture.

Born in 1877 in Philadelphia (the same year and place as fellow sculptor Meta Vaux Warrick Fuller), Mrs. Jackson was educated at J. Liberty Tadd's Art School in her native city, and at the Pennsylvania Academy. She had her own art studio in Washington, D. C. from 1902 until her death in 1931.

Her most representative busts include those of Paul Laurence Dunbar and Dean Kelly Miller of Howard University.

Her work has been exhibited at the National Academy of Design, the New York Emancipation Exposition, and the National Academy of Art in New York City.

In addition to lecturing and exhibiting, Mrs. Jackson taught sculpture at Howard University for a number of years.

DANIEL JOHNSON
Painter

Though he is a native of the Los Angeles Watts ghetto, Daniel Johnson does not attribute his creative instincts to his color. Instead, he believes that questions of race "are frivolous" and "have nothing to do with the consciousness of people who attempt to make art."

His own works, seen in prominent display at Manhattan's French & Co. in 1970, are painted sculptures which have already sold for upwards of $3,500. Critic Margit Rowell says of his work: "The sensation of a temporal, even acoustical experience—for which one was unprepared and which is intangible—is perhaps the most unsettling aspect of one's first encounter" with Johnson's work. Otherwise, the visual impact is one of strict sobriety—the total absence of extraneous forms and preoccupations.

Born in Los Angeles in 1938, Johnson holds a B.F.A. from Chouinard Art Institute (1960). For the past decade, he has divided his living time between New York,

Black artists Mel Edwards (left) and Vincent Smith (right) at the opening exhibition of The Studio Museum in Harlem.

Paris and Los Angeles. He has befriended, or studied with, such giants as Larry Rivers, Willem de Kooning and Giacometti. In 1961, he was awarded the Stanton Fellowship; within two years, he was touring the South collecting common objects for constructions. By 1966, he was fully involved in developing the technique of using high polishes for surface-painted wood.

Johnson has exhibited widely in Atlanta, at Howard University in Washington, D. C., in Pasadena and Los Angeles.

JACK JORDAN
Sculptor

Sculptor/painter Jack Jordan, born in Texas in 1925, is former head of the Art Department of Langston University in Langston, Oklahoma.

Jordan was educated at the State University of Iowa, and has studied under various private tutors. The artist has received many awards from Atlanta University and the National Conference of Artists.

JACOB LAWRENCE
Painter

Jacob Lawrence is generally considered to be the leading Negro painter in America today. Working in a two-dimensional style with egg tempera or oils, Lawrence has created several notable works dealing with episodes in Negro life and history.

Lawrence was born in 1917 in Atlantic City, and studied painting at the Harlem Art School and the American Artist School. He gained his initial fame through a series of biographical panels on Negro historical themes such as "The Life of Toussaint L'Ouverture" (41 panels—1937); "The Life of Frederick Douglass" (40 panels—1938); "The Life of Harriet Tubman" (40 panels—1939), and "The Negro Migration Northward in World War" (60 panels—1942).

Lawrence's work can be seen in the Metropolitan Museum of Art, the Whitney Museum, and the Museum of Modern Art. To the great Mexican painter Orozco, he is simply ". . . one of the few creative artists."

In his powerful renditions of everyday life in the ghettos of the North, Lawrence offers a vivid pictorial commentary of the post-depression shift in Negro population from the rural South to the urban North.

HUGHIE LEE-SMITH
Painter

During his career, Hughie Lee-Smith has received more than a dozen important prizes, including the Founders Prize of the Detroit Institute of Arts (1953) and the Emily Lowe Award (1957).

Born in Florida in 1915, Smith was awarded the Gilpin Players Scholarship at the Cleveland School of Art and later studied under Sarkis Sarkisian. He received his B.S. from Wayne University.

Smith is a member of Allied Artists of America, the Michigan Academy of Arts, Science & Letters, and the Artists Equity Association. He has had numerous one-man shows around the country.

EDMONIA LEWIS
1845-1890
Sculptor

Edmonia Lewis is important both aesthetically and historically in any review of the Negro's contribution to the fine arts. She was not only the first American Negro woman artist, but also the first of her race and sex to be recognized as a sculptor.

Born in 1845 in Greenhigh, Ohio, she was the daughter of a Chippewa Indian mother and a free Negro father. From 1859 to 1863, under the patronage of a number of abolitionists, she was educated at Oberlin College, the first American institution of higher learning to admit women on a non-segregated basis.

After completing her schooling, she moved to Boston where her interest in sculpture led to her studying with Edmund Brackett. While there, she met Colonel Robert Gould Shaw, the commander of the first Negro regiment raised in the state of Massachusetts during the Civil War, and did a bust of him.

In 1865, she traveled to Rome, where she soon became a prominent figure in the American colony. Returning to the United States, she fulfilled many commissions, including a bust of Henry Wadsworth Longfellow which was executed for the Harvard College Library.

Her best-known works include "Hiawatha" (1865); "The Marriage of Hiawatha" (1865); "Hagar in the Wilderness" (1866); "Madonna and Child" (1867); "Forever Free" (1867), and "The Death of Cleopatra" (1876). All are examples of the neo-classical sculp-

stones by Jacob Lawrence.

ture that was fashionable during her lifetime.

Miss Lewis died in Rome in 1890.

GERALDINE McCULLOUGH
Sculptor

One of the most promising new sculptors in America is Geraldine McCullough whose welded steel and copper abstraction "Phoenix" won the George D. Widener Gold Medal at the 1964 exhibition of the Pennyslvania Academy of Fine Arts. In capturing this award, her name was added to a roster of distinguished artists who have already won the same honor, including Jacques Lipchitz and Theodore Roszak. Of further note was the fact that this had been her first showing in a major national exhibition.

A native of Arkansas, Mrs. McCullough has lived in Chicago since she was three, and is a 1948 graduate of the Art Institute there.

She is currently teaching at Wendell Phillips High School in Chicago.

EARL MILLER
Painter

Among the most talented new Afro-American artists exhibiting in America since 1950 is Earl Miller, born in Seattle, Washington in 1930.

Miller studied in the United States until 1957, first at Pratt Institute in Brooklyn (1954-1956), later at the Art School of the Brooklyn Museum (1956) and, finally, at the Art Students League. He also attended the *Akademie der Bildenden Kunste* in Munich in 1963.

Miller has had several one-man exhibits, notably at New York's Phoenix Gallery (1961) and the Town Hall in Marbella, Spain (1962). In 1968 and 1969, he was among those featured at the American Greetings Gallery, the Lever House, the Museum of Modern Art, and Brooklyn College, all in New York.

Miller has won several awards, including the Grand Concourse Award for Painting offered by the Art Students League.

P'LLA MILLS
Painter
1918-1964

Painter P'lla Mills, born in Connersville, Indiana in 1918, first studied at the Chicago Art Institute and later worked under F. Carlton Ball at the University of Southern California. Miss Mills exhibited at the Heritage Gallery, Los Angeles Art Association and Paramount Studios. She died in 1964.

JOSEPH OVERSTREET
Painter

Born in Conehatta, Mississippi in 1934, Joe Overstreet studied at the California School of Arts and Crafts and participated in "New Black Artists," seen at the Brooklyn Museum in 1969.

Overstreet's canvases have of late eschewed racial themes to concentrate instead on vivid color and original configuration. Thus, many of his abstractions are based on a medley of African and Indian colors. When they are exhibited, the canvases are often held in place by guy wires.

Overstreet's work is equally memorable when it deals with racial subject matter. Noteworthy are *Jazz in 4/4 Time* (oil on canvas) and *Keep on Keeping On* (oil on canvas).

Joseph Overstreet.

Horace Pippin's "Buffalo Hunt"

HORACE PIPPIN
1888-1946
Painter

Horace Pippin was the greatest Negro primitive painter, and has been ranked in the company of Henri Rousseau as a self-taught artist.

Pippin was born in 1888 in West Chester, Pennsylvania, and painted steadily from 1920 until his death in 1946. Among his most vivid portrayals on canvas were the battle scenes which he remembered from his own experience in World War I, during which he was wounded and partially paralyzed.

Pippin's work was discovered in the late 1930's. From that time onward, he was championed by many critics as the finest Negro painter in America.

Apart from war scenes, Pippin dealt with a variety of other subjects as well. This can be seen in such important paintings as "John Brown Goes To His Hanging" (1942); "Flowers With Red Chair" (a still life); "Cabin in the Cotton" (1944), and "The Den" (1945)—both of which had domestic settings.

Before his death, Pippin won a Carnegie Exhibition award. Today, his work can be viewed in a number of major collections, such as those of the Whitney Museum and the Barnes Foundation.

AUGUSTA SAVAGE
1900-1962
Sculptor

One of the leading sculptors to emerge during the "Negro Renaissance" was Augusta Savage.

Born in Green Cove Spring, Florida in 1900, she was one of the artists represented in the first all-Negro exhibition in America, sponsored by the Harmon Foundation at International House in New York City. In 1939, her symbolic group piece "Lift Every Voice and Sing" was shown at the New York World's Fair Community Arts Building.

Miss Savage studied at Tallahassee State Normal School; at Cooper Union in New York City, and in France as the recipient of Carnegie and Rosenwald Fellowships. She was the first Negro to win acceptance in the National Association of Women Painters and Sculptors.

She died on March 27, 1962.

VINCENT SMITH
Painter

Black painter Vincent Smith, born in 1929, belongs to the social commentary school of artists, i.e., those who explore themes relating to the rise of black militancy and the aspirations of black youth.

A native of Brooklyn, Smith studied at the Art Students League (1953) and continued his training at the Brooklyn Museum School of Art. In 1957, he received a John Hay Whitney Fellowship.

Smith has exhibited widely in the East, and has even had several one-man shows. Among his best-known works are: *Molotov Cocktail* (1967) and *The People Cry Out* (1967).

HENRY OSSAWA TANNER
1859-1937
Painter

Alain Locke has called Henry Ossawa Tanner the leading talent of the "journeyman period" of American Negro art.

Born in Pittsburgh in 1859, Tanner chose painting rather than the ministry as a career, overcoming the strong objections of his father, an African Methodist Episcopal bishop. After attending the Pennsylvania Academy of Fine Arts, he taught at Clark University in Atlanta, supplementing his salary by working as a photographer. Some of Tanner's most compelling work—such as "The Banjo Lesson" (1890)—was produced during this period, with Tanner himself emerging as the most promising Negro artist of his day.

In 1891, however, Tanner abandoned Negro subject matter as such, and left the United States for Paris, where he began to concentrate on paintings with religious themes, the basis of his subsequent fame. In 1896, his "Daniel in the Lion's Den," a mixture of realism and mystical symbolism, won honorable mention at the Paris Salon. The following year, the French government purchased his "Resurrection of Lazarus."

In 1900, Tanner received the Medal of Honor at the Paris Exposition, and the Lippincott Prize as well. Among his most famous works are "Christ Walking on the Water," "The Disciples on the Road to Bethany," and "The Flight into Egypt."

Tanner died in 1937, having returned to the United States only once after his departure in 1891.

BOB THOMPSON
Painter

The death of Bob Thompson took from the black art world one of its outstanding painters, a man who had not only studied extensively here in the United States, but also travelled widely in Europe and North Africa, living in Paris (1961-1962), Ibiza (1962-1963) and Rome (1965-1966).

Born in Louisville, Kentucky in 1937, Thompson studied at the Boston Museum School in 1955 and later spent three years at the University of Louisville. In 1960, Thompson participated in a two-man show at Zabriskie Gallery and, two years later, received a John Hay Whitney Fellowship.

For the next several years, Thompson had several one-man exhibitions in such leading U. S. cities as New York and Chicago. His work was also seen abroad in Spain. Group exhibitions are too numerous to catalog.

A retrospective of Thompson's work was given at the New School Art Center in New York in 1969. Thompson's work is in several permanent collections around the country, including the Chrysler Museum in Provincetown, Massachusetts.

Among his most dynamic works are: *Ascension to the Heavens* (oil on canvas; 1961) and *Untitled Diptych* (gouache and crayon on paper, 1966).

LAURA WHEELER WARING
1887–1948
Artist, educator

Born in 1887 in Hartford, Connecticut, this portrait painter and illustrator received her first training at the Pennsylvania Academy of Fine Arts, where she studied for six years. In 1919, she won the Cresson Memorial Scholarship, which enabled her to continue her studies at the Academie de la Grande Chaumiere in Paris.

Mrs. Waring returned to the United States as an art instructor at Cheyney State Teachers College in Pennsylvania, eventually becoming head of the art department there. Her work, particularly portraits, has been exhibited at several leading American art galleries. In 1927, she received the Harmon Award for achievement in fine art.

Mrs. Waring was also the director in charge of the Negro art exhibits at the Philadelphia Exposition in 1926, and was a member of the national advisory board of Art Movements, Inc.

She died on February 3, 1948.

CHARLES WHITE
Painter

Charles White is one of the foremost exponents of the school of social art. His paintings have used as their subject matter both the notable achievements of famous American Negroes, as well as the suffering of the lowly and the anonymous.

White was born on April 2, 1918 in Chicago, and was influenced as a young boy by Alain Locke's critical review of the Harlem Renaissance: *The New Negro.*

At the age of 23, White won a Rosenwald Fellowship which enabled him to work in the South for two years, during which time he painted a celebrated mural depicting the Negro's contribution to American democracy. It is now the property of Hampton Institute in Virginia.

The bulk of his work is done in a black-and-white motif, one which he feels gives him the widest possible audience. His more famous works include: "Let's Walk Together," "Frederick Douglass Lives Again," "Women," and "Gospel Singer."

JACK WHITTEN
Painter

Painter Jack Whitten was born in Bessemer, Alabama in 1939 and studied at Tuskegee Institute and Southern University in Baton Rouge, Louisiana before coming North to receive his BFA degree from Cooper Union in New York.

Whitten, who currently teaches at Pratt Institute, received a Whitney Fellowship in 1964. His second one-man show was given at the Allan Stone Gallery in February 1970. He was also represented in the 1969 Whitney Museum of American Art Annual.

A poignant work of Charles White.

BEULAH WOODARD
1895-1955

Painter/Sculptor

Beulah Woodard's interest in African art predates the period during which black American culture made a conscious and concerted effort to return to its ancestral roots.

Born in Ohio in 1895, Miss Woodard received private lessons from a number of artists and also studied at the Los Angeles Art School and Otis Art Institute. During her lifetime, the artist worked in clay, plaster, wood, copper, bronze, oil paint and paper mache, capturing several distinctive African types in both painting and sculpture. Her primitive African masks were first exhibited at the Los Angeles County Museum, and she was later represented in numerous exhibits at both the local and national level. The recipient of several awards, Miss Woodard was, at the time of her death in 1964, working on an exhibit to be shown in Munich, Germany at the municipal museum.

HALE WOODRUFF
Painter

Hale Woodruff's paintings have been largely modernist landscapes and formal abstractions, but he has also done rural Georgia scenes evocative of the "red clay" country.

Born in 1900 in Cairo, Illinois, Woodruff is a graduate of the John Herron Art Institute in Indianapolis. Encouraged by a bronze award in the 1926 Harmon Foundation competition, Woodruff went to Paris to study at both the Académie Scandinave and the Académie Moderne, as well as with Henry Ossawa Tanner.

In 1931, he became art instructor at Atlanta University and, five years later, accepted a similar post at New York University. In 1939, he was commissioned by Talladega College to do "The Amistad Murals," an episodic depiction of a slave revolt.

That same year, Woodruff returned to Atlanta University and, in 1941, initiated the annual art shows which have continued to the present day.

Hale Woodruff's mural depicting the blacks' contribution to the growth of California from exploration and colonization through settlement.

OTHER NOTED NEGRO PAINTERS AND SCULPTORS

Name	*Place of Birth*	*Date of Birth*
Andrews, Benny	Madison, Georgia	1930
Artis, William E.*	New York, New York	1914
Bannarn, Henry W.	Wetunka, Oklahoma	1910
Bishop, Eloise*	Pittsburgh, Pennsylvania	1921
Blayton, Betty	Williamsburg, Virginia	1937
Burke, Selma H.*	Mooresville, North Carolina	—
Campbell, E. Simms	St. Louis, Missouri	1906
Catlett, Elizabeth*	Washington, D. C.	1915
Cortor, Eldzier	Chicago, Illinois	1915
Dawson, Charles C.	Brunswick, Georgia	1889
de Knight, Avel	New York City	1933
Delaney, Joseph	Knoxville, Tennessee	1904
Farrow, William McKnight	Dayton, Ohio	1885
Flemister, Fred C.	Atlanta, Georgia	1916
Freelon, Allan R.	Philadelphia, Pennsylvania	1895
Gammon, Reginald	Philadelphia, Pennsylvania	1921
Giles, William	South Carolina	1930
Goreleigh, Rex	Penllyn, Pennsylvania	1902
Greene, Stephen	New York City	1918
Harleston, Edward A.	Charleston, South Carolina	1882
Hayden, Palmer	Wide Water, Virginia	1893
Hines, Felrath	Indianapolis, Indiana	1918
Hollingsworth, Al	New York City	—
Johnson, Sargent C.*	Boston, Massachusetts	1888
Johnson, William H.	Florence, South Carolina	1901
Jones, Ben	Paterson, New Jersey	1941
Jones, Henry B.	Philadelphia, Pennsylvania	1889
Jones, Lois Mailou	Boston, Massachusetts	1906
Lewis, Larry	Selma, Alabama	1927
Lewis, Norman	New York, New York	1909
Lloyd, Tom	New York City	1929
Loper, Edward L.	Wilmington, Delaware	1916
Meeks, Leon	New York City	1940
Motley, Archibald	New Orleans, Louisiana	1891
Perkins, Marion*	Marche, Arkansas	1908
Porter, James A.	Washington, D.C.	1905
Prophet, Elizabeth	Providence, Rhode Island	1890
Scott, William Edouard	Indianapolis, Indiana	1884
Sebree, Charles	Madisonville, Kentucky	1914
Smith, Hughie Lee	Cleveland, Ohio	1914
Streat, Thelma Johnson	Yakima, Washington	1912
Wells, James L.	Atlanta, Georgia	1902
White, Jack	New York City	1940
Wilson, John	Boston, Massachusetts	1922

* Denotes sculptor; rest are primarily painters.

Benjamin Bannaker's

PENNSYLVANIA, DELAWARE, MARY-LAND, AND VIRGINIA

ALMANAC,

FOR THE

YEAR of our LORD 1795;

Being the Third after Leap-Year.

[Th]e title page of Benjamin Banneker's Almanac (1795)

PHILADELPHIA:

Printed for WILLIAM GIBBONS, Cherry Street

BLACK INVENTORS AND SCIENTISTS

Noted Black Inventors: Anonymity and Achievement
Inventions by Negroes: 1871-1900

In 1870, more than 80% of the Negroes in the United States were illiterate and, even 40 years later, more than one-third of the Negro population over 10 years of age had still never been to school. It is against this background of systematic educational deprivation that the achievements of the Negro inventor and scientist can be seen in their sharpest perspective.

In addition to this lack of formal schooling, the Negro inventor and scientist also encountered innumerable legal and social obstacles. In pre-Civil War days, for example, slaves were unable to obtain patents with the result that, today, there is no way of determining the actual number of Negro inventors who had their work expropriated by their masters. Even the inventions of free Negroes were often refused acceptance once the racial identity of the inventor became known. (See Garrett Morgan entry.)

Many inventions by Negroes have not, therefore, been identified as such; nonetheless, even if one considers only the *verifiable* ones, the total still runs into the thousands, ranging from simple household conveniences to more complex mechanical devices which have proved to be of vital importance to business and industry. Some are as familiar as the potato chip of Hyram S. Thomas, a Saratoga chef; the ice cream of Augustus Jackson, a Philadelphia confectioner known as the "man who invented ice cream" (1832); the golf tee of George F. Grant; the mop-holder of Thomas W. Stewart, and the player pianos of J. H. and S. L. Dickinson.

On the other hand, no commentary on Negro inventors and scientists could fail to make mention of the major accomplishments of such men as Granville Woods (the synchronous multiplex railway telegraph); Elijah McCoy (the automatic lubricator), and Jan Matzeliger (the shoe-last machine).

Nor should one forget that most of these achievements—whether large or small—were often made in the face of overwhelming odds, and frequently greeted with hostility and derision.

N. Rillieux.

Evaporating Pan.

No. 4,879

Patented Dec. 10, 1846

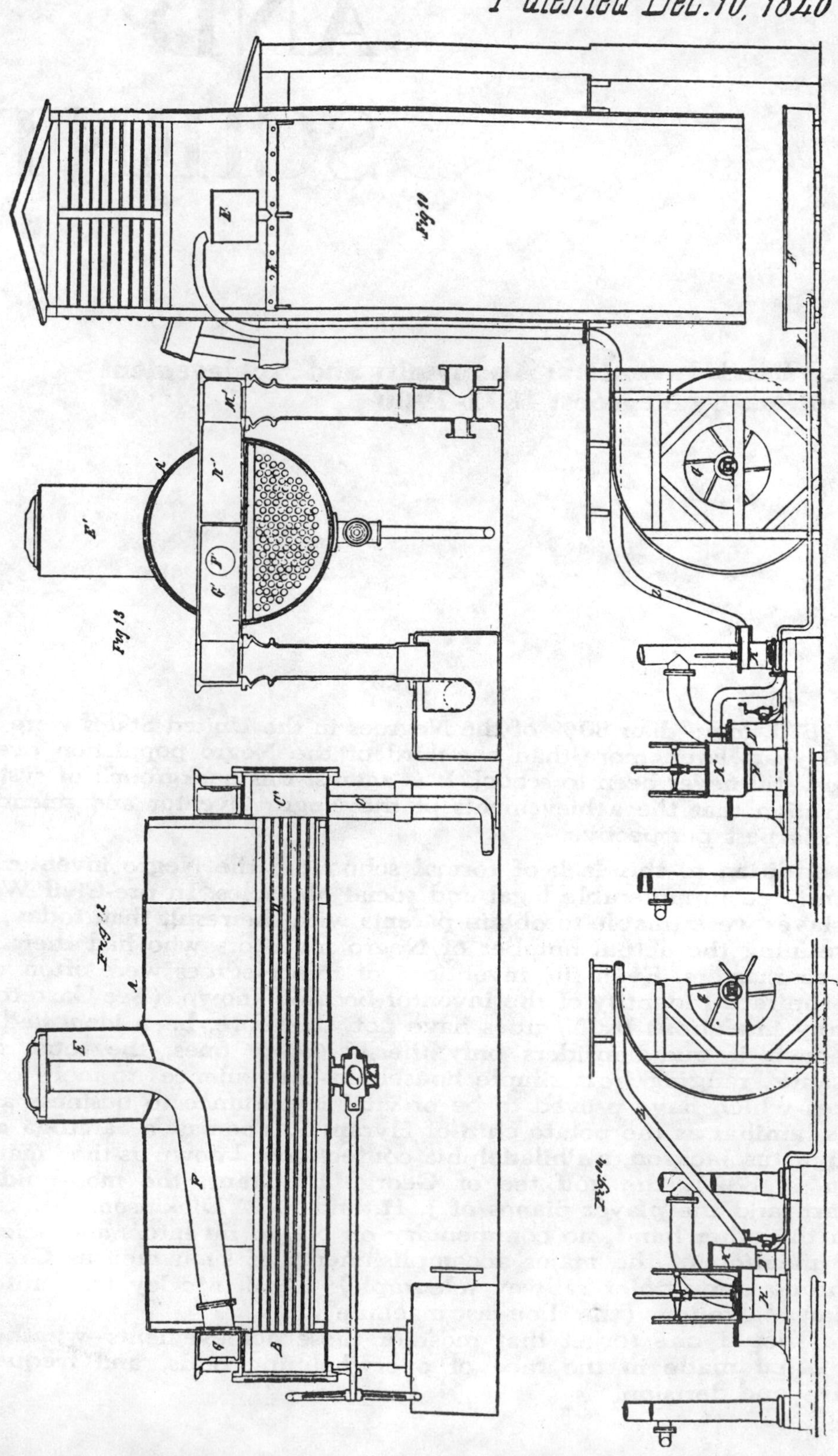

BENJAMIN BANNEKER
1731-1806
Inventor, mathematician, gazeteer

Benjamin Banneker's mechanical inventiveness led him, in 1761, to construct what was probably the first clock made in America—a wooden "striking" clock so accurate that it kept perfect time and struck each hour unfailingly for more than 20 years.

Born in Ellicott, Maryland on November 9, 1731 of a free mother and a slave father who ultimately purchased his own freedom, Banneker himself was considered free, and was thus able to attend an integrated private school, where he secured the equivalent of an eighth-grade education.

His aptitude in mathematics and his knowledge of astronomy enabled him to predict the solar eclipse of 1789. Within a few years, he began publishing an almanac which not only contained tide tables and data on future eclipses, but also listed a number of useful medicinal products and formulas as well. This almanac was the first scientific book written by an American Negro, and appeared annually for more than a decade.

Banneker's major reputation, however, stems from his service as a surveyor on the six-man team which helped lay out the blueprint for the eventual city of Washington, D. C. When the chairman of the committee, Major L'Enfant, abruptly resigned and returned to France with his plans, Banneker's precise memory enabled him to reproduce them in their entirety.

Banneker died in 1806.

ANDREW J. BEARD
Inventor

In 1897, Andrew J. Beard received $50,000 for an invention which has since prevented the death or maiming of countless numbers of railroad men.

While working in an Alabama railroad yard, Beard had all too often seen men lose hands, even arms, in serious accidents occurring during the manual coupling of railroad cars (a system, curiously enough, still used in some European countries). The system in use involved the dropping of a metal pin into place as two cars would crash together. It was not an utter rarity for a man himself to be caught between cars and crushed to death during this split-second operation.

Beard's invention, called the "Jenny Coupler," was an automatic device which secured two cars by merely bumping them together.

HENRY BLAIR
Inventor

On October 14, 1834, Henry Blair of Maryland was granted a patent for a corn-planting machine and, two years later, a second patent for a similar device used in planting cotton.

In the registry of the Patent Office, Blair was designated "a colored man"—the only instance of identification by race in these early records. Since slaves could not legally obtain patents, Blair was evidently a freedman, and is probably the first Negro inventor to receive a U. S. patent.

GEORGE WASHINGTON CARVER
1864-1943
Agricultural Scientist

George Washington Carver devoted his life to research projects connected primarily with Southern agriculture. The products he derived from the peanut and the soybean may be said to have revolutionized the economy of the South by liberating it from an excessive dependence on a single crop: cotton.

Born a slave in 1864 in Diamond Grove, Missouri, Carver was only an infant when he and his mother were abducted from his owner's plantation by a band of slave raiders. His mother was sold and shipped away, but her son was ransomed by his master in exchange for a race horse.

At the age of 13, Carver was already on his own. By working hard as a farm hand, he managed to obtain a high school education. After being turned down by many colleges, he was finally admitted as the first Negro student of Simpson College in Indianola, Iowa. He then attended Iowa Agricultural College (now Iowa State University) where, while working as the school janitor, he received a degree in agricultural science in 1894. Two years later, he received his master's degree from the same school, and became the first Negro to serve on its faculty. Within a short time, his fame had spread sufficiently for Booker T. Washington to offer him a post at Tuskegee.

Dr. Carver never patented any of the many discoveries he made while at Tuskegee. ("God gave them to me, how can I sell them to someone else?") In fact, in 1938, he donated over $30,000 of his life's savings to the George Washington Carver Foundation, and willed the rest of his estate to the same organization so that his work might be carried on after his death.

Carver died in 1943, and is buried alongside Booker T. Washington, his colleague of long standing. The Carver epitaph reads: "He could have added fortune to fame, but caring for neither, he found happiness and honor in being helpful to the world."

George Washington Carver was the most prominent black agricultural scientist of his day.

DR. ULYSSES GRANT DAILEY
1885-1961
Surgeon

Ulysses Grant Dailey served for four years (1908-1912) as surgical assistant to the famous Dr. Daniel Hale Williams, founder of Provident Hospital and noted heart surgeon.

Born in Donaldsonville, Louisiana in 1885, Dailey graduated in 1906 from the Northwestern University Medical School, where he was appointed a Demonstrator in Anatomy. He later studied in London, Paris and Vienna and, in 1926, set up his own hospital and sanitarium in Chicago. His name was soon widely associated with some of the outstanding achievements then being made in the fields of anatomy and surgery.

For many years an associate editor of the *Journal of the National Medical Association*, Dr. Dailey traveled around the world in 1933 under the sponsorship of the International College of Surgeons of which he was a Founder Fellow.

In 1951 and again in 1953, the U. S. State Department sent him to Pakistan, India, Ceylon and Africa. A year later, he was named honorary consul to Haiti.

Dr. Dailey died in 1961.

DR. CHARLES DREW
1904-1950
Blood plasma researcher

The techniques developed by Charles Richard Drew for separating and preserving blood, as well as his advanced research in the vital field of blood plasma, helped save countless lives during World War II.

Born in Washington, D. C. on June 3, 1904, Drew graduated from Amherst College in Massachusetts, where he received the Messman Trophy for having brought the most honor to the school during his four-year stay there. He was not only an outstanding scholar, but also the captain of the track team and star halfback on the football team.

After receiving his medical degrees from McGill University in 1933, Drew returned to Washington, D. C. to teach pathology at Howard University. In 1940, while taking his D. Sc. degree at Columbia University, he wrote a dissertation on "banked blood," and soon became such an expert in this field that the British government called upon his services to set up the first blood bank in England.

During World War II, Dr. Drew was appointed as director of the American Red Cross blood donor project and, later, served as chief surgeon of Freedmen's Hospital in Washington, D. C.

Dr. Charles Drew

He was killed in an automobile crash on April 1, 1950.

WILLIAM A. HINTON
1883-1959
Medical Scientist

Long one of the world's authorities on venereal disease, Dr. William A. Hinton is responsible for the development of the "Hinton test," a reliable method for detecting syphilis. During his lifetime, he also collaborated with Dr. J. A. V. Davies on what is now called the "Davies-Hinton test" for the detection of this same disease.

Born in Chicago on December 15, 1883, Hinton graduated from Harvard in 1905 and, seven years later, finished his studies at Harvard Medical School.

For three years after graduation, he served as a voluntary assistant in the pathological laboratory at Massachusetts General Hospital. This was followed by eight years of laboratory practice at the Boston Dispensary and at the Massachusetts Department of Public Health. Hinton then became an assistant lecturer in preventive medicine and hygiene at the Harvard University Medical School. In 1949, he became the first Negro to be granted a professorship there.

Though he lost a leg in an automobile accident, Dr. Hinton remained active in both his teaching and his work at the Boston Dispensary Laboratory, which he directed from 1916 to 1952.

He died on August 8, 1959 in Canton, Massachusetts.

PERCY JULIAN
Chemist

The research of Dr. Percy Julian has helped create derivative drugs which are in widespread use today by sufferers from arthritis.

Born in Montgomery, Alabama in 1898, Julian attended DePauw University in Greencastle, Indiana. He graduated Phi Beta Kappa and as valedictorian of his class after having lived during his college days in the attic of a fraternity house where he worked as a waiter.

For several years, Julian taught at Fisk and Howard universities, as well as at West Virginia State College, before attending Harvard and the University of Vienna.

He later headed the soybean research department of the Glidden Company, and then formed Julian Laboratories in order to specialize in the production of sterols, which he extracted from the oil of the soybean. The method perfected by Dr. Julian eventually lowered the cost of sterols to less than 20 cents a gram, and ultimately enabled millions of people suffering from arthritis to obtain relief from cortisone, a sterol derivative, at a price within their means.

In 1935, Dr. Julian successfully synthesized the drug physostigmine, which is used today in the treatment of glaucoma.

ERNEST E. JUST
1883-1941
Biologist

Dr. Ernest E. Just's pioneer investigations into the uncharted areas of egg fertilization and the biological phenomena relating to the structure of the living cell earned him rapid fame throughout the world of science.

Born of middle-class parents in 1883 in Charleston, South Carolina, he attended Dartmouth College, an Ivy League school, graduating *magna cum laude* and with Phi Beta Kappa honors. He later taught at Howard University.

Dr. Just wrote two major books and over 60 scientific dissertations relating to his field, and was the recipient of numerous grants and citations, including the first Spingarn Medal awarded by the NAACP (1915). A year later, he won his doctorate at the University of Chicago.

Just subsequently conducted research in marine biology for the U. S. government at Woods Hole, Massachusetts. He died in 1941.

LEWIS HOWARD LATIMER
1848-1928
Inventor, draftsman, engineer

Lewis Howard Latimer was employed by Alexander Graham Bell to make the patent drawings for the first telephone, and later went on to become chief draftsman for both the General Electric and Westinghouse Companies.

Born in Chelsea, Massachusetts on September 4, 1848, Latimer enlisted in the Union Navy at the age of 15, and began the study of drafting upon completion of military service. In 1881, he invented and patented the first incandescent electric light bulb with a carbon filament. Later, as an engineer for the Edison Company, he supervised the installation of electric light in New York, Philadelphia, Montreal, and London. He also wrote the first textbook on the lighting system used by this company.

Latimer died in 1928.

THEODORE K. LAWLESS
Dermatologist

Theodore K. Lawless is one of the leading skin specialists in the United States.

Born in 1892 in Thibodeaux, Louisiana, he was educated at Talladega College in Alabama, the University of Kansas, Columbia, and Harvard before receiving his M.D. from Northwestern University.

From 1924 until 1941, Dr. Lawless taught at the Northwestern School of Medicine, and did special research work in Vienna, Freiburg, and Paris, where he made valuable contributions to the scientific treatment of syphilis and leprosy.

The dermatology clinic at the Beilinson Hospital Center for Israel was erected largely through his efforts, and bears his name, as does a chapel at Dillard University in New Orleans.

Winner of the 1929 Harmon Award in medicine, and later awarded the Spingarn Medal (1954), Dr. Lawless continues his private practice in an office near Chicago's Provident Hospital where, for many years, he has served as senior attending physician.

JAN MATZELIGER
1852-1889
Inventor

The shoe-lasting machine invented by Jan Matzeliger, a Negro from Dutch Guiana, not only revolutionized the shoe industry, but also made Lynn, Massachusetts the "shoe capital of the world."

Born in Paramaribo, Dutch Guiana on September 15, 1852, Matzeliger found employment in the government machine works at the age of 10. Eight years later, he immigrated to the United States, settling at first in Philadelphia, where he worked in a shoe factory and learned the trade. He then left for New England, settling permanently in Lynn.

The Industrial Revolution then in progress in the United States had by this time resulted in the invention of a number of machines to cut, sew, and tack shoes, but none had been perfected to last a shoe. Seeing this, Matzeliger lost little time in designing and patenting just such a device, one which he refined over the years to such a point that it was able to adjust a shoe, arrange the leather over the sole, drive in the nails, and deliver the finished product—all in one minute's time.

Matzeliger's patent was subsequently bought by Sydney W. Winslow who established the United Shoe Machine Company, a multi-million dollar concern. The continued success of this business

J. E. MATZELIGER

LASTING MACHINE

No. 274,207. PATENTED MAR. 20, 1883

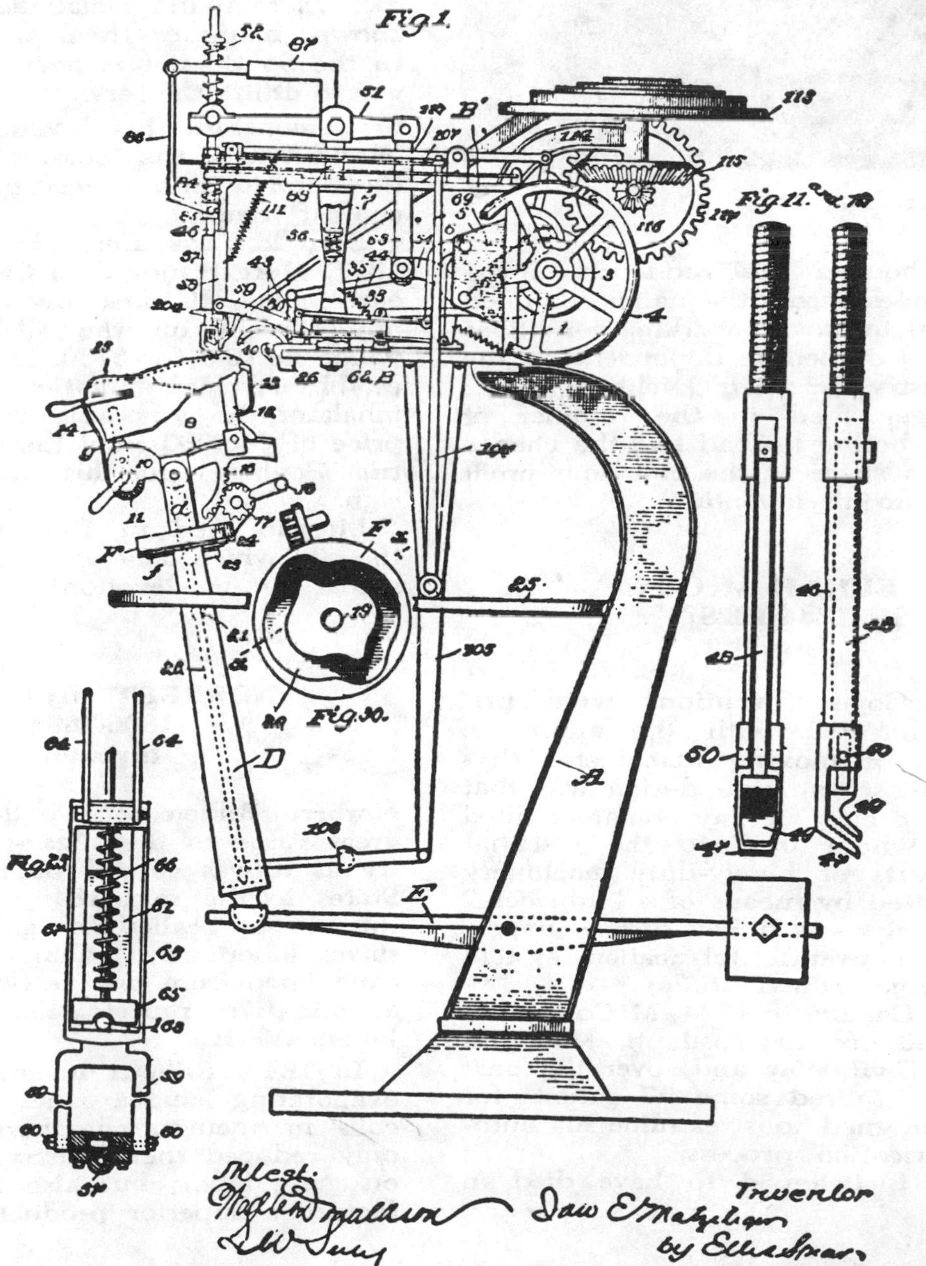

AN ILLUSTRATION SHOWING THE MODELS MADE BY MATZELIGER TO ILLUSTRATE HIS INVENTIONS IN SHOE MACHINES.

Jan E. Matzeliger

brought about a 50% reduction in the price of shoes across the nation, doubled wages, and improved working conditions for millions of people dependent on the shoe industry for their livelihood.

Matzeliger died in the summer of 1889 long before he had had the chance to realize a share of the enormous profit derived from his invention.

ELIJAH McCOY
1844-1928?
Inventor

Elijah McCoy's inventions were primarily connected with the automatic lubrication of moving machinery. Perhaps his most valuable design was that of the "drip cup," a tiny container filled with oil whose flow to the essential moving parts of heavy-duty machinery was regulated by means of a "stopcock." The drip cup was a key device in perfecting the overall lubrication system used in large industry today.

Born in Canada in 1844, McCoy established residence in Ypsilanti, Michigan after the Civil War and, over the next 40 years, acquired some 57 patents for devices designed to streamline his automatic lubrication process.

McCoy is believed to have died in 1928.

GARRETT A. MORGAN
1877-1963
Inventor

The value of Garrett Morgan's "gas inhalator" was first acknowledged during a successful rescue operation made necessary by a tunnel explosion which had trapped several men in the Cleveland Waterworks some 200 feet below the surface of Lake Erie. During the emergency, Morgan, his brother and two other volunteers—all wearing inhalators—were the only men able to descend into the smoke and gas-filled tunnel, and save several of the men from asphyxiation.

Orders for the Morgan inhalator soon began to pour into Cleveland from fire companies all over the nation but, as soon as Morgan's racial identity became known, many of them were cancelled. In the South, it was necessary for Morgan to utilize the services of a white man to demonstrate his invention. (During World War I, the Morgan inhalator was transformed into a gas mask used by combat troops.)

Born in Paris, Kentucky on March 4, 1877, Morgan moved to Cleveland at an early age. His first invention was an improvement on the sewing machine which he sold for $150. In 1923, having established his reputation with the gas inhalator, he was able to command a price of $40,000 from the General Electric Company for his automatic stop-sign.

Morgan died in 1963 in Cleveland, the city which once awarded him a gold medal for his devotion to public safety.

NORBERT RILLIEUX
1806-1894
Inventor

Norbert Rillieux's inventions were of great value to the sugar-refining industry as it was carried on in the United States in the mid 1840's. The method then in use called for gangs of Negro slaves laboriously ladling boiling sugar-cane juice from one kettle to another—a primitive process known as "The Jamaica Train."

In 1845, Rillieux invented a vacuum evaporating pan (a series of condensing coils in vacuum chambers) which not only reduced the industry's dependence on gang labor, but also helped manufacture a superior product at a greatly reduced cost. The first Rillieux evaporator was installed successfully at Myrtle Grove Plantation, Louisiana in 1845. In the following years, factories in Louisiana, Cuba, and Mexico converted to the "Rillieux system."

A native of New Orleans, Louisiana, Rillieux was born on March 17, 1806, the son of Vincent Rillieux, a wealthy engineer, and Constance Vivant, a slave on his plantation. Young Rillieux's higher education was obtained in Paris, where his extraordinary aptitude for engineering led to his appointment at the age of 24 as an instructor of applied mechanics at L'Ecole Central. Rillieux returned to Paris for good in 1854, securing a scholarship and working at the deciphering of hieroglyphics.

When his evaporator process was finally adopted in Europe, he returned to inventing with renewed interest—applying his process to the sugar beet. In so doing, he cut its production and refining costs in half.

Rillieux died in Paris on October 8, 1894, leaving behind a system which is in universal use throughout the sugar industry, and in the manufacture of soap, gelatin, glue, and many other products.

LEWIS TEMPLE
1800-1854
Inventor

The toggle harpoon invented by Lewis Temple so improved the whaling methods of the 19th century that it more than doubled the catch for this leading New England industry.

Little is known of Temple's early background, except that he was born in Richmond, Virginia in 1800, and had no formal education. As a young man, he moved to New England and settled in New Bedford, Massachusetts, then one of the major American whaling ports.

Finding work as a metalsmith, Temple soon made efforts to modify the design of the whalers' harpoon and, in the 1840's, manufactured a new version of the harpoon which allowed lines to be securely fastened to the whale. Using the "toggle harpoon," the whaling industry soon entered into a period of unprecedented prosperity.

Temple, who had never patented his harpoon, died destitute in 1854.

DANIEL HALE WILLIAMS
1856-1931
Surgeon

A pioneer in open heart surgery, Daniel Hale Williams was born in Holidaysburg, Pennsylvania in 1856. His father died when he was 11, and his mother deserted him after first apprenticing him to a cobbler. He later worked as a roustabout on a lake steamer and as a barber before finishing his education at the Chicago Medical College in 1883.

Williams opened his office on Chicago's South Side at a time when Chicago hospitals did not allow Negro doctors to use their facilities. In those days, operations were often performed on kitchen tables in tenements scattered through the Black Belt. Dr. Williams helped put an end to this practice by founding Provident Hospital, which was open to patients of all races.

It was at Provident Hospital in 1893 that Dr. Williams performed the operation upon which his later fame rests. On July 10 of that year, a patient was admitted to the emergency ward with a knife wound in an artery lying a fraction of an inch from the heart. With the aid of six staff surgeons, Williams made an incision in the patient's chest, and operated successfully on the artery.

Daniel Hale Williams

The invention of the toggle harpoon by Lewis Temple changed the nature of the whaling industry. New England added to its wealth as a result.

The operation performed by Williams was a delicate and astonishing feat of surgery. The doctor began by making a six-inch incision and detaching the fifth rib from the breastbone, so he could settle down to work through a 2"x1½" opening. After securing the left internal mammary artery, he then inspected the heart, noting instantly that the pericardium had been punctured by the knife. The heart muscle, too, had been nicked, but the wound here was not serious enough to require suturing or stitching. Williams then repaired the pericardium, sutured the chest opening, and completed the momentous operation.

For the next four days, the patient, James Cornish, lay near death, his temperature far above normal and his pulse dangerously uneven. An encouraging rally then brought him out of immediate danger, terminating the immediate crisis period. Three weeks later, minor surgery was performed by Williams to remove fluid from Cornish's pleural cavity. After recuperating for still another month, Cornish was fully recovered and able to leave the hospital, scarred but cured.

An uproar of publicity greeted Williams' later announcement that his heart surgery had been successful. Much of it was negative, in the sense that skeptics doubted a Negro doctor could have engineered such a significant breakthrough. Unaffected by the notoriety, Williams continued a full-time association with Freedmen's Hospital.

Dr. Williams died in 1931 after a lifetime devoted to his two main interests—the NAACP, and the construction of hospitals and training schools for Negro doctors and nurses.

Granville Woods

GRANVILLE T. WOODS
1856-1910
Inventor

During his lifetime, Granville T. Woods obtained some 50 patents, including one for an incubator which was the forerunner of present machines capable of hatching 50,000 eggs at a time.

Born in Columbus, Ohio on April 23, 1856, Woods attended school until he was 10. He was first employed in a machine shop. and continued to improve his mechanical aptitude by working on a railroad in 1872, in a rolling mill in 1874 and, later, by studying mechanical engineering at college. In 1878, Woods became an engineer aboard the *Ironsides*, a British steamer and, within two years, was handling a steam locomotive on the D & S Railroad.

In 1887, he patented the most advanced of his many inventions—the Synchronous Multiplex Railway Telegraph. This device was designed "for the purpose of averting accidents by keeping each train informed of the whereabouts of the one immediately ahead or following it, in communicating with stations from moving trains; and in promoting general social and commercial intercourse."

Woods marketed this product, as well as the others which followed it, through his own company. A perusal of the patent files in Washington, D. C. shows Woods to have been an extremely prolific inventor, as well as a highly important one. In the 20-year span between 1879 and 1899, no less than 23 separate inventions bear his name. In 1887 alone, he registered seven separate inventions with the Patent Office, all of them connected with the ingenious railway communications system he devised.

Woods died in New York City on January 30, 1910.

INVENTIONS BY NEGROES: 1871–1900

(In cases where an inventor has patented several variations on the same basic invention, a composite entry has been devised.)

INVENTOR	INVENTION	DATE	PATENT
Abrams, W. B.	Hame Attachment	Apr. 14, 1891	450,550
Allen, C. W.	Self-Leveling Table	Nov. 1, 1898	613,436
Allen, J. B.	Clothes Line Support	Dec. 10, 1895	551,105
Ashbourne, A. P.	Process for Preparing Coconut for Domestic Use	June 1, 1875	163,962
Ashbourne, A. P.	Biscuit Cutter	Nov. 30, 1875	170,460
Ashbourne, A. P.	Refining Coconut Oil	July 27, 1880	230,518
Ashbourne, A. P.	Process of Treating Coconut	Aug. 21, 1877	194,287
Bailes, Wm.	Ladder Scaffold-Support	Aug. 5, 1879	218,154
Bailey, L. C.	Combined Truss and Bandage	Sept. 25, 1883	285,545
Bailey, L. C.	Folding Bed	July 18, 1899	629,286
Bailiff, C. O.	Shampoo Headrest	Oct. 11, 1898	612,008
Ballow, W. J.	Combined Hatrack and Table	Mar. 29, 1898	601,422
Barnes, G. A. E.	Design for Sign	Aug. 19, 1898	29,193
Beard, A. J.	Rotary Engine	July 5, 1892	478,271
Beard, A. J.	Car-coupler	Nov. 23, 1897	594,059
Becket, G. E.	Letter Box	Oct. 4, 1892	483,525
Bell, L.	Locomotive Smoke Stack	May 23, 1871	115,153
Bell, L.	Dough Kneader	Dec. 10, 1872	133,823
Benjamin, L. W.	Broom Moisteners and Bridles	May 16, 1893	497,747
Benjamin, Miss M. E.	Gong and Signal Chairs for Hotels	July 17, 1888	386,286
Binga, M. W.	Street Sprinkling Apparatus	July 22, 1879	217,843
Blackburn, A. B.	Railway Signal	Jan. 10, 1888	376,362
Blackburn, A. B.	Spring Seat for Chairs	Apr. 3, 1888	380,420
Blackburn, A. B.	Cash Carrier	Oct. 23, 1888	391,577
Blair, Henry	Corn Planter	Oct. 14, 1834	—
Blair, Henry	Cotton Planter	Aug. 31, 1836	—
Blue, L.	Hand Corn Shelling Device	May 20, 1884	298,937
Booker, L. F.	Design Rubber Scraping Knife	Mar. 28, 1899	30,404
Boone, Sarah	Ironing Board	Apr. 26, 1892	473,653
Bowman, H. A.	Making Flags	Feb. 23, 1892	469,395
Brooks, C. B.	Punch	Oct. 31, 1893	507,672
Brooks, C. B.	Street-Sweepers	Mar. 17, 1896	556,711
Brooks, C. B.	Street-Sweepers	May 12, 1896	560,154
Brooks, Hallstead and Page	Street-Sweepers	Apr. 21, 1896	558,719
Brown, Henry	Receptacle for Storing and Preserving Papers	Nov. 2, 1886	352,036
Brown, L. F.	Bridle Bit	Oct. 25, 1892	484,994
Brown, O. E.	Horseshoe	Aug. 23, 1892	481,271
Brown & Latimer	Water Closets for Railway Cars	Feb. 10, 1874	147,363
Burr, J. A.	Lawn Mower	May 9, 1899	624,749
Burr, W. F.	Switching Device for Railways	Oct. 31, 1899	636,197
Burwell, W.	Boot or Shoe	Nov. 28, 1899	638,143
Butler, R. A.	Train Alarm	June 15, 1897	584,540
Butts, J. W.	Luggage Carrier	Oct. 10, 1899	634,611
Byrd, T. J.	Improvement in Holders for Reins for Horses	Feb. 6, 1872	123,328
Byrd, T. J.	Apparatus for Detaching Horses from Carriages	Mar. 19, 1872	124,790
Byrd, T. J.	Improvement in Neck Yokes for Wagons	Apr. 30, 1872	126,181
Byrd, T. J.	Improvement in Car-Couplings	Dec. 1, 1874	157,370

INVENTOR	INVENTION	DATE	PATENT
Campbell, W. S.	Self-Setting Animal Trap	Aug. 30, 1881	246,369
Cargill, B. F.	Invalid Cot	July 25, 1899	629,658
Carrington, T. A.	Range	July 25, 1876	180,323
Carter, W. C.	Umbrella Stand	Aug. 4, 1885	323,397
Certain, J. M.	Parcel Carrier for Bicycles	Dec. 26, 1899	639,708
Cherry, M. A.	Velocipede	May 8, 1888	382,351
Cherry, M. A.	Street Car Fender	Jan. 1, 1895	531,908
Church, T. S.	Carpet Beating Machine	July 29, 1884	302,237
Clare, O. B.	Trestle	Oct. 9, 1888	390,753
Coates, R.	Overboot for Horses	Apr. 19, 1892	473,295
Cook, G.	Automatic Fishing Device	May 30, 1899	625,829
Coolidge, J. S.	Harness Attachment	Nov. 13, 1888	392,908
Cooper, A. R.	Shoemaker's Jack	Aug. 22, 1899	631,519
Cooper, J.	Shutter and Fastening	May 1, 1883	276,563
Cooper, J.	Elevator Device	Apr. 2, 1895	536,605
Cooper, J.	Elevator Device	Sept. 21, 1897	590,257
Cornwell, P. W.	Draft Regualtor	Oct. 2, 1888	390,284
Cornwell, P. W.	Draft Regulator	Feb. 7, 1893	491,082
Cralle, A. L.	Ice-Cream Mold	Feb. 2, 1897	576,395
Creamer, H.	Steam Feed Water Trap	Mar. 17, 1895	313,854
Creamer, H.	Steam Trap Feeder	Dec. 11, 1888	394,463
(Creamer also patented five steam traps between 1887 and 1893.)			
Cosgrove, W. F.	Automatic Stop Plug for Gas Oil Pipes	Mar. 17, 1885	313,993
Darkins, J. T.	Ventilation Aid*	Feb. 19, 1895	534,322
Davis, I. D.	Tonic	Nov. 2, 1886	351,829
Davis, W. D.	Riding Saddles	Oct. 6, 1896	568,939
Davis ,W. R., Jr.	Library Table	Sept. 24, 1878	208,378
Deitz, W. A.	Shoe	Apr. 30, 1867	64,205
Dickinson, J. H.	Pianola	Detroit, Mich., 1899	
Dorsey, O.	Door-Holding Device	Dec. 10, 1878	210,764
Dorticus, C. J.	Device for Applying Coloring Liquids to Sides of Soles or Heels of Shoes	Mar. 19, 1895	535,820
Dorticus, C. J.	Machine for Embossing Photo	Apr. 16, 1895	537,442
Dorticus, C. J.	Photographic Print Wash	Apr. 23, 1895	537,968
Dorticus, C. J.	Hose Leak Stop	July 18, 1899	629,315
Downing, P. B.	Electric Switch for Railroad	June 17, 1890	430,118
Downing, P. B.	Letter Box	Oct. 27, 1891	462,093
Downing, P. B,	Street Letter Box	Oct. 27, 1891	462,096
Dunnington, J. H.	Horse Detachers	Mar. 16, 1897	578,979
Edmonds, T. H.	Separating Screens	July 20, 1897	586,724
Elkins, T.	Dining, Ironing Table and Quilting Frame Combined	Feb. 22, 1870	100,020
Elkins, T.	Chamber Commode	Jan. 9, 1872	122,518
Elkins, T.	Refrigerating Apparatus	Nov. 4, 1879	221,222
Evans, J. H.	Convertible Settees	Oct. 5, 1897	591,095
Faulkner, H.	Ventilated Shoe	Apr. 29, 1890	426,495
Ferrell, F. J.	Steam Trap	Feb. 11, 1890	420,993
Ferrell, F. J.	Apparatus for Melting Snow	May 27, 1890	428,670
(Ferrell also patented eight valves between 1890 and 1893.)			
Fisher, D. A.	Joiners' Clamp	Apr. 20, 1875	162,281
Fisher, D. A.	Furniture Castor	Mar. 14, 1876	174,794
Flemming, R. F., Jr.	Guitar*	Mar. 3, 1886	338,727
Goode, Sarah E.	Folding Cabinet Bed	July 14, 1885	322,177
Grant, G. F.	Golf-Tee	Dec. 12, 1899	638,920

INVENTOR	INVENTION	DATE	PATENT
Grant, W. S.	Curtain Rod Support	Aug. 4, 1896	565,075
Gray, R. H.	Baling Press	Aug. 28, 1894	525,203
Gray, R. H.	Cistern Cleaners	Apr. 9, 1895	537,151
Gregory, J.	Motor	Apr. 26, 1887	361,937
Grenon, H.	Razor Stropping Device	Feb. 18, 1896	554,867
Griffin, F. W.	Pool Table Attachment	June 13, 1899	626,902
Gunn, S. W.	Boot or Shoe*	Jan. 16, 1900	641,642
Haines, J. H.	Portable Basin	Sept. 28, 1897	590,833
Hammonds, J. F.	Apparatus for Holding Yarn Skeins	Dec. 15, 1896	572,985
Harding, F. H.	Extension Banquet Table	Nov. 22, 1898	614,468
Hawkins, J.	Gridiron	Mar. 26, 1845	3,973
Hawkins, R.	Harness Attachment	Oct. 4, 1887	370,943
Headen, M.	Foot Power Hammer	Oct. 5, 1886	350,363
Hearness, R.	Sealing Attachment for Bottles	Feb. 15, 1898	598,929
Hearness, R.	Detachable Car Fender	July 4, 1899	628,003
Hilyer, A. F.	Water Evaporator Attachment for Hot Air Registers	Aug. 26, 1890	435,095
Hilyer, A. F.	Registers	Oct. 14, 1890	438,159
Holmes, E. H.	Gage	Nov. 12, 1895	549,513
Hunter, J. H.	Portable Weighing Scales	Nov. 3, 1896	570,553
Hyde, R. N.	Composition for Cleaning and Preserving Carpets	Nov. 6, 1888	392,205
Jackson, B. F.	Heating Apparatus	Mar. 1, 1898	599,985
Jackson, B. F.	Matrix Drying Apparatus	May 10, 1898	603,879
Jackson, B. F.	Gas Burner	Apr. 4, 1899	622,482
Jackson, H. A.	Kitchen Table*	Oct. 6, 1896	569,135
Jackson, W. H.	Railway Switch	Mar. 9, 1897	578,641
Jackson, W. H.	Railway Switch	Mar. 16, 1897	593,665
Jackson, W. H.	Automatic Locking Switch	Aug. 23, 1898	609,436
Johnson, D.	Rotary Dining Table	Jan. 15, 1888	396,089
Johnson, D.	Lawn Mower Attachment	Sept. 10, 1889	410,836
Johnson, D.	Grass Receivers for Lawn Mowers	June 10, 1890	429,629
Johnson, I. R.	Bicycle Frame	Oct. 10, 1899	634,823
Johnson, P.	Swinging Chairs	Nov. 15, 1881	249,530
Johnson, P.	Eye Protector	Nov. 2, 1880	234,039
Johnson, W.	Velocipede	June 20, 1899	627,335
Johnson, W. A.	Paint Vehicle	Dec. 4, 1888	393,763
Johnson, W. H.	Overcoming Dead Centers	Feb. 4, 1896	554,223
Johnson, W. H.	Overcoming Dead Centers	Oct. 11, 1898	612,345
Johnson, W.	Egg Beater	Feb. 5, 1884	292,821
Jones & Long	Caps for Bottles	Sept. 13, 1898	610,715
Joyce, J. A.	Ore Bucket	Apr. 26, 1898	603,143
Latimer, L. H.	Manufacturing Carbons	June 17, 1882	252,386
Latimer, L. H.	Apparatus for Cooling and Disinfecting	Jan. 12, 1886	334,078
Latimer, L. H.	Locking Racks for Hats, Coats and Umbrellas	Mar. 24, 1896	557,076
Lavalette, W. A.	Printing Press*	Sept. 17, 1878	208,208
Lee, H.	Animal Trap	Feb. 12, 1867	61,941
Lee, J.	Kneading Machine	Aug. 7, 1894	524,042
Lee, J.	Bread Crumbing Machine	June 4, 1895	540,553
Leslie, F. W.	Envelope Seal	Sept. 21, 1897	590,325
Lewis, A. L.	Window Cleaner	Sept. 27, 1892	483,359
Lewis, E. R.	Spring Gun	May 3, 1887	362,096
Linden, H.	Piano Truck	Sept. 8, 1891	459,365

INVENTOR	INVENTION	DATE	PATENT
Little, E.	Bridle-Bit	Mar. 7, 1882	254,666
Loudin, F. J.	Sash Fastener	Dec. 12, 1892	510,432
Loudin, F. J.	Key Fastener	Jan. 9, 1894	512,308
Love, J. L.	Plasterers' Hawk	July 9, 1895	542,419
Love, J. L.	Pencil Sharpener	Nov. 23, 1897	594,114
Marshall, T. J.	Fire Extinguisher*	May 26, 1872	125,063
Marshall, W.	Grain Binder	May 11, 1886	341,599
Martin, W. A.	Lock	July 23, 1889	407,738
Martin, W. A.	Lock	Dec. 30, 1890	443,945
Matzeliger, J. E.	Mechanism for Distributing Tacks	Nov. 26, 1899	415,726
Matzeliger, J. E.	Nailing Machine	Feb. 25, 1896	421,954
Matzeliger, J. E.	Tack Separating Mechanism	Mar. 25, 1890	423,937
Matzeliger, J. E.	Lasting Machine	Sept. 22, 1891	459,899
McCoy, E.	Lubricator for Steam Engines	July 2, 1872	129,843
McCoy, E.	Lubricator for Steam Engines	Aug. 6, 1872	130,305
McCoy, E.	Steam Lubricator	Jan. 20, 1874	146,697
McCoy, E.	Ironing Table	May 12, 1874	150,876
McCoy, E.	Steam Cylinder Lubricator	Feb. 1, 1876	173,032
McCoy, E.	Steam Cylinder Lubricator	July 4, 1876	179,585
McCoy, E.	Lawn Sprinkler Design	Sept. 26, 1899	631,549
McCoy, E.	Steam Dome	June 16, 1885	320,354
McCoy, E.	Lubricator Attachment	Apr. 19, 1887	361,435
McCoy, E.	Lubricator for Safety Valves	May 24, 1887	363,529
McCoy, E.	Drip Cup	Sept. 29, 1891	460,215
(In addition, McCoy also held 16 different patents for lubricators designed between 1873 and 1899.)			
McCoy & Hodges	Lubricator	Dec. 24, 1889	418,139
McCree, D.	Portable Fire Escape	Nov. 11, 1890	440,322
Mendenhall, A.	Holder for Driving Reins	Nov. 28, 1899	637,811
Miles, A.	Elevator	Oct. 11, 1887	371,207
Mitchell, C. L.	Phoneterisin	Jan. 1, 1884	291,071
Mitchell, J. M.	Cheek Row Corn Planter	Jan. 16, 1900	641,462
Moody, W. U.	Game Board Design	May 11, 1897	27,046
Morehead, K.	Reel Carrier	Oct. 6, 1896	568,916
Murray, G. W.	Combined Furrow Opener and Stalk-knocker	Apr. 10, 1894	517,960
Murray, G. W.	Cultivator and Marker	Apr. 10, 1894	517,961
Murray, G. W.	Planter	June 5, 1894	520,887
Murray, G. W.	Cotton Chopper	June 5, 1894	520,888
Murray, G. W.	Fertilizer Distributor	June 5, 1894	520,889
Murray, G. W.	Planter	June 5, 1894	520,890
Murray, G. W,	Combined Cotton Seed	June 5, 1894	520,891
Murray, G. W.	Planter and Fertilizer Distributor Reaper	June 5, 1894	520,892
Murray, W.	Attachment for Bicycles	Jan. 27, 1891	445,452
Nance, L.	Game Apparatus	Dec. 1, 1891	464,035
Nash, H. H.	Life Preserving Stool	Oct. 5, 1875	168,519
Newman, Miss L. D.	Brush	Nov. 15, 1898	614,335
Newson, S.	Oil Heater or Cooker	May 22, 1894	520,188
Nichols & Latimer	Electric Lamp*	Sept. 13, 1881	247,097
Nickerson, W. J.	Mandolin and Guitar Attachment for Pianos	June 27, 1899	627,739
O'Conner & Turner	Alarm for Boilers	Aug. 25, 1896	566,612
O'Conner & Turner	Steam Gage	Aug. 25, 1896	566,613
O'Conner & Turner	Alarm for Coasts Containing Vessels	Feb. 8, 1898	598,572
Outlaw, J. W.	Horseshoes	Nov. 15, 1898	614,273
Perryman, F. R.	Caterers' Tray Table	Feb. 2, 1892	468,038

INVENTOR	INVENTION	DATE	PATENT
Peterson, H.	Attachment for Lawn Mowers	Apr. 30, 1889	402,189
Phelps, W. H.	Apparatus for Washing Vehicles	Mar. 23, 1897	579,242
Pickering, J. F.	Air Ship	Feb. 20, 1900	643,975
Pickett, H.	Scaffold	June 30, 1874	152,511
Pinn, T. B.	File Holder	Aug. 17, 1880	231,355
Polk, A. J.	Bicycle Support	Apr. 14, 1896	558,103
Pugsley, A.	Blind Stop	July 29, 1890	433,306
Purdy & Peters	Design for Spoons	Apr. 23, 1895	24,228
Purdy & Sadgwar	Folding Chair	June 11, 1889	405,117
Purdy, W.	Device for Sharpening Edged Tools	Oct. 27, 1896	570,337
Purdy, W.	Design for Sharpening Edged Tools	Aug. 16, 1898	609,367
Purdy, W.	Device for Sharpening Edged Tools	Aug. 1, 1899	630,106
Purvis, W. B.	Bag Fastener	Apr. 25, 1882	256,856
Purvis, W. B.	Hand Stamp	Feb. 27, 1883	273,149
Purvis, W. B.	Fountain Pen	Jan. 7, 1890	419,065
Purvis, W. B.	Electric Railway*	May 1, 1894	519,291
Purvis, W. B.	Magnetic Car Balancing Device	May 21, 1895	539,542
Purvis, W. B.	Electric Railway Switch	Aug. 17, 1897	588,176

(Purvis also patented 10 paper bag machines between 1884 and 1894.)

INVENTOR	INVENTION	DATE	PATENT
Queen, W.	Guard for Companion Ways and Hatches	Aug. 18, 1891	458,131
Ray, E. P.	Chair Supporting Device	Feb. 21, 1899	620,078
Ray, L. P.	Dust Pan	Aug. 3, 1897	587,607
Reed, J. W.	Dough Kneader and Roller	Sept. 23, 1884	305,474
Reynolds, H. H.	Window Ventilator for R. R. Cars	Apr. 3, 1883	275,271
Reynolds, H. H.	Safety Gate for Bridges	Oct. 7, 1890	437,937
Reynolds, R. R.	Non-Refillable Bottle	May 2, 1899	624,092
Rhodes, J. B.	Water Closets	Dec. 19, 1899	639,290
Richardson, A. C.	Hame Fastener	Mar. 14, 1882	255,022
Richardson, A. C.	Churn	Feb. 17, 1891	446,470
Richardson, A. C.	Casket Lowering Device	Nov. 13, 1894	529,311
Richardson, A. C.	Insect Destroyer	Feb. 28, 1899	620,362
Richardson, A. C.	Bottle	Dec. 12, 1899	638,811
Richardson, W. H.	Cotton Chopper	June 1, 1886	343,140
Richardson, W. H.	Child's Carriage	June 18, 1889	405,599
Richardson, W. H.	Child's Carriage	June 18, 1889	405,600
Richey, C. V.	Car Coupling	June 15, 1897	584,650
Richey, C. V.	Railroad Switch	Aug. 3, 1897	587,657
Richey, C. V.	Railroad Switch	Oct. 26, 1897	592,448
Richey, C. V.	Fire Escape Bracket	Dec. 28, 1897	596,427
Richey, C. V.	Combined Hammock and Stretcher	Dec. 13, 1898	615,907
Rickman, A. L.	Overshoe	Feb. 8, 1898	598,816
Ricks, J.	Horseshoe	Mar. 30, 1886	338,781
Ricks, J.	Overshoes for Horses	June 6, 1899	626,245
Robinson, E. R.	Electric Railway Trolley	Sept. 19, 1893	505,370
Robinson, E. R.	Casting Composite	Nov. 23, 1897	594,286
Robinson, J. H.	Life Saving Guards for Locomotives	Mar. 14, 1899	621,143
Robinson, J. H.	Life Saving Guards for Street Cars	Apr. 25, 1899	623,929
Robinson, J.	Dinner Pail	Feb. 1, 1887	356,852
Romain, A.	Passenger Register	Apr. 23, 1889	402,035
Ross, A. L.	Runner for Stops	Aug. 4, 1896	565,301

INVENTOR	INVENTION	DATE	PATENT
Ross, A. L.	Bag Closure	June 7, 1898	605,343
Ross, A. L.	Trousers Support	Nov. 28, 1899	638,068
Ross, J.	Bailing Press	Sept. 5, 1899	632,539
Roster, D. N.	Feather Curler	Mar. 10, 1896	556,166
Ruffin, S.	Vessels for Liquids and Manner of Sealing	Nov. 20, 1899	737,603
Russell, L. A.	Guard Attachment for Beds	Aug. 13, 1895	544,381
Sampson, G. T.	Sled Propeller	Feb. 17, 1885	312,388
Sampson, G. T.	Clothes Drier	June 7, 1892	476,416
Scottron, S. R.	Adjustable Window Cornice	Feb. 17, 1880	224,732
Scottron, S. R.	Cornice	Jan. 16, 1883	270,851
Scottron, S. R.	Pole Tip	Sept. 21, 1886	349,525
Scottron, S. R.	Curtain Rod	Aug. 30, 1892	481,720
Scottron, S. R.	Supporting Bracket	Sept. 12, 1893	505,008
Shanks, S. C.	Sleeping Car Berth Register	July 21, 1897	587,165
Shewcraft, Frank	Letter Box	Detroit, Mich.	
Shorter, D. W.	Feed Rack	May 17, 1887	363,089
Smith, J. W.	Improvement in Games	Apr. 17, 1900	647,887
Smith, J. W.	Lawn Sprinkler	May 4, 1897	581,785
Smith, J. W.	Lawn Sprinkler	Mar 22, 1898	601,065
Smith, P. D.	Potato Digger	Jan. 21, 1891	445,206
Smith, P. D.	Grain Binder	Feb. 23, 1892	469,279
Snow & Johns	Liniment	Oct. 7, 1890	437,728
Spears, H.	Portable Shield for Infantry	Dec. 27, 1870	110,599
Standard, J.	Oil Stove	Oct. 29, 1889	413,689
Standard, J.	Refrigerator	July 14, 1891	455,891
Stewart & Johnson	Metal Bending Machine	Dec. 27, 1887	375,512
Stewart, E. W.	Punching Machine	May 3, 1887	362,190
Stewart, E. W.	Machine for Forming Vehicle Seat Bars	Mar. 22, 1887	373,698
Stewart, T. W.	Mop	June 13, 1893	499,402
Stewart, T. W.	Station Indicator	June 20, 1893	499,895
Sutton, E. H.	Cotton Cultivator	Apr. 7, 1874	149,543
Sweeting, J. A.	Device for Rolling Cigarettes	Nov. 30, 1897	594,501
Sweeting, J. A.	Combined Knife and Scoop	June 7, 1898	605,209
Taylor, B. H.	Rotary Engine	Apr. 23, 1878	202,888
Taylor, B. H.	Slide Valve	July 6, 1897	585,798
Thomas, S. E.	Waste Trap	Oct. 16, 1883	286,746
Thomas, S. E.	Waste Trap for Basins, Closets, etc.	Oct. 4, 1887	371,107
Thomas, S. E.	Casting	July 31, 1888	386,941
Thomas, S. E.	Pipe Connection	Oct. 9, 1888	390,821
Toliver, George	Propeller for Vessels	Apr. 28, 1891	451,086
Tregoning & Latimer	Globe Supporter for Electric Lamps	Mar. 21, 1882	255,212
Walker, Peter	Machine for Cleaning Seed Cotton	Feb. 16, 1897	577,153
Walker, Peter	Bait Holder	Mar. 8, 1898	600,241
Waller, J. N.	Shoemaker's Cabinet or Bench	Feb. 3, 1880	224,253
Washington, Wade	Corn Husking Machine	Aug. 14, 1883	283,173
Watkins, Isaac	Scrubbing Frame	Oct. 7, 1890	437,849
Watts, J. R.	Bracket for Miners' Lamp	Mar. 7, 1893	493,137
West, E. H.	Weather Shield	Sept. 5, 1899	632,385
West, J. W.	Wagon	Oct. 18, 1870	108,419
White, D. L.	Extension Steps for Cars	Jan. 12, 1897	574,969
White, J. T.	Lemon Squeezer	Dec. 8, 1896	572,849
Williams, Carter	Canopy Frame	Feb. 2, 1892	468,280
Williams, J. P.	Pillow Sham Holder	Oct. 10, 1899	634,784

INVENTOR	INVENTION	DATE	PATENT
Winn, Frank	Direct Acting Steam Engine	Dec. 4, 1888	394,047
Winters, J. R.	Fire Escape Ladder	May 7, 1878	203,517
Winters, J. R.	Fire Escape Ladder	Apr. 8, 1879	214,224
Woods, G. T.	Steam Boiler Furnace	June 3, 1884	299,894
Woods, G. T.	Telephone Transmitter*	Dec. 2, 1884	308,8176
Woods, G. T.	Apparatus for Transmission of Messages by Electricity	Apr. 7, 1885	315,368
Woods, G. T.	Relay Instrument	June 7, 1887	364,619
Woods, G. T.	Polarized Relay	July 5, 1887	366,192
Woods, G. T.	Electro Mechanical Brake	Aug. 16, 1887	368,265
Woods, G. T.	Telephone System and Apparatus	Oct. 11, 1887	371,241
Woods, G. T.	Electro-Magnetic Brake Apparatus	Oct. 18, 1887	371,655
Woods, G. T.	Railway Telegraphy	Nov. 15, 1887	373,383
Woods, G. T.	Induction Telegraph System	Nov. 29, 1887	373,915
Woods, G. T.	Overhead Conducting System for Electric Railway	May 29, 1888	383,844
Woods, G. T.	Electro-Motive Railway System	June 26, 1888	385,034
Woods, G. T.	Tunnel Construction for Electric Railway	July 17, 1888	386,282
Woods, G. T.	Galvanic Battery	Aug. 14, 1888	387,839
Woods, G. T.	Railway Telegraphy	Aug. 28, 1888	388,803
Woods, G. T.	Automatic Safety Cut-out for Electric Circuits	Jan. 1, 1889	395,533
Woods, G. T.	Automatic Safety Cut-out for Electric Circuit	Oct. 14, 1889	438,590
Woods, G. T.	Electric Railway System	Nov. 10, 1891	463,020
Woods, G. T.	Electric Railway Supply System	Oct. 31, 1893	507,606
Woods, C. T.	Electric Railway Conduit	Nov. 21, 1893	509,065
Woods, G. T.	System of Electrical Distribution	Oct. 13, 1896	569,443
Woods, G. T.	Amusement Apparatus	Dec. 19, 1899	639,692
Wormley, James	Life Saving Apparatus	May 24, 1881	242,091

*Variation

Melba Moore (stage center) who won the coveted "Tony" award for her performance in Purlie.

THE BLACK ENTERTAINER IN THE PERFORMING ARTS

The Negro has made a truly prodigious contribution to the world of American entertainment. His presence has been felt to a degree far greater than could normally be expected given the clear population minority which he represents and the barely peripheral place which American society often provides him.

For more than a century, the most formidable obstacle faced by the Negro entertainer was the fact that he was often excluded—both as spectator and participant—from those public places of entertainment which are the logical training ground for any performer. Nevertheless, from the earliest days of slavery, entertainment was one of the few avenues of expression open to the Negro. As singers, dancers, or bones players, slaves were often called upon to perform for their masters and, if talented enough, were even hired out by them to entertain others. Such slave performers as "Blind Tom," a talented pianist, gained national fame in this manner.

Slaves also used the medium of religious songs (considered "safe" by the masters) to express their dissatisfaction with their lot. In this fashion, *Go Down Moses, Oh Freedom, God's Gonna Cut You Down* and many other spirituals have become part of the vast oral tradition created by the Negro musical artist. (After the Civil War, the Fisk Jubilee Singers extended the realm of the Negro spiritual to the international arena by going on a tour of Europe with "Negro" music as the basis of their repertoire.)

The Juba Dance: entertainment in Colonial America

Drama and Theatre

In Shakespeare's England, it seems apparent that the Negro on stage was thought of almost exclusively in the context of Othello, a man who was "black" and did not have "those soft parts of conversation that chamberers have." Shakespeare himself believed that Moors were Negroes, even without scientific verification. His investiture of Othello with the alleged personal attributes and moral characteristics of "the Negroes" of Elizabethan England was by no means accidental, nor was it even an unusual dramatic license for Shakespeare.

Othello was followed, in 1696, by *Oroonoko,* a tragedy written in five acts by Thomas Southerne. The hero was an African prince stolen from Angola during the reign of Charles II, and sold as a slave in the West Indies. On stage, Oroonoko had black skin and wooly hair, spoke in the stilted blank verse of the period, and manifested none of the traits and attributes that might safely be assigned to an African prince by an enlightened writer. He could, in other words, safely have been played by a chimney-sweeper in the throes of consumption.

Another stage Negro of dubious authenticity was Mungo, hero of the comic opera *The Padlock*. Mungo was the slave of Don Diego, a West Indian planter. The stage role was at least played by an Englishman who had studied the manners and dialect of the black man he was trying to impersonate. Still, the writing reflected little real contact with any black cultural context and, as such, perpetuated stereotypes with little genuine import. Mungo, for example, gets quite drunk in Act II, and is extremely profane and oafish throughout the performance. Still, critics seemed inclined to applaud the "truth" of the rendition, rarely—if at all—considering the criteria according to which such "truth" was being measured. Robinson Crusoe and the faithful Friday were two other characters endowed with stereotypical qualities on the English stage. Crusoe represented supremacy and power, even as Friday, clad in coffee-colored tights, appeared in the customary posture of the low-born savage.

In the United States, references to the black actor are rare in any setting prior to 1821. A unique handbill of "The African Company," at "The Theatre in Mercer Street, in the rear of the 1 Mile Stone, Broadway" refers to two dramatic offerings: *Tom and Jerry* and *Obi, or Three Fingered Jack*. This is believed to have been a company of Negro amateurs who played in New York about 1820 or 1821, but who have left no other significant mark upon the history of the stage. Historians know virtually nothing of the "theatre" they occupied. Broadway at Prince Street is one mile from City Hall, although the stone recording this fact has long since disappeared.

ANECDOTES, SONGS,

SKETCH OF THE LIFE,

Testimonials from the most Eminent Composers,

AND

OPINIONS OF THE AMERICAN AND ENGLISH PRESS,

OF

BLIND TOM,

THE MARVELLOUS MUSICAL PRODIGY,

THE NEGRO BOY PIANIST

(FROM AMERICA,)

Whose recent Performances at the Great St. James's and Egyptian Halls. London, have created such a profound sensation.

MUSICAL GUARDIAN OF "BLIND TOM," - - - - W. P. HOWARD, ESQ.

In the absence of anything like a complete and satisfactory history of black minstrelsy, it is not possible to discover its genesis adequately, although it is the only branch of the dramatic art which has had its origin in this country, while the melody it has inspired is certainly a uniquely American approach toward the creation of a national music.

Apart from minstrelsy, however, comic roles remained the forte of the white-turned-black actor. In 1823, at the Globe Theatre in Cincinnati, Edwin Forrest played a Negro in a farce called *The Tailor in Distress,* singing and dancing, and winning the compliment from a black onlooker that he was indeed "nigger all ober!" Forrest was by no means the only eminent American actor who hid his light behind a black mask. "Sol" Smith himself relates how, at 14, he became a supernumerary at the Green Street Theatre, in Albany, playing one of the blood-thirsty associates of *Three Fingered Jack* with a preternaturally smutty face, which he forgot to wash one eventful night, to the astonishment of his own family, who forced him to retire for a time to private life. At Vauxhall Garden, in the Bowery near Cooper Union, Bernard Flaherty, born in Cork, Ireland, sang Negro songs and danced Negro dances in 1838 to help support a widowed mother.

In 1850, when Edwin Booth was 17, and a year after his debut at the Boston Museum, he gave an entertainment with John S. Clarke, a youth of the same age, at the courthouse in Belair, Maryland. They read selections from *Richelieu, The Stranger,* and the quarrel scene from *Julius Caesar.* They also sang, with blackened faces, a number of Negro melodies, "using appropriate dialogue," as Mrs. Asia Booth Clarke records in the memoirs of her brother. Ralph Keeler is among the most prominent of the stage Negroes of later years. His *Three Years a Negro Minstrel,* first published in the Atlantic Monthly for July 1869, is instructive reading, and gives an excellent idea of the wandering minstrel life of that period.

Thomas D. Rice is generally conceded to have been the founder of so-called "Ethiopian minstrelsy." Although it did not originate with him, he made it popular on both sides of the Atlantic. The history of "Jim Crow Rice," as he was affectionately called for many years, was recounted, with particular vividness, in the columns of the New York *Times,* June 5, 1881. Rice first began "doing little Negro bits" between acts at a theatre in Cincinnati. Of particular merit was one sketch he had studied from life in Louisville the preceding summer. Back of the Louisville theatre was a livery-stable kept by a man named Crow. The actors could look into the stable-yard from the windows of their dressing-rooms, and were very fond of watching the movements of an old and decrepit slave who was employed by the proprietor to do all sorts of odd jobs. As was the custom among the Negroes, he had assumed his master's name, and called himself Jim Crow. He was very much deformed—the right shoulder was drawn up high, and the left leg was stiff and crooked at the knee. This gave him a painful, but at the same time ludricous, limp. He was in the habit of crooning an old tune, to which he had applied words of his own. At the end of each verse he gave a peculiar step, "rocking de heel" in the manner that has since become so general among the long generation of his delineators. The words of his refrain were as follows:

"Wheel about, turn about,
Do jis so,
An' ebery time I wheel about
I jump Jim Crow."

Rice closely watched this unconscious performer, and recognized in him a character entirely new to the stage. He wrote a number of verses, quickened and slightly changed the air (made up exactly like the original), and appeared before a Louisville audience, which reportedly went mad with delight, recalling him on the first night at least 20 times. And so Jim Crow jumped into fame and, indeed, immortality.

Apart from Rice, the first band of Negro minstrels was organized in the boarding-house of Mrs. Brooks, in Catherine Street, New York, late in the winter of 1842, and it consisted of "Dan" Emmet, "Frank" Brower, "Billy" Whitlock, and "Dick" Pelham. (The names of the "really great" Negro minstrels were always shortened in this familiar way.) They made their first appearance in public at the Chatham Theatre, New York, on February 17, 1843, and later toured other American cities, before going on to Europe.

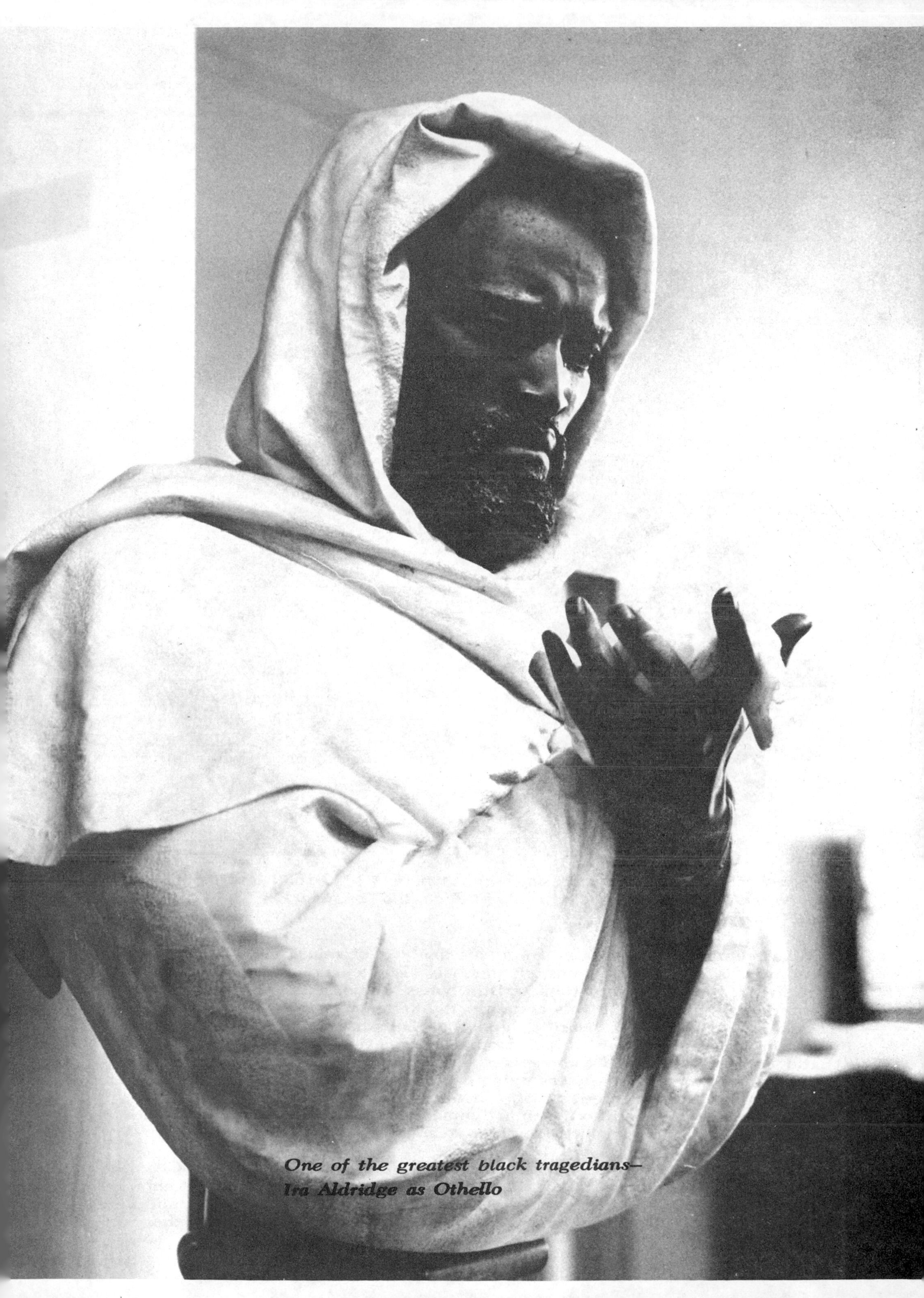

One of the greatest black tragedians—
Ira Aldridge as Othello

GEORGE CHRISTY.—From the collection of J. H. V. Arnold, Esq.

Portrayal of the black man on stage in the period 1830-1860 was largely the province of such white minstrels as (l. to r.) T. D. Rice (the "original Jim Crow"), George Christy, and "Charley" White.

What remains indisputable from this analysis of ministrelsy is that, though much popularity is due to the minstrel, much is also dependent on the Negro melody he introduced and upon the characteristic bones, banjo, and tambourine upon which he accompanied himself. It was certainly the song, not the singer, which once moved Thackeray to write: "I heard a humorous balladist not long since, a minstrel with wool on his head and an ultra-Ethiopian complexion, who performed a Negro ballad that I confess moistened these spectacles in a most unexpected manner. I have gazed at thousands of tragedy queens dying on the stage and expiring in appropriate blank-verse, and I never wanted to wipe them. They have looked up, be it said, at many scores of clergymen without being dimmed; and behold, a vagabond with a corked face and a banjo sings a little song, strikes a wild note, which sets the heart thrilling with happy pity."

As if to refute the famed English novelist, Southern folklorist Joel Chandler Harris argued, in the autumn of 1883, that he had never seen a banjo, or a tambourine, or a pair of bones, in the hands of the Negroes on any of the plantations of middle Georgia. Chandler's Uncle Remus, however, is not a travelled "darkie," and the existence of the banjo in other parts of the South has been clearly proved. George Washington Cable, in a pre Civil War work, quotes a Creole Negro ditty in which "Musieu Bainjo" is mentioned on every line; Maurice Thompson says the banjo is a common instrument among the field hands in North Georgia, Alabama, and Tennessee, and describes a rude banjo manufactured by its "dusky" performer out of a flat gourd, strung with horse-hair. In Jefferson's *Notes on Virginia,* printed in 1784, the following statement is worthy of note: "In music they (the blacks) are more generally gifted than the whites with accurate ears for tune and time, and they have been found capable of imagining a small catch." In a footnote, Jefferson adds: "The instrument proper to them is the banjar, which they brought hither from Africa." Their instrument . . . their old barnyard slave . . .

It was not until the 20th century that Negroes began to be treated with any seriousness on stage. On April 5, 1917, the production of three one-act plays by poet Ridgely Torrance, with music conducted and performed by Negroes, marked "the first time anywhere in the United States for Negro actors in the dramatic theatre to command the serious attention of the critics, the general press and public." Three years later, Charles Gilpin starred in Eugene O'Neill's *Emperor Jones* and, from then on, the Negro actor became a more accepted part of the American theatre. (Nevertheless, comparatively few Negro playwrights have been presented on Broadway in its entire history.)

Al Watts, Rex Ingram (center, wearing hat), Georgette Harvey, Leigh Whipper, Jack Carter, Edna Thomas in a scene from Stevedore

The Last Decade

There is, in the last decade of black drama, a curious and tragic ambivalence affecting both the artist and the actor. On the one hand, there is the success of being courted in public by the foundations; on the other, there is the realization that so many aborted lives have not yet made a reality of the change deemed so vital to the survival of the nation. Bitterness and redemption are qualities implicit in the work of black American dramatists who know they are right, but whose recognition is still being measured all too frequently by "patient" white standards. This, then, remains the gulf between the black dramatist and the white critic, the man who wrenches the truth from himself without being buried by violent rage and the man who analyzes that truth with a suave detachment that enables him to relegate the whole experience to some form of dramatic convention.

At the onset of the '60's, black playwright Loften Mitchell reflected on the situation of his peers with some optimism, noting that such fellow playwrights as William Branch, Alice Childress, Louis Peterson, Theodore Ward, Langston Hughes, Gertrude Jeanette, Harold Holifield, Charles Sebree, and Lorraine Hansberry were either

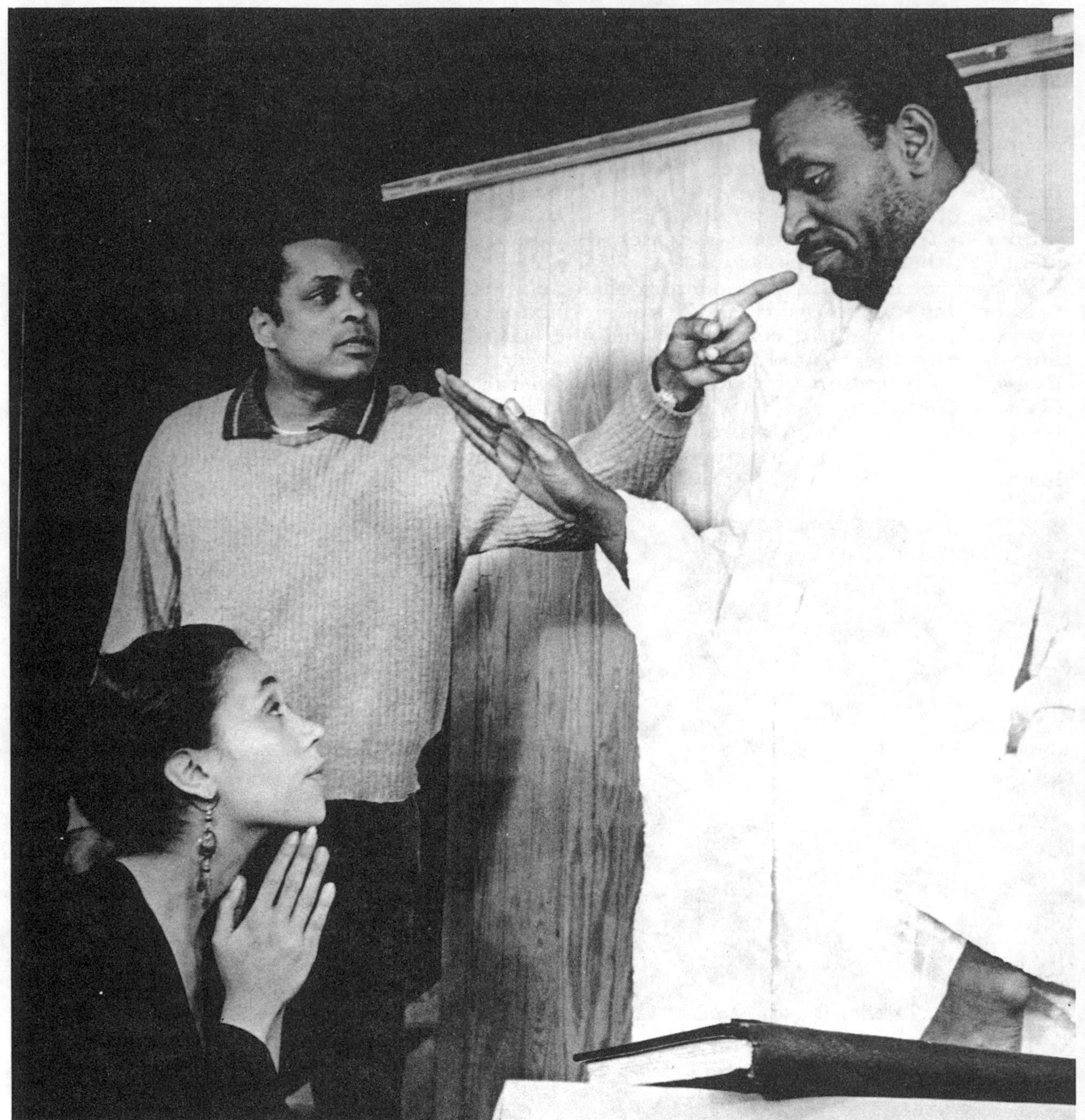

Members of The Negro Ensemble Company (l. to r.) Denise Nicholas, William Jay, and Moses Gunn in Daddy Goodness

in production or the beneficiaries of critical acclaim. Within six years, the burst of promise had deteriorated into a paean of despair. Lorraine Hansberry was dead after her second play *The Sign in Sidney Brustein's Window* had opened to mixed reviews; William Branch's *Wreath for Udomo* was performed successfully in Cleveland, but found little sympathy on the English stage; Alice Childress withdrew her *Trouble in Mind* when she grew disillusioned over the procrastination of the show's alleged producers; Ossie Davis' *Purlie Victorious* was successful, but not financially rewarding; Julian Mayfield's *417* found few dedicated backers; Louis Peterson suffered a heart attack and needed six months to recuperate. Loften Mitchell, though produced (*Tell Pharaoh* and *Ballad of the Winter Soldiers*), remained disillusioned. The difficulties, in other words, were not strictly racial, but they were not totally divorced from racial alienation either.

Big black names also made their impact during the period. James Baldwin's *Blues for Mr. Charlie* had a successful limited engagement on Broadway, white in the orchestra (some afraid; some appalled), and blacks in the balcony (quite inclined to agree, to cheer, or even to hiss). Leroi Jones' *Dutchman, The Toilet* and *The Slave* hit so hard that the white reviewers feared (or were convinced) that the playwright would consume himself with hatred. Langston Hughes had a number of plays on and off Broadway, but his was an idiom reflecting wit and wisdom rather than rage and rebuttal.

Douglas Turner Ward, a newcomer, had two one-act plays produced at the St. Marks Playhouse (Lower East Side) and gave impetus to an entire movement which culminated in the formation of the foundation-sponsored Negro Ensemble Company. The company found itself engaged in repertory and training, providing black character actors with an unparalleled opportunity to develop their talents. Robert Macbeth's New Lafayette Theatre (based in Harlem) enjoyed much the same opportunity.

By the late 60's, however, another depression set in. Branch's *Wreath for Udomo* found no backing, Childress' *Wedding Band* went unproduced, as did much of the work of Mitchell. Along came Howard Sackler with a play called *The Great White Hope*, an ideal vehicle for James Earl Jones in the role of the first black heavyweight champion, Jack Johnson. The play was a success though, in the words of Mitchell, it did not have "one well-constructed scene." It was followed by the catastrophic *Big Time Buck White* which not even Muhammad Ali could save.

Other controversial plays which spanked the white public exposed racism both historically and in contemporary terms. They took their raps, though this did not in any way alter their efficacy. Among those included in this category are: *Slave Ship* (Leroi Jones), *Ceremonies in Dark Old Men* (Lonne Elder), and *No Place to be Somebody* (Charles Gordone).

Despite the difficulties encountered in the past, there is little to indicate that a period of benign conformity is on the horizon. The abrasive spirit of the 60's is probably about to further escalate the tensions rampant in American society. If it does not resolve them, it will at least expose them.

Vaudeville

In the field of variety entertainment, the earliest commercial successes lay not with Negro song-and-dance men, but with white men performing their material in "blackface." Such groups as The Virginia Minstrels headed by Dan Emmett (the composer of *Dixie*) became popular in the 1840's and, for the next half century, America was entertained by the stereotyped image of the laughing, cake-walking, chicken-stealing, gin-guzzling, crap-shooting, razor-wielding Negro wearing any number of outlandish costumes. This is an image which the American Negro has been trying to overcome for many years. To cap the irony, when Negro performers did begin to share some of the commercial rewards of the variety stage, they too often worked in "blackface," thus imitating whites who were themselves imitating Negroes!

Movies

Until recent years, the Negro's role in movies has been a perpetuation of the clown figure. (The scene of the shiftless Negro walking through the graveyard rolling his eyes in terror and trying to whistle at the same time to allay his fears was for decades an American comedy staple.) This ludicrous image has probably been more damaging to the Negro in the long run than the threatening image of him as a terrorist. (In *The Birth of a Nation*, for example, one scene involves a Negro—played by a white man in blackface—who makes a fatal assault on the honor of a Southern white girl.)

Nowadays, more and more Negro actors in movies and television are being given opportunities to portray doctors, lawyers, mailmen—in short, the complete spectrum of available roles reflecting Negro life in the United States. Movie Oscars have been won by Negroes in both supporting and starring roles. On the concert stage, in grand opera, and in musical comedy, the Negro has also made notable strides toward the realization of his full potential.

Any list of outstanding performers could, therefore, run into the hundreds, and include great talents whose audience has been largely limited to Negro theatres. The list finally chosen by our editors represents an attempt to suggest the spectrum of talent ranging from concert, to theatre, to variety stage, as well as to most popular media of importance today.

Famous Performers

ALVIN AILEY
Dancer, Choreographer

Alvin Ailey, founder of the Alvin Ailey American Dance Theatre, has won international fame as both dancer and choreographer.

Ailey studied dancing after graduating from high school where he was a star athlete. With a short stint in college behind him, he formed his own dance group in 1961, and began giving four concerts annually. A year later, the Ailey troupe made an official State Department tour of Australia, and received accolades throughout the country. One critic called it "the most stark and devastating theatre ever presented in Australia."

After numerous appearances as a featured dancer with Harry Belafonte and others, Ailey performed in a straight dramatic role with Claudia McNeil in Broadway's *Tiger, Tiger Burning Bright*.

In 1965, Ailey took his group on one of the most successful European tours ever made by an American dance company. In London, it was held over six weeks to accommodate the demand for tickets and, in Hamburg, it received an unprecedented 61 curtain calls.

A German critic called this performance ". . . a triumph of sweeping, violent beauty, a furious spectacle. The stage vibrates. One has never seen anything like it."

THEATRE,
IN MERCER STREET,
In the rear of the 1 Mile Stone.
Broadway.
African Company.
Saturday Evening, June 7th,
Will be presented with new Scenery prepared expressly for this Piece the Musical Extravaganza of
Tom & Jerry,
Or, Life in London.
Got up under the Direction of Mr, Brown.
Scene I.
Life in the Country.
Corinthian Tom, Jerry Hawthorn — Mr, Williams, Jackson
Life on Foot
Logic, Tommy Green — Mr, Bates, Mr, Jackson
Life on Horse Back.
Honorable Dick Trifle, Gallon — Mr, Matthews, Mr, Bates
Life in Fancy.
Cap, Primefit, Miss Tartar, Jane — Mr. Dusenberry, Mr, Jackson, Miss Peterson, Miss Johnson
Life in the Dark.
Watchman, Dusty Bob — Mr, Smith, Mr, Johnson
Life in Rags,
Crib, African Sal — Mr, Wilson, Mr, Jackson
Life in Bond Street,
Cato, Sue — Miss Davis, Miss Foot
Life in Wapping
Mr, Davis — Miss Johnson
In The course of the Evening an additional Scene
Life in Limbo—Life in Love.
VANGO RANGE in Charleston
On the Slave *Market*.
Slaves, Auctioneer — By the Company, Mr, Smith
In the Course of the Evening a variety of
Songs & Dances.
The whole to conclude with the Pantomime of
OBI:
Or, Three Finger'd Jack.
Obi, Mr. Bates. | Planter, Mr. Johnson. Planter's Wife, - Miss Hicks.
Box Tickets 75 Cents, Pit. 50 Cents, Gallery 37 1-2.
On MONDAY Evening next,
Tom & Jerry, or. *Life in New-York,*
With an Additional Scene,
Life in Fulton-market!!!
And, FORTUNE'S FROLIC.
From the collection of Charles C. Moreau, Esq.

IRA ALDRIDGE
1807?-1867
Actor

Ira Aldridge was one of the leading Shakespearean actors of the 19th century. Although he was denied the opportunity to exhibit his talent to the American public, the fame which he won abroad is more than enough to establish him as one of the landmark figures in the annals of international theatre.

Aldridge's origins are obscure. Some accounts give his birthplace as Africa; others name Bel-Air, Maryland; still others list New York City. His birthdate ranges from 1804 to 1807. It seems clear that he attended the African Free School in New York until he was around 16, at which time he left home.

His early dramatic training centered around the *African Grove Theatre* in New York in 1821. His first role was in *Pizarro*, and he subsequently played a variety of small roles in classical productions before accepting employment as a steward on a ship bound for England.

After studying briefly at the University of Glasgow in Scotland, Aldridge went to London in 1825, appearing in the melodrama *Surinam, or A Slave's Revenge*. For the next eight years, he toured the provinces learning his craft. When he finally appeared in London's Theatre Royal in 1833, his Othello was acclaimed as brilliant by the critics. For the next three decades, he toured the continent with great success, appearing before several members of European royalty.

Aldridge died in Lodz, Poland on August 7, 1867. He is honored by a tablet housed in the New Memorial Theatre in Stratford-on-Avon, England.

EDDIE (ROCHESTER) ANDERSON
Comedian

For many years, Eddie Anderson was the only Negro performing regularly on a network radio show. As the character "Rochester" on the Jack Benny program, he became one of the most widely known American Negro entertainers.

Anderson was born in Oakland, California in 1906, the son of Big Ed Anderson, a minstrel performer, and Ella Mae, a tightwire walker. During the 1920's and early 1930's, Anderson traveled throughout the Middle and Far West singing, dancing and clowning in small clubs. On Easter Sunday, 1937, he was featured on Benny's radio show in what was supposed to be a "single-shot" appearance, but Anderson was such a hit that he quickly became a regular on the program.

Eddie Anderson, or "Rochester" as he was known to Jack Benny .

Anderson is best known for his work with Benny (in television, as well as on radio), but he has also appeared in a number of movies, including *Star-Spangled Rhythm* and *Cabin in the Sky.*

MARIAN ANDERSON
Contralto

At the peak of her career, Marian Anderson was regarded as the world's greatest contralto. When she made her Town Hall debut in New York on December 31, 1935, Howard Taubman, the New York *Times* reviewer, described it as "music-making that probed too deep for words."

Marian Anderson was born on February 27, 1902 in Philadelphia and, as a young choir girl, demonstrated her vocal talents by singing parts from soprano, alto, tenor and bass. At the age of 19, she began studying with Giuseppe Boghetti and, four years later, appeared as soloist with the New York Philharmonic. After a short engagement with the Philadelphia Symphony Orchestra, she traveled to Europe on a scholarship granted by the National Association of Negro Musicians.

It was on Easter Sunday in 1939 that Miss Anderson gave what is perhaps her most memorable concert—singing on the steps of the Lincoln Memorial after having been barred from making an appearance at Constitution Hall by the Daughters of the American Revolution (DAR).

In 1955, after years of successful concert work, she made her Metropolitan debut in Verdi's *The Masked Ball.* Two years later, a State Department tour took her around the world. In September of 1958, Miss Anderson was named to the U.S. delegation to the United Nations.

Now retired, she lives with her husband, Orpheus Fisher, in Danbury, Connecticut.

MARTINA ARROYO
Soprano

New York-born soprano Martina Arroyo is today one of a handful of black divas who have launched impressive and rewarding careers as operatic and orchestral soloists.

Miss Arroyo made her debut at the Metropolitan in February 1965 in the title role of "Aida," and has already sung engagements with opera houses in Vienna, Berlin, Buenos Aires, London and Hamburg. In addition to operatic appearances, she has also been a frequent guest soloist with many of the world's major orchestras.

In addition to Aida, Miss Arroyo's Metropolitan repertoire includes Donna Anna in *Don Giovanni*, Liu in *Turandot*, Leonora in *Il Trovatore*, Elsa in *Lohengrin*, and the title role of *Madame Butterfly*. These have been developed since 1958, the year she made her debut in Carnegie Hall in the American premiere of Pizzetti's *Murder in the Cathedral*. That same year, she made her Metropolitan debut as the celestial voice in *Don Carlos*.

Martina Arroyo

PEARL BAILEY
Singer

Pearl Bailey's easy style, impromptu wit (often aimed at herself) and informal communication with an audience have for many years endeared her to both the public and to her fellow performers.

Born on March 29, 1918 in Newport News, Virginia, she moved with her family in 1933 to Philadelphia, later making her professional debut in small clubs located in Scranton. After gaining additional experience in Washington, D.C. night spots, she became the vocalist with the Cootie Williams band and later with Count Basie.

In 1941, she had successful engagements in New York at the Village Vanguard and The Blue Angel, then toured with the U.S.O. throughout World War II. In 1946, she made her stage debut in *St. Louis Woman*, and won the Donaldson Award as the year's most promising new performer. In 1954, she appeared in the movie *Carmen Jones* and, later that same year, won acclaim for her starring performance in the Broadway musical *House of Flowers*.

To this day, she continues as a headliner in the country's leading night spots, and her countless television appearances have added significantly to her popularity. Her recorded hits include *Row, Row Row*; *Two to Tango*; *Tired*, and *Variety Girl*, a song she introduced in the Paramount movie of the same name.

JOSEPHINE BAKER
Chanteuse, stage star

A legend in her own time, and one of America's foremost entertainment expatriates, Josephine Baker first became an internationally famous variety show dancer and a celebrated music hall star in Paris during the 1920's. Since then, she has continued to win applause for her polished performances, her supple, lithe dance movements, and her sultry and engaging voice. By today's standards, her material would be considered only mildly risque; in the context of her time, however, it was considerably more bold and shocking.

Born in St. Louis on June 3, 1906, Miss Baker received little formal education, first leaving school at the age of eight to supplement the family income by working as a kitchen helper and baby-sitter. While still in elementary school, she took a part-time job as a chorus girl, a job she repeated at age 17 in Noble Sissle's musical comedy *Shuffle Along*, which played Radio City Music Hall in 1923. Her next show was *Chocolate Dandies*, followed by a major dancing part in *La Revue Nègre*, an American production that introduced Paris to *le jazz hot* in 1925.

Miss Baker later left the show to create her most sensational role, that of the "Dark Star" of the Folies Bergère. At the height of her act, she appeared topless on a mirror, clad only in a protective waist shield of rubber bananas. The spectacular dance made her an overnight star and a public figure with a rabid following. In true "star" tradition, she catered to her fans and to her success by adopting such flamboyant eccentricities as walking pet leopards down the Champs Elysees.

In 1930, after completing an around-the-world tour, she made her debut as a singing and dancing comedienne at the Casino de Paris. Critics called her a "complete artist, the perfect master of her tools." In time, she ventured into films, starring alongside French idol Jean Gabin,

With a style made up of frenzied wails and intricate, speedy dance steps, Brown has risen to the top of the "Rock" field. Annoyed by the fact that the American public was neglecting its native "down home" music while embracing its synthetic British imitations, Brown organized his own troupe to tour the country with the "genuine article."

With a 40-man ensemble known as "The James Brown Show," he played on the road for 340 days in 1965 and grossed over a million dollars. He drew crowds of 11,000 in Los Angeles; 15,000 in Annapolis, Maryland, and 27,000 in Atlanta. Estimates of future earnings run as high as $3,000,000 annually.

His hit songs include *Please, Please, Please; It's A Man's World,* and *I Feel Good.*

JOHN BUBBLES
Singer, Dancer

Song-and-dance man John Bubbles, once a top vaudeville star, is today in the midst of a comeback that many believe will even eclipse the notable success of his early career.

Bubbles was born in 1902 in Louisville and, at the age of seven, teamed with a fellow bowling alley pinboy, Ford (Buck) Washington, in what was soon to become one of the top vaudeville acts in show business. Throughout the 1920's and 1930's, Buck and Bubbles played the top theatres in the country at salaries of up to $1,750 a week.

The two appeared in several films, including *Cabin In The Sky.* Bubbles captured additional fame as Sportin' Life in the 1935 version of *Porgy and Bess.*

After Buck's death in 1955, Bubbles virtually disappeared from show business until 1964 when he teamed up with Anna Maria Alberghetti in a successful nightclub act. Since then, he has made numerous appearances with Johnny Carson, trouped to Vietnam with Bob Hope, and released several successful records.

GRACE BUMBRY
Mezzo-soprano

Grace Bumbry is the first black performer to have sung at the Wagner Festival in Bayreuth, Germany, and one of the few young singers who can boast of having

Grace Bumbry as "Carmen"

been called to play a command performance at the White House. Miss Bumbry, born in 1937, sang at a formal state dinner opening Washington's official social season as a guest of the Kennedys and the nation in 1962.

A native of St. Louis, Missouri, Miss Bumbry, like many black singers, had her first exposure to music in a church choir, singing with her brothers and her parents at the Union Memorial Methodist Church in St. Louis. After studying voice locally, she won a nationwide talent contest in 1954, and went on, with scholarship aid, to study successively at Boston and Northwestern Universities. At the latter school, she attended master classes in opera and lieder given by the famed teacher, Lotte Lehmann. Later competitions led to several important cash awards, as well as contacts with such important operatic personages as Marian Anderson.

Beginning in 1959, Miss Bumbry travelled to various European countries, performing in the operatic capitals of the world. On July 23, 1961, Wieland Wagner, grandson of Richard Wagner, shocked many traditionalists by selecting Miss Bumbry to sing the role of Venus in *Tannhauser*, a role which conventionally calls for a figure of so-called Nordic beauty, usually a tall and voluptuous blond. Miss

Bumbry proceeded to give a recital which won acclamation from both the harshest and the kindest of critics, all of whom praised her both for her physical radiance and her brilliant singing.

After her Washington engagement, Miss Bumbry returned to the United States for a concert debut at Carnegie Hall. Her recital was only moderately successful, however. Over the years, critics seemed to question her ability to evolve as a full-fledged interpreter of German *lieder*, many preferring instead to view her as the possessor of a big voice whose calibre and quality are more aptly suited for opera. To some extent, it would seem that she concurs in this analysis, being on record as having once said: "My style is really Verdi. This is my heart and soul."

HARRY T. BURLEIGH
1866-1949
Composer

Of Harry T. Burleigh, Alain Locke has said: "More than any other single person, Mr. Burleigh as arranger, composer, and baritone soloist played the role of a pathbreaking ambassador of Negro music to the musically elect." Burleigh's pioneer work in introducing Negro spirituals on the concert stage and his transcription of songs which had been previously transmitted only orally constitutes a major contribution to the field of American music.

Burleigh was born in Erie, Pennsylvania on December 2, 1866, the grandson of a blind slave who had been dismissed by his Maryland owners when he was unable to work. Burleigh's mother, a college graduate, supported the family after her husband's death by working as the janitor of a local school.

Singing in several choirs in Erie, Burleigh was urged to seek a scholarship to the National Conservatory of Music, one which he ultimately received with the aid of composer Edward MacDowell's mother. In 1900, he joined the choir of Temple Emanu-El in New York, the first Negro to have sung in that synagogue, one of the nation's largest.

Burleigh's concert tours included appearances before numerous presidents and members of royalty. In addition to his arrangements of such spirituals as *Deep River* and *Were You There*, he composed 250 original songs.

CAB CALLOWAY
Bandleader, singer

During the 1930's, Cab Calloway was one of the best-known Negro entertainers in the United States.

Calloway was born on Christmas Day in 1907 in Rochester, New York. At the age of 22, he was already being booked in New York's famous Cotton Club, a unique musical feat considering the number of well-known musicians active during this era. Calloway's band alternated with the Duke Ellington Orchestra at the Cotton Club throughout the 1930's. It was during this period that Calloway wrote and recorded the song which became an enormous international success and his personal theme song—*Minnie The Moocher*.

Calloway has been featured along with his band in such movies as *Big Broadcast*; *International House*, and *Stormy Weather*. Since 1948, he has worked with small groups, and has also been seen in such shows as the Broadway revival of *Porgy and Bess*, in which he played the part of Sportin' Life.

GODFREY CAMBRIDGE
Comedian

Godfrey Cambridge has gained considerable distinction in recent years—both as comedian and as actor.

Born in New York, Cambridge attended grammar school in Nova Scotia while living there with his grandparents. After finishing his schooling in New York at Flushing High School and Hofstra College, he began to study acting.

Cambridge made his Broadway debut in *Nature's Way*, and was featured in *Purlie Victorious*, both on stage and, later, on screen. He has also appeared off-Broadway in *Lost in the Stars*; *Take A Giant Step*, and *The Detective Story*. He won the Obie award for the 1960-1961 season's most distinguished performance in *The Blacks*.

As a comedian, he has appeared on the Jack Paar show, the Johnny Carson show, and many other variety hours. His material, drawn from the contemporary racial situation, is often presented in the style associated with the new wave of Negro comedians.

Godfrey Cambridge

Cambridge has also performed dramatically on many television series. In 1965, he starred in the stock version of *A Funny Thing Happened On the Way to the Forum.*

One of Cambridge's most memorable roles in recent years has been as the star of a serio-comic Hollywood film offering, *The Watermelon Man.* In it the comedian played a man who turns color overnight, a transformation which not only shocks his friends, but leaves his movie wife (Estelle Parsons) somewhat baffled. The action turned on Cambridge's zesty and unhesitating approach to the role.

DIAHANN CARROLL
Singer, actress

The stunning Diahann Carroll, the first black ingenue to star in a long-running network television offering, has had a diversified career in films, on stage, in nightclubs, and in the recording industry. Her most important dramatic role on live stage came in 1962 when she played opposite Richard Kiley as a lovesick fashion model sharing a writer's digs in Paris.

A native of the Bronx, Miss Carroll was born in July 1935, the daughter of a subway conductor and a nurse. She joined the Abyssinian Baptist Church choir as a Tiny Tot and, at the age of 10, won a Metropolitan Opera scholarship. Singing lessons held little appeal for her, however, so she continued her schooling at the High School of Music and Art, a "wonderful, beautiful oasis in my life." As a concession to her parents, she enrolled at New York University, where she was to be a sociology student, but stage fever quickly led her to audition for a part in an all-Negro revue. The show did not materialize, but it did lead to a further appearance on a television talent show netting her $1,000. A subsequent appearance at the Latin Quarter launched her professional career in earnest.

In 1954, Miss Carroll appeared in *House of Flowers,* winning favorable press notices as a refreshing personality, "with a rich, lovely, easy voice." Composer Richard Rodgers encountered her for the first time during the play, and resolved on the spot to write a show for her . . . someday.

Movie and television appearances kept her busy until 1958, the year she was slated to appear as an Oriental in Rodgers' *Flower Drum Song.* The part did not materialize, however, largely due to Miss Carroll's height and makeup problems.

Three years later, after seeing her on a nighttime TV show, Rodgers asked Miss Carroll about the kind of role she would like to perform on a Broadway stage. The result of the exchange was a subsequent commitment by Rodgers to cast her as a high-fashion model playing opposite a hesitant and troubled Pulitzer-prize author. The show was not a smashing success, although elements of it, including Miss Carroll's performance, received good notices.

The *Times* critic, Howard Taubman, singled out her special talent for putting across the show's rich melodies, alluding to her ability to create and sustain a mood of involvement. Miss Carroll herself is able to communicate with considerable fervor the knack of successful delivery. "[One] must be able . . . to make the audience feel," she says, "that the words have meaning to the singer, that you are not just repeating them, but that they come from your very being."

Miss Carroll's televison role as a nurse and war widow does not call for her to perform professionally as a singer.

Diahann Carroll

NAT "KING" COLE
1919-1965
Singer

The style and smooth delivery of Nat "King" Cole made him one of the most imitated singers ever produced in American popular music. His death from cancer in 1965 came after he had already enjoyed many successful years at the top of his profession.

Cole was born on March 17, 1919 in Montgomery, Alabama (the family name was Coles, but Cole dropped the "s" when he formed the *King Cole Trio* years later). When he was five, the family moved to Chicago, and he was soon playing piano and organ in the church where his father served as minister. While attending Phillips High School, Cole formed his own band, and also played with small combos, including one headed by his brother Edward, a bassist.

In 1936, Cole joined the touring company of *Shuffle Along*. When it folded in Los Angeles, he found work in small clubs there. In 1937, *The King Cole Trio* was formed quite by accident when the drummer in his quartet failed to appear for a scheduled performance. That same year, Cole made his singing debut when a customer insisted he sing *Sweet Lorraine* (a number he later recorded with great success).

Cole's first record was made in 1943. It was his own composition (*Straighten Up and Fly Right*), and sold more than 500,000 copies. Over the years, one hit followed another in rapid succession—*Paper Moon*; *Route 66*; *I Love You For Sentimental Reasons*; *Chestnuts Roasting On An Open Fire*; *Nature Boy*; *Mona Lisa*; *Too Young*; *Pretend*; *Somewhere Along the Way*; *Smile*, and many others.

BILL COSBY
Comedian

Bill Cosby is the first Negro actor ever to star in a network television series (*I Spy*), and also the first to win an Emmy.

A native of Philadelphia, Cosby dropped out of high school to become a medic in the Navy, obtaining his diploma while in service. On becoming a civilian, he entered Temple University, where he played football, and worked evenings as a bartender.

While doing this work, he began to entertain the customers with his comedy routines, and, encouraged by their reception, left Temple in 1962 to pursue a career in show business. He began by playing small clubs around Philadelphia and New York's Greenwich Village. Within two years, he was playing the top nightclubs around the country, and making television appearances on such shows as Johnny Carson (he acted as guest host during Carson's absence), Jack Paar and Andy Williams.

Cosby is the first Negro entertainer to star on network television in a role which is not racially motivated.

Bob Culp and Bill Cosby were partners in "I Spy."

RUPERT CROSSE
Actor

Actor Rupert Crosse's most important film role to date has been as Ned McCaslin, the black companion of Steve McQueen in the uproarious screen adaptation of William Faulkner's Pulitzer Prize-winning novel, *The Reivers*. Cross was nominated for an Academy Award as best supporting actor for his outstanding performance.

Born in Nevis, British West Indies, Crosse moved to Harlem at an early age, but returned to Nevis at the age of seven, after the death of his father. Reared by his grandparents and strongly influenced by his grandfather, a schoolmaster, Crosse received a solid education before returning to the United States, where he attended Benjamin Franklin High School. He later worked at odd jobs before spending two years in service in Germany and Japan.

Once out of service, Cross renewed his educational pursuits, finishing high school and entering Bloomfield College and Seminary in New Jersey. Though he intended to become a minister, it was obvious from the jobs he held — machinist, construction worker and recreation counsellor — that his career plans were not yet really definite.

Crosse subsequently enrolled at the Daykarhanora School for the stage, studying the acting craft and appearing in the Equity Library Theatre off-Broadway production, *Climate of Eden*. He then transferred to John Cassavetes' workshop, where he helped create *Shadows*, winner of a Venice Film Festival Award. Crosse's first Hollywood role was in a Cassavetes movie, *Too Late Blues*. Other film credits are: *The Wild Seed* and *Ride in the Whirlwind*.

Stage credits are also numerous, including appearances in *Sweet Bird of Youth, The Blood Knot*, and *Hatful of Rain*. Television viewers have seen Crosse in *Dr. Kildare, I Spy* and *The Man from U.N.C.L.E.*, as well as several other series. Crosse's big film break came in 1968 during an appearance at an Actors Studio production of *Echoes* at UCLA.

The actor has the ability to play American black roles and to interpret various African and West Indian characters. An ardent Yoga enthusiast and a practitioner of karate, Crosse believes his hobbies and experience broaden his ability to feel comfortable with a wide variety of roles.

upert Crosse, 1970 Academy Award nominee for "The Reivers"

OSSIE DAVIS, RUBY DEE
Acting Team

The Ossie Davis-Ruby Dee husband and wife team has won notable accolades in the American theatre. Acting together or separately, the Davises have also performed successfully on television, in movies and in cabarets.

Davis grew up in Waycross, Georgia, and attended Howard University in Washington, D.C., where Dr. Alain Locke suggested he try for an acting career in New York. After completing service in the Army, he landed his first role in 1946 in *Jeb*, the play in which he met Miss Dee. (Two years later, they were married.)

After appearing in the movie *No Way Out*, Davis won Broadway roles in *No Time for Sergeants*; *Raisin in the Sun*, and *Jamaica*. In 1961, he and Miss Dee starred in *Purlie Victorious*, which Davis himself had written. Two years later, they repeated their roles in the movie version *Gone Are the Days*.

Davis' other movie credits include *The Cardinal* and *Shock Treatment*. He has also written a number of TV scripts, and has acted on such television series as *The Defenders*, *The Nurses*, and *East Side, West Side*.

* * *

Ruby Dee was born in Cleveland, but grew up in Harlem, taking her undergraduate training at Hunter College in New York. In 1942, she appeared in *South Pacific* with Canada Lee and, five years later, met Ossie Davis while they were both playing in *Jeb*.

Her movies include *No Way Out*; *Edge of the City*; *Raisin in the Sun*, and *The Balcony*. She has appeared often on network television, and has starred in Shakespearean productions in Stratford, Connecticut.

The Davis-Dee team has often given stage and television readings of poetry by such noted Negro poets as Langston Hughes, Gwendolyn Brooks and Paul Laurence Dunbar.

SAMMY DAVIS, JR.
Singer, dancer, comedian, actor

Sammy Davis, Jr. is often called "the world's greatest entertainer"—a title which attests to his remarkable versatility as singer, dancer, actor, mimic and musician.

Davis was born in New York City on December 8, 1925 and, four years later, was appearing in vaudeville with his father and "uncle" in the Will Mastin Trio. In 1931, Davis made his movie debut with Ethel Waters in *Rufus Jones for President*, and followed this with an appearance in *Season's Greetings*.

Throughout the 1930's, the Will Mastin Trio continued to play vaudeville, burlesque, and cabarets. In 1943, Davis entered the Army and served for two years writing, directing, and producing camp shows. After his discharge, he rejoined the Trio which, in 1946, cracked the 'big-time' club circuit with a successful Hollywood engagement.

Davis has recorded a string of hits (*Hey There*; *Mr. Wonderful*; *Too Close for Comfort*) during his continued climb to the top of show business. In November 1954, he lost an eye in an automobile accident, but this did not in any way interfere with his career. He scored a hit in his first Broadway show *Mr. Wonderful* (1956), and later repeated this success in *Golden Boy*.

In 1959, he played Sportin' Life in the movie version of *Porgy and Bess*. Other Davis movies include *Oceans 11* and *Robin and the Seven Hoods*. In 1966, his autobiography *Yes, I Can* was a best seller, and he starred in his own network television series.

JAMES DE PREIST
Conductor

A gifted and versatile musician, James DePreist has been active in several areas of music as a performer, composer, arranger and conductor. It is in the last-named field that he has been most often acclaimed by musicians and critics alike as a young man of rare ability. This estimate was confirmed in 1965 when he was appointed assistant conductor of the New York Philharmonic.

Born in Philadelphia on November 21, 1936, DePreist studied piano and percussion from the age of 10, but did not decide on a musical career until he reached his early 20's. After graduating from high school, he entered the Wharton School of the University of Pennsylvania as a pre-law student, receiving a B.S. in 1958 and an M.A. in 1961.

DePreist also studied music history, the theory of harmony and orchestration at the Philadelphia Conservatory of Music, and composition with the distinguished American composer, Vincent Persichetti.

In 1962, the State Department sponsored a cultural exchange tour of the Near East and the Far East, engaging DePreist as an American specialist in music. During this tour, DePreist was stricken with polio, paralyzed in both legs, and flown home for intensive therapy.

Within six months, he had fought his way back to the point where he could walk with the aid of crutches and braces. Courage, determination and talent carried him to the semi-finals of the 1963 Dimitri Mitropoulos International Music Competition for Conductors.

After another overseas tour as conductor in residence in Thailand, DePreist returned to the United States, appearing with the Minneapolis Symphony Orchestra, the New York Philharmonic and the Philadelphia Orchestra.

In 1964, he recorded what is perhaps his most satisfying triumph, capturing first prize in the Mitropoulos International Competition. Another highlight of his career occurred on June 28, 1965 when he conducted Marian Anderson's farewell concert at Philadelphia's Robin Hood Dell.

DEAN DIXON
Conductor

In 1941, Dean Dixon became the first Negro and, at 26, the youngest musician ever to conduct the New York Philharmonic Orchestra.

Dixon was born in Manhattan on January 10, 1915, and graduated from DeWitt Clinton High School in 1932. Exposed to classical music by his parents (as a small boy he was regularly taken to Carnegie Hall), Dixon formed his own amateur orchestra at the Harlem YMCA while he was still in high school.

On the basis of a successful violin audition, he was admitted to the Juilliard Institute of Musical Art, where he received his B. S. in 1936. Three years later, he acquired his master's from Columbia.

The Dean Dixon Symphony Society, which he had formed in 1932, began to receive financial support from the Harlem community in 1937, and, in 1941, at the request of Eleanor Roosevelt, Dixon gave a concert at the Heckscher Theatre. He was later signed by the musical director of NBC to conduct the network's summer symphony in two concerts. Two months after the NBC concerts, he made his debut with the Philharmonic.

Dean Dixon

MATTIWILDA DOBBS
Coloratura Soprano

One of the world's most gifted coloratura soprano is Mattiwilda Dobbs. New residing in Sweden where she is a national favorite, Miss Dobbs has gained international fame with a voice which has been described as one "of often miraculous beauty . . . fascinating ease and uncanny accuracy."

Born in Atlanta, Georgia on July 11, 1925, Miss Dobbs graduated from Spelman College in 1946 as class valedictorian, having majored in voice training. After studying Spanish at Columbia, where she received her master's degree, she went to Paris for two years on a Whitney Fellowship.

In October 1950, competing against hundreds of singers from four continents, she won the International Music Competition held at Geneva. She made her professional debut in Paris, and then became the first Negro to sing a principal role at La Scala in Milan.

On March 8, 1954, she made her Town Hall debut in New York in the miniature opera *Ariadne auf Naxos*, and received a rousing ovation. A year later, she repeated the success with her first concert recital on the same stage.

Since then, she has made numerous recordings, including *The Pearl Fishers* and *Zaide*, and has toured the world with great success. She is currently a mainstay in the world of Swedish opera.

TODD DUNCAN
Actor, singer

Although thinking of himself primarily as a teacher, Todd Duncan has made notable contributions to the world of theatre and concert.

Duncan was born into a well-to-do family in Danville, Kentucky on February 12, 1903. He graduated from Butler University in Indianapolis in 1925, and began a teaching career—first at a junior high school and then in Louisville at the Municipal College for Negroes.

In 1930, he received his master's from Columbia. Since 1931, he has taught at Howard University, with an occasional hiatus to work in concerts or in the theatre.

In 1934, he appeared in New York in a single performance of an all-Negro version of the opera *Cavalleria Rusticana.* On the strength of this alone, he was auditioned less than a year later by George Gershwin, and received the role of Porgy in *Porgy and Bess.* He was such a success that he repeated his performance in the role in the 1938 and 1942 revivals of the play.

In 1940, he was a featured performer on Broadway in *Cabin in the Sky.* When the play closed, he headed for Hollywood to appear in the movie *Syncopation.* His concert repertoire includes German *Lieder* and French and Italian songs.

KATHERINE DUNHAM
Dancer, Choreographer

Katherine Dunham has for many years been one of the leading exponents of primitive dance in the world of modern choreography. She has used her training in anthropology and her study of primitive rituals from tropical cultures to create unique dance forms which blend native qualities with sophisticated Broadway stage settings.

Born in Chicago on June 22, 1910, Miss Dunham attended the University of Chicago, where she majored in anthropology. With the aid of a Rosenwald Fellowship, she was able to visit the Caribbean and Brazil to further her research in her chosen field.

In 1940, she appeared in *Cabin in the Sky,* a musical for which she had done the choreography. She later toured the United States with her own dance group and, after the war, also played to enthusiastic audiences in Europe.

Among her best-known choreographic pieces are *Bhahiana* and *Burrell House.* Under the pseudonym Kaye Dunn, Miss Dunham has written several articles and books on primitive dance.

Aretha Franklin

ARETHA FRANKLIN
Singer

The uncontested modern queen of "Soul," Aretha Franklin is a vigorous and talented performer who reigns over the pop music field. She has already reached the magic figure of one million sales on several singles and long-playing albums, all of which are characterized by a lively and pulsating rhythm and a compelling, infectious beat. Some of her music stems straight from the openly emotional jubilant gospel choir tradition in which her father, Rev. C. L. Franklin, was immersed during his evangelical years in Memphis and Detroit; she is, however, equally capable of delivering a warm blues number, or a rhythmically explosive solo reminiscent of her mentor, Ray Charles. Whatever the music calls for, her style radiates a relaxed natural honesty that critics regard as an admirable trademark.

Born in 1942, Miss Franklin moved to Detroit at the age of two, and grew up teaching herself the gospel songs and piano accompaniment which were to form the basis of her early career. Her success on the gospel circuit inspired her to test the pop music field, but she was only modestly successful until 1966, when she signed a contract with Atlantic Records, a company specializing in rhythm and blues performers.

In 1967 alone, she recorded four golden singles, went on her first European tour, and performed in New York's Lincoln Center, where she played before cheering, foot-stomping crowds. One of the secrets of her astonishing success was the breakthrough which black music itself was finally achieving. Much of it had been copied and adulterated by white artists familiar with its driving rhythms and throbbing vitality. When Miss Franklin came along, black artists were finally beginning to be appreciated nationally as the originators and prime interpreters of such music. In the words of one observer, it no longer needed to be "manicured" or "sanitized."

Thoroughly engrossed in her music and now in a position to command incredible concert fees, Miss Franklin remains an essentially unspoiled person, close to her family and childhood friends, finding that "it's just cool to be alive, to be around."

CHARLES GILPIN
1878-1930
Actor

Charles Gilpin has been described by Margaret Just Butcher as "the first modern American Negro to establish himself as a serious actor of first quality."

Gilpin was born in Virginia in 1878 and, after a brief period in school, began work as a printer's devil. In 1890, he began to travel with vaudeville troupes, a practice he continued for two decades, working as a printer, elevator operator, prizefight trainer, and porter during long interludes of theatrical unemployment.

Charles Gilpin as "Emperor Jones"

From 1911-1914, he toured with a group called the Pan-American Octette and, in 1914, had a bit part in *Old Ann's Boy*. Two years later, he organized and managed the Lafayette Theatre Company, one of the earliest Negro stock companies in New York.

After Eugene O'Neill saw Gilpin in *Abraham Lincoln*, he was chosen to play the lead in *Emperor Jones*, the role in which he starred from 1920-1924. (In 1921, he was named winner of the NAACP Spingarn Award for his theatrical accomplishment.)

Gilpin lost his voice in 1926, and was forced to earn his living once again as an elevator operator. He died in 1930.

DICK GREGORY
Comedian

Dick Gregory is one of America's best-known comedians and, more than anyone else, is responsible for creating the precedent which has since enabled other top-flight Negro humorists to present personal, racial humor to the general public.

Civil rights activist and comedian Dick Gregory

Born in St. Louis in 1932, Gregory struggled through the depths of the Depression, determined originally to escape from the ghetto on the strength of his athletic ability. As a high school miler, he won the Missouri State mile championship in 1951 and repeated this victory a year later.

He later attended Southern Illinois University on a track scholarship. While there, he was named the school's outstanding athlete in 1953, but he left after two years to join the army. Once in service, he began working as a comedian in Special Service shows.

After leaving Southern Illinois for the last time in 1956, he worked at various jobs while trying to establish himself in his chosen field. In 1960, part of his Chicago nightclub routine was seen on a television documentary, and he began to receive a few sporadic offers.

On January 13, 1961, he filled in at Chicago's Playboy Club for an ailing comedian and was such an astonishing success that he was held over, given special coverage in "Time" magazine, and booked into the country's top night spots.

Gregory has been an avid campaigner in the civil rights movement, often at great personal expense. While attempting to quiet the Watts rioters in 1965, he was shot in the leg, but was not seriously injured.

RERI GRIST
Coloratura Soprano

Reri Grist is today one of America's most promising coloratura sopranos. She has already sung at most of the world's great opera houses, including La Scala, Vienna State, and Covent Garden.

Miss Grist first came to national attention in the role of Consuela in Leonard Bernstein's *West Side Story*, and compounded this success in a performance of Mahler's Fourth Symphony with the New York Philharmonic.

When Dr. Herbert Graf, the former stage director of the Met, left in 1960 to become Director of the Zurich Opera, he persuaded many operatic talents, including Miss Grist, to accompany him there. While in Europe, Miss Grist was asked by Stravinsky to sing under his baton in *Le Rossignol*. In July 1964, she made a successful debut at the renowned Salzburg Festival in Austria.

Reri Grist

RICHARD B. HARRISON
1864-1935
Actor

Richard B. Harrison is one of the few actors to gain national prominence on the basis of one role, a feat which he accomplished with his characterization of "De Lawd" in *Green Pastures*.

Harrison was born in Canada in 1864, and moved to Detroit as a young boy. There, he worked as a waiter, porter, and handyman, using whatever money he could save to attend the theatrical offerings playing in town. After studying drama in Detroit, he made his professional debut in Canada in a program of readings and recitations.

For three decades, he entertained Negro audiences with one-man performances of *Macbeth*; *Julius Caesar*, and *Damon and Pythias*, as well as with poems by Shakespeare, Poe, Kipling, and Paul Laurence Dunbar. In 1929, while serving on the faculty of North Carolina A. & T. as a drama instructor, he was chosen for the part in *Green Pastures*.

When he died in 1935, Harrison had performed as "De Lawd" 1,656 times. His work had won him the 1930 Spingarn medal, and several honorary degrees as well.

ROLAND HAYES
Tenor

The success of Roland Hayes in the concert field played a great part in broadening the opportunities later afforded such singers as Paul Robeson and Marian Anderson.

Hayes was born of former slave parents in Curryville, Georgia on June 3, 1887. His tenant-farmer father was crippled by an accident, and died when Hayes was 12. Determined that her seven children would not share her illiteracy, Hayes' mother sent them to Chattanooga, Tennessee, where they set up a rotating system whereby one brother worked while the others attended school. Hayes was employed in a machine shop but, when his turn came to go to school, he passed it up, continuing to supply the family income while he studied at night.

Encouraged by a music student from Oberlin University who had heard him sing, Hayes set out for the Ohio school, but his money gave out in Nashville. He decided instead to enter Fisk University's preparatory department, and attended school for four years, while working as a servant in town and giving concerts as well. He was eventually asked to join the Fisk Jubilee Singers on a 1911 trip to Boston, the city which he made his home from then on while studying voice.

In 1917, he became the first Negro to give a recital in Boston's Symphony Hall. Three years later, he traveled to London and gave a royal command performance, following this up with other successes on the continent. Over the years, his rich, delicate tenor voice was used to good advantage in programs blended from Negro spirituals, folk songs, operatic arias, and German *Lieder*.

Hayes gave a well-received farewell concert at Carnegie Hall in New York on the occasion of his 75th birthday in 1962. Now retired, he lives in Massachusetts.

LENA HORNE
Singer, actress

Lena Horne has been called "the most beautiful woman in the world," an opinion which has been no small factor in the continued success of her stage, screen, and nightclub career.

Born on June 30, 1917, in Brooklyn, she joined the chorus line at the Cotton Club in 1933, and then left to tour as a dancer with Noble Sissle's Orchestra. She was given a leading role in *Blackbirds of 1939*, but the show folded quickly, whereupon she left to join Charlie Barnett's band as a singer. She made her first records (including the popular *Haunted Town*) with Barnett.

In the early 1940's, she worked at New York's Cafe Society Downtown and, from there, went to Hollywood where she was the first Negro woman ever to sign a term-contract in films.

Her films include *Panama Hattie* (1942); *Cabin in the Sky* (1943); *Stormy Weather* (1943); and *Meet Me in Las Vegas* (1956). In 1957, she took a break from her nightclub schedule to star in her first Broadway musical, *Jamaica*.

Her most popular recordings include *Stormy Weather*; *Blues in the Night*; *The Lady is a Tramp*, and *Mad About the Boy*.

Song stylist Lena Horne

EARLE HYMAN
Actor

When Earle Hyman made his debut in Eugene O'Neill's *Emperor Jones* in Oslo, Norway, he became the first American to perform a title role in a Scandinavian language. Hyman had originally become acquainted with Norway during a European trip made in 1957. He had planned to spend only two weeks in the Scandinavian country, but found himself so enchanted with it that he all but forgot the rest of Europe.

When he returned to New York, he resolved at once to learn Norwegian and, for practice, began to study the role of Othello (which he was doing for the Great Lakes Shakespeare Festival of 1962) in that language. By sheer coincidence, the director of *Den Nationale Scene* Theatre of Bergen, Norway invited him to play Othello there in the spring of the following year, a performance which marked Hyman's first success in the Norwegian theater.

Two years later, Hyman returned to Norway to play *Emperor Jones* for a different theater company, and was greeted with high critical acclaim for his portrayal. Due to the interest of the Norwegian people in his life, Hyman has been the subject of several radio broadcasts and numerous television interviews.

Born in North Carolina in 1926, Hyman began his acting career with the American Negro Theatre in New York, after which he appeared in eight Broadway productions, and over 100 television programs. He is also a five-year veteran of the American Shakespeare Festival at Stratford, Connecticut.

A bronze bust of the actor as Othello has been erected in the Norwegian theater where Hyman performed, and he has also been presented with an honorary membership in the Norwegian Society of Artists, the third foreigner and first American to be so honored.

After six years in Scandinavia, Hyman returned to the United States in 1970, accepting a featured role in *Les Blancs*, the Lorraine Hansberry play produced posthumously on Broadway. Among his other Broadway and off-Broadway credits are: *Mister Johnson*, *Waiting for Godot*, *No Time for Sergeants* and *St. Joan*. (In the last named vehicle, he played alongside Diana Sands at Lincoln Center.)

MAHALIA JACKSON
Gospel Singer

The rich contralto of Mahalia Jackson—with its great range and singular control

The voice of Mahalia Jackson has no equal in performing "gospel."

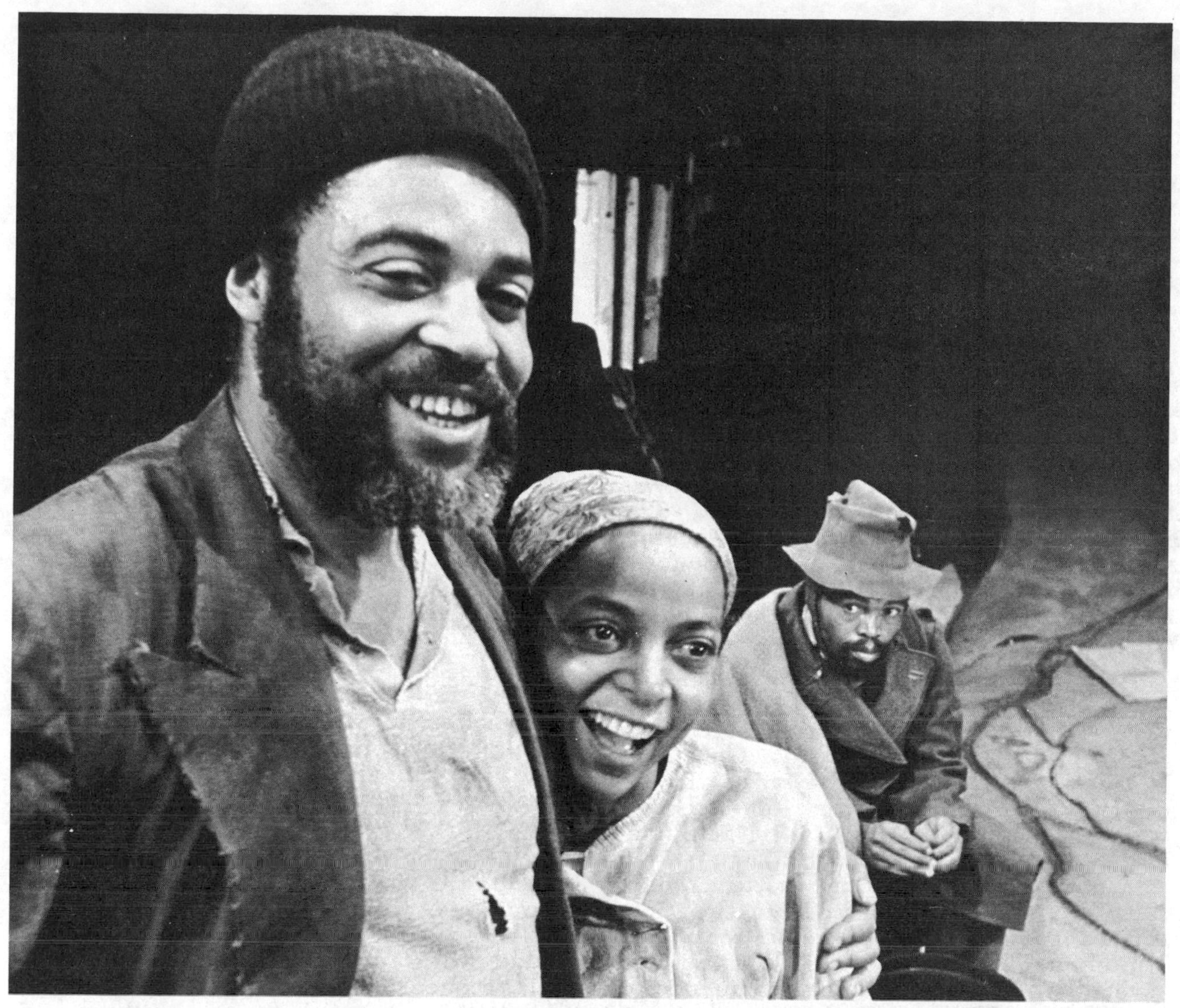

James Earl Jones and Ruby Dee: co-stars of Boesman and Lena

—has no equal in performing the original compositions of "gospel," a unique musical form produced by the style of worship prevalent in many Negro churches.

Mahalia Jackson was born in New Orleans on October 26, 1911. She was acquainted with the records of Bessie Smith and other blues singers but, at home, her preacher father confined the family's listening habits to strictly religious music.

She moved to Chicago at 16, and joined the Salem Baptist choir, saving enough from her work as a hotel maid to open her own beauty shop. In 1934, she made her first record *God Gonna Separate the Wheat from the Tares*, but she did not achieve national fame until 1945 with *Move On Up A Little Higher*, which ultimately sold over a million copies.

Over the next few years, her fame was even greater in Europe than at home. In 1950, however, she gave a highly successful concert at Carnegie Hall in New York City. Since then, she has had several hit records, and has made guest appearances on major television shows.

Her best-known record albums include *Bless This House*; *Sweet Little Jesus Boy*, and *The World's Greatest Gospel Singer*.

JAMES EARL JONES
Actor

James Earl Jones is one of the most prominent Negro actors in the United States today, having starred in a variety of Shakespearean roles, as well as a number of contemporary, avant-garde theatrical productions.

Jones (whose actor father was himself featured in the movie *One Potato, Two Potato*) was born in Tate County, Mississippi, and raised by his grandparents on a farm near Jackson, Michigan. He turned to acting after a brief period as a pre-medical student at the University of Michigan and upon completion of military service with the Army's Cold Weather Mountain Training Command in Colorado.

After drifting to New York, Jones studied at the American Theatre Wing, and made his off-Broadway debut in 1957 in *Wedding in Japan*. Since then, he has appeared in more than 30 plays on and off Broadway, including *Sunrise at Campobello*; *The Cool World*; *The Blacks*; *The Blood Knot*, and *Anyone, Anyone*. Jones holds a number of awards, including the 1961 Obie and the 1961-1962 Daniel Blum Theatre World Award.

Jones' progress as an actor was, in a sense, slow and deliberate, rather than meteoric, until he portrayed Jack Jefferson in the Broadway smash hit *The Great White Hope*. The play, based on the life of Jack Johnson, the first black heavyweight champion, invariably reminded audiences of the career of Muhammad Ali, the controversial deposed current champion. In 1969, Jones received the Tony Award for the best dramatic actor in a Broadway play, and the Drama Desk award for one of the best performances of the 1968-1969 New York season.

He has also appeared in films, notably in *Dr. Strangelove*.

HUDDIE (LEADBELLY) LEDBETTER
1888-1949
Folk Singer

One of the most legendary figures in the history of American entertainment is Huddie Ledbetter, known widely as "Leadbelly." The violence of Ledbetter's personal life sometimes tends to obscure the major contribution which he made to the folk music revival in the United States.

Ledbetter was born in Mooringsport, Louisiana in 1888, and raised in Texas where he learned to play accordion and guitar. From 1903 until 1917, he worked in the Louisiana-Texas area. In 1918, he was jailed for murder under the name Walter Boyd. Seven years later, he was pardoned, but, in 1930, he was jailed again for attempted homicide and, this time, served four years in prison. (There seems to be no basis for the legend that Ledbetter was freed by the governor of Louisiana because "he played the sweetest 12-string guitar in the whole wide world.")

Leadbelly

Discovered by folklorist Alan Lomax, Ledbetter recorded for the Library of Congress, and played numerous nightclub engagements during the 1940's. In 1949, he toured France successfully and, during this period, began to spark a general interest both at home and abroad in American folk music. Some of his songs, such as *On Top of Old Smoky* and *Irene Good Night*, became commercial successes when recorded by others.

He died in New York City on December 6, 1949.

CANADA LEE
1907-1951
Actor

Canada Lee is best known for his work in the 1941 Broadway version of *Native Son*, in which he played Bigger Thomas, and for his performance in the 1952 film *Cry the Beloved Country*.

Lee was born in Manhattan on May 3, 1907. After studying violin as a young boy, he ran off to Saratoga with the intention of becoming a jockey. Failing in this, he returned to New York and began a boxing career. By 1926, he had turned professional after winning 90 out of 100 fights, including the national amateur lightweight title.

Over the next few years, he won 175 out of some 200 fights against such top opponents as Jack Britton and Vince Dundee. In 1933, a detached retina brought an end to his ring career. (He had acquired his name when a ring announcer could not pronounce his real name–Lee Canetaga.)

In 1934, Lee was a struggling musician when he successfully auditioned at the Harlem YMCA for his first acting role in a WPA production of *Brother Mose.*

In 1941, Orson Welles, who had met him in the production of the Federal Theatre's Negro *Macbeth* chose nim to play Bigger Thomas in the stage version of Richard Wright's famed novel, *Native Son.* New York *Times* critic Brooks Atkinson called him "a superbly imaginative player."

In 1944, Lee served as narrator of a radio series called *New World A Comin'*, the first such series devoted to the race question. That same year, he also appeared in Alfred Hitchcock's film *Lifeboat*, and in the Broadway play *Anna Lucasta.*

Lee died in 1951.

Singer/actress Abbey Lincoln and her drummer husband Max Roach

ABBEY LINCOLN
Singer

"This is a WOMAN singing, and more specifically, it is a Negro woman, because part of this striking liberation of Abbey's singing has come from a renewed and urgent pride in herself as a Black Woman." This assessment of Abbey Lincoln's talent, style and direction, made by critic Nat Hentoff, places her among the great jazz singers of our time.

Born Anna Marie Wooldridge in Chicago, Miss Lincoln graduated from Kalamazoo Central High School in Kalamazoo, Michigan and later studied music for a number of years in Hollywood under several prominent vocal and dramatic coaches.

She began her professional career in Jackson, Michigan in 1950. Since then she has performed in movies (*Nothing But a Man*), made records (*Abbey is Blue*, *Straight Ahead*), played several prominent clubs, and appeared on nationwide television. More importantly, she has been hailed by many of the outstanding black jazz performers of our era, including Coleman Hawkins, Benny Carter and Charlie Mingus, as a singer to be classed with the likes of Billie Holiday.

JACKIE (MOMS) MABLEY
Comedienne

Although she is virtually unknown to the general public, Jackie (Moms) Mabley has been a favorite of Negro audiences for almost half a century. Within the last decade, her comedy record albums have made her "an overnight success after almost 50 years in show business."

Miss Mabley, who is "62 going on 72," was born Loretta Mary Aiken in North Carolina, and entered show business as a teenager when the team of Buck and Bubbles gave her a bit part in a vaudeville skit called *Rich Aunt From Utah*.

With the help of comedienne Bonnie Bell Drew, Miss Mabley developed a monologue, and was soon being booked on the Negro vaudeville circuit. Influenced by such teams as Butterbeans and Susie, she developed her own comic character, that of a world-weary old woman in a funny hat and droopy stockings, delivering her gags with a mixture of sassy folk-wisdom and sly insights. Her first big success came in 1923 at Connie's Inn in New York.

Her first record album *Moms Mabley at the U.N.* was a commercial success, and was followed by *Moms Mabley at the Geneva Conference*. In 1962, she made her Carnegie Hall debut on a program with Cannonball Adderley and Nancy Wilson. Her subsequent record successes promise to make her the favorite of a whole new generation.

JOHNNY MATHIS
Singer

Both records and nightclub engagements have combined to establish Johnny Mathis as one of the most successful popular singers of the last decade.

Mathis was born in San Francisco on September 30, 1935, and won an athletic scholarship to San Francisco State College, where he set a high-jump record. In 1955, while watching a friend perform in a San Francisco nightclub, he answered a request to sing, and was discovered by the club's owner. He was soon signed to a recording contract, and began to tour the nightclub circuit.

In 1958, he sang the title song and was featured in the movie *A Certain Smile*. Since then, he has made countless television appearances, and is one of the few singers on the current scene whose appeal is not limited to members of a single age-group.

His biggest hits include *Chances Are*; *It's Not For Me To Say*, and *Twelfth of Never*.

DOROTHY MAYNOR
Singer

Within a short time after her debut at New York's Town Hall in 1939, soprano Dorothy Maynor was being acclaimed by critics as a leading American singer. Since then, she has appeared as a soloist with almost every major symphony orchestra in the United States, and has made concert tours in Europe, Canada, and Latin America.

Born Dorothy Leigh Mayner (she changed the spelling of her last name when she became a singer) on September 3, 1910 in Norfolk, Virginia, she was raised in an atmosphere of music and singing. Nevertheless, she was originally intent on becoming a home economics teacher and, with this in mind, entered Hampton Institute at the age of 14. She

Johnny Mathis in a recording session

received her B. S. degree in 1933 and, shortly afterwards, was heard by the director of the Westminster Choir who made it possible for her to receive a scholarship at Westminster Choir College in Princeton, New Jersey.

In 1935, she graduated with a B. Mus. degree, and left for New York to study voice. After four years of directing a choir and teaching, she felt that she was ready for her New York debut, which took place in November of 1939. She had previously received support from Serge Koussevitzky, the conductor of the Boston Symphony Orchestra, who had once heard her sing and exclaimed: "The whole world must hear her!"

Miss Maynor has made several recordings for RCA Victor, and has been a guest artist on both radio and television. When not on tour, she lives in New York City with her husband, the Reverend S. A. Rooks of St. James Church.

HATTIE McDANIEL
1898-1952
Actress

The first Negro ever to win an "Oscar" was Hattie McDaniel who received the Motion Picture Academy's highest award in 1940 as the year's best supporting actress in *Gone With the Wind*.

Miss McDaniel was born on June 10, 1898 in Wichita, Kansas, and moved to Denver, Colorado as a child. After singing on Denver radio as an amateur for some time, she entered vaudeville professionally and, by 1924, was a headliner on the Pantages circuit.

By 1931, she had made her way to Hollywood where, after a slow start (during which time she supported herself as a maid and washer woman), she gradually began to get more movie roles. *Judge Priest*, *The Little Colonel*, and *Showboat* were some of the movies in which she appeared, along with *Saratoga* and *Nothing Sacred*. Her portrayal of a "mammy" figure in *Gone With the Wind*, is still regarded as a kind of definitive interpretation of this role.

In addition to her movie roles, she also had ample success on radio during the 1930's, particularly as Hi-Hat Hattie. She followed this in the 1940's in the title role of the very successful "Beulah" series.

Miss McDaniel died on October 26, 1952.

FLORENCE MILLS
1895-1927
Stage Performer

When Florence Mills died in New York City in November of 1927, she had been acclaimed as the leading Negro entertainer of her time. As a singing and dancing comedienne, she had become a star not only on Broadway but in London and Paris as well.

Miss Mills was born in Washington, D.C. on January 25, 1895, and made her debut there at the age of five in *Sons of Ham*. In 1903, the family moved to Harlem and, in 1910, she joined her sisters in an act known as *The Mills Trio*. She later appeared with a group called *The Panama Four*. (One of its members was Ada "Bricktop" Smith.)

In 1920, she appeared in *Shuffle Along*, a prototype among Negro musicals, and her success led to a long-time engagement at The Plantation, a New York night spot. After a successful appearance in London, she returned to the United States in 1924 to star in *From Dixie to Broadway*, the show in which she sang the song that became her trademark, "I'm Just A Little Blackbird Lookin' for a Bluebird." Later, her own "Blackbirds" revue was a great success in London and Paris.

Miss Mills returned to the United States in 1927. Exhausted by her work abroad, she entered the hospital on October 25 for a routine appendectomy, and died suddenly a few days later.

Florence Mills

Arthur Mitchell

ABBIE MITCHELL
1884–1960
Singer, actress

Most celebrated as a concert artist, Abbie Mitchell also displayed her versatility in the areas of serious acting and light musical comedy. At the age of 13, she came to New York City from Baltimore, joining Will Marion Cook's Clorindy company and, later, achieving her first real success with the Williams and Walker Company. (Miss Mitchell married Cook while still in her teens, and bore him a son, Mercer, now a diplomat in Africa.)

By 1923, Miss Mitchell had performed in nearly every European country, and returned home to give the first of her many voice concerts in the United States at the Mother A.M.E. Zion Church in New York.

Miss Mitchell also performed with many opera companies and acted in several plays, among them *Stevedore* in 1934, and *Coquette* with Helen Hayes. She also headed the voice department at Tuskegee Institute for three years.

She died in 1960 after a long illness.

ARTHUR MITCHELL
Dancer, choreographer

Although he was originally trained as a jazz and modern dancer, it is as a ballet soloist that Arthur Mitchell has made a truly remarkable contribution to the world of the performing arts. One of the mainstays of the New York City Ballet, Mitchell is the first black performer to have established himself as a principal dancer at one of the great ballet companies of the world. In recent years he has been especially acclaimed for his performance as Puck in George Balanchine's *A Midsummer Night's Dream.* His virtuosity was also tested by his City Center debut in Balanchine's *Western Symphony,* performed in 1958.

Born March 27, 1934 in New York City, Mitchell majored in dance at the High School of Performing Arts. After graduation, he chose to study at the School of American Ballet, which he attended on a scholarship. While there, he continued to perform as a modern dancer, making his first Broadway appearance in *House of Flowers*. Thereafter, he joined the John

Butler Company on tour in Europe, where he may well have remained to continue his studies, had not an invitation to join the New York City Ballet summoned him back home.

After his 1955 debut, he achieved an important second success in Stravinsky's *Agon*, a ballet in which Balanchine "explored most fully the possibilities of linear design in two extraordinarily supple . . . human bodies." Together, Mitchell and his co-star Diana Adams performed a technically challenging *pas de deux* which was regarded as the high point of the presentation. Only Mitchell's "unforgettable characterization" as the fumbling and mischievous Puck has elicited more gratifying reviews. Alternating between modern dance and classical performances, Mitchell was first faulted for lacking a clear point of view in his dancing. This difficulty has since disappeared in time, particularly now that he has begun to show a new boldness on stage and to explore his true potential with greater self-awareness.

Mitchell has also done choreography, and has taught dance classes in a number of schools, including the Jones-Haywood School of Ballet in Washington, D. C. Though he is the first black performer to achieve a measure of success in ballet, Mitchell is aware that obstacles continue to face the Negro in the field. His solution is to coax and encourage as many youngsters as possible to imitate him by taking the profession seriously and applying themselves with greater tenacity of purpose. Mitchell himself confesses to the hope that he will some day obtain the lead in a Broadway musical.

FREDERICK O'NEAL
Actor

Frederick O'Neal is the first Negro to hold the position of President of Actor's Equity. The honor of leading his profession's union is a fitting tribute to his long years of service to the American theatre as both actor and teacher.

O'Neal was born August 27, 1908 in Brookville, Mississippi. After his father's death in 1919, he moved with his family to St. Louis, finishing high school there, and then appearing in Urban League dramatic productions.

In 1927, with the help of some friends in St. Louis, O'Neal founded the Ira Aldridge Players, the second Negro acting group in America. For the next 10 years, he played in 30 of its productions. In 1937, he came to New York and, three years later, helped found the American Negro Theatre. Today, its alumni include such established stars as Sidney Poitier, Earle Hyman, Harry Belafonte, Ruby Dee, Ossie Davis, and Hilda Simms.

O'Neal himself starred in *Anna Lucasta*, and was later featured in *Take A Giant Step*; *The Winner*, and several other stage productions. In the 1944-1945 season, he won the Derwent Award and the Drama Critics Award for the best supporting performance by an actor on Broadway.

His films include *Pinky* and *The Man With the Golden Arm*. He has also appeared on several TV dramatic and comedy shows.

SIDNEY POITIER
Actor

In 1965, Sidney Poitier became the first Negro to win an Oscar for a starring role, receiving this award for his performance in *Lilies of the Field*. Seven years earlier, Poitier had been the first Negro actor nominated for the award for his portrayal of an escaped convict in *The Defiant Ones*.

Poitier was born on February 20, 1924 in Miami, but moved to the Bahamas with his family at a very early age. At 15, he returned to Miami, and later rode freight trains to New York City, where he found employment as a dishwasher. With the coming of Pearl Harbor, he enlisted in the Army and served on active duty for four years.

Back in New York, he auditioned for the American Negro Theatre, but was turned down by director Frederick O'Neal. After working diligently to improve his diction, Poitier was accepted in the theatre group and received acting lessons in exchange for performing backstage chores.

In 1950, he made his Hollywood debut in *No Way Out*, and followed this with successful appearances in *Cry the Beloved Country* (1952); *Red Ball Express* (1952); *Go, Man, Go* (1954); *Blackboard Jungle* (1956); *Goodbye, My Lady* (1956); *Edge of the City* (1957); *Band of Angels* (1957); *Something of Value* (1957), and *Porgy and Bess* (1959), among others.

Sidney Poitier is mobbed by fans and autograph-seekers.

Poitier starred on Broadway in 1959 in Lorraine Hansberry's award-winning *Raisin in the Sun*, and repeated this success in the later movie version of the play.

LEONTYNE PRICE
Lyric soprano

Leontyne Price is one of the world's leading lyric sopranos. Her career in concerts and opera has brought her the praise of public and critics alike.

Miss Price was born in Laurel, Mississippi on February 10, 1927, and received her B. A. in 1948 from the College of Education and Industrial Arts (now Central State College) in Wilberforce, Ohio. She later accepted a scholarship to Juilliard where she studied with Florence Page Kimball.

After seeing her in the student production of Verdi's *Falstaff*, Virgil Thomson, the noted critic, selected her to sing in the revival of his *Four Saints In Three Acts* which was performed on Broadway for two weeks in 1952. She then played the role of Bess in the 1952 revival of *Porgy and Bess*, and continued in the part on a tour sponsored by the U. S. State Department.

During the run of *Porgy and Bess*, she introduced works by Stravinsky, Henri Saguet, John La Montaine and others at such places as the Metropolitan Museum in New York and Constitution Hall in Washington, D. C.

In 1954, she gave a successful Town Hall recital and, the following year, did *Tosca* for the NBC-TV Opera Company. She later appeared on this network in *The Magic Flute* (1956); *Dialogues of the Carmelites* (1957), and *Don Giovanni* (1960).

Diva Leontyne Price opened the 1966 Met season in the role of Cleopatra.

Miss Price made her Metropolitan debut in *Il Trovatore* on January 27, 1961. Since then, she has made numerous recordings of operas and operatic arias. She is married to the noted Negro bass baritone, William Warfield.

Just one season after she had made her Met debut as Leonora in Verdi's *Il Trovatore,* Miss Price had her first Met opening in 1961 in the title role of Puccini's *The Girl of the Golden West.* Since then, she has made numerous recordings of operas and operatic arias.

In September of 1966, Miss Price opened the Metropolitan Opera season in the role of Cleopatra. The opera (*Antony and Cleopatra*) was said to have been written by composer Samuel Barber with her in mind.

In the world of opera, Miss Price ranks alongside Birgit Nilsson, Joan Sutherland and Renata Tebaldi as one of the most esteemed and celebrated sopranos of the contemporary era. Her voice is said to be the perfect Verdi voice; her *Aida* is often regarded as the paragon against which all others should be measured.

PEARL PRIMUS
Dancer

Along with Katharine Dunham, Pearl Primus stands as one of the towering figures in the world of primitive dance.

Born in Trinidad on November 29, 1919, Miss Primus moved to Manhattan, graduating from Hunter College in 1940 with a degree in biology. Unable to secure work in her chosen field, she joined a National Youth Administration dance group and, less than a year later, won a scholarship to the New Dance Group.

In 1943, she made her highly successful professional debut at the New York YMHA and, that same year, became a favorite nightclub performer at Cafe Society Downtown. The following year, she made her first Broadway appearance with her own troupe (four male dancers, a five-piece jazz combo, two drummers, two singers, and balladeer Josh White).

In 1947, Miss Primus opened her own dance school and later spent a year touring the Gold Coast, the Belgian Congo, French Equatorial Africa, and Nigeria, where she took part in court and social dances, and made a comprehensive study of native ritual. She continues to make extensive use of this material in her dance creations of today.

PAUL ROBESON
Actor, Singer

Paul Robeson has earned worldwide fame over the past four decades in a variety of roles—as athlete, actor, singer, and scholar.

Born in Princeton, New Jersey on April 9, 1898, Robeson is the son of a runaway slave who put himself through Lincoln University and later became a Presbyterian minister.

Robeson entered Rutgers on a scholarship, and won a total of 12 letters in track, football, baseball, and basketball. In 1917 and again in 1918, he was named All-American by Walter Camp who later called him "the greatest defensive end that ever tred the gridiron." In addition to his athletic exploits, his academic ability gained him Phi Beta Kappa honors in his junior year.

In 1923, Robeson won a law degree from Columbia, financing his schooling by playing professional football. While at Columbia, Robeson was seen by Eugene O'Neill in an amateur play. After making his professional debut in *Taboo* (1922), Robeson then appeared in O'Neill's *All God's Chillun Got Wings,* and *Emperor Jones.*

Called upon to whistle in the latter play, Robeson sang instead, and his voice met with instant acclaim. In 1925, he made his concert debut with a highly successful program of all-Negro music. He went on to such stage successes as

Paul Robeson as Emperor Jones *(1933)*

Show Boat; *Porgy*, and *Othello*. (When he did *Othello* in 1943 in New York, his ovation was called "one of the most prolonged and wildest . . . in the history of the New York theatre.")

A world traveller in the Soviet Union, Asia, and Europe, Robeson speaks several languages, including Chinese, Russian, Gaelic, and Spanish.

Robeson's political affiliations have at times tended to attract even more publicity than his artistic career. In 1950, for instance, he was denied a passport after refusing to sign an affidavit as to whether or not he had ever belonged to the Communist Party. Eight years later, the U.S. Supreme Court ruled that the refusal to sign such an affidavit was not valid grounds for denial of a passport. Robeson subsequently settled in London, making a number of trips to the continent (and to the U.S.S.R. as well) before returning to the United States in 1963.

BILL (BOJANGLES) ROBINSON
1878-1949
Dancer

Throughout his long career on stage and in movies, Bill Robinson was known as the "King of Tap Dancers."

Robinson was born on May 25, 1878 in Richmond, Virginia and, being orphaned early, was raised by his grandmother, a former slave. By the time he was eight, he was earning his own way dancing in the street for pennies and working as a stable boy.

In 1887, he toured the South in a show called *The South Before the War* and, the following year, moved to Washington, D.C. where he began working as a stable boy. By 1896, he had teamed up with George Cooper in vaudeville. This act had success on the Keith circuit until the slump of 1907 caused it to fold. Robinson returned to Richmond to work as a waiter, and, a year later, was discovered by a theatrical manager who soon had him working as a cabaret and vaudeville headliner.

In 1927, he starred on Broadway in *Blackbirds*, and in 1932, had top billing in *Harlem is Heaven*, the first all-Negro talking movie. Later, he scored a Hollywood success teaching his famous stair dance to Shirley Temple in *The Little Colonel*. All told, Robinson made 14 movies, including *The Littlest Rebel*; *In Old Kentucky*; *Rebecca of Sunnybrook Farm*; *Stormy Weather*, and *One Mile From Heaven*.

Robinson died on November 25, 1949.

NIPSEY RUSSELL
Comedian

One of the first "stand-up" comedians to gain success with jokes drawn from the contemporary racial situation is Nipsey Russell. Long before similar material had found its way to the general public via television appearances by various Negro comedians, Russell was delighting Harlem audiences with his routines at Smalls Paradise and the Baby Grand.

Born in Atlanta, Georgia, Russell at the age of six began to tour the South as a child performer. During his final years in high school, he lived in Cincinnati, and later attended college there, earning his B.A. in English in 1946 (with four years out for duty as an Army captain).

Russell has had a running part in television's *Car 54, Where Are You?*, and has been a frequent guest on Arthur Godfrey's show. He first came to national attention on the *Tonight* show when he was a guest of Orson Bean who was substituting for host Jack Paar. Paar subsequently had Russell on the show many times. He has also worked as a panelist on such shows as *Missing Links*.

PHILIPPA SCHUYLER
1932-1969
Pianist

Philippa Schuyler was at one time considered to be one of America's most outstanding musical prodigies. Now a mature concert pianist, she first gained national recognition as a child for her piano artistry and original compositions.

Born on August 21, 1932 in New York City, Miss Schuyler was already playing the piano at the age of two and began composing a year later. By the time she was eight, she had some 50 compositions to her credit. (Her published works include *Six Little Pieces* and *Eight Little Pieces*.)

At 12, her first symphonic composition (Manhattan Nocturne) was performed at Carnegie Hall, and, the following year, her scherzo (Rumplestiltskin) was written and subsequently performed by the Dean Dixon Youth Orchestra, the Boston Pops, the New Haven Symphony Orchestra, and the New York Philharmonic. Miss Schuyler herself was soloist with the last-named orchestra.

In 1953, she made her debut at Town Hall in New York. Since then, she has traveled in some 50 countries on good-will concert tours sponsored by the U.S. State Department.

Gifted also as a writer, Miss Schuyler is the author of such books as *Adventures in Black and White* (1960), and *Who Killed the Congo?* (1962).

George Shirley

GEORGE SHIRLEY
Tenor

Tenor George Shirley has sung more than 20 leading roles at the Metropolitan since his debut there as Ferrando in "Cosi fan tutte" on October 24, 1961.

Shirley, winner of the 1960-61 Metropolitan Opera auditions, was born April 18, 1934 in Indianapolis, and moved to Detroit in 1940. There he began giving vocal recitals in churches, deciding on a musical career after playing baritone horn in the Community band. In 1955, he graduated from Wayne State University in Detroit with a B.S. in musical education.

After his discharge from the Army in 1959, he began serious vocal studies with Themy S. Georgi. In June of that year, he made his operatic debut as Eisenstein in Strauss' "Die Fledermaus," performing with the Tunau Players in Woodstock. A year later, he won the American Opera Auditions, whereupon he journeyed to Milan, Italy, making his opera debut there in Puccini's "La Boheme."

In 1961, his career was given tremendous impetus by his victory in the Metropolitan Opera auditions. Recording, opera, and television engagements were numerous that year. In 1963, he made his debut at Carnegie Hall with the Friends of French Opera, singing opposite Rita Gorr in Massenet's "La Navarraise."

Since then, he has sung with several of the Met's leading divas, including Renata Tebaldi in "Simon Boccanegra" and Birgit Nilsson in "Salome." By now, Shirley has so broadened and refined his repertory that he is at home in virtually every major opera culture in Europe. He has made several European tours, performing with the leading orchestras on the continent and at the most prestigious opera houses there.

HILDA SIMMS
Actress

Hilda Simms was born Hilda Moses in Minneapolis, Minnesota, in 1920, the oldest of 13 children. Her family was very poor, and she worked at many odd jobs to help out before she won a scholarship to the University of Minnesota. After she had been in school for a year and a half, she left to marry William Simms and, shortly afterward, accepted a teaching fellowship at Hampton Institute in Virginia where she also worked for her B. S. degree.

Having completed her course of study at Hampton, Miss Simms left for New York City, working as a singer for several different radio stations before playing the lead in the 1944 production of *Anna Lucasta*, a role which was to make her famous.

The play was a production of the

American Negro Theater of Harlem, and was first performed in a tiny theater in the basement of the 135th Street public library in New York. It was subsequently brought to Broadway, where opening night reviewers had high praise for the "beauty and intelligence" of Miss Simms' characterization.

The actress also has an interest in writing (she has begun one novel), and has been an active worker in political campaigns. Most recently, she has become a featured columnist in "Tuesday" magazine.

NINA SIMONE
Singer, pianist

Nurtured in the tradition of Billie Holliday and fortified as well by years of classical training, Nina Simone is one of the most original and versatile black concert performers to have come along in the past decade. Implicit in her work is a deep-seated racial pride which burns through her music and suffuses her audiences with its liberating intensity and driving force. Her singing style is too individual to classify simply as jazz, popular, folk, gospel, etc. Like her piano playing, it is fraught with elements from many recognizable idioms, all of which are blended and contrasted in a highly evocative and spellbinding manner.

Born Eunice Kathleen Waymon on February 21, 1935 in Tryon, North Carolina, Miss Simone exhibited extraordinary virtuosity on the piano early in life, but found herself hampered by lack of money to pursue proper training. A dedicated and unselfish teacher soon moved to overcome the difficulty, establishing a fund which enabled her outstanding pupil to attend high school in North Carolina, where young Eunice excelled academically, in extracurricular activities, and in her musical development. She continued her education later at Juilliard and at the Curtis Institute of Music, but was finally forced to support herself by teaching piano privately.

The turning point in her career came in 1954 when she found a job in an Atlantic City nightclub, ostensibly as a performer on the piano, not as a vocalist. Her smashing success in both capacities convinced her that show business was a worthy career for her unique talents. Her first hit record thereafter was a haunting version of "I Love You Porgy," from the score of Gershwin's celebrated *Porgy and Bess.* At later recording sessions, she discovered a further gift for composition, and thus has come to write more than 50 of her own songs, including the bitter and controversial lament, "Wild Is the Wind."

Since 1960, the year she was named Most Promising Singer of the Year, Miss Simone has grown in stature as a concert and nightclub entertainer. She prefers the concert hall, where she feels she can "get more out of myself . . . call on every resource . . . give on a huge scale."

These widely acclaimed performances have placed her time and again among the top 10 performers in national and international jazz polls. In 1966, she was designated Woman of the Year by the Jazz at Home Club in New York City. The following year, the National Association of Television and Radio Announcers named ther Female Jazz Singer of the Year.

WILLIAM GRANT STILL
Composer

William Grant Still, one of the most prolific of American Negro composers, has had his works performed by major orchestras throughout the world.

Still was born in Woodville, Mississippi on May 11, 1895, and received his early musical training in Little Rock, Arkansas where his mother was a schoolteacher. He attended Wilberforce University and then studied at the Oberlin Conservatory of Music and the New England Conservatory. Since then, his creative efforts have been subsidized by both Guggenheim and Rosenwald Fellowships.

Still's early work was as an arranger for jazz orchestras, but he soon turned to composition, making use of his jazz background in a more classical framework. In 1926, the International Guild of Composers presented four of his songs, one of which was sung by Florence Mills.

A year later, his *Darker America*, a symphonic poem, was performed by the Rochester Symphony. In 1935, his *Afro-American Symphony* was played by the New York Philharmonic at the International Music Festival in Frankfurt, Germany and, two years after that, his *New Symphony in G Minor* was featured by the Philadelphia Symphony Orchestra.

In 1936, Still became the first Negro to conduct a major American orchestra when he gave a program of his own compositions at the Hollywood Bowl.

He has also written an opera, *Troubled Island* (libretto by Langston Hughes) and such successful musicals as *Running Wild* and *Dixie to Broadway*.

Leslie Uggams

THE SUPREMES
Popular singing group

Diana Ross, Florence Ballard, and Mary Wilson were all just high school girls who liked to sing when they appeared at the office of Motown president Berry Gordy, Jr. for an interview. Though Gordy liked them right away, he told them they would have to finish school before beginning a show business career in earnest.

Two years later, after cutting several "singles" which were largely unknown, the Supremes recorded their first big hit —"Where Did Our Love Go?" After that, as Gordy put it, "they could just about write their ticket with anybody else."

Since then, their hits have come with ever-increasing rapidity: the three are now America's most popular female vocal group, and have broken all records by amassing six consecutive number one hit records, five of them in 1965.

All three of the girls are products of the same Detroit area which has spawned several other Motown talents. Appealing to a wide range of audiences, the Supremes will earn over $400,000 in the next year, dividing their time between Motown recording sessions and national concert tours.

LESLIE UGGAMS
Singer, actress

Once dubbed a black Shirley Temple, scintillating Leslie Uggams has been a popular performer since her childhood. Nevertheless, abiding, undisputed fame did not come to the versatile entertainer until she opened on Broadway in the much-heralded musical *Hallelujah Baby*. The show was given the lift and verve it needed to survive by Miss Uggams' dynamic and impressive performance.

Born in the Washington Heights section of New York City in May of 1943, Miss Uggams enjoyed a comfortable childhood. She made her singing debut at the age of six, performing with the choir of St. James Presbyterian Church in New York, and followed shortly thereafter with her acting debut in the television series *Beulah*. Miss Uggams developed her poise and stage presence early in life, attending the Professional Children's School, where she was chosen student body president in her senior year.

Later, she won $25,000 on the popular quiz show, *Name That Tune*, gaining the opportunity as well to renew her interest in a singing career. In 1961, Miss Uggams became a regular on the Mitch Miller show, a variety offering featuring old favorites. She was at the time the only black performer appearing regularly on network television.

Throughout the '60s, Miss Uggams appeared in numerous nightclubs and filled several supperclub and television engagements. Her big break came when she was signed as a replacement for Lena Horne in *Hallelujah Baby*, a show which represented a kind of musical chronicle of the civil rights movement. Billed as "pure sunshine" and worth the price of admission by herself, Miss Uggams was elevated to instant stardom despite the lacklustre reviews attending the rest of the show.

Records and singing appear to be Miss Uggams' natural forte, but she feels less confident with the demands of the acting craft. As a result, she has done little dramatic work, preferring instead to concentrate on light escapist TV fare and variety appearances.

Miss Uggams has written a beauty book (*The Leslie Uggams Beauty Book*) dedicated to her two early mentors, Harry Salter and Mitch Miller, both of the *Name That Tune* era. The pair had "nothing to do with her beauty," one New York reporter once pointed out, "but a great deal to do with its intelligent exploitation."

SARAH VAUGHAN
Singer

When a high school junior from Newark, New Jersey, whose only previous singing experience had been with a church choir, stepped onto the stage of Harlem's Apollo Theater on Amateur Night in 1942 and sang "Body and Soul," the audience lost no time whistling and applauding her into first place.

Sarah Vaughan had agreed to enter the amateur contest purely by chance—on a dare from a girlfriend—and it was chance too that brought both Earl (Fatha) Hines and Ella Fitzgerald to the audience that night. Shortly afterwards, Miss Vaughan signed as vocalist with Hines' band, and stayed with him for two years until she was booked into Manhattan's Café Society Downtown, where she remained for a six-month engagement.

Sarah Vaughan

The next year, she met and married trumpeter George Treadwell, who left his job to become her agent. Since then, Miss Vaughan has become one of the most sought-after of jazz and popular artists, earning a six-figure income annually. Her first record, "It's Magic," sold over two million copies, and two others—"Don't Blame Me" and "I Cover the Waterfront"—have since become jazz standards.

SHIRLEY VERRETT
Mezzo-soprano

Mezzo-soprano Shirley Verrett is a striking and talented recitalist and opera performer whose most electrifying role has been in the title role of Bizet's *Carmen* which she has performed to rave notices in the great opera houses of the world.

Born of a musical family in New Orleans, Miss Verrett moved to California at the age of five, but had no formal voice training during her childhood, largely because her father felt singing would involve his daughter in too precarious a career. Still, he offered his daughter the opportunity to sing in church choirs under his direction, and provided her with an ample education at Ventura College, where she majored in business administration. By 1964, she was a prosperous real-estate agent, but her longing for an artistic career had become so acute that she decided to take voice lessons in Los Angeles and train her sights on the concert stage after all.

After winning a television talent show in 1955, she enrolled at the Juilliard School on a scholarship, taking her diploma in voice some six years later. Her debut at Town Hall in 1958 was not a sensational one, earning plaudits for her "sensitive, imaginative . . . comprehension," even as it inspired the conclusion that she was perhaps only an "earnest, conscientious" singer who was well coached and adequately prepared.

At Spoleto, Italy in 1962, she delivered an excellent *Carmen* and was praised for a "warm vibrant voice and earthy womanliness." A year later, she performed at Lincoln Center in New York, where her recital was said to be "simply without flaws, simply a great event in the annals of American music-making."

By 1964, her *Carmen* had improved so dramatically that the New York *Herald Tribune* critic was able to claim it was "the finest" performance "seen or heard

Shirley Verrett

in New York" for the past generation. Other performances in such roles as Orfeo in Gluck's *Orfeo ed Euridice* and as Ulrica in Verdi's *Un Ballo de Maschera* have been met with comparable acclaim.

Possessed of a remarkable range, Miss Verrett sustains a steady low register, a velvety middle register, and a clean, commanding, and opulent upper register. She does not add to her repertory too rapidly, lest she sacrifice true understanding of the character in whom the tones and the music are supposed to realize their ultimate importance.

WILLIAM WARFIELD
Singer

One of the most distinguished concert baritones in the world today is William Warfield, who made his debut at New York's Town Hall in March 1950.

Warfield was born in West Helena, Arkansas, and later moved with his family to Rochester, New York where he attended school. The son of a Baptist minister, he received early training in voice, organ and piano and, in 1938, while a student at Washington Junior High School, won the vocal competition at the Music Educators National Convention in St. Louis.

He then studied at the Eastman School of Music and the University of Rochester, receiving his A.B. while in the Army, where he worked in intelligence because of his fluency in Italian, French, and German. At the close of World War II, he returned to Eastman before spending a year traveling with the national company of *Call Me Mister*.

After his resounding New York debut in 1950, he made an unprecedented tour of Australia under the auspices of the Australian Broadcasting Commission. A year later, he made his movie debut in *Show Boat*.

Warfield then appeared on several major television shows and starred in the NBC television version of *Green Pastures*. Between 1952 and 1959, he made five international tours under the auspices of the U. S. State Department.

His performances as Porgy in the various revivals of *Porgy and Bess* in the last 15 years have made him the best-known singer in this role. Since 1952, he has been married to Leontyne Price, the brilliant opera star whom he met during a *Porgy and Bess* production.

ETHEL WATERS
Singer, actress

The distinguished career of Ethel Waters has spanned half a century, and made its mark in virtually every entertainment medium—stage, screen, television, and recordings.

Ethel Waters was born on October 31, 1900, and spent most of her childhood in Chester, Pennsylvania. At the age of 17, she was singing professionally at the Lincoln Theatre in Baltimore. During this early phase of her career, she became the first woman to perform W. C. Handy's *St. Louis Blues* on stage.

After several years in nightclubs and vaudeville, she made her Broadway debut in the 1927 revue, *Africana*. In 1930, she appeared in *Blackbirds* and, in 1931 and 1932, starred in *Rhapsody in Black*. The following year, she was featured with Clifton Webb and Marilyn Miller in Irving Berlin's *As Thousands Cheer*. In 1935, she co-starred with Bea Lillie in *At Home Abroad* and, three years later, played the lead in *Mamba's Daughters*.

In 1940, she created her greatest role in *Cabin in the Sky*, a triumph which she repeated in the 1943 movie version.

Her other films include *Rufus Jones for President* (1931); *Tales of Manhattan* (1941); *Cairo* (1942); *Stage Door Canteen* (1943), and *Pinky* (1949).

Her autobiography, *His Eye Is on the Sparrow*, was a 1951 Book-of-the-Month Club selection. The title is taken from a song which she sang during her memorable performance in the 1950 stage success *Member of the Wedding*.

ANDRE WATTS
Pianist

One of America's most gifted young pianists, Andre Watts has achieved a substantial degree of his fame while playing under the baton of Leonard Bernstein of the New York Philharmonic.

Born in Nuremberg, Germany of a Hungarian mother and an American G.I. father, Watts spent the first eight years of his life on Army posts in Europe before moving to Philadelphia, his current place of residence. By the time he was nine, he was already good enough to perform as a soloist with the Philadelphia Orchestra.

At the age of 17, Watts appeared on television in one of Leonard Bernstein's Young People's Concerts and was a huge success. After graduating from Lincoln Prep in Philadelphia, he enrolled at Baltimore's Peabody Conservatory of Music.

On one occasion, when Glenn Gould became ill just prior to a performance with the New York Philharmonic, Bernstein chose Watts as a last-minute replacement. At the conclusion of the concerto, Watts received a standing ovation not only from the audience but from the orchestra as well.

In June 1966, he made his debut in London, and, a month later, was the soloist for the two-day Philharmonic Stravinsky Festival at Lincoln Center.

BERT WILLIAMS
1876-1922
Vaudevillian

The legendary Bert Williams is considered by many to be the greatest Negro vaudeville performer in the history of the American stage. His considerable

Pianist Andre Watts at rehearsal

success extended into the realm of musical comedy as well.

Born in 1876 in the Bahamas, Williams moved to New York with his family, and then on to California, where he graduated from high school. After studying civil engineering for a time, he decided instead to try his hand at show business.

In 1895, he teamed with George Walker to form a successful vaudeville team. Five years later, they opened in New York in *The Sons of Ham*, and were acclaimed for the characterizations that became their stock-in-trade . . . Walker as a dandy, and Williams in blackface, complete with outlandish costumes and "Negro" comic dialect. The show ran for two years.

In 1902, their show *In Dahomey* was so popular that they took it to England, and met with equal success there. The partners continued to produce shows such as *The Policy Players*; *Bandanna Land*, and *Abyssinia* until Walker's death in 1909.

Thereafter, Williams worked as a featured single in the Ziegfeld Follies, touring America for 10 years in several versions of the show. His most famous songs were *Woodman, Spare That Tree*; *O, Death, Where is Thy Sting*; and *Nobody*, his own composition and trademark.

Williams died of pneumonia on March 4, 1922.

Comedian "Flip" Wilson has skyrocketed to stardom.

"FLIP" WILSON
Comedian

"Flip" Wilson has reached the pinnacle of stardom in the entertainment world with a series of original routines and ethnic characters rivalled only by Bill Cosby. Wilson's hilarious monologues have been seen on a number of network television shows, and have made him perhaps the most visible black comedian of 1970.

Born the tenth of 18 children in 1933, Wilson was a troublesome child during his youth in Jersey City. He ran away from reform school several times, and was ultimately raised in two foster homes.

Wilson' comic talents first surfaced during a hitch in the Air Force. While in service, he was sent overseas to the Pacific theatre, where he entertained his buddies with such preposterous routines as "The Sex Habits of the Coconut Crab."

Back in civilian life, he became a bellhop and part-time showman, but constant economic pressure left him without adequate time to refine his spontaneous material. Opportunity struck in 1959 when a Miami businessman gave him $50 a week for a year, thus enabling him to concentrate on the evolution of a successful style.

For the next five years or so, Wilson was a regular at the Apollo in Harlem. In 1965, he began a series of nationwide appearances on the *Tonight Show*. Long-term contracts and several hit records have followed in quick sequence since then, and Wilson has become firmly established as one of the big names and truly innovative talents in the comedy profession.

OTHER NEGRO PERFORMING ARTISTS

Name	*Area of Endeavor*	*Place of Birth*	*Dates of Birth and Death*
Mary Alice	actress	Indianola, Miss.	1941-
William Duncan Allen	pianist-accompanist	Portland, Ore.	1908-
Walter Anderson	composer, organist	Zanesville, Ohio	1915-
Joseph Attles	actor	Charleston, N.C.	1903-
Fran Bennett	actress	Malvern, Ark.	1935-
Leon Bibb	folk singer	Louisville, Ky.	1926-
Jules Bledsoe	singer	———	1900-1943
Carol Brice	concert singer	Indianapolis, Ind.	1918-
Annie Wiggins Brown	concert singer	Baltimore, Md.	1915-
Chelsea Brown	actress	Chicago, Ill.	—
Graham Brown	actor	New York City	1924-
Jim Brown	actor	Manhasset, N. Y.	1936-
Roscoe Lee Browne	actor	Woodbury, N. J.	1925-
Betty E. Burghardt	actress	Mount Vernon, N.Y.	1922-
Thelma Carpenter	actress	New York City	1922-
Diahann Carroll	actress, singer	New York City	
Ben Carter	actor	Fairfield, Iowa	1912-1946
"Chubby" Checker	singer	South Philadelphia, Pa.	1941-
Bob Cole	librettist, lyricist	———	1869-1912
Samuel Coleridge-Taylor	composer	England	1875-1912
Will Marion Cook	composer, orchestra leader	Washington, D.C.	1869-1944
Dorothy Dandridge	actress	Cleveland, Ohio	1924-1966
William Levi Dawson	composer, conductor	Anniston, Ala.	1899-
Peter de Anda	actor	Pittsburgh, Pa.	1941-
Carmen de Lavallade	dancer, actress	Port-of-Spain, Trinidad	1930-
R. Nathaniel Dett	composer	Canada	1882-1943
Nat Dickerson	singer	Waycross, Ga.	1920-
Carl Diton	composer	Philadelphia, Pa.	1886-
Arthur Duncan	dancer	Los Angeles, Calif.	—
Roy Felix Eaton	concert pianist	New York City	1930-
Billy Eckstine	singer	Pittsburgh, Pa.	1914-
Lillian Evanti	concert soprano	Washington, D.C.	
Stepin Fetchit	vaudeville	Key West, Fla.	1902-
Al Freeman, Jr.	actor	San Antonio, Tex	1934-
Louis Gossett	actor	New York City	1936-
"Rosey" Grier	actor	Cuthbert, Ga.	—
Moses Gunn	actor	St. Louis, Mo.	1929-
Ed Hall	actor	Roxbury, Mass.	1931-
Juanita Hall	actress, singer	Keyport, N.J.	1914-
Ena Hartman	actress	Moscow, Ark.	—
Lloyd Haynes	actor	South Bend, Ind.	—
George Hillman	actor	New York City	1906-
Geoffrey Holder	dancer	Port-of-Spain, Trinidad	1930-
Nora Holt	composer, music critic	Kansas City, Kan.	
Robert Hooks	actor	Philadelphia, Pa.	—
Rex Ingram	actor	Cairo, Illinois	1895-
Dots Johnson	actor, balladeer	Baltimore, Md.	1903-
Hall Johnson	choral conductor	Athens, Ga.	1888-
J. Rosamond Johnson	composer, actor	Jacksonville, Fla.	1873-1954
Ulysses Kay	composer	Tucson, Arizona	1917-

Name	Area of Endeavor	Place of Birth	Dates of Birth and Death
Woodie King	actor	Detroit, Mich.	1937-
Eartha Kitt	singer	Columbia, S.C.	1928-
Roger Lawson	actor	Tarrytown, N. Y.	1942-
Rosetta Lenoir	actress	New York City	1911-
Philip Lindsay	actor	Cairo, Ill.	1924-
Avon Long	dancer, songwriter	Baltimore, Md.	1910-
Barbara McNair	singer, actress	Chicago, Ill.	
Claudia McNeil	actress	Baltimore, Md.	1917-
William Marshall	actor	Gary, Ind.	1924-
Etta Moten	concert artist	San Antonio, Texas	
Denise Nicholas	actress	Detroit, Mich.	—
Odetta	singer	Birmingham, Ala.	1930-
Ron O'Neal	actor	Utica, N. Y.	1937-
Judy Pace	actress	Los Angeles, Calif.	—
Cecil Perrin	actress	Atlanta, Ga.	1945-
Brock Peters	actor	New York City	1927-
Muriel Rahn	soprano	Boston, Mass.	
Walter Raines	actor	Braddock, Pa.	1940-
Tracy Reed	actress	Fort Benning, Ga.	—
Felix Rice	actor	Washington, D. C.	1946-
Beah Richards	actress	Vicksburg, Miss.	
Roger Robinson	actor	Seattle, Washington	1941-
"Sugar Chile" Robinson	pianist	Detroit, Mich.	1939-
Percy Rodrigues	actor	Montreal, Can.	—
Diana Sands	actress	New York City	1934-
Harold Scott	actor	Morristown, N. J.	1935-
Hazel Scott	jazz pianist	Trinidad	1920-
Frank Silvera	actor	Kingston, Jamaica	1914-
Nat Simmons	actor	Richmond, Va.	1936-
Noble Sissle	orchestra leader, composer	Indianapolis, Ind.	1889-
Muriel Smith	actress, singer	New York City	1923-
Howard Swanson	composer	———	1909-
Clarice Taylor	actress	Buckingham Co., Va.	—
Helen Thigpen	soprano	Washington, D.C.	
Lois Towles	pianist	Texarkana, Texas	
Douglas Turner	actor	Burnside, La.	1930-
Vernon Washington	actor	Hartford, Conn.	1927-
Clarence Cameron White	composer, violinist	Clarkville, Tenn.	1880-1960
Jane White	actress	New York City	1921-
Josh White	folk singer	Greenville, S.C.	1908-
Camilla E. Williams	concert, opera singer	Danville, Va.	
Clarence Williams, III	actor	New York City	1939-
Andre Womble	actor	New York City	1940-
Allie Woods	actor	Houston, Tex.	1940-

Louis Armstrong, Cootie Williams (above), and John Coltrane (l. to r.).

THE JAZZ SCENE

The Medium and the Pioneers
The Last Decade: "The New Thing"
Outstanding Black Performers

Jazz is often referred to as "America's only original artistic contribution to the culture of the world." It is a musical form consisting mainly of West African rhythms, European harmonic structures, and American folk melodies. Although it has been influenced by a number of social factors (many of which are directly linked to racial injustice), it is not *racial* music as such. Its creation and reception have never been totally confined to the Negro, but the cultural environment in which jazz originated and developed during its early years was, for the most part, the Negro ghetto.

Although jazz was being created simultaneously in the Southwest and Midwest during the late 1800's, it is the Storeyville section of New Orleans which is generally accepted as its prime breeding ground. When Storeyville was closed by order of the U. S. Navy Department in 1919, jazz moved North and West, and soon began to effect a gradual transition from its Dixieland origins—evolving variations such as Boogie-Woogie, Swing, and Bop, to name but a few. In the process, it became a leading cultural export of the United States, often making its way around the world, and coming home with a host of strange instruments and unfamiliar sounds clinging to it. Today, it is still a vital force in the music of the world, but it remains a predominantly American phenomenon—one which, in many ways, continues to reflect the creative heritage of the Negro in the United States.

Throughout the 1960's, black jazz musicians continued to explore, expand, and extend the language of jazz. Consonant with their origins and experience, the new breed of performers, playing a style they called The New Thing, drew heavily on African sources, even as they recreated—at times furiously, at other times effortlessly—the turmoil of their private lives.

Tenor saxophonist John Coltrane won the admiration of his peers not only for his revolutionary "sheets of sound" technique, but for his quiet and convincing evangelical fervor—the manner of a priest, as one colleague described it. Now dead, Coltrane leaves behind Ornette Coleman, an alto sax virtuoso whose music is more consciously and deliberately angry rather than spiritual.

To other black musicans, jazz must remain true to both the innovations of the recent past and the gut-blues intensity of its revivalist origins. The religious energy and sense of elevated hysteria and euphoria which gripped hymn-chanting and foot-stomping black revivalists have penetrated the style of many contemporary black jazz figures, though their intellectual moorings are not totally obliterated or shattered by a healthy dosage of uplifting emotional ingredients. The origins, in a phrase, are incorporated into their own personal larger framework. Movement and mood do not simply overpower the creative performer who, like pianist Cecil Taylor, is seeking "a higher plane than he could ordinarily achieve." Taylor, for example, talks of accepting "the energy of God," rather than being strangled or dominated by it.

Today's black practitioners of jazz are more consciously nationalistic and humanistic

than ever before. They sense a kind of calling to be more than just talented or creative individuals, but rather interpreters of a people, musical spokesmen for a whole era of struggle and revolution.

Spatial limitations make it impossible to discuss all the great Negro jazz artists here. Those who have been included have been selected on the basis of their positions as landmark figures in the evolution of jazz—some because of their unique creativity, others because of their historical importance. Some were the first to make their particular instruments jazz vehicles; others were important bridges between different musical generations.

LOUIS ARMSTRONG
Trumpet

Born on the 4th of July at the turn of the 20th century, Louis Armstrong has been one of the most influential and durable of all jazz artists. He is, quite simply, one of the most famous people in the entire world.

On New Year's Eve in 1914, Armstrong was arrested in New Orleans for firing a pistol, and sent to the Colored Waifs Home. There, he first learned to play the cornet. His skill increased with the experience he gained from playing in the Home's band. When he was finally released from the institution, he was already proficient enough with the instrument to begin playing for money.

Befriended by his idol, King Oliver, Armstrong quickly began to develop the jazz skills which he had, until then, been able to admire only from a distance. When Oliver left for Chicago in 1919, a place was opened up for Armstrong as a member of the Kid Ory band in New Orleans.

In 1922, Oliver asked Armstrong to join him in Chicago as second cornet with his Creole Jazz Band. The duets between "Dippermouth," (as Armstrong was called) and "Papa Joe" (Oliver's nickname) soon became the talk of the Chicago music world.

Two years later, Armstrong joined the Fletcher Henderson band at the Roseland Ballroom in New York City where, at Henderson's suggestion, he switched from cornet to trumpet, the instrument he has played since. In 1925, he returned to Chicago to play with Erskine Tate. During the next four years, he made a series of recordings which brought him worldwide fame in musical circles.

In 1929, Armstrong returned to New York and there, in the revue "Hot Chocolates," scored his first triumph with a popular song (Fats Waller's "Ain't Misbehavin'"). This success was a turning point in his career inasmuch as he then began to front big bands, playing and singing popular songs rather than blues or original instrumentals.

In 1932, Armstrong headlined the show at the London Palladium, where he acquired the nickname "Satchelmouth" (since then abbreviated to "Satchmo"). From 1932 to 1935, he toured Europe, returning to the United States to film "Pennies from Heaven" with Bing Crosby. He continued to evolve from the status of musician to that of entertainer, and his singing soon became even more important than his playing. In 1947, he formed a small group which was an immediate success. Since then, he has continued to work in this context.

The influence of Louis Armstrong on the history of jazz is so all-pervasive that it has on occasion been blithely dismissed by those who have found fault with him for not "keeping up with the charges." It is clear, however, that Armstrong's continued success as a soloist and entertainer has helped make jazz a vital force in the general culture of the United States and, to some degree, of the entire world.

WILLIAM (COUNT) BASIE
Piano, bandleader

Count Basie is generally regarded as leader of the best jazz band in the United States and, consequently, one of the major influences on jazz as a whole.

His musical career ranges from a boyhood spent watching the pit band at the local movie theatre (he later learned the organ techniques of Fats Waller by crouching beside him in the Lincoln Theatre in Harlem) to his dual triumphs in 1957 when his became the first American band to play a royal command performance for the Queen of England, and the first Negro jazz band ever to play at the Waldorf Astoria Hotel in New York City.

During the early 1920's, Basie toured in vaudeville. Stranded in Kansas City, he joined Walter Page's Blue Devils. (Jimmy

Count Basie heads one of the leading jazz bands in the country.

Rushing was the singer.) After this band broke up, Basie joined Benny Moten and, in 1935, formed his own band at the Reno Club in Kansas City, where a local radio announcer soon dubbed him "Count."

At the urging of critic John Hammond, Basie brought his group to New York City in 1936. Within a year, he had cut his first record, and was well on his way to becoming an established presence in the jazz world.

The Basie trademark was a rhythm section which featured Basie's own clean, spare piano style, and outstanding soloists like Lester Young and Sweets Edison in the early years, and Lucky Thompson, J. J. Johnson, Clark Terry, and Benny Powell in the later period.

Except for the years 1950 and 1951 when he had a small group, Basie has led a big band for the last 30 years. In some way immune to changing fashion, the Basie band has completed numerous global tours and successful recording engagements without ever suffering an appreciable decline in its popularity.

SIDNEY BECHET
1897-1959
Soprano saxophone

Sidney Bechet was the first jazzman to achieve recognition on the soprano saxophone, and also one of the first to win acceptance in classical circles as a serious musician.

In 1919, Bechet played in England and on the Continent with Will Marion Cook's Southern Syncopated Orchestra. Even before this, his clarinet and soprano sax had been heard in the bands of King Oliver and Freddie Keppard.

During the early 1920's, Bechet made a series of records with Clarence Williams' *Blue Five;* worked briefly with Duke Ellington (one of his great admirers), and then returned to Europe. In the next decade, he played in Europe and the United States with Noble Sissle before forming his own trio. He took up residence in France toward the end of his career, and died there in 1959.

JIMMY BLANTON
1921-1942
Bass

CHARLIE CHRISTIAN
1917-1942
Electric guitar

(*Inasmuch as Jimmy Blanton and Charlie Christian established the bass and electric guitar, respectively, as solo instruments in jazz, their contributions can perhaps best be viewed within the framework of a single entry.*)

Jimmy Blanton was playing with the Fate Mirabile orchestra in St. Louis when he was discovered by Duke Ellington in 1939. Before that time, the bass was an instrument whose use was confined to the production of a steady, monotonous beat, one which was always subordinate to the more "glamorous" instruments.

Blanton, however, refused to be limited by quarter-note traditions. He improvised on his bass as freely as if it were a horn, using unique runs of eighth and sixteenth notes, and experimenting with ideas in melody and harmony that had never before been seriously considered for the bass. His technical skill was so great that no one seriously questions his designation as the first true bass master.

In 1941, Blanton contracted tuberculosis, and died the following year.

Sidney Bechet was an early innovator on the soprano saxophone.

Charlie Christian did for the electric guitar what Jimmy Blanton had done for the bass.

Christian joined Benny Goodman in 1939 and, after only two years with the Goodman sextet, achieved considerable fame as the first electric guitarist to use single-string solos. In his after-hour activities at such Harlem clubs as Minton's, he was an early contributor to the jazz revolution which would one day come to be called Bop. (Christian is even credited by some with having coined the actual word.)

In 1941, like Blanton, he contracted tuberculosis and, the following year, he too died.

BUDDY BOLDEN
1868-1931
Cornet

Buddy Bolden, a barber by trade, formed the first jazz band in the 1890's. By the turn of the century, his cornet was so popular that he was often called upon to sit in with a number of bands on a single evening.

His cornet style was the starting point for a chain of musicians from King Oliver to Louis Armstrong or, put another way, from New Orleans to Chicago. Since his career predated the recording of jazz, the only lasting memorial to his talent lies in the oral tradition which carries on his legend, and in the recorded successes of his proteges.

Bolden was committed to East Louisiana State Hospital in 1908, and remained there until his death in 1931.

OSCAR BROWN, JR.
Composer, singer

The many talents of Oscar Brown, Jr. make it necessary to view him as both a creative artist working behind the scenes and a dynamic interpreter delivering original and highly innovative "up-front" material to beguiled, and often enraptured, audiences.

Brown's talents first achieved nationwide recognition in the early 1960's. TIME Magazine characterized him as "the best new entertainer" in show business "since Belafonte" in 1962, quoting Ebony Magazine which viewed him as a "hip Negro

Jean Pace (l.) and Oscar Brown, Jr. performed together in Joy.

folk poet" and Lorraine Hansberry who called him "a startling genius."

Brown subsequently demonstrated the full measure of his jazz, folk music and blues talents in the off Broadway musical, *Joy*. *Times* critic Clive Barnes called composer/singer Brown "an artist of great merit" and "a major talent."

Brown, a native of Chicago, was born in 1926. He first gained a reputation as a jazzman playing Mister Kelly's there in the 1950's.

RAY CHARLES
Singer, Piano

Ray Charles is the vital link between contemporary jazz and the long-forgotten wellspring of early jazz. Charles uses what might be called a "down home" style to transmit contemporary musical ideas. He has succeeded to the point where he is one of the few musicians in our time to be acclaimed by jazz professionals and the general public alike.

Blinded at the age of six, Charles received his first musical training at a school for the blind in St. Augustine, Florida. Originally from Georgia, he left school there at the age of 15 to play local engagements. Two years later, he formed a trio which had some success in the Northwest. In 1954, he organized an even larger rhythm and blues group.

In 1957, his first LP was released, consisting of a potpourri of instrumentals drawn from pop, gospel and modern jazz sources. His singing and piano-playing found particular favor with a number of jazz artists who were reacting against what they felt was a growing tendency for jazz to become over-scored and underfelt. In Charles, they saw an artist who had restored both a sense of "soul" and instrumental "funkiness" to the jazz idiom.

Ray Charles

KENNY CLARKE
(Liaqat Ali Salaam)
Drums

Kenny Clarke was one of the "founding fathers" of the Bop movement. Along with Charlie Parker, Dizzy Gillespie and Thelonious Monk, Clarke made Minton's in Harlem *the* late-hour haunt for jazz buffs and musicians alike in the 1940's.

A pioneer figure in the use of drums as a solo instrument and not just as a background presence, he was the first musician to move away from the blatant use of cymbals to a more subtle style in which he maintained a steady rhythm with the top cymbal while "dropping bombs" with surprise bass-drum sounds.

Clarke hails from a musically inclined Pittsburgh family. While still in high school, he began the study of vibes, piano and trombone, as well as musical theory. His early professional experience was gained with Roy Eldridge and Edgar Hayes. (He traveled to Finland and Sweden with Hayes in 1937.)

In the early 1940's, he played with Teddy Hill and then moved into Minton's where his presence was strongly felt on the Bop scene. Throughout this decade, he continued to work with Dizzy Gillespie, Coleman Hawkins, Tadd Dameron and others. In 1951, he toured with Billy Eckstine and, the following year, helped organize the Modern Jazz Quartet, remaining with this group for the next three years. After free-lancing around New York for a year, he moved to France where he continued to work with a long list of visiting American talents.

Clarke's integrated use of the drums with other soloists has become a staple of contemporary jazz.

ORNETTE COLEMAN
Alto saxophone

It has often been said that the Bop revolution in jazz marked the beginning of a new musical era, but the music of Ornette Coleman has called that generalization into question. For all its intricacies, its radical harmonic departures which shocked those who first heard them, and its extremely free adherence to melodic lines, Bop may well have been the end of an old era rather than the beginning of a new one, since the core of its uniqueness was built around the concept of improvisation based on chord patterns.

Ornette Coleman

Ornette Coleman's style, however, represents a sharp break with this latter tradition. As a result of this, he has often been dismissed by many musicians (as well as by much of the general jazz public) as little more than "a noisemaker."

Coleman is largely self-taught on his alto. His early professional experience consisted of a series of irregular spots with rhythm and blues bands in New Orleans, Texas and California. While working as an elevator operator in Los Angeles in the mid 1950's, Coleman undertook a textbook study of harmony and theory before evolving a new style phase.

Arguments have raged since he completed his first major recording session in New York City in 1957. Some feel that the squeaks, bleats and other sounds which are produced with his plastic horn, not to mention the sounds he has recently begun to experiment with on violin, are meaningless. Others, however, (including John Lewis) are convinced that he is easily the most original and gifted jazz artist since Parker, Gillespie and Monk.

At this juncture, only time can provide the necessary perspective with which to pass judgment on the emerging school of harsh, atonal jazz, of which Coleman is undoubtedly a major exponent.

JOHN COLTRANE
1926-1967
Tenor saxophone

John Coltrane played tenor in a variety of settings during his musical career. In the 1940's, he was with a small combo featured in Philadelphia, then a U. S. Navy band playing in Hawaii and, lastly, a rhythm and blues group. Throughout the 1950's, he saw service with some of the greats of contemporary jazz: Dizzy Gillespie, Miles Davis and Thelonious Monk.

The music which Coltrane was creating —like that of Ornette Coleman, Archie Shepp and others—was the subject of great controversy in its heyday. Coltrane used his tenor to produce harsh, strange sounds which defied easy categorization. The overall effect of his music was regarded as unpleasant and unnerving by many of his listeners, including those who have always felt they were truly open to jazz experimentation.

Some always maintained that Coltrane's music was "meaningless," a charge which at least one fellow musician, J. J. Johnson, took great pains to refute, professing to see in the Coltrane-Monk relationship a parallel with that of Parker and Gillespie.

For all of the difficulty which his music presents to fellow musicians and critics, and likewise to the general listening public, Coltrane remained the most influential presence for young tenor men seeking to make their mark. The dissonance with which he was experimenting was a distinct keynote of jazz throughout the 1960's.

MILES DAVIS
Trumpet

Miles Davis has played a major role in effecting the transition from the hard, aggressive stance of Bop to the softer, more subtle shadings of the "cool school."

As a teen-age musician in St. Louis in the early 1940's, Davis sat in with his idols Charlie Parker and Dizzy Gillespie when they passed through town with the Billy Eckstine Band.

In 1945, his well-to-do father sent him to the Juilliard School of Music in New York. Within a short time, Davis was working the 52nd St. clubs with Parker and Coleman Hawkins, and touring with the bands of Billy Eckstine and Benny Carter.

In the late 1940's, Davis formed a nine-piece band of his own, including Lee Konitz, Gerry Mulligan, John Lewis and Max Roach. The group was highly praised by other musicians, but was a commercial failure.

Except for a brief hiatus due to illness, Davis has been an important jazz presence since 1950. In recent years, he has come to be regarded as the leading trumpet in the field.

DUKE ELLINGTON
Piano, bandleader, composer

Duke Ellington is believed by many critics to have made the most all-pervasive contribution to the development of jazz in the United States. Though the lion's share of Ellington's fame hinges on the numerous "standards" he has composed, it is his work as the leader of a jazz orchestra that has won him the respect and admiration of fellow musicians.

Ellington was born into a moderately well-to-do family in Washington, D.C. The name "Duke" was easily fitted to the dapper young man with the courtly manner. A gifted painter, Ellington was offered a scholarship to the Pratt Institute of Fine Arts in New York City, but he decided instead to play local music dates, and paint commercial signs. By 1918, he was doing well enough with his dance bands, featuring such talents as Sonny Greer on drums and Elmer Snowden on piano.

In 1923, at the urging of Fats Waller, Ellington made a trip to New York City, working in Harlem for Ada "Bricktop" Smith. He then became leader of his own group, and moved down to the Kentucky Club, where the band began to record under the name of Ellington's Kentucky Club Orchestra.

In 1924, Ellington wrote his first revue score for "Chocolate Kiddies," a show which ran for two years in Germany but never reached Broadway. From 1927 to 1932, Ellington and his orchestra held forth at the Cotton Club on Lenox Avenue (except for a brief hiatus in 1930 when he appeared in his first movie, Amos and Andy's *Check and Double Check*).

During the Cotton Club period, Ellington's orchestral genius gained him a national reputation, particularly through his

Miles Davis

records and his network broadcasts. Brilliant solo performances by such artists as Barney Bigard, Johnny Hodges and Cootie Williams set the pace for many later jazz orchestras. In the jazz world, however, it was his orchestrations—not his single-line melodies—which earned him the plaudits of his fellow musicians.

In 1927, Ellington introduced the wordless use of the voice as a jazz instrument and, in 1931, he broke through the traditional three-minute time limit set for commercial records. His later use of a miniature concerto context as a framework for compositions played by specific jazz soloists, and his creation of original works for new concerts are among the other significant contributions he has made to the realm of jazz.

Through European tours first begun in the 1930's, the Ellington sound was brought live to an international public which had, even then, long acclaimed his preeminence in the jazz domain. In 1943, his "Black, Brown and Beige" was regarded as the most important attempt of its time to fuse jazz elements with the formal concert idiom.

The roster of Ellington personnel through the years is among the most impressive in the history of jazz . . . Ben Webster, Juan Tizol, Ray Nance, Oscar Pettiford, Louis Bellson, Harry Carney, Johnny Hodges, etc. Even today, Ellington continues to exert a unique and powerful influence on the musical traditions of jazz, both here in the United States and abroad as well.

ELLA FITZGERALD
Singer

Ella Fitzgerald has emerged as the top female vocalist in virtually every poll conducted among jazz musicians during the last decade. No other jazz vocalist has been as unanimously acclaimed as she.

Discovered in 1934 by Chick Webb during an amateur contest at Harlem's Apollo Theatre in New York City, she cut her first side with Webb a year later. In 1938, she recorded "A Tisket, A Tasket," a novelty number which brought her commercial success and made her name widely known among the general public. Among musicians, however, her reputation stemmed from her singular ability to use her voice like an instrument, improvising effortlessly in a clear style filled with rhythmic subtleties.

Over the last 30 years, Ella Fitzgerald has been the leading jazz interpreter of the popular song.

Fitzgerald and Ellington, or "Ella" and "Duke" as they are known to thei- fans.

DIZZY GILLESPIE
Trumpet

Dizzy Gillespie and Charlie Parker were co-founders of the most revolutionary movement in jazz during the 1940's—the phenomenon known simply as Bop. The role which each played in this revolution has long been a subject of considerable controversy. Billy Eckstine, whose band at one time included both Gillespie and Parker, has defined Parker's role more as instrumentalist, and Gillespie's more as writer and arranger. Whatever their particular contributions were, however, it cannot be disputed that the sum total of their ideas has brought about a directional change in jazz which continues to the present time.

Gillespie studied harmony and theory at the Lauringburg Institute in North Carolina and, after moving to Philadelphia and gaining more professional experience there, he joined the Teddy Hill band where he replaced his early idol "Little Jazz" Roy Eldridge, who had moved to the Fletcher Henderson Orchestra.

He toured Europe with Teddy Hill during 1939 and, when he returned to New York to play with Mercer Ellington and Cab Calloway, his bop experimentation was already beginning to develop, and he had also begun his career as an arranger. After working with Ella Fitzgerald, Benny Carter, Charlie Barnet, Earl Hines and others, he joined Eckstine's band in 1944.

Since Bop has become nationally known, Gillespie has toured Europe, the Middle East, and Latin America with big bands and quintets, some of which have been subsidized by the U. S. State Department.

LIONEL HAMPTON
Vibraphone

Lionel Hampton was the first jazz musician to feature the vibes, an instrument which has since come to play a vital role in small-combo jazz. His first recorded solo on the instrument was in 1930 on "Memories of You" which featured Louis Armstrong, then fronting the Les Hite

Dizzy Gillespie

band in California.

Hampton later left Hite's band to form his own Los Angeles group. When Benny Goodman heard him in 1936, he used him on a record date with Teddy Wilson and Gene Krupa, and then persuaded him to sign on with the Goodman tour on a permanent basis.

Hampton played with the Goodman Quartet until 1940, the year he formed his own permanent orchestra. The following year, it scored its first big hit: "Flyin' Home."

Hampton enjoyed great commercial success in the 1940's and 1950's in such places as Israel, Europe, Australia and North Africa.

W. C. HANDY
1873–1958
Composer

Although he began as a cornetist and bandleader in the 1890's, W. C. Handy's fame as the "Father of the Blues" rests almost entirely on his work as a composer.

After studying at Kentucky Musical College, Handy toured with an assortment of musical groups, becoming the bandmaster of the Mahara Minstrels in 1896.

In 1909, during a political campaign in Memphis, Handy wrote *Mr. Crump*, a campaign song for E. H. "Boss" Crump. Three years later, the song was published as the *Memphis Blues*.

In 1914, Handy published his most famous song, *St. Louis Woman*, and, that same year, also wrote *Yellow Dog Blues*. Some others that have become perennial favorites are *Joe Turner Blues* (1915); *Beale Street Blues* (1916); *Careless Love* (1921), and *Aunt Hagar's Blues* (1922).

In the 1920's, Handy became a music publisher in New York. Despite his failing sight, he remained active until his death in 1958. His songs extended beyond the world of jazz to find their way into the general field of popular music in innumerable forms. Their popularity continues unabated even today.

COLEMAN HAWKINS
1904–1969
Tenor saxophone

With the position occupied by the tenor saxophone in jazz today, it is difficult to imagine that, until Coleman Hawkins came along, this instrument was not seriously considered as a suitable jazz vehicle. The full, rich tone which Hawkins brought to the tenor has helped make it one of the most vital instruments in the contemporary jazz ensemble.

When Hawkins took up the tenor at the age of nine, he had already had four years of training on piano and cello. He continued his studies at Washburn College in Topeka, Kansas and, in 1922, toured with Mamie Smith's Jazz Hounds. The following year, he began a 10-year stint with Fletcher Henderson's band.

Hawkins left Henderson in 1934 to tour England and the Continent, recording with Django Reinhardt, Benny Carter and others. When he returned to the United States in 1939, he recorded his first commercial hit, "Body and Soul," with his own band.

Unlike many of his contemporaries, Hawkins was open to the experimentations of the young musicians of the 1940's. In 1944, for example, he formed an all-star band for the first Bop record session, and he gave help and encouragement to Dizzy Gillespie, Charlie Parker, and others whom he admired.

With the advent of the "cool school," Hawkins lapsed into temporary decline, but, in recent years, the warmth of his style has been recognized anew by scores of young musicians attempting to duplicate his "soul" sound.

EARL (FATHA) HINES
Piano

Except for increased technical proficiency, the piano style of Earl "Fatha" Hines has barely changed from what it was in the late 1920's.

Hailing from a Pittsburgh background musically rounded out by his trumpeter father and organist mother. Hines originally planned to launch a concert career, but he was soon caught up in the world of jazz. Forming his own trio while still in high school, he began to play in local clubs before moving on to Chicago as a "single" (a solo act).

While there, he made a series of records with Louis Armstrong's *Hot Five*, and soon became known as "the trumpet-style pianist." Because of the exciting single-note use of his right hand, the intricacy of his style was well beyond that of any of his contemporaries, and served as a touchstone for a generation of succeeding pianists.

In 1928, Hines formed his own band at the Grand Terrace in Chicago. For the next 20 years, this band served as a proving ground for the best instrumentalists and innovators of the period (from Budd Johnson and Walter Fuller in the early era to Dizzy Gillespie and Charlie Parker in the later years).

From 1948 to 1951, Hines worked again with Armstrong. Since then, he has been active with his own small groups on the West Coast and has, on occasion, toured both the United States and the Continent.

BILLIE HOLIDAY
1915-1959
Singer

Billie Holiday, dubbed "Lady Day" by Lester Young, belongs to the great blues tradition dominated by such figures as Ma Rainey and Bessie Smith.

While still a young girl, she moved from her hometown of Baltimore to New York City and, in 1929, began her singing career in an assortment of Harlem night spots. Four years later, she cut her first sides with Benny Goodman and, from 1935 to 1939, established her reputation with a series of records made while she was vocalist with Teddy Wilson, Count Basie, Artie Shaw, and several other all-star bands.

Although Billie Holiday is often compared with Bessie Smith, her style and material were really far removed from those of the older singer. In fact, there is no earlier jazz artist who is known to have had a direct influence on Billie Holiday. What she shared with Bessie Smith and other blues singers was an ability to project a universal sense of loneliness—that feature which is thought to be at the core of true blues artistry.

In such classic records as "Strange Fruit" and "God Bless the Child," she departed from popular material to score her greatest artistic triumphs, depicting the harsh reality of Southern lynchings and the personal alienation she had experienced because of it.

Miss Holiday died of lung congestion and other ailments in Metropolitan Hospital, New York City. Once addicted to drugs and alcohol, she had written in her 1956 autobiography: "All dope can do for you is kill you—and kill you the long, slow, hard way."

J. J. JOHNSON
Trombone

J. J. Johnson stands alone as the unchallenged master of the jazz trombone. He is the first musician to have adapted this instrument to the demanding techniques called for by the advent of Bop.

Early in his career, Johnson displayed such skill in performing high-speed and intricate solos that those who knew him only from records found it hard to believe that he was actually using a slide—and not a valve—trombone.

Johnson spent the 1940's touring with Benny Carter, Count Basie, Woody Herman and Dizzy Gillespie. During these years, his trombone was as widely imitated as the trumpet and alto of Gillespie and Parker, respectively.

In the 1950's, Johnson retired for a time, only to return as part of Kai Winding's *Jay and Kai Quintet*. This group soon began to tour Europe and the United States with great commercial success.

For the last generation, Johnson's ability as a composer has also been widely praised. In 1959, he performed several of his works with the Monterey Festival Workshop Orchestra.

JAMES P. JOHNSON
1891-1955
Piano

The name of James P. Johnson is less known than that of his most famous protege, Fats Waller, but Johnson has, nonetheless, made a substantial contribution in the field of jazz piano and popular show music.

Johnson was the master of the "stride piano," an instrumental style which derives its name from the strong, striding left-hand style of the player. "Stride piano" came into its own during the 1920's, particularly in conjunction with the phenomenon known as the "rent party." Such a "party" was held for the purpose of raising rent money, and involved the payment of an admission fee which entitled a "patron" to food, drink, conviviality, and a "stride piano" session.

Duke Ellington and Count Basie were among the many who sharpened their skills in the "rent party" training ground. In fact, the influence of the "stride piano" was heard in popular music for

"Lady Day"—Billie Holiday

the next two decades. Johnson was also an early bridge between the worlds of jazz and Broadway. Numbered among his song hits are "If I Could Be With You," "Charleston," and "Runnin' Wild."

JOHN LEWIS
Piano, composer

John Lewis has become an international force in the world of jazz as an arranger, conductor, composer and instrumentalist.

Raised in a middle-class environment in Albuquerque, New Mexico, Lewis studied music and anthropology at the University of New Mexico until 1942. After three years in the Army, he went to New York City to become pianist and arranger with Dizzy Gillespie's band. Two years later at Carnegie Hall, Gillespie's band performed Lewis' first major work, "Toccata for Trumpet and Orchestra."

After a European tour with Gillespie, Lewis returned to the United States to play with Lester Young and Charlie Parker, and to arrange for Miles Davis. In 1952, after having finished his studies at the Manhattan School of Music, Lewis founded the group upon which a major part of his reputation rests: The Modern Jazz Quartet (MJQ). Throughout the 1950's, this group developed an international reputation in spite of some carping that its material was too charted to be truly called jazz.

Lewis has never confined his creativity to the MJQ, but has constantly assumed a variety of roles, ranging from conducting in Germany to serving as music director of the highly acclaimed Monterey Jazz Festival.

JIMMIE LUNCEFORD
1902–1947
Bandleader

"The Lunceford style"—although its originator himself never played an instrument while recording with his band (except on the record of *Liza*)—was one which influenced many bandleaders and arrangers up to the 1950's, including Sonny Dunham, Sonny Burke, and Tommy Dorsey. The Lunceford band reigned with those of Duke Ellington, Count Basie and Benny Goodman as the leading and most influential of the big jazz orchestras in the 1930's.

A native of Fulton, Missouri, Lunceford received his B.A. at Fisk University and later studied at City College in New York. After having become proficient on all reed instruments, Lunceford began his own career as a "leader" in Memphis in 1927. By 1934, he was already an established presence in the field of jazz. During the next decade, the Lunceford band was known as the best-disciplined and most showmanly Negro jazz ensemble in the nation.

The Lunceford vogue faded after 1942, by which time the band was already experiencing several changes of personnel. Lunceford himself died of a heart attack in 1947 while the band was on tour.

CHARLIE MINGUS
Bass, composer

Charlie Mingus is to the young jazz musician of the 1960's what Charlie Parker and Dizzy Gillespie were to this same generation in the two previous decades.

Mingus has emerged from classical training in Los Angeles on solfeggio and trombone to become one of jazz's most original bassists. His musical background ranges from five years of study with H. Rheinschagen of the New York Philharmonic to professional stints with Louis Armstrong, Kid Ory, Lionel Hampton, Red Norvo, Charlie Parker, Stan Getz, Duke Ellington, Bud Powell, and Art Tatum (a roster which literally spans the entire history of jazz).

Mingus came into his own as a composer in the mid 1950's. His experiments have always been directed at expanding the arbitrary limitations which he feels have been imposed on jazz. Some of the effects he creates (including atonalities and dissonances) have generated the same kind of furor which greeted the advent of Bop a decade earlier.

THELONIOUS SPHERE MONK
Piano

Thelonious Monk's popularity with the general public dates largely from the middle 1950's. However, within the world of professional jazz musicians themselves, his role as an important pioneer in the development of Bop had been acknowledged long before then.

Along with Charlie Parker and Dizzy Gillespie, Monk had been a vital member of the jazz revolution which took place in the early 1940's. Some musicians (among them Art Blakey) have felt that Monk actually predated his more renowned contemporaries. This view notwithstanding, Monk's piano technique and his talent as a composer in the new idiom have made him a leader in the development of modern jazz.

Aside from some brief work with the Lucky Millinder band and with Coleman Hawkins, Monk has spent the last 20 years as leader of his own small groups. He has been called "the most important jazz composer since Ellington." Many of his compositions, ("'Round about Midnight," "Ruby My Dear") have been established jazz standards for some time.

Monk's spare and serious piano style has spawned scores of imitators. He has managed, nonetheless, to remain unique as both an instrumentalist and composer, maintaining his own musical integrity and his melodic originality.

Thelonious Monk . . . "the most important composer since Ellington."

FERDINAND (JELLY ROLL) MORTON
1885-1941
Piano

Among the many controversial aspects of "Jelly Roll" Morton's life was his claim that he had "invented jazz in 1901." Although Morton's boast was often scorned by many, his talents as a soloist, composer and arranger place him in the forefront of the early jazz innovators.

A pianist in New Orleans from 1902 until the close of the Storeyville era, Morton lived in California from 1917 to 1922. Using the name "Morton's Red Hot Peppers" from 1926 to 1930, he cut a series of records which were to bring him a nationwide reputation. During this period of prosperity, Morton also became widely known for the diamond filling he wore in one of his teeth as a success symbol.

When jazz fashions changed in the 1930's, Morton fell into eclipse. By 1937, he was running an obscure nightclub in Washington, D. C.

In 1938, Morton made a number of recordings for the Library of Congress—playing, singing and narrating the major incidents of his life and career. These recordings brought him some renewed attention but, within two years, he had lapsed back into obscurity—this time in Los Angeles, where he died in 1941.

JOSEPH (KING) OLIVER
1885-1938
Cornet

Joe Oliver first earned the sobriquet "King" in 1917 after winning a kind of "open combat" solo contest against the likes of Freddie Keppard, Manuel Perez, and a host of other cornetists who filled the Storeyville nights with the first sounds of New Orleans jazz.

Strongly influenced by Buddy Bolden in the early part of his career, Oliver soon teamed up with Kid Ory, and organized what was to become the leading jazz band in New Orleans.

During the Storeyville era, Oliver met and befriended Louis Armstrong. Lacking a son of his own, he became Armstrong's "unofficial father," giving the boy his old horn, and sharing with him the musical knowledge which he had acquired over the years. In return for these favors, Armstrong treated him with great respect, referring to him always only as "Papa Joe."

With the closing of Storeyville, Oliver left for Chicago, whereupon Armstrong replaced him in Ory's band. By 1922, however, Oliver was in a position to summon Armstrong to play in his Creole Jazz Band as second cornetist.

In 1923, the Creole Jazz Band made the first series of recordings by a Negro jazz group. (Except for a few numbers by Kid Ory, almost no pure Negro jazz had ever been recorded.)

The duets of Oliver and Armstrong put Chicago on the jazz map of the United States. Some years later, however, changing tastes caused Oliver's music to decline in popularity so that, by the time he moved to New York in 1928, his best years were already behind him.

In the early 1930's, Oliver made an unsuccessful tour of the South before finally settling in Savannah, Georgia, where he worked in a poolroom until his death in 1938.

EDWARD (KID) ORY
Trombone

Kid Ory's musical career is in many ways emblematic of the story of jazz itself. Both reached a high point in New Orleans during the first two decades of this century; both moved North during the 1920's, only to lapse into obscurity in the 1930's before being revived in the next two decades.

Ory was the best known of the so-called "tailgate trombonists." He led his own band in Los Angeles until 1924 when he moved to Chicago to play with "King" Oliver and others. In 1926, together with Armstrong, he recorded his own composition "Muskrat Ramble."

He returned to the West Coast in 1929 and, after playing for a time with local bands, retired to run a successful chicken ranch from 1930 to 1939. In the 1940's, he returned gradually to music with Barney Bigard, Bunk Johnson, and other New Orleans notables. When "Muskrat Ramble" was commercially revived in 1956, Ory's name became known to a whole new generation.

He toured Europe successfully in 1956, and again in 1959, and has to this day continued to be a favorite in San Francisco nightclubs.

CHARLIE (BIRD) PARKER
1920-1955
Alto saxophone

The influence of Charlie Parker on the development of jazz has been felt not only in the realm of the alto saxophone which he dominated, but on the whole spectrum of jazz ideas. The astounding innovations which he introduced melodically, harmonically, tonally, and rhythmically made it virtually impossible for any jazz musician from the mid 1940's to the present time to develop his own style without reflecting some of Parker's tonal patterns, with or without acknowledgment.

Parker left school at 15 to become a professional, spending his early years with a group of fun-loving musicians in Kansas City, his hometown. After wandering about the Midwest for a time, Parker arrived in New York in 1939. Working sporadically in Harlem, he recorded his first sides with Jay McShann two years later. It was at this time that Parker met Dizzy Gillespie, who was developing parallel ideas and who would become known as co-founder with Parker of the bop movement some four years later.

In the early 1940's, Parker played with the bands of Noble Sissle, Earl Hines, Cootie Williams, Andy Kirk, as well as the original Billy Eckstine band—the first big band formed expressly to feature the new jazz style in both solos and arrangements.

In 1945, Parker formally launched the Bop movement by cutting a series of sides with Gillespie's rhythm section. Although Parker was soon revered by a whole host of younger musicians, his innovations met with a great deal of opposition from traditional jazz musicians and critics.

In 1946, Parker suffered a complete breakdown, and was confined to a state hospital in California. Six months later, he was back recording with Erroll Garner. From this point on until his death from a heart attack in 1955, he confined most of his activity to working with a quintet in the New York area, making his final appearance in 1955 at Birdland, the club which had been named in his honor.

OSCAR PETERSON
Piano

Oscar Peterson began classical study of the piano at the age of six in his native Canada and, in less than a decade, was playing regularly on a local radio show.

In 1944, he became a featured soloist with Johnny Holmes, one of the top

Oscar Peterson

bands in Canada, and his reputation soon spread throughout the United States jazz world. He continued to resist offers from Jimmie Lunceford and others to tour the States but, in 1949, was persuaded by Norman Granz to come to New York City for a Carnegie Hall appearance. The following year, he began to record and to tour the United States for Granz.

Peterson's international reputation stems from his annual European tours. His original group used bass (Ray Brown) and guitar (Barney Kessel, Herb Ellis) but, when Ellis left in 1958, Peterson hired drummer Ed Thigpen to fill out the trio.

The initial reaction to Peterson in the United States was often one of curt dismissal. He was first thought of as nothing but a composite of other pianists, but gradually it came to be recognized that he was forming a creative bridge between two jazz generations—Swing and Bop—using the very best elements of both to make his own highly personal statement.

OSCAR PETTIFORD
1922-1960
Bass

Oscar Pettiford was the leading bassist in the Bop era of jazz. Building his own style on the foundation which had been established by the late Jimmy Blanton, Pettiford achieved renown as the most technically capable and melodically inventive bassist in the jazz world of the late 1940's.

Pettiford was born on an Indian reservation and raised in Minneapolis. Until he was 19, he toured with the family band (father and 11 children), and was well known in the Midwest. In 1943, Charlie Barnet heard him in Minneapolis and hired him to team up with bassist Chubby Jackson.

Pettiford left Barnet later that year and became a regular at Minton's in the era during which Bop was being born. Later, he led his own group on 52nd Street and also played with Coleman Hawkins, Duke Ellington, and Woody Herman.

Pettiford's fame grew during the 1950's through his recordings and his tours of Europe and the Orient. In 1958, he settled permanently in Europe where he continued to work with a number of groups until his death in Copenhagen in 1960.

DON REDMAN
Saxophone, Composer

The first composer-arranger of any consequence in the history of jazz, Don Redman was known in the 1920's as a brilliant instrumentalist on several kinds of saxophones. He also made a number of records with Bessie Smith, Louis Armstrong, and other top-ranking jazz artists.

Born in Piedmont, West Virginia in 1900, Redman was a child prodigy who played trumpet at the age of three, joined a band at six, and later studied harmony, theory and composition at the Boston and Detroit Conservatories.

During most of the 1930's, Redman led his own band, regarded as one of the leading Negro orchestras of the day, and the first to play a sponsored radio series. In 1940, Redman went into the composing phase of his career with such bands as Paul Whiteman and Jimmy Dorsey.

Since 1951, Redman has been musical director for Pearl Bailey. From 1954 to 1955, he appeared in a small acting role in *House of Flowers* on Broadway. Thereafter, he returned to recording, cutting several albums for a number of companies.

JIMMY RUSHING
Singer

The song "Mister Five By Five," written in tribute to him, is an apt description of Jimmy Rushing, often called the greatest living male vocalist in jazz history.

Rushing played piano and violin as a boy, but he entered music professionally as a singer in the after-hours world of California in 1925. Over the years since then, Rushing has been linked with leading bands and musicians: with Walter Page from 1927 to 1928, Benny Moten in 1929 and, from 1935 to 1940, as a mainstay with the famed Count Basie band.

Rushing formed his own small group when he left Basie and, in the ensuing years, has worked most often as a "single." Since the rediscovery of the blues in the mid 1950's, Rushing has regained the widespread popularity he had achieved with earlier generations.

His nightclub and theatre engagements have been highly successful, and his world tours on his own and also with Benny Goodman have earned him critical acclaim and commercial success. His style has endured across four decades of jazz largely because it is noted for its great warmth, a sure, firm melodic line, and a swinging use of rhythm.

BESSIE SMITH
1894-1937
Singer

Bessie Smith rose from the most abject poverty to become the most popular Negro entertainer of her day.

Bessie was "discovered" at the age of 13 by Ma Rainey, the first of the great blues singers. Years later, while singing in Selma, Alabama, Bessie was heard by Frank Walker, the recording director of Columbia, a company which was then experiencing serious financial difficulties. In those days, most of the popular recordings of the blues had been so-called "urban blues," rendered by such singers as Mamie Smith (no relation). Walker's decision to record a less polished country blues singer created a furor of protest at Columbia, but it also established a personality who has since left a great imprint on the history of vocal jazz. In 1923, Bessie Smith recorded "Down Hearted Blues"—a number which sold over two million records in a single year.

From 1924 to 1927, Bessie Smith earned better than $2,000 a week, and was accompanied on her records by the top jazz musicians of her day, including Louis Armstrong and James P. Johnson. Within a short time, however, changing fashions, mismanagement of her funds, and other personal problems all combined to reduce her popularity, and bring her career to the brink of ruin.

In 1933, John Hammond arranged a recording session in tribute to her past greatness. Four years later, just before Hammond was to leave for Mississippi to bring her North, she met with a fatal automobile accident, bleeding to death after being refused admission to a segregated hospital in the South.

ART TATUM
1910-1956
Piano

In 1932, a young, almost-totally-blind pianist from Ohio—Art Tatum by name—arrived in New York City as an accompanist for Adelaide Hall. The first records he cut with her that year gave rise to questions of style which are still being debated today.

Within a year, Tatum's work at the Onyx Club on 52nd Street had made him the talk of the jazz world in New York. After a few years in Chicago, he went abroad in 1938, experiencing his greatest success in London. In his early years, Tatum worked almost exclusively as a soloist but, in 1943, he formed a trio (Slam Stewart on bass, Tiny Gaines on guitar), continuing to perform in this context until his death.

Tatum's emergence was extremely disconcerting to many musicians who felt that his style was far too classical to be truly placed in the category of jazz. Most musicians, however, recognized that Tatum's astounding technical skills and harmonic experimentations were simply years ahead of their time.

No one has yet equalled Tatum's technical virtuosity, though young pianists by the score have tried to do so. More important, however, Tatum seldom let his dexterity overshadow his basic jazz orientation. When he died of uremia in 1956, he had won the respect and acclaim reserved for those who totally dominate their art.

THOMAS (FATS) WALLER
1904-1943
Piano

The son of a former pastor of Harlem's Abyssinian Baptist Church, Thomas "Fats" Waller received his early training in the classical idiom.

Already an accompanist for Bessie Smith and other blues greats at the age of 15, Waller was also a piano and organ soloist in cabarets and theatres. He was the first to successfully use the organ as a jazz instrument. During the 1920's, Waller joined his idol James P. Johnson in touring the "rent parties" of Harlem, and in developing the "stride piano" which soon set the pace for a number of up-and-coming younger pianists. In 1932, while touring Europe, Waller and the eminent French organist Marcel Dupre gave a private recital in the Notre Dame Cathedral in Paris.

Waller's skill as a popular composer led to such hits as "Ain't Misbehavin'" and "Honeysuckle Rose."

LESTER (PREZ) YOUNG
1909-1959
Tenor Saxophone

It was Lester Young who gave Billie Holiday the name "Lady Day" when both were with Count Basie, and it was "Lady Day" in her turn who christened Lester Young as "President" (later shortened to "Prez").

Young spent his youth on the carnival circuit in the Midwest with his musical family, choosing to concentrate on the tenor saxophone, only one of the many instruments he was able to play.

When Young took over Coleman Hawkins' chair in Fletcher Henderson's orchestra, he was criticized for not having the same style as his predecessor. As a result of this, he returned to Kansas City to play with Andy Kirk, and then with Count Basie from 1936 to 1940. During the Basie years, Young and Hawkins were the two most vital influences on the tenor as a jazz instrument. Hardly a tenor man from the middle 1940's through the 1950's achieved prominence without building on the foundations laid by Lester Young. Young is considered to be a major figure involved in the transition between the big, rich tenor style and the quiet, moody "cool school."

Young suffered a complete breakdown in 1956, and died three years later after having made a brief European comeback.

OTHER NEGRO JAZZ ARTISTS

Name	*Place of Birth*	*Dates of Birth and Death*
Nat Adderley	Tampa, Fla.	1931-
Red Allen	Algiers, La.	1908-1969
Albert Ayler	Cleveland, Ohio	1936-
Benny Bailey	Cleveland, Ohio	1925-
Buster Bailey	Memphis, Tenn.	1902-
Dave Bailey	Portsmouth, Va.	1926-
Danny Barker	New Orleans, La.	1909-
Leon Berry	Wheeling, W. Va.	1941-
Denzil Best	New York City	1917-
George Braith	New York City	1939-
Oscar Brown, Jr.	Chicago, Ill.	1926-
Pete Brown	Baltimore, Md.	1906-
Donald Byrd	Detroit, Mich.	1932-
Cab Calloway	Rochester, N.Y.	1907-
Mutt Carey	New Orleans, La.	1948-
Bruno Carr	New York City	1928-
Scoops Carry	Little Rock, Ark.	1915-
Ron Carter	Ferndale, Mich.	1937-
Al Casey	Louisville, Ky.	1915-
Buddy Catlett	Long Beach, Calif.	1933-
Don Cherry	Oklahoma City, Okla.	1936-
Jimmy Cobb	Washington, D.C.	1929-
Hank Crawford	Memphis, Tenn.	1934-
Ted Curson	Philadelphia, Pa.	1935-
Richard Davis	Chicago, Ill.	1930-
Wild Bill Davis	Glasgow, Mo.	1918-
Eric Dolphy	Los Angeles, Calif.	1928-1964
Ed Durham	San Marcos, Tex.	1906-
Billy Eckstine	Pittsburgh, Pa.	1914-
Teddy Edwards	Jackson, Miss.	1924-
Ethel Ennis	Baltimore, Md.	1934-
Booker Ervin	Denison, Tex.	1930-
Gil Fuller	Los Angeles, Calif.	1920-
Victor Gaskin	New York City	1934-
Tyree Glenn	Corsicana, Tex.	1912-
Dexter Gordon	Los Angeles, Calif.	1923-

Name	Place of Birth	Dates of Birth and Death
Grant Green	Charleston, S.C.	1911-
Edward Hall	New Orleans, La.	1901-
Jimmy Hamilton	Dillon, S.C.	1917-
Herbie Hancock	Chicago, Ill.	1940-
Lil Hardin	Memphis, Tenn.	1903-
Eddie Harns	Chicago, Ill.	1934-
Louis Hayes	Detroit, Mich.	1937-
J. C. Heard	Dayton, Ohio	1917-
Percy Heath	Wilmington, N.C.	1923-
Fletcher Henderson	Cuthbert, Ga.	1898-1952
Joe Henderson	Lima, Ohio	1937-
Andrew Hill	Port au Prince, Haiti	1937-
Red Holt	Rosedale, Miss.	1932-
Darnell Howard	Chicago, Ill.	1892-
Freddie Hubbard	Indianapolis, Ind.	1938-
Paul Humphrey	Detroit, Mich.	1935-
Bobby Hutcherson	Los Angeles, Calif.	1941-
Quentin Jackson	Springfield, Ohio	1909-
Hilton Jefferson	Danbury, Conn.	1903-
Bud Johnson	Dallas, Tex.	1910-
James P. Johnson	New Brunswick, N.J.	1891-
Keg Johnson	Dallas, Tex.	1908-
Lonnie Johnson	New Orleans, La.	1889-
Elvin Jones	Pontiac, Mich.	1918-
Quincy Jones	Chicago, Ill.	1933-
Connie Kay	Tuckahoe, N.Y.	1927-
Wynton Kelly	Jamaica, West Indies	1931-
Al Killion	Birmingham, Ala.	1916-1950
John Kirby	Baltimore, Md.	1908-1952
Roland Kirk	Columbus, Ohio	1936-
Billy Kyle	Philadelphia, Pa.	1914-
Jusef Lateef	Chattanooga, Tenn.	1921-
Harland Leonard	Kansas City, Mo.	1904-
John Levy	New Orleans, La.	1912-
Ed Lewis	Eagle City, Okla.	1909-
Ramsey Lewis	Chicago, Ill.	1935-
Abbey Lincoln	Chicago, Ill.	1930-
John Lindsay	Algiers, La.	1894-1950
Melba Liston	Kansas City, Mo.	1926-
Johnny Lytle	Springfield, Ohio	1932-
Les McCann	Lexington, Ky.	1935-
Carmen McRae	New York City	1922-
John Mills*	Bellefonte, Pa.	1889-
Herbert Mills	Piqua, Ohio	1912-
Harry Mills	Piqua, Ohio	1913-
Donald Mills	Piqua, Ohio	1915-
George Mitchell	Louisville, Ky.	1899-
Hank Mobley	Eastman, Ga.	1930-
Lee Morgan	Philadelphia, Pa.	1938-
Bennie Moten	Kansas City, Mo.	1894-1935
Oliver Nelson	St. Louis, Mo.	1932-
David Newman	Dallas, Tex.	1933-
Albert Nicholas	New Orleans, La.	1900-
Joe Orange	New York City	1941-
Jimmy Owens	New York City	1943-
Walter Page	Gallatin, Mo.	1900-
John Patton	Kansas City, Mo.	1936-
Esther Phillips	Galveston, Tex.	1935-
Tommy Potter	Philadelphia, Pa.	1918-

Name	*Place of Birth*	*Dates of Birth and Death*
"Bud" Powell	New York City	1924-1966
Russell Procope	New York City	1908-
Lou Rawls	Chicago, Ill.	1935-
Jerome Richardson	Oakland, Calif.	1920-
Sam Rivers	El Reno, Okla.	1930-
Luis Russell	Careening Cay, Panama	1902-
Johnny St. Cyr	New Orleans, La.	1890-
Bud Scott	New Orleans, La.	1890-1949
Shirley Scott	Philadelphia, Pa.	1934-
Bola Sete	Rio de Janeiro, Brazil	1928-
Charlie Shavers	New York City	1917-
Orvell Shaw	St. Louis, Mo.	1923-
Archie Shepp	Ft. Lauderdale, Fla.	1937-
Wayne Shorter	Newark, N.J.	1933-
Ormer Simeon	New Orleans, La.	1902-
Tab Smith	Kingston, N.C.	1909-
Les Spann	Pine Bluff, Ark.	1932-
O'Neil Spencer	Springfield, Ohio	1909-1944
Billy Strayhorn	Dayton, Ohio	1915-1970
Maxine Sullivan	Homestead, Pa.	1911-
Buddy Tate	Sherman, Tex.	1915-
Art Tatum	Toledo, Ohio	1910-
Art Taylor	New York City	1929-
Cecil Taylor	New York City	1933-
John Tchicai	Copenhagen, Denmark	1936-
Clark Terry	St. Louis, Mo.	1920-
Walter Thomas	Muskogee, Okla.	1907-
"Lucky" Thompson	Detroit, Mich.	1924-
Stanley Torrentine	Pittsburgh, Pa.	1934-
McCoy Tyner	Philadelphia, Pa.	1938-
Mal Waldron	New York City	1926-
Clara Ward	Philadelphia, Pa.	1924-
Jack Washington	Kansas City, Mo.	1912-
Julius Watkins	Detroit, Mich.	1921-
Anthony Williams	Chicago, Ill.	1945-
John Williams	Cranford, Miss.	1903-
Marion Williams	Miami, Fla.	1927-
Nancy Wilson	Chillicothe, Ohio	1937-
Shadow Wilson	Yonkers, N.Y.	1919-
Phil Woods	Springfield, Mass.	1931-
Reggie Workman	Philadelphia, Pa.	1937-
Gene Wright	Chicago, Ill.	1923-
Lamar Wright	Texarkana, Tex.	1912-
Larry Young	Newark, N.J.	1940-

* Entries refer to the group which performed together as "The Mills Brothers."

Ossie Davis (l.) and Burt Lancaster in a scene from The Scalphunters

THE BLACK PERFORMER IN FILMS

A Survey of the Negro's Role in Motion Pictures from the Turn of the Century to the Present Day—List of Films with Negro themes and/or Negro Players

Negroes began to appear in films early in the silent era. A 1902 French production, *Off to Bloomingdale Asylum*, was the first to include a Negro role, and was soon followed by such American examples as *The Wooing and Wedding of a Coon, The Slave*, and the *Rastus* series. The Negro in these films was invariably cast either as an ignorant, superstitious, lazy, dim-witted buffoon or, in the "Uncle Tom" tradition, as a devoted slave who knows his place.

Films of the pre-World War I period which featured Negro characters invariably fell into one or the other of the following categories: the slapstick variety portraying the Negro as clown or fool, or the sentimental melodrama full of laughing, hymn-singing slaves toiling contentedly for their benevolent masters. With very few exceptions, these roles were played not by Negro actors, but by whites in blackface. Perhaps the most noteworthy film of this era was D. W. Griffith's 1915 production, *The Birth of A Nation*, in which the portrayal of the Reconstruction-period Negro as a corrupt, lawless villian invoked a storm of controversy and protest.

With the close of the war, Hollywood began casting actual Negro actors more frequently, though in roles showing no more latitude than before. The Negro servant, bell-hop, or ne'er-do-well was fast becoming an established fixture—a sure-fire device for inciting laughter and, in some cases, a measure of condescension and contempt. By 1922, with D. W. Griffith's *One Exciting Night*, a type had been born: the Negro as a blubbering, superstitious coward whose hair turned white at the approach of even the mildest form of danger. The other genre of Negro roles popular in the 1920's was the cannibalistic savage in jungle pictures about "darkest Africa." Probably the most true-to-life depiction of Negroes in this period was in Hal Roach's "Our Gang" comedies in which black and white children played together naturally, and generally, as equals.

The 1930's, when the sound film came into its own, ushered in the commercial exploitation of the Negro in yet another form: as song-and-dance man. Singers, dancers and jazz musicians from the New

York stage and nightclub circuit appeared in countless Hollywood musicals, usually in all-Negro productions, or in segregated sequences in otherwise all-white films. Integrated jazz groups were never shown. Performers such as Cab Calloway, Louis Armstrong, Lena Horne, and Hazel Scott became box-office names, with the musical serving as a vehicle for the discovery and popularization of much significant Negro talent. At the same time, the myth of the Negro as irrepressible "rhythm man" was being reinforced—a myth which found its most demeaning expression in the grinning, shuffling, eye-rolling antics of Stepin Fetchit, Mantan Moreland and Sleep 'n' Eat, among others. Even Negro films made independently of the major studios by Negro or, on occasion, white producers, followed Hollywood stereotypes of character and situation, although they at least utilized accurate local color motifs. Shoddily produced and acted, they made little effort to alter the already-distorted Negro film image.

The contributions of two directors, Mervyn LeRoy and Fritz Lang, offset the trends of this decade to some extent. In producing films which showed Negroes to possess the qualities and emotions of ordinary human beings, or which dealt with the theme of intolerance, they prepared the way for more understanding treatment and more realistic themes in the years to come. Documentary films of the early 1940's also helped correct many Hollywood stereotypes by showing Negroes at work, pursuing education, or in the armed services.

The new liberalism of the World War II years, with its concern for morale at home and its support of the country's fighting men of all colors, also had a corrective influence on the Negro's film image. In such pictures as *Of Mice and Men* and *Strange Incident* Negroes appeared as dignified American citizens, often as heroic or semi-heroic figures. Fewer films were made glorifying the Old South. The 1940's also saw increasingly vocal protest against Hollywood type-casting by the Negro and the liberal press, and by such groups as the NAACP and the International Film and Radio Guild. Pressure from these sources did much to eliminate offensive dialogue and character roles, and brought such major victories as the abandonment, in 1946, of plans for a new production of *Uncle Tom's Cabin.*

Gradually, since then, the worst racial offenses have begun to disappear from the scene. What once seemed to be an endless procession of scatterbrained maids, shuffle-foot janitors, and crazed savages has now tapered off considerably. Negro actors and actresses have begun to find roles worthy of their talent. In 1939, for example, Hattie McDaniel won an Academy Award for her supporting role as a stereotyped "Mammy" in *Gone With the Wind* whereas, by contrast, Sidney Poitier's 1965 best actor award was for a role (*Lilies of the Field*) which showed a Negro assuming his responsibilities with strength and skill in a natural, amicable relationship with a group of whites dependent on him.

Themes that were taboo well into the 1930's and beyond are now being dealt with more frankly: where once it was daring to examine the color bar with a story about Negroes "passing" for white, nowadays, a number of films have shown interracial love affairs and marriages. Moreover, the contemporary urban, educated Negro—sophisticated in speech, dress, and tastes—is more and more "visible" in both minor and major roles. In movies like *The Cool World,* honest attempts are made to understand the ghetto Negro in relation to his environment. And there have been a number of films, like *Pressure Point,* in which racial attitudes are frankly explored and amplified by allowing the Negro to express *his* ideas. As yet, however, only a handful of films have tried to deal meaningfully with the civil rights struggle across the country, particularly in the South.

Nevertheless, in today's films, one encounters a heightened flurry of activity involving black themes, black performers, and black behind-the-scenes men. Among the most prominent are: Gordon Parks, who wrote, scored, directed, and produced the film based on his autobiographical novel *The Learning Tree;* Melvin Van Peebles who directed *The Night the Sun Came Out;* Ossie Davis who directed the screen adaptation of Chester Himes' celebrated novel *Cotton Comes to Harlem* and Hugh Robertson, a film editor for the Academy award-winning film, *Midnight Cowboy.*

Besides performing in Hollywood films, many black actors are pooling their entrepreneurial talents to create films independently. Among them are Van Peebles himself, and actors Robert Hooks (director of the Negro Ensemble Company), Harry Belafonte, and Raymond St. Jacques.

The following list includes films

in which Negroes have either starred, played feature roles, or made significant contributions:

Off to Bloomingdale Asylum. 1902 (French). Produced by George Méliès. First appearance of Negroes in film. Slapstick comedy.

The Wooing and Wedding of a Coon. 1905. All-Negro. Undisguised mockery of Negro couple.

Fights of a Nation. 1905. Negro depicted as cake-walker, buck-dancer, and razor-thrower.

Godfrey Cambridge (l.) and Melvin Peebles, one of the few black directors to have made his mark in films

The Slave. Biograph, 1909. Directed by D. W. Griffith.

The Sambo Series. 1909-1911. Produced by Sigmund Lubin. All-Negro comedies similar to Rastus series.

The Rastus Series. About 1910. Produced by Sigmund Lubin. Series of all-Negro short comedies. Central character a Negro buffoon of small intelligence.

The Judge's Story. Thanhauser, 1911. A Southern judge moves a jury to leniency for an accused Negro. Probably first film to give a measure of sympathy to Negro character.

The Battle. Biograph, 1911. Directed by D. W. Griffith. The first of Griffith's glorifications of the Old South.

The Dark Romance of a Tobacco Can. Essanay, 1911. Man horrified to find girl he proposes to is Negro.

For Massa's Sake. Pathe, 1911. With Crane Wilbur. Devoted slave tries to sell himself to pay master's gambling debts.

The Debt. 1912. Tragedy of interracial love.

In Slavery Days. Rex, 1913. Directed by Otis Turner. With Robert Z. Leonard, Margarita Fischer, Edna Maison. Wicked octoroon foiled.

The Octoroon. Kalem, 1913. From the play by Dion Boucicault. With Guy Coombes, Marguerite Courtot. The tragedy of whites with Negro blood.

Coon Town Suffragettes. 1914. Produced by Sigmund Lubin. All-Negro. Southern "Mammys" try to keep their no-good husbands out of saloons.

Dark Town Jubilee. 1914. The first attempt to star a Negro, in this case Bert Williams, the well-known New York vaudevillian. Badly received by white audiences.

The Wages of Sin, The Broken Violin, etc. About 1914. Oscar Micheaux, independent producer. Series of all-Negro films.

Uncle Tom's Cabin. World, 1914. Directed by William R. Daly. From the novel by Harriet Beecher Stowe. With Sam Lucas, Irving Cummings, Marie Eline, and a cast of Negro players. The featuring of Negro actor Sam Lucas, rather than a white actor in blackface, created a precedent. This was the third film version of the novel; the first, in 1909, directed by Edwin S. Porter, seriously distorted the abolitionist intent of the book into a sentimental tale about slaves who "know their place." In 1927, Negro actor Charles Gilpin left the filming of a new production over a dispute about the characterization of Uncle Tom.

The Birth of a Nation. Epoch, 1915. Directed by D. W. Griffith. From the novel *The Clansman* by Thomas Dixon. With Mae Marsh, Lillian Gish, Henry B. Walthall, Robert Harron, Wallace Reid, George Seigmann, Walter Long, George Reed, Ralph Lewis, Elmo Lincoln, Elmer Clifton, Donald Crisp, Raoul Walsh, Joseph Henaberry, Eugene Pallette, Bessie Love, Jennie Lee, Howard Gaye, Tom Wilson, Erich von Stroheim, and others. Negroes as corrupt and brutal villains in Reconstruction-period South, with the Ku Klux Klan having a "just" triumph. Film caused storm of indignation in the North, was banned in some cities.

The Nigger. Fox, 1915. From the novel by Edward Sheldon. With William Farnum.

The "Our Gang" Comedies. Produced by Hal Roach. Negro children, including Farina, Stymie Beard, and Buckwheat, playing together with white.

The Greatest Thing in Life. 1918. Directed by D. W. Griffith. Includes episode of a white soldier in World War I kissing his Negro comrade-in-arms as he died. Griffith was accused of planting the scene to appease critics of his racially biased *Birth of a Nation*.

Ten Nights in a Bar-Room. Coloured Players Film Corporation, about 1920. All-Negro, with Charles Gilpin.

One Exciting Night. 1922. Directed by D. W. Griffith. First example of Negro as contemptible comic relief.

Broken Chains. 1924. Shows Negro as a murderous agitator.

The Florian Slappey Series. About 1925-1926. Written and produced by Octavus Roy Cohen, a Negro. All-Negro, "blackface" humor.

Melancholy Dame. 1929. Written and directed by Octavus Roy Cohen. All-

The "Our Gang" comedies depicted the mischievous antics of both Negro and white children.
(BETTMANN ARCHIVE)

Negro with Evelyn Preer, Eddie Thompson, Spencer Williams.

Hearts in Dixie. Fox. 1929. Directed by Paul Sloane. The first of Hollywood's all-Negro films, with Clarence Muse, Stepin Fetchit, Mildred Washington in stereotyped roles.

Hallelujah. M. G. M., 1929. Directed by King Vidor. From the novel by Wanda Tuchock. All-Negro, with Daniel Haynes, Nina Mae McKinney, Victoria Spivey, William Fountain, Harry Gray, Fannie Belle de Knight, Everett McGarritty. Usual stereotypes, though not as extreme as in *Hearts in Dixie*. Had very favorable press.

East of Borneo. Universal, 1932. Directed by George Melford. With Charles Bickford, Rose Hobart, Lupita Tovar, Noble Johnson. Typical Hollywood jungle film, in which Negro players were featured mostly as cannibals, head-hunters, and repulsive savages.

The Black King. Southland, 1932. Directed by Bud Pollard. From the story by Donald Heywood. With Vivian Baber, Harry Gray, Knolly Mitchell, Mary Jane Watkins. One of the first big independent all-Negro film productions.

Arrowsmith. 1932. Directed by John Ford. With Ronald Coleman, Clarence Brooks. Negro doctor given same stature as white doctor.

I Am a Fugitive from a Chain Gang. Warners, 1932. Directed by Mervyn LeRoy. With Paul Muni, Everett Brown. Sympathetic, realistic portrayal of Negro prisoner.

The Emperor Jones. Krimsky-Cochran, 1933. Directed by Dudley Murphy, under supervision of William C. DeMille. From the play by Eugene O'Neill. With Paul Robeson, Dudley Diggs, Frank Wilson, Rex Ingram, George Stamper, Fredi Washington, Ruby Elzy, Brandon Evans, Taylor Gordon. Significant in that it gave a Negro actor a leading part in a film also featuring whites. Dealt seriously with a Negro theme.

Hypnotized. World Wide, 1933. Directed by Mack Sennett. With George Moran, Charlie Mack, Ernest Torrence, Wallace Ford, Maria Alba. Typical of comedies featuring well-known "black-face" minstrels.

The Cabin in the Cotton. Warners, 1933. Directed by Michael Curtiz. From the novel by Henry Kroll. With Richard Barthelmess, Bette Davis, Dorothy Jordan, Henry B. Walthall, Clarence Muse, "Snowflake."

Judge Priest. Fox, 1935. Directed by John Ford. With Will Rogers, Tom Brown, Anita Louise, Henry B. Walthall, Rochelle Hudson, Hattie McDaniel, Stepin Fetchit.

Helldorado. Fox, 1935. Directed by James Cruze. With Richard Arlen, Madge Evans, Ralph Bellamy, James Gleason, Henry B. Walthall, Stepin Fetchit. Negro frightened by a "ghost," the butt of the humor.

Imitation of Life. Universal, 1935. Directed by John M. Stahl. From the novel by Fannie Hurst. With Claudette Colbert, Warren William, Ned Sparks, Louise Beavers, Fredi Washington, Rochelle Hudson, Sebie Hendricks, Dorothy Black, Alan Hale, Hazel Washington. A light-skinned Negro girl makes a desperate bid to pass as white. The film dealt seriously with this problem, but also had a "Mammy" role more in the foreground.

So Red the Rose. Paramount, 1935. Directed by King Vidor. With Margaret Sullivan, Walter Connolly, Randolph Scott, Daniel Haynes, Clarence Muse. Depicts the revolt against slavery as the work of a few Negro opportunists misleading the contented masses.

Show Boat. Universal, 1936. Directed by James Whale. From the operetta by Edna Ferber and Jerome Kern. With Irene Dunne, Paul Robeson, Allan Jones, Charles Winninger, Helen Morgan, Queenie Smith, Helen Westly, Donald Cook, Hattie McDaniel, Clarence Muse.

The Littlest Rebel. Twentieth-Century Fox, 1936. Directed by David Butler. With Shirley Temple, John Boles, Jack Holt, Bill Robinson, Karen Morley, Quinn Williams, Willie Best, Frank McGlynn Sr., Hannah Washington. Typical Hollywood Civil War picture, totally sympathetic to the South and Southerners.

The Singing Kid. Warners, 1936. Directed by William Keighley. With Al Jolson, Sybil Jason, Allen Jenkins, Lyle Talbot, Wini Shaw, Edward Everett Horton, Cab Calloway. Negro shown in natural, friendly relationship with white.

Spirit of Youth. Independent, 1937. With Joe Louis, Clarence Muse. Poor Negro fights his way to the top as a boxer.

The Black Legion. Warners, 1937. Directed by Archie Mays. With Humphrey Bogart, Dick Foran, Erin O'Brien Moore, Ann Sheridan, Robert Barrat, Joseph Sawyer, Paul Harvey, Henry Brandon, John Litel. An attack on the Ku Klux Klan.

The Green Pastures. Warners, 1937. Directed by William Keighley and Marc Connelly. All-Negro with Rex Ingram, Oscar Polk, Eddie Anderson, Frank Wilson, Ernest Whitman, William Cumby, Edna Mae Harris, Al Stokes, David Bethea, George Reed, Clinton Rosemond. Interprets the Negro idea of heaven. Did little to correct stereotypes, but gave many Negro actors chances for important roles.

Pennies from Heaven. Columbia, 1937. Directed by Norman McLeod. With Bing Crosby, Madge Evans, Edith Fellowes, Donald Meek, John Gallaudet, Louis Armstrong, Charles Wilson. Musical.

They Won't Forget. Warners, 1937. Directed by Mervyn LeRoy. Adapted from the Graham Greene novel, *Deep in the Deep South*. With Claude Rains, Allyn Joslyn, Gloria Dickson, Edward Norris, Clinton Rosemond. Indictment of Southern values, including treatment of Negro.

Mystery in Swing. Goldberg, independent, 1938. Produced and directed by Arthur Dreifuss. All-Negro with Monte Howley, Marguerite Whitten, Bob Webb, Sybil Lewis, Josephine Edwards, F. E. Miller, Haley Harding, Jess Lee Brooks. Murder of a famous jazz bandleader.

One Mile from Heaven. Twentieth-Century Fox, 1938. Directed by Allan Dwan. With Claire Trevor, Sally Blane, Douglas Fowley, Fredi Washington, Bill Robinson, Eddie Anderson. Fredi Washington as Negro foster-mother of a white child.

Mr. Creeps. Toddy Pictures, 1938. All-Negro, with Mantan Moreland, F. E. Miller. Comedy.

The Adventures of Huckleberry Finn. M. G. M., 1939 (earlier production, 1932). Directed by Richard Thorpe. From the novel by Mark Twain. With Mickey Rooney, Walter Connolly, William Frawley, Rex Ingram, Lynne Carver, Elizabeth Risdon, Victor Kilian, Minor Watson, Clara Blandick.

Harlem on the Prairie. Buell, 1939. Claimed as "the first independent all-Negro Western film."

Gone with the Wind. Selznick, 1939. Directed by Victor Fleming. From the novel by Margaret Mitchell. With Vivien Leigh, Clark Gable, Leslie Howard, Olivia de Haviland, Thomas Mitchell, Evelyn Keyes, Barbara O'Neill, Hattie McDaniel, Oscar Polk, Adrian Morris, Ben Carter, Eddie "Rochester" Anderson. Negro depicted in "Mammy" and "Uncle Tom" tradition. Hattie McDaniel won an Academy Award for best supporting actress.

Man About Town. Paramount, 1939. Directed by Mark Sandrich. With Jack Benny, Dorothy Lamour, Eddie "Rochester" Anderson, Binnie Barnes, Edward Arnold, Monty Woolley. Typical Benny-"Rochester" comedy of 1939-1944 period.

Bronze Venus. Toddy Pictures, 1940. All-Negro, with Lena Horne, Ralph Cooper. The life of a great musical star.

Chasing Trouble. Monogram, 1940. Directed by Howard Bretherton. From a screenplay by Mary McCarthy. With Frankie Darro, Mantan Moreland, Marjorie Reynolds, Milburn Stone, Cheryl Walker. White boy and Negro friend chase crooks together.

One Tenth of Our Nation. American Film Centre, 1940. Directed by Henwar Rodakiewiecz. Documentary showing inadequate conditions of education among Negroes in the South.

Of Mice and Men. Hal Roach, 1940. Directed by Lewis Milestone. From the play by John Steinbeck. With Burgess Meredith, Lon Chaney, Betty Field, Charles Bickford, Leigh Whipper. Dignified portrayal of Negro ranch worker.

Maryland. Twentieth-Century Fox, 1940. Directed by Henry King. With Walter Brennan, Fay Bainter, Brenda Joyce, John Payne, Charlie Ruggles, Hattie McDaniel, Marjorie Weaver, Sydney Blackmer, Clarence Muse, George Reed, Ben Carter, Ernest Whitman, Zack Williams, Thaddeus Jones, Clinton Rosemond, Jesse Graves. Romance of the South with several Negro players featured prominently as comic relief.

Murder on Lenox Avenue. Goldberg, independent, 1941. Directed by Arthur Dreifuss. All-Negro, with Mamie Smith, Alex Lovejoy, Dene Larry, Norman Astwood, Gus Smith, Edna Mae Harris, Alberta Perkins, George Williams.

A Place to Live. Philadelphia Housing Association, 1941. Directed by Irving Lerner. Documentary on housing conditions among Negroes and whites in Philadelphia.

Birth of the Blues. Paramount, 1941. Directed by Victor Scheitzinger. With Bing Crosby, Mary Martin, Brian Donlevy, Eddie "Rochester" Anderson, J. Carrol Naish, Warren Hymer, Horace MacMahon, Ruby Elzy.

Affectionately Yours. Warners, 1941. Directed by Lloyd Bacon. With Merle Oberon, Dennis Morgan, Rita Hayworth, Ralph Bellamy, George Tobias, James Gleason, Hattie McDaniel, Butterfly McQueen. Goodnatured "Mammy" types.

In This Our Life. Warners, 1942. Directed by John Huston. From the novel by Ellen Glasgow. With Bette Davis, Olivia de Havilland, George Brent, Dennis Morgan, Charles Coburn, Frank Craven, Billie Burke, Lee Patrick, Hattie McDaniel, Ernest Anderson. Dignified portrayal of young Negro studying to be lawyer, victimized by Southern prejudice and injustice. Placed on Honor Roll of Race Relations for 1942.

Henry Brown, Farmer. U. S. Dept. of Agriculture, 1942. Directed by Roger

Barlow. Narration by Canada Lee. Documentary on the life of a Negro farmer in Alabama.

Syncopation. R. K. O. Radio, 1942. Directed by William Dieterle. With Adolphe Menjou, Jackie Cooper, Bonita Granville, George Bancroft, Ted North, Todd Duncan. Negro trumpet player teaches jazz to white girl. Sympathetic handling of race relations.

Panama Hattie. M. G. M., 1943. Directed by Norman Z. McLeod. Based on the play by Herbert Fields and B. G. de Sylva. With Ann Sothern, Red Skelton, Rags Ragland, Ben Blue, Marsha Hunt, Virginia O'Brien, Carl Esmond, the Berry Brothers, Nyas, James and Warren, Lena Horne. Lena Horne's first major screen role.

Stormy Weather. Twentieth-Century Fox, 1943. Directed by Andrew Stone. With Lena Horne, Bill Robinson, Cab Calloway, Katherine Dunham, Harold and Fayard Nicholas, Ada Brown, Dooley Wilson, Babe Wallace, Ernest Whitman, Zuttie Singleton, F. E. Miller, Nicodemus Stewart. All-Negro musical.

Dixie. Paramount, 1943. Directed by Edward Sutherland. With Bing Crosby, Dorothy Lamour, Billy de Wolfe, Marjorie Reynolds, Lynne Overman, Raymond Walburn, Eddie Foy, Jr. Biography of Daniel Emmett, the first blackface minstrel and composer of "Dixie."

Tales of Manhattan. Twentieth-Century Fox, 1943. Directed by Julian Duvivier. With Charles Boyer, Rita Hayworth, Ginger Rogers, Henry Fonda, Charles Laughton, Edward G. Robinson, Paul Robeson, Eddie "Rochester" Anderson, Ethel Waters, Clarence Muse. Paul Robeson, enticed back from his self-imposed exile in Britain to make this film, was so disturbed by his "darky" role he declared he would never again accept such a part in a Hollywood film.

Cabin in the Sky. M. G. M., 1943. Directed by Vincente Minnelli. All-Negro, with Lena Horne, Eddie "Rochester" Anderson, Ethel Waters, Rex Ingram, Kenneth Spencer, Ernest Whitman, Mantan Moreland, Louis Armstrong, Oscar Polk, "Buck and Bubbles," Duke Ellington, John Sublett, Willie Best. Musical fantasy. Brought prominence to Lena Horne and to Katherine Dunham ballet.

Strange Incident. Twentieth-Century Fox, 1943. Directed by William Wellman. From the novel *The Ox Bow Incident*, by Walter V. T. Clark. With Henry Fonda, Dana Andrews, Anthony Quinn, and Leigh Whipper as Negro preacher who makes dignified, eloquent plea against lynching of white rustlers.

Bataan. M. G. M., 1943. Directed by Tay Garnett. With Robert Taylor, George Murphy, Thomas Mitchell, Lee Bowman, and Kenneth Spencer as Negro G. I. Won special award from NAACP.

Sahara. Columbia, 1944. Directed by Zoltan Korda. With Humphrey Bogart, Rex Ingram. Negro soldier in heroic role.

Carnival in Rhythm. Warners, 1944. A short film devoted to Katherine Dunham and her Negro ballet.

Lifeboat. Twentieth-Century Fox. 1944. Directed by Alfred Hitchcock. With Tallulah Bankhead, John Hodiak, Henry Hull, Walter Slezak, Canada Lee, Hume Cronyn, Mary Anderson, Heather Angel. Survivors in the lifeboat include an intelligent, heroic Negro.

Dr. George Washington Carver. M. G.-M., 1945. With Clinton Rosemond. Documentary based on the life and work of the Negro scientist.

The House I Live In. With Frank Sinatra. A plea for racial tolerance; won special Academy Award.

Jammin' the Blues. Warners, 1945. Directed and photographed by Gjon Mili. Semi-documentary of a "jam session" in a Negro club.

We've Come a Long, Long Way. "Negro Marches On," 1945. Produced and directed by Jack Goldberg. Narration by Elder Michaux. A documentary cavalcade of the Negro race.

Brewster's Millions. Edward Small, 1946. Directed by Alan Dwan. From the novel by George B. McCutcheon. With Dennis O'Keefe, Helen Walker, Eddie "Rochester" Anderson, June Havoc, Gail Patrick, Mischa Auer, Joseph Sawyer, John Litel, Herbert Dudley, Neil Hamilton. Film was banned in Memphis because Negro "acted too snappy and socialized too much with whites."

Ziegfeld Follies. M. G. M., 1946. Directed by Vincente Minnelli. With William Powell, Virginia O'Brien, Lucille Ball, Esther Williams, James Melton, Marion Bell, Victor Moore, Fred Astaire, Lucille

Bremer, Keenan Wynn, Lena Horne, Red Skelton, Judy Garland, Gene Kelly, Kathryn Grayson, Edward Arnold, Cyd Charisse, Robert Lewis, Avon Long.

Saratoga Trunk. Warners, 1946. Directed by Sam Wood. From the novel by Edna Ferber. With Ingrid Bergman, Gary Cooper, Flora Robson. In a psychological throwback to earlier days, Flora Robson played an important role in "blackface."

Mildred Pierce. Warners, 1946. Directed by Michael Curtiz. Based on the novel by James M. Cain. With Joan Crawford, Jack Carson, Zachary Scott, Eve Arden, Bruce Bennett, Ann Blyth, Lee Patrick. Butterfly McQueen, Moroni Olsen, Charles Trowbridge, Chester Clute. Butterfly McQueen in one of the "stupid maid" parts she subsequently announced she would no longer accept.

The Brotherhood of Man. Brandon, 1946. A color cartoon based on *The Races of Mankind by* Ruth Benedict and Gene Weltfish. Anti-prejudice message.

Till the End of Time. R. K. O. Radio, 1946. Directed by Edward Dmytryk. With Dorothy McGuire, Robert Mitchum, Guy Madison, Bill Williams, Tom Tully, Jean Porter, William Gargan. Sub-plot in which whites defend Negro against Fascist talk.

Song of the South. R. K. O. Radio-Disney, 1947. Produced by Walt Disney. Based on the "Uncle Remus" stories. With Ruth Warrick, James Baskett, Lucille Watson, Hattie McDaniel, Luana Patten, Bobby Driscoll. NAACP and IFRG tried to stop the filming because of stereotyped character of Uncle Remus.

Uncle Tom's Cabana. M. G. M., 1947. Produced by Fred Quimby. Typical comedy short film emphasizing the stereotype.

What a Guy. Toddy Pictures, 1947. All-Negro, with Ruby Dee.

The Burning Cross. Somerset-Screen Guild, 1947. Directed by Walter Colmes. With Hank Daniels, Virginia Patton, Joel Fluellyn, Dick Rich, Raymond Bond, Matt Willis. Ku Klux Klan exposé.

The Jackie Robinson Story. 1948. With Jackie Robinson, Ruby Dee, Joel Fluellyn, Louise Beavers. The story of Robinson's breakthrough to the major leagues and his early playing career.

Gangsters on the Loose. Toddy Pictures, 1948. All-Negro with Ralph Cooper, Teresa Thompson. Gangster picture about a double-crosser.

The Betrayal. Released by Astor Pictures, 1948. Produced by Oscar Micheaux. All-Negro cast in this story about a young Negro farmer in South Dakota who refuses the love of a woman he believes is white—only to marry her after discovering she is Negro.

Lost Boundaries. 1949. With Bill Greaves, Canada Lee, Beatrice Pearson. Concerns a New Hampshire physician "passing" for white, and his children who are unaware of their Negro blood.

Home of the Brave. 1949. With James Edwards as a Negro soldier torn by discrimination and hatred.

Pinky. 1949. With Ethel Waters, Jeanne Crain, Fred O'Neal, Kenny Washington, Nina Mae McKinney. A fair-skinned Negro girl refuses marriage with a white doctor.

The Quiet One. 1949. With Estelle Evans, Sadie Stockton, Donald Thompson. The juvenile delinquency problem.

Intruder in the Dust 1949. From the story by William Faulkner. With Juano Hernandez. A Negro is accused of murdering a white man.

Miracle in Harlem. 1949. Directed by Jack Kemp. Original screenplay and story by Vincent Valentini. All-Negro cast in this story about "murder and mayhem" in Harlem.

No Way Out. 20th-Century Fox, 1950. Produced by Darryl F. Zanuck. Sidney Poitier as a young doctor who fights racial animosity. Also stars Bobby Darin.

Stars in My Crown. 1950. Produced by William H. Wright for MGM. Juano Hernandez as an aged Negro in this film about a parson in a Southern town after the Civil War.

No Way Out. 1950. With Sidney Poitier, Linda Darnell, Mildred Joanne Smith, Fred O'Neal, Dots Johnson, Maude Simmons, Ruby Dee, Ossie Davis. The first Negro intern at a white hospital finds he must battle prejudice.

Show Boat. 1951. "Ole Man River" is sung by William Warfield in this revival

Jeanne Crain (right) and Ethel Waters in the 20-Century Fox film, "Pinky" (1949).

Juano Hernandez (center foreground) in a scene from "Intruder in the Dust" (1949).

of the 1927 stage production and the 1929 movie.

Bright Victory. 1951. With James Edwards. Concerns prejudice in a hospital for the blind once the white patients discover a blind Negro soldier is among them.

Native Son. 1951. With Richard Wright, Gloria Madison, Willa Pearl Curtiss. The movie version of Richard Wright's novel.

The Breaking Point. 1951. With Juano Hernandez. A white-Negro friendship.

The Well. 1951. With Maidie Norman, Ernest Anderson, Christine Larson, Bill Walker, Alfred Grant, Benjamin Hamilton. Rescue operations for a Negro child trapped in a mine shaft.

Tarzan's Perils. 1951. A Tarzan adventure film, with Dorothy Dandridge in the lead as an African princess.

Lydia Bailey. 1951 With Ken Renard, Juanita Moore, William Marshall. Story of Toussaint L'Ouverture, liberator of Haiti.

To Live Together. 1951. A documentary produced by B'nai B'rith. Depicts an interracial camp for Chicago children.

The Harlem Globetrotters. Columbia, 1951. With Thomas Gomez, Dorothy Dandridge, Bill Walker, Harlem Globetrotters team. Fiction plot, interspersed with Globetrotter games.

Member of the Wedding. Paramount, 1951. Stars Ethel Waters opposite Julie Harris in the screen version of Carson McCullers' play. Miss Waters gives a powerful portrayal of a cook who befriends a troubled young girl.

The Medium. 1951. Produced by Walter Lowenthal. Directed by Gian-Carlo Menotti, and based upon his play of the same name about a "phony" spiritualist. Leo Coleman, a Negro, plays the part of Toby, a mute gypsy boy.

The Steel Helmet. Lippert Pictures, 1951. Produced by Samuel Fuller. Features James Edwards in a low-budget picture about the adventures of an American infantry patrol detailed to occupy a Korean temple and set up an observation post. Edwards plays the part of a Negro medic.

Cry the Beloved Country. United Artists, 1952. Sidney Poitier along with Canada Lee in this screen version of Alan Paton's novel about South Africa.

Red Ball Express. Universal, 1952. Sidney Poitier as a member of Korea's famed trucking outfit.

Bright Road. MGM, 1953. Harry Belafonte, Dorothy Dandridge, Philip Hepburn in this story about a small, troubled boy and his schoolmaster.

The Joe Louis Story. United Artists, 1953. Stars Hilda Simms, Coley Wallace and others in a film based on the famous boxer's life.

Go Man, Go. United Artists, 1954. Sidney Poitier as a member of the Harlem Globetrotters, along with Dane Clark and actual players on the team.

New Faces: 20th-Century Fox, 1954. Eartha Kitt along with June Carroll, Ronny Graham and others in this screen version of the Broadway musical.

The Glenn Miller Story. Universal, 1955. Produced by Aaron Rosenberg. Louis Armstrong in this film biography of the famous bandleader.

Trial. MGM, 1955. Produced by Charles Schnee; directed by Mark Robson. Based on the novel by Don Mankiewicz, the screen version concerns the defense of a Mexican who is tried on a murder charge in a California town. Juano Hernandez is the judge.

Blackboard Jungle. MGM, 1956. Produced by Pancho S. Berman. Featuring Sidney Poitier in a film dealing with slum schools and juvenile delinquency.

Canada Lee (left) in the film version of the Alan Paton novel on South Africa, Cry the Beloved Country *(1952).*

Goodbye, My Lady. Warner Brothers, 1956. Sidney Poitier in a supporting role as a young farmer who is involved in the problems confronting sharecroppers in the Louisiana swamp country. Brandon De-Wilde and Phil Harris are also featured.

Safari. Columbia, 1956. Produced by Adrian D. Worker. Features Earl Cameron, Orlando Martins and Cy Grant in a story about hunting down the Mau Mau and life in Africa.

That Certain Feeling. Paramount, 1956. Produced and directed by Messrs. Norman Panama, Melvin Frank, I. A. L. Diamond and William Altman. Based on the play *The King of Hearts* by Jean Kerr. Features Pearl Bailey as a lyrical maid (she sings two numbers) in a comedy farce.

Edge of the City. United Artists, 1957. Sidney Poitier along with John Cassavetes and Jack Warden in a story about racial bigotry along the waterfront.

Island in the Sun. 1957. Produced by Darryl F. Zanuck. Harry Belafonte stars opposite Joan Fontaine in this story of interracial romance written by Alec Waugh.

Meet Me in Las Vegas. MGM, 1957. Produced by Joe Pasternak. Lena Horne is featured in this musical along with a host of other stars.

Something of Value. MGM, 1957. Stars Sidney Poitier in the screen adaptation of the Robert Ruark novel about the Mau Mau revolt in Kenya.

The Benny Goodman Story. Universal, 1957. Produced by Aaron Rosenberg. Stars Sammy Davis, Jr., Lionel Hampton, and Teddy Wilson in the life story of the famous jazzman.

The Defiant Ones. United Artists, 1957. Produced by Stanley Kramer. Involves the trials of two escaped convicts—one white, the other Negro. Sidney Poitier opposite Tony Curtis.

Anna Lucasta. United Artists, 1958. Produced by Sidney Harmon. Eartha Kitt, Sammy Davis, Jr., Frederick O'Neal, Rex Ingram, Henry Morgan star in this film about the problems of a young woman who has left home to become a streetwalker.

St. Louis Blues. Paramount, 1958. Produced by Robert Smith. All-Negro cast with Nat Cole, Eartha Kitt, Pearl Bailey, Cab Calloway, Ella Fitzgerald, Mahalia Jackson, Juano Hernandez, and Billy Preston in the life and times of W. C. Handy.

The Decks Ran Red. 1958. Dorothy Dandridge opposite Curt Jurgens in a film which deals with life aboard a slave ship.

The March of the Hawk. Universal-International, 1958. Sidney Poitier opposite Eartha Kitt in a story about the struggle for equality in Africa. Poitier plays a peaceful man at odds with his brother, the "hawk" who is dedicated to violence and war.

Black Orpheus. A Lopert Films release, 1959. Produced by Sacha Gordine. All-Negro cast in this story of a young couple who fall suddenly and rapturously in love, only to be separated by death as in the ancient Greek legend.

Night of the Quarter Moon. MGM, 1959. Produced by Albert Zugsmith. Stars Nat Cole, James Edwards, Marguerite Belafonte and Billy Daniels in a story of interracial love.

Odds Against Tomorrow. United Artists, 1959. Produced by Robert Wise. Stars Harry Belafonte, Carmen de Lavallade, along with Robert Ryan, Shelley Winters and Ed Begley. Story of the planning and execution of a crime, with three men (one a Negro). Musical score written by John Lewis. Screenplay by John O. Killens.

Porgy and Bess. Columbia, 1959. Produced by Samuel Goldwyn; directed by Otto Preminger. Based on the play by Dubose and Dorothy Heyward. Stars Sidney Poitier, Dorothy Dandridge, Sammy Davis, Jr., Pearl Bailey, and others.

Sapphire. J. Arthur Rank, 1959. Produced by Michael Ralph; directed by Basil Dearden. Featuring Earl Cameron, Gordon Heath, Harry Baird, Nigel Patrick, Yvonne Mitchell, Michael Craig and Paul Massie in a mystery with racial overtones. (The murdered girl turns out to be a Negro.)

Tamango. Hal Roach Release, 1959. Produced by Rene G. Vauttoux, Roland

Gerard, Sig Shore, and Joe Harris. Based on the novel by Prosper Merimée, with Dorothy Dandridge, Curt Jurgens, Jean Servais and Alex Cressah. Concerns the slave trade, and what happens on a slaver bound from Africa to Cuba.

The Sound and the Fury. 1959. Produced by Jerry Wald. Features Ethel Waters along with Margaret Leighton, Joanne Woodward, Yul Brynner and Jack Warden in the film version of the Faulkner novel. Miss Waters is Dilsey, the family cook.

The World, the Flesh and the Devil. 1959. Stars Harry Belafonte, along with Inger Stevens and Mel Ferrer. An interracial theme in a story which takes place at the end of the world.

All the Young Men. Columbia, 1960. Sidney Poitier, along with Alan Ladd and Mort Sahl, in this story about what happens to a small detachment of marines in Korea whose command is taken over by a Negro.

Let No Man Write My Epitaph. Columbia, 1960. Produced by Boris D. Kaplan. Bernie Hamilton appears in this film version of Willard Motley's novel.

Sergeant Rutledge. Warner Brothers, 1960. Produced and directed by John Ford. Stars Woody Strode in a tale of the Old West set in Arizona after the Civil War. The sergeant (Strode) is accused of violating and strangling a white girl, and of murdering her father, his commanding officer. Also features Jeffrey Hunter, Constance Towers and Billie Burke.

Shadows. 1960. Directed by John Cassavetes. Focuses on the rootlessness of the urban Negro in Greenwich Village.

Take a Giant Step. United Artists, 1960. Produced by Julius J. Epstein. Stars Johnny Nash, Ruby Dee, Frederick O'-Neal, Beah Richards in the screen version of Louis Peterson's play about a young man growing up.

The Adventures of Huckleberry Finn. MGM, 1960. Produced by Samuel Goldwyn, Jr. Archie Moore plays "Jim" in this modern version of the Mark Twain novel.

The Crowning Experience. Directed, produced and presented by Moral Rearmament, 1960. All-Negro cast in the screen version of the life of Mary McLeod Bethune.

A Raisin in the Sun. Columbia, 1961. Sidney Poitier, Claudia McNeil, Diana Sands in this film based on Lorraine Hansberry's award-winning play about an urban Negro family.

Biography of a Rookie. Wolper-Sterling Prod., 1961. Narrator, Mike Wallace. Story of the rise of Dodger baseball player Willie Davis to the major leagues.

Guns of the Trees. 1961. Produced by Jonas Mekas. This film juxtaposes the lives of two married couples, one white, the other Negro.

Paris Blues. United Artists, 1961. Sidney Poitier, Paul Newman, Joanne Woodward, Diahann Carroll in this film about two expatriate jazzmen living in Paris, and their romantic adventures with two American girls on the loose.

The Intruder. 1961. Produced by Roger Gorman. Based on a novel by Charles Beaumont, this film concerns an anti-integrationist who goes to a small Southern town to arouse the townspeople against integration in the local schools.

The Young One. 1961. Produced by George P. Werber. Stars Bernie Hamilton and Zachary Scott. A Negro (Hamilton) escapes to an isolated island over which Scott serves as a kind of warden.

A Taste of Honey. Continental Pictures, 1962. Produced by Tony Richardson. Features Paul Danquah as the Negro sailor who gets involved with a young white girl. Also seen are Dora Bryan and Rita Tushingham.

Carmen Jones. 20th-Century Fox, 1962. Produced and directed by Otto Preminger. Dorothy Dandridge, Harry Belafonte, Olga James, Pearl Bailey and Diahann Carroll in this revised version of Bizet's opera.

Oceans 11. 1962. Produced by Frank Sinatra. The famous "clan" with Sammy Davis, Jr. in a prominent role as a member of a daring gang that plans to hold up Las Vegas nightspots.

Pressure Point. United Artists, 1962. Sidney Poitier cast as a social worker who attempts to rehabilitate wrongdoer Bobby Darin.

The Connection. 1962. Vivid screen portrayal of Negroes in the narcotics underworld. Based on Jack Gelber's play.

An Affair of the Skin. 1963. Produced by Ben Maddow. Diana Sands as a Negro heroine in Greenwich Village. Featuring Viveca Lindfors, Kevin McCarthy.

Convicts 4. Allied Artists, 1963. Produced by A. Ronald Lubin. Sammy Davis, Jr. along with Richard Conte in a prominent role as a convict who contemplates escape.

Gone Are the Days. 1963. Directed by Nicholas Webster. Based on the play *Purlie Victorious* by Ossie Davis.

Sergeants 3. United Artists, 1963. Produced by Frank Sinatra. Stars Sammy Davis, Jr., along with Sinatra and Peter Lawford, as members of a U.S. Cavalry unit which fights a number of frontier battles.

The Cool World. 1963. Produced by Shirley Clarke. Based on Warren Miller's novel. An important film document about Negro life in Harlem.

The Greenwich Village Story. 1963. Produced by Jack O'Connell. Features Negroes as background presences in party sequences, street and restaurant scenes and, in general, as part of the Village milieu.

To Kill a Mockingbird. Universal, 1963. Produced by Alan J. Pakula; directed by Robert Mulligan. Based on Harper Lee's best-selling novel of 1960, this film has Brock Peters and Estelle Evans in prominent roles. The story concerns the defense of a Negro on trial for allegedly raping a white girl.

Black Like Me. 1964. Directed by Carl Lerner. Based on the novel of the same title by John Howard Griffin. A white man (James Whitmore) passes for Negro.

Free, White and 21. American International, 1964. Directed by Larry Buchanan; stars Frederick O'Neal. Carefree, wild, abandoned whites and their world of tinsel and gold.

Johnny Cool. United Artists, 1964. Producer-director William Asher. Based on the novel *The Kingdom of Johnny Cool* by John McPartland. Sammy Davis, Jr. in the role of "Educated," a sophisticated "hanger-on" in the underworld's gambling casinos. Plot turns on underworld life and intra-gang rivalry.

Lilies of the Field. United Artists, 1964. Sidney Poitier as a traveling vagabond who befriends a group of nuns and wins their friendship and understanding.

Living Between Two Worlds. 1964. Directed by Robert Johnson. Deals with a mother-son conflict within a Negro family in Los Angeles.

Nothing But A Man. 1964. Produced by Michael Roemer. The award-winning story of a Negro laborer and his romance. Stars Ivan Dixon and Abbey Lincoln.

One Potato, Two Potato. 1964. Directed by Larry Peerce. A love affair involving a Negro man and a white divorcee. The Negro is played by Bernie Hamilton.

The Long Ships. Columbia, 1964. Sidney Poitier as a powerful sultan in a costume drama. Also features Richard Widmark.

The Streets of Greenwood or Ivanhoe Donaldson. 1964. Directed by Harold Becher. A feature-length documentary illustrating the civil rights struggle in the U.S.

Cat Ballou. Columbia, 1965. Produced by Harold Hecht. Nat Cole is featured as a traveling minstrel.

Major Dundee. Columbia, 1965. Produced by Jerry Bresher. Brock Peters is featured as a member of the U.S. Cavalry.

None But the Brave. Warner Brothers, 1965. Produced and directed by Frank Sinatra. Rafer Johnson plays an Army officer on patrol in the South Pacific.

Synanon. Columbia, 1965. Produced and directed by Richard Quine. Features Eartha Kitt, Bernie Hamilton, Chuck Connors, Stella Stevens and Edmund O'Brien. The rehabilitation of drug addicts through the now-famous "synanon" method.

The Carpetbaggers. Paramount, 1965. Produced by Joseph E. Levine; based on the novel by Harold Robbins. Featuring Archie Moore in the role of Jedediah.

The Greatest Story Ever Told. 1965. The story of the ministry of Christ. Sidney

Poitier as the Ethiopian who is converted to Christianity.

The Hill. 1965. Produced by Sidney Lumet. Features Ossie Davis as a West Indian soldier-prisoner known as Jacko King. Based on the play by Ray Rigby about a British detention camp in North Africa during World War II.

The New Interns. Columbia, 1965. Ena Hartman in an important role as a nurse.

The Pawnbroker. Landau, 1965. Produced by Worthington Miner. This film with Brock Peters, Juano Hernandez and Rod Steiger depicts life in Harlem. One of the earliest films for which a Negro, Quincy Jones, wrote the musical score.

A Man Called Adam. 1966. Produced by Sammy Davis, Jr. Stars Sammy Davis, Jr., along with Cicely Tyson, Ossie Davis and Louis Armstrong in the story of a problem-ridden musician.

Blues for Lovers. 20th-Century Fox, 1966. Produced by Alexander Salkind. Features Ray Charles along with his orchestra and singers in a story about a small boy's need for understanding.

Booker T. Washington. Encyclopedia Britannica Films, 1966. Collaborator: John Hope Franklin. Tells the dramatic story of Washington's life and career.

Duel at Diablo. 1966. Sidney Poitier plays a feared gunslinger in this Western.

Hurry Sundown. 1966. Produced by Otto Preminger. Stars Diahann Carroll, Robert Hooks, Rex Ingram in a movie based on the best-selling novel.

Our Man Flint. 20th-Century Fox, 1966. Ena Hartman has a featured role as bigwig's (Lee J. Cobb) secretary.

Patch of Blue. MGM, 1966. Produced by Pancho S. Berman. A moving story about a blind girl befriended by a young Negro. Stars Sidney Poitier, Elizabeth Hartman, Shelley Winters, Ivan Dixon, Wallace Ford.

Rio Conchos. 20th-Century Fox, 1966. Produced by David Weisbart. Ex-football star Jim Brown, now an actor, as U.S. Cavalry Sergeant Ben Franklin, one of four men out to recover stolen rifles.

The Appaloosa. Universal, 1966. Frank Silvera in this modern Western starring Marlon Brando.

The Cincinnati Kid. MGM, 1966. Produced by Martin Ransohoff. Cab Calloway in a prominent role as a traveling card shark in a film about top-flight poker players.

The Girl Nobody Knew. Universal Studios, 1966. Ena Hartman is cast as a sophisticated New Yorker who moves in top social circles.

The Slender Thread. Paramount, 1966. Sidney Poitier opposite Anne Bancroft as the psychiatrist who saves her life.

The Bedford Incident. 1966. Sidney Poitier along with Richard Widmark in a story about life on a U.S. warship.

Dutchman. 1967. Produced by Gene Persson. Based on the off-Broadway play by Leroi Jones. Starring Shirley Knight and Al Freeman, Jr.

In the Heat of the Night. Mirisch Corporation. 1967. Director Norman Jewison presents a drama of racial hate and prejudice fictionally set in an ugly little Mississippi town. The stars Rod Steiger and Sidney Poitier (Virgil Tibbs) are well-realized characters. Quincy Jones composed the music and Ray Charles sang the title song.

Now Is the Time. 1967. Carousel Films. 36 minutes. WCAU-TV, Philadelphia. Chronicles the history of the American Negro and his emergence from a 300-year old "pagan" slave state. Shows him as of 1968, a crucial year in which he demands his rights and equal status. Combines the sounds and rhythms of the violence of race riots with folk, rock, and hymnal music. Features the works of Langston Hughes, Countee Cullen, James Baldwin, Malcolm X and Stokely Carmichael.

Some of My Best Friends are White. Robeck. 1967. Producer Michael Lathem. A provocative examination of America's racial problem as discussed from the point of view of the middle-class Negro involving his acceptance by society and the future of his children growing up in white suburbia. A BBC-TV Production.

***The talented comedian Godfrey Cambridge in a scene from the riotous* Cotton Comes to Harlem**

The Weapons of Gordon Parks. Color. 28 minutes. 1967. Contemporary — McGraw-Hill. The story of the internationally known black photographer seen at work, in his home, with his family, and on the streets of Harlem, as part of his past life is recreated. An inspiring and moving photographic essay. Directed by Warren Forma.

The President's Analyst. Paramount. 1967. Screenwriter/director Theodore J. Flicker came up with this smartly filmed Hollywood comedy with a distinctly intellectual turn. Godfrey Cambridge featured alongside James Coburn. The story is a take-off on governmental security, automation, and international intrigue involving U. S. and foreign agents.

A Time for Burning. 1967. Conceived, directed and edited by William C. Jersey and Barbara Connell, this film deals with a crisis that actually occurred in Omaha, Nebraska, when a Lutheran minister tried to inspire church members to destroy the barriers existing between themselves and the Negro ghetto.

Up the Down Staircase. Warner Brothers-Seven Arts. 1967. Director Robert Mulligan casts Jose Rodriguez in an adaptation of the best-selling novel about a big-city school system.

To Sir, With Love. Columbia. 1967. Director James Clavell here paints a picture of a Negro teacher who takes a post in a tough London school and battles to reach rebellious youngsters. Starring Sidney Poitier.

Doctor Dolittle. 20th Century Fox, 1967. Director Richard Fleisher has multi-talented Geoffrey Holder in this musical based on a series of stories bearing the same title. The film is one big colorful, imaginative burst of animal-people fun.

Portrait of Jason. Filmmakers. 1967. Director Shirley Clarke's intimate marathon interview with a self-described male prostitute, himself a Negro. The star bares his soul in an all-night camera session for director Clarke. The film comes off as a first-rate socio-psychological documentary.

The Dirty Dozen. MGM. 1967. Director Robert Aldrich has ex-football star Jim Brown in this tough, he-man, ribald film about war prisoners who are given a chance to redeem themselves by embarking on a perilous World War II mission.

The Night of the Living Dead. Walter Reade. 1968. Director, George A. Romero. The story involves corpses reawakened by radiation who roam the countryside killing and devouring cities. Stars Duane Jones.

The Scalphunters. United Artists. 1968. Directed by Sidney Pollack. Black power Western involving a furtrapper with a captured runaway slave stalking a scalp-hunting gang to retrieve stolen furs. A Negro, trying to gain his freedom by outwitting whites, proves that white supremacy isn't omnipotent. Ossie Davis is in this one along with Burt Lancaster.

Guess Who's Coming to Dinner. Columbia Pictures. 1968. Director Stanley Kramer draws on a top-level cast which includes Sidney Poitier, Spencer Tracy and Katherine Hepburn. The story deals with the question of interracial love and the problems of mixed marriage. The cast also includes Beah Richards.

For Love of Ivy. Cinerama. 1968. Director Daniel Mann. This film stars Sidney Poitier, Abbey Lincoln and Leon Bibb. A love affair between the luscious Ivy (Abbey Lincoln) and a suave businessman (Sidney Poitier). Quincy Jones composed the music.

Judy Pace (l.) and Raymond St. Jacques exemplify the new breed of black film star.

Sidney Poitier (l.), Spencer Tracy and Katherine Hepburn in a scene from the controversial **Guess Who's Coming to Dinner.**

Negro Kingdoms. Color. 16 minutes. 1968. Atlantis. Reveals the high level of culture and society of slavery existing in West Africa prior to the era of slavery through treatment of the changing climate of Africa, trans-Saharan trade, the growth of Islam, and the story of medieval Mali and Ghana.

If He Hollers, Let Him Go! (Cinerama Releasing, 1968.) Theme of this film is injustice to a black man hunted down following his escape from prison for a crime he did not commit. Stars Raymond St. Jacques, Barbara McNair, Dana Wynter and Kevin McCarthy.

P.J. Universal. 1968. Rough, tough, violent private-eye story directed by John Gulleria with Brock Peters in a top-level role.

Mingus. Filmmakers. 1968. Close-up of bassplayer and composer Charlie Mingus as he and his five-year-old daughter await eviction by the City of New York. The film is laced with intercuts of Mingus as a musician.

Dark of the Sun. MGM. 1968. Director Jack Cardiff off to the Congo on a story involving killing, gore, and double-dealing. Jim Brown prominent in this one.

Split Decision. Filmmakers. 1968. Fighter Jose Torres is followed in this film during preparations for his bout with Dick Tiger. The film manages to give some insight into the boxing profession.

The Story of a Three Day Pass. Sigma III. 1968. Black director Melvin Van Peebles tells a story of a young Negro on a three-day pass in Paris, of his weekend encounter with a white girl, as well as some white buddies from camp. This film gives tremendous insight in the gap between what people feel and what they encounter.

Robby. Bluewood. 1968. Writer/director Ralph C. Bluemke produces a sincere film about a white lad marooned on an island along with a Negro youngster. Both develop a friendship, only to be cruelly separated by racism after their rescue.

The Biggest Bundle of Them All. MGM. 1968. Director Ken Annakin produced this big caper spoof featuring an aging, exiled gangster in Italy who leads gang of amateurs in carefully planned heist. Starring Godfrey Cambridge.

Finian's Rainbow. Warner Brothers-Seven Arts, 1968. This long-time hit and favorite of Broadway's yesteryear is directed by Francis Ford Coppola and has a fresh movie look. Al Freeman, Jr. with Fred Astaire, Petula Clark, Tommy Steele and a completely integrated cast.

The Heart is a Lonely Hunter. Warner Brothers-Seven Arts, 1968. Robert Ellis Miller directed this poignant film based on Carson McCullers' novel about loneliness in a Southern town. Cicely Tyson featured with Percy Rodriguez.

Ice Station Zebra. MGM, 1968. Director John Sturges put Jim Brown in this suspenseful cold-war thriller about a U.S. nuclear war submarine on a secret mission to a polar region with an unknown saboteur aboard.

The Split. MGM, 1968. Director Gordon Fleming stars Jim Brown as a tough criminal who decides on one last caper before retiring—robbing the Los Angeles Coliseum.

Salt and Pepper. United Artists, 1968. Director Richard Donner put together this frantic comedy about London club owners caught in a plot to overthrow the British government. Peter Lawford is Pepper, and Sammy Davis, Jr. is Salt.

The Learning Tree. Warner Brothers-Seven Arts, 1969. Photo-journalist-musician Gordon Parks with a reflective film based upon his novel about a Negro youngster growing up in Kansas in the 1920's. Parks also composed the music. Stars include Kyle Johnson, Alex Clarke, Estelle Evans and Dana Elcar.

The Lost Man. Universal, 1969. Director Robert Alan Arthur cast Sidney Poitier as a hunted Negro militant in flight after a robbery to get funds for his movement fails. Also featuring Al Freeman, Jr. and Leon Bibb.

Float Like a Butterfly, Sting Like a Bee. Grove Films, 1969. Directed and filmed by William Klein, this film is a visually excellent, fascinating study of Cassius Clay, now Muhammad Ali. A factual biography with great moments from his ring career.

Putney Swope. Cinema V, 1969. Director Robert Downey tells what happens when a group of Negroes takes over an ad agency. Arnold Johnson, Laura Greene along with a huge amusing cast.

Terry Whitmore for Example. Grove Films, 1969. Director Bill Brodie presents a young Negro who, after having won a medal for heroism as a marine in Vietnam, defects to Sweden.

Ace High. Paramount, 1969. The world-famed Colizzi presents a western featuring intellectually attuned hombres, including Brock Peters.

Death of a Gunfighter. Universal, 1969. A marvelous western with an interracial marriage theme. Involves a town marshal who kills too easily and alienates his town. Lena Horne as the wife, Richard Widmark as her husband.

100 Rifles. 20th-Century Fox, 1969. Director Tom Gries presents a drama about the Mexican persecution of Yaqui Indians. The hero is big Jim Brown and the heroine is Raquel Welch.

Topaz. Alfred Hitchcock Universal Production Release, 1969. This is the film version of the Leon Uris' best-selling novel of the same title dealing with international espionage. Roscoe Lee Browne plays the role of an espionage agent.

Bye, Bye Braverman. Warner Brothers-Seven Arts, 1969. Director Sidney Lumet has Godfrey Cambridge in this film dealing with a slice of ethnic life in Brooklyn, New York.

Slaves. Walter Reade, 1969. This controversial drama takes a bold look at the system of slavery as it occurred in the United States and stars Ossie Davis along with Dionne Warwick.

Castle Keep. Columbia Pictures, 1969. Director Sydney Pollack casts Al Freeman, Jr. in this unusual war film about a small unit of U.S. servicemen who try to hold a castle against advancing Germans during World War II.

Change of Mind. Cinerama Release, 1969. Director Robert Stephens casts Raymond St. Jacques in this film about the brain of a white district attorney transplanted into the brain of a Negro man.

Two Gentlemen Sharing. American International Pictures, 1969. Director Ted Kotcheff put this film together about a young white man who shares a flat with an equally young Negro in London. An assortment of problems follows—equally shared by Robin Phillips and Hal Frederick.

Sweet Charity. Universal, 1969. Director Bob Fosse made the transition from stage to screen with singular intelligence, imagination and cinematic flair in this successful Broadway stage hit. Sammy Davis, Jr. is an appealing part of the action.

Up Tight. Paramount, 1969. Director/producer Jules Dassin set his locale in Cleveland, Ohio, to tell an honest, powerful drama of a poor, sincere Negro man caught in a changing world.

The Informer. Screen version of the Liam O'Flaherty story, 1969. The very able cast includes Raymond St. Jacques, Julian Mayfield, Ruby Dee, Frank Silvera, and Roscoe Lee Browne. Booker T. Jones composed the music.

Wild in the Streets. American International Pictures, 1969. Director Barry Shear put together this film about the explosive movement of the young to win the vote at age 15 and take over the U.S. government, with the "older generation" forcibly retired after age 35. Richard Pryor, comedian-turned-actor, plays a prominent role.

Joanna. 20th Century Fox, 1969. This well told British drama describes a world where life is free and easy. Its theme also covers an interracial love affair. Starring Glenna Forster Jones, Genevieve Waite and Calvin Lockhart.

The Comedians. MGM, 1969. Directed and produced by Peter Glenville. This film presents the sinister image of a rigid reign of terror in a Caribbean country under a black dictatorship. Negroes in top-level roles include Roscoe Lee Browne, George S Brown, James Earl Jones, Raymond St. Jacques, and Cicely Tyson.

Flame in the Streets. Atlantic, 1969 re-release (original 1962). Released again in 1969, this absorbing drama set in England deals with Negro and white civil, social and labor relationships, and the double-edged problem of mixed marriage. Stars Earl Cameron, Sylvia Sims, John Willis and Johnny Sekka.

The Riot. Paramount, 1969. Director Buzz Kulik made this film on location at the Arizona State Prison. Starring Jim Brown in a story about a prison break.

The Rievers. A Cinema Center Film Presentation, 1969. Director Mark Rydell based this film version on the Faulkner novel of the same title. The amusing story about the turn-of-the-century South co-starred Steve McQueen and Rupert Crosse, a Negro actor nominated for an Academy Award in a supporting role.

Hello Dolly. 20th Century Fox, 1969. Director Gene Kelly did the screen adaptation of this well-known Broadway play with finesse and great skill. The story hasn't changed. Dolly, a female jack-of-all-trades, is at it again. Barbra Streisand along with Walter Matthau, and Louis Armstrong.

First World Festival of Negro Arts. Color, 20 minutes. Contemporary-McGraw-Hill, 1969. Scenes of the first World Festival of Negro Arts held at Dakar in 1966, showing music, dance, sculpture, painting and the reciprocal influence of Negro art and culture in relation to the Western world.

I Have a Dream. 35 minutes. 1969. The biography of Martin Luther King made from newsreel footage of the civil rights movement during the 1950's and 1960's. Reveals his dedication to the movement and to the principles of nonviolence.

Martin Luther King: The Man and the March. 83 minutes. 1969. Produced by Public Broadcast Laboratory of NET. A documentary on the late Doctor Martin Luther King Jr.'s "Poor People's March." Shows Dr. King conferring with aides, speaking at rallies and traveling as he solicits support for, and develops the operational details of, the March. Indicates the methods used by his aides to create interest and support on a local level and with other ethnic groups.

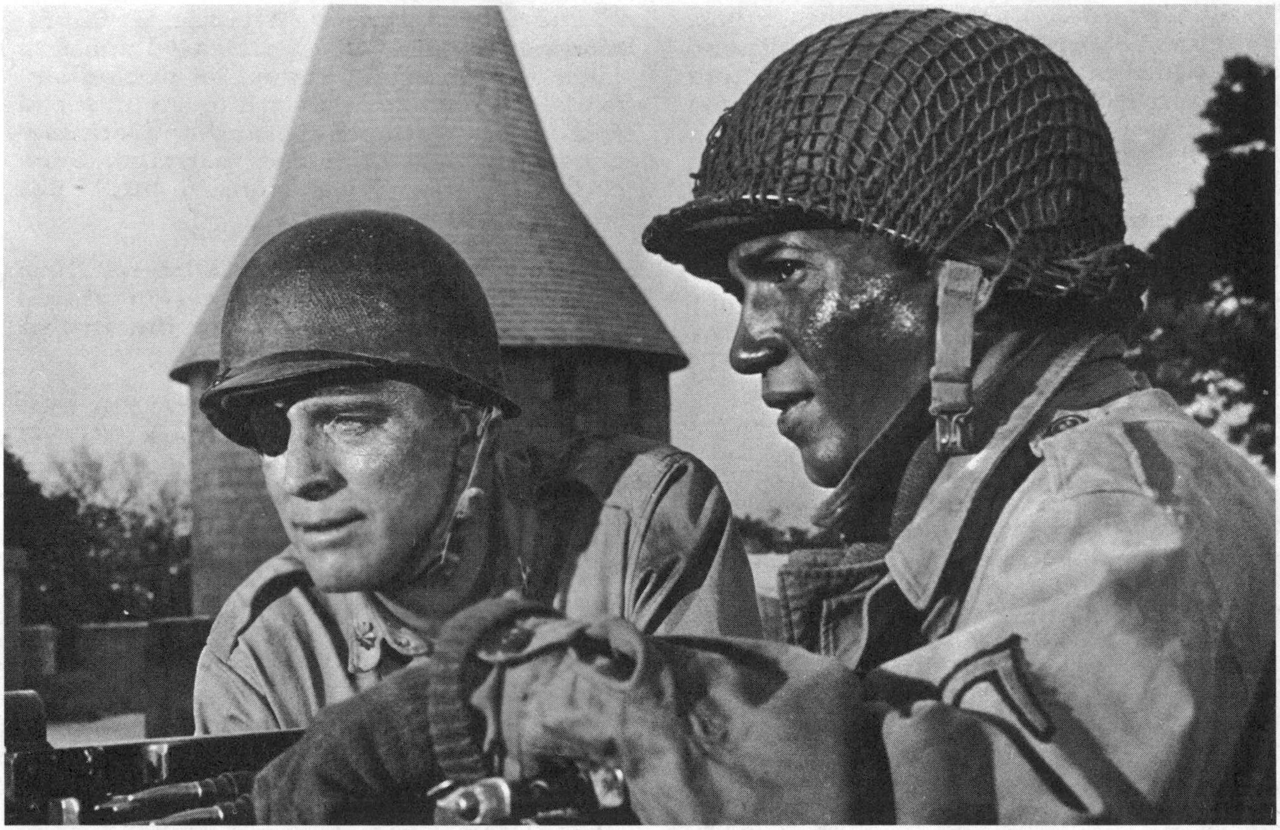

Burt Lancaster (l.) and Al Freeman, Jr. starred together in Castle Keep.

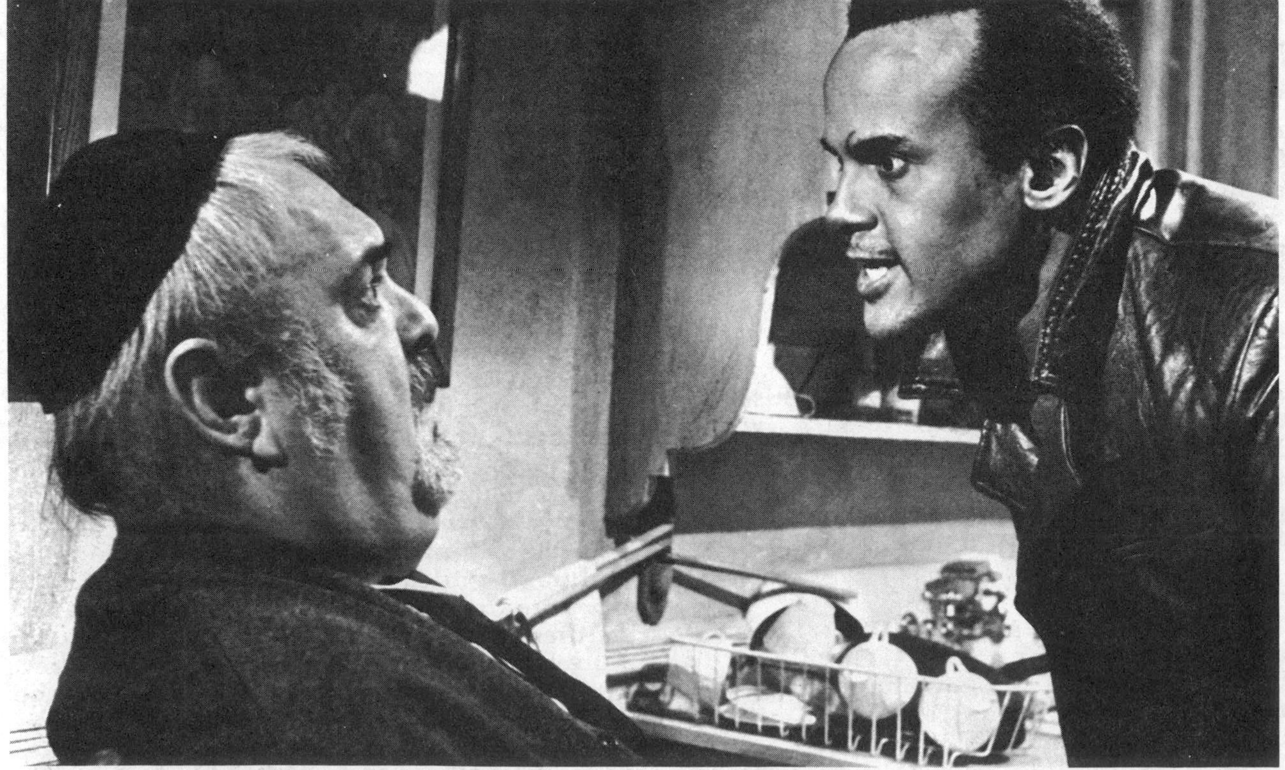

Harry Belafonte (r.) in a confrontation with Zero Mostel, as he tries to convince him that he is, in fact, The Angel Levine.

Three in the Attic. American International Pictures, 1969. Director Richard Wilson. This film tells the story of a campus Don Juan kidnaped and held in the attic by three of his girl friends. Judy Pace along with Christopher Jones.

No Vietnamese Ever Called Me Nigger. Bob Maurice Paradigm, 1969. 68 minutes. Three black G.I.'s discuss their experiences in Vietnam, the racism that exists in the armed forces, and their dissatisfaction with life in the U.S. upon their return.

The Watermelon Man, Columbia Pictures, 1970. Director Melvin Van Peebles (see also *The Story of a Three Day Pass,* 1969), in his American film debut, casts Godfrey Cambridge and Estelle Parsons in a film about a man who turns color overnight. What happens when that transformation becomes known to his associates and friends makes for a story perched on the fine edge between comedy and tragedy.

The Angel Levine. United Artists, 1970. Jon Kadar directed this film which casts Harry Belafonte as the angel opposite Zero Mostel whom he seeks to convince that he is for real.

Last of the Mobile Hot-Shots. Warner Bros., 1970. A Sidney Lumet Production. The film version of *The Seven Descents of Myrtle,* a play by Tennessee Williams adapted for the screen by Gore Vidal, tells the story of two brothers; one white, one black and the women they both love. Filmed largely on location in and around Baton Rouge, Louisiana. Stars Robert Hooks, Lynn Redgrave and James Coburn.

My Sweet Charlie. Universal, 1970. Directed by Lamont Johnson, this boy-meets-girl story initially premiered on NBC. Stars Patty Duke and Al Freeman, Jr.

End of the Road. Allied Artists Film, 1970. Directed by Aram Avakian. This film stars James Earl Jones as Doctor D. in a story involving one man's attempt to straighten out his life, only to find more difficulty lies at the end of the road.

Tick . . . Tick . . . Tick . . . MGM, 1970. Directed by Ralph Nelson. This new drama stars Jim Brown, George Kennedy, and Frederic March and centers around the aftermath of a bitter election campaign for sheriff in a small rural county in the Deep South.

Patton. Fox, 1970. A monumental performance by George C. Scott as World War II General George S. Patton. Karl Malden as General Bradley, along with the late James Edwards in his last film.

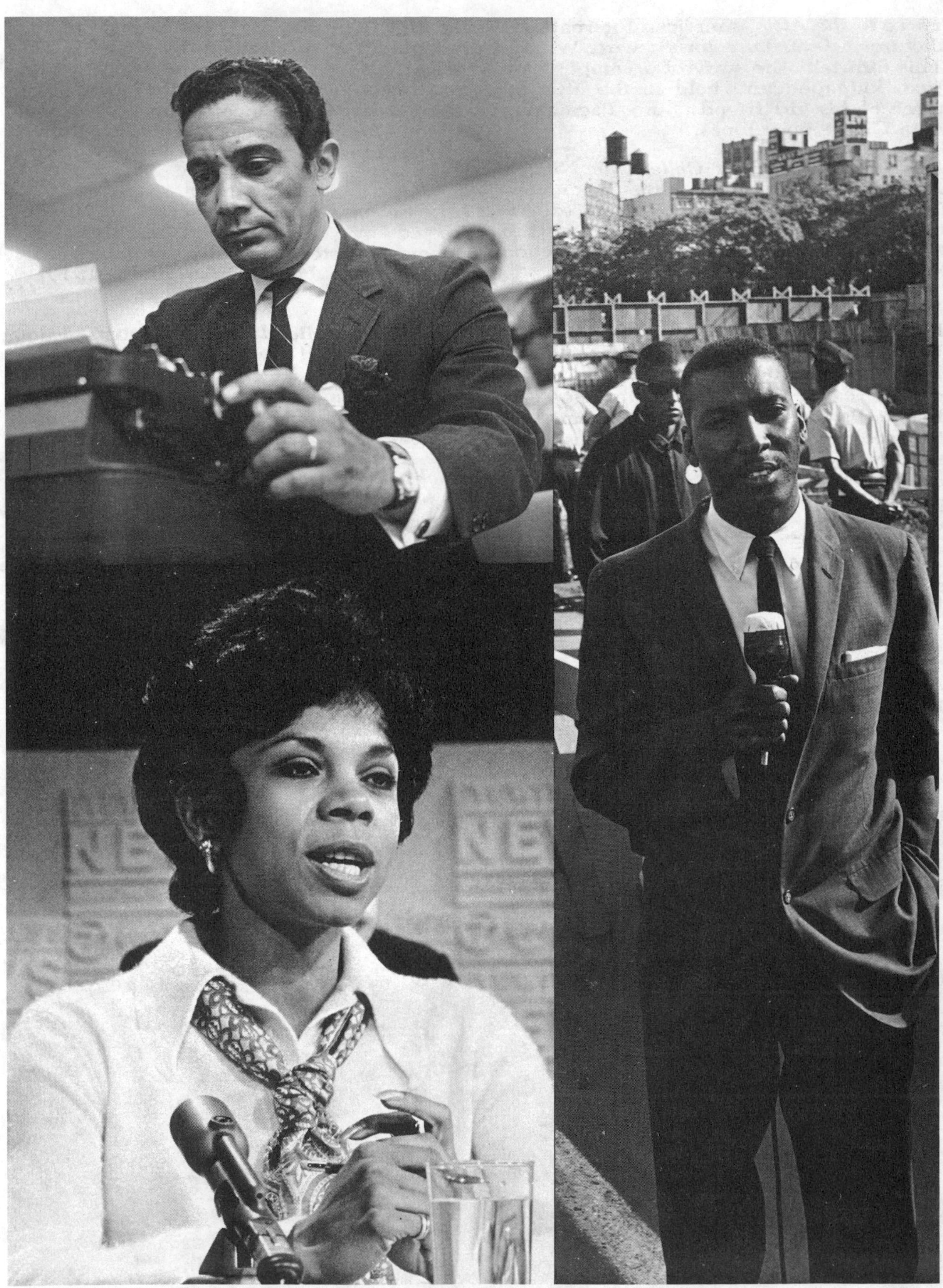

Chris Borgen, Melba Tolliver, and Bob Teague (l. to r.)

The Mass Media

The high visibility accorded the black man on network television is a direct outgrowth of several social factors, including the racial turbulence which scarred the nation's ghettos in 1967 and the assassination of Martin Luther King, Jr. a scant year later. Added to this however, is a growing maturity on the part of the stations themselves that they, like radio, have an ongoing responsibility to address a substantial portion of their programming to a vital segment of the listening audience.

Television shows featuring blacks enjoyed considerable popularity during the latter part of the 1960's. Among the most popular network shows (included under the term "network" is the independent complex of educational stations) were: *I Spy* and *The Bill Cosby Show* starring Bill Cosby; *Julia,* starring Diahann Carroll; *The Leslie Uggams Show,* starring Leslie Uggams; *Room 222,* starring Lloyd Haines and Denise Nicholas; *Mod Squad,* starring Clarence Williams, III, and *Black Journal,* hosted by Bill Greaves and Lou House.

The *I Spy* show ran for three years (Sept. 1965-Sept. 1968) and was a blend of espionage and intrigue in which Cosby played the "intellectual" member of two ostensible tennis bums. On the *Bill Cosby Show,* the talented comedian plays a high school gym teacher who doubles as a coach and confidante. *Julia* is a situation comedy dealing with a glamorous Viet Nam war widow who works as a nurse, has a young son, and lives in a middle-class setting. *The Leslie Uggams Show,* a variety offering, featured "the black Shirley Temple," but was short-lived, partly because of the stereotyped comedy routines which it attempted to perpetuate. *Room* 222 is set in an integrated high school and, in general, deals with the problems spawned by the generation gap, including racially motivated ones. *Mod Squad,* a slick detective vehicle, features the Afro-styled Clarence Williams, III; *Mission Impossible,* the dashing Greg Morris. *Black Journal* is a documentary series with a magazine format designed to probe behind the scenes of the black world—rural, urban, international. The show cuts across class lines and often brings comment on vital issues relating to, although not the exclusive concern of, the black community.

Other television programs geared toward black audiences are not of network scope, but do nonetheless generate considerable interest in the black community. Among these are: *For Black Only* (Chicago); *Black Horizons* (Pittsburgh); *Live in My Skin* (Spokane); *Black on Black* (Syracuse), and *Soul, Like It Is,* and *Bedford Stuyvesant* (New York). Says George Pryce of the variety show *Soul:* "[The program] was born out of a belief that television may very well reach a minority audience better with performance than with documentaries." *Like It Is,* produced by Emmy-award nominee Charles Hobson, features broad coverage of events of interest to the black community, and often uses on-location filming. Says Hobson: "We are going to pursue our policy of investigating situations and people in the black and Puerto Rican communities." Perhaps its most noteworthy achievement was an in-depth presentation of the perils of sickle-cell anemia, an incurable blood disease often affecting the rural black population in the U. S. *Inside Bedford Stuyvesant* provided an inside look at the second largest black ghetto in the United States.

Perhaps the most significant network documentary shows were seen on the *Of Black America* series, produced by CBS-TV in the summer of 1968. These consisted of seven half or one-hour programs entitled as follows: *Black History: Lost, Stolen, or Strayed; The Black Soldier; Black World; Body and Soul; The Heritage of Slavery; In Search of a Past,* and *Portrait in Black and White.* The series was hosted by Bill Cosby and featured black newsmen George Foster and Hal Walker.

Charles Hobson

The following is a list of "representative" people who work in responsible positions at NBC. It is, of necessity, selective rather than being all-inclusive:

NAME	*TITLE*	*LOCATION*
BOLDEN, J. TABER, JR.	DIRECTOR, MANAGEMENT DEVELOPMENT	NEW YORK
BURTON, CALVIN E.	ADMINISTRATOR, PROGRAMS	BURBANK
DOLAN, HARRY	WRITER	BURBANK
GRAHAM, GORDON	REPORTER	BURBANK
MATNEY, BILL	NEWS CORRESPONDENT	NETWORK
MATTHEWS, ROBERT W	NBC NEWS DUTY MANAGER	NEW YORK
MOSES, KENN	COMMUNITY RELATIONS MANAGER, WNBC RADIO	NEW YORK
QUARLES, NORMA	REPORTER	CLEVELAND
ROBERTSON, STAN	DIRECTOR, MOTION PICTURES FOR TELEVISION	BURBANK
SIMPSON, HELEN E.	PUBLIC RELATIONS ADMINISTRATOR	CLEVELAND
SYE, ROBERT J.	ADMINISTRATOR, PRESS AND PUBLICITY	BURBANK
TEAGUE, ROBERT	NEWSCASTER	NETWORK
TUCKER, LEM	NEWS CORRESPONDENT	NETWORK

Although she is no longer with CBS, Joan Murray was probably the most highly visible black news correspondent/show hostess ever employed by the station. Miss Murray is now executive vice president and co-owner of ZEBRA Associates, an advertising firm which specializes in developing ghetto accounts. Among those she left behind at the station were:

NAME	*TITLE*	*LOCATION*
BORGEN, CHRIS	NEWS CORRESPONDENT	NEW YORK
DUKE, STANLEY	SPORTS REPORTER	LOS ANGELES
FOSTER, GEORGE	REPORTER	CHICAGO
LOWRY, WILLIAM E.	HOST	CHICAGO
NICHOLS, RONN	PRODUCER	ST. LOUIS
PIERCE, PONCHITTA	REPORTER	NETWORK
PORTERFIELD, FRED	REPORTER/INTERVIEWER	ST. LOUIS
WALKER, HAL	NEWS CORRESPONDENT	NETWORK

ABC-TV also has a number of black on- and off-camera news personalities. They include:

NAME	*TITLE*	*LOCATION*
HOBSON, CHARLES	PRODUCER	NEW YORK
NOBLE, GIL	HOST	NEW YORK
ROBINSON, LAYHMOND	NEWS CORRESPONDENT	NETWORK
TOLLIVER, MELBA	NEWS CORRESPONDENT	NETWORK

On the National Education Television (NET) Network most black talent has gravitated toward the New York-based *Black Journal* series. The top personnel there include: William Greaves, executive producer; Lou House, co-host; Hazel Bright, managing editor; St. Clair Bourne, Phil Burton, Stan Lathan, and J. Robert Wagoner, producers; Jimmy McDonald and Peggy Pinn, associate producers; Angela Fontanez, program coordinator, and Joyce Shelton, production assistant.

WLIB AND LEON LEWIS

The Peabody Award citation received by Harlem radio station WLIB in 1966 was a milestone in the career of dialogue jockey Leon Lewis, now Ombudsman for WMCA's Call for Action. The WLIB show hosted by Lewis consisted of an early evening talk marathon (*Community Opinion*) in which ghetto residents could voice their grievances, air their feelings and, perhaps more importantly, take advantage of underpublicized community services available to deal with specific problems.

Lewis frequently cultivated relationships with local legal, educational, and political experts who often volunteered free advisory and consultative services. To their surprise and dismay, they often found themselves squirming nervously under a constant barrage of pointed questions. Lewis generally stayed out of the fray, except for an occasional quiet and philosophical remark which brought the confrontations to a satisfying close.

Still, by abating many tensions, WLIB, in the words of the Peabody citation, "gave Harlem a safety valve. It developed 'Community Opinion,' a radio program permitting citizens of Harlem to voice their feelings, frankly and openly, via a hot line telephone interview, heard not only by the Negro community, but by the entire city.

"In addition, the station provided details of how listeners could avail themselves of existing vital community services. At WLIB community involvement is more than just a station phrase." In recognition, WLIB received a Peabody Award for outstanding local radio education during 1966.

Veteran newsman Lewis, born in Troy, New York in 1917, has worked in a variety of radio and journalism jobs, including that of sales manager for an Albany station and circulation manager for the *Amsterdam News*. Glib and resourceful, he was not able to break into New York radio at first, but he found a ready career on the ethnic air waves.

After his success at WLIB, however, opportunity beckoned, and Lewis joined WMCA as Assistant Public Affairs Director in 1967. Over the years, several of his documentaries have won prestigious journalism awards, and have even led to a teaching career at Fordham University.

Nothing seems to satisfy Lewis better than his early-morning rendezvous with the unpredictable and fascinating potpourri of characters who vie for attention on his show, and constantly seek to either put him on the defensive or joke about his own idiosyncrasies.

For Lewis though, there has always been a discernible mission to be accomplished at his secluded outpost. While at WLIB, he once found succinct words to sum it up: "The walls of the ghetto are so high," he said, "that people can't see in and they can't see out. I'd like to see those walls come tumbling down."

Leon Lewis

BLACK RADIO STATIONS

The following is a state-by-state, city-by-city list of radio stations which broadcast music, news, and general interest shows with special relevance to the black community. Some stations are exclusively black in orientation; others offer black programing on a more limited scale.

ALABAMA

Andalusia

WCTA—920 kc.
WCTA (FM)—93.1 mc.
Andalusia Broadcasting Co., Inc.
Some Negro programming

Birmingham

WENN—1320 kc.
McLendon Birmingham Broadcasting Co., Inc.
All Negro programming

WJLD—1400 kc.
WJLD (FM)—104.7 mc.
Johnston Broadcasting Co.
All Negro programming

Decatur
WMSL—1400 kc.
Tennessee Valley Radio and Television Corp.
Some Negro programming

Huntsville
WEUP—1600 kc.
Garrett Broadcasting Service
All Negro programming

Jackson
WHOD—1290 kc.
WHOD (FM)—104.9 mc.
Jackson Broadcasting Co., Inc.
Some Negro programming

Mobile
WGOK—900 kc.
WGOK, Inc.
All Negro programming
WMOZ—960 kc.
Edwin H. Estes
All Negro programming
WUNI—1410 kc.
WUNI, Inc.
Some Negro programming

Montgomery
WRMA—950 kc.
WRMA Broadcasting Co., Inc.
All Negro programming

Selma
WGWC—1340 kc.
WGWC Radio-CBS
Some Negro programming
WHBB—1490 kc.
Talton Broadcasting Co.
Some Negro programming

Tuscaloosa
WTUG—790 kc.
Tri-Cities Broadcasting Co., Inc.
All Negro programming

Phoenix
KCAC—1010 kc.
KCAC Broadcasting Co., Inc.
All Negro programming

Tucson
KOLD—1450 kc.
Old Pueblo Broadcasting Co.
Some Negro programming

ARKANSAS

Little Rock
KOKY—1440 kc.
KOKY, Inc.
All Negro programming

Pine Bluff
KCAT—1530 kc.
J. B. Scanlon
All Negro programming

Texarkana
KOSY—790 kc.
KOSY (FM)—102.5 mc.
Gateway Broadcasting Co.
Some Negro programming

CALIFORNIA

Inglewood
KTYM-FM—103.9 mc.
Trans-American Broadcasting
Some Negro programming

Long Beach
KGER—1390 kc.
John Brown Schools of Calif.
Some Negro programming

Los Angeles
KDAY—1580 kc.
Continental Broadcasting of California, Inc. (Santa Monica) (Hollywood)
All Negro programming
KGFJ—1230 kc.
Tracy Broadcasting Co.
All Negro programming
KHOF (FM)—99.5 mc.
The Maple Chapel, Inc.
Some Negro programming

Oakland
KDIA—1310 kc.
KDIA, Inc.
All Negro programming

Paso Robles
KPRL—1230 kc.
KPRL, Inc.
Some Negro programming

Sacramento
KJML (FM)—106.5 mc.
Town and Country Broadcasters, Inc.
Some Negro programming

San Francisco
KSOL—1450 kc.
KSAN, Inc.
All Negro programming

COLORADO

Colorado Springs
KRDO—1240 kc.
Pikes Peak Broadcasting Co.
Some Negro programming

CONNECTICUT

Middletown
WCNX—1150 kc.
Middlesex Broadcasting Co.
Some Negro programming

Stamford
WSTC—1400 kc.
WSTC (FM)—96.7 mc.
The Western Connecticut Broadcasting Co.
Some Negro programming

DISTRICT OF COLUMBIA

Washington
WOOK—1340 kc.
United Broadcasting Co., Inc.
All Negro programming
WUST—1120 kc.
Atlantic Broadcasting Co.
All Negro programming

FLORIDA

Belle Glade
WSWN—900 kc.
Seminole Broadcasting Co., Inc.
Some Negro programming

Cocoa
WKKO—860 kc.
WKKO Radio, Inc.
Some Negro programming

Daytona Beach
WELE—1590 kc.
7 Cities Broadcasting Corp.
All Negro programming

Delray Beach
WDBF—1420 kc.
Sunshine Broadcasting Co.
Some Negro programming

Fort Lauderdale
WFTL—1400 kc.
WFTL Broadcasting Co.
Some Negro programming
WRBD—1470 kc.
Almardon, Inc. of Florida
All Negro programming

Gainesville
WGGG—1230 kc.
Radio Gainesville, Inc.
Some Negro programming

Chattahoochee
WSBP—1580 kc.
WSBP
Some Negro programming

Jacksonville
WRHC—1400 kc.
WRHC, Inc.
Some Negro programming

Madison
WMAF—1230 kc.
Norman O. Protsman
Some Negro programming

Miami
WAME—1260 kc.
WAME Broadcasting Co.
All Negro programming

Miami Beach
WMBM—1490 kc.
Community Service Broadcasters Inc.
All Negro programming

Ocala
WKOS—1370 kc.
WKOS, Inc.
All Negro programming

Panama City
WPCF—1430 kc.
Bay County Broadcasting Co.
Some Negro programming

Pensacola
WBOP—980 kc.
Tri-Cities Broadcasting Co., Inc.
All Negro programming

Sanford
WTRR—1400 kc.
WTRR, Box 1568, Seminole Broadcasting Center
Some Negro programming

Tampa
WTMP—1150 kc.
WTMP, Inc.
All Negro programming

Winter Garden
WOKB—1600 kc.
Everbach Broadcasting Co., Inc.
All Negro programming

GEORGIA

Albany
WJAZ—960 kc.
James S. Rivers, Inc.
Some Negro programming

Atlanta
WAOK—1380 kc.
WAOK Broadcasting Co.
All Negro programming
WERD—860 kc.
Radio Atlanta, Inc.
All Negro programming

Augusta
WAUG—1050 kc.
WAUG (FM)—105.7 mc.
Garden City Broadcasting Co., Inc.
All Negro programming
WTHB—1550 kc.
North Augusta Broadcasting Co., Inc.
All Negro programming

Blakely
WBBK—1260 kc.
Radio Blakely
Some Negro programming

Brunswick
WMOG–1490 kc.
Radio Brunswick, Inc.
Some Negro programming

Columbus
WCLS–1580 kc.
Muscogee Broadcasting Co., Inc.
All Negro programming
WOKS–1340 kc.
PAM Radio, Inc.
All Negro programming

Donalsonville
WSEM–1500 kc.
Radio Donalsonville
Some Negro programming

Eastman
WUFF (formerly WPFE)–710 kc.
Farnell O'Quinn
Some Negro programming

La Grange
WLAG–1240 kc.
WLAG (FM)–104.1 mc.
LaGrange Broadcasting Co.
Some Negro programming

Macon
WIBB–1280 kc.
Peach State Broadcasting Co., Inc.
All Negro programming

Madison
WYTH–1250 kc.
Central Georgia Broadcasting Co.
Some Negro programming

Savannah
WSOK–1230 kc.
WSOK, Inc.
All Negro programming

HAWAII

Hilo
KIPA–1110 kc.
Big Island Broadcasting Co., Ltd.
Some Negro programming

Honolulu
KUMU–1502 kc.
John Hutton Corp.
Some Negro programming

ILLINOIS

Belleville
WIBV–1260 kc.
Belleville Broadcasting Co.
Some Negro programming

Chicago
WAAF–950 kc.
Corn Belt Publishers, Inc.
(Drovers Journal Division)
All Negro programming
WSBC–1240 kc.
WSBC Broadcasting Co., Inc.
Some Negro programming

Chicago Heights
WMPP–1470 kc.
Seaway Broadcasting Co., Inc.
All Negro programming

Cicero
WVON–1450 kc.
L & P Broadcasting Corp.
All Negro programming

Decatur
WDZ–1050 kc.
Prairieland Broadcasters
Some Negro programming

INDIANA

Hammond
WJOB–1230 kc.
Colby Broadcasting Corp.,
Radio Center
Some Negro programming

Indianapolis
WGEE–1590 kc.
Rollins Broadcasting, Inc.
Some Negro programming

Michigan City
WIMS–1420 kc.
Northern Indiana Broadcasters, Inc.
Some Negro programming

IOWA

Des Moines
KWDN (FM)–93.3 mc.
SEQ Corp., Inc.
Some Negro programming

Waterloo
KXEL–1540 kc.
KXEL Broadcasting Co.
Some Negro programming

KANSAS

Leavenworth
KCLO–1410 kc.
KCLO, Inc.
Some Negro programming

KENTUCKY

Franklin
WFKN–1220 kc.
Franklin Favorite–WFKN, Inc.
Some Negro programming

Georgetown
WAXU–1580 kc.
WAXU Radio
Some Negro programming

Louisville
WLOU—1350 kc.
Rounsaville of Louisville, Inc.
All Negro programming

Madisonville
WTTL—1310 kc.
Hopkins County Broadcasters
Some Negro programming

Middlesboro
WMIK—560 kc.
Cumberland Gap Broadcasting Co.
Some Negro programming

Pineville
WMLF—1230 kc.
Ken-Te-Va Broadcasting Co., Radio Park
Some Negro programming

LOUISIANA

Bastrop
KTRY—730 kc.
Radio Station KTRY
Some Negro programming
KVOB—1340 kc.
Rainey-Ritchie Radio
Some Negro programming

Baton Rouge
WXOK—1260 kc.
WXOK, Inc.
All Negro programming

Bogalusa
WIKC—1490 kc.
Curt Siegelin
Some Negro programming

Farmerville
KTDL—1470 kc.
Union Broadcasting Co., Inc.
Some Negro programming

Jennings
KJEF—1290 kc.
Jennings Broadcasting Co.
Some Negro programming

Lake Charles
KAOK—1400 kc.
EJP Corp.
Some Negro programming

Lake Providence
KLPL—1050 kc.
Radio Services Co.
Some Negro programming

New Orleans
WBOK—1230 kc.
WBOK, Inc.
All Negro programming
WYLD—940 kc.
Rounsaville of New Orleans, Inc.
All Negro programming

Shreveport
KCIJ—980 kc.
Universal Broadcasting Corp.
Some Negro programming
KOKA—1550 kc.
KOKA Broadcasting Co., Inc.
All Negro programming
KWKH—1130 kc.
KWKH (FM)—94.5 mc.
International Broadcasting Corp. (The *Shreveport Times*)
Some Negro programming

Ville Platte
KVPI—1050 kc.
Ville Platte Broadcasting Co.
Some Negro programming

West Monroe
KUZN—1310 kc.
Howard E. Griffith
Some Negro programming

MARYLAND

Annapolis
WANN—1190 kc.
Annapolis Broadcasting Corp.
All Negro programming

Baltimore
WEBB—1360 kc.
1360 Broadcasting Co., Inc.
All Negro programming
WSID—1010 kc.
United Broadcasting Co.
All Negro programming
WWIN—1400 kc.
WWIN National City Bank Bldg.
All Negro programming

MASSACHUSETTS

Boston
WILD—1090 kc.
The Noble Broadcasting Corp.
Some Negro programming

MICHIGAN

Detroit
WGPR (FM)—107.5 mc.
WGPR, Inc.
Some Negro programming
WJLB—1400 kc.
Booth Broadcasting Co.
Some Negro programming

Flint
WAMM—1420 kc.
Mid-States Broadcasting Corp.
Some Negro programming

Inkster
WCHB—1440 kc.
Bell Broadcasting Co.
All Negro programming

Muskegon
WMUS—1090 kc.
WMUS (FM)—106.9 mc.
Greater Muskegon Broadcasters, Inc.
Some Negro programming

MINNESOTA

Minneapolis
KUXL—1570 kc.
Universal Broadcasting Co. of Minneapolis-St. Paul, Inc.
Some Negro programming

St. Paul
WMIN—1400 kc.
WMIN, Inc.
Some Negro programming

MISSISSIPPI

Canton
WMGO—1370 kc.
Canton Broadcasting Co.
Some Negro programming

Centreville
WLBS—1580 kc.
La-Miss Broadcasting Co.
Some Negro programming

Clarksdale
WROX—1450 kc.
Mrs. Eunice T. Imes
Some Negro programming

Greenville
WGVM—1260 kc.
Mid-America Broadcasting Co., Inc.
Some Negro programming

Hattiesburg
WXXX—1310 kc.
Echo Broadcasting Corp.
Some Negro programming

Jackson
WOKJ—1550 kc.
McLendon Jackson Broadcasting Co.
All Negro programming

Laurel
WAML—1340 kc.
New Laurel Radio Station, Inc.
Some Negro programming

Leland
WESY—1580 kc.
Miss-Ark Broadcasting Co.
All Negro programming

Magee
WSJC—790 kc.
Southeast Mississippi Broadcasting Co.
Some Negro programming

Meridian
WOKK—1450 kc.
New South Broadcasting Corp.
Some Negro programming
WQIC—1390 kc.
A. L. Royal
All Negro programming

Natchez
WNAT—1450 kc.
Old South Broadcasting Co., Inc.
Some Negro programming

Picayune
WRJW—1320 kc.
Tung Broadcasting Co.
Some Negro programming

MISSOURI

Fulton
KFAL—900 kc.
Robert W. Nickles
Some Negro programming

Kansas City
KPRS—1590 kc.
KPRS (FM)—103.3 mc.
KPRS Broadcasting Corp.
All Negro programming

St. Louis
KATZ—1600 kc.
Laclede Radio, Inc.
All Negro programming
KXLW—1320 kc.
Big Signal Radio Broadcasting Co., Inc.
All Negro programming

NEW JERSEY

Atlantic City
WMID—1340 kc.
Mid-Atlantic Broadcasting Co.
Some Negro programming

Newark
WNJR—1430 kc.
Continental Broadcasting, Inc.
All Negro programming
WHBI (FM)—105.9 mc.
Cosmopolitan Broadcasting Corp.
Some Negro programming

Plainfield
WERA—1590 kc.
Tri-County Broadcasting Corp.
Some Negro programming

Trenton
WTTM—920 kc.
Scott Broadcasting Co., Inc. of N. J.
Some Negro programming

NEW MEXICO

Albuquerque
KLOS—1580 kc.
B & M Broadcasters, Inc.
Some Negro programming

Hobbs
KWEW—1480 kc.
KWEW
Some Negro programming

NEW YORK

Buffalo
WUFO—1080 kc.
Dynamic Broadcasting, Inc.
All Negro programming

New York City
WADO—1280 kc.
Bartell Broadcasting Corp.
Some Negro programming
WLIB—1190 kc.
New Broadcasting Co., Inc.
Some Negro programming
WWRL—1600 kc.
WWRL, Inc.
Some Negro programming

North Syracuse
WSOQ—1220 kc.
WSOQ, Inc.
Some Negro programming

Poughkeepsie
WEOK—1390 kc.
WEOK Broadcasting Corp.
Some Negro programming

Rochester
WHEC—1460 kc.
WHEC, Inc.
Some Negro programming
WSAY—1370 kc.
The Federal Broadcasting System, Inc.
Some Negro programming

Syracuse
WOLF—1490 kc.
Ivy Broadcasting Co.
Some Negro programming

NORTH CAROLINA

Asheboro
WGWR—1260 kc.
WGWR (FM)—92.3 mc.
Asheboro Broadcasting Co.
Some Negro programming

Burlington
WBBB—920 kc.
WBBB (FM)—101.1 mc.
Alamance Broadcasting Co., Inc.
Some Negro programming

Charlotte
WGIV—1600 kc.
Charlotte Radio & Television Corp.
Some Negro programming
WRPL—1540 kc.
Voice of Charlotte, Incorporated
All Negro programming

Durham
WSRC—1410 kc.
Carolina Radio of Durham, Inc.
All Negro programming

Farmville
WFAG—1250 kc.
Farmville Broadcasting Co.
Some Negro programming

Greensboro
WEAL—1510 kc.
WEAL, Inc.
All Negro programming

Henderson
WHNC—890 kc.
WHNC (FM)—92.5 mc.
Henderson Radio Corp.
Some Negro programming

High Point
WHPE—1070 kc.
WHPE (FM)—95.5 mc.
The High Point Broadcasting Co.
Some Negro programming

Raleigh
WLLE—570 kc.
WLLE
All Negro programming

Scotland Neck
WYAL—1280 kc.
Pee Dee Broadcasting Co., Inc.
Some Negro programming

Mullins
WJAY—1280 kc.
Mullins & Marion Broadcasting Co.
Some Negro programming

North Augusta
WTHB—1550 kc.
North Augusta Broadcasting Co., Inc.
All Negro programming

Walterboro
WALD—1220 kc.
Walterboro Radiocasting Co., Inc.
Some Negro programming

York
WYCL—1580 kc.
York-Clover Broadcasting Co.
Some Negro programming

TENNESSEE

Bolivar
WBOL—1560 kc.
Savannah Broadcasting Service, Inc.
Some Negro programming

Chattanooga
WNOO—1260 kc.
WMFS, Inc.
All Negro programming

Clarksville
WDXN—540 kc.
Clarksville Broadcasting Co., Inc.
Some Negro programming

Humboldt
WIRJ—740 kc.
Gibson County Broadcasting Co.
Some Negro programming

Jackson
WJAK—1460 kc.
Jackson Broadcasting Co.
Some Negro programming

Memphis
WDIA—1070 kc.
WDIA, Inc.
All Negro programming
WLOK—1340 kc.
WLOK, Inc.
All Negro programming

Nashville
WVOL—1470 kc.
Rounsaville of Nashville, Inc.
All Negro programming

TEXAS

Beaumont
KJET—1380 kc.
KJET, Inc.
All Negro programming

Corsicana
KAND—1340 kc.
Alto, Inc.
Some Negro programming

Dallas-Fort Worth
KNOK—970 kc.
KNOK (FM)—107.5 mc.
KNOK Broadcasting Co., Inc.
Some Negro programming

Houston
KCOH—1430 kc.
Call of Houston, Inc.
All Negro programming
KYOK—1590 kc.
KYOK, Inc.
All Negro programming

Huntsville
KSAM—1490 kc.
Verla Cauthen
Some Negro programming

Statesville
WDBM—550 kc.
WDBM (FM)—96.9 mc.
Iredell Broadcasting Corp.
Some Negro programming

Wadesboro
WADE—1210 kc.
R. P. Lyon & Son, Radio Bldg.
Some Negro programming

Wilmington
WHSL—1490 kc.
The Progressive Broadcasting Corp.
Some Negro programming

OHIO

Cincinnati
WCIN—1480 kc.
Rounsaville of Cincinnati, Inc.
All Negro programming

Cleveland
WABQ—1540 kc.
Booth Broadcasting Co.
All Negro programming
WJMO—1490 kc.
UBC of Ohio
Some Negro programming

Columbus
WBNS—1460 kc.
RadiOhio, Inc.
Some Negro programming
WVKO—1580 kc.
Sky Way Broadcasting Corp.
All Negro programming

Dayton
WDAO (FM)—107.7 mc.
WAVI Broadcasting Corp.
All Negro programming

Youngstown
WBBW—1240 kc.
Mahoning Valley Broadcasting Corp.
Some Negro programming

OKLAHOMA

Edmond
KWHP (FM)—97.7 mc.
William H. Payne
Some Negro programming

El Reno
KELR—1460 kc.
C. P. Corporation, Inc.
Some Negro programming

Oklahoma City
KBYE—890 kc.
Great Empire Broadcasting Corp.
All Negro programming

Tulsa
KOCW (FM)—97.5 mc.
Grayhill, Inc.
Some Negro programming

PENNSYLVANIA

Philadelphia

WDAS—1480 kc.
Max M. Leon, Inc., WDAS Bldg.
All Negro programming

WHAT—1340 kc.
Independence Broadcasting Co., WHAT Radio Center
All Negro programming

Pittsburgh

WAMO—860 kc.
Dynamic Broadcasting, Inc.
All Negro programming

SOUTH CAROLINA

Anderson

WANS—1280 kc.
Radio Anderson, Inc.
Some Negro programming

Charleston

WPAL—730 kc.
WPAL, Inc.
All Negro programming

Columbia

WOIC—1320 kc.
WOIC, Inc.
All Negro programming

Florence

WYNN—540 kc.
WYNN, Inc.
All Negro programming

Greenville

WMUU (FM)—94.5 mc.
Bob Jones University
Some Negro programming

Greer

WCKI—1300 kc.
Sira-Pak Radio, Inc.
Some Negro programming

Midland

KJBC—1150 kc.
Radio KJBC
Some Negro programming

Sulphur Springs

KSST—1230 kc.
Hopkins County Broadcasting Co.
Some Negro programming

UTAH

Salt Lake City

KSXX—630 kc.
Star Broadcasting Co.
Some Negro programming

VIRGINIA

Altavista

WKDE—1280 kc.
Altavista Broadcasting Corp.
Some Negro programming

Chester

WIKI—1410 kc.
WIKI, Inc.
All Negro programming

Gretna

WMNA—730 kc.
WMNA (FM)—103.3 mc.
Central Virginia Broadcasting Co., Inc.
Some Negro programming

Lawrenceville

WLES—580 kc.
Harry A. Epperson, Law Bldg.
Some Negro programming

Norfolk

WRAP—850 kc.
Rollins Broadcasting, Inc.
All Negro programming

Richmond

WANT—990 kc.
The United Broadcasting Company
All Negro programming

Stuart

WHEO—1270 kc.
Gray Broadcasting Corp.
Some Negro programming

WASHINGTON

Seattle

KBLE 1050 kc.
Eastside Broadcasting Co.
Some Negro programming

KOMO—1000 kc.
Fisher's Blend Station, Inc.
Some Negro programming

KYAC—1460 kc.
Carl-Dek, Inc.
All Negro programming

WEST VIRGINIA

Beckley

WJLS—560 kc.
Joe L. Smith, Jr., Inc., WJLS Bldg.
Some Negro programming

Welch

WELC—1150 kc.
Pocahontas Broadcasting Co.
Some Negro programming

WISCONSIN

Wauwatosa

WTOS (FM)—103.7 mc.
Broadcast, Inc.
Some Negro programming

West Allis

WAWA—1590 kc.
Suburbanaire, Inc.
All Negro programming

REEDOM'S JOURNAL.

"RIGHTEOUSNESS EXALTETH A NATION."

NISH & RUSSWURM, Editors & Proprietors. NEW-YORK, FRIDAY, MARCH 16, 1827. VOL. I. NO

TO OUR PATRONS.

presenting our first number to our Pa-
, we feel all the diffidence of persons en-
upon a new and untried line of busi-
But a moment's reflection upon the no-

Samuel Cornish

ence has taught its subjects to be virtuous:
ny instances of poverty, because no suffi-
nt efforts accommodated to minds contrac-
by slavery, and deprived of early educa-
n have been made, to teach them how to
spend their hard earnings, and to secure to
mselves comforts.

Education being an object of the highest
portance to the welfare of society, we shall
deavour to present just and adequate views
it, and to urge upon our brethren the neces-
y and expediency of training their children,
ile young, to habits of industry, and thus
ming them for becoming useful members of
ciety. It is surely time that we should awake
m this lethargy of years, and make a con-
ntrated effort for the education of our youth.
e form a spoke in the human wheel, and it
necessary that we should underst
endence on the different parts, and
, in order to perform our part wi
y.

Though not desirous of dictating
el it our incumbent duty to dwell
ly upon the general principles and rules o
conomy. The world has grown too enlight-
ed, to estimate any man's character by hi
ersonal appearance. Though all men ac
nowledge the excellency of Franklin's max
s, yet comparatively few practise upo
hem. We may deplore when it is too la
he neglect of these self-evident truths, but
vails little to mourn. Ours will be the ta
f announcing our brethren on these point

The civil rights of a people being of the
greatest value, it shall ever be our duty to
vindicate our brethren,
nd to lay the case befor
hall also urge upon our
ualified by the laws of
he expediency of using
hise; and of making a
f the same. We wish the

works of trivial importance, we shall consider it a part of our duty to recommend to our young readers, such authors as will not only enlarge their stock of useful knowledge, but such as will also serve to stimulate them to higher attainments in science.

lso, that through the columns
om's Journal, many practi-
aving for their bases, the im-
our brethren, will be presented
the pens of many of our respect-
o have kindly promised their as-

rnest wish to make our Journal
intercourse between our breth-
ferent states of this great con-
through its columns an expres-
ntiments, on many interesting
h concern us, may be offered to
that plans which apparently are
y be candidly discussed and pro-
; if worthy, receive our cordial
if not, our marked disapproba-

wledge of every kind, and every
ates to Africa, shall find a ready
o our columns; and as that vast
omes daily more known, we trust
ngs will come to light, proving
es of it are neither so ignorant
they have generally been sup-

these important subjects shall
lumns of the Freedom's Jour-
ould not be unmindful of our brethren who are still in the iron fetters of bondage. They are our kindred by all the ties of nature; and though but little can be effected by us, still let our sympathies be poured forth, and our prayers in their behalf, ascend to Him who is able to succour them.

From the press and the pulpit we have suffered much by being incorrectly represented. Men, whom we equally love and admire have not hesitated to represent us disadvantageously, without becoming personally acquainted with the true state of things, nor discerning be
virtu
sevel
thing
Ou
rayed
by un

narrative which they have published; the establishment of the republic of Hayti after years of sanguinary warfare; its subsequent progress in all the arts of civilization; and the advancement of liberal ideas in South America, where despotism has given place to free governments, and where many of our brethren now fill important civil and military stations, prove the contrary.

The interesting fact that there are FIVE HUNDRED THOUSAND free persons of colour, one half of whom might peruse, and
the whole
the Journa
been devo
ment—tha
standard a
of few, ma
important
izens have
prove the
appearance

John B. Russwurm

It shall e
editorial de
offence to
farther fro
of any part
gion. Wh
been devot
ren; and
mainder m
service.

In concl
people, wil
the Fre
all the prin

And whi
be perform
Journal, w
merous frie
tions, and our coloured brethren to strengthen our hands by their subscriptions, as our labour is one of common cause, and worthy of their consideration and support. And we do most earnestly solicit the latter, that if at any time we should seem to be zealous, or too pointed in the inculcati
rtant lesson,
lly in-
e enga-
culiari-
t enga-

ORS.

of his countrymen he possessed s
superior to his condition; althou
diligent in the business of his
faithful to his interest, yet by gre
and economy he was enabled to pu
personal liberty. At the time the
several Indian tribes, who originall
ed the right of soil, resided in Mass
Cuffee became acquainted with a w
scended from one of those tribes, na
Moses, and married her. He co
habits of industry and frugality, a
terwards purchased a farm of 100 a
point in Massachusetts.
Cuffee and Ruth had a family o

and his brother John Cuffee, we
by the collector of the district, in
resided, for the payment of a pers
appeared to them, that by the la
stitution of Massachusetts, taxat
whole rights of citizenship were
the laws demanded of them the
the personal taxes, the same laws
sarily and constitutionally invest
the right of representing and b
sented in the state legislature. F
never been considered as entitled
ilege of voting at elections, nor of
ted to places of trust and honor.
circumstances they refused pay
demands. The collector resorted
of the laws, and after many del
tentions, Paul and his brother de
prudent to silence them by pay
mands; but they resolved, if it w
to obtain the rights which they b
connected with taxation. They
respectful petition to the state l
From some individuals it met w
most indignant opposition.
majority was, however,
object. They perceived t
justice of the petition, and
ble magnanimity, in defiance
of the times, they passed a
all free persons of color liable
rding to the established rat
and granting them all the pr
ng to the other citizens. T
ly honorable to the petitio
ature—a day which ought t
remembered by every pers
the boundaries of Massac
es of John and Paul C
d with its recollec
aused.

New-Y
the Su
state of
the Hous

THE BLACK PRESS

Guide to Negro Newspapers and Periodicals
Famous Negro Publishers and Journalists

The Negro press in the United States is heir to a great and, indeed, largely unheralded tradition. It began with the first Negro newspaper, *Freedom's Journal* (edited and published by Samuel Cornish and John B. Russwurm), which first appeared in New York City on March 16, 1827. Like many other Negro newspapers of later vintage—and several white abolitionist organs as well—*Freedom's Journal* sought to represent the Negro by pleading *his* case before the American public. *The North Star*, the newspaper of the celebrated abolitionist, Frederick Douglass, dedicated itself to much the same cause when its first edition rolled off the presses in Rochester, New York on December 3, 1847.

Negro journalism experienced a rapid growth in the era immediately following the Civil War. Several periodicals began publication but, more importantly, the "political" press came into its own, reflecting the Negro's new-found awareness of himself as a decision-maker in Congress, as well as in several state legislatures.

By the 1880's, the Negro's increasing social mobility, coupled with his ability to establish a substantial cultural environment in many cities of the North, led to the creation of a new wave of publications, including the Washington *Bee*, the Indianapolis *World*, the Philadelphia *Tribune*, the Cleveland *Gazette*, and the New York *Age*. By 1900, there were no less than three dailies, one each in Norfolk, Kansas City, and Washington, D.C.

Among the famous Negro editors associated with this era are W. M. Trotter, editor of the Boston *Guardian*, a self-styled "radical" paper which showed no sympathy for the so-called conciliatory stance of Booker T. Washington; Robert S. Abbott whose Chicago *Defender* pioneered in the use of headlines and other techniques of mass circulation, and T. T. Fortune of the New York *Age*, who championed free public schools in an age when many were opposed to the idea.

The Negro press at once set for itself the goal of keeping the Negro public informed of the vital issues of the day, as well as creating an appropriate forum for the voicing of Negro sentiment on such issues. Moreover, the press sought to expose political injustice and corruption, while at the same time exhorting the Negro to become more aware of his achievements and the opportunities open to him. While on the one hand it demanded that society as a whole provide better schools, improved sanitation, and more comprehensive police protection, it likewise threw its support behind Negro self-help groups like the NAACP and the National Negro Business League which themselves sought to better the Negro's lot in a variety of areas.

Realizing that urbanization, for all its drawbacks, still offered the Negro a more promising future than a rural environment, the Negro press backed migration to the North as a means of escaping Southern oppression. It is also important to remember that most Negro papers were behind American involvement in World War I, and sought actively to encourage Negroes to fight for their country.

Today, it would be difficult to label any single Negro newspaper as *the* most influential in the nation. By virtue of the very frequency of their appearance, if nothing else, the two dailies—the *Atlanta Daily World* and the *Chicago Daily Defender*—clearly deserve mention. So, too, do the *Pittsburgh Courier* and *Afro-American* chains. The weekly *Courier* has one national and several other editions which appear in such major cities as Chicago (8,259); Detroit (15,925); New York (13,016); Philadelphia (1,242) and Pittsburgh (14,550).* The *Afro-American*, founded in Baltimore in 1892, is now distributed in 43 states, and has a total circulation of 152,615.

Perhaps the most ambitious venture in recent years has been *Tuesday* magazine, a Sunday supplement with a circulation of 1,400,000 which is being carried in the newspapers of several leading American cities, and sold on newsstands as well. There are also, of course, high-quality weekly and monthly magazines like *Jet* and *Ebony* which have provided a better-rounded and more sophisticated view of Negro life in America.

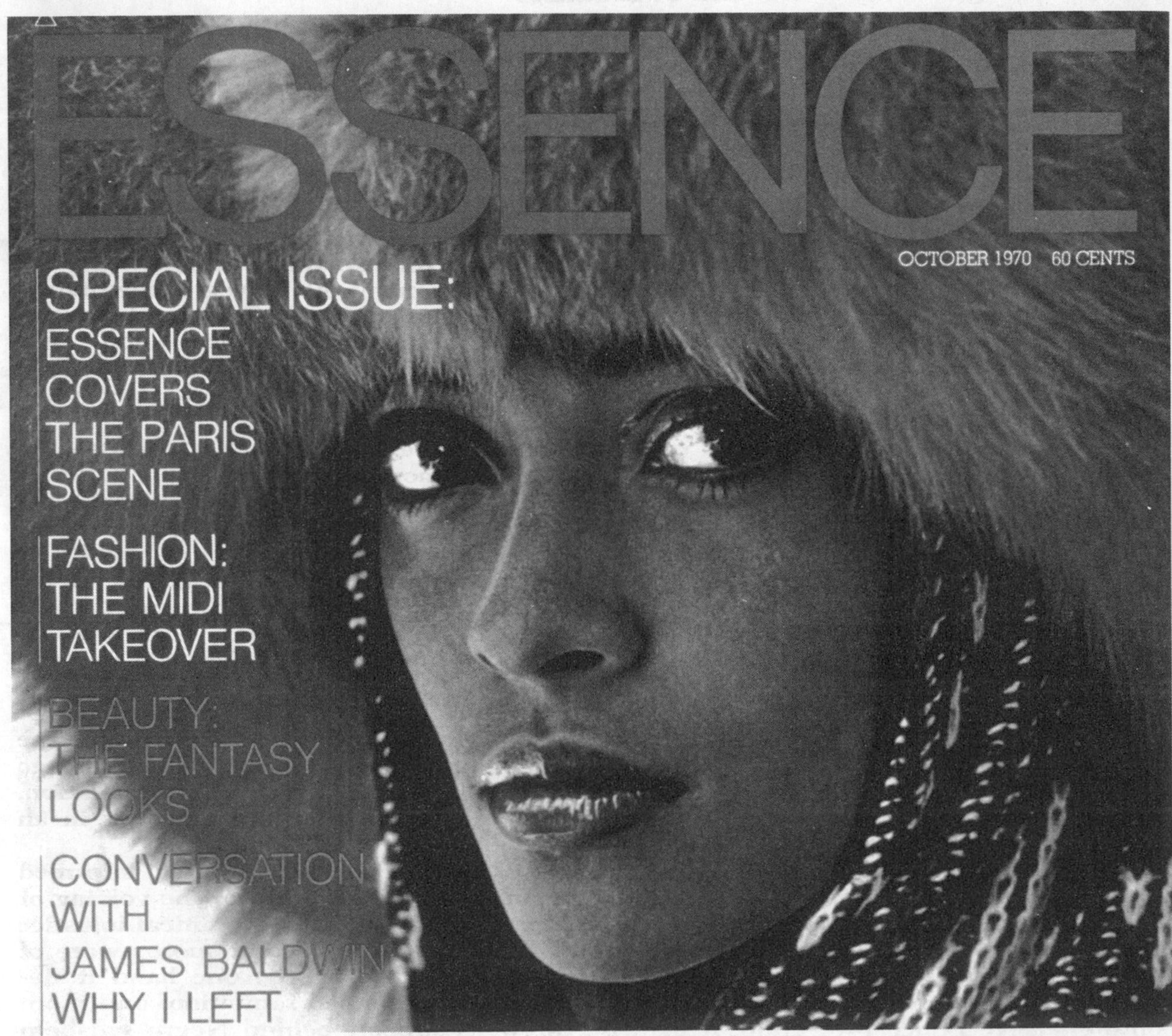

ESSENCE *is a new magazine featuring black arts, design concepts and cultural activities.*

As of 1968, publisher W. Leonard Evans was able to report that *Tuesday's* circulation had climbed another 100,000, with white readership representing some 15% of that total. "A medium confined to the ghetto will not work," Evans contended. "Civil rights is communicating and information has to flow not only in but also out. *Tuesday* interprets for the first time the positive side of the Negro community." The sleek graphic attractiveness of *Tuesday* was another factor promoting its growth.

Seeking the positive side and projecting the glamor implicit in the "black is beautiful" syndrome led to the founding in 1970 of another stylish monthly magazine called *Essence*. The magazine has borrowed heavily on the *Vogue* format, although editorial director Gordon Parks has on occasion lent it a *Ramparts* air with provocative pictures and hard-hitting commentary on aspects of black militancy. As the magazine progresses, however, youth, beauty and femininity may find themselves uneasily wedded to a heavy dosage of polemical writing.

Roy Innis and William Haddad are co-publishers of the **Manhattan Tribune.**

The New York newspaper *Manhattan Tribune,* founded in 1968, decided instead to adopt a strong editorial stance on vital community and urban issues, and to hammer away at themes designed to arouse controversy and rankle consciences. Co-editors Roy Innis and William Haddad fought it out weekly in print on the virtues, advantages, and possibilities of integration in American society, but they tackled concrete gut issues affecting Upper West Side and Harlem residents as well. Thus, they investigated consumer purchasing patterns, price discrepancies, and pervasive drug traffic as well. Constructively, the *Tribune* editors set aside ideological differences whenever the opportunity arose to benefit minority group members. Thus, the pair set up a training program for black and Puerto Rican journalism aspirants, and found willing helpers among an advisory committee from Time, Inc., Harper's and the New York *Times.*

To determine the journalism industry's own record in the field of minority group hiring, former newspaper and TV reporter Woody Klein, once press secretary under Mayor John Lindsay, studied the editorial stance and hiring patterns of the organizations which came forth to help fledgling ventures like the *Tribune.* His survey *News Media and Race Relations* showed that the media had become aware that it was not adequately conveying to its predominantly white audience a sense of the conditions and feelings of most of the black population. Klein concluded that the profession was showing "definite signs of progress" in what had at last become a stated goal: to study the black/white relationship (and the black/black relationship) on a regular, not on a "special" basis.

To facilitate this task, it was thought that newspaper and broadcasting titans in the field were under a special obligation to recruit more black reporters, editors, correspondents, and photographers. Surveys of such papers as the New York *Times* (13 blacks out of 374 editorial employees), the San Francisco *Chronicle* (four out of 150) and the Washington *Post* (19 out of 222) at least provided some statistical yardstick of black participation in determining the flow and tone of the news. News-gathering organizations like the United Press and the Associated Press, the natural training grounds for big-city reporters, released figures which could hardly be regarded as favorable. UPI claimed to have 10 black staffers among its 650 employees, whereas the Associated Press showed only 12 out of nearly 1,000 editorial employees. Among the networks, the percentages were better, particularly at NBC which estimated that about a dozen of its 60-odd nationwide correspondents were black. *Newsweek* and *Time* each showed 10 blacks filling assorted editorial capacities; *Life* and *Look* listed five each.

The lack of adequate encouragement from the "white" media is one of the reasons for the continuing success of the Johnson publishing empire and the uninterrupted growth of the black press. From the outset, Johnson realized that a magazine in tune with the pace of black progress would have an enormous market in the black community, and appeal as well to multiple advertisers anxious to expose their wares to a comparatively prosperous black buying public. Once *Ebony* gained a foothold as a black middle-class version of *Life,* Johnson was in a position to cultivate other identifiable markets in the ghetto community. *Tan* offered home-making advice and love stories; *Jet* offered inside dope, gossipy tidbits, and social news; *Black World* (formerly *Negro Digest*) sustained a literary and intellectual clientele, featuring analyses of protest movements and black power rhetoric. *Ebony* continues to turn huge profits (over $7,000,000 in ad revenues in 1967) with its durable format stressing both achievement and tumult.

Like *Ebony,* the black press in general—whether it be the large weeklies like the New York Amsterdam *News* or Detroit's Michigan *Chronicle,* or the established dailies like the Chicago *Defender* or the Atlanta *Daily World*—practices a moderate brand of militancy, even as it deliberately promotes a more conspicuous tone of black chauvinism. Most newspapers debunk the tactics of black power militants like Stokely Carmichael, and condemn violence and rioting with equal candor. They steer a cautious middle ground between alerting the white establishment to the legitimate grievances of the black community and prodding local citizens to exhibit more determination and resolve in dealing with some of the more readily surmountable problems.

The flourishing black press and the thawing white press cannot fail to agree with the analysis offered by black Washington *Post* columnist William Raspberry. "Even if you're covering something about subways or bridges," says Raspberry, "black people inevitably enter into the picture."

GUIDE TO NEGRO NEWSPAPERS AND PERIODICALS IN THE U.S.*

Newspapers

The Mirror
1517 Cooper Ave.,
Anniston, Ala.
Circ.—2,140 wkly.

Birmingham World
312 17th St., N.,
Birmingham, Ala.
Circ.—9,700 wkly.

The Mirror
1517 4th Ave., N.,
Birmingham, Ala.
Circ.—14,436 wkly.

The Mirror
230 Church St.,
Huntsville, Ala.
Circ.—3,160 wkly.

Mobile Beacon
415 S. Cedar St.,
Mobile, Ala.
Circ.—5,000 wkly.

Alabama Tribune
123½ Monroe St.,
Montgomery, Ala.
Circ.—1,500 wkly.

Tri-Cities Mirror
1013 E. 18th St.,
Sheffield, Ala.
Circ.—2,245 wkly.

Alaska Spotlight
P. O. Box 116,
Anchorage, Alas.
Circ.—1,000 wkly.

Arizona Sun
4014 S. Central St.,
Phoenix, Ariz.
Circ.—5,550 wkly.

Arizona Tribune
2137 E. Broadway St.,
Phoenix, Ariz.
Circ.—3,300 wkly.

California Eagle
2101 W. Vernon Ave.,
Los Angeles, Cal.
Circ.—27,500 wkly.

Herald-Dispatch
1431 W. Jefferson Blvd.,
Los Angeles, Cal.
Circ.—31,000 semi-wkly.

The Sentinel
1112 E. 43rd St.,
Los Angeles, Cal.
Circ.—38,612 wkly.

California Voice
814 27th St.,
Oakland, Cal.
Circ.—12,500 wkly.

Observer
P. O. Box 209,
Sacramento, Cal.
Circ.—7,410 wkly.

Outlook
1715 8th St.,
Sacramento, Cal.
Circ.—4,940 bi-wkly.

The Light House
2652 Imperial Ave.,
San Diego, Cal.
Circ.—8,500 wkly.

The Voice
1867 National Ave.,
San Diego, Cal.
Circ.—10,004 wkly.

The Independent
1555 Turk St.,
San Francisco, Cal.
Circ.—12,825 wkly.

The Sun-Reporter
1579 Post St.,
San Francisco, Cal.
Circ.—8,685 wkly.

The Blade
116 E. 20th Ave.,
Denver, Col.
Circ.—1,500 wkly.

The Star
3401 Columbine St.,
Denver, Col.
Circ.—1,200 wkly.

Wash. Afro-American
1800 11th St., N.W.,
Washington, D.C.
Circ.—152,615 semi-wkly.

The Spur
P. O. Box 8727,
Fort Lauderdale, Fla.
Circ.—1,700 wkly.

The Chronicle
1521 Avenue D,
Fort Pierce, Fla.
Circ.—9,879 wkly.

Florida Star-News
2323 Moncrief Dr.,
Jacksonville, Fla.
Circ.—25,374 wkly.

Florida Tattler
918 W. Union St.,
Jacksonville, Fla.
Circ.—16,500 wkly.

Miami Times
6740 N.W. 15th Ave.,
Miami, Fla.
Circ.—9,757 wkly.

Pensacola Citizen
508 W. Jackson St.,
Pensacola, Fla.
Weekly

Weekly Bulletin
P. O. Box 2510,
Sarasota, Fla.
Circ.—4,500 wkly.

Florida Sentinel-Bulletin
1511 Central Ave.,
Tampa, Fla.
Circ.—15,000 semi-wkly.

News Reporter
Box 2539, Tampa, Fla.
Circ.—4,920 wkly.

W. Palm Bch. Photo News
2108½ N. Tamarind Ave.,
West Palm Beach, Fla.
Circ.—1,871 wkly.

Southwest Georgian
517 Gordon Ave.,
Albany, Ga.
Circ.—2,900 wkly.

Atlanta Daily World
210 Auburn Ave., N.E.,
Atlanta, Ga.
Circ.—30,100 daily

Atlanta Inquirer
953 Hunter St., N.W.,
Atlanta, Ga.
Circ.—18,911 wkly.

Weekly Review
1540 12th St.,
Augusta, Ga.
Circ.—4,600 wkly.

Columbus News
Columbus, Ga.
Circ.—14,000 semi-wkly.

The Herald
808 Montgomery St.,
Savannah, Ga.
Circ.—5,015 wkly.

The Telegram
P. O. Box 1433,
Valdosta, Ga.
Circ.—10,000 wkly.

Illinois Times
202 Ellis Ave.,
Champaign, Ill.
Circ.—1,500 wkly.

Chicago Bulletin
Chicago, Ill.
Circ.—23,000 wkly.

Chicago Daily Defender
(daily edition)
2400 S. Michigan Ave.,

GUIDE TO NEGRO NEWSPAPERS AND PERIODICALS IN THE U.S.*—Cont.

Chicago, Ill.
Circ.—37,549 daily

Chicago Defender
(weekend edition)
2400 S. Michigan Ave.,
Chicago, Ill.
Circ.—39,959 wkly.

Muhammad Speaks
5335 S. Greenwood Ave.,
Chicago, Ill.

New Crusader
6429 S. Park Ave.,
Chicago, Ill.
Circ.—19,541 wkly.

The Beacon
2217 Missouri Ave.,
East St. Louis, Ill.
Circ.—3,500 wkly.

The Crusader
1600 Missouri Ave.,
East St. Louis, Ill.
Circ.—7,000 wkly.

The East Side Monitor
504 Alexander Place,
East St. Louis, Ill.
Circ.—7,500 wkly.

Negro Voice
807 E. Benton St.,
Joliet, Ill.
Circ.—4,500 wkly.

The Crusader
821 Winnebago St.,
Rockford, Ill.
Circ.—3,500 wkly.

Springfield Ill. Chronicle
1210 S. 16th St.,
Springfield, Ill.
Circ.—600 bi-wkly.

The American
2268 Broadway,
Gary, Ind.
Circ.—6,885 wkly.

The Crusader
1930 Broadway,
Gary, Ind.
Circ.—11,269 wkly.

Indiana Herald
Indianapolis, Ind.
Circ.—14,601 wkly.

Indianapolis Recorder
518 Indiana Ave.,
Indianapolis, Ind.
Circ.—10,758 wkly.

Iowa Bystander
223½ Locust St.,
Des Moines, Iowa
Circ.—2,592 wkly.

The Enlightener
2226 Mossman St.,
Wichita, Kan.
Circ.—2,400 wkly.

Louisville Defender
714 N. Chestnut St.,
Louisville, Ky.
Circ.—5,180 wkly.

News Leader
Alexandria, La.
Circ.—10,500 wkly.

Baton Rouge News Leader
P. O. Box 1921,
Baton Rouge, La.
Circ.—15,500 wkly.

The Hurricane
P. O. Box 5628,
Bossier City, La.
Circ.—2,375 wkly.

News Leader
Monroe, La.
Circ.—10,000 wkly.

Louisiana Weekly
640 S. Rampart St.,
New Orleans, La.
Circ.—18,621 wkly.

Shreveport Sun
1030 Texas Ave.,
Shreveport, La.
Circ.—12,748 wkly.

Afro-American
(national edition)
628 N. Eutaw St.,
Baltimore, Md.
Circ.—30,194 wkly.

Afro-American
(Tues., Sat. edition)
628 N. Eutaw St.,
Baltimore, Md.
Circ.—72,521 semi-wkly.

Boston Chronicle
794 Tremont St.,
Boston, Mass.
Circ.—10,509 wkly.

Boston (Roxbury) City News
Boston, Mass.
Circ.—19,328 wkly.

Boston Graphic
979 Tremont St.,
Boston, Mass.
Circ.—4,000 wkly.

The Orator
254 Seaver St.,
Boston, Mass.
Circ.—2,000 wkly.

The Times
169 Massachusetts Ave.,
Boston, Mass.
Circ.—12,000 wkly.

The Sun
235 Hancock St.,
Springfield, Mass.
Circ.—12,500 wkly.

Michigan Chronicle
479 Ledvard St.,
Detroit, Mich.
Circ.—54,744 wkly.

Michigan Scene
8335 Woodward Ave.,
Detroit, Mich.
Circ.—4,100 wkly.

The Tribune
970 Gratiot St.,
Detroit, Mich.
Circ.—28,700 wkly.

The Spokesman
3744 4th Ave., S.,
Minneapolis, Minn.
Circ.—10,416 wkly.

The Twin City Observer
23 S. 6th St.,
Minneapolis, Minn.
Circ.—2,000 wkly.

The Recorder
403 New York Bldg.,
St. Paul, Minn.
Circ.—8,322 wkly.

The Sun
809 Dayton Ave.,
St. Paul, Minn.
Circ.—2,000 wkly.

Greenville Delta Leader
1513 Alexander St.,
Greenville, Miss.
Weekly

Jackson Advocate
406½ Farish St., N.,
Jackson, Miss.
Circ.—4,000 wkly.

Jackson Enterprise
110 E. Monument St.,
Jackson, Miss.
Weekly

Mississippi Free Press
1072-1 W. Lynch St.,
Jackson, Miss.
Circ.—8,000 wkly.

New Albany Community Citizen
P. O. Box 213,

GUIDE TO NEGRO NEWSPAPERS AND PERIODICALS IN THE U.S.*—Cont.

New Albany, Miss.
Circ.—1,360 semi-mthly.

Kansas City Call
1715 E. 18th St.,
Kansas City, Mo.
Circ.—20,116 wkly.

Crusader
1025 Grand Ave.,
St. Louis, Mo.
Circ.—5,000 wkly.

New Citizen
4441 Kennerly St.,
St. Louis, Mo.
Circ.—3,100 bi-wkly.

New Crusader
5938 Plymouth St.,
St. Louis, Mo.
Circ.—4,100 wkly.

The American
3608 Cozens St.,
St. Louis, Mo.
Circ.—7,200 wkly.

The Argus
4595 Easton Ave.,
St. Louis, Mo.
Circ.—6,386 wkly.

Omaha Star
2216 N. 24th St.,
Omaha, Neb.
Circ.—5,600 wkly.

The Guide
2420 Grant St.,
Omaha, Neb.
Circ.—4,050 wkly.

Central Jersey Post
RFD 178A,
Asbury Park, N.J.
Circ.—7,500 wkly.

New Jersey Herald News
188 Belmont Ave.,
Newark, N.J.
Circ.—28,080 wkly.

Newark Afro-American
190 Clinton Ave.,
Newark, N.J.
Circ.—5,311 wkly.

Buffalo Empire Star
625 William St.,
Buffalo, N.Y.
Circ.—15,000 wkly.

Criterion
267 William St.,
Buffalo, N.Y.
Circ.—12,000 wkly.

Westchester County Press
61 Pinecrest Dr.,
Hastings-on-Hudson, N.Y.
Circ.—5,000 wkly.

Westchester Observer
905 S. 5th Ave.,
Mt. Vernon, N.Y.
Circ.—7,500 wkly.

New York Recorder
1650 Fulton St.,
Brooklyn, N.Y.
Circ.—17,750 wkly.

The Urban Life
560 Atlantic Ave.,
Brooklyn, N. Y.
Circ.—2,500 (est.), wkly.

East Elmhurst News & Queens Voice
95-18 Astoria Blvd.,
East Elmhurst, N.Y.
Weekly

Muhammad Speaks
113 Lenox Ave.,
New York, N.Y.
Circ.—50,000 (est.), bi-wkly.

New York Amsterdam News
2340 8th Ave.,
New York, N.Y.
Circ.—89,596 wkly.

The American Negro
Rochester, N.Y.
Circ.—7,000 wkly.

Progressive Herald
815 E. Fayette St.,
Syracuse, N.Y.
Circ.—9,300 wkly.

Charlotte Post
Charlotte, N.C.
Circ.—18,265 wkly.

Charlotte Queen City Gazette
Charlotte, N.C.
Circ.—2,750 wkly.

Carolina Times
436 E. Pettigrew St.,
Durham, N.C.
Circ.—22,004 wkly.

Future Outlook
505 E. Market St.,
Greensboro, N.C.
Circ.—8,762 wkly.

The Carolinian
518 E. Martin St.,
Raleigh, N.C.
Circ.—6,800 wkly.

Wilmington Journal
412 S. 7th St.,
Wilmington, N.C.
Circ.—6,025 wkly.

The Herald
3488 Reading Rd.,
Cincinnati, Ohio
Circ.—4,900 wkly.

Call & Post
P. O. Box 6237,
Cleveland, Ohio
Circ.—28,147 wkly.

Columbus Call & Post
1102 E. Long St.,
Columbus, Ohio
Circ.—6,658 wkly.

Ohio Sentinel
430 E. Long St.,
Columbus, Ohio
Circ.—3,862 wkly.

Bronze Raven
920 Collingswood Blvd.,
Toledo, Ohio
Circ.—9,500 wkly.

Buckeye Review
423 Oak Hill Ave.,
Youngstown, Ohio
Circ.—5,500 wkly.

Butler County American
422 S. Front St.,
Hamilton, Ohio
Circ.—2,650 wkly.

The Herald
325 N. 2nd St.,
Muskogee, Okla.
Circ.—1,500 wkly.

Black Dispatch
P. O. Box 1254
Oklahoma City, Okla.
Circ.—11,688 wkly.

Oklahoma Eagle
P. O. Box 1867
Tulsa, Okla.
Circ.—6,000 wkly.

Open Mike
1834 W. Girard Ave.,
Philadelphia, Pa.
Circ.—5,000 wkly.

Philadelphia Afro-American
427 S. Broad St.,
Philadelphia, Pa.
Circ.—5,005 wkly.

Philadelphia Independent
1708 Lombard St.,
Philadelphia, Pa.

GUIDE TO NEGRO NEWSPAPERS AND PERIODICALS IN THE U.S.*—Cont.

Circ.—12,067 wkly.

Philadelphia Tribune
524-526 S. 16th St.,
Philadelphia, Pa.
Circ.—71,014 semi-wkly.

The Pittsburgh Courier (national edition)
2628 Centre Ave.,
Pittsburgh, Pa.
Circ.—94,464 wkly. (all editions)

The Herald
407 Butler St.,
Anderson, S.C.
Circ.—5,000 wkly.

Palmetto Times
Columbia, S.C.
Circ.—4,000 wkly.

Carolina Sun
601 E. Main St.,
Kingstree, S.C.
Circ.—1,000 wkly.

Chattanooga Observer
124½ E. 9th St.,
Chattanooga, Tenn.
Circ.—4,200 wkly.

Flashlight Herald
506 College St., N.W.,
Knoxville, Tenn.
Circ.—3,700 wkly.

Knoxville Times
P. O. Box 281,
Knoxville, Tenn.
Circ.—2,495 wkly.

Memphis World
546 Beale St.,
Memphis, Tenn.
Circ.—6,000 semi-wkly.

Tri-State Defender
P. O. Box 311,
Memphis, Tenn.
Circ.—5,405 wkly.

Murfreesboro News
121 Vine St.,
Murfreesboro, Tenn.
Circ.—3,500 mthly.

Nashville Commentator
1909 Formosa St.,
Nashville, Tenn.
Circ.—2,500 wkly.

Dallas Express
2604 Thomas Ave.,
Dallas, Tex.
Circ.—6,621 wkly.

Dallas Post Tribune
2606 Forest Ave.,
Dallas, Tex.
Circ.—4,153 wkly.

Dallas World
Dallas, Tex.
Circ.—6,000 wkly.

Fort Worth Mind
805 Bryan St.,
Fort Worth, Tex.
Circ.—12,955 wkly.

Fort Worth Weekly
5529 Wellesley St.,
Fort Worth, Tex.
Circ.—2,000 wkly.

Forward Times
4411 Almeda Rd.,
Houston, Tex.
Circ.—12,000 wkly.

Informer
2418 Leeland Ave.,
Houston, Tex.
Circ.—9,037 semi-wkly.

Negro Labor News
P. O. Box 8055
Houston, Tex.
Circ.—20,000 mthly.

Sunnyside Digest
3306 Chenevert St.,
Houston, Tex.
Circ.—3,000 wkly.

The Messenger
P. O. Box 7,
Kendleton, Tex.
Circ.—2,100 wkly.

San Antonio Register
207 N. Centre St.,
San Antonio, Tex.
Circ.—9,924 wkly.

The Messenger
P. O. Box 2087,
Waco, Tex.
Circ.—3,400 wkly.

Charlottesville-Albemarle Tribune
1055 Grady Ave.,
Charlottesville, Va.
Circ.—2,271 wkly.

Journal & Guide
719 E. Olney Rd.,
Norfolk, Va.
Circ.—34,691 wkly.

Richmond Afro-American
301 E. Clay St.,
Richmond, Va.
Circ.—15,175 wkly.

Roanoke Tribune
312 First St., N.W.,
Roanoke, Va.
Circ.—15,200 wkly.

Gazette
2421 N. 3rd St.,
Milwaukee, Wis.
Circ.—11,010 wkly.

The Star
2334 N. 3rd St.,
Milwaukee, Wis.
Circ.—6,000 wkly.

Commercial Magazines and Journals

American News
5425½ S. Central Ave.,
Los Angeles, Cal.
Circ.—12,000 wkly.

Bronze America
2400 S. Western Ave.,
Los Angeles, Cal.
Circ.—25,000 (est.), six times yearly

Bronze California
3406 W. Washington Blvd.,
Los Angeles, Cal.
Circ.—30,000 (est.), mthly.

Elegant Magazine
8212 S. Western Ave.,
Los Angeles, Cal.
Circ.—60,000 (est.), bi-mthly.

Journal of Negro History
1538 Ninth St., N.W.,
Washington, D.C.
Circ.—5,000

Negro History Bulletin
1538 Ninth St., N.W.,
Washington, D.C.
Circ.—8,900 mthly.

GUIDE TO NEGRO NEWSPAPERS AND PERIODICALS IN THE U.S.*—Cont.

The Pyramid
1116 Rhode Island Ave.,
Washington, D.C.
Circ.—22,000

The Foundation
9 McDonough Blvd.,
Atlanta, Ga.
Circ.—1,500 qtrly.

Ebony Magazine
1820 S. Michigan Ave.,
Chicago, Ill.
Circ.—825,000 mthly.

Ivy Leaf
5211 S. Greenwood,
Chicago, Ill.
Circ.—10,000 qtrly.

Jet Magazine
1820 S. Michigan Ave.,
Chicago, Ill.
Circ.—371,000 wkly.

Tan Magazine
1820 S. Michigan Ave.,
Chicago, Ill.
Circ.—123,000 mthly.

On the Ball Magazine
754 East 169th St.,
Bronx, N.Y.
Circ.—5,000 qtrly.

African Heritage
79 Wall St.,
New York, N. Y.
Circ.—15,000 mthly.

African Opinion
8 W. 117th St.,
New York, N.Y.
Circ.—3,000 (est.),
bi-mthly.

Freedomways
799 Broadway,
New York, N. Y.
Circ.—5,000 qtrly.

Journal of the National Medical Association
30 Rockefeller Plaza,
New York, N.Y.
Circ.—3,600 bi-mthly.

Link Magazine
243 W. 125th St.,
New York, N. Y.
Monthly

News Illustrated
203 W. 138th St.,
New York, N. Y.
Circ.—4,000 mthly.

The Voice
200 W. 135th St.,
New York, N.Y.
Circ.—50,000 mthly.

Voice of Missions
112 W. 120th St.,
New York, N.Y.
Circ.—10,000 mthly.

Index to Selected Periodicals
Hallie Q. Brown Library,
Central State College,
Wilberforce, Ohio
Circ.—1,000 qtrly.

Journal of Human Relations
Central State College,
Wilberforce, Ohio
Circ.—1,200 qtrly.

Kappa Alpha Psi Journal
901 26th Ave., N.,
Nashville, Tenn.
Circ.—3,000 qtrly.

Bronze Thrills
Good Publishing Co.,
1220 Harding St.,
Fort Worth, Tex.
Circ.—400,000 combined
national distribution

Religious Publications

Baptist Leader
1621 Fourth Ave., N.,
Birmingham, Ala.
Circ.—2,112 wkly.

Campus Digest
P. O. Box HH,
Tuskegee, Ala.
Circ.—3,000 bi-wkly.

Journal of Religious Thought
The School of Religion,
Howard University,
Washington, D.C.
Circ.—1,500 semi-annual

The Center
Interdenominational
Theological Center,
Atlanta,Ga.
Circ.—1,500 qtrly.

St. Augustine's Messenger
Bay St. Louis, Miss.
Circ.—5,000 mthly.

Star of Zion
P. O. Box 1047,
Charlotte, N.C.
Circ.—4,500 wkly.

AME Church Review
5828 Race St.,
Philadelphia, Pa.
Circ.—5,000 qtrly.

Christian Index
109 Shannon St.,
Jackson, Tenn.
Circ.—5,000 wkly.

The Message Magazine
2119 24th Ave., N.,
Nashville, Tenn.
Circ.—50,000 mthly.

The Review
414 8th Ave., S.,
Nashville, Tenn.
Circ.—2,000 mthly.

Union Review
523 2nd Ave., N.,
Nashville, Tenn.
Circ.—5,000 wkly.

* Arranged in alphabetical order by city and state.

For further information, consult the latest editions of *Ayer's Directory of Newspapers and Periodicals* and the *Editor and Publisher's International Yearbook*. (Bellwether is grateful to both these publications for the assistance they have rendered.)

JOHNSON PUBLICATION

EBONY

Making Of Black America Par

THE WORLD OF THE SL

By Lerone Bennet

BLACK LAWMAKE IN CONGRE

P. ROBERT N. C. NIX

REP. CHARLES C. DIGGS

SEN. EDWARD W. BROOKE

REP. SHIRLEY CH

P. AUGUSTUS F. HAWKINS

HN CONYERS JR.

REP. LOUIS

REP. WILLIAM

P. CHARLES B. RANGEL

REP. RONALD V. DELLUMS

REP. RALPH H. METCALFE

REP. GEORGE W. COLLINS

REP. PARREN J. M

EBRUARY 1971 75c

FAMOUS PUBLISHERS AND JOURNALISTS

ROBERT S. ABBOTT
1870–1940
Founder of the Chicago *Defender*

One of the founding fathers of Negro journalism in the United States, Robert S. Abbott realized a lifelong dream when the first issue of his Chicago *Defender* rolled off the presses on May 5, 1905.

A native of St. Simon Island, Georgia, Abbott studied at Beach Institute in Savannah, and later did his undergraduate work at Claflin University in Orangeburg, South Carolina. Some 12 years after this, however, he took the advice of his stepfather, John J. Sengstacke, and learned the printing trade. Migrating to Chicago, he attended Kent Law School, and took a job in a printing house until he completed his law studies in 1899.

After wandering around the country for a time, Abbott returned to Chicago, and decided to devote all his energies to founding the *Defender* which he himself initially sold on a door-to-door basis. Over the next 15 years, the paper's circulation climbed into the hundreds of thousands.

Abbott died in 1940, whereupon the *Defender* was inherited by his nephew, John H. Sengstacke, who has since introduced a daily edition of the paper.

T. THOMAS FORTUNE
1856-1928
Author, Journalist

T. Thomas Fortune was, in his lifetime, one of the most prominent black journalists involved in the flourishing black press of the post Civil War era.

Born in Florida, the son of a Reconstruction politician, Fortune was particularly productive before his 30th year, having completed such important literature as *Black and White: Land, Labor and Politics in the South* and *The Negro in Politics* by the time he was only 29.

Fortune attended Howard University for two years, leaving to marry Miss Carrie Smiley of Jacksonville, Florida. The couple went to New York in 1878, with Fortune taking a job as a printer for the New York *Sun*. In time, Fortune caught the attention of *Sun* editor Charles A. Dana who eventually promoted him to the editorial staff of the paper.

Journalism claimed most of his professional time, however, particularly while he edited *The Globe*, a Negro daily, and later as chief editorial writer and polemicist on the staff of *The Negro World*. In 1900, he joined Booker T. Washington in helping to organize the successful National Negro Business League. His later activity gained him more notoriety and publicity than his fearless and outspoken writing, although the latter is clearly more vital in affording him an important niche in the history of black protest.

In 1883, Fortune founded the New York *Age*, the paper with which he sought to "champion the cause" of his race. In time, the *Age* became the leading Negro journal of opinion in the United States. One of Fortune's early crusades was against the practice of separate schools for the races in the New York educational system.

Fortune was later responsible for coining the term "Afro-American" as a substitute for Negro in New York newspapers. He also set up the Afro-American Council, an organization which he regarded as the precursor of the Niagara Movement. In 1907, Fortune sold the *Age*, although he remained active in journalism as an editorial writer for several Negro newspapers.

At the time of his death in 1928, Fortune was writing for the *Negro World*.

JOHN H. JOHNSON
Publisher

The nation's foremost black businessman, John H. Johnson sits at the head of the most prosperous and powerful black publishing empire in the United States. Beginning with *Ebony*, a picture-and-feature story magazine which first appeared in 1945, and ending in recent years with Johnson Publishing and Johnson Reprints, the affluent and influential publisher has built the most impressive chain of journalistic successes in the history of black publishing.

The company publishes three major magazines in addition to *Ebony*. These are: *Tan*, a women's service magazine with food, grooming, and child-care advice as well as "true confession" stories; *Jet*, a pocket-sized news weekly, and *Black World* (formerly *Negro Digest*), a literary vehicle for black militants, revisionist historians, and young writers. (Only the last-named magazine of the quartet does not turn a profit.)

Born in Arkansas City, Arkansas in 1918, Johnson at age six lost his father, a mill worker, and was raised by his mother and stepfather. His segregated schooling was obtained locally until he and the family moved to Chicago, where his father found a WPA job. Johnson attended DuSable High School in Chicago, excelling academically and in extracurricular activities, writing for the yearbook and school paper.

After graduation, an insurance executive heard a speech delivered by Johnson, and was so impressed by him that he decided to offer him a part-time scholarship at the University of Chicago. After two years, however, Johnson quit classes, although he returned to the Northwestern School of Commerce in 1938, studying for an additional two years before devoting his full energies to the Supreme Liberty Life Insurance Company.

While running the company's house organ, it occurred to Johnson that a digest of weekly or monthly gathered news items of special interest and importance to the black community might achieve a wide black readership. The idea resulted in the creation of *Negro Digest,* a periodical containing both news reprints and feature articles. Of the latter, perhaps the most beneficial to circulation was Eleanor Roosevelt's contribution, "If I were a Negro."

Buoyed by success, Johnson decided to approach the market with yet another offering, a pictorial magazine patterned after *Life*. The first issue of *Ebony* sold out its press run of 25,000 copies, and became a permanent staple in the world of journalism as soon as big companies began to advertise regularly in it. Johnson ran ads for both consumer merchandise and ethnic products, mainly hair- and skin-conditioning items. The world of "special markets" was born in earnest.

In style, tone, and format, *Ebony* glamorized American life and appealed both to middle-class citizens who felt they were already participating in the milieu he described, and to the poor black masses who modelled their aspirations on the world of fulfillment he so effectively created.

From its preoccupation with frothy glamor and eye-catching photographs, *Ebony* evolved over the years into a family-style magazine devoting much of its coverage to black success stories, show business personalities, and other unusual facets of black life. For a time, much of its material was so superficial and innocuous that it succeeded in alienating many black activists but, as its circulation grew and its outlook changed, it took a more aggressive editorial stance. Today, it produces more responsible articles dealing with racial issues and black-white controversies, and generally features some aspect of black history, often written by the accomplished journalist/historian, Lerone Bennett. Its circulation has now passed the one-million mark.

Success has brought Johnson numerous key appointments to civic and educational posts, and has earned for him as well numerous awards, including the Freedom Fun Award, the Horatio Alger Award, and the Order of Lincoln Award.

Married in 1941, Johnson and his wife have two adopted children, a boy and a girl. Despite his success, Johnson has not become a man of leisure, preferring instead the constant challenges of work and the thrill of putting a publication to bed. He insists on checking all major stories and exercising final editorial approval over them.

LOU LOMAX
Journalist

Lou Lomax, a prolific journalist, contributor to magazines, and author, was born in Valdosta, Georgia in 1922, and raised there under the guardianship of his grandmother, Rozena Lomax.

A graduate of Dasher High School and Paine College, Lomax began his professional career with the *Afro-American*, and later did graduate work at the American University. Lomax then joined the faculty of Georgia State College in Savannah, where he served as an assistant professor of philosophy. After studying for a time at Yale, he became a staff feature writer for the Chicago *American*.

Since then, Lomax's articles have appeared in such magazines as "Harper's," "Life," and "The Nation." In 1959, Lomax became the first Negro to appear on television as a newsman. Later, he was named Director of News for WNEW-TV in New York.

Lomax has authored a number of books, including *The Reluctant African* (1960) and *The Negro Revolt* (1962).

His last book, *To Kill A Black Man,*

covered the lives and assassinations of Malcolm X and Martin Luther King, Jr. Lomax was killed in an automobile crash in Santa Rosa, New Mexico on July 30, 1970.

GORDON PARKS
Novelist, Photographer, Composer

Gordon Parks, the internationally acclaimed photographer whose work has appeared in such leading magazines as "Life," is also well known as a composer (*First Concerto for Piano and Orchestra*) and novelist (*The Learning Tree*).

Born in Fort Scott, Kansas in 1912, Parks moved to St. Paul, Minnesota, and attended high school there for a time while engaging in a variety of odd jobs. Having chosen photography as a career in 1937, Parks went to Chicago, where he became closely associated with the South Side Community Art Center.

A one-man exhibit of his work eventually led to his being awarded a Rosenwald Fellowship, after which he accepted two government assignments, one of which was in the Overseas Division of the Office of War Information.

After World War II, Parks made a number of documentaries for a large New Jersey oil firm, and was later taken on as a staff photographer for "Life." Since then, he has traveled widely, lived abroad, and captured a number of impressive awards, including "Magazine Photographer of the Year" (1961) and the Newhouse Award from Syracuse University.

As a member of *Life* magazine's photographic team since 1949 he has achieved an international reputation. He has won awards not only for his photography but also for his writing. His subject matter has included such diverse topics as the Black Muslims, the Paris of the 1920's, and the plight of all oppressed peoples in U. S. ghettos. As a composer, his music has been performed in New York, Venice and Philadelphia.

In addition to *The Learning Tree*, Parks has written an autobiography entitled *A Choice of Weapons* (1965). For National Educational Television, he has produced three documentaries which focus on ghetto life. In 1968 he was the director of the motion picture version of *The Learning Tree*. His most recent book, *A Poet and His Camera* was published in 1968.

TED POSTON
1906-
Journalist

Primarily a newspaperman, Ted Poston is still active with the *Post*, an afternoon tabloid in New York. Earlier, he worked for the Pittsburgh *Courier*, and New York *Amsterdam News*.

Born in Hopkinsville, Kentucky, Poston attended local public schools, and went on to study at Tennessee A & I State College and New York University. Before beginning newspaper work, he had done a variety of odd jobs—everything from tobacco stemmer and shoeshine boy to dining car waiter and seaman. He also travelled abroad in an abortive attempt to produce motion pictures in Russia but, after spending some time in Germany, decided to return to the United States.

Much of Poston's writing is journalistic in tone and character, but much of it rises to the level of literature, particularly when he turns to writing sketches of black workers, and even short stories.

JOHN B. RUSSWURM
1799-1851
Co-Publisher, *Freedom's Journal*

John B. Russwurm is conventionally identified as the first Negro to have graduated from a U.S. College, although this claim has of late come to be disputed by some sources who maintain that Edward A. Jones graduated from Amherst some 11 days before he did in 1826.

At any rate, Russwurm took his degree at Bowdoin that year and, by 1827, was engaged in editing the first Negro newspaper, *Freedom's Journal*. His colleague in this effort was the Reverend Samuel E. Cornish, pastor of the African Presbyterian Church in New York. (The paper changed its name to *Rights of All* in 1830.)

In 1828, Russwurm migrated to Liberia, finding in the new colony a "promised land." He remained there until his death some 23 years later, eventually becoming superintendent of schools.

THE BLACK WOMAN

Historical Perspectives
Matriarchy and Current Trends
Outstanding Black Women
List of Additional Prominent Women

The civil rights struggle in the United States—often thought of as an attempt to allow the Negro male to assume his rightful place in American society—has at times tended to obscure the role of Negro women in shaping America's culture.

Historically, the roots of Negro women go back as far as any on American soil. Of the 20 African Negroes who arrived in Jamestown in 1619, at least two—Antony and Isabella—are reported later to have been married and, in 1624, to have become the parents of the first Negro child born in the English colonies of mainland America (William Tucker, named in honor of a local planter).

Until 1863, the Negro woman was as much governed by the slave system as the Negro man. Without rights of any kind, it was impossible for her to function as a woman—even to hold her own family intact when her children became old enough to be sold to other slaveowners. Nor could she assume her natural role as the emotionally supportive personality of the family, particularly since she herself was often forced to engage in such rigorous physical labor that the care of her own children became an immense burden. (Ironically, she was given special status as the nurse and confidante of her mistress' children, but was often deprived of the opportunity to shower the same appropriate attentions on her own children.)

Defined by countless stereotypes, the Negro woman was often denounced as an insensitive creature by the very people subjecting her to the oppressive circumstances which made such a generalization appear to be accurate.

If it is true that a woman has often had to work harder than a man to achieve the same recognition and earn the same money, then surely the Negro woman has often labored under a double burden. She has had to struggle for the emancipation of her race as a whole, while at the same time fighting for her rights as a woman as well.

On many occasions, the currents of these two streams—Negro rights and women's rights—crossed and merged with each other. The battles for the Negro vote and the vote for women, for Negro education and education for women, were often fought on the same ground. In the mid-19th century, for instance, Frederick Douglass and the Forten sisters, all Negroes, were fighting for Negro emancipation and the rights of women, and were aided in their work by a number of white abolitionists (e.g.

Sarah and Angelina Grimké). In Philadelphia and Boston especially, many Negro and white families united to form anti-slavery societies dedicated to the common cause of emancipation and education.

After Emancipation, one of the first discernible trends among Negro women was the development of a strong club movement, designed to improve their overall welfare and broaden the horizons open to them. At that time, such leading Negro educators as Fannie Jackson Coppin, Charlotte Hawkins Brown and Nannie Helen Burroughs came into prominence, only to be joined later by Mary McLeod Bethune and Mary Church Terrell, among others. These women were eventually to become famous among members of both races.

Matriarchy and Current Trends

Much has been written of the matriarchal structure of Negro society—from the post-war era down to the present day. Whatever conclusions are drawn, there can be little doubt that the Negro woman has often been called upon to compensate for the failure (through no fault of his own) of the Negro man to find suitable, dependable employment in an intensely competitive society. Cases in which women become the marginal family breadwinner—the sole financial support of the group—inevitably involve a certain reversal of roles for both partners, and assuredly contribute in some measure to the psychological hazards faced by the Negro family as a whole.

Nevertheless, Negro women have strengthened their positions considerably in the 20th century by their entry into more skilled and better-paying jobs made possible through higher educational achievement. As opportunities have opened up, the Negro woman has been quick to make the transition from low-paid, unskilled domestic, farm and operative jobs to employment in clerical, professional, technical, sales and service jobs.

Today, the role of the Negro woman in American life is as significant as it ever was, and more people than ever are becoming aware of the implications of this role. The last 20 years have seen important advances not only in the rights of the Negro in general, but also in the status of the Negro woman. The women included in our section are representative of a truly vast number which have been unavoidably omitted due to spatial limitations.

SADIE T. M. ALEXANDER
Lawyer

Born in Philadelphia, Pennsylvania in 1898, Sadie Alexander has set a series of precedents in pursuing her distinguished career as a lawyer. She is the first Negro woman to earn a Ph. D. degree in the United States and the first woman to earn a law degree from the University of Pennsylvania. In 1927, she became the first Negro women to be admitted to the bar in the state of Pennsylvania.

Before graduating with honors from the University of Pennsylvania in 1918, Mrs. Alexander had acted as the associate editor of the university's law review. She then received a scholarship for a year's graduate study, and was also awarded the Frances S. Pepper Fellowship in Economics for the year 1920–1921.

Besides belonging to several church and law associations, Mrs. Alexander has served on the Board of Directors of the New York City branch of the National Urban League. The author of several articles, she was the editor of *Who's Who Among Negro Lawyers* in 1949.

IDA B. WELLS BARNETT
1864–1931
Anti-lynching crusader

Born in Mississippi and educated at Rusk University, Ida Wells Barnett was one of the few women in the South who engaged in a vigorous campaign against the lynching practices common at that time. She was affiliated with several newspapers, most prominently as the editor of *Free Speech* in Memphis, Tennessee.

In 1895, her first pamphlet against lynching, *The Red Record*, was compiled. Mrs. Barnett also wrote several other pamphlets and articles during the years when her speaking engagements took her across the United States and to Europe as well.

After having become chairman of the Anti-Lynching Bureau of the National African Council, she organized and became the first president of the Negro Fellowship League in 1908. Five years

Ida B. Wells Barnett

later, her social work began to center around Chicago, where she was appointed probation officer. She left this post in 1915, having been elected Vice-President of the Chicago Equal Rights League. From then on, Mrs. Barnett devoted most of her time to civil rights activities.

She died in 1931.

CHARLOTTA A. BASS
Vice-presidential candidate

Chosen unanimously by the Progressive Party Convention in Chicago in 1952, Mrs. Charlotta A. Bass thus became the first Negro woman to run for the nation's second-highest political office—vice president of the United States.

Born in Little Compton, Rhode Island in 1890, Mrs. Bass studied at Brown University, Columbia University, and U.C.L.A. While a resident of Los Angeles, Mrs. Bass was the editor and publisher of the *California Eagle*, the oldest Negro newspaper on the West Coast.

Until 1948, Mrs. Bass was a member of the Republican party, and had even served as Western Regional Director for Wendell Wilkie in his 1940 presidential campaign. In 1950, however, Mrs. Bass ran for Congress in the 14th District of Los Angeles on the ticket of the Progressive party, which she herself had helped found two years earlier.

During her newspaper career, Mrs. Bass was known as a vigorous opponent of the Ku Klux Klan, and an outspoken foe of discrimination in employment.

DAISY BATES
Little Rock integrationist

Mrs. Daisy Bates first captured the national spotlight in 1957 during the Little Rock crisis in which President Dwight Eisenhower was forced to use federal troops to effect the admission of nine Negro children to Central High School. As Arkansas president of the NAACP, Mrs. Bates submitted to arrest and other gestures of intimidation while standing firm in the struggle to integrate the school.

Born in Huttig, Arkansas, Mrs. Bates attended school in Memphis, Tennessee, and later went to Philander Smith and Shorter Colleges in Little Rock. She married L. Christopher Bates in 1941, the same year they organized a weekly newspaper (The Arkansas *State Press*) which has since become one of the most influential of its kind in the South. In 1946, Mrs. Bates and her husband were convicted on contempt charges for criticizing a Circuit Court trial, but the Arkansas Supreme Court later reversed the decision.

Mrs. Bates has recounted her integration experiences in her book *The Long Shadow of Little Rock*, published in 1962.

MARY McLEOD BETHUNE
1875-1955
Administrator, Division of Negro Affairs, National Youth Administration (NYA)

Mary McLeod Bethune is such a major figure in American Negro history that no comprehensive discussion of it is possible without introducing her name in some context.

Born on July 10, 1875, she gained her special insight into the everyday problems of the average Negro youth while growing up on a farm in Mayesville, South Carolina. As a young woman, she

Dr. Mary McLeod Bethune

spent some seven years at Scotia Seminary in North Carolina and, later, did further study at the Moody Bible Institute in Chicago—all this with the intention of eventually becoming a missionary. But when this proved impossible (her application for a post in Africa was turned down by the Presbyterian Board of Missions in New York), she turned instead to teaching.

Herbert Hoover was the first American president to utilize her abilities when, in 1930, he invited her to a White House Conference on Child Health and Protection. Franklin D. Roosevelt was quick to follow his predecessor's lead by asking her to serve on the Advisory Committee of one of the organizations he helped establish—the National Youth Administration (NYA). In 1935, after a year on the job of laying the foundations and groundwork for the NYA, her work so impressed the President that he was persuaded to set up an Office of Minority Affairs, with Mrs. Bethune as administrator. This established a precedent, for it was the first post of its kind ever to be held by an American Negro woman.

Congressional appropriations for the NYA continued from 1936 through 1944, and Mary Bethune's title was soon changed to the more specific one of Director of the Division of Negro Affairs. Her duties consisted largely in granting funds to deserving students (particularly Negro) who could not otherwise have continued graduate study.

During the 1930's, she was one of the leading figures (and the only woman) in the unofficial "Black Cabinet" which had begun the fight for advanced integration in the U. S. government.

In later years, Mrs. Bethune was instrumental in establishing what is now known as Bethune-Cookman College, a merger of her own school (The Daytona Educational and Industrial School for Negro Girls) with the Cookman Institute.

Mrs. Bethune died in 1955 at the age of 80. Though she had been the holder of many important awards—among them, the 1935 Spingarn Medal—her greatest achievement was the legacy of a lifelong career dedicated to young people, one which won her worldwide recognition and acclaim.

CHARLOTTE HAWKINS BROWN
1882–1961
Educator

Although she was raised and educated in Cambridge, Massachusetts, Charlotte

Hawkins made yearly visits with her parents to her birthplace in Henderson, North Carolina, and, as she grew older, became interested in improving educational facilities for Negroes in the South

With the aid of her benefactor, Alice Freeman Palmer, she received training as a teacher at Salem (Mass.) Normal School and at Wellesley College, later accepting a position from the American Missionary Association as a teacher in a small school near Sedalia, North Carolina.

Due to lack of funds, however, the Association was forced to close the school in 1902. Conscious of the community's urgent need for educational facilities, Miss Hawkins decided to work in Sedalia without a salary, and to establish her own school there. By 1904, she had raised enough money to construct the first building of what was to become Palmer Memorial Institute.

In addition to her distinguished work as an educator, Mrs. Brown (she married Edward S. Brown in 1911) served as president of the Federation of Women's Clubs of North Carolina, and as vice-president of the National Association of Colored Women. She was also well-known as a lecturer on interracial subjects.

Dr. Brown resigned as president of Palmer in 1952, but remained as director of finance until 1955. She died in 1961 in Greensboro, North Carolina.

HALLIE Q. BROWN
1845?–1949
Teacher, elocutionist, writer

A distinguished lecturer and elocutionist who traveled throughout the United States and several European countries, Hallie Q. Brown was born in Pittsburgh, Pennsylvania, but moved with her family at an early age to Ontario, Canada. Having completed her early education, she returned to the United States and attended Wilberforce College in Ohio, graduating with a B. S. degree in 1873.

Before she began her lecture tours with the Wilberforce Grand Concert Company, Miss Brown taught for several years at plantation schools in the South, and later at Allen University (South Carolina) and Tuskegee Institute (Alabama). She also returned to her alma mater to teach and serve as a trustee.

Between 1905 and 1912, Miss Brown served as president of both the Ohio State Federation of Women and National Association of Colored Women, establishing the latter organization's scholarship fund.

Miss Brown was the author of several books, among them *First Lessons in Public Speaking*, and *Homespun Heroines and Other Women of Distinction*.

NANNIE HELEN BURROUGHS
1883–1961
Educator

Nannie Helen Burroughs began her career as a bookkeeper and associate editor of the Philadelphia *Christian Banner* but, because of her long-standing interest in the church, decided after a year to leave her position with the paper in order to devote all her energies to social service.

Working for the Association of Colored Women, she organized the Women's Industrial Club in Louisville, which specialized in teaching domestic skills to Negro girls. In 1907, she began her work with the National Baptist Convention, playing an important role in founding the National Training School for Women and Girls, which opened in 1909 with her as president.

Though most of her time was devoted to the school, Miss Burroughs was also particularly active as a member of both the National Association of Colored Women and the National Association for the Advancement of Colored People.

DR. ANNA JULIA COOPER
1858–1964
Eduator

This noted educator was, as early as the age of 11, acting as a student-teacher at St. Augustine Normal School, the institution which she attended in her native city of Raleigh, North Carolina. She was later to return there to teach for two years after she had become a full professor.

Dr. Cooper married the Reverend G. A. C. Cooper in 1877 and, four years later, left for Oberlin College in Ohio, where she taught and continued to pursue her own studies at the same time. Upon graduation in 1885, she became a professor of modern languages and science at Wilberforce University. However, her primary work in the field of educational administration came during her 50-year association with the old M Street High School in Washington, D. C., (later to become Dunbar). She served there as both instructor and principal.

In addition to her career as a teacher, Dr. Cooper wrote *A Voice from the South*, a well-received book on the racial problem which appeared in 1892. In 1925, at the age of 66, she received a Ph. D. from the Sorbonne in Paris, and later became president of Frelinghuysen University, a school for employed Negroes which she ran in her own home in Washington, D. C.

Dr. Cooper died on February 27, 1964 at the age of 105.

LOUISE M. DARGANS

Chief Clerk, House Committee on Education and Labor

Louise M. Dargans has been known as the "good right hand" of New York Congressman Adam Clayton Powell ever since joining his staff in 1946. Today, she is one of the two Negroes who heads a committee staff, and the only woman employed as chief clerk of a House committee.

The youngest of nine children, Miss Dargans was born in Daytona Beach, Florida, and moved to New York with her parents at the age of seven. In 1938, she graduated from Hunter College, and went on to work for the New York State Department of Labor, the Office of Price Administration, and the Internal Revenue Service.

CHRISTINE R. DAVIS

Staff Director, House Committee on Government Operations

Christine Ray Davis was born in Nashville, Tennessee, and began her education as a music major at Fisk University. However, she left Fisk in 1935 and completed her higher education at Tennessee State College, majoring in business administration.

Her first job was as secretary and research assistant in a Boston law firm. Later, she left for Washington, D. C. to become administrative assistant to Arthur W. Mitchell, the Democratic Congressman from Illinois. She held this position until 1942 when Mitchell retired, after which she began to work for his successor, William L. Dawson.

In 1949, Dawson became chairman of the Committee on Expenditures (now the Committee on Government Operations), and appointed Mrs. Davis chief clerk. When the Democrats won control of the House in 1954, Dawson appointed her Staff Director of the Committee.

Mrs. Davis has been the recipient of several awards for her work in government, among them the citation of "Outstanding Woman of the Year," given her by the National Council of Negro Women in 1949. She also holds the award for "distinguished achievement in government affairs" from the National Association of Colored Women's Clubs.

JULIETTE DERRICOTTE

1897–1931

Educator

Raised in Athens, Georgia, Juliette Derricotte was educated in the public schools there and at Talladega College, then a small school in Alabama operated by the American Missionary Association. Some 11 years after graduating from Talladega in 1918, Miss Derricotte became the first woman trustee of the college.

In the intervening years, she traveled across the United States, speaking at many colleges and educational conferences. In both 1924 and 1928, she was chosen to be a delegate representing American college students at the convention of the General Committee of the World's Student Christian Federation.

She later became the National Student Secretary for the Y.W.C.A., but resigned from this position in 1929 in order to become Dean of Women at Fisk University.

She died two years later in an automobile accident.

DR. DOROTHY B. FEREBEE

Physician

A physician who received her medical degree with honors from Tufts Medical School in Massachusetts, Dr. Dorothy Ferebee has been active all her life in civic and social affairs. She began her medical career in Washington, D. C., where she served for several years on the Board of Directors of the Southeast Settlement House.

For seven summers, she worked among Negro sharecroppers in Mississippi on a health project which was sponsored by the Alpha Kappa Alpha Sorority. Dr. Ferebee later became president of this society, and also succeeded Mary McLeod Bethune as president of the National Council of Negro Women.

In 1951, Dr. Ferebee was sent by the U. S. Labor Department to study the problems of women in Germany, and later visited Africa as a delegate to an international conference of women of African descent.

Besides maintaining her own medical practice, Dr. Ferebee acts as the head of the Student Health Service at Howard University, and is an assistant professor of preventive medicine at the Howard School of Medicine.

GLORIA GASTON
Human Resources Development Officer, Bureau of Latin America, Agency for International Development (AID)

Gloria Gaston is the first Negro woman to occupy a post of major importance in the Agency for International Development (AID). Miss Gaston is the Human Resources Development Officer for the Bureau of Latin America.

A graduate of the University of Washington where she received her B. A. in 1948, Miss Gaston has done graduate work at the New School for Social Research in New York City.

Her first government assignment was as a Peace Corps liaison officer (1962–1964). Later, she served in the Sudan with a Columbia research team gathering data on possible investment programs there.

Miss Gaston has also held a number of important posts with private organizations—among them the Bank Street College of Education and the National Conference of Christians and Jews.

A native of Dallas, she holds membership in several professional and cultural associations.

REGINA GOFF
Assistant Commissioner, Office of Education, Department of Health, Education and Welfare

A specialist in child development and welfare, Dr. Regina Goff worked in the field of education for many years before she assumed her position with the Department of Health, Education and Welfare.

Born in St. Louis in 1917, she received a B. A. in English from Northwestern University in 1936 and, later, both an M. A. and a Ph. D. in child development from Columbia University. She has taught both nursery school and kindergarten, and has served as chairman of the department of child development at Florida A. & M.; state supervisor of Negro elementary schools for the Florida Department of Education, and professor of education at Morgan State College in Baltimore, Maryland.

In 1955, Dr. Goff was appointed consultant to the Ministry of Education in Iran by the International Cooperation Administration (now the Agency for International Development). She returned to Morgan State for a year before accepting her present position.

JESSIE P. GUZMAN
Educator

The distinguished teaching career of Jessie P. Guzman, which began 47 years ago in the schools of Greensboro, North Carolina, came to an end in 1965 when she retired as professor of history and director of the Department of Records and Research at Tuskegee Institute in Alabama.

A native of Savannah, Georgia, Mrs. Guzman was educated at Clark College in Atlanta, Columbia University, and the University of Chicago. Before her appointment to the Tuskegee faculty in 1924, Mrs. Guzman had taught at Dillard University in New Orleans, and had served as a secretary to the New York City Bible Society. She left Tuskegee after one year to join the faculty of Alabama State Teachers College in Montgomery, but returned to the former school in 1930 to begin an uninterrupted 34-year tenure there. She served as teacher, research assistant, and dean of women at Tuskegee prior to accepting the positions she held at the time of her retirement.

A leader in the civic affairs of her community, Mrs. Guzman has also authored some 15 books, pamphlets, and articles. In 1947 and again in 1952, she was the editor of the *Negro Year Book*, and today serves as secretary to the Southern Conference Educational Fund and as director of the Tuskegee branch of the NAACP.

ANNA ARNOLD HEDGEMAN
Sociologist, educator, civil rights leader

From 1949 to 1953, Anna A. Hedgeman served as assistant to Oscar R. Ewing, administrator of the Federal Security Agency (now known as the Department of Health, Education and Welfare). In 1954, she became a member of Mayor Robert F. Wagner's cabinet in New York, serving for five years as liaison with eight city departments.

Born in Marshalltown, Iowa, Mrs. Hedgeman was educated at Hamline University, the University of Minnesota, and the New York School of Social Work. After teaching for two years in Mississippi, she decided to go North, working in various capacities for the Young Women's Christian Associations of Springfield, Ohio; Jersey City, New York, and Philadelphia.

She later served as consultant on racial problems for the Emergency Relief Bureau in Brooklyn. In 1944, she was asked to serve as executive director of the National Council for the Fair Employment Practices Commission, a position which she held for four years.

Her other activities include participation in the Council of Church Women, the National Conference of Christians and Jews, and the Commission on Race and Religion of the National Council of Churches.

DOROTHY I. HEIGHT
President, National Council of Negro Women

Before becoming the fourth president of the National Council of Negro Women, Dorothy Height had for many years served as a member of the organization's Board of Directors, later becoming its Executive Director.

Miss Height is also the Associate Director for Leadership Training Services for the Young Women's Christian Association of the United States. From 1952 to 1955, she served as a member of the Defense Advisory Committee on Women in the Services, having been appointed by General George C. Marshall.

A native of Richmond, Virginia, Miss Height holds a master's degree from New York University, and has also studied at the New York School of Social Work. In the fall of 1952, she served as a visiting professor at the Delhi School of Social Work in New Delhi, India.

Six years, later, Miss Height was appointed to the Social Welfare Board of New York by Governor Averell Harriman, and was reappointed by Governor Nelson Rockefeller in 1961 for another five years.

In 1960, Miss Height was sent to five African countries by the Committee on Correspondence to make a study of women's organizations there. In addition to the presidency of the National Council Of Negro Women, Miss Height also holds the office of vice-president of the National Council of Women of the United States.

AILEEN C. HERNANDEZ
Commissioner, Equal Employment Opportunity Commission

Aileen C. Hernandez is the only woman commissioner serving on the Equal Employment Opportunity Commission.

Born in New York City, Mrs. Hernandez attended Howard University in Washington, D. C., where she was active in student civil rights work. In 1959, she received an M. A. from Los Angeles State College, and has since studied at New York University, UCLA, and the University of Oslo in Norway.

She has had several years' experience with the educational program of the International Ladies Garment Workers' Union on the West Coast and, in the summer of 1960, toured six Latin American countries under the auspices of the State Department, giving lectures on labor education and reporting on the position of minority groups in the United States.

Mrs. Hernandez is a member of several national organizations, including the NAACP, the Urban League, and Americans for Democratic Action. In 1961, she was selected "Woman of the Year" by the Community Relations Conference of Southern California.

CHARLOTTE MOTON HUBBARD
Deputy Assistant Secretary of State for Public Affairs

Appointed in May of 1964 as Deputy Assistant Secretary of State for Public Affairs, Charlotte Hubbard now serves in the highest permanent federal position ever to be held by a Negro woman.

Born in Hampton, Virginia, Mrs. Hubbard received a junior college certificate in home economics from Tuskegee Institute, a B. S. in education at Boston University, and did graduate work both at

Chairman Franklin D. Roosevelt, Jr. presides over a meeting of the Equal Employment Opportunities Commission. Other members of the Commission include (l. to r.) Richard Graham, Aileen Hernandez, Samuel Jackson, and Luther Holcomb.

the latter school and at Bennington College. Before joining the government, she was an instructor and later an associate professor of physical education at Hampton Institute.

In 1942, Mrs. Hubbard—largely on the recommendation of Mrs. Eleanor Roosevelt—was named recreation representative in what is now the Department of Health, Education, and Welfare, her main job being that of organizing communities where a particular need for welfare and recreational facilities existed.

Some 10 years later, Mrs. Hubbard became the first Negro to be appointed to an important position with a television station (WTOP-TV) in Washington, D.C. From 1958 to 1963, she was public relations assistant of the United Givers Fund, an organization linking local and national welfare agencies.

JANE EDNA HUNTER
Social Worker

Jane Hunter spent the early years of her life in her home state of South Carolina, although she took nurses training in Virginia before migrating North in search of a better job. For two years, however, she had great difficulty finding suitable employment in Cleveland, and it was not until she met the secretary to the physician of John D. Rockefeller that she received any real help in securing a satisfactory position.

By this time, she was acutely aware of the need for an institution to aid other Negro women coming to Cleveland in search of employment. With this in mind, she called the first meeting of the Working Girls' Home Association (later renamed the Phillis Wheatley Association) in 1911. Although the early years of the Association were ones of hardship, it was able to expand both its boarding facilities and other services after receiving a substantial grant from Rockefeller in 1917.

Although much of her time was occupied by her obligations to the Association, Miss Hunter was able to study law for four years at Baldwin Wallace College. She was admitted to the bar in 1925, after which she continued her work with the Association. Under her guidance, several similar organizations have been established in leading cities across the country.

JEAN BLACKWELL HUTSON
Curator,
Schomburg Collection

For more than 20 years, Jean Blackwell Hutson has served as curator of the prestigious Schomburg Collection of Negro Life and History, a special non-circulating library and autonomous research division within the New York Public Library system. In recent years, the Schomburg has grown so phenomenally and been the source of so much lasting scholarship that it may prove a lifetime's work merely cataloguing the new output of erudition based largely on materials in the collection. Though buried in work, the staff headed by Miss Hutson realizes that the Schomburg is now a synonym for black history U.S.A.

A native of Summerfield, Florida, Mrs. Hutson was at first interested in a career in medicine. She studied for three years at the University of Michigan, transferring to Barnard College in New York where she earned her B.A. in 1935. A year later, she received a B.S. from the Columbia School of Library Service. Mrs. Hutson has worked as a high school librarian in Baltimore and a junior high school librarian in Englewood, New Jersey.

Her first assignment in the New York Public Library system was as branch librarian of Woodstock in the Bronx. She has been with Schomburg since 1948, although she took a leave of absence in 1964-1965 to serve as assistant librarian at the University of Ghana. After her return to New York, she served as chairman of the Harlem Cultural Council, only one of the numerous progressive and productive groups she has supported during her distinguished and diversified career.

Mrs. Hutson has been a lecturer at City College, and belongs to numerous cultural organizations which cultivate an interest in, and promote the study of the heritage of Africa. These include the American Society of African Culture and the African Studies Association. Mrs. Hutson is a Delta, and a member of the NAACP, the National Urban League, and the American Library Association.

Since her association with the Schomburg, the collection has grown immensely, largely due to her canny acquisitions, alert reading of the expanding relevance of black studies materials, and internationalist outlook. The Schomburg now has vertical files, microfilm, tapes and records, and photographs—in addition to books and periodicals from all over the world. It is the single most important repository on black culture and achievement in the U.S.

Mrs. Jean Blackwell Hutson, curator of the Schomburg Collection

SISSIERETTA JONES
1868–1933
Opera singer

One of the most famous opera stars of the late 19th century, Sissieretta Jones was born Matilda S. Joyner in Portsmouth, Virginia, and went to Providence, Rhode Island as a young girl to study at the Academy of Music there. Upon completing her studies, she received further training at the New England Conservatory in Boston.

Shortly afterwards, her professional career was launched when she appeared as the first Negro singer on the stage of Wallack's Theater in Boston. Upon returning from a subsequent tour of South America and the West Indies, she gave a featured performance at New York's Madison Square Garden, and received additional bookings for the concert stage in the United States.

In 1892, she sang at a White House

reception given by President Benjamin Harrison, after which she embarked on a successful year-long concert tour of Europe, where she was known to her audiences as the "Black Patti" (after the famous Italian soprano, Adelina Patti).

When she came back to New York, she left the concert stage to star in an all-Negro group, "Black Patti's Troubadours," which performed for 19 years in many Southern and Western cities.

CORETTA SCOTT KING
Civil rights activist

While her husband lived, it is not surprising that Coretta (Scott) King functioned mainly as a devoted wife and mother rather than as a vigorous and indefatigable public campaigner and crusader. This was the role which her marriage summoned her to fulfill, a personal mission made necessary by King's kaleidoscopic public career and exceptional commitment to humanity.

After King's assassination, those who know her were heartened at her ability to make a swift transition from a dedicated parent living in comparative seclusion to a dynamic civil rights and peace crusader in her own right. During her husband's life, she accommodated herself to the mother/wife role; with him gone, it seemed imperative that she carry on his life's work and perpetuate his ideals actively and publicly.

Born one of three children on April 27, 1927, Mrs. King is a native of Heiberger, Alabama. During the Depression years, she was forced to contribute to the family income by hoeing and picking cotton, but she resolved early to overcome adversity, seek treatment as an equal, and struggle to achieve a sound education.

In 1945, she attended Antioch College in Yellow Springs, Ohio on a scholarship, majoring in education and music. A teaching career appealed to her, but she became badly disillusioned when she was not allowed to do her practice teaching in the public schools of the town. No Negro had ever taught there, and she was not destined to be the first to break the tradition.

Musical training in voice and on piano absorbed much of her time, with the result that, upon graduation, she decided to continue her studies at the New England Conservatory of Music in Boston, attending on a modest fellowship which covered tuition, but made part-time work a necessity. Paradoxically, her financial situation improved when she began receiving state aid from Alabama. (Such aid was available to Negroes studying outside the state, but not for black applicants seeking to attend schools within the state itself.)

Her meeting with Martin Luther King thrust her into a whirlwind romance, and also presented her with the opportunity to marry an exceptional young minister whose intense convictions and concern for humanity brought her a measure of rare self-realization early in life. Sensing his incredible dynamism, she suffered no regrets at the prospect of relinquishing her own possible career.

Completing her studies in 1954, Mrs. King moved back South with her husband, who became pastor of Drexel Avenue Baptist Church in Montgomery, Alabama. Within a year, King had led the Montgomery bus boycott, and given birth to a new era of civil rights agitation in the South. Two years later, he was the head of the Southern Christian Leadership Conference (SCLC), a network of clergymen who coordinated new demonstrations and established policy for nonviolent confrontations throughout the South.

By 1964, Mrs. King was the mother of four children: Yolanda (born 1955); Martin Luther, III (born 1957); Dexter Scott (born 1961); and Bernice Albertine (born 1963). Despite the pressures of his public identity, his constant travel and his enormous undertakings, King attached great value to raising healthy, happy and normal children. Understandably, he entrusted the major responsibilities for this goal to the strong and compassionate woman who shared this outlook.

Over the years, Mrs. King did some teaching and fund-raising work for SCLC, and became more accustomed to the limelight, particularly after her trip to Oslo in 1964. It was more than such exposure, however, that gave her the strength, the courage, and the determination to deal with the assassination, to sense and accept her surrogate role during the Memphis march and, later, to deliver the speeches he had drafted in rough form.

Her speech on Solidarity Day, June 19, 1968, is often identified as a prime example of her emergence from the shadow of her husband's memory. In it, she called upon American women to "unite and form a solid block of women power" to fight the three great evils of racism, poverty, and war.

Much of her subsequent activity revolved around building plans for the creation of a Martin Luther King, Jr. Memorial in Atlanta. Mrs. King's other major preoccupation was with a commitment to write a book of reminiscences which has since appeared under the title *My Life with Martin Luther King, Jr.* The book is a tribute to his memory, as well as a ringing affirmation of her intention to keep his thoughts and principles intact in as many lives as she can hope to influence.

ELIZABETH DUNCAN KOONTZ
Educator, government official

Mrs. Elizabeth Duncan Koontz has devoted most of her professional life to the field of classrom education, having served as a teacher in the public schools of Salisbury, North Carolina from 1945 to 1968, the year she became president of the 1.1 million-member National Education Association (NEA). A year later, she was appointed Director of the Women's Bureau in the Department of Labor and, in a related assignment, named U.S. Delegate to the U.S. Commission on the Status of Women.

Born the youngest of seven children, Mrs. Koontz was reared by well-educated parents who instilled in their offspring a dutiful appreciation for, and respect of, the values of formal education. Like the rest of the family, Mrs. Koontz was attracted to a teaching career, taking her first job in the small lumbertown of Dunn, North Carolina where she found herself tackling the biggest assignment with the least experience. She quickly developed what has now become a lifelong interest in "supposedly mentally retarded" children, whom she herself generally classifies as slow learners needing only patience and understanding before they will develop the same rate of perception and level of skill as other less-neglected pupils.

Mrs. Koontz was once head of North Carolina's all-Negro N.E.A. affiliate, as well as the Association's largest division, the 820,000 member-strong Association of Classroom Teachers. Once in office as N.E.A. head, she made it clear that she anticipated trouble as soon as teachers began to organize, agitate, and strike for higher pay and improved conditions. When the N.E.A. did in fact stage strikes, she advised communities to adjust to teachers' demands, and support bonafide attempts to upgrade the calibre of teaching candidates by making the profession more lucrative.

It would appear from her latest appointment that she is becoming engrossed with an issue that only recently has come to occupy the national spotlight: women's liberation. Such an involvement would be consistent with her reputation as a fighting lady equally adept at practicing both careful, soothing tact and decisive, outspoken bluntness.

Elizabeth Duncan Koontz

LUCY LANEY
1854–1933
Educator

Lucy Craft Laney, born a slave in Macon, Georgia, rose to become the founder and principal of Haines Normal Institute in Georgia. Her work was made possible largely through the early efforts of her master's sister, who taught her to read at the age of four and later enabled her to enter Atlanta University.

After graduating from the first class there, Miss Laney taught for several years in the public schools of Savannah before accepting an invitation from the Presbyterian Board of Missions for Freedmen to start a private school in Atlanta. When the funds from the Board were not forthcoming, Miss Laney decided to raise the money for the school herself.

In 1886, the school was first opened in the remodeled basement of a church, and, though beset by financial difficulties, was able to accommodate over 200 pupils by its second year.

Such generous financial aid was received from Mrs. F. E. H. Haines of Milwaukee that it was soon decided to name the school after its benefactor. Further allocations from the Presbyterian Mission Board, together with donations of land from other sources, made it possible for Haines to expand from a one-room school to the prospering educational community of over 1,000 students which it is today.

MARJORIE LAWSON
Lawyer, social worker, judge

In August of 1962, Marjorie M. Lawson became the first Negro woman to be appointed to a judgeship by a president of the United States, and the first Negro woman ever to be approved by the Senate for a statutory appointment.

Born in Pittsburgh, Pennsylvania in 1912, Judge Lawson graduated from the University of Michigan in 1933, and received a Certificate in Social Work there the next year. In 1939, she earned the Bachelor of Law degree from the Terrell Law School in Washington, D. C. and, in 1950, from the Columbia University School of Law.

Admitted to the District of Columbia Bar in 1939, Judge Lawson engaged in private practice with her husband, Belford V. Lawson, Jr., until the time of her appointment to the bench. From 1943 to 1946, she was the assistant director and, later, the director of the Division of Review and Analysis of the President's Committee on Fair Employment Practice, and was also editor of the Committee's reports in 1944 and 1946. In addition, she wrote a weekly public affairs column for 15 years for the Pittsburgh *Courier*.

Judge Lawson has held a variety of social work positions, often employing her capacity as a lawyer to act as counsel for families in the Juvenile Court of the District of Columbia. She has also been active in several organizations dealing with housing and employment problems, among them the National Urban League.

In 1958, Judge Lawson became race relations advisor to Senator John F. Kennedy and, upon his nomination for the presidency, was named director of civil rights for his campaign. In 1962, Kennedy named her to his Committee on Equal Employment Opportunity.

In addition to her extensive social and political activities, Judge Lawson has worked as a volunteer in many local and national organizations, and has held the post of Vice-President of the National Council of Negro Women.

CONSTANCE BAKER MOTLEY
District Court Judge, New York State Senator, Manhattan Borough President

Born in Connecticut of West Indian parents, Constance Baker Motley was recently appointed by President Johnson to the U. S. District Court for Southern New York, thus becoming the nation's first Negro woman federal judge. The appointment marked the high point of her long career in politics and civic affairs.

While still a law student at Columbia University, Mrs. Motley began working with the NAACP Legal and Defense Educational Fund, Inc., beginning an association that was to make her famous as a defender of civil rights. After receiving her law degree, she began to work full-time with this organization, and eventually became one of its associate counsels.

Before leaving the organization in 1964 to run for the New York State Senate, Mrs. Motley had argued nine successful NAACP cases before the U. S. Supreme Court, having participated in almost every important civil rights case that had passed through the courts since 1954—from Autherine Lucy in Alabama to James Meredith in Mississippi. By winning election to the state senate in February of 1964, Mrs. Motley became the only woman among 58 senators and the first Negro woman in New York state history to sit in the upper chamber.

Then, one year later, the state senator ran for the position of Manhattan Borough President, emerging the victor by the unanimous final vote of the City Council. She thus became the first woman to serve as a city borough president, and therefore also the first woman on the

Constance Baker Motley is sworn in as Borough President of Manhattan by New York City Mayor Robert E. Wagner. Looking on are Mr. Motley and the couple's son.

Board of Estimate.

A resident of Manhattan's Upper West Side, where she lives with her husband and young son, Mrs. Motley hopes that her career "will be an inspiration to other Negro women," and feels that "it is important for women, and especially Negro women, to become involved and to hold public office."

DR. JEANNE NOBLE

Educator and guidance expert

With an extensive background in the fields of education and social service, Dr. Jeanne Noble was well-equipped to accept Sargent Shriver's 1964 offer to head a committee in drawing up plans for the Girls' Job Corps, a separate department within the federal government's anti-poverty program. The Corps recruits girls from poverty areas all over the country, and places them in residential centers where they receive training in such areas as home management, and assistance in finding suitable employment after completing their studies.

Herself a product of a poverty-stricken environment in Albany, Georgia, Dr. Noble graduated from Howard University before going on to take two post-graduate degrees at the Teachers College of New York's Columbia University. Having specialized in guidance and developmental psychology, Dr. Noble returned to her hometown to teach social science at Albany State College. She later was a visiting professor at Tuskegee Institute and the University of Vermont, and has since taught human relations at New York University.

Her activities in the field of social service include work with the Girl

Scouts, HARYOU-ACT in Harlem, the National Social Welfare Assembly, and the President's Commission on the Status of Women. She has also published articles in several professional journals, and has written one book, *The Negro Woman's College Education.*

In 1963, Dr Noble was named by "Ebony" magazine as "one of the 100 most influential Negroes of the Emancipation Centennial Year." She received the Bethune-Roosevelt Award in 1965 for service in the field of education.

Dr. Jeanne Noble

ELEANOR HOLMES NORTON
Civil liberties lawyer

Mrs. Eleanor Holmes Norton replaced Simeon Golar as head of the Human Rights Commission in the Spring of 1970. Head of the city's principal antidiscrimination agency, Mrs. Norton is also the highest-ranking Negro in the Administration of New York's Mayor John V. Lindsay.

Upon acknowledging her appointment, Mrs. Norton characterized the function of the Commission as one of assuring that "irrational" criteria of race, religion, or national origin be eliminated as grounds for evaluating the personal merits of job applicants.

At this time, Mrs. Norton included sex among the irrational factors which sometimes caused discrimination and pledged to remove this consideration from the list of acceptable job criteria.

In 1968, while serving as a Civil Liberties Attorney, Mrs. Norton demonstrated her dedication to principle by pressing for the right of George Wallace to hold an outdoor rally at Shea Stadium. She followed through on her stand despite stiff opposition from the mayor and noisy protests from other liberal quarters.

Born in Washington, D.C. in 1938, Mrs. Norton is a graduate of Antioch College, and holds masters and law degrees from Yale. A transplanted Manhattanite, she has had to search for a dependable formula enabling her to combine the rigors of bureaucratic life with the challenges of being a wife and mother. She seems capable of succeeding in both endeavors.

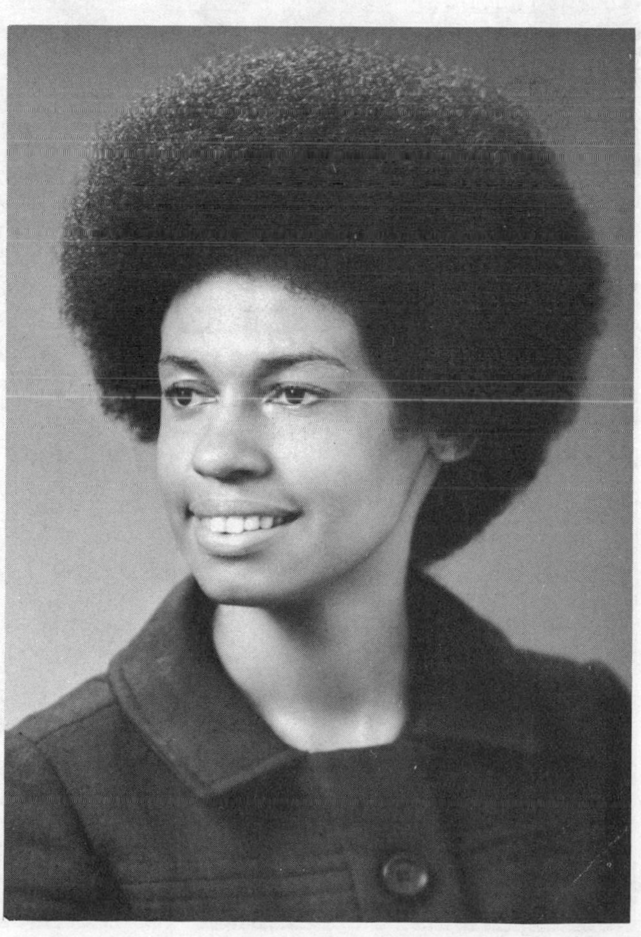

Eleanor Holmes Norton

ESTELLE MASSEY OSBORNE
Nurse

With her appointment in February of 1945 to the faculty of New York Unievrsity, Mrs. Estelle Osborne became the first Negro woman instructor at that school. She began her duties with the Department of Nursing Education in the spring of that year.

Prior to her appointment, Mrs. Osborne had already had a long career in nursing and allied fields. An instructor of nursing at Harlem and Lincoln Hospitals from 1929 to 1931, she later served as director of the Freedmen's Nursing School and of the Homer Phillips School in St. Louis. She was also a consultant on the staff of the National Nursing Council for War Service.

A native of Palestine, Texas, Mrs. Osborne received her education at Prairie View College, the Nursing School of City Hospital #2 in St. Louis, and Columbia University in New York. She taught for a short time in the public schools of Texas and of Kansas City, Missouri.

Active throughout her life in public health organizations, Mrs. Osborne has also served as vice-president of the National Council of Negro Women and as a member of the executive committee of the Committee of Women in World Affairs.

She has authored many articles which have appeared in several prominent publications, such as the "Journal of Negro Education," "Opportunity," and the "American Journal of Nursing." In 1943, the "Estelle Massey Scholarship" was established in her honor at Fisk University and, in 1946, Mrs. Osborne was the recipient of the Mary Mahoney Award in recognition of her contributions to nursing.

Rosa Parks

ROSA PARKS
Civil rights activist

There is about her name no discernible ring nor aura of distinction. There is about her dress and manner no singular, commanding, or memorable uniqueness. Her story, however, is one of the most inspirational to come out of the civil rights movement, a simple message to all that human dignity cannot interminably be undermined by brute force.

On the evening of December 1, 1955, Rosa Parks boarded a public bus in Montgomery, Alabama, took a seat with the other passengers, and prepared to relax for 15 minutes or so before arriving home. As the bus began to fill up, however, the number of seats dwindled until, within a few minutes, there were none left. As soon as the white bus driver noticed that a black woman was occupying a seat in the "white" section of the bus while a white passenger was standing, he ordered the "offender" to the rear.

The "offender" did not make a scene when she refused. She did not scream; she did not whine; she did not threaten; she did not exhort. She simply did not move, thus forcing those who would force her to move to make the next move.

Rosa Parks was arrested, jailed, and brought to trial while the rest of the once quiescent black community refused to ride public buses. Mrs. Parks was the catalyst in the Montgomery boycott, the first public confrontation which brought the name of Martin Luther King, Jr., into the ears of America.

Mrs. Parks paid dearly for her courage. Her husband, a barber, became ill from the pressure; the family ultimately moved to Detroit, where Parks resumed his profession. Mrs. Parks did sewing and alterations at home until she found a job as a dressmaker.

In Detroit, she has since become active in youth work, job guidance, cultural and recreational planning—the daily grind of a community activist. Dr. King, while he lived, once called her "the great fuse that led to the modern stride toward freedom."

She made the stride while sitting still.

VIRGINIA ESTELLE RANDOLPH
1876–1958
Social worker

Concerned with the problems of youth, Virginia E. Randolph was both a teacher and a social worker in the area of juvenile affairs. Born of slave parents in Richmond, Virginia, she was able to receive an education at the Bacon School and the City Normal School, both in her native city. At the age of 16, she took her first teaching job in Goochland County, Virginia, holding it for three years before moving to a small schoolhouse in Henrico County.

In 1908, she accepted an important appointment as the first supervisor of the Jeanes Fund, a philanthropic organization established by Anna Jeanes, a Philadelphia Quaker, to finance Negro rural schools in the South. Having for many years emphasized the importance of vocational training for youth, Miss Randolph often worked in conjunction with the Richmond Juvenile and Domestic Relations Court and, in 1926, received the Harmon Award in recognition of her outstanding social service.

She retired in 1948 as supervisor of education in Henrico County, and was honored the next year at an appreciation service given her by many educators of both races.

JUANITA STOUT
Municipal court judge

The first woman ever to reach the bench in Pennsylvania is Juanita Kidd Stout, who was appointed Judge of the Philadelphia Municipal Court by Governor David L. Lawrence in September of 1959. In November of that year, Judge Stout ran in a city-wide election and won a 10-year term, thus becoming the nation's first elected Negro woman judge.

Judge Stout earned her Master of Laws and Doctor of Jurisprudence degrees at the University of Indiana, and was admitted to the bar in the District of Columbia in 1950 and in Philadelphia in 1954.

Since 1959, she has served as a judge of Philadelphia's Juvenile Court, a position which at times has proven to be a dangerous one. Her safety has often been threatened by those who feel that her methods of dealing with delinquent youth are too severe, but she also has many supporters who feel that her stringent measures have done much to reduce Philadelphia's delinquency rate.

MARY CHURCH TERRELL
1863–1954
Women's rights advocate

An active leader all her life in the campaign for equal rights, Mary Church

Terrell was born the year the Emancipation Proclamation was issued, and died only a few months after segregation had been declared unconstitutional by the *Brown* v. *Board of Education* decision of 1954.

A graduate of Oberlin College in 1884, Mrs. Terrell was appointed to the District of Columbia school board in 1895 and, in the following year, became one of the charter members of the National Association of Colored Women. She was consistently active in politics, campaigning against the practice of segregation in the United States, and, on several occasions, acting as a delegate from her country to international conferences.

Born of ex-slave parents in Memphis, Tennessee, Mary Church Terrell chose to make her home in Washington, D. C., a city which remained segregated until 1953. In that year, she headed a committee of Washington citizens who demanded enforcement of a 75-year-old law prohibiting discrimination against "respectable persons" in restaurants. In the resulting test case, the U. S. Supreme Court ruled that the old law was still valid, thus paving the way for the beginning of integration in the public accommodations of the nation's capital.

A year later, having seen the initiation of a new policy which she herself had done much to bring about, Mary Church Terrell died in Annapolis, Maryland at the age of 90.

SOJOURNER TRUTH
Abolitionist
1797-1883

Isabella Baumfree—or Sojourner Truth as she is popularly known—became famous in her lifetime as a preacher, abolitionist and lecturer. Born, it is believed, in 1797 in Ulster County, New York, she is known to have been freed from slavery by the New York State Emancipation Act of 1827, and to have lived for a time in New York City.

Soon disillusioned with life there, she adopted the name Sojourner Truth (a name she felt God had given her), and assumed as her "mission" in life the task of traveling across the country and spreading "the truth." It was not long before this self-styled prophetess had become famous as an itinerant preacher. Wherever she appeared, huge crowds would gather to hear her, for she was reputed to have not only "mystical gifts" but great powers of oratory as well.

Since Negro women were early and active participants in the anti-slavery movement, it was not surprising that, before long, Sojourner Truth was addressing countless meetings in the abolitionist cause. Prior to the Civil War, she had already become friendly with such leading Northern white abolitionists as James and Lucretia Mott, as well as Harriet Beecher Stowe.

With the outbreak of hostilities, she raised money by her lecturing and singing to buy gifts for the soldiers, and went into the army camps to distribute them herself. She also aided those of her people who had managed to escape North, helping them to find work and places to live.

Even after the war was over, Sojourner Truth continued traveling up and down the country on behalf of her people, campaigning in particular for better educational opportunities. Her *Narrative*, published in 1875, recounts her war experiences, as well as a meeting with Abraham Lincoln.

Age and ill health soon began to overtake her, however, so that she was finally forced to give up traveling, and then even the less demanding schedule of lectures at Battle Creek Sanatarium.

She died in Michigan on November 26, 1883.

HARRIET ROSS TUBMAN
Underground Railroad Conductor
1820-1913

The greatest "conductor" on the Underground Railroad—an organized network of way-stations which helped Negro slaves escape from the South to the free states and as far North as Canada—was an ex-slave and a woman, Harriet Ross Tubman.

Believed to have been born about 1820 in Dorchester County, Maryland, Miss Tubman had a childhood similar to that of most other slave children—i.e. no schooling, little play, much hard work, and often severe punishment. In 1848, she finally succeeded in escaping from this life, even though it meant leaving behind her two brothers, as well as her own husband John Tubman, who threatened to report her to their master.

Once free, she began to devise practical ways to help other slaves escape. Over the next 10 years, she made some 20 trips from the North to the South,

I Sell the Shadow to Support the Substance.

SOJOURNER TRUTH.

Harriet Tubman (left, with pan) stands alongside a group of slaves which she helped escape via the Underground Railroad.

rescuing more than 300 slaves and eventually having a price of $40,000 set on her head.

Her reputation spread rapidly, and she won the respect of leading abolitionists like the Motts, the Horace Manns, the Bronson Alcotts, and Ralph Waldo Emerson. Many of her "passengers" were temporarily sheltered in the home of Susan B. Anthony.

One of her major disappointments was the ultimate failure of John Brown's raid on Harpers Ferry. She had met and aided Brown in recruiting soldiers for his cause (in fact, he called her "General Tubman"), and she was always to regard him, rather than Lincoln, as the true emancipator of her people.

In 1860, Harriet Tubman began to canvass the nation, appearing at anti-slavery meetings and speaking on behalf of women's rights. Shortly before the outbreak of the Civil War, she was forced for a time to leave for Canada, but she soon returned to the United States, serving the Union cause openly and actively as nurse, soldier, spy and scout. She was particularly valuable in this latter capacity, since her work on the "Railroad" had made her thoroughly familiar with much of the terrain.

Two years after the end of the war, John Tubman died and, in 1869, she married Nelson Davis, a war veteran. A year earlier, her biography had been written by Sarah Bradford, and the proceeds from the sales of the book were given to her to help ease her financial burden.

Despite her many honors and tributes (including a medal from Queen Victoria of England), Harriet Tubman spent her last years in poverty. She did not receive a pension until more than 30 years after the close of the Civil War. Awarded $20 a month for the remainder of her life, she used most of this money to help found a place for the aged and needy—later to be called The Harriet Tubman Home.

She died in Auburn in March 1913.

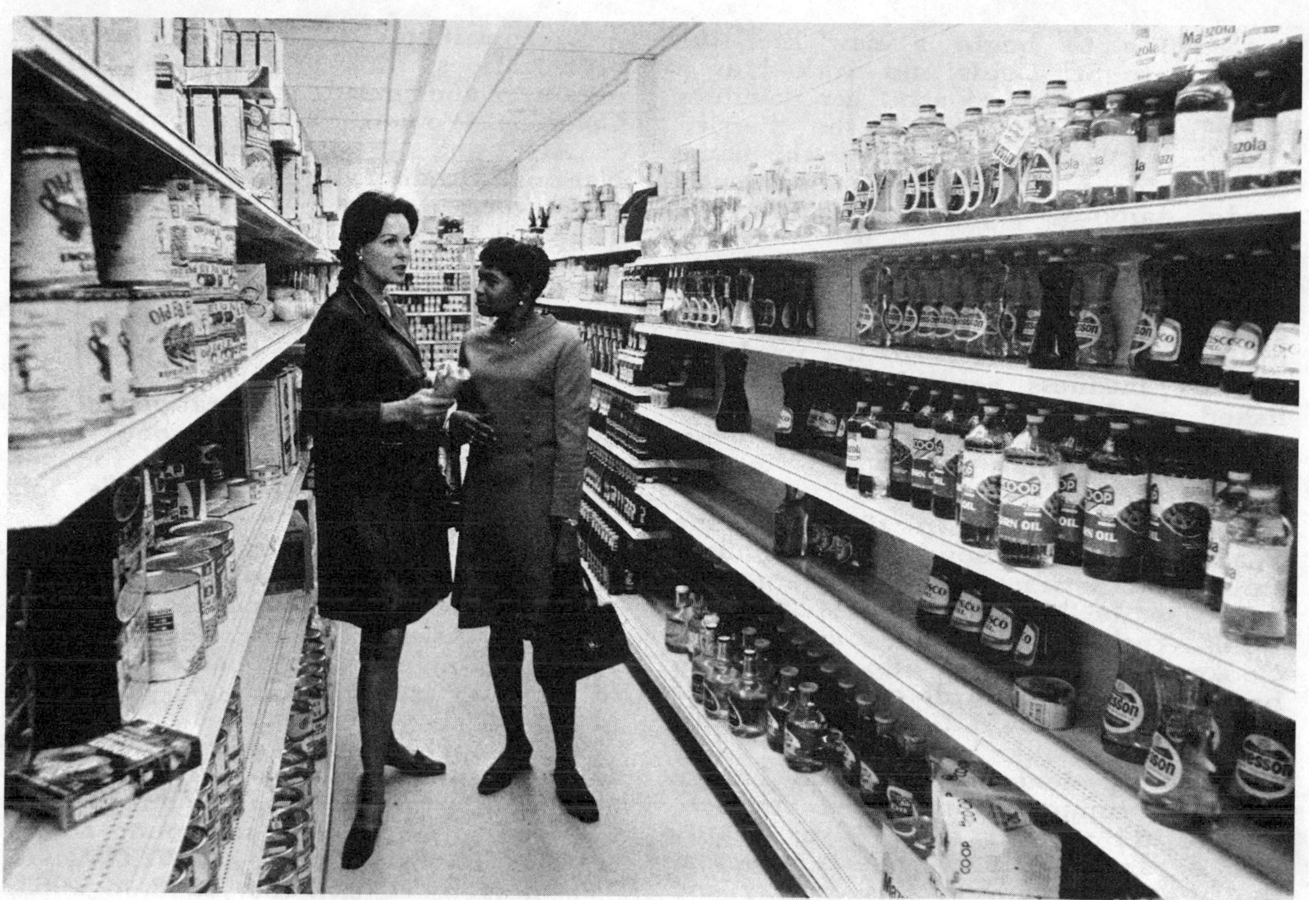

Cora Walker (Left) with Bess Myerson

CORA WALKER

Attorney, businesswoman

Cora Walker has brought to Harlem a cooperative supermarket which some have tried to undermine, but which the people have resolved to support. While others have spoken of philosophy, Mrs. Walker has concentrated on action—the action of self-help, self-improvement, self-respect.

Born in Charlotte, North Carolina, Mrs. Walker grew up in the Bronx, and educated herself there in the midst of poverty and hardship. She ultimately attended St. John's University in Brooklyn, and went on to study law. After graduating from law school, she opened up a practice, married, and had two sons.

Her public career has involved her in numerous legal and civic projects. She has often been quoted as a severe critic of the Harlem community, and has thus come under fire from many political regulars who feel her views are distorted. Many of these views, however, are now part of the new handbook of values being written by young militants who are pressing for such things as community ownership and local control of schools.

Mrs. Walker has been defeated in her bids for public office, but she has demonstrated a will to succeed, an admirable flexibility, and a tenacious resolve. The Harlem Co-op which she eventually masterminded is not only an asset to Harlem, but also a tribute to one who believes that self-generating momentum changes lives and forges destinies.

MADAME C. J. WALKER
1869–1919

Cosmetics manufacturer

Madame C. J. Walker who, because of her innovations in the cosmetics business, was to become one of the wealthiest and most famous women of her race experienced an early life of poverty and hardship. Born to ex-slave parents in Delta, Louisiana, Sarah McWilliams was orphaned at the age of seven, married at 14 and was left a widow with a small child at the age of 20.

Deciding to begin a new life, she traveled to St. Louis and worked as a laundress in order to send her daughter to school. In the 1890's, she married Charles J. Walker and, under the name of Madame C. J. Walker, subsequently made famous her new hair-styling formula.

In 1910, she went to Indianapolis to begin the manufacture of her hair preparations, later adding a complete line of toiletries and cosmetics to her products. As her business expanded, she established many Walker schools of beauty culture across the country. In the process, she became the first Negro woman millionaire.

Before her death in 1919, Madame Walker was well-known for her philanthropic activities: she made large bequests to the NAACP, the YMCA of St. Louis, Tuskegee Institute, and Bethune-Cookman College, and also stipulated in her will that two-thirds of the profits of her company should be given to charitable organizations.

Today, students from several foreign countries come to the United States to receive training at the Walker beauty schools, and over 2,000 agents represent the Walker system in this country and abroad.

MAGGIE LENA WALKER
1867–1934
Banker

Born in Richmond, Virginia, Maggie L. Walker had no specific training for the banking career in which she was later to achieve such notable success. After graduating from high school, she taught for several years before starting as secretary to the Independent Order of St. Luke, a Negro organization in Virginia.

During this time, she helped establish branches of the Order throughout Virginia and West Virginia. In 1899, she became secretary-treasurer of the organization. Under her guidance, the Order was restored to financial solvency, and grew to include an insurance concern and a banking establishment. The latter, which became known as the Consolidated Bank and Trust Company, functioned with Mrs. Walker serving as chairman of the board. She also established and supervised the *St. Luke Herald*, the newspaper which was the official organ of the Order of St. Luke.

A contributor to several charitable organizations, Mrs. Walker was also an organizer and president of the Council of Colored Women, a director of the NAACP and a board member of the National Urban League.

She died in 1934.

BENNETTA B. WASHINGTON
Director, Women's Job Corps
Office of Economic Opportunity

The background and education of Dr. Bennetta B. Washington was one which served her well in preparation for her role as director of the Women's Job Corps.

Born in Winston Salem, North Carolina, she moved as a child to Washington, D. C. with her parents. She received both B. A. and M. A. degrees from Howard University, and later a Ph. D. in sociology from the Catholic University of America.

In 1941, she began working as a counselor in the public school system of Baltimore, Maryland, leaving in 1944 to act as program director for young adults at the Phillis Wheatley Y.W.C.A. in Washington, D. C. From 1946 to 1965, Dr. Washington worked first as counselor in the Washington schools, then as principal of several different high schools.

In 1965, she assumed her present position as Director of the Women's Job Corps.

GERALDINE WHITTINGTON
White House Secretary

Born in West River, Maryland in 1931, Geraldine Whittington graduated from high school in Annapolis before taking a two-year secretarial course at Virginia State College in Petersburg.

In 1950, she began her career in government service as a secretary for the Veterans Administration, later leaving to join the Office of Public Health in the International Cooperation Administration. By 1961, she had become executive assistant to the Administrator of the Agency for International Development. That same year, she was called upon to work as secretary to Ralph Dungan, special assistant to President John F. Kennedy. She remained with Dungan until 1963, when she joined the staff of Bill Moyers, press secretary to Lyndon B. Johnson.

Dr. Bennetta Washington (Left) with members of her staff.

In December of that year, she accepted an invitation from President Johnson to become one of his secretaries, traveling and working with him during his subsequent campaign.

Miss Whittington later moved to the Office of the Chief of Protocol.

MARIA SELIKA WILLIAMS
Concert Star

One of the foremost Negro singers of the 19th century, Maria Selika Williams was also one of the few Negro performers to receive the training necessary to launch a legitimate career in opera.

Known as "Madame Selika" (she received her stage name from the Meyerbeer opera *L'Africaine*), she studied in Boston, and ultimately became proficient in French, Italian and German. After first winning favor in her own country, she toured Europe—receiving excellent press notices in such newspapers as the *Figaro* in Paris and the *Tagesblatt* in Berlin. In the latter city, it was said that she "roused the audience to the highest pitch of enthusiasm."

Upon her return to the United States, Madame Selika and her husband settled in Philadelphia. Later, she moved to New York City, becoming a voice teacher at the Martin-Smith School of Music in Harlem.

ADDITIONAL PROMINENT NEGRO WOMEN

Name	*Dates of Birth and Death*	*Place of Birth*	*Primary Activity*
Allen, Sarah	1764–1849	Virginia	home missions pioneer
Anderson, Dr. Caroline V. Still	1849–1919	Philadelphia, Pa.	physician
Baldwin, Maria Louise	1856–1922	Cambridge, Mass.	educator
Barrett, Janie Porter	1870–1949	Georgia	educator, clubwoman
Beasley, Delilah L.	1871–1934	Cincinnati, Ohio	historian, journalist
Beasley, Mother Matilda	1834–1903	New Orleans, La.	educator, social worker
Becraft, Ann Marie	1805–1833	Washington, D. C.	educator
Bergen, Flora Batson	1865– ?	Washington, D. C.	opera singer
Bowser, Rosa Dixon	1885–1931	Virginia	teacher, clubwoman
Brown, Sue M.	1877–1941	Virginia	club leader and organizer
Cary, Mary Ann Shadd	1823–1893	Wilmington, Dela.	educator, abolitionist, newspaper editor, journalist
Cook, Myrtle Foster	1870–1951	Ontario, Canada	teacher, social worker
Coppin, Fannie Jackson	1835–1912	Washington, D. C.	teacher, African missionary
Douglass, Anna Murray	? –1882	Maryland	abolitionist, Underground Railroad worker
Douglass, Sarah Mapps	1806–1882	Philadelphia, Pa.	educator, abolitionist
Eldridge, Elleanor	1785–1845	Warwick, R. I.	writer
Fayerweather, Sarah Harris	1820–1870	Canterbury, Conn.	abolitionist, Underground Railroad worker
Frazier, Susan E.	1864–1924	New York	President, Women's Auxiliary, New York National Guard
Gordon, Nora A.	1866–1901	Georgia	teacher, missionary
Gray, Dr. Ida	1867– ?	Tennessee	dentist
Greenfield, Elizabeth Taylor	1809–1876	Natchez, Miss.	opera singer ("The Black Swan")
Grimké, Charlotte Forten	1838–1914	Philadelphia, Pa.	teacher, writer, poet
Hackley, Emma Azalia	1867–1922	Detroit, Mich.	teacher, concert artist, writer
Hare, Maude Cuney	1874–1936	Texas	music teacher, writer
Holland, Annie Wealthy	1871–1934	Virginia	educator
Hudlun, Anna Elizabeth	1840–1914	Pennsylvania	social worker
Logan, Adella Hunt	1863–1915	Georgia	educator
Matthews, Victoria Earle	1861–1898	Georgia	social worker
Merritt, Emma Frances Grayson	1860–1933	Virginia	educator
Mitchell, Nellie Brown	1845–1924	New Hampshire	singer
Mossell, Gertrude Bustill	1855– ?	Philadelphia, Pa.	newspaper editor and writer
Mossell, Mary Ella	1853–1886	Baltimore, Md.	teacher, A.M.E. missionary in Haiti
Nelson, Alice Dunbar	1875–1935	New Orleans, La.	author, editor

Name	*Dates of Birth and Death*	*Place of Birth*	*Primary Activity*
Patterson, Mary Jane	1840–1894	Raleigh, N.C.	educator (first Negro woman college graduate: Oberlin, 1862)
Peake, Mary Smith Kelsey	1823–1862	Norfolk, Va.	teacher
Preston, Frances E. L.	1844–1929	Virginia	lecturer and temperance organizer
Putnam, Georgianna Frances	1839–1914	Salem, Mass.	teacher and principal
Pyles, Charlotta G.	1806–1880	—	abolitionist
Remond, Sarah	1815– ?	Salem, Mass.	abolitionist and physician
Ruffin, Josephine St. Pierre	1842–1924	Boston, Mass.	organizer of women's clubs
Shorter, Susie	1859–1912	Terre Haute, Ind.	teacher, writer
Simpson, Georgianna R.	1866–1944	Washington, D. C.	professor and linguist
Smith, Amanda Berry	1836–1915	Maryland	evangelist and African missionary
Stewart, Sallie W.	1881–1951	Tennessee	teacher, clubwoman
Talbert, Mary B.	1866–1923	Ohio	educator, social organizer
Vashon, Susan Paul	1838–1912	Boston, Mass.	teacher, nurse
Washington, Josephine Turpin	1861–1949	Virginia	journalist, teacher
Washington, Margaret Murray	1865–1925	Georgia	organizer of women's clubs
Washington, Olivia Davidson	1859–1889	Virginia	Tuskegee fund-raiser
Williams, Lulu	1874–1945	Michigan	teacher, social organizer
Yates, Josephine Silone	1852–1912	New York	educator, writer

THE BLACK RELIGIOUS TRADITION

Negro Denominations: The Baptists and the Methodists
Catholicism among Negroes
"White Churches"
Black Jews
Mormon Policy Toward Negroes
Non-affiliated Churches: The Evangelical Movement
The Negro Church
Negro Churchmen
The National Committee of Negro Churchmen
Gospel Music in the United States

"The . . . (Christian) . . . church is one outstanding institution of the community over which the Negroes themselves exercise control, and because it stands so alone in administering to their own conception of their needs, its function is varied. The religious emotions of the people demand some channel of formal expression, and find it in the church. But more than this, the church is the most important center for face-to-face relations. It is in a very real sense a social institution. It provides a large measure of the recreation and relaxation from the physical stress of life . . . Above this it holds out a world of escape from the hard experiences of Life *common to all* (emphasis added).

Charles S. Johnson in
Shadow of the Plantation
(University of Chicago Press, 1934)

From his earliest arrival in America, the Negro slave accepted Christianity as a vital spiritual force in his life. The acceptance of a new faith which, on the one hand, espoused the ideal of the brotherhood of all men and, on the other, tolerated and even encouraged the existence of slavery involved a gross contradiction. Most white Christians had little difficulty in resolving this dilemma inasmuch as spokesmen for their churches were not concerned with the slave's physical bondage, but rather with his commitment to Christian ideals. One is at a loss, however, to explain how Negro slaves were able to adjust to a faith which, in its early stages, held out little real hope for putting an end to their bondage. (In the context of the 19th century, such an adjustment is less surprising in view of the prevailing abolitionist sentiment which had taken root in much of the nation by then.)

Scholars investigating this problem have tended to become preoccupied with cultural antecedents in their belief that these are necessary for the acceptance of a new religious philosophy. Melville Herskovits, for example, has taken the position that

African survivals can be found in numerous phases of Negro life in the United States (including the Christian religion), and tends to be supported in this view by Harry V. Richardson who maintains that Africans were inclined to accept Christianity since they already possessed a highly developed religious tradition of their own. Frazier, on the other hand, exhorts readers of *The Negro Church in America* to recognize the fact that the enslaved African Negro was "practically stripped" of his social heritage, and indicates likewise in his *The Negro in the United States* that "it would be . . . difficult to establish any relation between African religious practices and the Negro church which developed on American soil."

Nevertheless, a discussion of African cultural antecedents does not of itself shed any light on the question of how the Negro resolved the basic dilemma of being a "Christian slave." Without becoming excessively preoccupied with this aspect of the matter, however, it is still possible to arrive at certain uniform conclusions regarding the growth and development of the Negro church. It seems clear, for example, that slavery was the paramount issue to be considered by all agencies which sought to deal with the Negro, including those desiring his conversion to Christianity. The work of the Society for the Propagation of the Gospel in Foreign Parts was clearly directed toward the conversion of Negro children, and was conducted, as Frazier suggests, under carefully controlled conditions acceptable to white slaveowners. The Quakers (Society of Friends), however, felt it far more important to take a *moral position* on slavery, rather than simply to bring Christianity to the slaves. Thus, it was they who not only condemned slavery as an institution, but also hastened to prevent their members from owning slaves.

Christian missionaries who originally found it difficult to circulate among Negroes were given some encouragement by the passage of a Virginia law which declared that the receipt of baptism could have no effect whatsoever on the legal status of the slave. As a result of this dictum, slaveowners throughout the 18th and early 19th centuries tended to feel more secure in their belief that Christianity itself would not automatically lead to the abolition of slavery.

The Christian message which was carried to the Negro in the 19th century by the missionary zeal of evangelical Methodist and Baptist sects was designed first and foremost to generate belief in a gospel of hope and future bliss, not to hold out the promise of an immediate end to earthly troubles.

Thus, even before the "great day," the fabric of Negro religious worship was organized around a program of Christianity which provided answers to all of the key questions underlying man's *eternal destiny*. Once emancipation came, bringing with it a tremendous release from earthly oppression, the Negro church quickly fell heir to the fruits of its own self-righteous position. In some way, it too could be credited with the victory won.

NEGRO DENOMINATIONS

Baptists: History and Worship

The Baptist church became a major force in Negro religious life in the years immediately following the Civil War. By 1870 (four years after North Carolina had launched the movement), Baptist state conventions had been organized throughout the South.

The Consolidated American Baptist Convention, organized in 1867 and lasting until 1880, represented the Negro's first attempt to create a national body independent of, and separate from, white-dominated groups. With the dissolution of this convention, three smaller ones sprang up in its place: the Foreign Mission Baptist Convention of the U.S.A. (1880); the American National Baptist Convention (1880), and the American National Educational Baptist Convention (1893). These organizations were then united as the National Baptist Convention of the U.S.A.

The National Baptist Convention of America, organized in 1880, and usually referred to as the "unincorporated" body, has a membership of 2,668,799 (though the figures reflect 1956 totals, they are the latest available), and is based in Jacksonville, Florida. Correspondence should be addressed to Corresponding Secretary Rev. Robert H. Wilson at 1058 Hogan Street in Jacksonville.

The National Baptist Convention, U.S.A., Inc. had a membership of 5.5 million as of 1958, the latest year for which official statistics have been compiled. Rev. J. H. Jackson (3101 South Parkway, Chicago 60616) has been president of the convention since 1953.

OFFICERS OF THE NATIONAL BAPTIST CONVENTION, U.S.A., INC.

Officers:

Pres.: Rev. J. H. Jackson,
405 E. 31st Street,
Chicago, Illinois 60616

Vice Pres. at Large: Rev. E. D. Billoups,
1678—79th Avenue,
Baton Rouge, Louisiana 70807

Vice Presidents: Rev. C. H. Hampton,
605 S. 32nd St., San Diego, Calif.

Rev. A. E. Campbell,
2500 Carnes Ave., Memphis, Tenn.

Rev. J. A. F. Finlayson,
3389 Charles Ave., Miami, Florida

Rev. Sandy Ray, 574 Madison St.,
Brooklyn, New York

Gen. Sec.: Rev. T. J. Jemison,
915 Spain Street,
Baton Rouge, Louisiana 70802

Treasurer: Rev. L. G. Carr,
5600 W. Girard Avenue,
Philadelphia, Pa. 19131

Statistician: Rev. B. J. Johnson,
1304 Hunter Street,
Atlanta, Georgia

Historiographer: Rev. E. T. Caviness,
10505 Tacoma Avenue,
Cleveland, Ohio

Editor: Rev. Caesar Clark,
902 North Good Street,
Dallas, Texas

The first Negro Baptist church in Savannah, Georgia

Other Organizations:

Foreign Mission Board:
Sec., Rev. William J. Harvey III
701 S. 19th Street,
Philadelphia, Pa. 19146

Homes Missions & Evangelism Board:
701-703 S. 19th Street,
Philadelphia, Pa. 19146
Ex. Sec., Rev. Charles P. Harris

Benefit Board:
Chmn., Rev. W. Herbert Brewster
903 Loney St., Memphis, Tennessee

Education Board:
Corr. Sec., Rev. W. H. Brewster

B.T.U. Board:
Sec., Rev. C. R. Williams
412 4th Avenue,
Nashville, Tenn. 37219

Sunday School Publishing Board:
330 Charlotte Ave., Nashville, Tenn.
Exec. Dir., Rev. D. C. Washington

Laymen's Movement: 399 McAllister St.,
San Francisco, California 14115
Corr. Sec., William H. Pryor

Woman's Auxiliary Convention:
Pres., Mrs. Mary O. Ross,
584 Arden Park,
Detroit, Michigan 48202

National S.S. and B.T.U. Congress:
Pres., Dr. O. Clay Maxwell
114 W. 120 St., N. Y., N. Y. 10027

OFFICERS OF THE NATIONAL BAPTIST CONVENTION OF AMERICA

Officers:

Pres.: Dr. J. C. Sams
1724 Jefferson Street,
Jacksonville, Florida

Vice Pres.: Rev. B. O. Byrd
5200 S. Central Avenue,
Los Angeles, California 90011

Recording Secretary: Rev. D. C. Cooksey
1227 N. Greenwood Avenue,
Tulsa, Oklahoma 74106

Corresponding Secretary:
Rev. Robert H. Wilson
1058 Hogan Street,
Jacksonville, Florida 32202

Official Reporter: Rev. William Downs
1017 East Boulevard,
Cleveland, Ohio 44108

Treasurer: Dr. A. A. Lucas
5109 Farmer Street,
Houston, Texas 77020

Statistician: Rev. John T. Walker
Denver, Colorado

Historiographer: Rev. Marvin C. Griffin
915 N. 6th Street, Waco, Texas 76707

Auditor: Rev. M. C. Allen
Virginia Seminary and College,
Lynchburg, Virginia

Other Organizations:

Benevolent Board:
Corr. Sec., Rev. George J. Johnson
Mary Allen College, Crockett, Texas

Benevolent Board:
Chmn., Rev. John W. Williams
1414 E. 15th Street,
Kansas City, Mo. 64106

Evangelical Board:
Chmn., Rev. H. H. Robinson
116 W. 8th Street,
Jacksonville, Florida 32206

Foreign Mission Board:
Chmn., Rev. F. D. Johnson
444 E. 50th St., Chicago, Ill. 60653

Home Mission Board:
Chmn., Rev. J. H. L. Smith
4501 Vincennes Avenue
Chicago, Illinois 60653

Publishing Board:
Chmn., Rev. J. B. Ridley, 319 21st St.,
Nashville, Tennessee 37206

Educational Board:
Chmn., Rev. P. S. Wilkinson
1011 Delaware Street,
San Antonio, Texas

B.Y.P.U. Board:
Chmn., Rev. L. W. Mingo,
217 E. Monroe St., Carbondale, Ill.

Senior Woman's Auxiliary:
Pres., Mrs. Fannie C. Thompson
516 E. Waverly Street, Tucson, Ariz.

Junior Woman's Auxiliary:
Pres., Mrs. Hattie L. E. Williams

National Baptist Brotherhood:
Pres., Mr. Ira L. Clark
3615 Rosedale St., Houston, Texas

National Baptist Youth Convention:
Pres., Rev. James J. Sutton
Oakland, California

OFFICERS OF THE PROGRESSIVE NATIONAL BAPTIST CONVENTION, INC.

Officers:

Pres.: Dr. E. R. Searcy
137 Boulevard, N.E.,
Atlanta, Georgia 30312

Vice Pres.: Dr. E. L. Harrison
1500—9th Street, N.W.,
Washington, D. C.

Exec. Sec.: Dr. L. V. Booth
630 Glenwood Avenue,
Cincinnati, Ohio 45229

Treas.: Dr. A. A. Banks, 441 Monroe Ave.,
Detroit, Michigan 48226

Dir. Publicity: Rev. George Lawrence
828 Green Ave., Brooklyn, N. Y.

Other Organizations:

Dcpt. of Christian Education:
Sec., Dr. S. D. Edwards
913 E. Myrtle Avenue,
Flint, Michigan 48505

National Sunday School &
B.T.U. Congress:
Pres., Dr. William C. Upshaw
470 Wooster Ave., Akron, Ohio 44307

Woman's Auxiliary:
Pres., Mrs. Minnie L. Bruce
4130 S. Indiana Avenue,
Chicago, Illinois 60653

Home Mission Board:
Chmn., Rev. Louis Johnson,
3900 Beaubien Avenue,
Detroit, Michigan 48201

Laymen's Dept.:
Pres., Chester E. Dixon
179 W. Washington Street, Room 907
Chicago, Illinois 48202

A preacher exhorts his black congregation in the African Church in Cincinnati, Ohio in 1853 .

Rev. Richard Allen

Methodists: History and Worship

Large numbers of Negroes joined the Methodist Church in colonial and pre-Revolutionary times. In some areas, they were organized into separate congregations presided over by white preachers while, in others, they participated in services on a segregated basis (occupying special seats, and taking communion only after their white counterparts had done so). Dissatisfaction with the latter system grew so pronounced that, by 1785, several influential members of Methodist churches in the North had voted to establish their own places of worship. The leader in this movement, Richard Allen, was himself a freedman and a convert to Methodism. By 1787, he and his followers were convinced that Negroes would best be served by a church of their own making. The resulting church proved to be a prototypical one, and spawned a whole new movement across the South. In 1816, the leaders of this movement called a conference in Philadelphia, where they established the African Methodist Episcopal Church, with Allen in the capacity of bishop.

The Negro Methodist movement experienced its first real flowering after the Civil War, at which time many rural churches in the South showed an inclination to accept its leadership. In part, this phenomenon was due to the greater mobility enjoyed by the Negro—both preacher and convert—as a result of emancipation. Despite its growth, however, the Methodist gospel never succeeded in matching the appeal generated by the Baptist movement. Nevertheless, the Methodists of today, although in three major denominations, lay claim to more than two million members.

As in the case of the Baptists, Methodist worship has tended to reflect the religious mentality and spiritual expectations of the Negro masses. As such, it is usually evangelistic in tone, and relies heavily on the dynamism and personality of the preacher, rather than on any strict adherence to the articles of faith he espouses.

A. *The AME Church*

In 1816, Richard Allen, then a deacon of Bethel Church, called together representatives of separate Negro churches which had been established in Delaware, Maryland and New Jersey. The meeting resulted in the formation of the African Methodist Episcopal (AME) Church—one of the earliest Negro Methodist denominations in the United States.

The AME Church—now divided into 18 episcopal districts spread across the United States, Africa, Canada, and the islands of the Caribbean—has approximately 1.1. million members attending close to 6,000 churches. Its chief governing bodies are the General Conference, the Council of Bishops, and the General Board. The main work of the church is carried out through a number of lesser boards and departments in charge of such fields as missionary endeavor, education and evangelism.

Headquarters of the church are at 1212 Fountain S.W., Atlanta 30314.

Bishop James Varick

AME OFFICIAL DIRECTORY FOR 1968-72 QUADRENNIUM

This church began in 1787 in Philadelphia when persons in St. George Methodist Episcopal Church withdrew as a protest against color segregation. In 1816 the denomination was started, led by Rev. Richard Allen, who had been ordained deacon by Bishop Asbury, and who was ordained elder and elected and consecrated bishop.

Officers:

President of Bishops' Council:
Bishop John Douglas Bright

Senior Bishop (Approvals Officer):
Bishop D. Ward Nichols

Chairman of The General Board:
Bishop William F. Ball, Sr.

Treasurer: Dr. A. G. Gaston

General Secretary: Dr. Russell S. Brown

Historiographer: Dr. Howard D. Gregg

Organizations:

Board of Missions: Sec., Rev. Ford Gibson —deceased, succeeded by
Dr. John W. P. Collier
475 Riverside Drive,
Room 1926, N.Y., N.Y. 10027

Department of Education:
Sec.-Treas:, Rev. S. L. Greene, Jr.
1461 Northgate Rd., Wash., D.C. 20012

A.M.E. Sunday School Union:
Sec.-Treas., Rev. Charles S. Spivey, Sr.
414 Eighth Ave., South,
Nashville, Tenn. 37203

A.M.E. Urban Ministry & Ecumenical Relations: Head, Bishop F. D. Jordan

Board of Church Extension: Sec.-Treas.

Division of Christian Education:
Gen. Sec., Rev. Andrew White
414 Eighth Ave., Nashville,
Tenn. 37203

Evangelism:
Dir., Rev. G. H. J. Thibodeaux
1150 Portland Ave.,
Shreveport, La. 71103

Woman's Missionary Society:
Pres., Mrs. Anne E. Heath
1541 14th St., N.W.,
Washington, D.C. 20005

Bishop William F. Ball is a prominent AME churchman.

Bishop Stephen G. Spottswood of the Ame Zion Church.

Pension Department:
Sec., Rev. J. M. Granberry
414 Eighth Ave., South,
Nashville, Tenn. 37203

Religious Literature:
Editor, Rev. Therion Cobb
414 Eighth Ave., South,
Nashville, Tenn. 37203

Periodicals:

A.M.E. Review:
Editor, Rev. Benjamin H. Hill
3004 North Cincinnati St.,
Tulsa, Oklahoma 74106

Christian Recorder:
Editor, Rev. B. J. Nolen
414 Eighth Ave., South,
Nashville, Tenn. 37203

Voice of Missions:
Editor, John W. P. Collier, Jr.

Woman's Missionary Recorder:
Editor, Mrs. A. B. Lynem
226 West 6th Street,
Lexington, Kentucky 40502

There are eighteen Districts in the A.M.E. Church which are presided over by the following bishops:

Bishop John D. Bright (1)*
1701 Arch Street—Room 420
Philadelphia, Pa. 19103

Bishop George W. Baber (2)
7508 16th Street, N.W.
Washington, D.C. 20012

Bishop W. R. Wilkes (3)
11009 Wade Park Avenue
Cleveland, Ohio 44106

Bishop H. Thomas Primm (4)
2820 Monaco Parkway
Denver, Colorado 80207

Bishop Harrison J. Bryant (5)
2804 Sewell Street
Kansas City, Kansas 66104

Bishop E. L. Hickman (6)
1212 Fountain Drive, S.W.
Atlanta, Georgia 30314

Bishop William F. Ball (7)
7530 N.W. 10th Avenue
Miami, Florida 33150

Bishop I. H. Bonner (8)
1937 Peniston Street
New Orleans, La. 70115

Bishop Hubert N. Robinson (9)
A. G. Gaston Building
1523 Fifth Avenue, N.
Birmingham, Alabama 35203

Bishop O. L. Sherman (10)
128 Garrison Street
Waco, Texas 76704

Bishop George N. Collins (11)
1706 Jefferson Street
Jacksonville, Florida 32209

Bishop D. Ward Nichols (12)
Shorter College
Little Rock, Arkansas

Bishop Carey A. Gibbs (13)
1011 W. 8th Street
Jacksonville, Fla. 32209

Bishop H. I. Bearden (14)
644 Skipper Dr., N.W.
Atlanta, Georgia 30318

Bishop G. Dewey Robinson (15)
28 Walmer Road
Woodstock, Cape Town, South Africa

Bishop G. Wayman Blakely (16)
6605 Lincoln Drive
Philadelphia, Pa. 19119

Bishop Henry W. Murph (17 & 18)
4103 Palmwood Drive—Apt. #4
Los Angeles, California 90008

Bishop Frederick D. Jordan
5151 Franklin Avenue
Hollywood, California 90027

Bishop Joseph Gomez
13855 Superior Road
(Forest Park Tower)
East Cleveland, Ohio 14118

*(The numbers in parentheses indicate the Episcopal District)

B. The AMEZ Church

In 1796, Bishop Francis Asbury acceded to the request of the Negro members of the Methodist Episcopal Church in New York for permission to hold meetings under their own auspices. Among those who participated in this movement were James Varick, Francis Jacobs, William Brown, Peter Williams, June Scott, Samuel Pontier, Thomas Miller, William Hamilton, Abraham Thompson, William Miller. They fitted out an old building on Cross Street, between Mulberry and Orange Streets, which had previously been used as a stable, as a place of worship. Thus was born the prototype of the "African Methodist Episcopal Zion Church." The founders, however, did not declare their underlying purpose at once and withheld their new name from the public until 1799.

Prominent among those who attended the meeting in 1799, when it was decided to make public their purpose and declare the name of the first African Methodist Church in America, were George E. Moore, Thomas Sipkins, David Bias, George White, Thomas Cook, John Teesman, and George Collins with those named above. The first Board of Trustees were: Francis Jacobs, William Brown, Thomas Miller, Peter Williams, Thomas Sipkins, William Hamilton, George Collins.

The first church frame was built in 1800 on the corner of Church and Leonard Streets. A year later, on Feb. 16, 1801, the Church was officially incorporated. The General Conference of the Methodist Episcopal Church, through Rev. John McClaskey, recognized the new body on April 6, 1801.

The first elders elected in the AMEZ Church were Abraham Thompson and James Varick. These, with Leven Smith, were ordained elders June 17, 1821, by Rev. James Covel, D.D., Rev. Sylvester Hutchinson, and Rev. William Stilwell, elders of the Methodist Episcopal Church. Local deacons, ordained by the Methodist Episcopal Conference, officiated in the African Methodist Episcopal Zion Church prior to 1800.

The first Conference was held in Zion Church, New York, June 21, 1821. Rev. William Phoebus, of the Methodist Church, presided. At this Conference a form of "Limited Episcopacy" was established, and James Varick was elected the first Bishop—then called "Superintendent." The first Discipline for the African Methodist Episcopal Zion Church was adopted October 25, 1820.

The first attempt to effect the "Organic Union" of the African Methodist Episcopal and African Methodist Episcopal Zion Churches was made August 17, 1820, at the residence of Mr. William Brown, Leonard Street, New York, by the officials of the African Methodist Episcopal Zion Church and Bishop Richard Allen. The merger was not accomplished, however.

The original title of the African Methodist Episcopal Zion Church was "The African Methodist Episcopal Church," the word "Zion" being used only accommodatively. Since the sister Church had adopted the same title, however, the General Conference of 1848 made the "Zion" a part of the corporate title to avoid confusion.

The policy of the church has been Episcopal Methodism in its entirety from its beginning. Changes have been minimal, except that in 1868 the limit of Episcopal tenure was extended during life or good behavior. The form of consecration also varied; and the imposition of hands was introduced.

The Church is the first Methodist Church to admit women to all functions, save for Ordination. It was also the only colored Methodist Church that declared against slavery, the measure being incorporated in her first Copy of Discipline, 1820. This action proved a means of keeping her out of the South till 1862-63.

Latest figures (1965) place the membership at 1.1 million. Church headquarters are at 1328 U St., N.W., Washington, D.C.

AFRICAN METHODIST EPISCOPAL ZION CHURCH

The A.M.E. Zion Church is an independent Methodist body, having been organized in New York City in 1796 as the result of withdrawing from the John Street Methodist Church because of racial discrimination and social proscription of black members in the John Street congregation.

AMEZ DIRECTORY OF BISHOPS AND EPISCOPAL DISTRICTS FOR 1968-72 QUADRENNIUM

I. Bishop Raymond Luther Jones, 916 Horah Street, Salisbury, North Carolina 28144: Western North Carolina, West Central North Carolina, and Tennessee Conferences.

II. Bishop Herbert Bell Shaw, 520 Red Cross Street, Wilmington, North Carolina 28401: New York, Western New York, Cape Fear, Bahamas, and Jamaica Conferences.

III. Bishop Stephen Gill Spottswood, 1931 16th Street, N.W., Washington, D.C. 20009: Michigan, New England, Philadelphia, Baltimore, Virgin Islands, Guyana Conferences.

IV. Bishop William Andrew Stewart, 2314 20th Street, N.W., Washington, D.C. 20009: Central North Carolina, North Carolina, and Virginia Conferences.

V. Bishop C. Ewbank Tucker, 1715 Ormsby Avenue, Louisville, Kentucky 40210: Indiana, South Mississippi, and Blue Ridge Conferences.

VI. Bishop Joseph Dixon Cauthen, 2843 Princess Ann Road, Norfolk, Virginia 23504: Pee Dee, Palmetto, South Carolina, and Missouri Conferences.

VII. Bishop Felix S. Anderson, 741 South 44th Street, Louisville, Kentucky 40211: Kentucky, North Alabama, East Tennessee-Virginia Conferences.

VIII. Bishop William Milton Smith, 1509 Basil Street, Mobile, Alabama 36603: West Alabama, New Jersey, Alabama, Florida, South Florida, and Albemarle Conferences.

IX. Bishop S. Dorme Lartey, Post Office Box 169, Monrovia, Liberia: Liberia, West Ghana, East Ghana, and Nigeria Conferences.

X. Bishop William A. Hilliard, 690 Chicago Boulevard, Detroit, Michigan 48202: Ohio, Allegheny, California, Southwest Rocky Mountain, Oregon-Washington, and Colorado Conferences.

XI. Bishop Alfred G. Dunston, 5901 Cobbs Creek Parkway, Philadelphia, Pennsylvania 19143: Central Alabama, South Alabama, Cahaba, West Tennessee, Mississippi, and Louisiana Conferences.

XII. Bishop Charles Herbert Foggie, 1200 Windermere Drive, Pittsburgh, Pennsylvania 15218: Arkansas, North Arkansas, Oklahoma, Georgia, Texas, and South Georgia Conferences.

Bishop William Jacob Walls (Retired), 4736 South Dr. Martin L. King Drive, Chicago, Illinois 60615.

General Officers and Departments

Dr. R. H. Collins Lee, General Secretary-Auditor, Department of Records and Research, 1326-28 You Street, N.W., Washington, D.C. 20009.

Mr. Richard W. Sherrill, Secretary, Department of Finance, P.O. Box 1047, Charlotte, N.C. 28201.

Rev. Durocher L. Blakey, General Manager, A.M.E. Zion Publishing House, P.O. Box 508, Charlotte, North Carolina 28201.

Rev. M. B. Robinson, Editor, The Star of Zion, P.O. Box 1047, Charlotte, North Carolina 28201.

Dr. David Bradley, Editor, A.M.E. Zion Quarterly Review, P.O. Box 146, Bedford, Pennsylvania 15522.

Dr. J. Clinton Hoggard, Secretary-Editor, Department of Foreign Missions and Missionary Seer, 475 Riverside Drive, Room 1910, New York, New York 10027.

Dr. A. P. Morris, Secretary-Treasurer, Department of Home Missions, Pensions and Relief, P.O. Box 10143, Charlotte, North Carolina 28201.

Rev. G. L. Blackwell, Secretary, Christian Education Department, 128 East 58th Street, Chicago, Illinois 60637.

Dr. Louis J. Baptiste, Editor, Department of Church School Literature, P.O. Box 10693, Charlotte, North Carolina 28201.

Mr. Lem Long, Jr., Secretary-Treasurer Department of Church Extension, A.M.E. Zion Publishing House, Room 105, P.O. Box 1047, Charlotte, North Carolina 28201.

Dr. J. Dallas Jenkins, Sr., Director, Department of Evangelism, 1326-28 U Street, N.W., Washington, D.C. 20009.

Mr. Alexander Barnes, Director, Public Relations Department, 4407 Columbia Street, Durham, N.C. 27707.

Dr. Samuel C. Coleman, M.D., Director, Department of Health, 126 Grove Street, Hot Springs National Park, Arkansas 71901.

Dr. F. George Shipman, President, Livingstone College, and Hood Seminary, Salisbury, N.C. 28144.

Dr. S. E. Duncan (Deceased), President, Livingstone College, and Hood Seminary, Livingstone College, Salisbury, N.C. 28144.

Dr. Walter R. Lovell (Deceased), Editor, The Star of Zion, P.O. Box 1047, Charlotte, North Carolina 28201.

Bishop Herbert Bell Shaw

General Officers of the Woman's Home and Foreign Missionary Society

Mrs. Emma B. Watson, General President, 7405 Monticello Street, Pittsburgh, Pennsylvania 15208.

Mrs. Rosanna Nelson, First Vice President, 84 North Munn Avenue, Newark, New Jersey 07106.

Mrs. Elizabeth Michael, Second Vice President, 4918 Walnut Street, Philadelphia, Pennsylvania 19139.

Mrs. Grace L. Holmes, Executive Secretary, 2565 Linden Avenue, Knoxville, Tennessee 37914.

Miss Susie M. Moore, Recording Secretary, 4268 East Capitol St., N.E., Washington, D.C. 20019.

Mrs. Minnie D. Hurley, Treasurer, 2026 7th Avenue, New York, N.Y. 10027.

Mrs. Lonia M. Gill, Secretary of Young Women, 2864 Whistler Street, Whistler, Alabama 36612.

Mrs. Willie B. Heath Bobo, Superintendent, Buds of Promise, 400 Caulder Avenue, Spartanburg, South Carolina 29301.

Mrs. Laura E. Small, Secretary of Supplies, 1326-28 You Street, N.W., Washington, D.C. 20009.

Mrs. Ann Walker, Chairman, Life Membership Council, 3427 South Kemper Road, Arlington, Virginia 22206.

Mrs. Maggie E. Sheppard, Editor, Women's Column, The Missionary Seer, 4260 Hopper Avenue, Los Angeles, California 90011.

GENERAL OFFICERS OF THE CONNECTIONAL LAYMEN'S COUNCIL

Mr. Arthur E. Brooks, General President, 778 Hobart Pl., N.W., Washington, D.C. 20001.

Mr. D. D. Garrett, Vice-President, P.O. Box 235, Greenville, N.C. 27834.

Mr. R. J. Harris, Sr., Treasurer, P.O. Box 685, Statesville, N.C.

Mrs. Betty V. Stith, Secretary, 21 Goldwin St., Rye, New York 10580.

Mrs. Essie R. McDaniels, Recording Secretary, P.O. Box 41-A, Tappahannock, Virginia.

Mr. Guy Mayzck, Chaplain, Rte. 7, Box 560, Durham, N.C.

C. The CME Church

The Christian Methodist Episcopal (CME) Church, known until 1956 as the Colored Methodist Episcopal Church, is the third largest Negro Methodist body in the United States.

Like many Negro churches, this particular one came into being after the Civil War when some 250,000 segregated or otherwise restricted Negroes belonging to the Methodist Episcopal (ME) Church South appealed to the General Conference for the right to form their own church. In 1870, an ME commission was appointed to study the situation, and recommended that the Negro members in question be allowed to set up such a church.

In December of that same year, the first General Conference of the CME Church was held in Jackson, Tennessee, where two Negro bishops—Henry Miles and Richard H. Vanderhorst—were elected. Since then, the two churches have cooperated in many ways, primarily in the field of education. (The CME Church operates three colleges, several secondary schools, and a seminary.)

Latest membership figures show a total of over 466,000 communicants. The secretary of the Conference is Rev. A. Ralph Davis, 6432 S. Green St., Apt. 1, Chicago 60621.

CME OFFICIAL DIRECTORY FOR 1968-72 QUADRENNIUM

Officer:
Bishop B. Julian Smith
(Senior Bishop—Approvals Officer)

Organizations:

Board of Missions:
Chmn., Bishop E. P. Murchison
Gen. Sec., Rev. Isaiah Scipio, Jr.

Board of Christian Education:
Chmn., Bishop B. Julian Smith
Gen. Sec., Rev. C. D. Coleman

Publishing Board:
Chmn., Bishop Henry C. Bunton
Pub. Agent, Rev. M. C. Pettigrew

Board of Finance:
  Chmn., Bishop J. Claude Allen
  Fin. Sec., Prof. O. T. Peeples
Board of Pension:
  Chmn., Bishop W. H. Amos
  Gen. Sec., Rev. D. S. Cunningham
Board of Evangelism:
  Chmn., Bishop P. R. Shy
  Gen. Sec., Rev. N. L. Linsey
Board of Lay Activities:
  Chmn., Bishop Norris S. Curry
  Gen. Sec., W. E. Solomon
Woman's Missionary Council:
  Pres., Mrs. Phyllis Bedford

The nine Districts in the Christian Methodist Episcopal Church which are presided over by the following Bishops: Bishop B. Julian Smith (Senior), Bishop E. P. Murchison, Bishop J. Claude Allen, Bishop J. A. Johnson, Bishop C. A. Kirkendoll, Bishop P. R. Shy, Bishop Henry C. Bunton, Bishop N. S. Curry, Bishop W. H. Amos, and Bishop B. W. Doyle (Retired).

Addresses of Bishops:

Bishop B. W. Doyle, (Retired)
  1982 Madison Lane,
  Gary, Indiana 46407

Bishop B. J. Smith, Senior,
  First Episcopal District
  564 East Frank Avenue,
  Memphis,Tennessee 38106

Bishop J. Claude Allen,
  Third Episcopal District
  755 West 26th Avenue,
  Gary, Indiana 46407

Bishop E. P. Murchison,
  Second Episcopal District
  6322 Elwynne Drive,
  Cincinnati, Ohio 45236

Bishop P. R. Shy,
  Sixth Episcopal District
  2780 Collier Drive, N. W.,.
  Atlanta, Georgia 30318

Bishop N. S. Curry, Secretary,
  Eighth Episcopal District
  2330 Sutter Street,
  Dallas, Texas 75216

Bishop W. H. Amos,
  Ninth Episcopal District
  2111 LaSalle Gardens, South,
  Detroit, Michigan 48206

Bishop Henry C. Bunton,
  Seventh Episcopal District
  6524 16th Street, N.W.,
  Washington, D.C. 20012

Bishop J. A. Johnson, Jr.,
  Fourth Episcopal District
  109 Holcomb Drive,
  Shreveport, Louisiana 71103

Bishop C. A. Kirkendoll,
  Fifth Episcopal District
  Lane College,
  Jackson, Tennessee 38301

General Officers:

Rev. John M. Exum,
  Editor, "The Christian Index"
  P.O. Box 6138,
  Memphis, Tennessee 38106

Rev. M. C. Pettigrew, Publishing Agent,
  P.O. Box 6447,
  Memphis, Tennessee 38106

Prof. O. T. Peeples, Financial Secretary
  Box 6276,
  Memphis, Tennessee 38106

Rev. C. D. Coleman, General Secretary,
  Board of Christian Education
  1474 Humber Street,
  Memphis, Tennessee 38106

Rev. D. S. Cunningham,
  General Secretary, Pension Fund Dept.
  531 S. Parkway, East,
  Memphis, Tennessee 38106

Rev. Isaiah Scipio, Jr., General Secretary,
  Board of Mission
  22241 Boston Blvd.,
  Detroit, Michigan 48206

Rev. N. Linsey,
  General Secretary of Evangelism
  164-B Rocky Ford Road, N.E.,
  Atlanta, Georgia 30317

Mr. W. E. Solomon,
  General Secretary of Lay Activities
  P.O. Box 4012,
  Columbia, South Carolina 29204

Rev. Alex. Chambers,
  Editor, "Eastern Index"
  P.O. Box 1575,
  Greenville, S. C. 29602

Rev. G. H. Carter, (Retired)
  140 Hill Drive,
  Homer, Louisiana 37104

Rev. W. Louis Smith,
  Editor, "Western Index"
  1455-75 Golden Gate Avenue,
  San Francisco, California 94115

Mrs. Phyllis Bedford, President,
  Woman's Missionary Council
  1152 Lansdown Street,
  Youngstown, Ohio 44504

Rev. J. W. Bonner, President,
  Ministers and Laymens Council
  1928 N. Palace Avenue,
  Tyler, Texas 75703

Catholicism

The data below testifies to the development of Catholicism among Negroes in recent decades. Missionary activities have grown in intensity—particularly in the past 25 years—with the result that Negro membership has nearly tripled during this latter period. As of 1963, the Catholic Church had 700,000 Negro members in more than 500 parishes which were served by some 800 priests. It was also maintaining over 300 schools with an enrollment of close to 100,000 students.

The above figures apply only to those churches which exist in all-Negro or predominantly Negro residential areas. Other figures—i.e. those reflecting membership in "mixed congregation" churches—are not available. Nevertheless, there is good cause to believe that the Catholic Church is today the third or fourth largest religious organization among American Negroes (exceeded only by the two Baptist conventions and the AME denomination).

NEGRO MISSIONS AND PARISHES (1965)*

DIOCESE	CATH-OLICS	CHURCHES	PRIESTS	—BAPTISMS— INFANTS	ADULTS	SCHOOLS	PUPILS
Albany	500	1	1	. . . .	. . . .	0	0
Alexandria	9,667	19	20	318	99	18	3,230
Amarillo	200	1	1	18	28	1	110
Atlanta	2,000	2	7	134	76	3	692
Austin	700	3	3	11	12	1	20
Baltimore	27,600	6	11	606	184	6	1,128
Baton Rouge	14,717	10	10	482	149	6	1,753
Belleville	2,400	1	1	28	49	0	0
Boston	2,500	1	1	. . . .	. . . .	0	0
Brooklyn	28,500	7	20	990	500	3	2,984
Buffalo	5,000	0	4	150	. . . .	. . . .	
Camden	2,875	3	5	165	72	2	590
Charleston	4,245	19	7	76	129	14	2,139
Chicago	45,000	24	75	135	1,290	24	8,352
Cincinnati	3,000	3	3	38	65	2	605
Cleveland	9,000	7	33	179	149	6	1,706
Columbus	885	1	2	45	40	1	209
Corpus Christi	462	1	1	9	0	0	0
Covington	450	2	2	15	11	0	0
Dallas-Fort Worth	1,153	7	6	40	26	5	1,628
Detroit	30,000	14	30	1,054	1,060	12	4,943
Erie	1,020	1	1	16	8	0	0
Evansville	450	1	1	32	34	1	149
Galveston-Houston	62,000	20	28	1,269	256	12	2,884
Gary	2,000	1	2	49	1	1	235
Indianapolis	4,948	3	6	235	164	3	893
Kansas City, Kansas	2,500	2	2	19	16	2	207
Kansas City-St. Joseph	7,900	8	13	375	245	8	2,628
Lafayette, Louisiana	77,988	65	56	2,861	115	19	5,884
Lansing	400	1	1	13	19	0	0
Little Rock	1,400	10	7	55	75	6	985
Los Angeles	40,000	10	14	1,733	618	12	3,471
Louisville	5,000	5	7	153	84	5	824
Miami	3,800	5	4	172	121	2	510
Milwaukee	5,521	4	8	353	195	4	985
Mobile-Birmingham	19,374	59	71	993	1,015	33	5,806
Monterey-Fresno	4,192	2	2	340	82	1	206

DIOCESE	CATH-OLICS	CHURCHES	PRIESTS	—BAPTISMS— INFANTS	ADULTS	SCHOOLS	PUPILS
Nashville	3,800	5	5	101	257	5	1,476
Natchez-Jackson	6,416	29	25	313	221	19	4,955
Newark	8,000	4	11	240	238	2	468
New Orleans	55,000	32	53	2,278	501	26	10,136
New York	62,678	5	18	2,691	1,209	5	8,916
Oakland	2,500	2	4			2	481
Oklahoma City-Tulsa	6,500	7	8	250	200	2	311
Omaha	900	1	2	32	20	1	186
Owensboro	500	2	2	16	24	1	107
Philadelphia	41,637	4	21	1,523	1,033	6	1,223
Pittsburgh	2,500	3	3	32	61	2	326
Portland, Oregon	550	0	0	28	15	0	0
Raleigh	3,962	23	22	180	122	16	2,631
Reno	722	1	1	52	23	0	0
Richmond	8,320	12	19	281	183	8	1,546
Sacramento	10,000	3	9	.....	.....	3	1,040
St. Augustine	2,889	9	6	123	89	5	818
St. Louis	24,700	17	42	725	796	16	4,883
St. Paul	1,500	2	3	0	16	2	242
San Antonio	550	1	1	26	12	1	215
San Diego	6,110	2	3	194	23	0	0
San Francisco	11,000	...	...	.....	.....	0	0
Savannah	3,650	9	12	157	205	8	2,328
Seattle	1,250	0	0	33	47	0	0
Toledo	700	0	0	.....	.....	0	0
Trenton	2,150	2	4	183	140	1	240
Tucson	800	1	1	9	3	0	0
Washington	65,832	23	39	2,695	1,129	10	3,197
Wichita	1,075	1	1	42	23	0	0
Wilmington	1,300	2	2	7	10	1	77
Total*	766,838	531	783	25,392	13,587	354	101,558

* The statistics presented here comprise the data compiled and supplied by the Ordinaries to whom funds were allotted, supplemented by data kindly supplied by pastors in charge of Negro parishes in the other dioceses. Data from the latter source are in some instances not complete in one or more categories.

"White Churches"

The term "white churches" is used to identify those churches which, though they have predominantly white congregations, have nonetheless admitted large numbers of Negroes into their places of worship on a predominantly non-segregated basis. Among others, these include: the Methodist Church (c. 370,000); the Protestant Episcopal Church (c. 78,000); Seventh Day Adventists (c. 50,000), and the Congregational Church (c. 38,000). Since not all churches base their tabulations of membership on a racial breakdown, it is hazardous to estimate the number of Negroes in such churches, although a figure of 800,000 has been advanced.

Negro members of "white churches" generally enjoy the rights of full participation. In the Methodist Church, for example, Negro bishops serve side by side, and on an equal footing, with their white counterparts.

The Black Jews

There are believed to be approximately 44,000 so-called "black Jews" (they are actually more appropriately classified as members of Ethiopian Hebrew congregations) in the United States. These Jews, located in such cities as Philadelphia, Boston, Chicago, Los Angeles and New York, are mainly natives of the West Indies or the American South, although they consistently trace their ancestry and heritage back to Africa.

Closely knit, clannish, and fully involved, the black Jews continue to live successfully in poor or lower middle-class neighborhoods, despite the high crime rates prevalent in settings such as these. Both their religious optimism and the strong parental authority exercised on offspring contribute to the inherent stability of the group. New York's Wentworth A. Matthew, leader of Harlem's Ethiopian Hebrew Congregation, credits the strength and solidarity of his group to the presence of a "towering" father figure and a tenacious mother who "sets the tone and the mood" of family life.

Like Jews everywhere, the Ethiopian Hebrew congregations observe the rituals and holidays stemming from ancient Jewish traditions. Thus, they too celebrate such joyous occasions as the liberation of the Jews from bondage in Egypt by reading the Passover stories and participating in the family *seder*.

Their form of worship, the Sephardic, originated with the Jews in Spain and Portugal and was carried by them to the lands of Latin America and the islands of the West Indies. Thus, the Spanish influence is evident in the ethnic composition of the congregations which often includes Spanish and Portuguese members.

Like many American Jews, the Ethiopians identify strongly with Israel. One member of the 4,000-strong New York congregation has already taken a dance troupe of four black and 20 white youngsters to Israel for a seven-week seminar. The group was so well received that it made an appearance on Israeli television.

Despite the Jewish values which suffuse their lives, young blacks in the congregation are becoming increasingly aware of the contemporary pressures to identify with the black movement. In most cases, however, cultural and philosophical preoccupations continue to eclipse racial matters as concerns which unify and connect the community.

A black rabbi stands in front of his Bronx-based congregation.

Race, however, is still an issue which tends to fragment the black Jews and becloud their status. Thus, some black Jews seek to identify with the universal Jewish world whose nationhood is centered in the state of Israel while others, sensing the suspicion and uneasiness that might be generated by their presence in many areas of the white (including the Jewish) world, prefer to remain in small, unrelated clusters or decentralized factions.

Though many have worshipped as Jews for years, they often cannot produce the necessary documents required to prove to a rabbinical court their eligibility to call themselves orthodox Jews. Some do not qualify as Jews in the strict religious sense of the term, i.e., they are neither persons born of a Jewish mother or brought into the faith by a properly ordained rabbi.

The isolation of the black Jews contributes to the difficulty of finding absolute verification of their Jewish origins. Most trace their forbears to West or East Africa and are linked in some way to the Ethiopian Jews known as Falashas.

Mormonism—

On January 9, 1970, Mormon leaders around the world were informed of church policy toward the Negro. The text of the official Mormon position follows:

In view of confusion that has arisen, it was decided at a meeting of the first presidency and the quorum of the twelve to restate the position of the church with regard to the Negro both in society and in the church.

First, may we say that we know something of the suffering of those who are discriminated against in a denial of their civil rights and constitutional privileges. Our early history as a church is a tragic story of persecution and oppression.

Our people repeatedly were denied the protection of the law. They were driven and plundered, robbed and murdered by mobs who in many instances were aided and abetted by those sworn to uphold the law. We as a people have experienced the bitter fruits of civil discrimination and mob violence.

We believe that the Constitution of the United States was divinely inspired, that it was produced by "wise men" whom God raised up for this "very purpose," and that the principles embodied in the Constitution are so fundamental and important that, if possible, they should be extended "for the rights and protection" of all mankind.

In revelations received by the first prophet of the church in this dispensation, Joseph Smith (1805-1844), the Lord made it clear that it is "not right that any man should be in bondage one to another." These words were spoken prior to the Civil War. From these and other revelations have sprung the church's deep and historic concern with man's free agency and our commitment to the sacred principles of the Constitution.

It follows, therefore, that we believe the Negro, as well as those of other races, should have his full constitutional privileges as a member of society, and we hope that members of the church everywhere will do their part as citizens to see that these rights are held inviolate. Each citizen must have equal opportunities and protection under the law with reference to civil rights.

However, matters of faith, conscience, and theology are not within the purview of the civil law. The first amendment to the Constitution specifically provides that "Congress shall make no law respecting an establishment of religion, or prohibiting the free exercise thereof."

The position of the Church of Jesus Christ of Latter-day Saints affecting those of the Negro race who choose to join the church falls wholly within the category of religion. It has no bearing upon matters of civil rights. In no case or degree does it deny to the Negro his full privileges as a citizen of the nation.

This position has no relevancy whatever to those who do not wish to join the church. Those individuals, we suppose, do not believe in the divine origin and nature of the church, nor that we have the priesthood of God. Therefore, if they feel we have no priesthood, they should have no concern with any aspect of our theology on priesthood so long as that theology does not deny any man his constitutional privileges.

A word of explanation concerning the position of the church: The Church of Jesus Christ of Latter-day Saints owes its origin, its existence, and its hope for the future to the principle of continuous revelation. "We believe all that God has revealed, all that He does now reveal, and we believe that He will yet reveal many great and important things pertaining to the Kingdom of God."

From the beginning of this dispensation, Joseph Smith and all succeeding presidents of the church have taught that Negroes, while spirit children of a common father, and the progeny of our earthly parents

Adam and Eve, were not yet to receive the priesthood, for reasons which we believe are known to God, but which He has not made fully known to man.

Our living prophet, President David O. McKay, has said, "The seeming discrimination by the church toward the Negro is not something which originated with man; but goes back into the beginning with God. Revelation assures us that this plan antedates man's mortal existence, extending back to man's pre-existent state."

President McKay has also said, "Sometime in God's eternal plan, the Negro will be given the right to hold the priesthood."

Until God reveals His will in this matter, to Him whom we sustain as a prophet, we are bound by that same will. Priesthood, when it is conferred on any man comes as a blessing from God, not of men.

We feel nothing but love, compassion, and the deepest appreciation for the rich talents, endowments, and the earnest strivings of our Negro brothers and sisters. We are eager to share with men of all races the blessings of the gospel. We have no racially segregated congregations.

Were we the leaders of an enterprise created by ourselves and operated only according to our own earthly wisdom, it would be a simple thing to act according to popular will. But we believe that this work is directed by God and that the conferring of the priesthood must await his revelation. To do otherwise would be to deny the very premise on which the church is established.

We recognize that those who do not accept the principle of modern revelation may oppose our point of view. We repeat that such would not wish for membership in the church, and therefore the question of priesthood should hold no interest for them.

Without prejudice they should grant us the privilege afforded under the Constitution to exercise our chosen form of religion just as we must grant all others a similar privilege. They must recognize that the question of bestowing or withholding priesthood in the church is a matter of religion and not a matter of constitutional right.

We extend the hand of friendship to men everywhere and the hand of fellowship to all who wish to join the church and partake of the many rewarding opportunities to be found therein.

THE NEGRO PREACHER.

Non-affiliated Churches: The Evangelical Movement

One of the byproducts of Negro migration from rural to urban areas has been the development of the so-called "store front" church, i.e. one which serves those poor who are forced to live within the confines of what is known as "the inner city," or in other ghetto quarters. Such churches are usually set up in vacant stores which lend themselves readily to adaptation as appropriate meeting places. In some cases, such groups are affiliated with larger bodies; in others, they are individual units maintained by a single, self-appointed evangelist.

Worship in these churches is highly emotional and marked by Biblical and often puritanical admonitions. "Moral" living is stressed, and little attention paid to the economic and social conditions in which the congregation lives. The "store front" church, however, for all its deficiencies, provides its members with some sense of belonging, as well as a temporary escape from the pressures of daily life. Moreover, it offers the isolated inner-city inhabitant an opportunity to join a group with which he can readily identify. (Peripherally, it may be said that such churches, by indirection, offer their own commentary on the ability of established, status-mindful churches to cope with the religious needs or the emotional fervor of many of their members.)

THE NEGRO CHURCH

The following is a list of Negro churches and religious organizations presently active in the United States. Inevitably, such a list can only aspire to being comprehensive, rather than claiming to be complete. It offers only a brief glimpse into the prevailing religious mood of the Negro churchgoer in the United States today.*

The *African Orthodox Church* was founded in 1921 by Archbishop George Alexander McGuire, once a priest in the Protestant Episcopal Church. At first associated with the Marcus Garvey movement, this church is today an autonomous and independent body adhering to an "orthodox" confession of faith. Its nearly 6,000 members worship in some 25 to 30 churches. The organization's headquarters are at 122 West 129th Street, New York City.

The *African Union First Colored Methodist Protestant Church, Inc.* grew out of the Methodist Episcopal Church in 1805, although it did not become a distinct denomination until fully eight years later. Today, it has more than 30 churches and a membership of some 5,000. Headquarters for the organization are at 602 Spruce Street, Wilmington, Delaware.

The *Apostolic Overcoming Holy Church of God* was incorporated in Alabama in 1919. Evangelistic in purpose, it emphasizes sanctification, holiness and the power of divine healing. As of 1956, it had a membership of 75,000 people in some 300 congregations. The headquarters of the organization are at 1807 S. Mott Drive, Mobile, Alabama 36617.

Christ's Sanctified Holy Church was organized in 1903 from among the members of a Negro Methodist church. The last available figures put church membership at 600. This church, which holds its annual conference in September, has its headquarters at South Cutting Avenue and East Spencer Street in Jennings, Louisiana.

The *Church of Christ, Holiness, U.S.A.* was organized by Bishop C. P. Jones in 1896. The avowed mission of this body is to proclaim the gospel, seek the conversion of sinners, and perfect them in their Christian belief. Some 150 churches belong to this group, which has a membership of about 7500. The organization, with headquarters at 329 East Monument Street, Jackson, Mississippi, has an annual national convention in August.

The *Church of God and Saints of Christ* was organized in 1896 in Lawrence, Kansas by William S. Crowdy, who held the belief that Negroes were descended from the 10 lost tribes of Israel. Crowdy's followers today observe the Old Testament calendar, using Hebrew terminology for the months, and are sometimes referred to as "Black Jews." National headquarters for the organization were established in Philadelphia in 1900. In 1917, international headquarters were set up at Belleville, R.F.D. 1, Portsmouth, Virginia, site of the quadrennial general conference. The organization's more than 200 churches have a membership of some 38,000.

The *Church of God in Christ* was organized in Arkansas in 1895 by Elders C. P. Jones and C. H. Mason. Today, the organization has over 4,000 churches, and a membership of better than 400,000. Annual conferences are held in the 5,000-seat Mason's Temple in Memphis, Tennessee. Headquarters are at 958 Mason Street, Memphis.

The *Church of the Living God* was founded in 1889 in Wrightsville, Arkansas by William Christian. Believers practice baptism by immersion, foot-washing and the use of water in the dispensation of the sacrament. The churches—or temples as they are called—are organized along fraternal order lines. A national assembly is held by the group on the second Tuesday in October on a biennial basis. The close-to-300 churches in the movement claim a membership of over 43,000.

The *Churches of God, Holiness* were organized by K. H. Burruss in Georgia in 1914. Headquarters are at 170 Ashby Street, N.W. Atlanta, Georgia. Membership in the group's 40-odd churches totals some 25,000.

The Negro churches of the *Cumberland Presbyterian Church* were established with their own ecclesiastical organization in 1869. Nowadays, the general assembly of the Second Cumberland Presbyterian Church in U. S. (formerly Colored Cumberland Presbyterian Church) meets annually in June. Total membership in the church's more than 100 places of worship in the United States stands at some 30,000.

The *Fire Baptized Holiness Church* was organized in Atlanta, Georgia in 1898. Its headquarters today are at 556 Houston Street, Atlanta, Georgia. The general council for its 50-odd churches (membership, c. 1,000) meets annually.

The *Free Christian Zion Church of Christ* was organized in 1905 at Redemption, Arkansas by a company of Negro ministers who were associated with a variety of Methodist-inclined denominations. Church membership today stands at approximately 20,000. Headquarters for the organization, which has an annual general assembly in November, are in Nashville, Arkansas.

The *House of God, Which Is the Church of the Living God, the Pillar and Ground of the Truth, Inc.* was organized by R. A. R. Johnson in 1918. A small body which meets annually in October, it has about 100 churches, and a membership approaching 2500.

The *Independent A.M.E. Denomination* was founded in Jacksonville, Florida in 1907 by 12 elders who had withdrawn from the A.M.E. Church. Information on this body is scant, although it is known that, as of 1940, it had 12 churches and an inclusive membership of 1,000.

The *Kodesh Church of Immanuel* was founded in 1929 by the Rev. Frank R. Killingsworth, leader of a group which had withdrawn from the African Methodist Episcopal Zion Church. According to its last report, it had nine churches, and a membership of 562.

The *National Baptist Evangelical Life and Soul Saving Assembly of U.S.A.* was founded in 1921 by A. A. Banks, who envisioned that it would become a charitable, educational and evangelical body. The church, with headquarters at 441 Monroe Avenue, Detroit, Michigan 48207, has a general assembly for its close to 60,000 members who worship in some 260 churches across the United States.

The *National David Spiritual Temple of Christ Church Union (Inc.), U.S.A.* was organized in 1921 by the Most Rev. David William Short, originally a Baptist minister. The organization's headquarters are at 545 W. 92nd Street, Los Angeles 44, California. A national assembly is held annually in August. Membership has already passed 40,000.

The *National Primitive Baptist Convention of the U.S.A.*, founded in 1907, differs from similar bodies in its general opposition to the notion of extensive organization. Headquarters of this body are at 2116 Clinton Avenue, West, Huntsville, Alabama 35805.

The *Reformed Methodist Union Episcopal Church* was founded in Charleston, South Carolina by a group which had withdrawn from the African Methodist Episcopal Church there. Doctrinally, this church closely resembles the Methodist Episcopal Church. Headquarters for the more than 30 churches are in Charleston, South Carolina; membership is estimated at over 11,000. The church also has an annual general conference.

The *Reformed Zion Union Apostolic Church*, organized in 1869 at Boydton, Virginia by a minister of the A.M.E. Zion Church (Elder James R. Howell of New York) espouses doctrines which are generally in accord with those of the Methodist Episcopal Church. Its annual conference, held in August, is superseded by a quadrennial general conference, the last of which was held in 1966. It has over 50 churches, and a membership of about 12,000.

Triumph the Church and Kingdom of God in Christ was organized in 1902 in

Georgia by the Elder E. D. Smith, who taught sanctification and the second coming of Christ. The church has quarterly and annual conferences, as well as a quadrennial international religious congress. Headquarters are at 213 Furrington Avenue, S.E. Atlanta, Georgia. Membership has grown rapidly in recent years, and is now approaching 60,000.

The *Union American Methodist Episcopal Church,* founded by Rev. Peter Spencer in Delaware in 1813, is reputed to be the first all-Negro Methodist denomination in the United States. Until 1850, the organization went by the name of the "Union Church of Africans." That year, however, a split occurred, whereupon the main body adopted the name by which it is currently known. The latest figures made available by the organization show it to have 256 churches and 27,560 members.

The *United Free Will Baptist Church* set up its organization in 1870, and has since maintained close ties with the Free Will Baptists. It has a general conference every three years and is headquartered at Kinston College, 1000 University Street, Kinston, North Carolina. Membership stands at about 100,000; churches number close to 900.

The *United Holy Church of America, Inc.* was founded in 1886 at Method, North Carolina. This body recognizes baptism by immersion and the Lord's Supper, and meets quadrennially. Its headquarters are at both 500 Gulley Street, Goldsboro, North Carolina and 31 Miami Avenue, Columbus 3, Ohio. Its membership is approaching 30,000, while its churches are nearing the 500 mark in number.

* Statistics on the number of Negroes who belong to local churches which have both Negro and white members in their congregations are not readily accessible. The following churches—apart from those already mentioned elsewhere in this section—fit into this category:

Evangelical and Reformed Church, Board of National Missions
The Evangelical United Brethren Church
Lutheran Synodical Conference
The Presbyterian Church in the U. S.
The Presbyterian Church in the U. S. A.
The Salvation Army
The United Presbyterian Church

For further information on any aspect of religious life in the United States, write the National Council of Churches of Christ in the U.S.A., 475 Riverside Drive, New York 27, New York. The annual Yearbook issued by this organization has been most helpful in the compilation of this section.

"We Shall Overcome" is still sung during black congregational services.

NEGRO CHURCHMEN

The Negro church as an institution cannot be properly understood without some reference to the scores of clergymen who have contributed to its development. The pioneer minister of the early churches was not only responsible for the spiritual needs of his congregation, but was also a primary force in promoting its material welfare.

By working with abolitionist societies, by helping to sponsor the Underground Railroad, and by directing a number of forums for the voicing of Negro protest sentiment, the Negro minister managed to establish his church as the focal point of every significant movement designed to improve the political and social status of his congregation.

Although the role of the Negro churchman is declining in importance today, there are still several major contemporary figures—Adam Clayton Powell, Jr., and Martin Luther King, Jr., to name just two—who continue to exert a good part of their influence on the national scene through the pulpit.

Our section takes into account both the historical importance of the personality in question, and the position he occupied within the framework of the religious belief he espoused.

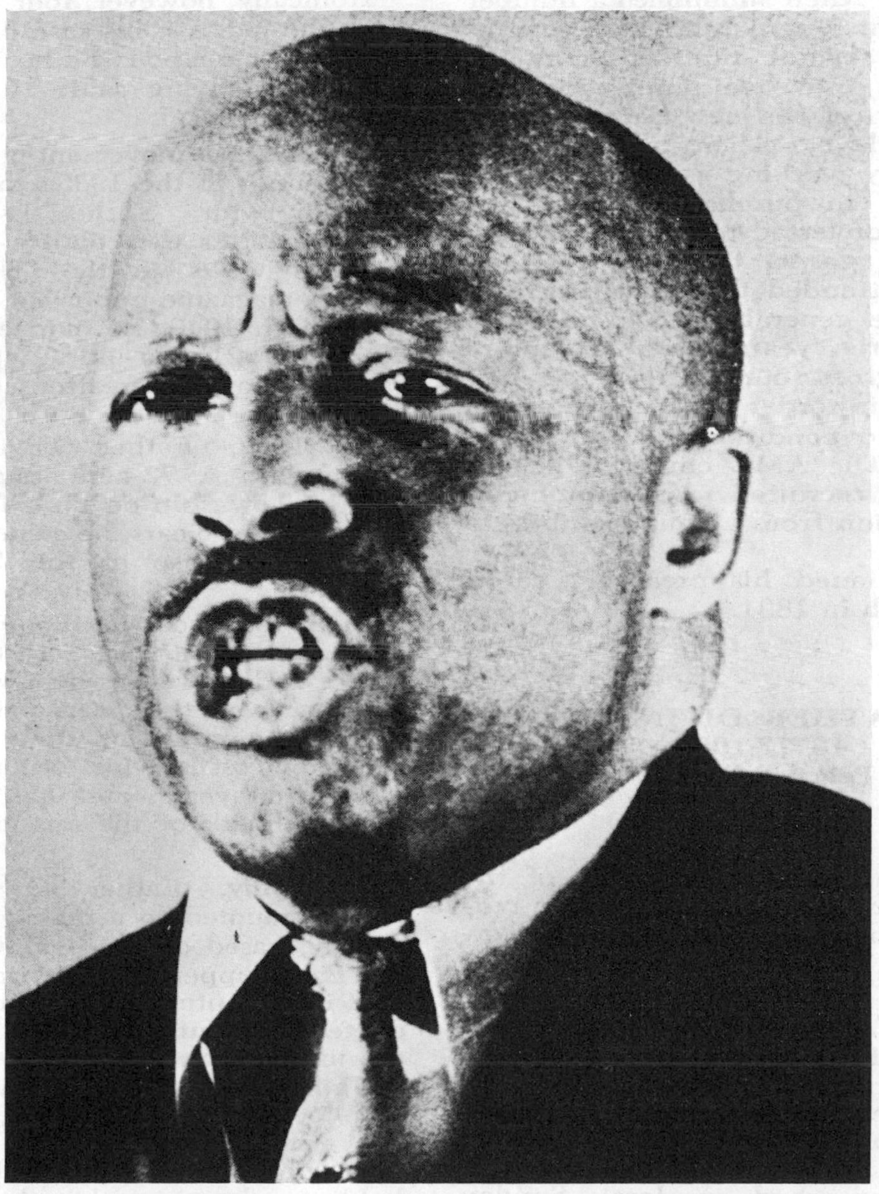

Father Divine believed he could "produce God and shake the earth with it."

RICHARD ALLEN
1760-1831
Founder, African Methodist Episcopal (AME) Church

The African Methodist Episcopal (AME) Church is the oldest Negro religious denomination in the United States, having been founded by Richard Allen in Philadelphia in 1787. That year, Allen and a group of his followers bolted from the St. George Methodist Church after having grown more and more impatient with the numerous restrictions placed upon Negro worshippers there.

Over the next two years, Philadelphia Negroes flocked to the newly founded Bethel Church in ever-increasing numbers. In 1816, Allen summoned a number of independent Negro Methodist congregations from several different states, organized them into one group, and was elected bishop of the new denomination.

Born a slave, Allen soon earned enough money working as a wood cutter and wagoner to purchase his freedom. After being converted to Christianity and preaching its gospel to Negro Pennsylvanians, he attended the organizing conference of the general Methodist Church in 1784. Three years later, he and a group of Negroes founded the Free African Society in order to improve social and economic conditions in the Negro community. The AME church which he later founded recruited a large number of its congregation from among members of this society.

Allen continued his preaching career until his death in 1831.

FATHER DIVINE
1877?-1965
The Peace Mission Cult

Father Divine was the founder of the Peace Mission Cult, a non-ritualistic religious movement whose followers worshipped their leader as God incarnate on earth.

Mystery shrouds the early identity and real name of Father Divine, although there is reason to believe he was born George Baker in 1877 on Hutchinson's Island in Georgia. Before the turn of the century, he lived in East Baltimore, where he preached in local Sunday schools. In 1907, he became a disciple of Sam Morris, a Pennsylvania Negro who called himself "Father Jehovia." Two years later, he switched over to John Hickerson's "Lift Ever, Die Never" group before returning to Georgia where he began his own campaign to promote himself as a "divine messenger."

Threatened by local authorities (he was once booked as "John Doe, alias God"), Father Divine left Georgia in 1914, and later settled in New York City, where he worked as a kind of employment agent for the few followers still loyal to him. Calling his meeting place "Heaven," he soon attracted a larger following and moved to Sayville, Long Island, where he was once sentenced to six months in jail as a public nuisance.

Ironically, however, four days after his trial, the judge in his case died of a heart attack, whereupon Father Divine was quoted as having said: "I hated to do it."

The Divine movement grew by leaps and bounds in the 1930's and 1940's, especially with "Father" speaking frequently across the country and publicizing his views in the "New Day," a weekly magazine published by his organization. In 1946, he married his "Sweet Angel," a 21-year-old Canadian stenographer, known thereafter as Mother Divine.

In 1953, Father Divine acquired Woodmont, a 73-acre estate in lower Merion Township on Philadelphia's Main Line. In later years, he came to refer to it as the showcase of the "Kingdom of Peace."

Many believers in the Father Divine cult pointed with pride to the way their leader had provided them with food and lodging over the years, at prices well within the range of their pocketbooks. The low-cost service originated in the Depression years, and has continued to be a hallmark of the missions ever since then.

Spiritually, Father Divine fostered what amounted to a massive cooperative agency, based on the communal spirit of the Last Supper. Services included songs and impromptu sermons and were conducted without Scripture readings and the use of a clergy.

Father Divine himself died peacefully at Woodmont on September 10, 1965. His wife has pledged to continue the work of the movement, whose property holdings alone are thought to be worth 10 million dollars.

JAMES AUGUSTINE HEALY
1830-1900
First Negro Catholic bishop

James Augustine Healy was the first Negro Catholic bishop in the United States. For 25 years, he presided over a diocese covering the states of Maine and New Hampshire.

A native of Macon, Georgia, Healy received his education in the North, first at Franklin Park Quaker School in Burlington, New York and, later, at Holy Cross in Worcester, Massachusetts. After graduating from the latter school with first honors, Healy continued his studies abroad, and was ordained at Notre Dame Cathedral in 1854. He then returned to the United States.

Pastor of a predominantly Irish congregation which was at first reluctant to accept him, Bishop Healy performed his priestly duties with devotion, and eventually won the respect and admiration of all his parishioners—particularly after performing his office during a typhoid epidemic.

Thereafter, he was made an assistant to Bishop John Fitzpatrick of Boston who appointed him chancellor and entrusted him with a wide variety of additional responsibilities. In 1875, he was named Bishop of Portland, Maine.

Bishop Healy died in 1900. (His brother, Patrick Francis Healy, was a Jesuit priest who served as president of Georgetown University from 1873 to 1882.)

DR. JOSEPH H. JACKSON
President, National Baptist Convention, U.S.A., Inc.

Dr. Joseph H. Jackson has been the leader of some five million U.S. Negro Baptists since 1953, the year he was elected to the presidency of the National Baptist Convention, U.S.A., Inc. Dr. Jackson has steered the organization into new spheres of influence, notably into a more activist role in the civil rights struggle.

One of the most ambitious ventures initiated under Dr. Jackson has been the Liberian land investment program whereby Baptists hope to develop extensive farms on some 100,000 acres of Liberian land, and thus raise additional funds to help sponsor their missionary labors in Africa. The Convention has also purchased 400 acres in Fayette County, Tennessee, and owns a Nashville publishing house with sales of close to one million dollars annually.

Dr. Jackson himself is a well-educated, widely traveled Baptist preacher; a member of the Central Committee of the World Council of Churches, and a vice president of the World Baptist Alliance. He has visited Asia, Africa, Europe and the Middle East, taped messages for the Voice of America, preached in Russia, written campaign literature for John F. Kennedy, and attended the 1962 Second Vatican Council in Rome.

Dr. Jackson is the pastor of Olivet Baptist Church in Chicago.

The Rev. Thomas Paul

THOMAS PAUL
1773-1831
Baptist leader

It is Thomas Paul who is credited with having begun the movement toward the establishment of independent Negro Baptist churches in the United States.

Organizing a congregation of free Negroes in a church on Jay Street in Boston (1805), Paul soon became a highly publicized preacher and religious exhorter. Within three years, he had become so famous that he was being invited to speak before white congregations in New York City where Negroes were maintained as "segregated brethren." The First Baptist Church soon granted 16 of its members the right to organize a separate congregation under Paul's leadership. (It later became known as Abyssinian Baptist Church.)

Paul also carried his message to the Caribbean, spending six months in Haiti under the auspices of the Massachusetts Baptist Society. He later returned to the United States, continuing his work in the North until his death in 1831.

HAROLD ROBERT PERRY
Auxiliary Bishop of New Orleans

Harold Robert Perry was consecrated a Bishop of New Orleans on January 6, 1966—and thus became the first Negro Catholic bishop to serve in the United States in the 20th century.

One of six children, Perry was born the son of a rice-mill worker and a domestic cook in Lake Charles, Louisiana. He entered the Divine Word Seminary in Mississippi at the age of 13, was ordained a priest in 1944, and spent the next 14 years in parish work. In 1958, he was appointed rector of the seminary.

Perry is serving in New Orleans, although his diocese includes Southeastern Louisiana and the city of Bogalusa, where civil rights opponents have mar-

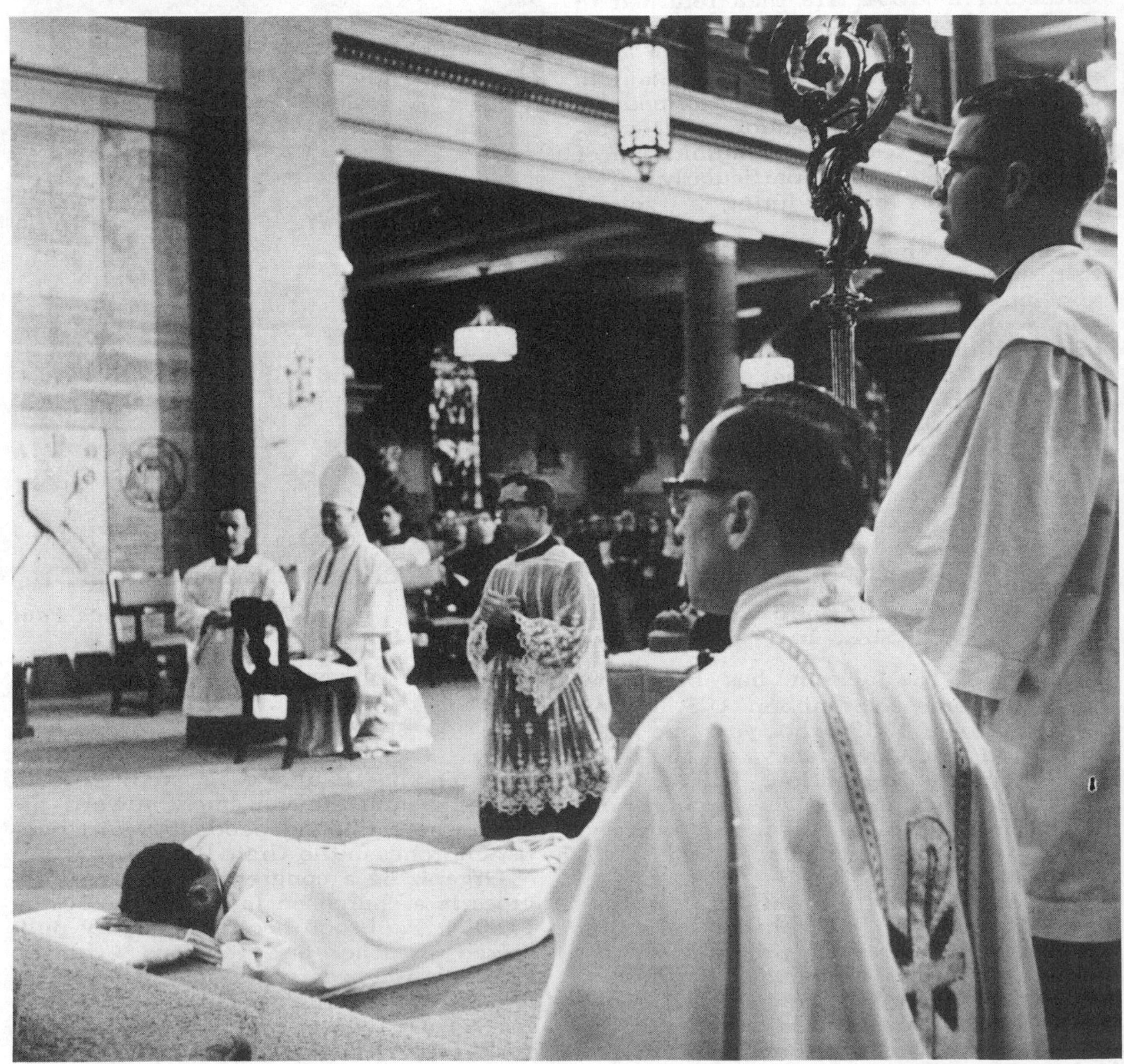

The consecration of Bishop Harold R. Perry, New Orleans, January 1966

tialled stiff resistance to attempts to desegregate public facilities. Louisiana itself has the largest concentration of Negro Catholics in the South, some 200,000 in all.

ADAM CLAYTON POWELL, SR. 1865-1953
Pastor of Abyssinian Baptist Church

Adam Clayton Powell, Sr.—father of the Harlem Congressman who is also his successor—was the man largely responsible for building Abyssinian Baptist Church into one of the most celebrated Negro congregations in the world.

Born in the backwoods of Virginia in 1865, Powell attended school locally and, between sessions, worked in the mines of West Virginia. After deciding to enter the ministry, he began his studies at Wayland Academy (now Virginia Union University), working his way through this school as a janitor and waiter. He later attended the Yale University School of Divinity, and served for a time as pastor of the Immanuel Baptist Church in New Haven.

Powell became pastor of Abyssinian in 1908—at a time when it had a membership of only 1,600 and an indebtedness of over $100,000. By 1921, the church had not only been made solvent, but was able to move into a $350,000 Gothic structure at its present location on 138th Street in Harlem.

During the Depression, Powell opened soup kitchens for Harlem residents, and served thousands of meals to the destitute and needy. Later, he and his son campaigned vigorously to expand job opportunities and city services in the Harlem community.

Powell retired from Abyssinian in 1937, and died in 1953, at which time the church was already being pastored by his son.

GOSPEL MUSIC IN THE UNITED STATES

Gospel music, a modern fusion of elements of the camp-meeting spiritual and certain characteristics of blues and jazz, has as its theme the uninhibited praise and joyous worship of God. The major rhythms of gospel pieces are up-tempo and syncopated, but their melodies remain simple enough to enable large numbers of untrained musicians to master the playing and singing. Their harmonies are generally uncomplicated, although they have of late begun to show the influence of other musical forms.

The main performer in gospel is an outstanding soloist who is usually backed by a combination of singers able to provide him with a moving foundation on which he can base his own improvisations. (This is, then, not unlike jazz where the group often forms a fabric around and through which the soloist may move.) Another major aspect of gospel is the highly repetitious "drive" which seeks to raise the fervor of the audience by building a hypnotic effect over it. The repeated phrases of the "drive" are intended to sway the listener, and create a mood which mounts to an apex of power.

Historical Roots

The rich, vibrant gospel music of the American Negro—an integral part of most traditional Negro religious services—can be grouped into two main styles or divisions: spirituals themselves, with their poignant and soulful quality (*Deep River*; *Were You There*; *Nobody Knows the Trouble I've Seen*), and camp-meeting songs, sung in part by a "leader" and then taken up by a "congregation" or chorus.

Along with traditional hymns, spirituals were sung during worship services in Negro Baptist or Methodist churches, and were also heard in conjunction with the work songs which the Negro devised to help him through his wearisome field labors. The "field holler," a combination of "yell" and "yodel" developed by Negro slaves in the South, eventually became a component of solo "blues," a musical diary through which the Negro expressed his sense of despair and hopelessness.

Spirituals, hymns and blues—these were the three ingredients which contributed most significantly to the development of gospel music in the post-Emancipation era. The Negro was free, but remained a creature apart from the rest of men, still clinging to the single institution around which much of his social life revolved: the church.

Choral or communal singing in the Negro church soon came to be a highly organized practice. Certain "arrangements" of traditional spirituals then began to incorporate ideas from the "blues" idiom, together with a more syncopated, up-tempo style. In the early 1900's, a "blues" pianist, Thomas A. Dorsey, was sufficiently impressed by some of this music to write his own original tunes using this form. Dorsey was later responsible for popularizing it across the country by going on tour with Sallie Martin, a religious singer.

The "leader-congregation" style eventually gave way to the "soloist-background" method of performing. In this way, several soloists began to gain widespread fame for their artistic achievement. In the late 1930's, for example, Miss Roberta Martin of Chicago brought together several young soloists of varying styles and outstanding ability, and formed a small, mixed group known as the Roberta Martin Singers. (This group is still in existence today.) Elsewhere in Chicago, Miss Mahalia Jackson was also on her way to becoming an international celebrity through her singular renditions of Negro gospel music. In the East, it was Clara Ward and the Ward Singers, given their original impetus by Mrs. Gertrude Ward. The Ward Singers introduced new techniques into their performances, employing all-female voices singing together in unusually high-pitched harmony and using synchronized theatrical motions and movements in their presentation.

Post-war Trends

During World War II, "jubilee" singing had a run of popularity, involving as it did male quartets who sang a type of arranged spiritual. Perhaps the most representative of these groups in this era was the Golden Gate Quartet. Radio appearances by such choral ensembles as The Wings Over Jordan group helped popularize the gospel style even further, and made thousands of people more acutely aware of a coming musical trend. Soon, the recording industry (Apollo and Gotham Records) took a more active interest in cultivating this brand of music. One of the first big recording successes for gospel was *Old Ship of Zion* by the Roberta Martin Singers, featuring the voice of Norsalus McKissick.

The music itself quickly became separated into two camps: gospel and quartet. Gospel included all-male, all-female, or mixed groups using piano or organ as accompanying instruments, whereas quartet involved all-male groups whose accompaniment was always provided by a guitarist. Gospel singers generally used colorful choir robes, whereas quartet groups were identified by conventional coat and trousers.

The first gospel recording which sold over a million copies—*Surely God Is Able* (Savoy Records)—was made during the late 1940's by Clara Ward and her group. Soon thereafter, the Alex Bradford Singers recorded *Too Close to Heaven* (Specialty Records), a tune which approximated the success of *Surely*. Gospel arrangers then began to pore through the pages of numerous hymnals in search of appropriate material for the growing number of programs, revivals, festivals, etc.

In the 1950's, the Davis Sisters came to dominate the gospel field, ushering in the era of "song battles" between competing groups which would try to outdo each other in the intensity and fervor of their performances. Some of the most popular tunes recorded by the Davis Sisters were: *Jesus*; *Reign in Jerusalem*; *He'll Understand*; *Plant My Feet on Higher Ground*, and *Twelve Gates to the City*. (Perhaps the "arch-rivals" of the Davis Sisters during these years were the Gospel Harmonettes of Birmingham, led by Dorothy Love. Among the leading tunes recorded by the Harmonettes were: *I'm Sealed*; *You Must Be Born Again*; *That's Enough*, and *Lord, You've Been Good to Me*.)

The leading "quartet" groups of this period included: The Dixie Hummingbirds; The Nightingales; The Harmonizing Four, and The Soul Stirrers. (Sam Cooke, later to gain great fame in the popular music field, was once a regular performer with the last-named group, and had such hits as *Nearer to Thee* and *Touch the Hem of His Garment*.)

The Impact of Gospel

Gospel has had profound effects on rock 'n' roll performers like Ray Charles and James Brown, both of whom retain the same inflections used by the gospel singer. In fact, many churches in which gospel music is sung have served as a kind of unintentional training ground for rock 'n' roll, popular, and jazz musicians whose trademark is something called "soul."

Over the years, gospel forms have often been incorporated into more programmed arrangements in an effort to blend the fervor and excitement of the music itself with the form and texture of classical

The Utterbach Concert Ensemble

and contemporary harmony. One of the more accomplished groups in this area has been the Utterbach Concert Ensemble, formed by Clinton Utterbach of New York City in 1961.

Moreover, gospel music has begun to achieve a degree of international recognition. (This development parallels the interest generated in Europe by the Fisk Jubilee Singers who went on tour there in the 1870's to popularize the Negro spiritual.) In the present case, the man most responsible for bringing gospel into the European spotlight is Negro poet-author Langston Hughes. Hughes has accomplished this feat through the creation of such song-plays as *Black Nativity, Jericho, Jim Crow*, and *Trumpets for the Lord*.

Nowadays, gospel is moving out of the churches into auditoriums across the country, and is likewise being heard by entertainment-conscious audiences at jazz festivals and folk shows throughout the world. Along with jazz and the spiritual, it is proving to be yet another contribution to the musical world for which the Negro deserves special recognition.

NATIONAL BLACK ORGANIZATIONS

List of Organizations
The National Council of Negro Women
Negro Banks
Negro Insurance Companies

As a rule, Negro organizations have been created by the political, social, economic and educational horizons open to the Negro in the United States during the 20th century. Although many barriers in racial communication have been breached over the years, it has, nonetheless, been necessary for Negroes to foster closer ties among themselves—partly in recognition of a discreet racial cleavage still operative at most levels of American society.

Organization	*Year of Founding*	*Chief Executive*	*Membership*
Alpha Kappa Alpha Sorority	1908	Mrs. Julia B. Purnell	40,000
Alpha Kappa Mu Honor Society	1937	Dr. Thomas Freeman	6,500
Alpha Phi Alpha Fraternity, Inc.	1906	Lionel H. Newson	35,000
American Teachers Association	—	R. J. Martin	40,000
Ancient and Accepted Scottish Rite Masons	1864	William J. Fitzpatrick	25,000
Ancient Egyptian Arabic Order, Nobles of the Mystic Shrine	—	Roscoe C. Washington	22,000
Benevolent Protective Order of Reindeer	1923	William C. Moore	2,000
Bible Way, Church of Our Lord Jesus Christ World Wide, Inc.	1957	Bishop Smallwood C. Williams	50,000
Central Intercollegiate Athletic Association	—	Dr. Samuel E. Barnes	18 member schools
Chi Delta Mu Fraternity	1913	Dr. J. C. Carr	800

Organization	*Year of Founding*	*Chief Executive*	*Membership*
Chi Eta Phi Sorority	1932	Mrs. L. P. Brown	600
Drifters, Inc.	—	Miss Mary E. Broomfield	200
Delta Sigma Theta Sorority	—		
Eta Phi Beta Sorority, Inc.	—	Mrs. Pennie L. Burden	500
Frontiers International	1936	Marcus Neustadter, Jr.	2,000
Gamma Phi Delta Sorority	1940	Mrs. Kay Davis	—
Girl Friends, Inc.	—	Mrs. A. Sampson Moore	500
Grand Temple Daughters, Improved Benevolent Protective Order of Elks of the World	1902	Mrs. Nettie B. Smith	150,000
Grand United Order of Odd Fellows	—	—	114,000
Imperial Court, Daughters of Isis	1910	Mrs. E. Harmon Moore	7,000
Improved Benevolent Protective Order of Elks of the World	1898	Hobson R. Reynolds	500,000
International Conference of Grand Chapters Order of the Eastern Star	1907	—	250,000
Jack and Jill of America, Inc.	—	Mrs. Margaret E. Simms	5,000
Kappa Alpha Psi Fraternity	1911	—	27,000
Knights of Peter Claver	1909	Shields G. Gilmore	15,000
Lambda Kappa Mu Sorority, Inc.	1937	Mrs. Marie G. Leatherman	900
Links, Inc.	1946	Mrs. Vivian Beamon	2,000
National Alumni Council of the United Negro College Fund	—	Moses S. Belton	145,000
National Association of Barristers Wives	1949		—
National Association of College Deans and Registrars	1926	Edwin M. Thorpe	250
National Association of Colored Women's Clubs Inc.	—	Mrs. Mamie B. Reese	100,000
National Association of Fashion and Accessory Designers, Inc.	1950	Mrs. Henrienne M. Vincent	300
National Association of Market Developers	1953	James S. Avery	500
National Association of Ministers' Wives	1941	Mrs. R. W. Lucas	400
National Association of Negro Business and Professional Women's Clubs	1935	Mrs. M. E. Bryant	5,000
National Association of Negro Musicians	1919	Clarence H. Williams	1,000
National Association of Real Estate Brokers	—	Q. V. Williamson	—

Organization	*Year of Founding*	*Chief Executive*	*Membership*
National Bankers Association	1926	B. Doyle Mitchell	15 member banks
National Bar Association	1925	—	2,500
National Beauty Culturists' League	1919	Dr. Katie E. Whickam	50,000
National Business League	1900	—	—
National Conference of Artists	1959	Jack Jordan	—
National Convention of Gospel Choirs and Choruses	1932	Dr. Thomas A. Dorsey	2,500
National Council of Negro Women	1935	Miss Dorothy Height	2,850,000
National Dental Association	1913	—	1,000
National Epicureans	1951	Mrs. Thelma G. Fields	280
National Funeral Directors and Morticians Association	—	—	2,000
National Grand Chapter of the Eastern Star	—	Dr. Julia C. Fitzpatrick	10,000
National Housewives' League of America	—	Mrs. Pearl L. Bell	2,250
National Insurance Association	1921	H. C. Gilliam, Jr.	11,000
National Medical Association	1895	Dr. Leonidas H. Berry	4,200
National Newspaper Publishers Association	1940	Frank C. Stanley, Sr.	50 newspapers
National Technical Association	1926	—	300
National United Church Ushers Association of America	1919	Leroy Johnson	35,000
Nationwide Hotel-Motel Association	—	Ellis L. Marsalis	
Omega Psi Phi Fraternity	1911	—	10,000
Phi Beta Sigma Fraternity	1914	Maurice A. Moore	12,000
Sigma Gamma Rho Sorority	—		
Tau Gamma Delta Sorority	1942	Mrs. Eliza Hamilton	500
United Mortgage Bankers of America, Inc.	—	Dempsey J. Travis	250
Women's Auxiliary to the Benevolent Protective Order of Reindeer	—	Mrs. Amy Gelwitz Sloan	1,800
Women's Auxiliary to the National Medical Association	—	Mrs. Murray B. Davis	—
Zeta Phi Beta Sorority			

THE NATIONAL COUNCIL OF NEGRO WOMEN

The National Council of Negro Women (NCNW) was founded in 1935 by the distinguished educator, Mary McLeod Bethune. In December of that year, Mrs. Bethune brought together 35 eminent women to map out a program for united planning and concerted action by various Negro women's organizations. A decision was ultimately reached to establish a new organization which would serve as a kind of clearing house for the activities of one million women.

Incorporated in the District of Columbia in 1936, the National Council of

Negro Women has since extended its influence into many parts of the world, concerning itself primarily with programs for the economic, social, cultural and educatonal welfare of Negro women in particular. The NCNW is affiliated with such organizations as the National Council of Women, the International Council of Women, and the Pan-Pacific Southeast Asia Women's Association of the United States.

In its silver anniversary year (1960), the NCNW pledged itself to erect a memorial in honor of Mrs. Bethune in Lincoln Park, Washington, D.C. The Memorial will also include a building and cultural center dedicated to the aims expressed in the NCNW pledge:

> **"It is our pledge to make a lasting contribution to all that is finest and best in America, to cherish and enrich her heritage of Freedom and progress by workng for the integration of all her people regardless of race, creed, or national origin, into her spiritual, social, cultural, civic and political life, and thus aid her to achieve the glorious destiny of a true and unfettered democracy."**

ALPHA KAPPA ALPHA

The Alpha Kappa Alpha Sorority was founded in 1908 by an undergraduate group at Howard University in Washington, D. C. Since then, it has grown into a nationwide organization whose members can be found in close to 200 chapters covering two-thirds of the country at more than 120 accredited colleges. Sorority historian Marjorie H. Parker indicates that the organization was "first conceived as an instrument to enrich the social and intellectual aspects of college life." Over the years, Alpha Kappa Alpha has reevaluated its original program so as to "discharge some of (its) responsibilities for bettering social and economic conditions in (its) expanding community." The periodic assemblies of the Sorority are called *Boules* after the name given the governing assembly in the ancient Greek city-states.

DELTA SIGMA THETA

Delta Sigma Theta is a "public service organization dedicated to a program of sharing membership skill and organizational services in the public interest." This noted sorority was founded in 1913 by 22 Howard University graduates who set high scholastic achievement as their standard for membership, and thus concentrated more on cultural and educational pursuits than on the social aspects of sorority activity. Delta has maintained a National Scholarship Program since 1921; a library project since 1937; job opportunity clinics since 1941, and a variety of volunteer programs on "vital public matters." The organization currently has 312 chapters in 48 states, and an interracial membership of 45,000 sorors. National headquarters for the organization are at 1814 M Street, N.W., Washington 6, D. C.

Freedom National Bank is Harlem's first Negro-chartered, Negro-owned bank.

NEGRO BANKS

Banking operations among Negroes began on March 3, 1865 when the U. S. Congress authorized the establishment of the Freedmen's Savings and Trust Company, which remained in business until 1874. Thereafter, the first banking institution organized and operated by Negroes was the Savings Bank of the Grand Fountain United Order of True Reformers, established in Richmond, Virginia in 1888.

In 1926, the National Bankers Association came into being, with Major R. R. Wright serving as its first president. There are now 12 member banks in the association.

BANK	CITY	YEAR OF INCORPORATION	PRESIDENT
Carver State Bank	Savannah, Ga.	1948	L. D. Perry
Citizens Savings Bank and Trust Company	Nashville, Tenn.	1904	W. G. Ferguson
Citizens and Southern Bank	Philadelphia, Pa.	1925	Marcel L. Vandenaiz
Citizens Trust Company	Atlanta, Ga.	1921	L. D. Milton
Consolidated Bank and Trust Company	Richmond, Va.	1903	J. J. Nickens
Douglas State Bank	Kansas City, Kan.	1947	E. E. Tillmon
First State Bank	Danville, Va.	1919	M. C. Martin
Industrial Bank of Washington, D. C.	Washington, D. C.	1934	B. Doyle Mitchell
Mechanics and Farmers Bank	Durham, N. C.	1907	J. H. Wheeler
Riverside National Bank	Houston, Tex.	1964	Edward D. Irons
Tri-State Bank	Memphis, Tenn.	1947	A. Maceo Walker
Victory Savings Bank	Columbia, S. C.	1921	Dr. H. D. Monteith

NEGRO INSURANCE COMPANIES

Most leading Negro insurance companies are members of the National Insurance Association (formerly the National Negro Insurance Association) which was first organized in 1921 by a group of nine men headed by business pioneer C. C. Spaulding. The permanent association was later formed at a meeting of 60 insurance men representing 13 companies.

The NIA seeks to raise the standards and practices of participating members, and to build confidence in insurance companies owned and controlled by Negroes. The following is a list of NIA members around the country.

AFRO-AMERICAN LIFE INSURANCE COMPANY (S)
101 East Union Street
Jacksonville, Florida 32203
Phone: ELgin 6-0441 Area Code: 305
President—Dr. James H. Lewis

AMERICAN WOODMEN, THE SUPREME CAMP OF (Fraternal)
2100 Downing Street, P. O. Box 987
Denver, Colorado 80205
Phone: 623-5305 Area Code: 303
President/Agency Director—
Lawrence H. Lightner

ATLANTA LIFE INSURANCE COMPANY (S)
148 Auburn Avenue, P. O. Box 897
Atlanta, Georgia 30312
Phone: JA. 1-0513 Area Code: 404
President/Treasurer—
N. B. Herndon

BENEVOLENT LIFE INSURANCE COMPANY (S).
1624 Milam Street
Shreveport, Louisiana 71103
Phone: 425-1522 Area Code: 318
President— H. D. Wilson

BOOKER T. WASHINGTON INSURANCE COMPANY (S)
1527 Fifth Avenue, North
P. O. Box 2621
Birmingham, Alabama 35202
Phone: 251-9195 Area Code: 205
President/Treasurer—
A. G. Gaston

BRADFORD'S INDUSTRIAL INSURANCE COMPANY (S)
1525 Seventh Avenue, North
P. O. Box 2015
Birmingham, Alabama 35201
Phone: 251-8373 Area Code: 205
President—
Marion Kennon Bradford (Mrs.)

CENTRAL LIFE INSURANCE COMPANY OF FLORIDA (S)
1416 North Boulevard, P. O. Box 3286
Tampa, Florida 33607
Phone: 251-1897 Area Code: 813
President—
Edward D. Davis

CHICAGO METROPOLITAN MUTUAL ASSURANCE COMPANY (M)
4455 South Parkway
Chicago, Illinois 60653
Phone: 285-3030 Area Code: 312
President—
George S. Harris

CHRISTIAN BENEVOLENT BURIAL ASSOCIATION, INC. (S)
452 St. Anthony Street, P. O. Box 511
Mobile, Alabama 36601
Phone: 432-8072 Area Code: 205
President—
Pearl Johnson Madison (Mrs.)

CRUSADER LIFE INSURANCE COMPANY, INC. (S)
845 Minnesota Avenue, P. O. Box 1249
Kansas City, Kansas 66116
Phone: DR. 1-6140 Area Code: 913
President—
James H. Browne

DOUGLASS LIFE INSURANCE COMPANY (S)
2203 Dryades Street, P. O. Box 52092
New Orleans, Louisiana 70113
President—
Joseph Bartholomew

GERTRUDE GEDDES WILLIS LIFE INSURANCE COMPANY (S)
2120 Jackson Avenue
New Orleans, Louisiana 70113
Phone: JA. 2-2276 Area Code: 504
President—
Gertrude Geddes Willis (Mrs.)

GOLDEN CIRCLE LIFE INSURANCE COMPANY (S)
39 Jackson Avenue, P. O. Box 293
Brownsville, Tennessee
Phone: 772-1472 Area Code: 901
President—
C. A. Rawls

GOLDEN STATE MUTUAL LIFE INSURANCE COMPANY (M)
1999 West Adams Boulevard
P. O. Box 2332, Terminal Annex
Los Angeles, California 90054
Phone: RE. 1-1131 Area Code: 213
President—
Norman O. Houston

GOOD CITIZENS LIFE INSURANCE COMPANY (S)
1809 Dryades Street, P. O. Box 50428
New Orleans, Louisiana 70113
Phone: JA. 2-5144 Area Code: 504
President—
Clifton H. Denson

GREAT LAKES MUTUAL LIFE INSURANCE COMPANY (M)
8401 Woodward Avenue
Detroit, Michigan 48202
Phone: 872-7870 Area Code: 313
President—
Louis C. Blount

GREAT LIBERTY LIFE INSURANCE COMPANY (S)
2527 Ross Avenue
Dallas, Texas
Phone: RI. 2-4155 Area Code: 214
President—
George L. Allen

GUARANTY LIFE INSURANCE COMPANY (S)
460 West Broad Street, P. O. Box 2247
Savannah, Georgia 31401
Phone: 233-4565 Area Code: 912
Executive Vice President/Secretary—
B. C. Ford

KEYSTONE LIFE INSURANCE COMPANY (S)
1503 St. Bernard Avenue
P. O. Box 51748
New Orleans, Louisiana 70150
Phone: WH. 7-2161 Area Code: 504
President— Dr. Ulric W. Pryce

LIGHTHOUSE LIFE INSURANCE COMPANY, INC. (S)
1544 Milam Street
Shreveport, Louisiana 71103
Phone: 423-5292 Area Code: 318
President—
Bunyan Jacobs

LINCOLN INDUSTRIAL INSURANCE COMPANY (M)
1801 Avenue C, Ensley
Birmingham, Alabama 35218
Phone: ST. 5-1126 Area Code: 205
President/Treasurer—
L. W. Stallworth, Jr.

MAJESTIC LIFE INSURANCE COMPANY (S)
1833 Dryades Street
New Orleans, Louisiana 70113
Phone: JA. 5-0375 Area Code: 504
President—
James V. Haydel

MAMMOTH LIFE AND ACCIDENT INSURANCE COMPANY (S)
608 West Walnut Street, P. O. Box 2099
Louisville, Kentucky, 40201
Phone: 585-4137 Area Code: 502
President—
J. E. Hankins

NORTH CAROLINA MUTUAL LIFE INSURANCE COMPANY (M)
114 West Parrish Street, P. O. Box 201
Durham, North Carolina 27702
Phone: 682-9201 Area Code: 919
President—
Asa T. Spaulding

PEOPLES LIFE INSURANCE COMPANY OF LOUISIANA (S)
901-07 North Claiborne Avenue
New Orleans, Louisiana 70116
Phone: WH. 9-7592 Area Code: 504
President—
H. J. Christophe

PEOPLE'S PROGRESSIVE BURIAL COMPANY (S)
109 Harrison Street, P. O. Box 426
Rayville, Louisiana
Phone: 728-4434 Area Code: 318
President—
Olivia Simms (Mrs.)

PILGRIM HEALTH & LIFE INSURANCE COMPANY (S)
1143 Gwinnett Street, P. O. Box 904
Augusta, Georgia 30903
Phone: PA. 2-5517/18 Area Code: 404
President—
W. S. Hornsby, Jr.

PROGRESSIVE INDUSTRIAL LIFE INSURANCE COMPANY (S)
1106 North Claiborne Avenue
New Orleans, Louisiana 70116
Phone: 529-1438 Area Code: 504
President—
C. L. Dennis

PROTECTIVE INDUSTRIAL INSURANCE COMPANY OF ALABAMA, INC. (M)
237 Graymont Avenue, North
P. O. Box 528
Birmingham, Alabama 35201
Phone: 323-5256 Area Code: 205
President—
Dr. V. L. Harris

PROVIDENT HOME INDUSTRIAL MUTUAL LIFE INSURANCE COMPANY (M)
731 South Broad Street
Philadelphia, Pennsylvania 19147
Phone: PE. 5-7477 Area Code: 215
President—
Joseph A. Faison

PURPLE SHIELD LIFE INSURANCE COMPANY (S)
407 South 13th Street, P. O. Box 386
Baton Rouge, Louisiana 70802
Phone: DI. 2-2284 Area Code: 501
President—
Homer J. Sheeler, Sr.

RICHMOND BENEFICIAL INSURANCE COMPANY (S)
700-02 North Second Street
P. O. Box 1400
Richmond, Virginia 23211
Phone: MI. 3-7306 Area Code: 703
President—
J. E. Harris

SECURITY LIFE INSURANCE COMPANY (S)
1328 Lynch Street, P. O. Box 1549
Jackson, Mississippi 39205
Phone: FL. 3-4954 Area Code: 601
President—
W. H. Williams

SOUTHERN AID LIFE INSURANCE COMPANY (S)
214 East Clay Street
Richmond, Virginia 23219
Phone: 648-7234 Area Code: 703
President— H. H. Southall

SOUTHERN LIFE INSURANCE COMPANY (S)
1841 Pennsylvania Avenue
Baltimore, Maryland 21217
Phone: PL. 2-2604 Area Code: 301
President—
William LeRoy Berry, M.D.

STANDARD LIFE INSURANCE COMPANY OF LOUISIANA (S)
1530 North Claiborne Avenue
New Orleans, Louisiana 70116
Phone: 945-1185 Area Code: 504
President—
C. C. Haydel, M.D., FICS

SUPREME INDUSTRIAL LIFE INSURANCE COMPANY, INC. (S)
1433 North Claiborne Avenue
New Orleans, Louisiana 70116
Phone: WH. 5-8846 Area Code: 504
President—
Lucien V. Alexis, Sr.

SUPREME LIFE INSURANCE COMPANY OF AMERICA (S)
3501 South Parkway
Chicago, Illinois 60653
Phone: KE. 8-5100 Area Code: 312
President—
Earl B. Dickerson

UNION MUTUAL LIFE, HEALTH & ACCIDENT INSURANCE COMPANY (M)
20th and Master Streets
Philadelphia, Pennsylvania 19121
Phone: PO. 5-4199/4200
Area Code: 215
President—
M. T. Somerville

UNION PROTECTIVE LIFE INSURANCE COMPANY (S)
1234 Mississippi Boulevard
P. O. Box 851
Memphis, Tennessee 38106
Phone: 948-2706 Area Code: 901
President—
Lewis H. Twigg

UNITED MUTUAL LIFE INSURANCE COMPANY (M)
310 Lenox Avenue
New York, New York 10027
Phone: EN. 9-4200 Area Code: 212
President—
Charles Buchanan

UNITY BURIAL AND LIFE INSURANCE COMPANY (S)
506 St. Michael Street
Mobile, Alabama 36602
Phone: 438-1671 Area Code: 205
President—
A. L. Herman

UNIVERSAL LIFE INSURANCE COMPANY (S)
480 Linden Avenue, P. O. Box 241
Memphis, Tennessee 38101
Phone: 525-3641 Area Code: 901
President—
A. M. Walker, Sr.

VICTORY MUTUAL LIFE INSURANCE COMPANY (M)
5601 South State Street
Chicago, Illinois 60621
Phone: MU. 4-6878 Area Code: 312
President—
Bindley C. Cyrus

VIRGINIA MUTUAL BENEFIT LIFE INSURANCE COMPANY (M)
214 East Clay Street
Richmond, Virginia 23219
Phone: MI. 3-0245 Area Code: 703
President/Treasurer/Public Relations Director—
B. T. Bradshaw, Jr.

WINSTON MUTUAL LIFE INSURANCE COMPANY (M)
1100 East 11th Street, P. O. Box 998
Winston-Salem, North Carolina
Phone: PA. 2-3466 Area Code: 919
President—
E. E. Hill

WRIGHT MUTUAL INSURANCE COMPANY (M)
2995 East Grand Boulevard
Detroit, Michigan 48202
Phone: TR. 1-2112 Area Code: 313
President/Impairment Officer/Public Relations Director—
Wardell C. Croft

(S)—Stock Company
(M)—Mutual Company

ASSOCIATIONS

CHICAGO INSURANCE ASSOCIATION
3420 South Cottage Grove (c/o Secretary)
Apartment 1201
Chicago, Illinois 60616

Phone: VI. 2-1314 Area Code: 312
President—
Wendell O. Haynes

LEXINGTON UNDERWRITERS ASSOCIATION
149 Deweese Street, P. O. Box 1078
Lexington, Kentucky 40501
Phone: 252-8644 Area Code: 606
President—
Mary E. Woodford

SOUTH CAROLINA INSURANCE ASSOCIATION
P. O. Box 1030
Sumter, South Carolina 29151
Phone: 773-2224
President—
J. L. Tyson

Gloria Smith—the first Miss Black America (1969)

BLACK 'FIRSTS'

Noteworthy Accomplishments by Negroes in Education, Military Affairs, Sports, Public Life, and the Fine Arts

A number of prominent 'firsts' are scattered throughout the pages of this book. This section has been designed to deal wth selected personalities who—for any number of reasons—are not discussed at length elsewhere. (Instances of 'firsts' appearing with biographical data on an individual are numerous. Jackie Robinson, for example, is the first Negro to play major league baseball. This fact can be ascertained by reading his biographical sketch.

FIRST COLLEGE HEAD IN NEW YORK

The first Negro to head a college in New York State (and possibly the first to head a "predominantly white" college in the United States) is Dr. James Allen Colston, president of Tennessee's Knoxville College. Dr. Colston has taken over as president of the two-year Bronx Community College in New York City.

FIRST COLLEGE GRADUATE

John Russwurm, the first Negro college graduate, received his degree from Bowdoin College in Maine in 1826.* Russwurm was one of the editors of *Freedom's Journal*, the first Negro newspaper printed in the United States.

FIRST SERVICE ACADEMY GRADUATES

Wesley A. Brown became the first Negro to graduate from the Naval Academy at Annapolis on June 3, 1949. Henry O. Flipper became the first Negro to graduate from West Point on June 15, 1877.

FIRST WARSHIP COMMANDER

By assuming command of the destroyer escort *U.S.S. Falgout* on January 31, 1962, Lieutenant Commander Samuel L. Gravely was said to have become the first Negro to command a U. S. warship.

* This claim is disputed in some sources, which maintain that Edward A. Jones graduated from Amherst a few days earlier than Russwurm.

FIRST ENSIGN IN THE U.S. NAVY

Bernard W. Robinson, a medical student at Harvard, became the first Negro to win a commission in the U. S. Navy on June 18, 1942. Robinson was the first Negro ensign in the U. S. Naval Reserve.

FIRST GENERAL IN THE U. S. ARMY

Benjamin O. Davis, Sr. was promoted to the rank of brigadier general in 1940, and thus became the first Negro to hold this post in the U. S. Army. A career man, Davis (born in 1877) re-enlisted in the Regular Army in 1899; made second lieutenant in 1901, and rose through the officers' ranks until he was promoted to full colonel in 1930. He retired in 1948. (His son, Benjamin O. Davis, Jr., was formerly a general in the Air Force. His last assignment was as chief of staff of U. S. Forces in Korea, and Chief of Staff of the U. N. Commission there. After World War II, Davis was the first Negro to command an air base—Godman Field in Kentucky. He became the first general in the history of the Air Force on October 27, 1954.)

Brig. Gen. Benjamin O. Davis

FIRST MILITARY AIDE IN THE WHITE HOUSE

One of the 20 bachelor officers who serve as military social aides in the White House, Lieutenant Commander Benjamin Wallace Cloud is unique for at least one reason: he is the first Negro to receive such an assignment. Cloud is attached to the Bureau of Naval Personnel, and has served a tour of duty in Vietnam, where he was awarded the Air Medal.

FIRST CASUALTY OF THE CIVIL WAR

The first Negro wounded in the Civil War—65-year-old Nicholas Biddle of Pottsville, Pennsylvania—was an escaped slave who had attached himself to a troop unit heading for the defense of Washington, D. C. On April 18, 1861, while marching through the slave-holding city of Baltimore, Biddle was stoned by an angry mob. His scalp cut to the bone, Biddle managed to escape further injury only with the aid of his white comrades-in-arms.

FIRST POSTAGE STAMP HONORING A NEGRO

The Booker T. Washington stamp, the first of its kind honoring a Negro, went on sale at Tuskegee Institute on April 7, 1940. Valued at 10 cents, the stamp belongs to the Famous American Series, and bears a picture of the head of Washington. Its issuance came at the culmination of a seven-year campaign which had originally been sponsored by Major R. R. Wright, president of the Citizens and Southern Bank and Trust Company of Philadelphia. (Seven years later, a stamp honoring George Washington Carver was put out on the fourth anniversary of the renowned scientist's death. The stamp is of three-cent denomination, and bears a picture of Carver's head.)

FIRST COIN HONORING A NEGRO

The first coin honoring a Negro was a 50-cent piece which bears a relief bust of Booker T. Washington, the founder of Tuskegee Institute. The coin was issued in May 1946.

FIRST LAWYER ADMITTED TO BAR

Macon B. Allen passed his examination in Worcester, Massachusetts on May 3, 1845, and thus became the first Negro formally admitted to the bar.

FIRST COACH OF A MAJOR LEAGUE TEAM

Bill Russell, star center of the world-champion Boston Celtics, became the first Negro to direct a major league sports team when he was named on April 18, 1966 to succeed Red Auerbach as coach. Russell will act as player-coach for the 1966-1967 season at a salary of well over $125,000. He will be the fourth coach of the Celtics since 1946.

FIRST UMPIRE IN THE MAJOR LEAGUES

Emmett Ashford, the first Negro umpire in the major leagues, made his debut on April 12, 1966 in the American League inaugural between the Cleveland Indians and the Washington Senators. Vice-President Hubert Humphrey was on hand to throw out the first ball.

Born in Los Angeles, Ashford attended Jefferson High School and Los Angeles City College. Before getting his major league assignment at the age of 51 (four years before compulsory retirement age), Ashford had umpired in the Dominican Republic for three winter seasons (1958, 1959, 1964), and in several other minor leagues as well, including the Pacific Coast League where he was umpire-in-chief as of September 1965.

FIRST NEGRO ADMITTED TO CONGRESSIONAL PRESS GALLERIES

Louis Lautier, Washington bureau chief of the Negro Newspaper Publishers Association, was the first Negro formally accredited to both the Senate and House press galleries. Lautier was admitted to the galleries in 1947, after a Senate Rules Committee overrode the refusal of the Standing Committee of Newspaper Correspondents to grant him the necessary credentials.

Emmett Ashford

Captain Lloyd Sealy

FIRST PHYSICIAN IN AMERICA

James Derham, born a slave in Philadelphia in 1762, is generally regarded as the first Negro physician in America. After learning medicine while serving as an assistant to his master (a doctor by profession), Derham purchased his freedom in 1783, and went on to establish a thriving practice with both Negro and white clientele. By 1788, he was considered to be one of the leading physicians in New Orleans. Dr. Benjamin Rush, a leading contemporary of Derham, once said of him: "I have conversed with him upon most of the acute and epidemic diseases of the country where he lives. I expected to have suggested some new medicines to him, but he suggested many more to me."

FIRST NEGRO OFFICER TO COMMAND A HARLEM PRECINCT

Holder of the highest post ever awarded a Negro in the New York City uniformed police, Lloyd Sealy is in charge of all uniformed forces in Brooklyn North, an area including Bedford-Stuyvesant, Brownsville, Downtown Brooklyn, and a portion of East New York. A native New Yorker, Sealy joined the force in 1942; later became a patrolman and sergeant in the Youth Division and, in 1959, was assigned to the Confidential Squad as a lieutenant. He became a captain in 1963.

FIRST WOMAN PRINCIPAL IN NEW YORK

Mrs. Gertrude Elise Ayer was the first Negro woman to serve as a school principal in the New York City public school system. A native of New York City, Mrs. Ayer was appointed to her post at P.S. 24 (Madison Avenue and 128th Street) in 1935.

FIRST BLACK "MR. AMERICA"

Chris Dickerson was born in 1939. So was the Mr. America contest. On June 14, 1970, at the Veterans Memorial Association in Los Angeles, California, Chris Dickerson became the first black man in the history of the contest to win the title "Mr. America." This is only one—albeit the most important—of 15 body-building titles which Dickerson has won to date. Among the others are: Mr. California, Mr. Eastern America, and Mr. Junior U.S.A. Born one of triplets in Montgomery, Alabama on August 25, 1939, Dickerson was an outstanding athlete throughout his school years, and showed an early interest in a singing career. The desire to improve his voice quality and breath control led him into body building in the mid 1960's. Dickerson appeared on the Johnny Carson show in 1970 after his notable achievement, and has since given talks, exhibitions, and demonstrations to various groups. He hopes ultimately to open and operate a gym of his own and thus "help . . . young Negro kids who are hopeful of winning the Mr. America contest some day." Dickerson's mother, a lawyer, resides in Anchorage, Alaska, where she practices her profession. His father works for the Cleveland Trust Company in Cleveland, Ohio.

FIRST NEGRO DEPUTY POLICE COMMISSIONER NEW YORK

William L. Rowe, appointed a member of the New Rochelle, N. Y. Human Rights Commission in February 1966, was the first Negro to hold the post of Deputy Police Commissioner in the history of the City of New York. He was appointed to this position on August 23, 1951 by Mayor Vincent Impellitieri, and completed his term of service in 1954 during the administration of Mayor Robert Wagner. Rowe was employed by the Pittsburgh Courier newspaper chain for some 16 years before entering government service. As an overseas correspondent he covered World War II from Guadalcanal to Tokyo and was cited for bravery in the Solomon Islands. Since then he has become president of a highly successful publicity firm, "Louis-Rowe Ent.," with such clients as Sammy Davis, Jr., Burlington-Socks, Louis Armstrong and Freedom National Bank.

FIRST WOMAN DOCTOR

The first Negro woman to enter the medical profession formally is believed to have been Dr. Susan McKinney (1848-1918).* A native of Brooklyn, New York, Dr. McKinney (born Susan Smith) began her studies at the New York Medical College, graduating in 1870 as an honors student. She completed her postgraduate work at Long Island College Hospital—the only female in the graduating class. Dr. McKinney practiced in Brooklyn for more than 20 years, and eventually came to maintain two offices, one in Manhattan, the other in Brooklyn (first at 205 DeKalb Avenue; later, at 178 Ryerson Street). Early in her career, she practiced homeopathy at a hospital and dispensary located on Myrtle and Grand Avenues in Brooklyn. The dispensary later moved to larger quarters, and was renamed the Memorial Hospital for Women and Children. At one time, it was granted some $4,000 in public funds.

Married to the Reverend William McKinney, Dr. McKinney became an organist and choir master at the Bridge Street AME Church. She was a board member of the Brooklyn Home for Aged Colored People. After her first husband's death (c. 1894), she married the Reverend T. G. Steward, an Army chaplain and instructor at Wilberforce University. By the time she left for Ohio, there was already another Negro woman physician in Brooklyn, a Dr. Verina Morton Jones, who had set up practice there in 1891.

* According to the medical college of the New York Infirmary, Dr. Rebecca Cole was the first Negro woman physician in the United States, having practiced from 1872 to 1881. In any case, Dr. McKinney is the first Negro woman to practice medicine in New York City.

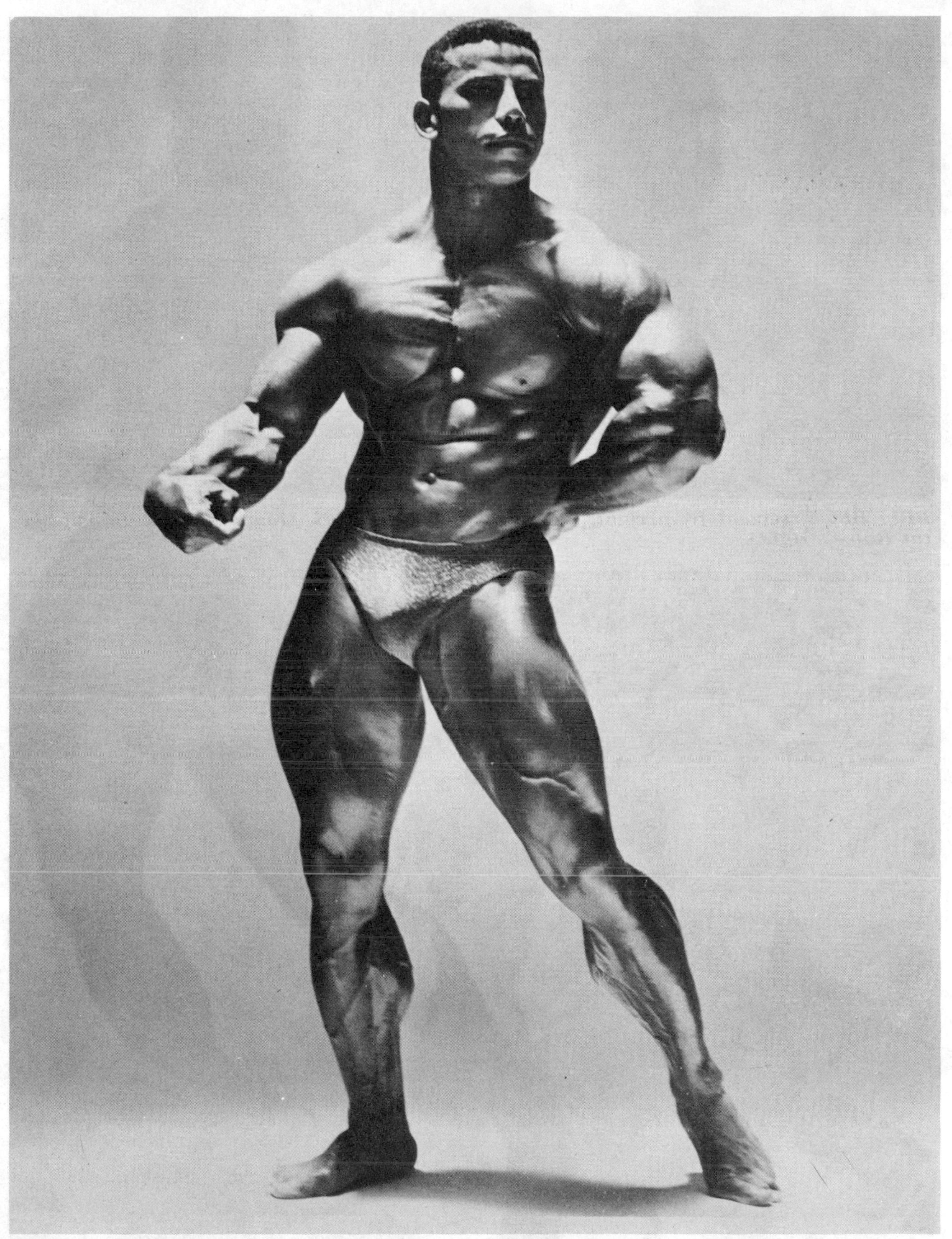

Chris Dickerson the first black man in history to win the title "Mr. America."

Billy Rowe (second from right) is sworn in by New York Mayor Vincent Impellitieri (at Rowe's right).

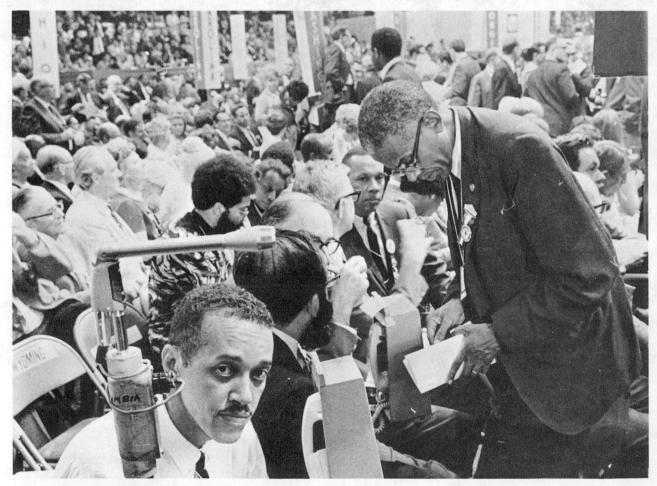

Channing Phillips—the first black major-party Presidential nominee in the 20th century. Phillips' name was entered at the 1968 Democratic convention.

FIRST MODERN-DAY CANDIDATE FOR GEORGIA GOVERNORSHIP

Forty-six-year-old C. B. King announced his candidacy for the Georgia governorship in December 1969. King (no relation to Martin Luther King, Jr.) did not indicate whether he would run under a party label, and professed support for what he called a "new politics" to take cognizance of the needs of blacks and whites alike.

FIRST MEMBER OF N. Y. STOCK EXCHANGE

The first black man proposed for a seat on the nation's leading securities market, Joseph L. Searles III was formerly an aide in the Lindsay Administration. Searles resigned to become one of the three floor traders, as well as a general partner, for Newburger, Loeb & Co.

FIRST PASTOR IN THE N Y. ARCHDIOCESE

Archbishop Terence J. Cooke named Rev. Harold A. Salmon the first Negro pastor within the Archdiocese and Vicariate Delegate for Harlem in 1968. Rev. Salmon was put in charge of Harlem's largest parish, St. Charles Borromeo's. The cardinal outlined Father Salmon's mission as taking responsibility for "the over-all planning and efforts of the seven Harlem parishes so that they may better serve the total community." Estimates of the number of black Catholics in Harlem range at less than 5% of the black population there. Altogether, black Catholics in New York number some 9% of the 1.2 million Negroes in the city.

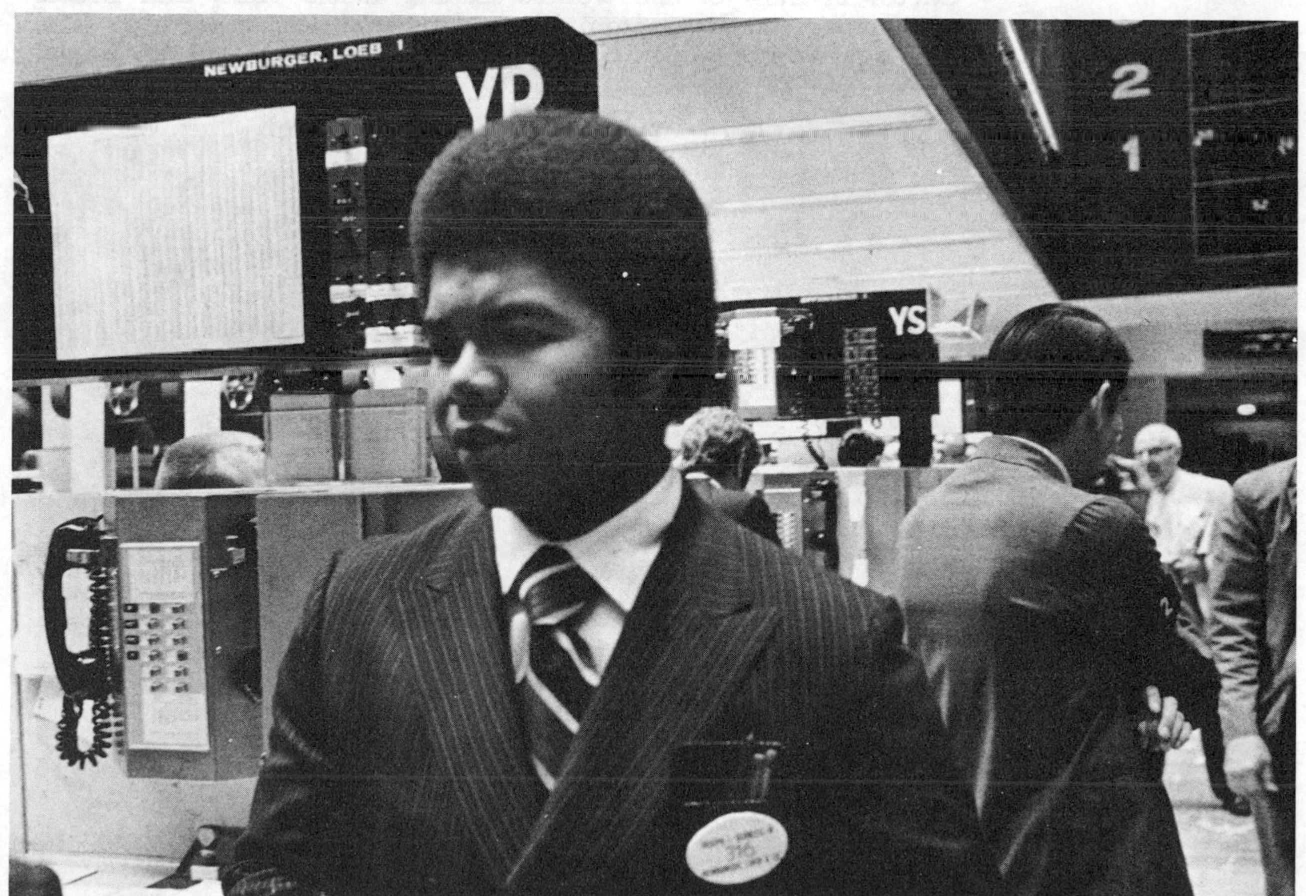

Joseph Searles on the floor of the N.Y. Stock Exchange

FIRST MUSIC DIRECTOR OF AN AMERICAN ORCHESTRA

Firsts have almost become second nature to Los Angeles born Henry Lewis, the first Negro musician to play regularly with a major U.S. orchestra (the Los Angeles Philharmonic) and, as of 1968, the first Negro named music director of an American orchestra (the Newark-based New Jersey Symphony). Other black conductors—Dean Dixon and Everett Lee—have found regular podiums in Europe; Lewis, however, is the first to be appointed in the U.S.

Born in 1932 in Los Angeles, Lewis demonstrated his musical talents in early childhood, beginning his piano studies at the age of five. By the time he entered junior high school he was already proficient with the baton, but he continued to study and master most of the standard instruments because he realized that a good conductor is required to know the capacities of orchestral instruments. His mastery of the double bass led to an audition with the Los Angeles Philharmonic, Alfred Wallenstein conducting. At 16, Lewis became the youngest person to be awarded a chair with the symphony. Lewis finished high school while a member of the famed orchestra, and was subsequently awarded a musical scholarship to the University of Southern California. In 1955, Lewis served overseas with the Seventh Army Symphony and was eventually chosen its musical director. It was here that he began regular appearances on the podium, giving three to five concerts a week for a whole year. Back in civilian life, Lewis continued to play with the Philharmonic until 1961, the year he first appeared as a substitute conductor for a pair of concerts scheduled to be given by Igor Markevitch. The event brought Lewis public and critical recognition. Nowadays, Lewis appears as guest conductor in most of the world's leading music halls, and makes numerous recordings from his wide symphonic repertoire. The Lewises live in Orange, New Jersey, and have a daughter, Angela.

Henry Lewis directs the New Jersey Symphony.

FIRST TRUSTEE OF YALE UNIVERSITY

Nearly 270 years elapsed before the first black man, Federal Judge A. Leon Higginbotham, Jr., was elected a trustee of Yale University. The judge, who succeeded New York's Mayor John Lindsay, defeated five other candidates in nationwide balloting in April and May 1969. Some 25,000 of Yale's 75,000 eligible alumni took part.

FIRST MUSICIAN WITH THE PHILADELPHIA ORCHESTRA

Renard Edwards became the first black musician to play for the Philadelphia Orchestra when he was hired as a violist for the 1970-71 season. Edwards was formerly with the Symphony of the New World, an integrated orchestra fully one-third to one-half of whose members are Negroes. The Boston Symphony has a Negro harpist; the Cleveland Orchestra, a Negro cellist, and the New York Philharmonic, a Negro violinist. Only the Chicago Orchestra of the so-called Big Five has not yet engaged a black performer.

FIRST VA. LEGISLATOR IN THE 20TH CENTURY

Lawrence Douglas Wilder, 38, became the first Negro to serve in the Virginia Senate since 1890 when he was elected over white Republican and white Democratic candidates. The last Negro in the legislature, Nathaniel E. M. Griggs, served in that body from 1887 to 1890. Wilder's election brings to three the number of Negroes in the legislature. The others are Dr. William Ferguson Reid and William P. Robinson, Sr.

FIRST WOMAN LEGISLATOR

Crystal Bird Fauset was the first Negro woman elected to a state legislature in the United States, acquiring this distinction when she was named to the Pennsylvania House of Representatives on November 8, 1938. Miss Fauset died on March 28, 1965.

FIRST PRIMA BALLERINA FOR METROPOLITAN

Janet Collins was the first Negro to dance for the Metropolitan Opera in New York. Miss Collins, signed by an agent of the company in 1951, made her debut in *Aida*.

FIRST BLACK PRESIDENTIAL NOMINEE OF A MAJOR PARTY

Chairman of the District of Columbia delegation, Rev. Channing Phillips, a favorite son, was placed in nomination at the 1968 Democratic convention in Chicago. Phillips received 67½ votes. At the same time, the Peace and Freedom Party of New York State announced that Dick Gregory and Mark Lane would actually run for this office on the state ballot.

SLAVERY IN THE WESTERN HEMISPHERE

Arguments for and against Slavery
Race Riots and Slave Conspiracies
Leaders of Slave Revolts

The slave trade in the Western Hemisphere began formally in 1517, the year the Spanish resolved to encourage immigration to Latin America by allowing each Spanish settler a quota of 12 Negro slaves.

The vast majority of these slaves (with the exception of some free Negroes who immigrated to the New World from Spain and Portugal) worked on plantations, in the mines of the Caribbean islands, and on Spanish and Portuguese settlements south of the Rio Grande River as well.*

The voyage from Africa to the Caribbean Sea, known as the "Middle Passage," was filled with misery and degradation for the slave. He slept in overcrowded quarters, was often mercilessly beaten, and was subject to disease and malnutrition. The mere fact that he survived the ordeal made him a valuable commodity. Time had proved that the enslaved Indian was unable to adjust to the rigors of the New World's complex agricultural economy. (Indians died in large numbers, either from disease, or from the constant pressure of forced labor.) The Negro, however, was able to survive a period of "seasoning" in the Caribbean islands be-

*** Negroes in the New World, however, were not exclusively utilized as slaves. Some accompanied the expeditions of such famed explorers and *conquistadores* as Balboa, Cortes, Alvarado, Pizarro, Coronado and Cabeza de Vaca through Central and South America, while others joined French Jesuit missionaries in their travels through much of North America.**

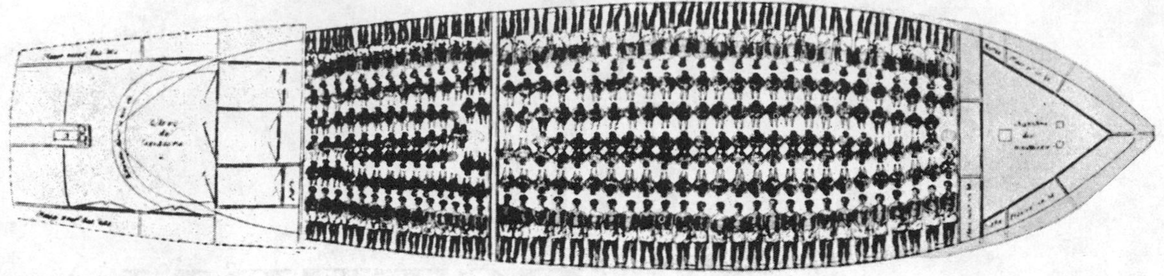

An overhead view of the interior of a slave ship.

fore being introduced onto the mainland itself.

There was, of course, constant Negro resistance to the system, either in the form of minor uprisings or of wholesale insurrections. In the 1550's, for example, there were frequent outbreaks of violence in Cartagena (Colombia). During the 17th century, similar upheavals occurred in Bahia and Rio de Janeiro (Brazil), despite the fact that the Negro in these areas enjoyed a relative measure of well-being.

Another important factor necessary for analyzing the slave experience in Latin America is an understanding of the role played by the Catholic Church. Christianity, as practiced in this era, theoretically involved some recognition of the dignity of the slave and the sanctity of his family relationship. Moreover, manumission was even condoned in certain cases. On the other hand, slavery was frequently justified on the grounds that it enabled pagans to learn the gospel of Christ. Various religious orders attempted to reduce illiteracy among Negroes as part of an ongoing program designed to impose European cultural values upon the Negro population. The fact that interracial marriages were fairly commonplace, particularly in Brazil, is another point which sheds considerable light on the position of the Negro in Latin American society.

Thus, the Negro in this part of the world had achieved some measure of social status and individual dignity even before being granted any kind of legal equality. (The reverse seems to be true of the Negro in North America, particularly in the United States.) Moreover, slavery as an institution was practiced with virtually no opposition *everywhere* in Latin America, whereas in North America it was *confined to a smaller area* and was, at least intermittently, under attack from outside forces.

The first European nation to abolish slavery in the New World was France (1794). The French proclamation provided for the theoretical, if not actual, emancipation of all slaves in the French West Indies. The distinction of having been the first nation in the Western Hemisphere to do away with slavery belongs to Haiti (1804). Slavery was abolished in England in 1772, and the British slave trade halted in 1807. It was not until 1833, however, that Parliament passed an act eliminating slavery (after payment of compensation to slaveowners) in all British overseas possessions—including Canada, the mainland colonies in Central and South America, and the island colonies in the Caribbean. The measure was not fully enforced until 1838.

On the Spanish and Portuguese mainland, the abolition of slavery was linked with the independence struggles of various subject territories. Slaves were freed in the United Provinces of Central America (1824); in Mexico (1829); in Latin America, to all intent and purpose, by 1855; in Cuba (1886); and in Brazil (1888).

The United States (1619-1865)

Slavery on the shores of what was to become the United States of America began with the arrival of Europeans from the Old World, and of Negroes from the Dark Continent.

The Europeans (chiefly of English, German and Scotch-Irish ancestry) who immigrated to the colonies as laborers came

A Dutch man-of-war lies at ...chor in Jamestown, the English ...olony into which slaves were ...troduced in the year 1619.

as "indentured servants"—men who had voluntarily bound themselves over to the service of a master for a number of years in payment for passage and board. (Those who came involuntarily were either debtors or paupers who had been deported and were obliged to work seven years before achieving their freedom, or else children who had been kidnapped, shipped to the colonies, and then sold into service.)

The 20 Negro servants who landed at Jamestown, Virginia in 1619 were not "slaves" in the strictest sense of the term. Some of them were assigned land upon the termination of their contracts, whereas others opted for the liberties and privileges associated with membership in the "free laboring class." Beginning in the 1640's, however, the Negro ceased to be regarded as a "servant" and, instead, came to be assigned the status of "chattel slave"—one who remained a fixed item of personal property for the duration of his life.

Negroes clustered into those areas of the South where agricultural produce—tobacco, rice, indigo, cotton—was the primary source of economic wealth. The slave population soon rose sharply due to the increased demand for cheap labor brought on by the westward expansion of the original colonies. The democratically inclined Northern states were less in need of slaves and so found it far easier to abolish the institution than did the agrarian-minded South. The cotton gin, the growth of foreign textile markets, and the development of cotton cultivation made the slave an indispensable unit within the economic framework of the "Old South."

With the passage of time, white indentured servants gradually disappeared from the colonial labor market, particularly after liberalized legislation enabled them to acquire freedom and land after a curtailed period of service. This only accelerated the flow of Negro workers into the colonies, and encouraged planters to institutionalize the notion of perpetual Negro servitude. Practical considerations for such a move included the fact that Negro runaways could be detected more easily than fugitive whites. Moreover, since the incoming Negro was not a Christian, he was consequently regarded as a product of a wholly primitive and savage culture, and hence fit for nothing better than a life of unbroken drudgery. (Even when the Negro later accepted Christianity, his status was in no way altered.) Color ultimately became the sole badge of complete social ostracism—the mark whch removed the Negro from the ranks of humanity and cast him, once and for all, into the immutable role of chattel slave.

The year 1763 was a most significant one in the history of the Negro slave inasmuch as it inaugurated an era during which anti-slavery sentiment began to gain a foothold in America, and to achieve widespread prominence in the public domain. For all practical purposes, the colonists, victimized by the tighter restrictions imposed upon them by the Crown, were forced by the very nature of their own struggle for representative institutions to agitate also for the rights of Negroes.

In his *Rights of the British Colonies* (1764), James Otis proved he was one man who did not fear the consequences of proclaiming the Negro's right to be free. In 1773, Reverend Isaac Skillman made the even more radical assertion that slaves should rebel against their masters. A year later, Thomas Jefferson described the abolition of slavery as one of the goals of the colonists, and accused Great Britain of blocking efforts to end the slave trade. Later, the Continental Congress passed a resolution not to import any slaves after December 1, 1775. Ultimately, the colonists—in the person of Thomas Jefferson—went so far as to include a violent denunciation of slavery in an early draft of the Declaration of Independence. (This clause was later eliminated and, to some critics, serves as proof positive that equality and independence were never meant to be extended to the Negro American.)

Anti-slavery and manumission activities continued throughout, and also after, the Revolutionary War. By 1787—the year it was abolished in the Northwest Territory—slavery had been banned in such states as Pennsylvania (1780); Massachusetts (1783); Connecticut and Rhode Island (1784); New York (1785) and New Jersey (1786).

However, the Constitution itself served to dampen the hopes of abolitionists by providing for the extension of the slave trade for a 20-year period, and for the return of fugitive slaves to their owners. The famous "three-fifths compromise," according to which five slaves were to be regarded as the equivalent of three nonslaves in terms of taxation and representation, further succeeded in safeguarding the pro-slavery interests in the United States.

In the 19th century, the slave population of the United States grew by leaps and bounds, reaching a figure of 4,000,000 prior to the outbreak of the Civil War. Democratic institutions within the country also developed on a broad scale, although the slave himself derived little practical advantage from such advances. In the South, slavery became a "way of life" for both plantation owner and field hand, particularly as the Cotton Kingdom became more firmly entrenched.

Although the African slave trade was technically discontinued in 1808 (it is estimated that, from that date until 1860, no less than 250,000 slaves were in fact imported, the ban notwithstanding), nothing prevented slaves from being bred and bartered within various territories of the United States proper. Virginia, for example, earned the title of the "Negro-raising state" by virtue of its being able to export over 6,000 slaves annually to such centers of trade as Baltimore, Washington, D.C., Charleston, Montgomery, Memphis and New Orleans.

On the larger plantations, slaves were generally divided into two categories: house servants and field hands. The former group was often charged with such assorted tasks as caring for the grounds and garden, keeping the house clean, and maintaining and repairing rigs. In many cases, house servants were allowed to learn trades (becoming smiths, carpenters, builders, etc.), as well as to develop other skills (doctoring, child care, and tutoring). Field hands, however, were forced to submit to the monotony of sowing and reaping, planting and picking, without respite or any prospect of change.

The bare necessities of life—a roof over one's head, food on one's table, clothes on one's back—were all that the slave could expect for his labor. The only break in this routine occurred at Christmas and on other holidays, or in those brief hours before the day's end when the slave might hunt, fish or garden.

Raiding an African village to capture people for the slave trade.

Though such a life may seem to have been immensely confining, slaves do not seem to have been docile and submissive creatures, as is so often popularly believed. Evidence of their rebelliousness and discontent can be found in the white man's need for creating strict codes which controlled almost all their movements and subordinated them completely to the will of the master.

The slave needed written permission—a veritable passport—to leave the plantation. He could not enter into a contract; hire out his services to other men; take a stand in court; defend himself, or read anything labeled "incendiary" literature. He was subject to whipping, branding, imprisonment or death for any of a number of minor offenses.

The abortive Nat Turner rebellion of 1831 must be regarded as another turning point in the history of the Negro slave. From this point until the outbreak of the Civil War and emancipation, the slave was relentlessly harassed by the stringent enforcement of slave codes, a further reduction in his educational opportunities, and the almost complete suspension of the practice of manumission.

This same period also marked a sharp decline in the "repatriation" movement which had been sponsored largely by the American Colonization Society. The idea of returning free Negroes to their "ancestral homeland" was in part motivated by sincere humanitarian impulses, but it also had its utilitarian side. By 1830, the more than 300,000 free Negroes in the United States constituted an important element in the population, particularly in the South where their presence caused considerable embarrassment to the planter aristocracy.

Of even greater significance to the Negro slave, however, was the creation of the New England Antislavery Society and the publication of the first issue of the crusading abolitionist journal, *The Liberator*. As colonization and manumission lost their momentum, abolition quickly sprang to the fore as a compelling moral alternative, drawing much of its strength from the dedication of an impressive array of white leaders, as well as a number of fiery and determined Negro spokesmen.

In the South, abolition only hardened the already congealed opinion of the slaveholding class. Slavery, it was said, was necessary for economic survival; it had enabled the white man to create a unique and progressive culture; it was even countenanced by Christianity as a means of converting the Negro pagan from abject heathenism. Above and beyond these rationalizations lay the ultimate racist ideology which has characterized the thinking of many white South-

This Harper's Weekly *illustration, done in 1861, depicts a slave auction in a Southern city.*

Henry 'Box' Brown emerges from the crate in which he escaped from Richmond, Virginia. The dimensions of the crate were three feet long, 2½ feet deep, and two feet wide.

erners throughout their history. The Negro was, in their view, biologically inferior—a fact which they would at times assert without any seeming malice.

As positions polarized and battle lines were drawn, the politics of the slavery question vaulted into the foreground of American life. The Fugitive Slave Act (1850), the Compromise of 1850, the publication of *Uncle Tom's Cabin* (1852), the Kansas-Nebraska Act (1854), the Dred Scott decision (1857), the Harpers Ferry raid (1859)—these and countless other events recounted in standard American history texts were in one way or another connected with the attempt to effect a final resolution of the slavery issue in the United States.

"Slavery" shared the spotlight with the "Preservation of the Union" as the paramount issues of the Civil War. It can perhaps be said that both questions had to be resolved simultaneously, or not at all. Abraham Lincoln, elected to the presidency as a racial moderate in 1860, came to power knowing full well that slavery was wrong, but arguing nonetheless that the federal government had no right to prohibit slavery in the South. He even went so far as to say the following:

"If I could save the Union without freeing any slave, I would do it; if I could save it by freeing all the slaves, I would do it; and if I could save it by freeing some and leaving others alone, I would also do that. What I do about slavery and the colored race, I do because I believe it helps save the Union. . . ."

As military pressures mounted, Lincoln sponsored the Confiscation Act of 1861, which provided for the emancipation of slaves who had been used for insurrectionary purposes in the South. Within two years, free Negro regiments were responding to the Union slogan that they could at last fight for their own freedom.

By May 1862, Lincoln was prepared to move even closer to the position advocated by the Radical Republicans: complete abolition. In September of that year, the President issued a preliminary Emancipation Proclamation—holding out to slaveowners the possibility of compensation, and continuing to suggest to freedmen the prospect of voluntary colonization in Africa.

On January 1, 1863, a further proclamation declared that all slaves living in the *seceded states* of the Confederacy were to be "thenceforward, and forever free." It conferred legal, though not actual, emancipation on three-fourths of the slave population, yet made no provisions for some 800,000 Negroes living outside the South who remained technically enslaved. Constitutional emancipation did not come *for all slaves* until 1865 with the passage of the 13th amendment—the single, all-embracing legislative enactment which brought the United States a step closer to its motto: "Land of the Free."

(The story of the Negro freedman during Reconstruction, and of the Negro population in general during the 20th century, belongs to another province of American history. For our purposes, slavery as a *legal* concept ended in the year 1865, although its repercussions continue to plague our society down to our very own time.)

THE GREAT DEBATE: ARGUMENTS FOR AND AGAINST SLAVERY

Civilized man has produced several arguments in favor of, or violently opposed to, the institution of slavery. We have attempted here to indicate them in summary form.

IN DEFENSE OF SLAVERY

1. Biology. The established classes within most ancient and medieval societies assumed that certain groups of people were inherently inferior. (In modern times, this theory is embodied in the term "white supremacy.")
2. Necessity. Agricultural and industrial surpluses could not be produced, nor could public works projects or cultural monuments be undertaken, without the use of slave labor. Slavery was needed to create wealth and grandeur.
3. Convenience. The advancement of culture, thought to be the natural province of the "leisure class" within a community, could not exist unless more menial and commonplace services were provided by a laboring class.
4. Status. Slave ownership was a primary attribute of power and distinction within certain societies.
5. Religion. Slavery was sanctioned by Christianity itself as a means of converting the slave from paganism.
6. Profit. Slavery was profitable to those engaged in the trade. Their well-being was not isolated, but contributed instead to the good fortune of others.

IN OPPOSITION TO SLAVERY

1. Biology. The inherent inferiority of any group of people cannot be scientifically demonstrated.
2. Freedom. Slavery was morally indefensible, since it involved the denial of two of Man's inalienable rights: personal freedom and equality of birth.
3. Brutality. Slavery was inhumane, awakening the most brutal instincts within the slaveowner.
4. Degradation. Slavery caused the physical, mental and moral degradation of the slave.
5. Religion. Slavery was contrary to such Christian principles as brotherly love and the sanctity of the individual in the sight of God.
6. Identity. Slavery deprived the slave of a sense of identity and pride, causing him to lose confidence in his own capacities—intellectual and otherwise.

RACE RIOTS AND SLAVE CONSPIRACIES IN THE UNITED STATES

This chronology is intended to shed some light on the nature and gravity of a number of race riots and slave conspiracies which have occurred in the United States since 1663. Of necessity, our list is selective, since it becomes difficult at times to characterize a particular event as either a riot or a conspiracy. Then, too, records of earlier uprisings sometimes reveal differences in documentation and interpretation among historians.

The causes of the riots and conspiracies vary with the times, but they do have one thing in common: they are all expressions of the Negro's discontent with his status and position in American society—first as a slave, and later in such roles as segregated student, laborer, soldier, resident, etc. Those outbreaks of more recent vintage reflect the Negro's increasing self-assertiveness and his impatient, smoldering rage at second-class citizenship and the economic hardship he is often forced to endure. Spreading to the overcrowded ghettos of the North in the post-World War II period, racial riots have generated great tension and unrest everywhere in the United States. The reason is elementary: they affect everyone, regardless of race, creed, color, or national origin.

CHRONOLOGY OF U.S. RACE RIOTS AND SLAVE CONSPIRACIES 1663–1970

YEAR	EVENT
1663	Servant betrays first serious plot of Negro slaves and white servants in Gloucester, Virginia.
1712	Slave revolt in New York results in the death of nine whites and the execution of 21 slaves.
1739	Slave revolt in Stono, South Carolina: 25 whites dead.
1741	Reports of slave conspiracy in New York City lead to the execution of 31 slaves and five whites.
1800	Conspiracy of Gabriel Prosser and some 1,000 followers betrayed by two slaves. Gabriel and 15 others hanged.
1811	Slave revolt in Louisiana suppressed by U.S. troops.
1822	Betrayal by a house slave of Denmark Vesey conspiracy involving thousands of Negroes in Charleston, South Carolina and environs. Four whites, 131 Negroes arrested; 37 hanged (including Vesey and five of his aides).
1829	Race riot in Cincinnati, Ohio. More than 1,000 Negroes migrate to Canada.
1831	Nat Turner Revolt in Southampton County, Virginia results in the death of 60 whites. Turner is captured and hanged.
1841	Slave revolt on "Creole," ship en route from Hampton, Virginia to New Orleans, Louisiana. The slaves sail the vessel to the Bahamas, where they are granted asylum and emancipated.
1859	John Brown and his followers (13 whites and five Negroes) attack Harpers Ferry. Of the five Negroes, two are killed, two are captured, and one escapes.
1863	The "Draft Riots," among the bloodiest in United States history, break out in New York City. Mobs sweep through the streets, murder Negroes, and hang them on lampposts. The Negro Orphan Asylum on Fifth Avenue is destroyed. Some 1,000 are killed. Estimated property damage: $1.5 million.
1866	Race riots in Memphis, Tennessee.
1868	Race riots in New Orleans, Opelousas and St. Bernard Parish—all in Louisiana.
1871	Race riot in Meridian, Mississippi.

1878 Colfax Massacre in Grant Parish, Lousiana results in the killing of more than 600 Negroes.

1898 Race riot in Wilmington, North Carolina. Eight Negroes slain.

1900 Race riot in New Orleans, with several people hurt. Property damage: one Negro school, 30 Negro homes burned.

1904 Race riot in Springfield, Ohio.

1906 Negro soldiers raid Brownsville, Texas in protest against racial insults. One white killed, two wounded. President Theodore Roosevelt musters three companies out of the Negro 25th Regiment.

Atlanta riots result in the death of 10 Negroes and two whites, injury to 70, and the proclamation of martial law.

Race riot in Springfield, Ohio.

1908 Race riot in Springfield, Illinois, triggered by alleged rape of a white woman by a Negro, is quelled by troops.

1917 Race riots in East St. Louis, Illinois, with estimates on numbers of Negroes killed ranging from 40 to 200. Martial law declared.

Race riot in Houston, Texas between soldiers of the 24th Infantry Regiment and white citizens. Two Negroes and 17 whites killed; 13 members of the regiment later hanged.

1918 Race riot in Chester, Pennsylvania results in five deaths.

Race riot in Philadelphia, Pennsylvania. Four dead and 60 injured.

1919 "Red Summer" of 1919.

Race riots in Longview and Gregg County, Texas.

Race riots in Washington, D.C., with six deaths and 150 injured.

Troops called out to suppress Chicago riot (15 whites and 23 Negroes killed; 537 injured).

Rioting in Elaine (Phillips County), Arkansas, with five whites and 25 to 50 Negroes killed.

1921 Race riot in Tulsa, Oklahoma causing death of 21 whites and 60 Negroes.

1942 Race riot at the Sojourner Truth Homes in Detroit, Michigan.

1943 Two dead in Beaumont, Texas race riot.

Race riot in Detroit, Michigan (34 dead).

Race riot in Harlem.

1946 Race riot in Columbia, Tennessee (two killed, 10 injured).

Race riot, Athens, Alabama (50 to 100 Negroes injured).

Race riot in Philadelphia.

1960 Race riot in Chattanooga, Tennessee during a sit-in demonstration.

Race riot in Biloxi, Mississippi after a wade-in by Negroes at a local beach.

Race riot in Jacksonville after 10 days of sit-ins.

1964 Riots in Harlem (one dead, 144 injured).

Riots in Rochester, New York (four dead, 350 injured).

Riots in Jersey City, Paterson, and Elizabeth, New Jersey (some 125 injured).

Riots in Chicago (341 injured).

Riots in Philadelphia.

1965 Riots in Watts, Los Angeles (see page 39).

1966 Renewed outbreak of violence in Watts, Los Angeles.

1967 Twenty-three persons are dead in the aftermath of the Newark riot—21 of them black and two, a policeman and a fireman, white. Six of the dead are women; two are children. Damage is more than 10 million dollars. More than 1,000 persons are injured; more than 1,600 are arrested, including poet/playwright Leroi Jones.

1967 Death and disaster tolls in the Detroit riot are even higher than they are in Newark. Of the 43 persons killed during the riot, 33 are black and 10 are white; 17 are looters, 15 of them black; 15 citizens (four of them white) die as a result of gunshot wounds. Property loss is placed at approximately 22 million dollars by the Kerner Commission.

1968 Three black youths are shot to death and more than 30 other

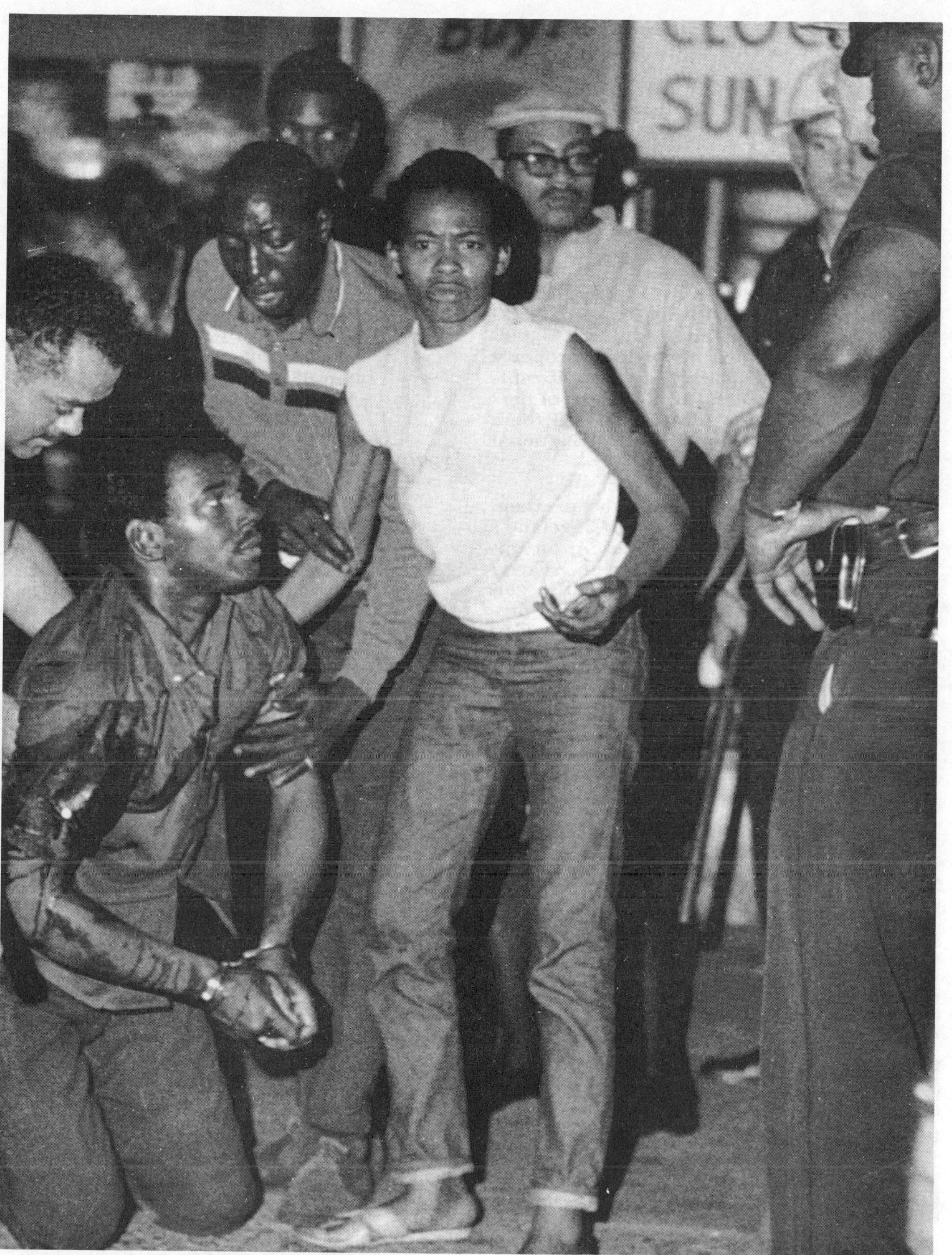

The 1964 Harlem riots.

persons are wounded in a race riot in Orangeburg, South Carolina. Cause of the riot is the refusal of a local bowling alley to admit black patrons in direct violation of the 1964 Civil Rights Act.

1968 More than 100 cities in 28 states and the District of Columbia are struck by violent disorders in the aftermath of Martin Luther King's assassination. There are 46 deaths, and 2,600 persons are injured. Over 20,000 arrests are recorded, property damage is estimated at 45 million dollars. Over 50,000 soldiers are involved, 21,000 of them federal troops, the rest National Guardsmen.

1968 Eleven persons, eight of them black, are killed in Cleveland's Glenville district during an uprising led by Ahmed (Fred) Evans, a black nationalist employed in the local poverty program. Cleveland Mayor Carl Stokes characterizes the incident as a deliberate premeditated attempt to attack police and initiate urban guerrilla warfare, the first stage of concerted revolutionary strife.

1969 After a comparatively quiet summer, with few concerted outbursts of uncontrolled violence and citizen involvement in ghetto policing efforts relieving tensions, the city of Hartford is the scene of ghetto disorders, including firebombings and sniper activity. Scores of people are arrested, but the strife is relatively brief and contained without wholesale loss of life and property. Other disturbances are recorded in Camden and Fort Lauderdale, but major cities are largely spared.

1970 Six Negroes are shot, all of them in the back, and 20 other persons are injured during a night of violence in Augusta, Georgia. Two black students are killed in Mississippi at Jackson State College, where witnesses charge that police spray bullets indiscriminately at the residence hall in a fit of hysteria and rage. The facade of the building, pockmarked with bullet holes, corroborates the claim.

Rioting broke out in Hartford in 1969. It was not as severe as in earlier years.

LEADERS OF SLAVE REVOLTS IN THE U.S.

GABRIEL PROSSER
1775?–1800
Slave insurrectionist

Not much is known of the early background of Gabriel Prosser beyond the fact that he was born around 1775, and was a coachman belonging to Thomas Prosser of Henrico County, Virginia.

The revolt which Prosser organized—the first of at least three major slave uprisings in the first half of the 19th century—was remarkable not only for the skill of its organization, but also for the large numbers of people who were to have taken part in it. The environs of Richmond, Virginia—chosen as the site of the rebellion—had some 32,000 slaves, but only 8,000 whites, including a number of Frenchmen and Quakers, groups which Prosser felt would be sympathetic to his cause.

Prosser planned the revolt for the end of August, reasoning that there would be plenty to eat at the harvest, and that his followers would thus be spared any shortage of important supplies. He intended to kill all slaveowners, but to spare the French, the Quakers, elderly women, and children. Eventually, he hoped that the remaining 300,000 slaves in Virginia would follow his lead, and take over the entire state.

The plans laid, it was decided to meet at the Old Brook Swamp outside of Richmond on the last night of August, and to martial forces there for the attack on the city. A severe rainstorm, however, made it impossible for many of the slaves to assemble at the appointed rendezvous, necessitating a postponement of plans. Before the slaves could reassemble, the plot was betrayed by a pair of slaves who did not wish their master killed.

Panic quickly swept Richmond, and martial law was declared. Most slaves implicated in the conspiracy were rounded up and hanged, at least until it became apparent that this procedure would soon decimate the area's slave population. Less severe sentences were then meted out by the courts.

Prosser himself was captured in the hold of the schooner *Mary* when it docked at Norfolk after a trip from Richmond. Brought back in chains, he was interrogated by the governor, but refused to divulge any information on the nature of his plans, or on the identities of his compatriots. Prosser was hanged on October 7, 1800.

DENMARK VESEY
1767–1822
Slave insurrectionist

The second serious uprising of the 19th century was led by Denmark Vesey, a slave who for 20 years had sailed with his master, Captain Vesey, to the Virgin Islands and Haiti, the latter an independent island ruled by Negroes.

Born in 1767, Vesey was sold by his master at an early age, but later repurchased because he was an epileptic. Vesey enjoyed a considerable degree of mobility in his native Charleston, South Carolina, and eventually secured his own freedom by paying his master $600 of a $1500 sum won in a lottery. He later became a Methodist minister, using his church as a base from which to recruit supporters for his plan to take over Charleston—a plan set to go into operation on the second Sunday in July of 1822.

As in the case of Prosser, the Vesey plan was betrayed by a slave who alerted the white authorities of the city. Hundreds of Negroes were quickly rounded up, and Vesey himself was taken prisoner after a two-day search.

Vesey, who was literate, was extremely adept at cross-examining witnesses at his trial, but was unable to deny that his intended purpose was the overthrow of the city. Sentenced to death, he was hanged with his compatriots on July 2, 1822.

NAT TURNER
1800–1831
Slave insurrectionist

The Nat Turner Revolt is the best-known of the three major slave uprisings which occurred in the South in the early decades of the 19th century.

Born in 1800, the year of the Prosser revolt, Turner was strongly drawn by a kind of visionary mysticism through which he heard "voices" and believed in a special destiny. An avid reader of the Bible, he also prayed and fasted often, and ultimately conceived a plan to conquer Southampton County in Virginia.

Nat Turner plotting the insurrection.

Nat Turner is taken prisoner in the Dismal Swamp.

Recruiting a handful of co-conspirators, Turner struck isolated white homes within his immediate area and, within 48 hours, had built up his band to 60 armed men. Terrorizing the county, they killed 55 whites before deciding to attack the county seat of Jerusalem.

While en route, Turner's men were overtaken by a posse and dispersed, with Turner himself taking refuge in the forbidding confines of what was known as the Dismal Swamp. Remaining there for six weeks, he was finally captured, brought to trial and, along with 16 other Negroes, sentenced to death by hanging.

A modern construction worker in Niger, with the traditional markings of tribal initiation on his face.

AFRICA: THE CHANGING CONTINENT

Chronology
3000 B.C. — 1970 A.D.
The Nations of Africa
French African Dependencies
Portuguese African Dependencies
South African Dependency
Spanish African Dependencies
United Kingdom African Dependencies

Africa—known through much of its history as the "Dark Continent"—has undergone a profound social, economic and political transformation since 1945. Vast areas once identified with European nations (*French* West Africa and *British* East Africa, to mention but two) have now been carved into a number of independent nations whose emergence is destined to have an enormous impact on the world of tomorrow.

The momentum of change in Africa has not gone unnoticed by Negro civil rights leaders in the United States. The American Negro is coming more and more to understand that the struggles of his cousins-across-the-seas—distant though they may be—in some way mirror his own; that their identity in some way is reflected in his; that their cultural values in some way have been carried over into his world.

This *sense of kinship* between the African and the American Negro is the rationale for our review of African nationalism in its most contemporary setting. By keeping the reader abreast of the most recent developments in the nations of Africa (both new and old), we hope to make him aware that there are sound, even compelling, reasons for the "Dark Continent" to be rechristened the "Changing Continent."

CHRONOLOGY OF IMPORTANT EVENTS IN AFRICAN HISTORY 3000 B.C.–1970 A.D.

Date	*Event*
3000 B.C.	Tasili Frescoes, rock murals located in southeast Algeria, give evidence of an early Negro pastoral civilization (believed to date back to 6000 B.C.).
1200 B.C.	Beginnings of Nok culture (in Nigeria): an advanced Negro civilization with a great tradition of terra cotta sculpture (lasting until 200 B.C.).
1100 B.C.	The Phoenicians found the city of Utica in Tunisia.
813 B.C.	The Phoenicians found the city of Carthage, a center of trade in North Africa, and later a bitter rival of the Roman Empire.
650 B.C.	Beginnings of the Kingdom of Axum in Ethiopia (lasting until 650 A.D.).
631 B.C.	The Greeks found the city of Cyrene in North Africa.
470 B.C.	Hanno of Carthage explores the coast of West Africa as far south as Sierra Leone.
350 B.C.	Meroe, the capital of ancient Nubia, falls to Ethiopia.
332 B.C.	Conquest of Egypt by Alexander the Great, who later builds the city of Alexandria.
168 B.C.	Colonization of Egypt by Rome.
100 A.D.	Introduction of Christianity into North Africa.
300	Beginnings of the Kingdom of Ghana in the Western Sudan.
320	Introduction of Christianity in the Kingdom of Axum (present-day Ethiopia).
800	Founding of Arab colonies in Madagascar and Zanzibar; organization of Arab expeditions into East Africa in search of slaves.
800	Zenith of the Negro kingdom of Ghana—extending from the Atlantic coast to Timbuktu, "the land of gold" (lasting until 1240).
1000	Zenith of the Great Zimbabwe civilization of Rhodesia, site of a highly developed Negro culture marked by architectural wonders.
1054	Beginnings of the conquest of West Africa by Moslem Berber tribes.
1100	Zenith of the Songhai Kingdom of West Africa, with its capital at Timbuktu.
1147	Conquest of portions of North Africa by the Almohades, fierce Berber Moslems who establish hegemony over the region.
1269	Fall of the Berbers' North African Empire.
1300–1500	Zenith of Ife, a holy city in Nigeria noted for its fine sculpture.
1307	West Africa ruled by Mandingo Empire, successor to the Ghana and Songhai kingdoms.
1350	Beginnings of Benin, seat of a royal court and Nigerian city famed for bronze sculpture (lasting until 1897).
1400	Emergence of a Baluba Kingdom in the Congo.

Date	Event
1415	Arrival of Portuguese in West Africa; beginnings (under Prince Henry the Navigator) of trade with, and exploration of, West Africa.
1471	Portuguese begin mining of precious metal on "Gold Coast."
1482	Portuguese colonize Angola.
1488	Portuguese explorer, Bartholomew Diaz, reaches Cape of Good Hope at the southern tip of Africa.
1491	Portuguese explorer, Vasco da Gama, rounds the Cape, and sails up the East African coast en route to Asia.
1493–1529	Defeat of Mandingos by the Songhai Empire, headed by Askia Mohammed.
1503–1507	Leo Africanus of Morocco explores the Sudan.
1508–1515	Portuguese colonize Mozambique.
1513–1517	Conquest of Hausa states by Songhai Empire; Negroes succeed Arabs, and form Hausa Confederation to carry on prosperous trade (West Africa).

Brass figurines representing West African "juju men."

Date	Event
1562	England's Sir John Hawkins plays active role in slave trade between Africa and the Americas.
1571–1603	Zenith of Kanem (Bornu) Empire in Lake Chad region, West Africa.
1590–1618	Defeat of Songhai by Moroccans who gain control over much of West Africa.
1618	Pedro Paez of Spain discovers the source of the Blue Nile in Ethiopia.
1652	Founding by the Dutch of Cape Town, South Africa.
1660	Rise of the Bambara Kingdom in Niger (West Africa).
1672	Founding in England of the Royal Africa Company for the cultivation of trade in West Africa.
1697–1893	Rise of Ashanti Kingdom (noted for its high-quality gold work) in what is now Ghana.
1713	Asiento Treaty enables British to monopolize slave trade to Latin America.
1787	Great Britain acquires Sierra Leone (West Africa) through treaties with local chieftains.
1795	England's Mungo Park explores Gambia, the Niger River regions, and the interior of West Africa.
1807	Great Britain abolishes the slave trade.
1808	Sierra Leone becomes a British Crown Colony, with Gambia falling under its administration.
1814	Great Britain secures possession of the Cape of Good Hope through the Peace of Paris.
1815	France, Spain and Portugal abolish the slave trade.
1821	Sierra Leone, Gold Coast and Gambia are united to form British West Africa.
1822–1827	Hugh Clapperton and Dixon Denham explore the Sudan, Nigeria, and other territories in West Africa.
1827	René Caillié of France reaches Timbuktu.
1835–1837	The Great Boer Trek from the Cape Colony to the Transvaal (South Africa).
1840–1870	Dr. David Livingstone explores Central Africa, discovering Lakes Ngami and Nyasa, and reaching the Upper Zambezi River.
1845–1855	Heinrich Barth of Germany leads scientific expeditions into the Sahara and the Sudan.
1847	Liberia becomes the first independent republic in Africa.
1858	Richard Burton and John Speke of England discover Lake Tanganyika.
1861–1864	Samuel Baker of England discovers Lake Albert and Murchison Falls; also explores the Nile's tributaries in Ethiopia.
1867–1871	The discovery of diamonds in South Africa, with Kimberly becoming the center of the diamond industry and the mecca for fortune hunters.
1869	Gustav Nachtigal of Germany explores the central Sahara.
1871	Great Britain annexes the Orange Free State (South Africa).
1873–1874	Great Britain conquers the Ashanti Kingdom of the Gold Coast region.
1874–1889	Henry Morton Stanley explores the Congo River from its source to its mouth.
1875–1883	Pierre de Brazza of France explores southern and western Africa; founds Brazzaville.

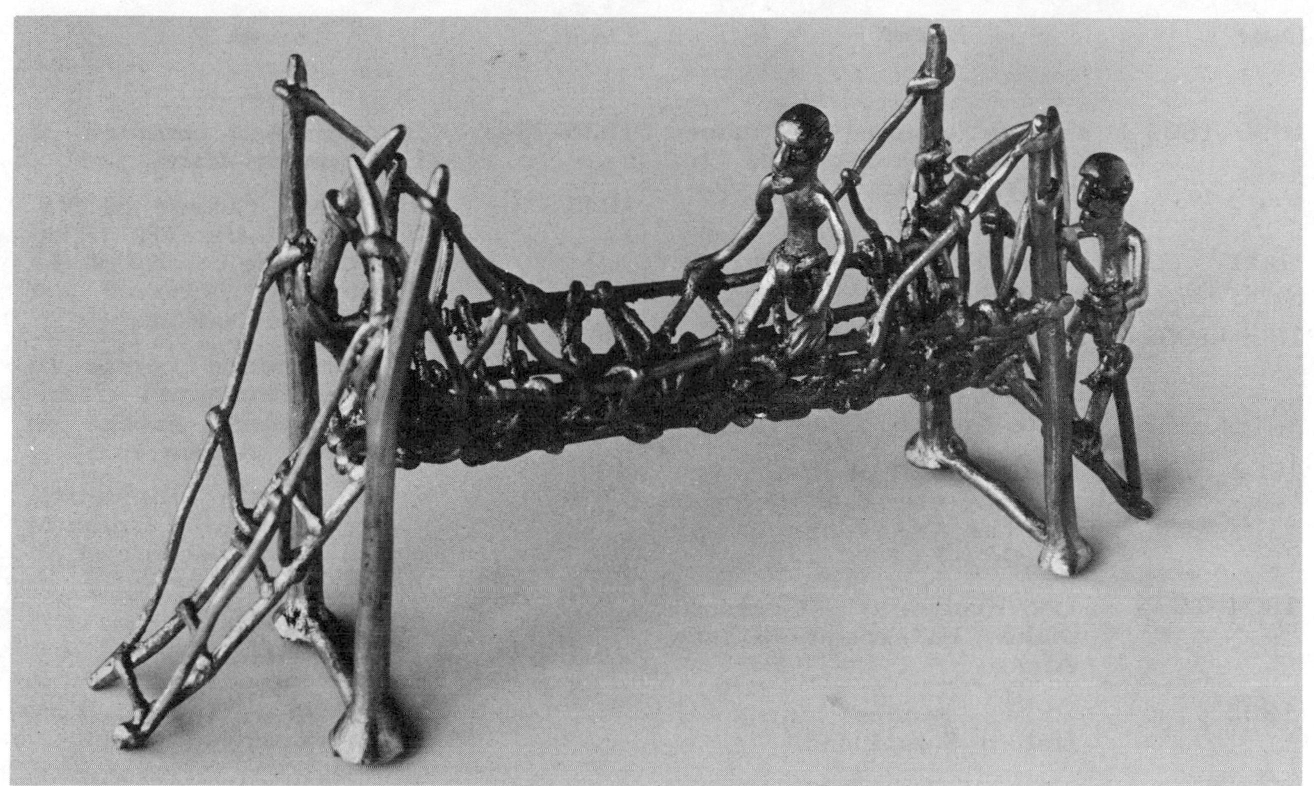

A miniature of a swinging suspension bridge, typical of Camerounian art in West Africa.

Date	Event
1876	Exploitation of the Congo begins under King Léopold II of Belgium.
1877	Annexation of the Transvaal (South Africa) by Great Britain.
1878–1890	Emin Pasha (Eduard Schnitzer) of Germany explores Central Africa.
1879	Outbreak of the British-Zulu war, with British winning decisive victory at Ulundi.
1880	Founding of Brazzaville in the Congo by France.
1881	Tunisia accepts status as French protectorate (Treaty of Bardo).
1884	Germany annexes Southwest Africa; also establishes control over Cameroons and Togoland.
1885	Germany proclaims a protectorate over Tanganyika.

Date	Event
1886	Gold rush to Witwatersrand in southern Transvaal (South Africa).
1888	Formation of the British East Africa Company.
1889	Germany relinquishes its claim on Uganda to Great Britain.
1890–1897	Cecil Rhodes, British diamond tycoon, becomes leading empire-builder in Africa.
1893	Great Britain establishes protectorate over Ashanti Kingdom (West Africa) and Nyasaland (Central Africa).
1896	Ethiopian forces, victorious in the Battle of Adua, force Italy to withdraw from Ethiopia.
1896–1925	Carl E. Ackley of the United States explores various parts of Africa.

Date	*Event*
1898–1899	France assigns the name "French West Africa" to its West African possessions.
1899	Nigeria becomes a British protectorate.
1899–1902	Great Britain defeats the Boers in South Africa; annexes the Orange Free State and the Transvaal.
1902	Louis Gentil of France explores portions of Morocco and the Atlas Mountains of North Africa.
1904–1935	Leo Frobenius of Germany makes 12 expeditions into Africa.
1905	Italy assumes control of Italian Somaliland.
1908	Belgium annexes the Congo Free State.
1910	Formation of the Union of South Africa (composed of Cape of Good Hope and Natal provinces, Transvaal and Orange Free State), with Louis Botha as first premier.
1911	Annexation of Libya by Italy.
1912	Partition of Africa completed (only Ethiopia and Liberia independent).
1914	France and Great Britain conquer German colonies of Togo and Cameroons.
1923	Rhodesia (named after Cecil B. Rhodes) is divided into Northern and Southern Rhodesia.
1926	Firestone Rubber Company purchases one million acres of land in Liberia to be used in the development of rubber plantations.
1930	Haile Selassie I is crowned as Emperor of Ethiopia.

Date	*Event*
1935–1942	Invasion and conquest of Ethiopia by Italy.
1945	Mandated League of Nations territories are transferred to the control of the Trusteeship Council of the United Nations.
1945–1966	**Independence comes to Africa; European domination ends, except in Southern Africa.**
1946	India breaks diplomatic relations with the Union of South Africa because of alleged mistreatment of its Indian minority.
1948	D. F. Malan and the National Party elected in South Africa on apartheid platform.
1950	Seretse Khama sent into exile from Bechuanaland.
1952	Independence for Libya (North Africa).
1952–1960	Mau-Mau violence in Kenya (East Africa).
1953	Egypt proclaims itself a republic.
1954	Revolt begins in Algeria.
1956	Tunisia and Morocco gain independence from France.
1956	Sudan proclaims itself a republic.
1957	Ghana becomes first independent "black dominion" in the British Commonwealth.
1958	First conference of independent African states convenes in Accra, Ghana.
1958	Arch supporter of apartheid, Henrik Verwoerd, is elected Prime Minister of South Africa.
1958	Guinea votes for independence from France; rest of French West Africa joins French Community.

Date	*Event*
1960	**Independence for Cameroun, Togo, Malagasy Republic, Congo (Léopoldville), Somali Republic, Dahomey, Niger, Upper Volta, Ivory Coast, Chad, Central African Republic, Congo (Brazzaville), Gabon, Senegal, Mali, Nigeria, and Mauritania.**
1960–1963	**Tribal war and anarchy prevail in the Congo until United Nations forces restore order; Premier Patrice Lumumba assassinated.**
1961	**Independence for Tanganyika.**
1961	**Death of Dag Hammarskjold, Secretary-General of the UN, in a plane crash in Northern Rhodesia.**
1961	**Sierra Leone becomes independent within the British Commonwealth.**
1962	**Independence for Algeria, Burundi, Rwanda, and Uganda.**
1963	**Independence for Kenya (with Jomo Kenyatta as prime minister) and Zanzibar.**
1964	**Independence for Malawi and Zambia.**
1964	**Tanzania (composed of Tanganyika and Zanzibar) united under Julius Nyerere.**
1964	**Moise Tshombe named premier of Congo.**
1965	**Independence for Gambia.**
1965	**Ahmed Ben Bella overthrown in Algeria by Colonel Houari Boumedienne.**
1965	**General Joseph Mobutu seizes power in Congo (Léopoldville); General Christophe Soglo ousts Sourou Migan-Apithy in Dahomey.**
1965	**Rhodesia declares unilateral independence from Great Britain.**
1966	**Colonel Jean-Bedel Bokassa overthrows President David Dacko of the Central African Republic; Lt. Col. Sangoule Lamizane seizes power in Upper Volta.**
1966	**Assassination of Abubakar Tafawa Balewa, chief of state in Nigeria; General Aguiyi Ironsi heads caretaker military government.**
1966	**Kwame Nkrumah overthrown in Ghana by Sandhurst-trained officers under the leadership of General Joseph A. Ankrah.**
1966	**Assassination of South African premier, Henrik Verwoerd.**
1966	**Independence for Basutoland (Lesotho) and for Bechuanaland (Botswana). Lesotho is ruled by Premier Leabua Jonathan, whereas Botswana has as its prime minister Seretse Khama.**
1967	**Congolese President Joseph Mobutu nationalizes the Union Minière du Haut-Katanga, the Belgian mining concern which produces three-fourths of the nation's mineral exports, and accounts for nearly one-half of his government's revenues. The company on the other hand, withholds more than 10 million dollars in royalties, and suspends its tax payments which normally run some two million dollars per month.**

Date	*Event*
1969	A new Rhodesian constitution severs all ties with Great Britain and institutionalizes white minority rule and racial supremacy for an indefinite period.
1969	Kenya's Economic Planning Commissioner Tom Mboya is assassinated in Nairobi, sparking sporadic clashes between Luo tribesmen and members of the Kikuyu.
1970	Two and a half years of civil war in Nigeria ends with the capitulation of the Biafran secessionists to federal authorities in Lagos. At the time of the surrender, Biafra has shrunk to a 3,000-square-mile area with a population of three million. On May 30, 1967, at the time it declared its independence, Biafra consisted of a 30,000 - square - mile area peopled by 14 million tribesmen, most of them Ibos. Announcement of the surrender is made by Maj. Gen. Philip Effiong, successor to Odumegwu Ojukwu who has fled the country. In an attempt to scotch rumors of an impending bloodbath, Nigerian commander Major General Yakubu Gowon declares a general amnesty "for all those misled into attempting to disintegrate the country." Gowon calls the surrender "one of the greatest moments in the history of our nation, a great moment of victory for unity and national reconciliation." As he talks, a million Biafran refugees search the scorched and barren countryside for food and shelter, victims of the political struggle which has caused widespread famine and mass starvation. Relief offers are rejected from nations deemed hostile by General Gowon, but the general expresses "warm appreciation" for U.S. and British gestures. Withal, Biafra remains etched in the memory of Western man as a grim chapter of human horror and barbarism, a reminder that not even the cries of innocent children for food will prevent men from clashing doggedly over divergent points of view.

Major Gen. Yakubu Gowon

Odumegwu Ojukwu

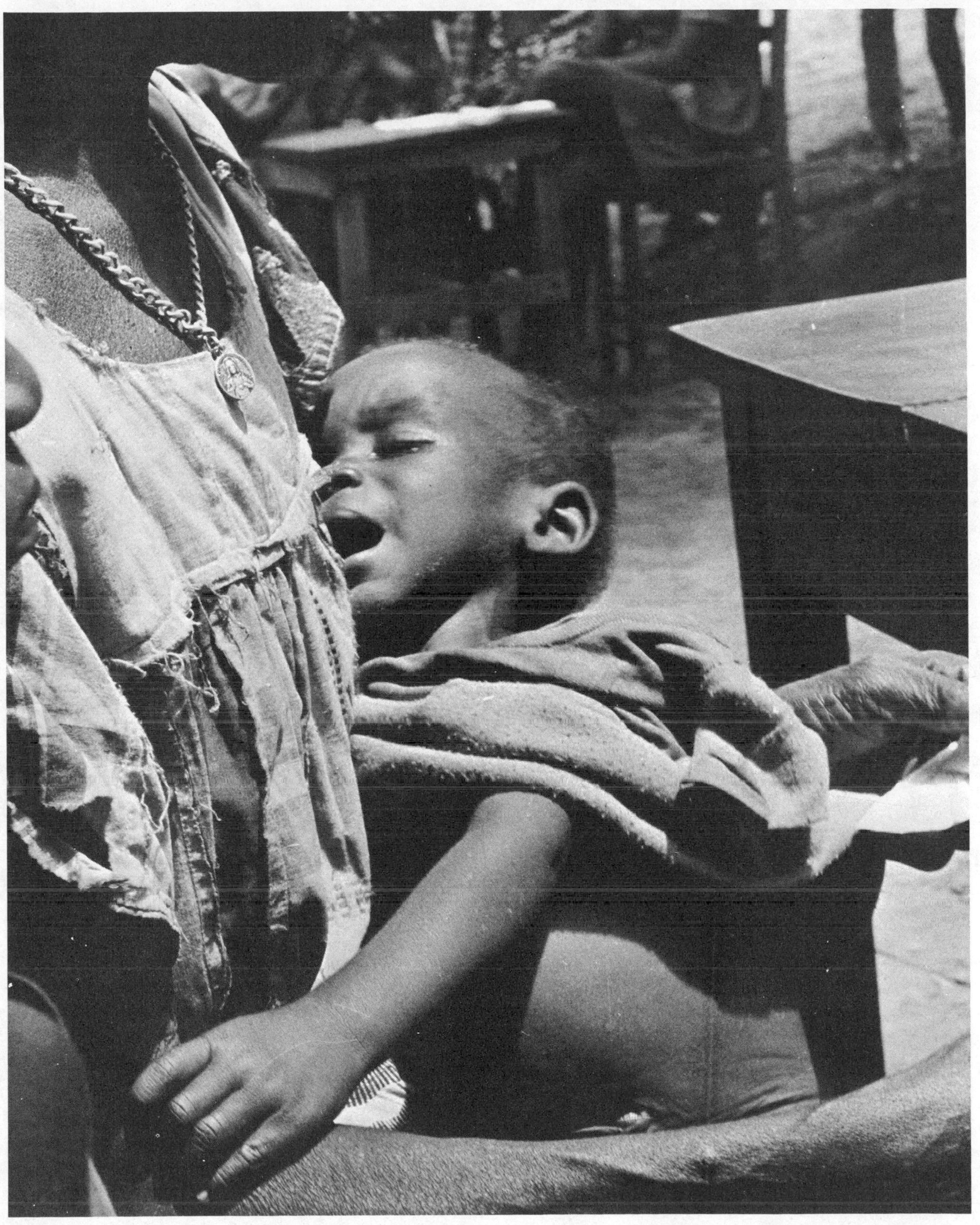

The price of civil war in Biafra

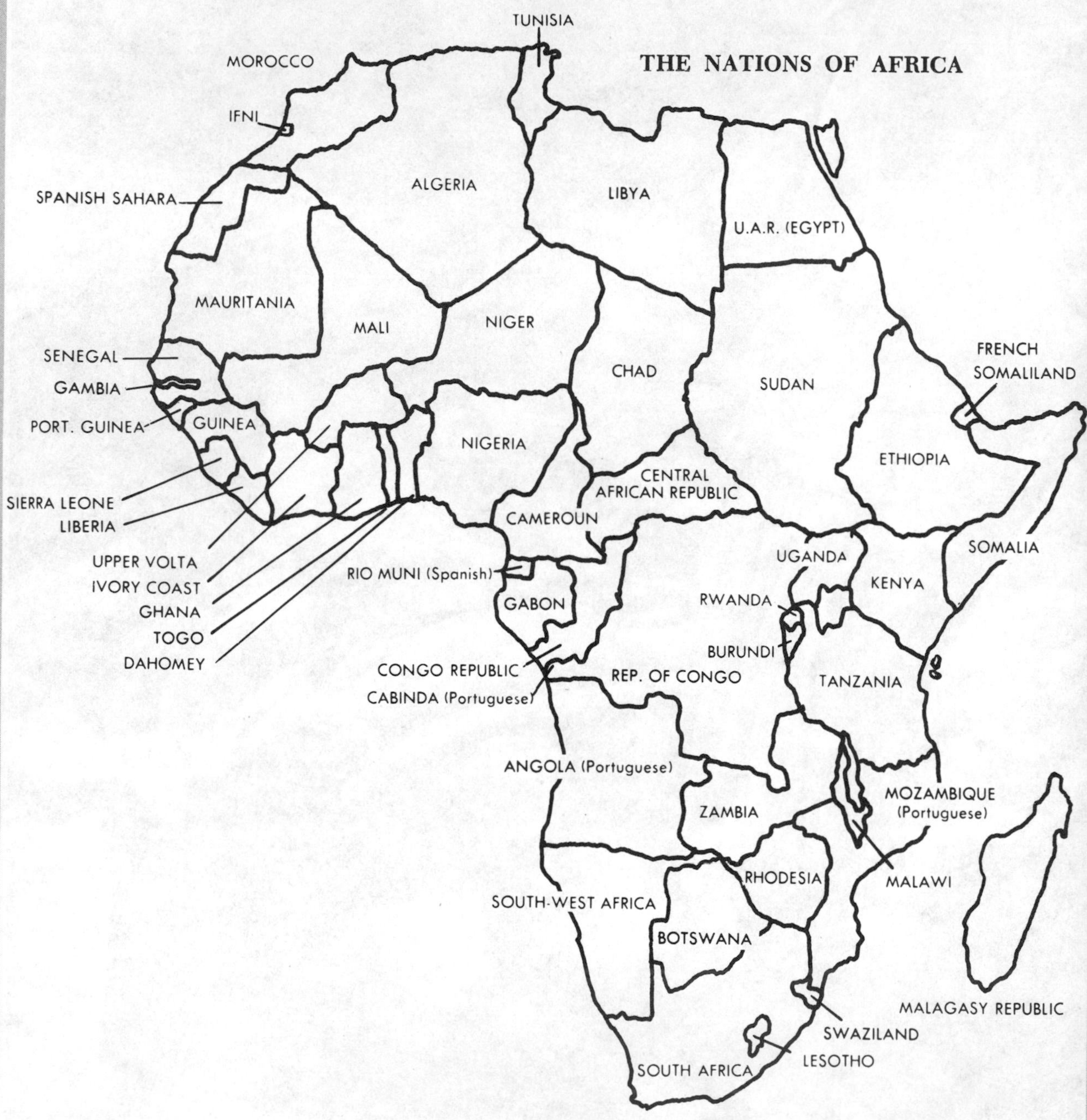
THE NATIONS OF AFRICA
TUNISIA
MOROCCO
IFNI
SPANISH SAHARA
ALGERIA
LIBYA
U.A.R. (EGYPT)
MAURITANIA
MALI
NIGER
CHAD
SUDAN
FRENCH
SOMALILAND
SENEGAL
GAMBIA
PORT. GUINEA
GUINEA
NIGERIA
ETHIOPIA
SIERRA LEONE
LIBERIA
CENTRAL
AFRICAN REPUBLIC
CAMEROUN
SOMALIA
UPPER VOLTA
IVORY COAST
GHANA
TOGO
DAHOMEY
RIO MUNI (Spanish)
UGANDA
KENYA
GABON
RWANDA
BURUNDI
CONGO REPUBLIC
CABINDA (Portuguese)
REP. OF CONGO
TANZANIA
ANGOLA (Portuguese)
ZAMBIA
MOZAMBIQUE
(Portuguese)
RHODESIA
MALAWI
SOUTH-WEST AFRICA
BOTSWANA
MALAGASY REPUBLIC
SWAZILAND
LESOTHO
SOUTH AFRICA

NATION: ALGERIA

Date of Independence: July 3, 1962
Area: 919,593 square miles
Population: 11,600,000
Capital: Algiers
Monetary Unit: The Algerian franc
Principal economic resources: oil, grapes, citrus fruits
Languages: French, Arabic
History at a glance:

Algeria (ancient Numidia) did not begin to exist as a unified territory until 1848, at which time the French finally subdued the Berber inhabitants from whom they had originally taken much of the fertile land along the coastal area. (Before this, Algeria had been ruled by Carthage, Rome, and a succession of Arab invaders, the most powerful of whom had established a Moorish empire uniting Algeria with Morocco and Spain.)

Effective control of Berber outposts in the Sahara region was not achieved by the French until the first decade of the 20th century. During World War II, many Algerian nationalists cooperated with the Allies in the hope of gaining a greater degree of self-autonomy. Having failed in this, a group of discontented factions united in 1954 under the banner of two revolutionary associations: the *Front de Liberation Nationale* (FLN) and the *Mouvement Nationale Algérien* (MNA). Both groups, though at odds with each other, began to undermine French interests in the territory—first by terrorism and subversion and, ultimately, by open revolt.

Politically, this revolt was instrumental in bringing about the fall of the Fourth French Republic in 1958 and the rise to power of Charles De Gaulle, hero of the French resistance during World War II and the man to whom the army and the *colons* (European colonists in Algeria) looked to as their savior. This group, which centralized its opposition to the Algerian nationalists in the Secret Army Organization (OAS), eventually (though unsuccessfully) sought to overthrow De Gaulle when he advocated negotiations with the FLN and self-determination for Algeria. Ultimately, the following choices were open to the rebels: absolute independence (with no ties to the mother country); incorporation into France as an overseas province, or federal autonomy involving closer ties with France. Algeria chose self-determination in a 1961 referendum and, a year later, voted for the third of the above alternatives.

A cease-fire was achieved in 1962, followed by the formation of a sovereign state headed by Premier Youssef Ben Khedda. He in turn was overthrown by a military coup d'etat which supported Ahmed Ben Bella, then vice-premier. Elected on a single-party slate in 1962, Ben Bella announced that Algeria would follow a socialist course of development, with a non-aligned foreign policy.

In 1965, Ben Bella was deposed in a bloodless, army-backed coup by Colonel Houari Boumedienne, now president and defense minister.

Algeria today is under the control of a 24-man Revolutionary Council, composed chiefly of active army officers. Colonel Boumediene heads the civilian cabinet, but it lacks decision-making authority. The country had made only modest economic strides since Ben Bella's ouster. It has of late revised its nationalization program to allow many small businesses to revert back to the hands of former owners.

NATION: BOTSWANA

Area: 238,605 square miles
Population: 629,000
Capital: Gaborone
Monetary Unit: The South African rand
Principal economic resources: livestock, asbestos, gold, silver
Language: English
History at a glance:

Bechuanaland became a British protectorate in 1885 at the request of Bechuana chieftains who sought protection against the Boers. Its boundaries were defined in 1891.

In March of 1965, Bechuanaland ceased to have the status of a high-commission territory, and was granted internal self-government. Since achieving independence, Botswana has been a constitutional democracy headed by Seretse Khama, who serves as chief executive and head of the armed forces.

Poor and landlocked, Botswana has been reliant on outside assistance to shore up its economy, but recent mineral discoveries may brighten the economic picture somewhat. Until the country develops a stronger economic position, however, there is little likelihood that Khama will alter his basic policy of peaceful accommodation with neighboring South Africa, whose racial policies he particularly deplores (Khama is married to a white woman), but cannot as yet hope to reverse.

NATION: **BURUNDI**
Date of Independence: July 1, 1962
Area: 10,747 square miles
Population: 2,650,000
Capital: Bujumbura
Monetary Unit: The Burundi franc
Principal economic resources: coffee, palm oil, barley, wheat
Languages: French, Kirundi
History at a glance:

The early history of Burundi strongly parallels that of its northern neighbor, Rwanda. The first-known inhabitants of both regions were the Twa, a tribe of pygmy hunters who were gradually pushed back into the jungle by the agriculturally inclined Hutu, a Bantu people.

In the 15th century, the Tutsi (of Hamitic stock) entered the area from the northeast, establishing a caste-oriented feudal society. Headed by an omnipotent chieftain, or mwami, the Tutsi became the ruling class, and obliged the Hutu to tend the fields and produce food for everyone.

In 1858, the English explorers, John Speke and Richard Burton, became the first white men in the area when they crossed Burundi in search of the headwaters of the Nile River. Thirteen years later, Stanley and Livingstone landed at Usumbura, and explored the Ruzizi River region. Ultimately, however, it was the Germans who succeeded in consolidating control over the territory as a result of agreements reached with other major European powers at the Berlin Conference (1884-1885).

During World War I, Belgium replaced Germany as the power administering the territory. In 1923, the League of Nations formalized this arrangement by granting the Belgian king a special mandate over the combined territory of Ruanda-Urundi. This mandate remained operant until 1946, at which time the United Nations substituted a system of trusteeship.

By this time, it was clear that Ruanda and Urundi were developing along separate paths which would, without proper supervision, lead to a possible collision course. To the north, Ruanda seemed bent on a republican form of government; to the south, Urundi continued to favor a monarchical structure. In the 1961 elections, Urundi expressed its preference for a constitutional monarchy, headed by Prince Rwagasore, a son of the mwami. Later that same year, the prince was assassinated by rival nationalists.

The UN stepped into the ensuing power vacuum, recommending that a united Ruanda-Urundi declare itself independent by July 1, 1962. With one significant exception, the deadline and the conditions were met by both territories. Ruanda became the Republic of Rwanda; Urundi, the Kingdom of Burundi. Since then, however, outbreaks of violence between the Tutsi and Hutu tribes have flared up on several occasions, threatening to engulf both countries in what some experts believe could become a literal bloodbath.

Since 1962, internal upheaval has in fact disrupted Burundi and undermined the welfare of her people. A measure of encouraging self-control and harmony followed upon the elimination of the monarchy and the substitution of a republican government dedicated to peace, social equality and economic development. Head of state is Colonel Michel Micombero, a Watusi who has dedicated himself to ridding the country of class and tribal conflict.

NATION: **CAMEROUN**
Date of Independence: January 1, 1960
Area: 183,569 square miles
Population: 4,560,000
Capital: Yaoundé
Monetary Unit: The CFA franc
Principal economic resources: cocoa, coffee, cotton, bananas
Language: French
History at a glance:

The first European to explore any part of present-day Cameroun was Fernando Po, a Portuguese who arrived in the territory in 1472. (Po was followed by a number of Portuguese navigators who found the territory's main waterways overloaded with prawn, a crustacean known in their language as "camarãos.") Portuguese interests soon gave way to those of the English and the Germans, respectively.

Germany had already established trading posts and factories at various points along the West African coast before becoming interested in basing her African colonial empire in the Cameroun. Thus, in 1884, with the approval of England, she placed the territory under protectorate status. Prior to World War I, the Germans concentrated on developing the resources of the interior, cultivating banana and coffee plantations, building roads and railroads, and establishing a communications network.

During World War I, the German Cameroons (as they were then called) were seized by French, British and Belgian troops. In 1915, the territory known as "New Cameroons" (an additional portion which had been ceded to Germany by France in 1911) was returned to France, and incorporated into French Equatorial Africa. Later that year, the French and the British agreed to rule the rest of the territory jointly, pending a more formal agreement, which was reached in 1919 with the Treaty of Versailles. (New Cameroons remained part of French Equatorial Africa; the eastern sector became East Cameroun, while the western area adjoining Nigeria was dubbed British Cameroons.)

Between the two world wars, the French contributed significantly to the development of the territory's resources, although they did little to encourage the inhabitants to develop self-sustaining political institutions. In 1946, the territory was placed under international trusteeship, and the possibility of reunification became the paramount question to be resolved.

In 1957, France granted Cameroun full internal autonomy. A year later, the Camerounian Legislative Assembly voted to declare the territory independent by 1960, with Ahmadou Ahidjo as chief of state. During this same period, John Foncha emerged as the key figure behind the independence movement in the British Cameroons. After a short period of unrest culminating with the appearance of French troops in East Cameroun, a national assembly was elected, and Ahidjo was returned to office as president of the newly created Republic of Cameroun.

In 1961, the Northern British Cameroons were incorporated into the Republic of Nigeria as the Sarduana Province,

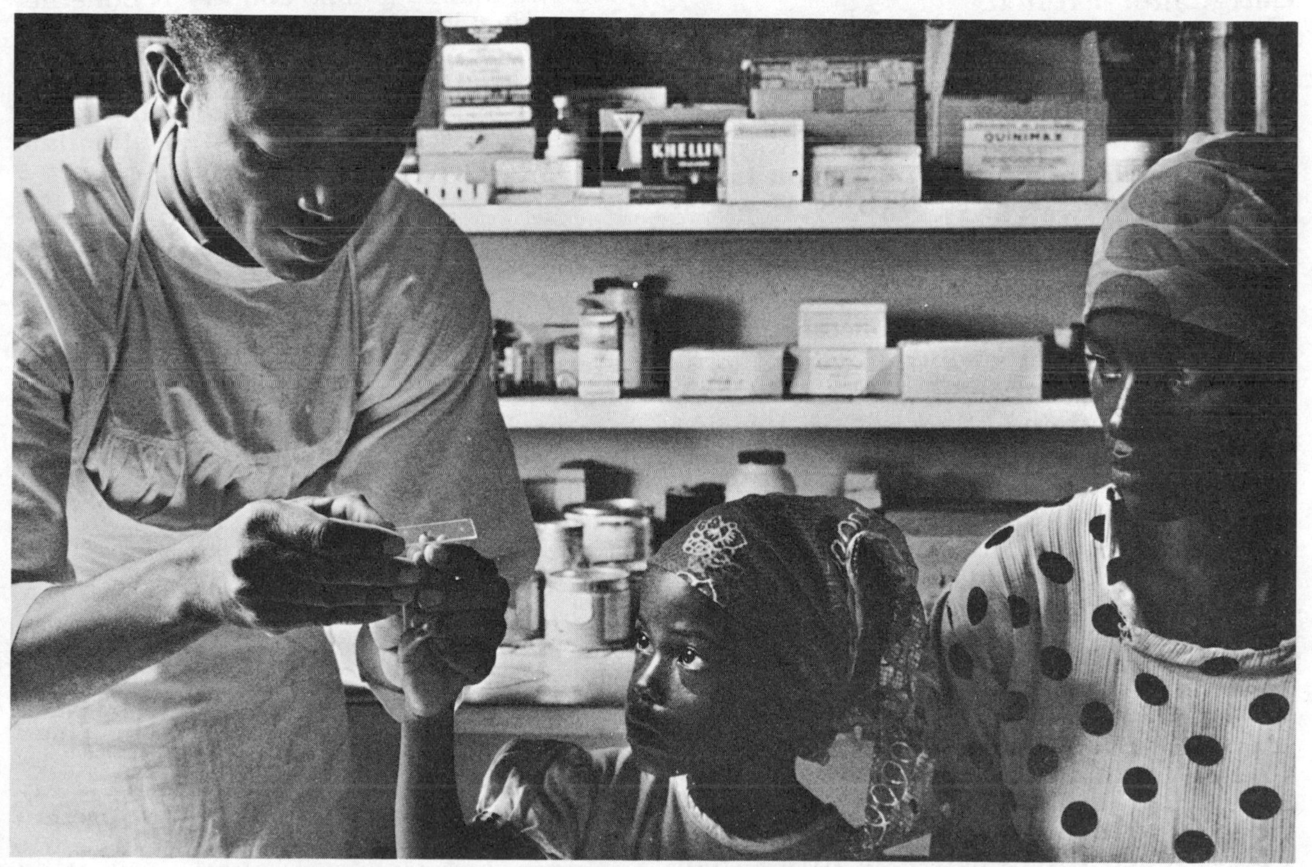

Improved medical facilities have been instrumental in eradicating malaria in the Cameroun. Here, a native girl s being given a blood test.

while the Southern British Cameroons joined the Cameroun Republic. After a constitution had finally been drafted and approved, the Cameroun Republic came into being as the combined states of East and West Cameroun. Ahidjo serves as president of the republic; Foncha, as vice-president.

Throughout the 1960's, Cameroun maintained close ties with France, its chief economic benefactor. Internationally, the country generally supports the Western bloc, although it has also signed economic and cultural agreements with the Soviet Union and its satellites.

NATION: CENTRAL AFRICAN REPUBLIC

Date of Independence: August 13, 1960
Area: 238,200 square miles
Population: 1,300,000
Capital: Bangui
Monetary Unit: The CFA franc
Principal economic resources: cotton, coffee, peanuts, diamonds, gold
Language: French

History at a glance:

The territory of what is now the landlocked Central African Republic was first settled by France in 1887 pursuant to the Berlin Conference (1884-1885) which had established French rights to all land lying beyond the right bank of the Congo River. Early French explorers of this region were particularly concerned with solidifying France's control over all territory between Brazzaville and Lake Chad. With this in mind, they set up the first French outpost of any major consequence at Bangui (the site of the present capital) in 1889. Within five years, the territory had become the French colony of Ubangi-Shari, a name derived from its two main rivers. In 1905, Ubangi-Shari was united with Chad and, five years later, became one of the four territories constituting French Equatorial Africa.

During both world wars, the territory was effectively utilized as a base for French military operations—in the first case, against the Germans in the Cameroons and then, in conjunction with the Free French forces active in Africa from 1940 to 1944.

Following World War II, Ubangi-Shari was granted a greater degree of autonomy, sending elected representatives to the French Senate and Chamber of Deputies in Paris. Under the 1946 constitution, all inhabitants of the region were officially designated as citizens of France. In 1958, Ubangi-Shari changed its name to the Central African Republic, and voted to join the French Community as an autonomous republic. Two years later, it voted for full independence with David Dacko as president.

Dacko introduced one-party rule and steered his regime toward a closer alignment with the government of Communist China. In 1964, this policy led to official recognition of the Chinese regime which, by then, had launched an ambitious program of economic aid in the Central African Republic.

Early in 1966, the Dacko regime was overthrown in a military coup d'etat led by Colonel Jean-Bedel Bokassa, now serving as head of an interim government with the announced intention of severing all ties with Communist China.

The Bokassa government has imposed balanced budgets, stable prices, and systematic planning. The country is nonetheless dependent on French aid to overcome its chronically unfavorable trade balance, but it is striving—through such facilities as a jet airport, an international hotel and resort and game facilities — to stimulate international tourism.

NATION: CHAD

Date of Independence: August 11, 1960
Area: 495,750 square miles
Population: 2,800,000
Capital: Fort Lamy
Monetary Unit: The CFA franc
Principal economic resources: cotton, groundnuts, fish
Language: French
History at a glance:

Ancient history records the existence of several African empires which flourished between the Niger River and the Upper Nile, particularly around the Lake Chad region. Both the Baguirmi and Wadai Empires are known to have held sway within the boundaries of the present Chadian republic. In the 14th century, Islamic invaders from North and West Africa penetrated as far south as Wadai, and used this land as a fertile hunting ground for the flourishing slave trade.

(One of the long-range results of this human exploitation has been the development of a deep-seated hostility between Chadian Negroes and their former Arab masters.)

Initial European contact with the territory dates back to 1822, although exploration did not begin in earnest until 1853. During the 1890's, the French pushed their way northwards from the Middle Congo region and, by 1897, had reached the shores of Lake Chad itself. Before the turn of the century, boundaries had been fixed between adjacent French, British and German territories in the area.

In 1910, Chad became one of the territories constituting French Equatorial Africa, but its economy developed slowly due to the lack of markets for its produce. By 1930, it was already being affected adversely by the onset of the world depression.

During World War II, the colony rallied to the side of the Free French and became an important staging area for Allied troops earmarked for battle on the North African front. As a reward for its loyalty, Chad was granted a greater degree of autonomy in 1946, and began sending elected representatives to the French National Assembly. In 1958, Chad became a member state of the French Community and, two years later, a fully independent republic with François Tombalbaye as chief of state.

Since he has been in office, Tombalbaye has attempted, with some success, to temper the antagonisms of the Moslem North and the pagan and Christian South. He has likewise found it expedient to maintain token French forces on Chadian soil, and to sign mutual cooperation agreements with France for the economic development of the country. Nonetheless, unlike France, Chad has refused to establish diplomatic relations with Red China.

Throughout the 1960's, Chad diversified its agriculture, particularly around Lake Chad, and moved to improve its industrial position as well. The country produces a sufficient supply of food—mainly grains, meat, and fish—to sustain the population.

NATION: **CONGO (BRAZZAVILLE)**
Date of Independence: August 15, 1960
Area: 132,046 square miles
Population: 1,000,000
Capital: Brazzaville
Monetary Unit: The CFA franc
Principal economic resources: palm products, timber

Language: French
History at a glance:

During the 16th century, the territory of today's Congo (Brazzaville) Republic was part of the so-called Congo Empire, which is believed to have extended as far south as Angola. Prior to this time, the sole Europeans in the area had been the Portuguese who discovered the mouth of the Congo River in 1484.

France established numerous trading companies during the 17th century, showing particular interest in slaves and ivory as items of commerce. Following the abolition of the slave trade, however, France undertook the exploration of the interior, a task hampered by its dense forests and barely navigable rivers. In 1880, a local chieftain signed a treaty with French explorer Pierre Savorgnan De Brazza, placing his domain under the protection of France. Five years later, the major European powers recognized French claims to the entire region lying beyond the right bank of the Congo River. In 1908, France installed a governor-general in Brazzaville, the present-day capital of the republic. Two years later, Middle Congo (as it was then called) was made a separate colony within the framework of French Equatorial Africa.

In 1940, Middle Congo joined Chad in declaring its support of the Free French forces under the leadership of Charles De Gaulle. During the war, it played a valuable strategic role in accommodating troops ultimately bound for combat in various parts of the Sahara Desert.

By 1956, Middle Congo had achieved full local autonomy. Two years later, it became an independent state within the French Community, changing its name to the Congo Republic. Fulbert Youlou, mayor of Brazzaville, was elected president in 1960, the same year the Congo opted for full independence. Youlou was deposed three years later in the wake of popular unrest following passage of a bill designed to institute one-party rule in the country.

Under Youlou's successor, Alphonse Massmba-Debat, the Congo cultivated close ties with Communist China, and sought to implement a national policy which Debat characterized as "scientific socialism." When Debat introduced Cuban advisers, however, utilizing them as a kind of private militia, the regular army staged a coup d'etat in 1968, installing President Marien Ngouabi as head of state.

NATION: **CONGO (Kinshasa)**
Date of Independence: June 30, 1960
Area: 905,562 square miles
Population: 15,007,000
Capital: Kinshasa (formerly Léopoldville)
Monetary Unit: The Congo franc
Principal economic resources: coffee, palm products, rubber, industrial diamonds, cobalt, uranium
Language: French
History at a glance:

The first known inhabitants of the Congo are believed to have been pygmy tribes who eventually came to be dominated by Bantu and Nilotic groups engaged in sedentary agriculture.

In 1482, the Portuguese explorer Diogo Cão visited the mouth of the Congo River, but penetration of the interior did not follow. The world became aware of the potential wealth of the territory only after Henry Stanley had made his fabled

Copper pits of the Union Miniere du Haut-Katanga, the combine which produces more than three-fourths of the Congo's total mining exports.

trip down the Congo River in 1877. Rumors of great riches induced King Léopold II of Belgium to commission Stanley to conduct further explorations, and to sign appropriate commercial treaties with local chieftains for access to the region. Within a year, Léopold had formed the International Association of the Congo, a development company in which he himself was the chief stockholder. At the Berlin Conference of 1884-1885, the major European powers recognized the Independent State of the Congo, with Léopold as its absolute monarch. However, a subsequent scandal concerning the treatment accorded Congolese mine and plantation workers was of such consequence that the king was forced to transfer his territory to Belgium in 1908. Rechristened the Belgian Congo, the territory was sufficiently stable to campaign against the Germans during World War I.

African nationalism did not emerge as a potent factor in the Congo for more than a decade after World War II had ended. The Congolese struck swiftly in their demands for independence, however. In 1959, rioting broke out in Léopoldville and soon spread to other parts of the territory. Belgium quickly indicated its willingness to establish a gradual, but specific, timetable for self-rule, but pressure from the Congolese eventually persuaded the Belgians to accept June 30, 1960 as the date for complete independence. At the time of the original agreements between both negotiating parties, it had been clearly established that Belgium would continue to provide technical and economic aid to the Congo *after* independence. Of even greater importance was the fact that Belgium was to assist in the training of Congolese administrators and politicians. (The Congolese had no national political organization apart from a conglomeration of over 200 minor groups split along religious, personal, tribal and regional lines.)

Independence on June 30, 1960 was followed by a complete collapse of national authority. Intertribal fighting broke out; secessionist movements gained momentum; the army dismissed its European officers and stood in open rebellion against the central government. Less than two weeks after independence, Moise Tshombe complicated matters even further by announcing the secession of the mineral-rich Katanga province. Even as this transpired, Belgian civil servants and professional men left the country *en masse,* thus creating an enormous vacuum in the government. Faced with chaos, the new republic quickly appealed to the United Nations, which responded with a massive aid program funneled through the hastily organized Fund for the Congo. The UN backed these measures with a multi-national armed force whose instructions were to avoid becoming embroiled in political and military controversies.

Politically, the initial struggle shaped up between the adherents of Patrice Lumumba, the Belgian-appointed first prime minister who advocated the creation of a strong centralized government, and the supporters of chief of state Joseph Kasavubu who favored a looser type federal system which allowed for a greater degree of provincial autonomy.

At one point, Lumumba and Kasavubu took turns dismissing each other, but parliament quickly rescinded both dismissals, only to see itself dismissed by Kasavubu whose military backers took Lumumba prisoner. Lumumba was then delivered into the hands of Katanga authorities who subsequently reported that he had been killed while trying to escape. (A UN investigating commission later disclosed that Lumumba had probably been put to death by a Belgian mercenary in the presence of Tshombe.) The UN then authorized its troops to use whatever force it deemed necessary to prevent renewed hostilities from breaking out.

In July of 1961, Cyrille Adoula, a moderate, was named premier. Adoula attempted to negotiate with Tshombe for the termination of Katanga's secession, an issue which involved the direct intervention of UN Secretary-General Dag Hammarskjold. (Hammarskjold was killed in an air crash in September of 1961 while en route to a meeting with Tshombe in Elisabethville.)

During the summer of 1962, the UN once again submitted reconciliation proposals to the disputing parties. It was not until the latter part of the year, however, that negotiators succeeded in convincing the reluctant Tshombe to end the secession of Katanga, and thus restore a measure of unity and stability to the country as a whole.

The followers of Patrice Lumumba, however, remained far from being pacified. Across the Congo River, in the Brazzaville Republic, they set up a self-styled "government in exile," headed by Christophe Gbenye. Guerrilla action and other

Fishing with a cast-net on the Niger River, Mali

subversive tactics soon spread to the eastern part of the Congo. Through its embassy in the tiny Kingdom of Burundi, Communist China gave the rebels substantial backing, whereas the Soviet Union began to funnel arms and other provisions to the rebels through Algeria and Egypt. Incidents of butchery and pillaging grew in number and severity; missionaries were slain; innocent civilians indiscriminately slaughtered.

In the summer of 1964, Tshombe returned to the Congo and was quickly sworn in as the nation's new premier. Within a short time, however, Stanleyville had fallen to the rebels, who consolidated their control over much of the eastern territory. Congo forces, aided by Belgian mercenaries, succeeded in stemming the tide toward the end of the year, at which time Belgian paratroopers liberated Stanleyville and rescued most of the white hostages being held there. Communist-bloc nations, as well as several other African and non-aligned countries, were quick to denounce the joint U.S.-Belgian action.

Within the year, Tshombe had once again been ousted from office—this time by President Joseph Kasavubu who installed Evariste Kimba (slain since then) as premier. The Kasavubu-Tshombe rivalry, however, had been closely watched by Colonel Joseph Mobutu, head of the army. In December of 1965, Mobutu deposed Kasavubu, canceled the scheduled presidential elections and installed himself as head of a "regime of exception" for a five-year term.

Early in 1966, Mobutu threatened to dissolve parliament if it attempted to nullify any of the ordinances which he had decreed upon seizing power. Mobutu made clear his intention to take the country out of the hands of contending politicians—at least for a time.

In 1969, when trouble erupted at the University of Lovanium, Mobutu curtailed his involvement with regional associations concerned with the rest of Africa, choosing instead to consolidate his power at home and keep in touch with internal political developments. As a result, he dismissed his popular foreign minister Justin Bomboko, replacing him with former premier Cyrille Adoula, considered a less ambitious and energetic politician. Mobutu has since visited the United States, and conferred with President Nixon regarding prospects for strengthening Union Miniere, the huge Belgian mining complex which has been nationalized.

NATION: **DAHOMEY**

Date of Independence: August 1, 1960

Area: 44,290 square miles

Population: 2,250,000

Capital: Porto Novo

Monetary Unit: The CFA franc

Principal economic resources: palm products and groundnuts

Language: French

History at a glance:

Long before the Portuguese arrived in the 16th century, the modern nation of Dahomey was already heir to a long and proud tradition—replete with mighty armies, glittering cities, and lavish palaces. At the height of its power, Dahomey (then much larger than it is today) exchanged ambassadors with the French court of King Louis XIV.

The Portuguese (who discovered Dahomey's ancient capital of Abomey) were soon followed by the Dutch, English, French and Spanish, all of whom shared a common interest: the slave trade.

In the 19th century, the French eventually emerged the victors over their competitors, and imposed protectorate status on the territory. In 1902, Dahomey was made part of the Federation of French West Africa. The territory's first real stride toward independence occurred under the constitution of 1946 when, as an overseas member of the French Union, it won the right to send representatives to the Chamber of Deputies in Paris. By 1952, a territorial assembly had been established. Four years later, under the *loi-cadre* (the Enabling Act which gave most French West African territories a greater share in self-government), universal suffrage was instituted.

Dahomey accepted French President Charles De Gaulle's constitution of 1958, and proclaimed itself an autonomous republic, with full membership in the French Community. Two years later, Dahomey opted for full independence, with Hubert Maga as president. The Maga government itself soon fell as a result of a wave of labor unrest which swept the country, and was temporarily replaced by a caretaker military regime headed by Colonel Christophe Soglo. An election in 1964 established Sourou Migan-Apithy as president of the republic.

Soglo, now a general, overthrew Apithy in 1965. When conditions did not improve, Emile-Derlin Zinsou assumed office as head of a new civilian administration three years later. Nominated by a military regime, Zinsou was approved as chief of state after a nationwide referendum.

NATION: **EQUATORIAL GUINEA**
(consisting of Rio Muni, Fernando Poo and Annobon)

Area: 10,830 square miles

Population: 286,000

Capital: Santa Isabel

Principal economic resources: coffee, cocoa, bananas

Language: Spanish, Fang

History at a glance:

Fernando Póo was discovered by Fernao de Po of Portugal in 1471, at which time it was given the name Formosa. (Annobón, an island lying some 400 miles to the southwest, was discovered a year later.) Portugal ceded both islands to Spain in 1778. From 1827 to 1843, Great Britain received permission from Spain to use Fernando Póo as a base for hunting down slave-runners. During this period, a number of Sierra Leonean Creoles and West Indian Maroons were liberated on the island. In 1904, Fernando Póo and Río Muni became known as the West African Territories and, later, as Spanish Guinea. This territory acquired the status of a province in 1960. *Río Muni* was ceded to Spain by Portugal in 1778 and reconfirmed as a Spanish possession at the Berlin Conference (1884-1885). Spain, however, did not take over its administration until about 1900.

Equatorial Guinea gained its independence from Spain in 1968, but it has been unable to sever economic ties with the former colonial power, not only due to tribal differences which militate against political stability, but also due to the inexperience of the country's new leadership.

President Francisco Macias Nguema is still largely dependent on Spain's willingness to accept more than 90% of the nation's foreign exports, and is likewise forced to depend on Spanish economic generosity to overcome national deficits. The 6,000 or so Spanish colonists have fared well in the country, and hold the key, for the moment at least, to the administrative stability of the nation.

NATION: **ETHIOPIA**
Area: 457,266 square miles
Population: 22,000,000
Capital: Addis Ababa
Monetary Unit: The Ethiopian dollar
Principal economic resources: coffee, tobacco, livestock, spices, quat, civet
Language: Amharic
History at a glance:

Ethiopia is easily one of the oldest nations in the world, and certainly the oldest in Africa south of the Sahara Desert. Its original settlers, the Cushites, were descendants of the Galla and Sidama tribes which occupied the territory prior to 1,000 B.C. From the 10th to the 7th centuries B.C., Semitic peoples from southern Arabia entered Ethiopia, and it is their offspring which became the lineal descendants of the Amhara and Tigrai tribes found there today. In the writings of the 5th century B.C. Greek historian Herodotus, one encounters a reference to the Ethiopians as "the most just men" and, even in Homer, they are spoken of as the "blameless race."

Traditionally, Menelik, the first son of King Solomon and the Queen of Sheba, is regarded as the founder of the Ethiopian Empire, which is said to date back to 1,000 B.C. The earliest authenticated history of the area describes Ethiopia as a pagan empire with its capital at Axum.

Christianity was first introduced in the 4th century A.D., and survived the onslaughts of Moslem hordes which in the 7th century imposed the religion of Islam on northeastern Africa. For a time, the Axum dynasty fell into decline and was even seriously threatened with extinction by the Zagwe dynasty which was founded by Takla Haimanot. In 1260, with the accession of Yekumo Amlak, the Axum line was restored and the reputed link with Solomon re-established. Emperor Amda Seyon I later imposed Ethiopian rule over the Moslem principalities which had sprung up to the east and south.

In the 16th century, however, Moslem power reasserted itself when the Somalis (with the aid of the Ottoman Turks) began a holy war that threatened to engulf the entire kingdom. Though the Ethiopians received some help from Portugal, they were saved largely due to the heroic exploits of their legendary emperor, Prester John.

The next three centuries, characterized by anarchy, cultural decadence, religious controversy, and other divisive influences, resulted in the partitioning of Ethiopia by a number of rival pretenders to the throne. Allegiance to a central government was not rekindled until 1855 when the Emperor Theodore II, himself a onetime petty chieftain, succeeded in subjugating a number of other dissident chieftains. However, when Theodore committed suicide in 1869, the country was once again plunged into internal strife.

In 1885, Italy capitalized on the discordant situation by capturing the seaport of Massawa, thus gaining a secure foothold in Eritrea. Menelik II, one of Ethiopia's great reform emperors, thereupon signed a face-saving treaty with Italy, maintaining that it was with his approval that a protectorate was being established over the country. However, Italy attempted to force the issue even further (to total conquest) by launching an invasion in 1895, but she was forced to withdraw after having suffered a humiliating defeat.

Menelik II turned his energies to the development of the interior of his country—building a rail line, establishing more schools, improving communications and introducing postal service. After the death of Menelik in 1913, his successor Lij Yassu embraced the Moslem faith—a gesture which led to his being deposed by Ras Tafari Menkonnen, a grandnephew of Menelik. Later Ras (prince) Tafari made Judith (Lij Yassu's aunt) empress, and assumed the role of regent until her death in 1930. He was then crowned as emperor in his own right, and ascended the throne as Haile Selassie I, the Lion of Judah.

Five years later, with the invasion of Ethiopia by Italy, he was forced to flee his country. His plea for international intervention, aired before the League of Nations, went largely unheeded, and he then took up his exile in Great Britain. On May 5, 1941, however, he triumphantly re-entered Addis Ababa at the head of a liberating army and was restored to his throne.

In 1952, with the approval of the UN, Eritrea was linked to Ethiopia as a federated state. (Ten years later, though, its status was changed to that of an Ethiopian province.)

During the post-war period, Ethiopia has modernized its institutions somewhat. A liberalized constitution has been put into effect, and Haile Selassie himself has attempted to function as a kind of moderating influence between firebrand African nationalists on the one hand, and the last heirs to the European colonial tradition on the other.

In Ethiopia itself, a coup d'etat was attempted in 1960 by members of the Imperial Guard under the leadership of Crown Prince Asfa Wassan. The revolt was quickly crushed, and its chief leaders (with the exception of the Crown Prince, the emperor's son) were executed.

Throughout the 1960's, Ethiopia has striven to establish itself as a political headquarters and cultural center for the rest of emergent Africa. This is symbolized in the pride of Addis Ababa, the imposing edifice known as Africa Hall, headquarters of the Organization of African Unity and the United Nations Economic Commission for Africa.

NATION: **GABON**
Date of Independence: August 17, 1960
Area: 103,089 square miles
Population: 456,000
Capital: Libreville
Monetary Unit: The CFA franc
Principal economic resources: gold, oil, lumber
Language: French
History at a glance:

The first Europeans to visit and explore the territory of Gabon were the Portuguese, who arrived toward the end of the 15th century and established trading posts at the mouth of the Ogowe River. French missionaries followed soon after, only to be succeeded by groups of European slave traders.

By 1815, the slave trade had been abolished, thus obliging the French to concentrate their energies on the exploitation of the territory's other resources, notably her forests. This policy brought about the development of several coastal ports, and the signing of a number of treaties with local rulers. The French agreed to protect the interests of these chieftains in return for access to the regions they controlled.

At the Congress of Berlin (1884-1885), the major European powers agreed to recognize French control over the land lying beyond the right bank of the Congo River (subsequently known as the French Congo). Five years later, Gabon became a part of this region, although it did not come to exist as a distinct administrative entity until 1893. In 1910, it achieved colonial status within what was then called French Equatorial Africa.

After World War II, Gabon was made an Overseas Territory of the French Union, and given the right to be represented in the French Parliament by a senator and a deputy of its own choice. In 1958, the colony voted to become fully autonomous within the framework of the French Community and, two years later, declared itself a fully independent republic, with Léon M'Ba as premier.

M'Ba was returned to office a year later, this time with the title of president of Gabon. In 1964, the Gabonese army temporarily overthrew the government, but the deposed M'Ba was reinstated by French President Charles De Gaulle who ordered French troops airlifted into Libreville to quell the rebellion.

In 1967, M'ba died, and was replaced by Albert-Bernard Bongo, who had been elected vice president in the spring of that year. Political stability has insured Gabon's continuing economic growth. Her mineral riches, her timber wealth, and her industrial expansion are bringing most Gabonese closer to a solid measure of economic security.

NATION: **GAMBIA**
Date of Independence: February 18, 1965
Area: 4,003 square miles

Population: 320,000
Capital: Bathurst
Monetary Unit: The Gambian pound
Principal economic resources: groundnuts
Language: English
History at a glance:

The first reference to Gambia in the historical records of antiquity occurs in the reports of voyages made by such Carthaginian explorers as Hanno, whose writings lend support to the theory that an entrance was made into the Gambian estuary as far back as 450 B.C. Modern-day archeologists are striving to establish some link between the Stone Circles found in the territory and the Carthaginian seafarers believed to have explored the region.

The first Europeans to set foot in Gambia were led by Alvise de Cadamosto and Antoniotto Usodimare, both of whom were in the service of Portugal's Prince Henry the Navigator (1455).

Later, Gambia became part of England's ambitious colonization schemes for West Africa, with a settlement being founded at Fort James, a small island some 20 miles from the mouth of the Gambia River. English merchants in increasing numbers were granted royal charters to trade in West Africa, often competing with their French counterparts. Not until the Treaty of Versailles (1783) did the English establish a clear-cut priority in the area.

In 1821, Gambia was placed under the control of a British colonial administration based in Sierra Leone. It did not finally become a colony in its own right until 1888, at which time it was provided with its own governor and legislative and executive councils.

Gambia's path to independence in the 20th century was a peaceful and gradual one. The nation's present constitution was introduced in 1960, and established a representative assembly headed by a chief minister. Modeling its governmental institutions on those of Great Britain, Gambia achieved final independence on February 18, 1965, with David K. Jawara as prime minister. On the first anniversary of its independence, Gambia opted for a republican form of government, thus becoming the smallest nation on the whole of the African continent.

Gambia has avoided the extravagant and, at times, grandiose economic projects which have brought some of her more famous neighbors to the brink of financial ruin. Careful and deliberate, the tiny country has met its budget in the past few years, and staked out realistic, rather than improbable, goals.

NATION: GHANA

Date of Independence: March 6, 1957
Area: 91,483 square miles
Population: 7,300,000
Capital: Accra
Monetary Unit: The cedi
Principal economic resources: cocoa, palm products, gold, diamonds, manganese
Language: English
History at a glance:

Modern Ghana takes its name from an ancient African empire which flourished in the Western Sudan from the 4th through the 12th centuries.

Ghana's first contact with the nations of Europe dates back to the 15th century when a band of Portuguese seafarers landed on the "Gold Coast," as it was then called, and began to trade in the area's plentiful gold dust. The Portuguese were followed by the Dutch, the Danes, the Swedes, the Prussians and, finally, by the English who in 1807 prohibited the lucrative slave trade which had begun to replace gold as the most profitable commodity in the territory.

The English remained the dominant European power in Ghana during the 19th century, although their hegemony was often threatened by the frequent tribal uprisings of the powerful and well-organized Ashanti Confederation. Ashanti territory, however, was annexed by the English in 1900, and thus was incorporated with the Northern Protectorates into the already-existing Gold Coast Colony. In 1922, Togoland, formerly under German control, was given over to Great Britain, which administered this territory, too, as part of the Gold Coast.

After World War II, Ghana gradually came to have more say about its political destiny, first by participating actively in the rewriting of a constitution, then by electing its own representatives to a duly-constituted parliament. On March 6, 1957, Ashanti, the Northern Protectorates, the Gold Coast and British Togoland declared their independence, adopted the name of Ghana, and immediately joined the British Commonwealth. Officially, Ghana became a republic on

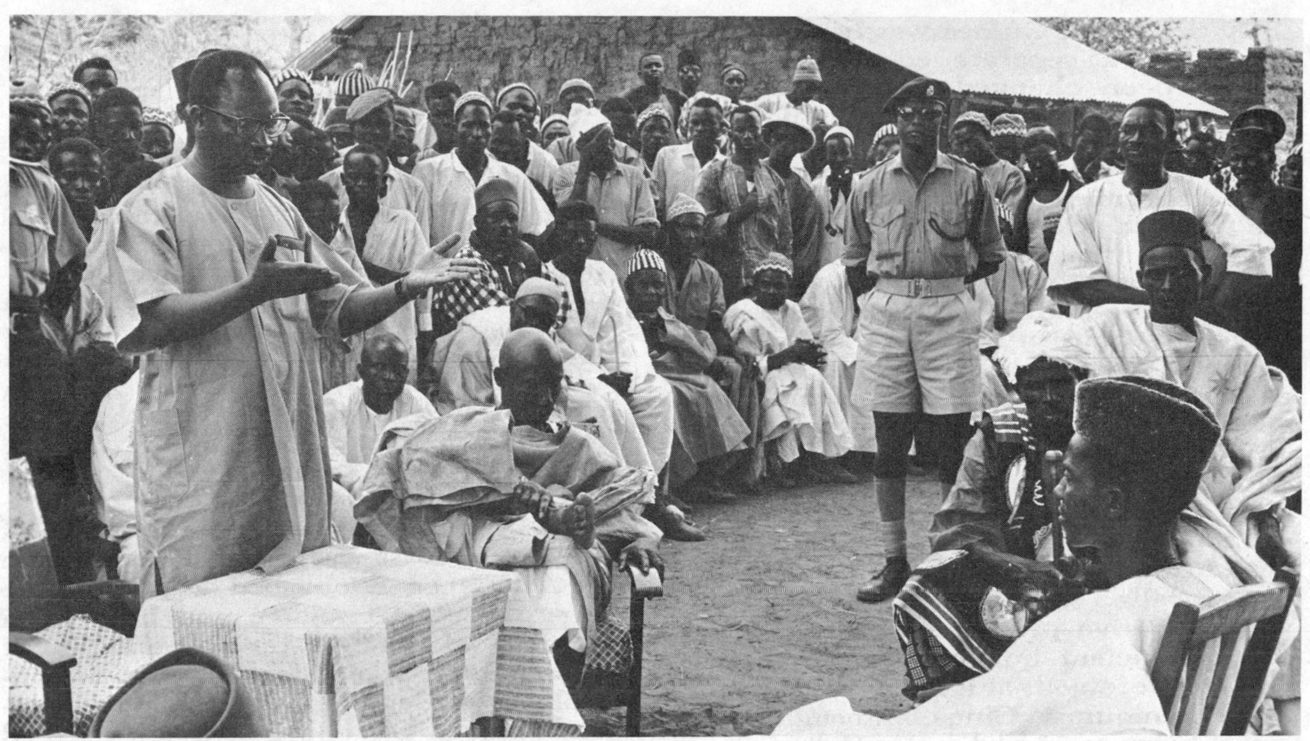

Prime Minister Dauda Jawara campaigning in Gambia.

July 1, 1960, continuing under the leadership of President Kwame Nkrumah, who held absolute power until he himself was overthrown on February 24, 1966 while on a visit to Red China.

The National Liberation Council then established a military government, installing J. A. Ankrah as head of state. Foreign debtors granted extensions on the loans negotiated by Nkrumah, though the new regime was not able to so revive the economy that money poured into the national coffers to liquidate these debts. Still, return to civilian rule was an encouraging sign. The current prime minister is Kofi A. Busia.

NATION: **GUINEA**
Date of Independence: October 2, 1958
Area: 94,926 square miles
Population: 3,400,000
Capital: Conakry
Monetary Unit: The Guinea franc
Principal economic resources: bananas, coffee, palm products, bauxite, diamonds
Language: French
History at a glance:

According to reputable scholars, modern-day Guinea is linked historically with the ancient Ghanaian kingdom of West Africa. The territory is believed to have been ruled by a succession of dynasties, the most celebrated of which was headed by the Malinke chieftain, Sundiata, founder of the Mali Empire. The last Malinke emperor was deposed in the 17th century, some two centuries after the first Europeans (the Portuguese) had begun to explore the area.

Portuguese, French and British traders were engaged in competitive trade along Guinea's coast long before the Peace of Paris (1814) secured for France the most advantageous position in the region. By 1849, the French had proclaimed a protectorate over the Guinea coast.

Opposition to French rule from the inhabitants of the interior was widespread during the last decades of the 19th century. In 1879, the famous Malinke chieftain, Almany Samoury Touré (a direct descendant of Guinean president Sekou Touré), seized Kankan in the Upper Guinea region, and began terrorizing French settlers in the area. On two occasions (in 1887 and in 1890), Touré signed peace treaties with the French, yet hostilities were soon renewed. Finally, in 1898, the Malinke leader was captured and sent into exile.

By that time, Guinea was being administered as a separate colony, its name having been changed from Rivières du Sud to French Guinea. Up until World War I, a number of chieftains from the hinterlands continued to harass the colonial authorities, but this did not prevent the French from holding together the federation they had imposed on their West African territories.

The inhabitants of Guinea became French citizens in 1946, but first won the right to vote in 1957. A year later, the electorate rejected an offer of independence within the French Community, preferring instead complete independence with Sekou Touré as president. This situation had serious repercussions, however, inasmuch as the French immediately withdrew all economic and financial aid, and recalled the trained technical and administrative personnel needed to operate an efficient bureaucracy. For a time, Guinea received aid from the U.S.S.R. and Communist China, although it has since been assisted by the United States and other Western nations as well. Since their independence, Guinea, Ghana and Mali have been closely allied as members of the Union of African States.

Although he is an avowed Marxist, Touré has followed a foreign policy of non-alignment, and cultivated particularly close ties with Kwame Nkrumah (deposed as president of Ghana in 1966).

Toure offered Nkrumah a huge welcome after the latter entered Guinea in exile, naming him co-president. U.S. black power advocate Stokely Carmichael has also taken up residence in Guinea, where he is reported to be studying French and readying himself for a leading role as a Pan-Africanist. Toure himself has shown a certain fondness for this role, but he has never been able to cultivate a consistent diplomatic outlook toward his neighbors. The Toure dictum is based on complete independence. The country, Toure says, "prefers poverty in freedom to riches in slavery."

NATION: **IVORY COAST**
Date of Independence: August 7, 1960
Area: 124,503 square miles
Population: 3,665,000
Capital: Abidjan
Monetary Unit: The CFA franc
Principal economic resources: coffee, cocoa, timber, bananas, industrial diamonds, bauxite
Language: French
History at a glance:

The first Europeans to establish themselves in what is today the Ivory Coast were the Portuguese, whose commercial activities there date back to the 15th century. Other European nations (principally Holland and England) soon began to compete for their share of the thriving slave market, and for gold, ivory and spices as well. With different aims in view, French missionaries established a foothold in this region by settling at Assinie in 1687.

It was not until the 19th century, however, that the economic exploitation of the Ivory Coast was begun in earnest. In 1842, France established a protectorate over the coastal region, and built up a number of trading posts, primarily at Assinie and Grand Bassam. French control was gradually extended into the interior through a number of treaties signed with various local chieftains. In 1893, the territory was placed under the control of a French governor. The administrative organization and military pacification of the area engaged the energies of the French until 1912.

After World War I, the colony flourished as a producer of hardwoods, cocoa, coffee and bananas. Both European planters and African cultivators shared in the wealth produced by these exports.

In 1933, France linked Upper Volta with the Ivory Coast in the hope of inducing the former territory to provide a source of cheap labor for the latter. The plan failed, however, and the Ivory Coast was soon returned to its original status.

At the close of World War II, the Ivory Coast officially became an overseas territory of the French Union. By 1956, it had gained self-autonomy; by 1958, it had become an independent republic and a member of the French Community and, by 1960, it had attained complete independence, with a republican form of government. It was headed by a popularly elected president, Félix Houphouët-Boigny.

Since then, the Ivory Coast has retained close economic ties with France, disavowing all help from countries with alleged Communist affiliations. Foreign companies operate relatively free of the restrictions which are so often typical of other African nations. As of 1963, Boigny claimed that he had discovered and suppressed at least two plots on his life, lay-

A watchman stands guard at the construction site of this modern dam in Bouake, Ivory Coast.

ing the blame for them on neighboring Ghana, as well as on "certain foreign powers."

The antithesis of Guinea and its leader Sekou Toure, the Ivory Coast and Houphouet-Boigny have relied heavily on foreign investment to modernize the capital, improve public health, and eliminate primitive housing. The country seems likely to outstrip its neighbors in economic prosperity.

NATION: **KENYA**
Date of Independence: December 12, 1963
Area: 224,960 square miles
Population: 9,104,000
Capital: Nairobi
Monetary Unit: The East African shilling
Principal economic resources: sisal, coffee, pyrethrum
Languages: Swahili, English
History at a glance:

Kenya has been the site of several archeological excavations which have shed considerable light on the nature of ancient civilizations and the toolmaking capacity of early man. Bones, instruments, and several other artifacts (some of which may be 30,000 years old) have been discovered in the Great Rift Valley, and it has been determined that the earliest known inhabitants of the region buried their dead ceremoniously—a practice generally associated with a relatively advanced culture. Archeologists have also linked Kenya with an Iron Age civilization of a later vintage.

Long before the Portuguese arrived in Africa in the 15th century, the region is known to have been visited by Greek merchants and Arab slave traders. With the arrival of Vasco da Gama in 1498, the Portuguese established new trading posts and succeeded in suppressing Arab influence for the next two centuries. In 1729, however, the Arabs regained the upper hand, exercising sway for more than 150 years, during which time a kind of Arab empire was established throughout East Africa.

European explorers again became active in the area in the 19th century, particularly in the persons of the Englishmen Rebman and Kraft, as well as of John Speke who discovered Lake Victoria in 1858. During the next few decades, Great Britain and France put into effect what has been called the "spheres of influence policy" of partitioning East and Central Africa. In 1887, Great Britain obtained a lease on the main coastal dominion of the Sultan of Zanzibar, the island from which the Arabs exercised considerable control over Kenya. Eight years later, Kenya (including the Sultan's coastal strip) was declared a British protectorate.

Beginning in the 20th century, settlement of the territory was undertaken on a large scale by the British, the South Africans, and the Asians (most of whom were from the Indian subcontinent). As a rule, white Europeans acquired exclusive rights over the most desirable land in Kenya: the so-called "White Highlands." After World War I, the protectorate became a British Crown Colony, and the coastal strip was given the status of a protectorate.

During the next three decades, sharp divisions between the Crown, the settlers (both white and Indian) and the natives resulted in a potentially explosive situation—culminating in 1952 with the outbreak of the so-called "Mau Mau" rebellion. This uprising was characterized by savage butchery on all sides and eventually claimed some 12,000 lives. When the state of emergency was finally declared at an end in 1960, some 80,000 suspected "Mau Mau" members were in prison, including Jomo Kenyatta, convicted leader of the rebellion.

Majority rule by the Africans was in the process of being introduced even as the "Mau Mau" revolt raged. In 1954, however, Tom Mboya, leader of the elected Africans, expressed his dissatisfaction with the existing political arrangement, and even went so far as to reject a newly proposed constitution. In 1960, a conference was held in London's Lancaster House, where an African delegation finally accepted the British blueprint for a transitional government. A year later, Kenyatta was released from prison, and quickly returned to the leadership of the Kenya African National Union (KANU). In 1963, KANU won control of the legislature and, with British approval, introduced a program of internal self-government. In October of the same year, the Sultan of Zanzibar relinquished all rights to his mainland dominion. A month later, Kenya became an independent republic within the British Commonwealth.

In the right foreground stands Kenya's prime minister, Jomo Kenyatta, wearing a beaded cap. Other African leaders include (l. to r.): Milton Obote (Uganda); Cyrille Adoula (former premier of the Congo) and, at far right in traditional African dress, Kenneth Kaunda of Zambia. The occasion is the opening meeting of the Pan-African Movement for East and Central Africa (PAFMECA).

Tribalism continues to be a problem in modern Kenya. Most recently, it found expression in the murder of Economics Minister Tom Mboya, a Luo, who was killed by a Kikuyu tribesman. Still, on overall merits, Kenya has achieved startling progress since independence. Its tourist industry is booming, its program of "Africanizing" business and industry (though this is placing considerable pressure on the Asian population) has been successful, and it is compensating for lack of mineral wealth by developing smaller industries that are attracting foreign capital.

NATION: **LESOTHO**
Area: 11,716 square miles
Population: 1,000,000
Capital: Maseru
Monetary Unit: The South African rand
Principal economic resources: wool, mohair, livestock, wheat, beans
Language: English
History at a glance:

An enclave within the Republic of South Africa, Basutoland first became a battleground in 1831, when Basuto tribes engaged in open warfare against the Boers who were advancing northward from South Africa. In 1867, having been defeated by the Boers, the Basuto asked for and received British protection in return for granting England full sovereignty rights. In 1964, Basutoland won internal autonomy and, at the same time, made known its intention of becoming independent as the Kingdom of Lesotho in October of 1966. (Its prime minister is Chief Leabua Jonathan.)

Until then, the territory was governed by a paramount chief and by a British high commissioner in charge of defense, foreign affairs and internal security.

Upon assuming independence, Prime Minister Jonathan pursued policies of peaceful co-existence with her larger, richer and more potent neighbor, South Africa. The relationship was not without some uneasiness, however. In the words of Jonathan, the country has been desirous of "choosing our friends," while at the same time "living with our neighbors."

NATION: **LIBERIA**
Date of Independence: July 26, 1847
Area: 42,990 square miles
Population: 1,040,000
Capital: Monrovia
Monetary Unit: The Liberian dollar
Principal economic resources: rubber, iron ore, diamonds
Language: English
History at a glance:

Portuguese adventurers of the 15th century were most likely the first white men to see and explore the Liberian coast from Cape Mount to Cape Palmas.

The first permanent settlement of this territory at Cape Mesurado in 1822 was sponsored by the American Colonization Society, a private corporation which financed the return of emancipated Negroes to Africa. By 1839, the group of settlements which had sprung up in the interim had found it mutually advantageous to join forces and to establish a commonwealth. Liberia's first governor was Thomas Buchanan, a cousin of James Buchanan, the 15th president of the United States. Eight years later, on July 26, the commonwealth proclaimed itself an independent republic.

For the remainder of the 19th century, Liberia was ruthlessly carved up by a host of European nations, which were interested not only in exploiting its natural resources, but also in preventing it, as a nation of free Negroes, from becoming a base for the dissemination of what could readily become politically dangerous ideas to colonial territories in adjacent areas.

Soon after the turn of the century, the United States directly intervened to save the country from financial ruin, made imminent as a result of a series of disastrous foreign loans negotiated largely through British concessionaires. Particularly hard-hit by the Depression of the 1930's, Liberia found itself further humiliated by an international scandal involving a number of corrupt government officials who were condoning a thriving forced-labor trade.

Due to its strategic value, Liberia became an important base for Allied military operations in Africa during World War II. The country did not become financially solvent, however, until its defaulted loans were paid off by the Firestone Corporation, which then invested heavily in the development of many new rubber plantations. The wealth flowing out from this booming industry has helped to improve public-health and educational facilities in the country,

President William V. S. Tubman rides in an official state limousine during a parade in Monrovia, Liberia.

which is now ruled, for the most part, by some 15,000 Americo-Liberian descendants of the early settlers.

Historically, there is an interesting comparison to be made between their patronizing attitude toward the "uncivilized" tribes of the interior, and the attitudes of the planter group among which their ancestors had originally lived. According to some reliable historians, the "natives" of the interior have been exploited by the Americo-Liberians in much the same way as their forebearers had once been at the hands of Southern slaveholders.

Since 1943, William V. S. Tubman has held the office of president of Liberia. Last elected in 1967, Tubman has since been a leading supporter of the concept of a West African common market. Such an arrangement would be especially beneficial to Liberia because of its free port of Monrovia and the enormous cargoes it could handle.

NATION: **LIBYA**

Date of Independence: December 24, 1951

Area: 679,343 square miles

Population: 1,200,000

Capitals: Benghazi and Tripoli

Monetary Unit: The Libyan pound

Principal economic resources: olives, dates, oil

Language: Arabic

History at a glance:

Both Carthage and Rome left their imprint on Libya in the pre-Christian era—Carthage along the Tripolitania coast, and Greece in the portion known as Cyrenaica. By the third century B.C., Rome had replaced Greece as the dominant power in the region and, with the destruction of Carthage, went on to become the sole empire builder throughout most of North Africa.

In the third century A.D., with Rome already in a state of decline, Emperor Diocletian assigned Tripolitania to the western part of the Roman Empire and Cyrenaica to the eastern portion of it. By 431, however, Rome could no longer protect these outlying territories, and they were overrun by hordes of Vandal invaders. In the 6th century, Emperor Justinian's military commander, Belisarius, conquered the territory and placed it under the suzerainty of the Byzantine Empire. The first of what were to become frequent Arab invasions occurred in 643, the year which ushered in three centuries of almost continuous religious and dynastic conflicts. During this period, Tripolitania manifested a tendency to identify itself with the Western world, whereas Cyrenaica became more closely associated with Egypt to the east.

In 1510, Tripoli was seized by the Spanish who were in turn overcome by Ottoman Turks. From 1711 to 1835, Libyan territory was controlled by the Karamanli family, which wrested virtual autonomy from the Turks whose capital was in Constantinople. Ultimately, the Turks regained their power, only to lose it again in 1911 to Italy. Over the next two decades, the Italians worked their way inland with marked effectiveness.

During World War II, Libya was occupied by British and Free French forces. When the war ended, the United Nations voted to create an independent state—a decision which was put into effect two years later with the establishment of a federated kingdom embracing Tripolitania and Cyrenaica (now known as Fezzan and Barquah).

With the discovery of oil in recent years, Libya has improved her chronically desperate economic situation, and is now pressing hard for the removal of British and American forces stationed on her soil in World War II.

Libya's King, Muhammad Idris a-Mahdi al-Sanusi was overthrown in 1969, and replaced by Premier Mahmoud Soliman al-Maghreby.

NATION: **MALAGASY REPUBLIC**
Date of Independence: June 26, 1960
Area: 230,036 square miles
Population: 6,180,000
Capital. Tananarive
Monetary Unit: The CFA franc
Principal economic resources: coffee, rice
Languages: French, Malgasy
History at a glance:

The language, customs and culture of the Malagasy Republic (formerly known as Madagascar) are closely associated with those of other Indonesian peoples who are believed to have migrated in great numbers to the island even before the Christian era. Arab traders and African slaves began arriving in the 7th century A.D., and thus added their own blood to the distinctive racial stock which has since emerged there.

Portuguese explorers first became aware of the island's existence in the 15th century, and they were followed in short

Sheepherding in Libya.

order by French, Dutch and English traders. In the 17th century, France attempted for a time to establish her own colonies in the southern portion of the island, but she abandoned this area in favor of more suitable locales. This left open the way for Malagasy to become a popular pirate haunt. (Even the famous Captain Kidd laid over there on occasion.)

By this time, the three main kingdoms on the island—the Merina, the Sakalava, and the Betsimisaraka—were establishing themselves in the central, western and eastern reaches of the island. Near the end of the 18th century, the Merina kingdom, headed by its greatest ruler, Andrianampoinimerina, made a first attempt to extend its dominion over the entire island. Radama I not only continued in his father's footsteps but went even further—imposing a ban on the slave trade. Opposition to French influence hardened after the death of Radama I; Christian persecution intensified, and European settlers were eventually obliged to leave the island altogether.

By 1885, France had reasserted itself in the territory with the establishment of a protectorate that was recognized in 1890 by Great Britain in return for French recognition of British control in Zanzibar. French forces occupied the capital in 1895, but were not wholly successful in stamping out opposition in the south until 10 years later.

The move toward independence showed signs of gaining momentum in Madagascar as far back as the post-World War I decade. In 1940, British troops occupied the territory, maintaining themselves there until French administration could be restored under General De Gaulle's Free French government.

In 1946, Madagascar became an overseas territory of France, a move which was denounced by various nationalist elements. A bloody rebellion broke out against French rule in 1947. Before peace was restored, a year had elapsed, and some 60,000-90,000 Malagasy had lost their lives. As a result of this violence, conservative business and political interests on the island gained support and, in 1958, succeeded in leading the territory to independence within the framework of the French Community. Two years later, the Malagasy Republic became a sovereign independent nation, retaining close ties with its mother country, France.

The republic's first president, Philibert Tsiranana, leader of the pro-French Social Democratic Party, was last returned to office in March of 1965. His seven-year term is not scheduled to expire until 1972. Tsirinana has spent much of his time assuaging ethnic rivalries between the Merina people (Protestants) and the *cotiers* (Roman Catholics).

NATION: MALAWI

Date of Independence: July 6, 1964

Area: 46,066 square miles
Population: 3,753,000
Capital: Zomba
Monetary Unit: Malawi pound
Principal economic resources: tobacco, tea, tung oil, iron ore, bauxite
Language: English

History at a glance:

Malawi, known as Nyasaland prior to its independence, was first settled by an agricultural people of Bantu origin who appeared in the Lake Nyasa area some 2,000 years ago and then moved southward to the Shire River Valley. Later migrations by the Yao and Nyanja peoples from the neighborhood of the southern Congo eventually led to population pressures and tribal conflicts in the Lake Nyasa region.

The lake itself is said to have been sighted for the first time in 1616 by a Portuguese, Casper Boccaro, but the actual discovery of it is credited to David Livingstone, the Scotch explorer who arrived there in 1859. By this time, Nyasaland was already an important base for Arab slave traders, whose operations were not checked until a number of Christian missionaries appeared in the area.

British influence in Nyasaland reached its zenith during the last four decades of the 19th century. The African Lakes Company, having followed the missionaries into the territory in 1878, quickly became enbroiled in sharp competition with the Arab ivory traders on the northern end of Lake Nyasa. By 1891, the British had fully consolidated their political position in the region and given it protectorate status.

Hostility to British colonial policies first manifested itself in Nyasaland in 1915 when John Chilembwe (an American-trained African religious leader) led an armed revolt which, though unsuccessful, nonetheless helped crystallize the political aspirations of the African inhabitants. After World War II, it became increasingly apparent that Great Britain would attempt to establish a federation made up of its three important Central African territories—Northern Rhodesia, Southern Rhodesia and Nyasaland. Thus, despite its opposition to the idea, Nyasaland was forced in 1953 to join the federation, a move which only fanned the growing flames of nationalist fervor in the territory. Nyasaland lost no time in protesting to the Queen herself, maintaining that the federation of which it was a part was dominated by a white minority intent on institutionalizing the notion of perpetual European political superiority. Fearing likewise that the federation might achieve complete independence from Great Britain, Nyasaland became ripe for revolt—particularly with the return of Dr. Hastings Banda in 1958. Within a year, an uprising did occur, and several Africans were killed. As a consequence, the Nyasaland African Congress (NAC), the main nationalist party, was outlawed, and its leaders, including Dr. Banda himself, were imprisoned.

In 1960, with Ian MacLeod serving as England's Colonial Secretary, the British government accepted the fact-finding report of an investigating commission which maintained that the original uprising had been caused by popular dissatisfaction with the idea of federation.

Upon his release from prison, Dr. Banda formed the Malawi Congress Party (MCP) which won widespread support at the polls. This encouraged England to institute certain constitutional reforms leading to internal autonomy for Nyasaland. The latter seceded from the federation in 1963 and became an independent state, adopting the name "Malawi" a year later.

In 1967, Malawi took the initiative among black African republics in establishing trade relations with the white-dominated nations of southern Africa. Despite the criticism he incurred, Banda remained steadfast in his convictions that Malawi should trade "with the devil" if that becomes necessary to improve the economic status of the nation.

NATION: **MALI**

Date of Independence: September 22, 1960

Area: 464,873 square miles

Population: 4,394,000

Capital: Bamako

Monetary Unit: The Mali franc

Principal economic resources: groundnuts, rice, cotton

Language: French

History at a glance:

What is now known as Mali was, in the 4th century A.D., only a portion of the larger and far more influential empire of Ghana. By the 8th century, Ghana was known to the Moslem Arab world as the land of gold. It later became a source of wealth for Spain and North Africa before entering into a period of decline which culminated in its overthrow in the mid 13th century by a Moslem empire named Mali.

Perhaps the most famous of Mali's many emperors was the fabled Mansa Musa, who conquered Timbuktu and the vast regions of the Middle Niger. On one of his pilgrimages to Mecca, he is reported to have taken along some 500 slaves and to have distributed 50,000 ounces of gold. On his return from Mecca, he brought with him a number of Moslem tutors and men of learning, and thus fostered the growth of Timbuktu as a center of medieval African scholarship.

Due to persistent pressure on its frontiers, Mali declined in power in the 14th and 15th centuries, eventually giving way to the Songhai kingdom of Gao which, in its turn, was overcome by armed hosts from Morocco. During the 19th century, the territory finally achieved a degree of unity under the banner of Islam, but this was short-lived due to French military intervention and the extension of French administrative control.

Mali was known at this time as the French Soudan, a vast and underdeveloped country which was to have little importance until World War II when it became a rallying point for the Free French. Even in 1958, the Soudan was still only one of the numerous French West African territories which accepted the De Gaulle Constitution and voted for membership in the French Community.

A year later, Soudan, Senegal, Dahomey and Upper Volta drafted their own constitution calling for the creation of a Federation of Mali. Only Senegal and Soudan, however, ratified the document. Shortly thereafter, the Mali Federation appealed to France for recognition by, and complete sovereignty within, the French Community. Although this request was granted, the federation collapsed almost immediately, largely because of the sharp differences existing between key politicians in each territory.

Under the leadership of Modibo Keita, Mali then declared itself an independent state, and embarked on its own program of development.

In 1965, Bamako was the site of an epoch-making conference between the heads of state of Ghana, Algeria and Mali, all nations desirous of creating a closely knit Pan African group to rival the French-oriented Afro-Malagasy Common Organization.

Keita subsequently set the nation on a course of strict alignment with the Red Chinese brand of "socialism." The economy fell completely into the hands of state enterprises operated with the help of more than 1,000 technicians. The bankruptcy of this policy produced a counter-revolutionary fervor among a group of young Army officers who, in 1968, overthrew Keita, and installed a National Liberation Committee, headed by Lieutenant Moussa Trauore.

NATION: **MAURITANIA**

Date of Independence: November 28, 1960

Area: 419,229 square miles

Population: 780,000

Capital: Nouakchott

Monetary Unit: The CFA franc

Principal economic resources: livestock, gum, salt

Language: French

History at a glance:

In its early history, Mauritania was the scene of successive waves of southward migration by Arabs and Berbers, both of whom conquered the indigenous Negro inhabitants. Perhaps the most important invaders were the nomadic Tuareg Berbers who often carried out raids on the Morocco-Ghana caravan route, and thus disrupted the commerce between the great Negro empires of the Western Sudan in the 11th century. Islam became a potent force in this area during the 14th and 15th centuries when Arab invaders from Egypt drove out the Berbers. Attracted by the gum trade, the Portuguese arrived in the 15th century, setting up trading posts along Mauritania's southern boundary—the Senegal River. For the next four centuries, the French slowly pushed their way northward from Senegal and, by signing appropriate treaties with several Moorish chieftains, came to exercise hegemony over most of the desert zone of Mauritania.

The French retaliated against the frequent raids of Moorish tribes early in the 20th century by extending their authority over more and more of the territory. By 1909, to cite one example, they had added the Adrar region, bordering on the Spanish Sahara, to their dominion. The territory of Mauritania was established as an administrative unit in 1920, at which time the city of Saint-Louis in Senegal was made its capital. At the same time, Mauritania also became a part of French West Africa, a loosely knit federation set up in the French colonial holdings.

After World War II, Mauritania received the same colonial concessions from France as did the other territories in the region. In 1946, it assumed partial control of its own affairs through the election of its own assembly, and sent representatives to the French National Assembly in Paris, as well as to the Assembly of the French Union. Work was begun on the new capital of Nouakchott in 1957. A year later, Mauritania approved the constitution of the Fifth French Republic, and decided in favor of membership within the French Community. Complete independence was not achieved until 1960.

Since then, Mauritania has been wholly reliant on French financial aid to shore up its economy. Its ruling class is composed of an elite group of chieftains who themselves are largely dependent upon French support.

The president of the Islamic Republic of Mauritania is Moktar Ould Daddah.

The capital Nouakchott has made appreciable strides toward modernization since 1958, but it is still fringed with clusters of nomadic settlements suggestive of the desert ways that are still prevalent in the rest of the country.

NATION: **MAURITIUS**

Area: 720 square miles

Population: 810,000

Capital: Port Louis

Monetary Unit: The Mauritius rupee

Principal economic resources: sugar, tea, tobacco, aloe fibers

Language: English

History at a glance:

Mauritius was discovered by Portuguese sailors in the early 16th century, but it was first settled by the Dutch who gave it its name in 1598. After the Dutch withdrew in 1710, the French claimed the island (renaming it Ile de France), but they lost it to British forces in 1810. Four years later, British sovereignty was recognized by the Peace of Paris. With the abolition of slavery in the British Empire in 1834, Mauritius absorbed large numbers of migrant laborers from the Asian subcontinent. (Today, some 200,000 Mauritians are of mixed French and African origin; the remainder, mostly Indo-Mauritians.)

Great Britain is represented on the island by a resident governor. In recent years, however, representative institutions have developed to such a degree that the question of independence has already been discussed in London (1965).

In 1967, Mauritius became self-governing, with Labour party leader Seewoosagur Ramgoolam being appointed prime minister. Racial and labor unrest involving the island's Creole and Moslem population followed almost immediately thereafter, but the island maintained sufficient equilibrium to declare its independence in 1968.

NATION: MOROCCO

Date of Independence: March 2, 1956
Area: 171,305 square miles
Population: 12,959,000
Capital: Rabat
Monetary Unit: The Moroccan dirham
Principal economic resources: fish, grapes, wool, cork, iron, coal, phosphates
Languages: Arabic, French, Spanish
History at a glance:

Morocco shares with the rest of North Africa a long history of domination by foreign powers. However, it differs from its neighbors in that it was never completely overrun by either Rome or the Ottoman Empire.

In ancient times, the Berbers, the earliest known inhabitants of Morocco, were invaded by Phoenicians and Carthaginians. In the early centuries of the Christian era, they suffered the same fate at the hands of the Vandals, Byzantines and Arabs. In 683, Morocco fell under the potent influence of Islam but, for all its unifying effect, religion did not succeed, in the next four centuries, in eliminating the grounds for conflict between numerous petty chieftains.

From the 11th to the 13th centuries, Morocco was ruled by the Almoravid, Almohade and Marinid dynasties, and enjoyed a period of relative political stability and intellectual development. Under the Sa'adi kings, Morocco experienced its period of greatest prosperity. Its strong military defenses and its reorganized army protected it from Turkish invasions, while its own spoils of victory enabled its rulers to build a magnificent capital at Marrakesh.

By the middle of the 16th century, however, Europe began to cast its first shadow over Morocco. Soon, Spain and England controlled most of the country's major seaports. Were it not for the tenacity of the Filali dynasty, these nations would certainly have attempted to gain control of the interior as well. The Filali king Mawlay Isma'il (1672-1727) managed for a time to preserve Moroccan independence by driving the Spanish from Lavache and the English from Tangier.

The establishment of diplomatic relations with France in 1682 led to an expansion of Moroccan trade during the following two centuries and, ultimately, to French military occupation (1844). In 1860, Spain invaded and occupied northern Morocco, necessitating the signing in 1880 of an international agreement to guarantee Morocco's territorial integrity. By 1904, however, France and Spain had secretly agreed to divide up all of Morocco between themselves. Two years later, the Act of Algeciras established the principle of commercial equality for European nations trading in the region, although policing of the act's provisions was left to France and Spain. In 1912, Morocco was divided into French Morocco (a protectorate with Rabat as its capital); Spanish Morocco (a protectorate with Tetuan as its capital); Southern Morocco (administered as part of Spanish Sahara), and the international zone of Tangier.

In 1921, Berber nationalism reached fever pitch, culminating in the Rif War during which Abd el-Krim inflicted several crucial defeats on both the French and Spanish before himself being captured and exiled in 1926. Guerrilla fighting continued until 1934.

During World War II, Allied forces landed in Morocco, where they were soon joined by large detachments of Moroccan troops who fought on the side of the Free French. At the war's end, Sultan Sidi Mohammed demanded independence for his country, but was exiled instead in 1952—a gesture which triggered massive anti-French demonstrations lasting for nearly two years. What with her already humiliating defeat in Indo-China, France was now forced to loosen her grip on Morocco, to allow Sidi Mohammed to return in 1955, and to grant the territory (including Tangier and the French and Spanish zones) complete independence a year later. Muhammad V then ascended the throne as the first modern-day king of Morocco.

After his death in 1961, the king was succeeded by his son, Hassan II. Since then, Hassan has had great difficulty—both in winning popular support and in maintaining a stable government. Opposition to his rule is strong, and he has more than once been forced (most recently, during a general strike in 1965) to reshuffle his cabinet and declare a state of emergency.

Apart from political and economic woes, Morocco has had her share of disputes with neighboring Arab states, notably Algeria and Mauritania.

Early in 1969, Morocco persuaded Spain to surrender the tiny enclave of Ifni on the Mediterranean, signed an accord minimizing political and military frictions with its leftist neighbor Algeria, and worked out terms with the European Common Market to achieve associate status.

NATION: **NIGER**
Date of Independence: August 3, 1960
Area: 489,189 square miles
Population: 3,190,000
Capital: Niamey
Monetary Unit: The CFA franc
Principal economic resources: livestock, hides, skins, peanuts
Language: French
History at a glance:

The territory known today as Niger was, for most of its early history, a crossroads for migration between the white peoples of North Africa and the black peoples of the Lake Chad region. The Kanem-Bornu Empire was only one of several powerful states which came into flower in this area during the 8th and 9th centuries. This empire was overthrown in the 10th century by the Hausa states which lay in the southern reaches of Niger, and by the Songhai Kingdom which held sway in the western half of the country until the 16th century, when it was itself destroyed by an invading Moroccan army.

The first European explorer in the area was the fabled Scot, Mungo Park (1805). Later, Major Dixon Denham and Lieutenant Hugh Clapperton who were sent by Great Britain to explore the Niger River and reached Lake Chad after crossing the Sahara Desert from Tripoli.

By 1900, the French had pushed their way eastward despite fierce opposition from the Tuareg tribe. In 1901, Niger was declared a military district and thus became part of a larger territorial unit known as Haut-Senegal et Niger. Sporadic revolts continued right up until the eve of World War I, at which time they were finally quelled with the aid of British forces from Nigeria. In 1922, Niger was officially declared a French colony.

Due to its lack of strategic importance, the territory remained virtually unaffected by World War II. Nationalism and, with it, the growth of political parties became inevitable once France had made it clear that she intended to offer her West African territories a greater share in self-government. In 1958, Niger approved the new French Constitution and, within two years, had become a fully independent state.

The president of Niger, Hamani Diori, has embarked upon an ambitious economic program which calls for long-term cooperation with France. He has already survived one assassination attempt, made in April 1965.

In 1967, Niger was found to be rich in uranium ore, and plans were begun to process the deposits by 1971. The discovery of more than 100,000 tons of iron ore added still more to the potential wealth of the country.

Niger is still heavily dependent on France for export markets and foreign aid. Though independent politically, it has no diplomatic relations with Communist nations.

NATION: **NIGERIA**
Date of Independence: October 1, 1960
Area: 356,668 square miles
Population: 55,600,000
Capital: Lagos
Monetary Unit: The Nigerian pound
Principal economic resources: cocoa,

peanuts, cotton, rubber, columbite, tin, oil
Languages: English, Hausa
History at a glance:

Little is known of the history of the early peoples who inhabited Nigeria. During the Middle Ages, Northern Nigeria was in contact with the kingdoms of the western Sudan, and with the nations lying to the north of the Sahara Desert as well. Islam was established as the major religion in Nigeria during the 15th century, by which time the Ife and Benin kingdoms were already flourishing.

Contact between the coastal peoples of Nigeria and the nations of Europe was based upon the profitable exploitation of slaves who were removed from the territory in astounding numbers. The British abolished the slave trade in 1807 and, with the discovery of the mouth of the Niger River in 1830, began instead to extend their economic influence into the interior. In 1861, they annexed the island of Lagos, an important center in the palm oil trade. Toward the end of the century, they swept into the eastern regions of Nigeria, establishing both the Oil Rivers Protectorate (1885) and the Niger Coast Protectorate (1893).

British influence in Nigeria was formally recognized by the Berlin Conference of 1884-1885. Over the next 15 years, Great Britain gained control of an even more substantial piece of territory in Northern Nigeria, where still a third protectorate was established.

In 1914, these separate administrative areas were combined into the Colony and Protectorate of Nigeria, governed by Sir Frederick (later Lord) Lugard. Lugard was instrumental in introducing a system of indirect rule which enabled powerful local chieftains to exercise a significant degree of control over their own affairs.

Nationalism became a potent force in Nigeria after World War II, primarily under the leadership of Nnamdi Azikiwe, Obafemi Awolowo and Alhaji Sir Abubakar Tafawa Balewa. In 1960, Nigeria became a fully independent federation within the framework of the British Commonwealth and, three years later, opted for a republican form of government.

Early in 1966, Nigeria was the scene of the bloodiest military coup any black African nation has suffered to date. Prime

Boys playing on lawn in front of the Parliament building in Lagos.

Minister Tafawa Balewa was assassinated, and a military government headed by General J. Aguiyi-Ironsi seized power. This government abolished the existing constitution; eliminated the offices of president and prime minister, and dismissed the premiers of Nigeria's four semi-autonomous regions (the Northern, the Western, the Eastern and the Midwestern).

Later that year, Aguiyi-Ironsi was deposed by Lieutenant Colonel Yakubu Gowon, head of a new military junta. When anti-Ibo rioting began anew late in 1966, Ibos from all over the nation began flocking back to their homeland in the Eastern Region. Soon the new state of Biafra was created, and civil war engulfed the country. War dragged on for three years until the rebel Ibos were finally starved into submission at the beginning of 1970.

NATION: **RHODESIA**

Date of Independence: November 11, 1965

Area: 105,333 square miles

Population: 4,210,000

Capital: Salisbury

Monetary Unit: The Rhodesian pound

Principal economic resources: tobacco, corn, livestock, asbestos, gold, copper, coal, chrome, tin, iron

Language: English

History at a glance:

The Rhodesian plateau is believed to have been settled some 2,000 years ago by a group of farmers who had mastered the use of iron. After the 8th century A.D., descendants of this group began trading gold and ivory with the Arabs on the east coast of Africa. The great stone structures of Zimbabwe, near Fort Victoria, are believed to have been built some time between the 11th and 15th centuries, shortly before the Vakaranga tribe moved northward—there to establish a state which extended over the northern and eastern Rhodesian plateau, as well as over the Mozambique lowlands.

The Portuguese were the first Europeans in the region, carrying out their explorations between 1514 and 1569. At the end of the 17th century, the Monomatapa tribe and their Portuguese overlords were defeated by the Changamires who then held sway until the 19th century, the time of the great Zulu emigration from Natal. This emigration ushered in the era of Matabele rule at much the same time that David Livingstone, the Scottish missionary and explorer, was opening up the entire region to European exploitation. Livingstone's reports in 1875-1876 were chiefly responsible for the establishment of two Scottish missions in the territory of Nyasaland.

British entry into this region precipitated a series of immediate conflicts with the Portuguese who had already laid claim to the whole of Central Africa in the hope of linking Angola on the west with Mozambique on the east. Cecil B. Rhodes, holder of the controlling interest in the diamond mines of South Africa, soon sent his agents into the territory to sign treaties with, and obtain mining concessions from, a number of the local chieftains. In 1888, Lobengula, the powerful and legendary chief of the Matabele, signed such a treaty with the British, thus preventing any Portuguese or Boer (South African) penetration. Within a year, the discovery of extensive gold deposits enabled Rhodes to acquire a charter giving him the right to form the British South Africa Company and to exploit the area.

In 1890, the company sent a group of European settlers into Mashonaland, where they founded the town of Salisbury, site of the present capital. Meanwhile, Lobengula had granted Edward A. Lippert, a German concessionaire, the sole right to dispose of land in the territory he controlled. This did not stop Rhodes from buying the concession and from continuing to send in settlers until 1893, the year of the unsuccessful Matabele rebellion. In 1897, the Mashona uprising was crushed by the British, and Rhodes was able to promote the development of the territory without any interference whatsoever.

For the next 20 years, conflicts arose between the settlers who sought an increasing degree of self-government and the British South Africa Company, which was subject only to the supervisory control of the high commissioner in South Africa. In 1922, the settlers finally won the right to establish a government separate from that of South Africa. A year later, the territory was annexed to the Crown, a move which made British subjects of all African inhabitants.

Southern Rhodesia (as it was then called) then set itself the task of dividing its total land mass into two basic areas: mining and industrial regions (for European settlement), and native reserves, forest lands, etc. (for Africans only). Through this system, the Europeans received some 52 million acres of the choicest land, while the Africans were confined to what remained.

After World War II, nationalism took a firm foothold in neighboring Northern Rhodesia and Nyasaland. This led European settlers in both these regions, and in Southern Rhodesia as well, to close ranks behind the idea of a federation embracing the three territories. The Federation of Rhodesia and Nyasaland came into being in 1953, and had a stormy life for the 10 years it survived. African resentment in Nyasaland flared into violence in 1959, during which time a state of emergency was declared. Within a few years, the success of African nationalist parties at the polls, coupled with the growth in influence of the Afro-Asian UN bloc, sealed the final doom of the federation. In Nyasaland and Northern Rhodesia, African-controlled governments came into being and succeeded in getting Great Britain to agree to independence talks.

In 1962, the UN General Assembly censured Southern Rhodesia in an official resolution calling for the passage of a new constitution there. This pressure only led to the creation of a right-wing, white-supremacist government headed by Prime Minister Ian Smith, who was to defy Great Britain late in 1965 by declaring unilateral independence and withdrawing from the British Commonwealth. Economic sanctions imposed in 1966 by Great Britain and other members of the UN did not succeed in breaking the determination of Rhodesia's white minority to maintain its hold on the country.

Three years later, the predominantly white electorate of Rhodesia voted overwhelmingly in a referendum to abandon all pretext at professing loyalty to the Queen and to support a constitution guaranteeing white supremacy indefinitely.

NATION: **RWANDA**
Date of Independence: July 1, 1962
Area: 10,169 square miles
Population: 2,634,000
Capital: Kigali
Monetary Unit: The Rwanda-Burundi franc
Principal economic resources: cotton, coffee, cattle, hides
Language: French
History at a glance:

The more recent history of Rwanda, a tiny country adjacent to the Congo (Léopoldville), has been largely one involving the strained relatonship between the Tutsi and the Hutu tribes.

A nomadic pastoral people, the Tutsi first entered Rwanda in the 15th century, subjugating its inhabitants, the Hutu and Twa. The Tutsi instituted a caste system, and came to function as the feudal overlords of the Hutu tribe, which was composed mainly of farmers. The Twa, on the other hand, slowly retired into the surrounding jungle in search of wild game.

The first white men to pass through Rwanda were the English explorers, John Speke and Richard Burton, who crossed the territory in 1858 during their search for the southernmost source of the river Nile. In 1871, Stanley and Livingstone landed at Usumbura (now in Burundi) after having first explored the Ruzizi River region. They were soon to be followed by German explorers and by Roman Catholic missionaries.

The status of both Rwanda (originally spelled Ruanda) and Burundi (then known as Urundi) was first determined by the Berlin Conference of 1884-1885. Ultimately, Rwanda was made a distinct colony by Germany and given its own administrative headquarters at Kigali, the present capital.

Following World War II, Germany was forced to surrender this territory to Belgium, which was awarded a mandate over once-again-united Ruanda-Urundi by the League of Nations. In 1946, although it continued to be administered from the Belgian Congo, it was made a trust territory by the United Nations.

During the next decade, fierce tribal clashes became more frequent in Ruanda-Urundi. The politically awakened Hutu tribe, in particular, grew more militant and self-assertive toward its aristocratic Tutsi overlords. Finally, in 1960, an outbreak of violence caused large numbers of Tutsi to flee to neighboring countries. That same year, Belgium withdrew from the Congo, and thus served notice of her intention to sever formal political ties with her African colonies. A year later, a UN commission called for legislative elections and a referendum to decide on the fate of the mwami (a tribal king with absolute power). The people voted to abolish the mwami's major governing powers, and to set up instead a republican form of government.

On July 1, 1962, with Gregoire Kayibanda as its president, Rwanda declared its independence and formally separated itself from Burundi which, by contrast, retained a monarchist form of government.

Due largely to its limited size, its landlocked position, and its meagre resources, Rwanda has continued to depend on agriculture and tourism as the most likely activities for upgrading its economic status. Progress has not been startling, but Rwanda has shown dogged determination to grow and prosper.

NATION: **SENEGAL**
Date of Independence: August 20, 1960
Area: 76,085 square miles
Population: 3,400,000
Capital: Dakar
Monetary Unit: The CFA franc
Principal economic resources: groundnuts, titanium, cement, phosphates
Languages: French, Wolof
History at a glance:

Parts of what is today Senegal were at different times in the past ruled by the empires of Tekrur, Ghana, and Mali, the last of which reached the zenith of its power in the 14th century.

The first Europeans to arrive in this general area—along the Cape Verde peninsula and in the estuary of the Gambia River—were the Portuguese, who were soon followed by the English and the French. French activity was concentrated around the trading post of Saint-Louis and the island of Gorée, just outside the city of Dakar.

In the 19th century, the French began cultivating peanuts in the valleys of Senegal, and this crop came to be the staple of a predominantly agricultural economy. On the political front, four large municipalities (Saint-Louis, Gorée, Dakar and Rufisque) won the right to choose a single deputy to be seated in the French parliament. However, the first African deputy was not elected until 1914. At the end of World War II, Senegal, as part of the French Union, was permitted by the parent government to send two representatives to the Chamber of Deputies in Paris.

In 1946, a constitution was drawn up, and a territorial assembly established. By 1957, universal suffrage had been introduced. A year later, Senegal ratified the new constitution of French president

Sierra Leone has had its own television transmitter since 1962. Particular stress is laid on educational programs.

Charles De Gaulle, thus becoming an autonomous republic within the French Community.

Senegal joined the short-lived Mali Federation in 1959, only to withdraw a year later when the Legislative Assembly declared the country independent. Since then, the president of the country has been Léopold Sédar Senghor, widely considered to be one of the leading intellectuals on the African continent.

Re-elected in 1968, Senghor has not been able to produce economic miracles for Senegal. He has been hampered by declining prices for the country's economic staple, peanuts, and has been faced with recurrent budget deficits.

NATION: SIERRA LEONE

Date of Independence: April 27, 1961
Area: 27,925 square miles
Population: 2,183,000
Capital: Freetown
Monetary Unit: The leone
Principal economic resources: palm products, iron ore, diamonds
Language: English
History at a glance:

Founded in 1787 by Granville Sharp, an English abolitionist, Sierra Leone was first settled by Negro slaves who had been brought to England and freed there.

Granted a royal charter in 1799, Sierra Leone ("The Province of Freedom") was first governed by a town council, complete with a mayor and aldermen. However, after several attacks on the settlement by hostile tribes, Great Britain decided to bring the colony under the direct administration of the Crown. When the English parliament ruled the slave trade illegal in 1807, Sierra Leone came to be utilized as a base from which slave runners could be hunted down.

The frontiers of Sierra Leone were not settled until late in the 19th century. At this time, the hinterlands of the territory were declared a British protectorate, a move which caused considerable tribal unrest. The Mende and Temne peoples in particular were opposed to a hut tax imposed by the officials of the Crown.

In 1924, the constitution under which the colony had been governed was revised so as to provide for the election of three Sierra Leoneans to posts on the Legislative Council. Again, in 1951, a new constitution was promulgated, ushering in a system of party rule through a duly-elected African majority, whose decisions, however, were still subject to the veto of an English resident. Five years later, the Legislative Council gave way to a House of Representatives, consisting of 39 members and 12 chiefs.

In 1958, Dr. Milton Margai formed the first cabinet and, three years later, the country achieved full independence within the British Commonwealth. Prime Minister Margai died in 1964, and was succeeded by his brother, Milton, who was, in turn, overthrown in 1967 by Siaka Stevens, head of the All People's Congress. Stevens was temporarily overthrown by an army coup, but was reinstated in 1968.

NATION: SOMALIA

Date of Independence: July 1, 1960
Area: 246,201 square miles
Population: 2,300,000
Capital: Mogadiscio
Monetary Unit: The Somali shilling
Principal economic resources: hides, skins, salt, gum
Language: Arabic
History at a glance:

As part of what is called the "Horn of East Africa," Somalia has been involved, throughout its history, in the territorial and expansionist schemes of several empires. The ancient Egyptians visited Somalia ("Land of Aromatics") during the pre-Christian era in search of incense and aromatic herbs.

From 900-1400 A.D., the eastern coast of the territory was part of the Zenj Empire which finally fell in the 15th century to Portugal. Later, Arabs from Muscat and Oman asserted their control over Somalia's major coastal centers, only to be replaced in the 19th century by the Sultan of Zanzibar.

European contact with this region dates back to 1839, the year that Aden came under the domination of Great Britain. Effective control was not established, however, until the English managed, between 1884 and 1886, to sign a number of "protectorate" treaties with various Somali chieftains in the north. The Italians, meanwhile, began to expand into southern Somalia in 1885, establishing administrative control and consolidating their territory by extensive military operations. For her part, Great Britain first began to administer her protectorate through the Colonial Office in 1905, and was embroiled in conflict with a rebellious local chief until 1920.

From 1934 to 1936, Italy used Somalia as a staging area for the invasion of Ethiopia, establishing at the same time a colonial government to administer most of Somalia, as well as Ogaden (the eastern portion of Ethiopia and the home of many Somalis).

During World War II, Italian troops occupied British Somaliland, but lost control of this region with their defeat in 1941 at the hands of the British. Italian Somaliland was itself occupied by British troops until 1950, at which time it was returned to Italy under a ten-year United Nations trusteeship arrangement. By then, the UN had already decided that Italian Somaliland should receive its independence by 1960. (In 1954, matters had been complicated somewhat by the transference of a portion of British-controlled Ogaden to Ethiopia.) Unification of the two territories, and their subsequent independence was achieved in 1960.

Since then, Somali-inhabited sections of both Kenya and Ethiopia have repeatedly expressed a desire to be reunited with Somalia. In 1963, diplomatic relations were severed with Kenya over this issue and, two years later, fighting broke out with Ethiopia over much the same question. As might be expected, Somalia has also advocated self-determination for the inhabitants of French Somaliland, including the port of Djibouti, terminus of the Ethiopian railroad.

Somalia's chief of state is Abdirizak Hagi Hussein.

In 1969, President Abdirashid Ali Shermarke was assassinated, whereupon the army took power. It appointed Mukhtar Mohammed Hussein acting head of state.

NATION: SOUTH AFRICA

Date of Independence: May 31, 1910
Area: 471,818 square miles
Population: 17,474,000
Capital: Cape Town (legislative)
Pretoria (administrative)
Bloemfontein (judicial)
Monetary Unit: The South African rand
Principal economic resources: diamonds, gold, platinum, sugar cane, tobacco, cotton, pineapples
Languages: English, Afrikaans

History at a glance:

Fossils discovered in South Africa lend evidence to archeological speculation that the country is one of the earliest homes of mankind. Before the Europeans made contact with it in the 15th century (Bartholomew Diaz of Portugal discovered the Cape of Good Hope in 1488), this huge area was inhabited by Bushmen (nomadic hunters confined to the western uplands) and by Hottentots (a pastoral people settled largely in its southern and eastern coastal sectors). At the same time, however, it became the scene of increased migration from the north by Bantu-speaking peoples who are today still firmly entrenched there, primarily in the "reserves" set aside for them by the government.

On Christmas Day in 1497, Vasco da Gama discovered Natal, bordering on the Mozambique Channel, but South Africa itself did not come to be settled by Europeans until 1652. In that year, Jan van Riebeeck brought the first colonists into the Cape of Good Hope region under the sponsorship of the Dutch East India Company. The settlers began to import slaves from West Africa almost immediately and, what with the scarcity of European women, eventually entered into mixed marriages which produced the so-called "Cape Colored" people. The Dutch, who were known as Boers or "farmers," were soon joined by French, Scandinavian and German immigrants who adopted the name "Afrikaaners" to distinguish themselves from the rest of the population.

The first contacts with Bantu-speaking Africans were made along the Great Fish River in the 1730's. By 1778, boundaries had been set up to separate the settlers from the Africans. Within the year, the first Kaffir War had broken out between the Xhosa tribesmen and the colonists. (Between then and 1812, three more such wars were fought.)

In 1795, Great Britain took charge of the Cape region and, by 1815, pursuant to the Treaty of Vienna, had extended official control over the territory. English settlers began arriving in 1820. From the outset, England granted the free "Cape Colored" people the same legal and political privileges as white people and, in fact, abolished slavery in 1834. Two years later, the Dutch (Boers), alienated by these policies, undertook their great northward trek, defeating Bantu tribesmen in the interior and going on to found the Natal, Transvaal and Orange Free State territories.

The British, however, followed close on the heels of the Boers, annexing Natal in 1843; Kaffraria in 1847; Griqualand West in 1873; Bechuanaland in 1885, and Zululand and Tongaland in 1887. In 1848, the Orange Free State was taken over by the British, only to regain its independence six years later. The Transvaal was made independent in 1852, annexed in 1877, and returned to independence in 1881, the same year in which Swaziland achieved this status.

Despite the preponderance of British political influence, economic factors in the territory accounted for much of its social development during the 19th century. For one thing, the growth of the sugar cane plantations in Natal led to the importation of thousands of East Indians who worked off their period of indenture and then remained in the territory as tradesmen and fishermen. For another, the discovery of diamonds along the Orange and Vaal Rivers (1868) and of gold on the Witwatersrand (1886) hastened the fanatically systematic creation of separate white and African communities. Within the white communities, however, friction between the Dutch farmers and the "outsiders" (English and others) soon led to armed conflict (the Jameson Raid of 1895), and culminated in the Boer War, which was won by the British in 1902.

The Union of South Africa was formed in 1910, and consisted of the two Boer republics (which by then had been granted self-government by the British) and the Cape and Natal provinces. (In 1926, South Africa was given equal legal status with Great Britain, as well as the right to associate freely with the sovereign members of the Commonwealth of nations.)

Despite the restoration of peace, Boer-English relations continued to be marked by wholesale bitterness and recrimination. Two political parties emerged—the Unionists on the one hand advocating cooperation with Great Britain, and the Boer supremacists (the group in power today) who ultimately conceived and executed the policy of "apartheid," or separate racial development.

During both world wars, Boer nationalists attempted to prevent South Africa from participating on the Allied side. They first managed to consolidate effective control over the country in 1948, the year in which Prime Minister Daniel Malan came to power. Since then, white-supremacist politics has become even more firmly entrenched, particularly now that industrial development has brought a tremendous improvement in the living standards of white South Africans.

In 1959, the Nationalists passed the **Promotion of Bantu Self-Government Act** which provided for the creation of eight separate autonomous states for black Africans only. Two years later, concurrent with its withdrawal from the British Commonwealth, South Africa opted for a republican form of government, although its constitution barely changed.

Since then, South Africa has continued to refine its program of apartheid, turning a deaf ear to the protests of the UN, the rest of Africa, and most of the civilized world. The state, headed by Prime Minister Hendrik F. Verwoerd, has taken sterner measures in recent years to suppress all forms of political opposition, censoring the press and other media, imprisoning citizens for up to six months with no formal charges and without a trial—in short, declaring all forms of objectionable activity Communist-inspired.

(Late in 1966, Prime Minister Verwoerd was assassinated by a white man, Dimitrio Tsafendas who, ironically, thought that Verwoerd was doing too much for the Negro population.)

Since then, under prime minister Balthazar J. Vorster, South Africa has strengthened its defense establishment in anticipation of stepped-up guerrilla activity and possible sea and air attacks emanating from its black neighbors to the North. At the same time, the UN has sought desperately to take control of South-West Africa due to South Africa's imposition of apartheid there, but it has been unable to dislodge the republic from the mandated territory.

NATION: **SUDAN**

Date of Independence: January 1, 1956

Area: 967,498 square miles

Population: 13,372,000

Capital: Khartoum

Monetary Unit: The Sudanese pound

Principal economic resources: cotton, livestock

Language: Arabic

History at a glance:

Sudanese history reflects the country's

natural division between the predominantly Arab North (which for centuries has lived in close contact with the civilizations of Egypt, Rome, Byzantium, Turkey, etc.) and the Negro-dominated South (which has been virtually isolated from significant contact with North African and Near Eastern culture).

The earliest known references to the country are to be found in ancient Egyptian inscriptions and in the Old Testament. In antiquity, the center of Sudan lay in what is today the eastern portion of the territory—i.e., in the vicinity of the kingdom of Meroe (750 B.C.-300 A.D.) which even ruled Egypt for a time.

Beginning in the 9th century A.D., nomadic tribes from neighboring Egypt penetrated other areas of the Sudan, intermarrying with the indigenous peoples of the Upper Nile region. From 1500 to 1820, control over most of central and northern Sudan rested with a confederation of tribes ruled and administered by the "Black Sultans" of the Funj dynasty.

In 1820, Sudan was conquered by the Ottoman viceroy of Egypt, Mohammed Ali. Some 50 years passed before the Khedive Ismail led a campaign against the slave trade and, as a result, moved down the Nile into the southern Sudan.

Soon after, several Sudanese tribes rallied to the side of Muhammad Ahmad who proclaimed himself the Mahdi (a religious leader believed to be acting under the inspiration of Allah), and led a number of Sudanese tribes in a successful revolt against Anglo-Egyptian rule. The Mahdi took possession of Khartoum and put to death the British governor, General Charles Gordon. In 1898, Anglo-Egyptian forces under General Kitchener

A Sudanese girl winnows rice after it has been hand-threshed. The Food and Agriculture Organization (FAO) and other UN specialized agencies are carrying out programs in the Sudan to help raise the living standards of the country's tribesmen.

defeated the Mahdi's successor in the battle of Obdurman. British rule was then established through a nominal Anglo-Egyptian condominium (a jointly ruled territory) which remained in effect until 1955. This arrangement was threatened seriously on only one occasion—during the celebrated Fashoda Incident when a French attempt to seize portions of the Sudan was foiled by Kitchener.

Sudanese nationalism became a viable force after World War I at a time when differences were growing more pronounced between the Moslem Northerners and the Negro tribes of the South who were falling under the influence of Christian missionaries and the British educational system. The split gradually widened between those seeking union with Egypt and those advocating the establishment of a separate state.

During World War II, British-led Sudanese troops compiled an outstanding combat record, particularly against vastly superior and better equipped Italian forces. Later, several schemes for a unified state encompassing the entire Nile Valley were advanced, but substantial agreement was not reached by the negotiating parties (Great Britain, Egypt and the Sudan) until 1953, the year Egypt's King Farouk was deposed.

The new republic of Sudan came into being three years later. Within a short time, the government had launched its Arabization-of-the-South program which had widespread repercussions, and led to the eventual overthrow of the existing parliamentary regime by a military junta headed by Lieutenant General Ibrahim Abbud. In 1964, a popular revolution swept the army aside but, by this time, the crucial question of Sudanese unity threatened to plunge the nation into civil war.

Though secessionist activity subsided in the late 1960's, the Sudan was still troubled by internal political turmoil and a growing financial deficit. The nation relinquished American aid in 1967 after breaking ties with the U.S. over the Arab-Israeli war. Two years later, a military coup headed by Gafaar Muhammed al-Nimeiry took over the state and set it on a socialist course.

NATION: SWAZILAND
Area: 6,705 square miles
Population: 375,000
Capital: Mbabane
Monetary Unit: The South African rand
Principal economic resources: rice, cotton
Language: English
History at a glance:

Swaziland was settled in the early 19th century by the Swazi, a people of Bantu stock who had been driven from their homelands in northern Zululand by the Zulus. Swazi independence was guaranteed by Great Britain in 1881 and, three years later, by the Republic of South Africa. In 1890, a joint British-South African-Swazi government was established, with South Africa declaring a protectorate over the territory four years later. After the Boer War, Swaziland was administered by the governor of Transvaal. In 1907, it was placed under the control of the British High Commissioner for South Africa.

The commissioner continues to exercise authority over the territory, although he is now assisted by executive and legislative councils.

In 1967, Swaziland won a measure of self government under a new constitution and, a year later, achieved full independence under King Sobhuza II. Remarkably free of tribal frictions, Swaziland felt its stability would encourage Great Britain to offer it more economic aid than was in fact forthcoming. As a result, Swaziland expanded its trade with its southern and eastern African neighbors to boost revenues.

NATION: TANZANIA (Tanganyika and Zanzibar)
Dates of Independence: December 9, 1961; December 10, 1963.
Area: 362,720 square miles
Population: 10,300,000
Capital: Dar es Salaam
Monetary Unit: The East African shilling
Principal economic resources: sisal, cotton, coffee, diamonds, cloves
Language: English
History at a glance:

Since 1959, Tanzania has been able to lay an authoritative claim to the distinction of being the aboriginal home of mankind. It was in this year that Dr. L.S.B. Leakey discovered *homo zinjan-*

thropus in the Olduvai Gorge near Serengeti National Park. Knowledge of the early history of the region is scant, although it is certain that East Africa as a whole was involved in trade with Greece, Arabia, Persia, India, and even China.

The coastal region of Tanzania (then known as Tanganyika) first attracted Arab colonists from Oman in the 8th century A.D. and Persian settlers a century later. For the next 500 years, a number of coastal towns enjoyed considerable commercial prosperity. During this period, Islam gained a secure foothold along the coast, and the Swahili language and culture developed among the Bantu tribes of the region.

Portugal first came on the scene in the 16th century, wresting the Indian Ocean trade from the Arabs and conquering the coastal towns under the latter's control. The Portuguese themselves were driven from their coastal holdings during the next two centuries by Arab slave traders based in Zanzibar and loyal to the Omani sultans. The height of Arab influence on the mainland occurred in the 19th century under the Iman Seyyid Said. The plantation system introduced by Zanzibar around 1840 inevitably led to an extension of the slave trade which brought about considerable tribal unrest and warfare.

The first Europeans to explore the interior of Tanzania were the Englishmen Burton and Speke, who crossed the territory in 1857 in search of the headwaters of the Nile River. After the Berlin Conference of 1884-1885, Tanzania came under the influence of Germany, which established a protectorate extending over the areas of Rwanda and Burundi (German East Africa). In 1890, Germany purchased a portion of the coast from the Sultan of Zanzibar, and gradually began to extend its influence farther into the interior, encountering stiff resistance from the African population. The Germans established plantations, built railways, improved communications, and substituted a system of forced labor for the slave trade which they abolished.

After Germany's defeat in World War I, Tanzania was mandated to Great Britain by the League of Nations, and retained this status until it was taken over by the United Nations after World War II.

By 1954, African nationalism had reached such fever pitch in the territory that the Tanganyika African National Union (TANU) petitioned the UN to persuade Great Britain to establish a timetable for the specific steps leading to independence. In September 1960, Julius Nyerere became Tanganyika's chief minister. By the end of 1961, the territory had become fully independent.

Meanwhile, Zanzibar had likewise begun to press Great Britain for full internal autonomy. In 1964, shortly after Zanzibar had won its independence under an Arab-controlled government, a popular revolt was staged by the African-supported Afro-Shirazi party. Both the sultan and the prime minister were deposed, and a republican government headed by Abeid Karume installed. Three months later, Zanzibar merged its political fortunes with those of Tanganyika, creating what was at first called the United Republic of Tanganyika and Zanzibar and, what has since come to be known as Tanzania. The merger was regarded as an effective measure to neutralize the growing influence of Communist China in Zanzibar. President Nyerere has remained on friendly terms with this Asian power, even exchanging official visits with Premier Chou-En-lai, but Zanzibar has been prevented—at least for the time being—from becoming what one observer called a potential "Cuba of Africa."

In 1967, Nyerere undertook an extensive program of nationalization that covered banks, trading companies, insurance firms and the food-processing industry. Despite the program, the President emphasized that private investment would still be welcome in his country, operating in partnership with the National Development Corporation.

NATION: **TOGO**
Date of Independence: April 27, 1960
Area: 21,853 square miles
Population: 1,600,000
Capital: Lomé
Monetary Unit: The CFA franc
Principal economic resources: cocoa, cotton, coffee, groundnuts, palm products, phosphate
Language: French
History at a glance:

Togo was first settled by the Ewe people who migrated there from the Niger Valley between the 12th and the 14th centuries.

During the next two centuries, the territory was frequently visited by the

Portuguese who instituted a thriving slave trade in Grand Popo and Petit Popo, two of Togo's coastal villages. The Portuguese were then displaced, first by the French who established trading posts in the area, and then by the Germans who ultimately won control over the territory by signing a treaty with the chief of Togo, then only a village on the coast. (The Germans later applied the name Togo to the entire territory.)

The Togolese capital of Lomé was established in 1897 and, within a few years, boundary settlements had been arranged with England and France. These agreements paid scant attention to existing tribal unities, with the result that a number of groups found themselves simultaneously incorporated into three distinct colonial areas—Ghana, Togo and Dahomey.

During World War I, England took over control of the coastal areas (British Togoland), whereas France administered Togo's interior (French Togoland). In 1922, the League of Nations gave official sanction to this war-time arrangement.

In 1945, at the end of World War II, both England and France relinquished their holds on Togo to the United Nations. Two years later, the Ewe people sent the first of a number of petitions to the UN requesting assistance in the achievement of tribal and national unification. After nine years of debate (differences had to be resolved not only between England and France, but also between a number of conflicting tribes), a plebiscite was held in British Togoland, which was incorporated into the Republic of Ghana when that nation became independent in 1957.

On the other hand, French Togoland voted for full autonomy within the French Community, a decision opposed at first by the UN. In 1960, the Republic of Togo became a sovereign nation, with Sylvanus Olympio as prime minister. When Olympio was assassinated in 1963, Nicholas Grunitzky (living in exile in Dahomey at the time) became the new prime minister.

In 1967, Lieutenant Colonel Etienne Eyadema overthrew the Grunitzky government, naming himself president and instituting military rule. After a year, Eyadema postponed a referendum for a new constitution and a return to civilian control. In 1969, he "acceded to the popular will" after staging demonstrations in which the people ostensibly demanded his continuation in office.

NATION: **TUNISIA**

Date of Independence: March 20, 1956

Area: 38,332 square miles

Population: 4,565,000

Capital: Tunis

Monetary Unit: The Tunisian dinar

Principal economic resources: olives, grapes, cork

Language: Arabic

History at a glance:

Tunisia is the site of the ancient empire of Carthage, which once vied with Rome for power in the Mediterranean and in North Africa, but was finally defeated in 146 B.C. in the last of the three Punic Wars. Tunisia was occupied by the Vandals in the 5th century A.D.; by the Byzantines a century later, and by the Arabs for many centuries thereafter. The Arabs, in fact, held sway until the coming of the Ottoman Turks, and used Tunisia as a base from which to extend their power and the religion of Islam south and west into sub-Sahara Africa, and northwards across the Mediterranean to Sicily.

The Turks seized Tunisia in 1574, holding it for the next three centuries, a period of time during which the territory was ruled either by governors from Istanbul or by descendants of the Husayn dynasty.

In the late 19th century, due to Tunisia's precarious financial position, France felt it incumbent upon itself to impose a protectorate over the territory by armed force. By this time (c. 1880), Great Britain, Italy and France had established a control commission to supervise Tunisia's tottering finances. Once France had a clear field, though, she proceeded with a program of heavy investments which helped Tunisia modernize itself. In return, she benefited from Tunisia's unstinting loyalty during World War I.

Tunisian nationalism was an outgrowth of a moderate reform movement begun by the Destour Party in the 1920's. Led by Habib Bourguiba, the Neo-Destour Party of the next decade was more activist in character, and able to negotiate with France from a position of strength after World War II.

In 1951, the French rejected a Tunisian demand for internal autonomy, a decision which touched off a wave of unrest punctuated by terrorism. In 1955,

Ghana's Prime Minister Dr. K. A. Busia shaking hands with Secretary General U Thant.

a Franco-Tunisian treaty was signed in Paris and, a year later, Tunisia was granted full independence. A new constitution, with Bourguiba as the first president, went into effect in 1959.

Two years later, Tunisia attempted a blockade of the French naval base at Bizerte, a move which immediately provoked the armed intervention of France and led to the massacre of several Tunisian civilians. The tension eased off gradually and, in 1963, the base was evacuated by France.

Since then, Tunisia has nationalized all foreign-owned land in an effort to initiate a program of internal reform. This policy has been vigorously opposed by the French, who have withdrawn their technical experts, suspended financial aid and eliminated export subsidies. The United States has taken up part of the slack by donating some of its surplus grain, and by supporting a large public works program which is still in operation.

In recent years, Tunisia has made remarkable strides toward modernizing its industry, extending basic rights to all of the populace (women in particular have received more ample legal protection), improving health facilities, and educating its young people. The Bourguiba regime, though it discourages opposition, has proved to be enlightened and progressive. Bourguiba was last returned to office in 1969.

NATION: UGANDA

Date of Independence: October 9, 1962
Area: 93,181 square miles
Population: 7,270,000
Capital: Kampala
Monetary Unit: The East African shilling
Principal economic resources: cotton, coffee, maize, groundnuts, copper
Language: English
History at a glance:

According to the testimony of contemporary archeologists, tiny landlocked Uganda was the site of a highly developed African civilization long before European explorers opened up this portion of the African continent. Negro Africans of Bantu stock built up a relatively advanced Iron Age civilization there. It remained intact until Hamitic peoples from the northeast overcame the Bantu in armed conflict.

The two mightiest kingdoms in the area were the Buganda to the north and the Bunyoro to the south. Arab slave traders took advantage of the clash between these two groups, which reached a climactic stage in the mid 19th century.

In 1862, John Hanning Speke and Captain J. A. Grant explored the territory for Great Britain, as did Samuel Baker who discovered Lake Albert. (Baker later returned to Uganda as a foreign agent for Egypt which had its own expansionist interests in the regions of the lower Nile.) In 1875, Henry Stanley arrived in Uganda, and was followed by a host of Christian missionaries seeking to win favor with the Kabaka (the king of Buganda).

In 1894, consistent with the role it had assigned itself in the carving up of Africa into different "spheres of influence," Great Britain established a formal protectorate over Buganda, and consolidated its influence there in short order. In 1900, Sir Harry Johnstone negotiated the Uganda Agreement, giving the Buganda Kingdom a privileged position within the British-controlled territory. A year later, similar agreements were concluded with the kingdoms of Toro and Ankole.

In the first decade of the 20th century, Sir Hesketh Bell, the British commissioner, drafted a program designed to assist the peasant in the cultivation and development of cotton as a staple crop. Thus, Uganda was spared the upheaval which later afflicted neighboring Kenya, where the predominant system of free speculation in land allowed the white European to win control of the choicest land and to establish a plantation-based economy.

As in the rest of Africa, nationalism took hold in Uganda after World War II. Buganda, however, refused to endorse a republican form of government, advocating instead the establishment of a federation which would allow each territory to maintain its autonomy.

In 1962, a coalition government headed by A. Milton Obote was voted into power. Agreement with the petty kingdoms of the territory as to their status and representation was reached before the end of the year when independence came.

In 1966, President Obote moved to unify Uganda by removing Mutesa, suspending the Constitution, abolishing the federal system, and assuming all ruling power. A year later, the traditional kingdoms were abolished, and Obote was named president under a new republican constitution. Obote has shown himself a tough and uncompromising leader willing to resort to severe measures to insure the success of his policies.

NATION: **UNITED ARAB REPUBLIC (Egypt)**

Date of Independence (as republic): June 18, 1953

Area: 386,102 square miles

Population: 28,359,000

Capital: Cairo

Monetary Unit: The Egyptian pound

Principal economic resources: cotton, livestock, manganese, phosphates, salt, iron ore, petroleum

Language: Arabic

History at a glance:

The site of one of the oldest civilizations in the world, Egypt was a name in recorded history long before its upper and lower kingdoms were united (c. 3200 B.C.). Such milestones of human endeavor as the great tombs of the Pharaohs, the pyramids and the sphinx are irretrievably associated with this ancient land. The "golden age" of Egypt was reached during the 18th dynasty or about 1570 B.C., at which time the New Empire superceded it. As this kingdom weakened, invasion by foreign conquerors, particularly the Assyrians, the Persians (525 B.C.) and the Macedonians under Alexander the Great (332 B.C.), became more and more devastating.

For the next three centuries, Egypt was effectively ruled by the Ptolemaic dynasty which fell to Rome in 31 B.C. when Caius Octavius (later to become the Emperor Augustus) defeated the combined forces of Cleopatra and Marc Antony at the Battle of Actium.

In 340 A.D., Egypt was made part of the Eastern Roman Empire (Byzantium). Three centuries later, it fell under Arab control and became a center of the Islamic world. Arab domination was not ended until 1250 when the Mamelukes, slaves of non-Arabic stock, gained supremacy, only to be engulfed in their own turn by the Ottoman Empire, centered in Constantinople (1517). In 1798, the armies of Napoleon Bonaparte occupied Egypt but, within three years, they had been ousted by British and Turkish forces. In 1805, the Ottoman Turks appointed Mohammed Ali pasha, or governor, of the territory. Backed by the power of the Turks, he was able, by 1811, to eliminate the last vestiges of Mameluke influence in Egypt. The dynasty which Mohammed Ali founded eventually proved to be the last royal line of Egypt.

The 19th century was a time of ambitious planning in Egypt. Land reform and improved methods for cotton cultivation were introduced, and construction was begun on the Suez Canal, linking the Mediterranean with the Red Sea. With the opening of the canal to water traffic in 1869, Egypt became a transportation center of international significance—so much so that, in 1882, Great Britain sent in troops to quell a threatened rebellion there. In the process, she also took over the Egyptian government, solidifying her rule over all the territory as far south as the Sudan.

With the outbreak of World War I, Great Britain established a protectorate over this area as well. By 1922, Egypt had won back a degree of nominal sovereignty. England, continued, however, to exercise control over foreign affairs, defense, communications, and the Anglo-Egyptian Sudan to the South.

Between wars, Egyptian nationalism was centered in the Wafd Party, first led by Sa'ad Zaghul Pasha and later by Dahas Pasha. In 1936, the year Farouk I ascended the throne, an Anglo-Egyptian treaty was signed under which Britain restricted its occupation forces only to specified areas—mainly those along the Suez Canal route.

During World War II, Cairo became the Middle Eastern headquarters for British forces and a key military staging ground for the Allies. In 1948, fighting broke out between Egypt and Israel which had only just acquired its independence. After nine months in which the Egyptians were severely beaten, a truce was declared, but army dissatisfaction continued to smolder. In 1952, a group called the Society of Free Officers revolted against the monarchy. Led by General Mohammed Naguib (although the guiding genius was Colonel Gamal Abdel Nasser), the coup forced Farouk to abdicate and led to the establishment of a republic on June 18, 1953. Within a year, Nasser had gained absolute control of the country, and entered into a series of agreements with the United States, Great Britain and other United Nations members to help build a new dam at Aswan. At the same time, Nasser also negotiated with the Soviet Union for economic aid and arms shipments, a move which finally caused the United States to withhold its promised financial assistance. Nasser, however, countered this move by seizing and nationalizing the Suez Canal on July 26, 1956. This action was followed by an Israeli invasion of the Sinai Peninsula, and by British and French military intervention in the Port Sa'id area. However, a Soviet ultimatum, backed in part by the United States, led to the forced withdrawal of these troops, and to the subsequent restoration of peace and order by UN forces.

In 1958, Egypt and Syria combined their states into a single entity—the United Arab Republic (UAR), a federation under one chief of state, governed by a common legislature and defended by a unified army. That same year, Yemen joined the federation which came to be known as the United Arab States (UAS). The union lasted until 1961, when the Syrian army revolted, causing the withdrawal of Syria from the federation. By the end of the year, Egypt had broken off relations with Yemen as well.

Since then, renewed efforts have been made by several Arab states to form closer ties with each other, and even to establish a federal union. To date, however, despite agreement in principal, no effective measures have been undertaken by any of the proposed participants (Syria, Yemen, Iraq, Algeria) to bring about such a union.

The United Arab Republic was badly drubbed by Israeli military forces in the six-day war of 1967, and has since sought desperately to retain its position of preeminence in the Arab world. With Russian help, it has stabilized its fortunes somewhat, but many Arab leaders sense that Nasser is growing increasingly vulnerable. The 1970 cease-fire suspending periodic artillery and air assaults between Israel and Egypt may bring unforeseen results in Cairo, as it already has in Jordan.

NATION: **UPPER VOLTA**
Date of Independence: August 5, 1960
Area: 95,444 square miles
Population: 4,760,000
Capital: Ouagadougou
Monetary Unit: The CFA franc

Principal economic resources: livestock, shea nuts
Language: French
History at a glance:

The early history of Upper Volta is largely concerned with the exploits of the Mossi people who, according to tradition, migrated from the east between the 11th and 13th centuries. During the following two centuries, there is evidence indicating that the Mossi conducted highly successful raids on the wealthy trading cities along the Niger River. Checked eventually by the armed might of the Songhai Empire, the Mossi organized the territorial spoils they had acquired into the states of Tenkodogo, Yatenga, and Ouagadougou, each of which was ruled by a moro naba (king). Of the three reigning kingdoms, Ouagadougou was unquestionably the most powerful.

The Mossi finally settled down to a life of commerce, engaging profitably in the export of gold, kola nuts, and slaves. In the 18th century, the Ashanti (from Ghana) made significant military inroads into Mossi territory. The rest of it was conquered in 1896 by a French lieutenant in command of a single infantry battalion.

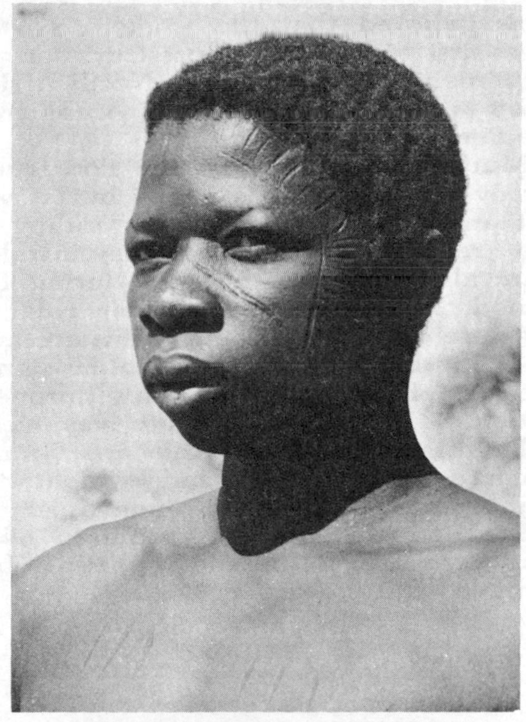

Tribal markings of a member of the Mossi in Upper Volta. In the old Mossi Empire, no person bearing these scars could be enslaved.

Governed at first as part of the Ivory Coast, Upper Volta was separated from this territory in 1919 and made a single administrative unit. In 1933, it was parcelled up among Niger, French Soudan, and the Ivory Coast.

After World War II, however, Upper Volta was again reconstituted as a separate territory—partly in response to the wishes of the Mossi, and partly to curb the growth of the African Democratic Rally, an interterritorial political party which was gaining widespread support throughout West Africa. Upper Volta accepted the French Constitution of 1958, thereby becoming an autonomous unit within the French Community. Two years later, the territory became completely independent, although retaining close ties with metropolitan France.

In 1966, Maurice Yaméogo, president of Upper Volta, was deposed by Lieutenant Colonel Sangoule Lamizane after several days of rioting in Ouagadougou concerning the issue of pay cuts for government employees.

Throughout the late 1960's, chief of staff Lamizana effectively headed the country and prevented any further erosion of its precarious financial position. The colonel has barred political activity until the country's economic house is in order.

NATION: **ZAMBIA**
Date of Independence: October 24, 1964
Area: 288,130 square miles
Population: 3,500,000
Capital: Lusaka
Monetary Unit: The Zambian pound
Principal economic resources: copper, zinc, lead, tobacco
Language: English
History at a glance:

Archeological discoveries in the Gwembe Valley near Lusaka in 1964 shed considerable light on the nature of the earliest known civilization in what is today the African nation of Zambia. Explorations currently in progress have uncovered such artifacts as copper wire, pottery specimens and iron gongs. It is also believed that the people of this period (850-1000) were skilled in the art of weaving cloth.

The first European to explore the territory was the Scotsman, David Livingstone. He was soon followed by representatives of the British South Africa Company which gradually edged its way across the Zambezi River until, by 1924, it had extended its influence as far north as the Belgian Congo.

Since the mineral wealth of Northern Rhodesia (as it was then called) was not immediately apparent, the British did not feel it necessary to give the territory colonial status, particularly since it was under the direct jurisdiction of the Colonial Office. In 1925, however, the rich ore deposits in what is today known as the Copper Belt were discovered, and Europeans literally flocked northward to search out their fortunes.

The political tactics of the European settler had a two-fold objective: to minimize the authority of the British Crown in the territory and, at the same time, to prevent the Africans from uniting behind a political, economic and educational program.

The political strength of the African crystallized slowly in Northern Rhodesia. It was not until 1948 that he won the right to be represented by non-Europeans. (Five years later, it should be mentioned, the British government decided to include the territory in a newly created federation, consisting of Northern and Southern Rhodesia as well as Nyasaland.)

In 1959, an investigating commission of the Crown reported that the majority of the population in both Northern Rhodesia and Nyasaland were violently opposed to union with Southern Rhodesia on the grounds that racial discrimination was institutionalized there. The European-dominated United Federal Party (UFP) contested the findings of the commission, and took issue with the pro-African United National Independence Party (UNIP) over the question of dissolving the federation.

With the eventual withdrawal of Nyasaland, relations between the two Rhodesias became even more strained. Subsequent elections did little to heal the breach, and the federation was officially dissolved in 1963.

A year later, Northern Rhodesia became independent as Zambia, with Kenneth Kaunda as its premier. Late in 1965, following Rhodesia's unilateral declaration of independence from Great Britain, Zambia, as a member of the British Commonwealth, requested and received the protection of British troops, as well as access to British armaments.

Reelected in 1968, Zambian President Kenneth Kaunda has diminished his country's dependence on imports obtained from Rhodesia, but he has purchased heavily in South Africa, where racial segregation is probably more thorough and repugnant than anywhere else in the world. It is Kaunda's policy, however, to be more concerned with the ownership of resources in Zambia than with external trade. All firms in Zambia are now obliged to sell the government a major interest. Whether this policy will ultimately discourage foreign investment remains yet to be seen.

FRENCH AFRICAN DEPENDENCIES

TERRITORY: *Comoro Islands (Grande Comore, Anjouan, Mohéli, Mayotte)*
Area: 838 square miles
Population: 207,000
Capital: Moroni
Monetary Unit: The CFA franc
Principal economic resources: coconuts, cloves, vanilla, copra, sisal
Language: French
History at a glance:

It is believed that the Comoro Islands were first visited in the pre-Christian era by Phoenician traders from North Africa. They were later invaded by Arabs from the Persian Gulf region.

Much later (in 1503), the Portuguese discovered the islands anew, but it was not until 1517 that an actual landing by the French took place. Malagasy invaders were also active in the area during this period. In 1843, the Malagasy ruler of Mayotte ceded that island to France and, in 1865, the local rulers of Mohéli signed a treaty of friendship with this European nation. A French protectorate was eventually established over Anjouan, Grande Comore and Mohéli, islands which were administered jointly with Madagascar.

In 1946, the Comoros acquired overseas territorial status and, by 1961, had achieved full internal autonomy.

TERRITORY: *French Somaliland*
Area: 8,494 square miles
Population: 80,000
Capital: Djibouti

Monetary Unit: The Djibouti franc
Principal economic resources: dates, vegetables, hides, salt
Language: French
History at a glance:

French control over this portion of Somaliland dates back to an omnibus treaty signed by France and a number of Danakil tribal chieftains in 1862. Seven years later, concurrent with the opening of the Suez Canal, a number of French development companies were established in the region. In 1896, France annexed the territory as a colony after having signed additional treaties with Danakil and Issa chieftains. The all-important railroad which links Addis Ababa (Ethiopia) to the sea was completed in 1917.

After World War II, French Somaliland became an overseas territory, and gained complete internal autonomy in 1956. Two years later, the local assembly voted to retain its territorial status.

In 1964, a conference of non-aligned nations placed the issue of French Somaliland on its agenda, and called upon France to grant the territory immediate independence. The Somalian delegate to the United Nations later asked that body to take up the same question, but political leaders within the territory itself rejected this proposal on the grounds that it involved "annexationist designs." Consequently, French Somaliland reaffirmed its loyalty to France.

TERRITORY: *Réunion*
Area: 969 square miles
Population: 370,000
Capital: Saint Denis
Monetary Unit: The CFA franc
Principal economic resources: sugar cane, geranium, vetiver
Language: French
History at a glance:

Réunion was an uninhabited volcanic island at the time of its discovery in 1528 by Pedro de Mascarenhas, a Portuguese explorer. By 1649, it had fallen under the control of France and was called "Bourbon Island." Having served originally as a French penal colony, it was later settled by Negroes, Malays, Indo Chinese, Chinese and Malabar Indians.

In 1665, the French East India Company established an outpost there. Coffee, which by 1715 had become the major agricultural staple of the island, was replaced in importance after 1800 by sugar cane.

Réunion, which received its present name in 1793, was made an overseas department of France in 1947.

PORTUGUESE AFRICAN DEPENDENCIES

TERRITORY: *Angola*
Area: 481,351 square miles
Population: 5,119,000
Capital: Luanda
Principal economic resources: coffee, sisal, corn, timber, fish, diamonds, iron ore, oil
Language: Portuguese
History at a glance:

The Congo River (the northern border of Angola) was discovered in 1482 by the Portuguese navigator Diogo Cão, who was followed by a number of other Portuguese explorers. Settlements were soon established and, by 1575, the town of Luanda had already been founded. Except for a brief period between 1641 and 1648 during which it was under Dutch control, Angola has been one of Portugal's major overseas dominions and a primary source of tropical products and raw materials.

Until the abolition of the slave trade in 1836, Angola served as the chief supplier of all slaves bound for Brazil and other parts of South America. The territory's boundaries were first fixed by an international treaty signed by the major European powers at the Berlin Conference of 1884-1885.

The tribes of the Angolan interior were gradually pacified during the first two decades of the 20th century and, by 1951, Portugal had imposed the status of an overseas province upon the territory. However, African representation in government and equal citizenship rights were so slow in coming to Angola that radical groups soon sprang up, carrying their campaign to the point of an open revolt which broke out in 1961. Although brutally suppressed, the revolt received such unfavorable publicity that it ultimately led to an investigation by the United Nations. While a government-in-exile was being formed in 1962 under the Angolan leader, Holden Roberto, the UN warned Portugal to eliminate its "repressive measures," and even went so far as to condemn Portugal's "colonial war."

TERRITORY: *Cape Verde Islands (São Tiago, São Antao, Fogo, São Vicente)*
Area: 1,557 square miles
Population: 218,000
Capital: Praia
Principal economic resources: coffee, fish, salt, bananas
Language: Portuguese
History at a glance:

The Cape Verde Islands, uninhabited when they were discovered by the Portuguese in 1456, were first settled toward the end of the 16th century, when African slaves were brought in from Portuguese Guinea to work the land. In 1587, the islands were placed under the administration of a colonial governor.

For the next two centuries, the population of the island grew steadily, particularly with the influx of Genoese and Spanish immigrants. Great Britain established a coaling station on the island of São Vicente in the 18th century, a move which also involved the founding of a settlement. On occasion, famine has caused some of the islands' inhabitants to emigrate to the African mainland or to the United States.

To this day, the territory has continued to be administered by a governor, although he is now assisted by two local councils. Some 60% of the inhabitants are of mixed Portuguese and African extraction.

TERRITORY: *Mozambique*
Area: 302,227 square miles
Population: 6,914,000
Capital: Lourenço Marques
Principal economic resources: sugar, cotton, cashew nuts, copra, sisal
Language: Portuguese
History at a glance:

Mozambique was first visited by the Portuguese explorer, Vasco da Gama, in the course of his voyage to India and the Far East in 1498. Settlements along the coastal areas were established in the 16th century, during which time the slave trade also prospered. By 1878, this trade had been abolished, and boundary settlements reached between adjacent British and German territories.

In 1951, the territory's status was changed to that of an overseas Portuguese province. African nationalism in Mozambique was slow to develop, with no definite trend in evidence until 1962 when the Mozambique Liberation Front was formed. Some fighting broke out in 1964 but, within a year, the Portuguese had largely succeeded in fragmenting the movement and in forcing it underground. Several thousand Mozambique nationalists have since sought asylum in neighboring African states which have already gained their independence.

TERRITORY: *Portuguese Guinea*
Area: 13,948 square miles
Population: 524,000
Capital: Bissau
Principal economic resources: oil seeds
Language: Portuguese
History at a glance:

Portuguese sailors first visited this portion of Guinea in 1446, some 100 years before it was to become a source of slaves. Cape Verdians set up trading posts there and, by the 19th century, had imposed their administration over the entire territory. The tribes of the interior, however, were not fully subjugated until after World War I—and only then with difficulty—so that it was hardly a surprise that nationalism quickly sprang to life during the Angola uprising of the 1960's.

Reports from conflicting sources have made it difficult to determine the exact situation in the territory at present. Some say that the rebels have cut the province in two, and that the Portuguese have been driven out of all areas—save for the most important towns and the coastal sectors.

The appointed governor of the territory is responsible to Portugal's Minister for Overseas Territories.

TERRITORY: *São Tomé and Príncipe*
Area: 372 square miles
Population: 56,000
Principal economic resources: cocoa,

coconuts, coffee, copra, palm oil, cinchona
Language: Portuguese
History at a glance:

Most of the people inhabiting São Tomé and Príncipe are descendants of the original Portuguese colonists and African slaves who hailed from Gabon and other parts of the Guinea coast as far south as Angola. The Angolares, descendants of Angolan slaves shipwrecked in the 16th century, live along the south and west coast of São Tomé. They have been joined there by a large number of migrant laborers who have come from other Portuguese territories on the mainland for the purpose of working on the numerous plantations scattered through the islands. São Tomé and Príncipe are ruled by an appointed governor.

SOUTH AFRICAN DEPENDENCY

TERRITORY: **NAMIBIA**
Area: 325,608 square miles
Population: 564,000
Capital: Windhoek
Monetary Unit: The South African rand
Principal economic resources: diamonds, copper, lead, zinc, manganese, fish
Language: English
History at a glance:

Great Britain was the first European nation to set foot in what is now the territory of South-West Africa, having gained control of a number of offshore islands, as well as the Walvis Bay region, by 1878. Germany established a protectorate over the mainland in 1884, and acquired a number of trading concessions there. However, she did not establish full administrative control until 1908.

Captured by South African troops in 1915, South-West Africa became a South African mandated territory in 1920, retaining this status until the close of World War II. At this point, South Africa sought unsuccessfully to annex the territory outright, rather than place it under the trusteeship of the United Nations as other colonial powers had done.

Soon thereafter, representatives of the African population in the territory were sent as petitioners to air their grievances before the United Nations. In 1962, Ethiopia and Liberia brought suit against South Africa before the International Court of Justice at the Hague, Netherlands, maintaining that the rights of the South-West African population had consistently been violated by the administering power.

On July 18, 1966, the Court dismissed the suit on the grounds that Ethiopia and Liberia did not have sufficient legal interest to obtain a judgment on the case's merits. This setback was regarded as a severe blow to the foes of apartheid.

The territory, governed by a South African administrator, is divided into the police zone (white settlement areas) and the reserve area (for native inhabitants only).

In 1966, the UN General Assembly declared that the South African mandate was terminated and, within a year, appointed a council to administer the territory until independence. In 1968, the territory was renamed Namibia.

South Africa, however, refused to relinquish administration. It currently appoints an administrator and elects an all-white legislative assembly and six members who sit in the South African House. Apartheid was extended to the area in 1966.

SPANISH AFRICAN DEPENDENCIES

TERRITORY: *Ifni*
Area: 579 square miles
Population: 50,000
Capital: Sidi Ifni
Principal economic resources: fish, barley, wheat and corn
Language: Spanish
History at a glance:

The tiny enclave of Ifni in West Africa was ceded to Spain "in perpetuity" by Morocco in 1860, but its exact boundaries with Morocco were not fixed until 1912, and Spain did not come to administer and occupy the territory until 1934. In recent years, Morocco has demanded its return from Spam, and it has been the scene of occasional armed clashes between the two nations.

TERRITORY: *Spanish North Africa,* consisting of CEUTA and MELILLA
Area: 12 square miles
Population: 157,000
Principal economic resource: fish
Language: Spanish
History at a glance:

Built on the site of an ancient Phoenician colony, *Ceuta* is believed to have been the locale of one of the fabled Pillars of Hercules. It was taken over from the Arabs by Portugal in 1415, only to fall under Spanish control in 1580. *Melilla,* the site of the initial uprising which launched the Spanish Civil War in 1936, has belonged to Spain since 1496.

A Togolese woman making pottery. Togo was once known as British Togoland.

TERRITORY: *Spanish Sahara,* consisting of RÍO DE ORO and SAGUIA EL HAMRA
Area: 102,702 square miles
Population: 42,000
Capital: El Aiún
Principal economic resources: barley, fish, livestock
Language: Spanish
History at a glance:

The three administrative districts of Spanish Sahara (with their centers at El Aiún, Villa Cisneros, and La Aguera) were organized as a province in 1958.

UNITED KINGDOM AFRICAN DEPENDENCIES

TERRITORY: *St. Helena**

Area: 47 square miles
Population: 5,000
Capital: Jamestown
Monetary Unit: The pound
Principal economic resources: hemp, timber
Language: English
History at a glance:

St. Helena was sighted by the Portuguese explorer Juan de Nova Castella in 1502, but was first claimed by the Dutch in 1633. By 1659, it was garrisoned by the British East India Company which withstood an armed attack by the Dutch in 1673.

Perhaps St. Helena's major claim to fame is the fact that Napoleon was exiled there in 1815, the year of his disastrous defeat at Waterloo. He remained there until his death in 1821.

In 1834, St. Helena became a British Crown Colony. It is now administered by a governor, who is assisted by executive and advisory councils.

TERRITORY: *Seychelles*
Area: 156 square miles
Population: 45,000
Capital: Port Victoria
Monetary Unit: The Seychelles rupee
Principal economic resources: coconuts, copra, cinnamon, patchouli oil, vanilla, guano, phosphates
Language: English
History at a glance:

Discovered by Portugal in 1505, the Seychelles became a pirates' base until they were settled by France in the mid-18th century. In 1794, Great Britain took control of the islands and, by 1810, had made them a dependency of the British colony of Mauritius. Four years later, at the signing of the Peace of Paris, the French officially ceded them to Great Britain. In 1903, the Seychelles became a separate colony, with a governor as well as executive and legislative councils.

* Includes the following dependencies: Tristan da Cunha (40 square miles; population, 250); Ascension Island (34 square miles; population, 475); and Gough, Nightingale and Inaccessible Islands (40 square miles; all uninhabited).

Loading bananas in Jamaica for export

THE NEGRO IN THE WESTERN HEMISPHERE

North America
Central America
South America
The Negro in the Caribbean
- **Independent Nations**
- **French American Dependencies**
- **Netherlands American Dependencies**
- **United Kingdom American Dependencies**
- **U.S. American Dependencies**

It is one of the many accidents of nature (in this case, color) that the Negro, with rare exception, is identifiable as such wherever he happens to be found. His considerable presence in the United States and the condition under which he lives in his adopted land have already received enormous publicity the world over. In the process, however, the fact that thousands of Negroes inhabit other parts of the Western Hemisphere is one which has often been largely overlooked. For this reason, the editors of this volume have attempted to bring into sharper focus those areas, particularly in the Caribbean, where Negroes form a substantial portion of the population, and are thus able to effect a material and/or cultural impact upon any given social order.

A. NORTH AMERICA

Canada. The Negro population of Canada has remained stable for most of the 20th century, hovering around a figure of from 16,000 to 20,000. Most Negroes there are of West Indian extraction, descendants of immigrants who entered the country through the ports of Halifax and St. John. They are settled, for the most part, in the provinces of Nova Scotia and Ontario; in cities like Toronto, Montreal and Windsor.

Mexico. Only 1% of the population of Mexico is Negro. Negroes are found almost exclusively in Veracruz and Acapulco.

The United States. About one-ninth of the total continental U. S. population is classified as Negro—the greatest concentration being in the South and in the large urban centers of the North and West. In the 20th century, the Negro has been involved in two major migratory movements: one to the North beginning in 1915 ("The Great Migration"), and the other to the West in the 1940's. Greater job opportunities and the desire to escape an all-pervasive discrimination were the major causes of both migrations.

B. CENTRAL AMERICA

British Honduras. About 60% of the inhabitants of British Honduras are of mixed Negro-white parentage. Most of the Negroes are of West Indian origin.

Costa Rica. Only 2% of the population of Costa Rica is Negro. Most Negroes are of Jamaican origin and, together with a small number of mulattoes, are settled in the Límon Province.

Guatemala. The relatively few Negroes and mulattoes in Guatemala inhabit the Caribbean and Pacific lowland areas.

Honduras. Some 2% of the Honduras population is Negro. The dominant strain is a mixture of Spanish and Indian blood.

Nicaragua. The Negro, comprising some 9% of the population in sparsely inhabited Nicaragua, is settled mainly along the Miskito Coast.

The docks at Cartagena.

Panama. Roughly 65% of the inhabitants of Panama are classified as mestizo or mulatto—i.e., mixed white and Indian, or mixed white and Negro.

C. SOUTH AMERICA

Bolivia. About 2% of the population of Bolivia is classified as Negro. Cultural factors, primarily those involving the Spanish and Indian population, are of greater import in this country than the race question.

Brazil. Brazil is the "melting pot" of South America, differing most significantly from the United States in that racial intermarriage has never been tabooed there. As a result, the Brazilian heritage is a compound of several diverse elements—millions of Negroes from Africa, Asians from Japan, Caucasians from Europe, as well as the aboriginal Indian population.

Colombia. Some 4% of Colombia's 15,000,000 people are Negroes, and an additional 3% are Zambo (a mixture of Indian and Negro blood). Negroes and mulattoes are most heavily settled in the coastal regions and tropical valleys. Originally introduced as slaves during the colonial era, Negroes have continued to immigrate to Colombia, in particular from the West Indies.

Ecuador. Ecuador's 4.8 million people are a basic mixture of white, Indian and Negro strains. Those people classified as Negro comprise 5% of the population,

A banana market in Colombia.

and live mainly in the northern coastal province.

Guayana. See page 225

Peru. There are more than 500,000 people classified as Negroes in Peru, although the Indians are by far the largest group there.

Uruguay. Negro influence in Uruguay is minimal. It is estimated that only one person in 10 has any trace of either Negro or Indian blood.

Venezuela. Bordering as it does on the Caribbean, it is not surprising that Venezuela has a sizable Negro population (7%). The Negro in this country originally provided the labor needed to run the large plantations which were granted to the Spanish conquistadores by the Crown. As in many other parts of the Caribbean, the original Indians died out almost entirely from disease (smallpox), war or brutality.

THE NEGRO IN THE CARIBBEAN

With some few exceptions, the Negro has been a potent force in the development of the Caribbean. The overwhelming majority of Haitians and Jamaicans, for instance, are of African descent. The Negro strain also predominates in Trinidad and Tobago, as it does in many of the American, Dutch, English and French dependencies in the Caribbean.

The following territories are discussed in this section.

Barbados
Cuba
Dominican Republic
Guyana (in South America)
Haiti
Jamaica
Trinidad and Tobago

French American Dependencies
- French Guiana (in South America)
- Guadeloupe
- Martinique

Netherlands American Dependencies
- Netherlands Antilles
- Surinam (in South America)

United Kingdom American Dependencies
- Bahamas
- Bermuda
- British Virgin Islands
- Cayman Islands
- Leeward Islands
- Turks and Caicos Islands
- Windward Islands

United States Dependencies
- Corn Islands
- Panama Canal Zone
- Puerto Rico
- Swan Islands
- Virgin Islands of the U. S.

NATION: **BARBADOS**

Area: 166 square miles
Population: 243,000
Capital: Bridgeton
Principal economic resources: sugar, rum, molasses, tourism
Language: English
History at a glance:

The most easterly of the Caribbean Islands, Barbados was originally the home of the Arawak Indians, although it was more than likely uninhabited when the first British settlers arrived in 1627. The land patents once granted to members of the English nobility were returned to the Crown in 1652. Though slavery was abolished in 1834, the last of the slaves were not liberated until four years later.

The constitution of Barbados, among the oldest in the Commonwealth, is based largely on convention. Universal adult suffrage was introduced in 1951; elected ministers in 1954; a cabinet system in 1958, and full internal autonomy in 1961. The bicameral legislature was headed by a Crown-appointed governor, who in turn appointed a premier enpowered to name a five-member cabinet.

Despite the coming of independence in November 1966, the "bajans" have retained strong political and cultural ties with England. Though an independent parliamentary democracy, they have remained within the British Commonwealth and preserved their allegiance to Queen Elizabeth II who is represented in the country by Sir Winston Scott.

About 75% of the inhabitants of Barbados are Negroes, with an additional 17% being of mixed origin. Only 5% is European.

NORTH AMERICA
ALASKA
CANADA
UNITED STATES
MEXICO
BR. HONDURAS
HONDURAS
GUATEMALA
NICARAGUA
EL SALVADOR
COSTA RICA
PANAMA

NATION: CUBA
Date of Independence: May 20, 1902
Area: 44,218 square miles
Population: 7,336,000 (73% white; 12% Negro; 15% mestizos)
Capital: Havana
Monetary Unit: The Cuban peso
Principal economic resources: sugar, tobacco, coffee, nickel, chrome, copper, iron, manganese
Language: Spanish
History at a glance:

The island of Cuba was discovered by Christopher Columbus during his first voyage to America. In 1511, the Spanish appointed a governor in the person of Diego Velasquez, who established Santiago as the capital and founded Havana just south of where it lies today. By 1523, the African slave had become a familiar sight on the island. Yet, during this period, Cuba was of even greater importance as an embarkation point for Spanish explorers bound for the Central and South American mainlands. The treasures of Mexico obtained by the conquistadores invariably passed through Havana on their way back to Europe, with the result that the northern coast of Cuba was often despoiled by French and English pirates preying on Spanish shipping. In 1762, the English occupied Havana, and held Cuba for nearly a year before returning it to Spain in exchange for Florida. Among the advantages brought on by the English occupation was the fact that it encouraged a greater spirit of national unity, and stimulated free trade.

Although the rest of Spanish America managed to win its independence from the mother country in the early decades of the 19th century, Cuba proved to be an exception to this trend. In 1868, Carlos Manuel de Cespedes, a wealthy planter, granted his slaves their freedom and agitated for a revolution against Spain. For the next decade or so, guerrillas were holed up in the hills of eastern Cuba, but their efforts against the combined strength of the colonial government and the Spanish army proved largely fruitless. In 1892, while in exile in the United States, Jose Marti founded the Cuban Revolutionary Party and, three years later, issued the famous *grito de Baire* (call to arms) which ushered in another civil war. The insurrection lasted for three years, despite the fact that Marti was killed in the initial engagement against Spanish forces.

The cause of the revolutionaries aroused considerable sympathy in the United States, both in private and official circles. Consequently, it hardly came as a surprise when the United States declared war on Spain after the U. S. battleship *Maine* was blown up in Havana harbor on February 15, 1898. Spanish resistance on both land and sea was easily overcome, and Cuba was declared independent—even though the U. S. Army occupied the island for a three-year period (1899-1902).

The United States, however, did force Cuba to ratify the Platt Amendment which specified that it could intervene in the island's internal affairs in the event it became necessary to insure the maintenance of law and order. In addition to this, much of Cuba's wealth, natural and otherwise, was soon in the hands of a number of American absentee owners. Revolts against Yankee imperialism brought about the periodic intervention of U. S. Marines—in 1906, 1912, and again in 1920. Finally, in 1934, during the first administration of Franklin D. Roosevelt, the Platt Amendment was abrogated. (The United States, however, retained possession of a naval base at Guantanamo Bay.)

During World War I, Cuba had enjoyed a brief period of prosperity due to the growth of its gold reserves; but sugar prices soon declined, giving rise to widespread unemployment and national hardship. In 1925, Gerardo Machado began an eight-year reign as a virtual dictator. His successor was overthrown in 1934 by an army sergeant, Fulgencio Batista y Zaldivar. More clever than his predecessor, Batista held power by installing puppet presidents whom he then deposed at will. In 1940, he had himself elected president, and allowed a new constitution to be passed. After his four-year term was over, he continued, nonetheless, to be a potent force in Cuban politics—a fact borne out by his seizure of power in 1952.

On July 26, 1953, a group of young firebrands staged an abortive raid on the army barracks at Fort Moncada. Led by Fidel Castro, the uprising was quickly suppressed, and Castro himself thrown into prison. He was released under a 1954 presidential amnesty, only to begin the immediate organization of what he came to term the sequel to the "26th of July" movement. Two years later, he and a small group of revolutionary forces (including his trusted aide, Ernesto

South America
VENEZUELA
GUYANA
SURINAM
FRENCH GUIANA
COLOMBIA
ECUADOR
PERU
BRAZIL
BOLIVIA
PARAGUAY
CHILE
ARGENTINA
URUGUAY

"Che" Guevara of Argentina) landed in Oriente province, where they holed up in the wilds of the Sierra Maestra Mountains. The rebellion thus launched soon spread across the island and, within three years, Batista had been forced into exile. The "26th of July" movement swept Castro into power as premier.

Members of the revolutionary cabinet then undertook to rule the country by decree, ostensibly until those reforms to which the movement had been dedicated could be put into effect. Castro himself disavowed any ties with Communism, and was given the status of a hero throughout most of Latin America.

By 1960, however, it had become apparent that Communist influence in Cuba was growing, particularly as the government plunged ahead with an ever-bolder and more comprehensive scheme of land expropriation, one which affected U. S. property holdings with disturbing frequency. Anti-Communist cabinet members were soon purged, and Cuba became a base for subversion, as well as a clearing-house for other Latin American revolutionary movements.

The United States, at this time still Cuba's chief hemispheric customer, ultimately decided to sever diplomatic relations with the Castro regime in retaliation for the nationalization of most U. S.-owned property on the island. The Cuban government countered this move by nationalizing U. S. oil refineries for having refused to process Soviet crude oil, whereupon the United States decided in its turn to eliminate Cuba's sugar quota. Trade and general relations with Soviet-bloc nations and Communist China offset some of the deficit incurred by the loss of U. S. markets. Late in 1960, Castro labeled Cuba a socialist country and, within a year, declared himself to be a follower of Marxist-Leninist doctrine.

In 1961, a group of Cuban exiles—financed, trained and organized by the Central Intelligence Agency (CIA)—undertook an amphibious invasion of the island at the Bay of Pigs. Within three days, however, Cuban military forces defeated the invaders, taking some 1,200 men prisoner. (The captives were later used by Castro as human barter for U. S. supplies.)

By 1962, a Soviet-style economic system was so firmly entrenched on the island that all major means of production and distribution, as well as communication and other public services, were in the hands of the state.

That same year, evidence gathered from U. S. aerial reconnaissance photographs of Cuba established the fact that the Soviet Union had begun to install ballistic missiles capable of reaching American soil. Moving decisively, President Kennedy quickly initiated a blockade of the island, and issued an ultimatum calling for the immediate withdrawal of all such offensive weapons. This action brought the world to the brink of war, averted only after the Russians backed down in the face of Kennedy's demand.

Castro remained in control, however, and continued to spread revolutionary propaganda throughout the rest of Latin America. In 1965, he instituted a program whereby all Cubans wishing to go to the United States (excepting those males eligible for military service) would be permitted to do so.

Castro has since reported that 1970 was a turning point in Cuban affairs. Viewing a decade of revolution, he assured the people that agricultural programs would continue to put plenty of food on their tables and on the shelves of their stores. He also maintained that Cuban industry was making remarkable strides and would bring the country out of its underdeveloped status before 1975.

NATION: **DOMINICAN REPUBLIC**

Date of Independence: February 27, 1809

Area: 18,816 square miles

Population: 3,452,000 (28% white; 12% Negro; 60% mestizos and mulattoes

Capital: Santo Domingo

Principal economic resources: sugar, coffee, tobacco, bananas, bauxite, iron, nickel

Language: Spanish

History at a glance:

The eastern portion of Hispaniola, the portion which forms today's Dominican Republic, was originally known as Quisqueya, i.e. "mother of all lands." It was first settled by the warlike Carib Indians, who were succeeded by the peace-loving and agriculturally inclined Arawaks.

In 1492, Christopher Columbus became the first European to land on the island, claiming it for Spain and giving it the name by which it was known for several centuries thereafter—Hispaniola. Within the next two decades, Hispaniola became a base from which Spain initiated her conquest of the Caribbean and, indeed, the entire New World. By 1517, cattle and horses were being raised on the island, and sugar cane had become the staple of its agricultural economy. At that time, the population was estimated to be about 60,000, a substantial portion of which were Negro slaves. Following the discovery of Mexico and Peru, and due also to the ravages of a smallpox epidemic and to the excesses of Dutch, English and French buccaneers, the population declined considerably, and Hispaniola soon outlived its usefulness as a staging ground for the Spanish conquest of the New World.

In 1697, Spain was forced by the Treaty of Ryswick to acknowledge French dominion over the western third of the island (Haiti). A century later, it also lost control of the eastern two-thirds of Hispaniola (Santo Domingo) in the aftermath of a serious slave uprising. Toussaint L'Ouverture, the Negro liberator of Haiti, conquered Santo Domingo as well in 1801, but the Dominicans, fearing Negro rule, backed a French force which soon succeeded in overcoming the Haitians. Haiti achieved independence in 1804, but Saint Domingue (as it was rechristened by the French) remained under French control until 1809 when Juan Sánchez Ramirez defeated the French at Palo Hincado and proclaimed the founding of the first Dominican Republic.

Spain regained control of this territory under the Treaty of Paris (1814) but, in 1821, another republic was founded, this time by Jose Muñez de Caceres. Within a year, however, Santo Domingo was once again overrun by Haiti, which then occupied the territory for some 22 years, a period marked by the departure of most land-owning whites, by fierce racial and cultural animosities, and by an atmosphere heavy with oppression and violence. In 1884, a secret group known as La Trinitaria organized a successful revolt which once more restored the independent republic of Santo Domingo.

For the next 20 years, Dominican history ran an unpredictable course, punctuated by petty internecine rivalries, further threatened invasions by Haiti and several changes of government. In 1861, President General Santana invited Spain to annex the country and, for the next four years, it was administered as a Spanish colony. Spanish troops withdrew in 1865, ushering in still another period of almost continuous revolution and widespread governmental corruption.

In 1870, Santo Domingo was on the verge of being annexed by the United States, but the U. S. Senate refused to ratify the necessary treaty. By 1905, the country teetered on the brink of bankruptcy and political chaos. That year, however, the United States assumed control of Dominican customs. In 1915, following a presidential assassination and the overthrow of several chief executives, the United States set up an economic council to stabilize the island's economy. A year later, a military government under Captain H. S. Knapp was established. This government remained in power until 1924 when Dominican sovereignty was restored, and U. S. forces withdrawn. (The customs control mission remained until 1941.)

In 1930, Rafael Leonidas Trujillo Molina was elected president, and ushered in a 30-year period of rule during which Santo Domingo became, as it were, his personal property. Aided by his family, Trujillo became an absolute dictator who quashed all attempts at resistance by murder, imprisonment and other grisly forms of intimidation. Reelected in 1934, 1940 and 1947, Trujillo did manage to improve economic conditions in his country; achieve administrative stability; balance the budget and free the nation from domestic and foreign debt. In the process, however, he accumulated an enormous private fortune, estimated at from 900 million to 1.5 billion dollars. Moreover, he completely suppressed all those human rights traditionally associated with democratic principles and freedom of expression.

In 1961, Trujillo was assassinated, and a wave of terror swept the island as his son, Air Force General Rafael Trujillo Martinez, seized power. Special investigators from the Organization of American States (OAS) reported that the new repressions were even more ruthless than the old.

Over the next four years (once the influence of the Trujillo family had finally been eradicated), the country was ruled by two presidents, two councils of state, and two juntas. Coup and counter-coup verged on the order of the day. The situation was further complicated by near-war with Haiti and by guerrilla activity sponsored by pro-Castro Dominicans.

In 1965, the ruling civilan junta was overthrown in a military uprising which triggered a civil war involving rebel forces laced with Castroite supporters and hard-core Communists. Almost at once, the United States intervened militarily, ostensibly on the grounds that it was protecting American nationals. In May of that year, an inter-American contingent was created by the OAS, and dispatched to the scene to serve as an occupational force until constitutional government could be restored. The major factions agreed on the installation of Hector Garcia-Godoy as provisional president in the summer of 1965. A year later, Joaquín Balaguer was elected president, whereupon U.S. combat troops were withdrawn from the island.

Balaguer has kept the nominal allegiance of the military, but at a remarkably high price. The national budget currently allocates more than 17% of its operating expenditures to military upkeep. The expansion of the U.S. sugar quota has helped the country, but political unrest, labor problems, and dwindling tourism have offset much of the gain from this source.

NATION: **GUYANA** (formerly British Guiana)
Date of Independence: May 26, 1966
Area: 83,000 square miles
Population: 628,000 (50% East Indian; 33% Negro; 17% Mixed, European, Chinese)
Capital: Georgetown
Principal economic resources: bauxite, gold, diamonds, manganese
Language: English
History at a glance:

Little can be said of the pre-European history of what is today the independent nation of Guyana. Spanish sailors first charted the coastline in 1499, but the territory itself was not settled until 1620, and then only by the Dutch West Indies Company. By 1746, the Dutch had founded settlements in Essequibo, Demerara, and Berbice; but they lost control of these areas to the English—first in 1796, then in 1803 and, finally, in 1814. The colony of British Guiana was formed in 1831.

With the abolition of slavery in 1837, most Negroes either settled down on the land they had worked, or else migrated to the towns. This being the case, the aristocratic planter class exerted pressure on the government for the importation of indentured servants from India to work on the plantations. (Today, most of the sugar workers are East Indians, whereas the urban population is predominantly of Negro origin—a factor of great importance in evaluating current political trends in the country.)

In 1928, British Guiana was granted limited representative government along with a new constitution. (This latter replaced the charter under which the colony had been administered while it was a Dutch possession.) In 1953, another constitution was put into effect, this one calling for the establishment of a bicameral legislature and for an increase in the elected majority of the lower house. Because of charges of Communist subversion, however, England was obliged to suspend the elections, instituting instead an interim government which ruled until 1957 when new elections were held. Victory went to the People's Progressive Party (PPP), headed by Dr. Cheddi Jagan, who was named minister of trade and industry.

In 1961, British Guiana was granted full autonomy. That same year, elections held under still another constitution resulted again in a majority victory for the PPP which controlled the Legislative Assembly. A year later, Dr. Jagan (by then the premier) submitted an austerity program calling for compulsory savings and for a property tax. Announcement of this program triggered a violent general strike, which could not be put down until British troops arrived on the scene.

In 1963, there was further unrest as an aftermath of a labor relations bill which appeared to make it possible for Dr. Jagan to favor the interests of certain unions. Racial friction heightened between the East Indian followers of Dr. Jagan and the Negro-dominated urban population, many of whom occupied civil service posts. Strikes and even more violent upheavals seriously affected Guiana's economy, and large losses were suffered by the sugar and bauxite industries.

Late in 1964, the People's National Congress (PNC), headed by Forbes Burnham, wrested control from the PPP by winning the national elections. (The PNC, however, was only able to form a government with the aid of the United Force Party, a right-wing, business-oriented group encouraging close ties with the West.) British Guiana became independent under its new name of Guyana on May 26, 1966, with Burnham remaining in power as the duly-elected prime minister.

Since then, Guyana has been involved in a running feud with its western neighbor, Venezuela, which has laid claim to more than half the entire territory of the new republic. As a result, Guyana has reluctantly abandoned some of her ambitious economic plans to concentrate instead on defense measures. Outlays for military preparedness now absorb 20% of the national budget.

NATION: **HAITI**
Date of Independence: January 1, 1804
Area: 10,714 square miles
Population: 4,551,000 (95% Negro, 5% mulatto)
Capital: Port-au-Prince
Monetary Unit: The gourde
Principal economic resources: Coffee, tourism
Language: French
History at a glance:

Christopher Columbus discovered the island of Hispaniola (the western half of which is today called Haiti) in 1492, and established a settlement on the north coast near the present city of Cap Haitien. The Spanish colonists lost little time in wiping out the island's Indian inhabitants, a policy which eventually made it necessary for the Spanish crown to import Negro slaves from Africa for plantation labor.

By 1625, French privateers, operating from the island of Tortuga, had been successful in expelling the Spanish along the northern coast, and in paving the way for French colonies to spring up there. With sugar as the basis of the plantation economy, the French found it necessary to continue the practice the Spanish had introduced, and so brought more and more slaves from West Africa. In 1697, under the Treaty of Ryswick, Spain ceded the western portion of Hispaniola to France. Under French rule, St. Domingue (as this area was then called) became one of the most prosperous territories in the entire Caribbean.

By the 18th century, four distinct social groupings had emerged on the island: the white French planter; the Creole; the freed Negro, and the Negro slave. The Creoles—sandwiched, as it were, between the white and the Negro—found themselves striving desperately, on the one hand, for the privileges accorded the white minority while living, on the other, in an almost constant fear of being overrun by the blacks.

It was not until the French Revolution in 1789 that the explosive potential inherent in such a social situation began to reveal itself, as Haiti's half a million Negro slaves became increasingly imbued with a desire for freedom. In 1791, an abortive Negro uprising was suppressed by the French, but the movement, as a whole, never lost its momentum thanks largely to the fervor and genius of a self-educated Negro slave and former soldier, Toussaint L'Ouverture. Within two years, Toussaint had shocked the French not only by conquering the entire island, but also by promulgating a new constitution and abolishing slavery. In 1802, however, a huge force sent by Napoleon recaptured the island. Toussaint himself was betrayed and, after being taken prisoner, was shipped to France where he died.

However, his successor, Jean Jacques Dessalines (another Negro general who had risen in the ranks) continued this struggle and finally overcame the French forces in 1803. A year later, Dessalines proclaimed the independence of St. Domingue, and restored to it the original Indian name of Haiti ("land of mountains"), in the process taking for himself the title of emperor.

When Dessalines was assassinated in 1806, the nation soon became divided into a northern kingdom ruled by Henri Christophe and a southern republic administered by Alexandre Sabès Pétion, a mulatto. (France lost control of Santo Domingo, the eastern portion of the island, in 1808.)

The next decade was marked by widespread agricultural reform (the liquidation of the estates), and by internal political manipulation which accomplished little for any of the principals involved in it.

In 1820, when Christophe committed suicide, the ensuing power vacuum was quickly filled by Jean Boyer who, after conquering Santo Domingo in 1822, introduced compulsory labor in all parts of the island. In 1843, Boyer was finally ousted, and Santo Domingo regained its independence a year later. Six years later, Faustin Elie Soulouque, the Negro president of Haiti, proclaimed himself Emperor Faustin. Within the next decade, however, he was dethroned by Nicholas Fabre Geffard who re-established a republic, and later signed an agreement with the Vatican whereby Roman Catholicism became the national religion.

For the next 50 years, Haiti remained on the brink of political chaos and national bankruptcy. Saddled with a crushing foreign debt, it lapsed slowly back into an archaic agricultural economy. In 1905, the United States took over receivership of its customs and later persuaded the Haitian Congress to relinquish its control of the country. While the American occupation, which lasted until 1934, did bring economic progress to the island, it also provoked bitter protests from other Latin American nations. In 1935, under President Stenio Vincent, a new constitution was proclaimed but, within two years, relations with neighboring Santo Domingo were severely strained. The latter, however, agreed to pay Haiti an indemnity to settle a Haitian claim that thousands of her citizens had been massacred in Santo Domingo.

The almost constant instability of Haiti's government was again made manifest in 1950, when General Paul Magloire overthrew the government in a coup d'etat. Though Magloire's policies led to a serious depression, he did promulgate a constitution which institutionalized universal suffrage. In 1956, he resigned as constitutional president, only to be returned to power almost at once by the Haitian army. This, however, led to a general strike which forced Magloire's ultimate resignation. Interim president Daniel Fignolé was then kidnapped by the army and deported. Finally, in 1951, the head of the army, Major General Antoine Kebreau, held an election which, though boycotted by many, was won by a middle-class Negro physician, François Duvalier.

Since then, Duvalier has consolidated his complete control over the island, ruling as a dictator by absolute fiat and with the support of the dreaded police force (*tontons macoute*). Without recourse to any constitutional process, he has had himself re-elected to the presidency, and has even gone so far as to have himself designated as president for life.

Duvalier remains such a pervasive influence in the country that it is virtually impossible to consider any activity outside of the context of his approval. Recurrent invasion attempts by Duvalier's enemies in exile have been repulsed handily. The strength of the regime has, to some extent, revitalized the tourist industry.

NATION: JAMAICA

Date of Independence: August 6, 1962
Area: 4,411 square miles
Population: 1.7 million (90% Negro; 10% Mixed, East Indian, European, Chinese)
Capital: Kingston
Monetary Unit: Jamaican pound of 20 shillings
Principal economic resources: bananas, rum, bauxite, tourism
Language: English
History at a glance:

The island of Jamaica was discovered by Christopher Columbus on May 2, 1494, while on his second voyage to the New World. Some 15 years later, it was settled by the Spanish who systematically exterminated its original inhabitants, the Arawak Indians, replacing them with slaves brought from Africa to work the plantations.

The English conquered the island in 1655, at which time a group of slaves (the Maroons) fled into the interior, where they established a number of strongholds from which they made sporadic raids on the English settlers. This situation lasted until 1740, the year the Maroons were granted virtual autonomy over their own lands.

Jamaica soon became a base of operations for buccaneers raiding the Spanish Main. On the whole, however, the English continued to maintain a slave-operated plantation economy based on such crops as sugar, cocoa, and coffee. With the abolition of slavery in 1834, the settlers were forced to recruit other sources of cheap labor, resorting to the importation of East Indian and Chinese farm hands. In 1846, the removal of the tariff protection for colonial produce entering the British market set off a violent dispute between the planter-dominated Jamaican legislature and the Crown on the one hand, and the planter-dominated administration and the Jamaican freedmen on the other. This conflict culminated in the Morant Bay uprising of 1865, which led to the imposition of Crown-colony status one year later. The growth of banana cultivation, the improvement of internal transportation and communication, and much-needed reform in the political administration improved the status of the islanders somewhat, although insurmountable barriers continued to separate most groups within Jamaican society, which was largely class-centered.

The Depression of the 1930's aggravated already-existing problems in Jamaica to such an extent that England felt it necessary to dispatch a royal investigating commission to the island. The commission's report led to the drafting of the 1944 constitution which permitted Jamaicans a wider degree of self-government.

Cabinet government was introduced in 1953, five years before the island became a member of the West Indies Federation. (Jamaica withdrew from this organization in 1961.) Full self-government followed in 1959, with independence within the British Commonwealth being achieved three years later. Thereafter, the Prime Minister was Sir Alexander Bustamante, leader of the Jamaican Labour Party (JLP). Bustamante was succeeded in office in 1967 by Prime Minister Hugh Shearer.

An open-air market in Kingston, Jamaica.

NATION: **TRINIDAD AND TOBAGO**
Date of Independence: August 31, 1962
Area: 1,980 square miles
Population: 922,000 (43% Negroes; 37% East Indians; 17% Mixed; 3% Whites, Chinese)
Capital: Port of Spain
Monetary Unit: The West Indian dollar
Principal economic resources: oil, asphalt, cocoa, sugar, molasses, rum, tourism
Language: English
History at a glance:

Christopher Columbus discovered Trinidad and Tobago on July 31, 1498, bestowing the name "La Trinidad" (Spanish for "The Trinity") on the larger of the two islands. A Spanish governor was not placed in charge of Trinidad until 1522, at which time the island became a kind of supply station for ships en route to South America. Settlers attempting to colonize Trinidad during these years met with opposition from the Carib Indians, and were likewise harassed by British buccaneers then active in the Caribbean. (Sir Walter Raleigh, for example, burned St. Joseph in 1595.)

In time, however, the Spanish did manage to establish settlements, and to introduce a plantation-based economy heavily dependent on the importation of slave labor from West Africa. In 1725, a severe blight all but wiped out the cocoa crop, with the result that agriculture was at a virtual standstill for the next 50 years. In 1783, the Spanish government began inviting immigrants of other nationalities to help colonize the islands, an offer which attracted many Frenchmen who thus acquired free land grants. (The distinctive French-Creole flavor in today's Trinidad is directly traceable to this influx of French settlers.)

Trinidad itself was captured by the British in 1797, and was formally ceded to Great Britain by Spain five years later (The Treaty of Amiens). Trinidad then became a Crown Colony, and was linked to Tobago in 1888.

In the 19th century, sugar proved to be the island's agricultural staple. Cultivation of this crop was made possible by the utilization of slave labor but, when slavery was abolished in 1834, the landowners resorted to the importation of more than 150,000 Hindu and Moslem "contract workers" from India. A good number of them remained in Trinidad once their contracts had expired, finding work in the cocoa industry which experienced a revival in the late 19th century. Since then, sugar and petroleum have grown in importance as major sources of foreign exchange.

Independence was granted Trinidad and Tobago jointly in 1962, with Dr. Eric Williams serving the new nation both as prime minister and head of the majority party, The Peoples National Movement.

* * *

After its discovery by Columbus, Tobago too went virtually ignored until 1616, when colonists from Great Britain first appeared among the island's Carib Indian inhabitants. England gained permanent possession of Tobago in 1814, and ruled it for much of the 19th century from the Windward Island of Grenada. Tobago became a Crown Colony in 1877, and was linked to Trinidad in 1888. Since then, it has remained associated with the latter in all phases of its political, economic and social development.

FRENCH AMERICAN DEPENDENCIES

TERRITORY: ***French Guiana***
Area: 35,135 square miles
Population: 35,000
Capital: Cayenne
Principal economic resources: hardwoods, tantalite, gold, bauxite, rum
Language: French
History at a glance:

French Guiana first began to be colonized in 1604, although it was not formally awarded to France until 1667 by the Peace of Breda. During the French Revolution, it served both as a penal colony and a place of exile. The territory's permanent borders were not settled until 1854.

Since 1947, French Guiana has been an overseas department of France, exercising the privilege of being represented in the French parliament by one senator and one deputy. The territory of Inini, included within it, has a status equivalent to that of a Parisian arrondissement (an administrative district).

Most of the inhabitants are of mixed Negro and white stock, although there are several tribes of aboriginal Indians in the interior. Most descendants of freed or fugitive Negro slaves have settled along the rivers and coastal lowlands.

TERRITORY: *Guadeloupe* (Basse-Terre, Grand Terre)
Dependencies: Marie Galante, Les Saintes, Désirade, Saint-Barthelemy, Saint Martin
Area: 687 square miles
Population: 297,000
Capital: Basse-Terre
Principal economic resources: sugar cane, bananas, rum, tourism
Language: French
History at a glance:

Guadeloupe was discovered by Christopher Columbus in 1493 during his second voyage to the New World. A permanent colony was established there by France in 1635. Since then, with the exception of two brief periods during which the island was occupied by Great Britain, Guadeloupe has been in the hands of the French without interruption. An overseas department of France since 1946, it is represented in Paris by three deputies and two senators.

The inhabitants of Guadeloupe are either Negroes, or a mixture of Negroes and the French settlers who first arrived in the 17th century.

TERRITORY: *Martinique*
Area: 425 square miles
Population: 303,000
Capital: Fort-de-France
Principal economic resources: sugar, bananas, rum, tourism
Language: French
History at a glance:

Christopher Columbus discovered the island of Martinique in 1502, but it was first colonized by the French in 1635. It has remained under the control of France for all but two short periods of its history: from 1762 to 1763, during the Seven Years War, and from 1794 to 1815, during the Napoleonic Wars. In both these instances, Great Britain temporarily occupied the island.

In 1902, a terrible catastrophe took place on the island when Mount Pelée erupted and completely destroyed the city of St. Pierre, together with its 30,000 inhabitants.

Martinique is represented in the French parliament by three deputies and two senators. An appointed prefect is chief administrator, and is assisted by a 36-member general council. The island has been an overseas department of France since 1946.

The people of Martinique are mostly Negro, or of Carib Indian or European stock.

NETHERLANDS AMERICAN DEPENDENCIES

TERRITORY: *Netherlands Antilles*
Territorial Units: LEEWARD ISLANDS—
Aruba, Bonaire, Curaçao
WINDWARD ISLANDS—
Saba, St. Eustatius, St. Maarten (shared with France)
Area: 371 square miles
Population: 202,000
Capital: Willenstad (Curaçao)
Principal economic resources: oil (Aruba and Curaçao); fishing, boatbuilding (Saba); cotton, sugar cane, tropical fruits (Saint Maarten); agriculture (St. Eustatius); tourism
Language: Dutch
History at a glance:

Curaçao, the largest of the Netherlands Antilles, was discovered in 1499 by Alonso de Ojeda and Amerigo Vespucci, but Spain did not begin colonizing the island until 1527. In 1634, the Dutch, under Johannes van Walkeeck, seized the islands (including Aruba and Bonaire) and installed Peter Stuyvesant as their first governor. During the Napoleonic Wars, the English occupied them, but they were restored to the Netherlands in 1816.

Saba was first occupied by the Dutch in the 17th century, while St. Eustatius, in the hands of the Dutch since 1632, served as a supply depot for England's American colonies before and during the Revolutionary War. (It is traditionally credited with having been the first foreign post to render a salute to the Ameri-

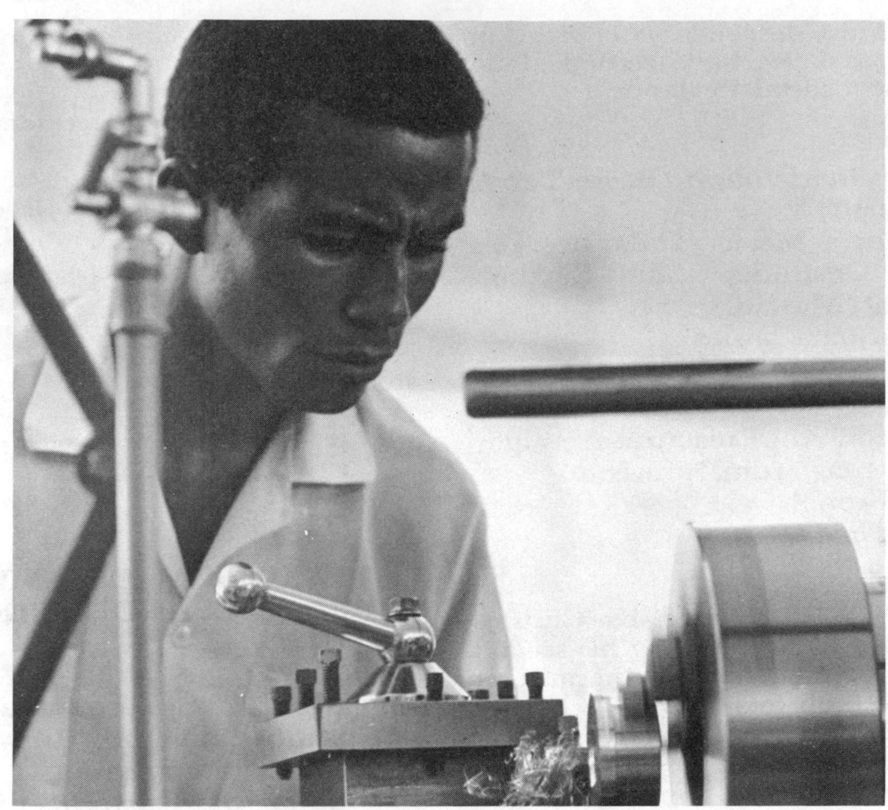

A student at the University of the West Indies in Trinidad operates a lathe in the workshop of the engineering faculty.

can flag in 1776.) The island changed hands several times before being permanently restored to the Netherlands in 1841. Saint Maarten, occupied by the Dutch and French in 1648, was later divided between them.

The Netherlands Antilles, a part of the kingdom of the Netherlands, has had complete internal autonomy since 1954. Executive power is wielded by a governor who represents the Dutch sovereign.

The people are about 85% mestizo, i.e. a mixture of Negro, Indian, Spanish and Dutch strains.

TERRITORY: *Surinam* (Dutch Guiana)
Area: 55,144 square miles
Population: 358,000
Capital: Paramaribo
Principal economic resources: bauxite, rice, sugar cane, citrus fruits, coconuts, bananas
Language: Dutch
History at a glance:

In the 16th century, Spaniards in search of gold were the first Europeans to set foot on Surinam, but they left as soon as it became apparent that treasure was not to be found there. In 1625, the British, French and Dutch began simultaneously to take an interest in, and ultimately to vie for control of, the territory. Under the Treaty of Breda (1667), Great Britain agreed to cede it to the Netherlands in return for the colony of New Amsterdam (later New York). Dutch control, however, was not recognized by other European powers until the Treaty of Paris at the end of the Napoleonic Wars.

In 1954, Surinam was granted full internal autonomy in accordance with the provisions of a new statute put into effect by the king of the Netherlands. (This charter united the Netherlands, Surinam, and the Netherlands Antilles on a basis of equality and as constituents of a single kingdom.) Surinam is administered by a governor who is assisted by a cabinet and by an elected legislative council.

The Negro inhabitants of Surinam (representing about 10% of the population) are descendants of fugitive slaves who were imported from Africa before 1865. Other major groups include: Indians (from the Asian subcontinent); Indonesians; Creoles (persons of mixed blood), and aboriginal Indians.

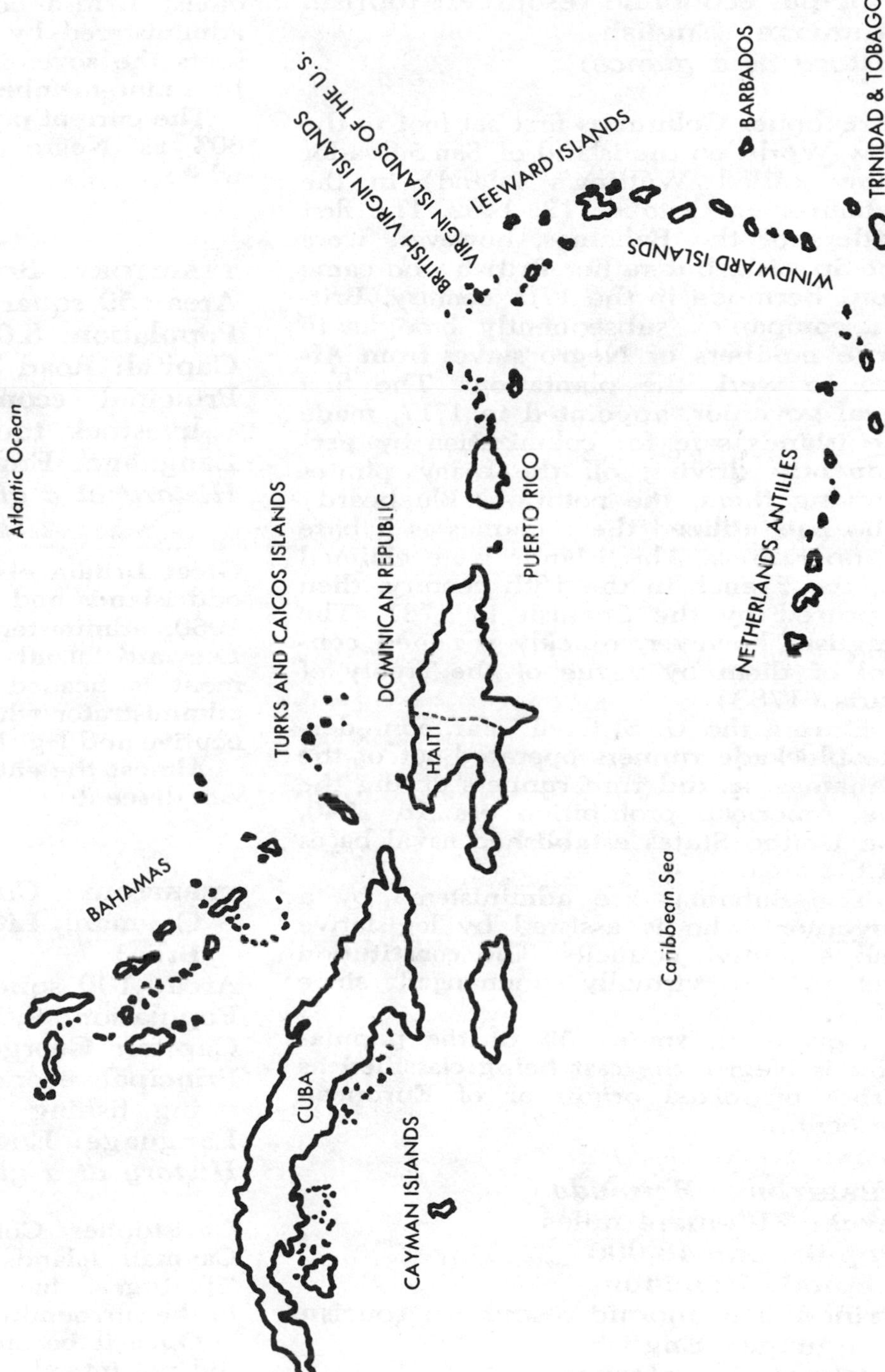
Caribbean
Atlantic Ocean
BAHAMAS
TURKS AND CAICOS ISLANDS
CUBA
CAYMAN ISLANDS
HAITI
DOMINICAN REPUBLIC
PUERTO RICO
BRITISH VIRGIN ISLANDS
VIRGIN ISLANDS OF THE U.S.
LEEWARD ISLANDS
WINDWARD ISLANDS
BARBADOS
TRINIDAD & TOBAGO
NETHERLANDS ANTILLES
Caribbean Sea

UNITED KINGDOM AMERICAN DEPENDENCIES

TERRITORY: *Bahamas*
Area: 4,400 square miles
Population: 131,000
Capital: Nassau
Principal economic resources: tourism
Language: English
History at a glance:

Christopher Columbus first set foot in the New World on the island of San Salvador (now called Watling's Island) in the Bahamas on October 12, 1492. The first settlers of the Bahamas, however, were not Spanish, but rather British who came from Bermuda in the 17th century. British companies subsequently brought in large numbers of Negro slaves from Africa to work the plantations. The first royal governor, appointed in 1717, made the islands safe for colonization by permanently driving off the many pirates (among them, the notorious Bluebeard) who had utilized the Bahamas as a base of operations. The islands were claimed by the French in the 18th century, then captured by the Spanish in 1781. The English, however, quickly regained control of them by virtue of the Treaty of Paris (1783).

During the U. S. Civil War, confederate blockade runners operated out of the Bahamas, as did rum runners during the the American prohibition era. In 1940, the United States established naval bases in the area.

The Bahamas are administered by a governor, who is assisted by legislative and executive councils. The constitution has existed virtually unchanged since 1729.

Nowadays, some 75% of the population is Negro, the rest being classified as either of mixed origin or of European descent.

TERRITORY: *Bermuda*
Area: 21 square miles
Population: 48,000
Capital: Hamilton
Principal economic resources: tourism
Language: English
History at a glance:

Discovered in 1515 by the Spaniard Juan de Bermudez, Bermuda was first settled by a group of British colonists who had been shipwrecked in 1609 while en route to Virginia. The islands were officially acquired by the British Crown in 1684.

In modern times, the British have established a naval base on Ireland Island, while the United States has leased sites for military bases on two of the other islands.

A Crown Colony, Bermuda has the oldest British colonial legislature. It is administered by a governor who represents the sovereign, and who is assisted by a nine-member executive council.

The current population breakdown lists 60% as Negro or mixed, and 40% as white.

TERRITORY: *British Virgin Islands*
Area: 59 square miles
Population: 8,000
Capital: Road Town
Principal economic resources: fish, livestock, tourism
Language: English
History at a glance:

Great Britain obtained title to these 40-odd islands and islets in 1666 and, until 1960, administered them as part of the Leeward Islands. At present, the government is headed by a Crown-appointed administrator who is assisted both by executive and legislative councils.

Almost the entire population is of African descent.

TERRITORY: *Cayman Islands* (Grand Cayman, Little Cayman, Cayman Brac)
Area: 100 square miles
Population: 9,000
Capital: Georgetown
Principal economic resources: farming, fishing
Language: English
History at a glance:

Christopher Columbus discovered the Cayman Islands in 1503, naming them "Tortugas" due to the profusion of turtles in the surrounding waters.

Once it became clear that the Spanish did not intend to colonize them, the British sent in settlers from nearby Jamaica. Until 1959, the islands remained a dependency of Jamaica but, when this island became independent in 1962, they became subject to a new constitution providing for a Crown-appointed administrator, a legislative assembly, and an executive council.

One out of every five Cayman Islanders is classified as Negro; approximately half of the population is of mixed blood; the rest is European.

TERRITORY: *Leeward Islands*
Territorial Units: Antigua, Barbuda, Redonda, St. Kitts-Nevis-Arguilla, Montserrat
Area: 356 square miles
Population: 137,000
Principal economic resources: agriculture, tourism
Language: English
History at a glance:

When the Leeward Islands were discovered by Christopher Columbus in 1493, they were inhabited by Carib Indians. St. Kitts was the first English settlement in the Caribbean (1623); Nevis was colonized five years later, and Montserrat in 1632. The French captured some of the islands in 1666 and again in 1782, but they were returned to the British under the Treaty of Versailles (1783).

Significant constitutional changes were first introduced in the 19th century, particularly after the abolition of the slave trade (1808) and of slavery itself (1838). Although suffrage was extended, the small farmer and the laboring class still found themselves not truly represented.

In 1956, the separate colonies were united to form the territory of the Leeward Islands and, two years later, were incorporated into the Federation of the West Indies which lasted until 1962.

Today, each territorial unit has a Crown-appointed administrator, as well as executive and legislative councils.

Most of the population is an intermixure of European settlers and the descendants of West African slaves.

TERRITORY: *Turks* (Grand Turk; Salt Cay) and *Caicos* (South Caicos; North Caicos) *Islands*
Area: 166 square miles
Population: 6,000
Capital: Grand Turk
Principal economic resources: salt, crayfish, sisal, conch products
Language: English
History at a glance:

Though discovered by Ponce de Leon in 1512, the Turks and Caicos Islands remained uninhabited until 1678, at which time the Bermudians settled there to mine salt. They were expelled by the Spanish in 1710, but soon returned, only to survive several Spanish and French attacks.

In 1848, the islands became a separate colony under the administration of Jamaica before being annexed by the latter in 1873. They were again separated from Jamaica when that island became independent in 1962. Since then, they have been administered by a British resident who is assisted by an executive council and a legislative assembly.

Most of the inhabitants are either of African descent, or of mixed blood.

TERRITORY: *Windward Islands*
Territorial Units: Dominica; Grenada; Saint Lucia; Saint Vincent
Area: 825 square miles
Population: 335,000
Principal economic resources: livestock, fish
Language: English
History at a glance:

The Windward Islands were inhabited by Indians when they were discovered by Columbus in 1493. Later settled by the English, they soon became a battleground between the indigenous Caribs, the English, and the French. Carib opposition was, to all intent and purpose, eliminated toward the beginning of the 18th century, when the remaining Indians were deported to areas lying near Honduras. During much the same period, Great Britain won important territorial concessions under the Treaty of Versailles (1783) and at the Congress of Vienna (1815).

Africans worked the fields until slavery was abolished, at which time they were replaced by East Indians and Portuguese. Despite the introduction of limited voting rights, the descendants of the land-working class remained essentially unrepresented until the 20th century.

In 1956, the four territories—Dominica, Grenada, Saint Lucia, and Saint Vincent—were combined to form the Windward Islands and, two years later, incorporated into the Federation of the West Indies (dissolved in 1962).

The islands are governed by a Crown-appointed administrator, aided by executive and legislative councils.

The population is an intermixture of European settlers, the descendants of West African slaves and Carib Indians.

UNITED STATES DEPENDENCIES

TERRITORY: *Corn Islands*
Area: four square miles
Population: uninhabited
Principal economic resources: coconuts
Language: English
History at a glance:

The Corn Islands (Great Corn and Little Corn) were leased to the United States by Nicaragua in 1916 as a means of protecting a contemplated canal across the latter country. The lease was signed for a 99-year period.

TERRITORY: *Panama Canal Zone*
Area: 372 square miles
Population: 53,900
Principal Cities: Balboa, Cristobal
Principal economic resources: (economy dependent on canal operation)
Languages: English, Spanish
History at a glance:

The Canal Zone is a 50-mile-long, five-mile-wide strip lying between the Atlantic and Pacific Oceans, on both sides of the Panama Canal. It was granted in perpetuity to the United States by virtue of a U. S.-Panamanian treaty signed in 1903. The United States pays in the neighborhood of two million dollars annually for control of the zone, which is governed as an independent agency under the supervision of the Secretary of the Army. The President-Governor (at present Robert J. Fleming) is appointed by the President of the United States, and exercises administrative and executive authority. In times of crisis or emergency, however, his role is subordinate to that of the resident U. S. military commander.

The canal is currently operated by the U. S.-owned Panama Canal Company under the terms of the Panama Canal Act of 1950. The governor of the zone is also the president of the company. Canal Zone legislation remains in the hands of the U. S. Congress.

Since 1959, the residents of the zone (half of whom were born in the continental U. S., the rest coming either from Panama or the zone itself) have grown more vehement in their demands for its restoration to Panama. On occasion, student demonstrations have even flared to the point of violence before being suppressed.

By 1967, U.S. and Panamanian negotiators produced draft treaties that would provide for Panamanian participation in canal management, profit-sharing between Panama and the U.S., and a measure of dual sovereignty. The treaties were obstructed by the forceful overthrow of Panamanian President Arnulfo Arias in 1968.

TERRITORY: *Puerto Rico* (Culebra, Mona, Vieques)
Area: 3,435 square miles
Population: 2,584,000
Capital: San Juan
Principal economic resources: coffee, tobacco, sugar cane, manufacturing industries, dairy farming, tourism
Languages: English, Spanish
History at a glance:

Discovered by Columbus in 1493 on his second voyage to the New World, Puerto Rico was soon conquered by the Spaniard Ponce de Leon, who was appointed governor of the island in 1509. The indigenous Carib Indians, almost all of whom were utilized by the Spaniards as plantation laborers, were eventually wiped out—only to be replaced in 1513 by Negro slaves. Puerto Rico was held by the English in 1598, and San Juan was besieged by the Dutch in 1625. Otherwise, Spanish control remained unchallenged until the Spanish-American War.

The island was captured by U. S. forces during this conflict and ceded outright to the United States under the Treaty of Paris (1898). In 1900, Congress established a local administration—with a governor appointed by the American president, an executive council, and an elected house of delegates. Puerto Ricans were granted U. S. citizenship in 1917.

After World War II, Congress pro-

The limbo dance of the Caribbean

vided that the governor of the island be an elected official, whereupon, in 1948. Luis Muñoz Marín was chosen for this office. In 1950, a further Act of Congress enabled Puerto Rico to draft its own constitution and, in three years time, it became a member of the U. S. Commonwealth.

Since then, Puerto Rican politics have been dominated by Muñoz Marín and the Popular Democratic Party. (Marín's handpicked successor, Roberto Sanchez Villela, was elected in January 1965.) This party is committed to the retention of Commonwealth status, inasmuch as the island has experienced considerable prosperity within this framework. This is particularly attributable to "Operation Bootstrap," a program which has succeeded in bringing into Puerto Rico a large number of American industries. Emigration to the mainland, a major factor in the 1950's, has declined in recent years. Despite the preponderance of popular support for the Democrats, two other parties have managed to gain some foothold: the Statehood Republican Party, which advocates statehood for the island, and the Independence Party, which seeks complete independence for Puerto Rico.

Many Puerto Ricans today are of mixed Negro and Spanish ancestry. For the most part, the original Indian inhabitants of the island were exterminated in the 16th century.

In 1968, Luis A. Ferre, long an advocate of statehood, was elected governor of the island as a candidate of the New Progressive party. Ferre made it clear, however, that statehood would depend on a separate plebiscite which would be run apart from the general election.

TERRITORY: *Swan Islands*
Area: four square miles
Population: less than 100 (Big Swan)
Principal economic resources: guano
Language: English
History at a glance:

The Swan Islands (Big Swan and Little Swan) were discovered in the early 16th century, and have been in the possession of the United States ever since 1863, although the Central American republic of Honduras has laid claim to them. The islands, now the site of a lighthouse and a radio station, are believed to be a base of operations for the Central Intelligence Agency.

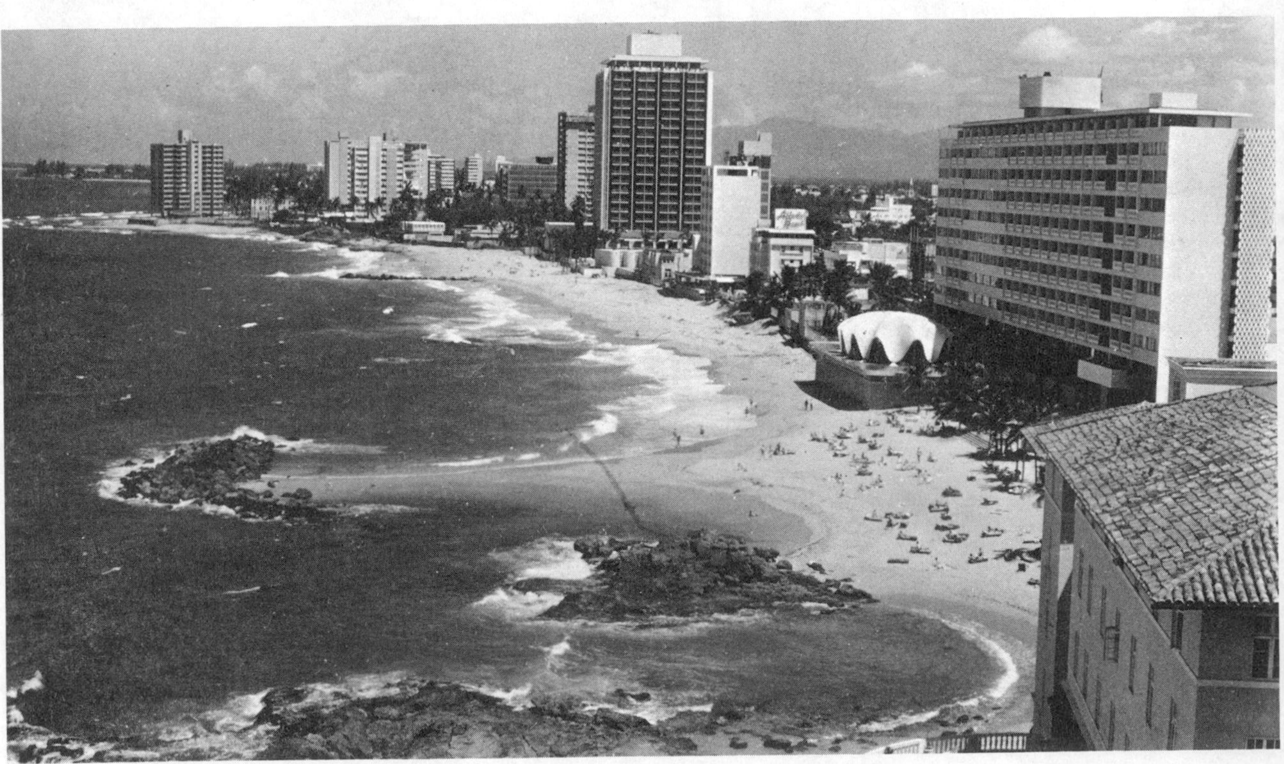

Hotels dot the beachfront in sunny Puerto Rico.

One of Puerto Rico's most fascinating and famed points of interest is El Morro, which rises dramatically from the sea at the northwest tip of old San Juan.

TERRITORY: *Virgin Islands of the U. S.* (St. Croix, St. Thomas, St. John)
Area: 132 square miles
Population: 40,600
Capital: Charlotte Amalie
Principal economic resources: fish, sugar cañe, tourism
Language: English
History at a glance:

Discovered by Christopher Columbus in 1493, the Virgin Islands (an archipelago of 74 islands) is now divided into two distinct clusters: the U. S. Virgin Islands (three main islands; 65 islets) and the British Virgin Islands (six main islands).

The American group was originally owned by Denmark and settled by the Danish West India Company, which first colonized St. Thomas in 1672. In 1683, St. John was likewise claimed by this company and, by 1733, St. Croix had been acquired from France. Some 20 years later, the holdings of this company were taken over by the Danish crown, which then reconstituted them as a royal colony (The Danish West Indies).

The United States bought the territory from Denmark in 1917 for some 25 million dollars, and granted citizenship to its inhabitants (40% of whom are Negro) 10 years later. In 1931, its administration was transferred from the U. S. Navy Department to the Department of the Interior.

Limited self-government for the territory dates back to 1936, although the internal administration of the islands continues to be in the hands of a governor appointed by the President of the United States. (The first Negro governor, William H. Hastie, was appointed in 1946.) Under the terms of the 1954 Revised Organic Act of the Virgin Islands, local legislative power rests in the hands of a unicameral chamber composed of 11 popularly elected senators.

Under the terms of the constitution now in effect, the United States retains the authority to introduce and enact the legislation needed to govern the territory. The courts are also controlled by the United States, with an American district judge serving as the territory's highest judicial officer.

Pursuant to a bill passed by Congress in 1968, the governor of the island is an elected, rather than an appointed official. (Dr. Melvin Evans, the first native black governor, came to office in mid 1969.)

"SOUL FOOD" RECIPES

The culinary art of the Negro, as expressed in an assortment of favorite dishes

The isolation of the Negro has been a major factor in creating a climate for much of what he has produced. Cooking is one of the areas in which this phenomenon can be most readily observed. Negro recipes are largely Southern in origin, but there is "something extra" about them—something Negroes themselves call "soul"—which places them in a distinctive category all their own. There are canning and bottling procedures known largely to Negro women of the older generation, there are ways of preparing and seasoning food which have often been passed on during on-the-job training sessions involving the older and the younger generations. The "flavor of soul" is hopefully suggested by the following recipes, the first of which are reprinted here with the permission of the "Soul Food" column in "Tuesday" magazine. Some are for main courses; others are for desserts; still others are for items especially reserved for festive times of the year.

Smithfield Ham

Scrub skin to remove excess pepper and molds. Soak in cold water, covering, at least 18 hours, possibly more depending upon the age of the ham. Change the water several times during the soak period. Boil in fresh water to which has been added:

1 cup brown sugar or molasses	3 bay leaves
few slivers of lemon rind	1 whole peach
8 peppercorns	1 cup apple cider
1 cinnamon stick	1 tbs: Worcestershire sauce
	celery tops

Boil gently, 25 minutes to the pound, keeping ham covered with water. Add hot water when needed. Cool. Save about ½. cup of liquid for crust. Remove skin, leaving at least ¼ inch of fat on the ham.

Golden Crust

3 egg yolks	1 cup cracker meal
1 tsp. dry mustard	1 tbs. Worcestershire sauce
¼ cup brown sugar	

Mix all 5 ingredients together, add water that ham was cooked in to make a paste. Spread evenly over ham. Place ham in preheated oven (450 degrees). Let brown quickly to a golden crust. When serving, slice thin (the thinner the better).

Baked Ham

Requires one eight- to 10-pound picnic ham. Proceed as follows:

1. Rinse in cold water. Plunge into hot boiling water for 30 minutes. Cut off outside skin. (This skin may be used in making crackling for crackling corn bread.)
2. Cover with brown sugar and cloves.
3. Pour two cups of warm cider over ham while cooking.
4. Bake in slow oven for 1½ hours.

One may dress up ham by using pineapple slices, cloves and cherries. A possible substitute for brown sugar is honey. Cinnamon sticks can also be boiled with your cider. Serve with crackling corn bread, red kidney beans, or rice.

Red Ribs

3 to 4 lbs. spareribs
salt and pepper to taste
1 and ½ cups prepared barbecue sauce*
2 cups water
4 tbs. vinegar
2 to 3 tsp. of any hot sauce made with Louisiana red peppers

Preheat oven to 325 deg. Wipe a rack of spareribs with damp cloth, sprinkle with salt and pepper. Cook slowly in shallow pan lined with foil until brown (50 minutes), basting often with vinegar and water mixture. (Use a brush to baste rather than spooning the mixture over the ribs as you want them to bake—not steam—slowly and brown evenly without drying out. If you don't have a brush, wrap the end of a wooden spoon with several layers of cheesecloth and tie.) Then cover with sauce and let cook 30-40 minutes more.

If you parboil ribs, omit basting with vinegar and water. Bake until brown (about 30 mins.), then baste with sauce for another 20 minutes.

Never boil ribs in plain water! Boil water first then add ½ tsp. each of marjoram, thyme, oregano and 1 tsp. each of garlic powder and salt, and 8 peppercorns—then add ribs.

*There are on the market some excellent prepared barbecue sauces to suit your individual taste—you may want to experiment with these.

Rib Marinade

Ingredients A:
Sauce for marinating:
2 cups oil
1 tsp. onion powder
1 tsp. garlic powder
¾ c. wine vinegar
½ tsp. oregano
½ tsp. basil
¼ tsp. thyme
2 tsp. crushed red pepper
salt and pepper to taste

Ingredients B:
4 cloves garlic crushed

Ingredient C:
½ cup tomato sauce or catsup

Wipe ribs with damp cloth. Cut into serving pieces. Combine ingredients A and B for marinade. Cover ribs with sauce and let marinate in the refrigerator for at least 24 hrs., occasionally turning so that all sides are thoroughly marinated. Place on rack in roasting pan in preheated 350 deg. oven brush with marinade or other barbecue sauce occasionally and let cook for 1 hour or until ribs are crispy.

A commercial salad dressing of oil, vinegar and herbs may be substituted for ingredients A.

Ingredient C is optional and may be added to either the marinade or basting sauce.

Sweet Barbecue Sauce

1 cup catsup or tomato sauce
¼ cup vinegar
2 tsp. olive oil
1 tbs. brown sugar or molasses
1 tsp. salt
1 tsp. dry mustard
¼ tsp. Tabasco
dash cayenne pepper
¼ tsp. garlic powder
1 clove garlic minced
1 onion medium, chopped
2 tsp. sweet pickle relish (optional)

Simmer slowly until hot, stir thoroughly.

This sauce may be made hot for "Red Ribs" by adding 2 tsp. red peppers or increasing the Tabasco to taste.

Fried Pork Chops

Take 2 lbs. of chops, add pepper and salt to taste, and dip in sweet milk. Bread chops in one cup of cracker meal or corn bread. Fry in deep hot fat approximately ¼ inch deep until golden brown. (Note: Oil or lard may be used.) Serve with gumbo or black-eyed peas, rice and greens, corn bread and pecan pie.

Pigs Feet and Tails

Ingredients:
6 feet, 8 tails
1½ cups vinegar
2½ onions
3½ tsp. salt
celery stalks & tops
hot sauce
8 pepper corns
2½ cloves garlic
5 bay leaves
3 lemons
1 potato
1 cucumber

Steps to follow:

1. Wash thoroughly and scrub with a brush.
2. Cook feet and tails together.
3. Cook feet in water with vinegar, onion, celery and tops and salt until meat falls from bone.
4. Squeeze juice from lemons and add spices and one cup pot likker.

(Around New Year's, it is customary to fix pig tails in black-eyed peas.) Serve with black-eyed peas and greens, hoe cake and pot likker. (For pot likker, you may add carrots and potatoes and snow peas to make a soup.) Flapjacks for dessert.

Fried Chicken

Ingredients:
5 lbs. of chicken
1½ cups lard to ½ cup pork grease

Cut chicken into desired parts. Sprinkle with salt, pepper and garlic powder. Pour into brown paper bag 1½ cups flour, 3 tbs. salt, 4 tbs. pepper. Flour parts individually in bag by folding top of bag and shaking thoroughly. Heat lard and pork grease until very hot. Fry chicken for 25 minutes, keeping covered for first 15 minutes, and removing cover for last 10 minutes, allowing to brown. Drain chicken on paper towel and serve. Serve with beets, hash brown potatoes, watermelon.

Chicken Feet Stew

Ingredients:

2 lbs. chicken feet	1 cup day-old string beans
4 onions (quartered)	salt & pepper to taste
5 potatoes (cut into eighths)	3 bay leaves
3 carrots sliced horizontally	1 clove garlic

Sever skin in the middle of the bristle on leg and pull off. Cut nails. Cover with water in cast-iron Dutch oven. Add all ingredients, and cook until chicken feet are tender. Serve with hoe cake or corn bread and black molasses.

Rabbit, Muskrat, Squirrel

Disjoint and soak in salt water and vinegar for one hour. Clean as other fowl. Make a batter of: 1 cup corn meal, ½ cup flour, ¾ cup milk, one egg. Season animal with salt and pepper. Dip in batter. Fry in deep hot fat (seasoned, or used). Serve with fried okra, tomatoes and onions.

Candied Yams

6 medium-sized yams	4 tbs. butter
6 cups water	1½ tsp. cinnamon
3 cups sugar	½ tsp. cloves
	½ tsp. nutmeg

Wash yams, cover with water and bring to a fast boil. Cook 5 minutes longer. Drain and cool. Peel and slice in half lengthwise. Place in 4-quart saucepan. Add sugar, spices, butter and water. Cook uncovered for 1½ hours until thick syrup has almost cooked away. Serves 8.

Catfish

Four easy steps to prepare catfish:

1. To skin the fish, draw a sharp knife around it behind the gills and pull off the skin with a pair of pliers.
2. Clean as you would any other fish, discarding tail and head, or using both as base for a fish pot likker soup. To do so, boil with onion, garlic, cloves, salt and pepper.
3. Cut into catfish steaks. Season with lemon, salt and pepper, and cayenne pepper, and roll in meal.
4. Fry in deep hot fat in heavy cast iron skillet.

Chitterlings
(usually pronounced "chitlins")

10 lbs. chitterlings—Clean very carefully in warm water, removing all the lining and leaving a bit of the fat.

Cover in pot with cold water adding 1 onion, 1 cup vinegar, 1 small potato (to absorb odor, not to eat), 2 tsp. crushed red pepper, salt, clove garlic, tsp. dried parsley.
Cover and cook about four hours until well done.

Drain off liquid, leaving a little in the pot. Remove chitterlings, and cut them into small pieces. Add black pepper and:

1. Put back in pot with 2 tbs. vinegar. Simmer gently for 20 minutes.
   or
2. Saute gently with 1 tbs. vinegar in bacon drippings until most of liquid is cooked away.
   or
3. Dip pieces in beaten egg and cracker crumbs, and fry in deep fat to golden brown.

Serves 6

Collard Greens and Ham Hocks

9 lbs. collard greens (or collard turnip, mustard mixed)
6 medium-sized smoked hamhocks, or 1 lb. piece of bacon
salt
2 tsp. crushed red pepper

Slice leaves off stalks. Place in cold water. Sprinkle with salt (this aids in washing out sand).

Wash thoroughly twice, then rinse through without salt.

Slice leaves across into three slices. Leave soaking for an hour or more.

Rinse hamhocks. Place in three quarts of water. Sprinkle with crushed red pepper, or two fresh hot peppers.

Cook covered for 2½ hours. Mix lightly once to turn greens so that all cook evenly.

Serves 10

Corn Bread

2 cups white cornmeal
2 eggs
1 tbs. sugar
1 tsp. salt
2 tsp. baking powder
2 tbs. drippings or shortening
2½ cups milk or buttermilk

Put cornmeal, sugar, salt and baking powder into mixing bowl. Add eggs and milk. Melt drippings or shortening in baking pan in oven. Stir into batter. Pour batter into pan and bake 20-25 minutes at 450°.

Corn Bread with Salt

Follow corn bread recipe. Dice salt pork, and brown in oven. Use drippings in batter, pour batter over salt pork in baking pan. Bake 25-30 minutes at 450°.

(The following recipes are supplied through the courtesy of Mrs. Birdie Dillahunty of Louisville, Kentucky.)

Corn Pudding

2 cups creamed corn
1 egg beaten slightly
3 tablespoons flour
3 tablespoons butter
salt and pepper to taste

Combine ingredients and mix thoroughly. Place mixture in baking dish. Bake in moderate oven (350° F.) 45 minutes, or until knife inserted in center comes out clean. Serve with sliced tomatoes.

Spoon Bread

Scald cornmeal with 2 cups boiling water. Boil five minutes, stirring constantly. Remove from fire. Add and mix ingredients of corn bread, except for eggs and baking powder. Add beaten eggs, and mix in baking powder. Cook 25-30 minutes at 425°.

Corn Bread Stuffing

Dice the following ingredients:

2½ large onions
2 large seeded green (Bell) peppers
½ stalk celery
2 cups fresh mushrooms

Combine ingredients and saute in bacon drippings or peanut oil. Add one- or two-day-old corn bread and hoe cakes crumbled. Add one cup crushed walnuts. Season with 2 tablespoons pepper, and same measure of thyme, sage and poultry seasoning. Salt to taste. Makes enough to stuff a 16-18 pound turkey.

Crackling Corn Bread

½ cup flour
1 cup yellow corn meal
1½ tsp. baking powder
1 tsp. salt
½ tsp. baking soda
2 tbs. sugar
1 cup butter milk
1 egg, beaten
½ cup crushed pork crackling

Pre-heat oven for 10 minutes to 450°. Mix and sift all dry ingredients. Add buttermilk, egg, crackling, and stir well. Pour into 9" skillet and bake for 20 minutes.

Hush Puppies

1½ cups corn meal
1 egg
½ tsp. sugar
pinch of salt
1 cup fish stock
medium onion chopped

Mix all ingredients and mold into hand-sized cakes. Fry in one inch of hot fat.

Hoe Cake

2 handfuls (2½ cups) sifted corn meal
⅛ tsp. baking soda
⅛ tsp. salt
1 cup sweet milk
3 tbs. melted bacon drippings

Mix all ingredients. Pour into hot greased black #6 cast-iron skillet. Bake in oven at 450° for 20 minutes until golden brown or, if preferred, cook on top of stove. (Note: This is especially good with "pot likker"—chicken, beef, pork—or black molasses and thick strips of bacon.)

Hoecake Stuffing

Crumble one hoecake. Add one small chopped onion, one chopped Bell pepper, and ½ cup beef broth. Mix, mold and stuff bird—turkey, chicken, or game fowl. (Note: To enhance flavor still further, add bits of roast pork, bits of roast chopped sausages, and scrapple.)

Pecan Pie

Boil one cup sugar and 1½ cups corn syrup for three minutes. Add three beaten eggs to mixture. Add the following: ¼ lb. butter, two to three tbs. vanilla, one tbs. corn starch, 2½ cups broken or shelled pecan nuts. Turn into unbaked pie shell and bake 45 minutes at 350°.

Sweet Potato Pie

1½ lbs. sweet potatoes (or two large ones)
2 cups sugar
¼ lb. butter
2 teaspoons vanilla
1 teaspoon cinnamon
½ teaspoon nutmeg
4 slightly beaten eggs

Boil sweet potatoes in jackets until tender. Drain. Remove skin and mash with butter. Combine sugar, vanilla, cinnamon, nutmeg and eggs. Beat for five minutes. Bake in moderate oven (350° F.) 45 minutes, or until knife inserted in center comes out clean. Makes one (nine-inch) pie.

Watermelon Preserves

Take rind from one small watermelon. Peel off green portion. Soak in lime water overnight and one full day. Remove from lime water and soak in fresh water for two hours, then for two more hours in salt water. Rinse rinds and cook in fresh water for 40 minutes. Add 1½ cups water, add sugar to the rind in the proportion one pound of sugar to one melon. Boil until clear. Put up in mason jars.

A SELECTED BIBLIOGRAPHY

The Afro-American Africa and the Caribbean

In recent years, the enormous amount of material published on the Negro—not only in connection with civil rights, but in terms of his general culture—has made it necessary to compile ever larger and more comprehensive bibliographical lists. Mr. Ernest Kaiser has long been justly considered the reigning expert in this field and this bibliography is his compilation. The most recent compilation of value in book form is *The Negro in the United States, A Selected Bibliography* compiled by Dorothy Porter, the librarian of the Moorland Collection at Howard University. Published by the Library of Congress in Washington, D.C., in 1970, it is available from the Superintendent of Documents, U.S. Government Printing Office, Washington, D.C. 20402. The price is $3.25. The Miles M. Jackson list, *Bibliography of Negro History and Culture for Young People,* fills a need in the children's market, as does what is undoubtedly the most comprehensive and important juvenile list, *The Black Experience in Children's Books,* compiled by Augusta Baker, Coordinator of Children's Services, New York Public Library. Published in 1971, the book is available for 50¢ from the NYPL, 8 East 40th Street, New York 10016.

—A—

A. Philip Randolph Institute. New York: A. Philip Randolph Institute.
1. *Civil Rights: The Movement Reexamined.*
2. *New Careers: A Basic Strategy Against Poverty* (Frank Riessman).
3. *Our Urban Poor: Promises to Keep and Miles to Go.* (St. Clair Drake).
4. *The City in Crisis.*
5. *Separation or Integration: Which Way for America? A Dialogue.* Robert S Browne and Bayard Rustin.

Aaron, Henry. (as told to Furman Bisher). *"Aaron, r.f."* New York: World, 1968.

Abramson, Doris. *Negro Playwrights in the American Theatre: 1925-1959.* New York: Columbia University Press, 1969.

Adams, A. John and Joan M. Burke. *Civil Rights: A Current Guide to the People, Organizations and Events.* New York: Bowker, 1970.

Adams, Russell L. *Great Negroes Past and Present.* Chicago: Afro-Am, 1969.

Adams, William, Peter Conn and Barry Sleplan (eds.). *Afro-American Literature: Drama, Fiction, Non-fiction.* Boston: Houghton Mifflin, 1969.

Addison, Lloyd. *The Aura & the Umbra.* (Distributed by Broadside Press, Detroit, Mich.). London: Paul Bremen, 1970.

Adoff, Arnold (ed.). *I Am the Darker Brother: An Anthology of Poems by Negro Americans.* New York: Macmillan, 1968.

——— (ed.). *Black on Black: Commentaries by Negro Americans.* New York: Macmillan, 1968.

——— (ed.). *Black Out Loud.* New York: Macmillan, 1970.

Adventures in Negro History (3 vols.). New York: Pepsi Cola.

Afro-American History and Culture. New York: Folkways Scholastic.

Ahmann, Matthew (ed.). *The New Negro.* Notre Dame: Fides, 1961.

Ahmann, Matthew and Margaret Roach (eds.). *The Church and the Urban Racial Crisis.* Techny: Divine Word Publications, 1967.

Alex, Nicholas. *Black in Blue: A Study of the Negro Policeman.* New York: Appleton-Century-Crofts, 1969.

Alexander, Rae Pace (compiler). *What It Means to Be Young and Black in America.* New York: Random House, 1970.

Alexander, Richard D., et al. *The Management of Racial Integration in Business.* New York: McGraw Hill, 1964.

Alhamisi, Ahmed and Harum Kofi Wangara (eds.). *Black Arts: An Anthology of Black Creations.* Detroit: Broadside Press, 1969.

Allen, Robert L. *Black Awakening in Capitalist America: An Analytic History.* New York: Doubleday, 1969.

Allen, Walter C. and Brian A. L. Rust. *King Joe Oliver.* London: Sidgwick & Jackson, 1958.

Altschuler, Alan. *Community Control: The Black Demand for Participation in Large American Cities.* New York: Pegasus, 1970.

America in Crisis. Text by Mitchel Levitas. Photographs by Magnum. New York: Holt, Rinehart & Winston, 1969.

The American Negro: His History and Literature. New York: Arno, 1968- . (A series of reprints of important black literature, with William Loren Katz as General Editor, and a group of black scholars as consultants. More than 100 titles already released.)

Ames, William C. *The Negro Struggle for Equality in the 20th Century.* Boston: Heath, 1965.

Amis, Lola Jones. *3 Plays: The Other Side of the Wall; The Places of Wrath, and Helen.* New York: Exposition Press, 1965.

Amistad I: Writings on Black History and Culture. New York: Random House.

Anderson, Margaret. *The Children of the South*. New York: Farrar Strauss, 1966.

Angelou, Maya. *I Know Why the Caged Bird Sings*. New York: Random House, 1970.

Anthony, Earl. *Picking Up the Gun: A Report on the Black Panthers*. New York: Dial, 1970.

Aptheker, Herbert. *American Negro Slave Revolts*. New York: International, 1963.

———. *And Why Not Every Man?: Documentary Story of the Fight Against Slavery in the U.S.* New York: International, 1970.

———. *Dr. Martin Luther King: Vietnam and Civil Rights*. New York: New Outlook, 1966.

———. *A Documentary History of the Negro People in the United States from Colonial Times Through the Civil War*. New York: Citadel Press, 1969.

———. *Nat Turner's Slave Revolt: The Environment, the Event, the Effects*. New York: Humanities, 1965.

———. *One Continual Cry: David Walker's "Appeal to the Colored Citizens of the World, 1829."* New York: Humanities, 1965.

———*Soul of the Republic: The Negro Today*. New York: Marzani & Munsell, 1964.

———. *To Be Free: Studies in American Negro History*. New York: International, 1968.

Archer, Jules. *Angry Abolitionist: William Lloyd Garrison*. New York: Julian Messner, 1969.

Argument: The History-Making Decision That Spurred the Civil Rights Revolution in the United States. New York: Chelsea House.

Armstrong, Louis. *Satchmo (My Life in New Orleans)*. New York: New American Library, 1971.

Armstrong, William H. *Sounder*. New York: Harper & Row, 1969.

Ashe, Arthur. *Advantage Ashe*. New York: Coward-McCann, 1967.

Asinof, Eliot. *People vs. Blutcher. Black Men and White Law in Bedford-Stuyvesant*. New York: Viking Press, 1970.

Atkins, James A. *The Age of Jim Crow*. New York: Vantage Press, 1964.

Atkins, Russell. *Phenomena*. Wilberforce: Wilberforce University Press, 1961.

Aukofer, Frank A. *City With a Chance*. Milwaukee: Bruce Publishing, 1968.

Austin, Edmund O. *The Black Challenge*. New York: Vantage Press, 1958.

—B—

Bacote, Clarence. *The Story of Atlanta University, 1865 to 1965: A Century of Service*. Atlanta: Atlanta University Bookstore, 1969.

Bailey, Harry A., Jr. *Negro Politics in America*. Columbus: Charles E. Merrill Books, 1967.

Bailey, Hugh C. *Hinton Rowan Helper: Abolitionist - Racist*. University: University of Alabama Press, 1965.

Bailey, Pearl. *The Raw Pearl*. New York: Harcourt, Brace & World, 1968.

Baldwin, James. *The Amen Corner*. New York: Dial Press, 1968.

———. *Blues for Mister Charlie*. New York: Dial Press, 1964.

———. *Going to Meet the Man*. New York: Dell, 1966.

———. *Tell Me How Long the Train's Been Gone*. New York: Dial Press, 1968.

Banks, James A. *March Toward Freedom: A History of Black Americans*. Palo Alto: Fearon Publishers, 1970.

Barbour, Floyd B. (ed.). *The Black Power Revolt*. Boston: Porter Sargent Publisher, 1968.

———. *The Black Seventies*. Boston: Porter Sargent Publisher, 1970.

Bardolph, Richard (ed.). *The Civil Rights Record: Black Americans and the Law, 1849-1970*. New York: Thomas Y. Crowell, 1970.

———. *The Negro Vanguard*. New York: Rinehart, 1959.

Barndt, Joseph R. *Why Black Power?* New York: Friendship Press, 1968.

Barnwell, William H. *In Richard's World: The Battle of Charleston*. Boston: Houghton Mifflin, 1969.

Barrett, Russell H. *Integration at Ole Miss*. Chicago: Quadrangle Books, 1965.

The Basic Afro-American Reprint Library. New York: Johnson Reprint Corp., 1968- . (The first series was 23 volumes selected from Clarence L. Holte's private library in N.Y.C.)

Bass, Charlotta. *Forty Years, Memoirs from the Pages of a Newspaper*. Los Angeles: The Author, 1960.

Bates, Daisy. *The Long Shadow of Little Rock: A Memoir*. New York: David McKay, 1962.

Baughman, E. Earl and W. Grant Dahlstrom. *Negro and White Children: A Psychological Study in the Rural South*. New York: Academic Press, 1968.

Bayliss, John C. (ed.) *Black Slave Narratives*. New York: Macmillan, 1970.

Bayton, James A. *Tension in the Cities: Three Programs for Survival*. Philadelphia: Chilton Books, 1969.

Beam, Lura. *He Called Them by the Lightning: A Teacher's Odyssey in the Negro South, 1908-1919*. Indianapolis: Bobbs-Merrill, 1967.

Bearden, Romare and Carl Holty. *The Painter's Mind: A Study of the Relations of Structure and Space in Painting*. New York: Crown Publishers, 1969.

Beasley, Delilah L. *The Negro Trail Blazers of California*. San Francisco, R. & E. Research Associates, 1968.

Beckham, Barry. *My Main Mother*. New York: Walker and Co., 1969.

Beckwourth, James P. *The Life and Adventures of James P. Beckwourth*. New York: Arno, 1969.

Beecher, John. *Hear the Wind Blow! Poems of Protest and Prophecy*. New York: International Publishers, 1969.

Belafonte, Harry. *Songs Belafonte Sings*. New York: Duell, Sloan and Pearce, 1962.

Belfrage, Sally. *Freedom Summer*. New York: Viking Press, 1965.

Bell, Inge P. *C.O.R.E. and the Strategy of Nonviolence*. New York: Random House, 1968.

Benedict, Steward H. (ed.). *Backlash*. New York: Popular Library, 1970.

Benjamin, Joseph L. and Anita Honis. *And the Truth Shall Make Us Free*. New York: Carlton Press, 1964.

Bennett, Alving. *God the Stonebreaker*. London: Heinemann, 1964.

Bennett, Hal. *The Black Wine*. New York: Doubleday, 1968.

———. *Lord of Dark Places*. New York: Norton, 1970.

Bennett, Lerone, Jr. *Before the Mayflower. A History of Black America*. Chicago: Johnson, 1969.

———. *Black Power USA: The Human Side of Reconstruction 1867-1877*. Chicago: Johnson, 1967.

———. *Confrontation: Black and White*. Chicago: Johnson, 1965.

———. *The Negro Mood and Other Essays*. Chicago: Johnson, 1964.

———. *Pioneers in Protest*. Chicago: Johnson, 1968.

———. *What Manner of Man: The Life of Martin Luther King, Jr.* Chicago: Johnson, 1964.

Berger, Morroe. *Equality by Statute: The Revolution in Civil Rights*. New York: Doubleday, 1967.

Bergman, Peter M. and Mort N. (compilers). *The Chronological History of the Negro in America*. New York: Harper and Row, 1970.

Bergman, Peter M. and Jean McCarroll (compilers). *The Negro in the Continental Congress, 1774-1789*. New York: Bergman Publishers, 1970.

Bernard, Jacqueline. *Journey Toward Freedom: The Story of Sojourner Truth*. New York: W. W. Norton, 1967.

Bernard, Jessie S. *Marriage and Family Among Negroes*. Englewood Cliffs: Prentice-Hall, 1965.

Bernstein, Saul. *Alternatives to Violence: Alienated Youth and Riots, Race and Poverty*. New York: Association Press, 1967.

Berrigan, Philip. *No More Strangers*. New York: Macmillan, 1965.

Bertol, Roland. *Charles Drew*. New York: Thomas Y. Crowell, 1970.

Berube, Maurice and Marilyn Gittel (eds.). *Confrontation at Ocean Hill-Brownsville: The New York School Strikes of 1968*. New York: Praeger.

Berwanger, Eugene H. *The Frontier Against Slavery: Western Anti-Negro Prejudice and the Slavery Extension Controversy*. Urbana and Chicago: University of Chicago, 1967.

Bigsby, C. W. E. (ed.). *The Black American Writer: Vol. 1—Fiction: Vol. 2—Poetry and Drama*. Deland: Everett / Edwards, 1970.

Billingsley, Andrew. *Black Families in White America*. Englewood Cliffs: Prentice-Hall, 1968.

Birch, Herbert C. and Joan Dye Gussow. *Disadvantaged Children: Health, Nutrition and School Failure*. New York: Harcourt, Brace & World, 1970.

Bittle, William E. *The Longest Way Home*. Detroit: Wayne State University, 1964.

Black Algernon D. *The People and the Police*. New York: McGraw-Hill, 1968.

Black, Algernon D. *The People Days to the Present*. (Text by Jon Kurt Wilkman.) New York: Universal Publishing and Distributing.

Black Autobiographies: Adaptations Especially for Ghetto High-School Students of Forgotten Black Men and Women: *In Chains to Louisiana: Solomon Northup's Story; the Slave Who Bought His Freedom; Equiano's Story*. New York: Richard W. Baron, 1970.

The Black Experience in America. New York: Negro Universities Press (Greenwood Publishing). (A series of important reprints of out-of-print titles)

The Black Heritage Library Collection. Freeport: Books for Libraries, 1969- (A reprint series of over 200 titles of black history and literature from the black collection of Fisk University)

Black History in White America. Greenwich: Grade Teacher, 1969.

Black Misery. (Drawings by Suzanne Heller. Text by Langston Hughes.) New York: Eriksson, 1969.

The Black Panthers Speak. (ed. by Philip S. Foner). Philadelphia: Lippincott, 1970.

Black Poetry: A Supplement to Anthologies Which Exclude Black Poets. (ed. by Dudley Randall). Detroit: Broadside Press, 1970.

A Black Quartet: Four New Black Plays by Ben Caldwell, Ronald Milner, Ed Bullins and Leroi Jones. New York: New American Library, 1971.

Black Review No. 1. (ed. by Mel Watkins). New York: William Morrow, 1971.

The Black Revolution. (An *Ebony* Special Issue). Chicago: Johnson, 1970.

Black Studies Program in Reprint: Literature of the Black Experience. New York: AMS Press. 1969. (A series of reprints of early novels by Negroes, Negroes in Wars, etc.).

Black Titan: W. E. B. DuBois: An Anthology. Boston: Beacon Press, 1970.

The Black Tradition in American Fiction: College Park: McGrath, 1970. (A collection of 24 novels, plays, poems and short stories by blacks.)

Black Voices: Anthology of Afro-American Literature. New York: St. Martin's Press, 1970.

Black Voices from Prison. (by Etheridge Knight and other inmates of Indiana State Prison). New York: Pathfinder Press, 1970.

Black Woman. (Photographs by Chester Higgins, Jr., text by Harold McDougall). New York: McCall Publishing, 1970.

The Black Woman: An Anthology. (ed. by Toni Cade). New York: New American Library, 1970.

Black Writing in the U.S.A.: A Bibliographic Guide. Brockport: Drake Memorial Library, 1970.

Blacking, John. *Black Background*. New York: Abelard Schuman, 1964.

Blair, Lewis H. *A Southern Prophecy*. Boston: Little, Brown, 1964.

Blaustein, Albert P. and Robert L. Zangrando (eds.). *Civil Rights and The American Negro: A Documentary History*. New York: Trident Press, 1968.

Bleiweiss, Robert M. (et al.) *Marching to Freedom: the Life of Martin Luther King, Jr.* Middletown: American Education, 1968.

Boeckman, Charles. *Cool, Hot and Blue: A History of Jazz for Young People*. New York: Washington Square Press, 1970.

Boggs, James. *Racism and the Class Structure: Further Pages from a Black Worker's Notebook*. New York: Monthly Review Press, 1970.

Boles, Robert. *Curling*. Boston: Houghton Mifflin, 1967.

Bond, Frederick W. *The Negro and the Drama: The Direct and Indirect Contribution Which the American Negro Has Made to Drama and the Legitimate Stage, with the Underlying Conditions Responsible*. College Park: McGrath, 1970.

Bond, Horace Mann. *Negro Education in Alabama: A Study in Cotton and Steel*. New York: Atheneum, 1969.

Bond, Jean Carey. *Brown Is a Beautiful Color*. New York: Franklin Watts, 1970.

Bone, Robert. *Richard Wright*. Minneapolis: University of Minnesota, 1969.

———. *The Negro Novel in America*. New Haven: Yale University, 1965.

Boning, Richard A. *Profiles of Black Americans* (two vols.). Rockville Centre: Dexter and Westbrook, Ltd., 1970. (250 photographs and biographical sketches).

Bontemps, Arna. (ed.). *American Negro Poetry*. New York: Hill and Wang, 1963.

——— and Jack Conroy. *Anyplace But Here*. New York: Hill & Wang, 1966.

———. *Black Thunder*. Boston: Beacon Press, 1968.

———. *Famous Negro Athletes*. New York: Dodd, Mead, 1964.

———. *Frederick Douglass: Slave, Fighter, Freeman*. New York: Alfred A. Knopf, 1959.

———. *Great Slave Narratives*. Boston: Beacon Press, 1970.

———. *One Hundred Years of Negro Freedom*. New York: Dodd, Mead, 1961.

Booker, Simeon. *Black Man's America*. Englewood Cliffs: Prentice-Hall, 1964.

———. *Susie King Taylor: Civil War War Nurse*. New York: McGraw-Hill, 1970.

Books for Friendship: A List of Books Recommended for Children. (ed. by Mary Esther McWhirter). New York: Anti-Defamation League.

Borland, Kathryn K. and Helen R. Speicher. *Phillis Wheatley: Young Colonial Poet*. Indianapolis: Bobbs-Merrill, 1968.

Boskin, Joseph (ed.). *Urban Racial Violence in the Twentieth Century*. Beverly Hills: Glencoe Press, 1970.

Boulware, Marcus H. *The Oratory of Negro Leaders: 1900-1968*. New York: Negro Universities Press, 1970.

Boyd, Malcolm, Bruce Roberts and Eric Sevareid. *You Can't Kill the Dream*. Richmond: John Knox Press, 1968.

Bracey, John H., Jr., August Meier, and Elliott Rudwick (eds.). *Black Nationalism in America*. Indianapolis and New York: Bobbs-Merrill, 1970.

Bradford, Amory. *Oakland's Not for Burning*. New York: McKay, 1968.

Bradford, Perry. *Born with the Blues*. New York: Oak Publications, 1965.

Bradford, Sarah. *Harriet Tubman, the Moses of Her People*. New York: Corinth Books, 1961.

Branch, Hettye W. *The Story of "80 John."* New York: Greenwich, 1960.

Brandon, Brumsie, Jr. *Luther Tells It as It Is*. New York: Eriksson, 1970.

Brasmer, William and Dominick Consolo (eds.). *Black Drama: An Anthology*. Columbus, Ohio: Charles E. Merrill, 1970.

Brawley, Benjamin G. *Negro Builders and Heroes*. Chapel Hill: University of North Carolina, 1937. (Still in print.)

Breitman, George (ed.). *Malcolm X Speaks*. New York: Merit, 1965.

Brewer, J. Mason. *American Negro Folklore*. Chicago: Quadrangle Books, 1968.

———. *Worser Days and Better Times*. Chicago: Quadrangle Books, 1965.

Brink, William and Louis Harris. *The Negro Revolution in America*. New York: Simon and Schuster, 1964.

———. *Black and White*. New York: Simon and Schuster, 1967.

Brisbane, Robert H. *The Black Vanguard: Origins of the Negro Social Revolution 1900-1960*. Valley Forge: Judson Press, 1970.

Bristow, Robert O'Neil. *Time for Glory*. New York: William Morrow, 1968.

Broderick, Francis L. and August Meier (eds.). *Negro Protest Thought in the Twentieth Century*. Indianapolis: Bobbs-Merrill, 1965.

Bronz, Stephen H. *Roots of Negro Racial Consciousness*. New York: Libra Publications, 1964.

Brooks, Gwendolyn. *In the Mecca*. New York: Harper and Row, 1968.

———. *Selected Poems*. New York: Harper and Row, 1963.

Broom, Leonard and Norval D. Glenn. *Transformation of the Negro American*. New York: Harper and Row, 1965.

Brotz, Howard (ed.). *Negro Social and Political Thought, 1850-1920: Representative Texts*. Basic Books, 1966.

Brown, Cecil. *The Life and Loves of Mr. Jiveass Nigger*. New York: Farrar, Straus and Giroux, 1970.

Brown, Claude. *Manchild in the Promised Land*. New York: Macmillan, 1965.

Brown, H. Rap. *Die Nigger Die! A Political Autobiography*. New York: Dial Press, 1969.

Brown, Jimmy (with Myron Cope). *Off My Chest*. New York: Doubleday, 1964.

Brown, Marion. *Marion Brown's Southern Cookbook*. New York: Pocket Book.

Brown, Turner, Jr. *Black Is*. New York: Grove Black Cat Press, 1969.

Brown, William Wells. *The Black Man, His Antecedents, His Genius, His Achievements*. New York: Arno, 1969.

Browne, Rose Butler and James W. English. *Love My Children: An Autobiography*. New York: Meredith Press, 1969.

Bryant, Lawrence C. (ed.). *Negro Lawmakers in the South Carolina Legislature, 1869-1902*. Orangeburg: South Carolina State College, 1968.

———. *Negro Senators and Representatives in the South Carolina Legislature, 1868-1902*. Orangeburg: South Carolina State College, 1968.

Buckler, Helen. *Daniel Hale Williams: Negro Surgeon*. New York: Pitman, 1968.

Buckmaster, Henrietta. *Flight to Freedom: Story of the Underground Railroad.* New York: Crowell, 1958.

———. *Freedom Bound.* New York: Macmillan, 1965.

Budd, Edward C. (ed.). *Inequality and Poverty.* New York: Norton, 1967.

Bullins, Ed. *Five Plays.* Indianapolis: Bobbs-Merrill, 1969.

———. *How Do You Do: A Nonsense Drama.* Mill Valley: Illumination Press, 1968.

——— (ed.). *New Plays for the Black Theatre: An Anthology.* New York: Bantam Books, 1970.

Bullock, Henry Allan. *A History of Negro Education in the South: From 1619 to the Present.* Cambridge: Harvard University, 1967.

Bullock, Paul (ed.). *Watts—The Aftermath: An Inside View of the Ghetto, by the People of Watts.* New York: Grove Press, 1970.

Bullock, Ralph W. *In Spite of Handicaps.* Freeport: Books for Libraries Press, 1968.

Burchard, Peter. *Bimby.* New York: Coward-McCann.

———. *One Gallant Rush.* New York: St. Martin's Press, 1965.

Burke, Lily. *Search for Accord.* New York: Comet Press, 1959.

Burley, Dan. *Diggeth Thou?* Chicago: Cross, 1960.

Burns, W. Haywood. *The Voices of Negro Protest in America.* London: Oxford University, 1963.

Burt, McKinley, Jr. *Black Inventors of America.* Portland: National Book Co., 1970.

Burt, Olive W. *Negroes in the Early West.* New York: Julian Messner, 1970.

Buswell, James O. *Slavery, Segregation and Scripture.* Grand Rapids: Eerdmans, 1964.

Butcher, Margaret Just. *The Negro in American Culture.* New York: Alfred A. Knopf, 1957.

Byrd, James W. *J. Mason Brewer, Negro Folklorist.* Austin: Steck-Vaughn, 1967.

—C—

Cable, George W. *The Negro Question.* New York: Doubleday, 1958.

Cade, John Brother. *Holsey, the Incomparable.* New York: Pageant Press, 1964.

Caldwell, Erskine. *In Search of Bisco.* New York: Farrar, Straus, 1965.

Callcott, Margaret Law. *The Negro in Maryland Politics 1870-1912.* Baltimore: Johns Hopkins Press, 1969.

Campanella, Roy. *It's Good to Be Alive.* Boston: Little, Brown, 1959.

Campbell, Moses, Jr. *Cash and Credit.* New York: Vantage Press, 1964.

Cameron, Lou. *The Block Busters.* New York: David McKay, 1964.

Cantor, Louis. *A Prologue to the Protest Movement: The Missouri Share-Cropper Roadside Demonstrations of 1939.* Durham: Duke University Press, 1969.

Cantor, Milton (ed.). *Black Labor in America.* Westport: Greenwood Publishing, 1970.

Carawan, Guy, and Candie Carawan. *Ain't You Got a Right to the Tree of Life?* New York: Simon & Schuster, 1966.

——— (eds.). *Freedom Is a Constant Struggle: Songs of the Freedom Movement.* New York: Oak Publications.

Carmichael, Peter A. *The South and Segregation.* Washington, D.C.: Public Affairs Press, 1965.

Carmichael, Stokely and Charles V. Hamilton. *Black Power: The Politics of Liberation in America.* New York: Random House, 1967.

Carruth, Ella Kaiser. *She Wanted to Read: The Story of Mary McLeod Bethune.* Nashville: Abingdon Press, 1969.

Carson, Josephine. *Silent Voices: The Southern Negro Woman Today.* New York: Delacorte Press, 1969.

Carter, Dan T. *Scottsboro: Tragedy of the American South.* Baton Rouge: Louisiana State University, 1969.

Carter, Robert and others. *Equality.* New York: Pantheon Books, 1965.

Carter, Wilmoth A. *The New Negro of the South: A Portrait of Movements and Leadership.* New York: Exposition Press, 1967.

———. *The Urban Negro in the South.* New York: Vantage Press, 1961.

Caughey, John W., John Hope Franklin and Ernest R. May. *Land of the Free—A History of the United States.* New York: Benziger, 1966.

Cayton, Horace R. *Long Old Road.* New York: Trident Press, 1965.

Cepeda, Orlando (with Charles Einstein). *My Ups and Downs in Baseball.* New York: Putnam's.

Chace, William M. and Peter Collier (eds.). *Justice Denied: The Black Man in White America.* New York: Harcourt, Brace & World.

Chalmers, David M. *Hooded Americanism: The First Century of the Ku Klux Klan.* New York: Doubleday, 1965.

Chalmers, Bradford (ed.). *Chronicles of Negro Protest: A Background Book for Young People Documenting the History of Black Power.* New York: Parents Magazine Press, 1968.

Chambers, Bradford and Rebecca Moon (eds.). *Right On! An Anthology of Black Literature.* New York: New American Library, 1970.

Chametzky, Jules and Sidney Kaplan (ed.). *Black and White in American Culture: An Anthology from the Massachusetts Review.* Amherst: University of Massachusetts Press, 1969.

Chapman, Abraham (ed.). *Black Voices.* New York: New American Library, 1968.

Charters, Ann. *Nobody: The Story of Bert Williams.* New York: Macmillan, 1970.

Charters, Samuel. *The Bluesmen: The Story and the Music of the Men Who Made the Blues.* New York: Oak Publications, 1967.

Chase, W. M. and Peter Collier (eds.). *Justice Denied: The Black Man in White America.* New York: Harcourt, Brace and World, 1970.

Cheek, William F. *Black Resistance Before the Civil War.* Beverly Hills: Glencoe Press, 1970.

Cherry, Gwendolyn, Ruby Thomas and Pauline Willes. *Portraits in Color. The Lives of Colorful Negro Women.* New York: Pageant Press, 1962.

Chesnutt, Charles W. *The Marrow of Tradition.* Ann Arbor: University of Michigan Press, 1969.

———. *The Wife of His Youth and Other Stories of the Color Line.* Ann Arbor: University of Michigan Press, 1968.

Chesnutt, Helen M. *Charles Waddell Chesnutt; Pioneer of the Color Line.* Chapel Hill: University of North Carolina Press, 1962.

Chevigny, Paul. *Police Power.* New York: Pantheon Books, 1969.

Child, Lydia. *The Freedmen's Book.* New York: Arno Press, 1968.

Chisholm, Shirley. *Unbought and Unbossed.* Boston: Houghton Mifflin, 1970.

Clark, Kenneth B. *Dark Ghetto.* New York: Harper and Row, 1965.

———. *Prejudice and Your Child.* Boston: Beacon Press, 1963.

——— (ed.). *A Relevant War Against Poverty: A Study of Community Action Programs and Observable Social Change.* New York: Metropolitan Applied Research Center, 1969.

Clark, Mary T. *Discrimination Today.* New York: Hobbs, Dorman, 1966.

Clark, Septima P. and LeGette Blyth. *Echo in My Soul.* New York: Dutton, 1962.

Clarke, John H. (ed.). *American Negro Short Stories.* New York: Hill and Wang, 1966.

——— (ed.). *Harlem.* New York: New American Library, 1970.

——— (ed.). *Malcolm X: The Man and His Times.* New York: Macmillan, 1969.

——— and Vincent Harding (eds.). *Slave Trade and Slavery.* New York: Holt, Rinehart & Winston, 1970.

——— (ed.). *William Styron's Nat Turner: Ten Black Writers Respond.* Boston: Beacon Press, 1968.

Claspy, Everett. *The Negro in Southwestern Michigan: Negroes in the North in a Rural Environment.* Dowagiac, Michigan. Author.

Clay, Cassius (with Jack Olsen). *Black Is Best.* New York: Putnam, 1967.

Clayton, Edward T. *Martin Luther King: The Peaceful Warrior.* Englewood Cliffs: Prentice-Hall, 1964.

———. *The Negro Politician: His Success and Failure.* Chicago. Johnson, 1964.

Cleage, Albert B., Jr. *The Black Messiah.* New York: Sheed and Ward, 1968.

Cleaver, Eldridge. *Eldridge Cleaver: Post-Prison Writings and Speeches.* New York: Random House, 1969.

———. *Soul on Ice.* New York: McGraw-Hill, 1968.

Clifton, Lucille. *Good Times.* New York: Random House, 1969.

Clift, Virgil, Archibald A. Anderson, and H. Gordon Hullfish. *Negro Education in America.* New York: Harper, 1962.

Cobb, Charlie. *Charlie Cobb's Rage.* Tougaloo Flute Publications, 1968.

Cogan, Lee. *Negroes for Medicine: Report of a Macy Conference.* Baltimore: Johns Hopkins Press, 1968.

Cohen, Harry Rabbi. *Justice, Justice: A Jewish View of the Negro Revolt.* New York: Union of American Hebrew Congregations, 1968.

Cohen, Nathan (ed.). *The Los Angeles Riots: A Socio-Psychological Study.* New York: Praeger, 1970.

Cohen, Tom. *Three Who Dared.* New York: Doubleday, 1969.

Coleman, James S. *Equality of Educational Opportunity.* Washington, D. C.: Department of Health, Education and Welfare, 1966.

Coles, Robert. *Children of Crisis: A Study of Courage and Fear.* Boston: Little, Brown, 1967.

———. *Still Hungry in America.* New York: New American Library, 1969.

———. *Uprooted Children: The Early Life of Migrant Farm Workers.* Pittsburgh: University of Pittsburgh Press, 1970.

Collier Paperback Series. New York: 1970. (Mostly novels by Africans, Afro-Americans and West Indians)

Colter, Cyrus. *The Beach Umbrella.* Iowa City: University of Iowa Press.

Commager, Henry S. (comp.). *The Struggle for Racial Equality; A Documentary Record.* New York: Harper and Row, 1967.

Cone, James H. *Black Theology & Black Power.* New York: Seabury Press, 1969.

———. *Black Theology of Liberation.* New York: Lippincott, 1970.

Conot, Robert. *Rivers of Blood, Years of Darkness.* New York: Bantam, 1967.

Conrad, Earl. *Harriet Tubman.* New York: Eriksson, 1969.

———. *The Invention of the Negro.* New York: Hill & Wang, 1967.

———. *Everything and Nothing: Dorothy Dandridge.* New York: Abelard Schuman, 1970.

Cook, Mercer and Stephen E. Henderson. *The Militant Black Writer in Africa and the United States.* Madison: University of Wisconsin Press, 1969.

Cooke, Paul. *Civil Rights in the U. S.* Washington, D. C.: Meridian House, 1966.

Coombs, Orde (ed.). *We Speak as Liberators: Young Black Poets.* New York: Dodd, Mead, 1970.

Cooper, Clarence L., Jr. *The Farm.* New York: Crown, 1967.

Copeland, Vincent. *The Crime of Martin Sostre.* New York: McGraw-Hill, 1970.

Cornish, Sam and Lucian W. Dixon (eds.). *Chicory: Young Voices from the Black Ghetto.* New York: Association Press, 1969.

Corson, William. *Promise or Peril: The Black College Student in America.* New York: Norton, 1970.

Cotton, Ella E. *Queen of Persia.* New York: Exposition Press, 1960.

———. *A Spark for My People.* New York: Exposition Press, 1964.

Cottrell, John. *Muhammad Ali, Who Once was Cassius Clay.* New York: Funk and Wagnalls, 1968.

Couch, William, Jr. (ed.). *New Black Playwrights: An Anthology.* Baton Rouge: Louisiana State University Press, 1968.

Courlander, Harold. *Negro Folk Music, U. S. A.* New York: Columbia University Press, 1963.

Covin, Kelly. *Hear That Train Blow! A Novel About the Scottsboro Case.* New York: Delacorte Press, 1970.

Cox, Archibald, M. D. Howe and J. R. Wiggins. *Civil Rights, The Constitution and the Courts.* Cambridge: Harvard University Press, 1967.

Cox, Joseph Mason Andrew. *The Collected Poetry of J. M. A. Cox.* Francestown: The Golden Quill Press, 1970.

Cox, Oliver C. *Capitalism and American Leadership.* New York: Philosophical Library, 1962.

———. *Capitalism as A System.* New York: Monthly Review Press, 1965.

Cronon, Edmund Davis. *Black Moses.* Madison: University of Wisconsin Press, 1962.

Cross, Theodore L. *Black Capitalism: Strategy for Business in the Ghetto,* New York: Atheneum, 1969.

Crouchett, Lawrence. *The Negro in United States History.* Concord: Diablo Valley College, 1969.

Crow, Lester D., Walter I. Murray and Hugh H. Smythe. *Educating the Culturally Disadvantaged Child: Principles and Programs.* New York: David McKay, 1966.

Crowe, Charles (ed.). *The Age of Civil War and Reconstruction, 1830-1900: A Book of Interpretive Essays.* Homewood: Dorsey Press.

Cruden, Robert. *The Negro in Reconstruction.* Englewood Cliffs: Prentice-Hall, 1969.

Crump, Paul. *Burn, Killer, Burn!* Chicago: Johnson, 1962.

Cruse, Harold. *The Crisis of the Negro Intellectual.* New York: Morrow, 1967.

Cruz, Victor Hernandez. *Snaps.* New York: Random House, 1969.

Cuney-Hare, Maud. *Negro Musicians and Their Music.* Washington, D. C.: Associated, 1936.

Cunningham, Sis (ed.). *Broadside* (Vol. 2). New York: Oak Publications.

Curry, Gladys J. (ed.). *Viewpoints from Black America.* Englewood Cliffs: Prentice-Hall.

Curtin, Philip D. *The Atlantic Slave Trade: A Census.* Madison: University of Wisconsin Press, 1969.

Curtis, George M. *Bellhop Blues.* New York: Carlton Press, 1960.

Curtis, James C. and Lewis L. Gould (eds.). *The Black Experience in America. Selected Essays.* Austin: The University of Texas Press, 1970.

—D—

Dahl, Mary B. *Free Souls.* Boston: Houghton, 1969 (deals with the 1840 slave mutiny on the *Amistad*)

Dalfume, Richard M. *Desegregation of the U.S. Armed Forces: Fighting on Two Fronts 1939-1953.* Columbia: University of Missouri, 1969.

Damerell, Reginald G. *Triumph in a White Suburb: The Dramatic Story of Teaneck, N.J., The First Town in the Nation to Vote for Integrated Schools.* New York: William Morrow, 1968.

Dance, Stanley. *The World of Duke Ellington.* New York: Scribner's, 1970.

Dancy, John C. *Sand Against the Wind.* Detroit: Wayne State, 1966.

Daniel, Bradford. *Black, White & Gray.* New York: Sheed & Ward, 1964.

Daniels, Roger and Kitano, Harry H. *American Racism: Exploration of the Nature of Prejudice.* Englewood Cliffs: Prentice-Hall, 1970.

Danner, Margatet. *To Flower, Poems.* Hemphill Press, 1963.

DaSilva, Benjamin, M. Finkelstein and A. Loshin. *The Afro-American in United States History.* New York: Globe Book, 1969.

David, Jay (ed.). *Growing Up Black.* New York: William Morrow, 1968.

Davis, Benjamin J. *Communist Councilman from Harlem: Autobiographical Notes Written in a Federal Penitentiary.* New York: International Publishers, 1969.

Davis, Charles T. and Daniel Walden (eds.). *On Being Black: Writings by Afro-Americans from Frederick Douglass to the Present.* New York: Fawcett, 1970.

Davis, John P. (ed.). *The American Negro Reference Book.* Englewood Cliffs: Prentice-Hall, 1965.

Davis, Ossie. *Purlie Victorious, A Comedy in Three Acts.* New York: French, 1961.

Davis, Sammy, Jr., with Jane and Burt Boyar. *Yes I Can.* New York: Farrar Straus, 1965.

Dawson, Helaine. *On the Outskirts of Hope: Educating Youth from Poverty Areas.* New York: McGraw-Hill, 1968.

Day, Charles U. (ed.). *The Media and the Cities.* Chicago: University of Chicago, 1969.

DeCarava, Roy and Langston Hughes. *The Sweet Flypaper of Life.* New York: Hill & Wang, 1968.

Decker, Sunny. *An Empty Spoon.* New York: Harper and Row, 1969.

DeCoy, Robert H. *The Big Black Fire.* Los Angeles: Holloway House, 1969.

DeKnight, Freda. *The Ebony Cookbook, A Date With a Dish.* Chicago: Johnson, 1962.

Delany, Martin R. *Blake, or the Huts of America.* Boston: Beacon Press, 1970.

Delany, Martin R. and Robert Campbell. *Search for a Place: Black Separatism and Africa. 1860.* Ann Arbor: University of Michigan, 1969.

Delany, Samuel R. *The Einstein Intersection.* New York: Ace Books, 1968.

Delbanco, Nicholas. *News.* New York: William Morrow, 1970.

Demby, William. *The Catacombs.* New York: Pantheon Books, 1965.

Dennis, R. Ethel. *The Black People of America: Illustrated History.* New Haven: Readers Press, 1970.

Dennison, Tim, Sr. *The American Negro and His Amazing Music.* New York: Vantage Press, 1963.

Dent, Thomas C. and Richard Schechner (eds.). *The Free Southern Theatre.* New York: Bobbs-Merrill, 1969.

Dentler, Robert, Bernard and Warshauer, Marrev Ellen (eds.). *The Urban R's: Race Relations as the Problem in Urban Education.* New York: Praeger, 1968.

Diggs, Brother Alfred. *Naturally Black.* Chicago: Author, 1969.

Dionisopoulos, P. Allan. *Rebellion, Racism, and Representation: The Adam Clayton Powell Case and Its Antecedents.* DeKalb: Northern University, 1970.

Dobler, Lavinia and Edgar A. Toppin. *Pioneers and Patriots: The Lives of Six Negroes in the Revolutionary Era.* New York: Doubleday Zenith, 1965.

Dorman, Michael. *We Shall Overcome*. New York: Delacorte Press, 1964.

Douglas, William O. *Mr. Lincoln and the Negroes*. New York: Atheneum, 1963.

Douglass, Frederick. *Life and Times of Frederick Douglass*. New York: Collier, 1962.

———. *The Mind and Heart of Frederick Douglass: Excerpts from Speeches of the Great Negro Orator*. New York: Crowell, 1968.

———. *My Bondage and My Freedom*. New York: Arno, 1969. Chicago: Johnson, 1970.

———. *Narrative of the Life of Frederick Douglass, An American Slave*. Cambridge: Harvard University, 1960. N.Y.: Doubleday, 1963.

Douty, Esther M. *Forten the Sailmaker: Pioneer Champion of Negro Rights*. Chicago: Rand McNally, 1968. (Biography of James Forten.)

Dover, Cedric. *American Negro Art*. Greenwich: New York Graphic Society, 1960.

Downey, Fairfax. *The Buffalo Soldiers in the Indian Wars*. New York: McGraw-Hill, 1969.

Drama Review. (ed. by Ed Bullins). Summer, 1968.

Draper, Theodore. *The Rediscovery of Black Nationalism*. New York: Viking Press, 1970.

Drayton, Thomas. *A Grain of Sand*. New York: The Little Hut, 1970.

Drimmer, Melvin. *Black History: A Reappraisal*. New York: Doubleday, 1968.

Drisko, Carol F. and Edgar A. Toppin. *The Unfinished March*. New York: Doubleday, 1967.

Drotning, Phillip T. *A Guide to Negro History in America*. New York: Doubleday, 1968.

——— and Wesley South. *Up From the Ghetto*. New York: Cowles, 1970.

DuBois, W. E. B. *An A B C of Color*. New York: International, 1970.

———. *The Autobiography of W. E. B. DuBois*. New York: International, 1968.

———. *Black Reconstruction in America, 1860-1880*. New York: Atheneum, 1969.

———. *Darkwater: Voices from Within the Veil*. New York: Schocken, 1968.

———. *Dusk of Dawn: An Essay Toward an Autobiography of a Race Concept*. New York: Schocken, 1968.

———. *The Gift of Black Folk: The Negroes in the Making of America*. New York: Washington Square, 1970.

———. *John Brown*. New York: International, 1962.

———. *The Philadelphia Negro: A Social Study*. New York: Schocken, 1967.

———. *Souls of Black Folk*. New York: New American Library, 1969. New York: Dodd, 1970.

———. *The World and Africa*. New York: International, 1965.

Duberman, Martin (ed.). *The Anti-slavery Vanguard: New Essays on the Abolitionists*. Princeton: Princeton University, 1965.

Ducas, George (ed.) with Charles Van Doren. *Great Documents in Black American History*. New York: Praeger, 1970.

Dumond, Dwight L. *America's Shame and Redemption*. Marquette: Northern Michigan Universities Press, 1965.

Dunbar, Ernest (ed.). *The Black Expatriates: A Study of American Negroes in Exile*. New York: Dutton, 1968.

Dunham, Katherine. *A Touch of Innocence*. New York: Harcourt, Brace, 1959.

Durham, Philip and Everett L. Jones. *The Adventures of the Negro Cowboys*. New York: Bantam, 1969.

———. *The Negro Cowboys*. New York: Dodd, Mead, 1970.

Duster, Alfreda M. (ed.). *Crusade for Justice: The Autobiography of Ida B. Wells*. Chicago: University of Chicago, 1970.

— E —

Ebony. *The Black Revolution*. Chicago: Johnson, 1970.

———. *The Negro Handbook*. Chicago: Johnson, 1966.

———. *The White Problem in America*. Chicago: Johnson, 1966.

Ebony Classics. Chicago: Johnson, 1970. (First series of six historical volumes by blacks.)

Edwards, G. Franklin (ed.). *E. Franklin Frazier on Race Relations, Selected Papers*. Chicago: University of Chicago Press, 1968.

Edwards, Harry. *Black Students*. New York: The Free Press, 1970.

———. *The Revolt of the Black Athlete*. New York: The Free Press, 1969.

Edwards, Junius. *If We Must Die*. New York: Doubleday, 1963.

Egerton, John. *State Universities and Black Americans: An Inquiry into Desegregation and Equity for Negroes in 100 Public Universities*. Atlanta: Southern Education Foundation, 1969.

Ehle, John. *The Free Men*. New York: Harper & Row, 1965.

Elder III, Lonne. *Ceremonies in Dark Old Men*. New York: Farrar, 1968.

Elliott, Lawrence. *George Washington Carver: The Man Who Overcame*. Englewood Cliffs: Prentice-Hall, 1965.

Ellis, William W. *White Ethics and Black Power*. Chicago: Aldine Publishing, 1970.

Ellison, Ralph. *Invisible Man*. New York: New American Library, 1969.

———. *Shadow and Act*. New York: New American Library, 1966.

Elman, Richard. *Ill-at-Ease in Compton*. Compton: Pantheon, 1967.

Emanuel, James A. and Theodore L. Gross (eds.). *Dark Symphony: Negro Literature in America*. New York: The Free Press, 1968.

———. *Langston Hughes*. New York: Twayne, 1967.

———. *Panther Man*. Detroit: Broadside, 1970.

———. *The Treehouse and Other Poems*. Detroit: Broadside, 1968.

Endleman, Shalom (ed.). *Violence in the Streets*. Chicago: Quadrangle, 1969.

English, James W. *Handyman of the Lord*. New York: Meredith, 1967.

Epstein, Sam and Beryl. *Harriet Tubman: Guide to Freedom*. Champaign: Garrard Publishing, 1969.

Epstein, Sam. *George Washington Carver: Negro Scientist*. Champaign: Garrard Publishing, 1960.

Equal Educational Opportunity. Cambridge: Harvard University, 1969.

Erlich, Lillian. *What Jazz Is All About*. New York: Messner, 1962.

Essien-Udom, E. U. *Black Nationalism: A Search for an Identity in America*. New York: Dell, 1964.

Etzkowitz, Henry and Gerald M. Schaflander. *Ghetto Crisis: Riots or Reconciliation?* Boston: Little, Brown, 1969.

Evans, Mari. *I Am A Black Woman*. New York: Morrow, 1970.

Evers, Myrlie and William Peters. *For Us, the Living*. New York: Doubleday, 1967.

Ewers, Carolyn H. *The Long Journey: A Biography of Sidney Poitier*. New York: New American Library, 1969.

— F —

Faber, Doris. *I Will Be Heard: The Life of William Lloyd Garrison*. New York: Lothrop, 1970.

Factor, Robert L. *The Black Response to America*. Reading: Addison-Wesley, 1970.

Fager, Charles. *White Reflections on Black Power*. New York: Eerdmans, 1967.

Fair, Ronald L. *Hog Butcher*. New York: Harcourt, Brace, 1966.

———. *Many Thousand Gone: An American Fable*. New York: Harcourt, Brace, 1965.

———. *World of Nothing*. New York: Harper & Row, 1970.

Fairbairn, Ann. *Call Him George*. New York: Crown Publishers, 1970.

———. *Five Smooth Stones*. New York: Crown, 1968.

Farmer, James. *Freedom—When?* New York: Random House, 1966.

Farr, Finis. *Black Champion: The Life and Times of Jack Johnson*. New York: Scribner, 1964. New York: Fawcett, 1969.

Farrison, William Edward. *William Wells Brown: Author and Reformer*. Chicago: University of Chicago Press, 1969.

Fast, Howard. *Freedom Road*. New York: Crown, 1969.

Fauset, Arthur Huff and Nellie Rathbone Bright. *America: Red, White, Black, Yellow*. Philadelphia: Franklin Publishing, 1969.

Fax, Elton. *Contemporary Black Leaders*. New York: Dodd, 1970.

Feldman, Eugene P. R. *Black Power in Old Alabama: The Life and Stirring Times of James Rapier, Black Congressman from Alabama*. Chicago: Museum of African American History, 1968.

———. *Figures in Negro History*. Chicago: Museum of Negro History and Art, 1964.

Feldstein, Stanley. *Once A Slave: The Slaves' View of Slavery*. New York: Morrow, 1971.

Felton, Harold W. *Jim Beckwourth: Negro Mountain Man*. New York: Dodd, Mead, 1966.

———. *John Henry and His Hammer*. New York: Alfred A. Knopf, 1950.

———. *Nat Love, Negro Cowboy*. New York: Dodd, Mead, 1969.

———. *Edward Rose: Negro Trail Blazer*. New York: Dodd, Mead, 1967.

Fenderson, Lewis H. *Thurgood Marshall: Fighter for Justice*. New York: McGraw-Hill, 1969.

Ferguson, Blanche E. *Countee Cullen and the Negro Renaissance*. New York: Dodd, Mead, 1966.

Ferman, Louis A., Joyce L. Kernbluh, and J. A. Miller (eds.). *Negroes and Jobs: A Book of Readings*. Ann Arbor: University of Michigan Press, 1968.

———, and Alan Haber. *Poverty in America: A Book of Readings*. Ann Arbor: University of Michigan Press, 1968.

Ferris, Louanne. *I'm Done Crying*. New York: Evans, 1970.

Filler, Louis. *The Crusade Against Slavery: 1830-1860*. New York: Harper, 1960.

Fischer, John H., et al. *Education Parks: Appraisals of Plans to Improve Educational Quality and Desegregate the Schools*. Washington, D.C.: U.S. Commission on Civil Rights, 1967.

Fishel, Leslie and Benjamin Quarles (eds.). *The Black American: A Documentary History*. New York: Morrow, 1968.

Fisher, Miles M. *Negro Slave Songs in the United States*. New York: Citadel, 1963.

Fisher, Paul L. and Ralph L. Lowenstein. *Race and the News Media*. New York: Praeger, 1967.

Flipper, Henry O. *The Colored Cadet at West Point*. New York: Arno, 1969.

———. *Negro Frontiersman*. El Paso: Western College Press, 1963.

Flood, Curt (with Richard Carter). *The Way It Is*. New York: Trident Press, 1971.

Flynn, James J. *Negroes of Achievement in Modern America*. New York: Dodd, 1970.

Foley, Albert S. *Bishop Healy: Beloved Outcast*. New York: Farrar, Strauss, 1954.

———. *God's Men of Color*. New York: Arno, 1969.

Foner, Eric (ed.). *America's Black Past: A Reader in Afro-American History*. New York: Harper & Row, 1970.

Foner, Philip S. *Frederick Douglass*. New York: Citadel, 1964.

——— (ed.). *W. E. B. DuBois Speaks: Speeches and Addresses 1890-1963*. (2 vols.). New York: Pathfinder Press, 1970.

Fontaine, William T. *Reflections on Segregation, Desegregation, Power and Morals*. Springfield: Thomas, 1968.

Ford, Hugh (ed.). *Nancy Cunard: Brave Poet, Indomitable Rebel, 1896-1965*. Philadelphia: Chilton Books, 1968.

Ford, Jesse Hill. *The Liberation of Lord Byron Jones*. Boston: Little, Brown, 1965.

Ford, N. A. *The Contemporary Negro Novel*. College Park: McGrath, 1970.

Forer, Lois G. *No One Will Lissen: How Our Legal System Brutalizes the Youthful Poor*. New York: John Day, 1970.

Forman, James. *Sammy Younge, Jr.: The First Black College Student to Die in the Black Liberation Movement*. New York: Grove Press, 1968.

Forten, Charlotte L. *A Free Negro in the Slave Era*. New York: Collier, 1961.

Fox, Stephen. *The Guardian of Boston: William Monroe Trotter*. New York: Atheneum Press, 1970.

Franklin, John Hope (ed.). *Color and Race*. Boston: Houghton Mifflin.

———. *The Emancipation Proclamation*. New York: Doubleday, 1963.

——— (ed.). *A Fool's Errand*. Cambridge: Belknap Press, 1961.

———. *From Slavery to Freedom: A History of American Negroes*. (3rd ed.). New York: Alfred A. Knopf, 1967.

———. *An Illustrated History of Black Americans*. New York: Time-Life, 1970.

———, and Isidore Starr (eds.). *The Negro in Twentieth Century America: A Reader on the Struggle for Civil Rights*. New York: Random House, 1967.

———. *Reconstruction: After the Civil War*. Chicago: University of Chicago Press, 1961.

Frazier, E. Franklin. *Black Bourgeoisie*. New York: Collier, 1962.

———. *The Negro Church in America*. New York: Schocken Books, 1963.

———. *The Negro Family in the United States*. 1966.

———. *The Negro in the United States*. New York: Macmillan, 1957.

———. *Negro Youth at the Crossways: Their Personality Development in the Middle States*. New York: Schocken Books, 1967.

Frazier, Thomas R. (ed.). *Afro-American History: Primary Sources*. New York: Harcourt, Brace & World, 1970.

Frederickson, George M. (ed.). *William Lloyd Garrison*. Englewood Cliffs: Prentice Hall, 1969.

Freed, Leonard. *Black in White America*. New York: Grossman Publishers, 1969.

Freedman, Frances S. *The Black American Experience*. New York: Bantam, 1970.

Freuchen, Peter. *The Legend of Daniel Williams*. New York: Messner, 1956.

Friedman, Lawrence J. *The White Savage: Racial Fantasies in the Post-Bellum South*. Englewood Cliffs: Prentice Hall, 1970.

Friedman, Leon G. *Civil Rights Reader*. New York: Walker, 1967.

——— (ed.). *Southern Justice*. New York: Pantheon Books, 1965.

Fry, John R. *Fire and Blackstone*. New York: Lippincott, 1970.

Fulks, Bryan. *Black Struggle: A History of the Negro in America*. New York: Dell, 1970.

Fullinwider, S. P. *Negro Intellectuals in the 20th Century*. Homewood: Dorsey Press, 1970.

— G —

Gaines, Ernest J. *Bloodline*. New York: Dial Press, 1968.

———. *Catherine Carmier*. New York: Atheneum Press, 1964.

———. *Of Love and Dust*. New York: Dial Press, 1967.

Garland, Phyl. *The Sound of Soul*. Chicago: Regnery, 1970.

Garvey, Amy Jacques. *Garvey and Garveyism*. New York: Collier Books, 1970.

Gaskins, Ruth L. *A Good Heart and a Light Hand*. New York: Simon & Schuster, 1969.

Gayle, Addison, Jr. (ed.). *The Black Aesthetics*. New York: Doubleday, 1970.

———. *Black Expression: Essays By and About Black Americans in the Creative Arts*. New York: Weybright and Talley, 1969.

———. *The Black Situation*. New York: Horizon Press, 1970.

———. *Bondage, Freedom and Beyond: The Prose of Black Americans*. New York: Doubleday Zenith, 1971.

Genovese, Eugene D. *The Political Economy of Slavery*. New York: Pantheon, 1965.

Gettleman, M. E. and D. Mermelstein (eds.). *The Great Society Reader: The Failure of American Liberalism*. New York: Random House, 1967.

Ghetto Schools: Problems and Panaceas. New York: New Republic Book, 1968.

Gibson, Althea (with Ed Fitzgerald). *I Always Wanted to be Somebody*. New York: Harper, 1958.

——— (with Richard Curtis). *So Much to Live For*. New York: Putnam, 1968.

Gibson, Bob (with Phil Pepe). *From Ghetto to Glory: The Story of Bob Gibson*. New York: Englewood Cliffs: Prentice-Hall, 1968. New York: Popular Library, 1968.

Gibson, D. Parke. *The $30 Billion Negro*. New York: Macmillan, 1969.

Gilbert, Ben W. (ed.). *Ten Blocks from the White House*. New York: Praeger, 1968.

Giles, L. H. and L. F. Holmes. *Color Me Brown*. Chicago: Johnson, 1963.

Gillett, Charlie. *The Sound of the City: The Rise of Rock and Roll*. New York: Outerbridge and Dienstfrey, 1970.

Gillon, Adam (ed.). *Poems of the Ghetto: A Testament of Lost Men*. New York: Twayne, 1970.

Ginger, Ann Fagan (ed.). *Minimizing Racism in Jury Trials: The Voir Dire Conducted by Charles R. Garry in People of Calif. v. Huey P. Newton*. Berkely: National Lawyers Guild, 1970.

——— and Louis H. Bell. *Trials: Police Miscounduct, Litigation —Plaintiff's Remedies*. Berkeley: Civil Liberties Library, 1970.

Ginsburg, Ralph. *100 Years of Lynchings*. New York: Lancer Books, 1970.

Ginzberg, Eli (ed.). *The Negro Challenge to the Business Community*. New York: McGraw Hill, 1964.

——— and A. S. Eichner. *The Troublesome Presence*. New York: Free Press of Glencoe, 1964.

——— (ed.). *Business Leadership and the Negro Crisis*. New York: McGraw-Hill, 1968.

———. *The Middle-Class Negro in the White Man's World*. New York: Columbia University, 1967.

Giovanni, Nikki. *Black Feeling, Black Tale, Black Judgment*. New York: Morrow, 1970.

———. *Black Judgment*. Detroit: Broadside Press, 1969.

———. *Re-Creation*. Detroit: Broadside, 1970.

Gitler, Ira. *Jazz Masters of the Forties*. New York: Macmillan, 1966.

Gladwin, Thomas. *Poverty U.S.A.* Boston: Little, Brown, 1967.

Glock, Charles Y. and Ellen Siegelman (eds.). *Prejudice U.S.A.* New York: Praeger, 1969.

Golden, Harry. *Mr. Kennedy and the Negroes*. Cleveland: World, 1964.

Goldman, Peter. *Report from Black America*. New York: Simon and Schuster, 1970.

Goldwin, Robert A. (ed.). *100 Years of Emancipation*. Chicago: Rand McNally, 1964.

Gonzales, Juan, and Peter Quinn: *Mayerson, Charlotte, Two Blocks Apart*. New York: Holt, 1965.

Good, Paul. *The American Serfs: A Report on Poverty in the Rural South*. New York: Putnam, 1969.

Goodman, Morris C. *A Junior History of the American Negro Vol. I—Discovery to the Civil War, Vol. II—Civil War to Civil Rights War*. New York: Fleet Press, 1970.

Goodman, Walter. *Black Bondage: The Life of Slaves in the South*. New York: Farrar, Straus & Giroux, 1969.

Goodmans, Mary Ellen. *Race Awareness in Young Children*. Cambridge: Addison-Wesley, 1952.

Gordon, Milton. *Assimilation in American Life. The Role of Race, Religion and National Origins*. New York: Oxford University, 1964.

Gordone, Charles. *No Place to Be Somebody: A Black Black Comedy*. Indianapolis: Bobbs-Merrill, 1970.

Goro, Herb. *The Block*. New York: Random House, 1970.

Gossett, Thomas S. *Race: The History of an Idea in America*. Dallas: Southern Methodist University Press, 1963.

Gould, Jean. *That Dunbar Boy*. New York: Dodd, 1958.

Gourlay, Jack G. *The Negro Salaried Worker*. New York: American Management Association, 1965.

Graham, Hugh Davis. *Crisis in Print: Desegregation and the Press in Tennessee*. Nashville: Vanderbilt University Press, 1968.

——— and Ted Robert Gurr (eds.). *The History of Violence in America*. New York: Praeger & Bantam, 1969.

Graham, Lorenz. *North Town*. New York: Crowell, 1965.

Graham, Shirley. *Booker T. Washington*. New York: Messner, 1955.

——— (and George D. Lipscomb). *Dr. George Washington Carver, Scientist*. New York: Messner, 1944.

———. *Jean Baptiste Pointe Du Sable*. New York: Messner, 1953.

———. *Paul Robeson, Citizen of the World*. New York: Messner, 1946.

———. *The Story of Phillis Wheatley*. New York: Archway Paperbacks, 1968.

———. *There Was Once a Slave: The Heroic Story of Frederick Douglass*. New York: Messner, 1947.

———. *Your Most Humble Servant*. New York: Messner, 1949.

———. *Black Protest*. New York: Fawcett, 1968.

Grant, Joanne. *Confrontation on Campus: The Columbia Pattern for the New Protest*. New York: New American Library, 1969.

Gregory, Dick. *From the Back of the Bus*. New York: Avon, 1962.

——— (with Robert Lipsyte). *Nigger*. New York: E. P. Dutton, 1964.

———. *No More Lies*. New York: Harper, 1970.

———. *The Shadow That Scares Me*. New York: Doubleday, 1968.

———. *What's Happening?* New York: E. P. Dutton, 1965.

———. *Write Me In!* New York: Bantam Books, 1968.

Green, Constance McL. *The Secret City: A History of Race Relations in the Nation's Capital*. Princeton: Princeton University Press, 1967.

Green, Robert L. (ed.). *Racial Crisis in American Education*. Chicago: Follett, 1970.

Greenberg, Polly. *The Devil Has Slippery Shoes: A Biased Biography of the Child Development Group of Mississippi*. New York: Macmillan, 1969.

Greene, Lorenzo. *The Negro in Colonial New England, 1620-1776*. New York: Atheneum, 1968.

Greenlee, Sam. *The Spook Who Sat by the Door*. New York: Richard W. Baron, 1970.

Greenwood, Elma L. *How Churches Fight Poverty: 60 Successful Local Projects*. New York: Friendship Press, 1968.

Greenwood, Theresa. *Psalms of a Black Mother*. Anderson: Warner Press, 1970.

Grier, William H. and Price M. Cobbs. *Black Rage*. New York: Basic Books, 1968.

Griffin, John Howard. *Black Like Me*. New York: New American Library, 1962.

———. *The Church and the Black Man*. Dayton: George A. Pflaum Publishing, 1970.

Grimshaw, Allen D. (ed.). *Racial Violence in the United States*. Chicago: Aldine Publishing, 1970.

Gross, Martha. *The Possible Dream: 10 Who Dared*. Philadelphia: Chilton, 1970.

Gross, Seymour and John Edward Henry (eds.). *Images of the Negro in American Literature*. Chicago: University of Chicago Press, 1966.

Grossman, Barney, with Gladys Groom and the pupils of P.S. 150, Bronx, N. Y. *Black Means . . .* New York: Hill & Wang, 1970.

Grosvenor, Kali. *Poems by Kali*. New York: Doubleday, 1970.

Grosvenor, Verta Mae. *The Vibration Cookbook*. New York: 1970.

Guy, Rosa. *Bird At My Window*. New York: Lippincott, 1966.

———. *Children of Longing*. New York: Bantam, 1970.

—H—

Haas, Ben. *KKK*. Evanston: Regency Books, 1963.

———. *Look Away, Look Away*. Simon & Schuster, 1964.

Haber, Louis. *Black Pioneers of Science and Invention*. New York: Harcourt, Brace & World, 1970.

Haddad, William F. and G. Douglas Pugh (eds.). *Black Economic Development*. Englewood Cliffs: Prentice Hall, 1970.

Halliburton, Warren J. and William L. Katz. *American Majorities and Minorities: A Syllabus of United States History for Secondary Schools*. New York: Arno Press, 1970.

Hamilton, Virginia. *The House of Dies Drear*. New York: Macmillan, 1969.

———. *Zeely*. New York: Macmillan, 1968.

Hannerz, Ulf. *Soulside: Inquiries into Ghetto Culture and Community*. New York: Columbia University, 1970.

Hano, Arnold. *Willie Mays*. New York: Grosset, 1966.

Hansberry, Lorraine. *The Movement: Documentary of the Struggle for Equality*. New York: Simon & Schuster, 1964.

———. *A Raisin in the Sun*. New York: Random House, 1959.

———. *The Sign in Sidney Brustein's Window*. New York: Random House, 1965.

———. *To Be Young, Gifted and Black*. Adapted by Robert Nemiroff. New York: New American Library, 1970.

Hardwick, Richard. *Charles Richard Drew: Pioneer in Blood Research*. New York: Scribners, 1967.

Hare, Maud C. *Norris Wright Coney*. Austin: Steck-Vaughn, 1968.

Hare, Nathan. *The Black Anglo-Saxons*. New York: Collier, 1970.

Harper, Michael S. *Dear John, Dear Coltrane: Poems*. Pittsburgh: University of Pittsburgh, 1970.

Harris, Abram L. *The Negro as Capitalist: A Study of Banking and Business Among American Negroes*. College Park: McGrath, 1970.

Harris, Janet. *The Long Freedom Road. The Civil Rights Story*. New York: McGraw-Hill, 1967.

———. *Students in Revolt*. New York: McGraw-Hill, 1970.

——— and Julius Hobson. *Black Pride*. New York: McGraw-Hill, 1969.

Harris, Middleton A. *A Negro History Tour of Manhattan*. New York: Negro University Press: Greenwood Publishing Co., 1968.

Harris, Paul N. *Base Company 16*. New York: Vantage Press, 1963.

Harris, Robert J. *The Quest for Equality*. Baton Rouge: Louisiana State University, 1960.

Harris, Sara. *Father Divine: Holy Husband*. New York: Doubleday: Permabooks, 1971.

Harrison, Delores. *The Bannekers of Bannaky*. New York: Hawthorn Books, 1970.

——— (ed.). *We Shall Live in Peace: The Teachings of Martin Luther King, Jr.* New York: Hawthorn Books, 1968.

Haskins, Jim. *Diary of a Harlem Schoolteacher*. New York: Grove Press, 1970.

Hatch, James V. *Black Image on the American Stage: A Bibliography of Plays and Musicals 1770-1970*. New York: Drama Book Specialists, 1970.

Havens, Murray Clark; Carl Leiden, Karl M. Schmitt. *The Politics of Assassination*. Englewood Cliffs: Prentice-Hall, 1970.

Hawkins, Hugh (ed.). *Booker T. Washington and His Critics: The Problem of Negro Leadership*. Boston: D. C. Heath, 1963.

Hayden, Robert (ed.). *Kaleidoscope: Poems by American Negro Poets*. New York: Harcourt, Brace, 1967.

———. *Selected Poems*. New York: October House, 1966.

———. *Words in the Morning Time*. New York: October House, 1971.

Hayden, Tom. *Rebellion in Newark: Official Violence and the Ghetto Response*. New York: Random House, 1967.

Heard, J. Norman. *The Black Frontiersmen: Adventures of Negroes Among American Indians 1528-1918*. New York: John Day, 1969.

Heard, Nathan C. *Howard Street*. New York: Dial Press, 1968.

Hedgeman, Anna Arnold. *The Trumpet Sounds: A Memoir of Negro Leadership*. New York: Holt, Rinehart & Winston, 1964.

Helper, Rose. *Racial Policies and Practices of Real Estate Brokers*. Minneapolis: University of Minnesota, 1968.

Henderson, David. *De Mayor of Harlem*. New York: E. P. Dutton, 1970.

———. *Felix of the Silent Forest*: New York: The Poets Press, 1967.

Hendin, Herbert. *Black Suicide*. New York: Basic Books, 1970.

Henson, Josiah. *Father Henson's Story of His Own Life*. New York: Corinth Books, 1962.

Henson, Matthew A. *Black Explorer at the North Pole*. New York: Walker & Co., 1969.

Hentoff, Nat. *The Jazz Life*. New York: Dial Press, 1963.

———. *The New Equality*. New York: Viking Press, 1964.

———. *Call the Keeper*. New York: Viking Press, 1966.

Herbers, John. *The Lost Priority*. New York: Funk & Wagnalls, 1970.

Hercules, Frank. *Where the Hummingbird Flies*. New York: Harcourt, Brace, 1961.

———. *I Want a Black Doll*. New York: Simon & Schuster, 1967.

Herndon, Angelo. *Let Me Live*. New York: Arno Press, 1970.

Herndon, James. *The Way It Spozed to Be: A Report on the Classroom War Behind the Crisis in Our Schools*. New York: Simon & Schuster, 1968.

Hernton, Calvin S. *Sex and Racism in America*. New York: Doubleday, 1964.

———. *White Papers for White Americans*. New York: Doubleday, 1966.

Herschler, Mildred Barger. *Frederick Douglass*. Chicago: Follett, 1969.

Hersey, John. *The Algiers Motel Incident*. New York: Knopf, 1968.

Herskovits, Melville J. *The Myth of the Negro Past*. New York: Harper, 1964.

Hesslink, George K. *Black Neighbors: Negroes in a Northern Rural Community*. Indianapolis: Bobbs-Merrill, 1968.

Heuman, William. *Famous Pro Basketball Stars*. New York: Dodd, 1970.

Hickey, Neil and Ed Edwin. *Adam Clayton Powell and the Politics of Race*. New York: Fleet, 1965.

Highbee, Jay Anders. *Development and Administration of the New York State Law Against Discrimination*. University: University of Alabama, 1968.

Higginson, Thomas W. *Army Life in a Black Regiment*. New York: Collier, 1963.

Hill, Herbert (ed.). *Anger and Beyond*. New York: Harper, 1966. New York: Perennial Library, 1968.

———. *Soon One Morning*. New York: Knopf, 1963.

Hill, Roy L. *Who's Who in the American Negro Press*. Dallas: Royal, 1960.

Hilton, Bruce. *The Delta Ministry*. New York: Macmillan, 1969.

Himes, Chester. *Cast the First Stone*. New York: Coward-McCann, 1952.

———. *The Big Gold Dream and All Shot Up*. New York: Avon, 1960.

———. *Cotton Comes to Harlem*. New York: G. P. Putnam, 1965.

———. *Pinktoes*. New York: G. P. Putnam & Stein and Day, 1965.

Hirsch, Phil (ed.). *Listen White Man, I'm Bleeding*. New York: Pyramid, 1970.

Hirschberg, Al. *Basketball's Greatest Teams*. New York: Putnam, 1965.

———. *Henry Aaron: Quiet Superstar*. New York: Putnam, 1969.

Hodges, Carl G. and Helene H. Levene. *Illinois Negro Historymakers*. Chicago: Illinois Emancipation Centennial Commission, 1964.

Holiday, Billie (with William Duffy). *Lady Sings the Blues*. New York: Popular Library, 1969.

Holland, Jerome H. *Black Opportunity*. New York: Weybright & Talley, 1970.

Holloway, Harry. *The Politics of the Southern Negro: From Exclusion to Big City Organization*. New York: Random House, 1969.

Holt, Len. *The Summer That Didn't End*. New York: Morrow, 1965.

Holt, Rackham. *George Washington Carver*. New York: Doubleday, 1963.

———. *Mary McLeod Bethune*. New York: Doubleday, 1964.

Hooper, Sr., Cliff. *Black Father, Black Faith*. Seattle: Author, 1970.

Hoover, Dwight W. (ed.). *Understanding Negro History*. Chicago: Quadrangle Books, 1968.

Horne, Lena, with Richard Schickel. *Lena*. New York: Doubleday, 1965.

Horwitz, George D. *La Causa: The California Grape Strike*. New York: Macmillan, 1970.

Horwitz, Julius. *The W.A.S.P.* New York: Atheneum Press, 1967.

Hough, Jr., Joseph. *Black Power and White Protestants: A Christian Response to the New Negro Pluralism*. New York: Oxford University, 1968.

Howard, Elston. *Catching*. New York: Viking Press, 1966.

Howard, John R. (ed.). *Awakening Minorities: American Indians, Mexican Americans, Puerto Ricans*. Chicago: Aldine Publishing Co., 1970.

Howell, Jinxy Red (Dressler LaMarr). *All the Hairs on My Head Hurt*. New York: Exposition Press, 1964.

Howell, Leon. *Freedom City*. Richmond: John Knox Press, 1969.

Hoyt, Edwin P. *Paul Robeson: The American Othello*. Cleveland: World, 1967. (A very poor book on Robeson.)

Hughes, Langston. *Ask You Mama, 12 Moods for Jazz*. New York: Knopf, 1961.

———. *The Best of Simple*. New York: Hill and Wang, 1961.

——— (ed.). *Best Short Stories by Negro Writers: An Anthology From 1899 to the Present*. Boston: Little, Brown, 1967.

———. *The Big Sea*. New York: Hill and Wang, 1963.

——— and Milton Meltzer. *Black Magic: A Pictorial History of the Negro in American Entertainment*. Englewood Cliffs: Prentice-Hall, 1967.

——— (and Arna Bontemps). *The Book of Negro Folklore*. New York: Dodd, Mead, 1958.

———. *Don't You Turn Back*. New York: Knopf, 1969.

———. *Famous Negro Heroes of America*. New York: Dodd, Mead, 1958.

———. *Fight for Freedom: The Story of the NAACP*. New York: Norton, 1962.

———. *Five Plays*. Bloomington: Indiana University Press, 1963.

———. *I Wonder as I Wander*. New York: Rinehart, 1956.

———. *The Langston Hughes Reader*. New York: Braziller, 1958.

——— (ed.). *New Negro Poets, U.S.A.* Bloomington: Indiana University Press, 1964.

———. *The Panther and the Lash: Poems of Our Times*. New York: Knopf, 1967.

——— (with Milton Meltzer and C. Eric Lincoln). *A Pictorial History of the Negro in America*. New York: Crown, 1968.

——— and Arna W. Bontemps (eds.). *The Poetry of the Negro 1746-1970*. New York: Doubleday, 1970.

———. *Selected Poems*. New York: Knopf, 1959.

———. *Simple's Uncle Sam*. New York: Hill and Wang, 1965.

———. *Something in Common and Other Stories*. New York: Hill and Wang, 1963.

Huie, William Bradford. *Three Lives for Mississippi*. New York: New American Library, 1968.

———. *He Slew the Dreamer: My Search for the Truth About James Earl Ray and the Murder of Martin Luther King*. New York: Delacorte Press, 1970.

———. *The Klansmen*. New York: Delacorte Press, 1967.

Human, Harold M. (ed.). *The Radical Republicans and Reconstruction*. Indianapolis: Bobbs-Merrill, 1968.

Hundley, Mary Gibson. *The Dunbar Story*. New York: Vantage Press, 1965.

Hunger USA: A Report by the Citizens' Board of Inquiry into Hunger and Malnutrition in the United States. Boston: Beacon Press, 1969.

Hunter, Kristin. *God Bless the Child*. New York: Scribner, 1964.

———. *The Soul Brothers and Sister Lou*. New York: Scribner, 1968.

Hunton, George K. *All of Which I Saw, Part of Which I Was*. New York: Doubleday, 1967.

Hurley, Rodger. *Poverty & Mental Retardation: A Causal Relationship*. New York: Random House, 1970.

—I—

I Was A Black Panther (as told to Chuck Moore). New York: Doubleday, 1970.

Ianniello, Lynne (ed.). *Milestones Along the March*. New York: Praeger, 1965.

Images of Dignity: The Drawings of Charles White. Los Angeles: The Ward Ritchie Press, 1967.

Iman, Brother. *War in America: The Malcolm X Doctrine*. Detroit: Malcolm X Society, 1968.

International Library of Negro Life and History. Dr. Charles H. Wesley (Editor-in-Chief). Washington, D.C.: United Publishing Corp., 1967-1969.

Isaacs, Edith J. *The Negro in the American Theatre*. College Park: McGrath, 1970. (There are many books in the McGrath reprint series on black literature, business, college, etc.)

Isaacs, Harold R. *The New World of Negro Americans.* New York: John Day, 1963.

Ivanov, Robert F. *The Struggles of Negroes for Land and Freedom in the Southern U.S.A., 1865-1877.* Moscow: Publishing House of the Academy of Science of the U.S.S.R., 1958.

— J —

Jackson, Bruce (ed.). *The Negro and His Folklore in Nineteenth Century Periodicals.* Austin: University of Texas, 1968.

Jackson, Clyde Owen. *The Songs of Our Years: A Study of Negro Folk Music.* New York: Exposition Press, 1968.

Jackson, Florence and J. B. Jackson. *The Black Man in America. 1619-1790.* New York: Franklin Watts, 1970.

Jackson, George. *Soledad Brother: The Prison Letters of George Jackson.* New York: Coward-McCann, 1970. New York: Bantam, 1970.

Jackson, James E. *The View From Here.* New York: Publishers New Press, 1963.

Jackson, Jesse. *Tessie.* New York: Harper & Row, 1968.

Jackson, Kenneth T. *The Ku Klux Klan in the City 1915-1930.* New York: Oxford University, 1967.

Jackson, Mahalia (with Evan McLeod). *Movin' On Up.* New York: Hawthorne, 1966. New York: Avon, 1969.

Jackson, Miles M. (compiler & ed.). *A Bibliography of Negro History and Culture.* Atlanta: Atlanta University, 1969.

Jackson, Robert B. *Earl the Pearl: the Story of Earl Monroe.* New York: Walck, 1969.

Jacobs, Paul. *Prelude to Riot: A View of Urban America from the Bottom.* New York: Random House, 1968.

——— and Saul Landau, with Eve Pell (eds.). *To Serve the Devil:* Vol. I, *Natives and Slaves;* Vol. II, *Colonials and Sojourners.* New York: Random House, 1971.

Jacobson, Julius (ed.). *The Negro and the American Labor Movement.* New York: Doubleday, 1969.

Jaffe, A. J., Walter Adams and Sandra G. Meyers. *Negro Higher Education in the 1960's.* New York: Praeger, 1968.

James, Beauregard. (pseud.). *The Road to Birmingham.* New York: Bridgehead, 1965.

James, Charles L. (ed.). *From the Roots: Short Stories by Black Americans.* New York: Dodd, Mead, 1970.

Jarry, Hawke. *Black Schoolmaster.* New York: Exposition Press, 1970.

Jeffers, Lance. *My Blackness is the Beauty of This Soul.* Detroit: Broadside, 1970.

Joans, Ted. *Black Pow-Wow: Jazz Poems.* New York: Hill & Wang, 1970.

———. *The Hipsters.* New York: Citadel, 1961.

John, Frank. *Black Songs.* London: Longmans, Ltd., 1970.

Johnson, B. B. *Black is Beautiful.* New York: Paperback Library, 1970.

Johnson, Haynes. *Dusk at the Mountain.* New York: Doubleday, 1963.

Johnson, Jack. *Jack Johnson in the Ring and Out.* Chicago: National Sports Publishing, 1927.

Johnson, James Hugo. *Race Relations in Virginia and Miscegenation in the South, 1776-1860.* Amherst: University of Massachusetts, 1970.

Johnson, James Weldon. *Along This Way.* New York: Viking, 1968.

———. *The Autobiography of an Ex-Coloured Man.* New York: Hill and Wang, 1960.

———. *Black Manhattan.* New York: Arno Press, 1968.

——— (ed.). *The Book of American Negro Poetry.* New York: Harcourt, Brace & World, 1958.

——— and J. Rosamond Johnson. *Lift Every Voice and Sing.* New York: Hawthorne, 1970.

Johnson, Jesse, Jr. *Ebony, Brass: An Autobiography of Negro Frustration Amid Aspiration.* New York: William-Frederick Press, 1968.

Johnson, Marvin E. *Down Under the Sun, U.S.A.* New York: Carlton Press, 1964.

Johnson, Philip A. *Call Me Neighbor, Call Me Friend.* New York: Doubleday, 1965.

Johnson, William M. *The House on Corbett Street.* New York: William-Frederick Press, 1968.

Johnston, Johanna. *Paul Cuffee: America's First Black Captain.* New York: Dodd, 1970.

———. *Runaway to Heaven: The Story of Harriet Beecher Stowe.* New York: Doubleday, 1963.

Johnston, Percy E. (ed.). *Afro American Philosophies: Selected Readings, From Jupiter to Eugene C. Holmes.* Upper Montclair: Montclair State College, 1970.

Jones, Cleon (with Ed Hershey). *Cleon.* New York: Coward-McCann, 1970.

Jones, E. H. *A Pleasant Encounter, and Other Poems.* New York: Vantage, 1964.

Jones, Edward Allen. *A Candle in the Dark: A History of Morehouse College.* Valley Forge: Judson Press, 1967.

Jones, Jymi. *Guerrilla Warfare in Philly.* Elkins Park: Uhuru Publications, 1970.

Jones, Leroi. *The Baptism and the Toilet.* New York: Grove, 1967.

——— and Larry Neal (eds.). *Black Fire: An Anthology of Afro-American Writing.* New York: Morrow, 1968.

———. *Black Magic. Sabotage, Target Study, Black Art, Collected Poetry, 1961-1967.* Indianapolis: Bobbs-Merrill, 1969.

———. *Black Music.* New York: Morrow, 1967.

———. *Blues People. Negro Music in White America.* New York: Morrow, 1963.

———. *The Dead Lecturer.* New York: Grove, 1964.

———. *Dutchman and the Slave.* New York: Morrow, 1964.

———. *Four Black Revolutionary Plays.* Indianapolis: Bobbs-Merrill, 1970.

———. *Home: Social Essays.* New York: Morrow, 1966.

——— and Billy Abernathy. *In Our Terribleness: Some Elements and Meanings in Black Style.* New York: Bobbs-Merrill, 1970.

———. *It's Nation Time.* Chicago: Third World Press, 1970.

——— (Imamu Amiri Baraka). *Jello.* Chicago: Third World Press, 1970.

——— (ed.). *The Moderns: An Anthology of New Writings in America.* New York: Corinth Books, 1963.

———. *Preface to A Twenty-Volume Suicide Note: Poems.* New York: Citadel, 1961.

———. *The System of Dante's Hell.* New York: Grove Press, 1966.

———. *Tales.* New York: Grove, 1967.

Jones, Lewis Wade. *Cold Rebellion: The South's Oligarchy in Revolt.* London: MacGibbon & Kee, 1962.

Jones, Ruth Fosdick. *Escape to Freedom.* New York: Random House, 1958.

Jordan, June (ed.). *Soulscript: Afro-American Poetry.* Garden City: Doubleday, 1970.

——— and Terri Bush (eds.). *The Voice of the Children.* New York: Holt, 1971.

———. *Who Look At Me.* New York: Crowell, 1970.

Jordan, Lewis G. *Negro Baptist History U.S.A.* Nashville: Sunday School Publishing Board, 1930.

Jordan, Winthrop D. *White Over Black: American Attitudes Toward the Negro 1550-1812.* Chapel Hill: University of North Carolina, 1968.

Joseph, Stephen M. (ed.). *The Me Nobody Knows: Children's Voices From the Ghetto.* New York: Avon, 1968.

Josey, E. J. (ed.). *The Black Librarian in America.* Metuchen: Scarecrow Press, 1970.

— K —

Kahn, Tom. *Unfinished Revolution.* New York: Socialist Party, 1960.

Kain, John F. (ed.). *Race and Poverty: The Economics of Discrimination.* Englewood Cliffs: Prentice-Hall, 1970.

Kaiser, Inez Y. *Soul Food Cookery.* New York: Pitman, 1968.

Kaland, William J. (ed.). *The Great Ones: Ten Remarkable Black Americans.* New York: Washington Square Press, 1970.

Kalven, Harry, Jr. *The Negro and the First Amendment.* Columbus: Ohio State University, 1965.

Kaplan, Edith. *Voices of the Revolution.* Philadelphia: Author, 1967.

Katz, Bernard (ed.). *The Social Implications of Early Negro Music in the United States.* New York: Arno Press, 1969.

Katz, Schlomo (ed.). *Negro and Jew: An Encounter in America.* New York: Macmillan, 1969.

Katz, William L. *Eyewitness: The Negro in American History.* New York: Pitman, 1967.

———. *Five Slave Narratives.* New York: Arno Press, 1969.

———. *Teachers' Guide to American Negro History.* Chicago: Quadrangle Books, 1970.

Kearns, Francis E. (ed.). *The Black Experience: An Anthology of American Literature for the 1970s.* New York: Viking Press, 1970.

Keating, Edward M. *Free Huey!* New York: Dell, 1970.

Keats, Ezra Jack. *Whistle for Willie.* New York: Viking Press, 1964.

Keckley, Elizabeth. *Behind the Scenes.* New York: Arno, 1968.

Keech, William R. *The Impact of Negro Voting: The Role of the Vote in the Quest for Equality.* Chicago: Rand McNally, 1969.

Keil, Charles. *Urban Blues.* Chicago: University of Chicago, 1966.

Kelley, William Melvin. *Dancers on the Shore.* New York: Doubleday, 1964. New York: Bantam, 1966.

———. *A Different Drummer*. New York: Doubleday, 1962. New York: Bantam, 1964.

———. *A Drop of Patience*. New York: Doubleday, 1965.

———. *Dunfords Travels Everywhere*. New York: Doubleday, 1970.

Kellogg, Charles F. *NAACP: A History of the National Association for the Advancement of Colored People*. Baltimore: Johns Hopkins Press, 1967.

Kelsey, George D. *Racism and the Christian Understanding of Man*. New York: Scribners, 1965.

Killens, John Oliver. *And Then We Heard the Thunder*. New York: Knopf, 1963.

———. *Black Man's Burden*. New York: Trident Press, 1965. New York: Pocket Books, 1969.

———. *Cotillion*. New York: Trident Press, 1970.

———. *'Sippi*. New York: Trident, 1967.

———. *Slaves*. New York: Pyramid, 1969.

——— (ed.). *The Trial Record of Denmark Vesey*. Boston: Beacon, 1970.

———. *Youngblood*. New York: Pocket Books, 1955. New York: Trident, 1970.

Killian, Lewis M. *The Impossible Revolution: Black Power and The American Dream*. New York: Random House, 1968.

Kimbrough, Jess. *Defender of the Angels: A Black Policeman in Old Los Angeles*. New York: Macmillan, 1969.

King, Martin Luther, Jr. *The Measure of a Man*. New York: Harper, 1970.

———. *Strength to Love*. New York: Harper & Row, 1963. New York: Pocket Books, 1964.

———. *Stride Toward Freedom*. New York: Harper, 1958. New York: Ballantine, 1969.

———. *The Trumpet of Conscience*. New York: Harper & Row, 1968.

———. *Where Do We Go From Here: Chaos or Community?* New York: Harper, 1967. New York: Bantam, 1968.

———. *Why We Can't Wait*. New York: Harper and Row, 1964. New York: New American Library, 1964.

Kingsley, Michael J. *Black Man, White Man, Dead Man*. New York: Random House, 1970.

Kissin, Eva H. (ed.). *Stories in Black and White*. Philadelphia: Lippincott, 1970.

Kitt, Eartha. *Thursday's Child*. New York: Duell, Sloan and Pearce, 1956.

Klein, Herbert S. *Slavery in the Americas: A Comparative Study of Virginia and Cuba*. Chicago: University of Chicago, 1967.

Klein, Larry. *Jim Brown: The Running Back*. New York: Putnam, 1965.

Knight, Etheridge. *Poems from Prison*. Detroit: Broadside, 1968.

Knowles, Louis L. and Kennith Prewitt (eds.). *Institutional Racism in America*. Englewood Cliffs: Prentice-Hall, 1970.

Koblitz, Minnie W. *The Negro in Schoolroom Literature: Resource Materials for the Teacher of Kindergarten Through the Sixth Grade*. New York: Center for Urban Education, 1967.

Kofsky, Frank. *Black Nationalism and the Revolution in Music*. New York: Pathfinder, 1970.

Kohl, Herbert and Victor Hernandez Cruz (eds.). *Stuff: A Collection of Poems, Visions and Imaginative Happening from Young Writers in Schools—Open and Closed*. New York: World Publishing, 1970.

———. *36 Children*. New York: New American Library, 1967.

Konvitz, Milton R. *A Century of Civil Rights*. New York: Columbia University, 1961.

Kovel, Joel. *White Racism: A Psychohistory*. New York: Pantheon Books, 1970.

Kozol, Jonathan. *Death at an Early Age*. Boston: Houghton Mifflin, 1967.

Kraditor, Aileen S. *Means and Ends in American Abolitionism: Garrison and His Critics on Strategy and Tactics, 1834-1850*. New York: Pantheon, 1968.

Krislov, Samuel. *The Negro in Federal Employment: The Quest for Equal Opportunity*. Minneapolis: University of Minnesota, 1968.

Kugelmass, J. Alvin. *Ralph J. Bunche: Fighter for Peace*. New York: Messner, 1952.

Kunstler, William. *Deep in My Heart*. New York: Morrow, 1966.

Kvaraceus, William C. *Negro Self-Concept-Implications for School and Citizenship*. New York: McGraw-Hill, 1965.

— L —

Lacy, Leslie Alexander. *Cheer The Lonesome Traveler: The Life of W. E. B. DuBois*. New York: Dial Press, 1970.

Ladenburg, Thomas J. and William S. McFeely. *The Black Man in the Land of Equality*. New York: Hayden Book Co., 1970.

Larkin, Rochelle. *Soul Music*. New York: Lancer Books, 1970.

Larner, Jeremy, and Irving Howe (eds.). *Poverty: Views from the Left*. New York: Morrow, 1968.

Larson, Richard and James Olson (eds.). *I Have A Kind of Fear: Confessions From the Writings of White Teachers and Black Students in City Schools*. Chicago: Quadrangle Books, 1970.

Larsson, Clayton (ed.). *Marriage Across the Color Line*. Chicago: Johnson, 1965.

Latimore, Jewel C. (Johari Amini). *Black Essence*. Chicago: Third World Press, 1970.

———. *Folk Fable*. Chicago: Third World Press, 1970.

———. *Images in Black*. Chicago: Third World Press, 1970.

———. *Let's Go Somewhere*. Chicago: Third World Press, 1970.

Lawrence, Jacob (illus.). *Harriet and the Promised Land*. New York: Simon and Schuster (Windmill), 1968.

Leckie, William H. *The Buffalo Soldiers: A Narrative of the Negro Cavalry in the West*. Norman: University of Oklahoma, 1967.

Lecky, Robert S. and Elliott H. Wright. *Black Manifesto: Religion, Racism and Reparations*. New York: Sheed and Ward, 1970.

Lee, Alfred McClung and N. D. Humphrey. *Race Riot*. New York: Octagon, 1968.

Lee, Audrey. *The Clarion People*. New York: McGraw-Hill, 1968.

Lee, Calvin B. T. *One Man, One Vote: WMCA and the Struggle for Equal Representation*. New York: Scribners, 1968.

Lee, Don L. *Black Pride*. Detroit: Broadside Press, 1967.

———. *Don't Cry, Scream*. Detroit: Broadside Press, 1969.

———. *Dynamite Voices. Black Poets of the 1970's*. Detroit: Broadside, 1971.

———. *For Black People*. Chicago: Third World Press, 1970.

———. *Think Black*. Detroit: Broadside, 1967.

———. *We Walk the Way of the New World*. Detroit: Broadside, 1970.

Lee, Irvin H. *Negro Medal of Honor Men*. Dodd, 1967.

Leggett, John C. *Class, Race, and Labor: Working-Class Consciousness in Detroit*. New York: Oxford University, 1971.

Leinwand, Gerard (comp.). *The Negro in the City*. New York: Washington Square Press, 1968.

Lens, Sidney. *Poverty: America's Enduring Paradox: A History of the Richest Nation's Unwon War*. New York: Thomas Y. Crowell, 1969.

Lentz, Perry. *The Falling Hills*. New York: Scribners, 1967.

Leonard, Neil. *Jazz and the White Americans*. Chicago: University of Chicago, 1962.

Lerner, Gerda. *The Grimke Sisters From South Carolina: Rebels Against Slavery*. Boston: Houghton Mifflin, 1967.

Lester, Julius. *Black Folktales*. New York: Dial Press, 1969.

———. *Look Out, Whitey! Black Power's Gon' Get Your Mama*. New York: Dial Press, 1968.

———. *Revolutionary Notes*. New York: Richard W. Baron, 1969.

———. *Search for the New Land: History as Subjective Experience*. New York: Dial Press, 1970.

———. *The Seventh Son*. New York: Dial Press, 1971.

——— (ed.). *To Be A Slave*. New York: Dial Press, 1968.

Levenson, Dorothy. *Reconstruction*. New York: Franklin Watts, 1970.

Levine, Naomi (with Richard Cohen). *Ocean Hill-Brownsville: A Case History of Schools in Crisis*. New York: Popular Library, 1969.

Levy, Charles. *Voluntary Servitude: Whites in the Negro Movement*. New York: Appleton-Century-Crofts, 1968.

Levy, Gerald E. *Ghetto School: Class Warfare in an Elementary School*. New York: Pegasus Publishers, 1970.

Levy, Mimi Cooper. *Corrie and the Yankee*. New York: Viking, 1959.

———. *Whaleboat Warriors*. New York: Viking, 1963.

Lewison, Paul. *Race, Class and Party: A History of Negro Suffrage and White Politics in the South*. New York: Russell, 1963.

Lewis, Anthony. *Portrait of a Decade: The Second American Revolution*. New York: Random House, 1964.

Lewis, Claude. *Adam Clayton Powell*. Greenwich: Fawcett, 1963.

———. *Benjamin Banneker: The Man Who Saved Washington*. New York: McGraw-Hill, 1970.

———. *Cassius Clay. A No-Holds-Barred Biography of Boxing's Most Controversial Champion*. New York: Macfadden-Bartell, 1965.

Lewis, David L. *King: A Critical Biography*. New York: Praeger, 1970.

Lewis, Samella S. and Ruth Waddy (eds.). *Black Artists on Art Vol I.* Los Angeles: Contemporary Crafts Publishers, 1970.

Libarley, Marc and Tom Seligson. *The High School Revolutionaries.* New York: Random House, 1969.

The Liberator. Documents of Upheaval: Selections from William Lloyd Garrison's The Liberator, 1831-1865. New York: Hill & Wang, 1966.

Libby, Bill. *The Dick Bass Story.* New York: Messner, 1969.

Lichello, Robert. *Pioneer in Blood Plasma: Dr. Charles Richard Drew.* New York: Julian Messner, 1968.

Liebow, Elliott. *Tally's Corner; A Study of Negro Streetcorner Men.* Boston: Little, Brown, 1967.

Lightfoot, Claude M. *Black America and the World Revolution.* New York: New Outlook Publishers, 1970.

———. *Black Power and Liberation: A Communist View.* New York: New Outlook Publishers, 1967.

———. *Ghetto Rebellion to Black Liberation.* New York: International Publishers, 1968.

Lincoln, C. Eric. *The Blackamericans.* New York: Bantam, 1969.

———. *The Black Muslims in America.* Boston: Beacon, 1961.

——— (ed.). *Is Anybody Listening to Black America?* New York: Seabury Press, 1968.

——— (ed.). *Martin Luther King, Jr.: A Profile.* New York: Hill & Wang, 1970.

———. *My Face is Black.* Boston: Beacon, 1964.

———. *The Negro Pilgrimage in America.* New York: Bantam, 1969.

——— and Meltzer, Milton. *A Pictorial History of the Negro in America.* New York: Crown Publishers, 1968.

———. *Sounds of the Struggle: Persons and Perspectives in Civil Rights.* New York: Morrow, 1967.

Lincoln, James H. *The Anatomy of a Riot: A Detroit Judge's Report.* New York: McGraw-Hill, 1969.

Lindenmeyer, Otto. *Black and Brave: The Black Soldier in America.* New York: McGraw-Hill, 1970.

———. *Black History: Lost, Stolen or Strayed.* New York: Avon Books, 1970.

Litwack, Leon F. *North of Slavery: The Negro in the Free States, 1790-1860.* Chicago: University of Chicago, 1961.

Locke, Alain. *The Negro and His Music* (and) *Negro Art: Past and Present.* New York: Arno, 1969.

———. *The Negro in Art.* New York: Hacker Art Books, 1970.

——— (ed.). *The New Negro: An Interpretation.* New York: Arno, 1968. New York: Atheneum, 1969.

——— and Montgomery Gregory (eds.). *Plays of Negro Life.* New York: Harper & Row, 1970.

Locke, Hubert G. *The Detroit Riot of 1967.* Detroit: Wayne State University, 1970.

Lockwood, Lee. *Conversations with Eldridge Cleaver/Algiers.* New York: McGraw-Hill, 1970.

Loftis, N. J. *Exiles and Voyages.* New York: Black Market Press, 1970.

Logan, Frenise. *The Negro in North Carolina 1876-1894.* Chapel Hill: University of North Carolina, 1964.

Logan, Rayford W. and Irving S. Cohen. *The American Negro: Old World Background and New World Experience.* Boston: Houghton Mifflin, 1970.

———. *The Betrayal of the Negro From Rutherford B. Hayes to Woodrow Wilson.* New York: Collier Books, 1965.

———. *Howard University: The First Hundred Years, 1867-1967.* New York: New York University, 1970.

———. *The Negro in the United States.* Princeton: Van Nostrand, 1957.

Loguen, J. W. *The Rev. J. W. Loguen, as a Slave and as a Freeman.* Syracuse: Truair, 1859.

Lokos, Lionel. *House Divided.* New Rochelle: Arlington House, 1968.

Lomax, Alan and Raoul Abdul (eds.). *3,000 Years of Black Poetry: An Anthology.* New York: Dodd, Mead, 1970.

Lomax, Louis E. *The Negro Revolt.* New York: Harper, 1962. New York: New American Library, 1963.

———. *The Reluctant African.* New York: Harper, 1960.

———. *Thailand: The War That Is, The War That Will Be.* New York: New American Library.

———. *To Kill a Black Man.* Los Angeles: Holloway House, 1968.

———. *When the Word is Given. A Report of Elijah Muhammad, Malcolm X, and the Black Muslim World.* Cleveland: World Publishing, 1963. New York: New American Library, 1964.

Longsworth, Polly. *Charlotte Forten, Black and Free.* New York: Crowell, 1970.

Lord, Walter, *Peary to the Pole.* New York: Harper, 1963.

Lorde, Audre. *Cables to Rage.* Detroit: Broadside Press, 1970.

———. *The First Cities.* New York: The Poets Press, 1968.

Lott, Albert J. and E. Bernice. *Negro and White Youth.* New York: Holt, Rinehart and Winston, 1962.

Louis, Debbie. *And We Are Not Saved: A History of the Movement as People.* New York: Doubleday, 1970.

Love, Nat. *The Life and Adventures of Nat Love, Better Known in the Cattle Country as "Deadwood Dick."* New York: Arno Press, 1968.

Love, Rose Leary (ed.). *A Collection of Folklore for Children in Elementary School and at Home.* New York: Vantage Press, 1964.

Lowe, David. *KKK: The Invisible Empire.* New York: Norton, 1967.

Lowe, Jeanne R. *Cities in a Race With Time: Progress and Poverty in America's Renewing Cities.* New York: Random House, 1967.

Lucas, Bob. *Black Gladiator. A Biography of Jack Johnson.* New York: Dell, 1970.

Lucas, Lawrence. *Black Priest White Church: Catholics and Racism.* New York: Random House, 1970.

Lutz, Alma. *Crusade for Freedom: Women in the Antislavery Movement.* Boston: Beacon Press, 1968.

Lyle, Jack (ed.). *The Black American and the Press.* Los Angeles: The Ward Ritchie Press, 1969.

Lynch, John Roy. *Reminiscences of an Active Life: The Autobiography of John Roy Lynch.* (ed. by John Hope Franklin). Chicago: University of Chicago Press, 1970.

Lynd, Staughton. *Class Conflict, Slavery and the United States Constitution, Ten Essays.* New York: Bobbs-Merrill, 1967.

Lynn, Conrad J. *How to Stay Out of the Army.* New York: Grove Press, 1968.

—M—

McCague, James. *The Second Rebellion: The Story of the New York City Draft Riots of 1863.* New York: Dial Press, 1968.

McCall, Dan. *The Example of Richard Wright.* New York: Harcourt, Brace & World, 1969.

———. *The Man Says Yes.* New York: Viking, 1969.

McCarthy, Agnes and L. D. Reddick. *Worth Fighting For: A History of the Negro in the United States During the Civil War and Reconstruction.* New York: Doubleday Zenith, 1965.

McConnell, Roland C. *Negro Troops of Antebellum Louisiana.* Baton Rouge: Louisiana State University Press, 1968.

McCord, William, John Howard, Bernard Friedberg and Edwin Harwood. *Life Styles in the Black Ghetto.* New York: Norton, 1969.

McCullough, Norman Verle. *The Negro in English Literature.* Devon: Stockwell, 1962.

McDougall, Marion Gleason. *Fugitive Slaves 1619-1865.* New York: Berman Publishers, 1968.

McFarland, Harry S. *Missing Pages.* Boston: Forum, 1964.

McGhee, Reginald (ed.). *The World of James Van Der Zee. A Visual Record of Black Americans.* New York: Grove Press, 1970.

McGill, Ralph. *The South and the Southerner.* Boston: Little, Brown, 1963.

McGinnis, Frederick A. *The Education of Negroes in Ohio.* Wilberforce: author, 1964.

McGovern, Ann. *Black is Beautiful.* New York: Four Winds Press, 1969.

———. *Runaway Slave.* New York: Scholastic, 1965.

McGrath, Earl J. *The Predominantly Negro Colleges and Universities in Transition.* New York: Teachers College Press (Columbia University), 1965.

McKay, Claude. *Banana Bottom.* Chatham: The Chatham Bookseller, 1970.

———. *Home to Harlem.* New York: Avon, 1966.

McKissick, Floyd. *Three-Fifths of a Man.* New York: Macmillan, 1969.

McManus, Edgar J. *A History of Negro Slavery in New York.* New York: Syracuse University Press, 1966.

McPherson, James Alan. *Hue and Cry.* Boston: Little, Brown, 1969.

McPherson, James M. *Marching Toward Freedom: The Negro in the Civil War, 1861-1865.* New York: Alfred A. Knopf, 1968.

McQuilkin, Frank. *Think Black: An Introduction to Black Political Power.* New York: Bruce Publishing, 1970.

Mabee, Carleton. *Black Freedom: The Nonviolent Abolitionists from 1830 through the Civil War.* New York: Macmillan, 1970.

Mack, Raymond W. (ed.). *Our Children's Burden: Studies of Desegregation in Nine American Communities.* New York: Random House, 1968.

———. *Prejudice and Race Relations.* Chicago: Quadrangle, 1969.

Madian, Jon. *Beautiful Junk: A Story of the Watts Towers.* Boston: Little, Brown, 1968.

Maddox, James G. et al. *The Advancing South: Manpower Prospects and Problems.* New York: The Twentieth Century Fund, 1968.

Magdol, Edward. *Owen Lovejoy.* New Brunswick: Rutgers, 1967.

Magoun, F. Alexander. *Amos Fortune's Choice.* Freeport: Bond Wheelwright, 1964.

Mahone, Barbara. *Sugarfields Poems.* Detroit: Broadside, 1970.

Mahoney, William. *Black Jacob.* New York: Macmillan, 1969.

Major, Clarence. *All-Night Visitors.* New York: Olympia Press, 1969.

———. *Dictionary of Afro-American Slang.* New York: International, 1970.

——— (ed.). *The New Black Poetry.* New York: International, 1969.

———. *Swallow the Lake.* Middletown: Wesleyan University Press, 1970.

Malcolm X. *The Autobiography of Malcolm X.* New York: Grove Press, 1966.

———. *By Any Means Necessary: Speeches, Interviews, and a Letter by Malcolm X.* New York: Pathfinder Press, 1970.

———. *Malcolm X Speaks.* New York: Merit, 1965.

———. *The Speeches of Malcolm X at Harvard.* New York: William Morrow, 1968.

Malone, Mary. *Actor in Exile: The Life of Ira Aldridge.* New York: Crowell-Collier, 1969.

Mannix, D. P. and Malcolm Cowley. *Black Cargoes: History of the Atlantic Slave Trade, 1518-1865.* New York: Viking, 1962.

Marcus, Lloyd. *The Treatment of Minorities in Secondary School Textbooks.* New York: Anti-Defamation League, 1961.

Margolies, Edward. *The Art of Richard Wright.* Carbondale: Southern Illinois University Press, 1969.

———. *Native Sons: A Critical Study of Twentieth-Century Negro American Authors.* New York: Lippincott, 1968.

———. *A Native Sons Reader.* Philadelphia: Lippincott, 1970.

Marine, Gene. *The Black Panthers.* New York: New American Library, 1969.

Marris, Peter and Martin Rein. *Dilemmas of Social Reform: Poverty and Community Action in the United States.* New York: Atherton Press, 1967.

Marshall, F. Ray and Vernon M. Briggs. *The Negro and Apprenticeship.* Baltimore: Johns Hopkins Press, 1967.

———. *The Negro and Organized Labor.* New York: Wiley, 1965.

Marshall, Herbert and Mildred Stock. *Ira Aldridge: The Negro Tragedian.* Carbondale: Southern Illinois University Press, 1968.

Marshall, Paule. *The Chosen Place, the Timeless People.* New York: Harcourt, Brace & World, 1969.

———. *Soul Clap Hands and Sing.* New York: Atheneum, 1961.

Marvin X. *Black Man Listen.* Detroit: Broadside, 1969.

Marx, Gary T. *Protest and Prejudice: A Study of Belief in the Black Community.* New York: Harper and Row, 1967.

Masotti, Lewis H. and Don R. Bowen (eds.). *Riots and Rebellion: Civil Violence in the Urban Community.* New York: Sage Publications, 1968.

——— and Jerome R. Corsi. *Shoot-out in Cleveland: Black Militants and the Police.* New York: Praeger, 1969.

Massey, Joe C. *Singing Stars.* New York: Greenwich, 1964.

Masuoka, Jitsuichi and Preston Valien. *Race Relations: Problems and Theory.* Chapel Hill: University of North Carolina Press, 1964.

Mather, Melissa. *One Summer in Between.* New York: Harper, 1967.

Mathews, Marcia. *Richard Allen.* Baltimore: Helicon Books, 1963.

———. *Henry O. Tanner—American Artist.* Chicago: University of Chicago Press, 1969.

Matthews, Donald R. and James W. Prothro. *Negroes and the New Southern Politics.* New York: Harcourt, 1966.

Matthiessen, Peter. *Sal Si Puedes: Cesar Chavez and the New American Revolution.* New York: Random House, 1970.

Mayfield, Julian. *The Grand Parade.* New York: Vanguard Press, 1961.

———. *Nowhere Street (The Grand Parade).* New York: Paperback Library, 1968.

Mayhew, Leon H. *Law & Equal Opportunity: A Study of the Massachusetts Commission Against Discrimination.* Cambridge: Harvard University Press, 1968.

Mays, Benjamin E. *Disturbed About Man.* Richmond: John Knox Press, 1969.

Mays, Willie. *Born to Play Ball.* New York: Putnam, 1955.

———. *My Life In and Out of Baseball.* New York: Dutton, 1966.

———. *My Secrets of Playing Baseball.* New York: Viking, 1967.

Meier, August and Elliott Rudwick (eds.). *Black Protest in the Sixties.* Chicago: Quadrangle Books, 1970.

———. *From Plantation to Ghetto: An Interpretive History of American Negroes.* New York: Hill and Wang, 1966.

———. *The Making of Black America: Essays in Negro Life and History: Vol. I, The Origins of Black Americans; Vol. II, The Black Community in Modern America.* New York: Atheneum, 1969.

———. *Negro Thought in America, 1880-1915: Racial Ideologies in the Age of Booker T. Washington.* Ann Arbor: University of Michigan Press, 1968.

Meltzer, Milton (ed.). *In Their Own Words: A History of the American Negro, 1619-1865; 1865-1916; 1916-1966.* (3 vols.). New York: Thomas Y. Crowell, 1964-1967. (Also in paper.)

———. *Langston Hughes: A Biography.* New York: Thomas Y. Crowell, 1968.

——— and August Meier. *Time of Trial, Time of Hope. The Negro in America, 1919-1941.* New York: Doubleday, 1966.

Mendelsohn, Jack. *The Martyrs.* New York: Harper and Row, 1965.

Meredith, James. *Three Years in Mississippi.* Bloomington: Indiana University Press, 1966.

Meriwether, Louise. *Daddy Was a Number Runner.* Englewood Cliffs: Prentice-Hall, 1970. New York: Pyramid, 1971.

Messner, Gerald (ed.). *Another View: To Be Black in America.* New York: Harcourt, Brace and World, 1970.

Metcalf, George R. *Black Profiles.* New York: McGraw-Hill, 1970.

Meyer, Howard N. *Colonel of the Black Regiment: The Life of Thomas Wentworth Higginson.* New York: Norton, 1967.

——— (ed.). *Integrating America's Heritage. A Congressional Hearing to Establish a National Commission on Negro History and Culture.* College Park: McGrath, 1970.

Millea, Rev. Thomas. *Ghetto Fever.* Milwaukee: Bruce Publishing, 1968.

Millender, Dolly. *Yesterday in Gary: A Brief History of the Negro in Gary 1900-1967 (Vol. I).* Gary: Author, 1967.

Miller, Abie. *The Negro and the Great Society.* New York: Vintage, 1967.

Miller, Floyd. *Ahdoolo! The Biography of Matthew A. Henson.* New York: Dutton, 1963.

Miller, Kelly. *Radicals and Conservatives: and Other Essays on the Negro in America.* New York: Schocken Books, 1968.

Miller, Loren. *The Petitioners.* New York: Pantheon Books, 1966.

Miller, May. *Into the Clearing.* Washington, D.C.: Charioteer Press, 1959.

Miller, William Robert. *Martin Luther King, Jr.: His Life, Martyrdom, and Meaning for the World.* New York: Weybright and Talley, 1968.

Mills, Earl. *Dorothy Dandridge: A Portrait in Black.* Los Angeles: Holloway House, 1970.

Mississippi Black Paper: Fifty-Seven Negro and White Citizens' Testimony of Police Brutality, the Breakdown of Law and Order, and the Corruption of Justice in Mississippi. New York: Random House, 1965.

Mitchell, Glenford E. and William H. Peace, III (eds.). *The Angry Black South.* New York: Citadel, 1962.

Mitchell, Henry H. *Black Preaching.* Philadelphia: Lippincott, 1970.

Mitchell, J. Paul. *Race Riots in Black and White.* Englewood Cliffs: Prentice-Hall, 1970.

Mitchell, Loften. *Black Drama: The Story of the American Negro in the Theatre.* New York: Hawthorn, 1967.

———. *Land Beyond the River.* Cody: Pioneer Drama Service, 1963.

Moellering, Ralph. *Christian Conscience and Negro Emancipation.* Philadelphia: Fortress Press, 1965.

Mokray, William G. *Basketball Stars of 1961.* New York: Pyramid Books, 1961.

Monte, Anita and Gerald Leinwand. *Riots.* New York: Washington Square Press, 1970.

Montgomery, David. *Beyond Equality: Labor and the Radical Republicans, 1862-1872.* New York: Alfred A. Knopf, 1968.

Montgomery, Elizabeth R. *William C. Handy: Father of the Blues.* Champaign: Garrard Publishing, 1968.

Moody, Anne. *Coming of Age in Mississippi: An Autobiography.* New York: Dial Press, 1968.

Moore, Archie. *The Archie Moore Story.* New York: McGraw-Hill, 1960.

Moore, Carmen. *Somebody's Angel Child: The Story of Bessie Smith.* New York: Thomas Y. Crowell, 1970.

Moore, Maria Edith. *Unmasked. The Story of My Life on Both Sides of the Race Barrier.* New York: Exposition Press, 1964.

Moore, Richard B. *The Name "Negro": Its Origin and Evil Use.* New York: Afro-American, 1960.

Morris, Carl. *The Black Mood in Pittsburgh.* Pittsburgh: New Pittsburgh Courier, 1968.

Morrison, Toni. *The Bluest Eye.* New York: Holt, Rinehart & Winston, 1970.

Morrow, E. Frederic. *Black Man in the White House. A Diary of the Eisenhower Years.* New York: Coward-McCann, 1963.

Morsbach, Mabel. *The Negro in American Life.* New York: Harcourt, Brace and World, 1967.

Moseley, J. H. *60 Years in Congress and 28 Out.* New York: Vantage, 1960.

Muhammad, Elijah. *Message to the Black Man in America.* Chicago: Muhammad's Mosque No. 2, Book Division, 1965.

Mulzac, Hugh. *A Star to Steer By.* New York: International, 1963.

Murphy, Beatrice M. and Nancy L. Arnez. *The Rocks Cry Out.* Detroit: Broadside, 1969.

——— (ed.). *Today's Negro Voices: An Anthology by Young Negro Poets.* New York: Julian Messner, 1970.

Murphy, Raymond J. and Howard Elinson (eds.). *Problems and Prospects of the Negro Movement.* Belmot: Wadsworth Publishing, 1968.

Murray, Albert. *The Omni-Americans. New Perspectives on Black Experience and American Culture.* New York: Outerbridge and Dienstfrey, 1970.

Murray, Andrew E. *Presbyterians and the Negro: A History.* Philadelphia: Presbyterian Historical Society, 1968.

Murray, Joan. *The News.* New York: McGraw-Hill, 1968.

Murray, Pauli. *Proud Shoes.* New York: Harper, 1956.

Muse, Benjamin. *The American Negro Revolution.* Bloomington: Indiana University Press, 1968.

———. *Ten Years of Prelude: The Story of Integration Since the Supreme Court's 1954 Decision.* New York: Viking Press, 1964.

Myrdal, Gunnar. *An American Dilemma. The Negro Problem and Modern Democracy.* New York: Harper, 1962.

—N—

Nash, Gary B. and Richard Weiss (eds.). *The Great Fear: Race in the Mind of America.* New York: Holt, Rinehart and Winston, 1970.

Nathan, Hans. *Dan Emmett and the Rise of Early Negro Minstrels.* Norman: University of Oklahoma, 1962.

Neal, Larry. *Black Boogaloo (Notes on Black Liberation).* San Francisco: Journal of Black Poetry Press, 1969.

Nearing, Scott. *Black America.* New York: Schocken Books, 1969.

Negro: An Anthology (Edited by Nancy Cunard). New York: Unger, 1970.

Negro Heritage Library. Yonkers: Educational Heritage, 1964-1966.

Negro History and Literature: A Selected Annotated Bibliography. New York: The Anti-Defamation League, 1968.

The Negro in American History. Vol. I: Black Americans 1587-1854. Vol. II: A Taste of Freedom 1854-1927. Vol. III: Slaves and Masters 1928-1968. New York: Praeger, 1970.

Negro-Jewish Relations in the United States: A Symposium. New York: Citadel, 1966.

Nelson, Bernard. *The Fourteenth Amendment and the Negro Since 1920.* New York: Russell and Russell, 1967.

Nelson, Jack and Jack Bass. *The Orangeburg Massacre.* New York: World, 1970.

Nelson, Truman. *The Right of Revolution.* Boston: Beacon Press, 1968.

———. *The Sin of the Prophet.* Boston: Little, Brown, 1952.

———. *The Torture of Mothers.* Boston: Beacon Press, 1965.

New Jersey and the Negro, 1715-1966. Trenton: New Jersey Library Assoc., 1966.

Newby, I. A. *Challenge to the Court: Social Scientists and the Defense of Segregation.* Baton Rouge: Louisiana State University, 1967.

———. *Jim Crow's Defense: Anti-Negro Thought in America, 1900-1930.* Baton Rouge: Louisiana State University, 1965.

———. *Segregationists: Readings in the Defense of Segregation and White Supremacy.* Homewood: Dorsey Press, 1968.

Newman, Shirlee. *Marian Anderson: Lady from Philadelphia.* Philadelphia: Westminster, 1965.

Nichols, Charles H. *Many Thousand Gone.* New York: Citadel.

Nilon, Charles H. *Faulkner and the Negro.* New York: Citadel Press, 1965.

Nolen, Claude H. *The Negro's Image in the South: The Anatomy of White Supremacy.* Lexington: University of Kentucky, 1967.

Norholt-Scholte, J. W. *The People That Walk in Darkness.* New York: Ballantine, 1956. (Still in print.)

Norman, John C. (ed.). *Medicine in the Ghetto.* New York: Appleton-Century-Crofts: Meredith Press, 1970.

Northwood, Lawrence King and Ernest A. T. Barth. *Urban Desegregation: Negro Pioneers and Their White Neighbors.* Seattle: University of Washington, 1965.

Nye, Russell B. *Fettered Freedom.* East Lansing: Michigan State University Press, 1964.

—O—

O'Gorman, Ned. *The Storefront: A Community of Children on 129th Street and Madison Avenue.* New York: Harper & Row, 1970.

Oakes, Theresa and Jerry M. Weiss. *The Unfinished Journey: Themes From Contemporary Literature.* New York: McGraw-Hill, 1967.

Ofari, Earl. *The Myth of Black Capitalism.* New York: Monthly Review, 1970.

Okpaku, Joseph. *Verdict! The Exclusive Picture of the Trial of the Chicago 8.* New York: Third Press, 1970.

Oliver, Paul. *Aspects of the Blues Tradition.* New York: Oak Publications, 1970.

———. *Bessie Smith.* New York: Barnes, 1961.

———. *Blues Fell This Morning: The Meaning of the Blues.* New York: Horizon, 1961.

———. *Conversation with the Blues.* New York: Horizon Press, 1965.

Olmstead, Frederick Law. *The Slave States.* New York: Putnam, 1959.

Olsen, Jack and the editors of Time-Life Books. *The Black Athletes: A Shameful Story: The Myth of Integration in American Sport.* New York: Time-Life Books, 1968.

——— *Black Is Best: The Riddle of Cassius Clay.* New York: Putnam, 1967. New York: Dell, 1967.

Olsen, Otto. *Carpetbagger's Crusade: The Life of Albion W. Tourgee.* Baltimore: Johns Hopkins, 1965.

——— (ed.). *The Thin Disguise: Turning Point in Negro History. Plessy v. Ferguson: A Documentary Presentation (1864-1896).* New York: Humanities Press, 1968.

One Year Later: An Assessment of the Nation's Response to the Crisis Described by the National Advisorg Commission on Civil Disorders by Urban America, Inc. and the Urban Coalition. New York, 1969.

Oppenheimer, Martin. *The Urban Guerrilla.* Chicago: Quadrangle Books, 1969.

Orem, R. C. (ed.). *Montessori for the Disadvantaged: An Application of Montessori Educational Principles to the War on Poverty.* New York: Putnam, 1968.

Orr, Jack. *The Black Athlete: His Story in American History.* New York: The Lions Press, 1969.

Osborne, William. *The Segregated Covenant: Race Relations and American Catholics.* New York: Herder & Herder, 1967.

Osofsky, Gilbert. *Harlem: The Making of a Ghetto.* New York: Harper, 1966.

——— (ed.). *The Burden of Race: A Documentary History of Negro-White Relations in America.* New York: Harper & Row, 1967.

——— (ed.). *Puttin' On Ole Massa: The Slave Narratives of Henry Bibb, William Wells, and Solomon Northrup.* New York: Harper, 1969.

Otis, Johnny. *Listen to the Lambs.* New York: Norton, 1968.

Ottley, Roi. *The Lonely Warrior. The Life and Times of Robert S. Abbott.* Chicago: Regnery, 1955.

——— and William J. Weatherby (ed.). *The Negro in New York: An Informal Social History.* New York: Oceana, 1967.

———. *New World A-Coming.* New York: Arno, 1969.

Ovington, Mary W. *The Walls Came Tumbling Down.* New York: Harcourt, 1947.

Owens, William B. *Black Mutiny*. Philadelphia: United Church Press, 1968.

— P —

Pain, William. *To Do Justice: The Heroic Struggle for Human Rights*. New York: Pyramid, 1965.
Panger, Daniel. *Ol' Prophet Nat*. Winston-Salem: John F. Blair, 1967.
Parker, Seymour and Robert J. Kleiner. *Mental Illness in the Urban Negro Community*. New York: Macmillan, 1966.
Parks, David. *G.I. Diary*. New York: Harper & Row, 1968.
Parks, Gordon. *A Choice of Weapons*. New York: Harpers, 1966. New York: Berkeley, 1967.
———. *The Learning Tree*. New York: Harper & Row, 1963. New York: Fawcett, 1964.
———. *Gordon Parks: A Poet and His Camera*. New York: Viking Press, 1968.
———. *Gordon Parks: Whispers of Intimate Things*. New York: Viking, 1970.
Parsons, Talcott, and Kenneth B. Clark (eds.). *The Negro Americans*. Boston: Houghton Mifflin, 1966.
Passow, A. Harry (ed.). *Education in Depressed Areas*. New York: Teachers College, Columbia University, 1963.
Patrick, John J. *The Progress of the Afro-Americans*. Westchester: Benefic, 1968.
Patterson, Floyd (with Milton Gross). *Victory Over Myself*. New York: Geis, 1962.
Patterson, Katheryn. *No Time for Tears*. Chicago: Johnson, 1964.
Patterson, Raymond. *26 Ways of Looking at a Black Man and Other Poems*. New York: Award Books, 1969.
Patterson, William L. *Ben Davis: Crusader for Negro Freedom and Socialism*. New York: New Outlook, 1967.
——— (ed.). *We Charge Genocide: The Crime of Government Against the Negro People*. New York: International Publishers, 1970.
Pauli, Hertha E. *Her Name Was Sojourner Truth*. New York: Appleton-Century-Crofts, 1962.
Pease, Jane and William. *The Antislavery Argument*. Indianapolis: Bobbs-Merrill, 1965.
———. *Black Utopia: Negro Communal Experiments in America*. Madison: State Historical Society of Wisconsin, 1964.
Pelt, Rev. Owen D. and R. L. Smith. *The Story of the National Baptists*. New York: Vantage, 1960.
Pepe, Phil. *The Incredible Knicks*. New York: Popular Library, 1970.
———. *Stand Tall: The Lew Alcindor Story*. New York: Grosset, 1970.
Perry, Charles. *Portrait of a Young Man Drowning*. New York: Simon & Schuster, 1962. New York: New American Library, 1963.
Peskin, Allan (ed.). *North into Freedom. The Autobiography of John Malvin, Free Negro, 1795-1880*. Cleveland: Western Reserve, 1967.
Peters, Margaret. *The Ebony Book of Black Achievement*. Chicago: Johnson, 1970.
Peterson, Robert. *Only the Ball Was White*. Englewood Cliffs: Prentice-Hall, 1970.
Petry, Ann. *Harriet Tubman: Conductor of the Underground Railroad*. New York: Crowell, 1955.
———. *Tituba of Salem Village*. New York: Crowell, 1964.
Pettigrew, Thomas F. *A Profile of the Negro American*. Princeton: Van Nostrand, 1964.
———. *Epitaph for Jim Crow*. New York: ADL, 1964.
Pharr, Robert Deane. *The Book of Numbers*. New York: Doubleday, 1969.
Pickard, Kate R. *The Kidnapped and the Ransomed: The Narrative of Peter and Vina Still After 40 Years of Slavery*. Philadelphia: Jewish Publication Society of America, 1970.
Pinkney, Alphonso. *Black Americans*. Englewood Cliffs, Prentice-Hall, 1969.
Place, Marian. *Mountain Man: The Life of Jim Beckworth*. New York: Crowell-Collier, 1970.
———. *Rifles and War Bonnets: Negro Cavalry of the West*. New York: Ives Washburn, 1968.
Ploski, Harry A. and Roscoe C. Brown (eds.). *The Negro Almanac*. New York: Bellwether Publishing, 1967.
Plumpp, Sterling C. *Half Black, Half Blacker*. Chicago: Third World Press, 1970.
———. *Portable Soul*. Chicago: Third World Press, 1970.
Poinsett, Alex. *Black Power Gary Style: The Making of Mayor Richard Gordon Hatcher*. Chicago: Johnson, 1970.
Polite, Carlene Hatcher. *The Flagellants*. New York: Farrar, Strauss & Giroux, 1967.
Political Participation: A Report of the U. S. Commission on Civil Rights. Washington, D.C.: May, 1968.
The Political Thought of James Forman. Detroit: Black Star Publishing, 1970.
Pool, Rosey (ed.). *Beyond the Blues, New Poems by American Negroes*. Kent: Hand and Flower Press, 1962.
Porter, Dorothy B. *The Negro in the United States, A Selected Bibliography*. Washington, D.C.: Library of Congress, 1970.
———. *North American Negro Poets: A Bibliographical Checklist of Their Writings, 1760-1944*.
Porter, James A. *Modern Negro Art*. New York: Arno, 1969.
———. *Ten Afro-American Artists of the 19th Century*. Washington, D.C.: Howard University, 1967.
Powell, Adam Clayton. *Keep the Faith, Baby*. New York: Trident Press, 1967.
Powledge, Fred. *Black Power, White Resistance: Notes on the New Civil War*. New York & Cleveland: World, 1967.
Preston, Edward. *Martin Luther King: Fighter for Freedom*. New York: Doubleday, 1968.
Problems of American Society. New York: Washington Square Press, 1969.
Proctor, Samuel D. *The Young Negro in America, 1960-1980*. New York: Association Press, 1966.

— Q —

Quarles, Benjamin. *Black Abolitionists*. New York: Oxford University, 1969.
———. *Frederick Douglass*. Washington: Associated, 1948.
——— (ed.). *Frederick Douglass*. Englewood Cliffs: Prentice-Hall, 1968.
——— (with Dorothy Sterling). *Lift Every Voice*. New York: Doubleday, 1965.
———. *Lincoln and the Negro*. New York: Oxford University, 1962.
———. *The Negro in the American Revolution*. Chapel Hill: University of North Carolina, 1961.
———. *The Negro in the Civil War*. Boston: Little, Brown, 1969.
———. *The Negro in the Making of America*. New York: Collier, 1968.

— R —

Raab, Earl (ed.). *American Race Relations Today*. New York: Doubleday, 1962.
Race Relations in the U.S.A.: 1954-1968: Keesing's Research Report. New York: Scribner's, 1970.
Racism and American Education: A Dialogue and Agenda for Action. New York: Harper & Row, 1970.
Racism in America: And How to Combat It. Washington, D.C.: U. S. Commission on Civil Rights, 1967.
Rainwater, Lee (ed.). *Soul*. Chicago: Aldine, 1970.
——— and William L. Yancey. *The Moynihan Report and the Politics of Controversy*. Cambridge: MIT Press, 1967.
Randall, Dudley. *Cities Burning*. Detroit: Broadside, 1968.
——— and Margaret G. Burrough (eds.). *For Malcolm: Poems on the Life and Death of Malcolm X*. Detroit: Broadside, 1967.
———. *Love You*. Detroit: Broadside, 1970.
Randel, William P. *The Ku Klux Klan*. New York: Chilton, 1965.
Read, Florence Matilda. *The Story of Spelman College*. Atlanta: Spelman College, 1961.
Reddick, L. D. *Crusader Without Violence*. New York: Harper, 1959.
Redding, Saunders. *The Lonesome Road*. New York: Doubleday, 1958.
———. *The Negro*. Washington, D.C.: Potomac Books, 1967.
———. *No Day of Triumph*. New York: Harper, 1970.
———. *Stranger and Alone*. New York: Harper, 1970.
———. *They Came in Chains*. New York: Lippincott, 1969.
———. *To Make A Poet Black*. College Park: McGrath, 1970.
Redkey, Edwin S. *Black Exodus: Black Nationalist and Back-to-Africa Movements, 1890-1910*. New Haven: Yale University Press, 1970.
Reed, Ishmael. *The Free-Lance Pallbearers*. New York: Doubleday, 1967. New York: Bantam, 1969.
——— (ed.). *19 Necromancers from Now: An Anthology of Original American Writing for the 1970's*. New York: Doubleday, 1970.
———. *Yellow Back Radio Broke-Down*. New York: Doubleday, 1969. New York: Bantam, 1970.
Reilly, John M. (ed.). *Twentieth Century Interpretations of Invisible Man: A Collection of Critical Essays*. Englewood Cliffs: Prentice-Hall, 1970.
Reimers, David. *White Protestantism and the Negro*. New York: Oxford, 1965.
Reisner, Robert G. *Bird*. New York: Citadel, 1962.

Reissman, Frank and Hermine I. Popper. *Up from Poverty: New Career Leaders for Nonprofessionals*. New York: Harper and Row, 1969.
Reitzes, Dietrich. *Negroes and Medicine*. Cambridge: Harvard University Press, 1958.
Report of the National Advisory Commission on Civil Disorders. New York: E. P. Dutton, 1968. New York: Bantam, 1968.
Rex, Barbara. *Vacancy on India Street*. New York: Norton, 1967.
Richardson, Ben. *Great American Negroes*. New York: Crowell, 1956.
Richette, Lisa Aversa. *The Throwaway Children*. Philadelphia and New York: Lippincott, 1969.
Riessman, Frank. *Strategies Against Poverty*. New York: Random House, 1969.
Ripley, Sheldon N. *Matthew Henson: Arctic Negro*. Boston: Houghton Mifflin, 1966.
Ritz, Joseph P. *The Despised Poor: Newburgh's War on Welfare*. Boston: Beacon Press, 1966.
Rivelli, Pauline and Robert Levin (eds.). *The Black Giants*. New York: World, 1970.
———. *The Rock Giants*. New York: World, 1970.
Rivers, Conrad Kent. *The Still Voice of Harlem*. London: Paul Bremen, Ltd., 1969. (Distributed by Broadside Press).
———. *These Black Bodies and This Sunburnt Face*. Cleveland: Free Lance Press, 1963.
Roberts, Joan I. (ed.). *School Children in the Urban Slum: Readings in Social Science Research*. New York: The Free Press, 1968.
Robinson, Armstead L., Craig C. Foster and Donald H. Ogilvie (eds.). *Black Studies in the University: A Symposium*. New Haven: Yale University Press, 1969.
Robinson, Donald L. *Slavery in the Structure of American Politics, 1765-1820*. New York: Harcourt, 1971.
Robinson, Frank (with Al Silverman). *My Life is Baseball*. New York: Doubleday, 1968.
Robinson, Jackie. *Baseball Has Done It*. Philadelphia: J. B. Lippincott, 1964.
——— (and Alfred Duckett). *Breakthrough to the Big League*. New York: Harper and Row, 1965.
Robinson, Louis, Jr. *Arthur Ashe: Tennis Champion*. New York: Doubleday, 1970.
Robinson, Rose. *Eagle in the Air*. New York: Crown, 1969.
Robinson, Sugar (with Dave Anderson). *Sugar Ray*. New York: Viking, 1970.
Robinson, William M., Jr. (ed.). *Early Black American Poets*. Dubuque: William C. Brown, 1970.
Rodgers, Carolyn. *Paper Soul*. Chicago: Third World Press, 1970.
———. *Songs of a Black Bird*. Chicago: Third World Press, 1970.
———. *Two Love Raps*. Chicago: Third World Press, 1970.
Rogers, J. Overton. *Blues and Ballads of a Black Yankee*. New York: Exposition Press, 1965.
Rohrer, John H. and Munro S. Edmonson (eds.). *The Eighth Generation*. New York: Harper, 1960.
Rollins, Charlemae H. *Black Troubadour: Langston Hughes*. Chicago: Rand, 1970.
———. *Christmas Gif'*. Follett, 1963.
———. *Famous American Negro Poets*. New York: Dodd, Mead, 1965.
———. *Famous Negro Entertainers of Stage, Screen, and TV*. New York: Dodd, Mead, 1967.
———. *They Showed the Way*. New York: Crowell, 1964.
Rose, Arnold Marshall. *De Facto School Segregation*. New York: National Conference of Christians and Jews, 1964.
——— (ed.). *Assuring Freedom to the Free*. Detroit: Wayne State University Press, 1964.
Rose, Thomas (ed.). *Violence in America: A Historical and Contemporary Reader*. New York: Random House, 1970.
Ross, Arthur M. and Herbert Hill (eds.). *Employment, Race and Poverty*. New York: Harcourt, Brace and World, 1967.
Roth, R. S. *Negro Heroes Show the Way*. Miami: International Book, 1969.
Roucek, Joseph S. and Thomas Kiernan (eds.). *The Negro Impact on Western Civilization*. New York: Philosophical Library, 1970.
Roy, Jessie H. and Geneva C. Turner. *Pioneers of Long Ago*. Washington, D.C.: Associated, 1951.
Rozwenc, Eugene C. (ed.). *Slavery as a Cause of the Civil War*. Boston: Heath, 1963.
Rubinstein, Annette T. (ed.). *Schools Against Children: The Case for Community Control*. New York: Monthly Review Press, 1970.
Ruchames, Louis. *The Abolitionists. A Collection of Their Writings*. New York: Putnam, 1963.
——— (ed.). *Racial Thought in America: Vol. I—From the Puritans to Abraham Lincoln: A Documentary History*. Amherst: University of Massachusetts Press, 1970.
Rudwick, Elliott M. *Race Riot at East St. Louis, July 2, 1917*. Carbondale: Southern Illinois University Press, 1964.
———. *W. E. B. DuBois: Propagandist of the Negro Protest*. New York: Atheneum Press, 1968.
Russell, Bill (with William McSweeney). *Go Up for Glory*. New York: Coward-McCann, 1966. New York: Berkeley, 1966.
Russell, Cazzie L., Jr. *Me, Cazzie Russell*. Westwood: Fleming H. Revell, 1969.
Russell, Patrick. *The Tommy Davis Story*. New York: Doubleday, 1969.
Rutland, Eva. *The Trouble with Being a Mama*. New York: Abingdon Press, 1964.

— S —

Sabin, Lou and Dave Sendler. *Stars of Pro Basketball*. New York: Random House, 1970.
Salk, Erwin A. *A Layman's Guide to Negro History*. New York: McGraw-Hill, 1967.
Salzman, Jack and Barry Wallenstein (eds.). *Years of Protest: A Collection of American Writings of the Nineteen Thirties*. New York: Pegasus, 1969.
Samuel, Howard D. (ed.). *Toward a Better America*. New York: Macmillan, 1968.
Sanchez, Sonia. *Homecoming*. Detroit: Broadside, 1969.
———. *We a BaddDDD People*. Detroit: Broadside, 1970.
Sarratt, Reed. *The Ordeal of Desegregation: The First Decade*. New York: Harper and Row, 1966.
Saunders, Doris E. (ed.). *The Day They Marched*. Chicago: Johnson, 1964.
———. *The Kennedy Years and the Negro*. Chicago: Johnson, 1964.
Schatz, Walter (ed.). *Directory of Afro-American Resources*. New York: Bowker, 1970.
Schechter, William. *History of Negro Humor in America*. New York: Fleet Publishing, 1970.
Scheiner, Seth M. *Negro Mecca: A History of the Negro in New York City, 1865-1920*. New York: New York University Press, 1965.
Schoener, Allon (ed.). *Harlem on My Mind. Cultural Capital of Black America 1900-1968*. New York: Random House, 1969.
Schollianos, Alva. *Call to Greatness*. New York: William-Frederick Press, 1963.
Schrag, Peter. *Village School Downtown: Politics and Education—A Boston Report*. Boston: Beacon Press, 1968.
Schuchter, Arnold. *Reparations: The Black Manifesto and Its Challenge to White America*. Philadelphia: Lippincott, 1970.
———. *White Power/Black Freedom: Planning the Future of Urban America*. Boston: Beacon Press, 1969.
Schulberg, Budd (ed.). *From the Ashes; Voices of Watts*. New York: New American Library, 1967.
Schuller, Gunther. *Early Jazz: Its Roots and Musical Development*. New York: Oxford University Press, 1968.
Schulz, David A. *Coming Up Black: Patterns of Ghetto Socialization*. Englewood Cliffs: Prentice-Hall, 1969.
Schwartz, Barry N. and Robert Disch (eds.). *White Racism: Its History, Pathology and Practice*. New York: Dell, 1970.
Scott, Benjamin. *The Coming of the Black Man*. Boston: Beacon Press, 1969.
Scott, Nathan A., Jr. (ed.). *Adversity and Grace: Studies in Recent American Literature*. Chicago: University of Chicago Press, 1968.
——— (ed.). *Form of Extremity in the Modern Novel*. Richmond: John Knox, 1965.
———. *Negative Capability: Studies in the New Literature and the Religious Situation*. New Haven: Yale University Press, 1969.
———. *Reinhold Niebuhr*. Minneapolis: University of Minnesota, 1963.
Scott, Robert L. and Wayne Brockriede (eds.). *The Rhetoric of Black Power*. New York: Harper and Row, 1969.
Seale, Bobby. *Seize the Time: The Story of the Black Panther Party and Huey P. Newton*. New York: Random House, 1970.
Selby, John. *Beyond Civil Rights*. New York: World, 1966.
Seligman, Ben B. *Permanent Poverty: An American Syndrome*. Chicago: Quadrangle, 1968.

Sellers, Charles Grier (ed.). *The Southerner as an American.* Chapel Hill: University of North Carolina Press, 1960.

Shackelford, Jane Dabney. *The Child's Story of the Negro.* Washington, D. C.: Associated, 1956.

Shade, William G. and Roy C. Herrenkohl (eds.). *Seven on Black: Reflections on the Negro Experience in America.* Philadelphia: Lippincott, 1970.

Shapero, Fred C. and James W. Sullivan. *Race Riots.* New York: Crowell, 1964.

Shapiro, Fred C. *Whitmore.* Indianapolis: Bobbs-Merrill, 1969.

Shapiro, Milton J. *The Hank Aaron Story.* New York: Messner, 1961.

———. *Jackie Robinson of the Brooklyn Dodgers.* New York: Messner, 1963.

———, *The Willie Mays Story.* New York: Messner, 1963.

Shaw, Arnold. *Belafonte.* Philadelphia: Chilton, 1960. New York: Pyramid, 1970.

———. *The World of Soul: Black America's Contribution to the Pop Music Scene.* New York: Cowles, 1970.

Shepherd, George W., Jr. *Racial Influences on American Foreign Policy.* New York: Basic Books, 1971.

Sherman, Richard B. (ed.). *The Negro and the City.* Englewood Cliffs: Prentice-Hall, 1970.

Sherrard, O. A. *Freedom from Fear.* New York: St. Martin's, 1959.

Sherrill, Robert. *Gothic Politics in the Deep South: Stars of the New Confederacy.* New York: Grossman Publishers, 1968.

Shirley, Kay and Frederick Diggs (eds.). *The Book of Blues.* New York: Crown, 1963.

Silberman, Charles E. *Crisis in Black and White.* New York: Random House, 1964.

Silver, James W. *Mississippi: The Closed Society.* New York: Harcourt, Brace & World, 1964.

Silverman, Jerry. *Folk Blues: 110 American Folk Blues.* New York: Oak Publications, 1969.

Simmons, Herbert A. *Man Walking on Eggshells.* Boston: Houghton, Mifflin, 1962.

Sleeper, C. Freeman. *Black Power and Christian Responsibility.* Nashville: Abingdon Press, 1969.

Sloan, Irving J. *The American Negro: A Chronology and Fact Book.* Dobbs Ferry: Oceana, 1965.

———. *The Negro in Modern American History Textbooks.* Chicago: American Federation of Teachers, 1966.

Smith, Ed. *Where To, Black Man?* Chicago: Quadrangle, 1967.

Smith, Elbert B. *The Death of Slavery: The United States, 1837-'65.* Chicago: University of Chicago Press, 1967.

Smith, Frank E. *Congressman from Mississippi.* New York: Pantheon Books, 1964.

Smith, Lillian. *Our Faces, Our Words.* New York: Norton, 1964.

Smith, Robert Collins. *They Closed Their Schools: Prince Edward County, Va.* Chapel Hill: University of North Carolina Press, 1965.

Smith, Samuel D. *The Negro in Congress, 1870-1901.* Chapel Hill: University of North Carolina Press, 1967.

Smith, Willie the Lion (with George Haefer). *Music on my Mind: the Memoirs of an American Pianist.* New York: Doubleday, 1964.

Snyder, Louis L. *The Idea of Racialism. Its Meaning and History.* Princeton: Van Nostrand, 1962.

Sobel, Lester A. (ed.). *Civil Rights, 1960-1966.* New York: Facts on File, 1967.

Southern, Eileen. *The Music of Black Americans.* New York: Norton, 1971.

Spangler, Earl. *Bibliography of Negro History.* Minneapolis: Ross & Haines, 1963.

———. *The Negro in Minnesota.* Minneapolis: Denison, 1961.

Spear, Allan H. *Black Chicago: The Making of a Negro Ghetto, 1890-1920.* Chicago: University of Chicago Press, 1967.

Spellman, A. B. *Four Lives in the Bebop Business.* New York: Random House, 1966.

Spike, Robert W. *The Freedom Revolution and the Churches.* New York: Association Press, 1965.

Stahl, David, F. B. Sussman and N. J. Bloomfield (eds.). *The Community and Racial Crisis.* New York: Practicing Law Institute, 1966.

Stainback, Berry. *Football Stars of 1967.* New York: Pyramid Books, 1968.

Stampp, Kenneth M. *The Peculiar Institution.* New York: Alfred A. Knopf, 1956.

——— and Leon F. Litwack (eds.). *Reconstruction: An Anthology of Revisionist Writings.* Baton Rouge: Louisiana State University Press, 1969.

Starobin, Robert S. *Industrial Slavery in the Old South.* New York: Oxford University Press, 1971.

Staupers, Mabel K. *No Time for Prejudice: A Study of the Integration of Negroes in Nursing in the United States.* New York: Macmillan, 1961.

Stavis, Barrie. *Harpers Ferry: A Play About John Brown.* New York: A. S. Barnes, 1970.

———. *John Brown: The Sword and the Word.* New York: A. S. Barnes, 1970.

Stearns, Marshall and Jean. *Jazz Dance: The Story of American Vernacular Dance.* New York: Macmillan, 1969.

———. *The Story of Jazz.* New York: New American Library, 1958.

Stephany, *Moving Deep.* Detroit: Broadside, 1969.

Sterling, Dorothy. *Captain of the Planter.* New York: Washington Square, 1968.

——— (with Benjamin Quarles). *Lift Every Voice: The Lives of Booker T. Washington, W. E. B. DuBois, Mary Church Terrell, and James Weldon Johnson.* New York: Doubleday Zenith, 1965.

———. *Tear Down the Walls: A History of the American Civil Rights Movement.* New York: Doubleday, 1968.

Sterling, Philip and Rayford Logan. *Four Took Freedom.* New York: Doubleday, 1967.

Stern, Harold. *Blackland.* New York: Doubleday, 1970.

Stern, Leni and Philip. *O, Say Can You See, by "the Dawn's Urban Blight."* Indianapolis: Bobbs-Merrill, 1969.

Sternsher, Bernard (ed.). *The Negro in Depression and War: Prelude to Revolution, 1930-1945.* Chicago: Quadrangle Books, 1970.

Sterne, Emma Gelders. *I Have A Dream.* New York: Knopf, 1965.

———. *The Long Black Schooner.* Chicago: Follett, 1969.

———. *Mary McLeod Bethune.* New York: Alfred A. Knopf, 1957.

———. *They Took Their Stand.* New York: Crowell-Collier, 1968.

Stevenson, Janet. *Spokesman for Freedom: The Life of Archibald Grimke.* New York: Crowell-Collier, 1970.

Stillman, Richard J. *Integration of the Negro in the U. S. Armed Forces.* New York: Praeger, 1968.

Stone, Chuck. *Black Political Power in America.* Indianapolis: Bobbs-Merrill, 1969.

———. *Tell It Like It Is.* New York: Trident Press, 1967.

Storing, Herbert J. (ed.). *What Country Have I? Political Writings by Black Americans.* New York: St. Martin's Press, 1970.

Strauss, Frances. *Where Did the Justice Go? The Story of the Giles-Johnson Case.* Boston: Gambit Press, 1970.

Stringfellow, William. *My People is the Enemy. An Autobiographical Polemic.* New York: Holt, Rinehart and Winston, 1964.

Strother, Horatio T. *The Underground Railroad in Connecticut.* Middletown: Wesleyan University Press, 1962.

Studies in American Negro Life. New York: Atheneum, 1969. (A series of reprints of old books).

Sugarman, Tracy. *Stranger at the Gates.* New York: Hill & Wang, 1966.

Sullivan, George. *Wilt Chamberlain.* New York: Grosset, 1966, 1967.

Sullivan, Leon H. *Build Brother, Build: From Poverty to Economic Power.* Philadelphia: Macrae Smith, 1969.

Sullivan, Neil V. *Bound for Freedom.* Boston: Little, Brown, 1965.

The Supplemental Studies for the National Advisory Commission on Civil Disorders. Washington, D. C.: U. S. Government Office, 1969.

Szwed, John F. (ed.). *Black America.* New York: Basic Books, 1970.

—T—

Tabb, William K. *The Political Economy of the Black Ghetto.* New York: Norton, 1970.

Taeuber, Karl E. and Alma F. *Negroes in Cities: Residential Segregation and Neighborhood Change.* Chicago: Aldine, 1965.

Tannenbaum, Frank. *Slave and Citizen: The Negro in the Americas.* New York: Alfred A. Knopf, 1947.

Tarry, Ellen. *Martin de Porres: Saint of the New World.* New York: Farrar, Strauss, 1963.

———. *The Third Door.* New York: McKay, 1955. New York: Guild Press, 1966.

———. *Young Jim: The Early Years of James Weldon Johnson.* New York: Dodd, Mead, 1967.

Taylor, Julius H. (ed.). *The Negro in Science.* Baltimore: Morgan State College Press, 1955.

Teague, Robert L. *The Climate of Candor*. New York: Pageant Press, 1962.

———. *Letters to a Black Boy*. New York: Walker & Co., 1969.

Ten Broek, Jacobus. *Equal Justice Under Law*. New York: Collier, 1965.

Teodori, Massimo (ed.). *The New Left: A Documentary History*. Indianapolis: Bobbs-Merrill, 1970.

Thomas, Jesse O. *My Story in Black and White: The Autobiography of Jesse O. Thomas*. New York: Exposition Press, 1967.

Thomas, John L. (ed.). *Slavery Attacked: the Abolitionist Crusade*. Englewood Cliffs: Prentice-Hall, 1965.

Thomas, Piri. *Down These Mean Streets*. New York: Knopf, 1967.

Thompson, Carolyn. *Frank*. Detroit: Broadside, 1970.

Thompson, Daniel C. *The Negro Leadership Class*. Englewood Cliffs: Prentice-Hall, 1963.

——— and Herbert Nipson. *White on Black*. Chicago: Johnson, 1963.

Thornbrough, Emma Lou (ed.). *Booker T. Washington*. Englewood Cliffs: Prentice-Hall, 1969.

———. *A Short History of Indiana Negroes*. Indianapolis: Indiana Division of the Emancipation Centennial Authority, 1964.

Thorpe, Earl E. *Black Historians: A Critique*. New York: Morrow, 1971.

———. *The Mind of the Negro: An Intellectual History of Afro-Americans*. Baton Rouge: Ortlieb Press, 1971.

Three Negro Classics: Up from Slavery; The Souls of Black Folk; The Autobiography of an Ex-Colored Man. New York: Avon, 1965.

Thurman, Howard. *Disciplines of the Spirit*. New York: Harper & Row, 1963.

———. *The Inward Journey*. New York: Harper and Brothers, 1961.

———. *The Luminous Darkness, A Personal Interpretation of the Anatomy of Segregation and the Ground of Hope*. New York: Harper & Row, 1965.

———. *Why I Believe There Is a God*. Chicago: Johnson, 1965.

Thurman, Sue Bailey. *Pioneers of Negro Origin in California*. San Francisco: Acme, 1952.

Thurman, Wallace. *The Blacker the Berry*. New York: Macmillan, 1970.

A Time to Listen . . . A Time to Act: Voices from the Ghettos of the Nation's Cities. Washington, D.C.: U.S. Commission on Civil Rights, 1969.

Tindall, George Brown. *South Carolina Negroes: 1877-1900*. Baton Rouge: Louisiana State University Press, 1969.

To Establish Justice, To Insure Domestic Tranquility. New York: Praeger, 1970.

To Gwen with Love. An Anthology Dedicated to Gwendolyn Brooks. Chicago: Johnson, 1971.

Toomer, Jean. *Cane*. New York: University Place Press. 1969. New York: Harper, 1969.

Toure, Askia Muhammad. *Juju*. Chicago: Third World Press, 1970.

Trefousse. Hans L. *The Radical Republicans: Lincoln's Vanguard for Social Justice*. New York: Alfred A. Knopf, 1969.

Treworgy, Mildred L. and Paul B. Foreman. *Negroes in the United States. A Bibliography of Materials for Schools*. University Park: Pennsylvania State University, 1967.

Trillin, Calvin. *An Education in Georgia*. New York: Viking Press, 1964.

Trotter, James M. *Music and Some Highly Musical People*. New York: Johnson Reprint Corp., 1968.

Troop, Cornelius V. *Distinguished Negro Georgians*. Dallas: Royal Pub. Co., 1962.

Trubowitz, Julius. *Changing the Racial Attitudes of Children: The Effects of an Activity Group Program in NYC Schools*. New York: Praeger, 1970.

Trubowitz, Sidney A. *A Handbook for Teaching in the Ghetto School*. Chicago: Quadrangle Books, 1968.

Truth, Sojourner. *Narrative of Sojourner Truth*. Chicago: Johnson, 1970. New York: Arno, 1968.

Tucker, Sterling. *Beyond the Burning: Life and Death of the Ghetto*. New York: Association Press, 1969.

The Tuesday Magazine Soul Food Cookbook. New York: Bantam Books, 1970.

Tuotti, Joseph Dolan. *Big Time Buck White. A Play*. New York: Grove Press, 1969.

Turner, Darwin T. *Afro-American Writers*. New York: Appleton-Century-Crofts, 1970.

Tyack, David. *Nobody Knows: Black Americans in the Twentieth Century*. New York: Macmillan, 1970.

— U —

Ullman, Victor. *Look to the North Star: A Life of William King*. Boston: Beacon Press, 1969.

Umbra: Anthology 1967-1968. (Edited by David Henderson.) New York: Umbra, 1968.

Urban Riots: Violence and Social Change. (Preface by Robert H. Connery.) New York: Columbia University, 1969.

— V —

Van Dyke, Henry. *Blood of Strawberries*. New York: Farrar, Straus & Giroux, 1969.

Van Peebles, Melvin. *A Bear for the F.B.I.* New York: Trident Press, 1968. New York: Pocket Books, 1969.

Van Vechten, Carl. *Nigger Heaven*. New York: Avon, 1951.

Vance, Samuel. *The Courageous and the Proud: A Black Man in the White Man's Army*. New York: Norton, 1970.

Vanguard Society of America. *The Civil War Centennial and the Negro*. Los Angeles: Vanguard Society of America, 1961.

Vlock, Laurel F. and Joel A. Levitch. *Contraband of War: William Henry Singleton*. New York: Funk and Wagnalls, 1970.

Voegeli, V. Jacque. *Free But Not Equal: The Midwest and the Negro During the Civil War*. Chicago: University of Chicago, 1967.

Vroman, Mary E. *Harlem Summer*. New York: Putnam, 1967.

———. *Shaped to Its Purpose: Delta Sigma Theta—The First 50 Years*. New York: Random House, 1965.

— W —

Wade, Richard C. (ed.). *The Negro in American Life*. Boston: Houghton Mifflin, 1968.

Wagandt, C. L. *The Mighty Revolution: Negro Emancipation in Maryland*. Baltimore: Johns Hopkins Press, 1965.

Wagner, Jane. *J.T.* New York: Van Nostrand-Reinhold, 1970.

Wagstaff, Thomas. *Black Power: The Radical Response to White America*. Beverly Hills: Glencoe Press, 1969.

Wakefield, Dan. *Revolt in the South*. New York: Grove Press, 1960.

Wakin, Edward. *At the Edge of Harlem*. New York: Morrow, 1965.

Walker, Alice. *Once*. New York: Harcourt, Brace & World, 1969.

———. *The Third Life of Grange Copeland*. New York: Harcourt, Brace & Jovanovich, 1970.

Walker, Margaret. *For My People*. New Haven: Yale University Press, 1969.

———. *Jubilee*. Boston: Houghton Mifflin, 1966.

———. *Prophets for a New Day*. Detroit: Broadside, 1970.

Walser, Richard. *The Black Poet: Being the Remarkable Story of George Moses Horton, A North Carolina Slave*. New York: Philosophical Library, 1966.

Walton, Hanes, Jr. *The Negro in Third-Party Politics*. Philadelphia: Dorrance, 1969.

Ward, Douglas Turner. *Happy Ending* and *Day of Absence*. New York: Dramatist Play Service, 1967.

Warren, Robert Penn. *Who Speaks for the Negro?* New York: Vintage, 1966. Dodd, Mead, 1965.

Washington, Joseph R., Jr. *Black and White Power Subseption*. Boston: Beacon Press, 1967.

———. *Black Religion: The Negro and Christianity in the United States*. Boston: Beacon Press, 1964.

———. *Marriage in Black and White*. Boston: Beacon, 1971.

———. *The Politics of God*. Boston: Beacon Press, 1967.

Waskow, Arthur L. *Running Riot*. New York: Herder and Herder, 1970.

Waters, Ethel (with Charles Samuels). *His Eye Is on the Sparrow*. New York: Bantam, 1967.

Watkins, Mel and Jay David (eds.). *To Be a Black Woman: Portraits in Fact and Fiction*. New York: Morrow, 1970.

Watters, Pat and Reese Cleghorn. *Climbing Jacob's Ladder: The Arrival of Negroes in Southern Politics*. New York: Harcourt, Brace and World, 1968.

———. *The South and the Nation*. New York: Pantheon Books, 1970.

Weaver, Robert C. *Dilemmas of Urban America*. Cambridge: Harvard University Press, 1965.

———. *The Urban Complex: Human Values in Urban Life*. New York: Doubleday, 1964.

Webb, Constance. *Richard Wright: A Biography*. New York: G. P. Putnam's Sons, 1968.

Weinberg, Arthur and Lila (eds.). *Instead of Violence*. New York: Grossman Publishers, 1963.

Weinberg, Kenneth G. *Black Victory: Carl Stokes and the Winning of Cleveland*. Chicago: Quadrangle Books, 1969.

Weinberg, Meyer (ed.). *Integrated Education*. Beverly Hills: Glencoe Press, 1968.

———. *School Integration: A Comprehensive Classified Bibliography of 3,100 References.* Chicago: Integrated Education Associates, 1967.

———. *W. E. B. DuBois: A Reader.* New York: Harper and Row, 1970.

Weiner, Sandra. *It's Wings That Make Birds Fly.* New York: Pantheon Books, 1969.

Weinstein, Allen and Frank Otto Gatell (eds.). *American Negro Slavery: A Modern Reader.* New York: Oxford University Press, 1969.

———. *The Segregation Era, 1863-1954: A Modern Reader.* New York: Oxford University Press, 1970.

Weissman, Harold H. *Community Councils and Community Control: The Workings of Democratic Mythology.* Pittsburgh: University of Pittsburgh Press, 1970.

Werstein, Irving. *The Draft Riots: July 1863.* New York: Messner, 1971.

———. *The Plotters: The New York Conspiracy of 1741.* New York: Scribner's, 1969.

———. *A Proud People: Black Americans.* Philadelphia: Lippincott, 1970.

Wertheim, Bill (ed.). *Talkin' About Us: Writings by Students in the Upward Bound Program.* New York: Hawthorn, 1970.

Wesley, Charles, and Carter G. Woodson. *The Negro in Our History.* Washington, D.C.: Associated, 1962.

———. *Ohio Negroes in the Civil War.* Columbus: Ohio State University, 1962.

———. *Year's Pictorial History of the Black American.* Maplewood: Hammond, 1968.

Westin, Alan F. (ed.). *Freedom Now! The Civil Rights Struggle in America.* New York: Basic Books, 1964.

White, Charles. *Images of Dignity.* Los Angeles: Ritchie Press, 1967.

White, Josh (ed. by Robert Shelton). *The Josh White Song Book.* Chicago: Quadrangle Books, 1963.

Whitfield, Mal and A. S. Young. *Welcome Home Stranger.* New York: McKay, 1963.

Whitten, Norman E., Jr. and John F. Szwed (eds.). *Afro-American Anthropology: Contemporary Perspectives.* New York: Free Press, 1970.

Wideman, John Edgar. *A Glance Away.* New York: Harcourt, Brace and World, 1967.

Wiggins, Jefferson. *White Cross—Black Crucifixion: Conflict on the College Campus. A Social Commentary.* New York: Exposition Press, 1970.

Wiggins, Sam P. *The Desegregation Era in Higher Education.* Berkelev: McCutcheon Publishing, 1967.

Wilev, Joseph Harold, Kenneth Jeffries and Charles T. Brooker. *From Nowhere to Somewhere.* Philadelphia: Chilton Books, 1970.

Williams, Edward G. *Not Like Niggers.* New York: St. Martin's Press, 1970.

Williams, Eric. *Capitalism and Slavery.* Chapel Hill: University of North Carolina Press, 1964.

Williams, Jamye Coleman and Donald Williams (eds.). *The Negro Speaks: The Rhetoric of Contemporary Black Leaders.* New York: Noble and Noble, 1970.

Williams, John A. (ed.). *Beyond the Angry Black.* New York: Cooper Square Publishers, 1966.

———. *The King God Didn't Save: Reflections on the Life and Death of Martin Luther King, Jr.* New York: Coward-McCann, 1970.

———. *The Man Who Cried I Am.* Boston: Little, Brown, 1967. New York: New American Library, 1968.

———. *The Most Native of Sons. A Biography of Richard Wright.* New York: Doubleday, 1970.

Williams, Kenny J. *They Also Spoke: An Essay on Negro Literature in America, 1787-1930.* Nashville: Townsend, 1970.

Williams, Martin. *The Jazz Tradition.* New York: Oxford University Press, 1970.

Williams, Robert F. *Negroes with Guns.* New York: Marzani & Munsell, 1963.

Williamson, Henry. *Hustler!* New York: Doubleday, 1965.

Williamson, Joel. *After Slavery.* Chapel Hill: University of North Carolina Press, 1965.

Williamson, Stanford Winfield. *With Grief Acquainted.* Chicago: Follett, 1964.

Wills, Gary. *The Second Civil War: Arming for Armageddon.* New York: The New American Library, 1968.

Wills, Maury and Steve Gardner. *It Pays to Steal.* Englewood Cliffs: Prentice-Hall, 1963.

Wilson, Theodore B. *The Black Codes of the South.* Birmingham: University of Alabama Press, 1965.

Wilson, Walter (ed.). *The Selected Writings of W. E. B. DuBois.* New York: New American Library, 1970.

Winders, Gertrude Hacker. *Harriet Tubman: Freedom Girl.* Indianapolis: Bobbs-Merrill, 1970.

Wish, Harvey (ed.). *The Negro Since Emancipation.* Englewood Cliffs: Prentice-Hall, 1964.

Wolff, Miles. *Lunch at the Five and Ten: The Greensboro Sit-ins—A Contemporary History.* New York: Stein and Day, 1970.

Wolters, Raymond. *Negroes and the Great Depression.* Westport: Greenwood Publishing, 1970.

Wood, Forrest G. *Black Scare: The Racist Response to Emancipation and Reconstruction.* Berkeley: University of California Press, 1969.

Woodson, Carter G. *The Mind of the Negro as Reflected in Letters Written During the Crisis, 1800-1860; Negro Orators and Their Orations; and A Century of Negro Migration.* New York: Russell and Russell, 1969.

———. *The Mis-Education of the Negro.* Washington, D.C.: Associated Publishers, 1970.

——— and Charles H. Wesley. *Negro Makers of History.* Washington, D.C.: Associated, 1958.

Woodward, C. Vann. *Origins of the New South, 1877-1913.* Baton Rouge: Louisiana State University Press, 1951.

———. *Reunion and Reaction.* New York: Doubleday, 1956.

———. *The Strange Career of Jim Crow.* New York: Oxford, 1957.

Wormley, Stanton L. and Lewis H. Fenderson (eds.). *Many Shades of Black.* New York: William Morrow, 1969.

Wright, Charles. *The Messenger.* New York: Farrar, Strauss, 1963.

Wright, Dale. *They Harvest Despair. The Migrant Farm Worker.* Boston: Beacon Press, 1965.

Wright, Nathan, Jr. *Black Power and Urban Unrest.* New York: Hawthorn, 1967.

———. *Let's Work Together.* New York: Hawthorn Books, 1969.

———. *Ready to Riot.* New York: Holt, Rinehart & Winston, 1968.

———. *What Black Educators Are Saying.* New York: Hawthorn, 1970.

Wright, Richard. *Black Boy.* New York: New American Library, 1968.

———. *Eight Men.* New York: Avon Press, 1961.

———. *Lawd Today.* New York: Walker, 1963.

———. *The Long Dream.* New York: Doubleday, 1958.

———. *Native Son.* New York: Harper & Brothers, 1957.

———. *Uncle Tom's Children.* New York: World, 1943.

Wright, Richard R. *The Bishops of the AME Church.* Nashville: A.M.E., 1963.

Wright, Sarah. *This Child's Gonna Live.* New York: Delacorte Press, 1969.

Wyatt-Brown, Bertram. *Lewis Tappan and the Evangelical War Against Slavery.* Cleveland: Case Western Reserve University, 1969.

Wyman, Walter D., and John D. Hart. *The Legend of Charlie Glass: Negro Cowboy on the Colorado-Utah Range.* River Falls: River Falls State University Press, 1970.

Wynes, Charles E. (ed.). *Forgotten Voices: Dissenting Southerners in the Age of Conformity.* Baton Rouge: Louisiana State University Press, 1967.

———. *The Negro in the South Since 1865.* University: University of Alabama Press, 1965.

— Y —

Yates, Elizabeth. *Amos Fortune, Free Man.* New York: Aladdin, 1950.

Yerby, Frank. *Goat Song: A Novel of Ancient Greece.* New York: Dial Press, 1969.

Yette, Samuel F. *The Choice: The Issue of Black Survival in America.* New York: Putnam, 1971.

Young, Margaret B. *Black American Leaders.* New York: Watts, 1969.

———. *The First Book of American Negroes.* New York: Watts, 1966.

———. *The Picture Life of Thurgood Marshall.* New York: Watts, 1971.

Young, Whitney M., Jr. *Beyond Racism: Building an Open Society.* New York: McGraw-Hill, 1969.

———. *To Be Equal.* New York: McGraw-Hill, 1964.

— Z —

Zilversmit, Arthur. *The First Emancipation: The Abolition of Negro Slavery in the North.* Chicago: University of Chicago, 1967.

Zinn, Howard. *SNCC: The New Abolitionists.* Boston: Beacon Press, 1964.

———. *The Southern Mystique.* New York: Knopf, 1964.

AFRICA AND THE CARIBBEAN

— A —

Abir, Modechai. *Ethiopia — The Era of the Princes: The Challenge of Islam and the Reunification of the Christian Empire, 1769-1855.* New York: Praeger, 1969.

Abrahams, Peter. *This Island, Now.* New York: Alfred A. Knopf, 1967.

Abrash, Barbara (compiler). *Black African Literature in English Since 1952: Works and Criticism.* New York: Johnson Reprint, 1967.

Abruquah, Joseph. *The Torment.* New York: Humanities Press, 1969.

Achebe, Chinua. *A Man of the People.* New York: John Day, 1966.

Addo, Peter Eric Adotey (translator-editor). *Ghana Folk Tales: Ananse Stories from Africa.* New York: Exposition Press, 1969.

Ajayi, J. F. Ade and Ian Espire (eds.). *A Thousand Years of West African History: A Handbook for Teachers and Students.* London: Thomas Nelson, 1965.

African and Afro-American Studies. New York: Oxford University Press, 1969.

Africana Catalog No. 1. New Books Published. January 1967-October 1968. New York: International University Booksellers, 1969.

Ahmed, Rollo. *The Black Art.* New York: Paperback Library, 1967.

Anderson, Rosa Claudette. *River, Face Homeward (Suten dan W'ani Hive Fie): An Afro-American in Ghana.* New York: Exposition Press, 1969.

Andreski, Iris. *Old Wives Tales: Life-Stories from Ibibioland.* New York: Schicken, 1970.

Anene, Joseph C. and Godfrey Brown (eds.). *Africa in the 19th and 20th Centuries.* Edinburgh: Nelson and Sons, 1966.

———. *The International Boundaries of Nigeria, 1885-1960.* New York: Humanities Press, 1970.

Anthony, Michael. *The Games Were Coming.* Boston: Houghton Mifflin, 1968.

Appiah, Peggy. *Ananse the Spider: Tales from an Ashanti Village.* New York: Pantheon, 1966.

Archer, Jules. *Congo: The Birth of a New Nation.* New York: Messner, 1970.

Arikpo, Okoi. *The Development of Modern Nigeria.* Baltimore: Penguin Books, 1967.

Armah, Ayi Kwei. *The Beautiful Ones Are Not Yet Born.* Boston: Houghton Mifflin, 1969.

The Art of Central Africa: Sculpture and Tribal Masks. New York: New American Library, 1969.

The Art of Western Africa. New York: New American Library, 1969.

Ayandele, E. A. *The Missionary Impact on Modern Nigeria, 1842-1914: A Political and Social Analysis.* New York: Humanities Press, 1968.

— B —

Balandier, George. *Daily Life in the Kingdom of the Kongo.* New York: Pantheon, 1968.

———. *The Sociology of Black Africa: Social Dynamics in Central Africa.* New York: Praeger, 1970.

Banfield, Beryle. *Africa in the Curriculum: A Teacher's Guide.* New York: Edward W. Blyden, 1968.

Barbadiana. A List of Works Pertaining to the History of the Island of Barbados. Prepared in the Public Library to Mark the Attainment of Independence. Bridgetown: Barbados Public Library, 1966.

Barnes, Leonard. *African Renaissance.* Indianapolis: Bobbs-Merrill, 1969.

Beier, Ulli. *African Poetry: An Anthology of Traditional African Poems.* New York: Cambridge University, 1966.

———. *Contemporary Art in Africa.* New York: Praeger, 1968.

——— (ed.). *Introduction to African Literature.* Evanston: Northwestern University, 1967.

——— (ed.). *Three Nigerian Plays.* New York: Humanities, 1968.

Bell, Patricia. *Puerto Rico—Island Paradise of U.S. Imperialism.* New York: New Outlook, 1968.

Bell, Wendell (ed.). *The Democratic Revolution in the West Indies: Studies in Nationalism, Leadership and the Belief in Progress.* Cambridge: Schenkman, 1967.

ben-jochannan, Yosef, Hugh Brooks and Kempton Webb. *Africa: The Land, The People, The Culture.* New York: Wm. H. Sadlier, 1969.

———. *African Origins of the Major Western Religions.* New York: Author, 1970.

———. *Black Man of the Nile: Contributions to European Civilization and Thought.* New York: Author, 1970.

Bennett, Louise. *Jamaica Labrish.* Jamaica, West Indies: Sangster's Book Stores, 1966.

Bennett, Norman R. (ed.). *Leadership in Eastern Africa: Six Political Biographies.* Boston: Boston University, 1970.

———. *Mirambo of Tanzania, 1840-1884.* New York: Oxford University Press, 1971.

Berrian, Albert H. and Richard A. Long (eds.). *Negritude: Essays and Studies.* Hampton: Hampton Institute, 1967.

Beshir, Mohamed Omer. *The Southern Sudan: Background to Conflict.* New York: Praeger, 1969.

Biebuyck, Daniel and Kahombo C. Mateene (eds.). *The Mwindo Epic.* Berkeley: University of California, 1969.

Bethell, Leslie. *The Abolition of the Brazilian Slave Trade.* New York: Cambridge University, 1970.

The Black Man in Search of Power: A Survey of the Black Revolution Across the World. New York: Thomas Nelson, 1969.

Bleeker, Sonia. *The Ibo of Biafra.* New York: Morrow, 1969.

Blyden, Edward W. *Christianity, Islam and the Negro Race.* Chicago: Aldine, 1967.

Boahen, A. Adu. *Topics in West African History.* London: Longmans, 1966.

Bodrogi, Tibor. *Art in Africa.* New York: McGraw-Hill, 1968.

Boetie, Dugmore. *Familiarity is the Kingdom of the Lost.* New York: Faucett, 1970.

Bond, Jean Carey. *A Is for Africa.* New York: Franklin Watts, 1969.

Brau, Maria M. *Island in the Crossroads: The History of Puerto Rico.* New York: Doubleday, Zenith, 1969.

Braithwaite, E. R. *Choice of Straws.* Indianapolis: Bobbs-Merrill, 1966.

Braithwaite, Edward. *Islands.* New York: Oxford University, 1969.

———. *Masks.* New York: Oxford University, 1968.

———. *Rights of Passage, Poems.* New York: Oxford University, 1967.

Brench, A. C. *The Novelists' Inheritance in French Africa: Writers from Senegal to Cameroon.* New York: Oxford University, 1967.

Brokensha, David and Michael Crowder. *Africa in the Wider World.* Elmsford: Pergamon, 1969.

Brown, Evelyn S. *Africa's Contemporary Art and Artists: A Review of Creative Activities in Painting, Sculpture, Ceramics and Crafts of More than 300 Artists Working in the Modern Industrialized Society of Some of the Countries of Sub-Saharan Africa.* New York: Harmon Foundation, 1966.

Brutus, Dennis. *Letters to Martha and Other Poems from a South African Prison.* New York: Humanities, 1969.

Bull, Theodore. *Rhodesia: Crisis of Color.* (Intro. by Gwendolyn Carter.) Chicago: Quadrangle Books, 1968.

— C —

Carroll, David. *Chinua Achebe.* New York: Twayne, 1970.

Carter, Gwendolen M., Thomas and Stultz Karis, and M. Newell. *South Africa's Transkei: The Politics of Domestic Colonialism.* Evanston: Northwestern University Press, 1967.

Cartey, Wilfred and Martin Kilson (eds.). *The Africa Reader: Vol. I — Independent Africa; Vol. II—Colonial Africa.* New York: Random House, 1970.

——— (ed.). *Palaver. Modern African Writings.* New York: Nelson, 1970.

———, *Whispers from a Continent: The Literature of Contemporary Black Africa.* New York: Random House, 1969.

Cassell, C. Abayomi. *Liberia: History of the First African Republic.* New York: Fountainhead, 1971.

Caute, David. *Frantz Fanon.* New York: Viking, 1970.

Chilcote, Ronald H. *Portuguese Africa.* Englewood Cliffs: Prentice-Hall, 1967.

Clark, John Pepper. *Ozidi: A Play.* London: Oxford University Press, 1968.

———. *A Reed in the Tide.* London: Longmans, 1966.

Clark, Leon E. (ed.). *Through African Eyes: Cultures in Change.* New York: Praeger, 1970.

Clarke, Austin. *The Echo at Coole.* Chester Springs: Dufour Editions, 1969.

Clegern, Wayne M. *British Honduras: Colonial Dead End.* Baton Rouge: Louisiana State University Press, 1967.

Cole, Ernest. *House of Bondage.* New York: Random House, 1967.

Cole, Hubert. *Christophe, King of Haiti.* New York: Viking Press, 1967.

Collins, Harold R. *Amos Tutuola.* New York: Twayne, 1969.

Collins, Robert O. and Robert L. Tignor. *Egypt and the Sudan.* Englewood Cliffs: Prentice-Hall, 1967.

——— (ed.). *Problems in African History.* Englewood Cliffs: Prentice-Hall, 1969.

Color and Race. Cambridge: Harvard University (Journal of the American Academy of Arts and Sciences), 1968.

Comitas, Lambros. *Caribbeana 1900-1965: A Topical Bibliography.* Seattle: University of Washington Press, 1968.

Contemporary African Art. New York: Africana Publishing Corp., 1970.

Courlander, Harold. *The African.* New York: Crown, 1967.

Courlander, Harold and Remy Bastien. *Religion and Politics in Haiti: Essays.* Washington, D.C.: Institute for Cross-Cultural Research, 1967.

Curtin, Philip D. and others (eds.). *Africa Remembered: Narratives by West Africans from the Era of the Slave Trade.* Madison: University of Wisconsin Press, 1967.

—D—

Daniel, W. W. *Racial Discrimination in England.* Baltimore: Penguin, 1969.

Dathrone, D. R. and Willfried Feuser (eds.). *Africa in Prose.* Baltimore: Penguin, 1969.

Davidson, Basil. *A History of West Africa to the 19th Century.* New York: Doubleday Anchor, 1966.

———. *Africa: History of a Continent.* New York: Macmillan, 1966.

———. *Africa in History: Themes and Outlines.* New York: Macmillan, 1969.

———. *The African Genius: An Introduction to African Social and Cultural History.* Boston: Atlantic-Little, Brown, 1970.

——— and Editors of Time-Life Books. *African Kingdoms.* New York: Time-Life, 1966.

——— (with J. E. F. Mhina and Betwell A. Ogot). *East and Central Africa to the 19th Century.* New York: Doubleday Anchor, 1968.

Davies, Oliver. *West Africa before the Europeans: Archaeology and Prehistory.* New York: Barnes and Noble, 1968.

de Craemer, Willy and Renee C. Fox. *The Emerging Physician: A Sociological Approach to the Development of a Congolese Medical Profession.* Stanford: The Hoover Institution, 1969.

deGraft-Johnson, J. C. *African Glory: The Story of Vanished Negro Civilizations.* New York: Walker & Co., 1967.

de Lusignan, Guy. *French-Speaking Africa Since Independence.* New York: Praeger, 1969.

Delany, Martin R. and Robert Campbell. *Search for a Place: Black Separatism and Africa.* Ann Arbor: University of Michigan, 1969.

Desai, R. and L. Szabo. *African Society and Culture.* New York: International University Booksellers, 1969.

Diederich, Bernard and Al Burt. *Papa Doc: The Truth About Haiti Today.* New York: McGraw-Hill, 1969.

Dietz, Betty Warner and Michael B. Olatunji. *Musical Instruments of Africa: Their Nature, Use and Place in the Life of a Deeply Musical People.* New York: John Day, 1965.

Doob, Leonard. *A Crocodile Has Me by the Leg: African Poems.* New York: Walker and Co., 1968.

Dormu, Alfonso K. *The Constitution of the Republic of Liberia and the Declaration of Independence.* New York: Exposition Press, 1970.

Dostert, Pierre E. *Africa 1967.* Washington, D.C.: Stryker-Post Publications, 1968.

DuBois, W. E. B. *The Negro* (new introduction by George Shepperson). New York: Oxford University Press, 1970.

——— *The Suppression of the African Slave Trade to the United States of America, 1638-1870.* Baton Rouge: Louisiana State University, 1970.

Duffy, James. *A Question of Slavery: Labour Policies in Portuguese Africa and the British Protest 1850-1920.* Cambridge: Harvard University Press, 1967.

Dunham, Katherine. *Island Possessed.* New York: Doubleday, 1969.

—E—

An East African Childhood: Three Versions. Edited by Lorene K. Fox and written by A. Lijembe, Anna Apoki and J. Mutuku Nzioki. New York: Oxford University, 1966.

Edwards, Paul (ed.). *Equiano's Travels: The Interesting Narrative of the Life of Olaudah Equiano or Gustavus Vassa the African.* New York: Praeger, 1967.

Emmerson, Donald K. (ed.). *Students and Politics in Developing Nations.* New York: Praeger, 1968.

—F—

Fagan, Brian M. (ed.). *A Short History of Zambia. From the Earliest Times Until A.D. 1900.* New York: Oxford University Press, 1968.

Fage, J. D. (ed.). *Africa Discovers Her Past.* New York: Oxford University Press, 1970.

Fagg, William. *African Tribal Images.* Cleveland: Cleveland Museum of Art, 1969.

Fanon, Frantz (translated by Charles Lam Markmann). *Black Skin, White Masks.* New York: Grove Press, 1967.

———. *Studies in a Dying Colonialism.* New York: Grove Press, 1969.

———. *Toward the African Revolution: Political Essays.* New York: Monthly Review Press, 1967.

———. *The Wretched of the Earth.* New York: Grove Press, 1968.

Feelings, Muriel. *Zamani Goes to Market.* New York: Seabury, 1970.

Feit, Edward. *African Opposition in South Africa.* Stanford: Stanford University, 1967.

Fernandes, Florestan. *The Negro in Brazilian Society.* New York: Columbia University, 1969.

Fieldhouse, D. K. *The Colonial Empires: A Comparative Survey from the Eighteenth Century.* New York: Delacorte Press, 1966.

Fisher, Allan G. B. and Humphrey J. *Slavery and Muslim Society in Africa: The Institution in Saharan and Trans-Saharan Trade.* New York: Doubleday, 1971.

Forde, Daryll and Phyllis M. Kaberry (ed.). *West African Kingdoms in the Nineteenth Century.* New York: Oxford University, 1967.

Fox, Lorene K. (ed.). *An East African Childhood: Three Versions.* New York: Oxford University, 1967.

Frank, Andre Gunder. *Capitalism and Underdevelopment in Latin America: Historical Studies of Chile and Brazil.* New York: Monthly Review Press, 1969.

—G—

Gabel, Creighton and Norman R. Bennett (eds.). *Reconstructing African Culture History.* Boston: Boston University Press, 1968.

Gardner, Brian. *The Quest for Timbuctoo.* New York: Harcourt, Brace, 1969.

Gardi, Rene. *African Crafts and Craftsmen.* Princeton: Van Nostrand Reinhold, 1971.

Gbadamosi, Bakare and Ulli Beier. *Not Even God Is Ripe Enough —Yoruba Stories.* New York: Humanities Press, 1969.

Geismar, Peter. *Fanon.* New York: Dial, 1971.

Grade Teacher (magazine), October 1968. *Africa for the Elementary Grades.* New York: Teachers Publishing Corp., 1968.

Graham, Lorenz. *Every Man Heart Lay Down.* New York: Crowell, 1970.

Grant, Douglas. *The Fortunate Slave: An Illustration of African Slavery in the Early Eighteenth Century.* New York: Oxford University, 1969.

Green, Reginald H. and Ann Seidman. *Unity or Poverty. The Economics of Pan-Africanism.* Baltimore: Penguin Books, 1968.

Green, Reginald H. and K. G. V. Krishna. *Economic Cooperation in Africa: Retrospect and Prospect.* New York: Oxford University Press, 1967.

Gutteridge, William F. *The Military in African Politics.* New York: Barnes and Noble, 1969.

—H—

Hallett, Robin. *Africa to 1875: A Modern History.* Ann Arbor: University of Michigan, 1969.

Hammond, Dorothy and Alta Jablow. *The Africa That Never Was: Four Centuries of British Writing About Africa.* New York: Twayne, 1970.

Hance, William A. *Southern Africa and the United States.* New York: Columbia University Press, 1968.

Handyside, Richard (ed.). *Revolution in Guinea: Selected Texts by Amilcar Cabral.* New York: Monthly Review Press, 1970.

Hargreaves, John D. *West Africa: The Former French States.* Englewood Cliffs: Prentice-Hall, 1967.

Haslow, Vincent and E. M. Chilvers (eds.). *History of East Africa* (3 vols.). New York: Oxford University, 1968-.

Haskins, Sam. *African Image.* New York: Grosset and Dunlap, 1967.

Hatch, John. *The History of Britain in Africa, from the 15th Century to the Present.* New York: Praeger, 1970.

Head, Bessie. *When Rain Clouds Gather.* New York: Simon and Schuster, 1969.

Heady, Eleanor B. *When the Stones Were Soft: East African Fireside Tales*. New York: Funk and Wagnalls, 1968.

Heckert, Eleanor Louise. *Muscavado*. New York: Doubleday, 1967.

Heinz, G. and H. Donnay. *Lumumba: The Last Fifty Days*. New York: Grove Press, 1970.

Helleiner, Gerald K. *Peasant Agriculture, Government and Economic Growth in Nigeria*. Homewood: Richard D. Irwin, 1966.

Hess, Robert L. *Ethiopia: The Modernization of Autocracy*. Ithaca: Cornell University, 1970.

Hill, Adelaide Cromwell and Martin Kilson (eds.). *Apropos of Africa: Sentiments of Negro American Leaders on Africa from the 1800's to the 1950's*. New York: Humanities Press, 1969.

Hodgson, Eva N. *Second Class Citizens; First Class Men*. Hamilton: Amalgamated Bermuda Union of Teachers, 1967.

Hoetink, H. *The Two Variants in Caribbean Race Relations: A Contribution to the Sociology of Segmented Societies*. New York: Oxford University Press, 1967.

Holbrook, Sabra. *The American West Indies: Puerto Rico and the Virgin Islands*. New York: Meredith, 1963.

Holden, Edith. *Blyden of Liberia: An Account of the Life and Labors of Edward Wilmot Blyden, LL.D.* New York: Vantage Press, 1966.

Holly, James T. and J. D. Harris. *Black Separatism and the Caribbean, 1860*. Ann Arbor: University of Michigan, 1970.

Hooker, James R. *Black Revolutionary: George Padmore's Path from Communism to Pan-Africanism*. New York: Praeger, 1967.

—I—

Ijimere, Obotunde. *The Imprisonment of Obatala and Other Plays*. New York: Humanities Press, 1969.

Iliffe, John. *Tanganyika Under German Rule, 1905-1912*. New York: Cambridge University, 1969.

Irvine, Keith. *The Rise of the Colored Races*. New York: W. W. Norton, 1970.

—J—

Jackson, John G. *Introduction to African Civilizations*. New York: University Books, 1970.

Jagan, Cheddi. *The West on Trial: My Fight for Guyana's Freedom*. New York: International, 1967.

Jahn, Janheinz. *Bibliography of Creative African Writing*. New York: Kraus Reprint, 1971.

———. *Neo-African Literature: A History of Black Writing*. New York: Grove Press, 1970.

James, Louis (ed.). *The Islands in Between: Essays on West Indian Literature*. New York: Oxford University, 1968.

John, Errol. *Screenplays: Force Majeure, The Dispossessed, Hasta Luego*. London: Faber and Faber, 1968.

Johnson, Willard R. *The Cameroon Federation: Political Integration in a Fragmentary Society*. Princeton: Princeton University, 1970.

Joseph, Helen. *Tomorrow's Sun: A Smuggled Journal from South Africa*. New York: John Day, 1968.

July, Robert W. *A History of the African People*. New York: Scribners, 1967.

———. *The Origins of Modern African Thought: Its Development in West Africa During the Nineteenth and Twentieth Century*. New York: Praeger, 1968.

—K—

Kahn, E. J., Jr. *The Separated People: A Look at Contemporary South Africa*. New York: Norton, 1969.

Kamarck, Andrew M. *The Economics of African Development*. New York: Praeger, 1967.

Kaunda, Kenneth. *A Humanist in Africa: Letters to Colin Morris from Kenneth Kaunda, President of Zambia*. Nashville: Abingdon Press, 1967.

Kay, F. George. *The Shameful Trade*. New York: A. S. Barnes, 1968.

Keating, Bern. *Chaka: King of the Zulus*. New York: Putnam's, 1969.

Kedounie, Elie (ed.). *Nationalism in Asia and Africa*. New York: World, 1970.

Kgositsile, Keorapetse. *For Melba*. Chicago: Third World Press, 1970.

———. *Spirits Unchained*. Detroit: Broadside, 1968.

Kilson, Martin. *Political Change in a West African State: A Study of the Modernization Process in Sierra Leone*. Cambridge: Harvard University Press, 1966.

Klein, Herbert S. *Slavery in the Americas: A Comparative Study of Cuba and Virginia*. Chicago: University of Chicago Press, 1967.

Klineberg, Otto and Mansa Zavalloni. *Nationalism and Tribalism Among African Students: A Study of Social Identity*. New York: Humanities Press, 1969.

Konadu, Asare. *Ordained by the Oracle*. New York: Humanities Press, 1969.

Kunst, Hans-Joachim. *The African in European Art*. Bad Godesberg: Inter Nationes, 1967.

—L—

Lacy, Leslie A. *Black Africa on the Move*. New York: Franklin Watts, 1970.

Lang, D. M. (ed.). *The Penguin Companion to Literature: Oriental and African*. Baltimore: Penguin, 1969.

Laurence, Margaret. *Long Drums and Cannons: Nigerian Dramatists and Novelists*. New York: Praeger, 1969.

———. *New Wind in a Dry Land*. New York: Knopf, 1964.

Leins, Michel and Jacqueline Delange. *African Art*. New York: Golden Press, 1969.

Lemarchand, Rene. *Rwanda and Burundi*. New York: Praeger, 1970.

Leroy, Jules. *Ethiopian Painting in the Late Middle Ages and During the Gondar Dynasty*. New York: Praeger, 1967.

Le Vine, Victor T. *Political Leadership in Africa*. Stanford: Hoover Institution, 1967.

Levi-Strauss, Claude. *The Savage Mind*. Chicago: University of Chicago, 1966.

Lewis, Gordon. *The Growth of the Modern West Indies*. New York: Monthly Review, 1968.

———. *Puerto Rico: Freedom and Power in the Caribbean*. New York: Harper Torchbook, 1968.

Levitt, Leonard. *An African Season*. New York: Simon and Schuster, 1967.

Lewis, I. M. *The Modern History of Somaliland*. London: Weidenfeld and Nicolson, 1965.

Ling, Dwight L. *Tunisia, from Protectorate to Republic*. Bloomington: Indiana University, 1967.

Lips, Juliua E. *The Savage Hits Back, or the White Men Through Native Eyes*. New Hyde Park: University Books, 1966.

Little, Tom. *Modern Egypt*. New York: Praeger, 1967.

Litto, Frederic M. (ed.). *Plays from Black Africa*. New York: Hill and Wang, 1969.

Liyong, Tabanlo. *Eating Chiefs: Luo Culture from Lolwe to Malkal*. New York: Humanities Press, 1971.

———. *Fixions and Stories by a Ugandan Writer*. New York: Humanities Press, 1969.

Lloyd, P. C. *Africa in Social Change: West African Societies in Transition*. New York: Praeger, 1968.

Lynch, Hollis R. *Edward Wilmot Blyden: Pan-Negro Patriot*. New York: Oxford University, 1967.

Lynd, G. E. *The Politics of African Trade Unionism*. New York: Praeger, 1968.

—M—

McCloy, Shelby T. *The Negro in the French West Indies*. Lexington: University of Kentucky, 1966.

McEwan, P. J. M. (ed.). *Twentieth Century Africa*. New York: Oxford University, 1968.

McKown, Robin. *Lumumba: A Biography*. New York: Doubleday, 1969.

Makeba, Miriam. *The World of African Song*. Chicago: Quadrangle, 1971.

Marcum, John. *The Angolan Revolution. Vol. I*. Cambridge: M.I.T., 1968.

Markovitz, Irving Leonard (ed.). *African Politics and Society*. New York: Free Press, 1970.

———. *Leopold Sedar Senghor and the Politics of Negritude*. New York: Atheneum, 1969.

Marshall, Anthony D. *Africa's Living Arts*. New York: Franklin Watts, 1969.

Mayer, Emerico Jamassa. *Ghana: Past and Present*. New York: Arco Publishing, 1968.

Mbiti, John S. *African Religions and Philosophy*. New York: Praeger, 1969.

———. *Concepts of God in Africa*. New York: Praeger, 1970.

Mboya, Tom. *The Challenge of Nationhood: A Collection of Speeches and Writings of Tom Mboya*. New York: Praeger, 1970.

Meauze, Pierre. *African Art: Sculpture*. New York: World Publishing, 1968.

Menkiti, Ifeanyi. *Affirmations*. Chicago: Third World Press, 1970.

Mertens, Alice. *South West Africa and Its Indigenous Peoples*. New York: Taplinger, 1966.

Miner, Horace (ed.). *The City in Modern Africa*. New York: Praeger, 1968.

Mitchison, Naomi. *African Heroes*. New York: Farrar, Straus & Giroux, 1969.

Montejo, Esteban. *The Autobiography of a Runaway Slave*. New York: Pantheon Books, 1969.

Moore, Clark D. and Ann Dunbar (eds.). *Africa Yesterday and Today*. New York: Bantam, 1968.

Morgan, Gordon D. *African Vignettes: Notes of an American Negro Family in East Africa*. Jefferson City: New Scholars Press, 1968.

Motley, Mary P. *Africa: Its Empires, Nations, and People*. Detroit: Wayne State, 1970.

Moumouni, Abdou. *Education in Africa*. New York: Praeger, 1968.

Mphahlele, Ezekiel (ed.). *African Writing Today*. Baltimore: Penguin, 1967.

Mulford, David C. *Zambia: The Politics of Independence, 1957-1964*. New York: Oxford University, 1967.

Murphy, E. Jefferson. *Understanding Africa*. New York: Crowell, 1969.

Mwase, George Simeon. *Strike a Blow and Die: A Narrative of Race Relations in Colonial Africa*. Cambridge: Harvard University, 1967.

— N —

Newton, A. P. *The European Nations in the West Indies*. New York: Barnes and Noble, 1967.

Nkrumah, Kwame. *Axioms of Kwame Nkrumah*. New York: International, 1970.

———. *Challenge of the Congo*. New York: International, 1967.

———. *Class Struggle in Africa*. New York: International, 1970.

———. *Dark Days in Ghana*. New York: International, 1968.

———. *Handbook of Revolutionary Warfare: A Guide to the Armed Phase of the African Revolution*. New York: International, 1969.

———. *Neo-Colonialism: The Last Stage of Imperialism*. New York: International, 1969.

Nolen, Barbara. *Ethiopia*. New York: Franklin Watts, 1971.

Nyerere, Julius K. *Freedom and Socialism / Uhuru Na Ujamaa*. New York: Oxford University, 1970.

———. *Freedom and Unity (Uhuru Na Umoha): A Selection from Writings and Speeches, 1952-1965*. New York: Oxford University, 1967.

— O —

Odinga, Oginga. *Not Yet Uhuru: An Autobiography*. New York: Hill and Wang, 1967.

Ogot, B. A. and J. A. Kieran (eds.). *Zamani: A Survey of East African History*. New York: Humanities, 1969.

Okpaku, Joseph (ed.). *New African Literature and the Arts. Vols. 1 and 2*. New York: Thomas Y. Crowell, 1970, 1971.

Oliver, Roland and Anthony Atmore. *Africa Since 1800*. New York: Cambridge University, 1967.

Omer, Cooper R. *The Zulu Aftermath: A Nineteenth-Century Revolution in Bantu Africa*. London: Longmans, Green, 1967.

Ottaway, David and Marina. *Algeria: The Politics of a Social Revolution*. Berkeley: University of California, 1970.

Oxaal, Ivar. *Black Intellectuals Come to Power: The Rise of Creole Nationalism in Trinidad and Tobago*. Cambridge: Schenckman Publishing, 1968.

The Oxford Library of African Literature. New York and London: Oxford University Press, 1966-. 12 or more volumes.

1. *The Zande Trickster*. Edited by E. E. Evans-Pritchard.
2. *Chaga Childhood*. By O. F. Raum.
3. *African Integration and Disintegration*. Edited by Arthur Hazelwood.
4. *Rhodesia: The Road to Rebellion*. By James Barber.
5. *The Medicine Man*. By Bwana Hasani bin Ismail.

— P —

Patterson, H. Orlando. *The Sociology of Slavery: An Analysis of the Origins, Development and Structure of Negro Slave Society in Jamaica*. Rutherford: Fairleigh Dickinson University Press, 1969.

Pfefferman, Guy. *Industrial Labor in the Republic of Senegal*. New York: Praeger, 1969.

Pierson, Donald. *Negroes in Brazil: A Study of Race Contact at Bahia*. Carbondale: Southern Illinois University Press, 1967.

Pike, John G. *Malawi: A Political and Economic History*. New York: Praeger, 1969.

Plotnicov, Leonard. *Strangers to the City: Urban Man in Jos, Nigeria*. Pittsburgh: University of Pittsburgh Press, 1967.

Polatnick, Florence T. and Alberta L. Saletan. *Shapers of Africa*. New York: Messner, 1969.

Pope-Hennessy, James. *Sins of the Fathers: A Study of the Atlantic Slave Traders*. New York: Alfred A. Knopf, 1967.

— R —

Radin, Paul (ed.). *African Folktales*. Princeton: Princeton University, 1970.

Ramchand, Kenneth. *The West Indian Novel and Its Background*. New York: Barnes and Noble, 1970.

Ransford, Oliver. *Livingstone's Lake: The Drama of Nyasa, Africa's Inland Sea*. New York: Thomas Y. Crowell, 1967.

Rice, Berkeley. *Enter Gambia: The Birth of an Improbable Nation*. Boston: Houghton Mifflin, 1967.

Rive, Richard. *Modern African Prose*. London: Heinemann, 1968.

Robins, Eric. *The Ebony Ark: Black Africa's Battle to Save Its Wildlife*. New York: Taplinger, 1970.

Robbins, Warren M. *African Art in American Collections*. New York: Praeger, 1966.

Rodman, Seldon. *The Caribbean*. New York: Hawthorn Books, 1969.

Rosenthal, Rita (Ricky). *The Splendor That Was Africa*. Dobbs Ferry: Oceana, 1967.

Rotberg, Robert I. *A Political History of Tropical Africa*. New York: Harcourt, Brace & World, 1967.

——— and Ali A. Mazrui (eds.). *Protest and Power in Black Africa*. New York: Oxford University, 1970.

Ruhumbika, Gabriel. *Village in Uhuru*. New York: Humanities Press, 1970.

— S —

Salih, Tayeb. *The Wedding of Zein and Other Stories*. New York: Humanities Press, 1969.

Schwarz-Bart, Andre and Simone. *A Plate of Pork with Green Bananas*. Paris: Editions Du Seuil, 1965.

Segal, Ronald. *The Race War: The World-Wide Clash of White and Non-White*. New York: Viking, 1966.

Seligman, C. G. *Races of Africa*. New York: Oxford University, 1966.

Sellassie, B. M. Sahle. *The Afersata: An Ethiopian Novel*. New York: Humanities, 1969.

Shaloff, Stanley. *Reform in Leopold's Congo*. Richmond: John Knox, 1970.

Shelton, Austin J. (ed.). *The African Assertion: A Critical Anthology of African Literature*. New York: Odyssey Press, 1969.

Sherlock, Philip. *West Indies*. New York: Walker, 1966.

Shinnie, P. L. *Meroe: A Civilization of the Sudan*. New York: Praeger, 1967.

Shore, Herbert L. and Megchelina Shore-Bos (eds.). *Come Back Africa!* New York: International, 1969.

Sik, Endre. *The History of Black Africa* (2 vols.). Budapest: Publishing House of the Hungarian Academy of Sciences, 1966.

Singleton, F. Seth and John Shingler. *Africa in Perspective*. New York: Hayden Book, 1967.

Sithole, Ndabaningl. *African Nationalism*. New York: Oxford University, 1968.

Smith, Robert S. *Kingdoms of the Yoruba*. New York: Barnes and Noble, 1969.

Snowden, Frank M., Jr. *Blacks in Antiquity: Ethiopians in the Greco-Roman Experience*. Cambridge: Harvard University, 1970.

Southern Africa: A Time for Change. New York: Friendship, 1969.

Soyinka, Wole. *Five Plays*. New York: Oxford University, 1966.

———. *Idanre and Other Poems*. New York: Hill, 1969.

Spiro, Herbert J. (ed.). *Patterns of African Development: Five Comparisons*. Englewood Cliffs: Prentice-Hall, 1967.

Stevens, Richard P. *Lesotho, Botswana and Swaziland: The Former High Commission Territories in Southern Africa*. New York: Praeger, 1967.

Stevenson, Robert P. *Population and Political Systems in Tropical Africa*. New York: Columbia University, 1968.

Stokes, Eric and Richard Brown (eds.). *The Zambesian Past: Studies in Central African History*. New York: Humanities. 1966.

Sub-Saharan Africa: A Guide to Serials. Washington, D.C.: Library of Congress, 1970.

Sudan, Nazzam Al. *Sudan Rajuli Samia/Black Man Listen*. Burlington: Al Kitab Sudan Publications, 1967.

Sweeney, James Johnson (ed.). *African Sculpture*. Princeton: Princeton University Press, 1970.

— T —

Taylor, Sidney (ed.). *The New Africans: A Guide to the Contemporary History of Emergent Africa and Its Leaders*. New York: Putnam's, 1967.

Thompson, Vincent Bakpetu. *Africa and Unity: The Evolution of Pan-Africanism*. New York: Humanities Press, 1969.

Tindall, P. E. N. *A History of Central Africa*. New York: Praeger, 1969.

Tolson, Melvin B. *Libretto for the Republic of Liberia*. New York: Collier, 1970.

Tracey, Hugh. *The Lion on the Path and Other African Stories*. New York: Praeger, 1968.

Trimingham, J. Spencer. *The Influence of Islam upon Africa*. New York: Praeger, 1969.

Trowell, Margaret and Hans Nevermann. *African and Oceanic Art*. New York: Harry N. Abrams, 1969.

Tuck, Jay Nelson. *Heroes of Puerto Rico*. New York: Fleet Press, 1969.

Tucker, Martin. *Africa in Modern Literature: A Survey of Contemporary Writing in English*. New York: Frederick Ungar, 1967.

— U —

U'Tam'si, Tchicaya. *Selected Poems*. New York: Humanities Press, 1970.

— V —

Vansina, Jan. *Kingdoms of the Savanna: A History of the States of Central Africa*. Madison: University of Wisconsin, 1966.

Vlahos, Olivia. *African Beginnings*. New York: Viking Press, 1969.

— W —

Waddell, D. A. G. *The West Indies and the Guianas*. Englewood Cliffs: Prentice-Hall, 1967.

Wallerstein, Immanuel. *Africa: The Politics of Unity*. New York: Random House, 1967.

Ward, W. E. F. *The Royal Navy and the Slaves: The Suppression of the Atlantic Slave Trade*. New York: Pantheon, 1969.

Warner, Esther. *The Crossing Fee: A Story of Life in Liberia*. Boston: Houghton Mifflin, 1968.

Wassing, Rene S. *African Art: Its Background and Tradition*. New York: Harry N. Abrams, 1969.

Waterfield, Gordon (ed.). *Letters from Egypt*. New York: Praeger, 1969.

Wauthier, Claude. *The Literature and Thought of Modern Africa: A Survey*. New York: Praeger, 1967.

Weatherby, William J. *Out of Hiding*. New York: Doubleday, 1966.

Webster, J. B., A. A. Boahen and H. O. Idowu. *Growth of African Civilization: West Africa Since 1800*. London: Longmans, Green, 1969.

Weinstein, Brian. *Gabon: Nation-Building on the Ogooue*. Cambridge: MIT Press, 1966.

Wellard, James. *Lost Worlds of Africa*. New York: Dutton, 1967.

White, Stanhope. *Dan Bana: The Memoirs of a Nigerian Official*. New York: Heinemann, 1966.

Willett, Frank. *African Art*. New York: Praeger, 1971.

———. *Ife in the History of West African Sculpture*. New York: McGraw-Hill, 1967.

Williams, Eric. *British Historians and the West Indies*. New York: Scribner's, 1964.

———. *Inward Hunger: The Education of a Prime Minister*. London: Deutsch, 1970.

Willis, A. J. *An Introduction to the History of Central Africa*. New York: Oxford University Press, 1964.

Wilson, Charles M. *Liberia: Black Africa in Microcosm*. New York: Harper, 1971.

Windsor, Rudolph R. *From Babylon to Timbuktu*. New York: Exposition, 1969.

Woddis, Jack. *An Introduction to Neo-Colonialism*. New York: International, 1968.

Woodson, Carter G. *The African Background Outlined: or, Handbook for the Study of the Negro*. Westport: Negro Universities Press, 1969.

— Y —

Young, B. A. *Bechuanaland*. New York: British Information Service, 1966.

— Z —

Zagoren, Ruby. *Venture for Freedom: The True Story of an African Yankee*. Cleveland: World, 1969.

APPENDIX

List of Tables
List of Charts
List of Illustrations

LIST OF TABLES

LIST OF CHARTS

LIST OF ILLUSTRATIONS

Picture Credits

A 767–AL 936–ALH, JR. 721–AM 779–AN 615, 653, 659, 872–AP Inc. 295–AT 685–BA 793, 823, 888, 947–BC 519–BHAC 12–BM 921–BNR 798–BSNY 220–C 758, 794, 799, 821, 868–CBH and MC 191–CC 877–CG of J 234–CJ 206–CMA 762–CMB 715, 718–CN 39, 624, 631, 648, 654, 882, 914, 937, 955–CO 389–CP 837–CPI 761, 763–CR 797, 808, 810–CWMAA 717–DDMC 582–DG 326–DGA 686–DM and C 666-681–DNC 325–DPL 177, 187–EEOC 891–FA of A–682–FD 801–GS 901–H and Br. 699–HB 766–HS 491, 714–JM 772–LC 7, 13, 14, 15, 16, 20, 109, 125, 183, 198, 205, 282, 308, 562, 563, 575, 577, 586, 588, 611–LH 941–LM 668, 675, 684–MGMUR 804–MOA, Inc. 756, 759, 769, 785, 789–MR 788, 803–NA op 1, 4, 8, 17, 21, 96, 130, 185, 197, 274, 347, 348, 484, 485, 486, 487, 489, 493, 494, 495, 496, 497, 558, 559, 566, 568, 569, 570, 571, 572, 602, 603, 695, 697, 726, 728, 729, 731, 854, 871, 935, 940, 944, 946, 949, 950, 951, 956, 958–NAACP 27–NBC 388, 755, 757, 782, 791, 842–NEA 880–NET 482–NEWM 734, 735–NHA 187–NUL 216, 319, 320, 322, 384–NYDN 909–NYHS 190, 887–NYPL 94, 103, 113, 120, 127, 176–NYT 857, 883–OPS 5–P 805–PBNY 878–PC 521–RRD and HV 393–SAC 812–SO of NJ 884–T 702, 704, 705, 712, 713–TSA 204–UA 680, 818, 840–U Inc. 652 –UN 168, 341, 960, 963, 965, 969, 973, 976, 978, 983, 985, 986, 988, 989, 995, 998, 1006, 1009, 1014, 1019, 1028–UNCF 498, 517, 523, 530–UP 828–UPI 31, 34, 35, 38, 42, 49, 52, 54, 59, 61, 62, 65, 67, 68, 71, 75, 80, 83, 84, 87, 229, 239, 290, 294, 332, 336, 387, 390, 392, 396, 503, 605, 612, 617, 619, 623, 634, 638, 640, 650, 658, 662, 665, 787, 889, 932–US 771–USA 25, 576, 578, 583, 591, 594, 595, 599, 934–USAF 580, 609, 610–WHCU of OK 201–WIP 842–WMCA 845–WPMC 573–WW 29, 32, 37, 56, 255, 278, 390, 625, 643, 657, 661, 769–ZP 744, 773

Key to Picture Credits

A.—Atlantic
A.L.—American League
A.L.H. Jr.—Alfred L. Hathaway, Jr.
A.M.—Arthur Mitchell
A.N.—Amsterdam News
A.N.L.—Amsterdam News Library
A.P.—Acme Photo
A.P. Inc.—Associated Publishers, Inc.
A.T.—Al Thompson
B.A.—Bettman Archives
B.C.—Bishop College
B.H.A.C.—Berber's History of Amistad Captives
B.N.R.—Blue Note Records
B.P., N.U.L.—Brush Photos, National Urban League
B.S.N.Y.—Blackstone Shelburne, N.Y.
C.—Courier
C.B.H. & M.C.—Custer Battlefield Historical & Museum Collection
C.C.—Charles Caldweer
C.G. of J.—Consulate General of Jamaica
C.J.—Courier Journal
C.M.A.L.—Creative Management Association Limited
C.M.B.—Chase Manhattan Bank
C.N.—Carl Nessfield
Co.—Core Photo
C.P.—Columbia Pictures
C.P.I.—Columbia Pictures Industries
C.R.—Columbia Records
C.W.M.A.A.—Whitney Museum of American Art, Collection of
D.D.M.C.—Defense Dept.—Marine Corps.
D.G.—Dave Green
D.GA.—Dave Gahr
D.M. & Co.—Dodd Mead & Co.
D.N.C.C.—Democratic Nat'l. Congressional Committee
D.P.L., W.C.—Denver Public Library, Western Collection
E.E.O.C.—Equal Employment Opportunity Center, Wash., D.C.
E.H., R.M.—Educational Heritage, Roland Mitchell
F.A. of A.—Free Academy of Art, Berlin
F.C., W.W.—Fred Canley, Wide World
F.D.—Flying Dutchman
G.S.—Glamour Studios
G.S.M.I.—Golden State Mutual Insurance
H. & Bros.—Harper & Brothers
H.B.—Herbert Breslin
H.S.—Head Start
H.S.—Howard Smith
J.M.—Jim Marshall
K.B.—Kunstlammlung, Basel
L.C.—Library of Congress
L.H.—Leroy Henderson
L.M.—Leroy McLucas
McG.H.F.—McGraw Hill Films
M. Chic.—Morrison, Chicago
M.E.—Morton Englebert
MGM V.R.—MGM Verve Records
M.H.S.—Montana Historical Society
M.O.A. Inc.—Metropolitan Opera Association, Inc.
M.P.K.—Motion Picture "King"
M.R.—Mercury Records
N.A.—Negro Almanac (Private Collection)
NAACP—National Association Advancement of Colored People
NBC—National Broadcasting Company
N.E.A.J.D.D.—National Education Association, Joe DiDio
N.E.T.—National Education Television
N.E.W.M.—New England Whaling Museum
N.H.A.—Negro History Associates
N.U.L.—National Urban League
N.Y.D.N.—New York Daily News
N.Y.H.S.—New York Historical Society
N.Y.P.L.—New York Public Library
N.Y.T.—New York Times
O.P.S.—Old Print Shop
P.—Philips
P.B.N.Y.—Pach Bros., N.Y.
P.C.—Peace Corps.
R.R.D. & H.U.—Rocke Robertson, Drug & Hospital Union
S.A. Corp.—Shaw Artists Corp.
T.—Time
T.C.F.—Twentieth Century Fox
T.S.A.—Texas State Archives
U.A.—United Artists
U. Inc.—Uniroyal, Inc.
U.N.—United Nations
U.N.C.F.—United Negro College Fund
U.P.—Universal Pictures
U.P.I.—United Press International
U.S.—Universal Studios
U.S.A.—United States Army
U.S.A.F.—United States Air Force
U.S.A.S.C.—United States Army Signal Corps.
U.S.N.—United States Navy
W.H.—White House, Wash., D.C.
W.H.C., U. of OK. Lib.—Western History Collections, Univ. of Oklahoma Library
W.I.—Wagner International
W.M.C.A.—W.M.C.A. N.Y.C.
W.P.M.C.—West Point Museum Collection
W.W.—Wide World
Z.P.—Zodiac Photographers

INDEX

— A —

—B—

—C—

—D—

— E —

—F—

— G —

—H—

—I—

— J —

—K—

—L—

—M—

— N —

—O—

— P —

—S—

— U —

—V—

—W—